THE SCOUTING NOTEBOOK 2005

Editors/The Scouting Notebook
THOM HENNINGER
TONY NISTLER
DON ZMINDA

The photographs which appear in *The Scouting Notebook 2005* are courtesy of the following Major League Baseball teams, whose cooperation is gratefully acknowledged: Anaheim Angels, Baltimore Orioles, Boston Red Sox, Chicago White Sox/Ron Vesely, Cleveland Indians, Detroit Tigers, Kansas City Royals, Minnesota Twins, New York Yankees, Oakland Athletics, Courtesy Seattle Mariners, Tampa Bay Devil Rays, Texas Rangers, Toronto Blue Jays, Arizona Diamondbacks, Atlanta Braves (Courtesy of Atlanta National Baseball Club, Inc. ©2004. All rights reserved) , Chicago Cubs, Cincinnati Reds, Colorado Rockies, Florida Marlins/Dennis Bancroft, Houston Astros, Los Angeles Dodgers, Milwaukee Brewers, Montreal Expos, Mark S. Levine/New York Mets, Philadelphia Phillies, Pittsburgh Pirates, St. Louis Cardinals, San Diego Padres and San Francisco Giants.

ON THE COVER: Top: Alex Rodriguez photo by Jon Dunn for The Sporting News; bottom left to right: Eric Gagne by John Cordes/The Sporting News, Ivan Rodriguez by John Cordes/The Sporting News, Mark Prior by Jay Drowns/The Sporting News; spine: Gary Sheffield by Bob Leverone for The Sporting News; back: Jim Edmonds by Albert Dickson for The Sporting News.

Cover Design: Chad Painter/The Sporting News.

Major league statistics compiled by STATS, Inc., a News Corporation Company, 8130 Lehigh Avenue, Morton Grove, IL 60053. STATS is a trademark of Sports Team Analysis and Tracking Systems, Inc.

ISBN: 0-89204-768-2

10 9 8 7 6 5 4 3 2 1

Table of Contents

The Scouting Staff

The scouting reports on each team's ballpark, manager and significant players were written by the following people, in conjunction with our editors:

Anaheim Angels	Mark Saxon *Orange County Register*
Baltimore Orioles	Rick Wilton *Sports Weekly Hot Sheet*
Boston Red Sox	Matt Brown *STATS, Inc.*
Chicago White Sox*	Phil Rogers *Chicago Tribune/* *Baseball America*
Cleveland Indians	Paul Hoynes *Cleveland Plain Dealer*
Detroit Tigers	Pat Caputo *Oakland (Mich.) Press/* *Baseball America*
Kansas City Royals*	Marc Bowman *STATS, Inc.*
Minnesota Twins	Jim Souhan *Minneapolis* *Star Tribune*
New York Yankees	Matt Mahoney *STATS, Inc.*
Oakland Athletics*	Lawr Michaels *www.creativesports.com*
Seattle Mariners	Corey Brock *The News Tribune (Tacoma)/* *Baseball America*
Tampa Bay Devil Rays	Marc Topkin *St. Petersburg Times/* *Baseball America*
Texas Rangers*	Evan Grant *Dallas Morning News*
Toronto Blue Jays	Jeff Blair *Globe and Mail*
Arizona Diamondbacks*	Ed Price *East Valley Tribune* *(Mesa, Ariz.)*
Atlanta Braves*	Bill Ballew *Baseball America*
Chicago Cubs	Bruce Miles *Daily Herald*
Cincinnati Reds	Peter Pascarelli *ESPN*
Colorado Rockies*	Tracy Ringolsby *Rocky Mountain News* *(Denver)/Baseball America*
Florida Marlins*	Mike Berardino *South Florida Sun-Sentinel*
Houston Astros	Jim Carley *Sporting News*
Los Angeles Dodgers*	Don Hartack *STATS, Inc.*
Milwaukee Brewers*	Ron Thompson *STATS, Inc.*
New York Mets*	Bill Ballew *Baseball America*
Philadelphia Phillies*	Paul Hagen *Philadelphia Daily News*
Pittsburgh Pirates*	John Perrotto *Beaver County (Pa.) Times/* *Baseball America*
St. Louis Cardinals	Peter Pascarelli *ESPN*
San Diego Padres*	Trace Wood *www.longgandhi.com*
San Francisco Giants	Joe Roderick *Contra Costa Times*
Washinton Nationals*	Trace Wood *www.longgandhi.com*

The minor league prospect reports were written by Thom Henninger (AL), Jim Henzler (Reds, Astros, Cardinals, Giants), Ron Thompson (Tigers, Brewers, Yankees), Dan Ford (Cubs) and the individual team writers as noted with an asterisk (*). We'd like to thank the player-development personnel who were willing to discuss their teams' farm systems. *Baseball America's* Jim Callis also was a big help when it came to filling in blanks. The "Other Anaheim Angels," etc., were written by the STATS, Inc. publications staff. I'd also like to thank Norm DeNosaquo, Don Hartack, Brian Hogan, Matt Mahoney, Jacob Nuesser, Corey Roberts, John Strougal and Don Zminda for their integral roles in helping to get this edition to print.

—Tony Nistler

Introduction

Welcome to the 11th edition of *The Scouting Notebook*. This is the 16th annual book of scouting reports that STATS, Inc. has created. We get several prominent baseball analysts and have them give us detailed reports on every major league player who saw significant action last season. We think you'll agree that our scouting staff features some of the top baseball minds around. Special thanks to Marc Bowman, Paul Hoynes and John Perrotto, who have contributed to all 16 books.

This is an encyclopedia of contemporary major league baseball. We tell you about the strengths and weaknesses of hundreds of players. Our analysis extends beyond major league players, too, covering each club's top minor league prospects. We study the statistics and we talk to the scouts. We look for the true ability that may have been exaggerated or obscured by the hype.

The Ballparks

We report on each club's ballpark. We detail how each stadium affects hitters, pitchers and fielders in general, as well as which players it helps and hurts the most. We also project what the park will do to rookies and other newcomers in 2005. We provide vital statistics for each park, such as its dimensions, capacity, elevation, playing surface and the amount of foul territory.

We also present our trademark park indexes. In a variety of statistical categories, we show how the home team and its opponents performed at the park and on the road. Interleague games aren't included. By comparing the overall totals at the park and on the road, we get a measure of the stadium's impact. We divide the home totals by the road totals and multiply by 100 to get the park index. An index of greater than 100 shows that the park favors a particular statistic, while an index of less than 100 means the opposite.

Most of the indexes are calculated on a per at-bat basis. Runs, hits, errors and infield errors are figured on a per-game basis. For most parks, we present data for both 2004 and the last three years overall. If the park's configuration has changed since the end of the 2002 season, we present the data for the different setups separately.

Most of the abbreviations are common, with these exceptions:

E-Infield: Infield errors.

LHB-Avg: Batting average by lefthanded hitters.

LHB-HR: Home runs by lefthanded hitters.

RHB-Avg: Batting average by righthanded hitters.

RHB-HR: Home runs by righthanded hitters.

We also list any indexes in which the park ranked in the top or bottom three in its league in 2004.

The Managers

On these pages, we analyze each manager's strengths and weaknesses, style and strategy, and outlook for 2005. We present his 2004 and career managerial record, and we also show how often he used starting pitchers on various days of rest. In determing days rest, each pitcher's first start of the year is excluded, as are any relief appearances. We compare his use and the performance of his starters to the league average.

We also provide statistical breakdowns detailing his handling of his pitching staff and his use of strategies like the sacrifice, the hit-and-run and defensive substitutions. To qualify for the rankings, a manager had to have his team for at least 100 games in 2004. Some of the terms listed in the statistics and rankings sections may be unfamiliar. They include:

Hit & Run Success %: The percentage of hit-and-runs resulting in baserunner advancement with no double play.

Platoon Pct.: Frequency that the manager gets his hitters the platoon advantage (lefty vs. righty and vice versa). Switch-hitters always are considered to have the advantage.

Defensive Subs: The number of straight defensive substitutions with the team leading by four runs or fewer.

High-Pitch Outings: The number of times a manager's starting pitchers threw more than 120 pitches in a ballgame.

Quick/Slow Hooks: A Quick Hook occurs when a pitcher is removed after having pitched less than six innings and given up three runs or fewer. A Slow Hook occurs when a pitcher works more than nine innings, allows seven or more runs, or his total innings and runs equal 13 or more.

First-Batter Platoon Percentage: The percentage of times a manager's relievers had a platoon advantage over the first hitter they faced (lefty vs. lefty, righty vs. righty).

Mid-Inning Changes: The number of times the manager changed pitchers in the middle of an inning.

Pitchouts with a Runner Moving: The number of times the opposition was running when the manager called a pitchout.

Sacrifice Bunt Percentage: The percentage of bunts resulting in sacrifices or hits with runners on.

Starting Lineups Used: Based on batting order, 1-8 for National Leaguers, 1-9 for American Leaguers.

2+ Pitching Changes in Low-Scoring Games: The number of times a manager used at least three pitchers in a game in which his team allowed two runs or fewer.

The Players

For each major league team, we give extensive reports on 22 players. Twelve of them get a full page of scouting information, while 10 receive half-page reports. Because we like to get this book into your hands as soon as possible, players are listed with their 2004 clubs. We keep abreast of postseason transactions, and all player moves that took place through December 13, 2004 are noted. If you can't find a particular player, check the detailed index in the back.

Pages for primary players have two columns. The left column provides an in-depth report by an analyst. The right column contains statistical information:

Position: The first position shown is the player's most common position in 2004. Positions at which he played 10 or more games also are shown. For pitchers, SP stands for starting pitcher and RP for relief pitcher.

Bats and Throws: L represents for lefthanded, R stands for righthanded, and B represents both (switch-hitter).

Ht: Height.

Wt: Weight.

Opening Day Age: This is the player's age on April 1, 2005.

Born: Birthdate and birthplace.

ML Seasons: This number indicates the number of different major league seasons in which the player has appeared. For example, if a player was called up to play in September in each of the last three seasons, the number shown would be 3. This is different from major league service, which is used to determine arbitration and free-agency eligibility.

Overall Statistics: These are traditional major league statistics for the player's 2004 season and his career.

Where He Hits The Ball

For every major league game in 2004, STATS reporters entered into our computers every single ball hit into play. They kept track of the type of batted balls—grounders, flyballs, popups, line drives and bunts—as well as the distance each ball traveled. Direction was tracked by dividing the field into 26 "wedges" projecting out from home plate. Distance was measured in 10-foot increments outward from home plate.

Below are the 2003 hitting diagrams for righthanded-hitting Adrian Beltre of the Los Angeles Dodgers. The chart on the left shows where Pierre hit the ball against lefthanders, while the chart on the right shows what he did against righties.

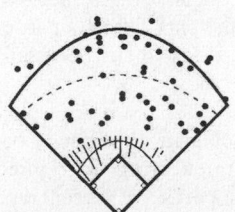 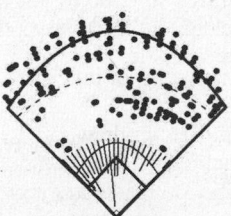

Vs. LHP   **Vs. RHP**

In the diagrams, groundballs and short line drives are shown by the lines of various lengths in the infield. The longer the line, the more groundballs and line drives were hit in that direction. As you can see from the charts above, Beltre showed power to all fields in his breakout 2004 season with the Dodgers. He was successful both at home and away, batting .326 and slugging .611 at pitcher-friendly Dodger Stadium last year.

New Dodgers hitting coach Tim Wallach had Beltre using the whole field more in 2004, and that's apparent when you compare the third baseman's hitting charts for 2003 to last year's. While Beltre tended to pull grounders, his 2004 hitting charts show more balls landing in short right field and many more traveling deep to right. He often went the opposite way off righthanders. Clearly Beltre hit more longballs to all fields in 2004, when he hit a major league-best 48 home runs, more than double his previous career high.

A lot of experimentation went into producing the hitting diagrams. When we first started, we tried to show every single batted ball that was put into play by each player. We found that the charts became very cluttered for everyday players, so we began experimenting with trying to show only the most meaningful information. When all was said and done, here's what we ended up with:

a. Popups and bunts are excluded. We excluded popups because 95 percent of these are caught regardless of how fielders are positioned. We excluded bunts because defensing a bunt is an entirely different strategy primarily used against a select number of players or in specific situations.

b. For groundballs and short line drives, we include all batted balls.

c. For balls hit to the outfield, we excluded isolated points only if the chart contains more than 125 batted balls to the outfield. In such cases, if a player hits only one ball to a given area and had no other batted balls in the vicinity all season, we exclude it because it doesn't give a true indication of a tendency.

Other notes of interest:

The field is drawn to scale, with the outfield fence reaching 400 feet in center and 330 feet down the lines. Ballparks are configured differently, so a dot inside of the fence might have been a home run. Similarly, a dot outside the fence might actually have been in play.

Line drives under 170 feet are part of the infield. We give responsibility for short liners to the infielders.

No distinction is made between hits and outs.

2004 Pitching Profiles

Past readers of the *Scouting Notebook* may notice a change to our full-page reports for major league pitchers. We have replaced the charts that displayed how often a pitcher threw strikes with a more extensive breakdown of a given pitcher's performance in eight common categories, and compared them to the 2004 league averages.

The first two categories, **Overall Strike %** and **1st Pitch Strike %**, include swinging strikes, taken strikes, foul balls and balls put in play. STATS reporters tracked every pitch thrown in a major league game in 2004. Though not all batted balls come on pitches thrown within the strike zone, our theory is that most are and the ones that aren't would be difficult to judge. Our numbers reflect these assumptions.

Another statistic that may require further explanation is **Ratio**, which is the number of baserunners allowed by a pitcher per inning: ((hits + walks)/IP). This category also is commonly referred to as WHIP.

One additional note: For the category of **Groundball/Flyball Ratio**, groundballs include hits, outs and errors, while flyballs *exclude* line drives.

2004 Situational Stats

There are eight situational breakdowns for every primary player. *Home* and *Road* show performance in his home ballpark and on the road. *First Half* and *Scnd Half* show performance before and after the 2004 All-Star break. For hitters, *LHP* and *RHP* show how the player hit against lefthanders and righthanders. For pitchers, *LHB* and *RHB* show how the opposition lefthanders and righthanders hit against the pitcher. *Sc Pos* shows batting or pitching performance with runners in scoring position. *Clutch* shows batting or pitching performance in clutch situations, defined as the seventh inning or later with the batting team ahead by one run, tied or with the tying run on base, at bat or on deck. Our definition is consistent with save situations.

2004 Rankings

This section shows how the player ranked in his league and among his teammates. Because of space considerations, we omitted some of the less interesting rankings when a player placed high in numerous categories.

We include many less traditional categories. The Definitions and Qualifications section below provides details for these statistics.

Definitions and Qualifications

The following are definitions and qualifications for the Major League Leaders and Rankings.

Definitions:

Times on Base — Hits plus walks plus hit-by-pitch.

Groundball-Flyball Ratio — Groundballs hit divided by the total of flyballs and popups hit. Bunts and line drives are excluded.

Runs/Times on Base — Runs scored divided by times on base.

Clutch — A player's batting average in the late innings of close games, defined as the seventh inning or later with the batting team ahead by one run, tied or with the tying run on base, at bat or on deck.

Bases Loaded — A player's batting average in bases-loaded situations.

GDP per GDP situation — Groundball double plays divided by groundball double-play situations, defined as a man on first base with less than two out.

Percentage of Pitches Taken — The percentage of pitches a player lets go by without swinging.

Percentage Swings Put In Play — The percentage of swings resulting in a batted ball into fair territory or a foul-ball out.

Run Support per Nine Innings — The number of runs scored for a pitcher while he was pitching, scaled to a nine-inning figure.

Baserunners per Nine Innings — The total of hits, walks and hit batsmen allowed per nine innings.

Strikeout-Walk Ratio — Strikeouts divided by walks.

Stolen-Base Percentage Allowed — Stolen bases divided by stolen-base attempts.

Save Percentage — Saves divided by save opportunities. Save opportunities include saves plus blown saves.

Blown Saves — A blown save is charged any time a pitcher enters a game in a save situation and loses the lead. A save situation is defined as any time a reliever enters the game with a lead, isn't the pitcher of record and either a) pitches at least one inning with a lead of no more than three runs; b) enters the game with the potential tying run on base, at bat or on deck; or c) pitches effectively for at least three innings.

Holds — A hold is given to a pitcher when he enters a game in a save situation and is removed before the end of the game while maintaining his team's lead. The pitcher must retire at least one batter to get a hold.

Percentage of Inherited Runners Scored — Percentage of runners already on base when a pitcher enters a game that he allows to score.

First Batter Efficiency — The batting average allowed by a reliever to the first batter he faces in a game.

Qualifications:

In order to be ranked, a player had to qualify with a minimum number of opportunities. Minimums for league rankings are listed below. Minimums for team rankings are 60 percent of the figure for league rankings unless noted otherwise.

Batters

Batting average, slugging percentage, on-base percentage, home run frequency, groundball-flyball ratio, runs scored per time reached base and pitches seen per plate appearance — 3.1 plate appearances per team game

Percentage of pitches taken, lowest percentage of swings that missed and percentage of swings put into play — 9.26 pitches seen per team game

Percentage of extra bases taken as a runner — .25 opportunities to advance per team game

Stolen-base percentage — .12 stolen-base attempts per team game

Runners in scoring position — .62 plate appearances with runners in scoring position per team game

Clutch — .31 plate appearances in the clutch per team game

Bases loaded — .06 plate appearances with the bases loaded per team game

GDP per GDP situation — .31 plate appearances in GDP situations per team game

BA vs. LHP — .77 plate appearances against left-handers per team game

BA vs. RHP — 2.33 plate appearances against righthanders per team game

BA at home — 1.55 plate appearances at home per team game

BA on the road — 1.55 plate appearances on the road per team game

Leadoff on-base percentage — .93 plate appearances in the No. 1 lineup spot per team game

Cleanup slugging percentage — .93 plate appearances in the No. 4 lineup spot per team game

BA on 3-1 count — .06 plate appearances with a 3-1 count per team game

BA with 2 strikes — .93 plate appearances with two strikes per team game

BA on 0-2 count — .12 plate appearances with an 0-2 count per team game

BA on 3-2 count — .25 plate appearances with a 3-2 count per team game

Pitchers

Earned run average, run support per nine innings, baserunners per nine innings, batting average allowed, slugging percentage allowed, on-base percentage allowed, home runs per nine innings, strikeouts per nine innings, strikeout-walk ratio, stolen-base percentage allowed, GDPs per nine innings, pitches thrown per batter and groundball-flyball ratio against—one inning per team game

Winning percentage — .09 decisions per team game

GDPs induced per GDP situation — .19 batters faced in GDP situations per team game

BA allowed, runners in scoring position — .93 batters faced with runners in scoring position per team game

ERA at home — .5 innings at home per team game

ERA on the road — .5 innings on the road per team game

BA vs. LHB — .77 lefthanders faced per team game

BA vs. RHB — 1.39 righthanders faced per team game

Relievers

ERA, batting average allowed, baserunners per nine innings, strikeouts per nine innings — .93 relief innings per team game (same for team rankings)

Save percentage — .12 save opportunities per team game

Percentage of inherited runners scoring — .19 inherited runners per team game

First batter efficiency — .25 games in relief per team game

Fielders

Percentage caught stealing by catchers — .43 stolen-base attempts per team game

Fielding percentage — .67 games at a position per team game (1 inning per team game for pitchers, .5 games per team game for catchers)

Other Players

Some players didn't play enough to merit a full- or half-page essay, and aren't young enough or good enough to deserve a prospect report. But they did play in the majors last year, so we give them a brief evaluation. Following the half-page reports for each team, you'll find a page devoted to these part-timers under the heading "Other Anaheim Angels," etc. Each player gets a short summary and his 2005 Outlook is graded as follows:

A — Should be an important contributor.

B — Should play most of the season in the majors and contribute.

C — Unlikely to play much in the majors or contribute much if he does.

D — Unlikely to play in the majors.

Minor League Prospects

We present two pages of minor league prospects for each team. Prospect writers spoke directly to major league player-development personnel and also looked beyond athletic tools by analyzing statistics. Each club has seven or eight featured prospects. We try to include most of the top phenoms, but our primary emphasis is on advanced players with the best chance of contributing in the majors in 2005.

We also include an organizational overview for each team, which gives you a glimpse into the current state of each club's minor league system. In addition, we summarize a few more notable prospects per team in a section called "Others to Watch."

Where we mention that managers voted a player as the best in a specific category in his league, our source is *Baseball America*.

Major League Leaders

After the team sections, we provide a complete listing of MLB leaders for the 2004 season. The top three players in each category are shown for the American and National Leagues. You'll notice a STATS flavor to these leaders. Not only do we show the leaders for the common categories such as batting average, home runs and ERA, but you'll also find less traditional categories like steals of third and total pitches thrown.

American League Players

Offense

One of the reasons the Angels didn't dominate at Angel Stadium last season is that two of their top pitchers, Bartolo Colon and Jarrod Washburn, rely on flyballs, and those carry well on warm summer days. Colon had a 5.42 ERA and allowed 26 home runs at home while Washburn had a 5.76 ERA there and gave up 12 home runs in 65.2 innings.

Defense

Vladimir Guerrero embarrassed himself several times in the quirky dimensions of Angel Stadium's right field, and he didn't get much help from Garret Anderson, who was nursing an assortment of leg injuries and didn't always run full-speed for flyballs in the large dimensions of center. The Angels tend to play crisply on the infield at home.

Who It Helps the Most

Although Angel Stadium tends to favor pitchers, in part because they play so few day games, Guerrero seemed to like hitting there just fine. He drove in a majority of his runs at home. Part of the reason is that the ball carries well to center field and Guerrero has prodigious power in that direction.

Who It Hurts the Most

Some of the Angels' pitchers consider the mound at Angel Stadium to be among the worst in the league, and it shows in their numbers. Anderson didn't have the same bat speed in 2004, in part due to an assortment of injuries, and the high wall in right-center field cost him some home runs. He hit just four of his 14 home runs at home.

Rookies & Newcomers

Dallas McPherson should benefit from the relatively short dimensions in right, although with his raw power, few parks will contain him when he connects. Francisco Rodriguez will be feeling the heat of being the full-time closer now, but he was murderously tough to hit at home last year.

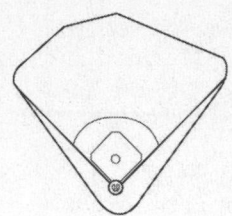

Dimensions: LF-330, LCF-387, CF-400, RCF-370, RF-330

Capacity: 45,030

Elevation: 160 feet

Surface: Grass

Foul Territory: Average

Park Factors

2004 Season

| | Home Games | | | Away Games | | | |
	Angels	Opp	Total	Angels	Opp	Total	Index
G	72	72	144	72	72	144	
Avg	.287	.268	.278	.282	.262	.272	102
AB	2429	2556	4985	2588	2408	4996	100
R	357	331	688	404	312	716	96
H	698	686	1384	730	630	1360	102
2B	111	128	239	131	140	271	88
3B	11	8	19	21	13	34	56
HR	73	83	156	75	63	138	113
BB	187	221	408	214	220	434	94
SO	405	524	929	421	507	928	100
E	45	41	86	37	63	100	86
E-Infield	32	35	67	32	57	89	75
LHB-Avg	.277	.282	.280	.291	.261	.275	102
LHB-HR	19	46	65	20	27	47	134
RHB-Avg	.294	.255	.276	.276	.263	.270	102
RHB-HR	54	37	91	55	36	91	103

2002-2004

| | Home Games | | | Away Games | | | |
	Angels	Opp	Total	Angels	Opp	Total	Index
G	217	217	434	215	215	430	
Avg	.277	.258	.268	.278	.258	.269	100
AB	7294	7610	14904	7642	7116	14758	100
R	1035	927	1962	1126	963	2089	93
H	2024	1966	3990	2127	1838	3965	100
2B	375	374	749	418	349	767	97
3B	40	20	60	44	42	86	69
HR	194	226	420	210	238	448	93
BB	588	679	1267	648	671	1319	95
SO	1105	1455	2560	1177	1339	2516	101
E	129	119	248	124	161	285	86
E-Infield	102	98	200	109	132	241	82
LHB-Avg	.279	.257	.267	.291	.256	.274	98
LHB-HR	75	112	187	89	107	196	92
RHB-Avg	.276	.260	.268	.268	.260	.264	102
RHB-HR	119	114	233	121	131	252	94

2004 Rankings (American League)

- Second-highest LHB home-run factor
- Third-highest home-run factor
- Second-lowest triple factor
- Third-lowest double factor
- Third-lowest walk factor
- Third-lowest infield-error factor

Mike Scioscia

2004 Season

At times last season, Mike Scioscia seemed mystified at the lack of production his star-laden offense was providing. The Angels led the league with a .282 batting average, but finished seventh in runs scored. It was due in part to a failure to hit in the clutch, but it was fueled by an offense skewed in favor of free swingers. While most teams are drifting toward a "Moneyball" approach favoring hitters who take walks, Scioscia and GM Bill Stoneman cling stubbornly to the belief that the best way to score is to swing aggressively and to pressure defenses on the bases.

Offense

The Angels led the league once again in stolen bases, and they finished second to the White Sox in sacrifice bunts. Scioscia's belief in aggressive baserunning goes back to his days as a catcher with the Dodgers in the 1980s, particularly having to try to contain the baserunners of the ultra-quick St. Louis Cardinals. His style stands out as nearly unique in the American League these days.

Pitching & Defense

Scioscia took some rare heat for using Jarrod Washburn to face David Ortiz after Ortiz ended Anaheim's short playoff run with an opposite-field home run on Washburn's first pitch. But Scioscia's feel for his bullpen generally was unmatched, thanks in part to some of the finest relief arms in baseball. For the first time in Scioscia's six-year tenure, he won't have Troy Percival to rely on in the ninth inning. Then again, he will have Francisco Rodriguez.

2005 Outlook

After a serious clash that resulted in outfielder Jose Guillen being suspended for the final week of the season and the playoffs, Scioscia may have to regain the trust of some of the Angels' Latin players. That has never before been a problem for Scioscia, who speaks conversant Spanish and began his career as Fernando Valenzuela's personal catcher. If Vladimir Guerrero, Bartolo Colon and Rodriguez aren't happy, the Angels aren't going anywhere.

Born: 11/27/58 in Upper Darby, PA

Playing Experience: 1980-1992, LA

Managerial Experience: 5 seasons

Manager Statistics

Year	Team, Lg	W	L	Pct	GB	Finish
2004	Anaheim, AL	92	70	.568	–	1st West
5 Seasons		425	385	.525	–	–

2004 Starting Pitchers by Days Rest

	<=3	4	5	6+
Angels Starts	5	81	54	16
Angels ERA	5.40	4.37	5.01	4.55
AL Avg Starts	2	82	47	21
AL ERA	5.36	4.87	4.65	4.93

2004 Situational Stats

	Mike Scioscia	AL Average
Hit & Run Success %	38.9	36.8
Stolen Base Success %	75.7	68.6
Platoon Pct.	56.6	61.6
Defensive Subs	31	21
High-Pitch Outings	4	5
Quick/Slow Hooks	19/14	20/16
Sacrifice Attempts	75	53

2004 Rankings (American League)

- 1st in stolen base attempts (189), steals of second base (123), steals of home plate (1), double steals (8), hit-and-run attempts (131) and starts on three days rest
- 2nd in stolen-base percentage, steals of third base (19), sacrifice bunt attempts, squeeze plays (7), pitchouts (35), pitchouts with a runner moving (7) and saves with over 1 inning pitched (11)
- 3rd in defensive substitutions and 2+ pitching changes in low-scoring games (32)

Garret Anderson

2004 Season

The Angels locked up one of their homegrown talents just as injuries began to slow down his stellar career. Garret Anderson had bouts with arthritis and some stubborn tendinitis in his left knee that cost him 43 games and much of his power and outfield range. In part because of the injuries, the Angels are committed to moving their best left-handed hitter to left field to avoid the wear and tear of running down balls in center.

Hitting

Anderson's home-run totals were cut roughly in half, down to 14, in 2004. Most scouts attributed his lack of pop to injuries. There has never before been reason to doubt his durability. He played in at least 156 games every year from 1998-2003. He still has a knack for clutch hitting, and he had the game-winning RBI single against Oakland October 2 that clinched the Angels' first division title since 1986. If he bats cleanup again, he could be searching for protection without Troy Glaus and Jose Guillen around him.

Baserunning & Defense

Anderson was one of the best left fielders in the league two years ago, but he was only a so-so center fielder. The reasons: lack of range and leg injuries that cost him much of his once-solid speed. Anderson's future will be as a left fielder. His instincts and intelligence mean he rarely does dumb things in the outfield or on the bases. Considering the Angels have several players who do, those are important traits.

2005 Outlook

With the Angels signing Steve Finley to a two-year deal to play center field, Anderson will move back to left in 2005. If he can return to playing more than 155 games and to hitting more than 25 home runs, he could provide a big boost to this team. However, his arthritic knee condition likely won't go away and injuries could continue to plague him. The Angels made a big investment in Anderson, locking him up through 2008, and they need him to be the player he used to be. With Troy Percival gone and Tim Salmon's career in jeopardy, Anderson is now Mr. Angel.

Position: CF/DH
Bats: L **Throws:** L
Ht: 6' 3" **Wt:** 225

Opening Day Age: 32
Born: 6/30/72 in Los Angeles, CA
ML Seasons: 11

Overall Statistics

	G	AB	R	H	D	T	HR	RBI	SB	BB	SO	Avg	OBP	Slg
'04	112	442	57	133	20	1	14	75	2	29	75	.301	.343	.446
Car.	1477	5897	760	1766	369	28	207	947	68	280	807	.299	.329	.477

Where He Hits the Ball

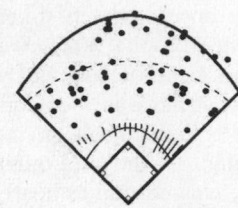 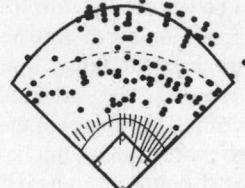

Vs. LHP   **Vs. RHP**

2004 Situational Stats

	AB	H	HR	RBI	Avg		AB	H	HR	RBI	Avg
Home	219	59	4	32	.269	LHP	149	39	2	27	.262
Road	223	74	10	43	.332	RHP	293	94	12	48	.321
First Half	177	56	7	26	.316	Sc Pos	130	36	5	57	.277
Scnd Half	265	77	7	49	.291	Clutch	61	21	2	13	.344

2004 Rankings (American League)

- 6th in batting average in the clutch
- 7th in fewest GDPs per GDP situation (3.4%)
- 10th in cleanup slugging percentage (.493)
- Led the Angels in batting average in the clutch

Bartolo Colon

Position: SP
Bats: R **Throws:** R
Ht: 5'11" **Wt:** 250

Opening Day Age: 31
Born: 5/24/73 in
Altamira, DR
ML Seasons: 8
Pronunciation:
bar-TOE-loh ko-LONE

2004 Season

Bartolo Colon's year was a tale of two seasons. The first was awful, the second stellar. It's fair to say the Angels were appalled at Colon's first-half struggles, particularly since there were serious questions about his conditioning in spring training. At the All-Star break, Colon had a 6.38 ERA, the worst in the league. But he got a few days to rest his aching left ankle and he went 12-4 with a 3.63 ERA in the second half to fuel hopes that he can be the front-of-the-rotation pitcher the Angels paid $51 million to get.

Pitching

For all the talk about Colon's velocity, he hasn't struck out as many as 200 batters in a season since 2001 and his strikeouts dipped last year. As Colon's girth grows, his velocity seems to decline. He rarely threw consistently in the upper 90s and there were times he struggled to break 90 MPH. However, when he is locating his pitches on the edges of the plate, he is tough to hit. One distressing trend: batters are taking him deep more and more.

Defense

He's not exactly the Big Cat, but Colon moves fairly well for a man of his size. He takes up so much space in the center of the diamond, batters have trouble sneaking groundballs into center field. Colon has a quick release to home plate, making it a challenge to run on him.

2005 Outlook

The Angels will know by February how committed their No. 1 starter is to being their ace. Colon will have to show up in Tempe, Ariz., in better shape than he did last year, in order to win back the respect of some of his teammates. He has shown a tendency to pitch better in the final months of a season, which is convenient for a team making a pennant run, but the Angels can't afford another early-season flop.

Overall Statistics

	W	L	Pct.	ERA	G	GS	Sv	IP	H	BB	SO	HR	Avg
'04	18	12	.600	5.01	34	34	0	208.1	215	71	158	38	.265
Car.	118	74	.615	4.01	247	245	0	1597.0	1537	596	1278	186	.254

2004 Pitching Profile

	Bartolo Colon	AL Average
Overall Strike %	64.1	62.3
1st Pitch Strike %	62.3	58.1
Ratio	1.37	1.42
Strikeouts per 9 IP	6.83	6.45
Walks per 9 IP	3.07	3.34
Home Runs per 9 IP	1.64	1.15
Strikeout/Walk Ratio	2.23	1.93
Groundball/Flyball Ratio	0.91	1.17

2004 Situational Stats

	W	L	ERA	Sv	IP		AB	H	HR	RBI	Avg
Home	10	8	5.42	0	119.2	LHB	455	124	22	69	.273
Road	8	4	4.47	0	88.2	RHB	355	91	16	46	.256
First Half	6	8	6.38	0	104.1	Sc Pos	160	39	4	65	.244
Scnd Half	12	4	3.63	0	104.0	Clutch	26	7	2	3	.269

2004 Rankings (American League)

- 2nd in home runs allowed
- 3rd in wins, games started and most run support per nine innings (7.0)
- 4th in lowest stolen-base percentage allowed (33.3) and most home runs allowed per nine innings (1.64)
- 5th in highest ERA at home
- 8th in highest slugging percentage allowed (.472)
- 9th in lowest groundball-flyball ratio allowed (0.9)
- 10th in pitches thrown (3,405) and lowest fielding percentage at pitcher (.927)
- Led the Angels in wins, games started, innings pitched, hits allowed, batters faced (897), home runs allowed and lowest stolen-base percentage allowed (33.3)

Anaheim

David Eckstein

2004 Season

It's so easy to like David Eckstein, because he plays the game the way everybody swears they would if they could play in the majors. He doesn't do dumb things and he makes all the routine plays. His .988 fielding percentage led major league shortstops, though his limited range and lack of offensive oomph mean he'll never be considered for a Gold Glove. At the plate, he was what he always has been: an annoying hitter to face. He struck out once every 13 plate appearances, the second-best ratio in the league.

Hitting

Unlike in 2003, Eckstein was healthy last year. Unfortunately for him, that fact simply exposed his shortcomings as a hitter. He is simply too small to inspire any fear in a pitcher, and he is an aggressive swinger, so he's not prone to drawing walks. The best thing Eckstein has going for him is Mike Scioscia's love of the hit-and-run, as he is one of the best in the league at handling the bat.

Baserunning & Defense

Eckstein's rag arm is infamous by now, but it was amazing how few times it seemed to cost the Angels last year. He has become amazingly adept at getting rid of the ball quickly, and he and Adam Kennedy were impressive as a double-play tandem. However, Eckstein rarely makes spectacular plays because of his limited range, and his size further limits his ability to stop balls by diving. He's beginning to slow down a bit on the bases, though he matched his 2003 steals total with 16 last season.

2005 Outlook

With no appreciable baseball skills other than heart and determination, Eckstein's job likely never is secure. And in his second year of arbitration eligibility, he no longer comes cheap, either. That could spell a slipping grip on his everyday job, as the Angels would like to bring in a harder-hitting shortstop. Eckstein might be needed to play second base while Kennedy is recovering from knee surgery.

Position: SS
Bats: R **Throws:** R
Ht: 5' 7" **Wt:** 165

Opening Day Age: 30
Born: 1/20/75 in Sanford, FL
ML Seasons: 4
Pronunciation: eck-STYNE

Overall Statistics

	G	AB	R	H	D	T	HR	RBI	SB	BB	SO	Avg	OBP	Slg
'04	142	566	92	156	24	1	2	35	16	42	49	.276	.339	.332
Car.	567	2208	340	614	94	10	17	170	82	166	198	.278	.347	.353

Where He Hits the Ball

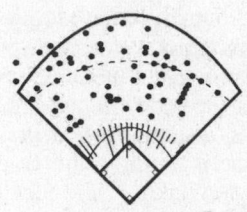 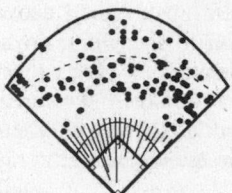

Vs. LHP   **Vs. RHP**

2004 Situational Stats

	AB	H	HR	RBI	Avg		AB	H	HR	RBI	Avg
Home	286	86	2	18	.301	LHP	179	50	2	12	.279
Road	280	70	0	17	.250	RHP	387	106	0	23	.274
First Half	280	82	0	18	.293	Sc Pos	126	26	0	32	.206
Scnd Half	286	74	2	17	.259	Clutch	66	14	0	4	.212

2004 Rankings (American League)

- 1st in lowest percentage of swings that missed (7.5), lowest percentage of swings on the first pitch (11.2), fielding percentage at shortstop (.988), lowest slugging percentage and lowest HR frequency (283.0 ABs per HR)
- 4th in singles, sacrifice bunts (14) and highest percentage of swings put into play (52.9)
- 6th in hit by pitch (13) and lowest batting average with runners in scoring position
- 7th in lowest on-base percentage for a leadoff hitter (.343)
- Led the Angels in singles, sacrifice bunts (14), lowest percentage of swings that missed (7.5), highest percentage of swings put into play (52.9) and lowest percentage of swings on the first pitch (11.2)

Darin Erstad

2004 Season

A lot of people wondered if Darin Erstad's magical 2000 season was a fluke, but he answered many of his critics with a solid 2004 campaign. He became the first player to win a Gold Glove in the infield and the outfield when he collected his third award overall—his first as a first baseman. The main thing Erstad did in 2004 was to stay healthy for the better part of the year, something he didn't do in 2003.

Hitting

Erstad readily admits he is not a home-run hitter, and the numbers prove him right. He set unrealistic expectations when he bashed 25 in 2000, but he has reached double figures just once since then. Still, Erstad drove in 69 runs often batting high in the order, so he has a knack for hitting with runners on base. He got in one of the longest hot streaks of his career, batting .346 from June through August before fatigue finally caught up to him in September.

Baserunning & Defense

While Erstad no longer is the stolen-base threat he once was, he runs hard and with intelligence at all times. It would be hard to play first base more effectively than Erstad did, considering one of his four errors came on an over-the-shoulder catch attempt on a foul popup. He saved the left side of the Angels' infield many errors with adept scoops, and his range is the best in the business for first basemen.

2005 Outlook

The Angels figured moving Erstad to first base would keep him healthy, and they were generally correct. They will keep him at first, as they signed Steve Finley to a two-year deal in December to play center field. They know they are lucky to have a player capable of winning Gold Gloves at either position, and one who was willing to be shuttled back and forth.

Position: 1B
Bats: L **Throws:** L
Ht: 6' 2" **Wt:** 210

Opening Day Age: 30
Born: 6/4/74 in Jamestown, ND
ML Seasons: 9
Pronunciation: ER-stad

Overall Statistics

	G	AB	R	H	D	T	HR	RBI	SB	BB	SO	Avg	OBP	Slg
'04	125	495	79	146	29	1	7	69	16	37	74	.295	.346	.400
Car.	1127	4554	724	1318	238	26	107	554	159	366	669	.289	.344	.424

Where He Hits the Ball

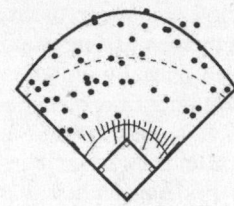

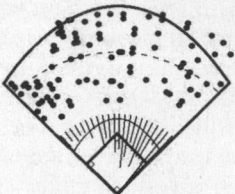

Vs. LHP   **Vs. RHP**

2004 Situational Stats

	AB	H	HR	RBI	Avg		AB	H	HR	RBI	Avg
Home	217	65	3	28	.300	LHP	166	42	2	23	.253
Road	278	81	4	41	.291	RHP	329	104	5	46	.316
First Half	216	64	2	29	.296	Sc Pos	127	38	4	60	.299
Scnd Half	279	82	5	40	.294	Clutch	57	13	1	12	.228

2004 Rankings (American League)

- 3rd in fielding percentage at first base (.996)
- 4th in highest groundball-flyball ratio (2.1)
- 5th in lowest percentage of swings on the first pitch (12.9)
- 8th in lowest HR frequency (70.7 ABs per HR)
- Led the Angels in highest groundball-flyball ratio (2.1), stolen-base percentage (94.1), highest percentage of pitches taken (58.8) and batting average with the bases loaded (.556)
- Led AL first basemen in batting average

Kelvim Escobar

2004 Season

Kelvim Escobar firmly established himself as one of the more capable starters in the American League with his most consistent season yet. The fact that he had a sub-.500 record shouldn't fool anyone. Escobar was the ace of the staff, leading the club in innings pitched and strikeouts. He ranked in the top 10 in the league in ERA, strikeouts, opponent batting average and Ks per nine innings—what manager Mike Scioscia calls his "internal numbers." The 3.9 runs of support the Angels mustered for him was the primary culprit in keeping Escobar off the national radar during his stellar season.

Pitching

With Bartolo Colon having lost something on his fastball, Escobar was the Angels' most imposing power arm in the rotation. He typically works in the mid-90s all game long. He doesn't rely on his fastball nearly as much as Colon does, mixing in an array of breaking pitches. He throws a change-up, curveball, cutter and a split-finger pitch. It's one of the most impressive repertoires in the game, though the hits can pile up quickly when Escobar begins to struggle.

Defense

Also unlike Colon, Escobar keeps in tip-top physical condition. He jogs nearly every day, something he has done since he was a kid in Venezuela. One of the results of Escobar's hard work is that he has not been on the disabled list since 1998. Another is that he seems to have some of his best stuff late in a season. He moves quickly off the mound, though he doesn't work fast to home plate and can be easily victimized by basestealers.

2005 Outlook

If Escobar gets a little more luck, he has enough talent to emerge as a Cy Young contender in 2005. Then again, he also could content himself with being a solid, well-paid No. 3 starter. It will depend on how much he wants to distinguish himself. Considering how badly the Angels need an ace, especially if Colon falters again early, they hope he'll take on the challenge.

Position: SP
Bats: R **Throws:** R
Ht: 6' 1" **Wt:** 210

Opening Day Age: 28
Born: 4/11/76 in La Guaria, VZ
ML Seasons: 8

Overall Statistics

	W	L	Pct.	ERA	G	GS	Sv	IP	H	BB	SO	HR	Avg
'04	11	12	.478	3.93	33	33	0	208.1	192	76	191	21	.244
Car.	69	67	.507	4.45	334	134	58	1057.1	1038	470	935	105	.256

2004 Pitching Profile

	Kelvim Escobar	AL Average
Overall Strike %	62.4	62.3
1st Pitch Strike %	58.1	58.1
Ratio	1.29	1.42
Strikeouts per 9 IP	8.25	6.45
Walks per 9 IP	3.28	3.34
Home Runs per 9 IP	0.91	1.15
Strikeout/Walk Ratio	2.51	1.93
Groundball/Flyball Ratio	1.14	1.17

2004 Situational Stats

	W	L	ERA	Sv	IP		AB	H	HR	RBI	Avg
Home	4	8	3.95	0	114.0	LHB	405	102	6	38	.252
Road	7	4	3.91	0	94.1	RHB	381	90	15	43	.236
First Half	5	5	3.91	0	103.2	Sc Pos	181	48	5	55	.265
Scnd Half	6	7	3.96	0	104.2	Clutch	46	8	1	1	.174

2004 Rankings (American League)

- 1st in fielding percentage at pitcher (1.000)
- 2nd in least run support per nine innings (3.9)
- 3rd in pickoff throws (150) and most strikeouts per nine innings (8.3)
- 4th in strikeouts, stolen bases allowed (24) and highest stolen-base percentage allowed (85.7)
- 5th in pitches thrown (3,431)
- 6th in lowest slugging percentage allowed (.388)
- 7th in fewest home runs allowed per nine innings (.91) and most pitches thrown per batter (3.91)
- 8th in games started and lowest batting average allowed (.244)
- Led the Angels in innings pitched, walks allowed, strikeouts, pitches thrown (3,431), pickoff throws (150) and stolen bases allowed (24)

Troy Glaus

Position: DH/3B
Bats: R **Throws:** R
Ht: 6' 5" **Wt:** 240

Opening Day Age: 28
Born: 8/3/76 in Tarzana, CA
ML Seasons: 7
Pronunciation: gloss

2004 Season

Things started so promisingly for Troy Glaus, as winter laser eye surgery was letting him see the ball better than ever in spring training. But a decision to forego another surgery, to his right shoulder, came back and punished Glaus and the Angels. He re-injured his shoulder in May against the Yankees on a swing and wound up missing nearly four months. Still, he came back and proved he's one of the elite young sluggers, mashing seven home runs in September to help the Angels reach the playoffs.

Hitting

As long as he's healthy, Glaus should be able to hit 30 home runs a year without much effort. He has the potential to hit 50 or more, having smashed 47 to lead the league in 2000. The key, as always, is staying healthy. He insists on playing third base and that could lead to further injuries down the road, as his 245 pounds diving for balls can tend to strain tendons, ligaments and muscles. The other issue is the long slumps he can stumble into, typically around early June.

Baserunning & Defense

Glaus makes the routine plays and he once had a strong throwing arm. However, there is a serious question mark about his throwing after he spent the winter rehabilitating from shoulder surgery. His range seems to decrease year by year, making him just an average third baseman. He is surprisingly nimble around the bases for such a large man, though he never will be a basestealer.

2005 Outlook

The Angels decided it was too risky a bet to give Glaus a long-term contract after shoulder surgery, so they decided to go with promising rookie Dallas McPherson for the league minimum. In December, Glaus signed a four-year, $45 million deal to play third base for the Arizona Diamondbacks. While his slipping defense and a tendency to get hurt are concerns, he will continue to put up big power numbers based in a hitter-friendly ballpark.

Overall Statistics

	G	AB	R	H	D	T	HR	RBI	SB	BB	SO	Avg	OBP	Slg
'04	58	207	47	52	11	1	18	42	2	31	52	.251	.355	.575
Car.	827	2962	523	748	165	7	182	515	49	470	784	.253	.357	.497

Where He Hits the Ball

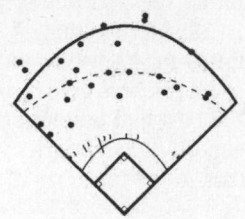
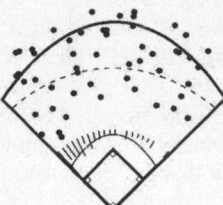

Vs. LHP   **Vs. RHP**

2004 Situational Stats

	AB	H	HR	RBI	Avg		AB	H	HR	RBI	Avg
Home	83	24	9	21	.289	LHP	62	15	5	15	.242
Road	124	28	9	21	.226	RHP	145	37	13	27	.255
First Half	108	32	11	28	.296	Sc Pos	58	17	5	24	.293
Scnd Half	99	20	7	14	.202	Clutch	22	5	2	4	.227

2004 Rankings (American League)

- Did not rank near the top or bottom in any category

Vladimir Guerrero

2004 Season

Vladimir Guerrero smashed all sorts of Angels records in his first season with the club, including runs scored, batting average for a righthanded hitter and total bases. And he did it when it counted, batting .536 with six home runs and 11 RBI in the final seven games as the Angels wiped out a three-game deficit to win the division. In other words, it was an MVP season in Guerrero's first year in the American League, and he joined Don Baylor (1979) as the only other Angel to win the award.

Hitting

In his eighth full season, Guerrero has made it clear he isn't going to change his approach. He swings at nearly every pitch he sees, particularly the first one in an at-bat. Considering that, it's amazing he walks 50-80 times in a season most years. That's how much respect pitchers give him. He continues to be one of the best bad-ball hitters in baseball, so pitching around him can be tricky. He doesn't need to see strikes to get hits.

Baserunning & Defense

Nobody mixes the spectacular with the spectacularly bad as well as Guerrero. He can throw runners out at third base flat-footed from the warning track as easily as he can drop flyballs or overthrow cutoff men. His mistakes usually are errors of aggression, especially when he tries to throw out runners he has no chance of getting. He also makes shockingly bad decisions on the bases from time-to-time, but he never lacks for effort.

2005 Outlook

Guerrero has proven to be one of the game's great offensive machines, and the Angels need him to keep it up. He and Jose Guillen were the only consistent power sources in the lineup, and Guillen is gone. Guerrero's back held up fine, but he had a nagging knee problem that limited him at times. If he keeps up the pace for a couple of more years, he's a lock for the Hall of Fame.

Position: RF/DH
Bats: R **Throws:** R
Ht: 6' 3" **Wt:** 220

Opening Day Age: 29
Born: 2/9/76 in Nizao Bani, DR
ML Seasons: 9
Pronunciation: guh-RAR-oh

Overall Statistics

	G	AB	R	H	D	T	HR	RBI	SB	BB	SO	Avg	OBP	Slg
'04	156	612	124	206	39	2	39	126	15	52	74	.337	.391	.598
Car.	1160	4375	765	1421	265	36	273	828	138	433	558	.325	.390	.589

Where He Hits the Ball

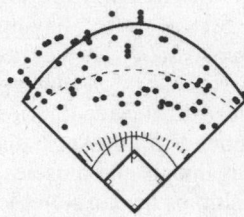
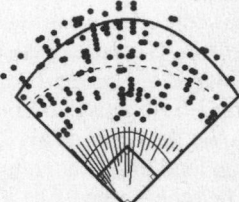

Vs. LHP   **Vs. RHP**

2004 Situational Stats

	AB	H	HR	RBI	Avg		AB	H	HR	RBI	Avg
Home	302	102	19	72	.338	LHP	155	53	15	32	.342
Road	310	104	20	54	.335	RHP	457	153	24	94	.335
First Half	345	119	20	77	.345	Sc Pos	169	53	9	85	.314
Scnd Half	267	87	19	49	.326	Clutch	73	24	1	11	.329

2004 Rankings (American League)

- 1st in runs scored, total bases (366), fewest pitches seen per plate appearance (3.17), lowest percentage of pitches taken (41.3) and highest percentage of swings on the first pitch (54.0)
- 2nd in batting average on the road, errors in right field (9) and lowest fielding percentage in right field (.973)
- 3rd in batting average, hits and slugging percentage
- 4th in home runs, RBI, sacrifice flies (8), intentional walks (14) and times on base (266)
- Led the Angels in at-bats, runs scored, hits, doubles, RBI, walks, intentional walks (14), GDPs (19), slugging percentage, on-base percentage, and HR frequency
- Led AL right fielders in home runs and RBI

Jose Guillen

2004 Season

When Jose Guillen isn't turning a clubhouse into a soap opera, he is one of the more talented righthanded hitters around. Guillen followed a 31-homer showing in 2003 by bashing 27 longballs last year while driving in more than 100 runs for the first time in his career. However, a tirade on the field and later in the clubhouse after being pulled for a pinch-runner led to him being suspended for the final eight games of the season and the playoffs.

Hitting

Guillen is from the Vladimir Guerrero mold. If he can see the ball, he probably will swing at it. However, he made some strides away from his reputation as a wild hacker and managed to walk 37 times. He also struck out 92 times. When he is seeing the ball well, he has outstanding power to center and right field, as well as one of the quicker bats in the game. His good hands and his strength allow him to see the ball a long time before swinging.

Baserunning & Defense

Guillen was about 15 pounds overweight all season and it showed in his baserunning and defense. The move that caused him to be suspended—being lifted for a pinch-runner—came about because he has only average speed as a runner these days. He was slowed in part because of injuries caused by having been hit by pitches 15 times. He has one of the best outfield arms in baseball, and putting him in left was almost unfair.

2005 Outlook

The Angels were intent on trading Guillen by spring training because of the animosity between him and manager Mike Scioscia. They were able to swing a deal in mid-November with the Washington Nationals, sending Guillen to D.C. in exchange for Juan Rivera and Maicer Izturis. The move could be good for all involved, as the Angels get a pair of talented up-and-comers while Guillen gets a chance at a fresh start on a team that is making a fresh start of its own.

Position: LF/DH
Bats: R **Throws:** R
Ht: 5'11" **Wt:** 190

Opening Day Age: 28
Born: 5/17/76 in San Cristobal, DR
ML Seasons: 8
Pronunciation: GHEE-yen

Anaheim

Overall Statistics

	G	AB	R	H	D	T	HR	RBI	SB	BB	SO	Avg	OBP	Slg
'04	148	565	88	166	28	3	27	104	5	37	92	.294	.352	.497
Car.	898	3100	404	850	158	17	110	458	20	157	566	.274	.322	.443

Where He Hits the Ball

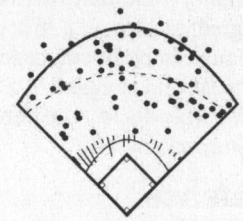
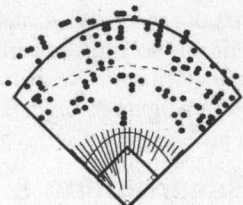

Vs. LHP	**Vs. RHP**

2004 Situational Stats

	AB	H	HR	RBI	Avg		AB	H	HR	RBI	Avg
Home	292	92	13	51	.315	LHP	144	43	7	31	.299
Road	273	74	14	53	.271	RHP	421	123	20	73	.292
First Half	322	97	15	65	.301	Sc Pos	150	49	6	74	.327
Scnd Half	243	69	12	39	.284	Clutch	71	21	4	15	.296

2004 Rankings (American League)

- 3rd in hit by pitch (15) and lowest fielding percentage in left field (.979)
- 4th in errors in left field (6)
- 5th in fewest pitches seen per plate appearance (3.47)
- Led the Angels in hit by pitch (15), batting average with runners in scoring position and cleanup slugging percentage (.589)

Adam Kennedy

2004 Season

What began as a frustrating season grew even more aggravating when Adam Kennedy tore knee ligaments two weeks before the start of the play-offs. He had just begun finding his batting stroke, too, having hit .333 in August and .328 in September. Kennedy was trying to field an Ichiro Suzuki grounder to his right on September 20 when his right leg slid and he tore his ACL and MCL. He had surgery in mid-October and was expected to be out for 6-10 months.

Hitting

Kennedy's unusual upper-cut stroke tends to drive some purists crazy, but he's sticking with it after a few good seasons in the majors. He tends to be streaky, but he has made great strides as a hitter. For one torrid week in August, nobody could get Kennedy out. He batted .619 and slugged .952 from August 23-29. His 92 strikeouts last year are a problem for a guy with limited power.

Baserunning & Defense

The Angels were unhappy Kennedy didn't win his first Gold Glove, and argued that he certainly deserved it more than Bret Boone. As fatigue overtook Kennedy near the end of the season, he made four errors in his last 20 games after going the previous 54 games without a miscue. His range is exceptional and he gets the shortstop the ball where he can handle it for double plays. Kennedy isn't overly fast, but he makes good decisions on the bases.

2005 Outlook

It's doubtful Kennedy will be back before June, at the earliest, while he rehabs from his October surgery. That will leave a big hole in the Angels' infield and a smaller hole in their lineup. With Kennedy out, David Eckstein might be forced to shift to second base, and Anaheim brass will be talking to many of the free-agent shortstops, including Orlando Cabrera.

Position: 2B
Bats: L **Throws:** R
Ht: 6' 1" **Wt:** 185

Opening Day Age: 29
Born: 1/10/76 in Riverside, CA
ML Seasons: 6

Overall Statistics

	G	AB	R	H	D	T	HR	RBI	SB	BB	SO	Avg	OBP	Slg
'04	144	468	70	130	20	5	10	48	15	41	92	.278	.351	.406
Car.	757	2569	348	713	137	27	46	277	88	163	397	.278	.329	.406

Where He Hits the Ball

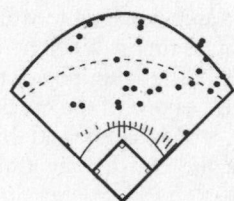
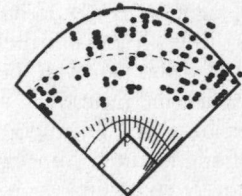

Vs. LHP   **Vs. RHP**

2004 Situational Stats

	AB	H	HR	RBI	Avg		AB	H	HR	RBI	Avg
Home	223	54	5	20	.242	LHP	108	27	2	11	.250
Road	245	76	5	28	.310	RHP	360	103	8	37	.286
First Half	280	74	5	31	.264	Sc Pos	119	23	3	37	.193
Scnd Half	188	56	5	17	.298	Clutch	63	11	1	6	.175

2004 Rankings (American League)

- 3rd in lowest batting average with runners in scoring position
- 4th in errors at second base (12)
- 5th in lowest fielding percentage at second base (.982)
- 6th in hit by pitch (13)
- Led the Angels in most pitches seen per plate appearance (3.96)

John Lackey

2004 Season

After John Lackey won Game 7 of the 2002 World Series, he appeared to be a young star on the rise. Now, he looks like the epitome of a mediocre starter. Lackey followed a 16-loss season in 2003 with another ho-hum effort. He showed flashes of dominance, including a three-hit shutout of Tampa Bay on May 7. But Lackey allows a lot of hits, and he struggled badly on the road. He hasn't exactly shown the consistency the Angels would like to see from their first pick in the 1999 draft.

Pitching

Lackey seems to do best on the biggest stages, but he has a tendency to let his concentration ebb for long stretches of the season. He had an ERA of better than 5.00 in three of the five months last season, meaning he has yet to blossom into more than the team's No. 4 starter. He went to his developing changeup more last year and, at times, he showed promise combining that with a good curveball against young, aggressive teams. However, he left too many fastballs in hittable places, and the results often weren't pretty.

Defense

Lackey is a good athlete who played first base in high school and college, and he fields his position well. His pickoff move is only so-so, however, and basestealers have a tendency to exploit his fairly slow delivery. Opposing thieves succeed at a 2-1 margin against him.

2005 Outlook

If the Angels get strong performances from the lead men in their rotation, Lackey can be a good complementary player. In his fourth season, it's pretty clear he likely won't be a No. 1 starter. He doesn't have overpowering velocity or a great strikeout pitch, so he relies on his fielders. On the other hand, he can be counted on for around 200 innings per year, and he doesn't back down from hitters. His rotation spot is secure, but the Angels would love to see him take some strides.

Position: SP
Bats: R **Throws:** R
Ht: 6' 6" **Wt:** 235

Opening Day Age: 26
Born: 10/23/78 in Abilene, TX
ML Seasons: 3

Anaheim

Overall Statistics

	W	L	Pct.	ERA	G	GS	Sv	IP	H	BB	SO	HR	Avg
'04	14	13	.519	4.67	33	32	0	198.1	215	60	144	22	.278
Car.	33	33	.500	4.44	84	83	0	510.2	551	159	364	63	.276

2004 Pitching Profile

	John Lackey	AL Average
Overall Strike %	62.9	62.3
1st Pitch Strike %	64.3	58.1
Ratio	1.39	1.42
Strikeouts per 9 IP	6.53	6.45
Walks per 9 IP	2.72	3.34
Home Runs per 9 IP	1.00	1.15
Strikeout/Walk Ratio	2.40	1.93
Groundball/Flyball Ratio	1.11	1.17

2004 Situational Stats

	W	L	ERA	Sv	IP		AB	H	HR	RBI	Avg
Home	7	5	3.48	0	93.0	LHB	419	127	13	50	.303
Road	7	8	5.72	0	105.1	RHB	355	88	9	45	.248
First Half	7	8	4.76	0	107.2	Sc Pos	163	57	7	76	.350
Scnd Half	7	5	4.57	0	90.2	Clutch	52	6	0	1	.115

2004 Rankings (American League)

- 1st in fielding percentage at pitcher (1.000)
- 2nd in highest batting average allowed with runners in scoring position
- 5th in highest ERA on the road
- 6th in losses, wild pitches (11) and least run support per nine innings (4.4)
- 8th in wins
- Led the Angels in losses, hits allowed and hit batsmen (8)

2004 Season

Each season that goes by, it becomes harder and harder for one of the most consistent closers of all time to do his job. But each year, Troy Percival finds a way. After dealing with a degenerative hip condition in 2003, he had inflammation in his right elbow last year that kept him out for most of June. But after struggling in May and June, Percival returned with a vengeance. He converted 21 of his final 22 save chances while picking up his 300th save along the way. Percival is one of only five pitchers to reach 300 saves with one team.

Pitching

Percival has learned to rely on guile as much as pure talent. Still, he consistently works in the 92-94 MPH range, and his occasional changeup helps complement the fastball and curveball. He never has worked as tidily as Mariano Rivera, but his career numbers stack up pretty favorably to the Yankees' future Hall of Famer. One worrisome trend for Percival is that he struck out only 33 batters last year, less than one-third the number Francisco Rodriguez did and a sharp decline over his 2003 numbers.

Defense

Percival's leg kick makes it easy to run on him, but few closers hold runners on well. Although he is a converted catcher, he is not particularly graceful fielding his position. In the past, opponents have hit him so rarely, none of that has mattered. Now that they are finally hitting him at about a .230 rate, his fielding and ability to hold runners might become more of an issue.

2005 Outlook

Just as Percival once took over for an aging Lee Smith, he now yields to Francisco Rodriguez. The Angels announced in early November that they would not be offering Percival a contract extension after 10 seasons in Anaheim. They felt Rodriguez was ready for the job, and that's probably a wise business move as well. Percival signed a two-year, $12 million deal to work the ninth inning for the Detroit Tigers.

Position: RP
Bats: R **Throws:** R
Ht: 6' 3" **Wt:** 235

Opening Day Age: 35
Born: 8/9/69 in Fontana, CA
ML Seasons: 10
Pronunciation: PURR-si-vul
Nickname: Percy

Overall Statistics

	W	L	Pct.	ERA	G	GS	Sv	IP	H	BB	SO	HR	Avg
'04	2	3	.400	2.90	52	0	33	49.2	43	19	33	7	.230
Car.	29	38	.433	2.99	579	0	316	586.2	393	253	680	63	.186

2004 Pitching Profile

	Troy Percival	AL Average
Overall Strike %	64.6	62.3
1st Pitch Strike %	55.5	58.1
Ratio	1.25	1.42
Strikeouts per 9 IP	5.98	6.45
Walks per 9 IP	3.44	3.34
Home Runs per 9 IP	1.27	1.15
Strikeout/Walk Ratio	1.74	1.93
Groundball/Flyball Ratio	0.64	1.17

2004 Situational Stats

	W	L	ERA	Sv	IP		AB	H	HR	RBI	Avg
Home	1	2	2.81	18	25.2	LHB	101	22	5	13	.218
Road	1	1	3.00	15	24.0	RHB	86	21	2	10	.244
First Half	2	1	4.37	15	22.2	Sc Pos	47	13	2	18	.277
Scnd Half	0	2	1.67	18	27.0	Clutch	126	31	3	19	.246

2004 Rankings (American League)

- 4th in saves
- 5th in lowest save percentage (86.8)
- Led the Angels in saves, games finished (48), save percentage (86.8) and relief losses (3)

Jarrod Washburn

2004 Season

Jarrod Washburn threw the Angels' final pitch of the season, a slider on the outside part of the plate that David Ortiz hit over Fenway Park's Green Monster to end Anaheim's short playoff run. It was Washburn's first relief appearance in four years, but it was also emblematic of a so-so season for the veteran lefthander. Washburn had a serious injury to the cartilage in his ribcage and missed six weeks, then pitched inconsistently—going 1-3 in September. Washburn is a competitive guy who may have rushed back in order to help the Angels reach the playoffs.

Pitching

Washburn once relied on his fastball nearly 90 percent of the time, but he has learned to trust his so-so breaking ball and a changeup a little bit more. That helped keep hitters off-balance, but Washburn still needs to rely on location and decent velocity to get hitters out. He is a flyball pitcher, which seemed to hurt him at Angel Stadium. He isn't overly fond of the mound at home and had a 5.76 ERA there.

Defense

Washburn is a good athlete. He easily is the best hitter among Angels pitchers and fields his position better than any of the other starters. He also has one of the best pickoff moves in the game, meaning basestealers usually don't try to test him. Because Washburn doesn't have overwhelming stuff, he relies on his total game to get through an outing.

2005 Outlook

Each season that goes by, the Angels' only left-handed pitcher grows more expensive. He was arbitration-eligible again for the final time over the winter and reaches free agency following this season. All of which could induce Anaheim to trade Washburn, and interest in him should be high. He is among the most solid lefty starters in the league, and he still is relatively young. He doesn't turn 31 until August.

Position: SP
Bats: L **Throws:** L
Ht: 6' 1" **Wt:** 195

Opening Day Age: 30
Born: 8/13/74 in La Crosse, WI
ML Seasons: 7

Overall Statistics

	W	L	Pct.	ERA	G	GS	Sv	IP	H	BB	SO	HR	Avg
'04	11	8	.579	4.64	25	25	0	149.1	159	40	86	20	.269
Car.	67	49	.578	4.07	164	154	0	976.0	938	297	605	131	.252

2004 Pitching Profile

	Jarrod Washburn	AL Average
Overall Strike %	63.6	62.3
1st Pitch Strike %	62.2	58.1
Ratio	1.33	1.42
Strikeouts per 9 IP	5.18	6.45
Walks per 9 IP	2.41	3.34
Home Runs per 9 IP	1.21	1.15
Strikeout/Walk Ratio	2.15	1.93
Groundball/Flyball Ratio	0.96	1.17

2004 Situational Stats

	W	L	ERA	Sv	IP		AB	H	HR	RBI	Avg
Home	4	4	5.76	0	65.2	LHB	142	32	6	21	.225
Road	7	4	3.76	0	83.2	RHB	448	127	14	54	.283
First Half	9	4	4.62	0	101.1	Sc Pos	122	37	3	51	.303
Scnd Half	2	4	4.69	0	48.0	Clutch	19	8	0	3	.421

2004 Rankings (American League)

- 9th in lowest ERA on the road
- Led the Angels in GDPs induced (14), lowest ERA on the road, most run support per nine innings (7.1) and fewest walks per nine innings (2.4)

Jeff DaVanon

Position: CF/RF/LF/DH
Bats: B **Throws:** R
Ht: 6' 0" **Wt:** 200

Opening Day Age: 31
Born: 12/8/73 in San Diego, CA
ML Seasons: 5
Pronunciation: duh-VAN-un

Overall Statistics

	G	AB	R	H	D	T	HR	RBI	SB	BB	SO	Avg	OBP	Slg
'04	108	285	41	79	11	4	7	34	18	46	54	.277	.372	.418
Car.	294	753	111	198	32	7	26	94	37	103	155	.263	.348	.428

2004 Situational Stats

	AB	H	HR	RBI	Avg		AB	H	HR	RBI	Avg
Home	154	42	4	16	.273	LHP	22	3	0	0	.136
Road	131	37	3	18	.282	RHP	263	76	7	34	.289
First Half	168	50	4	22	.298	Sc Pos	83	21	2	29	.253
Scnd Half	117	29	3	12	.248	Clutch	56	13	0	4	.232

2004 Season

The Angels were at their best when Jeff DaVanon wasn't playing. That's no knock on DaVanon, as he's one of the more useful utility outfielders in the league. But when he was playing every day, that meant Garret Anderson, Vladimir Guerrero or Jose Guillen wasn't. That said, he was a solid replacement for short stretches.

Hitting, Baserunning & Defense

DaVanon can be streaky, which isn't always a good thing for a role player, and he might want to consider giving up righthanded hitting. He hit all-seven of his home runs from the left side. He takes awkward routes to flyballs and, every once in a while, drops one. But he generally is a serviceable outfielder and one of the fastest, shrewdest bases-tealers on the team.

2005 Outlook

DaVanon no longer harbors hopes of being an everyday player, and that might help his career as he focuses on preparing himself to be a quality role player. He has missed time in two of the past three seasons with lower-back problems, so that bears watching. The Angels were forced to play DaVanon every day in the playoffs, but their line-up looks a lot more ferocious when he is listed under reserves.

Brendan Donnelly

Position: RP
Bats: R **Throws:** R
Ht: 6' 3" **Wt:** 240

Opening Day Age: 33
Born: 7/4/71 in Washington, DC
ML Seasons: 3

Overall Statistics

	W	L	Pct.	ERA	G	GS	Sv	IP	H	BB	SO	HR	Avg
'04	5	2	.714	3.00	40	0	0	42.0	34	15	56	5	.224
Car.	8	5	.615	2.12	149	0	4	165.2	121	58	189	9	.201

2004 Situational Stats

	W	L	ERA	Sv	IP		AB	H	HR	RBI	Avg
Home	2	0	2.75	0	19.2	LHB	76	16	2	7	.211
Road	3	2	3.22	0	22.1	RHB	76	18	3	12	.237
First Half	1	2	3.72	0	9.2	Sc Pos	34	12	1	15	.353
Scnd Half	4	0	2.78	0	32.1	Clutch	45	11	2	7	.244

2004 Season

Other than a broken nose and a car accident in spring training, followed by right elbow tendinitis, Brendan Donnelly had an easy year. Then again, nothing ever came easy for the 33-year-old. After missing the first 65 games because of the broken nose and repeated nosebleeds, Donnelly kept cementing himself as one of the game's best relievers upon his return.

Pitching & Defense

Donnelly could always throw the ball hard, but it took him 10 seasons bouncing around the minor leagues before he figured out that location is the key. He has good velocity, but it's the movement on his fastball, slider and split-finger pitch that makes him so effective. He lets his fielders handle the glove work, and he has yielded exactly two stolen bases in each of his three MLB seasons.

2005 Outlook

Donnelly was a great supporter of closer Troy Percival, but his return to the setup role was guaranteed by Percival's departure. If Francisco Rodriguez struggles, the Angels would likely give Donnelly first crack at closing. For the Angels' bullpen to be as effective as it was in '04, Donnelly will have to pitch as well as Rodriguez did in the eighth. That's hard to do.

Chone Figgins

Position: 3B/CF/2B/SS
Bats: B **Throws:** R
Ht: 5' 8" **Wt:** 160

Opening Day Age: 27
Born: 1/22/78 in Leary, GA
ML Seasons: 3
Pronunciation: shawn

Overall Statistics

	G	AB	R	H	D	T	HR	RBI	SB	BB	SO	Avg	OBP	Slg
'04	148	577	83	171	22	17	5	60	34	49	94	.296	.350	.419
Car.	234	829	123	244	32	21	5	88	49	69	137	.294	.346	.402

2004 Situational Stats

	AB	H	HR	RBI	Avg		AB	H	HR	RBI	Avg
Home	269	79	3	30	.294	LHP	169	53	1	18	.314
Road	308	92	2	30	.299	RHP	408	118	4	42	.289
First Half	296	91	2	28	.307	Sc Pos	148	46	1	51	.311
Scnd Half	281	80	3	32	.285	Clutch	80	25	0	11	.313

2004 Season

Chone Figgins looked so indecisive and unsure of himself in the playoffs, it nearly erased the memory of his strong emergence as an everyday player. But not quite. Manager Mike Scioscia said repeatedly that he considered Figgins one of his top three most valuable players, because he played so well and at so many positions.

Hitting, Baserunning & Defense

Figgins is one of the fastest players in baseball, but he doesn't bunt well enough to fully exploit it. Still, he turns routine doubles into routine triples. On any ball hit into a gap, he is likely to try for third. As fast as he is, he isn't an instinctual basestealer and he was caught 13 times in 2004. His best position is second, but playing every day tends to expose his defensive weaknesses.

2005 Outlook

The Angels' ideal scenario is to land a front-line everyday shortstop, switch David Eckstein to second while Adam Kennedy is out and leave Figgins in center field. Then again, injuries have tended to scramble their plans in the past. And that's why Figgins is such a luxury. If Figgins continues to improve, he could establish himself as one of the best speed guys in the game.

Kevin Gregg

Position: RP
Bats: R **Throws:** R
Ht: 6' 6" **Wt:** 220

Opening Day Age: 26
Born: 6/20/78 in Corvallis, OR
ML Seasons: 2

Overall Statistics

	W	L	Pct.	ERA	G	GS	Sv	IP	H	BB	SO	HR	Avg
'04	5	2	.714	4.21	55	0	1	87.2	86	28	84	6	.255
Car.	7	2	.778	4.01	60	3	1	112.1	104	36	98	9	.245

2004 Situational Stats

	W	L	ERA	Sv	IP		AB	H	HR	RBI	Avg
Home	4	1	4.23	0	44.2	LHB	173	45	2	20	.260
Road	1	1	4.19	1	43.0	RHB	164	41	4	25	.250
First Half	3	0	3.42	1	52.2	Sc Pos	103	23	0	37	.223
Scnd Half	2	2	5.40	0	35.0	Clutch	78	25	1	8	.321

2004 Season

Kevin Gregg's season started so promisingly, it looked like the Angels had another Brendan Donnelly on their hands. But after Gregg made his first Opening Day roster and posted a 1.39 ERA for April and May, he had a 5.86 ERA thereafter. Still, for a guy who had pitched in all of five games before the season, Gregg established himself as a major leaguer in 2004.

Pitching & Defense

Gregg has above-average velocity and a good split-finger pitch. But that is sometimes his dilemma, as he occasionally has no idea where the splitter is headed. His 13 wild pitches were second in the AL. And on July 25 in Seattle, he threw four wild pitches in one inning to tie a major league record. Last season was his first full year as a reliever, and he seemed to pitch worse as his appearances mounted by June.

2005 Outlook

With Troy Percival gone, everybody moves up a notch in the bullpen. That means Gregg will be relied on to pitch in similar spots Scot Shields did in 2004. Gregg isn't quite as durable as Shields, but if he can give the Angels another 87.2 innings of serviceable work, they'll be happy.

Bengie Molina

Position: C
Bats: R **Throws:** R
Ht: 5'11" **Wt:** 220

Opening Day Age: 30
Born: 7/20/74 in Rio Piedras, PR
ML Seasons: 7

Overall Statistics

	G	AB	R	H	D	T	HR	RBI	SB	BB	SO	Avg	OBP	Slg
'04	97	337	36	93	13	0	10	54	0	18	35	.276	.313	.404
Car.	597	2074	205	557	91	2	50	293	2	91	190	.269	.304	.387

2004 Situational Stats

	AB	H	HR	RBI	Avg		AB	H	HR	RBI	Avg
Home	172	47	5	27	.273	LHP	103	26	3	11	.252
Road	165	46	5	27	.279	RHP	234	67	7	43	.286
First Half	177	52	5	31	.294	Sc Pos	97	31	5	46	.320
Scnd Half	160	41	5	23	.256	Clutch	40	12	2	7	.300

2004 Season

Bengie Molina's string of two successive Gold Gloves was snapped by Pudge Rodriguez. Besides that, injuries and perhaps poor conditioning led to a slightly disappointing season. Though Molina's skills stayed sharp, a strained left calf and a broken right index finger cost him time on the DL.

Hitting, Baserunning & Defense

Molina is one of the better contact hitters in the AL. In part because of that, he is one of the Angels' best hitters with runners in scoring position. On the other hand, he probably is the slowest baserunner in the AL, and therefore one of the easiest double-play victims around. His defense, other than his lack of mobility, is practically flawless. However, his success rate against basestealers dropped sharply last year.

2005 Outlook

The Angels picked up their $3 million option on Molina in mid-November, but they will need him to report to camp in better condition than the year before. He had leg problems starting in spring training that some feel were caused by him reporting overweight. He can remain one of the best catchers and most underrated players in the league. Few catchers hit .280 every year while providing stalwart work behind the plate.

Ramon Ortiz

Position: RP/SP
Bats: R **Throws:** R
Ht: 6' 0" **Wt:** 175

Opening Day Age: 31
Born: 5/23/73 in Cotui, DR
ML Seasons: 6
Pronunciation: or-TEEZ

Overall Statistics

	W	L	Pct.	ERA	G	GS	Sv	IP	H	BB	SO	HR	Avg
'04	5	7	.417	4.43	34	14	0	128.0	139	38	82	18	.280
Car.	59	49	.546	4.60	157	137	0	893.2	905	325	590	136	.262

2004 Situational Stats

	W	L	ERA	Sv	IP		AB	H	HR	RBI	Avg
Home	2	2	4.32	0	66.2	LHB	259	79	15	39	.305
Road	3	5	4.55	0	61.1	RHB	237	60	3	22	.253
First Half	3	5	4.18	0	60.1	Sc Pos	131	34	3	38	.260
Scnd Half	2	2	4.66	0	67.2	Clutch	26	8	1	4	.308

2004 Season

Two years ago, Ramon Ortiz won 16 games. That just obscured what wasn't a very good year, and his downhill trend continued in 2004. Ortiz won the fifth-starter job in spring training, but lost it after April. After that, Ortiz was relegated to the bullpen, where he wasn't very happy. Ortiz grumbled, demanding a trade at several points, but was actually fairly solid as a reliever.

Pitching & Defense

Although Ortiz has good stuff, he continues to struggle to consistently get major league hitters out. Some scouts feel it's because he throws a relatively straight fastball, which generally is in the low to mid-90s. He is only 6-feet tall, so he has trouble getting downward tilt on his pitches. His slider can be very good, but it can also be mediocre. He is erratic with the glove, but he did manage three pickoffs last year.

2005 Outlook

The Angels declined Ortiz' $5 million option for 2005, making him a free agent. It appears his future will lie elsewhere, because the Angels have plans to upgrade their rotation and won't need Ortiz as a long reliever either. There's no reason he can't rebound and be a solid starter on another team.

Robb Quinlan

Position: 3B/1B
Bats: R **Throws:** R
Ht: 6' 1" **Wt:** 200

Opening Day Age: 28
Born: 3/17/77 in St. Paul, MN
ML Seasons: 2

Overall Statistics

	G	AB	R	H	D	T	HR	RBI	SB	BB	SO	Avg	OBP	Slg
'04	56	160	23	55	14	0	5	23	3	14	26	.344	.401	.525
Car.	94	254	36	82	18	2	5	27	4	20	42	.323	.375	.469

2004 Situational Stats

	AB	H	HR	RBI	Avg		AB	H	HR	RBI	Avg
Home	79	29	3	12	.367	LHP	59	23	3	7	.390
Road	81	26	2	11	.321	RHP	101	32	2	16	.317
First Half	68	17	0	5	.250	Sc Pos	38	14	1	18	.368
Scnd Half	92	38	5	18	.413	Clutch	26	11	0	1	.423

2004 Season

Quietly, one of the more meaningful injuries to the Angels happened when Robb Quinlan tore an oblique muscle taking early batting practice on August 17. At that point of the season, he had been carrying the Angels. Filling in for injured Troy Glaus, Quinlan had batted .442 during a 21-game hitting streak from July 7 to August 10.

Hitting, Baserunning & Defense

Quinlan sacrifices home-run power to make contact. He has only once hit as many as 20 home runs in a season, but he is also a lifetime .323 hitter. He is not fast, but he runs the bases well enough at least to fit into the Angels' aggressive style. He plays a surprisingly serviceable third base when pressed into service, having spent his entire career as a first baseman and occasional left fielder.

2005 Outlook

As well as Quinlan played in 2004, the Angels likely won't consider him for an everyday job. That's because they have young slugger Dallas McPherson ready to break out at third and Darin Erstad planted firmly at first. Still, Quinlan and Jeff DaVanon will be Anaheim's two most-used bench players. Quinlan likely will be satisfied just to spend a full season in the majors for the first time in his career.

Francisco Rodriguez (Unhittable

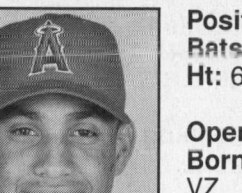

Position: RP
Bats: R **Throws:** R
Ht: 6' 0" **Wt:** 185

Opening Day Age: 23
Born: 1/7/82 in Caracas, VZ
ML Seasons: 3

Overall Statistics

	W	L	Pct.	ERA	G	GS	Sv	IP	H	BB	SO	HR	Avg
'04	4	1	.800	1.82	69	0	12	84.0	51	33	123	2	.172
Car.	12	4	.750	2.36	133	0	14	175.2	104	70	231	14	.172

2004 Situational Stats

	W	L	ERA	Sv	IP		AB	H	HR	RBI	Avg
Home	3	1	1.93	5	42.0	LHB	155	33	1	12	.213
Road	1	0	1.71	7	42.0	RHB	142	18	1	12	.127
First Half	1	1	1.34	7	47.0	Sc Pos	83	15	1	23	.181
Scnd Half	3	0	2.43	5	37.0	Clutch	217	32	1	21	.147

2004 Season

Francisco Rodriguez already has proven he is one of the most intimidating pitchers in the AL. For most of 2004, he simply was impossible to hit. He skipped the early struggles of 2003 and went right to dominating. He also proved he can pitch the ninth inning, filling in for a month for Troy Percival, and made his first All-Star team.

Pitching & Defense

Some people grumble that Rodriguez relies too heavily on his slider, but he made great strides in 2004 throwing it for a strike. A hitter has the choice of guessing whether he'll see the slider—Rodriguez has two types—or the fastball. Angels manager Mike Scioscia would like to see Rodriguez work on pitching more efficiently, which means concentrating less on the strikeout. Rodriguez is so amped up on the mound, he sometimes looks silly fielding his position.

2005 Outlook

The Angels will now hand the ball to this 23-year-old in the ninth inning after Troy Percival had taken it for nine straight seasons. The pressure will be great, but nothing in Rodriguez' cocky personality suggests he'll be overwhelmed by it. It's likely he will have some bumpy innings, but he has the stuff to get out of anything he creates.

Aaron Sele

Position: SP
Bats: R **Throws:** R
Ht: 6' 5" **Wt:** 230

Opening Day Age: 34
Born: 6/25/70 in Golden Valley, MN
ML Seasons: 12
Pronunciation: SEE-lee

Overall Statistics

	W	L	Pct.	ERA	G	GS	Sv	IP	H	BB	SO	HR	Avg
'04	9	4	.692	5.05	28	24	0	132.0	163	51	51	16	.310
Car.	131	92	.587	4.52	321	316	0	1880.0	2068	706	1268	191	.280

2004 Situational Stats

	W	L	ERA	Sv	IP		AB	H	HR	RBI	Avg
Home	4	3	5.27	0	70.0	LHB	267	79	6	32	.296
Road	5	1	4.79	0	62.0	RHB	259	84	10	47	.324
First Half	5	0	4.27	0	71.2	Sc Pos	123	40	4	57	.325
Scnd Half	4	4	5.97	0	60.1	Clutch	2	2	0	0	1.000

2004 Season

Few statistics are more misleading than Aaron Sele's 9-4 record, as the Angels had astonishingly little confidence in the 11-year veteran. Sele started 24 games and only twice was able to get through seven innings. When the pennant race heated up, manager Mike Scioscia was simply hoping to get a lead in the first six innings, then yank Sele in favor of the bullpen.

Pitching & Defense

Sele is a professional pitcher and the one thing he offers is the knowledge of how to win games. Somehow, some way, he often finds a way to navigate through a lineup even though his curveball is far less effective than it once was and his fastball barely sneaks into the high 80s. He does an excellent job of controlling the running game, but he will commit the occasional miscue in the field.

2005 Outlook

Despite an injury-riddled tenure with the Angels, Sele is likely to catch on somewhere because of his track record. He isn't likely to start for a contender, but he'll get a chance with a team in need of pitching help. The shoulder surgery he had in October 2002 appears to have sapped his right arm of whatever it had left.

Scot Shields

Position: RP
Bats: R **Throws:** R
Ht: 6' 1" **Wt:** 170

Opening Day Age: 29
Born: 7/22/75 in Fort Lauderdale, FL
ML Seasons: 4

Overall Statistics

	W	L	Pct.	ERA	G	GS	Sv	IP	H	BB	SO	HR	Avg
'04	8	2	.800	3.33	60	0	4	105.1	97	40	109	6	.238
Car.	18	11	.621	2.81	141	14	5	313.2	274	106	257	22	.234

2004 Situational Stats

	W	L	ERA	Sv	IP		AB	H	HR	RBI	Avg
Home	4	1	2.93	2	55.1	LHB	200	47	1	19	.235
Road	4	1	3.78	2	50.0	RHB	207	50	5	25	.242
First Half	5	2	3.07	3	58.2	Sc Pos	95	23	3	37	.242
Scnd Half	3	0	3.66	1	46.2	Clutch	152	29	2	13	.191

2004 Season

Considering the Angels had four starters win at least 10 games and Francisco Rodriguez was all but unhittable, it might seem odd that manager Mike Scioscia called Scot Shields his pitching MVP. But that's how valuable the versatile righthander was. Shields provided solid relief work in the middle innings and saved four games.

Pitching & Defense

Shields throws hard, has a good slider and occasionally mixes in a changeup and curveball. His stuff is good enough that he registered 109 strikeouts and allowed just 97 hits in 105.1 innings. For the first time in three seasons, Shields did not get a spot start—largely because he was too valuable in the bullpen. He fields his position with aplomb and holds runners far better than most relievers.

2005 Outlook

Shields has established himself as a must-have commodity. He and Brendan Donnelly will have jobs getting the ball to Rodriguez. That could mean Shields isn't as available to pitch three-inning stints, as he often did in 2004. Other Anaheim relievers call Shields the "Human Rubber Band" because of his arm's ability to bounce back from long appearances and working on back-to-back days.

Alfredo Amezaga (**Pos**: SS/2B/3B, **Age**: 27, **Bats**: B)

	G	AB	R	H	D	T	HR	RBI	SB	BB	SO	Avg	OBP	Slg
'04	73	93	12	15	2	0	2	11	3	3	24	.161	.212	.247
Car.	122	211	30	44	7	2	4	20	6	12	48	.209	.264	.318

Amezaga batted .347 at Triple-A Salt Lake in 2003. But the dependable defender looks less like a prospect and more like a bench player. 2005 Outlook: C

Dusty Bergman (**Pos**: LHP, **Age**: 27)

	W	L	Pct.	ERA	G	GS	Sv	IP	H	BB	SO	HR	Avg
'04	0	0	—	13.50	1	0	0	2.0	4	1	1	0	.444
Car.	0	0	—	13.50	1	0	0	2.0	4	1	1	0	.444

The southpaw enjoyed his best Triple-A season in 2004. It led to his big league debut in June, but being the only lefty in the Anaheim pen wasn't enough to keep him around. 2005 Outlook: C

Scott Dunn (**Pos**: RHP, **Age**: 26)

	W	L	Pct.	ERA	G	GS	Sv	IP	H	BB	SO	HR	Avg
'04	0	0	—	9.00	3	0	0	3.0	7	1	2	0	.438
Car.	0	0	—	9.00	3	0	0	3.0	7	1	2	0	.438

Dunn hasn't been able to ditch his high walk rate. He won 10 games with a 3.21 ERA as a swingman at Triple-A Salt Lake, but allowed 56 walks in 89.2 innings before a September callup. 2005 Outlook: C

Andres Galarraga (**Pos**: DH, **Age**: 43, **Bats**: R)

	G	AB	R	H	D	T	HR	RBI	SB	BB	SO	Avg	OBP	Slg
	7	10	1	3	0	0	1	2	0	0	3	.300	.364	.600
	2257	8096	1195	2333	444	32	399	1425	128	583	2003	.288	.347	.499

Galarraga signed with Anaheim in August and surfaced in September, in pursuit of his 400th career home run at age 43. He fell one short. 2005 Outlook: C

Shane Halter (**Pos**: 3B, **Age**: 35, **Bats**: R)

	G	AB	R	H	D	T	HR	RBI	SB	BB	SO	Avg	OBP	Slg
'04	46	114	10	23	5	0	4	13	1	7	30	.202	.248	.351
Car.	690	1899	201	468	93	18	45	197	17	146	414	.246	.303	.385

Halter enjoyed a solid 2001 season as a regular with Detroit, but his playing time and hitting percentages have been on a steady decline. 2005 Outlook: C

Matt Hensley (**Pos**: RHP, **Age**: 26)

	W	L	Pct.	ERA	G	GS	Sv	IP	H	BB	SO	HR	Avg
'04	0	2	.000	4.88	16	0	0	27.2	32	7	30	5	.294
Car.	0	2	.000	4.88	16	0	0	27.2	32	7	30	5	.294

Hensley moved from the rotation to the pen for his third season at Triple-A Salt Lake. An excellent Triple-A stint led to a lengthy big league audition. 2005 Outlook: B

Jose Molina (**Pos**: C, **Age**: 29, **Bats**: R)

	G	AB	R	H	D	T	HR	RBI	SB	BB	SO	Avg	OBP	Slg
'04	73	203	26	53	10	2	3	25	4	10	52	.261	.296	.374
Car.	180	443	54	108	21	2	5	41	4	21	105	.244	.281	.334

Molina serves as Anaheim's backup catcher behind older brother Bengie, but he's not the youngest catching Molina anymore. Not since younger brother Yadier has come on the scene. 2005 Outlook: B

Raul Mondesi (**Pos**: LF/RF, **Age**: 34, **Bats**: R)

	G	AB	R	H	D	T	HR	RBI	SB	BB	SO	Avg	OBP	Slg
	34	133	10	32	9	0	3	15	0	13	31	.241	.313	.376
	1484	5672	892	1559	312	48	267	843	229	463	1095	.275	.332	.488

Mondesi left the Pirates in May to address a personal issue in the Dominican Republic. He signed with Anaheim, injured a quad and was released when he missed a rehab appointment in July. 2005 Outlook: C

Josh Paul (**Pos**: C, **Age**: 29, **Bats**: R)

	G	AB	R	H	D	T	HR	RBI	SB	BB	SO	Avg	OBP	Slg
'04	46	70	11	17	3	0	2	10	2	7	17	.243	.308	.371
Car.	194	425	65	109	22	2	6	52	11	37	91	.256	.316	.360

Paul spent all of 2004 in the bigs. Neither backup, Paul nor Jose Molina, generated an OPS that was within 100 points of Barry Bonds' slugging mark. 2005 Outlook: C

Curtis Pride (**Pos**: LF, **Age**: 36, **Bats**: L)

	G	AB	R	H	D	T	HR	RBI	SB	BB	SO	Avg	OBP	Slg
'04	35	40	5	10	3	0	0	3	1	0	11	.250	.268	.325
Car.	388	758	124	192	36	12	19	80	29	79	199	.253	.329	.408

Pride, an inspiration for reaching the majors despite being deaf, surfaced with his fourth big league team in five seasons. He signed a new minor league deal with the Angels in November. 2005 Outlook: C

Adam Riggs (**Pos**: LF, **Age**: 32, **Bats**: R)

	G	AB	R	H	D	T	HR	RBI	SB	BB	SO	Avg	OBP	Slg
'04	16	36	2	7	3	0	0	3	1	1	10	.194	.216	.278
Car.	61	153	18	33	9	1	3	10	6	16	30	.216	.290	.346

Riggs managed just three extra-base hits in 16 games with the Angels. An opportunity slipped away, and the Angels released him in October. He signed to play in Japan in 2005. 2005 Outlook: D

Tim Salmon (**Pos**: DH, **Age**: 36, **Bats**: R)

	G	AB	R	H	D	T	HR	RBI	SB	BB	SO	Avg	OBP	Slg
	60	186	15	47	7	0	2	23	1	14	41	.253	.306	.323
	1596	5723	956	1618	331	22	290	989	48	941	1316	.283	.386	.500

A productive career may be over for Salmon, who faced surgery on his left knee and left shoulder. Rehab will keep him out for all of 2005. 2005 Outlook: D

Derrick Turnbow (**Pos**: RHP, **Age**: 27)

	W	L	Pct.	ERA	G	GS	Sv	IP	H	BB	SO	HR	Avg
'04	0	0	—	0.00	4	0	0	6.1	2	7	3	0	.105
Car.	2	0	1.000	3.17	39	1	0	59.2	45	46	43	7	.213

The hard-thrower worked four scoreless outings for the Angels in 2004 before Milwaukee claimed him off waivers in October. 2005 Outlook: C

Ben Weber (**Pos**: RHP, **Age**: 35)

	W	L	Pct.	ERA	G	GS	Sv	IP	H	BB	SO	HR	Avg
'04	0	2	.000	8.06	18	0	0	22.1	37	15	11	4	.363
Car.	19	8	.704	3.58	218	0	7	271.2	285	96	154	19	.272

After posting a 2.61 ERA and grabbing a championship ring in 2002 and 2003 with the Angels, Weber executed an improbable slide to oblivion. 2005 Outlook: C

Anaheim Angels Minor League Prospects

Organization Overview:

The Anaheim system has lacked depth and hasn't generated much impact talent over the last few years, but that is changing. Casey Kotchman, Dallas McPherson and Jeff Mathis could be anchoring the heart of the Angels' batting order soon, with the two corner infielders possibly securing starting jobs in the spring. Middle infielders Erick Aybar and Albert Callaspo were all-star teammates in 2002 and 2003, and they could settle into the Anaheim infield together in a couple of years. Injuries have been a curse to many an Anaheim pitching prospect in recent seasons, but there's hope in the development of Ervin Santana and Steve Shell. A host of others could emerge from an Angels system that is better stocked than it was a few short years ago.

Erick Aybar

Position: SS
Bats: B **Throws:** R
Ht: 5' 10" **Wt:** 165

Opening Day Age: 21
Born: 1/14/84 in Bani, DR

Recent Statistics

	G	AB	R	H	D	T	HR	RBI	SB	BB	SO	Avg
2003 A Cedar Rapds	125	496	83	153	30	10	6	57	32	17	54	.308
2004 A Rancho Cuca	136	573	102	189	25	11	14	65	51	26	66	.330

Following two impressive seasons as a pro, Aybar reached career highs in most offensive categories at high Class-A Rancho Cucamonga in 2004. The switch-hitting leadoff man led the California League in hits and stolen bases, though he was caught 36 times in 87 tries. While he has first-step quickness and speed, he must learn to read pitchers on the bases. Aybar was stronger in 2004 and showed more over-the-fence pop. He's a free swinger who neither walks nor strikes out much, so the Angels are not tampering with his aggressive approach. His range, arm strength and instincts make for a promising shortstop prospect. Among Anaheim's crop of young shortstops, Aybar has the most promise.

Alberto Callaspo

Position: SS
Bats: B **Throws:** R
Ht: 5' 10" **Wt:** 155

Opening Day Age: 21
Born: 4/19/83 in Maracay, VZ

Recent Statistics

	G	AB	R	H	D	T	HR	RBI	SB	BB	SO	Avg
2003 A Cedar Rapds	133	514	86	168	38	4	2	67	20	42	28	.327
2004 AA Arkansas	136	550	76	155	28	2	6	48	15	47	25	.282

Not only did Callaspo bypass high Class-A ball for Double-A Arkansas in 2004, he also shifted from second base to shortstop, as the Angels broke up their all-star middle-infield combo of Callaspo and Erick Aybar. Callaspo got the higher assignment because he was the more advanced hitter with a better understanding of the strike zone. Despite skipping a level, Callaspo ranked among Texas League leaders in hits and batted .282. His bat control is impressive, but he may need to show more patience against more advanced pitching. While Callaspo has the tools to handle shortstop, he could be moved back to second base. His size may be better suited for second, and perhaps he and Aybar are meant to play side by side in Anaheim's infield.

Maicer Izturis

Position: SS-2B
Bats: B **Throws:** R
Ht: 5' 8" **Wt:** 155

Opening Day Age: 24
Born: 9/12/80 in Barquisimeto, VZ

Recent Statistics

	G	AB	R	H	D	T	HR	RBI	SB	BB	SO	Avg
2004 AAA Edmonton	99	376	65	127	19	2	3	36	14	57	30	.338
2004 NL Montreal	32	107	10	22	5	2	1	4	4	10	20	.206

After six years in the Cleveland system, Izturis was dealt to Montreal before his breakout year at Triple-A Edmonton in 2004. In November, he was traded to Anaheim for veteran Jose Guillen. The younger brother of the Dodgers' Cesar Izturis shares the same excellent defensive qualities—a quick first step with excellent range in all directions, soft hands, a strong accurate arm and a quick release. Maicer is a good contact hitter with gap power from both sides of the plate. He also can bunt. Izturis handles fielding duties at second and short equally well and is unflappable on the pivot. More advanced pitchers busting him inside will give him trouble, but he could claim Anaheim's starting shortstop job this spring.

Casey Kotchman

Position: 1B
Bats: L **Throws:** L
Ht: 6' 3" **Wt:** 210

Opening Day Age: 22
Born: 2/22/83 in St. Petersburg, FL

Recent Statistics

	G	AB	R	H	D	T	HR	RBI	SB	BB	SO	Avg
2004 AA Arkansas	28	114	19	42	11	0	3	18	0	10	7	.368
2004 AAA Salt Lake	49	199	32	74	22	0	5	38	0	14	25	.372
2004 AL Anaheim	38	116	7	26	6	0	0	15	3	7	11	.224

Confirming his status as a premier prospect, Kotchman batted .370 and slugged .550 in the high minors in 2004. Called up in early May, he went 48 major league plate appearances before striking out, and he ripped it up for Salt Lake, after he was demoted in June to get his first taste of Triple-A pitching. His plate patience puts him in counts that allow him to drive baseballs to all fields, and his classic lefthanded stroke may generate more power as he matures. He's also advanced defensively and looks like Gold Glove material. His injury history is a concern. Wrist and shoulder strains, similar to those he has suffered in past years, sidelined him for most of July.

Jeff Mathis

Position: C   **Opening Day Age:** 22
Bats: R **Throws:** R   **Born:** 3/31/83 in
Ht: 6' 0" **Wt:** 180   Marianna, FL

Recent Statistics

	G	AB	R	H	D	T	HR	RBI	SB	BB	SO	Avg
2003 A Rancho Cuca	97	378	73	122	28	3	11	54	5	35	74	.323
2003 AA Arkansas	24	95	19	27	11	0	2	14	1	12	16	.284
2004 AA Arkansas	117	432	57	98	24	3	14	55	2	49	101	.227

During the first half of 2004, Mathis built on his promising three years as a pro, excelling with Casey Kotchman and Dallas McPherson in the Double-A Arkansas lineup. After his teammates were promoted to higher levels, Mathis didn't get much to hit and turned more pull-conscious, possibly trying to show more power with the other run producers gone. His hitting and defensive game went on a slide, perhaps equally affected by the Texas heat that seemed to wear him down. The tools are still there: good catch-and-throw skills, soft hands, impressive bat speed and the athleticism to excel in all aspects of the game.

Dallas McPherson

Position: 3B   **Opening Day Age:** 24
Bats: L **Throws:** R   **Born:** 7/23/80 in
Ht: 6' 4" **Wt:** 230   Greensboro, NC

Recent Statistics

	G	AB	R	H	D	T	HR	RBI	SB	BB	SO	Avg
2004 AA Arkansas	68	262	53	84	17	6	20	69	6	34	74	.321
2004 AAA Salt Lake	67	259	54	81	19	8	20	57	6	23	95	.313
2004 AL Anaheim	16	40	5	9	1	0	3	6	1	3	17	.225

Kotchman and McPherson could be key middle-of-the-order guys for years to come in Anaheim. In 2004, McPherson combined for 40 homers and 126 RBI at Double-A Arkansas and Triple-A Salt Lake. Calling on his raw power, he crushes fastballs, though he's still learning how to handle good breaking stuff. His swing now has more loft, leading to more tape-measure shots but also lots of strikeouts. Defensively, there have been questions about McPherson's footwork and a tendency to rush his throws at third base. Yet, while at Anaheim in September, he fielded and threw without hesitation, and he didn't commit an error in 31 chances. With free agent Troy Glaus leaving the Angels, McPherson is in line to claim the third-base job this spring.

Kendry Morales

Position: OF   **Opening Day Age:** 21
Bats: B **Throws:** R   **Born:** 6/20/83 in
Ht: 6' 1" **Wt:** 225   Fomento, Cuba

Recent Statistics

	G	AB	R	H	D	T	HR	RBI	SB	BB	SO	Avg
Has not played in minor leagues												

Morales is a switch-hitting outfielder who defected from Cuba last summer. Widely considered the most gifted Cuban to defect since the Cuban revolution in 1959, Morales shows power from both sides of the plate. Defensively, he's a solid corner outfielder with a good arm. He made a name for himself in 2002, as a star player for Cuba's national team. After Morales worked out in the Dominican Republic for big league clubs, the Angels signed him to a six-year deal in November. The Angels see a middle-of-the-order hitter who could make the club out of spring training. The only question is whether he will struggle with cultural adjustments. The success stories among Cuban defectors are few beyond Livan and Orlando Hernandez.

Ervin Santana

Position: P   **Opening Day Age:** 22
Bats: R **Throws:** R   **Born:** 1/10/83 in La
Ht: 6' 2" **Wt:** 150   Romana, DR

Recent Statistics

	W	L	ERA	G	GS	Sv	IP	H	R	BB	SO	HR
2003 A Rancho Cuca	10	2	2.53	20	20	0	124.2	98	44	36	130	9
2003 AA Arkansas	1	1	3.94	6	6	0	29.2	23	15	12	23	4
2004 AA Arkansas	2	1	3.30	8	8	0	43.2	41	19	18	48	3

Santana has generated more than a strikeout an inning in four pro seasons. He's called on a smooth, effortless motion that generates mid-90s heat and a tight slider. At least until shoulder stiffness sidelined him for the first six weeks of 2004. When he was ready, Santana was impressive and threw in the low 90s. But the righthander quickly developed elbow tendinitis and made only eight starts all season for Double-A Arkansas. The Angels were being cautious with their top pitching prospect, and by instructional league, Santana's offerings were showing their typical explosiveness, and he should be ready to go in the spring. A better changeup could spark a rapid rise by Santana.

Others to Watch

Righthanded-hitting outfielder **Nick Gorneault** (25) has an unorthodox swing that isn't pretty, but he has power potential and a knack for making hard contact. While he also misses and strikes out a lot, he enjoyed a .280-21-81 season at Double-A Arkansas in 2004. . . After missing 2003 with a torn rotator cuff and labrum that was rehabbed without surgery, southpaw **Joe Saunders** (23) returned, made 27 starts at two stops and reached Double-A Arkansas. He was 13-10 (4.04) while regaining his velocity during the season. He attacks hitters with a late-moving low-90s two-seamer, an improving curve and a changeup with good fade. . . Righthander **Steven Shell** (22) enjoyed a career year in his second go-round at high Class-A Rancho Cucamonga. En route to a 12-7 (3.59) season, he led the Cal League with 190 strikeouts. His command of a low-90s fastball and curve were exceptional. . . Lefty **Jake Woods** (23) works with a moving fastball and big-breaking curve. His changeup isn't as far along, but he went 9-2 (2.60) in 14 starts at Double-A Arkansas before a 6-4 (6.07) finish at Triple-A Salt Lake. He needs more time to learn how to take off or add on to his fastball.

Oriole Park at Camden Yards

Offense

In recent seasons, Oriole Park at Camden Yards has gone from a run-challenged ballpark to one that is now about average and has little effect on batting average. It has its share of nook and crannies, yet it plays stingy for triples and doubles. Righthanded hitters have a slight advantage over lefthanded hitters, as the right-center field gap and 25-foot wall in right field combined to keep many balls in the ballpark. Righthanded hitters get a boost in the warm weather months when the ball travels further out to left, especially down the line. Major league batters consider the Camden Yards' hitting background one of the best.

Defense

The Orioles continue to keep the infield grass slightly longer than most teams, and that benefits both the infielders and pitchers. Even with its share of odd angles, Oriole Park doesn't produce difficult plays for outfielders. Foul territory is about average and doesn't aid pitchers. Though the ballpark is close to the water, the wind is fairly predictable, rarely causing problems for fielders.

Who It Helps the Most

While Baltimore hitters tend to generate more power and hit for a higher average on the road, Javy Lopez and Larry Bigbie enjoyed a slight but not significant power advantage at Camden Yards.

Who It Hurts the Most

Brian Roberts set a team record with 50 doubles last season, but recorded only 21 at home. Jerry Hairston hit 73 points higher on the road than at home. For Miguel Tejada the difference was 15 points. For B.J. Surhoff, 34 points.

Rookies & Newcomers

The Orioles brought in Javy Lopez and Miguel Tejada, and both players followed the ballpark's trend and fared better away from Camden Yards. The Orioles will give Matt Riley, John Maine and other young pitchers a long look this season. They'll receive a noticeable benefit in pitching at home.

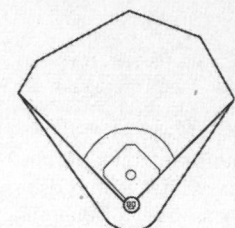

Dimensions: LF-333, LCF-364, CF-400, RCF-373, RF-318

Capacity: 48,286

Elevation: 20 feet

Surface: Grass

Foul Territory: Average

Park Factors

2004 Season

	Home Games Orioles	Opp	Total	Away Games Orioles	Opp	Total	Index
G	72	72	144	72	72	144	
Avg	.282	.272	.277	.287	.256	.272	102
AB	2465	2591	5056	2613	2398	5011	101
R	375	411	786	397	322	719	109
H	695	704	1399	750	613	1363	103
2B	143	113	256	150	103	253	100
3B	4	12	16	10	12	22	72
HR	74	79	153	78	65	143	106
BB	217	315	532	253	296	549	96
SO	371	471	842	455	484	939	89
E	59	52	111	34	56	90	123
E-Infield	54	44	98	32	48	80	123
LHB-Avg	.263	.278	.270	.295	.256	.278	97
LHB-HR	28	37	65	37	26	63	103
RHB-Avg	.300	.267	.282	.279	.255	.267	106
RHB-HR	46	42	88	41	39	80	108

2002-2004

	Home Games Orioles	Opp	Total	Away Games Orioles	Opp	Total	Index
G	216	216	432	217	217	434	
Avg	.268	.265	.266	.265	.274	.269	99
AB	7302	7657	14959	7662	7366	15028	100
R	992	1072	2064	1029	1076	2105	99
H	1958	2027	3985	2027	2020	4047	99
2B	384	346	730	425	378	803	91
3B	20	25	45	35	48	83	54
HR	223	270	493	207	241	448	111
BB	623	792	1415	637	761	1398	102
SO	1164	1337	2501	1302	1364	2666	94
E	137	162	299	124	144	268	112
E-Infield	118	132	250	108	125	233	108
LHB-Avg	.261	.269	.265	.277	.270	.273	97
LHB-HR	81	129	210	79	119	198	105
RHB-Avg	.272	.261	.267	.257	.278	.266	100
RHB-HR	142	141	283	128	122	250	115

2004 Rankings (American League)

- Third-highest error factor
- Lowest strikeout factor

Lee Mazzilli

2004 Season

In his first season as a major league manager, Lee Mazzilli's Orioles failed to reach the .500 mark after investing heavily in the free-agent market. At the core of his team's struggles was a subpar pitching staff. He pulled his starters quicker than most American League managers, but that said more about their struggles than his managerial style. He worked well with both young players and veterans, displaying patience in tough times.

Offense

Mazzilli prefers to go with a set lineup whenever possible, rather than mixing and matching his roster against the starting pitcher. His team can be aggressive on the bases, but he prefers to pick his spots to run, resulting in a good success rate in stealing bases. He is aggressive using the hit-and-run to jump-start his lineup, but is less is not afraid to insert a young player into the lineup on a regular basis.

Pitching & Defense

Mazzilli shows patience with starters who keep his team in the game, but will pull a pitcher who can't throw strikes more quickly. His starters rarely work deep into the game because of poor performance. Mazzilli shows confidence in his closer and prefers one reliever in the ninth-inning role. When the situation calls for it, he'll match up his bullpen specialists with opposing hitters late in the game. He leaned toward a lineup with offense punch over defensive prowess in 2004. He utilizes pinch-hitters and defensive replacements less frequently than most of his AL peers.

2005 Outlook

At the end of the season, there were grumblings that Mazzilli could be replaced by a more experienced manager. That didn't happen and he'll get a second chance in 2005. If the front office adds some veteran depth and quality to the pitching staff—both the rotation and the bullpen—the Orioles have a solid shot at finishing above .500.

Born: 3/25/55 in New York, New York

Playing Experience: 1976-1989, NYM, NYY, Tex, Pit, Tor

Managerial Experience: 1 season
Pronunciation: muh-ZILL-ee

Manager Statistics

Year	Team, Lg	W	L	Pct	GB	Finish
2004	Baltimore, AL	78	84	.481	23.0	3rd East
1 Season		78	84	.481	–	–

2004 Starting Pitchers by Days Rest

	<=3	4	5	6+
Orioles Starts	2	82	44	22
Orioles ERA	5.40	5.36	5.17	4.07
AL Avg Starts	2	82	47	21
AL ERA	5.36	4.87	4.65	4.93

2004 Situational Stats

	Lee Mazzilli	AL Average
Hit & Run Success %	36.1	36.8
Stolen Base Success %	71.1	68.6
Platoon Pct.	59.1	61.6
Defensive Subs	12	21
High-Pitch Outings	2	5
Quick/Slow Hooks	29/22	20/16
Sacrifice Attempts	58	53

2004 Rankings (American League)

- 2nd in steals of third base (19), slow hooks and quick hooks
- 3rd in relief appearances (452) and 2+ pitching changes in low-scoring games (32)

Erik Bedard

2004 Season

Eric Bedard is now two-plus years removed from Tommy John surgery. Expectations were low for 2004, in light of his recovery and inexperience at the major league level. Bedard pitched better in the first half, recording a decent 4.01 ERA in 15 starts. He faded after the All-Star break, running out of gas after pitching a career-high 133.1 innings as a pro by mid-September. Bedard was shut down until October 2 as a precaution.

Pitching

Bedard throws his fastball in the 90-92 MPH range. He does a good job of spotting the pitch on both sides of the plate and pushing hitters off the dish. He has a slightly above-average curveball, though it's not the 12-to-6 variety. Often it's more like a slurve since his surgery. Once his curveball regains its pre-surgery break, it will be an out pitch. Bedard has good arm action when throwing his changeup, but it's a below-average offering right now. When he's inconsistent, Bedard struggles to repeat his release point. He also doesn't fare as well after reaching the 60-pitch count level. Bedard doesn't always trust his stuff, preferring to nibble at the corners. When he pitches aggressively, he's much more effective.

Defense

His move to first base to keep runners close is nothing special, though Bedard is a good athlete who gets off the mound quickly. He fields bunts and slow rollers with ease and confidence. He's quick to get over to first base when he's needed to cover the bag.

2005 Outlook

The Orioles are counting on Bedard to step it up a level this season. He's shown he can pitch and not get hurt, so he's over that hurdle. Improved arm strength and stamina will allow him to work deeper into games. If he can tighten the break of his curveball and show consistency with his release point, Bedard could prove to be the second-best pitcher on Baltimore's staff by season's end.

Position: SP
Bats: L **Throws:** L
Ht: 6' 1" **Wt:** 189

Opening Day Age: 26
Born: 3/6/79 in Navan, ON, Canada
ML Seasons: 2

Overall Statistics

	W	L	Pct.	ERA	G	GS	Sv	IP	H	BB	SO	HR	Avg
'04	6	10	.375	4.59	27	26	0	137.1	149	71	121	13	.270
Car.	6	10	.375	4.63	29	26	0	138.0	151	71	122	13	.272

2004 Pitching Profile

	Erik Bedard	AL Average
Overall Strike %	61.3	62.3
1st Pitch Strike %	55.7	58.1
Ratio	1.60	1.42
Strikeouts per 9 IP	7.93	6.45
Walks per 9 IP	4.65	3.34
Home Runs per 9 IP	0.85	1.15
Strikeout/Walk Ratio	1.70	1.93
Groundball/Flyball Ratio	0.92	1.17

2004 Situational Stats

	W	L	ERA	Sv	IP		AB	H	HR	RBI	Avg
Home	2	6	5.02	0	57.1	LHB	112	31	2	16	.277
Road	4	4	4.28	0	80.0	RHB	439	118	11	58	.269
First Half	3	3	4.01	0	76.1	Sc Pos	154	34	6	57	.221
Scnd Half	3	7	5.31	0	61.0	Clutch	4	0	0	0	.000

2004 Rankings (American League)

- 2nd in losses among rookies
- 4th in wins among rookies
- 5th in balks (2)
- 7th in lowest batting average allowed with runners in scoring position and lowest winning percentage
- Led the Orioles in balks (2), fewest home runs allowed per nine innings (.85) and most strikeouts per nine innings (7.9)

Larry Bigbie

2004 Season

Injuries and off seasons by other players opened the door to more playing time for Larry Bigbie. With the exception of a poor July, when he hit .219, Bigbie responded with a solid season and was consistent from month to month. He was most productive in September, when he batted .340 and drove in 15 runs, including seven against Minnesota on September 17. Yet, Bigbie struck out at a higher rate than in 2003, when he was part-time player.

Hitting

In some ways, Bigbie's swing is similar to teammate B.J. Surhoff's. It's level and he uses it to hit to all fields. Bigbie has the ability to inside out an inside pitch and drive it down the left-field line. His home-run power is from left-center to right-center only. With regular playing time, Bigbie struggles against southpaws. His bat speed and approach to hitting make it difficult for him to get around inside hard stuff. Bigbie hits much better at the bottom of the order, where there isn't a lot of pressure on him.

Baserunning & Defense

Bigbie has slightly above-average speed that doesn't translate into many stolen bases. He still needs to work on reading pitchers to get better jumps. He's fast enough to score from second on most hits to right field and into the gaps. He's an intelligent runner who rarely makes a mistake on the bases. Bigbie doesn't always get a great jump when in the outfield, and that relegates him to a corner-outfield spot. He can play center in a pinch. His speed comes in handy in cutting off balls hit into the gap and charging hits in front of him. His throws are accurate and strong enough to keep most runners honest.

2005 Outlook

The Orioles have lots of options in the outfield, and that doesn't bode well for Bigbie. Unless he can reduce his strikeouts and generate more power, he's likely to be demoted to the fourth-outfielder role this season.

Position: LF/CF
Bats: L **Throws:** R
Ht: 6' 4" **Wt:** 207

Opening Day Age: 27
Born: 11/4/77 in Hobart, IN
ML Seasons: 4
Pronunciation: BIGG-bee

Overall Statistics

	G	AB	R	H	D	T	HR	RBI	SB	BB	SO	Avg	OBP	Slg
'04	139	478	76	134	23	1	15	68	8	45	113	.280	.341	.427
Car.	285	930	135	257	45	2	26	113	20	92	226	.276	.340	.413

Where He Hits the Ball

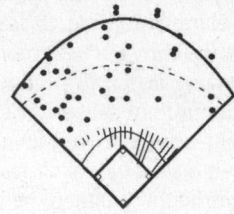 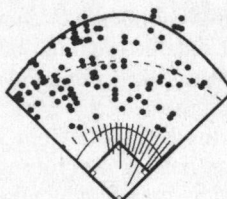

Vs. LHP   **Vs. RHP**

2004 Situational Stats

	AB	H	HR	RBI	Avg		AB	H	HR	RBI	Avg
Home	236	65	8	26	.275	LHP	148	32	6	22	.216
Road	242	69	7	42	.285	RHP	330	102	9	46	.309
First Half	276	72	7	36	.261	Sc Pos	132	32	4	52	.242
Scnd Half	202	62	8	32	.307	Clutch	65	15	2	7	.231

2004 Rankings (American League)

- 3rd in highest groundball-flyball ratio (2.1) and fielding percentage in left field (.991)
- 6th in lowest batting average vs. lefthanded pitchers
- Led the Orioles in strikeouts and highest groundball-flyball ratio (2.1)

Jay Gibbons

2004 Season

A strained left hip flexor curtailed Jay Gibbons' season and his effectiveness at the plate. Gibbons picked up 16 RBI in 20 April contests and enjoyed his best month in September. In between, he rarely showed the offensive production that had made him an effective middle-of-the-order hitter. His limited mobility reduced the range he had in the outfield and at first base.

Hitting

When healthy, Gibbons has a compact swing that allows him to pull inside offerings to right field. He uses his short stroke to take pitches on the outside of the plate to left. When he's fooled with an inside pitch, he can inside-out it and go the other way. Gibbons has enough plate discipline to lay off outside breaking balls in the dirt. He's learned to work the count and not swing at the first good pitch he sees. Over the past couple of seasons, his swing has gone from a slight uppercut to a level one that has him hitting down on the ball at times. Even though he makes consistent contact, he's rarely used in a hit-and-run situation.

Baserunning & Defense

With a logjam at first base, his natural position, Gibbons has garnered most of his playing time in right field. His range is limited there, especially with an injury like a hip flexor. To his credit, Gibbons handles almost all of the chances within his range. His arm is accurate but limited in the outfield. When playing first base, his range is slightly above average and his glove work around the bag is a plus. Gibbons is a station-to-station runner when he's on base. He rarely scores from second unless the ball is deep into the gap.

2005 Outlook

Rafael Palmeiro will be back in 2005, which may limit Gibbons' time at his preferred position. More time at first base also would take some stress off his troublesome hip and back. Still, a healthy Gibbons should return to his pre-injury level of offensive production.

Position: RF/DH/1B
Bats: L **Throws:** L
Ht: 6' 0" **Wt:** 197

Opening Day Age: 28
Born: 3/2/77 in Rochester, MI
ML Seasons: 4

Overall Statistics

	G	AB	R	H	D	T	HR	RBI	SB	BB	SO	Avg	OBP	Slg
'04	97	346	36	85	14	1	10	47	1	29	64	.246	.303	.379
Car.	466	1686	214	432	92	4	76	252	2	140	258	.256	.315	.451

Where He Hits the Ball

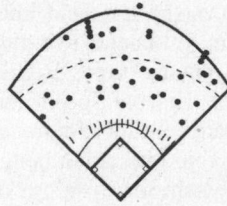 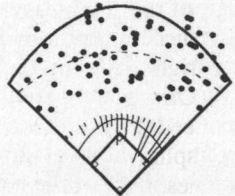

Vs. LHP   **Vs. RHP**

2004 Situational Stats

	AB	H	HR	RBI	Avg		AB	H	HR	RBI	Avg
Home	163	39	4	23	.239	LHP	109	28	2	14	.257
Road	183	46	6	24	.251	RHP	237	57	8	33	.241
First Half	197	44	6	28	.223	Sc Pos	85	22	3	38	.259
Scnd Half	149	41	4	19	.275	Clutch	57	13	1	9	.228

2004 Rankings (American League)

- Did not rank near the top or bottom in any category

Jerry Hairston Jr.

2004 Season

For the second straight season, Jerry Hairston Jr. lost a considerable amount of time to injuries. In early March, he fractured a finger on his right hand. His season ended in mid-August when he suffered a fractured left ankle. In between the injuries, Hairston was moved to center field after Brian Roberts' fine play secured the second-base job. Hairston was a productive hitter in 86 games.

Hitting

Even with all the time lost to injuries the past couple of seasons, Hairston continues to improve. He values a walk more than at any time in his career, and he has developed average plate patience. Pitchers still use the breaking ball on the outside part of the plate to get him out. But with increasing success, Hairston is driving the pitch to right and right-center field. If he can stay healthy, he is the Orioles' best leadoff hitter. Hard work has reduced his tendency to swing at high fastballs and splitters in the dirt. Hairston still tends to pull pitches, but he attempts to hit the ball to all fields more than ever. Though he has top-of-the-order speed, he's never developed into an above-average bunter.

Baserunning & Defense

Hairston is still a threat to steal when he's on base. He uses a quick first step, rather than above-average speed, to steal bases. He scores from second on hits to right field and gap hits to left-center. Hairston is one of the best on the Baltimore roster at going from first to third. That quick first step helps him get a good jump on the ball, whether he's playing second base or center field. His ability to turn the double play is above average.

2005 Outlook

If Hairston returns to the Orioles this season, he'll share time with Luis Matos in center field and Brian Roberts at second base. Two straight seasons with significant injuries raise concerns that he is injury prone. In November, he underwent surgery to have the talus bone removed from the left ankle he fractured in August. If he can stay healthy in 2005, Hairston should remain a solid top-of-the-order hitter and basestealer.

Position: RF/DH/CF/2B/LF
Bats: R **Throws:** R
Ht: 5'10" **Wt:** 183

Opening Day Age: 28
Born: 5/29/76 in Naperville, IL
ML Seasons: 7

Overall Statistics

	G	AB	R	H	D	T	HR	RBI	SB	BB	SO	Avg	OBP	Slg
'04	86	287	43	87	19	1	2	24	13	29	29	.303	.378	.397
Car.	530	1825	241	477	98	12	26	160	94	162	229	.261	.334	.371

Where He Hits the Ball

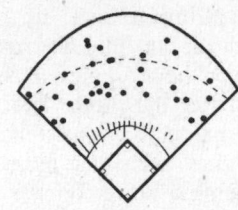
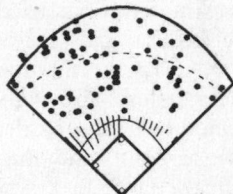

Vs. LHP   **Vs. RHP**

2004 Situational Stats

	AB	H	HR	RBI	Avg		AB	H	HR	RBI	Avg
Home	136	36	0	11	.265	LHP	98	31	0	6	.316
Road	151	51	2	13	.338	RHP	189	56	2	18	.296
First Half	185	60	1	19	.324	Sc Pos	63	18	0	20	.286
Scnd Half	102	27	1	5	.265	Clutch	39	6	0	4	.154

2004 Rankings (American League)

- 3rd in batting average with two strikes (.280)
- 7th in lowest stolen-base percentage (61.9)
- 10th in fewest GDPs per GDP situation (4.3%)
- Led the Orioles in lowest percentage of swings that missed (9.0), batting average on the road and lowest percentage of swings on the first pitch (9.3)

Jorge Julio

2004 Season

Jorge Julio opened the 2004 season with a stellar April, posting an 0.82 ERA and saving three games. He struggled some in May and nearly lost his job after posting a 9.72 ERA in June. Julio regrouped nicely before faltering again in September. A loss of command often sparked his trouble spots. As in 2003, Julio seemed in jeopardy of losing his job, but the Orioles have very few options to replace him.

Pitching

Julio throws an above-average four-seem fastball that regularly is clocked at 96-98 MPH. He struggles controlling the movement and location of the pitch, which is when he gets into trouble. The coaching staff has tried to get him to back off a few MPH to gain better control, but Julio reverts to throwing his hardest when he struggles. His slider usually is clocked in the high 80s. Sometimes Julio battles to maintain a consistent release point, and that plagues his slider more than the fastball. Despite being a power pitcher, he doesn't pitch inside enough. This allows hitters to lean out over the plate and cover the outside corner. Julio has improved his approach against left-handed hitters and no longer struggles against them.

Defense

With a slightly below-average move to first base, Julio negates the advantage of being a power pitcher. Baserunners were 11-for-13 against him when stealing in 2004. Julio gets a good jump to first base when he covers on grounders to the right side. Otherwise, he's average in fielding his position, with a fall off toward first base at the end of his pitching motion.

2005 Outlook

Although just 26, Julio has been the Orioles' closer for three seasons. Despite his youth, he needs to become more consistent or he'll risk losing the closer's job. If the Orioles can find another closer option in spring training or at some point in the 2005 season, look for Julio to face a battle to keep his job.

Position: RP
Bats: R **Throws:** R
Ht: 6' 1"   **Wt:** 232

Opening Day Age: 26
Born: 3/3/79 in Caracas, VZ
ML Seasons: 4
Pronunciation:
HOR-hay HOO-lee-oh

Overall Statistics

	W	L	Pct.	ERA	G	GS	Sv	IP	H	BB	SO	HR	Avg
'04	2	5	.286	4.57	65	0	22	69.0	59	39	70	11	.228
Car.	8	19	.296	3.64	214	0	83	220.0	199	109	199	28	.237

2004 Pitching Profile

	Jorge Julio	AL Average
Overall Strike %	60.8	62.3
1st Pitch Strike %	56.0	58.1
Ratio	1.42	1.42
Strikeouts per 9 IP	9.13	6.45
Walks per 9 IP	5.09	3.34
Home Runs per 9 IP	1.43	1.15
Strikeout/Walk Ratio	1.79	1.93
Groundball/Flyball Ratio	0.94	1.17

2004 Situational Stats

	W	L	ERA	Sv	IP		AB	H	HR	RBI	Avg
Home	2	4	6.28	11	38.2	LHB	137	32	6	20	.234
Road	0	1	2.37	11	30.1	RHB	122	27	5	15	.221
First Half	1	2	4.58	12	35.1	Sc Pos	64	14	0	22	.219
Scnd Half	1	3	4.54	10	33.2	Clutch	156	33	8	23	.212

2004 Rankings (American League)

- 4th in lowest save percentage (84.6)
- 6th in games finished (50)
- 7th in saves
- Led the Orioles in saves, games finished (50), stolen bases allowed (11), lowest batting average allowed vs. righthanded batters and save percentage (84.6)

Javy Lopez

2004 Season

Javy Lopez was signed as a free agent last winter after recording his most productive season with Atlanta in 2003. Baltimore wanted a catcher who could play every day and provide punch in the middle of the lineup, and Lopez delivered. Among American League catchers, he finished near the top in every offensive category. He also posted personal bests in at-bats and games played.

Hitting

Lopez has good power to left and left-center field, and can drive the ball out to right-center occasionally. When Lopez is in a hitting groove, he is more likely to work the count to his advantage. His ability to coax a walk is among the best at his position. He still has a tendency to chase pitches low and outside the strike zone when he's pressing. Lopez makes much better contact and produces more power in games under the lights than day games. His swing is more level than in past years, and as a result, he's hitting more doubles than at any point in his career.

Baserunning & Defense

Now that his knees are healthy again, Lopez' overall defense has rebounded. Lopez can be inconsistent in blocking pitches in the dirt, sometimes using good fundamentals, only to get lazy and stab at pitches with his glove. His throws to second base are accurate but lack velocity. His quicker than normal release to second helps keep runners honest. Lopez gets out of his crouch quickly to handle bunts out in front of the plate. His baserunning is below average and he struggles to go from first to third on anything but extra-base hits into the gaps. He's not a threat to steal a base.

2005 Outlook

The Orioles look for production similar to last season's. Now that Lopez knows American League pitchers, the hope is he'll take advantage of the smaller American League ballparks and generate more power. As long as he remains healthy, Lopez should be at least as productive as he was in 2004.

Position: C/DH
Bats: R **Throws:** R
Ht: 6' 3" **Wt:** 224

Opening Day Age: 34
Born: 11/5/70 in Ponce, PR
ML Seasons: 13
Pronunciation: HAH-vee LOE-pezz

Overall Statistics

	G	AB	R	H	D	T	HR	RBI	SB	BB	SO	Avg	OBP	Slg
'04	150	579	83	183	33	3	23	86	0	47	97	.316	.370	.503
Car.	1306	4582	591	1331	223	17	237	780	8	318	825	.290	.341	.502

Where He Hits the Ball

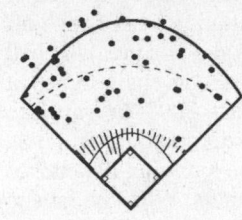 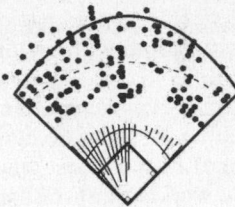

Vs. LHP   **Vs. RHP**

2004 Situational Stats

	AB	H	HR	RBI	Avg		AB	H	HR	RBI	Avg
Home	298	96	14	44	.322	LHP	150	47	8	20	.313
Road	281	87	9	42	.310	RHP	429	136	15	66	.317
First Half	330	106	12	42	.321	Sc Pos	156	41	5	65	.263
Scnd Half	249	77	11	44	.309	Clutch	94	26	2	12	.277

2004 Rankings (American League)

- 3rd in lowest percentage of runners caught stealing as a catcher (22.7)
- Led AL catchers in batting average

Rodrigo Lopez

2004 Season

Rodrigo Lopez was coming off a very disappointing 2003 campaign. He began the 2004 season in the bullpen, where he dominated American League hitters and posted a 0.55 ERA. He slowly worked his way back into the starting rotation, based on his performance and the struggles by others. In September, he was 4-0 with a 2.57 ERA. By season's end, his 2004 campaign looked very similar to his surprising rookie season in 2002.

Pitching

Lopez' fastball rarely tops out above 88 MPH, but it does have good movement. Lopez uses it to keep hitters off the plate and set up his other pitches. He has a knack for taking just enough off a pitch to keep hitters off stride. His breaking ball is more like a slurve than a curveball. When it flattens out like it often did in 2003, he gets into trouble. Because he lacks a dominating out pitch, Lopez is at his best when he's mixing his pitches and working just off the corners. When he fails to do so, he is likely to struggle the second time through the order. Lopez gives up a lot of home runs to righthanded batters when he lacks sharp movement on his pitches.

Defense

His move to first base is above average, helping to slow down the opponents' running game. Lopez does a solid job moving to his left and right to field bunts and slow rollers. Occasionally he'll get a slow jump off the mound in covering first base and bunts dropped in front of home plate.

2005 Outlook

The big question is, which Lopez will show up this season. Lopez has shown he can be one of the better starters in the American League. He's unlikely to get better than what he displayed in 2004 because his pitching repertoire won't dominate hitters. As long as he maintains his control and command, however, he'll be effective. Lopez should come close to duplicating his 2002 and 2004 campaigns.

Position: SP/RP
Bats: R **Throws:** R
Ht: 6' 1" **Wt:** 190

Opening Day Age: 29
Born: 12/14/75 in Tlalnepantla, Mexico
ML Seasons: 4
Pronunciation: rod-REE-go

Overall Statistics

	W	L	Pct.	ERA	G	GS	Sv	IP	H	BB	SO	HR	Avg
'04	14	9	.609	3.59	37	23	0	170.2	164	54	121	21	.252
Car.	36	31	.537	4.42	102	83	0	539.0	564	172	377	73	.270

2004 Pitching Profile

	Rodrigo Lopez	AL Average
Overall Strike %	63.5	62.3
1st Pitch Strike %	60.5	58.1
Ratio	1.28	1.42
Strikeouts per 9 IP	6.38	6.45
Walks per 9 IP	2.85	3.34
Home Runs per 9 IP	1.11	1.15
Strikeout/Walk Ratio	2.24	1.93
Groundball/Flyball Ratio	1.33	1.17

2004 Situational Stats

	W	L	ERA	Sv	IP		AB	H	HR	RBI	Avg
Home	7	6	3.55	0	88.2	LHB	337	87	7	25	.258
Road	7	3	3.62	0	82.0	RHB	314	77	14	36	.245
First Half	6	6	3.89	0	83.1	Sc Pos	132	26	6	43	.197
Scnd Half	8	3	3.30	0	87.1	Clutch	62	13	1	2	.210

2004 Rankings (American League)

- 1st in fielding percentage at pitcher (1.000)
- 4th in lowest batting average allowed with runners in scoring position
- 6th in ERA
- 7th in lowest on-base percentage allowed (.310)
- 8th in wins, lowest slugging percentage allowed (.392) and lowest ERA on the road
- Led the Orioles in ERA, wins, pickoff throws (106), runners caught stealing (4), highest strikeout-walk ratio (2.2), lowest batting average allowed (.252), lowest on-base percentage allowed (.310), lowest ERA at home, lowest ERA on the road and fewest walks per nine innings (2.8)

Melvin Mora

2004 Season

Melvin Mora's season began with a rash of errors at his new full-time position—third base. It ended as his most productive season in the majors. He finished with the second-highest batting average and the best on-base percentage in the American League. Mora's 27 home runs and 104 RBI were major surprises to the Orioles. A torrid May had Mora hitting .391 as late as May 28, and he showed more power during the second half.

Hitting

Mora's late-developing swing is a lot more level than it was just a few seasons ago. He now generates a high rate of line drives and fewer popups and lazy flyballs to the outfield. Almost all of his home-run power is to left and left-center field. Mora has become one of the best in the American League at working the count to his advantage. He doesn't lean out over the plate as much as he did a few seasons ago, and he isn't hit by pitches nearly as frequently. This also allows him to handle inside fastballs much more effectively. While Mora has above-average speed, he is reluctant to lay down a bunt.

Baserunning & Defense

Nor has Mora made an effort to study pitchers, which would aid him in stealing bases. Still, he's an above-average baserunner going from first to third and scoring from second base. Occasionally a loss of focus on the bases leads to a lost opportunity to move up one bag. He improved and became more consistent at third base as the season wore on. His range at third is about average and his throws to first are accurate.

2005 Outlook

Mora will be the Orioles' starting third baseman this season with two more years left on a three-year deal. The 33-year-old Mora won't sneak up on American League pitchers this season, and he shouldn't be expected to improve upon his 2004 performance. Look for his batting average to drop closer to the .300 mark.

Position: 3B
Bats: R **Throws:** R
Ht: 5'11" **Wt:** 200

Opening Day Age: 33
Born: 2/2/72 in Agua Negra, VZ
ML Seasons: 6
Pronunciation: MORE-a

Overall Statistics

	G	AB	R	H	D	T	HR	RBI	SB	BB	SO	Avg	OBP	Slg
'04	140	550	111	187	41	0	27	104	11	66	95	.340	.419	.562
Car.	711	2332	380	654	138	10	76	312	58	265	452	.280	.367	.446

Where He Hits the Ball

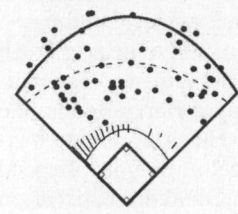
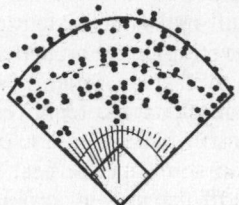

Vs. LHP **Vs. RHP**

2004 Situational Stats

	AB	H	HR	RBI	Avg		AB	H	HR	RBI	Avg
Home	253	90	15	43	.356	LHP	132	40	8	27	.303
Road	297	97	12	61	.327	RHP	418	147	19	77	.352
First Half	259	90	12	43	.347	Sc Pos	161	52	3	70	.323
Scnd Half	291	97	15	61	.333	Clutch	71	21	1	6	.296

2004 Rankings (American League)

- 1st in on-base percentage, batting average at home and batting average with two strikes (.293)
- 2nd in batting average, batting average vs. righthanded pitchers, errors at third base (21) and lowest fielding percentage at third base (.948)
- 4th in batting average on the road
- 5th in slugging percentage
- Led the Orioles in runs scored, hit by pitch (11), times on base (264), slugging percentage, most pitches seen per plate appearance (4.11), highest percentage of pitches taken (59.6), batting average with the bases loaded (.533), and batting average at home
- Led AL third basemen in batting average

Rafael Palmeiro

2004 Season

Rafael Palmeiro returned to Baltimore, where he recorded some of his best seasons in a long and distinguished major league career. He registered his lowest output for home runs and RBI since 1994. His .258 batting average was his lowest since the 1997 season. The highlight of his season came in September, when he batted .318, belted nine home runs and drove in 23 runs. In the end, though, his season was a disappointment. Clearly age has caught up with him as he nears the end of his career.

Hitting

In an effort to maintain his power, Palmeiro continues to sacrifice his batting average. While he still makes consistent contact against southpaws, he struggles to hit better than .200 or deliver much power against them. Palmeiro remains very pull-conscious and teams employ a Barry Bonds-like shift when he's at the plate. He's still able to handle some of the best fastballs, though offspeed stuff causes him problems. Breaking balls in on the hands tie him up because he tries pulling nearly every pitch. Palmeiro still hits much better in day games than at night.

Baserunning & Defense

Cranky knees have reduced Palmeiro to mostly a station-to-station runner on the bases. He seldom scores from second base on base hits to right field and doubles are needed to get him home. Palmeiro rarely goes from first to third unless the ball is hit into the gaps. In the field, he's no more than an average fielder these days because of his troublesome knees. His range is limited going into the second-base hole and coming in on slow rollers. He hasn't lost his ability to scoop bad throws out of the dirt.

2005 Outlook

Palmeiro signed a one-year, $3 million deal to return, most likely as a designated hitter and fill-in at first base. His struggles against southpaws may cut into his playing time. It's conceivable he'll hit 20 homers again, though he's nothing more than an average hitter.

Position: 1B/DH
Bats: L **Throws:** L
Ht: 6' 0" **Wt:** 214

Opening Day Age: 40
Born: 9/24/64 in Havana, Cuba
ML Seasons: 19
Pronunciation: pahl-MARE-oh
Nickname: Raffy

Overall Statistics

G	AB	R	H	D	T	HR	RBI	SB	BB	SO	Avg	OBP	Slg
154	550	68	142	29	0	23	88	2	86	61	.258	.359	.436
2721	10103	1616	2922	572	38	551	1775	95	1310	1305	.289	.372	.517

Where He Hits the Ball

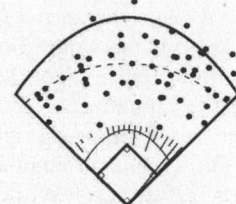 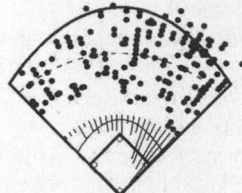

Vs. LHP   **Vs. RHP**

2004 Situational Stats

	AB	H	HR	RBI	Avg		AB	H	HR	RBI	Avg
Home	292	70	12	46	.240	LHP	159	30	5	20	.189
Road	258	72	11	42	.279	RHP	391	112	18	68	.286
First Half	299	74	13	52	.247	Sc Pos	154	36	3	60	.234
Scnd Half	251	68	10	36	.271	Clutch	72	14	3	9	.194

2004 Rankings (American League)

- 1st in lowest batting average vs. lefthanded pitchers
- 2nd in intentional walks (15)
- 3rd in sacrifice flies (9), errors at first base (8) and lowest fielding percentage at first base (.993)
- 4th in lowest batting average at home
- 5th in lowest groundball-flyball ratio (0.7)
- 6th in walks
- 7th in lowest cleanup slugging percentage (.423)
- 9th in lowest percentage of swings that missed (10.3)
- Led the Orioles in walks and intentional walks (15)

Sidney Ponson

2004 Season

Free agent Sidney Ponson returned to Baltimore before the 2004 season. Despite a career year in 2003, he recorded his worst single-season ERA and allowed a career-high 265 hits in 215.2 innings. Needless to say, Ponson was a big disappointment in Baltimore last summer. He opened the season without the control or command he displayed in 2003. He showed glimpses of his 2003 form in July and September, but otherwise Ponson struggled to put together two solid starts in a row.

Pitching

When Ponson is pitching well, his fastball can reach 92-94 MPH, but he often works in the 90-92 range. One reason for the drop in velocity is a lack of conditioning that also affects his stamina. The key to his 2003 success was an improved slider. When he's able to throw a sharp slider with good command, it helps set up his other pitches. He's not afraid to throw inside to keep hitters off the plate. Ponson used to throw an average forkball, but recent elbow and shoulder woes have forced him to abandon the pitch. Without the forkball and the velocity he once had, he needs to keep the ball down in the strike zone to stay out of trouble. Poor control and pitches high in the zone were a problem in 2004.

Defense

Due to his large frame, Ponson is slow getting off the mound to field his position. When he reaches slow rollers in front of him, he handles them without problems. He is average in getting over to first base when the ball is hit to the first baseman. His move to first is deliberate and barely keeps hitters honest.

2005 Outlook

If Ponson is to approach his 2003 form, he must improve his conditioning. If the righthander enters the 2005 season in decent shape, the Orioles should see improved stamina and performance. The onus is on Ponson to prove that 2003 wasn't a fluke, and that he can be a decent No. 2 or 3 starter.

Position: SP
Bats: R **Throws:** R
Ht: 6' 1" **Wt:** 266

Opening Day Age: 28
Born: 11/2/76 in Noord, Aruba
ML Seasons: 7
Pronunciation: pon-SONE

Baltimore

Overall Statistics

	W	L	Pct.	ERA	G	GS	Sv	IP	H	BB	SO	HR	Avg
'04	11	15	.423	5.30	33	33	0	215.2	265	69	115	23	.305
Car.	69	80	.463	4.67	210	199	1	1313.0	1416	435	802	170	.277

2004 Pitching Profile

	Sidney Ponson	AL Average
Overall Strike %	63.8	62.3
1st Pitch Strike %	59.7	58.1
Ratio	1.55	1.42
Strikeouts per 9 IP	4.80	6.45
Walks per 9 IP	2.88	3.34
Home Runs per 9 IP	0.96	1.15
Strikeout/Walk Ratio	1.67	1.93
Groundball/Flyball Ratio	1.63	1.17

2004 Situational Stats

	W	L	ERA	Sv	IP		AB	H	HR	RBI	Avg
Home	5	7	5.09	0	106.0	LHB	455	146	12	70	.321
Road	6	8	5.50	0	109.2	RHB	413	119	11	50	.288
First Half	3	12	6.29	0	113.0	Sc Pos	228	71	8	91	.311
Scnd Half	8	3	4.21	0	102.2	Clutch	46	19	3	7	.413

2004 Rankings (American League)

- 1st in complete games (5), shutouts (2) and hits allowed
- 2nd in batters faced (954) and GDPs induced (36)
- 3rd in losses
- 4th in highest batting average allowed (.305) and highest on-base percentage allowed (.361)
- 5th in balks (2) and fewest pitches thrown per batter (3.47)
- 7th in most GDPs induced per GDP situation (18.8%)
- Led the Orioles in losses, games started, complete games (5), shutouts (2), innings pitched, hits allowed, batters faced (954), home runs allowed, hit batsmen (8), balks (2), pitches thrown (3,310), GDPs induced (36), highest groundball-flyball ratio allowed (1.6) and fewest pitches thrown per batter (3.47)

Brian Roberts

2004 Season

Brian Roberts was expected to serve as a backup in the middle infield. He got out of the gate quickly, however, subbing for the injured Jerry Hairston Jr. After batting .305 with eight doubles and seven steals in April, he struggled before turning it around in July. A red-hot August, with 10 doubles and 10 RBI, was followed by a subpar September. Despite a hot-and-cold season, Roberts broke the Orioles' single-season doubles record with 50.

Hitting

Roberts has a short, level swing that allows him to spray the ball to all fields. When he gets good wood on the ball, he can drive it into both gaps. He has the ability to coax a walk when he's patient at the plate. Roberts struggles at times with low-and-outside breaking balls. He'll also climb the ladder to chase a fastball. The switch-hitter struggles against southpaws who constantly pitch him away. He's a good bunter but rarely is called on to sacrifice. When he does bunt for a base hit, he has good bat control and placement.

Baserunning & Defense

Roberts' speed is above average and he can score from second on most hits to the outfield. He also is effective going from first to third. When he's on base, his steals are more about pure speed than an ability to read pitchers. That should change with experience. Roberts can play both second base and short, though he's better suited at second. His arm is adequate and his throws to first are accurate. He handles his responsibilities at second with confidence and turns the double play with regularity. Simply put, he's solid in the field.

2005 Outlook

At times last season, Roberts played like an All-Star, only to fall into a long slump. If he's going to retain the starting second-base job, he must develop consistency. In his defense, he's still a relatively inexperienced player. A healthy and productive spring training by Jerry Hairston Jr. is likely to push Roberts back into a utility role this season.

Position: 2B
Bats: B **Throws:** R
Ht: 5' 9" **Wt:** 176

Opening Day Age: 27
Born: 10/9/77 in Durham, NC
ML Seasons: 4

Overall Statistics

	G	AB	R	H	D	T	HR	RBI	SB	BB	SO	Avg	OBP	Slg
'04	159	641	107	175	50	2	4	53	29	71	95	.273	.344	.376
Car.	384	1502	232	397	90	9	12	122	73	145	210	.264	.328	.360

Where He Hits the Ball

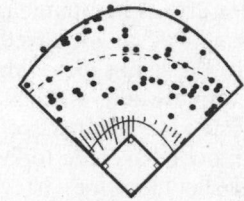 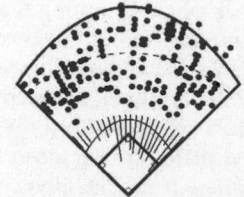

Vs. LHP   **Vs. RHP**

2004 Situational Stats

	AB	H	HR	RBI	Avg		AB	H	HR	RBI	Avg
Home	316	82	0	19	.259	LHP	200	43	0	15	.215
Road	325	93	4	34	.286	RHP	441	132	4	38	.299
First Half	339	86	2	29	.254	Sc Pos	120	33	2	49	.275
Scnd Half	302	89	2	24	.295	Clutch	81	21	1	11	.259

2004 Rankings (American League)

- 1st in doubles and pitches seen (2,908)
- 2nd in lowest HR frequency (160.3 ABs per HR)
- 3rd in sacrifice bunts (15), plate appearances (736), bunts in play (29), fielding percentage at second base (.988) and lowest slugging percentage
- 4th in stolen bases
- Led the Orioles in doubles, sacrifice bunts (15), stolen bases, caught stealing (12), pitches seen (2,908), plate appearances (736), bunts in play (29), steals of third (6), fewest GDPs per GDP situation (2.9%), and on-base percentage for a leadoff hitter (.346)

Miguel Tejada

2004 Season

Miguel Tejada was inked to a six-year free-agent deal last winter to anchor the middle of the Orioles' lineup, and he didn't disappoint. His 2004 season was a model of consistency from start to finish. He tied his career high in home runs and set a personal best in RBI, leading the major leagues with 150 ribbies. With Alex Rodriguez moving to third base and Nomar Garciaparra in the National League, Tejada now is the Junior Circuit's most productive shortstop.

Hitting

Tejada generates his home-run power to left and left-center field. His doubles power ranges from foul line to foul line. Tejada's swing is more compact that it used to be, yet he struggles with soft-tossers. Finesse pitchers are able to keep him off stride and reduce his power. His slight uppercut swing allows groundball pitchers to keep the ball in the park and have success against him. Tejada remains one of the better hitters in the American League with runners in scoring position. He's more productive batting fourth than in the No. 3 spot.

Baserunning & Defense

While Tejada generated 24 errors in 2004, he still is considered one of the American League's top shortstops. His range is among the best in the league, especially going into the hole. Tejada has a plus arm and can make all the required throws. He's adept at turning the double play, recording a league-leading 118 at short last season. While he rarely steals a base, he can go from first to third on singles to right field. His speed allows him to score from second on most hits to the outfield.

2005 Outlook

Tejada continues to be one of the marquee hitters in the American League. If the Orioles can add more depth to the lineup, his run production should remain close to his 2004 level. At age 28, he's entering the peak years of his career and could improve upon his 2004 season. Tejada is a perennial MVP candidate.

Position: SS
Bats: R **Throws:** R
Ht: 5' 9" **Wt:** 209

Opening Day Age: 28
Born: 5/25/76 in Bani, DR
ML Seasons: 8
Pronunciation: mee-GHEL tay-HA-duh

Baltimore

Overall Statistics

	G	AB	R	H	D	T	HR	RBI	SB	BB	SO	Avg	OBP	Slg
'04	162	653	107	203	40	2	34	150	4	48	73	.311	.360	.534
Car.	1098	4237	681	1171	231	13	190	754	53	335	615	.276	.336	.472

Where He Hits the Ball

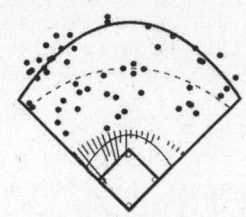 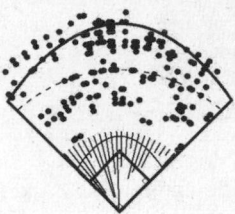

Vs. LHP   **Vs. RHP**

2004 Situational Stats

	AB	H	HR	RBI	Avg		AB	H	HR	RBI	Avg
Home	320	97	17	87	.303	LHP	159	52	11	40	.327
Road	333	106	17	63	.318	RHP	494	151	23	110	.306
First Half	344	107	15	75	.311	Sc Pos	208	67	12	113	.322
Scnd Half	309	96	19	75	.311	Clutch	90	29	4	17	.322

2004 Rankings (American League)

- 1st in RBI, sacrifice flies (14), games played and GDPs (24)
- 2nd in cleanup slugging percentage (.591) and lowest percentage of swings on the first pitch (12.1)
- 3rd in at-bats, total bases (349) and errors at shortstop (24)
- 4th in hits, plate appearances (725) and lowest fielding percentage at shortstop (.971)
- Led the Orioles in home runs, at-bats, hits, singles, total bases (349), HR frequency (19.2 ABs per HR), highest percentage of swings put into play (50.4), batting average in the clutch, and cleanup slugging percentage (.591)
- Led AL shortstops in home runs and RBI

Kurt Ainsworth

Position: SP
Bats: R **Throws:** R
Ht: 6' 3" **Wt:** 208

Opening Day Age: 26
Born: 9/9/78 in Baton Rouge, LA
ML Seasons: 4
Pronunciation: ANES-werth

Overall Statistics

	W	L	Pct.	ERA	G	GS	Sv	IP	H	BB	SO	HR	Avg
'04	0	1	.000	9.68	7	7	0	30.2	39	20	20	6	.320
Car.	6	8	.429	5.19	29	22	0	126.2	136	61	90	16	.278

2004 Situational Stats

	W	L	ERA	Sv	IP		AB	H	HR	RBI	Avg
Home	0	1	11.41	0	23.2	LHB	64	20	4	22	.313
Road	0	0	3.86	0	7.0	RHB	58	19	2	10	.328
First Half	0	1	9.68	0	30.2	Sc Pos	36	15	4	30	.417
Scnd Half	0	0	—	0	0.0	Clutch	3	0	0	0	.000

2004 Season

Baltimore had high hopes for Kurt Ainsworth, who came into spring training with 15 pounds of extra muscle and a healed right shoulder blade. His elbow started bothering him early in the season and required surgery in June to clean out bone chips. Despite an aggressive rehab, he wasn't able to get healthy enough to return in 2004.

Pitching & Defense

Ainsworth has a four-seem fastball that can reach 95 MPH, though it's more effective in the 90-92 MPH range. It's not an out pitch because it lacks movement. Ainsworth uses it to set up his sinker, slider and changeup. None of his pitches stand out, so he needs to mix them up and locate them down in the zone to be effective. Ainsworth fields his position as needed and does a good job in getting over to first to cover. His move to first is average.

2005 Outlook

After two straight injury-plagued seasons, Ainsworth's immediate future is up in the air. Will the Orioles look elsewhere for starting pitching or give him another chance? Can he stay healthy and show the improvement he demonstrated with San Francisco? Ainsworth has the skills to be a consistent and above-average starter, but staying healthy is the question.

Daniel Cabrera

Position: SP
Bats: R **Throws:** R
Ht: 6' 7" **Wt:** 230

Opening Day Age: 23
Born: 5/28/81 in San Pedro de Macoris, DR
ML Seasons: 1

Overall Statistics

	W	L	Pct.	ERA	G	GS	Sv	IP	H	BB	SO	HR	Avg
'04	12	8	.600	5.00	28	27	1	147.2	145	89	76	14	.259
Car.	12	8	.600	5.00	28	27	1	147.2	145	89	76	14	.259

2004 Situational Stats

	W	L	ERA	Sv	IP		AB	H	HR	RBI	Avg
Home	3	4	5.60	0	53.0	LHB	293	73	10	47	.249
Road	9	4	4.66	1	94.2	RHB	267	72	4	35	.270
First Half	6	3	2.90	1	77.2	Sc Pos	131	45	5	65	.344
Scnd Half	6	5	7.33	0	70.0	Clutch	13	4	1	2	.308

2004 Season

Daniel Cabrera earned a callup from Double-A Bowie early in May and stuck with the Orioles the rest of the season. His best month was June, when he posted a 2.83 ERA and opponents hit just .204 against him. Cabrera's season went south when his control deserted him early in the year.

Pitching & Defense

The Orioles like Cabrera's mid-90s fastball, which has been clocked at 97 MPH at times. The fastball is an out pitch for Cabrera, but he has trouble controlling it. His big curveball, already an above-average offering, breaks sharply. His changeup is a below-average work in progress, rarely needed or used before reaching the majors. An inconsistent release point sometimes leads to high walk totals. In time he should harness his mechanics and cut down on walks. Because of his 6-foot-7 frame, Cabrera tends to be slow fielding his position.

2005 Outlook

The Orioles needed a power pitcher. Cabrera got the call, but wasn't as polished as they had hoped. His two power pitches are a solid foundation as a starter. He only needs to improve his mechanics and changeup. We'll see more on-the-job training in 2005. Cabrera is at least a year away from making his mark at the major league level.

Eric DuBose

Position: SP
Bats: L **Throws:** L
Ht: 6' 3" **Wt:** 216

Opening Day Age: 28
Born: 5/15/76 in Bradenton, FL
ML Seasons: 3
Pronunciation: dew-BOWES

Overall Statistics

	W	L	Pct.	ERA	G	GS	Sv	IP	H	BB	SO	HR	Avg
'04	4	6	.400	6.39	14	14	0	74.2	76	44	48	12	.263
Car.	7	12	.368	5.02	35	24	0	154.1	143	70	96	19	.246

2004 Situational Stats

	W	L	ERA	Sv	IP		AB	H	HR	RBI	Avg
Home	2	2	5.59	0	38.2	LHB	60	10	2	5	.167
Road	2	4	7.25	0	36.0	RHB	229	66	10	42	.288
First Half	4	6	6.39	0	74.2	Sc Pos	72	20	3	35	.278
Scnd Half	0	0	–	0	0.0	Clutch	14	3	0	0	.214

2004 Season

Eric Dubose opened 2004 with a great first month. He won three times, posted a 3.06 ERA and held opposing batters to a .190 batting average. In May, the roof caved in, and by mid-June, bone chips in his pitching elbow landed him on the disabled list. Arthroscopic surgery on July 1 ended the lefthander's season.

Pitching & Defense

DuBose has a sharp-breaking curveball. While it isn't a 12-to-6 curve, it is very effective because of its quick break. He's effective when he spots it over the outside corner, rather than in the middle of the plate. His fastball usually arrives in the 88-90 MPH range. DuBose knows how to use it to set up his breaking ball and give hitters a different look. His changeup is solid average and he uses it just to show hitters a different speed. He lacks an effective pitch against righthanded batters. DuBose has a good move to first, but is no more than an average fielder.

2005 Outlook

After going the entire 2003 season without an arm injury, the injury-prone DuBose was hurt again in 2004. The Orioles are wondering if he can stay healthy. If he can, he showed in April that he can pitch at the major league level.

John Maine

Position: SP
Bats: R **Throws:** R
Ht: 6' 4" **Wt:** 193

Opening Day Age: 23
Born: 5/8/81 in Fredericksburg, VA
ML Seasons: 1

Overall Statistics

	W	L	Pct.	ERA	G	GS	Sv	IP	H	BB	SO	HR	Avg
'04	0	1	.000	9.82	1	1	0	3.2	7	3	1	1	.438
Car.	0	1	.000	9.82	1	1	0	3.2	7	3	1	1	.438

2004 Situational Stats

	W	L	ERA	Sv	IP		AB	H	HR	RBI	Avg
Home	0	1	9.82	0	3.2	LHB	9	4	1	3	.444
Road	–	–	–	–	–	RHB	–	–	–	–	–
First Half	0	0	–	0	0.0	Sc Pos	6	1	0	2	.167
Scnd Half	0	1	9.82	0	3.2	Clutch	0	0	0	0	–

2004 Season

John Maine made the jump from Double-A Bowie to the Orioles' Triple-A team in Ottawa by throwing strikes and keeping the ball in the park. While he struggled with his control at Ottawa, he showed he could compete at that level in just his third pro season. He debuted with an emergency start against Minnesota in July.

Pitching & Defense

While his fastball can reach the mid-90s, Maine is more comfortable and effective throwing it in the 92-93 MPH range. His fastball has solid sinking action, limiting the number of home runs he allows. He continues to improve his sharp slider and it's close to being an out pitch. Maine also throws a curveball and changeup, though he's inconsistent in keeping them in the strike zone. Because of his lanky frame, his move to first is mechanical and he's no more than an adequate fielder.

2005 Season

Maine has made a quick ascent to the majors. He's expected to vie for a starting rotation spot in spring training. His limited experience and inconsistent mechanics will make for some rough stretches in 2005. Yet, we'll see some promising efforts based on his natural ability alone.

Luis Matos

Position: CF
Bats: R **Throws:** R
Ht: 6' 0" **Wt:** 208

Opening Day Age: 26
Born: 10/30/78 in Bayamon, PR
ML Seasons: 5
Pronunciation: MAH-tose

Overall Statistics

	G	AB	R	H	D	T	HR	RBI	SB	BB	SO	Avg	OBP	Slg
'04	89	330	36	74	18	0	6	28	12	19	60	.224	.275	.333
Car.	318	1080	143	273	55	6	24	103	48	71	216	.253	.307	.381

2004 Situational Stats

	AB	H	HR	RBI	Avg		AB	H	HR	RBI	Avg
Home	175	42	2	16	.240	LHP	105	14	2	7	.133
Road	155	32	4	12	.206	RHP	225	60	4	21	.267
First Half	312	73	6	27	.234	Sc Pos	78	16	0	19	.205
Scnd Half	18	1	0	1	.056	Clutch	53	7	0	1	.132

2004 Season

Based on Luis Matos' 2003 performance at the plate, the Orioles had high hopes for him. His 2004 season began, however, with a very small stress fracture in his right shin, an injury that plagued him most of the season. The fracture reappeared in July and his season was over.

Hitting, Baserunning & Defense

When he's healthy, Matos is a line-drive hitter who generates his power from a quick swing. More times than not, he's a dead pull hitter who doesn't use the entire field enough. His weakness at the plate is swinging at fastballs up in the strike zone and low-and-outside breaking balls. While Matos hits righthanders, he struggles against southpaws when they paint the outside corner. He has above-average speed that garners steals, but he doesn't study pitchers enough to improve his technique and success rate. Defensively, Matos covers a lot of ground, especially in the gaps, and throws accurately.

2005 Outlook

Matos should be ready for spring training with his leg ailments behind him. This multitalented outfielder should rebound and approach his 2003 performance in 2005. Look for Matos to be the starting center fielder.

David Newhan

Position: DH/RF/LF/3B
Bats: L **Throws:** R
Ht: 5'10" **Wt:** 180

Opening Day Age: 31
Born: 9/7/73 in Fullerton, CA
ML Seasons: 4

Overall Statistics

	G	AB	R	H	D	T	HR	RBI	SB	BB	SO	Avg	OBP	Slg
'04	95	373	66	116	15	7	8	54	11	27	72	.311	.361	.453
Car.	158	459	83	130	18	7	11	63	13	37	96	.283	.339	.425

2004 Situational Stats

	AB	H	HR	RBI	Avg		AB	H	HR	RBI	Avg
Home	171	51	3	26	.298	LHP	101	30	1	10	.297
Road	202	65	5	28	.322	RHP	272	86	7	44	.316
First Half	85	36	4	17	.424	Sc Pos	99	34	1	39	.343
Scnd Half	288	80	4	37	.278	Clutch	52	14	0	9	.269

2004 Season

David Newhan exercised a clause in his contract with the Texas Rangers on June 15, making him a free agent when he wasn't recalled by the Rangers. He signed with the Orioles and hit a pinch-hit home run in his first game as an Oriole on June 18. The 31-year-old journeyman made the most of his playing time, providing both power and speed from the left side of the plate.

Hitting, Baserunning & Defense

Newhan hits pitchers from both sides of the rubber equally well, though he generates more of his power against righthanders. His swing is compact and level, mostly generating line drives and groundballs. Newhan uses a quick first step and hustle to steal bases, rather than pure speed. He can play any infield position except short, as well as both corner outfield spots. His range is average both in the infield and outfield, and he throws accurately with an arm that isn't particularly strong.

2005 Outlook

Newhan is a free agent who will garner interest from the Orioles, who want to re-sign him, and other teams looking for a low-cost investment. Depending on where he lands, Newhan may duplicate his 2004 success, but it's unlikely.

John Parrish

Position: RP
Bats: L **Throws:** L
Ht: 5'11" **Wt:** 192

Opening Day Age: 27
Born: 11/26/77 in Lancaster, PA
ML Seasons: 4

Overall Statistics

	W	L	Pct.	ERA	G	GS	Sv	IP	H	BB	SO	HR	Avg
'04	6	3	.667	3.46	56	1	1	78.0	68	55	71	4	.238
Car.	9	10	.474	4.44	94	10	1	160.0	147	115	134	17	.247

2004 Situational Stats

	W	L	ERA	Sv	IP		AB	H	HR	RBI	Avg
Home	6	1	2.49	0	43.1	LHB	103	25	3	20	.243
Road	0	2	4.67	1	34.2	RHB	183	43	1	22	.235
First Half	5	3	3.75	1	50.1	Sc Pos	103	26	2	40	.252
Scnd Half	1	0	2.93	0	27.2	Clutch	27	3	0	1	.111

2004 Season

John Parrish showed flashes of the talent that once had him high on the Orioles' prospect lists. He struggled at times early in the season by not throwing strikes consistently. Still, he provided quality depth to the bullpen and won five times before the All-Star break. In the second half, Parrish averaged more than a strikeout per inning and posted a 2.93 ERA.

Pitching & Defense

Parrish uses a 91-93 MPH fastball to keep hitters from leaning over the plate. His offspeed pitch is average at best. His breaking ball is sharp but inconsistent, but he can be deceptive because of a quick motion to the plate. An inconsistent release point often plagues Parrish, and that can cause his command and control to desert him. Parrish is a good athlete who fields his position well. He successfully covers first base on grounders to the right side. His move to first is average.

2005 Outlook

Unless he has a poor spring training, Parrish should stick at the major league level, but as a reliever. He lacks three quality pitches and the control to warrant a move to the rotation. A more consistent release point could spark some improvement in his performance.

Matt Riley

Position: SP
Bats: L **Throws:** L
Ht: 6'1" **Wt:** 221

Opening Day Age: 25
Born: 8/2/79 in Antioch, CA
ML Seasons: 3

Overall Statistics

	W	L	Pct.	ERA	G	GS	Sv	IP	H	BB	SO	HR	Avg
'04	3	4	.429	5.63	14	13	0	64.0	60	44	60	11	.244
Car.	4	4	.500	5.40	19	18	0	85.0	84	62	74	16	.257

2004 Situational Stats

	W	L	ERA	Sv	IP		AB	H	HR	RBI	Avg
Home	2	2	5.58	0	40.1	LHB	44	14	3	12	.318
Road	1	2	5.70	0	23.2	RHB	202	46	8	22	.228
First Half	1	3	8.39	0	34.1	Sc Pos	58	16	4	26	.276
Scnd Half	2	1	2.43	0	29.2	Clutch	7	0	0	0	.000

2004 Season

After Tommy John surgery in 2000, Matt Riley is inching closer to his pre-surgical level. While a May trip to the disabled list and two stints at Triple-A Ottawa limited his big league innings, he closed with a 2-1 record and 2.43 ERA in five September starts.

Pitching & Defense

When Riley is on, he's repeating his delivery with all his pitches, but that doesn't happen often enough and his control and command will desert him. His curveball can be one of the best in the Orioles' system, but he struggles to keep it in the strike zone. His 92-94 MPH fastball doesn't have a lot of movement. He's improving a changeup that should become a plus pitch. Riley's move to first is quick, but he sometimes loses focus with a fast runner aboard. He's able to get to bunts and slow rollers, but tends to rush his throws.

2005 Outlook

Riley has shown glimpses of being the top southpaw prospect he was before his elbow injury, and the Orioles believe he'll make major strides in his consistency this season. While Riley is very talented and will improve as a full-time member of the Orioles' rotation, there will be growing pains.

B.J. Ryan

Position: RP
Bats: L **Throws:** L
Ht: 6' 6" **Wt:** 249

Opening Day Age: 29
Born: 12/28/75 in Bossier City, LA
ML Seasons: 6

Overall Statistics

	W	L	Pct.	ERA	G	GS	Sv	IP	H	BB	SO	HR	Avg
'04	4	6	.400	2.28	76	0	3	87.0	64	35	122	4	.200
Car.	15	15	.500	3.79	336	0	6	311.0	253	169	365	25	.221

2004 Situational Stats

	W	L	ERA	Sv	IP		AB	H	HR	RBI	Avg
Home	2	3	2.00	3	45.0	LHB	106	10	2	7	.094
Road	2	3	2.57	0	42.0	RHB	214	54	2	24	.252
First Half	3	2	1.75	1	46.1	Sc Pos	102	18	1	27	.176
Scnd Half	1	4	2.88	2	40.2	Clutch	215	42	2	24	.195

2004 Season

B.J. Ryan posted career highs in holds (21), ERA and strikeouts in 2004, demonstrating that he has become one of the best lefthanded relievers in the American League. After the best stretch of pitching in his career during the first half, Ryan was called on as more than just a situational lefty by manager Lee Mazzilli. Ryan allowed opponents to bat just .200 against him, one of the best marks in the AL.

Pitching & Defense

Ryan has deceptive pitching motion that is tough on hitters. His best pitch is a sharp-breaking slider. Lefthanded hitters struggle mightily, as the pitch starts in the strike zone and breaks sharply down and in. Until last season, Ryan used his low-90s fastball simply to set up the slider. Now, with increased movement on the pitch, hitters must respect it. It's a reason he is more effective retiring righthanded batters, leading to an expanded role.

2005 Outlook

Ryan's steady improvement over the last three seasons makes him one of the best lefty relievers in the game. He could assume the closer role in 2005, as the Orioles' confidence in Jorge Julio has eroded the last two seasons. A solid spring could turn ninth-inning duties over to Ryan.

B.J. Surhoff

Position: RF/LF/DH/1B
Bats: L **Throws:** R
Ht: 6' 1" **Wt:** 210

Opening Day Age: 40
Born: 8/4/64 in Bronx, NY
ML Seasons: 18

Overall Statistics

	G	AB	R	H	D	T	HR	RBI	SB	BB	SO	Avg	OBP	Slg
	100	343	49	106	12	1	8	50	2	30	46	.309	.365	.420
	2222	7955	1032	2248	429	40	183	1119	141	629	807	.283	.334	.416

2004 Situational Stats

	AB	H	HR	RBI	Avg		AB	H	HR	RBI	Avg
Home	171	50	4	26	.292	LHP	99	33	1	14	.333
Road	172	56	4	24	.326	RHP	244	73	7	36	.299
First Half	137	44	3	19	.321	Sc Pos	94	32	3	44	.340
Scnd Half	206	62	5	31	.301	Clutch	58	18	0	5	.310

2004 Season

B.J. Surhoff seemed to find the fountain of youth. The 40-year-old outfielder posted his first .300 average since 1999. While his power numbers dropped off, he still provided key hits over the course of the season. Only a strained left calf muscle kept Surhoff from topping 400 at-bats.

Hitting, Baserunning & Defense

While Surhoff doesn't pull the ball as much as he once did, he still can get around on most inside pitches. This savvy lefthanded hitter actually hits southpaws as well as he does righthanded pitchers, and he's at his best going the other way to the gap. His basestealing days are over, but he can't be ignored at first base. Surhoff still can score from second base on hits to the gaps and right field. He can play first base or the corner outfield spots, where he uses his experience and a quick first step to get the job done. His throws are accurate to any base.

2005 Outlook

After a solid 2004 season, Surhoff's indecision about 2005 didn't last long. In early December, he agreed to a one-year, $1.1 million deal to return to the Orioles. If Surhoff remains healthy, there isn't any reason he can't approach his 2004 performance.

Other Baltimore Orioles

Rick Bauer (**Pos**: RHP, **Age**: 28)

	W	L	Pct.	ERA	G	GS	Sv	IP	H	BB	SO	HR	Avg
'04	2	1	.667	4.70	23	2	0	53.2	49	20	37	4	.238
Car.	8	13	.381	4.39	120	9	1	231.2	226	89	141	28	.257

Statistically, Bauer has posted very similar seasons the last two summers. A key difference is that he closed 2004 with a pair of decent starts, including six shutout innings versus Toronto. He's a longshot to join the Orioles' rotation, but he's another option for the young O's. 2005 Outlook: B

Dave Borkowski (**Pos**: RHP, **Age**: 28)

	W	L	Pct.	ERA	G	GS	Sv	IP	H	BB	SO	HR	Avg
'04	3	4	.429	5.14	17	8	0	56.0	65	15	45	6	.289
Car.	5	13	.278	6.33	51	21	0	167.2	192	77	126	23	.287

With little big league success in his history, Borkowksi beat the Rays and shut out Boston for seven innings in two of his first four 2004 starts in July. He was better as a starter (3-4, 4.63 ERA), but struggled after August 15 (10.64 ERA in 11 IP) as his magic slipped away. 2005 Outlook: C

Bruce Chen (**Pos**: LHP, **Age**: 27)

	W	L	Pct.	ERA	G	GS	Sv	IP	H	BB	SO	HR	Avg
'04	2	1	.667	3.02	8	7	0	47.2	39	16	32	7	.220
Car.	22	20	.524	4.44	163	68	0	501.0	473	210	432	90	.248

Chen seemed to be in pursuit of Mike Morgan's record for big league teams, as the lefthander has played for eight clubs since 2000. His 1-1 (3.22) performance in seven starts with Baltimore was his best since his 2000 season with Atlanta and Philadelphia. Maybe he's found a home. 2005 Outlook: C

Darwin Cubillan (**Pos**: RHP, **Age**: 32)

	W	L	Pct.	ERA	G	GS	Sv	IP	H	BB	SO	HR	Avg
'04	0	0	–	5.40	7	0	0	10.0	13	7	8	3	.302
Car.	1	0	1.000	6.85	56	0	0	69.2	96	44	54	13	.330

After a two-year absence from the majors, Cubillan spent three weeks with Baltimore during the first half. He didn't show any more than he had in previous trials with Toronto, Texas and Montreal. Lots of walks and home runs allowed tell the story. 2005 Outlook: C

Jack Cust (**Pos**: DH, **Age**: 26, **Bats**: L)

	G	AB	R	H	D	T	HR	RBI	SB	BB	SO	Avg	OBP	Slg
'04	1	1	0	0	0	0	0	0	0	0	1	.000	.000	.000
Car.	66	141	15	31	9	0	5	19	0	23	58	.220	.331	.390

After slugging 48 doubles and 50 homers at two Triple-A Pacific Coast League stops in 2001-02, the power prospect has 33 doubles and 26 homers (in 124 fewer AB) in the Triple-A International League the last two years. He lacks a position and his hitting percentages are sliding. 2005 Outlook: C

Karim Garcia (**Pos**: RF/CF, **Age**: 29, **Bats**: L)

	G	AB	R	H	D	T	HR	RBI	SB	BB	SO	Avg	OBP	Slg
'04	85	258	33	59	7	2	10	33	3	14	50	.229	.265	.388
Car.	488	1463	180	352	44	13	66	212	10	81	330	.241	.279	.424

Garcia didn't rebound from a bad night in a Fenway Park bullpen late in 2003. He didn't produce in a golden opportunity as a Mets starter last spring, was displaced by Richard Hidalgo, dealt to Baltimore and released in August. He has signed to play for the Orix Blue Wave in Japan. 2005 Outlook: D

Geronimo Gil (**Pos**: C, **Age**: 29, **Bats**: R)

	G	AB	R	H	D	T	HR	RBI	SB	BB	SO	Avg	OBP	Slg
'04	12	32	1	9	2	0	0	4	0	3	5	.281	.343	.344
Car.	208	681	59	164	27	0	15	71	2	41	134	.241	.289	.347

After serving as the Orioles' starting catcher in 2002 and spending most of 2003 as a backup, Gil didn't reach Baltimore until September in 2004. He wasn't productive offensively at Triple-A Ottawa, and it's unlikely he'll ever be the Orioles' starter again. 2005 Outlook: C

Jason Grimsley (**Pos**: RHP, **Age**: 37)

	W	L	Pct.	ERA	G	GS	Sv	IP	H	BB	SO	HR	Avg
'04	5	7	.417	3.86	73	0	0	63.0	61	35	39	4	.251
Car.	40	54	.426	4.74	511	72	4	887.0	900	481	602	74	.264

A solid 2001 with the Royals reinvigorated his career, but Grimsley has been on the decline. He blew all nine of his save chances in 2004, and at the end of the season it was revealed that he needed Tommy John surgery and would miss all of 2005. At his age, he may not return to the majors. 2005 Outlook: D

Buddy Groom (**Pos**: LHP, **Age**: 39)

	W	L	Pct.	ERA	G	GS	Sv	IP	H	BB	SO	HR	Avg
'04	4	1	.800	4.78	60	0	0	52.2	67	16	32	6	.309
Car.	30	31	.492	4.63	739	15	26	693.2	774	248	474	68	.284

Groom's stunning 2002 season at age 37—a 1.60 ERA and 0.94 baserunners per inning over 62 frames—was an aberration. He has a 5.05 ERA with 1.62 baserunners per inning over the last two summers, and his 40th birthday awaits him in July. 2005 Outlook: C

Ken Huckaby (**Pos**: C, **Age**: 34, **Bats**: R)

	G	AB	R	H	D	T	HR	RBI	SB	BB	SO	Avg	OBP	Slg
'04	24	50	4	7	3	0	0	0	0	5	12	.140	.218	.200
Car.	118	335	34	76	10	1	3	24	0	14	59	.227	.258	.290

Through a decade of part-time catching duties at the Triple-A level, Huckaby has managed a cup of coffee in the majors in each of the last four seasons. Offensively, he didn't do anything in 2004 to warrant a part-time job at a higher level when the new season begins. 2005 Outlook: C

Jose Leon (Pos: 1B, Age: 28, Bats: R)

	G	AB	R	H	D	T	HR	RBI	SB	BB	SO	Avg	OBP	Slg
'04	31	66	4	12	2	0	2	8	0	2	19	.182	.203	.303
Car.	88	209	18	47	5	0	5	18	1	8	57	.225	.262	.321

Leon enjoyed his best Triple-A season in four tries in 2004. He didn't do anything with the Orioles that would make him a contender for a reserve role as a corner infielder in the spring, but the Pirates signed him to a minor league deal in December. 2005 Outlook: C

Luis Lopez (Pos: SS/3B, Age: 34, Bats: B)

	G	AB	R	H	D	T	HR	RBI	SB	BB	SO	Avg	OBP	Slg
'04	56	88	7	16	5	0	1	8	0	3	20	.182	.211	.273
Car.	704	1593	171	384	82	7	22	149	10	99	337	.241	.294	.343

Lopez continues to surface in the majors as a backup infielder, though only in 2000 with Milwaukee did he show some of the pop that scouts thought might be hidden in his bat. He's been below the Mendoza line in 197 at-bats the last two seasons, and he may be running out of chances. 2005 Outlook: C

Robert Machado (Pos: C, Age: 31, Bats: R)

	G	AB	R	H	D	T	HR	RBI	SB	BB	SO	Avg	OBP	Slg
'04	37	73	5	11	3	0	1	3	0	4	18	.151	.195	.233
Car.	253	636	66	146	36	2	11	61	0	45	135	.230	.282	.344

Machado has batted better than .300 with solid hitting percentages as a part-time catcher in Triple-A ball the last two seasons. He's never hit that well in the majors, but that didn't stop the Rangers from inking him to a minor league deal in late November. 2005 Outlook: C

Darnell McDonald (Pos: RF, Age: 26, Bats: R)

	G	AB	R	H	D	T	HR	RBI	SB	BB	SO	Avg	OBP	Slg
'04	17	32	3	5	1	0	0	1	1	2	6	.156	.206	.188
Car.	17	32	3	5	1	0	0	1	1	2	6	.156	.206	.188

McDonald arguably had his worst Triple-A season since reaching the level in 2001. A toolsy guy, he hasn't transformed his gifts into major league skills. Now he's a six-year minor league free agent in search of a new organization in which to try to have that breakout season. 2005 Outlook: C

Chad Mottola (Pos: LF, Age: 33, Bats: R)

	G	AB	R	H	D	T	HR	RBI	SB	BB	SO	Avg	OBP	Slg
'04	6	14	2	2	1	0	1	3	0	2	3	.143	.250	.429
Car.	49	109	14	21	4	0	4	12	2	10	25	.193	.264	.339

Mottola, who has spent a decade at the Triple-A level, came up and hit his first major league home run since 1996. He was with the Reds then, his original organization, but he's passed through seven minor league systems since leaving the Reds. 2005 Outlook: C

Keith Osik (Pos: C, Age: 36, Bats: R)

	G	AB	R	H	D	T	HR	RBI	SB	BB	SO	Avg	OBP	Slg
'04	11	25	0	2	0	0	0	0	0	0	7	.080	.080	.080
Car.	450	1119	96	259	55	4	13	108	6	111	200	.231	.309	.323

Osik won the backup catcher's job in spring training, but he was released in late May as part of a roster shakeup in Baltimore. He later played Triple-A ball for the Marlins' and D-Rays' affiliates and didn't fare well at the plate. He'll battle for a backup job again in the spring. 2005 Outlook: C

Tim Raines Jr. (Pos: CF, Age: 25, Bats: R)

	G	AB	R	H	D	T	HR	RBI	SB	BB	SO	Avg	OBP	Slg
'04	48	94	14	24	6	0	0	5	7	4	16	.255	.293	.319
Car.	75	160	24	34	9	1	0	7	10	9	36	.213	.263	.281

Raines has taken a long time developing, but he had a much better 2003 season in the high minors. He wasn't as good at Triple-A Ottawa in 2004, but became very familiar with flying between Ottawa and Baltimore. He may need time to adjust in the majors and may never be a regular. 2005 Outlook: C

Aaron Rakers (Pos: RHP, Age: 28)

	W	L	Pct.	ERA	G	GS	Sv	IP	H	BB	SO	HR	Avg
'04	0	0	—	4.15	3	0	0	4.1	5	1	3	0	.278
Car.	0	0	—	4.15	3	0	0	4.1	5	1	3	0	.278

Rakers also has taken time to develop in the minors, but he was impressive at Triple-A Ottawa and may be ready to help in the Orioles' bullpen in 2005. With Ottawa, he posted a 2.75 ERA in 78.2 innings, while allowing 65 hits and 25 walks and fanning 80. He could surprise. 2005 Outlook: C

Eddy Rodriguez (Pos: RHP, Age: 23)

	W	L	Pct.	ERA	G	GS	Sv	IP	H	BB	SO	HR	Avg
'04	1	0	1.000	4.78	29	0	0	43.1	36	30	37	5	.231
Car.	1	0	1.000	4.78	29	0	0	43.1	36	30	37	5	.231

Visa problems delayed his spring prep, but Rodriguez was a pleasant surprise when he joined the O's in May. A Double-A closer in 2003, he posted a 2.52 ERA in 15 games through the All-Star break and got his first big league "W." Then he struggled with the O's and at Triple-A, too. 2005 Outlook: C

David Segui (Pos: DH, Age: 38, Bats: B)

	G	AB	R	H	D	T	HR	RBI	SB	BB	SO	Avg	OBP	Slg
'04	18	59	8	20	3	0	1	7	0	5	13	.339	.400	.441
Car.	1456	4847	683	1412	284	16	139	684	17	524	687	.291	.359	.443

The end of Segui's four-year, $28 million contract with Baltimore finally has arrived, and the veteran managed just 670 at-bats over the life of the contract because of injuries. He may have to take a minor league deal with an invite to spring training to stick around in the majors. 2005 Outlook: C

Todd Williams (Pos: RHP, Age: 34)

	W	L	Pct.	ERA	G	GS	Sv	IP	H	BB	SO	HR	Avg
'04	2	0	1.000	2.87	29	0	0	31.1	26	9	13	2	.232
Car.	5	3	.625	4.45	79	0	0	85.0	93	38	45	8	.278

Williams' first year as a Triple-A closer was 1993, and he gets few saves any more. Still, he pitched well enough at his second Triple-A stop of 2004 to join and be successful with the Orioles. It was his first big league job since 2001, his fifth with five teams since 1995. 2005 Outlook: C

Baltimore Orioles Minor League Prospects

Organization Overview:

The Orioles' system hasn't yielded much in the way of major league talent in recent seasons, but that could be changing and soon. Outfielder Val Majewski is an all-around talent who played in last year's Futures Game. Righthander John Maine made solid strides last season and is expected to garner a starting spot with the parent club in 2005. Baltimore also has more help on the way, including third baseman Tripper Johnson, who has solid power potential but needs to improve his plate awareness, and second baseman Mike Fontenot, who may be ready to contribute immediately if not for the O's current logjam at the keystone. Overall, the system is adding depth, though the cupboard remains bare of top-notch prospects.

Dave Crouthers

Position: P
Bats: R **Throws:** R
Ht: 6' 3" **Wt:** 190

Opening Day Age: 25
Born: 12/18/79 in
Edwardsville, IL

Recent Statistics

	W	L	ERA	G	GS	Sv	IP	H	R	BB	SO	HR
2003 A Frederick	7	5	3.59	18	18	0	92.2	83	47	43	82	1
2003 AA Bowie	4	2	3.80	9	9	0	45.0	37	20	18	29	4
2004 AA Bowie	9	9	5.03	27	27	0	139.2	134	81	68	138	23

Crouthers struck out 138 in 139.2 innings at Double-A Bowie last season. He throws almost effortlessly, and his fastball usually sits around 93-95 MPH. What is missing so far is a consistent release point. He struggles to repeat his delivery, especially with his slider—a plus-type pitch—and changeup. His command deserted him at times last season, and he saw a huge increase in the amount of home runs he allowed (23). He also walked 68 batters. Before climbing further up the organizational ladder, Crouthers will need to improve his command, learn to keep the ball down in the strike zone and develop his changeup. He's a couple years away from helping the parent club, but he could move quickly with improved consistency.

Mike Fontenot

Position: 2B
Bats: L **Throws:** R
Ht: 5' 8" **Wt:** 167

Opening Day Age: 24
Born: 6/9/80 in New Iberia, LA

Recent Statistics

	G	AB	R	H	D	T	HR	RBI	SB	BB	SO	Avg
2003 AA Bowie	126	449	63	146	24	5	12	66	16	50	89	.325
2004 AAA Ottawa	136	524	73	146	30	10	8	49	14	48	111	.279

If Fontenot can learn to cut down his strikeouts a bit, he could be a valuable asset as a No. 2 hitter. He has gap power to all fields and is learning to hit offspeed offerings with more consistency. That said, offensively Fontenot is ready for the majors. He has racked up impressive extra-base totals in each of the past two seasons. The two hurdles standing in his way are his position and his barely adequate defense. Fontenot is a second baseman who has Brian Roberts and possibly Jerry Hairston Jr. in front of him on the big league roster. Fontenot struggles with his footwork and inconsistent play around the second-base bag, but his arm isn't strong enough for a permanent move to third. He'll help the big league team this season, but most likely in a reserve role.

David Haehnel

Position: P
Bats: L **Throws:** L
Ht: 6' 4" **Wt:** 180

Opening Day Age: 22
Born: 7/21/82 in Wheeling, IL

Recent Statistics

	W	L	ERA	G	GS	Sv	IP	H	R	BB	SO	HR
2004 A Aberdeen	3	1	1.69	28	0	15	37.1	23	8	11	61	1

The Orioles see Haehnel as a potential closer, though he lacks the dominating out pitch that many major league closers have. He relies on a low-90s fastball and a slider that can look like a cutter at times. He hides his pitches well, and that gives him the ability to keep hitters off stride. His offspeed offering is promising and has the potential to be a plus pitch as he develops more consistency. Baltimore believes this southpaw has as a high ceiling as any reliever in the organization. All Haehnel needs is experience and consistency. It's unlikely he'll be moved into a starting role, as he's targeted to close again in Class-A ball.

Tripper Johnson

Position: 3B
Bats: R **Throws:** R
Ht: 6' 1" **Wt:** 195

Opening Day Age: 22
Born: 4/28/82 in Bellevue Wa

Recent Statistics

	G	AB	R	H	D	T	HR	RBI	SB	BB	SO	Avg
2003 A Frederick	123	417	43	114	25	3	5	50	7	46	92	.273
2004 A Frederick	129	465	62	125	19	2	21	74	14	51	93	.269

The talented Johnson has yet to make significant improvement after five years in the Baltimore system. He has flashed good power (21 homers at high Class-A Frederick last season), but a back injury in 2003 and a aggressive swing at the plate in 2004 hurt his overall numbers. Johnson is a streaky hitter who continues to produce too many unproductive at-bats. Effort is not the problem, however, as he pushes himself too hard at times and is prone to slumps. Once he gets better control of his strikeouts, his production should increase. At the hot corner, Johnson displays above-average footwork and his throws are accurate. At present, his defense is ahead of his offense. A true test comes this season at Double-A Bowie.

Adam Loewen

Position: P **Opening Day Age:** 20
Bats: L **Throws:** L **Born:** 4/9/84 in Surrey,
Ht: 6' 6" **Wt:** 219 Canada

Recent Statistics

	W	L	ERA	G	GS	Sv	IP	H	R	BB	SO	HR
2003 A Aberdeen	0	2	2.70	7	7	0	23.1	13	7	9	25	0
2004 A Delmarva	4	5	4.11	20	19	0	85.1	77	47	58	82	3
2004 A Frederick	0	2	6.75	2	2	0	8.0	7	6	9	3	2

Loewen remains Baltimore's top pitching prospect, even though he torn the labrum in his pitching shoulder late in the year. If he avoids surgery, he could pitch a half season in the minors. If surgery is required, he'll miss the 2005 campaign. This former first-rounder's calling card is a 12-to-6 curveball in the mold of Barry Zito's, though it isn't nearly as sharp or consistent. Loewen's fastball ranges from 90-95 MPH, but he has better control throwing it 90-92 MPH. His changeup is average but could develop into a plus pitch. Loewen is a very good athlete, and the Orioles believe that if healthy, he has the skills and makeup to be a top-of-the-rotation starter.

Val Majewski

Position: OF **Opening Day Age:** 23
Bats: L **Throws:** L **Born:** 6/19/81 in New
Ht: 6' 2" **Wt:** 200 Brunswick, NJ

Recent Statistics

	G	AB	R	H	D	T	HR	RBI	SB	BB	SO	Avg
2004 AA Bowie	112	433	71	133	24	5	15	80	14	33	68	.307
2004 AL Baltimore	9	13	3	2	1	0	0	1	0	0	1	.154

The Orioles' Minor League Player of the Year, Majewski posted another very good, if not dominant, season, this time at Double-A Bowie. He uses the whole field to his advantage as he goes with where the pitch is located. His power is starting to develop, and it should improve as he learns to turn on inside pitches more than trying to inside-out them. Majewski played center field last year, and while he could play there in the majors, he's better suited as a corner outfielder. What really sets him apart from other Baltimore prospects is his aggressive attitude. He rarely gets down on himself and is polished beyond his years. Majewski is close to sticking with the Orioles for good.

Nick Markakis

Position: OF **Opening Day Age:** 21
Bats: L **Throws:** L **Born:** 11/17/83 in
Ht: 6' 1" **Wt:** 170 Woodstock, GA

Recent Statistics

	G	AB	R	H	D	T	HR	RBI	SB	BB	SO	Avg
2003 A Aberdeen	59	205	22	58	14	3	1	28	13	30	33	.283
2004 A Delmarva	96	355	57	106	22	3	11	64	12	42	66	.299

Markakis, a former first-round selection and potential pitching prospect, already has shown he can hit. While most major league teams thought he was a better pitch-er, Baltimore liked his short, compact swing. He has good plate coverage, gap power that should continue to improve and a major league attitude about his craft. In the field, Markakis has a plus-arm to go along with good outfield instincts, especially for a player with limited pro experience. Even with that limited experience, he handled the move to Class-A Delmarva without a problem. Markakis could make his way to Double-A Bowie by the end of 2005 if he handles the anticipated jump to high Class-A Frederick.

Walter Young

Position: 1B **Opening Day Age:** 25
Bats: L **Throws:** R **Born:** 2/18/80 in
Ht: 6' 5" **Wt:** 305 Hattiesburg, MS

Recent Statistics

	G	AB	R	H	D	T	HR	RBI	SB	BB	SO	Avg
2003 A Lynchburg	117	431	76	120	15	2	20	87	2	35	88	.278
2004 AA Bowie	133	486	88	133	28	1	33	98	2	47	145	.274

Young could be considered a larger version of Calvin Pickering: monster home-run power that turns heads in batting practice and in games when he connects. That ability makes him a potential DH candidate down the road. The downside of all that power is a very long swing. Young gets tied up on inside fastballs and he chases too many fastballs up in the zone. The Orioles believe his high strikeout totals can be greatly reduced if he tightens up his swing and improves his plate discipline. Because of his size, the jury still is out as to whether he can contribute much in the field. His towering home runs may get him to the majors late in the upcoming season, but the question will be whether his bat alone can keep him in the big leagues.

Others to Watch

Shortstop **Bryan Bass** (22) has the skills to be one of the best in the organization. But inconsistent contact at the plate and poor fundamentals in the field get him into trouble. If the light were to come on, he would move quickly through the system. . . Righthanded starter **Freddy Deza** (22) teamed with Hayden Penn to form a solid starting duo in Class-A ball last season. Deza is not quite as polished as Penn, but the former has solid upside. . . Southpaw **Rommie Lewis** (22) took a step back last season, as concerns about his durability led to a move to the bullpen. He has a low-90s fastball, which is above-average velocity for a lefty. The problem is a lack of aggressiveness in going after hitters. . . Righthander **Hayden Penn** (20) finished the 2004 season at high Class-A Frederick. He showed very good control and a knack for setting up hitters. Experience and refinement of his pitches are the only things that stand between Double-A and reaching Triple-A in 2005. . . The Orioles believe righty **Chris Ray** (23) has a major league-caliber split-finger pitch and a solid enough fastball to earn him a big league starting job in time. He also has a decent slider, but difficulty repeating his delivery gets him into trouble.

Fenway Park

Offense

Fenway Park is a renowned hitters' park, especially for hitters who can utilize the left-field wall. Though it remains a fairly good home-run park, it is more doubles-friendly and not the long-ball paradise it was in decades past. Righthanded power hitters traditionally benefit from Fenway's cozy confines, but lefties who can hit to the opposite field also thrive here. Foul territory is tiny, further favoring offense.

Defense

Fenway's dimensions present a unique challenge to each outfield position. Left field, of course, has the Green Monster. Its caroms can baffle visiting players, but its closeness to the plate can mask a lack of range in left fielders, such as Boston's Manny Ramirez, if they learn the bounces. Right field may be the most challenging. There is plenty of ground to cover, with a 302-foot foul pole arcing back to a 380-foot power alley. Fenway's right field also gets harsh sun in the early innings of summer night games. Center field juts to 420 feet from home plate at its deepest.

Who It Helps the Most

Kevin Millar takes full advantage of the left-field wall, and hit more than 100 points better at home than on the road last season. Jason Varitek also thrives here, hitting well to all fields. Curt Schilling rode generous run support and a penchant for strikeouts to a 12-1 mark at home in his first season in Boston.

Who It Hurts the Most

The park can be hard on lefty hurlers, and few pitchers have an easy time at Fenway. Righthanders Keith Foulke and Bronson Arroyo struggled here in 2004, with ERAs two runs higher than on the road. David Ortiz sees his home runs decline a bit because of the deep right-center field, but he generates a higher batting average at home.

Rookies & Newcomers

Southpaw Abe Alvarez is one of the few upper-level prospects who could surface in Boston in 2005. He has little margin for error with his stuff, and Fenway would provide a great challenge for him.

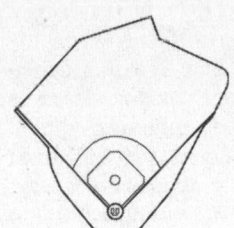

Dimensions: LF-310, LCF-379, CF-420, RCF-380, RF-302

Capacity: 35,095

Elevation: 21 feet

Surface: Grass

Foul Territory: Small

Park Factors

2004 Season

| | Home Games | | | Away Games | | | |
	Red Sox	Opp	Total	Red Sox	Opp	Total	Index
G	72	72	144	72	72	144	
Avg	.306	.255	.280	.257	.256	.257	109
AB	2534	2553	5087	2557	2430	4987	102
R	469	350	819	381	329	710	115
H	776	650	1426	658	622	1280	111
2B	193	164	357	138	123	261	134
3B	8	12	20	13	16	29	68
HR	102	69	171	98	71	169	99
BB	291	196	487	297	192	489	98
SO	515	520	1035	533	480	1013	100
E	59	53	112	44	42	86	130
E-Infield	51	47	98	36	36	72	136
LHB-Avg	.311	.255	.281	.249	.243	.246	115
LHB-HR	44	28	72	47	29	76	94
RHB-Avg	.302	.255	.279	.265	.271	.267	104
RHB-HR	58	41	99	51	42	93	104

2002-2004

| | Home Games | | | Away Games | | | |
	Red Sox	Opp	Total	Red Sox	Opp	Total	Index
G	216	216	432	216	216	432	
Avg	.298	.255	.276	.268	.252	.260	106
AB	7429	7561	14990	7778	7316	15094	99
R	1279	1005	2284	1177	974	2151	106
H	2217	1927	4144	2084	1844	3928	105
2B	530	455	985	439	370	809	123
3B	39	35	74	36	52	88	85
HR	268	188	456	297	211	508	90
BB	827	560	1387	776	635	1411	99
SO	1274	1543	2817	1434	1504	2938	97
E	161	151	312	130	124	254	123
E-Infield	136	127	263	108	106	214	123
LHB-Avg	.297	.248	.272	.258	.251	.255	107
LHB-HR	114	77	191	144	109	253	76
RHB-Avg	.300	.261	.281	.277	.253	.266	106
RHB-HR	154	111	265	153	102	255	105

2004 Rankings (American League)

- Highest batting-average factor
- Highest hit factor
- Highest double factor
- Highest error factor
- Highest infield-error factor
- Highest LHB batting-average factor
- Second-highest run factor

Boston

Terry Francona

2004 Season

Terry Francona couldn't take offense when his players called him an idiot. The Red Sox called themselves "the idiots," and Francona deserves credit for fostering a relaxed clubhouse atmosphere. When the Red Sox played .500 ball from May through July, Francona took heat for everything from his game management to his refusal to criticize players. But Boston caught fire, going 42-18 after August 1 and winning its first World Series since 1918.

Offense

In Francona's first season in Boston, he managed an offense that would do Earl Weaver proud. The bunt was a mere afterthought, as the club registered a meager 12 sacrifice hits all season. Even with speedsters Johnny Damon and Pokey Reese on the roster, Francona played station-to-station baseball more often than he gave runners the green light. He used 141 different starting lineups, the second-highest total in the league, but much of that was due to injuries and an ever-evolving roster.

Pitching & Defense

After the Red Sox upgraded their defense at the trading deadline, Francona began using a late-inning "hands team," with Doug Mientkiewicz, Pokey Reese and Gabe Kapler providing defensive upgrades to hold late leads. Otherwise, Francona seemed loathe to keep the big bats out of the lineup. He clearly had established "A" and "B" sets of relievers, which worked well to hold leads but often turned deficits into blowouts. His adherence to pitch counts depended on the starting pitcher. He was not inclined to issue intentional walks.

2005 Outlook

Francona may be the first Red Sox manager in recent memory not to begin the season on the hot seat. Nonetheless, fickle Red Sox Nation demands success, and a poor start to the campaign could put pressure on Francona. Although the Red Sox have several high-profile free agents, Francona will be expected to win again with Curt Schilling as his ace, and Manny Ramirez and David Ortiz returning to the heart of the lineup.

Born: 4/22/59 in Aberdeen, SD

Playing Experience: 1981-1990, Mon, ChC, Cin, Cle, Mil

Managerial Experience: 5 seasons

Manager Statistics

Year	Team, Lg	W	L	Pct	GB	Finish
2004	Boston, AL	98	64	.605	3.0	2nd East
5 Seasons		383	427	.473	–	–

2004 Starting Pitchers by Days Rest

	<=3	4	5	6+
Red Sox Starts	0	77	64	13
Red Sox ERA	–	4.48	4.30	3.50
AL Avg Starts	2	82	47	21
AL ERA	5.36	4.87	4.65	4.93

2004 Situational Stats

	Terry Francona	AL Average
Hit & Run Success %	21.2	36.8
Stolen Base Success %	69.4	68.6
Platoon Pct.	65.1	61.6
Defensive Subs	53	21
High-Pitch Outings	3	5
Quick/Slow Hooks	11/25	20/16
Sacrifice Attempts	20	53

2004 Rankings (American League)

- 1st in defensive substitutions and slow hooks
- 2nd in fewest caught stealings of third base (2) and starting lineups used (141)
- 3rd in pitchouts with a runner moving (6)

Orlando Cabrera

2004 Season

Orlando Cabrera arrived in Boston with some mighty shortstop shoes to fill, acquired from Montreal in the deadline deal that shipped Nomar Garciaparra out of town. Cabrera filled the bill, perhaps better than expected, providing the Red Sox with a strong performance and a breath of fresh air in the clubhouse. The midseason change of scenery seemed to do his bat good. He hit .294 after joining Boston, with as many RBI (31) in 58 games as he'd had in 103 games for the Expos. He drove in 11 runs in 14 postseason games, and batted .379 in the ALCS.

Hitting

Cabrera steps to the plate for one reason, and it's not to admire the scenery. He hacks with reckless abandon, especially at fastballs. Cabrera is a line-drive hitter who can slap the ball to all fields from seemingly any location. He has good reflexes and nearly always puts the ball in play, seldom walking or striking out. Curveballs and offspeed pitches can frustrate him. He has good power for a player his size, most of it to left field.

Baserunning & Defense

In Cabrera's first game with the Red Sox, his error allowed the winning run to score. That was an aberration. Cabrera is among the better defensive shortstops in baseball. He has fantastic range and an arm lively enough to make a strong throw, even after diving for a ball. He turns the double play quickly and effectively. Cabrera is a fast runner with the potential to steal lots of bases, but he deferred to Boston's offensive strategy and attempted just five steals.

2005 Outlook

Cabrera seemed happy in Boston and the Red Sox would like him back, but he will test the waters in his first crack at free agency. The market will be good for a top-flight fielding shortstop who can hit around .300. Cabrera is in his prime and should provide several more reliable seasons. If he stays in Boston, he may settle in as the No. 2 hitter behind Johnny Damon.

Position: SS
Bats: R   **Throws:** R
Ht: 5'10"   **Wt:** 190

Opening Day Age: 30
Born: 11/2/74 in Cartagena, Colombia
ML Seasons: 8
Pronunciation: kah-BRAY-rah

Overall Statistics

	G	AB	R	H	D	T	HR	RBI	SB	BB	SO	Avg	OBP	Slg
'04	161	618	74	163	38	3	10	62	16	39	54	.264	.306	.383
Car.	962	3516	440	944	233	23	72	412	97	244	321	.268	.316	.409

Where He Hits the Ball

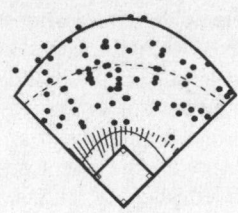
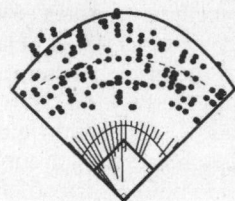

Vs. LHP   **Vs. RHP**

2004 Situational Stats

	AB	H	HR	RBI	Avg		AB	H	HR	RBI	Avg
Home	308	78	2	30	.253	LHP	193	57	3	15	.295
Road	310	85	8	32	.274	RHP	425	106	7	47	.249
First Half	329	78	4	23	.237	Sc Pos	144	37	3	47	.257
Scnd Half	289	85	6	39	.294	Clutch	91	25	2	9	.275

2004 Rankings (American League)

- 1st in lowest batting average with the bases loaded (.000)

Johnny Damon

2004 Season

Johnny Damon garnered headlines for his Captain Caveman hairdo in 2004, but he made plenty of news with his best offensive season as Boston's leadoff hitter and everyday center fielder. Damon set career highs in home runs and RBI, and batted better than .300 for the first time since 2000. In an early-July hot streak, he enjoyed seven straight multihit games. In the ALCS, he awakened from a swoon to hit two home runs in Game 7, including a second-inning grand slam that propelled the Red Sox into the World Series.

Hitting

Damon is among the game's most patient hitters, unafraid to take several pitches before he sees something he likes. Capable of handling almost any type of pitch, Damon is equally adept at pulling inside pitches or taking outside pitches the opposite way. He takes full advantage of Fenway Park's short right-field porch, frequently wrapping home runs around Pesky's Pole. He loses some power against lefthanded pitching, but as a groundball and line-drive gap hitter, he loses little in overall effectiveness.

Baserunning & Defense

After consecutive 30-steal seasons in Boston, Damon swiped only 19 bags last season in 27 attempts. In the postseason, though, he demonstrated the klepto's touch, with five steals in 14 games. With the wheels Damon possesses, he covers plenty of ground in center field and usually gets a good jump on the ball. Damon is a risk-taker. He will go all-out after a shallow liner, sometimes producing a great catch, but sometimes letting the ball get by him. Damon's throwing arm is below average, but accurate.

2005 Outlook

Damon's role on the team is as secure as any player's on the roster. He will fill the leadoff and center-field roles, and the Red Sox have no desire to replace a player of his caliber. He's also remarkably durable, having played 145 games or more in each of his nine full seasons in the majors. He may not quite match his 2004 production, but it's a safe bet he will approach it.

Position: CF
Bats: L **Throws:** L
Ht: 6' 2" **Wt:** 190

Opening Day Age: 31
Born: 11/5/73 in Fort Riley, KS
ML Seasons: 10
Pronunciation: DAY-mun

Overall Statistics

	G	AB	R	H	D	T	HR	RBI	SB	BB	SO	Avg	OBP	Slg
'04	150	621	123	189	35	6	20	94	19	76	71	.304	.380	.477
Car.	1407	5553	956	1592	291	74	120	625	263	545	635	.287	.351	.431

Where He Hits the Ball

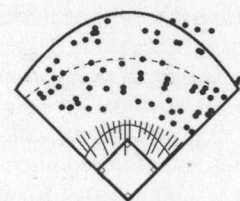 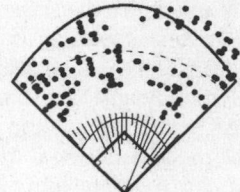

Vs. LHP   **Vs. RHP**

2004 Situational Stats

	AB	H	HR	RBI	Avg		AB	H	HR	RBI	Avg
Home	303	100	9	41	.330	LHP	223	62	3	29	.278
Road	318	89	11	53	.280	RHP	398	127	17	65	.319
First Half	340	109	10	46	.321	Sc Pos	155	55	4	77	.355
Scnd Half	281	80	10	48	.285	Clutch	72	24	3	18	.333

2004 Rankings (American League)

- 2nd in runs scored, pitches seen (2,893) and on-base percentage for a leadoff hitter (.385)
- 3rd in times on base (267)
- 4th in batting average with runners in scoring position and lowest fielding percentage in center field (.986)
- Led the Red Sox in at-bats, runs scored, hits, singles, triples, stolen bases, caught stealing (8), times on base (267), plate appearances (702), highest groundball-flyball ratio (1.5), batting average with runners in scoring position, batting average in the clutch, lowest percentage of swings on the first pitch (14.6) and batting average with two strikes (.274)
- Led AL center fielders in RBI

Keith Foulke

Position: RP
Bats: R **Throws:** R
Ht: 6' 0" **Wt:** 210

Opening Day Age: 32
Born: 10/19/72 in Rapid City, SD
ML Seasons: 8
Pronunciation: FOLK

2004 Season

The Red Sox brought in free agent Keith Foulke to solidify a bullpen that had been the team's biggest weakness. He delivered. Aside from a brief midseason hiccup, Foulke owned the ninth inning (and sometimes the eighth) all season long, notching 32 saves and pitching especially well on the road. Where Foulke really paid off was in the postseason, when he allowed just one run and seven hits in 14 innings en route to Boston's World Series crown.

Pitching

As a closer, Foulke doesn't come from central casting. He isn't overly tall and doesn't overpower, but he is very effective. His fastball creeps into the low 90s, and he couples it with a great slow change, also tossing in an occasional slider. He likes to work on the outside part of the plate, and generally does so with excellent control. The rare times when Foulke gets hit usually occur when he has trouble locating his fastball. In each of the last two seasons, he has been tougher against lefties. He allows more flyballs than grounders, but does well keeping hitters in the yard.

Defense

Defense is yet another reason for fans not to sweat when Foulke is on the mound. He has gone 384 consecutive appearances since 1999 without committing an error, the fourth-longest active streak for any major league pitcher. After a couple of seasons in which he struggled to hold baserunners, Foulke allowed only three stolen bases in five attempts last season.

2005 Outlook

If Foulke does nothing else in a Boston uniform, Red Sox Nation will remember him fondly for recording the final out in the World Series. But for Foulke to do nothing else would be shocking. He is one of the top closers in the game, and pitching for the talented Red Sox, he should continue to get plenty of save opportunities. His ability to throw more than one inning at a time, and on minimal rest, only enhances his value.

Overall Statistics

	W	L	Pct.	ERA	G	GS	Sv	IP	H	BB	SO	HR	Avg
'04	5	3	.625	2.17	72	0	32	83.0	63	15	79	8	.206
Car.	33	28	.541	3.04	501	8	175	660.1	519	156	625	70	.214

2004 Pitching Profile

	Keith Foulke	AL Average
Overall Strike %	67.2	62.3
1st Pitch Strike %	65.7	58.1
Ratio	0.94	1.42
Strikeouts per 9 IP	8.57	6.45
Walks per 9 IP	1.63	3.34
Home Runs per 9 IP	0.87	1.15
Strikeout/Walk Ratio	5.27	1.93
Groundball/Flyball Ratio	0.70	1.17

2004 Situational Stats

	W	L	ERA	Sv	IP		AB	H	HR	RBI	Avg
Home	4	3	3.00	15	45.0	LHB	168	31	3	8	.185
Road	1	0	1.18	17	38.0	RHB	138	32	5	17	.232
First Half	2	2	1.53	13	47.0	Sc Pos	68	13	2	18	.191
Scnd Half	3	1	3.00	19	36.0	Clutch	180	37	5	19	.206

2004 Rankings (American League)

- 1st in fewest GDPs induced per GDP situation (0.0%)
- 2nd in lowest batting average allowed vs. lefthanded batters
- 3rd in blown saves (7) and lowest save percentage (82.1)
- 4th in games finished (61)
- 5th in saves, relief ERA (2.17) and fewest baserunners allowed per nine innings in relief (9.1)
- 7th in first batter efficiency (.171)
- Led the Red Sox in saves, games finished (61), lowest batting average allowed vs. lefthanded batters, save percentage (82.1), blown saves (7), relief wins (5), relief innings (83.0), relief ERA (2.17), lowest batting average allowed in relief (.206), most strikeouts per nine innings in relief (8.6) and fewest baserunners allowed per nine innings in relief (9.1)

Derek Lowe

2004 Season

After deeming a contract offer from the Red Sox insulting in spring training, Derek Lowe posted a 6.02 ERA through July 4, while bristling at suggestions he lacked mental toughness. He then won seven of eight decisions in a late-summer run, before faltering again in September. After manager Terry Francona initially left him out of the postseason rotation, a revitalized Lowe resurfaced to win the clinching games in all three playoff series, allowing one run in 14 innings.

Pitching

Lowe is known for his sinker, which he throws most of the time. When it's on, it is a thing of beauty. He can vary the speed of it through the 80s, and hitters usually beat it into the ground or miss it entirely. Lowe also throws effective sliders and curves to complement his primary offering. Whatever he throws, he almost always keeps the ball down. Lowe produces roughly three times as many groundballs as flyballs, making his success as dependent on his infield defense as any pitcher in the game. Last season, one defensive miscue behind him often snowballed into a big inning, leading to questions about his mental makeup.

Defense

With Lowe inducing so many groundballs, he's had more than 60 total chances in each of the last two seasons. Although Lowe is generally a reliable fielder, he committed three errors in 2004. Lowe is slow to the plate, and his pickoff move is average at best. As a result, stolen bases against him have become a major problem. He allowed a major league-high 34 steals last season, while only two runners were caught.

2005 Outlook

Lowe's stellar postseason outings may have salvaged his stock as a free agent. Prior to Lowe's October renaissance, it was widely assumed Boston would not bring him back. For whoever signs him, Lowe represents an intriguing gamble. He has the stuff to win 16-18 games with an ERA in the threes. Or he could repeat his spotty 2004 performance and win fewer games with less run support.

Position: SP
Bats: R **Throws:** R
Ht: 6' 6" **Wt:** 210

Opening Day Age: 31
Born: 6/1/73 in Dearborn, MI
ML Seasons: 8

Overall Statistics

	W	L	Pct.	ERA	G	GS	Sv	IP	H	BB	SO	HR	Avg
'04	14	12	.538	5.42	33	33	0	182.2	224	71	105	15	.299
Car.	72	59	.550	3.88	396	120	85	1090.0	1083	332	712	80	.259

2004 Pitching Profile

	Derek Lowe	AL Average
Overall Strike %	62.1	62.3
1st Pitch Strike %	58.7	58.1
Ratio	1.61	1.42
Strikeouts per 9 IP	5.17	6.45
Walks per 9 IP	3.50	3.34
Home Runs per 9 IP	0.74	1.15
Strikeout/Walk Ratio	1.48	1.93
Groundball/Flyball Ratio	2.87	1.17

2004 Situational Stats

	W	L	ERA	Sv	IP		AB	H	HR	RBI	Avg
Home	8	4	4.55	0	87.0	LHB	413	126	7	61	.305
Road	6	8	6.21	0	95.2	RHB	335	98	8	53	.293
First Half	7	8	5.57	0	93.2	Sc Pos	238	73	7	94	.307
Scnd Half	7	4	5.26	0	89.0	Clutch	30	6	2	4	.200

2004 Rankings (American League)

- 1st in stolen bases allowed (34), highest groundball-flyball ratio allowed (2.9), highest stolen-base percentage allowed (94.4) and highest ERA on the road
- 2nd in most run support per nine innings (7.3)
- 3rd in fewest home runs allowed per nine innings (.74) and highest on-base percentage allowed (.365)
- 4th in lowest strikeout-walk ratio (1.5)
- 5th in GDPs induced (28)
- 6th in highest ERA
- 7th in highest batting average allowed (.299)
- 8th in wins, games started and highest walks per nine innings (3.5)
- Led the Red Sox in losses, games started, hits allowed, walks allowed, pickoff throws (77), stolen bases allowed (34), GDPs induced (28), highest groundball-flyball ratio allowed (2.9) and fewest home runs allowed per nine innings (.74)

Pedro Martinez

2004 Season

Most major league starting pitchers would pine for the season Pedro Martinez had in 2004, but by the three-time Cy Young Award winner's standards, it was a mixed bag. Martinez won 16 games, but his 3.90 ERA was the highest of his career. He struck out more than a batter per inning, but rarely appeared dominant and pitched more than seven innings only four times. He did save his best for last, hurling seven shutout innings to win World Series Game 3.

Pitching

As most power pitchers must do, Martinez has evolved. He still lives off his fastball, which now tops out from the high 80s to mid 90s, depending on his stuff. Martinez is less capable of dialing up his heater to blow away hitters, and as a result, his changeup sometimes serves as his strikeout pitch. The book on Martinez for years has been to be patient, foul off pitches, drive up his pitch count and get him out of the game. That's an easier task now than it used to be. His somewhat-fragile arm is most effective if kept on a strict pitch count and given full rest.

Defense

Martinez is quick around the mound and always has been a good fielding pitcher. He made just one error in 2004 and has only three in the past five seasons. He likes to look runners back to first base as opposed to throwing over, but he allowed 19 stolen bases last year, way up from the five steals he'd yielded in 2003.

2005 Outlook

If 2004 was Pedro Martinez' final season in Boston, he achieved his long-stated goal of bringing the city a championship. The free agent has said publicly he wants to remain with the Red Sox, but a bidding war may ensue, pricing him beyond what Boston believes he is worth. Martinez is no longer the same pitcher who dominated baseball a few years ago, but he's still good enough to be a No. 1 starter for many clubs.

Position: SP
Bats: R **Throws:** R
Ht: 5'11" **Wt:** 180

Opening Day Age: 33
Born: 10/25/71 in Manoguayabo, DR
ML Seasons: 13

Overall Statistics

W	L	Pct.	ERA	G	GS	Sv	IP	H	BB	SO	HR	Avg
16	9	.640	3.90	33	33	0	217.0	193	61	227	26	.238
182	76	.705	2.71	388	321	3	2296.0	1746	615	2653	175	.209

2004 Pitching Profile

	Pedro Martinez	AL Average
Overall Strike %	65.0	62.3
1st Pitch Strike %	56.3	58.1
Ratio	1.17	1.42
Strikeouts per 9 IP	9.41	6.45
Walks per 9 IP	2.53	3.34
Home Runs per 9 IP	1.08	1.15
Strikeout/Walk Ratio	3.72	1.93
Groundball/Flyball Ratio	0.91	1.17

2004 Situational Stats

	W	L	ERA	Sv	IP		AB	H	HR	RBI	Avg
Home	9	3	3.22	0	111.2	LHB	449	106	15	43	.236
Road	7	6	4.61	0	105.1	RHB	363	87	11	47	.240
First Half	9	3	3.67	0	117.2	Sc Pos	173	34	2	53	.197
Scnd Half	7	6	4.17	0	99.1	Clutch	55	10	2	5	.182

2004 Rankings (American League)

- 2nd in hit batsmen (16), strikeouts and most strikeouts per nine innings (9.4)
- 3rd in lowest batting average allowed (.238) and lowest batting average allowed with runners in scoring position
- 4th in pitches thrown (3,491) and lowest on-base percentage allowed (.301)
- 5th in stolen bases allowed (19) and highest strikeout-walk ratio (3.7)
- 6th in wins and innings pitched
- 7th in winning percentage
- Led the Red Sox in games started, strikeouts, pitches thrown (3,491), lowest batting average allowed (.238), lowest ERA at home, lowest batting average allowed with runners in scoring position and most strikeouts per nine innings (9.4)

Boston

Kevin Millar

2004 Season

For Kevin Millar, the ringleader of the 2003 "Cowboy Up" Red Sox, 2004 began inauspiciously. His first-half power production and RBI were down, and by June he was hearing regular boos from the Fenway fans who'd once adored him. When his playing time briefly waned, he offered the season's most public criticism of manager Terry Francona's use of lineups. Then, just before the All-Star break, Millar caught fire. He batted .322 with 53 RBI from July 1 on, pushing his full-season numbers into their typical range while providing his usual enthusiasm.

Hitting

Millar's 2004 fortunes reversed themselves when he opened up his stance at the start of July. Inside pitches had been tying him up, but he began driving them off and over the left-field wall. Millar hits fastballs very well, but has less success against breaking balls. He is a flyball pull hitter at heart, but he can slap pitches on the outside corner the opposite way. Millar is a fairly patient hitter, but tends to grow more impatient as the count progresses. He sometimes has trouble holding back on the high fastball out of the strike zone.

Baserunning & Defense

Millar looks like a lovable beer-league softball player, and his defensive play can reinforce the stereotype. He performs best at first base, where his limited range is less of a factor. He is adequate at best at handling throws. In the outfield, Millar possesses a subpar arm, and his lack of speed hurts him at cutting off balls in the gap. It also limits his baserunning.

2005 Outlook

Millar may be best suited to a full-time DH role, but that won't happen in Boston with David Ortiz on the roster. Still, Millar's bat is strong enough that the Red Sox are willing to live with his shaky glove. Millar is streaky, but barring a prolonged slump, he should be a fixture in the fifth or sixth spot in the Red Sox' lineup again.

Position: 1B/RF/LF
Bats: R **Throws:** R
Ht: 6' 0" **Wt:** 210

Opening Day Age: 33
Born: 9/24/71 in Los Angeles, CA
ML Seasons: 7
Pronunciation: mi-LAR

Overall Statistics

	G	AB	R	H	D	T	HR	RBI	SB	BB	SO	Avg	OBP	Slg
'04	150	508	74	151	36	0	18	74	1	57	91	.297	.383	.474
Car.	798	2551	362	744	177	13	102	421	5	273	454	.292	.366	.491

Where He Hits the Ball

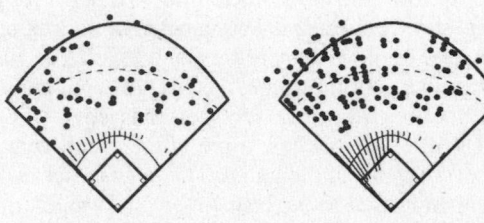

Vs. LHP   **Vs. RHP**

2004 Situational Stats

	AB	H	HR	RBI	Avg		AB	H	HR	RBI	Avg
Home	260	91	12	53	.350	LHP	154	46	3	17	.299
Road	248	60	6	21	.242	RHP	354	105	15	57	.297
First Half	282	79	5	25	.280	Sc Pos	128	40	5	57	.313
Scnd Half	226	72	13	49	.319	Clutch	67	16	3	10	.239

2004 Rankings (American League)

- 1st in hit by pitch (17)
- 3rd in batting average at home
- 4th in errors at first base (6)
- 6th in errors in right field (3)
- 8th in lowest batting average on the road
- 10th in lowest groundball-flyball ratio (0.8)
- Led the Red Sox in hit by pitch (17) and batting average at home

Bill Mueller

2004 Season

Bill Mueller couldn't produce an encore of his 2003 batting title, but the Red Sox probably didn't expect one. His production returned to its career norms, which meant he provided Boston with a decent average, occasional power and very steady defense at third base. Mueller missed all of June after undergoing knee surgery, but returned to the lineup and rekindled his 2003 spark in August, batting .380 for the month. Mueller performed well in postseason play, with seven multi-hit games and 10 runs scored in 14 contests.

Hitting

The switch-hitting Mueller moved around the order in 2004, doing his best work out of the eighth spot, where he hit .354. He is largely a line-drive hitter who can spray the ball to all fields from either side of the plate. He's felt comfortable at home in Fenway Park, where he utilizes the left-field wall and has batted .343 the last two seasons. Mueller possesses a good eye, makes consistent contact and does not strike out often.

Baserunning & Defense

Rarely spectacular but always steady, Mueller makes the plays he should make, calling on adequate range and an accurate third baseman's arm. He also has quick reflexes grabbing balls hit down the line. Mueller can play second base, where he was pressed into duty in a career-high 14 games last season. He has enough speed not to embarrass himself on the basepaths, though he is not a threat to steal. His two stolen bases in 2004 were his most in four seasons.

2005 Outlook

The Red Sox wasted no time in exercising Mueller's option following the World Series. His steady play would make any manager confident penciling his name into the lineup each day. Knee problems have plagued him in the past, and at age 34, he and the Red Sox will have to hope those problems don't grow more frequent. Otherwise, Mueller likely won't win another batting title, but will provide the same quality, blue-collar production he's offered throughout his career.

Position: 3B/2B
Bats: B **Throws:** R
Ht: 5'10" **Wt:** 180

Opening Day Age: 34
Born: 3/17/71 in Maryland Heights, MO
ML Seasons: 9
Pronunciation: MILL-er
Nickname: Ferris, Muley

Overall Statistics

	G	AB	R	H	D	T	HR	RBI	SB	BB	SO	Avg	OBP	Slg
'04	110	399	75	113	27	1	12	57	2	51	56	.283	.365	.446
Car.	1034	3597	582	1049	224	19	72	416	19	467	488	.292	.374	.425

Where He Hits the Ball

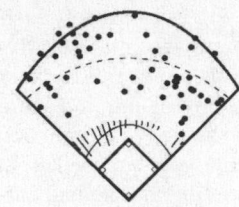 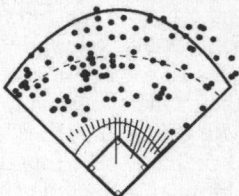

Vs. LHP   **Vs. RHP**

2004 Situational Stats

	AB	H	HR	RBI	Avg		AB	H	HR	RBI	Avg
Home	195	67	9	36	.344	LHP	137	35	4	18	.255
Road	204	46	3	21	.225	RHP	262	78	8	39	.298
First Half	172	49	6	28	.285	Sc Pos	108	25	5	41	.231
Scnd Half	227	64	6	29	.282	Clutch	60	15	1	5	.250

2004 Rankings (American League)

- 1st in lowest batting average with the bases loaded (.000)
- 5th in errors at third base (14)
- 10th in lowest percentage of swings that missed (10.6)
- Led the Red Sox in lowest percentage of swings that missed (10.6) and highest percentage of swings put into play (48.8)

Boston

61

David Ortiz

2004 Season

Given his 2004 postseason heroics, David Ortiz may never pay for a drink in Boston again. The slugging designated hitter batted .400 in the play-offs with five homers and 19 RBI, highlighted by dramatic walkoff longballs in ALDS Game 3 and ALCS Game 4. The October stage merely showed a national audience what Red Sox Nation already knew: Ortiz has blossomed into a monster power hitter with a knack for producing in the clutch. He and Manny Ramirez combined for 269 RBI, the most of any duo in baseball.

Hitting

Ortiz often draws comparisons with Mo Vaughn in his prime. Still, Ortiz is more of a pull hitter and a pure home-run hitter. He lives off low fast-balls, which he commonly turns into majestic fly-balls down the line or into the right-field power alley. One approach to beat Ortiz is jamming him with offspeed pitches, but no strategy is a safe bet. Ortiz has worked hard, and largely succeeded, at eliminating the holes in his swing that he had ear-lier in his career. His strikeouts rose significantly last season, but so did his average and power numbers, so it is likely no cause for alarm.

Baserunning & Defense

Neither baserunning nor defense elevated Ortiz to the majors. At his size, he lumbers down the line, though he rarely makes foolish mistakes on the basepaths. Ortiz is hindered by limited range when he does play first base, but he fields balls and throws a bit better than one might assume. He adequately manned first base in the road games of the World Series without incident.

2005 Outlook

The Red Sox inked Ortiz to a two-year, $12.5 mil-lion extension last May, which looks like a steal, given what he produced for them. Ortiz enjoys playing in Boston, and his friendly persona plays well in the clubhouse and community. If he isn't slowed by an August shoulder injury, which forced Ortiz to take cortisone shots down the stretch and bypass winter ball, another season with 40 homers and 130 RBI is within his reach. So is contending for an MVP Award.

Position: DH/1B
Bats: L **Throws:** L
Ht: 6' 4" **Wt:** 230

Opening Day Age: 29
Born: 11/18/75 in Santo Domingo, DR
ML Seasons: 8
Pronunciation: or-TEEZ

Overall Statistics

	G	AB	R	H	D	T	HR	RBI	SB	BB	SO	Avg	OBP	Slg
'04	150	582	94	175	47	3	41	139	0	75	133	.301	.380	.603
Car.	733	2507	388	697	194	8	130	478	4	319	555	.278	.359	.517

Where He Hits the Ball

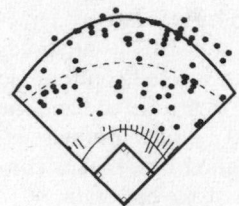
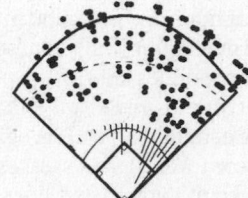

Vs. LHP   **Vs. RHP**

2004 Situational Stats

	AB	H	HR	RBI	Avg		AB	H	HR	RBI	Avg
Home	305	99	17	64	.325	LHP	196	49	10	43	.250
Road	277	76	24	75	.274	RHP	386	126	31	96	.326
First Half	345	105	23	78	.304	Sc Pos	160	56	7	90	.350
Scnd Half	237	70	18	61	.295	Clutch	71	23	5	18	.324

2004 Rankings (American League)

- 2nd in home runs, total bases (351), RBI and slugging percentage
- 3rd in doubles, HR frequency (14.2 ABs per HR) and cleanup slugging percentage (.570)
- 4th in sacrifice flies (8)
- 5th in batting average with runners in scoring position
- 6th in batting average vs. righthanded pitchers
- 8th in strikeouts and pitches seen (2,668)
- 9th in lowest groundball-flyball ratio (0.8)
- 10th in errors at first base (4) and lowest percentage of swings put into play (37.1)
- Led the Red Sox in doubles, total bases (351), RBI, sacrifice flies (8) and batting average vs. righthanded pitchers

Manny Ramirez

2004 Season

Following an offseason in which the Red Sox nearly traded him for Alex Rodriguez and put him through waivers at one point, Manny Ramirez produced perhaps his finest season in a Boston uniform. He enjoyed a torrid April, hitting .388, and never let up until he won the World Series MVP Award. He had at least one hit in all 14 post-season games.

Hitting

Simply put, Ramirez arguably is the best all-around righthanded hitter in the league. He hits lefties and righties equally well, has tremendous power, even to the opposite field, and is not afraid to take the occasional free pass. His quick hands and good bat speed mean he is able to turn on most any pitch. Opposing pitchers will nibble around the corners against him with sliders and curves, not because Ramirez can't hit them, but because anything over the middle to him is asking for trouble.

Baserunning & Defense

The occasional brain cramps both on the bases and in the field are part of the equation with Ramirez, and Bostonians lovingly refer to the mishaps as "Manny's moments." Ramirez actually has made himself a better fielder, as he's grown accustomed to playing under the Green Monster. His arm is above average. His range is not as bad as it sometimes appears, but he tends to judge balls poorly and get bad jumps. Ramirez' long strides make him look lackadaisical running the bases, but he does give a full effort. He is not, however, a threat to steal or take an extra base.

2005 Outlook

He may have appeared aloof for much of his career, but Ramirez seems to have matured and become more approachable to his teammates, fans and media. At one point last season, he even offered to give up part of his contract if it would help the Red Sox re-sign Pedro Martinez. Manager Terry Francona's relaxed style also seems to mesh well with Ramirez. He will continue to pose the biggest offensive threat in a Boston lineup filled with them.

Position: LF/DH
Bats: R **Throws:** R
Ht: 6' 0" **Wt:** 213

Opening Day Age: 32
Born: 5/30/72 in Santo Domingo, DR
ML Seasons: 12
Pronunciation: ruh-MEER-ez

Overall Statistics

G	AB	R	H	D	T	HR	RBI	SB	BB	SO	Avg	OBP	Slg
152	568	108	175	44	0	43	130	2	82	124	.308	.397	.613
1535	5572	1067	1760	381	14	390	1270	33	874	1230	.316	.411	.599

Where He Hits the Ball

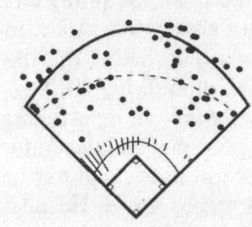 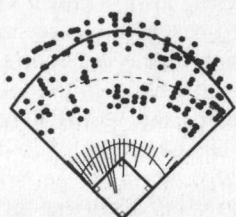

Vs. LHP   **Vs. RHP**

2004 Situational Stats

	AB	H	HR	RBI	Avg		AB	H	HR	RBI	Avg
Home	289	91	23	72	.315	LHP	160	49	13	41	.306
Road	279	84	20	58	.301	RHP	408	126	30	89	.309
First Half	314	108	26	77	.344	Sc Pos	156	53	11	85	.340
Scnd Half	254	67	17	53	.264	Clutch	75	21	3	8	.280

2004 Rankings (American League)

- 1st in home runs, slugging percentage, HR frequency (13.2 ABs per HR), cleanup slugging percentage (.621) and lowest fielding percentage in left field (.967)
- 2nd in intentional walks (15) and errors in left field (7)
- 3rd in RBI
- 4th in doubles and total bases (348)
- Led the Red Sox in batting average, home runs, intentional walks (15), GDPs (17), games played, slugging percentage, on-base percentage, HR frequency (13.2 ABs per HR), cleanup slugging percentage (.621) and batting average on the road
- Led AL left fielders in batting average, home runs and RBI

Curt Schilling

2004 Season

Returning to the club that originally drafted him, Curt Schilling won his first seven decisions at Fenway Park en route to a 21-6 mark. While dominant only occasionally, Schilling always was solid, pitching six or more innings in 28 starts. He did this while battling various ailments that never placed him on the disabled list. Schilling's fortitude was best displayed when he won games in the ALCS and World Series, despite pitching with a torn ankle tendon that bled through his sock.

Pitching

Schilling is a power pitcher first and foremost, and he starts most counts off with his fastball. He nearly always gets it over the plate. Schilling has led baseball in percentage of first-pitch strikes in each of the last four seasons. His heater consistently clocks in the low 90s, though he still possesses the 95-MPH heat to blow it by a hitter when he needs it. Schilling gets ahead in the count before trying to get a hitter to chase a splitter or slow curveball out of the strike zone. He also throws a changeup and a slider with good downward movement. Control is Schilling's game, as he consistently fans five times as many hitters as he walks.

Defense

Opposing baserunners rarely try to run on Schilling, who gets the ball to the plate quickly. They attempted only seven steals against him in all of 2004. He is an adequate fielder, though not fleet of foot, and he lumbers down the line if he needs to cover first base on a grounder.

2005 Outlook

By the end of last season, Schilling had supplanted Pedro Martinez as Boston's ace. His torn right-ankle tendon required surgery in November, putting his status for Opening Day in doubt. Schilling is under contract through 2006 with a mutual option in 2007. He fits right in with rabid Red Sox Nation, as his frequent "Curt in a car" calls to Boston radio shows attest. He's not getting any younger, but Schilling's conditioning and competitive fire mean he should remain one of the league's top pitchers for another couple of years.

Position: SP
Bats: R **Throws:** R
Ht: 6' 5" **Wt:** 235

Opening Day Age: 38
Born: 11/14/66 in Anchorage, AK
ML Seasons: 17
Pronunciation: SHILL-ing

Overall Statistics

W	L	Pct.	ERA	G	GS	Sv	IP	H	BB	SO	HR	Avg
21	6	.778	3.26	32	32	0	226.2	206	35	203	23	.239
184	123	.599	3.32	482	370	13	2812.2	2492	638	2745	286	.236

2004 Pitching Profile

	Curt Schilling	AL Average
Overall Strike %	69.9	62.3
1st Pitch Strike %	69.2	58.1
Ratio	1.06	1.42
Strikeouts per 9 IP	8.06	6.45
Walks per 9 IP	1.39	3.34
Home Runs per 9 IP	0.91	1.15
Strikeout/Walk Ratio	5.80	1.93
Groundball/Flyball Ratio	1.04	1.17

2004 Situational Stats

	W	L	ERA	Sv	IP		AB	H	HR	RBI	Avg
Home	12	1	3.45	0	127.2	LHB	462	110	6	39	.238
Road	9	5	3.00	0	99.0	RHB	399	96	17	40	.241
First Half	11	4	3.16	0	125.1	Sc Pos	181	40	3	53	.221
Scnd Half	10	2	3.38	0	101.1	Clutch	42	11	1	9	.262

2004 Rankings (American League)

- 1st in wins, winning percentage, highest strikeout-walk ratio (5.8), most run support per nine innings (7.5) and fielding percentage at pitcher (1.000)
- 2nd in ERA and lowest on-base percentage allowed (.271)
- 3rd in innings pitched, strikeouts and fewest walks per nine innings (1.4)
- 4th in lowest batting average allowed (.239), lowest ERA on the road and highest stolen-base percentage allowed (85.7)
- Led the Red Sox in ERA, wins, complete games (3), innings pitched, batters faced (910), winning percentage, highest strikeout-walk ratio (5.8), lowest slugging percentage allowed (.387), lowest on-base percentage allowed (.271), lowest ERA on the road, most run support per nine innings (7.5) and fewest walks per nine innings (1.4)

Jason Varitek

2004 Season

He might not have generated the most ink or hit the most home runs, but it's doubtful the Red Sox could have won the World Series without Jason Varitek. The catcher was a rock of consistency, appearing in 137 games and posting career highs in batting average and on-base percentage. In contrast to previous seasons when he wore down late, Varitek was at his best in August, batting .449 with 20 RBI. He caught all but two innings of Boston's marathon ALCS series vs. the Yankees.

Hitting

While always a professional hitter, Varitek now is downright lethal from the right side of the plate, as he slugged .569 off southpaws last season. Batting lefthanded, curveballs tailing inside can tie him up, but from either side of the plate he has few holes and possesses good power to all fields. Varitek is a patient hitter who averaged more than four pitches per plate appearance in 2004. Yet, he hacks if he sees a first pitch he likes. He batted .521 last season when putting the first pitch in play.

Baserunning & Defense

Varitek is one of the most respected signal callers in the majors. He also has a strong arm and throws well to second base. While opposing baserunners stole at a 79.4-percent clip against him in 2004, pitchers on the mound had more to do with that than Varitek's throwing ability. He never has been fleet of foot, but Varitek was in great shape last year, picking his spots to the tune of 10 stolen bases, most among American League catchers.

2005 Outlook

Varitek has been called the heart and soul of the Red Sox so many times that it seems almost cliché, but it really is the case. The Red Sox will go all out to keep their backstop, but bidding could get fierce, as Varitek is the lone elite catcher on the free-agent market. Whoever signs him will get their money's worth. Varitek is a consistent performer in every facet of the game.

Position: C
Bats: B **Throws:** R
Ht: 6' 2" **Wt:** 230

Opening Day Age: 32
Born: 4/11/72 in Rochester, MI
ML Seasons: 8
Pronunciation: VAIR-eh-teck

Overall Statistics

	G	AB	R	H	D	T	HR	RBI	SB	BB	SO	Avg	OBP	Slg
'04	137	463	67	137	30	1	18	73	10	62	126	.296	.390	.482
Car.	832	2708	363	733	182	7	97	418	21	298	576	.271	.347	.451

Where He Hits the Ball

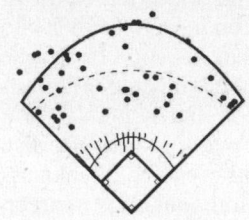 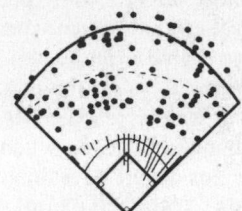

Vs. LHP **Vs. RHP**

2004 Situational Stats

	AB	H	HR	RBI	Avg		AB	H	HR	RBI	Avg
Home	229	77	8	41	.336	LHP	137	48	6	26	.350
Road	234	60	10	32	.256	RHP	326	89	12	47	.273
First Half	262	72	10	34	.275	Sc Pos	139	40	4	54	.288
Scnd Half	201	65	8	39	.323	Clutch	69	13	1	11	.188

2004 Rankings (American League)

- 1st in lowest percentage of runners caught stealing as a catcher (20.6)
- 2nd in batting average vs. lefthanded pitchers
- Led the Red Sox in stolen-base percentage (76.9) and batting average vs. lefthanded pitchers

Boston

Tim Wakefield

2004 Season

For the second consecutive season, Tim Wakefield spent the entire year in Boston's starting rotation and produced respectable results. Yet there were ups (six wins in seven starts in late July and August) and downs (a record six home runs allowed at Detroit on August 8). In an unselfish act likely to be forgotten over time, Wakefield volunteered 3.1 innings of relief in a painful 19-8 ALCS Game 3 loss, saving the staff and making a series comeback possible.

Pitching

Hitters have long known what to expect from Wakefield—the knuckleball. They just don't know where to expect the knuckler to float. Wakefield can vary speeds on it, from the 60s into the low 70s, and when he has his good floater, he seems to sail through a game with ease. His fastball barely reaches 80 MPH and is purely for a change of pace or when he needs a strike. He also mixes in an occasional slow curve. Streakiness has followed him throughout his career. Wakefield can appear unhittable for weeks at a time, then struggle mightily for a spell.

Defense

Wakefield doesn't induce ulcers when the ball comes to him, but he's not as agile as he was in his younger years. He made four errors last season, tying his career high from 1993. He still does a good job covering first base on grounders. With a pitch as slow as the knuckleball, opponents will run on Wakefield. His 33 steals allowed in 2004 were second in baseball; only teammate Derek Lowe gave up more. Wakefield tries to compensate with a sneaky pickoff move, which worked three times last year.

2005 Outlook

A Red Sox fixture since 1995, Wakefield is the team's senior member. The Sox once again will look to him to eat valuable innings near the back end of the rotation. Wakefield's versatility, durability and willingness to shift roles at a moment's notice are the secrets to his value in Boston. Don't be surprised if Wakefield has a few quality seasons left in him.

Position: SP
Bats: R **Throws:** R
Ht: 6' 2" **Wt:** 210

Opening Day Age: 38
Born: 8/2/66 in Melbourne, FL
ML Seasons: 12

Overall Statistics

W	L	Pct.	ERA	G	GS	Sv	IP	H	BB	SO	HR	Avg
12	10	.545	4.87	32	30	0	188.1	197	63	116	29	.264
128	111	.536	4.29	424	283	22	2066.2	2009	829	1439	261	.254

2004 Pitching Profile

	Tim Wakefield	AL Average
Overall Strike %	64.9	62.3
1st Pitch Strike %	59.9	58.1
Ratio	1.38	1.42
Strikeouts per 9 IP	5.54	6.45
Walks per 9 IP	3.01	3.34
Home Runs per 9 IP	1.39	1.15
Strikeout/Walk Ratio	1.84	1.93
Groundball/Flyball Ratio	1.23	1.17

2004 Situational Stats

	W	L	ERA	Sv	IP		AB	H	HR	RBI	Avg
Home	6	6	4.99	0	113.2	LHB	346	78	10	44	.225
Road	6	4	4.70	0	74.2	RHB	400	119	19	62	.298
First Half	5	5	4.17	0	105.2	Sc Pos	186	46	7	76	.247
Scnd Half	7	5	5.77	0	82.2	Clutch	23	6	2	2	.261

2004 Rankings (American League)

- 2nd in hit batsmen (16) and stolen bases allowed (33)
- 5th in errors at pitcher (4) and lowest fielding percentage at pitcher (.905)
- 7th in highest stolen-base percentage allowed (80.5)
- 9th in runners caught stealing (8)
- 10th in fewest pitches thrown per batter (3.61)
- Led the Red Sox in home runs allowed, wild pitches (9), pickoff throws (77), runners caught stealing (8) and fewest pitches thrown per batter (3.61)

Terry Adams

Position: RP
Bats: R **Throws:** R
Ht: 6' 3" **Wt:** 220

Opening Day Age: 32
Born: 3/6/73 in Mobile, AL
ML Seasons: 10

Overall Statistics

	W	L	Pct.	ERA	G	GS	Sv	IP	H	BB	SO	HR	Avg
'04	6	4	.600	4.76	61	0	3	70.0	84	28	56	10	.302
Car.	51	60	.459	4.04	558	41	42	856.0	865	370	687	60	.263

2004 Situational Stats

	W	L	ERA	Sv	IP		AB	H	HR	RBI	Avg
Home	4	2	3.62	3	37.1	LHB	158	36	3	17	.228
Road	2	2	6.06	0	32.2	RHB	120	48	7	34	.400
First Half	4	4	4.38	3	39.0	Sc Pos	88	26	2	41	.295
Scnd Half	2	0	5.23	0	31.0	Clutch	103	36	3	16	.350

2004 Season

The Red Sox acquired Terry Adams from Toronto in late July to help shore up an overtaxed bullpen. As it turned out, his main contribution simply was easing the workload of Boston's top relief arms, rather than providing quality innings himself. After posting a 12.79 ERA in August, he didn't appear in many key situations. The Red Sox left Adams off their postseason roster.

Pitching & Defense

Adams throws a fastball in the low 90s, complemented by a slider with some bite to it. He is a pitcher who likes to keep the ball down and force groundballs. Adams has allowed more than twice as many groundballs as flies in each season of his career. Somewhat alarmingly, Adams yielded a career-high 10 home runs in 2004, even exceeding his totals from his seasons as a starter. With 14 career errors, fielding has never been Adams' strong suit, though he has allowed only four stolen bases in the last two seasons.

2005 Outlook

For the second consecutive season, Adams finds himself a free agent. His best bet may be to latch on with a small- or medium-market club, where he could resurface as a key middle reliever. He remains young enough to regain his old form.

Bronson Arroyo

Position: SP
Bats: R **Throws:** R
Ht: 6' 5" **Wt:** 190

Opening Day Age: 28
Born: 2/24/77 in Key West, FL
ML Seasons: 5
Pronunciation: ah-ROY-yoh

Overall Statistics

	W	L	Pct.	ERA	G	GS	Sv	IP	H	BB	SO	HR	Avg
'04	10	9	.526	4.03	32	29	0	178.2	171	47	142	17	.249
Car.	19	23	.452	4.63	91	58	1	383.0	398	136	267	40	.267

2004 Situational Stats

	W	L	ERA	Sv	IP		AB	H	HR	RBI	Avg
Home	3	5	5.35	0	75.2	LHB	357	96	10	40	.269
Road	7	4	3.06	0	103.0	RHB	331	75	7	42	.227
First Half	3	7	4.09	0	88.0	Sc Pos	158	40	3	61	.253
Scnd Half	7	2	3.97	0	90.2	Clutch	34	13	3	10	.382

2004 Season

Bronson Arroyo entered the season with no clear role on the Boston staff, but established himself as one of baseball's more reliable fifth starters. A victim of spotty run support and bad luck, he pitched better than his record suggests. He grew stronger as the season progressed, going 8-2 with a 3.58 ERA after July 1.

Pitching & Defense

Arroyo offers a four-seam fastball that tops out in the high 80s to low 90s. His most effective pitches are his curve and slider, especially when he can get opposing hitters to chase them. He allows roughly an equal mix of flyballs and grounders, and usually exhibits good control. For whatever reason, he pitched much better on the road last season than in Fenway Park. The wiry Arroyo is a fine fielder, and his quick delivery makes him one of Boston's better pitchers at holding runners.

2005 Outlook

Manager Terry Francona showed growing confidence in Arroyo by placing him in the starting rotation to open the postseason. The affable Arroyo is a favorite in the clubhouse and, at age 28, appears to be harnessing his stuff and entering his prime. His slot in Boston's rotation for 2005 seems secure.

Mark Bellhorn

Position: 2B/3B
Bats: B **Throws:** R
Ht: 6' 1" **Wt:** 205

Opening Day Age: 30
Born: 8/23/74 in Boston, MA
ML Seasons: 7

Overall Statistics

	G	AB	R	H	D	T	HR	RBI	SB	BB	SO	Avg	OBP	Slg
'04	138	523	93	138	37	3	17	82	6	88	177	.264	.373	.444
Car.	509	1540	253	372	82	11	53	188	27	258	516	.242	.354	.412

2004 Situational Stats

	AB	H	HR	RBI	Avg		AB	H	HR	RBI	Avg
Home	265	75	11	52	.283	LHP	181	54	7	33	.298
Road	258	63	6	30	.244	RHP	342	84	10	49	.246
First Half	314	84	11	50	.268	Sc Pos	135	41	6	63	.304
Scnd Half	209	54	6	32	.258	Clutch	59	16	2	12	.271

2004 Season

Projected to fill a utility role for the Red Sox, Mark Bellhorn became a regular early on due to injuries, and he held on to the second-base job after the club got healthy. He showed a knack for the clutch hit, highlighted by three big postseason home runs.

Hitting, Baserunning & Defense

Bellhorn is a *Moneyball* player taken to an illogical extreme. His career on-base percentage is more than 100 points higher than his batting average. Nearly half of his 2004 plate appearances produced a strikeout, walk or home run. The lack of contact makes him an unorthodox No. 2 hitter, but that's where manager Terry Francona used him most often. Bellhorn succeeds at hitting fastballs on the outer part of the plate. Curves give him trouble. He is an average fielder and often gets replaced late in games. He has decent speed.

2005 Outlook

Francona stuck with Bellhorn amidst an early postseason slump and a media clamor for Pokey Reese. While Bellhorn's offense earned him a starting role, he will need to maintain his batting average near his 2004 mark. If Bellhorn doesn't, the Red Sox may turn to another candidate who provides better defense up the middle.

Alan Embree

Position: RP
Bats: L **Throws:** L
Ht: 6' 2" **Wt:** 190

Opening Day Age: 35
Born: 1/23/70 in The Dalles, OR
ML Seasons: 11
Pronunciation: EMM-bree

Overall Statistics

	W	L	Pct.	ERA	G	GS	Sv	IP	H	BB	SO	HR	Avg
'04	2	2	.500	4.13	71	0	0	52.1	49	11	37	7	.244
Car.	28	28	.500	4.40	568	4	7	515.1	478	203	480	65	.247

2004 Situational Stats

	W	L	ERA	Sv	IP		AB	H	HR	RBI	Avg
Home	1	0	4.18	0	23.2	LHB	104	25	4	14	.240
Road	1	2	4.08	0	28.2	RHB	97	24	3	12	.247
First Half	2	1	4.32	0	33.1	Sc Pos	53	14	2	19	.264
Scnd Half	0	1	3.79	0	19.0	Clutch	99	21	4	11	.212

2004 Season

The primary situational lefthander for the Red Sox, Alan Embree grew stronger as the summer wore on. He hit a rough patch in May and June, but rebounded and wound up with numbers virtually identical to his 2003 season. He pitched his best ball after Boston acquired fellow southpaw Mike Myers, posting a 3.46 ERA after August 6.

Pitching & Defense

Embree throws a four-seam fastball in the low to mid-90s, and his cut fastball tops out closer to 90 MPH. He also possesses a slider, often thrown away to get hitters to chase it. He seems to have his best stuff and good velocity when he's rested. Unlike most lefthanded relievers, Embree is nearly as effective facing righthanded batters as he is against lefties. He can be Houdini-like when he enters a jam. He stranded 34 of the 44 baserunners he inherited in 2004. Embree also is a good fielder.

2005 Outlook

Along with Mike Timlin, Embree forms half of the Red Sox' 1-2 middle-relief punch to get the game to Keith Foulke. There's no reason to expect Embree's numbers to drop off, barring an injury, although his results may be better if another reliable lefty is in the bullpen to ease his workload.

Byung-Hyun Kim

Position: RP
Bats: R **Throws:** R
Ht: 5' 9" **Wt:** 180

Opening Day Age: 26
Born: 1/19/79 in Gwangju, South Korea
ML Seasons: 6
Pronunciation: bee-yung hee-yun

Overall Statistics

	W	L	Pct.	ERA	G	GS	Sv	IP	H	BB	SO	HR	Avg
'04	2	1	.667	6.23	7	3	0	17.1	17	7	6	1	.258
Car.	31	28	.525	3.37	299	16	86	419.2	315	176	455	39	.206

2004 Situational Stats

	W	L	ERA	Sv	IP		AB	H	HR	RBI	Avg
Home	1	1	5.79	0	9.1	LHB	40	12	1	7	.300
Road	1	0	6.75	0	8.0	RHB	26	5	0	1	.192
First Half	1	1	6.17	0	11.2	Sc Pos	18	4	0	7	.222
Scnd Half	1	0	6.35	0	5.2	Clutch	7	0	0	0	.000

2004 Season

The 2004 season would be forgettable for Byung-Hyun Kim if it weren't so unusual. He spent April on the disabled list with a shoulder strain. Then he was sent to the minors after a pair of ineffective starts for Boston. Kim finally resurfaced in the Red Sox' bullpen in late September. He even spent some time in his native Korea in an effort to get straightened out.

Pitching & Defense

Kim possesses a unique sidearm delivery that can baffle hitters when he's on. He gets his fastball into the 90s, an impressive feat for a submariner. His fastball, sinker and changeup all have good action on them. Manager Terry Francona suggested Kim was not being as aggressive on the mound in 2004 as in previous seasons. Kim is agile and an effective fielder, although his long delivery is a disadvantage at holding runners.

2005 Outlook

Kim's once-promising career is at a crossroads. He has no clear role, either as a starter or closer, and did not ingratiate himself to Red Sox management last season. With Kim's impressive stuff, and considering his young age, it's possible a strong comeback could be in store. It's also possible Kim might not be long for the major leagues.

Doug Mientkiewicz

Position: 1B
Bats: L **Throws:** R
Ht: 6' 2" **Wt:** 206

Opening Day Age: 30
Born: 6/19/74 in Toledo, OH
ML Seasons: 7
Pronunciation: mint-KAY-vich

Overall Statistics

	G	AB	R	H	D	T	HR	RBI	SB	BB	SO	Avg	OBP	Slg
'04	127	391	47	93	24	1	6	35	2	48	56	.238	.326	.350
Car.	692	2254	286	613	152	7	44	276	11	310	326	.272	.363	.404

2004 Situational Stats

	AB	H	HR	RBI	Avg		AB	H	HR	RBI	Avg
Home	206	52	1	20	.252	LHP	123	27	1	10	.220
Road	185	41	5	15	.222	RHP	268	66	5	25	.246
First Half	275	67	5	23	.244	Sc Pos	91	23	2	28	.253
Scnd Half	116	26	1	12	.224	Clutch	58	13	0	5	.224

2004 Season

After arriving in Boston at the trading deadline, Doug Mientkiewicz assumed a defensive-replacement role at first base. The lack of playing time didn't please him, but he did little offensively to work his way into the lineup. He batted just .215 in 107 at-bats for the Red Sox, and his .238 average for the season was his lowest since 1999, his rookie year.

Hitting, Baserunning & Defense

When Mientkiewicz is on his offensive game, he somewhat resembles a poor man's Mark Grace. Though he seldom shows power, he reliably makes contact. His career batting averages against lefties and righties are identical (.272). Mientkiewicz' first-base defense is his claim to fame. A Gold Glover in 2001 with Minnesota, he is agile around the bag and excellent at fielding throws. He is an average baserunner.

2005 Outlook

Mientkiewicz is entering his contract year, and he wants to be a full-time player again. That's unlikely to happen in Boston, as the Red Sox like the power Kevin Millar provides at first base. The possibility exists that Mientkiewicz could be dealt. If not, the Red Sox can afford an extra glove, and they'll be glad to have him back.

Boston

Trot Nixon

Position: RF
Bats: L **Throws:** L
Ht: 6' 2" **Wt:** 211

Opening Day Age: 30
Born: 4/11/74 in
Durham, NC
ML Seasons: 8

Overall Statistics

	G	AB	R	H	D	T	HR	RBI	SB	BB	SO	Avg	OBP	Slg
'04	48	149	24	47	9	1	6	23	0	15	24	.315	.377	.510
Car.	744	2496	424	698	151	27	112	404	27	341	506	.280	.367	.496

2004 Situational Stats

	AB	H	HR	RBI	Avg		AB	H	HR	RBI	Avg
Home	70	24	3	13	.343	LHP	15	2	0	0	.133
Road	79	23	3	10	.291	RHP	134	45	6	23	.336
First Half	65	15	3	9	.231	Sc Pos	35	9	0	15	.257
Scnd Half	84	32	3	14	.381	Clutch	21	4	0	2	.190

2004 Season

Despite Boston's success, 2004 was a trying season for Trot Nixon. Back and quadriceps problems originally thought to be minor kept him out of action until June. The quad injury forced him back onto the disabled list in late July. He returned in September and received regular postseason playing time. He batted .357 in the World Series.

Hitting, Baserunning & Defense

Nixon is a flyball hitter with medium power who usually pulls the ball down the line or to the right-field power alley. Hitting lefthanders continues to be a problem, and he was a platoon player in 2004. He hits fastballs well, but struggles when he gets behind in the count. Defensively, Nixon generally gets good jumps on balls and makes the occasional highlight-reel catch. His arm is above average. Nixon is not a major basestealing threat, but he is an aggressive baserunner with average to above-average speed.

2005 Outlook

Nixon's bat got hot at the end of the season, which may mean his injury woes are behind him. If he's healthy, he should provide his usual mix of timely hitting, solid defense and all-around hard-nosed baseball. How often he will play against left-handers is less certain.

Pokey Reese (Great Range)

Position: SS/2B
Bats: R **Throws:** R
Ht: 5'11" **Wt:** 180

Opening Day Age: 31
Born: 6/10/73 in
Columbia, SC
ML Seasons: 8

Overall Statistics

	G	AB	R	H	D	T	HR	RBI	SB	BB	SO	Avg	OBP	Slg
'04	96	244	32	54	7	2	3	29	6	17	60	.221	.271	.303
Car.	856	2833	366	704	128	17	44	271	144	226	531	.248	.307	.352

2004 Situational Stats

	AB	H	HR	RBI	Avg		AB	H	HR	RBI	Avg
Home	114	26	3	14	.228	LHP	85	19	1	13	.224
Road	130	28	0	15	.215	RHP	159	35	2	16	.220
First Half	214	50	3	26	.234	Sc Pos	66	16	0	24	.242
Scnd Half	30	4	0	3	.133	Clutch	21	5	0	3	.238

2004 Season

Pokey Reese began the season as Boston's starting shortstop, replacing the injured Nomar Garciaparra. The diminutive infielder gained minor cult-hero status with flashy glove work and a two-homer effort against Kansas City on May 8. A ribcage injury sidelined Reese for most of the second half, and he had only four hits in 49 at-bats after July 1.

Hitting, Baserunning & Defense

Simply put, hitting is not the reason Reese is in the major leagues. He steps up to the plate hacking, and often pops up or chases bad pitches and strikes out. If Reese's offense was a bit better, he might draw annual Gold Glove attention for his magnificent defense. His range is fantastic at both middle-infield positions, and his arm is accurate and strong. Reese has good speed, but didn't utilize it often in 2004, attempting only eight steals.

2005 Outlook

Reese finds himself a free agent for the second consecutive season. His game might be a good fit in Boston, but manager Terry Francona clearly favored Mark Bellhorn's offense in the pennant drive. If the Red Sox don't bring him back, Reese could surface as a starter with a club looking for an old-school, defense-first middle infielder.

Dave Roberts ⟨Great Bunter⟩

Position: LF/CF/RF
Bats: L **Throws:** L
Ht: 5'10" **Wt:** 180

Opening Day Age: 32
Born: 5/31/72 in
Okinawa, Japan
ML Seasons: 6

Overall Statistics

	G	AB	R	H	D	T	HR	RBI	SB	BB	SO	Avg	OBP	Slg
'04	113	319	64	81	14	7	4	35	38	38	48	.254	.337	.379
Car.	422	1294	213	335	39	19	11	99	135	141	158	.259	.335	.344

2004 Situational Stats

	AB	H	HR	RBI	Avg		AB	H	HR	RBI	Avg
Home	172	43	2	19	.250	LHP	56	10	0	3	.179
Road	147	38	2	16	.259	RHP	263	71	4	32	.270
First Half	206	54	2	19	.262	Sc Pos	57	15	2	29	.263
Scnd Half	113	27	2	16	.239	Clutch	34	8	0	2	.235

2004 Season

Dave Roberts began 2004 as the Dodgers' leadoff man, and ended it mostly as a pinch-runner for the Red Sox. Boston utilized Roberts extensively in that role in the postseason after acquiring him at the trading deadline. He stole a base and scored the game-tying run late in ALCS Game 4, keeping Boston's hopes alive.

Hitting, Baserunning & Defense

Roberts is a classic slap hitter with speed. He has very little power, but excellent bunting ability, making him a strange fit on a 2004 Boston team that had the fewest bunts in the majors. Roberts is a patient hitter with a good eye. He has great speed, and his career stolen-base percentage is better than 80 percent. His speed helps him get a good jump on balls in the outfield, but his arm does not scare opposing baserunners.

2005 Outlook

Given his previous status as an everyday player, Roberts may not readily accept the limited role he filled in Boston. But it's difficult to envision him as a regular in an outfield with the depth and power of Boston's. Barring a trade, the Red Sox may be happy to use his speed off the bench again.

Mike Timlin ⟨Rubber Arm⟩

Position: RP
Bats: R **Throws:** R
Ht: 6' 4" **Wt:** 210

Opening Day Age: 39
Born: 3/10/66 in
Midland, TX
ML Seasons: 14
Pronunciation:
TIM-lin

Overall Statistics

	W	L	Pct.	ERA	G	GS	Sv	IP	H	BB	SO	HR	Avg
'04	5	4	.556	4.13	76	0	1	76.1	75	19	56	8	.257
Car.	56	59	.487	3.61	812		4	117	955.1| 898| 307	720	93	.249

2004 Situational Stats

	W	L	ERA	Sv	IP		AB	H	HR	RBI	Avg
Home	3	1	3.41	0	34.1	LHB	134	36	3	20	.269
Road	2	3	4.71	1	42.0	RHB	158	39	5	26	.247
First Half	4	3	3.57	1	45.1	Sc Pos	90	22	6	38	.244
Scnd Half	1	1	4.94	0	31.0	Clutch	124	30	2	15	.242

2004 Season

For the second consecutive season, Mike Timlin spent the year as Boston's top setup man. And for the second consecutive season he was effective in the role. His ERA of 4.13 was more than half a run higher than in 2003, but he rarely got lit up, registering 20 holds.

Pitching & Defense

Timlin's bread-and-butter pitch is a sinking fastball that reaches the low to mid-90s. He mixes in an occasional slider for good measure. The 19 walks he issued more than doubled his total from 2003, but still indicate a pitcher with excellent control. He induces a good deal of groundballs, and opposing hitters grounded into nine double plays against him last season. His greatest value may be his capacity for a heavy workload. He pitched on consecutive days 21 times in 2004. Timlin, a big man, is fair but unspectacular defensively, both in fielding balls and holding runners.

2005 Outlook

After several years as a journeyman, Timlin has found a home in the Red Sox' bullpen. His workload may need to be monitored, as he appeared worn down at times in midsummer and got hit in the postseason. Timlin may hold up better in 2005 with Boston's signing of Matt Mantei.

Other Boston Red Sox

Jimmy Anderson (Pos: LHP, Age: 29)

	W	L	Pct.	ERA	G	GS	Sv	IP	H	BB	SO	HR	Avg
'04	0	0	–	5.17	12	0	1	15.2	19	6	6	0	.306
Car.	25	47	.347	5.42	122	96	1	574.2	672	240	241	58	.295

Anderson was dealt from the Cubs to the Red Sox in early July, and then back to the Cubs in early August. He didn't have the control to be especially valuable to either team, or its Triple-A affiliate. 2005 Outlook: C

Pedro Astacio (Pos: RHP, Age: 35)

	W	L	Pct.	ERA	G	GS	Sv	IP	H	BB	SO	HR	Avg
'04	0	0	–	10.38	5	1	0	8.2	13	5	6	2	.342
Car.	118	109	.520	4.61	351	304	0	1979.2	2050	658	1544	260	.269

Shoulder woes in 2001 and 2002 led to labrum surgery in June 2003. Astacio returned last summer to pitch 26.2 innings in the minors and with Boston. Much better in the minors, the righthander should hook on somewhere. 2005 Outlook: C

Jamie Brown (Pos: RHP, Age: 28)

	W	L	Pct.	ERA	G	GS	Sv	IP	H	BB	SO	HR	Avg
'04	0	0	–	5.87	4	0	0	7.2	15	4	6	1	.417
Car.	0	0	–	5.87	4	0	0	7.2	15	4	6	1	.417

A fastball-changeup pitcher, Brown has posted some tantalizing strikeout-walk ratios at Triple-A, and he finally got his first taste of the majors. But he doesn't have many chances left. 2005 Outlook: C

Ellis Burks (Pos: DH, Age: 40, Bats: R)

G	AB	R	H	D	T	HR	RBI	SB	BB	SO	Avg	OBP	Slg
11	33	6	6	0	0	1	1	2	3	8	.182	.270	.273
2000	7232	1253	2107	402	63	352	1206	181	793	1340	.291	.363	.510

Burks has retired. He missed nearly all of 2004 with a knee injury, but the 1983 Red Sox draft pick earned his first World Series ring in Boston's historic season. Burks leaves with a .291 average and 352 homers in 2,000 games. He says he'd like to manage Triple-A Pawtucket in 2005. 2005 Outlook: D

Frank Castillo (Pos: RHP, Age: 36)

	W	L	Pct.	ERA	G	GS	Sv	IP	H	BB	SO	HR	Avg
'04	0	0	–	0.00	2	0	0	1.0	1	1	0	0	.333
Car.	82	103	.443	4.55	296	267	2	1591.0	1656	501	1097	190	.268

Castillo has forged a long career with an excellent changeup and a mid-80s fastball. But he's nearly four years removed from his last decent year in the majors. He signed a minor league deal with the Marlins in November. 2005 Outlook: C

Cesar Crespo (Pos: SS/2B, Age: 25, Bats: B)

	G	AB	R	H	D	T	HR	RBI	SB	BB	SO	Avg	OBP	Slg
'04	52	79	6	13	2	1	0	2	2	0	20	.165	.165	.215
Car.	132	261	38	50	10	1	4	14	11	28	76	.192	.270	.284

Three stints in the majors have Crespo living below the Mendoza line. The middle infielder-outfielder still is fairly young, but he hasn't shown enough offensively in four Triple-A seasons to expect an emergence. 2005 Outlook: C

Brian Daubach (Pos: 1B, Age: 33, Bats: L)

	G	AB	R	H	D	T	HR	RBI	SB	BB	SO	Avg	OBP	Slg
'04	30	75	9	17	8	0	2	8	0	10	21	.227	.326	.413
Car.	646	2000	267	522	137	10	92	330	5	229	536	.261	.342	.478

Daubach came back to Boston after spending 2003 with the White Sox. It wasn't a joyous homecoming, as the first baseman spent most of the summer hitting the ball well for Triple-A Pawtucket. 2005 Outlook: C

Lenny DiNardo (Pos: LHP, Age: 25)

	W	L	Pct.	ERA	G	GS	Sv	IP	H	BB	SO	HR	Avg
'04	0	0	–	4.23	22	0	0	27.2	34	12	21	1	.298
Car.	0	0	–	4.23	22	0	0	27.2	34	12	21	1	.298

A Rule 5 pick from the Mets' system a year ago, DiNardo spent about half of the season on the disabled list. The DL time kept him on the Boston roster all year, and he probably heads to Double-A Portland in the spring. 2005 Outlook: C

Andy Dominique (Pos: 1B, Age: 29, Bats: R)

	G	AB	R	H	D	T	HR	RBI	SB	BB	SO	Avg	OBP	Slg
'04	7	11	0	2	0	0	0	1	0	0	3	.182	.182	.182
Car.	7	11	0	2	0	0	0	1	0	0	3	.182	.182	.182

Dominique made a few trips between Pawtucket and Boston in 2004, though he managed just 11 at-bats to go along with his 888 games and 3,201 at-bats in the minors. Those 11 with Boston will be the ones he'll always remember. 2005 Outlook: C

Ricky Gutierrez (Pos: 2B, Age: 34, Bats: R)

	G	AB	R	H	D	T	HR	RBI	SB	BB	SO	Avg	OBP	Slg
'04	45	103	8	22	3	0	0	8	1	8	14	.214	.277	.243
Car.	1119	3632	471	967	141	25	38	357	50	364	586	.266	.338	.350

Gutierrez went to camp with Cleveland and was dealt to the Mets in late March. Released in May, he was signed by the Cubs, then dealt to Boston in July. Got all that? Now he's a free agent. 2005 Outlook: C

Adam Hyzdu (Pos: LF, Age: 33, Bats: R)

	G	AB	R	H	D	T	HR	RBI	SB	BB	SO	Avg	OBP	Slg
'04	17	10	3	3	2	0	1	2	0	1	2	.300	.364	.800
Car.	190	318	52	74	16	0	19	57	0	36	89	.233	.314	.462

Hyzdu first surfaced at the Triple-A level in 1994, and in his third stint at Pawtucket last summer, he posted hitting percentages of .301/.413/.568. He fared pretty well in his September callup, too. 2005 Outlook: C

Bobby M. Jones (Pos: LHP, Age: 32)

	W	L	Pct.	ERA	G	GS	Sv	IP	H	BB	SO	HR	Avg
'04	0	1	.000	5.40	3	0	0	3.1	3	8	3	1	.273
Car.	14	21	.400	5.77	99	47	0	324.2	366	195	229	45	.288

The southpaw version of Bobby Jones appeared in the majors for the first time since he was released by the Padres in September 2002, the day before the team released the righthanded version. He had been decent enough at the Triple-A in 2003, but didn't resurface after Boston designated him for assignment last April. 2005 Outlook: C

Gabe Kapler (**Pos**: RF/LF/CF, **Age**: 29, **Bats**: R)

	G	AB	R	H	D	T	HR	RBI	SB	BB	SO	Avg	OBP	Slg
'04	136	290	51	79	14	1	6	33	5	15	49	.272	.311	.390
Car.	742	2198	326	598	126	13	61	281	66	199	348	.272	.332	.424

Kapler was a dependable backup during Boston's championship season. He was most productive in June and July, batting .341 with 11 of his 21 extra-base hits for the season. He has signed a 2005 contract to play in Japan for the Yomiuri Giants. 2005 Outlook: D

Curtis Leskanic (**Pos**: RHP, **Age**: 36)

	W	L	Pct.	ERA	G	GS	Sv	IP	H	BB	SO	HR	Avg
'04	3	5	.375	5.19	51	0	4	43.1	47	30	37	8	.280
Car.	50	34	.595	4.36	603	11	55	712.2	678	362	641	80	.253

The Royals needed a closer last spring, and Leskanic was one of several Royals who weren't up to the task. He was released with an 8.04 ERA in mid-June, only to sign with Boston and pitch much better. From August 1 on, he posted a 1.29 ERA. 2005 Outlook: B

Mark Malaska (**Pos**: LHP, **Age**: 27)

	W	L	Pct.	ERA	G	GS	Sv	IP	H	BB	SO	HR	Avg
'04	1	1	.500	4.50	19	0	0	20.0	21	12	12	2	.266
Car.	3	2	.600	3.75	41	0	0	36.0	34	24	29	2	.252

Malaska has needed time to climb the developmental ladder and has been homer-prone in Triple-A ball. Walks have been a bigger problem in parts of two big league seasons, but he's lefthanded and should get a few more chances. Fenway isn't the best place for a lefty looking for work. 2005 Outlook: C

Anastacio Martinez (**Pos**: RHP, **Age**: 26)

	W	L	Pct.	ERA	G	GS	Sv	IP	H	BB	SO	HR	Avg
'04	2	1	.667	8.44	11	0	0	10.2	13	6	5	2	.289
Car.	2	1	.667	8.44	11	0	0	10.2	13	6	5	2	.289

Armed with a mid-90s fastball, Martinez has fared quite well in the high minors the last two seasons, but he was roughed up in four of his 11 big league outings in 2004. Better command of his pitches, which include a curve and changeup, would help him stick in Boston. 2005 Outlook: C

Sandy Martinez (**Pos**: C, **Age**: 34, **Bats**: L)

	G	AB	R	H	D	T	HR	RBI	SB	BB	SO	Avg	OBP	Slg
'04	4	6	0	0	0	0	0	0	0	0	3	.000	.000	.000
Car.	218	564	39	130	32	4	6	51	1	37	147	.230	.284	.333

Martinez surfaced in the majors for the first time since grounding into a double play for Montreal on Opening Day 2001. While he posted a career-high 17 homers in just 62 games at Triple-A Buffalo last season, he's never been brought to the majors for his bat. He may never return. 2005 Outlook: C

Dave McCarty (**Pos**: 1B, **Age**: 35, **Bats**: R)

	G	AB	R	H	D	T	HR	RBI	SB	BB	SO	Avg	OBP	Slg
'04	89	151	24	39	8	1	4	17	1	14	40	.258	.327	.404
Car.	619	1489	180	360	68	8	36	173	9	124	367	.242	.304	.371

McCarty stuck with the Red Sox in the spring when Trot Nixon's back injury opened a roster spot. He enjoyed a red-hot May, but wasn't a key player for much of the season. A cyst in his right wrist was a second-half factor. 2005 Outlook: C

Ramiro Mendoza (**Pos**: RHP, **Age**: 32)

	W	L	Pct.	ERA	G	GS	Sv	IP	H	BB	SO	HR	Avg
'04	2	1	.667	3.52	27	0	0	30.2	25	7	13	3	.225
Car.	59	40	.596	4.29	341	62	16	796.0	889	181	462	81	.282

Shoulder tendinitis sidelined Mendoza for most of the first half. He struggled in September, which damaged his chances of contributing much in the postseason. 2005 Outlook: B

Doug Mirabelli (**Pos**: C, **Age**: 34, **Bats**: R)

	G	AB	R	H	D	T	HR	RBI	SB	BB	SO	Avg	OBP	Slg
'04	59	160	27	45	12	0	9	32	0	19	46	.281	.368	.525
Car.	395	1023	124	248	61	2	41	147	1	125	267	.242	.331	.426

Mirabelli put up some nifty hitting percentages last season. He was a .364 hitter with runners in scoring position for the Red Sox. And he served as Tim Wakefield's personal catcher. 2005 Outlook: B

Mike Myers (**Pos**: LHP, **Age**: 35)

	W	L	Pct.	ERA	G	GS	Sv	IP	H	BB	SO	HR	Avg
'04	5	1	.833	4.64	75	0	0	42.2	45	23	32	5	.274
Car.	17	21	.447	4.40	684	0	14	419.1	407	210	359	46	.258

Myers went from worst to first in an August trade, departing the Mariners, who went on to lose 99 games, for the Red Sox. He posted a 4.20 ERA in a Boston pen that was in a constant search of a useful arm last summer. 2005 Outlook: C

Joe Nelson (**Pos**: RHP, **Age**: 30)

	W	L	Pct.	ERA	G	GS	Sv	IP	H	BB	SO	HR	Avg
'04	0	0	–	16.88	3	0	0	2.2	4	3	5	0	.364
Car.	0	0	–	25.07	5	0	0	4.2	11	5	5	1	.478

Nelson received his first taste of the big leagues since 2001 in July. While he coughed up runs in two of three relief appearances with the Sox, he enjoyed a pretty solid 2004 season in the high minors. 2005 Outlook: C

Phil Seibel (**Pos**: LHP, **Age**: 26)

	W	L	Pct.	ERA	G	GS	Sv	IP	H	BB	SO	HR	Avg
'04	0	0	–	0.00	2	0	0	3.2	0	5	1	0	.000
Car.	0	0	–	0.00	2	0	0	3.2	0	5	1	0	.000

Seibel earned his first big league promotion. He didn't allow a run in two relief appearances. 2005 Outlook: C

Earl Snyder (**Pos**: 3B, **Age**: 28, **Bats**: R)

	G	AB	R	H	D	T	HR	RBI	SB	BB	SO	Avg	OBP	Slg
'04	1	4	0	1	0	0	0	0	0	0	1	.250	.250	.250
Car.	19	59	5	12	2	0	1	6	0	4	23	.203	.277	.288

Snyder produced career bests at Triple-A Pawtucket in runs (85), doubles (43), homers (36), RBI (104) and slugging (.558). The Devil Rays signed him to a minor league deal in December. 2005 Outlook: C

Scott Williamson (**Pos**: RHP, **Age**: 29)

	W	L	Pct.	ERA	G	GS	Sv	IP	H	BB	SO	HR	Avg
'04	0	1	.000	1.26	28	0	1	28.2	11	18	28	0	.115
Car.	25	24	.510	2.98	269	10	55	371.1	258	208	429	27	.196

Bothered by elbow pain for much of the season, Williamson was facing offseason surgery—possibly the Tommy John procedure for the second time. He was fairly effective when the pain allowed him to pitch. 2005 Outlook: C

Boston Red Sox Minor League Prospects

Organization Overview:

It wasn't much of a farm system inherited by new Red Sox owners John Henry and Tom Werner. Neither the drafts nor the international signings by the previous regime proved fruitful, and the Red Sox have been trading prospects in recent years to stay close to the New York Yankees. Those kinds of trades, and the acumen of general manager Theo Epstein in assembling the 2004 club, paid off with a World Series title for the first time in 86 years. In the aftermath, the Red Sox' system resembles the Yankees'. There's little that might provide immediate assistance, but there is good talent working its way through the pipeline that could provide a payoff in a few years. For now, the Red Sox will have to keep buying or trading for what they need.

Abe Alvarez

Position: P   **Opening Day Age:** 22
Bats: L **Throws:** L   **Born:** 10/17/82 in
Ht: 6' 2" **Wt:** 190   Los Angeles, CA

Recent Statistics

	W	L	ERA	G	GS	Sv	IP	H	R	BB	SO	HR
2004 AA Portland	10	9	3.66	26	26	0	135.1	133	65	32	108	13
2004 AL Boston	0	1	9.00	1	1	0	5.0	8	5	5	2	2

A second-round pick in 2003, Alvarez didn't allow an earned run in his nine-start debut at short-season Lowell. He jumped to Double-A Portland last spring and made an emergency start for Boston in late July, 13 months after signing out of Long Beach State. Alvarez has an exceptional feel for an 86-88 MPH fastball that he can locate anywhere. He also uses a 78-82 MPH changeup just as effectively. Despite the slight difference in velocity between his two top pitches, they work because of his solid fastball-like arm action on the change. He also was more confident using his curveball in nearly any count in 2004. In his Boston start, Alvarez found he must work inside effectively against righthanded hitters to succeed in the majors.

Jon Lester

Position: P   **Opening Day Age:** 21
Bats: L **Throws:** L   **Born:** 1/7/84 in Tacoma,
Ht: 6' 4" **Wt:** 200   WA

Recent Statistics

	W	L	ERA	G	GS	Sv	IP	H	R	BB	SO	HR
2003 A Augusta	6	9	3.65	24	21	0	106.0	102	54	44	71	7
2004 A Sarasota	7	6	4.28	21	20	0	90.1	82	46	37	97	2
2004 R GC Red Sox	0	0	0.00	1	1	0	1.0	0	0	2	1	0

A second-rounder in 2002, Lester played full-season ball in 2003, showing an advanced feel for pitching and decent command of three pitches. With a power arm for a lefthander, he now works consistently in the low 90s with his fastball and pinpoints it well. Lester also uses a slurvy curveball and changeup and added a cut fastball last summer. He quickly established the cutter as a valuable option, but the consistency of his curve and change waver, despite good arm action on the change-up. With a smooth and deliberate delivery that he repeats successfully, Lester keeps the ball down and in the park. Polishing his secondary pitches will be a priority at Double-A Portland in 2005.

Brandon Moss

Position: OF   **Opening Day Age:** 21
Bats: L **Throws:** R   **Born:** 9/16/83 in Monroe,
Ht: 6' 0" **Wt:** 180   GA

Recent Statistics

	G	AB	R	H	D	T	HR	RBI	SB	BB	SO	Avg
2003 A Lowell	65	228	29	54	15	4	7	34	7	15	53	.237
2004 A Augusta	109	433	66	147	25	6	13	101	19	46	75	.339
2004 A Sarasota	23	83	16	35	2	1	2	10	2	7	15	.422

A 2002 pick, Moss struggled to hit for average and get on base during his first two pro seasons, but he emerged with a terrific 2004. Most of his raw numbers last summer were better than his previous two-year totals. How the hard-working Moss approached at-bats, both physically and mentally, was better. He laid the foundation for the Class-A Sally League batting title and MVP honors, before moving up to high Class-A Sarasota and batting .422 in 23 games. Moss also showed a propensity to work counts well and draw walks. He has a quick stroke that has yet to fully tap into his raw power. Defensively, he's developing into a solid fielder after moving from shortstop to the outfield in 2003.

Jon Papelbon

Position: P   **Opening Day Age:** 24
Bats: R **Throws:** R   **Born:** 11/23/80 in Baton
Ht: 6' 4" **Wt:** 220   Rouge, LA

Recent Statistics

	W	L	ERA	G	GS	Sv	IP	H	R	BB	SO	HR
2003 A Lowell	1	2	6.34	13	6	0	32.2	43	23	9	36	2
2004 A Sarasota	12	7	2.64	24	24	0	129.2	97	43	43	153	6

A reliever at Mississippi State, Papelbon has been converted to a starter since signing as a fourth-round pick in 2003. Over the course of the 2004 season, Papelbon showed the command and stuff that could land him near the top of a big league rotation. An offseason conditioning program left him in terrific shape last spring, boosting his stamina as he made the transition to a starter. He tended to rely on his low-90s fastball at high Class-A Sarasota, but eventually he called on a slider he picked up last summer and his changeup more as the season progressed. By season's end, he was featuring three plus pitches on most nights. He also has a curve he can throw for a strike, but the slider is a true weapon.

Dustin Pedroia

Position: SS   **Opening Day Age:** 21
Bats: R **Throws:** R   **Born:** 8/17/83 in
Ht: 5' 9" **Wt:** 180   Sacramento, CA

Recent Statistics

	G	AB	R	H	D	T	HR	RBI	SB	BB	SO	Avg
2004 A Augusta	12	50	11	20	5	0	1	5	2	6	3	.400
2004 A Sarasota	30	107	23	36	8	3	2	14	0	13	4	.336

A second-round pick last June, Pedroia is a classic grinder with good instincts. His bat control and strike-zone judgment were key assets in his first pro season, and he understands what pitchers are trying to do when he's at the plate. He has some pop, which should translate into plenty of doubles as he matures. Defensively, the Arizona State product is fundamentally sound with good hands as a shortstop, though it may take time to know if he has the arm and range to stay at the position. Pedroia, who takes pride in his defensive work, didn't commit a single error. An emphasis on conditioning would give Pedroia an edge. Though he's athletic, he doesn't have the classic physique for baseball.

Hanley Ramirez

Position: SS   **Opening Day Age:** 21
Bats: R **Throws:** R   **Born:** 12/23/83 in
Ht: 6' 1" **Wt:** 174   Samana, DR

Recent Statistics

	G	AB	R	H	D	T	HR	RBI	SB	BB	SO	Avg
2003 A Augusta	111	422	69	116	24	3	8	50	36	32	73	.275
2004 A Sarasota	62	239	33	74	8	4	1	24	12	17	39	.310
2004 R GC Red Sox	6	20	5	8	0	1	0	7	1	2	3	.400
2004 AA Portland	32	129	26	40	7	2	5	15	12	10	26	.310

Ramirez is a tremendous athlete, a premier shortstop prospect with a five-tool package. He suffered a hairline fracture in his left wrist in May. When he returned after six weeks in June, Ramirez went on a tear between high Class-A Sarasota and Double-A Portland. He has the quick bat to handle any fastball, and he recognizes pitches successfully enough that he can handle or lay off breaking stuff. He's abandoned switch-hitting in favor of batting from the right side. Defensively, he has the attributes to be an exceptional defender, and he's become very consistent on routine plays.

Kelly Shoppach

Position: C   **Opening Day Age:** 24
Bats: R **Throws:** R   **Born:** 4/29/80 in Fort
Ht: 5' 11" **Wt:** 210   Worth, TX

Recent Statistics

	G	AB	R	H	D	T	HR	RBI	SB	BB	SO	Avg
2003 AA Portland	92	340	45	96	30	2	12	60	0	35	83	.282
2004 AAA Pawtucket	113	399	62	93	25	0	22	64	0	46	138	.233

A 2001 second-rounder, Shoppach made a successful jump to Double-A Portland in 2003, despite offseason rotator cuff surgery. He threw out 33 percent of base-stealers with his plus arm, quick release and throwing accuracy, and he showed good power. Shoppach is fundamentally sound as a catcher and exhibits solid leadership skills. He was challenged by working with more advanced pitchers at Triple-A Pawtucket in 2004. It was a learning experience and his work with the Pawtucket staff was better late in the season. He generated more homers, but also more strikeouts and a lower batting average. He may never hit for average, but the Red Sox hope a more consistent approach at the plate will bring down the whiffs. He needs more Triple-A time.

Kevin Youkilis

Position: 3B   **Opening Day Age:** 26
Bats: R **Throws:** R   **Born:** 3/15/79 in
Ht: 6' 1" **Wt:** 220   Cincinnati, OH

Recent Statistics

	G	AB	R	H	D	T	HR	RBI	SB	BB	SO	Avg
2004 AAA Pawtucket	38	154	25	41	12	0	3	18	2	19	28	.266
2004 A Lowell	2	4	1	3	1	1	0	0	0	2	0	.750
2004 AL Boston	72	208	38	54	11	0	7	35	0	33	45	.260

A bit shy in tools, Youkilis developed the abilities to make consistent contact and control the strike zone in the minors, and those skills carried him to Boston in 2004. After struggling in his Triple-A debut late in 2003, Youkilis fared much better at Pawtucket last summer. He joined Boston in May, when third baseman Bill Mueller needed knee surgery. Inserted into Boston's lineup, Youkilis reached base in his first 10 games, batting .313 with a .452 OBP and 12 runs scored. He reached safely in 21 of 22 contests before a July slide, when he no longer played regularly. At third, Youkilis caught the ball and made the routine plays. His range is limited, but he should improve at positioning himself and reading balls off the bat with experience.

· Others to Watch

Righthander **Manny Delcarmen** (23) had Tommy John surgery in May 2003. He returned last May and worked 73 innings at high Class-A Sarasota with no ill effects. His low-90s velocity has returned, and he was getting good action on his curve, a pitch that had ranked among the best in the Boston system. . . Switch-hitting short-stop **Christian Lara** (19) controlled the bat well in his first tour of North America, making good contact and showing impressive plate discipline. A solid fielder who makes the plays, Lara batted .433 in rookie ball and held his own at short-season Lowell. . . Another top young shortstop, **Luis Soto** (19) has a sweet swing from both sides of the plate and serious power potential, perhaps as much as anyone in the Boston system. He showed good pop in the rookie-level Gulf Coast League in 2004. . . Lefthander **Billy Traber** (25) has worked with four solid offerings, including a splitter as his out pitch, but he underwent Tommy John surgery in September 2003 after his rookie season with Cleveland. He was claimed off waivers in November, an unlikely scenario before surgery, and Traber could surface in Boston's rotation or bullpen at some point in 2005.

U.S. Cellular Field

Offense

These days, AL power hitters start salivating as soon as the wheels of the team charter touch down at O'Hare Airport. The White Sox' home field has been a bandbox since Jerry Reinsdorf decided to move the fences in after the 2000 season. There were 3.4 home runs per game at the Cell last season, the most by far in the AL. The 2003 average at U.S. Cellular had been 2.7. It's possible that the increase reflects shifted wind patterns since the club lowered the height of the upper deck.

Defense

Outfield arms are emphasized here, because fielders must play so deep with balls flying toward the walls. Fielders can be made to look silly on windy days as balls get blown around.

Who It Helps the Most

Frank Thomas is going to miss this park like crazy if he ever leaves. He has hit 99 home runs at home and 36 on the road over the last five years. This will not be a selling point for him if he is forced onto the free-agent market after this season. Paul Konerko also mashes at the Cell—29 of 41 homers last year.

Who It Hurts the Most

Mark Buehrle has had a good career based at U.S. Cellular, but it caught up to him last year. He gave up 22 homers there compared to 11 on the road. His ERA was 5.02 at home and 2.63 on the road. Freddy Garcia had 2004 ERAs of 5.37 at U.S. Cellular and 2.61 at Safeco Field, his old home park.

Rookies & Newcomers

The White Sox have begun to cultivate a strong stable of hitting prospects. Outfielders Brian Anderson and Ryan Sweeney, third baseman Josh Fields and first baseman Casey Rogowski are some of the prospects who could benefit from the favorable conditions at U.S. Cellular. It is not a plus for young pitchers, however.

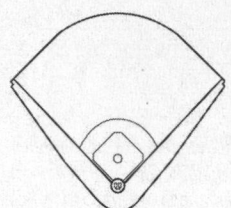

Dimensions: LF-330, LCF-377, CF-400, RCF-372, RF-335

Capacity: 40,615

Elevation: 595 feet

Surface: Grass

Foul Territory: Average

Park Factors

2004 Season

	Home Games CWS	Opp	Total	Away Games CWS	Opp	Total	Index
G	72	72	144	72	72	144	
Avg	.268	.279	.274	.262	.260	.261	105
AB	2421	2548	4969	2492	2367	4859	102
R	390	374	764	359	343	702	109
H	650	710	1360	652	615	1267	107
2B	114	124	238	126	119	245	95
3B	9	9	18	8	10	18	98
HR	121	110	231	90	82	172	131
BB	231	221	452	200	250	450	98
SO	427	479	906	465	427	892	99
E	42	45	87	47	56	103	84
E-Infield	32	40	72	43	49	92	78
LHB-Avg	.239	.287	.268	.256	.256	.256	105
LHB-HR	25	48	73	28	38	66	115
RHB-Avg	.281	.272	.277	.265	.263	.264	105
RHB-HR	96	62	158	62	44	106	140

2002-2004

	Home Games CWS	Opp	Total	Away Games CWS	Opp	Total	Index
G	216	216	432	216	216	432	
Avg	.273	.261	.267	.263	.261	.262	102
AB	7171	7443	14614	7546	7101	14647	100
R	1180	1002	2182	1047	1055	2102	104
H	1957	1942	3899	1983	1851	3834	102
2B	366	373	739	409	369	778	95
3B	28	28	56	33	30	63	89
HR	356	268	624	246	232	478	131
BB	687	679	1366	661	726	1387	99
SO	1187	1405	2592	1325	1272	2597	100
E	104	140	244	152	143	295	83
E-Infield	89	124	213	133	114	247	86
LHB-Avg	.264	.269	.267	.249	.273	.263	102
LHB-HR	80	134	214	72	111	183	121
RHB-Avg	.276	.253	.266	.269	.249	.261	102
RHB-HR	276	134	410	174	121	295	137

2004 Rankings (American League)

- Highest home-run factor
- Highest RHB home-run factor
- Third-highest batting-average factor
- Third-highest hit factor
- Third-highest LHB batting-average factor
- Third-highest RHB batting-average factor
- Third-lowest error factor

Ozzie Guillen

2004 Season

After six years away from Chicago's South Side, Ozzie Guillen returned last year to the organization where he had been Rookie of the Year in 1985. Guillen's bubbly personality helped in marketing campaigns that contributed to a much-needed increase at the gate, but he was unable to get more out of team built around slow, righthanded hitters than had his predecessor, Jerry Manuel. Guillen had the White Sox out of the gate fast, but they faded in the second half, in part because of failures in head-to-head play against Minnesota. This was the pattern he is expected to break.

Offense

Guillen talks about the importance of manufacturing runs, but he has not been able to win many games with that approach. The White Sox remained an all-or-nothing team built around power hitters but Guillen vows that will change in 2005. He tries to use the speed he does have, making Willie Harris a pet project. However, he sometimes seemed to force the running game last year. From August 1 to the end of the season, Sox baserunners were thrown out in 23 of their 47 steal attempts.

Pitching & Defense

As expected, Guillen had trouble handling a pitching staff. He twice accidentally waved for the wrong pitcher and once got stuck with him. The next day, he had large labels on his arm showing which was left and which was right. Give him credit for a sense of humor. Guillen is slower to go to the bullpen than Manuel, allowing his starters to get deeper into games. Mark Buehrle threw 17 more innings than any other AL pitcher last year.

2005 Outlook

Guillen came to the White Sox with a two-year contract and an option for a third season. It will be interesting to see if Jerry Reinsdorf exercises the 2006 option early or makes his old friend prove himself by winning 90-plus games and seriously contending for a playoff spot.

Born: 1/20/64 in Ocumare del Tuy, Venezuela

Playing Experience: 1985-2000, CWS, Bal, Atl, TB
Managerial Experience: 1 season
Pronunciation: GHEE-un

Manager Statistics

Year	Team, Lg	W	L	Pct	GB	Finish
2004	Chicago, AL	83	79	.512	9.0	2nd Central
1 Season		83	79	.512	–	–

2004 Starting Pitchers by Days Rest

	<=3	4	5	6+
White Sox Starts	4	95	36	16
White Sox ERA	5.48	4.97	4.90	5.22
AL Avg Starts	2	82	47	21
AL ERA	5.36	4.87	4.65	4.93

2004 Situational Stats

	Ozzie Guillen	AL Average
Hit & Run Success %	34.2	36.8
Stolen Base Success %	60.5	68.6
Platoon Pct.	55.3	61.6
Defensive Subs	13	21
High-Pitch Outings	5	5
Quick/Slow Hooks	8/22	20/16
Sacrifice Attempts	90	53

2004 Rankings (American League)

- 1st in sacrifice bunt attempts and pinch-hitters used (132)
- 2nd in slow hooks and starts on three days rest
- 3rd in squeeze plays (6)

Mark Buehrle

2004 Season

Few major league pitchers are as consistent as White Sox ace Mark Buehrle. He may not match up with other elite pitchers in terms of pure stuff, but his durability and command make him a cornerstone for a team trying to remodel itself from a power plant to one built around pitching and defense. Buehrle not only led the American League in innings pitched—he threw 17 innings more than anyone else, in part because Ozzie Guillen skipped the No. 5 starter whenever possible. Minnesota's Johan Santana and Brad Radke were the only AL pitchers with more quality starts than Buehrle, who had 23.

Pitching

Buehrle succeeds by keeping it simple. He attacks hitters with a low-90s fastball and a plus-plus changeup, working fast and throwing strikes. He used those two primary pitches to set up a cut fastball that sometimes comes and goes, but was generally in his 2004 arsenal. Buehrle yields a lot of home runs, in part because he is based at U.S. Cellular, and can give up ringing hits against batters who know he is going to challenge them in hitter's counts. He very rarely beats himself.

Defense

Buehrle is a steady fielder with quick reactions. He sometimes wants to force the action on bunts but has developed more patience with experience. He has an excellent pickoff move and is difficult to run on.

2005 Outlook

Buehrle continues to handle a heavy workload and still hasn't shown serious signs of wear and tear. One good sign for future seasons is that he increased his ratio of strikeouts per nine innings to 6.1 last season after it had dropped the three previous years. His mind seems free after signing a long-term contract, which has allowed his leadership skills to blossom. He remains a better bet for 16-18 wins and 225-plus innings than anyone else in the American League.

Position: SP
Bats: L **Throws:** L
Ht: 6' 2" **Wt:** 220

Opening Day Age: 26
Born: 3/23/79 in St. Charles, MO
ML Seasons: 5
Pronunciation: BURR-lee

Overall Statistics

	W	L	Pct.	ERA	G	GS	Sv	IP	H	BB	SO	HR	Avg
'04	16	10	.615	3.89	35	35	0	245.1	257	51	165	33	.271
Car.	69	45	.605	3.76	164	139	0	987.1	986	240	581	109	.261

2004 Pitching Profile

	Mark Buehrle	AL Average
Overall Strike %	65.0	62.3
1st Pitch Strike %	61.1	58.1
Ratio	1.26	1.42
Strikeouts per 9 IP	6.05	6.45
Walks per 9 IP	1.87	3.34
Home Runs per 9 IP	1.21	1.15
Strikeout/Walk Ratio	3.24	1.93
Groundball/Flyball Ratio	1.50	1.17

2004 Situational Stats

	W	L	ERA	Sv	IP		AB	H	HR	RBI	Avg
Home	9	7	5.02	0	129.0	LHB	202	58	6	25	.287
Road	7	3	2.63	0	116.1	RHB	745	199	27	83	.267
First Half	9	2	4.03	0	127.1	Sc Pos	179	54	6	73	.302
Scnd Half	7	8	3.74	0	118.0	Clutch	45	10	1	1	.222

2004 Rankings (American League)

- 1st in games started, innings pitched, batters faced (1,016) and pitches thrown (3,697)
- 2nd in hits allowed and lowest ERA on the road
- 3rd in GDPs induced (33)
- 4th in complete games (4)
- 5th in home runs allowed, lowest stolen-base percentage allowed (38.5), fewest walks per nine innings (1.9) and errors at pitcher (4)
- 6th in wins and most run support per nine innings (6.6)
- Led the White Sox in ERA, wins, hits allowed, hit batsmen (8), strikeouts, pickoff throws (110), highest strikeout-walk ratio (3.2), highest groundball-flyball ratio allowed (1.5), lowest stolen-base percentage allowed (38.5), fewest pitches thrown per batter (3.64), lowest ERA at home, fewest home runs allowed per nine innings (1.21) and fewest walks per nine innings (1.9)

Jose Contreras

2004 Season

Seemingly to his relief, José Contreras was traded from the New York Yankees to the White Sox at the July 31 trading deadline. The deal came only one week after his latest loss to Boston, and there's little doubt that a career ERA of 13.50 against the Red Sox was a primary motivation for the Yankees, who agreed to pay $5 million of the $17 million due Contreras in 2005 and '06. Contreras won three of his first four starts with the Sox but then showed the inconsistency that caused him to be considered a major disappointment by the Yankees, who had outbid Boston to sign him after he fled Cuba.

Pitching

Contreras' split-finger pitch is among the best in the majors, but hitters have begun to sit on it. The White Sox want Contreras to re-establish his fastball, which he can throw in the 94-95 MPH range, but Contreras struggles with spotting the pitch. As a result he often beats himself with walks and gives up long homers on fastballs right over the middle. He averaged 17.6 pitches per innings last year, meaning the bullpen was often on call.

Defense

Contreras is a big man who moves slowly. He can hurt his own cause by not being quick enough to get double plays on comebackers to the mound and not doing a good job holding runners on base.

2005 Outlook

Contreras is a huge X-factor for the White Sox. He has No. 1 starter stuff if they can harness it, but he won't even be adequate in the No. 3 or 4 spot if he doesn't improve from last season. He should be more comfortable than he's ever been, in large part because his wife and children joined him in the United States last year. He could still make the Yankees regret giving up on him so soon.

Position: SP
Bats: R **Throws:** R
Ht: 6' 4" **Wt:** 224

Opening Day Age: 33
Born: 12/6/71 in Havana, Cuba
ML Seasons: 2

Overall Statistics

	W	L	Pct.	ERA	G	GS	Sv	IP	H	BB	SO	HR	Avg
'04	13	9	.591	5.50	31	31	0	170.1	166	84	150	31	.253
Car.	20	11	.645	4.85	49	40	0	241.1	218	114	222	35	.239

2004 Pitching Profile

	Jose Contreras	AL Average
Overall Strike %	59.0	62.3
1st Pitch Strike %	54.1	58.1
Ratio	1.47	1.42
Strikeouts per 9 IP	7.93	6.45
Walks per 9 IP	4.44	3.34
Home Runs per 9 IP	1.64	1.15
Strikeout/Walk Ratio	1.79	1.93
Groundball/Flyball Ratio	1.07	1.17

2004 Situational Stats

	W	L	ERA	Sv	IP		AB	H	HR	RBI	Avg
Home	5	4	4.72	0	74.1	LHB	366	92	14	52	.251
Road	8	5	6.09	0	96.0	RHB	291	74	17	47	.254
First Half	6	3	5.64	0	68.2	Sc Pos	158	39	5	64	.247
Scnd Half	7	6	5.40	0	101.2	Clutch	23	6	0	1	.261

2004 Rankings (American League)

- 1st in wild pitches (17) and highest walks per nine innings (4.4)
- 2nd in runners caught stealing (11)
- 3rd in stolen bases allowed (29), most pitches thrown per batter (3.95) and highest ERA on the road (6.09)
- 4th in highest ERA (5.50)
- 5th in walks allowed (84), most home runs allowed per nine innings (1.64) and lowest fielding percentage at pitcher (.905)
- 7th in most strikeouts per nine innings (7.9)
- 10th in home runs allowed (31) and most run support per nine innings (6.3)
- Led the White Sox in stolen bases allowed (10)

Chicago (AL)

Joe Crede

2004 Season

The best one can say about Joe Crede's effort in 2004 is that he never lost his job. He definitely tried the patience of White Sox manager Ozzie Guillen and hitting coach Greg Walker, failing to provide the kind of production needed in a lineup that was often missing Magglio Ordonez and Frank Thomas. Hitting only .205 at the end of May, Crede couldn't dig himself out of that hole despite good months in June and September. He did wind up with a career-high 21 home runs, but that was very little consolation for a disappointing season.

Hitting

In his two full seasons, Crede has established himself as little more than a streak hitter. He endures long slumps, like the stretch in which he had only one home run over 91 at-bats. He fights a tendency to try to pull the ball with a swing that gets long, leaving big holes in his strike zone. He does his damage on pitches over the middle or on the outside half, seldom handling those on the inside corner. Strike zone judgment is also a problem for Crede, who chases too many bad breaking pitches. He hasn't developed the confidence to willingly go deep into counts. His walks are rare events.

Baserunning & Defense

An ability to make all the plays at third base is the saving grace in Crede's game. He has a solid arm and generally makes accurate throws. He has good instincts and moves well, especially to his left. Crede is another station-to-station runner in a lineup that has more than its share.

2005 Outlook

Citing the recent emergence of Adrian Beltre, the White Sox do not want to give up too soon on Crede. But this is a key season for him, as 2004 first-round pick Josh Fields could be pushing for big league consideration by the end of this season. His production numbers need to be much better than they've been.

Position: 3B
Bats: R **Throws:** R
Ht: 6' 1" **Wt:** 200

Opening Day Age: 26
Born: 4/26/78 in Jefferson City, MO
ML Seasons: 5
Pronunciation: CREE-dee

Overall Statistics

	G	AB	R	H	D	T	HR	RBI	SB	BB	SO	Avg	OBP	Slg
'04	144	490	67	117	25	0	21	69	1	34	81	.239	.299	.418
Car.	372	1290	166	330	68	3	52	189	3	77	210	.256	.304	.434

Where He Hits the Ball

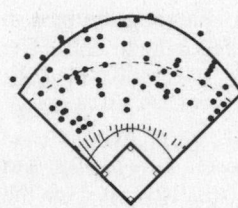 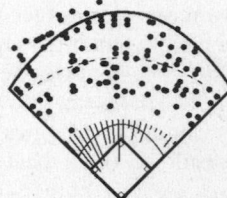

Vs. LHP   **Vs. RHP**

2004 Situational Stats

	AB	H	HR	RBI	Avg		AB	H	HR	RBI	Avg
Home	234	61	12	45	.261	LHP	164	42	4	20	.256
Road	256	56	9	24	.219	RHP	326	75	17	49	.230
First Half	278	67	12	39	.241	Sc Pos	122	29	4	44	.238
Scnd Half	212	50	9	30	.236	Clutch	70	18	3	16	.257

2004 Rankings (American League)

- 2nd in lowest on-base percentage and lowest batting average on the road
- 3rd in lowest batting average
- 5th in fielding percentage at third base (.965)
- Led the White Sox in hit by pitch (10)

Carl Everett

2004 Season

Injuries and a trade contributed to an alarming downturn for Carl Everett, whose conditioning was cited as a problem by two managers, Montreal's Frank Robinson and the White Sox' Ozzie Guillen. Everett did not appear to take care very good care of himself while spending a month on the disabled list after tearing tissue in his right shoulder sliding headfirst into second base on April 14. He put on so much weight that Guillen did not feel he could use him in the outfield after the Sox acquired him in a midseason trade for the second season in a row. They've given up five minor-leaguers in those deals, including pitchers Frankie Francisco, who was among three players sent to Texas in 2003, and Jon Rauch, who went to Montreal last year.

Hitting

Everett seemed to be affected by the injured shoulder all season. He hit the ball on the ground much more often than normal, and had no power from the right side (zero homers in 90 at-bats against lefthanders). He's always been better lefthanded than righthanded, and that trend continued.

Baserunning & Defense

Everett has never been considered a strong fielder, but he was adequate in center for the White Sox in 2003, benefiting from the small square footage of the U.S. Cellular outfield. However, he wasn't in shape to play the outfield when the Sox got him a second time. He was a full-time designated hitter for them last season, playing only one game in the outfield. He didn't try to steal a base until September 8, and when he did he pulled his hamstring. He played only one more game the rest of the season.

2005 Outlook

Everett exercised a $4 million player option to return to the White Sox, who don't know what they'll do with him. If he doesn't shape up, he'll be an expensive bench player, as Frank Thomas figures to be the DH.

Position: DH/LF/RF
Bats: B **Throws:** R
Ht: 6' 0" **Wt:** 215

Opening Day Age: 33
Born: 6/3/71 in Tampa, FL
ML Seasons: 12

Overall Statistics

	G	AB	R	H	D	T	HR	RBI	SB	BB	SO	Avg	OBP	Slg
'04	82	281	29	73	17	1	7	35	1	16	45	.260	.319	.402
Car.	1178	4011	612	1111	233	24	168	672	102	371	865	.277	.348	.473

Where He Hits the Ball

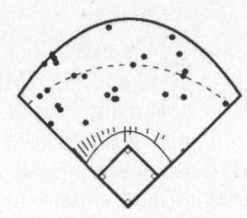
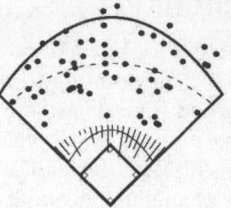

Vs. LHP   **Vs. RHP**

2004 Situational Stats

	AB	H	HR	RBI	Avg		AB	H	HR	RBI	Avg
Home	173	41	3	16	.237	LHP	90	21	0	10	.233
Road	108	32	4	19	.296	RHP	191	52	7	25	.272
First Half	117	31	2	13	.265	Sc Pos	62	19	1	26	.306
Scnd Half	164	42	5	22	.256	Clutch	35	10	0	2	.286

2004 Rankings (American League)

- Did not rank near the top or bottom in any category

Freddy Garcia

2004 Season

After contract negotiations broke down in Seattle, Freddy Garcia became a bargaining chip in the Mariners' rebuilding plans. He was sent to the White Sox in a trade on June 28, bringing catcher Miguel Olivo and prospects Jeremy Reed and Michael Morse in return. Garcia pitched better while with the Mariners but benefited from superior run support after the deal, going 9-4 in 16 starts with the Sox to finish the season with a winning record. He has an 85-54 career record but has been 25-25 the last two seasons. Garcia missed a pair of starts late in the season with a tight forearm, but returned to make his last five starts, easing concerns about 2005.

Pitching

Garcia looked like an ace early in his career but was disappointing for Seattle in 2002 and '03. He turned himself around in early '04, using one of the majors' best collection of quality pitches—a 92-93 MPH fastball, a good two-seamer, a quality changeup and both a curveball and slider—to frustrate hitters. He can struggle against lineups stacked with lefthanded batters, but was almost as tough on them as righthanded batters last year. Few pitchers are as durable as Garcia.

Defense

Garcia has slower reactions than you would like but has become an adequate fielder. He is adept at starting double plays and did not commit an error last season. He has developed a decent pickoff move but can be slow to home plate, making it possible to run on him.

2005 Outlook

Garcia carries large expectations after receiving a three-year contract from the White Sox shortly after the trade. He will be considered a disappointment if he doesn't improve the 4.46 ERA he posted after changing addresses. Ozzie Guillen should be able to count on 200-plus innings from his close friend. He has worked at least 200 innings in each of the last four seasons.

Position: SP
Bats: R **Throws:** R
Ht: 6' 4" **Wt:** 240

Opening Day Age: 29
Born: 6/10/75 in Caracas, VZ
ML Seasons: 6

Overall Statistics

	W	L	Pct.	ERA	G	GS	Sv	IP	H	BB	SO	HR	Avg
'04	13	11	.542	3.81	31	31	0	210.0	192	64	184	22	.242
Car.	85	54	.612	3.94	186	185	0	1199.1	1131	421	921	133	.248

2004 Pitching Profile

	Freddy Garcia	AL Average
Overall Strike %	60.5	62.3
1st Pitch Strike %	54.4	58.1
Ratio	1.22	1.42
Strikeouts per 9 IP	7.89	6.45
Walks per 9 IP	2.74	3.34
Home Runs per 9 IP	0.94	1.15
Strikeout/Walk Ratio	2.88	1.93
Groundball/Flyball Ratio	1.15	1.17

2004 Situational Stats

	W	L	ERA	Sv	IP		AB	H	HR	RBI	Avg
Home	5	7	3.99	0	117.1	LHB	420	99	14	43	.236
Road	8	4	3.59	0	92.2	RHB	375	93	8	39	.248
First Half	6	8	3.45	0	127.2	Sc Pos	179	39	5	56	.218
Scnd Half	7	3	4.37	0	82.1	Clutch	56	13	2	4	.232

2004 Rankings (American League)

- 1st in fielding percentage at pitcher (1.000)
- 3rd in least run support per nine innings (3.9)
- 5th in strikeouts (184), lowest batting average allowed (.242), lowest on-base percentage allowed (.303) and lowest batting average allowed with runners in scoring position (.218)
- 7th in ERA (3.81), lowest slugging percentage allowed (.389) and lowest ERA on the road (3.59)
- 9th in highest strikeout-walk ratio (2.9) and most strikeouts per nine innings (7.9)
- 10th in fewest home runs allowed per nine innings (.94)
- Led the White Sox in winning percentage (.692), lowest batting average allowed (.247), lowest slugging percentage allowed (.422), lowest on-base percentage allowed (.311), lowest batting average allowed with runners in scoring position (.233),and most strikeouts per nine innings (8.9)

Jon Garland

2004 Season

If a movie was made about Jon Garland's career, it might be entitled "Same Time, Next Year." While the White Sox have remained optimistic about Garland's potential, his disappointing performances keep repeating themselves. He had been expected to take a step forward in 2004, in part because new manager Ozzie Guillen promised to give him more rope than had predecessor Jerry Manuel, but it didn't happen. Garland was just as mediocre as in other seasons. In fact, his earned run average jumped one-third of a run per game and his ratio of strikeouts per nine innings dropped for the second year in a row.

Pitching

Garland has a solid sinking fastball in the low-90s but has been unable to complement it with another plus pitch. His curveball can be a good pitch, but he does not command it well enough. He does not do a good job of changing speeds and winds up in too many hitters' count, which helps explains how a sinkerballer could give up the fourth-most home runs in the AL.

Defense

Two errors in 2004 were Garland's first since '01. He is a solid fundamental fielder who has good instincts, seldom trying to force the action. Teams do not run on him much, but that may be because they're willing to take their chances hitting him.

2005 Outlook

On the plus side, Garland did set a career high for innings pitched and had as many or more quality starts as Barry Zito, Tim Hudson and Javier Vazquez. The White Sox are likely to point out those facts as they shop him to other teams for possible trades. They do not want to open the season with Garland as more than their No. 5 starter. Although the righthander's salary is beginning to get expensive for that role, the two sides quickly came to terms on a one-year, $3.4 million contract in mid-November. Whether Garland stays or goes, this is a critical season for his career.

Position: SP
Bats: R **Throws:** R
Ht: 6' 6" **Wt:** 210

Opening Day Age: 25
Born: 9/27/79 in Valencia, CA
ML Seasons: 5

Overall Statistics

	W	L	Pct.	ERA	G	GS	Sv	IP	H	BB	SO	HR	Avg
'04	12	11	.522	4.89	34	33	0	217.0	223	76	113	34	.269
Car.	46	51	.474	4.68	149	127	1	788.0	804	328	436	111	.268

2004 Pitching Profile

	Jon Garland	AL Average
Overall Strike %	62.2	62.3
1st Pitch Strike %	57.1	58.1
Ratio	1.38	1.42
Strikeouts per 9 IP	4.69	6.45
Walks per 9 IP	3.15	3.34
Home Runs per 9 IP	1.41	1.15
Strikeout/Walk Ratio	1.49	1.93
Groundball/Flyball Ratio	1.27	1.17

2004 Situational Stats

	W	L	ERA	Sv	IP		AB	H	HR	RBI	Avg
Home	5	6	5.27	0	94.0	LHB	446	117	19	69	.262
Road	7	5	4.61	0	123.0	RHB	383	106	15	50	.277
First Half	7	5	4.41	0	114.1	Sc Pos	180	47	10	84	.261
Scnd Half	5	6	5.44	0	102.2	Clutch	48	15	4	10	.313

2004 Rankings (American League)

- 4th in home runs allowed
- 5th in lowest strikeout-walk ratio (1.5)
- 6th in innings pitched
- 7th in batters faced (923), highest ERA at home and fewest strikeouts per nine innings (4.7)
- 8th in games started and pitches thrown (3,412)
- 10th in walks allowed and most home runs allowed per nine innings (1.41)
- Led the White Sox in losses, home runs allowed and walks allowed

Chicago (AL)

Paul Konerko

2004 Season

Following a disappointing season in 2003, the White Sox shopped Paul Konerko to try to ease their glut of righthanded hitters. They were lucky that no one was biting, as Konerko wound up being the key to a lineup that was without Magglio Ordonez and Frank Thomas for almost all of the second half. Konerko hit a career-high 41 home runs, and also avoided the long slumps that have dogged him in previous years. He's a pleasant guy who is popular with fans and good in an often-dysfunctional clubhouse.

Hitting

Konerko goes through painful contortions in the on-deck circle and sometimes looks wooden at the plate. Yet he gets solid plate coverage from a high-maintenance swing that requires constant work in the batting cage. He has good strike-zone judgment but sometimes lacks the bat speed to catch up with good fastballs, especially when they're in on his hands. Konerko hit 29 of his 41 homers at U.S. Cellular, which has become a bandbox since the fences were brought in after 2000.

Baserunning & Defense

There are no Gold Gloves in his trophy case, but Konerko has improved defensively at first base in recent seasons, particularly in scooping throws. He is capable of making the reaction catch on liners but overall lacks range. He is a base-clogger who struggles to go from first to third on most singles.

2005 Outlook

This is a big season for Konerko, as he's eligible for free agency at the end of the year. The White Sox will consider trade offers for him, as they are committed to balancing a lineup heavy on righthanded hitters and also adding speed and defense. Ross Gload is available as a first base option, but it's hard to see how the Sox can lose both Ordonez and Konerko in the same year. Konerko might not duplicate his 2004 totals, but there's no reason he shouldn't hit 30-plus homers and drive in 100 runs.

Position: 1B/DH
Bats: R **Throws:** R
Ht: 6' 2" **Wt:** 215

Opening Day Age: 29
Born: 3/5/76 in Providence, RI
ML Seasons: 8
Pronunciation: kun-ERR-coe

Overall Statistics

	G	AB	R	H	D	T	HR	RBI	SB	BB	SO	Avg	OBP	Slg
'04	155	563	84	156	22	0	41	117	1	69	107	.277	.359	.535
Car.	965	3420	482	952	172	5	170	592	4	319	500	.278	.345	.481

Where He Hits the Ball

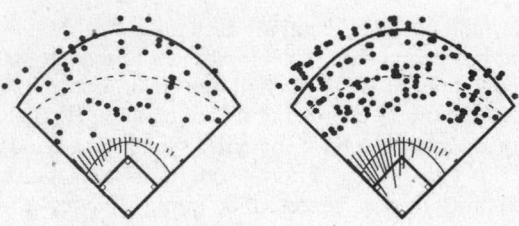

Vs. LHP	Vs. RHP

2004 Situational Stats

	AB	H	HR	RBI	Avg		AB	H	HR	RBI	Avg
Home	278	88	29	70	.317	LHP	163	47	13	38	.288
Road	285	68	12	47	.239	RHP	400	109	28	79	.273
First Half	284	84	22	59	.296	Sc Pos	140	44	10	77	.314
Scnd Half	279	72	19	58	.258	Clutch	71	19	2	9	.268

2004 Rankings (American League)

- 2nd in home runs and HR frequency (13.7 ABs per HR)
- 3rd in GDPs (23)
- 4th in errors at first base (6)
- 5th in fielding percentage at first base (.995) and lowest batting average on the road
- 6th in RBI and batting average with the bases loaded (.556)
- 7th in most GDPs per GDP situation (18.5%)
- Led the White Sox in home runs, RBI, walks, intentional walks (5), GDPs (23), pitches seen (2,557), games played and batting average at home
- Led AL first basemen in home runs

Carlos Lee

2004 Season

A steady run producer throughout his career, Carlos Lee has averaged 27 home runs and 94 RBI since 2000. He responded to the frequent absences of Magglio Ordonez and Frank Thomas by having his best season for the White Sox. Lee matched his 31 home runs from 2003 and hit better wire to wire than he had that season, even though his RBI total dropped by 14. He set career highs for batting average, hitting over .300 in every month except April, and on-base percentage. All in all, he had a very solid season.

Hitting

Lee has always been a dangerous hitter but has become a tougher out, in large part because he doesn't chase as many bad pitches as in previous seasons. He shortened his stroke as the season went on, generating as much power as at any time in his career (one homer every 13.4 at-bats after the All-Star break). He likes the first pitch, hitting .396 on it last season. He was as good against righthanded pitchers as lefthanders last year.

Baserunning & Defense

While not on the short list for an outfield Gold Glove, Lee is becoming a good outfielder. His range is average, but he does a good job making running catches and did not commit an error last season after making seven in 2003. He has an average arm but got 11 assists last season. Lee runs well and can steal a base when pitchers don't pay attention to him.

2005 Outlook

Lee signed a three-year contract before the 2004 season. He appeared to be a cornerstone in a lineup that would be without Magglio Ordonez in 2005 and possibly without both Frank Thomas and Paul Konerko after '05. Despite his consistency as a run producer, Lee was dealt to Milwaukee at the close of the winter meetings, in exchange for center fielder Scott Podsednik, reliever Luis Vizcaino and a player to be named. Lee becomes a key component of a Brewers lineup in need of power.

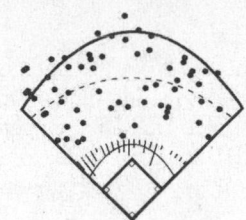

Position: LF
Bats: ⊓ **Throws:** ⊓
Ht: 6' 2" **Wt:** 240

Opening Day Age: 28
Born: 6/20/76 in Aguadulce, Panama
ML Seasons: 6

Overall Statistics

	G	AB	R	H	D	T	HR	RBI	SB	BB	SO	Avg	OBP	Slg
'04	153	591	103	180	37	0	31	99	11	54	86	.305	.366	.525
Car.	880	3328	533	957	192	10	152	552	64	255	501	.288	.340	.488

Where He Hits the Ball

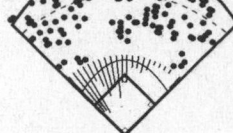

Vs. LHP   **Vs. RHP**

2004 Situational Stats

	AB	H	HR	RBI	Avg		AB	H	HR	RBI	Avg
Home	291	88	17	45	.302	LHP	156	48	10	24	.308
Road	300	92	14	54	.307	RHP	435	132	21	75	.303
First Half	324	94	11	50	.290	Sc Pos	147	44	7	65	.299
Scnd Half	267	86	20	49	.322	Clutch	77	22	4	12	.286

2004 Rankings (American League)

- 1st in fielding percentage in left field (1.000)
- 2nd in lowest groundball-flyball ratio (0.7)
- 4th in cleanup slugging percentage (.567)
- 8th in total bases (310)
- Led the White Sox in at-bats, runs scored, hits, singles, total bases (310), sacrifice flies (6), times on base (241), plate appearances (658), steals of third (2), batting average vs. lefthanded pitchers and cleanup slugging percentage (.567)

Magglio Ordonez

2004 Season

You can't say Magglio Ordonez is unwilling to play with pain. Following a full-speed collision with second baseman Willie Harris chasing an Omar Vizquel bloop on May 19, Ordonez missed only one game, then played in the next four games, three on the turf at the Metrodome, before it was discovered that he needed arthroscopic surgery on his left knee. Ordonez had the procedure on June 5, then returned to active duty on July 9. He played in 10 more games before being lost for the season with continued swelling in his left knee, which was diagnosed as bone marrow edema. Typically, he was 2-for-2 with a walk in the last game he played.

Hitting

There are few hitters who can drive the ball as effortlessly as Ordonez, who uses all fields and does a good job making contact. He had averaged 32 home runs and 118 RBI in the five seasons prior to 2004. He has a short, quick swing generated from a stance that has his weight on his back foot when the pitch is delivered. Ordonez can be slowed by righthanded pitchers but is dangerous against even the best. He is a clutch hitter, batting .352 with runners in scoring position last season.

Baserunning & Defense

Ordonez is solid if somewhat unconventional in right field. He is skilled at sliding to make catches in front of him, which allows him to play a step or two deeper. He has an average arm but it is accurate, which makes runners think twice before challenging him. Ordonez had slowed on the bases even before injuring his knee. He could be a station-to-station runner in the future.

2005 Outlook

Ordonez declined a five-year offer from the White Sox last season and enters free agency at a vulnerable time. Perhaps he will have to sign a one-year contract before he gets a chance at a multi-year deal that would garner an annual salary that approaches the $14 million he earned in 2004. He won't be returning to the White Sox, who didn't offer him salary arbitration. The process was likely to produce an eight-figure decision.

Position: RF
Bats: R **Throws:** R
Ht: 6' 0" **Wt:** 215

Opening Day Age: 31
Born: 1/28/74 in Caracas, VZ
ML Seasons: 8
Pronunciation: or-DOAN-yez
Nickname: Mags

Overall Statistics

	G	AB	R	H	D	T	HR	RBI	SB	BB	SO	Avg	OBP	Slg
'04	52	202	32	59	8	2	9	37	0	16	22	.292	.351	.485
Car.	1001	3807	624	1167	240	15	187	703	82	333	431	.307	.364	.525

Where He Hits the Ball

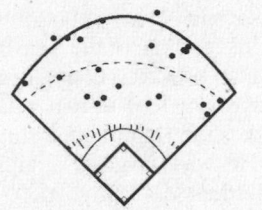 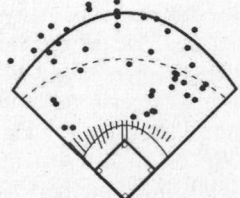

Vs. LHP **Vs. RHP**

2004 Situational Stats

	AB	H	HR	RBI	Avg		AB	H	HR	RBI	Avg
Home	94	28	4	19	.298	LHP	59	20	2	7	.339
Road	108	31	5	18	.287	RHP	143	39	7	30	.273
First Half	179	54	8	35	.302	Sc Pos	54	19	3	27	.352
Scnd Half	23	5	1	2	.217	Clutch	25	6	1	2	.240

2004 Rankings (American League)

- Did not rank near the top or bottom in any category

Aaron Rowand

2004 Season

After being relegated to fourth outfielder status in previous seasons, Aaron Rowand established himself as a regular. Those who looked closely saw one of the best center fielders in the American League in the second half of the season. Rowand was batting .213 on May 17 while sharing time with Willie Harris and Timo Perez, but he batted .332 the rest of the season. He finished with a .905 OPS, which was tops among AL center fielders. Because Rowand is popular in the clubhouse and community, many welcomed his emergence.

Hitting

With his confidence growing by the week, Roward began to drive pitches he had been happy just to put into play in previous seasons. He used the whole ballpark, going the opposite way against tough pitchers while jerking hangers into the seats. He's always been an aggressive hitter who swings early in the count, but he did a better job at spoiling filthy pitches. He figures to get more respect from pitchers, which could result in an increase in walks.

Baserunning & Defense

Roward is fun to watch in center field, but he does not cover ground like the Carlos Beltran guys with their long, smooth strides. He doesn't fit the mold, but he gets good jumps off the bat. He has quickened his release and overall his arm is considered adequate. After having only five steals in his first three seasons, Rowand responded to Ozzie Guillen's desire to force the action by stealing 17 bases.

2005 Outlook

Rowand returns as a regular and should hit high in the order, either leadoff or in the No. 2 hole. The only question is whether GM Ken Williams will look to add speed and a lefthanded bat in center field, which would prompt Guillen to shift Rowand to a corner. He could become an All-Star if he stays in center, where the hitting standard is lower.

Position: CF/RF
Bats: R **Throws:** R
Ht: 6' 0" **Wt:** 205

Opening Day Age: 27
Born: 8/29/77 in Portland, OR
ML Seasons: 4

Overall Statistics

	G	AB	R	H	D	T	HR	RBI	SB	BB	SO	Avg	OBP	Slg
'04	140	487	94	151	38	2	24	69	17	30	91	.310	.361	.544
Car.	422	1069	178	310	67	4	41	142	22	64	194	.290	.342	.475

Where He Hits the Ball

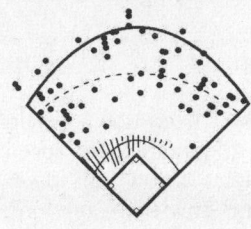 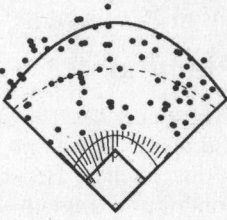

Vs. LHP　　　　**Vs. RHP**

2004 Situational Stats

	AB	H	HR	RBI	Avg		AB	H	HR	RBI	Avg
Home	244	74	12	36	.303	LHP	179	54	11	27	.302
Road	243	77	12	33	.317	RHP	308	97	13	42	.315
First Half	208	62	9	21	.298	Sc Pos	107	31	7	44	.290
Scnd Half	279	89	15	48	.319	Clutch	74	21	6	15	.284

2004 Rankings (American League)

- 2nd in lowest fielding percentage in center field (.980)
- 3rd in errors in center field (6)
- 4th in highest percentage of swings on the first pitch (38.3)
- 5th in lowest percentage of pitches taken (46.5)
- 7th in slugging percentage
- Led the White Sox in batting average, doubles, hit by pitch (10), stolen-base percentage (77.3), steals of third (2), batting average vs. righthanded pitchers, on-base percentage for a leadoff hitter (.369), and batting average on the road
- Led AL center fielders in home runs

Shingo Takatsu

2004 Season

Searching for a new challenge, Shingo Takatsu left Japan, where he was the career saves leader, to sign a one-year deal plus an option with the White Sox. Takatsu got hit hard in spring training and opened the season as the fourth righthander in Ozzie Guillen's bullpen, but by June he had replaced Billy Koch as the closer. Takatsu showed the funky stuff and mental toughness that earned him the nickname "Mr. Zero" while with the Yakult Swallows. He allowed only three of 25 inherited runners to score, went 19-for-20 in save situations and became a cult hero for fans at U.S. Cellular Field. In a remarkable stretch from late April through late June he went 24 appearances without allowing a run while holding batters to 10 hits in 26.1 innings.

Pitching

Everything Takatsu throws is from down under, and there's almost no way to anticipate the speed of his pitches. He sometimes throws his dive-bombing changeup in the low-60s—pitching coach Don Cooper says "it looks like it can defy a little gravity sometimes"—and can hit 90 with a fastball, which he generally throws in on hitters' hands. He rarely beats himself with walks and held opponents to a .182 batting average, including a .150 mark for righthanded hitters. He has a variety of pitches, but the key is how many speeds he throws his changeup and fastball.

Defense

Takatsu is tough to run on because he's so unorthodox. He permitted only one stolen base last season. He is a well-schooled fielder who handles his position.

2005 Outlook

Takatsu will get a chance to establish himself as one of the AL's top closers. Teams will have a better scouting report on him, but his strong September showed he doesn't depend on the element of surprise. Look for 30-plus saves and a possible trip to the All-Star Game in Detroit.

Position: RP
Bats: R **Throws:** R
Ht: 6' 0" **Wt:** 180

Opening Day Age: 36
Born: 11/25/68 in Hiroshima, Japan
ML Seasons: 1
Pronunciation: tah-kott-soo

Overall Statistics

	W	L	Pct.	ERA	G	GS	Sv	IP	H	BB	SO	HR	Avg
'04	6	4	.600	2.31	59	0	19	62.1	40	21	50	6	.182
Car.	6	4	.600	2.31	59	0	19	62.1	40	21	50	6	.182

2004 Pitching Profile

	Shingo Takatsu	AL Average
Overall Strike %	60.8	62.3
1st Pitch Strike %	54.7	58.1
Ratio	0.98	1.42
Strikeouts per 9 IP	7.22	6.45
Walks per 9 IP	3.03	3.34
Home Runs per 9 IP	0.87	1.15
Strikeout/Walk Ratio	2.38	1.93
Groundball/Flyball Ratio	0.85	1.17

2004 Situational Stats

	W	L	ERA	Sv	IP		AB	H	HR	RBI	Avg
Home	5	3	2.14	10	33.2	LHB	107	23	5	15	.215
Road	1	1	2.51	9	28.2	RHB	113	17	1	3	.150
First Half	4	1	1.30	5	34.2	Sc Pos	40	8	2	12	.200
Scnd Half	2	3	3.58	14	27.2	Clutch	126	22	4	15	.175

2004 Rankings (American League)

- 1st in save percentage (95.0)
- 2nd in first batter efficiency (.143)
- 3rd in fewest baserunners allowed per nine innings in relief (9.1)
- 4th in wins among rookies and lowest batting average allowed in relief (.182)
- 8th in relief ERA (2.31)
- 9th in relief wins (6) and games finished (45)
- 10th in saves
- Led the White Sox in saves, games finished (45), save percentage (95.0), lowest percentage of inherited runners scored (12.0), first batter efficiency (.143), relief wins (6), relief ERA (2.31), lowest batting average allowed in relief (.182),and fewest baserunners allowed per nine innings in relief (9.1)

Frank Thomas

2004 Season

For the second time in four years, Frank Thomas was sidelined for the season with an injury that at first did not appear to be a major concern. He did not play after July 6 because of a stress fracture in his left ankle. The initial diagnosis was inflammation in the ankle, and GM Ken Williams criticized Thomas for not making himself available at least as a pinch-hitter in the days following the injury. The Sox expected to get him back after he went on the disabled list, but the ankle never improved. Thomas eventually underwent surgery on October 6 and was expected to be in a cast for eight weeks.

Hitting

Before the injury, Thomas was as dangerous as ever, showing the ability to drive the ball along with patience at the plate. Thomas loves to jerk pitches into the left-field seats at U.S. Cellular, where he is a much more productive hitter than on the road. Fourteen of his 18 home runs were at home, bringing the total to 67 of 88 at home over the last three years.

Baserunning & Defense

While Thomas can play first base, he is primarily a designated hitter. He did not run well before the surgery and could be a major liability on the bases after surgery.

2005 Outlook

Many thought managing Thomas would be a major challenge for Ozzie Guillen, but the two got along well during Guillen's rookie season as manager. The October surgery to repair the navicular bone in his left ankle could slow Thomas' preparation for the 2005 season in spring training. Still, the White Sox are counting on him to give them a big season. Jermaine Dye has been signed to take over in right field, but he may not be the run producer that the departing Magglio Ordonez was in a typical year. This is the final season that Thomas has a player option, so it could be his last with the White Sox. They hold the option on his contract in 2006, and Williams seems more likely to give him a $3.5 million buyout than to pay him $10 million.

Position: DH
Bats: R **Throws:** R
Ht: 6' 5" **Wt:** 275

Opening Day Age: 36
Born: 5/27/68 in Columbus, GA
ML Seasons: 15
Nickname: Big Hurt

Overall Statistics

G	AB	R	H	D	T	HR	RBI	SB	BB	SO	Avg	OBP	Slg
74	240	53	65	16	0	18	49	0	64	57	.271	.434	.563
1925	6851	1308	2113	444	11	436	1439	32	1450	1134	.308	.429	.567

Where He Hits the Ball

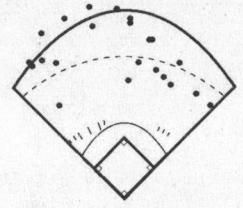
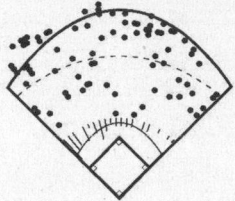

Vs. LHP   **Vs. RHP**

2004 Situational Stats

	AB	H	HR	RBI	Avg		AB	H	HR	RBI	Avg
Home	127	34	14	26	.268	LHP	50	10	3	7	.200
Road	113	31	4	23	.274	RHP	190	55	15	42	.289
First Half	240	65	18	49	.271	Sc Pos	66	18	5	32	.273
Scnd Half	0	0	0	0	–	Clutch	31	6	3	7	.194

2004 Rankings (American League)

- 8th in cleanup slugging percentage (.523)
- Led the White Sox in slugging percentage, on-base percentage, HR frequency (13.3 ABs per HR), most pitches seen per plate appearance (4.23), highest percentage of pitches taken (64.8), fewest GDPs per GDP situation (1.2%), and batting average with two strikes (.221)

Chicago (AL)

Roberto Alomar

Position: 2B
Bats: B **Throws:** R
Ht: 6' 0" **Wt:** 190

Opening Day Age: 37
Born: 2/5/68 in Ponce, PR
ML Seasons: 17
Pronunciation: AL-loh-mar
Nickname: Robby

Overall Statistics

G	AB	R	H	D	T	HR	RBI	SB	BB	SO	Avg	OBP	Slg
56	171	18	45	6	2	4	24	0	14	31	.263	.321	.392
2379	9073	1508	2724	504	80	210	1134	474	1032	1140	.300	.371	.443

2004 Situational Stats

	AB	H	HR	RBI	Avg		AB	H	HR	RBI	Avg
Home	102	29	4	20	.284	LHP	42	12	1	9	.286
Road	69	16	0	4	.232	RHP	129	33	3	15	.256
First Half	80	23	1	12	.288	Sc Pos	38	14	2	21	.368
Scnd Half	91	22	3	12	.242	Clutch	26	5	0	2	.192

2004 Season

It was the third down season in a row for Roberto Alomar, whose quest for 3,000 hits has slowed to a crawl. Alomar at least had an excuse this time around. A Ben Sheets pitch broke his right hand in April as a Diamondback, and a bad back sidelined him in September, when he was with the White Sox. He had spent the offseason improving his conditioning, but played in only 56 games. He's hit a pedestrian .262 over the last three seasons.

Hitting, Baserunning & Defense

Once feared for his ability to drive the ball, Alomar has become a slap hitter. He's generally been better lefthanded than righthanded but had no significant platoon differential last season. He has average speed and rarely tries to steal bases anymore. Alomar remains a fundamentally solid second baseman with a quick release on his throws. However, he sometimes seems lazy in the field.

2005 Outlook

Alomar appears to still have a desire to play and hoped to alleviate his back problems by shutting himself down in September. Finding a job will not be easy; his value as a bench player is dubious because he hasn't played anywhere other than second base since 1990.

Neal Cotts

Position: RP
Bats: L **Throws:** L
Ht: 6' 2" **Wt:** 200

Opening Day Age: 25
Born: 3/25/80 in Belleville, IL
ML Seasons: 2

Overall Statistics

	W	L	Pct.	ERA	G	GS	Sv	IP	H	BB	SO	HR	Avg
'04	4	4	.500	5.65	56	1	0	65.1	61	30	58	13	.247
Car.	5	5	.500	6.06	60	5	0	78.2	76	47	68	14	.255

2004 Situational Stats

	W	L	ERA	Sv	IP		AB	H	HR	RBI	Avg
Home	2	0	4.58	0	37.1	LHB	104	28	7	26	.269
Road	2	4	7.07	0	28.0	RHB	143	33	6	14	.231
First Half	1	3	5.64	0	30.1	Sc Pos	62	17	5	29	.274
Scnd Half	3	1	5.66	0	35.0	Clutch	64	19	5	12	.297

2004 Season

While Neal Cotts spent the full season in the big leagues, it was hardly a total success. Ozzie Guillen liked the way Cotts took his lumps and still wanted the ball, but he was hit harder than the White Sox had imagined a year ago, when he was dominating Double-A hitters. Cotts was scored on in 26 of his 56 outings as a long and middle reliever. He gave up one homer every five innings, including nine longballs away from hitter-friendly U.S. Cellular Field.

Pitching & Defense

A starter his whole career, Cotts struggled last year to set up his changeup, his best pitch. His fastball doesn't get much above 90 and his deceptive motion was not a big issue for lefthanded batters, who hit him surprisingly hard. Cotts was up with too many pitches last season, allowing more homers than he had in his minor-league career. He needs to work on his move to first base as he was easy to run on a year ago.

2005 Outlook

Cotts figures to return to the White Sox' bullpen in a secondary role. He needs to improve his command if he is to get consideration for a spot in the starting rotation, which once seemed to be his destiny.

Ben Davis

Position: C
Bats: B **Throws:** R
Ht: 6' 4" **Wt:** 225

Opening Day Age: 28
Born: 3/10/77 in Chester, PA
ML Seasons: 7

Overall Statistics

	G	AB	R	H	D	T	HR	RBI	SB	BB	SO	Avg	OBP	Slg
'04	68	193	22	40	9	0	6	18	1	12	49	.207	.256	.347
Car.	486	1512	168	358	77	2	38	204	9	153	385	.237	.306	.366

2004 Situational Stats

	AB	H	HR	RBI	Avg		AB	H	HR	RBI	Avg
Home	82	17	3	5	.207	LHP	58	10	1	5	.172
Road	111	23	3	13	.207	RHP	135	30	5	13	.222
First Half	40	3	0	2	.075	Sc Pos	40	6	1	11	.150
Scnd Half	153	37	6	16	.242	Clutch	28	4	0	4	.143

2004 Season

Needing a change of scenery, Ben Davis got one when Seattle sent him to the White Sox in the Freddy Garcia trade. He helped fill the hole left behind by Miguel Olivo, who had been the Sox' regular catcher. Davis, who had been relegated to Triple-A with the Mariners, started 44 games for Chicago. He got off to a fast start with the White Sox but disappeared late in the season, hitting .145 after August 31.

Hitting, Baserunning & Defense

A tall switch-hitter, Davis looks dangerous at the plate. Looks are deceiving, however, as he has huge holes in his swing and shaky strike zone judgment. He's a little better from the left side than the right. He has power but doesn't often get to use it. Davis is a marginal receiver and has become a target for basestealers, stopping only 24.5 percent of their steal attempts last season after getting 31.9 percent in 2003 and 44 percent in '02. He runs like a catcher.

2005 Outlook

The White Sox ended the season with Davis and Jamie Burke as their catchers, but were expected to upgrade over the winter. If he returns, Davis is likely to compete against Burke for a spot on the bench.

Ross Gload

Position: 1B/RF/LF/DH
Bats: L **Throws:** L
Ht: 6' 0" **Wt:** 185

Opening Day Age: 28
Born: 4/5/76 in Brooklyn, NY
ML Seasons: 3

Overall Statistics

	G	AB	R	H	D	T	HR	RBI	SB	BB	SO	Avg	OBP	Slg
'04	110	234	28	75	16	0	7	44	0	20	37	.321	.375	.479
Car.	154	296	36	89	17	1	9	51	0	26	54	.301	.357	.456

2004 Situational Stats

	AB	H	HR	RBI	Avg		AB	H	HR	RBI	Avg
Home	115	38	3	21	.330	LHP	40	17	2	6	.425
Road	119	37	4	23	.311	RHP	194	58	5	38	.299
First Half	105	28	2	20	.267	Sc Pos	58	23	2	37	.397
Scnd Half	129	47	5	24	.364	Clutch	39	13	0	6	.333

2004 Season

After showcasing himself at Triple-A Charlotte in 2003, Ross Gload spent his first full season in the big leagues as a role player for the White Sox varsity. He was productive in a difficult role, getting limited playing time before he got an extended look in late August. He got starts at first base and all three outfield positions, including 15 starts in right field.

Hitting, Baserunning & Defense

Gload is a solid hitter who can drive a fastball or hanging curve. He will go to the opposite field and does not often get himself out swinging at bad pitches. Few lefthanded pitchers intimidate him. Gload is strong defensively at first base, with quick reactions and soft hands, and solid in the outfield. His arm is a liability. He ran occasionally in the minors but has been timid on the bases in the big leagues.

2005 Outlook

Gload has earned his stripes with Ozzie Guillen. He hopes to get more at-bats in 2005 and could pick up some with the expected departure of Magglio Ordonez. A midseason trade is possible for Paul Konerko, who is approaching free agency, and the Sox are looking to get more lefthanded hitters into the lineup.

Chicago (AL)

Willie Harris

Position: 2B/CF
Bats: L **Throws:** R
Ht: 5' 9" **Wt:** 170

Opening Day Age: 26
Born: 6/22/78 in Cairo, GA
ML Seasons: 4

Overall Statistics

	G	AB	R	H	D	T	HR	RBI	SB	BB	SO	Avg	OBP	Slg
'04	129	409	68	107	15	2	2	27	19	51	79	.262	.343	.323
Car.	266	733	104	176	23	3	4	44	39	70	135	.240	.305	.296

2004 Situational Stats

	AB	H	HR	RBI	Avg		AB	H	HR	RBI	Avg
Home	202	49	2	13	.243	LHP	72	13	1	4	.181
Road	207	58	0	14	.280	RHP	337	94	1	23	.279
First Half	225	61	0	13	.271	Sc Pos	77	21	0	24	.273
Scnd Half	184	46	2	14	.250	Clutch	50	9	1	2	.180

2004 Season

Despite being made the personal project of manager Ozzie Guillen, Willie Harris failed to establish himself last season as anything more than an extra player. He got into 129 games and raised his batting average by 58 points over 2003, but has a .240 career average and lingering questions. A dynamic offensive player in the minors, Harris hasn't made much of an impact with the White Sox.

Hitting, Baserunning & Defense

Harris has not mastered lefties, which forces him to be platooned. He hits the ball on the ground, but has found it hard to get those grounders through the infield. He had a nice on-base percentage against righthanders last year. Harris is a gifted athlete who has terrific range at second base, especially covering ground to his left and toward the foul line on popups. His arm is below average. Harris can play center and left fields, which gives him value as a utility man. He's a quality basestealer and can fly going first to third.

2005 Outlook

Harris' situation depends largely on whether Juan Uribe is written into the lineup at shortstop or second base. If the Sox acquire a middle infielder in the offseason, Harris could be little more than an insurance policy.

Damaso Marte

Position: RP
Bats: L **Throws:** L
Ht: 6' 2" **Wt:** 200

Opening Day Age: 30
Born: 2/14/75 in Santo Domingo, DR
ML Seasons: 5
Pronunciation: da-muh-so mar-TAY

Overall Statistics

	W	L	Pct.	ERA	G	GS	Sv	IP	H	BB	SO	HR	Avg
'04	6	5	.545	3.42	74	0	6	73.2	56	34	68	10	.217
Car.	11	10	.524	3.10	241	0	27	258.2	200	104	269	26	.217

2004 Situational Stats

	W	L	ERA	Sv	IP		AB	H	HR	RBI	Avg
Home	5	2	3.92	3	41.1	LHB	98	14	2	10	.143
Road	1	3	2.78	3	32.1	RHB	160	42	8	20	.263
First Half	3	2	2.45	4	40.1	Sc Pos	56	9	1	19	.161
Scnd Half	3	3	4.59	2	33.1	Clutch	171	40	8	24	.234

2004 Season

After allowing only three homers in 2003, Damaso Marte gave up bombs to Carlos Beltran and Mendy Lopez on Opening Day, leaving him with a loss in Kansas City. It set a bad tone for the season, which would be a disappointment for a guy who had been one of the best bullpen lefties in the AL. Marte set a career high for appearances, but often seemed to struggle with his command. He was hard to hit but left too many pitches over the middle of the plate.

Pitching & Defense

Marte is generally a two-pitch pitcher, with a low-90s fastball and a slider that acts like a slurve. He has dabbled with a cut fastball but does not really need a third pitch in the relief role. Marte is a migraine for lefthanded batters, holding them to less than a .150 average in two of the last three seasons. He is not especially quick in handling comebackers but hasn't committed an error in 241 career games. Opposing basestealers can take advantage of him.

2005 Outlook

Marte has two guaranteed years and a 2007 option left on the deal he signed last year. He is likely to remain as the top lefthanded setup man for closer Shingo Takatsu, again appearing in 60-75 games.

Cliff Politte

Position: RP
Bats: R **Throws:** R
Ht: 5'11" **Wt:** 200

Opening Day Age: 31
Born: 2/27/74 in St. Louis, MO
ML Seasons: 7
Pronunciation: po-LEET

Overall Statistics

	W	L	Pct.	ERA	G	GS	Sv	IP	H	BB	SO	HR	Avg
'04	0	3	.000	4.38	54	0	1	51.1	52	22	48	6	.261
Car.	13	20	.394	4.50	232	16	14	314.0	304	135	270	40	.254

2004 Situational Stats

	W	L	ERA	Sv	IP		AB	H	HR	RBI	Avg
Home	0	0	3.07	1	29.1	LHB	74	26	4	15	.351
Road	0	3	6.14	0	22.0	RHB	125	26	2	15	.208
First Half	0	2	4.11	1	30.2	Sc Pos	56	17	0	23	.304
Scnd Half	0	1	4.79	0	20.2	Clutch	62	20	1	11	.323

2004 Season

The White Sox found out what the Blue Jays and Phillies had learned before them, that Cliff Politte is solid in the sixth and seventh innings but can't handle the pressure of getting the last three outs. He made 54 appearances and lowered his career ERA, bouncing back from a subpar 2003 in Toronto. His season ended early due to an appendectomy.

Pitching & Defense

Politte is a powerful pitcher. He hits the mid-90s on the radar gun and has a plus two-seamer, which has good sink. He throws a hard slider and occasionally mixes in a changeup. Control can be a problem, as he struggles to get himself back on track when his mechanics are off. He is Tom Gordon-tough on righthanded batters but has little margin for error against lefthanded hitters. He doesn't stop many hot shots up the middle but has a decent pickoff move.

2005 Outlook

Politte allowed the White Sox to restructure his 2005 option from $1.3 million to $1 million, and in exchange was given an option for '06. He will be in a middle-relief role, ideally as the No. 3 or 4 righthander.

Scott Schoeneweis

Position: SP
Bats: L **Throws:** L
Ht: 6' 0" **Wt:** 195

Opening Day Age: 31
Born: 10/2/73 in Long Branch, NJ
ML Seasons: 6
Pronunciation: SHOW-en-wice

Overall Statistics

	W	L	Pct.	ERA	G	GS	Sv	IP	H	BB	SO	HR	Avg
'04	6	9	.400	5.59	20	19	0	112.2	129	49	69	17	.291
Car.	36	41	.468	5.16	223	93	1	710.0	768	275	394	83	.277

2004 Situational Stats

	W	L	ERA	Sv	IP		AB	H	HR	RBI	Avg
Home	2	4	5.98	0	55.2	LHB	86	21	0	7	.244
Road	4	5	5.21	0	57.0	RHB	357	108	17	60	.303
First Half	5	7	4.71	0	93.2	Sc Pos	105	32	4	47	.305
Scnd Half	1	2	9.95	0	19.0	Clutch	13	3	0	1	.231

2004 Season

In a case of be-careful-what-you-ask-for, the White Sox gave Scott Schoeneweis his wish to start last season. He got off to a fast start but then crashed, possibly because of arm stress. He tried to pitch through pain in his elbow before undergoing arthroscopic surgery on August 13. He hoped to get back in time to showcase himself to other teams, but only had a chance to work one inning on the next-to-last day of the season.

Pitching & Defense

Schoeneweis spent spring training working on his changeup and experimenting with a cut fastball. Both pitches worked for him early in the year, complementing his 90-MPH fastball and high-80s sinker. His downfall was an inability to keep righthanded hitters off balance. They homered off him once every 21 at-bats. He kept baserunners off balance with his motion, allowing his catchers to throw out 10 of 20 baserunners trying to steal.

2005 Outlook

Schoeneweis filed for free agency after the season. He might have to sign a minor league contract to get another chance, and should consider moving to the National League. His stuff is not suited for U.S. Cellular and some of the other hitter-friendly parks in the American League.

Juan Uribe

(Great Range)

Position: 2B/SS/3B
Bats: R **Throws:** R
Ht: 5'11" **Wt:** 175

Opening Day Age: 25
Born: 7/22/79 in Bani, DR
ML Seasons: 4
Pronunciation: ooh-REE-bay

Overall Statistics

	G	AB	R	H	D	T	HR	RBI	SB	BB	SO	Avg	OBP	Slg
'04	134	502	82	142	31	6	23	74	9	32	96	.283	.327	.506
Car.	448	1657	228	440	90	27	47	209	28	91	331	.266	.307	.438

2004 Situational Stats

	AB	H	HR	RBI	Avg		AB	H	HR	RBI	Avg
Home	260	82	16	42	.315	LHP	178	47	12	34	.264
Road	242	60	7	32	.248	RHP	324	95	11	40	.293
First Half	302	84	12	37	.278	Sc Pos	99	32	5	51	.323
Scnd Half	200	58	11	37	.290	Clutch	69	19	3	14	.275

2004 Season

After coming over from Colorado in a trade for second baseman Aaron Miles, Juan Uribe took advantage of the chance to play for a Hispanic manager and to hit in a ballpark almost as good for batters as Denver's Coors Field. He established himself by hitting .335 through the end of May, then finished strong after a 32-for-173 slump at midseason.

Hitting, Baserunning & Defense

Working with Sox hitting coach Greg Walker, Uribe smoothed out his two-piece swing somewhat. He has surprising power and enjoyed hitting at U.S. Cellular. However, Uribe often swings at the first strike he sees and rarely works the count. Uribe is a skilled middle infielder with range, sure hands and a strong arm. He showed his versatility by starting 19 games at third base, where he had never previously played. Ozzie Guillen pushed Uribe to use his speed, but he was thrown out in 11 of his 20 stolen-base attempts.

2005 Outlook

The second-base and shortstop jobs were open heading into the winter, but Uribe seems certain to start at short after GM Ken Williams was unable to land Omar Vizquel in the free-agent market. Uribe should get 500-plus at-bats either way.

Jose Valentin

Position: SS
Bats: L **Throws:** R
Ht: 5'10" **Wt:** 195

Opening Day Age: 35
Born: 10/12/69 in Manati, PR
ML Seasons: 13
Pronunciation: val-en-TEEN

Overall Statistics

G	AB	R	H	D	T	HR	RBI	SB	BB	SO	Avg	OBP	Slg
125	450	73	97	20	3	30	70	8	43	139	.216	.287	.473
1434	4842	781	1179	263	35	226	722	125	547	1157	.243	.321	.452

2004 Situational Stats

	AB	H	HR	RBI	Avg		AB	H	HR	RBI	Avg
Home	207	45	16	39	.217	LHP	136	26	7	16	.191
Road	243	52	14	31	.214	RHP	314	71	23	54	.226
First Half	252	64	18	48	.254	Sc Pos	105	26	8	40	.248
Scnd Half	198	33	12	22	.167	Clutch	54	15	6	10	.278

2004 Season

Despite a declining batting average and the availability of Juan Uribe as a replacement, Jose Valentin remained the White Sox' primary shortstop for the fourth time in the last five seasons. A solid, all-around player when the White Sox won the AL West in 2000, he has become one-dimensional, with his only plus tool being power. He hit 30 homers but batted just .162 after June.

Hitting, Baserunning & Defense

Long considered a threat lefthanded and an easy out righthanded, Valentin stopped being stubborn and hit exclusively lefthanded. He did raise his average slightly against lefties, but only to .191. He piles up strikeouts swinging for the fences. At shortstop he is error-prone but maintains a strong arm. His range has decreased because of frequent hamstring and groin strains. He is a good baserunner with excellent instincts but has slowed down, stealing only eight bases last season.

2005 Outlook

Having finished a four-year, $20-million deal with the Sox, Valentin filed for free agency. Despite having averaged 27 homers and 76 RBI in his five years in Chicago, Valentin is at a crossroads. He could be valuable as a reserve. He should consider managing once his playing days are over.

Jon Adkins (**Pos**: RHP, **Age**: 27)

	W	L	Pct.	ERA	G	GS	SV	IP	H	BB	SO	HR	Avg
'04	2	3	.400	4.65	50	0	0	62.0	75	20	44	13	.305
Car.	2	3	.400	4.67	54	0	0	71.1	83	27	47	14	.299

Adkins made the White Sox out of spring training and pitched reasonably well through June. He was torched in the second half. He'll have to do better to survive another full season in Chicago. 2005 Outlook: C

Sandy Alomar Jr. (**Pos**: C, **Age**: 38, **Bats**: R)

	G	AB	R	H	D	T	HR	RBI	SB	BB	SO	Avg	OBP	Slg
'04	50	146	15	35	4	0	2	14	0	11	13	.240	.298	.308
Car.	1277	4272	500	1168	233	10	111	557	25	204	470	.273	.310	.411

Alomar's hitting percentages continued to slide in 2004. A groin injury in August and a .163 average after starting catcher Miguel Olivo was dealt to Seattle in June limited his playing time. He signed with Texas in December. 2005 Outlook: C

Jamie Burke (**Pos**: C, **Age**: 33, **Bats**: R)

	G	AB	R	H	D	T	HR	RBI	SB	BB	SO	Avg	OBP	Slg
'04	57	120	22	40	9	0	0	15	0	10	13	.333	.386	.408
Car.	72	153	23	44	9	0	0	17	0	10	15	.331	.379	.398

Burke bounced through four systems with stops at four Triple-A locales before surfacing in Chicago and hitting surprisingly well after starting catcher Miguel Olivo's departure in a July trade. He will play more in 2005 if he and Ben Davis share duties. 2005 Outlook: C

Felix Diaz (**Pos**: RHP, **Age**: 24)

	W	L	Pct.	ERA	G	GS	Sv	IP	H	BB	SO	HR	Avg
'04	2	5	.286	6.75	18	7	0	49.1	62	16	33	13	.310
Car.	2	5	.286	6.75	18	7	0	49.1	62	16	33	13	.310

Diaz had a strong second season at Triple-A Charlotte, going 10-2 with 2.97 ERA. One of many who auditioned to be the Sox' No. 5 starter, he beat the crosstown Cubs with a quality start in his third big league outing, but his only other good one was a September win over Seattle. 2005 Outlook: C

Kelly Dransfeldt (**Pos**: SS, **Age**: 29, **Bats**: R)

	G	AB	R	H	D	T	HR	RBI	SB	BB	SO	Avg	OBP	Slg
'04	15	30	5	10	0	0	0	4	0	0	6	.333	.333	.333
Car.	51	112	10	23	3	0	1	11	0	4	32	.205	.233	.259

Dransfeldt has done little offensively in six Triple-A seasons, but he got the call in April when Jose Valentin was hurt briefly. While he did his best big league hitting this time around, Dransfeldt wasn't heard from again after a mid-June demotion. 2005 Outlook: C

Jason Grilli (**Pos**: RHP, **Age**: 28)

	W	L	Pct.	ERA	G	GS	Sv	IP	H	BB	SO	HR	Avg
'04	2	3	.400	7.40	8	8	0	45.0	52	20	26	11	.294
Car.	5	5	.500	6.78	15	14	0	78.1	93	33	46	17	.303

Grilli was a Rule 5 pick of the Sox a year ago, though the Marlins didn't take him back when offered. He was better and less homer-prone at Triple-A Charlotte (9-9, 4.83 ERA) than Chicago. 2005 Outlook: C

Mike Jackson (**Pos**: RHP, **Age**: 40)

	W	L	Pct.	ERA	G	GS	Sv	IP	H	BB	SO	HR	Avg
'04	2	0	1.000	5.01	45	0	0	46.2	55	15	26	7	.294
Car.	62	67	.481	3.42	1005	7	142	1188.1	983	464	1006	127	.226

We haven't seen the best of Jackson since 1998. He hooked on with the Sox after being out of organized baseball in 2003, but he was given his release in late August. 2005 Outlook: C

Arnie Munoz (**Pos**: LHP, **Age**: 22)

	W	L	Pct.	ERA	G	GS	Sv	IP	H	BB	SO	HR	Avg
'04	0	1	.000	10.05	11	1	0	14.1	20	12	11	4	.339
Car.	0	1	.000	10.05	11	1	0	14.1	20	12	11	4	.339

A small lefthander with a big curveball, Munoz went from reliever to starter in the high minors last summer. He was impressive at Double-A (7-2, 2.05), but was throttled in his big league debut in June before faring a bit better in the Sox' bullpen. 2005 Outlook: C

Timo Perez (**Pos**: RF/LF/CF, **Age**: 29, **Bats**: L)

	G	AB	R	H	D	T	HR	RBI	SB	BB	SO	Avg	OBP	Slg
'04	103	293	38	72	12	0	5	40	3	15	29	.246	.285	.338
Car.	475	1371	159	369	73	8	23	154	20	71	124	.269	.306	.384

Perez is an adept outfielder, but he once again didn't get on base enough to make use of his speed. The numbers would be worse if not for an impressive June in which he hit .339 and scored 14 runs in 18 games. 2005 Outlook: C

Josh Stewart (**Pos**: LHP, **Age**: 26)

	W	L	Pct.	ERA	G	GS	Sv	IP	H	BB	SO	HR	Avg
'04	0	1	.000	15.26	3	2	0	7.2	16	3	5	3	.444
Car.	1	3	.250	8.10	8	7	0	33.1	44	19	18	7	.317

Stewart doesn't have much Triple-A experience and didn't dominate at Charlotte in 2004. Yet, he got a brief crack at the fifth-starter role that Chicago struggled to fill. Perhaps he'll be better equipped the next time the opportunity arises. 2005 Outlook: C

Dan Wright (**Pos**: RHP, **Age**: 27)

	W	L	Pct.	ERA	G	GS	Sv	IP	H	BB	SO	HR	Avg
'04	0	4	.000	8.15	4	4	0	17.2	24	11	6	5	.320
Car.	20	26	.435	5.65	70	64	1	366.2	393	167	225	65	.276

Wright's grip on a rotation spot slipped away when he started 0-4 after a 1-7 (6.15 ERA) showing in 2003. Then arm troubles last May led to a diagnosis of a labrum tear as well as Tommy John surgery. The Sox released him in December. 2005 Outlook: D

Kelly Wunsch (**Pos**: LHP, **Age**: 32)

	W	L	Pct.	ERA	G	GS	Sv	IP	H	BB	SO	HR	Avg
'04	0	0	–	0.00	3	0	0	2.0	2	1	1	0	.286
Car.	10	5	.667	3.64	212	0	1	153.1	116	83	123	12	.210

Wunsch started the year battling shoulder inflammation that compromised his velocity significantly. He pitched well at Triple-A Charlotte while working his way back, but he spent more time on the disabled list and never returned to Chicago. 2005 Outlook: B

Chicago (AL)

Chicago White Sox Minor League Prospects

Organization Overview:

Trying to end a pennant drought that dates to 1959, the White Sox annually are among the most aggressive middle-market teams in terms of trades. General manager Ken Williams is willing to use minor leaguers in rentals for veterans, with David Wells, Bartolo Colon, Freddy Garcia, Carl Everett and Roberto Alomar among the players he's acquired during his four seasons with the Sox. Yet owner Jerry Reinsdorf's commitment to scouting has allowed the Sox to continually restock their shelves. They haven't developed a real impact player of their own since Mark Buehrle, but feel there could be several on the way. The 2004 draft produced third baseman Josh Fields, who could soon challenge Joe Crede, and several high-ceiling pitchers.

Brian Anderson

Position: OF   **Opening Day Age:** 23
Bats: R **Throws:** R   **Born:** 3/11/82 in Tucson,
Ht: 6' 2" **Wt:** 205   AZ

Recent Statistics

	G	AB	R	H	D	T	HR	RBI	SB	BB	SO	Avg
2003 R Great Falls	13	49	6	19	2	1	2	13	3	9	10	.388
2004 A Winston-Sal	69	254	43	81	22	4	8	46	10	29	44	.319
2004 AA Birmingham	48	185	26	50	9	3	4	27	3	19	30	.270

Perhaps the highest compliment that can be paid to Brian Anderson is that the White Sox thought highly enough of him to include Jeremy Reed in the deal that brought Freddy Garcia from Seattle. Reed had been regarded as the organization's best prospect entering 2004, but he now has been supplanted by the 23-year-old Anderson, who like Reed is a center fielder. The Sox believe Anderson projects as a 20-30 homer player, which gives him the flexibility to fit in at any of the three outfield positions. For now, he is a solid center fielder with a plus arm. He's not likely to arrive before September but could stick around a long time.

Joe Borchard

Position: OF   **Opening Day Age:** 26
Bats: B **Throws:** R   **Born:** 11/25/78 in
Ht: 6' 5" **Wt:** 220   Panorama City, CA

Recent Statistics

	G	AB	R	H	D	T	HR	RBI	SB	BB	SO	Avg
2004 AAA Charlotte	82	301	44	80	21	0	16	48	4	30	68	.266
2004 AL Chicago	63	201	26	35	4	1	9	20	1	19	57	.174

Before waving farewell to a prospect to whom they awarded a $5.3 million signing bonus, the White Sox will give Joe Borchard every benefit of the doubt. That's why he could figure into their 2005 outfield after hitting just .174 in 63 games, when he took over right field after Magglio Ordonez' season-ending injury last year. Borchard flashed his potential with nine home runs, including a 504-foot shot onto the right-field concourse at U.S. Cellular Field off Philadelphia's Brett Myers, but he continued to struggle mightily with making contact. He did not seem to press when given the chance, which provided hope that he may yet make the adjustments to consistently hit big league pitching.

Josh Fields

Position: 3B   **Opening Day Age:** 22
Bats: R **Throws:** R   **Born:** 12/14/82 in
Ht: 6' 2" **Wt:** 210   Stillwater, OK

Recent Statistics

	G	AB	R	H	D	T	HR	RBI	SB	BB	SO	Avg
2004 A Winston-Sal	66	256	36	73	12	4	7	39	0	18	74	.285

Like Joe Borchard, Josh Fields was a star quarterback in college (Oklahoma State), who decided to pursue a professional career in baseball. The Sox used the 18th pick overall in the 2004 draft to get Fields and were thrilled with the early returns. He appears to have enough power to contribute as a third baseman and has shown solid fielding skills. He became a full-time third baseman in 2002 at OSU, so he still needs work at the position, but the team loves his approach. Fields helped push high Class-A Winston-Salem into the playoffs after receiving a $1.55 million bonus to sign. His play in 2005 could help determine whether the Sox try to sign Joe Crede to a long-term contract or deal him.

Pedro Lopez

Position: SS   **Opening Day Age:** 20
Bats: R **Throws:** R   **Born:** 4/28/84 in Moca,
Ht: 6' 1" **Wt:** 159   DR

Recent Statistics

	G	AB	R	H	D	T	HR	RBI	SB	BB	SO	Avg
2003 A Kannapolis	109	390	40	103	23	0	0	33	24	26	43	.264
2003 A Winston-Sal	4	13	1	3	0	0	0	0	0	1	0	.231
2004 A Winston-Sal	111	430	62	124	13	0	4	35	12	23	35	.288
2004 AA Birmingham	7	23	3	5	0	1	0	0	2	5	2	.217

The Sox have not had a homegrown regular at shortstop since they traded Bucky Dent to the Yankees after the 1976 season. They believe they have two solid candidates to fill that void in Pedro Lopez and Robert Valido, who is a rung behind Lopez in the system. Lopez had been overshadowed by Andy Gonzalez in his first three years of pro ball, but shot past him when he got the chance to shift from second base to short, his natural position. The White Sox love Lopez' range and defensive skills. He has long been praised for his bat control, but made strides in 2004 that have some in the organization believing he could develop into a leadoff man or run producer. Lopez, will go to Double-A Birmingham in 2005 after spending spring training getting to know Ozzie Guillen.

Brandon McCarthy

Position: P **Opening Day Age:** 21
Bats: R **Throws:** R **Born:** 7/7/83 in
Ht: 6' 7" **Wt:** 180 Glendale, CA

Recent Statistics

	W	L	ERA	G	GS	Sv	IP	H	R	BB	SO	HR
2003 R Great Falls	9	4	3.65	16	15	0	101.0	105	49	15	125	7
2004 A Kannapolis	8	5	3.64	15	15	0	94.0	80	41	21	113	10
2004 A Winston-Sal	6	0	2.08	8	8	0	52.0	31	12	3	60	3
2004 AA Birmingham	3	1	3.46	4	4	0	26.0	23	10	6	29	2

A middle-round pick in the 2002 draft, all Brandon McCarthy has done since signing with the White Sox is win in workmanlike fashion. He led the Arizona and Pioneer leagues in both innings pitched and strikeouts in 2002 and '03, and would have continued that trend had his talent not taken him to three different levels last year. He does not have any eye-popping tools, which is why he slid to the 17th round. His 91-92 MPH fastball is enough to set up a sinker, a curveball and a much improved changeup. The guy knows how to pitch and compete, and his durability is an added bonus. He'll start 2005 at Double-A Birmingham but could easily reach the big leagues before season's end.

Ryan Sweeney

Position: OF **Opening Day Age:** 20
Bats: L **Throws:** L **Born:** 2/20/85 in Cedar
Ht: 6' 4" **Wt:** 200 Rapids, IA

Recent Statistics

	G	AB	R	H	D	T	HR	RBI	SB	BB	SO	Avg
2003 R Bristol	19	67	11	21	3	0	2	5	3	7	10	.313
2003 R Great Falls	10	34	0	12	2	0	0	4	0	2	3	.353
2004 A Winston-Sal	134	515	71	146	22	3	7	66	8	40	65	.283

A natural hitter, Ryan Sweeney was the talk of camp after he hit .367 in 14 big league games last spring. He was only 19 and barely nine months out of Xavier High School in Cedar Rapids, Ia. Long-time White Sox executive Roland Hemond says he got the same kind of goosebumps watching Sweeney that he had when he saw Harold Baines in the minors. Sweeney held his own at the plate in high Class-A last season and is likely to move to Double-A at age 20. He's a gifted fielder blessed with a cannon. He figures to develop into a high-average hitter with gap power. There are no sure things, but Sweeney is about as safe a bet as it gets.

Wilson Valdez

Position: SS **Opening Day Age:** 26
Bats: R **Throws:** R **Born:** 5/20/78 in Nizao,
Ht: 5' 11" **Wt:** 160 DR

Recent Statistics

	G	AB	R	H	D	T	HR	RBI	SB	BB	SO	Avg
2004 AAA Albuquerque	66	285	36	91	11	3	2	25	19	16	35	.319
2004 AAA Charlotte	70	281	37	85	7	2	2	15	13	12	40	.302
2004 AL Chicago	19	43	8	10	1	0	1	4	1	2	5	.233

Acquired from Florida in a deal for Billy Koch, Wilson Valdez is coming off a strong season as a Triple-A shortstop. Many doubt Valdez can hit enough to play regularly in the big leagues, but manager Ozzie Guillen sees him as potentially filling the role of backup middle infielder. He is the kind of player the White Sox say they need more of—fast and with solid fielding skills. He'll be involved in spring competition for the 25-man roster, with his bat determining whether he sticks or goes back to Charlotte.

Chris Young

Position: OF **Opening Day Age:** 21
Bats: R **Throws:** R **Born:** 9/5/83 in Houston,
Ht: 6' 2" **Wt:** 180 TX

Recent Statistics

	G	AB	R	H	D	T	HR	RBI	SB	BB	SO	Avg
2003 R Bristol	64	238	47	69	18	3	7	28	21	23	40	.290
2003 R Great Falls	10	34	5	6	3	0	0	0	0	1	10	.176
2004 A Kannapolis	135	465	83	122	31	5	24	56	31	66	145	.262

You wouldn't know it by looking at him, but the slightly built, baby-faced Chris Young has as much raw power as anyone in the White Sox' organization. He is also among the top handful of players in terms of speed. That combination adds up to a tremendously high ceiling, but Young has not yet established the consistency and plate discipline that makes him a good bet to fulfill that potential. He has good range and an accurate arm in center field. If he gets it all together, Young could have a major impact. The Sox figure to be patient with him, and he will spend most or all of 2005 at high Class-A Winston-Salem.

Others to Watch

Righthander **Jeff Bajenaru** (27) excelled in the high minors last season and could work his way into the Sox' bullpen mix. He tired in September, when he got his first look with the Sox. . . **Gio Gonzalez** (19), a high schooler from Miami, joined collegians Ray Liotta, Tyler Lumsden and Wes Whisler in an impressive haul of lefthanders in the 2004 draft. . . Switch-hitting catcher **Francisco Hernandez** (19) has a strong arm and hit third for his short-season team last year. He's a long way away but has tremendous potential. . . Righty **Kris Honel** (22) was the organization's most highly regarded pitching prospect before mysterious shoulder problems kept him off the mound for most of 2004. He didn't need surgery and used the time off to work on his mechanics. . . Center fielder **Michael Spidale** (23) is a baseball player, not a tools guy. He hit .304 with 26 stolen bases at Double-A and is the kind of guy who could benefit from the organization's emphasis on speed and defense. . . Righthander **Sean Tracey** (24) might have the best fastball in the organization but has lacked command. He seemed to turn a corner while working with high Class-A Winston-Salem pitching coach J.R. Perdew, but the Sox need to see him repeat the improvements that allowed him to give up only three earned runs in a 45-inning stretch late last season.

Jacobs Field

Offense

Lefthanded power hitters who pull the ball straight down the line can make a good living at Jacobs Field. When the weather warms in late June and July, a consistent wind from left field to right-center field can turn flyballs into homers. Overall, however, the park is tough to homer in for most players, but Jacobs is a good doubles park. The ball gets into the gaps quickly, can take tricky bounces off the 19-foot wall that runs from left to left-center and gives outfielders fits when it reaches the corners.

Defense

Day games, played in the sunshine, favor the pitcher because at times it's difficult to pick up the ball. Outfielders have to back up each other in left and center field on wall balls. Catchers can climb the chicken-wire fencing in front of the field suites in pursuit of foul pops, but they can get tangled. The infield dirt gives a fair bounce and the infield and outfield grass is kept at a medium length.

Who It Helps the Most

Lefty Travis Hafner, who hits balls from left-center field to the right-field foul pole, used a consistent swing to bat .302 with 29 doubles, seven homers and 51 RBI at Jacobs Field. Righthander Jake Westbrook, a sinkerball pitcher, kept the ball on the ground and went 7-2 at Jacobs Field.

Who It Hurts the Most

Jody Gerut, who held his own at the Jake as a rookie, hit .241 with three homers last season as he lost his swing and confidence. Late in the year he tore the ACL in his right knee chasing a ball in the right-field corner.

Rookies & Newcomers

Third baseman Aaron Boone and shortstop Jhonny Peralta will get their first extended look at Jacobs Field this year in a season in which the Indians are supposed to contend. Both are line-drive hitters with medium power and could do well here.

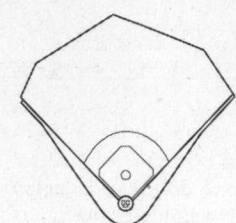

Dimensions: LF-325, LCF-370, CF-405, RCF-375, RF-325

Capacity: 43,389

Elevation: 660 feet

Surface: Grass

Foul Territory: Small

Park Factors

2004 Season

| | Home Games | | | Away Games | | | |
	Indians	Opp	Total	Indians	Opp	Total	Index
G	72	72	144	72	72	144	
Avg	.267	.272	.269	.281	.274	.278	97
AB	2400	2578	4978	2632	2517	5149	97
R	357	380	737	403	396	799	92
H	640	700	1340	740	690	1430	94
2B	156	155	311	136	148	284	113
3B	12	12	24	15	16	31	80
HR	62	81	143	105	98	203	73
BB	290	255	545	257	255	512	110
SO	437	507	944	459	470	929	105
E	45	68	113	46	42	88	128
E-Infield	35	53	88	41	34	75	117
LHB-Avg	.278	.268	.274	.283	.264	.275	99
LHB-HR	39	40	79	63	45	108	72
RHB-Avg	.251	.274	.265	.279	.281	.280	95
RHB-HR	23	41	64	42	53	95	73

2002-2004

| | Home Games | | | Away Games | | | |
	Indians	Opp	Total	Indians	Opp	Total	Index
G	216	216	432	216	216	432	
Avg	.255	.266	.261	.266	.275	.270	97
AB	7192	7637	14829	7641	7324	14965	99
R	991	1083	2074	1075	1145	2220	93
H	1835	2034	3869	2033	2011	4044	96
2B	408	431	839	383	418	801	106
3B	27	36	63	45	53	98	65
HR	210	218	428	284	252	536	81
BB	703	765	1468	714	735	1449	102
SO	1329	1501	2830	1386	1238	2624	109
E	138	193	331	162	112	274	121
E-Infield	117	164	281	141	97	238	118
LHB-Avg	.261	.269	.264	.267	.275	.270	98
LHB-HR	138	99	237	168	104	272	86
RHB-Avg	.249	.265	.258	.265	.274	.270	95
RHB-HR	72	119	191	116	148	264	74

2004 Rankings (American League)

- Highest walk factor
- Second-highest double factor
- Second-highest error factor
- Lowest home-run factor
- Lowest LHB home-run factor
- Lowest RHB home-run factor
- Third-lowest hit factor
- Third-lowest RHB batting-average factor

Eric Wedge

2004 Season

The Indians performed better than expected in Eric Wedge's second season, improving from 68 to 80 victories thanks largely to an offense that scored 858 runs compared to 699 in 2003. Wedge has a vision for the Indians and last year he convinced the players to embrace it. The tone was set late in spring training when Milton Bradley, the club's starting center fielder and cleanup hitter, was traded to Los Angeles following a confrontation with Wedge.

Offense

Wedge's offensive mantra is "one through nine." He asked his players to work counts, draw walks and never give up an at-bat. It worked last season, as each of the top eight spots in the lineup produced 73 or more RBI. Wedge considers the stolen base an overrated stat for good reason. The Indians led the big leagues last year with 55 caught stealings. His ideal leadoff hitter reaches base by any means possible. Wedge makes liberal use of the sacrifice bunt and stabilized his batting order after using 145 different lineups in 2003.

Pitching & Defense

Wedge feels a team's success begins with starting pitching and goes out of his way to protect his starters, rarely letting a player throw more than 105 pitches. He prefers to use one closer and likes defined roles for the rest of the pen. Wedge will stay with a hot hitter over a defensive specialist, but will bolster the defense when he has a lead in the late innings.

2005 Outlook

The Indians, trying to rebuild on the quickstep, have identified 2005 as their year to re-emerge as a contender. Wedge has the tools offensively, but he went into the offseason seeking another starter and a quality closer. The defense could be young and unsettled with Jhonny Peralta at shortstop, Coco Crisp probably in left field and Grady Sizemore in center. Another question mark defensively could be third baseman Casey Blake moving to second or right field to make room for Aaron Boone.

Born: 1/27/68 in Fort Wayne, Indiana

Playing Experience: 1991-1994, Bos, Col

Managerial Experience: 2 seasons

Manager Statistics

Year	Team, Lg	W	L	Pct	GB	Finish
2004	Cleveland, AL	80	82	.494	12.0	3rd Central
2 Seasons		148	176	.457	–	–

2004 Starting Pitchers by Days Rest

	<=3	4	5	6+
Indians Starts	1	100	26	24
Indians ERA	3.38	4.87	4.63	4.70
AL Avg Starts	2	82	47	21
AL ERA	5.36	4.87	4.65	4.93

2004 Situational Stats

	Eric Wedge	AL Average
Hit & Run Success %	29.5	36.8
Stolen Base Success %	63.1	68.6
Platoon Pct.	72.0	61.6
Defensive Subs	13	21
High-Pitch Outings	2	5
Quick/Slow Hooks	21/10	20/16
Sacrifice Attempts	57	53

2004 Rankings (American League)

- 1st in sacrifice-bunt percentage (93.0%) and relief appearances (479)
- 2nd in intentional walks (33)
- 3rd in pitchouts with a runner moving (6) and one-batter pitcher appearances (39)

Cleveland

Ronnie Belliard

2004 Season

The Indians signed Ronnie Belliard to a $1.1 million deal last year and he paid big dividends. Belliard, who finished with 61 extra-base hits, set career highs in hits, doubles and homers. He hit .417 in April and .304 in the first half to join four other Indians on the All-Star team. The Indians intially wanted Belliard to keep second base warm for prospect Brandon Phillips, but instead he revitalized his career.

Hitting

Belliard is a line-drive hitter with more than enough power to reach the gaps. He batted leadoff against lefties and wore them out, helping stabilize the top of the lineup by making contact and showing patience. He concentrated on driving the ball from gap to gap. In the past, Belliard has gotten into trouble trying to pull fastballs, but power wasn't his big concern last year. He didn't hit his first homer until June 4 and still set a career high. Righthanders with good breaking balls down and away give him trouble.

Baserunning & Defense

One scout had a great description of Belliard, who is short and thick. "He looks fat, but he doesn't play fat," said the scout. No one on the Indians ran from home to first harder than Belliard. He wore down in September because of a virus that made him dizzy and weak. Belliard played an interesting second base, moving back into short right field against slow-footed batters. It improved his range and allowed him to steal countless hits because of his strong throwing arm. He has soft hands, quick feet and turns a fast double play.

2005 Outlook

As well as Belliard played last year, the Indians were unsure if they could afford him for 2005. He was arbitration-eligible and in line for a decent raise. The Indians were considering trading Belliard, overpaying him for a year in arbitration or making him a free agent by not offering him a contract on December 20.

Position: 2B
Bats: R **Throws:** R
Ht: 5' 8" **Wt:** 197

Opening Day Age: 29
Born: 4/7/75 in Bronx, NY
ML Seasons: 7
Pronunciation: BELL-ee-yard

Overall Statistics

	G	AB	R	H	D	T	HR	RBI	SB	BB	SO	Avg	OBP	Slg
'04	152	599	78	169	48	1	12	70	3	60	98	.282	.348	.426
Car.	757	2732	394	736	181	19	50	294	28	308	423	.269	.344	.404

Where He Hits the Ball

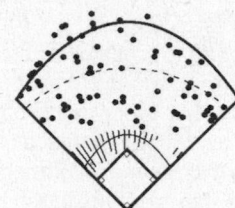 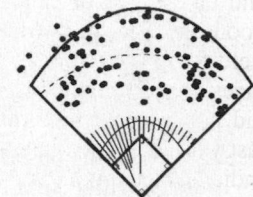

Vs. LHP   **Vs. RHP**

2004 Situational Stats

	AB	H	HR	RBI	Avg		AB	H	HR	RBI	Avg
Home	281	74	4	35	.263	LHP	204	65	7	23	.319
Road	318	95	8	35	.299	RHP	395	104	5	47	.263
First Half	339	103	5	37	.304	Sc Pos	141	40	4	58	.284
Scnd Half	260	66	7	33	.254	Clutch	95	30	1	12	.316

2004 Rankings (American League)

- 2nd in doubles and errors at second base (14)
- 3rd in on-base percentage for a leadoff hitter (.384)
- 4th in lowest fielding percentage at second base (.981)
- Led the Indians in at-bats, hits, doubles, games played and on-base percentage for a leadoff hitter (.384)
- Led AL second basemen in batting average

Casey Blake

2004 Season

The Indians gave veteran minor leaguer Casey Blake a chance to play every day in 2003, and he continued to take advantage of the opportunity last year, setting career highs in hits, doubles, homers and RBI. Blake ranked fourth among AL third basemen with 28 homers and 88 RBI, but also led American League third sackers with 26 errors.

Hitting

Blake is patient at the plate, sometimes too patient. He averaged more than four pitches an at-bat last year, the most in the AL, but still struck out 139 times. He's a guess hitter late in the count and takes a lot of called third strikes. Blake has good bat control, but his power is from the left-field foul pole to center field. Blake's power surfaces against righthanders more than lefties. He did not hit well with runners in scoring position last year and failed when given a shot at being the Indians' cleanup hitter.

Baserunning & Defense

Most of Blake's 26 errors came on fielding plays. He's played 304 of a possible 324 games over the last two year and tends to wear down. He has a strong, accurate arm and has more range going to his left than his right. Blake is one of the Indians' better baserunners when it comes to going from first to third and second to home. He's not a burner, but he gets good leads and knows when to gamble. Stealing is another story. He was thrown out eight times in 13 attempts.

2005 Outlook

Blake is in for an interesting year. With Aaron Boone expected to play third, Blake will be moving to second base or right field because the Indians want to keep his bat in the lineup. Blake spent a couple of days working out at second in the Florida Instructional League after last season. He was eligible for arbitration, and the Indians were talking to him about a multiyear deal.

Position: 3B
Bats: R **Throws:** R
Ht: 6' 2" **Wt:** 210

Opening Day Age: 31
Born: 8/23/73 in Des Moines, IA
ML Seasons: 6

Overall Statistics

	G	AB	R	H	D	T	HR	RBI	SB	BB	SO	Avg	OBP	Slg
'04	152	587	93	159	36	3	28	88	5	68	139	.271	.354	.486
Car.	353	1256	185	328	77	3	47	162	15	117	281	.261	.331	.439

Where He Hits the Ball

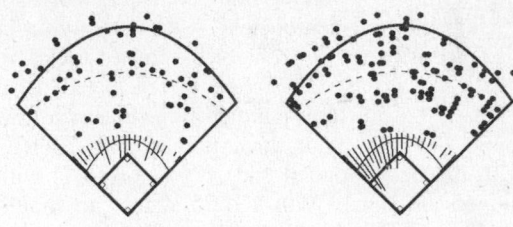

Vs. LHP   **Vs. RHP**

2004 Situational Stats

	AB	H	HR	RBI	Avg		AB	H	HR	RBI	Avg
Home	281	74	13	38	.263	LHP	189	46	11	25	.243
Road	306	85	15	50	.278	RHP	398	113	17	63	.284
First Half	305	82	14	46	.269	Sc Pos	173	44	3	56	.254
Scnd Half	282	77	14	42	.273	Clutch	116	37	6	21	.319

2004 Rankings (American League)

- 1st in most pitches seen per plate appearance (4.26), errors at third base (26), lowest cleanup slugging percentage (.333) and lowest fielding percentage at third base (.939)
- 3rd in pitches seen (2,844)
- 5th in strikeouts
- 6th in lowest percentage of swings on the first pitch (14.5)
- Led the Indians in home runs, total bases (285), strikeouts, pitches seen (2,844), games played, most pitches seen per plate appearance (4.26), highest percentage of pitches taken (61.2) and lowest percentage of swings on the first pitch (14.5)

Ben Broussard

2004 Season

After going 0-for-27 in late May, Ben Broussard not only turned his season around, but might have saved his job. When the Indians signed third baseman Aaron Boone in June, there was talk that Casey Blake would move from third to first and take Broussard's job. It didn't happen because Broussard hit .290 (87-for-300) with 16 homers and 64 RBI from May 30 through the end of the season. The surge included two pinch-hit grand slams.

Hitting

Broussard is learning. In his rookie year of 2003, he hit .175 against lefties. Last year he hit .362 against them by making more contact and driving the ball into left-center field. After coming out of his 0-for-27 slump, Broussard seemed to relax in clutch situations. He started to reach and drive fastballs before they jammed him. Broussard hit .636 (7-for-11) with three homers and 23 RBI with the bases loaded and .404 (19-for-47) with runners on third. With a fluid swing, he should develop additional power the more he pulls the ball.

Baserunning & Defense

A year's experience helped not only Broussard's offense, but also his defense at first base. He reduced his error total from nine in 2003 to six last year. Broussard has decent range, especially going to his right, and starts the 3-6-3 double play well. He has improved on scooping throws in the dirt. On the bases, Broussard has average speed, but he sometimes gambles when he shouldn't.

2005 Outlook

At the end of the 2004 season, manager Eric Wedge had questions about all of his infield positions except first base. He said Broussard was his guy for 2005. The next thing Broussard has to do is show management that he can play every day and that they don't need to platoon at first. Broussard's batting average, runs, homers and RBI have improved for two straight years. That trend should continue this year.

Position: 1B
Bats: L **Throws:** L
Ht: 6' 2" **Wt:** 220

Opening Day Age: 28
Born: 9/24/76 in Beaumont, TX
ML Seasons: 3
Pronunciation: brew-SARD

Overall Statistics

	G	AB	R	H	D	T	HR	RBI	SB	BB	SO	Avg	OBP	Slg
'04	139	418	57	115	28	5	17	82	4	52	95	.275	.370	.488
Car.	294	916	120	238	53	8	37	146	9	91	195	.260	.337	.456

Where He Hits the Ball

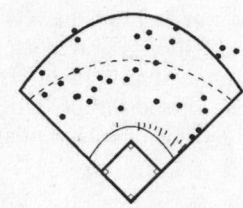 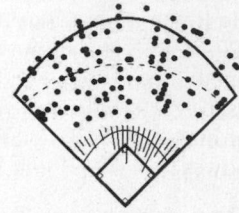

Vs. LHP   **Vs. RHP**

2004 Situational Stats

	AB	H	HR	RBI	Avg		AB	H	HR	RBI	Avg
Home	220	55	9	42	.250	LHP	69	25	3	22	.362
Road	198	60	8	40	.303	RHP	349	90	14	60	.258
First Half	208	52	4	39	.250	Sc Pos	118	34	7	67	.288
Scnd Half	210	63	13	43	.300	Clutch	84	27	4	23	.321

2004 Rankings (American League)

- 2nd in batting average with the bases loaded (.636)
- 4th in errors at first base (6) and lowest fielding percentage at first base (.994)
- Led the Indians in triples, batting average with the bases loaded (.636) and batting average vs. lefthanded pitchers

Coco Crisp

2004 Season

Coco Crisp spent most of April and May on the bench as the Indians gave Alex Escobar and Jody Gerut a chance to win the center-field job. When Escobar was sent to Triple-A Buffalo in mid-June and Gerut moved back to right field, Crisp got his chance. He hit .318 after the All-Star break and showed unexpected power. Crisp moved to left field late in the season as prospect Grady Sizemore played center.

Hitting

Crisp is a switch-hitting, line-drive hitter who chokes up on the bat, sprays the ball around and likes to bunt. If Crisp walked more, he would be an ideal leadoff hitter. But patience is a problem. He likes to swing early in the count, hitting .380 (27-for-71) on the first pitch. The Indians felt they put too much pressure on Crisp in 2003 when they asked him to hit leadoff. Last year, he spent most of his time in the ninth spot. Pitchers try to over-power the deceptively strong Crisp with fastballs.

Baserunning & Defense

Crisp stole 20 bases in 2004, but he still needs to work on his leads and knowledge of pitchers. With his speed, he should be better than a 61-percent basestealer. The Indians consider Crisp to be an above-average left fielder and an intriguing center fielder because he can hit with more power than most players who man the position. In left field, he comes in and goes back well on balls and is not afraid of the wall.

2005 Outlook

Sizemore is Cleveland's center fielder of the future, but Crisp outplayed him last year. At the end of the season, the Indians were saying Crisp would be an everyday outfielder in 2005, and they made room for him in left by trading Matt Lawton to Pittsburgh during the winter meetings. Crisp reinvented himself last season, and he better stay on the same path this year. The Indians considered him a fourth outfielder and trade bait before he changed their minds in 2004. Crisp has a golden opportunity to establish himself in the majors this year.

Position: CF/LF
Bats: B **Throws:** R
Ht: 6' 0" **Wt:** 185

Opening Day Age: 25
Born: 11/1/79 in Los Angeles, CA
ML Seasons: 3

Overall Statistics

	G	AB	R	H	D	T	HR	RBI	SB	BB	SO	Avg	OBP	Slg
'04	139	491	78	146	24	2	15	71	20	36	69	.297	.344	.446
Car.	270	1032	149	289	48	10	19	107	39	70	139	.280	.324	.401

Where He Hits the Ball

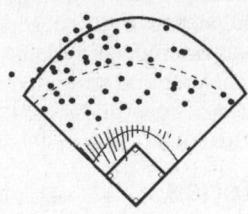 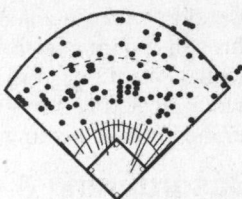

Vs. LHP   **Vs. RHP**

2004 Situational Stats

	AB	H	HR	RBI	Avg		AB	H	HR	RBI	Avg
Home	224	69	8	42	.308	LHP	177	55	8	32	.311
Road	267	77	7	29	.288	RHP	314	91	7	39	.290
First Half	224	61	5	32	.272	Sc Pos	128	37	6	59	.289
Scnd Half	267	85	10	39	.318	Clutch	82	28	2	14	.341

2004 Rankings (American League)

- 2nd in caught stealing (13)
- 5th in lowest stolen-base percentage (60.6)
- 6th in errors in center field (4)
- 7th in batting average in the clutch
- 9th in bunts in play (22)
- Led the Indians in caught stealing (13), highest groundball-flyball ratio (1.5), batting average in the clutch and batting average at home

Jody Gerut

2004 Season

Jody Gerut followed an impressive rookie season in 2003 with one that featured inconsistency and injury. Gerut had a 17-game hitting streak from April 25 through May 15, but hit .229 in his last 88 games of the season. His campaign ended September 17 when he tore the ACL in his right knee.

Hitting

Gerut worked hard to end his long slump, but it didn't happen. He went from making three or four hard outs a week to continually getting jammed and not hitting the ball out of the infield. Gerut, who follows his own workout and pregame preparation routines, took the same approach to hitting. He didn't take a lot of advice and tried to get through it on his own. He was dominated by left-handers for the second straight year and struggled with runners in scoring position. A gap-to-gap hitter, he knows how to work the count.

Baserunning & Defense

Gerut played all three outfield positions but spent most of the time in right field. He's a good defender, specializing in diving catches while going toward the right-field line. He was a little more cautious after tearing the rotator cuff in his left shoulder diving for a ball in 2003. The injury may have bothered Gerut's throwing early in the season, but he eventually showed his old accuracy and strength. An average runner, Gerut will break up a double play at second and steal a base when needed.

2005 Outlook

Team doctors say Gerut probably won't be ready to play until late May or June. When he is healthy, his playing time may be limited. Third baseman Casey Blake, who hit 28 homers last year, could end up in right field. So could Ryan Ludwick, who missed much of last season after knee surgery. Gerut would make a good fourth outfielder, but his status as a starter is in jeopardy.

Position: RF/CF
Bats: L **Throws:** L
Ht: 6' 0" **Wt:** 190

Opening Day Age: 27
Born: 9/18/77 in Elmhurst, IL
ML Seasons: 2
Pronunciation: GARE-et

Overall Statistics

	G	AB	R	H	D	T	HR	RBI	SB	BB	SO	Avg	OBP	Slg
'04	134	481	72	121	31	5	11	51	13	54	59	.252	.334	.405
Car.	261	961	138	255	64	7	33	126	17	89	129	.265	.335	.450

Where He Hits the Ball

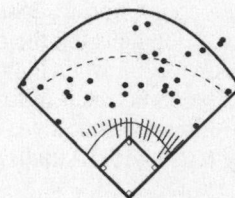 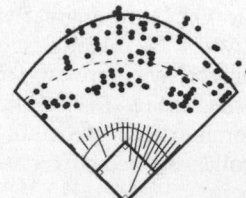

Vs. LHP   **Vs. RHP**

2004 Situational Stats

	AB	H	HR	RBI	Avg		AB	H	HR	RBI	Avg
Home	232	56	3	23	.241	LHP	149	31	2	15	.208
Road	249	65	8	28	.261	RHP	332	90	9	36	.271
First Half	323	83	7	33	.257	Sc Pos	131	27	3	38	.206
Scnd Half	158	38	4	18	.241	Clutch	84	19	2	8	.226

2004 Rankings (American League)

- 4th in lowest batting average vs. lefthanded pitchers
- 5th in errors in right field (4), fielding percentage in right field (.984), lowest batting average with runners in scoring position and lowest batting average at home
- Led the Indians in triples, highest percentage of swings put into play (50.8) and fewest GDPs per GDP situation (7.8%)

Travis Hafner

2004 Season

Travis Hafner played much of last year with a right elbow injury that required surgery, but you'd never know it. In the defining moment of a fine season, Hafner hit five homers and drove in 11 runs in consecutive games against the Angels on July 19-20. The 11 RBI in back-to-back contests tied a franchise record set in 1930. Hafner's .993 OPS (on-base plus slugging percentage) was second in the American League to Manny Ramirez.

Hitting

Hafner's nickname is Pronk. It stands for half project and half donkey. This donkey has quite a kick. Hafner can be beaten inside with fastballs, but lo to the pitchers who miss. He's a patient hitter who will work the count and doesn't give ground. Hafner was hit by pitches 17 times, tying him for the AL lead. Lefthanders neutralized him with sliders and breaking balls, but he made up for it against righthanders. He likes to drive the ball to left-center. Some young players resent being a DH, but Hafner uses the time on the bench to study video of his previous at-bats and to take swings in the batting cage.

Baserunning & Defense

Hafner made 10 starts at first base and didn't make an error in 90 total chances. He works hard on his defense, but his actions are stiff and he doesn't have the softest hands. Hafner, whose throwing was limited by his sore right elbow, had bone chips removed from it after the season. Hafner weighs 240 pounds, but does not clog the bases.

2005 Outlook

Team doctors think Hafner will be fully recovered from elbow surgery by the start of spring training. He helped to stablize the middle of the Tribe's lineup last year, and there's no reason he shouldn't continue to do the same this year. The Indians, who control Hafner's contract for four more years, were considering offering him a multiyear deal after last season, but declined because of his elbow surgery. He'll be eligible for arbitration after this year.

Position: DH/1B
Bats: L **Throws:** R
Ht: 6' 3" **Wt:** 240

Opening Day Age: 27
Born: 6/3/77 in Jamestown, ND
ML Seasons: 3
Pronunciation: HAF-ner

Overall Statistics

	G	AB	R	H	D	T	HR	RBI	SB	BB	SO	Avg	OBP	Slg
'04	140	482	96	150	41	3	28	109	3	68	111	.311	.410	.583
Car.	254	835	137	239	64	7	43	155	5	98	207	.286	.376	.534

Where He Hits the Ball

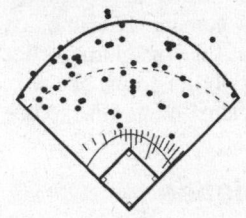 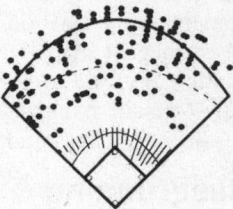

Vs. LHP **Vs. RHP**

2004 Situational Stats

	AB	H	HR	RBI	Avg		AB	H	HR	RBI	Avg
Home	252	76	7	51	.302	LHP	156	38	3	24	.244
Road	230	74	21	58	.322	RHP	326	112	25	85	.344
First Half	275	86	10	61	.313	Sc Pos	153	45	7	79	.294
Scnd Half	207	64	18	48	.309	Clutch	86	20	3	13	.233

2004 Rankings (American League)

- 1st in hit by pitch (17)
- 3rd in on-base percentage and batting average vs. righthanded pitchers
- 4th in slugging percentage
- 6th in doubles and batting average on the road
- Led the Indians in batting average, home runs, RBI, sacrifice flies (6), hit by pitch (17), slugging percentage, on-base percentage, HR frequency (17.2 ABs per HR), batting average vs. righthanded pitchers and batting average on the road

Matt Lawton

2004 Season

Spurred by a intense offseason conditioning program, Matt Lawton played so well in the first half that he made the All-Star team for the second time in his career. After hitting .305 with 15 homers and 49 RBI at the break, Lawton slumped, going .239-5-21 the rest of the way. After two injury-filled years, he played 150 games last year.

Hitting

Pitchers try to work Lawton away with fastballs, but he has an interesting theory to combat that. Rather than take those fastballs, Lawton tries to drive them to left-center field. He calls it turning a weakness into a strength. Lawton did an excellent job in the leadoff spot, hitting .299 with 16 homers and a .380 on base percentage. He finds an extra gear of patience at the top of the order and is not afraid to hit deep in the count or walk. Lawton said balance problems with his stance hurt him in the second half.

Baserunning & Defense

Lawton covered more ground last year following knee surgery, but remained a defensive liability in left and right field. He covered the gap decently, but any ball hit over his head or toward the line was an adventure. He underwent a serious operation on his right shoulder after the 2002 season and runners have been taking liberties against him ever since. Lawton is a good baserunner and the weight he lost last winter helped him steal 23 bases and score a career-high 109 runs.

2005 Outlook

It was feared that Lawton's second-half slump might kill the possibility of trading him, as he heads into the final year of a bad four-year, $27 million deal. During the winter meetings, however, the Indians dealt him to Pittsburgh for left-handed reliever Arthur Rhodes. After trading their leadoff hitter, Jason Kendall, to Oakland in late November, the Pirates are looking to Lawton to fill that role and play one of the corner outfield spots.

Position: LF/RF
Bats: L **Throws:** R
Ht: 5'10" **Wt:** 195

Opening Day Age: 33
Born: 11/3/71 in Gulfport, MS
ML Seasons: 10
Pronunciation: LAW-ton

Overall Statistics

	G	AB	R	H	D	T	HR	RBI	SB	BB	SO	Avg	OBP	Slg
'04	150	591	109	164	25	0	20	70	23	74	84	.277	.366	.421
Car.	1182	4236	684	1139	237	16	125	577	147	610	534	.269	.370	.421

Where He Hits the Ball

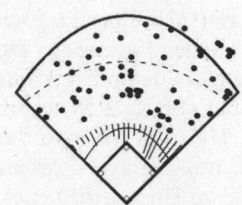 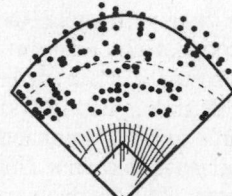

Vs. LHP   **Vs. RHP**

2004 Situational Stats

	AB	H	HR	RBI	Avg		AB	H	HR	RBI	Avg
Home	278	79	10	32	.284	LHP	191	50	6	25	.262
Road	313	85	10	38	.272	RHP	400	114	14	45	.285
First Half	348	106	15	49	.305	Sc Pos	142	34	5	53	.239
Scnd Half	243	58	5	21	.239	Clutch	101	22	2	12	.218

2004 Rankings (American League)

- 4th in on-base percentage for a leadoff hitter (.380)
- 5th in fielding percentage in left field (.988), GDPs (21) and most GDPs per GDP situation (21.0%)
- Led the Indians in runs scored, stolen bases, walks, times on base (249), GDPs (21), plate appearances (680) and steals of third (4)

Cliff Lee

2004 Season

Cliff Lee's first full season in the big leagues was one of extremes. The lefthander went 10-1 in his first 11 decisions before going 0-6 in his next nine starts. Suffering from a dead arm, Lee was given nine days rest and finished the season by winning his last three starts to tie for the team lead in victories with 14. He led the Indians with 161 strikeouts and 81 walks.

Pitching

Lee throws four pitches, along with various subgroups. He throws a fastball, curveball, slider and change. He'll use a cut fastball against righthanders and works in a four-seam fastball as well. He throws between 87-93 MPH, with his normal velocity at 90-91 MPH. Lee has a smooth delivery and a competitive nature that can get him into trouble. He challenged hitters with his fastball during his 10-1 run, but they started to turn around the heat in the second half. Lee allowed 30 homers, including 18 after the All-Star break. His control was another problem. He had too many three-ball counts, which prevented him from getting deep into games.

Defense

Lee didn't make an error in 33 starts last year. He has good range when it comes to getting off the mound for bunts and hustles to cover first. Being lefthanded, Lee has a built-in advantage in controlling runners at first. He did an average job controlling the running game, permitting nine steals in 14 attempts. His pickoff move can use some work.

2005 Outlook

The Indians want Lee to be their No. 4 starter this year behind C.C. Sabathia, Jake Westbrook and a potential free-agent starter. They also want him to reduce his walks and be more consistent with his pitches. Lee definitely should be stronger and smarter this year, as a hernia operation at the end of the 2003 season limited his offseason conditioning heading into last season. He also learned how to handle the first extended dead-arm period of his career.

Position: SP
Bats: L **Throws:** L
Ht: 6' 3" **Wt:** 190

Opening Day Age: 26
Born: 8/30/78 in Benton, AR
ML Seasons: 3

Overall Statistics

	W	L	Pct.	ERA	G	GS	Sv	IP	H	BB	SO	HR	Avg
'04	14	8	.636	5.43	33	33	0	179.0	188	81	161	30	.268
Car.	17	12	.586	4.88	44	44	0	241.2	235	109	211	37	.255

2004 Pitching Profile

	Cliff Lee	AL Average
Overall Strike %	62.6	62.3
1st Pitch Strike %	59.8	58.1
Ratio	1.50	1.42
Strikeouts per 9 IP	8.09	6.45
Walks per 9 IP	4.07	3.34
Home Runs per 9 IP	1.51	1.15
Strikeout/Walk Ratio	1.99	1.93
Groundball/Flyball Ratio	0.76	1.17

2004 Situational Stats

	W	L	ERA	Sv	IP		AB	H	HR	RBI	Avg
Home	7	4	5.29	0	85.0	LHB	143	33	2	15	.231
Road	7	4	5.55	0	94.0	RHB	559	155	28	88	.277
First Half	9	1	3.77	0	107.1	Sc Pos	149	47	9	75	.315
Scnd Half	5	7	7.91	0	71.2	Clutch	21	5	0	0	.238

2004 Rankings (American League)

- 1st in fielding percentage at pitcher (1.000) and lowest groundball-flyball ratio allowed (0.8)
- 2nd in most pitches thrown per batter (3.96)
- 3rd in highest walks per nine innings (4.1)
- 5th in most strikeouts per nine innings (8.1) and highest ERA
- 6th in highest ERA at home
- 7th in walks allowed, highest ERA on the road and most home runs allowed per nine innings (1.51)
- Led the Indians in wins, games started, home runs allowed, walks allowed, hit batsmen (11), strikeouts, pitches thrown (3,175), highest strikeout-walk ratio (2.0) and most strikeouts per nine innings (8.1)

Victor Martinez

2004 Season

Victor Martinez could do little wrong in his first full season in the big leagues. He went to the All-Star game, set a new RBI record for Indians catchers and had the best offensive night by a Tribe catcher in franchise history. He shared the Silver Slugger award for American League catchers with Ivan Rodriguez.

Hitting

The Indians were certain Martinez would hit for average in the big leagues based on his minor league track record, but they weren't sure about his power. Martinez ended that debate when he was put in the cleanup spot May 3. He hit .286 with 19 homers and 99 RBI the rest of the season. The switch-hitting Martinez, with more power lefthanded, swings for contact and would just as soon get a runner home from third on a grounder as a hit. He has a quick, even swing from both sides of the plate, but can be beaten by splitters and sliders.

Baserunning & Defense

Controlling the running game is Martinez' biggest weakness. He calls a good game and has soft hands, but his throws to the bases, especially second, are often high and off target. Martinez threw out only 22 percent of the basestealers he faced, though he improved after starting the season 1-for-21. Martinez blocks the plate well, but was charged with nine passed balls. He was slowed on the bases by hamstring and ankle problems.

2005 Outlook

There are some who say Martinez should move to third or first base before the rigors of catching ruin his offense. But the club puts a high value on having premium players in the middle of the diamond. The Indians will try to reduce Martinez' workload this year by using backup Josh Bard more, and they are expected to give Martinez playing time at first base because they felt he wore down late last year. Martinez certainly played like a premium player last year and should only get better.

Position: C
Bats: B **Throws:** R
Ht: 6' 2" **Wt:** 190

Opening Day Age: 26
Born: 12/23/78 in Ciudad Bolivar, VZ
ML Seasons: 3

Overall Statistics

	G	AB	R	H	D	T	HR	RBI	SB	BB	SO	Avg	OBP	Slg
'04	141	520	77	147	38	1	23	108	0	60	69	.283	.359	.492
Car.	202	711	94	202	43	1	25	129	1	76	92	.284	.355	.453

Where He Hits the Ball

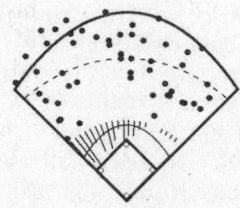 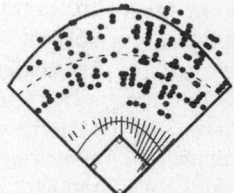

Vs. LHP **Vs. RHP**

2004 Situational Stats

	AB	H	HR	RBI	Avg		AB	H	HR	RBI	Avg
Home	260	76	8	55	.292	LHP	170	48	6	28	.282
Road	260	71	15	53	.273	RHP	350	99	17	80	.283
First Half	286	83	12	63	.290	Sc Pos	164	50	6	84	.305
Scnd Half	234	64	11	45	.274	Clutch	90	21	4	9	.233

2004 Rankings (American League)

- 2nd in lowest percentage of runners caught stealing as a catcher (21.9)
- Led the Indians in sacrifice flies (6), intentional walks (11), batting average with runners in scoring position and cleanup slugging percentage (.490)
- Led AL catchers in home runs and RBI

C.C. Sabathia

2004 Season

C.C. Sabathia made his second All-Star team in 2004, but the year was mostly about personal loss and professional frustration. In the span of six months, Sabathia's father, uncle and cousin died. On the field, he argued with umpires, injured the biceps tendon in his left arm on April 22 and had his season end September 16 because of a strained left hamstring. Sabathia won his 50th game July 27, six days after he turned 24.

Pitching

Sabathia's 11 victories are the fewest he's had in four big-league seasons, but he's still the youngest pitcher in the Cleveland rotation. A power pitcher who throws a fastball, curveball, slider and changeup, he throws between 92-99 MPH, but his normal range is 94-95 MPH. Sabathia's main difficulty is keeping his composure on the mound. He argued three times with plate umpires over the strike zone. When he got mad, he became a thrower instead of a pitcher and didn't stick around long. Sabathia averaged six innings per start and saw the bullpen blow six of his leads.

Defense

After doing a good job controlling the running game in 2003, Sabathia regressed last year. The opposition stole 17 bases in 23 tries with him on the mound. He developed a good pickoff move after advice from Terry Mulholland, but didn't use it much last year. The 290-pound Sabathia doesn't have good range and struggles at times to cover first, but he didn't make an error in 30 starts last year.

2005 Outlook

The Indians need Sabathia to keep his temper in check on the mound this year. He had a 5.56 ERA over his last 15 starts, and he's a much better pitcher than that. The club wants him to be focused and consistent pitch to pitch. Sabathia hired a personal trainer for the offseason. If he stays healthy this year, he will easily vest his $7 million club option for 2006.

Position: SP
Bats: L **Throws:** L
Ht: 6' 7" **Wt:** 290

Opening Day Age: 24
Born: 7/21/80 in Vallejo, CA
ML Seasons: 4
Pronunciation: sa-BATH-ee-a

Overall Statistics

	W	L	Pct.	ERA	G	GS	Sv	IP	H	BB	SO	HR	Avg
'04	11	10	.524	4.12	30	30	0	188.0	176	72	139	20	.252
Car.	54	35	.607	4.12	126	126	0	776.0	713	321	600	75	.247

2004 Pitching Profile

	C.C. Sabathia	AL Average
Overall Strike %	61.6	62.3
1st Pitch Strike %	57.0	58.1
Ratio	1.32	1.42
Strikeouts per 9 IP	6.65	6.45
Walks per 9 IP	3.45	3.34
Home Runs per 9 IP	0.96	1.15
Strikeout/Walk Ratio	1.93	1.93
Groundball/Flyball Ratio	0.98	1.17

2004 Situational Stats

	W	L	ERA	Sv	IP		AB	H	HR	RBI	Avg
Home	5	5	5.02	0	84.1	LHB	151	40	7	22	.265
Road	6	5	3.39	0	103.2	RHB	548	136	13	63	.248
First Half	5	4	3.33	0	105.1	Sc Pos	168	39	3	61	.232
Scnd Half	6	6	5.12	0	82.2	Clutch	30	6	1	6	.200

2004 Rankings (American League)

- 1st in fielding percentage at pitcher (1.000)
- 4th in most pitches thrown per batter (3.95)
- 6th in lowest ERA on the road
- 8th in stolen bases allowed (17)
- 10th in lowest batting average allowed (.252) and highest walks per nine innings (3.4)
- Led the Indians in losses, runners caught stealing (6) and lowest ERA on the road

Omar Vizquel

2004 Season

When Omar Vizquel made his seventh error on May 8, it looked like the two surgeries on his right knee in 2003 had sapped the juice from the nine-time Gold Glove Award-winning shortstop. But Vizquel pulled his game together and had another impressive offensive and defensive season. He recorded his 2,000th hit on April 22 against Kansas City. On August 31 against the Yankees, Vizquel went 6-for-7, with six-straight hits in a 22-0 victory.

Hitting

The switch-hitting Vizquel is an ideal No. 2 hitter. He led the American League with 20 sacrifice bunts and was the fifth-toughest man in the league to strike out. Lefthanders can get him out with high fastballs and breaking balls down and away. Vizquel is much more dangerous against righthanders, with a knack for finding the left- and right-field lines for doubles. He tends to lunge at pitches, but when he stays back he can hit the occasional homer.

Baserunning & Defense

Vizquel still plays shortstop like an acrobat. He makes the diving play behind second and in the hole, leaps over runners while turning the double play and covers shallow left field like a glove. After the slow start last year, he made only four errors in his final 119 games. He needed a day off here and there to stay sharp, but he still played 148 games. He does have trouble making throws from the hole and on slow rollers. Vizquel, who still runs well, stole 19 bases and ranks second in Indians franchise history at 279.

2005 Outlook

The Indians did not pick up Vizquel's $5 million option for this year, and he signed a three-year, $12.25 million contract with San Francisco. He'll be 38 in April and it will be interesting to see how he adjusts to the National League after spending 16 years in the AL. If Vizquel stays productive for two more seasons, he should draw consideration for the Hall of Fame.

Position: SS
Bats: B **Throws:** R
Ht: 5' 9" **Wt:** 175

Opening Day Age: 37
Born: 4/24/67 in Caracas, VZ
ML Seasons: 16
Pronunciation: viz-KELL

Overall Statistics

G	AB	R	H	D	T	HR	RBI	SB	BB	SO	Avg	OBP	Slg
148	567	82	165	28	3	7	59	19	57	62	.291	.353	.388
2138	7819	1129	2147	348	54	66	715	318	785	794	.275	.341	.358

Where He Hits the Ball

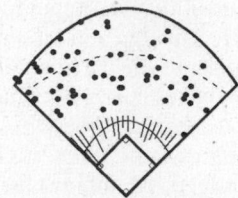
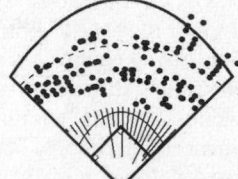

Vs. LHP   **Vs. RHP**

2004 Situational Stats

	AB	H	HR	RBI	Avg		AB	H	HR	RBI	Avg
Home	284	80	2	29	.282	LHP	190	49	1	23	.258
Road	283	85	5	30	.300	RHP	377	116	6	36	.308
First Half	314	94	4	38	.299	Sc Pos	133	40	1	46	.301
Scnd Half	253	71	3	21	.281	Clutch	85	22	0	9	.259

2004 Rankings (American League)

- 1st in sacrifice bunts (20)
- 3rd in fielding percentage at shortstop (.982)
- 5th in bunts in play (26)
- 6th in lowest HR frequency (81.0 ABs per HR)
- 7th in singles and batting average with two strikes (.269)
- 8th in lowest slugging percentage
- Led the Indians in singles, sacrifice bunts (20), sacrifice flies (6), stolen-base percentage (76.0), bunts in play (26), lowest percentage of swings that missed (10.8), steals of third (4) and batting average with two strikes (.269)

Jake Westbrook

Position: SP
Bats: R **Throws:** R
Ht: 6' 3" **Wt:** 185

Opening Day Age: 27
Born: 9/29/77 in
Athens, GA
ML Seasons: 5

2004 Season

Jake Westbrook lost his job in the starting rotation in spring training, but regained it on April 19 with seven perfect innings of relief against Detroit. It was the first time a pitcher worked seven perfect innings in relief since 1969. Westbrook regained his spot in the rotation after that appearance and went on to win a career-high 14 games while making the All-Star team. He finished third in the American League with a 3.38 ERA.

Pitching

Westbrook's breakout season was a matter of trust and a good sinker. He always had a good sinking fastball, but he wouldn't throw it for strikes. Last year, he threw the sinker over the plate and let it work. He complemented it with a slider, change-up and a cut fastball to lefties. Westbrook throws between 89-91 MPH as a starter and can hit 94 MPH when he relieves. He threw five complete games and 215.2 innings, both career highs, last year. He was able to keep his pitch count down because he gets so many outs on grounders early in the count. He induced 29 double plays.

Defense

Westbrook not only is a good fielder, but also a busy one because of his sinker. His groundball-flyball ratio was the second highest in the American League. He made three errors last year, but handled 76 total chances, the most on the staff. He also started six double plays, most among AL pitchers. Westbrook showed improvement against the running game in 2004, as 43 percent (6 of 14) of the basestealers who challenged him were thrown out.

2005 Outlook

After starting last season as a long man, Westbrook will open this season as the Tribe's No. 2 starter. He may not throw as many innings again, but he seems completely recovered from the elbow problems that hounded him early in his career. Westbrook could become a perennial 12-15 game winner.

Overall Statistics

	W	L	Pct.	ERA	G	GS	Sv	IP	H	BB	SO	HR	Avg
'04	14	9	.609	3.38	33	30	0	215.2	208	61	116	19	.255
Car.	26	28	.481	4.37	104	64	0	461.2	494	155	243	41	.277

2004 Pitching Profile

	Jake Westbrook	AL Average
Overall Strike %	62.5	62.3
1st Pitch Strike %	57.5	58.1
Ratio	1.25	1.42
Strikeouts per 9 IP	4.84	6.45
Walks per 9 IP	2.55	3.34
Home Runs per 9 IP	0.79	1.15
Strikeout/Walk Ratio	1.90	1.93
Groundball/Flyball Ratio	2.72	1.17

2004 Situational Stats

	W	L	ERA	Sv	IP		AB	H	HR	RBI	Avg
Home	7	2	2.36	0	91.1	LHB	428	112	12	55	.262
Road	7	7	4.13	0	124.1	RHB	389	96	7	29	.247
First Half	6	4	3.21	0	106.2	Sc Pos	215	48	5	66	.223
Scnd Half	8	5	3.55	0	109.0	Clutch	66	14	1	6	.212

2004 Rankings (American League)

- 1st in complete games (5) and lowest ERA at home
- 2nd in highest groundball-flyball ratio allowed (2.7)
- 3rd in ERA
- 4th in GDPs induced (29) and lowest slugging percentage allowed (.386)
- 5th in fewest home runs allowed per nine innings (.79)
- Led the Indians in wins, innings pitched, hits allowed, batters faced (895), pickoff throws (74), runners caught stealing (6), GDPs induced (29), lowest on-base percentage allowed (.308), lowest stolen-base percentage allowed (57.1), fewest pitches thrown per batter (3.51), lowest ERA at home, most run support per nine innings (6.5), lowest batting average allowed with runners in scoring position, and fewest walks per nine innings (2.5)

Cleveland

Rafael Betancourt

Position: RP
Bats: R **Throws:** R
Ht: 6' 2" **Wt:** 200

Opening Day Age: 29
Born: 4/29/75 in
Cumana, VZ
ML Seasons: 2

Overall Statistics

	W	L	Pct.	ERA	G	GS	Sv	IP	H	BB	SO	HR	Avg
'04	5	6	.455	3.92	68	0	4	66.2	71	18	76	7	.268
Car.	7	8	.467	3.27	101	0	5	104.2	98	31	112	12	.243

2004 Situational Stats

	W	L	ERA	Sv	IP		AB	H	HR	RBI	Avg
Home	2	2	4.76	4	34.0	LHB	136	37	4	16	.272
Road	3	4	3.03	0	32.2	RHB	129	34	3	18	.264
First Half	3	4	4.50	2	36.0	Sc Pos	67	21	2	26	.313
Scnd Half	2	2	3.23	2	30.2	Clutch	167	49	6	25	.293

2004 Season

Rafael Betancourt, a converted shortstop with a metal plate and six screws in his right elbow, went from setup man to closer to setup man last year. He did a nice job as a setup man, but was charged with seven blown saves, third most in the American League.

Pitching & Defense

A hard-throwing strikeout pitcher, Betancourt was overworked early in the year because he was one of the Indians' few effective relievers. The extra work put him on the disabled list in late June with biceps tendinits and made him vulnerable to pitching on consecutive days for the rest of the year. Betancourt's best pitch is a 92-95 MPH fastball. He topped out at 97 MPH when he closed, but he needs a better breaking ball. Betancourt slows the game down with runners on base and that seems to work against him. He fielded his position without incident but did not hold runners well.

2005 Outlook

The Indians received much more than they expected from Betancourt over the last two seasons. They signed him as a minor league free agent, and he's turned out to be a useful and inexpensive part of their bullpen. But it would not be a surprise if he doesn't make the club this year.

Aaron Boone

Position: 3B/2B
Bats: R **Throws:** R
Ht: 6' 2" **Wt:** 200

Opening Day Age: 32
Born: 3/9/73 in La
Mesa, CA
ML Seasons: 7

Overall Statistics

	G	AB	R	H	D	T	HR	RBI	SB	BB	SO	Avg	OBP	Slg
'04				Did Not Play										
Car.	722	2572	358	694	154	14	92	393	91	202	458	.270	.332	.448

2004 Situational Stats

	AB	H	HR	RBI	Avg		AB	H	HR	RBI	Avg
Home	–	–	–	–	–	LHB	–	–	–	–	–
Road	–	–	–	–	–	RHB	–	–	–	–	–
First Half	–	–	–	–	–	Sc Pos	–	–	–	–	–
Scnd Half	–	–	–	–	–	Clutch	–	–	–	–	–

2004 Season

Aaron Boone's lost season began with a torn ACL in his left knee suffered in a pickup basketball game in January. The Yankees voided his $5.75 million contract because of the injury, but the Indians signed him to a two-year, deal in June with an option for 2006. He needed a second surgery on the knee and didn't play.

Hitting, Baserunning & Defense

Boone doesn't have great numbers against left-handers, but his power increased in 2002-03 because he started pulling the ball more. He's not a high average hitter—his average has dropped steadily from .294 in 2001, while his strikeouts have climbed—but his run production has kept improving. He has problems with breaking balls out of the strike zone, but can take those pitches to right field. Boone, who can play short, second and third, has a good, accurate arm and was a high-percentage basestealer before the two knee surgeries.

2005 Outlook

If Boone is healthy, he's going to get the bulk of playing time at third base. The question is, how healthy is he going to be on a left knee that's been operated on three times since 2001? Boone was scheduled to start playing in exhibition games in mid-March.

Jason Davis

Position: SP
Bats: R **Throws:** R
Ht: 6' 6" **Wt:** 210

Opening Day Age: 24
Born: 5/8/80 in Chattanooga, TN
ML Seasons: 3

Overall Statistics

	W	L	Pct.	ERA	G	GS	Sv	IP	H	BB	SO	HR	Avg
'04	2	7	.222	5.51	26	19	0	114.1	148	51	72	13	.311
Car.	11	18	.379	4.86	56	48	0	294.1	332	102	168	39	.286

2004 Situational Stats

	W	L	ERA	Sv	IP		AB	H	HR	RBI	Avg
Home	1	4	4.62	0	62.1	LHB	233	71	8	29	.305
Road	1	3	6.58	0	52.0	RHB	243	77	5	39	.317
First Half	2	6	6.00	0	102.0	Sc Pos	154	42	2	53	.273
Scnd Half	0	1	1.46	0	12.1	Clutch	14	4	0	1	.286

2004 Season

Jason Davis traveled a rocky road last year. He opened the season as the Indians' No. 2 starter, but was optioned to Triple-A Buffalo on July 7 with a 2-6 record and a 6.00 ERA. He returned to make one start in September before being moved to the bullpen, where he had success.

Pitching & Defense

Davis is a power pitcher who throws a fastball, slider and splitter. He throws between 92-100 MPH, most frequently around 94-95 MPH. As a starter, Davis had difficulties maintaining his stuff into the middle and late innings. He was prone to walks, balks and wild pitches. The Indians think they can reduce his margin of error in the bullpen, where he can throw between 95-100 MPH for one or two innings. In his seven appearances as a reliever, Davis had a 1.23 ERA. Davis is a defensive disaster. Despite a limited workload, he allowed a staff-high 18 stolen bases in 21 attempts, and his lifetime fielding percentage is .890

2005 Outlook

Davis is expected to open the season in the bullpen. He has future closer written all over him. Davis likes the idea, and certainly throws hard enough to close, but he needs to get control of the strike zone and his emotions.

Scott Elarton

Position: SP
Bats: R **Throws:** R
Ht: 6' 8" **Wt:** 240

Opening Day Age: 29
Born: 2/23/76 in Lamar, CO
ML Seasons: 6

Overall Statistics

	W	L	Pct.	ERA	G	GS	Sv	IP	H	BB	SO	HR	Avg
'04	3	11	.214	5.90	29	29	0	158.2	164	62	103	33	.265
Car.	39	38	.506	5.22	164	110	3	716.2	732	288	518	122	.263

2004 Situational Stats

	W	L	ERA	Sv	IP		AB	H	HR	RBI	Avg
Home	3	6	6.36	0	99.0	LHB	318	72	16	46	.226
Road	0	5	5.13	0	59.2	RHB	301	92	17	55	.306
First Half	0	8	8.33	0	67.0	Sc Pos	144	40	9	66	.278
Scnd Half	3	3	4.12	0	91.2	Clutch	9	2	0	1	.222

2004 Season

Scott Elarton started the season with Colorado, but was released after going 0-6 in eight starts. The Indians signed him and brought him to Cleveland on June 12. He didn't win his first game until July 28, breaking a winless streak of 17 straight starts.

Pitching & Defense

Elarton is a finesse pitcher who throws a fastball, curveball and changeup. He throws between 88-92 MPH. The 6-foot-8 righthander has some deception because he short arms the ball, but too often he leaves his fastball up in the zone. When he does, he's very hittable, yielding 33 homers in only 158.2 innings last year. To be successful, Elarton needs to mix his three pitches. His change-up was particularly effective in the second half, when he went 3-3 in 15 starts. Coming off shoulder surgery in 2002, Elarton did a good job controlling the running game. He's a decent fielder.

2005 Outlook

The Indians were so impressed with Elarton's work last year that they re-signed him to a one-year deal for $850,000. He'll go into spring training competing with Jason Davis and others for the last spot in the rotation. With Davis probably headed for the pen, Elarton should be favored to win the job.

Cleveland

Bob Howry

Position: RP
Bats: L **Throws:** R
Ht: 6' 5" **Wt:** 220

Opening Day Age: 31
Born: 8/4/73 in Phoenix, AZ
ML Seasons: 7
Pronunciation: HOW-ree

Overall Statistics

	W	L	Pct.	ERA	G	GS	Sv	IP	H	BB	SO	HR	Avg
'04	4	2	.667	2.74	37	0	0	42.2	37	12	39	5	.228
Car.	18	22	.450	3.79	355	0	49	387.1	349	152	343	47	.242

2004 Situational Stats

	W	L	ERA	Sv	IP		AB	H	HR	RBI	Avg
Home	3	0	3.22	0	22.1	LHB	79	23	2	9	.291
Road	1	2	2.21	0	20.1	RHB	83	14	3	5	.169
First Half	1	0	1.04	0	8.2	Sc Pos	42	5	0	9	.119
Scnd Half	3	2	3.18	0	34.0	Clutch	68	18	4	9	.265

2004 Season

Bob Howry joined the Indians' bullpen on June 29 following a slow recovery from surgery on his right elbow in 2003. He quickly moved into the setup role, allowing only five earned runs in his first 25 appearances. Howry, who hadn't pitched regularly since 2002, struggled in September.

Pitching & Defense

Howry is a big-bodied power pitcher who throws a fasball and slider. He has a splitter as well, but didn't throw it much last year because of his elbow surgery. Howry throws between 91-93 MPH, topping out at 96 MPH. He's a strikeout pitcher who has closed in the past, but is probably better suited for the setup role right now until he proves he's 100 percent. Howry showed he could pitch two and three days in a row, but wore down in September. He had trouble with lefties. He's a good fielder and holds runners adequately.

2005 Outlook

Howry was eligible for arbitration, but the Indians signed him to a one-year deal worth an estimated $750,000. They liked what he did as a setup man, and think he'll only get stronger as he continues to recover from elbow surgery. Howry is also a safety net in case the Indians run into problems at closer.

Jhonny Peralta

Position: SS
Bats: R **Throws:** R
Ht: 6' 1" **Wt:** 185

Opening Day Age: 22
Born: 5/28/82 in Santiago, DR
ML Seasons: 2
Pronunciation: pah-RALL-tah

Overall Statistics

	G	AB	R	H	D	T	HR	RBI	SB	BB	SO	Avg	OBP	Slg
'04	8	25	2	6	1	0	0	2	0	3	6	.240	.321	.280
Car.	85	267	26	61	11	1	4	23	1	23	71	.228	.297	.322

2004 Situational Stats

	AB	H	HR	RBI	Avg		AB	H	HR	RBI	Avg
Home	4	0	0	0	.000	LHP	9	2	0	2	.222
Road	21	6	0	2	.286	RHP	16	4	0	0	.250
First Half	0	0	0	0	–	Sc Pos	9	2	0	2	.222
Scnd Half	25	6	0	2	.240	Clutch	7	1	0	2	.143

2004 Season

Jhonny Peralta, the Indians' shortstop in waiting, pleaded his case well at Triple-A Buffalo last year. He hit .326 with 44 doubles, 15 homers and 86 RBI. After helping Buffalo win the International League championship and being named league MVP, Peralta joined the Indians and hit .240 in eight games.

Hitting, Baserunning & Defense

Peralta made some adjustments in his swing last year. The changes, which included lowering his hands, allowed him to keep the bat in the strike zone longer and opened the right side of the field. Breaking balls on the outside part of the plate continue to give him problems. Peralta, who bounced between third and short at Buffalo, made 27 errors. He made three more when he joined Cleveland and seemed to have trouble making the backhand play at short. Peralta has decent range and an accurate arm. He needs to improve as a basestealer.

2005 Outlook

Peralta replaced the injured Omar Vizquel for 77 games in 2003. This year, he can replace Vizquel for good, as Vizquel signed a three-year deal with the Giants in November. Brandon Phillips will compete in spring training at short, but the job is Peralta's to lose.

Josh Phelps

Position: DH/1B
Bats: R **Throws:** R
Ht: 6' 3" **Wt:** 220

Opening Day Age: 26
Born: 5/12/78 in
Anchorage, AK
ML Seasons: 5

Overall Statistics

	G	AB	R	H	D	T	HR	RBI	SB	BB	SO	Avg	OBP	Slg
'04	103	371	51	93	19	2	17	61	0	22	93	.251	.304	.450
Car.	305	1045	152	281	57	4	52	186	2	82	296	.269	.337	.480

2004 Situational Stats

	AB	H	HR	RBI	Avg		AB	H	HR	RBI	Avg
Home	169	50	9	34	.296	LHP	152	47	12	32	.309
Road	202	43	8	27	.213	RHP	219	46	5	29	.210
First Half	271	66	9	45	.244	Sc Pos	95	27	4	41	.284
Scnd Half	100	27	8	16	.270	Clutch	51	13	2	6	.255

2004 Season

The Indians acquired Josh Phelps from Toronto in a waiver trade on August 6 for minor leaguer Eric Crozier. Phelps was hitting .237 but leading the Blue Jays with 51 RBI at the time of the deal. He made the most of his opportunities with the Indians, hitting .303 with five homers and 10 RBI.

Hitting, Baserunning & Defense

Long and lean, Phelps has good plate coverage and generates a lot of power when he keeps his swing short and compact. When the swing gets long, which it has a tendency to do, Phelps is an easy strikeout victim. Pitchers try to work Phelps away and then come inside with fastballs. After joining the Tribe, Phelps made seven starts at first base, where he needs work. The Indians worked him out in left field and talked to him about catching. The big man is faster than he looks but no threat to steal.

2005 Outlook

The Indians spent much of last year looking for a righthanded hitter to help them against lefties. Phelps was just what they wanted, but he couldn't get many at-bats because of DH Travis Hafner and first baseman Ben Broussard. The situation probably won't change much this year, and Phelps could be traded.

David Riske

Position: RP
Bats: R **Throws:** R
Ht: 6' 2" **Wt:** 190

Opening Day Age: 28
Born: 10/23/76 in
Renton, WA
ML Seasons: 5
Pronunciation:
RISK-ee

Overall Statistics

	W	L	Pct.	ERA	G	GS	Sv	IP	H	BB	SO	HR	Avg
'04	7	3	.700	3.72	72	0	5	77.1	69	41	78	11	.240
Car.	14	8	.636	3.68	229	0	15	244.2	210	120	270	33	.233

2004 Situational Stats

	W	L	ERA	Sv	IP		AB	H	HR	RBI	Avg
Home	4	0	1.45	4	37.1	LHB	143	32	7	24	.224
Road	3	3	5.85	1	40.0	RHB	145	37	4	17	.255
First Half	4	2	4.12	4	43.2	Sc Pos	84	22	4	30	.262
Scnd Half	3	1	3.21	1	33.2	Clutch	148	33	3	15	.223

2004 Season

David Riske opened the season at closer for injured Bob Wickman, but couldn't hold the job. He blew seven saves in two different tries at closer. Riske righted himself as a setup man by going 7-2 with a 2.19 ERA over his last 60 appearances, winning seven straight during that stretch.

Pitching & Defense

Riske pitches with his fastball and heart. He throws between 88-92 MPH, but he's usually between 90-91 MPH. He has good deception on the fastball and offsets it with a splitter. Riske always has been able to get both lefties and righties out, which makes him more than a matchup reliever. Lefties had a lower batting average against him than righties last year, but they hit seven of the career-high 11 homers he allowed. Possessing a quick move home, Riske knows how to control the running game. He did not make an error in a career-high 72 appearances.

2005 Outlook

Riske struggled early last season, in part because of some family issues. Those have passed, and the Indians expect him to return to being one of the best late-inning relievers in baseball. Riske is eligible for arbitration, but it's likely the Indians will sign him before going through that process.

Kazuhito Tadano

Position: RP
Bats: R **Throws:** R
Ht: 6' 0" **Wt:** 180

Opening Day Age: 24
Born: 4/25/80 in Tokyo, Japan
ML Seasons: 1

Overall Statistics

	W	L	Pct.	ERA	G	GS	Sv	IP	H	BB	SO	HR	Avg
'04	1	1	.500	4.65	14	4	0	50.1	55	18	39	6	.272
Car.	1	1	.500	4.65	14	4	0	50.1	55	18	39	6	.272

2004 Situational Stats

	W	L	ERA	Sv	IP		AB	H	HR	RBI	Avg
Home	0	0	4.43	0	22.1	LHB	90	20	3	12	.222
Road	1	1	4.82	0	28.0	RHB	112	35	3	16	.313
First Half	1	0	5.65	0	28.2	Sc Pos	58	16	3	23	.276
Scnd Half	0	1	3.32	0	21.2	Clutch	9	5	1	5	.556

2004 Season

Bouncing between Cleveland and Triple-A Buffalo, Kazuhito Tadano made a good impression with the Indians until a bulging disc ended his season in early September. He struck out nine in a June 26 relief appearance against Colorado. Then he struck out 10 in a seven-inning start against Cincinnati on July 2.

Pitching & Defense

Tadano, who has a deceptive motion, throws a fastball, slider, changeup and blooper ball. He throws his fastball between 87-91 MPH and will use a 50-70 MPH changeup to a big hitter on occasion. Tadano has a good knowledge of pitching, and knows how to exploit hitters. He would like to start, but the Indians aren't convinced he can handle the workload. He is the best fielding pitcher in the organization and covers first easily. Four of five basestealers were successful with Tadano on the mound in 2004, but generally he does good work in that area.

2005 Outlook

The Indians love Tadano's versatility. That versatility may allow him to break camp in the bullpen. He can pitch long, middle and late relief, or make a spot start. When he was shut down in September, surgery was contemplated, but not needed.

Bob Wickman

Position: RP
Bats: R **Throws:** R
Ht: 6' 1" **Wt:** 240

Opening Day Age: 36
Born: 2/6/69 in Green Bay, WI
ML Seasons: 12

Overall Statistics

	W	L	Pct.	ERA	G	GS	Sv	IP	H	BB	SO	HR	Avg
'04	0	2	.000	4.25	30	0	13	29.2	33	10	26	4	.282
Car.	59	47	.557	3.70	657	28	169	892.2	887	377	665	65	.261

2004 Situational Stats

	W	L	ERA	Sv	IP		AB	H	HR	RBI	Avg
Home	0	2	3.45	6	15.2	LHB	65	23	3	9	.354
Road	0	0	5.14	7	14.0	RHB	52	10	1	4	.192
First Half	0	0	0.00	0	3.0	Sc Pos	35	9	1	9	.257
Scnd Half	0	2	4.73	13	26.2	Clutch	74	19	2	8	.257

2004 Season

Bob Wickman went to spring training with the Indians' closer job in his back pocket. However, he re-injured a ligament in his right elbow that had been repaired by Tommy John surgery and didn't join the Indians until the beginning of July. Wickman reclaimed the closer's job in the second half and converted 13 of 14 opportunities.

Pitching & Defense

Wickman is a sinker-slider pitcher. He throws between 88-94 MPH, but his regular velocity is 90-92 MPH. When he first came off the DL in July after missing almost two years, Wickman was throwing hard, but he couldn't locate his slider. Lefthanders really made him pay. He never regained his location, and when he got up in the bullpen, the Indians made sure he got into the game because they knew he might not be able to pitch the next day. Wickman has trouble covering first base. He's pretty easy to run on.

2005 Outlook

Wickman, who turns 36 this February, talked retirement at the end of last year, and the Indians were looking elsewhere for a closer. They were concerned about him getting through the 2005 season healthy. Then Wickman called the team to say he wanted to pitch, the Indians signed him to a $2.75 million deal.

Jason Anderson (**Pos**: RHP, **Age**: 25)

	W	L	Pct.	ERA	G	GS	Sv	IP	H	BB	SO	HR	Avg
'04	0	0	—	45.00	1	0	0	1.0	1	4	1	1	.250
Car.	1	0	1.000	6.12	29	0	0	32.1	34	23	17	6	.272

Anderson was claimed off waivers twice last season, jumping from the Mets to the Indians and back to his original organization, the Yankees. He seems least likely to secure a bullpen job with the veteran Yankees, and he pitched the best for Cleveland's Triple-A Buffalo club. 2005 Outlook: C

Josh Bard (**Pos**: C, **Age**: 27, **Bats**: B)

	G	AB	R	H	D	T	HR	RBI	SB	BB	SO	Avg	OBP	Slg
'04	7	19	5	8	2	0	1	4	0	3	0	.421	.478	.684
Car.	122	412	39	102	20	1	12	52	0	29	66	.248	.294	.388

A switch-hitting catcher with a little pop, Bard missed the first half of 2004 after surgery for a sports hernia. The Indians think they have a potential big league regular in Bard, but he may have to change organizations with Victor Martinez' emergence last summer. 2005 Outlook: C

Cliff Bartosh (**Pos**: LHP, **Age**: 25)

	W	L	Pct.	ERA	G	GS	Sv	IP	H	BB	SO	HR	Avg
'04	1	0	1.000	4.66	34	0	0	19.1	22	11	25	4	.275
Car.	1	0	1.000	4.66	34	0	0	19.1	22	11	25	4	.275

Bartosh was dominant in Triple-A Buffalo's bullpen, allowing just 26 hits and eight walks in 35.1 innings while fanning 46. He posted a 2.80 ERA. The left-hander was roughed up early in Cleveland's pen, but he showed in September that he might be of some value this season. 2005 Outlook: C

Jack Cressend (**Pos**: RHP, **Age**: 29)

	W	L	Pct.	ERA	G	GS	Sv	IP	H	BB	SO	HR	Avg
'04	0	1	.000	6.32	11	0	0	15.2	22	10	8	4	.333
Car.	5	5	.500	4.20	122	0	0	160.2	172	60	104	17	.277

Cleveland tried anyone and everyone in its struggling bullpen last season, but Cressend wasn't the answer after pitching well there in 2003. At Triple-A Buffalo, he didn't pitch nearly as well as his 10-1 record suggests. 2005 Outlook: C

Jeff D'Amico (**Pos**: RHP, **Age**: 29)

	W	L	Pct.	ERA	G	GS	Sv	IP	H	BB	SO	HR	Avg
'04	1	2	.333	7.63	7	7	0	30.2	45	6	16	6	.333
Car.	45	52	.464	4.61	139	131	0	784.0	832	221	498	120	.272

D'Amico is a former first-round pick, a terrific pitching prospect felled by injuries. He hasn't been very effective since going 12-7 (2.66) with Milwaukee in 2000, and a chance to ressurect his career with a rebuilding Cleveland club ended with a back injury and his June release. 2005 Outlook: C

Joe Dawley (**Pos**: RHP, **Age**: 33)

	W	L	Pct.	ERA	G	GS	Sv	IP	H	BB	SO	HR	Avg
'04	0	0	—	5.40	2	2	0	8.1	7	7	8	1	.233
Car.	0	0	—	10.91	8	2	0	15.2	22	10	17	4	.324

The long-time minor leaguer got the call in late May, but went on the disabled list with a tender elbow in early June and didn't return. Dawley had posted solid Triple-A numbers and might have spent some time in the bigs if not for his elbow woes. 2005 Outlook: C

Alex Escobar (**Pos**: CF/RF, **Age**: 26, **Bats**: R)

	G	AB	R	H	D	T	HR	RBI	SB	BB	SO	Avg	OBP	Slg
'04	46	152	20	32	8	2	1	12	1	23	42	.211	.318	.309
Car.	92	301	39	69	11	2	9	34	3	33	94	.229	.309	.369

The tools-rich Escobar has been slow to develop his skills, but shared center field with Coco Crisp when the Tribe dealt Milton Bradley last April. Escobar was better at Triple-A Buffalo, but suffered a season-ending foot fracture in July and was claimed off waivers by the White Sox. 2005 Outlook: C

Raul Gonzalez (**Pos**: RF, **Age**: 31, **Bats**: R)

	G	AB	R	H	D	T	HR	RBI	SB	BB	SO	Avg	OBP	Slg
'04	7	11	0	1	0	0	0	0	0	0	4	.091	.091	.091
Car.	168	348	41	81	15	2	5	33	7	34	65	.233	.301	.330

Gonzalez enjoyed another decent Triple-A season, this time with Buffalo, but he went 1-for-11 with Cleveland and had his season end in August. He broke his right fibula in an aborted slide at home plate with Buffalo, where he posted hitting percentages of .310/.346/.491 in 56 games. 2005 Outlook: C

Jose Jimenez (**Pos**: RHP, **Age**: 31)

	W	L	Pct.	ERA	G	GS	Sv	IP	H	BB	SO	HR	Avg
'04	1	7	.125	8.42	31	0	8	36.1	45	14	21	6	.296
Car.	24	44	.353	4.92	329	38	110	521.1	572	186	319	46	.278

Jimenez was the Rockies' closer for four seasons before a 2003 meltdown. He had a chance to rebuild his career in a more pitcher-friendly environment, but he struggled along with his mates in the Cleveland pen. He was cut loose near midseason. 2005 Outlook: C

Tim Laker (**Pos**: C, **Age**: 35, **Bats**: R)

	G	AB	R	H	D	T	HR	RBI	SB	BB	SO	Avg	OBP	Slg
'04	43	117	12	25	2	0	3	17	0	7	28	.214	.262	.308
Car.	277	637	65	143	27	2	11	77	5	44	157	.224	.276	.325

Laker had been in Cleveland's system since December 2000, and served as the Indians' backup catcher the last two years. With Victor Martinez and Josh Bard passing him by, it appears he'll be moving on after hitting just .229 and slugging .341 those two summers. 2005 Outlook: C

Cleveland

Dave Lee (Pos: RHP, Age: 32)

	W	L	Pct.	ERA	G	GS	Sv	IP	H	BB	SO	HR	Avg
'04	0	0	–	10.38	4	0	0	4.1	8	4	4	0	.348
Car.	5	2	.714	4.37	96	0	1	115.1	117	72	97	14	.266

Lee wasn't all that effective at Triple-A Buffalo in 2004, but he got a crack at a job in a stumbling Indians bullpen in April. He was much better in the hitter-friendly Pacific Coast League in 2003, and he'll try to recapture his Las Vegas luck somewhere else in the spring. 2005 Outlook: C

Mark Little (Pos: CF, Age: 32, Bats: R)

	G	AB	R	H	D	T	HR	RBI	SB	BB	SO	Avg	OBP	Slg
'04	11	20	0	4	0	0	0	2	0	0	7	.200	.261	.200
Car.	148	247	46	61	11	3	3	22	8	18	66	.247	.332	.352

Little enjoyed a solid first half at Triple-A Buffalo, hitting .314 with good power, but he did little with his opportunity in Cleveland in July. He was released at the end of July and didn't resurface until signing a minor league deal with the Florida Marlins in November. 2005 Outlook: C

Ryan Ludwick (Pos: RF, Age: 26, Bats: R)

	G	AB	R	H	D	T	HR	RBI	SB	BB	SO	Avg	OBP	Slg
'04	15	50	3	11	2	0	2	4	0	2	14	.220	.278	.380
Car.	85	293	30	70	16	1	10	39	4	21	86	.239	.294	.403

A promising prospect who can't ditch the injury bug, Ludwick spent the first half rehabbing from April surgery to remove scar tissue from a previous procedure. He reached Cleveland in late August, before getting grazed by the stray bullet that hit Kyle Denney on a team bus. What luck. 2005 Outlook: C

John McDonald (Pos: SS/2B, Age: 30, Bats: R)

	G	AB	R	H	D	T	HR	RBI	SB	BB	SO	Avg	OBP	Slg
'04	66	93	17	19	5	1	2	7	0	4	11	.204	.237	.344
Car.	285	623	76	144	26	5	4	33	6	26	103	.231	.269	.308

Never much of a hitter in the majors, McDonald steered clear of the Mendoza line by batting .353 in 10 August contests, but went 0-for-14 in September. He was traded to the Blue Jays in December for RHP Thomas Mastny. 2005 Outlook: C

Lou Merloni (Pos: 1B, Age: 33, Bats: R)

	G	AB	R	H	D	T	HR	RBI	SB	BB	SO	Avg	OBP	Slg
'04	71	190	25	55	12	1	4	28	1	14	41	.289	.343	.426
Car.	409	1061	136	290	66	7	14	123	8	85	206	.273	.334	.388

The big difference between John McDonald and Merloni as utilitymen is that Merloni gets on base far more frequently. Most of his 2004 production came in June and July, when he batted .318 with three homers and 21 RBI. 2005 Outlook: C

Matt Miller (Pos: RHP, Age: 33)

	W	L	Pct.	ERA	G	GS	Sv	IP	H	BB	SO	HR	Avg
'04	4	1	.800	3.09	57	0	1	55.1	42	23	55	1	.216
Car.	4	1	.800	3.02	61	0	1	59.2	47	25	60	1	.224

The final numbers look pretty solid by themselves, but if you remove his stats from July, when he struggled mightily, Miller posted a 1.28 ERA in 42.1 innings over the other four months he was in the majors. An impressive rookie year for a late bloomer. 2005 Outlook: B

Lou Pote (Pos: RHP, Age: 33)

	W	L	Pct.	ERA	G	GS	Sv	IP	H	BB	SO	HR	Avg
'04	0	0	–	9.00	2	0	0	3.0	3	1	5	0	.250
Car.	4	4	.500	3.56	129	2	6	219.2	199	88	167	23	.242

Pote started the year at Oakland's Triple-A affiliate, pitching well enough to get a May trade to Cleveland, where he wasn't a solution for a struggling bullpen. The Rangers signed him to a minor league deal after the season. 2005 Outlook: C

Jake Robbins (Pos: RHP, Age: 28)

	W	L	Pct.	ERA	G	GS	Sv	IP	H	BB	SO	HR	Avg
'04	0	0	–	5.40	2	0	0	1.2	3	0	0	1	.375
Car.	0	0	–	5.40	2	0	0	1.2	3	0	0	1	.375

The long-time Yankees minor leaguer turned in a solid season at Triple-A Buffalo, going 6-1 with a 3.15 ERA, mostly in relief. The Cleveland bullpen needs all the help it can get, and Robbins could be in the mix. 2005 Outlook: C

Jeriome Robertson (Pos: LHP, Age: 28)

	W	L	Pct.	ERA	G	GS	Sv	IP	H	BB	SO	HR	Avg
'04	1	1	.500	12.21	8	0	0	14.0	22	9	6	5	.349
Car.	16	12	.571	5.71	51	32	0	184.1	215	78	111	32	.297

Robertson won 15 games as a rookie in 2003, thanks to a boatload of run support. The magic wasn't there in 2004, and he spent most of the year spinning a 6.75 ERA at a pair of Triple-A stops. The Reds signed him to a minor league deal in November. 2005 Outlook: C

Jason Stanford (Pos: LHP, Age: 28)

	W	L	Pct.	ERA	G	GS	Sv	IP	H	BB	SO	HR	Avg
'04	0	1	.000	0.82	2	2	0	11.0	12	5	5	0	.279
Car.	1	4	.200	3.10	15	10	0	61.0	60	21	35	5	.252

A sleeper in the Indians' system, Stanford enjoyed a promising debut in 2003 and made two excellent starts last April before forearm discomfort put him on the shelf. He had Tommy John surgery in July. He may return during the second half, but he won't be fully healthy until 2006. 2005 Outlook: C

Rick White (Pos: RHP, Age: 36)

	W	L	Pct.	ERA	G	GS	Sv	IP	H	BB	SO	HR	Avg
'04	5	5	.500	5.29	59	0	1	78.1	88	29	44	15	.293
Car.	33	45	.423	4.30	449	18	13	684.1	721	222	444	76	.273

White was a solid setup guy with the Rays and Mets in 2000 and 2001. He signed with Colorado as a free agent before 2002 and hasn't been the same since, except during very brief stints with the Cards (2002) and Astros (2003). He has a 5.51 ERA over the last two seasons. 2003 Outlook: C

Ernie Young (Pos: DH, Age: 35, Bats: R)

	G	AB	R	H	D	T	HR	RBI	SB	BB	SO	Avg	OBP	Slg
'04	3	4	0	2	0	0	0	0	0	1	2	.500	.600	.500
Car.	288	796	108	179	33	4	27	90	10	90	213	.225	.310	.378

Young has a nice collection of tools, but only his defensive game has emerged as major league caliber. He's made some phenomenal on-the-run catches over parts of eight big league seasons, but his bat hasn't been good enough. 2005 Outlook: C

Cleveland Indians Minor League Prospects

Organization Overview:

The Indians believe they have a bona fide major leaguer developing at every position within the system, and the organization is as rich as any in prospects. Credit general manager Mark Shapiro with some astute trading, especially in 2002, when few teams were parting with top prospects in trade deadline deals because labor strife threatened to shut down the season. Still, Shapiro acquired Travis Hafner, Ben Broussard, Brandon Phillips, Grady Sizemore, Cliff Lee, Coco Crisp and Francisco Cruceta that year. On top of that, assistant GM John Mirabelli has used the amateur draft to fill the system with promising talent in recent years. More of it will surface in 2005.

Michael Aubrey

Position: 1B **Opening Day Age:** 22
Bats: L **Throws:** L **Born:** 4/15/82 in
Ht: 6' 1" **Wt:** 195 Shreveport, LA

Recent Statistics

	G	AB	R	H	D	T	HR	RBI	SB	BB	SO	Avg
2003 A Lake County	38	138	22	48	13	0	5	19	0	14	22	.348
2004 A Kinston	60	218	34	74	14	1	10	60	3	27	26	.339
2004 AA Akron	38	134	13	35	7	0	5	22	0	15	18	.261

One of the more advanced hitters drafted in 2003, Aubrey earned an invite to big league spring training with an impressive debut at Class-A Lake County. He fit in with his demeanor, work ethic and maturity, and the gifted pure hitter looked like a major leaguer at the plate. Aubrey enjoyed a terrific 2004 at high Class-A Kinston before a second-half promotion to Double-A Akron. With his quick hands, Aubrey makes regular contact and drills the ball all over the field. A low-maintenance guy who can flat out hit, he seemed to tire down the stretch in his first full pro season. He's a promising fielder with a strong arm, though his footwork around the first-base bag needs work.

Fernando Cabrera

Position: P **Opening Day Age:** 23
Bats: R **Throws:** R **Born:** 11/16/81 in Toja
Ht: 6' 4" **Wt:** 170 Baja, PR

Recent Statistics

	W	L	ERA	G	GS	Sv	IP	H	R	BB	SO	HR
2004 AAA Buffalo	4	3	3.84	44	0	5	75.0	57	37	43	92	9
2004 AL Cleveland	0	0	3.38	4	0	0	5.1	3	3	1	6	0

In 2003, this 1999 draft pick was the hardest thrower in a Double-A Akron rotation of Cleveland's best pitching prospects. Calling on a mid-90s fastball, splitter, slider and changeup, Cabrera assumed Akron's closer duties partway through that season. He quickly showed he had the stuff and makeup to be Cleveland's ninth-inning guy after some big league seasoning. Cabrera often was dominant Triple-A Buffalo in 2004, working consistently at 95-96 MPH with a fastball he locates effectively and a splitter that is a solid second offering. He struck out well more than a batter an inning, and the Indians say that a first-pitch strike from Cabrera meant an out in 2004. He can punch out hitters quickly and should be a key guy in Cleveland's pen in 2005.

Francisco Cruceta

Position: P **Opening Day Age:** 23
Bats: R **Throws:** R **Born:** 7/4/81 in La Vega,
Ht: 6' 2" **Wt:** 180 DR

Recent Statistics

	W	L	ERA	G	GS	Sv	IP	H	R	BB	SO	HR
2004 AA Akron	4	8	5.28	15	15	0	88.2	89	58	33	45	11
2004 AAA Buffalo	6	5	3.25	14	14	0	83.0	78	35	36	62	6
2004 AL Cleveland	0	1	9.39	2	0	0	7.2	10	9	4	9	1

Acquired in the Paul Shuey trade with Los Angeles in 2002, Cruceta emerged with a 13-9 season at Double-A Akron in 2003, while leading his league in strikeouts. He didn't start as well at Akron in 2004, often battling to locate his low-90s fastball early in games while trying to establish his secondary pitches. His slider was better in the second half, and he allowed three earned runs or less in 12 of his 14 Triple-A starts for Buffalo. Cruceta had his secondary pitches working there, including a splitter he added over the summer. His fastball command will determine if he remains a starter or becomes a reliever in the majors. He will compete for a job in Cleveland's rotation in the spring.

Kyle Denney

Position: P **Opening Day Age:** 27
Bats: R **Throws:** R **Born:** 7/27/77 in Prague,
Ht: 6' 2" **Wt:** 195 OK

Recent Statistics

	W	L	ERA	G	GS	Sv	IP	H	R	BB	SO	HR
2004 AAA Buffalo	10	5	4.41	24	24	0	134.2	134	74	39	113	17
2004 AL Cleveland	1	2	9.56	4	4	0	16.0	32	17	8	13	3

A 26th-rounder in 1999, Denney endured Tommy John surgery in 2001 and has struggled with fastball command since then. It was improved from the start in 2004, as Denney was lights out early on at Triple-A Buffalo before straining a knee ligament several weeks into the season. With a four-pitch arsenal that was effective against lefties and righties—90-MPH fastball, curve, slider and changeup—Denney was destined for Cleveland before he went down. He wasn't as effective when he returned, but he was near peak form again by season's end. While he lacks stunning radar readings and blow-away stuff, he could excel based on the consistency of his stuff and his ability to throw strikes. Commanding the lower half of the strike zone is key to Denney's success.

Cleveland

Franklin Gutierrez

Position: OF
Bats: R **Throws:** R
Ht: 6' 2" **Wt:** 175

Opening Day Age: 22
Born: 2/21/83 in Caricuao, VZ

Recent Statistics

	G	AB	R	H	D	T	HR	RBI	SB	BB	SO	Avg
2003 A Vero Beach	110	425	65	120	28	5	20	68	17	39	111	.282
2003 AA Jacksnville	18	67	12	21	3	2	4	12	3	7	20	.313
2004 AAA Buffalo	7	27	4	4	1	0	1	3	0	1	11	.148
2004 AA Akron	70	262	38	79	24	2	5	35	6	23	77	.302

After a breakout year with two Dodger affiliates in 2003, Gutierrez was dealt to Cleveland in the Milton Bradley trade in April 2004. Gutierrez shined at Double-A Akron before he was hit by a pitch that dislodged bone chips in his elbow. He struggled following a promotion to Triple-A Buffalo, but bothered by the elbow, he wasn't at his best for his first taste of Triple-A pitching. Gutierrez didn't need surgery, but played little in the second half. A five-tool talent with speed and a strong arm, Gutierrez is a terrific center fielder, though Grady Sizemore may move him to right. The free-swinging Gutierrez has impressive bat speed and power potential, but will chase breaking stuff.

Adam Miller

Position: P
Bats: R **Throws:** R
Ht: 6' 4" **Wt:** 180

Opening Day Age: 20
Born: 11/26/84 in Plano, TX

Recent Statistics

	W	L	ERA	G	GS	Sv	IP	H	R	BB	SO	HR
2003 R Burlington	0	4	4.96	10	10	0	32.2	30	20	9	23	2
2004 A Lake County	7	4	3.36	19	19	0	91.0	79	39	28	106	7
2004 A Kinston	3	2	2.08	8	8	0	43.1	29	17	12	46	1

The 31st overall pick in 2003, Miller showed good command of his fastball in his pro debut at short-season Burlington. In 2004, the teenager maintained his 94-96 MPH velocity more consistently en route to high Class-A Kinston. His fastball has excellent movement, and with an 87-MPH slider that is just as nasty, Miller advanced on the strength of excellent command on both sides of the plate. His explosive stuff is remarkable enough, but the Indians are equally impressed by Miller's maturity. His workman-like approach and his desire to excel are key assets for a power pitcher with his tools. He will work on his changeup at Double-A Akron.

Brandon Phillips

Position: 2B
Bats: R **Throws:** R
Ht: 5' 11" **Wt:** 185

Opening Day Age: 23
Born: 6/28/81 in Raleigh, NC

Recent Statistics

	G	AB	R	H	D	T	HR	RBI	SB	BB	SO	Avg
2004 AAA Buffalo	135	521	83	158	34	4	8	50	14	44	56	.303
2004 AL Cleveland	6	22	1	4	2	0	0	1	0	2	5	.182

Drafted by Montreal in 1999, Phillips showed the tools and promise of a top prospect by climbing to the Double-A level as a teenager. Cleveland acquired him in the Bartolo Colon trade in June 2002, and gave him the second-base job the next spring. Expected to struggle offensively, Phillips was more overmatched than expected and also crashed at Triple-A Buffalo. Prior to 2004, he was challenged to make adjustments and responded well, using the whole field more and driving the ball the other way at Buffalo. The Indians want him to use his bat control to do the little things as well as drive the ball. He is solid defensively and could claim the second-base job in the spring.

Grady Sizemore

Position: OF
Bats: L **Throws:** L
Ht: 6' 2" **Wt:** 200

Opening Day Age: 22
Born: 8/2/82 in Seattle, WA

Recent Statistics

	G	AB	R	H	D	T	HR	RBI	SB	BB	SO	Avg
2004 AAA Buffalo	101	418	73	120	23	8	8	51	15	42	72	.287
2004 AL Cleveland	43	138	15	34	6	2	4	24	2	14	34	.246

Another top prospect acquired from Montreal for Bartolo Colon in June 2002, Sizemore has hit .289 in the minors and developed a power stroke since the deal. He has what it takes to be a star—from work ethic and makeup to instincts, speed, plate discipline and a terrific swing. Last spring, Sizemore dropped 15 pounds to a stomach virus and started slowly at Triple-A Buffalo. Despite the setback, Sizemore, though just 21, excelled at the Triple-A level and reached Cleveland in late July. He hit .304 with 11 RBI in his first 19 games before a 2-for-33 slide landed him back in Buffalo. He was recalled again in September, possibly for good, as he could take over center field for the Indians in 2005.

Others to Watch

Despite Tommy John surgery in 2000 and elbow surgery for bone chips in 2003, righthander **Andrew Brown** (24) throws a mid-90s fastball that can be exceptional. Acquired last spring in the Milton Bradley deal with Los Angeles, Brown's arm strength wasn't 100 percent in the high minors, but he could surface in Cleveland in 2005. . . Among the upper-level pitching prospects featured in these pages, **Fausto Carmona** (21) may have the most upside. He throws strikes and induces loads of grounders, though he may have thrown too many hittable strikes at three levels in 2004. Still, he reached Triple-A Buffalo and finished 10-10 with a 4.09 ERA. . . Catcher-first baseman **Ryan Garko** (24) lacks a natural position, but the righthanded hitter made hard contact all season in his first full pro season. The 2003 pick hit .330 with 33 doubles and 22 homers at three levels, including Triple-A Buffalo, and he may not be in the minors long enough to learn a position. . . Another 2003 pick, **Brad Snyder** (22), reached high Class-A Kinston last summer, where he hit .355 with 21 RBI in 29 games. The lefty outfielder, who projects as a plus major league hitter, may advance quickly through the system.

Offense

Comerica Park remains one of the most spacious fields in the major leagues and is the best park to hit a triple in. The Tigers, even though they do not have much team speed, easily led the AL in triples last season. Balls into the gaps take awhile to retrieve. Left field is more reasonable for righthanded power hitters to reach with the fence in, but it is not a bandbox, either. Lefthanded pull hitters have a distinct advantage because right field stays straight from the foul pole for an extended span.

Defense

Outfielders with range are important for success at Comerica Park. The ability to hit the cutoff man with throws also is key. One bobble and a triple can result in a run. The infield is slow, so middle infielders with range and strong arms thrive at Comerica.

Who It Helps the Most

The Tigers have several hitters who use all fields and benefit greatly from Comerica Park. They do not have a consistent lefthanded pull hitter, but if they ever develop one with a lot of power, he will thrive at Comerica. Finesse pitchers such as Mike Maroth do their best work at Comerica Park because the infield is slow and the outfield spacious.

Who It Hurts the Most

Righthanded power hitters and fielders lacking range struggle here. Comerica is not a place where you can hide a subpar outfielder such as Rondell White in either corner outfield position. It hurts Bobby Higginson the most among the hitters, because he can't pull the ball and his drives to the gaps usually are outs.

Rookies & Newcomers

The Tigers have three hard-throwing righthanded pitching prospects—Kyle Sleeth, Humberto Sanchez and Joel Zumaya—who reached the Double-A level last season. They should all benefit from the size of Comerica.

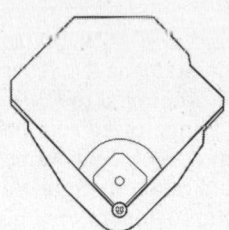

Dimensions: LF-345, LCF-370, CF-420, RCF-365, RF-330

Capacity: 40,120

Elevation: 585 feet

Surface: Grass

Foul Territory: Average

Park Factors

2004 Season

| | Home Games | | | Away Games | | | |
	Tigers	Opp	Total	Tigers	Opp	Total	Index
G	72	72	144	72	72	144	
Avg	.271	.277	.274	.271	.277	.274	100
AB	2444	2578	5022	2551	2425	4976	101
R	335	382	717	399	369	768	93
H	663	715	1378	691	671	1362	101
2B	99	130	229	146	128	274	83
3B	33	21	54	12	11	23	233
HR	76	88	164	105	85	190	86
BB	230	234	464	229	229	458	100
SO	462	450	912	551	421	972	93
E	58	32	90	72	48	120	75
E-Infield	44	27	71	57	39	96	74
LHB-Avg	.263	.260	.262	.259	.262	.260	101
LHB-HR	34	34	68	49	29	78	86
RHB-Avg	.279	.289	.284	.281	.287	.284	100
RHB-HR	42	54	96	56	56	112	85

2002-2003

| | Home Games | | | Away Games | | | |
	Tigers	Opp	Total	Tigers	Opp	Total	Index
G	143	143	286	144	144	288	
Avg	.242	.275	.259	.245	.297	.271	96
AB	4756	5162	9918	4913	4858	9771	102
R	501	747	1248	554	877	1431	88
H	1150	1422	2572	1205	1444	2649	98
2B	176	267	443	249	317	566	77
3B	44	57	101	20	41	61	163
HR	119	142	261	130	187	317	81
BB	340	448	788	386	466	852	91
SO	860	733	1593	1013	665	1678	94
E	118	90	208	136	71	207	101
E-Infield	96	70	166	106	62	168	100
LHB-Avg	.262	.287	.273	.256	.306	.279	98
LHB-HR	76	79	155	75	87	162	95
RHB-Avg	.217	.267	.246	.233	.290	.264	93
RHB-HR	43	63	106	55	100	155	67

2004 Rankings (American League)

- Highest triple factor
- Lowest double factor
- Lowest infield-error factor
- Second-lowest error factor
- Third-lowest home-run factor
- Third-lowest strikeout factor
- Third-lowest LHB home-run factor
- Third-lowest RHB home-run factor

Detroit

Alan Trammell

2004 Season

The Tigers made significant progress during Alan Trammell's second year as their manager. After going 43-119 in 2003, Detroit improved to 72-90 and even found itself on the fringe of contention in the American League Central until floundering during late July. Trammell had much more talent to work with. The Tigers improvement can be traced to acquiring Ivan Rodriguez, Carlos Guillen, Rondell White and Ugueth Urbina. Some of the Tigers young talent also came on strong last season.

Offense

Trammell plays it by the book most of the time. He does like to hit-and-run, but will not overuse that tactic. He is conservative when it comes to stealing bases. He will, however, give the green light to his faster players, especially if the pitcher is not doing a good job of holding runners.

Pitching & Defense

Trammell gets criticized a lot for the way he handles his bullpen, but in truth, he has not had much to work with. He tends to use his relievers for periods of time instead of situationally. But again, that's because the Tigers have not had enough depth where somebody such as Jamie Walker can be used strictly as a situational lefty, as he would be on a stronger staff. With his starters, Trammell has a quick hook in the later innings. However, he will stick with starters through a rough inning early in games.

2005 Outlook

Last season was the first time Trammell actually got a chance to manage, and his inexperience showed at times, especially during interleague games when he made a number of questionable moves. He clearly needs to be quicker-minded running a game, but he made progress in that regard late last season. The best thing Trammell does is give order to the clubhouse and dugout. He is a good teacher and a calm hand at the wheel who does not play mind games or have agendas.

Born: 2/21/58 in Garden Grove, California

Playing Experience: 1977-1996, Det

Managerial Experience: 2 seasons

Manager Statistics

Year	Team, Lg	W	L	Pct	GB	Finish
2004	Detroit, AL	72	90	.444	20.0	4th Central
2 Seasons		115	209	.355	–	–

2004 Starting Pitchers by Days Rest

	<=3	4	5	6+
Tigers Starts	1	84	54	16
Tigers ERA	3.86	5.42	4.36	5.15
AL Avg Starts	2	82	47	21
AL ERA	5.36	4.87	4.65	4.93

2004 Situational Stats

	Alan Trammell	AL Average
Hit & Run Success %	38.2	36.8
Stolen Base Success %	63.2	68.6
Platoon Pct.	66.9	61.6
Defensive Subs	18	21
High-Pitch Outings	3	5
Quick/Slow Hooks	28/16	20/16
Sacrifice Attempts	69	53

2004 Rankings (American League)

- 1st in squeeze plays (11)
- 3rd in sacrifice bunt attempts, sacrifice-bunt percentage (85.5%), quick hooks and mid-inning pitching changes (201)

Jeremy Bonderman

2004 Season

Jeremy Bonderman closed his second big league season strong, going 5-3 with a 2.33 ERA during his final eight starts. He struck out 60 hitters in 58 innings and allowed just 42 hits in those outings. At the All-Star break, Bonderman had an ERA of 6.03, but it was misleading. He pitched deep into most of his starts, averaging nearly six innings per outing. He struggled avoiding one big inning during many of his first-half starts, but was more consistent later in the season.

Pitching

Bonderman has an excellent fastball. He usually pitches at 95 MPH, but will hit as high as 98 MPH on his best days. He commands his fastball well for a younger pitcher, working it effectively around the strike zone. During the first half of last season, Bonderman sometimes was too fine with his fastball early in the count, fell behind and paid for it later. He improved in that regard during the second half. His slider is another plus pitch. It has a lot of break, giving it almost a slurve look. He throws it relatively hard, in the mid-80s, and commands it well, especially when working the outer half of the plate to righthanded hitters. Bonderman sometimes has a bad habit of relying too much on his slider. His worst pitch is his changeup, but it's not really a bad pitch. He sometimes throws it too hard, but he made strides in that regard during the second half last season.

Defense

Bonderman is a good athlete who fields his position well. He pays attention to runners and is quick to the plate. His pickoff move is average, however, and baserunners can get a good jump on his delivery.

2005 Outlook

Not only does Bonderman have a live arm and good command, but he also has a strong mental makeup. That, along with potentially three plus pitches, give Bonderman a chance to be a legitimate No. 1 starter. Based on the way he finished 2004, it could be as soon as this season.

Position: SP
Bats: R **Throws:** R
Ht: 6' 2" **Wt:** 210

Opening Day Age: 22
Born: 10/28/82 in Kennewick, WA
ML Seasons: 2

Overall Statistics

	W	L	Pct.	ERA	G	GS	Sv	IP	H	BB	SO	HR	Avg
'04	11	13	.458	4.89	33	32	0	184.0	168	73	168	24	.242
Car.	17	32	.347	5.20	66	60	0	346.0	361	131	276	47	.267

2004 Pitching Profile

	Jeremy Bonderman	AL Average
Overall Strike %	62.3	62.3
1st Pitch Strike %	55.5	58.1
Ratio	1.31	1.42
Strikeouts per 9 IP	8.22	6.45
Walks per 9 IP	3.57	3.34
Home Runs per 9 IP	1.17	1.15
Strikeout/Walk Ratio	2.30	1.93
Groundball/Flyball Ratio	1.44	1.17

2004 Situational Stats

	W	L	ERA	Sv	IP		AB	H	HR	RBI	Avg
Home	4	6	5.07	0	76.1	LHB	404	103	16	64	.255
Road	7	7	4.76	0	107.2	RHB	291	65	8	27	.223
First Half	6	6	6.03	0	94.0	Sc Pos	162	39	4	64	.241
Scnd Half	5	7	3.70	0	90.0	Clutch	18	6	1	3	.333

2004 Rankings (American League)

- 1st in shutouts (2)
- 3rd in lowest batting average allowed vs. righthanded batters and highest stolen-base percentage allowed (86.7)
- 4th in most strikeouts per nine innings (8.2)
- 6th in losses, strikeouts and highest walks per nine innings (3.6)
- 7th in lowest batting average allowed (.242) and lowest fielding percentage at pitcher (.906)
- 8th in complete games (2)
- Led the Tigers in complete games (2), shutouts (2), walks allowed, hit batsmen (10), strikeouts, stolen bases allowed (13), lowest batting average allowed (.242), lowest slugging percentage allowed (.406), lowest on-base percentage allowed (.321), lowest batting average allowed vs. righthanded batters and most strikeouts per nine innings (8.2)

Carlos Guillen

2004 Season

Acquired before the 2004 season in a trade with Seattle for middle infielder Ramon Santiago and a minor leaguer, Carlos Guillen had by far his best campaign. He more than doubled his previous best single-season total for home runs, and nearly doubled his previous best RBI output. A .264 lifetime hitter entering last season, he batted .318 and was named to the American League All-Star squad. Guillen's numbers would have been even better if it weren't for a torn ACL suffered September 11 while sliding into third base. It put him on the disabled list for the remainder of the season.

Hitting

A switch-hitter, Guillen hits for much better average on the left side, although he has a bit more power from the right. Either way, he uses the whole field. If pitched away, he will take the ball to the opposite field. He is patient and will wait out the count. Guillen has gotten stronger to the point where he will turn on a mistake pitch and drive it out of the ballpark.

Baserunning & Defense

Guillen has exceptional range to his glove side. He makes play after play on balls hit up the middle that most other shortstops just wave at. His range isn't quite as good to the hole, although it's still above average. His throwing arm is strong and accurate. Guillen has average speed for a major league middle infielder. He does not steal a lot of bases and has average instincts on the basepaths.

2005 Outlook

The Tigers liked what they saw from Guillen, so much so that in June they signed him to a three-year, $14 million contract extension. The reasons go beyond his performance on the field. He is an excellent leader in the clubhouse and a hardnosed player who is not afraid to get on a teammate when it is needed. He underwent knee surgery at the end of September to repair his ACL, and the 4-6 month recovery period should have him on track to be ready by Opening Day.

Position: SS
Bats: B **Throws:** R
Ht: 6' 1" **Wt:** 204

Opening Day Age: 29
Born: 9/30/75 in Maracay, VZ
ML Seasons: 7
Pronunciation: GEY-un

Overall Statistics

	G	AB	R	H	D	T	HR	RBI	SB	BB	SO	Avg	OBP	Slg
'04	136	522	97	166	37	10	20	97	12	52	87	.318	.379	.542
Car.	624	2187	361	605	117	26	49	308	27	235	399	.277	.346	.421

Where He Hits the Ball

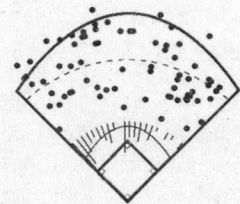 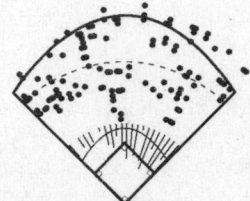

Vs. LHP   **Vs. RHP**

2004 Situational Stats

	AB	H	HR	RBI	Avg		AB	H	HR	RBI	Avg
Home	256	82	7	39	.320	LHP	197	53	6	35	.269
Road	266	84	13	58	.316	RHP	325	113	14	62	.348
First Half	330	107	13	65	.324	Sc Pos	132	41	5	77	.311
Scnd Half	192	59	7	32	.307	Clutch	76	19	0	11	.250

2004 Rankings (American League)

- 1st in batting average with the bases loaded (.667)
- 3rd in triples
- 6th in batting average and fielding percentage at shortstop (.974)
- Led the Tigers in runs scored, doubles, triples, total bases (283), RBI, times on base (220), plate appearances (583), slugging percentage, stolen-base percentage (70.6), batting average with the bases loaded (.667), and batting average vs. righthanded pitchers
- Led AL shortstops in batting average

Bobby Higginson

2004 Season

Bobby Higginson did not have a good season. He had a nice three-game series at Chicago in August where he tore up White Sox pitching with four home runs and 10 RBI. Take those games out of the equation and his lack of production offensively is even more alarming than it appears from his underwhelming overall statistics. From May on, Higginson had 46 RBI in 385 at-bats despite being in the middle of a potent lineup.

Hitting

There was a time when Higginson turned on low inside fastballs and drove them deep into the night. That time, however, has passed. His bat speed has slowed considerably. He is simply not the same hitter he was in 2000, when he had 30 home runs and 102 RBI while hitting .300. Higginson misses pitches he used to hit out. He seldom drives the ball and is not particularly effective using the entire field. He remains a patient hitter who will draw walks, and he does not strike out that much.

Baserunning & Defense

Higginson has below-average speed for a major league outfielder. However, he is a smart baserunner who does not run his team out of innings. Also, if the pitcher totally ignores him, he will steal second. Higginson has been playing right field the last two years. His best position, however, is left field. Despite his lack of speed, he gets a good jump and has average range, but he catches what he reaches. His arm strength and throwing accuracy remain above-average tools. He tied for the AL lead with 13 outfield assists in 2004.

2005 Outlook

Entering the final year of a five-year, $36 million contract, Higginson will get paid more than $8 million this season. He is nowhere near the caliber of player his salary suggests. He is not bad defensively and will put the ball in play at the plate, but that's all he offers at this point of his career.

Position: RF
Bats: L **Throws:** R
Ht: 5'11" **Wt:** 195

Opening Day Age: 34
Born: 8/18/70 in Philadelphia, PA
ML Seasons: 10

Overall Statistics

	G	AB	R	H	D	T	HR	RBI	SB	BB	SO	Avg	OBP	Slg
'04	131	448	63	110	24	2	12	64	5	70	84	.246	.353	.388
Car.	1352	4884	735	1334	270	33	187	708	91	648	791	.273	.359	.457

Where He Hits the Ball

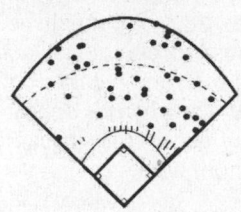 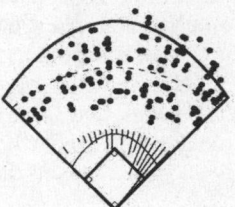

Vs. LHP   **Vs. RHP**

2004 Situational Stats

	AB	H	HR	RBI	Avg		AB	H	HR	RBI	Avg
Home	241	61	4	28	.253	LHP	116	27	0	16	.233
Road	207	49	8	36	.237	RHP	332	83	12	48	.250
First Half	255	66	5	37	.259	Sc Pos	112	33	3	50	.295
Scnd Half	193	44	7	27	.228	Clutch	65	14	1	3	.215

2004 Rankings (American League)

- 3rd in errors in right field (6), highest percentage of pitches taken (62.6) and lowest fielding percentage in right field (.975)
- 6th in lowest batting average and lowest batting average vs. righthanded pitchers
- Led the Tigers in walks, highest percentage of pitches taken (62.6), lowest percentage of swings that missed (11.6) and lowest percentage of swings on the first pitch (21.8)

Omar Infante

2004 Season

Following a dismal rookie season in 2003, Omar Infante was a long shot to make the major league club out of spring training. But after a good spring, he stuck as a utilityman. Then he received an opportunity in mid-May to play every day at second base when Fernando Vina was sidelined for the year by a hamstring injury. Infante responded by playing solid defense at second base, showing surprising power at the plate and establishing himself as a major league regular.

Hitting

Infante has gotten stronger. He has excellent bat speed and a quick trigger, and he likes fastballs up in the strike zone. That was the pitch most of his home runs were hit on. He still is an unpolished hitter when it comes to pitch recognition. Good pitchers who mix up their offerings continue to puzzle him, and there are times when he appears utterly confused at the plate. Those times became fewer as last season moved on, however.

Baserunning & Defense

Infante is an excellent athlete with exceptional range for a second baseman. He makes the play up the middle very well. He has sure hands and his concentration level in the field, so poor during 2003, has improved. He turns the double play equally well from second or short. He also played center field a couple times last season and was more than adequate. Infante has an average arm and always seems to be fighting off some kind of sore arm. He has above-average speed, but has yet to develop a knack for stealing bases.

2005 Outlook

Veteran Tigers shortstop Carlos Guillen has taken Infante under his wing, and the two have developed an excellent chemistry as a double-play combination. Infante's potential is unlimited. A downside is a history of back problems, but if those do not recur, Infante has chance to be a special player.

Position: 2B/SS/3B
Bats: R **Throws:** R
Ht: 6' 0" **Wt:** 176

Opening Day Age: 23
Born: 12/26/81 in Puerto la Cruz, VZ
ML Seasons: 3
Pronunciation: in-fahn-TAY

Overall Statistics

	G	AB	R	H	D	T	HR	RBI	SB	BB	SO	Avg	OBP	Slg
'04	142	503	69	133	27	9	16	55	13	40	112	.264	.317	.449
Car.	229	796	97	206	36	10	17	69	19	61	159	.259	.310	.393

Where He Hits the Ball

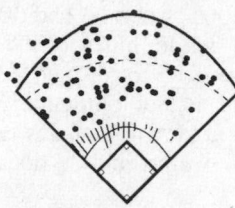
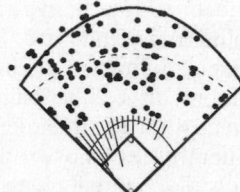

Vs. LHP   **Vs. RHP**

2004 Situational Stats

	AB	H	HR	RBI	Avg		AB	H	HR	RBI	Avg
Home	224	61	7	22	.272	LHP	188	52	5	20	.277
Road	279	72	9	33	.258	RHP	315	81	11	35	.257
First Half	214	61	7	28	.285	Sc Pos	114	30	3	38	.263
Scnd Half	289	72	9	27	.249	Clutch	75	21	2	5	.280

2004 Rankings (American League)

- 1st in lowest on-base percentage for a leadoff hitter (.271)
- 4th in triples and errors at second base (12)
- 7th in lowest on-base percentage
- 9th in lowest stolen-base percentage (65.0)
- 10th in lowest batting average with the bases loaded (.100) and lowest batting average with two strikes (.149)
- Led the Tigers in games played

Jason Johnson

2004 Season

Signed to a two-year, $7 million contract as a free agent prior to the season, Jason Johnson started to come on in June and July as if he was going to develop into the Tigers' No. 1 starter. He was remarkably consistent during those months, going 5-2 with a 2.95 ERA. However, as has been the case throughout his career, Johnson was not able to maintain his success. From the beginning of August until the close of the season, he was 0-7 with a 7.13 ERA, allowing 86 hits in 59.1 innings.

Pitching

Johnson has an above-average fastball. He usually pitches in the 92-MPH range, but will touch 94 MPH. His fastball has a sinking action to it, and he also has a straighter version he commands well. His breaking ball, a slider, is another good pitch and his changeup can be effective. "Stuff" is not an issue with Johnson. Durability is. He always seems to wear down. Some scouts think it is because he is a diabetic, although he is now allowed to wear an insulin pack when he pitches. Johnson also faces a constant struggle with blisters on the index finger of his pitching hand.

Defense

Johnson is poor athlete. He does not move well on the mound, and does not help himself out at all with the glove. He is a catcher's nightmare because he is slow to the plate and not athletic enough to display a quick, effective pickoff move.

2005 Outlook

Johnson presents a frustrating situation for his manager and pitching coach. There are times when what he brings with him to the mound is electric. But just when he is being counted on, his performance level drops considerably. It is why he will have a major league job deep into the future, but also likely why he never will pitch at the top of the rotation for a contending team.

Position: SP
Bats: R **Throws:** R
Ht: 6' 6" **Wt:** 217

Opening Day Age: 31
Born: 10/27/73 in Santa Barbara, CA
ML Seasons: 8

Overall Statistics

	W	L	Pct.	ERA	G	GS	Sv	IP	H	BB	SO	HR	Avg
'04	8	15	.348	5.13	33	33	0	196.2	222	60	125	22	.284
Car.	44	73	.376	4.95	182	166	0	1002.2	1096	402	643	139	.277

2004 Pitching Profile

	Jason Johnson	AL Average
Overall Strike %	64.5	62.3
1st Pitch Strike %	59.9	58.1
Ratio	1.43	1.42
Strikeouts per 9 IP	5.72	6.45
Walks per 9 IP	2.75	3.34
Home Runs per 9 IP	1.01	1.15
Strikeout/Walk Ratio	2.08	1.93
Groundball/Flyball Ratio	1.68	1.17

2004 Situational Stats

	W	L	ERA	Sv	IP		AB	H	HR	RBI	Avg
Home	4	10	5.98	0	105.1	LHB	430	121	10	56	.281
Road	4	5	4.14	0	91.1	RHB	353	101	12	47	.286
First Half	7	7	4.24	0	116.2	Sc Pos	172	59	4	74	.343
Scnd Half	1	8	6.41	0	80.0	Clutch	67	18	0	8	.269

2004 Rankings (American League)

- 2nd in highest ERA at home
- 3rd in losses
- 4th in lowest winning percentage, least run support per nine innings (4.2), highest batting average allowed with runners in scoring position and lowest fielding percentage at pitcher (.900)
- 7th in highest groundball-flyball ratio allowed (1.7)
- 8th in games started and complete games (2)
- 9th in highest stolen-base percentage allowed (78.6)
- 10th in GDPs induced (24) and highest ERA
- Led the Tigers in losses, games started, complete games (2), highest groundball-flyball ratio allowed (1.7), lowest ERA on the road and fewest home runs allowed per nine innings (1.01)

Detroit

Mike Maroth

2004 Season

After becoming the first major league pitcher in more than two decades to lose 20 games in a season in 2003, Mike Maroth found a level of consistency last year. He averaged nearly seven innings per start and did not have any real poor stretches during the season. He also benefited from improved run support. Maroth is not a dominant pitcher, but he did have a dominant performance, shutting out the Yankees on one hit during July. He did his best work early in the season and late in the season, and did not pitch all that bad during the span in between.

Pitching

Maroth does not have an overpowering arm, and his typical fastball sits at 86 MPH. What he does is throw four pitches—two- and four-seam fastballs, a curveball and a change—each of which he commands well. His changeup and two-seamer are his best offerings. He uses his changeup as an out pitch. The key for him is getting ahead early in the count with his fastball so he can set up his change. He uses his two-seamer as a cutter to work inside against righthanded hitters. Maroth locates the ball well early in the count. He throws strikes, but does not throw the ball over the heart of the plate often. He also has an exceptional mental makeup. Losing 21 games in 2003 only made him a better pitcher, and he bounces back quickly from bad outings.

Defense

Maroth moves well around the mound and is surehanded. He is overall a good fielder. He takes advantage of being lefthanded with a good pickoff move to first.

2005 Outlook

Maroth is one of those pitchers who proves that radar-gun readings often are misleading. In the minors, when he struggled, he threw 90 MPH consistently. He does not throw that hard anymore because it is counterproductive for him to do so. What he does understand is the art of upsetting the timing of a hitter, and he is getting better at it every year.

Position: SP
Bats: L **Throws:** L
Ht: 6' 0" **Wt:** 190

Opening Day Age: 27
Born: 8/17/77 in Orlando, FL
ML Seasons: 3
Pronunciation: mah-ROTH

Overall Statistics

	W	L	Pct.	ERA	G	GS	Sv	IP	H	BB	SO	HR	Avg
'04	11	13	.458	4.31	33	33	0	217.0	244	59	108	25	.288
Car.	26	44	.371	4.86	87	87	0	539.0	611	145	253	66	.289

2004 Pitching Profile

	Mike Maroth	AL Average
Overall Strike %	61.0	62.3
1st Pitch Strike %	60.7	58.1
Ratio	1.40	1.42
Strikeouts per 9 IP	4.48	6.45
Walks per 9 IP	2.45	3.34
Home Runs per 9 IP	1.04	1.15
Strikeout/Walk Ratio	1.83	1.93
Groundball/Flyball Ratio	1.38	1.17

2004 Situational Stats

	W	L	ERA	Sv	IP		AB	H	HR	RBI	Avg
Home	6	3	3.14	0	97.1	LHB	195	52	4	13	.267
Road	5	10	5.26	0	119.2	RHB	652	192	21	79	.294
First Half	5	7	5.02	0	113.0	Sc Pos	207	54	9	68	.261
Scnd Half	6	6	3.55	0	104.0	Clutch	56	14	0	5	.250

2004 Rankings (American League)

- 1st in fielding percentage at pitcher (1.000)
- 2nd in runners caught stealing (11)
- 5th in hits allowed, batters faced (928) and fewest strikeouts per nine innings (4.5)
- 6th in losses, innings pitched and lowest ERA at home
- 7th in GDPs induced (27)
- 8th in games started, complete games (2), wild pitches (10) and pickoff throws (129)
- 9th in fewest pitches thrown per batter (3.60)
- Led the Tigers in ERA, games started, complete games (2), innings pitched, hits allowed, batters faced (928), pitches thrown (3,344), pickoff throws (129), runners caught stealing (11), GDPs induced (27), lowest stolen-base percentage allowed (50.0), fewest pitches thrown per batter (3.60) and fewest walks per nine innings (2.4)

Craig Monroe

2004 Season

After getting off to a disappointing start, Craig Monroe closed with a flurry. He went on the 15-day disabled list July 21 because of a strained hamstring muscle but returned in early August and put together two strong months to close the season. In his final 188 at-bats, Monroe hit .314 with 14 home runs and 38 RBI. After playing mostly left-field with the Tigers, he saw much of his duty in center field late in the season because Alex Sanchez was injured.

Hitting

Monroe is a pull hitter. Every one of his home runs and most of his extra-base hits last season were to center field or left field. He hooks the ball foul too much and tries to pull outside pitches. He can be worked effectively around the strike zone because he does not take the ball the other way. Monroe does have a lot of power and will drive mistake pitches deep into the left-field stands. He was more patient at the plate and struck out less after he returned from the DL in August.

Baserunning & Defense

Although he made a lot of errors last season, Monroe is an average major league outfielder. He gets a good jump on the ball and has some speed. It gives him slightly better-than-average range for a corner outfielder. He is fluid in his movements for a strong player. His arm is average in terms of strength and accuracy, and he throws to the right base. He is not an ideal center fielder but can play the position adequately over an extended period. Early in his minor league career, Monroe stole a lot of bases, but he rarely has been asked to steal in the major leagues.

2005 Outlook

Monroe has enough tools to play regularly in the bigs. Coming off a 23-homer performance in 2003, his start last season was disappointing. The way he closed 2004 was encouraging, however. It will be important for Monroe to open this season the way he closed 2004.

Position: LF/RF/CF
Bats: R **Throws:** R
Ht: 6' 1" **Wt:** 220

Opening Day Age: 28
Born: 2/27/77 in Texarkana, TX
ML Seasons: 4

Overall Statistics

	G	AB	R	H	D	T	HR	RBI	SB	BB	SO	Avg	OBP	Slg
'04	128	447	65	131	27	3	18	72	3	29	79	.293	.337	.488
Car.	296	949	127	247	47	4	44	148	9	62	191	.260	.307	.457

Where He Hits the Ball

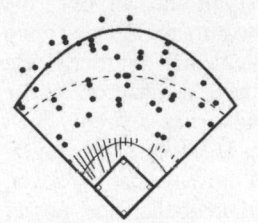
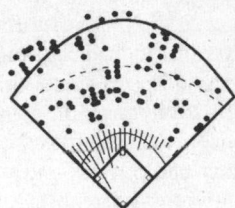

Vs. LHP   **Vs. RHP**

2004 Situational Stats

	AB	H	HR	RBI	Avg		AB	H	HR	RBI	Avg
Home	220	67	9	28	.305	LHP	160	41	5	21	.256
Road	227	64	9	44	.282	RHP	287	90	13	51	.314
First Half	251	68	3	32	.271	Sc Pos	115	30	5	48	.261
Scnd Half	196	63	15	40	.321	Clutch	58	16	1	12	.276

2004 Rankings (American League)

- 1st in errors in left field (8)
- 6th in errors in right field (3)

Carlos Pena

Position: 1B
Bats: L **Throws:** L
Ht: 6' 2" **Wt:** 215

Opening Day Age: 26
Born: 5/17/78 in Santo Domingo, DR
ML Seasons: 4
Pronunciation: PAIN-yuh

2004 Season

Carlos Pena closed last season by hitting 14 homers and driving in 29 runs during his final 52 games. It made his overall power and run production look better than the impact it actually had on his club throughout the season. When the Tigers surprisingly found themselves on the fringes of contention in the American League Central, Pena often was benched. Raising his batting average was a struggle. He did drive in a lot of runs early in the season, but he slumped badly in the middle.

Hitting

Pena does not have a quick bat. There were times last season when he could not handle even an average major league fastball thrown over the heart of the plate. But throw him an offspeed pitch without much on it, and Pena will murder it. He has good power and will drive the ball out of the park to right field. Pena also has a pretty good concept of the strike zone. He does not swing at many bad pitches and will draw walks. However, he swings through a lot of fastballs most power hitters drive with authority.

Baserunning & Defense

When the Tigers acquired Pena from Oakland early in the 2002 season, one of the major reasons was his fielding. Supposedly he was a great fielder. It has not turned out that way. In 2003, he was awful defensively. He made 13 errors, often on routine plays. Last season, Pena was better in the field, cutting his errors to six and making far fewer mental mistakes. Although he still has a ways to go to match his advance billing defensively, Pena was more than adequate last season. He has below-average speed, but seems to be making better decisions on the bases.

2005 Outlook

Pena's future looked bleak until his power surge late last season. He needs to display that kind of power earlier this year—when the games mean something to his team in regard to the standings—in order to solidify his spot as a regular.

Overall Statistics

	G	AB	R	H	D	T	HR	RBI	SB	BB	SO	Avg	OBP	Slg
'04	142	481	89	116	22	4	27	82	7	70	146	.241	.338	.472
Car.	410	1392	189	340	64	15	67	196	13	174	397	.244	.331	.456

Where He Hits the Ball

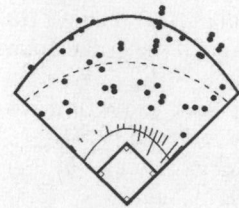 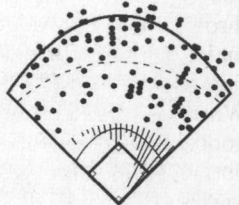

Vs. LHP   **Vs. RHP**

2004 Situational Stats

	AB	H	HR	RBI	Avg		AB	H	HR	RBI	Avg
Home	236	60	10	43	.254	LHP	147	36	8	30	.245
Road	245	56	17	39	.229	RHP	334	80	19	52	.240
First Half	257	60	11	47	.233	Sc Pos	119	28	5	52	.235
Scnd Half	224	56	16	35	.250	Clutch	65	13	5	13	.200

2004 Rankings (American League)

- 2nd in lowest percentage of swings put into play (32.7)
- 3rd in strikeouts, highest percentage of swings that missed (27.8), lowest batting average vs. righthanded pitchers and lowest batting average with two strikes (.133)
- 4th in errors at first base (6), lowest batting average and lowest batting average on the road
- 6th in fielding percentage at first base (.995)
- Led the Tigers in home runs, walks, strikeouts, pitches seen (2,271), games played and most pitches seen per plate appearance (4.04)

Nate Robertson

2004 Season

Nate Robertson entered last season just a handful of innings shy of being eligible for rookie status, but early in the year he pitched like a veteran. He anchored the Tigers' surprisingly good start by compiling a 9-4 record through July 18. Robertson hit a wall after that, struggling to get through five innings in several starts. A low point came when he had a nasty verbal confrontation with catcher Ivan Rodriguez in Anaheim on August 14. He did win three straight decisions after the incident, and his dozen wins led the staff.

Pitching

Robertson has a good fastball that is in the low 90s most of the time. His slider is another pitch he throws with good velocity. It is an above-average major league pitch and makes him capable of getting righthanded hitters out on a consistent basis. What he struggles with is finishing. He starts out good in many games, but then can wear down during the later innings. Robertson has a tendency to elevate his fastball as the game goes on, and he gets hit hard. There is a certain lack of consistency Robertson displays that is maddening. He also needs to gain a better grip on his emotions and handle success better.

Defense

Robertson hurt himself defensively last season. He does not move well on the mound, has poor hands and his concentration tends to wane. In just 34 chances, he made five errors. He also needs to do a better job of holding runners.

2005 Outlook

What Robertson did last season was open eyes. Despite his arm strength, he never really had been considered much of a prospect as a minor leaguer. That perception changed last season. He was able to establish himself as a legitimate major league starter. To keep himself out of the bullpen, Robertson will have to prove he can repeat pitches later in games and repeat good performances later in the season.

Position: SP
Bats: R **Throws:** L
Ht: 6' 2" **Wt:** 215

Opening Day Age: 27
Born: 9/3/77 in Wichita, KS
ML Seasons: 3

Overall Statistics

	W	L	Pct.	ERA	G	GS	Sv	IP	H	BB	SO	HR	Avg
'04	12	10	.545	4.90	34	32	1	196.2	210	66	155	30	.274
Car.	13	13	.500	5.23	48	41	1	249.2	280	93	191	39	.284

2004 Pitching Profile

	Nate Robertson	AL Average
Overall Strike %	63.2	62.3
1st Pitch Strike %	56.9	58.1
Ratio	1.40	1.42
Strikeouts per 9 IP	7.09	6.45
Walks per 9 IP	3.02	3.34
Home Runs per 9 IP	1.37	1.15
Strikeout/Walk Ratio	2.35	1.93
Groundball/Flyball Ratio	1.67	1.17

2004 Situational Stats

	W	L	ERA	Sv	IP		AB	H	HR	RBI	Avg
Home	6	7	5.19	0	102.1	LHB	143	36	2	21	.252
Road	6	3	4.58	1	94.1	RHB	623	174	28	87	.279
First Half	8	4	4.11	1	105.0	Sc Pos	166	50	4	70	.301
Scnd Half	4	6	5.79	0	91.2	Clutch	44	11	1	4	.250

2004 Rankings (American League)

- 1st in lowest fielding percentage at pitcher (.853)
- 2nd in errors at pitcher (5)
- 7th in GDPs induced (27)
- 8th in highest groundball-flyball ratio allowed (1.7) and highest ERA at home
- 9th in most run support per nine innings (6.4)
- Led the Tigers in wins, home runs allowed, GDPs induced (27), winning percentage, highest strikeout-walk ratio (2.3) and lowest stolen-base percentage allowed (50.0)

Ivan Rodriguez

2004 Season

After signing a complicated four-year contract full of incentives and escape clauses that could be worth as much as $40 million eventually, Ivan Rodriguez made everyone wonder why the Tigers were his only real suitors. At the All-Star break, he was hitting .369 with 12 home runs and 59 RBI. In June, he was incredible, hitting .500. After the break, Pudge hit .284 with seven home runs and 27 RBI. He suffered a hip flexor strain in July, a month where he hit just .244, and he banged up his knee in early September. Neither injury forced him out of the lineup for an extended period, but they hindered his play.

Hitting

Rodriguez appears to be one of those hitters who will be better in his mid-30s than he was in his mid-20s. He is stronger than he used to be and pulls the ball with power more often than he used to. Yet, he still uses the entire field with his inside-out swing. Rodriguez has excellent plate coverage and recognizes pitches particularly well.

Baserunning & Defense

Rodriguez, who won his 11th Gold Glove last season, has a strong, accurate arm and moves well behind the plate. His percentage throwing out basestealers, 28.6 last season and 32.2 in 2003, has dropped from the days when he routinely threw out more than 50 percent. Part of that is not being quite the same receiver he used to be. Part also is attributed to a pitching staff that does not hold runners well. Rodriguez' pitch calls still come into question at times, although the Tigers' and Marlins' staffs both improved with him behind the plate. He is not a threat to steal, but Rodriguez still runs well for a catcher.

2005 Outlook

Rodriguez has blown away any notion he is going to hit some sort of wall in his early 30s. He remains an elite player who through 14 big league seasons has produced nice round totals of 250 homers, 1,000 RBI and 400 walks.

Position: C
Bats: R **Throws:** R
Ht: 5' 9" **Wt:** 218

Opening Day Age: 33
Born: 11/30/71 in Vega Baja, PR
ML Seasons: 14
Pronunciation: rod-RI-gez
Nickname: Pudge

Overall Statistics

G	AB	R	H	D	T	HR	RBI	SB	BB	SO	Avg	OBP	Slg
135	527	72	176	32	2	19	86	7	41	91	.334	.383	.510
1758	6694	1014	2051	412	33	250	1000	97	400	946	.306	.347	.490

Where He Hits the Ball

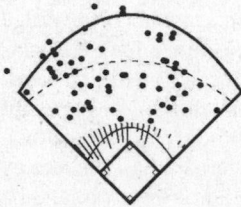

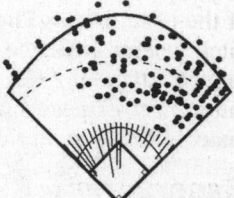

Vs. LHP   **Vs. RHP**

2004 Situational Stats

	AB	H	HR	RBI	Avg		AB	H	HR	RBI	Avg
Home	243	86	7	40	.354	LHP	175	60	5	30	.343
Road	284	90	12	46	.317	RHP	352	116	14	56	.330
First Half	312	115	12	59	.369	Sc Pos	133	48	5	67	.361
Scnd Half	215	61	7	27	.284	Clutch	74	18	2	6	.243

2004 Rankings (American League)

- 1st in errors at catcher (11)
- 2nd in batting average with runners in scoring position, batting average at home and lowest fielding percentage at catcher (.987)
- 3rd in fewest pitches seen per plate appearance (3.44) and lowest percentage of pitches taken (46.0)
- 4th in batting average
- 5th in batting average vs. lefthanded pitchers
- 8th in batting average on the road
- Led the Tigers in batting average, at-bats, hits, singles, intentional walks (6), times on base (220), GDPs (15), on-base percentage, batting average with runners in scoring position, batting average at home, batting average on the road and batting average with two strikes (.227)

Rondell White

2004 Season

A free agent who signed a two-year, $6 million contract to play with his sixth team in five seasons, Rondell White started out quickly and faded fast. During the first six weeks of the 2004 campaign, White had seven home runs and 30 RBI. But over the final 18 weeks of the season, he had just 12 home runs and 37 RBI. In mid-May, his batting average was .331. By the end of the year, it was .270. He also missed some time in September with a strained hip flexor.

Hitting

White has an exceptionally quick bat. He murders fastballs on the inner half of the strike zone, and he jumps at mediocre fastballs that cross the heart of the plate. He also has good power. If he gets a pitch where he likes it, White is capable of driving the ball a long way. Although a better fastball hitter than offspeed hitter, he still is the consummate professional at the plate.

Baserunning & Defense

Although he was used extensively in left field last season, on a good team White is strictly a designated hitter. His throwing arm probably is the weakest of any major league outfielder in recent memory. Opposing teams run on his arm at will. He lacks range, especially on balls hit directly over his head. His eight assists over the past two seasons are offset by eight errors. Despite knee problems and advancing age, White has average speed on the bases.

2005 Outlook

There is a role for White in the major leagues, but it is not as an outfielder. He can be the regular DH on a winning club, but it is not a good sign for a club when he is playing in the outfield. Teams keep trading for or signing White because they like his bat, but the honeymoon is often short because of his struggles in the field.

Position: LF/DH
Bats: R **Throws:** R
Ht: 6' 1" **Wt:** 225

Opening Day Age: 33
Born: 2/23/72 in Milledgeville, GA
ML Seasons: 12

Overall Statistics

	G	AB	R	H	D	T	HR	RBI	SB	BB	SO	Avg	OBP	Slg
'04	121	448	76	121	21	2	19	67	1	39	77	.270	.337	.453
Car.	1240	4537	667	1300	251	30	175	657	92	326	804	.287	.342	.471

Where He Hits the Ball

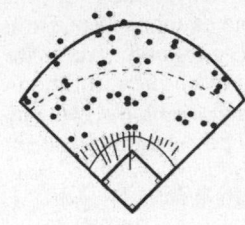
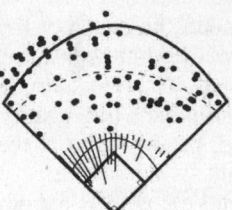

Vs. LHP   **Vs. RHP**

2004 Situational Stats

	AB	H	HR	RBI	Avg		AB	H	HR	RBI	Avg
Home	213	49	5	26	.230	LHP	157	46	3	19	.293
Road	235	72	14	41	.306	RHP	291	75	16	48	.258
First Half	299	83	12	49	.278	Sc Pos	121	39	4	48	.322
Scnd Half	149	38	7	18	.255	Clutch	69	13	2	9	.188

2004 Rankings (American League)

- 6th in errors in left field (3)
- 10th in lowest batting average in the clutch
- Led the Tigers in hit by pitch (8) and cleanup slugging percentage (.491)

Dmitri Young

2004 Season

In the second game, Dmitri Young suffered a broken bone in his lower right leg while making a tag play at first base. The injury put him on the disabled list until May 31. When he returned, Young put together a season typical of his past performances. His batting average was 21 points lower than his career mark, but his other numbers matched up in just about every other way across the board when the nearly two months he missed is considered.

Hitting

A switch-hitter, Young has fast hands and loves to jump on first-pitch fastballs. His hand-eye coordination is excellent. For a hitter who does not walk much, he does not strike out much, either. He is balanced in his stance and covers both side of the plate well. He takes the ball to all different fields. Young is a better hitter lefthanded than righthanded, but he might have more power righthanded.

Baserunning & Defense

Young has gotten bigger with age, but he remains a good athlete. Last season, he was thrust mostly in the role of DH upon his return from the disabled list. His best position is first base—he did not make an error there in 25 games last season. In 2003, Young played 61 games in the outfield, but last season, because he was coming off a leg injury, it was just two. He is a below-average outfielder, but he will make the routine play and throw to the right base. Young's worst position is third. Putting him there is a stretch at this stage of his career. He has below-average speed, but he is a smart baserunner who runs hard at all times.

2005 Outlook

Young is entering the fourth year of a four-year, $28.5 million contract. As he gets older, he seems to be getting categorized more as a DH. It probably will be his primary role this season. Yet, he still is capable of playing every day at first base, and in the outfield for shorter periods if needed.

Position: DH/1B
Bats: B **Throws:** R
Ht: 6' 2" **Wt:** 245

Opening Day Age: 31
Born: 10/11/73 in Vicksburg, MS
ML Seasons: 9

Overall Statistics

	G	AB	R	H	D	T	HR	RBI	SB	BB	SO	Avg	OBP	Slg
'04	104	389	72	106	23	2	18	60	0	33	71	.272	.336	.481
Car.	1004	3511	496	1030	228	24	126	504	23	295	630	.293	.351	.480

Where He Hits the Ball

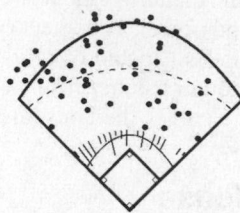 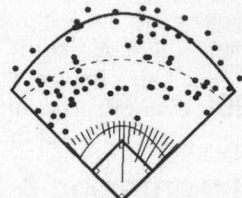

Vs. LHP　　　　**Vs. RHP**

2004 Situational Stats

	AB	H	HR	RBI	Avg		AB	H	HR	RBI	Avg
Home	196	49	8	28	.250	LHP	137	34	8	23	.248
Road	193	57	10	32	.295	RHP	252	72	10	37	.286
First Half	129	38	6	21	.295	Sc Pos	107	24	5	40	.224
Scnd Half	260	68	12	39	.262	Clutch	52	12	3	7	.231

2004 Rankings (American League)

- 9th in lowest batting average with runners in scoring position

Nate Cornejo

Position: SP
Bats: R **Throws:** R
Ht: 6' 5" **Wt:** 245

Opening Day Age: 25
Born: 9/24/79 in Wellington, KS
ML Seasons: 4
Pronunciation: cor-NAY-ho

Overall Statistics

	W	L	Pct.	ERA	G	GS	Sv	IP	H	BB	SO	HR	Avg
'04	1	3	.250	8.42	5	5	0	25.2	42	11	12	4	.375
Car.	12	29	.293	5.41	56	56	0	313.0	404	115	103	38	.318

2004 Situational Stats

	W	L	ERA	Sv	IP		AB	H	HR	RBI	Avg
Home	1	2	6.06	0	16.1	LHB	62	23	4	10	.371
Road	0	1	12.54	0	9.1	RHB	50	19	0	8	.380
First Half	1	3	8.42	0	25.2	Sc Pos	31	11	0	12	.355
Scnd Half	0	0	-	0	0.0	Clutch	5	2	1	1	.400

2004 Season

Nate Cornejo won his first start, but did not win another decision and was routinely shelled until being placed on the 15-day DL on May 5 because of inflammation in his right shoulder. On June 27, he was moved to the 60-day DL, and he eventually had surgery to repair a slight tear in the labrum.

Pitching & Defense

When he won 20 games combined at the Double-A, Triple-A and major league levels in 2001, Cornejo consistently hit 92 MPH with his fastball, topping out at 94. That was with a nasty sinking action that drew comparisons to Kevin Brown. He also featured a late-breaking slider he commanded well. The Tigers then-coaching staff changed the grip on his breaking ball and he has never recaptured its effectiveness, even when going with his old grip. His velocity was down to the low to mid-80s last season. Even for a groundball pitcher, it is alarming how few bats he misses. Cornejo is an excellent athlete with a quick pick-off move that is one of the best among righthanded pitchers in baseball.

2005 Outlook

Cornejo, expected to fully recover by the start of spring training, must regain his velocity. Otherwise his major league career will be short.

Brandon Inge

Position: 3B/C/CF
Bats: R **Throws:** R
Ht: 5'11" **Wt:** 195

Opening Day Age: 27
Born: 5/19/77 in Lynchburg, VA
ML Seasons: 4
Pronunciation: inj

Overall Statistics

	G	AB	R	H	D	T	HR	RBI	SB	BB	SO	Avg	OBP	Slg
'04	131	408	43	117	15	7	13	64	5	32	72	.287	.340	.453
Car.	409	1248	115	283	56	13	28	133	11	89	293	.227	.283	.360

2004 Situational Stats

	AB	H	HR	RBI	Avg		AB	H	HR	RBI	Avg
Home	213	58	9	36	.272	LHP	168	55	7	27	.327
Road	195	59	4	28	.303	RHP	240	62	6	37	.258
First Half	165	50	7	30	.303	Sc Pos	109	31	3	49	.284
Scnd Half	243	67	6	34	.276	Clutch	53	10	2	6	.189

2004 Season

Scheduled to be the Tigers' catcher before they signed Ivan Rodriguez, Brandon Inge, a shortstop and bullpen closer in college at Virginia Commonwealth, made the best of the situation. During the season, he caught 39 games, played in the outfield and ended the season as the regular third baseman. He also emerged as a hitter, with production not thought possible considering his .198 career average entering 2004.

Hitting, Baserunning & Defense

Inge is small in stature, but strong and athletic. He stopped tinkering and went with "a see the ball, hit the ball" approach at the plate last season. Inge is a good fastball hitter, but he struggles mightily against righthanders with good offspeed pitches. Inge is gifted defensively, both at catcher and third base. He has an exceptional arm and quick feet, and made several brilliant plays at third last season. He is an adequate outfielder and has average speed.

2005 Outlook

Inge's greatest value is as a catcher, but not in Detroit with Rodriguez blocking his way. If Inge hits like he did last season, it is more than good enough for him to be a regular third baseman. But is it wise to tie him to a position other than catcher when he is so versatile?

Detroit

Gary Knotts

Position: SP/RP
Bats: R **Throws:** R
Ht: 6' 4" **Wt:** 230

Opening Day Age: 28
Born: 2/12/77 in
Decatur, AL
ML Seasons: 4

Overall Statistics

	W	L	Pct.	ERA	G	GS	Sv	IP	H	BB	SO	HR	Avg
'04	7	6	.538	5.25	36	19	2	135.1	142	58	81	20	.267
Car.	13	16	.448	5.45	86	38	2	267.1	281	122	162	41	.267

2004 Situational Stats

	W	L	ERA	Sv	IP			AB	H	HR	RBI	Avg
Home	5	2	5.25	1	73.2	LHB		270	58	11	37	.215
Road	2	4	5.25	1	61.2	RHB		261	84	9	38	.322
First Half	5	3	5.06	0	80.0	Sc Pos		105	39	5	56	.371
Scnd Half	2	3	5.53	2	55.1	Clutch		27	8	1	1	.296

2004 Season

Gary Knotts had a rough stretch in July, after which he was placed on the 15-day disabled list because of a shoulder ailment. Before and after that period, he pitched relatively well while moving in and out of Detroit's starting rotation. Upon returning from the disabled list, Knotts pitched out of bullpen. Then he was moved back into the starting rotation in September, but manager Alan Trammell had a quick hook with him. That was until his final two starts, decisions Knotts won.

Pitching & Defense

Knotts has three pitches that are at least average for the major league level. His fastball is consistently at 92-93 MPH. He has a good curveball in terms of depth and bite and a respectable change-up. The key for Knotts is locating his fastball. If he does that, he starts dropping his curveball and changeup on hitters late in the count and becomes effective. Knotts is slow to the plate and does not have a good pickoff move. He has slow reactions as a fielder.

2005 Outlook

Knotts is an emotional sort who must control those emotions better to get full use of his tools. His future may be in the bullpen. How he reacts to that move may decide his fate.

Wilfredo Ledezma

Position: SP
Bats: L **Throws:** L
Ht: 6' 4" **Wt:** 212

Opening Day Age: 24
Born: 1/21/81 in
Guarico, VZ
ML Seasons: 2

Overall Statistics

	W	L	Pct.	ERA	G	GS	Sv	IP	H	BB	SO	HR	Avg
'04	4	3	.571	4.39	15	8	0	53.1	55	18	29	3	.272
Car.	7	10	.412	5.24	49	16	0	137.1	154	53	78	15	.288

2004 Situational Stats

	W	L	ERA	Sv	IP			AB	H	HR	RBI	Avg
Home	1	2	4.85	0	26.0	LHB		44	10	0	8	.227
Road	3	1	3.95	0	27.1	RHB		158	45	3	20	.285
First Half	0	0	–	0	0.0	Sc Pos		52	18	1	26	.346
Scnd Half	4	3	4.39	0	53.1	Clutch		8	2	0	3	.250

2004 Season

After spending the entire 2003 season in the major leagues because he was a Rule 5 draft choice from Boston's organization, Wilfredo Ledezma was placed at Double-A Erie to begin last season. He dominated the Eastern League with a 10-3 record. The Tigers called him back to Detroit in mid-July and he more than held his own, though his starts and innings were limited in the major leagues to prevent Ledezma from being overworked.

Pitching & Defense

Ledezma has an excellent fastball. He not only throws it between 92-95 MPH, but he cuts across the ball with his fingers so it tails in on lefthanded hitters. His changeup is another top-of-the-line pitch that he uses effectively against righthanded batters. The Tigers kept Ledezma in the minor leagues so long last season so he could develop a better breaking ball. It is more of a slurve than anything else, and he did use it successfully in the major leagues last season.

2005 Outlook

Unless he falls on his face during spring training, Ledezma is slated to be part of the Tigers' starting rotation. With his solid makeup and arm, it is not out of the realm of possibility that he will be a top-of-the-rotation starter someday.

Eric Munson

Position: 3B
Bats: L **Throws:** R
Ht: 6' 3" **Wt:** 225

Opening Day Age: 27
Born: 10/3/77 in San Diego, CA
ML Seasons: 5

Overall Statistics

	G	AB	R	H	D	T	HR	RBI	SB	BB	SO	Avg	OBP	Slg
'04	109	321	36	68	14	2	19	49	1	29	90	.212	.289	.445
Car.	246	764	71	164	26	3	40	111	4	73	184	.215	.287	.414

2004 Situational Stats

	AB	H	HR	RBI	Avg		AB	H	HR	RBI	Avg
Home	164	38	13	34	.232	LHP	66	15	5	13	.227
Road	157	30	6	15	.191	RHP	255	53	14	36	.208
First Half	202	47	12	34	.233	Sc Pos	76	20	6	31	.263
Scnd Half	119	21	7	15	.176	Clutch	45	10	3	7	.222

2004 Season

There were moments when Eric Munson was brilliant. He hit a 457-foot home run to straightaway center field at Comerica Park to win a June game against Arizona. He also turned on a Johan Santana fastball, driving a two-run homer to right in a 2-0 victory over Minnesota in July. Those moments were few and far between. Mostly Munson slumped. He lost his starting third-base spot to Brandon Inge and was bypassed on the depth chart at first base by Carlos Pena.

Hitting, Baserunning & Defense

Munson is a mystery. He has an exceptionally quick bat and extraordinary power. But his plate coverage is poor. He swings at too many bad pitches and does not take the ball to the opposite field enough. A catcher in college at USC, Munson is a below-average fielder. His range is lacking at both corner infield positions. His arm is erratic, and he is a slow runner.

2005 Outlook

A lot of people have waited a long time for Munson, the third overall pick in the 1999 draft, to break loose. It simply has not happened. He offers little defensively, so he has to hit to be in the lineup. So far, he has not hit, so his future is uncertain.

Alex Sanchez (Great Speed)

Position: CF
Bats. L **Throws:** L
Ht: 5'10" **Wt:** 180

Opening Day Age: 28
Born: 8/26/76 in Havana, Cuba
ML Seasons: 4

Overall Statistics

	G	AB	R	H	D	T	HR	RBI	SB	BB	SO	Avg	OBP	Slg
'04	79	332	41	107	9	3	2	26	19	7	50	.322	.335	.386
Car.	365	1351	161	395	45	20	4	95	114	68	199	.292	.327	.364

2004 Situational Stats

	AB	H	HR	RBI	Avg		AB	H	HR	RBI	Avg
Home	158	52	1	7	.329	LHP	141	49	1	15	.348
Road	174	55	1	19	.316	RHP	191	58	1	11	.304
First Half	292	95	2	23	.325	Sc Pos	60	18	0	22	.300
Scnd Half	40	12	0	3	.300	Clutch	48	14	1	5	.292

2004 Season

Alex Sanchez got off to a fast start. Then he strained his right hamstring muscle and his production dropped sharply. He was placed on the disabled list in early July. He returned later in the month, but by August 9 his season was over because of a strained right quadriceps.

Hitting, Baserunning & Defense

Sanchez has much better than average speed and tries to take advantage of it by playing small ball. He is an excellent bunter and always is a threat to lay one down. He slaps the ball the other way. He is not an ideal leadoff hitter despite his speed and bunting ability because he does not draw walks. He is wildly inconsistent as a center fielder. Sanchez will make some good plays, but he is mostly a miscue about to occur. There were numerous times in 2004 when he did not get to balls because of poor jumps or wayward routes. He also has poor instincts on the bases.

2005 Outlook

Sanchez is eligible for arbitration for the first time and would be due a huge raise from the $385,000 he made last season. Because he is so hauntingly inconsistent, he may have trouble finding someone willing to give him that raise.

Marcus Thames

Position: LF/RF
Bats: R **Throws:** R
Ht: 6' 2" **Wt:** 205

Opening Day Age: 28
Born: 3/6/77 in Louisville, MS
ML Seasons: 3
Pronunciation: timms

Overall Statistics

	G	AB	R	H	D	T	HR	RBI	SB	BB	SO	Avg	OBP	Slg
'04	61	165	24	42	12	0	10	33	0	16	42	.255	.326	.509
Car.	98	251	38	60	15	0	12	39	0	24	64	.239	.313	.442

2004 Situational Stats

	AB	H	HR	RBI	Avg		AB	H	HR	RBI	Avg
Home	68	20	5	18	.294	LHP	81	23	6	17	.284
Road	97	22	5	15	.227	RHP	84	19	4	16	.226
First Half	39	8	2	3	.205	Sc Pos	37	15	3	25	.405
Scnd Half	126	34	8	30	.270	Clutch	25	5	2	3	.200

2004 Season

Marcus Thames got off to an incredibly productive start at Triple-A Toledo. It forced Detroit to call him up, and he played his first game June 22. He proceeded to go 1-for-20 until hitting a home run at Colorado. It was the first of six home runs in 42 at-bats for Thames. He was used mostly against lefthanded starters after he cooled down in late July.

Hitting, Baserunning & Defense

Thames has one good tool. It is power. He is capable of driving the ball a long way. He is an odd hitter in that many times he does nothing with fastballs that pierce the heart of the plate. Yet, he will drive an offspeed pitch out of the strike zone at odd times. He does not draw many walks and is a free swinger who strikes out a lot. Defensively, Thames is an average corner outfielder. He plays hard, will catch most of what he reaches and he throws to the right base. He does not run well.

2005 Outlook

Thames was exposed when he got hot last season and pitchers worked him more carefully. At best, he's a backup outfielder who provides power at times. At worst, he had his 15 minutes of fame last season.

Ugueth Urbina

Position: RP
Bats: R **Throws:** R
Ht: 6' 0" **Wt:** 205

Opening Day Age: 31
Born: 2/15/74 in Caracas, VZ
ML Seasons: 10
Pronunciation: oo-get oor-bee-NAH

Overall Statistics

	W	L	Pct.	ERA	G	GS	Sv	IP	H	BB	SO	HR	Avg
'04	4	6	.400	4.50	54	0	21	54.0	38	32	56	7	.194
Car.	39	43	.476	3.42	502	21	227	617.2	483	268	717	74	.212

2004 Situational Stats

	W	L	ERA	Sv	IP		AB	H	HR	RBI	Avg
Home	3	3	3.77	12	28.2	LHB	89	17	2	15	.191
Road	1	3	5.33	9	25.1	RHB	107	21	5	14	.196
First Half	3	3	4.63	14	35.0	Sc Pos	54	11	3	24	.204
Scnd Half	1	3	4.26	7	19.0	Clutch	131	23	4	19	.176

2004 Season

After drawing limited interest on the free-agent market, Ugueth Urbina signed a one-year, $3.5 million contract with Detroit in late March. Less than a month later, he became the Tigers' closer and converted 21-of-24 save opportunities. Urbina's season came to unfortunate end the first week of September when his mother was kidnapped in his native Venezuela and he left the team.

Pitching & Defense

Urbina is a much different pitcher than early in his career when he was a hard-thrower with Montreal. Now his fastball is from 88-90 MPH. He shoots for the corners early in the count to set up his slider and changeup, which are both excellent pitches, late in the count. Urbina's mindset is his great strength. He does not give in to hitters. It's why he yields so few hits and strikes out such a high ratio of hitters despite a mediocre fastball, and why he walks a lot of hitters.

2005 Outlook

While he no longer lights up the radar gun, Urbina still is a serviceable major league closer. He is crafty and unafraid. The Tigers picked up their $4 million option on Urbina's contract for 2005 before signing Troy Percival to close. Urbina could set up or be traded.

Jamie Walker

Position: RP
Bats: L **Throws:** L
Ht: 6' 2" **Wt:** 195

Opening Day Age: 33
Born: 7/1/71 in
McMinnville, TN
ML Seasons: 5

Overall Statistics

	W	L	Pct.	ERA	G	GS	Sv	IP	H	BB	SO	HR	Avg
'04	3	4	.429	3.20	70	0	1	64.2	69	12	53	8	.263
Car.	11	12	.478	4.24	261	2	5	233.2	238	61	177	37	.259

2004 Situational Stats

	W	L	ERA	Sv	IP		AB	H	HR	RBI	Avg
Home	2	0	2.06	1	35.0	LHB	115	23	1	12	.200
Road	1	4	4.55	0	29.2	RHB	147	46	7	24	.313
First Half	1	3	3.15	0	34.1	Sc Pos	89	21	1	26	.236
Scnd Half	2	1	3.26	1	30.1	Clutch	126	35	4	18	.278

2004 Season

Jamie Walker continued to work out of the bullpen as the Tigers' situational lefthander. The Tigers badly lacked bullpen depth, so he often was taken out of that role and made a setup man out of necessity. It was the second straight season Walker worked 70 or more games.

Pitching & Defense

Walker is much more effective against lefthanded hitters than righthanded hitters. In an ideal world, manager Alan Trammell never would have him face righties. Walker does not throw hard, topping out in the high 80s. He gets by mostly on deception and by using four pitches—fastball, curveball, slider and changeup—with equal effectiveness to keep hitters off balance. Walker fields the position cleanly, but basestealers are a perfect 14-for-14 on his watch over the past three years.

2005 Outlook

Walker is a valuable member of Detroit's bullpen, and he was rewarded with a one-year, $900,000 contract for this season with an option for 2006. The Tigers would love to improve their bullpen depth to the point that Walker is used strictly as a situational lefthander. But if they do not, they are comforted by the fact that Walker always is more than willing to take the ball.

Esteban Yan

Position: RP
Bats: R **Throws:** R
Ht: 6' 4" **Wt:** 255

Opening Day Age: 29
Born: 6/22/75 in
Campina del Seibo, DR
ML Seasons: 9
Pronunciation:
YAHN

Overall Statistics

	W	L	Pct.	ERA	G	GS	Sv	IP	H	BB	SO	HR	Avg
'04	3	6	.333	3.83	69	0	7	87.0	92	32	69	8	.274
Car.	31	38	.449	5.17	396	23	50	591.1	656	220	484	89	.281

2004 Situational Stats

	W	L	ERA	Sv	IP		AB	H	HR	RBI	Avg
Home	1	3	2.55	5	53.0	LHB	165	42	1	18	.255
Road	2	3	5.82	2	34.0	RHB	171	50	7	31	.292
First Half	0	2	4.14	2	50.0	Sc Pos	114	35	3	42	.307
Scnd Half	3	4	3.41	5	37.0	Clutch	170	49	3	28	.288

2004 Season

Detroit signed Esteban Yan to a minor league contract in January and invited him to the major league camp for spring training. He pitched well enough during exhibition games to make the major league club to start the season. He was used as one of Detroit's closers during the first three weeks before closer Ugueth Urbina arrived, and during the final month of the season after Urbina left because of a family emergency. Yan had seven saves in 17 opportunities.

Pitching & Defense

Yan has a great arm. It was not uncommon for him to hit 98 MPH last season. He also has a good split-finger pitch. His problems stem from inconsistency. One game he has excellent command, the next none at all. Between those periods as closer, Yan was used as Urbina's primary setup man, with mixed results. He is a very poor fielder who does not hold runners well, though he is not often in situations that call for a steal.

2005 Outlook

Yan still throws hard and is going to dazzle at times, but his inconsistency is maddening and he's not closer material. A free agent after last season, Yan signed a two-year deal to work in the middle of the Anaheim bullpen.

Detroit

Other Detroit Tigers

Steve Colyer (**Pos**: LHP, **Age**: 26)

	W	L	Pct.	ERA	G	GS	Sv	IP	H	BB	SO	HR	Avg
'04	1	0	1.000	6.47	41	0	0	32.0	33	24	31	8	.270
Car.	1	0	1.000	5.05	54	0	0	51.2	55	33	47	8	.281

Colyer has an electric mid-90s fastball and the makeup to work the ninth inning, but he must gain command of his heater to establish himself in the pen. 2005 Outlook: B

Craig Dingman (**Pos**: RHP, **Age**: 31)

	W	L	Pct.	ERA	G	GS	Sv	IP	H	BB	SO	HR	Avg
'04	2	2	.500	6.75	24	0	0	29.1	33	22	16	3	.295
Car.	2	2	.500	7.74	41	0	1	47.2	62	28	26	8	.325

The 31-year-old righthander has been pitching at the Triple-A level since 2000. He was recalled for the first time since 2001 and did little to warrant a longer look this spring. 2005 Outlook: C

John Ennis (**Pos**: RHP, **Age**: 25)

	W	L	Pct.	ERA	G	GS	Sv	IP	H	BB	SO	HR	Avg
'04	0	0	–	8.44	12	0	1	16.0	20	5	13	3	.290
Car.	0	0	–	7.65	13	1	1	20.0	25	8	14	3	.305

Ennis enjoyed his best season in the minors in 2004, going 9-5 with a 3.59 ERA as a swingman for Toledo. He picked up 10 saves there and added another with Detroit. He'll battle for a relief role. 2005 Outlook: C

Franklyn German (**Pos**: RHP, **Age**: 25)

	W	L	Pct.	ERA	G	GS	Sv	IP	H	BB	SO	HR	Avg
'04	1	0	1.000	7.36	16	0	0	14.2	17	11	8	4	.279
Car.	4	4	.500	5.73	68	0	6	66.0	67	58	55	9	.265

While he posted 27 saves at Triple-A Toledo, German was less dominant than he was the previous two seasons. The potential closer was inconsistent and homer-prone with the Tigers. 2005 Outlook: C

Al Levine (**Pos**: RHP, **Age**: 36)

	W	L	Pct.	ERA	G	GS	Sv	IP	H	BB	SO	HR	Avg
'04	3	4	.429	4.58	65	0	0	70.2	83	24	32	10	.295
Car.	24	33	.421	3.85	407	7	10	565.0	581	232	274	68	.269

Levine joined his sixth big league club in 2004 and posted his highest ERA since 1997 with the White Sox. He allowed just one run in 13.1 innings in July, but otherwise wasn't very effective. 2005 Outlook: C

Nook Logan (**Pos**: CF, **Age**: 25, **Bats**: B)

	G	AB	R	H	D	T	HR	RBI	SB	BB	SO	Avg	OBP	Slg
'04	47	133	12	37	5	2	0	10	8	13	24	.278	.340	.346
Car.	47	133	12	37	5	2	0	10	8	13	24	.278	.340	.346

Logan climbed quickly through the Tigers' system. He batted .329 for Detroit in 26 games in July and August before slumping in September. He'll vie for playing time as the Tigers rebuild. 2005 Outlook: C

Greg Norton (**Pos**: 3B, **Age**: 32, **Bats**: B)

	G	AB	R	H	D	T	HR	RBI	SB	BB	SO	Avg	OBP	Slg
'04	41	86	9	15	1	0	2	2	0	12	21	.174	.276	.256
Car.	722	1651	211	404	88	8	61	228	13	198	416	.245	.326	.419

Returning to the AL didn't work in Norton's favor. He went on a rehab assignment for an inflammed knee in July and never was summoned back. 2005 Outlook: C

Danny Patterson (**Pos**: RHP, **Age**: 34)

	W	L	Pct.	ERA	G	GS	Sv	IP	H	BB	SO	HR	Avg
'04	0	4	.000	4.75	37	0	2	41.2	44	16	24	7	.282
Car.	24	22	.522	4.14	350	0	9	384.1	418	112	250	35	.282

The Tigers lacked a closer at the start of 2004, but Patterson struggled and was released in August. He posted a 6.75 ERA for the Cards' Triple-A club the rest of the way. 2005 Outlook: C

Chris Shelton (**Pos**: DH, **Age**: 24, **Bats**: R)

	G	AB	R	H	D	T	HR	RBI	SB	BB	SO	Avg	OBP	Slg
'04	27	46	6	9	1	0	1	3	0	9	14	.196	.321	.283
Car.	27	46	6	9	1	0	1	3	0	9	14	.196	.321	.283

After batting .359 with 21 homers as a Class-A player in the Pirates' system in 2003, Shelton was lost to Detroit in the Rule 5 draft a year ago. He stuck with the Tigers all season and probably starts 2005 in the high minors. 2005 Outlook: C

Jason Smith (**Pos**: 2B/SS, **Age**: 27, **Bats**: L)

	G	AB	R	H	D	T	HR	RBI	SB	BB	SO	Avg	OBP	Slg
'04	61	155	20	37	7	4	5	19	1	8	37	.239	.280	.432
Car.	90	225	29	51	8	6	6	25	4	10	62	.227	.263	.396

Injuries to Fernando Vina and Carlos Guillen allowed Smith to surface in Detroit. Despite decent speed and some pop, Smith didn't make enough contact to stick, just as he hadn't with Tampa Bay. 2005 Outlook: C

Andres Torres (**Pos**: CF, **Age**: 27, **Bats**: B)

	G	AB	R	H	D	T	HR	RBI	SB	BB	SO	Avg	OBP	Slg
'04	3	0	1	0	0	0	0	0	1	0	0	–	–	–
Car.	81	238	31	51	5	4	1	12	8	16	51	.214	.264	.282

Torres opted for free agency in April when he was designated for assignment, and then posted a .295 average and .371 OBP with the White Sox' Triple-A affiliate in Charlotte. He signed a minor league deal with Texas after the season. 2005 Outlook: C

Lino Urdaneta (**Pos**: RHP, **Age**: 25)

	W	L	Pct.	ERA	G	GS	Sv	IP	H	BB	SO	HR	Avg
'04	0	0	–	–	1	0	0	0.0	5	1	0	0	1.000
Car.	0	0	–	–	1	0	0	0.0	5	1	0	0	1.000

A Rule 5 pick from Cleveland a year ago, Urdaneta spent most of 2004 on the disabled list with elbow inflammation. He doesn't fit into the Tigers' plans for 2005, but he'll be in their system. 2005 Outlook: C

Fernando Vina (**Pos**: 2B, **Age**: 35, **Bats**: L)

	G	AB	R	H	D	T	HR	RBI	SB	BB	SO	Avg	OBP	Slg
'04	29	115	21	26	5	0	0	7	2	9	9	.226	.308	.270
Car.	1148	4240	627	1196	194	49	40	343	116	288	292	.282	.348	.379

Vina's hitting percentages have been on a steady decline. A bad right hamstring and a tendon tear in his left knee limited him to 29 games in 2004. He's under contract for another year. 2005 Outlook: C

Detroit Tigers Minor League Prospects

Organization Overview:

GM Dave Dombrowski didn't inherit much in the system when he took over the Tigers in 2002. Now, nearly three years later, only three Tigers are on *Baseball America*'s list of Top 20 prospects in their respective minor leagues. But since the big league club was awful in 2001, 2002 and 2003, Detroit had premium picks the following seasons. Dombrowski and Scouting Director Greg Smith used those picks to select Kenny Baugh, Preston Larrison and Ryan Raburn in 2001, Curtis Granderson and Joel Zumaya in 2002, Kyle Sleeth and Tony Giarratano in 2003, and Justin Verlander in 2004. The club still is very thin on hitting prospects, however, and it looks like it will be years before the Tigers can expect to compete for postseason play.

Tony Giarratano

Position: SS	Opening Day Age: 22
Bats: B Throws: R	Born: 11/29/82 in
Ht: 6' 0" Wt: 180	Queens, NY

Recent Statistics

	G	AB	R	H	D	T	HR	RBI	SB	BB	SO	Avg
2003 A Oneonta	47	189	31	62	11	4	3	27	9	12	22	.328
2004 A W Michigan	43	165	20	47	6	1	1	13	11	25	22	.285
2004 A Lakeland	53	202	30	76	11	0	5	25	14	16	38	.376

Giarratano is one of the Tigers' two best hitting prospects, a switch-hitting shortstop with excellent athletic ability. Of the five tools, he ranks excellent in all but power. Drafted in the third round out of Tulane University in 2003, he got a $500,000 signing bonus. Since then, he has moved quickly up the lower rungs of the Tigers' system, starting in the short-season New York-Penn League and moving in 2004 through the Class-A leagues. Giarratano has hit for excellent average with some power in both of his professional seasons. With his speed and plate discipline, he's well suited to leading off or hitting second. He could arrive in Detroit by the middle of next year.

Curtis Granderson

Position: OF	Opening Day Age: 24
Bats: L Throws: R	Born: 3/16/81 in Blue
Ht: 6' 1" Wt: 185	Island, IL

Recent Statistics

	G	AB	R	H	D	T	HR	RBI	SB	BB	SO	Avg
2004 AA Erie	123	462	89	140	19	8	21	93	14	80	95	.303
2004 AL Detroit	9	25	2	6	1	1	0	0	0	3	8	.240

Granderson had a breakout season at Double-A Erie in 2004, hitting for power and average, and establishing his credentials as the Tigers' best outfield prospect. Selected in the third round of the 2002 draft, Granderson signed quickly, and hit .344 in the short-season New York-Penn League. Skipping the low

Class-A level, he posted good numbers at high Class-A Lakeland in 2003. Granderson has above-average but not outstanding speed. With an average throwing arm, his most likely major league position is center field, although the power he showed in 2004 could make a move to left possible. After a September cup of coffee, Granderson will try to win a roster slot in spring training. If that doesn't happen, he'll likely start at Triple-A.

Preston Larrison

Position: P	Opening Day Age: 24
Bats: R Throws: R	Born: 11/19/80 in
Ht: 6' 4" Wt: 215	Aurora, IL

Recent Statistics

	W	L	ERA	G	GS	Sv	IP	H	R	BB	SO	HR
2003 AAA Toledo	0	1	3.38	1	1	0	5.1	3	3	2	3	1
2003 AA Erie	4	12	5.61	24	24	0	126.2	161	89	59	53	10
2004 AA Erie	5	4	3.05	20	20	0	118.0	122	54	36	59	12

For Larrison, 2004 offered the chance to recover from a very disappointing 2003 season. In '03, he almost made the major league club to start the season, and was the winning pitcher in the Futures Game, but struggled mightily in the second half at Double-A Erie. He responded with an acceptable season back at Erie last year, but he still seems to be at least a full year away from contributing at the major league level. The Tigers selected Larrison with the 55th choice in the 2001 draft. He features an excellent sinking fastball and a good changeup, but has yet to develop a consistent breaking ball. Larrison will likely join the rotation at Triple-A Toledo to begin 2005.

Roberto Novoa

Position: P	Opening Day Age: 25
Bats: R Throws: R	Born: 8/15/79 in Las
Ht: 6' 5" Wt: 200	Matas de Farfan, DR

Recent Statistics

	W	L	ERA	G	GS	Sv	IP	H	R	BB	SO	HR
2004 AA Erie	7	0	2.96	41	0	4	79.0	63	32	18	59	7
2004 AL Detroit	1	1	5.57	16	0	0	21.0	25	15	6	15	4

Novoa was one of the players acquired from Pittsburgh in the November 2002 trade for Randall Simon. The Pirates had signed Novoa as an undrafted free agent in his native Dominican Republic. He is a tall righthander who throws his fastball around 94 MPH. He has shown outstanding control throughout his minor league career, posting a strikeout-walk ratio of 3.1:1. A starter until 2004, Novoa's lack of a third pitch resulted in his moving to the bullpen. He made the transition at Double-A Erie, with excellent results. That led to a second promotion to the majors, where he continued his impressive strikeout-walk totals. Novoa is expected to compete for a bullpen slot in spring training.

Ryan Raburn

Position: 3B
Bats: R **Throws:** R
Ht: 6' 0" **Wt:** 185

Opening Day Age: 23
Born: 4/17/81 in Tampa, FL

Recent Statistics

	G	AB	R	H	D	T	HR	RBI	SB	BB	SO	Avg
2004 A Lakeland	3	11	1	3	1	0	1	3	0	1	6	.273
2004 AA Erie	98	366	66	110	29	4	16	63	3	47	96	.301
2004 AL Detroit	12	29	4	4	1	0	0	1	1	2	15	.138

Although Raburn hit well at Double-A Erie in 2004, he really struggled in making the transition from third base to second. The Tigers drafted him in the fifth round in 2001, but injuries limited him to 409 at-bats in his first two seasons. In 2004, he committed 27 errors at Erie, though he played better in a September major league callup. If Raburn can't make it as an infielder, he might return to the outfield, his position in junior college. He's still young, and his hitting stats are promising, but he needs to be more consistent at the plate and cut down on his strikeouts. His defense currently presents a major obstacle in his path to the big leagues.

Kyle Sleeth

Position: P
Bats: R **Throws:** R
Ht: 6' 5" **Wt:** 205

Opening Day Age: 23
Born: 12/20/81 in Thornton, CO

Recent Statistics

	W	L	ERA	G	GS	Sv	IP	H	R	BB	SO	HR
2004 A Lakeland	5	4	3.31	11	11	0	68.0	60	29	18	65	3
2004 AA Erie	4	4	6.30	13	13	0	80.0	93	58	34	57	14

The Tigers paid a $3.35 million bonus to sign the third overall pick in the 2003 draft, Wake Forest righthander Kyle Sleeth. He did not sign until August, and made his pro debut in 2004. Success at high Class-A Lakeland led to a midseason promotion to Double-A Erie, where he struggled. At Lakeland, he showed excellent control. Sleeth is an aggressive pitcher, who features an excellent fastball and a plus curve. He's still making improvements to his slider and changeup. He likely will return to Erie to start 2005. If he pitches well there, he could move quickly to the major leagues. Once established in the AL, he figures to be the Tigers' rotation anchor for years to come.

Juan Tejeda

Position: 1B
Bats: R **Throws:** R
Ht: 6' 2" **Wt:** 195

Opening Day Age: 23
Born: 1/26/82 in Tamboril, DR

Recent Statistics

	G	AB	R	H	D	T	HR	RBI	SB	BB	SO	Avg
2003 A Lakeland	125	461	63	129	28	4	10	76	6	56	68	.280
2004 AA Erie	125	457	71	132	29	3	23	92	0	51	102	.289

Power was the missing element in Tejeda's game entering the 2004 season, but he answered his critics with a home-run total better than his combined production in 2002 and 2003. A native of the Dominican Republic, the first baseman was signed by the Tigers as an undrafted free agent at age 17. In 2002, at age 20, he led the Class-A Midwest League with 106 RBI. In 2004, his first year at Double-A ball, Tejeda showed excellent power and plate discipline. Over the course of his minor league career, he has more RBI than strikeouts. With nothing left to prove in Double-A, he figures to start 2005 at Triple-A Toledo, and has a shot at a mid-season callup.

Joel Zumaya

Position: P
Bats: R **Throws:** R
Ht: 6' 3" **Wt:** 215

Opening Day Age: 20
Born: 11/9/84 in Chula Vista, CA

Recent Statistics

	W	L	ERA	G	GS	Sv	IP	H	R	BB	SO	HR
2003 A W Michigan	7	5	2.79	19	19	0	90.1	69	35	38	126	3
2004 A Lakeland	7	7	4.36	20	20	0	115.2	90	60	58	108	10
2004 AA Erie	2	2	6.30	4	4	0	20.0	19	20	10	29	6

Selected at age 17 by the Tigers in the 11th round of the 2002 draft, Zumaya features a fastball that reaches into the high 90s, and an excellent hard curveball. In 2003, Zumaya averaged 12.5 strikeouts per nine innings, but he missed six weeks with back problems and a strained oblique muscle. In 2004, at high Class-A Lakeland and Double-A Erie, he continued to average more than a strikeout per frame. He figures to start 2005 back at Erie, pitching in the rotation, but has the tools to move up quickly. With the Troy Percival signing, Zumaya likely will start his major league career in the Detroit rotation, but his skills and size mark him as a possible closer.

Others to Watch

Righthander **Kenny Baugh** (26) was the 11th overall choice in the 2001 draft. Arthroscopic surgery to repair a torn labrum cost him all of 2002, and he struggled in 2003, but recovered to pitch well at Double-A Erie in 2004. . . With the bullpen an annual concern of the Tigers, **Eulogio de la Cruz** (21) will be on the team's radar. The righthander is just 5-foot-11, but threw in the high 90s as Class-A West Michigan's closer, with decent control for his age and velocity readings. . . Acquired by trade in July 2002, former Cincinnati Reds first-round choice **David Espinosa** (23) made the move to the outfield from second base in 2004, hitting .264 with 19 homers and 20 stolen bases for Double-A Erie. . . Third baseman **Kody Kirkland** (21) was acquired in the Randall Simon trade with Pittsburgh in 2002. A draft and follow that year, he hit well in short-season ball in 2003. But 2004 was a disappointment, as he hit .236 and committed 29 errors at Class-A West Michigan. . . After the minor league season ended, the Tigers signed the second man picked in the 2004 draft, **Justin Verlander** (22), to a major league contract. The righthander has a great curve and a fastball that approaches triple digits. He'll likely start 2005 at high Class-A Lakeland.

Ewing M. Kauffman Stadium

Offense

Kauffman Stadium is an equal opportunity offensive enhancement for hitters—just about every type of hitter gets a boost. Excellent sight lines make for an ideal hitting environment, increasing batting averages and reducing strikeouts. Power hitters, however, took a hit when the outfield fences were moved back 10 feet prior to the start of the season. The large outfield expanse lets balls get to the wall for doubles and triples. Recently-added luxury boxes even do their part in prolonging at-bats by occasionally taking away access to foul balls.

Defense

The decison to move back the fences not only cut home-run power a bit, but also made the need for fleet-footed outfielders even more acute. Corner outfielders have to be wary of the very slight angles at the foul poles, as sharply hit balls down the lines tend to hug the walls and scoot by for triples. Glove men enjoy an immaculately groomed infield that produces few bad hops.

Who It Helps the Most

Speedy gap hitters and righthanded power hitters benefit the most from Kauffman's wide outfield expanses and the way the ball carries in the summer. Pitchers who can keep the ball down in the strike zone can take advantage of the well-groomed infield and avoid the most damaging aspects of the park's offensive tendencies.

Who It Hurts the Most

Pitchers who work high in the strike zone will be hurt by extra-base hits more in Kauffman than almost anywhere else. Hitters who rely on beating the ball into the turf and outrunning infielders' throws work against the offensive advantages available at Kauffman. Outfielders who have less than average range will find Kauffman wearing.

Rookies & Newcomers

The aggressive slash-hitting, speed-and-defense style of David DeJesus will be rewarded by Kauffman. Zack Greinke should succeed more often at home with offspeed stuff. The superior infield will assist Andres Blanco's glove work, but his hitting style will not be helped.

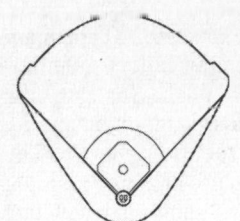

Dimensions: LF-330, LCF-385, CF-410, RCF-385, RF-330

Capacity: 40,785

Elevation: 750 feet

Surface: Grass

Foul Territory: Average

Park Factors

2004 Season

| | Home Games | | | Away Games | | | |
	Royals	Opp	Total	Royals	Opp	Total	Index
G	71	71	142	73	73	146	
Avg	.265	.283	.274	.257	.296	.276	99
AB	2356	2530	4886	2572	2504	5076	99
R	313	378	691	336	433	769	92
H	624	717	1341	662	741	1403	98
2B	105	163	268	131	159	290	96
3B	13	18	31	10	13	23	140
HR	51	84	135	83	106	189	74
BB	215	209	424	201	235	436	101
SO	413	418	831	532	370	902	96
E	46	40	86	69	58	127	70
E-Infield	41	35	76	55	50	105	74
LHB-Avg	.258	.290	.274	.249	.322	.284	96
LHB-HR	21	28	49	30	40	70	76
RHB-Avg	.269	.280	.275	.263	.280	.271	101
RHB-HR	30	56	86	53	66	119	73

2002-2003

| | Home Games | | | Away Games | | | |
	Royals	Opp	Total	Royals	Opp	Total	Index
G	143	143	286	145	145	290	
Avg	.276	.291	.284	.250	.265	.258	110
AB	4854	5220	10074	4986	4811	9797	104
R	754	891	1645	627	654	1281	130
H	1342	1520	2862	1248	1276	2524	115
2B	267	301	568	225	265	490	113
3B	38	30	68	34	30	64	103
HR	135	211	346	127	154	281	120
BB	451	491	942	432	486	918	100
SO	689	772	1461	939	838	1777	80
E	88	114	202	116	97	213	96
E-Infield	71	102	173	97	83	180	97
LHB-Avg	.274	.296	.285	.243	.273	.257	111
LHB-HR	64	90	154	67	65	132	112
RHB-Avg	.279	.287	.283	.257	.259	.258	110
RHB-HR	71	121	192	60	89	149	126

2004 Rankings (American League)

- Third-highest triple factor
- Lowest error factor
- Second-lowest home-run factor
- Second-lowest infield-error factor
- Second-lowest LHB home-run factor
- Second-lowest RHB home-run factor
- Third-lowest LHB batting-average factor

Tony Pena

2004 Season

After the euphoria of an unexpected 2003 pennant chase, the Royals added veteran hitters in anticipation of another playoff push. Instead, the wheels came off early, the losses mounted and by midseason the club was in rebuilding mode. The Royals went all year without sweeping a single series and won more than two games in a row just three times. Manager Tony Pena's geniality and patience were tested as his team set a club record with 104 losses.

Offense

Because the Royals often lack power in their line-up, Pena utilizes many one-run strategies, even sacrificing early in the game. He expects every hitter to know how to bunt and contribute to the high-pressure speed tactics. Pena believes players have to play every day to make necessary adjustments in the majors, so he'll usually stick a newcomer in the lineup right away for an extended period while asking him to focus on specific goals. He makes very little use of pinch-hitters or pinch-runners.

Pitching & Defense

Pena is very protective of young arms, keeping strict pitch counts for young starters and limiting use of young relievers. He'll give veteran starters longer leashes and make them work out of their own jams. He focuses more on roles than situational matchups when selecting relievers. Fundamentals are elemental to Pena's defensive approach, and players are more likely to be benched for poor fundamentals than for any other problem.

2005 Outlook

The Royals are committed to Pena, so the record-setting disappointment of 2004 is no threat to his job security. The front office is supplying him with a steady stream of youngsters, relying on Pena's teaching abilities to mold a winner eventually. He'll be expected to build the team around players like Zack Greinke, David DeJesus and John Buck, while finding useful roles for other young players. Any veteran additions more likely will be role players or those who can fill gaps until the club develops from within.

Born: 6/04/57 in Monte Cristi, Dominican Republic

Playing Experience: 1980-1997, Pit, StL, Bos, Cle, CWS, Hou

Managerial Experience: 3 seasons

Manager Statistics

Year	Team, Lg	W	L	Pct	GB	Finish
2004	Kansas City, AL	58	104	.358	34.0	5th Central
3 Seasons		190	260	.422	–	–

2004 Starting Pitchers by Days Rest

	<=3	4	5	6+
Royals Starts	1	62	58	29
Royals ERA	3.60	5.84	5.30	4.99
AL Avg Starts	2	82	47	21
AL ERA	5.36	4.87	4.65	4.93

2004 Situational Stats

	Tony Pena	AL Average
Hit & Run Success %	42.7	36.8
Stolen Base Success %	58.3	68.6
Platoon Pct.	57.0	61.6
Defensive Subs	12	21
High-Pitch Outings	3	5
Quick/Slow Hooks	20/21	20/16
Sacrifice Attempts	59	53

2004 Rankings (American League)

- 2nd in hit-and-run attempts (96) and intentional walks (33)
- 3rd in hit-and-run success percentage and starting lineups used (140)

Jeremy Affeldt

2004 Season

After struggling through eight starts at the beginning of the season, Jeremy Affeldt was shifted once again to bullpen stopper. He again found success as a closer, converting eight of 10 saves before losing almost two months due to a right ribcage strain. Affeldt returned late in August and resumed his role as closer, although he pitched in limited action because there were scant few leads to protect.

Pitching

Affeldt makes heavy use of two outstanding pitches: a mid-90s four-seam fastball, and a slow, 12-to-6 curve that bends hitters' knees. He'll also toss an occasional slider to lefties, but it is just for show. The fastball is strong enough to blow by hitters high in the strike zone and makes his curve look even slower. He throws both pitches for strikes, although he sometimes has problems getting umpires' strike calls with the curveball. When Affeldt mixes both pitches it is an especially effective combination, as they work well against a hitter's timing. He generally gives lefthanded hitters more trouble, but also succeeds against righthanders because he can throw either pitch to either side of the plate. Persistent blistering on the middle finger of his pitching hand and other nagging injuries have limited Affeldt's durability over the course of the season.

Defense

Affeldt has a decent pickoff move, but he hasn't had much success in limiting basestealers, especially when they run against his breaking pitches. He has experimented with a slide step, with marginal results. Affeldt moves well off the mound but is not an adept fielder.

2005 Outlook

Health rather than ability is the primary focus for Affeldt. He has the stuff to succeed, but he needs to remain fully healthy all year to reach his full potential. Although he has a strong enough repertoire for the rotation, he's likely to remain in short relief as a means of staying off the disabled list. Given a full season, Affeldt can emerge as a strong bullpen ace.

Position: RP
Bats: L **Throws:** L
Ht: 6' 4" **Wt:** 215

Opening Day Age: 25
Born: 6/6/79 in Phoenix, AZ
ML Seasons: 3
Pronunciation: AFF-felt

Overall Statistics

	W	L	Pct.	ERA	G	GS	Sv	IP	H	BB	SO	HR	Avg
'04	3	4	.429	4.95	38	8	13	76.1	91	32	49	6	.302
Car.	13	14	.481	4.40	108	33	17	280.0	302	107	214	26	.276

2004 Pitching Profile

	Jeremy Affeldt	AL Average
Overall Strike %	62.5	62.3
1st Pitch Strike %	58.4	58.1
Ratio	1.61	1.42
Strikeouts per 9 IP	5.78	6.45
Walks per 9 IP	3.77	3.34
Home Runs per 9 IP	0.71	1.15
Strikeout/Walk Ratio	1.53	1.93
Groundball/Flyball Ratio	1.47	1.17

2004 Situational Stats

	W	L	ERA	Sv	IP		AB	H	HR	RBI	Avg
Home	3	2	4.95	8	36.1	LHB	70	19	4	12	.271
Road	0	2	4.95	5	40.0	RHB	231	72	2	33	.312
First Half	2	3	4.70	8	61.1	Sc Pos	95	24	1	34	.253
Scnd Half	1	1	6.00	5	15.0	Clutch	81	27	2	15	.333

2004 Rankings (American League)

- 2nd in balks (3)
- 9th in highest batting average allowed vs. righthanded batters
- Led the Royals in saves, games finished (26), balks (3), save percentage (76.5), blown saves (4) and relief wins (3)

Brian Anderson

2004 Season

Expected to be the staff ace and lead the Royals into contention, Brian Anderson started the season poorly and got worse. As the losses mounted, Anderson lost his spot in the rotation, then struggled with spotty command out of the bullpen before correcting a mechanical flaw and regaining his form over the last couple of months. Overall, he placed near the bottom in many league pitching categories.

Pitching

With a fastball that reaches only the low 90s, Anderson has to stay out of the middle of the plate. He succeeds when he can spot his fastball on the corners to get ahead, setting up an above-average changeup thrown down and away. Anderson has developed a cut fastball to keep righthanded hitters from crowding the plate; he throws it in the upper 80s, but usually not for strikes. He works quickly and throws strikes, and has good control of most of his pitches. Anderson has the pitching smarts to make adjustments during a game, but struggles with his command for lengthy stretches each season. Durability over the course of the season has been an issue for Anderson, although usually due to injuries unrelated to his pitching arm.

Defense

One of the game's best at controlling the running game, Anderson makes frequent throws to first and has two different pickoff moves, one to keep runners close and the other to pick them off. He is a steady fielder whose athletic ability shows, as he is quick off the mound and in reacting to grounders through the middle.

2005 Outlook

For a contending team, Anderson would be relegated to long relief and spot start duties. With a second-division club, he should compete for a mid-rotation job. He's neither as bad as he looked in 2004, nor as good as he seemed to be in 2003. With a bit more consistency, Anderson can be a useful starter, although he would be miscast as a staff ace.

Position: SP
Bats: R **Throws:** L
Ht: 6' 1" **Wt:** 185

Opening Day Age: 32
Born: 4/26/72 in Portsmouth, VA
ML Seasons: 12

Overall Statistics

	W	L	Pct.	ERA	G	GS	Sv	IP	H	BB	SO	HR	Avg
'04	6	12	.333	5.64	35	26	0	166.0	217	53	70	33	.320
Car.	81	81	.500	4.69	285	239	1	1516.1	1704	333	706	257	.287

2004 Pitching Profile

	Brian Anderson	AL Average
Overall Strike %	61.2	62.3
1st Pitch Strike %	61.1	58.1
Ratio	1.63	1.42
Strikeouts per 9 IP	3.80	6.45
Walks per 9 IP	2.87	3.34
Home Runs per 9 IP	1.79	1.15
Strikeout/Walk Ratio	1.32	1.93
Groundball/Flyball Ratio	0.86	1.17

2004 Situational Stats

	W	L	ERA	Sv	IP		AB	H	HR	RBI	Avg
Home	3	7	5.71	0	93.0	LHB	169	57	8	25	.337
Road	3	5	5.55	0	73.0	RHB	510	160	25	88	.314
First Half	1	8	7.23	0	79.2	Sc Pos	169	51	7	75	.302
Scnd Half	5	4	4.17	0	86.1	Clutch	25	11	0	3	.440

2004 Rankings (American League)

- 1st in lowest stolen-base percentage allowed (20.0) and highest batting average allowed (.320)
- 2nd in highest ERA, lowest strikeout-walk ratio (1.3), highest slugging percentage allowed (.545), highest on-base percentage allowed (.366) and fewest strikeouts per nine innings (3.8)
- 3rd in lowest winning percentage and most home runs allowed per nine innings (1.79)
- 4th in highest ERA at home and highest batting average allowed vs. lefthanded batters
- 5th in home runs allowed
- 7th in lowest groundball-flyball ratio allowed (0.9)
- 8th in complete games (2) and highest batting average allowed vs. righthanded batters
- Led the Royals in GDPs induced (22), lowest stolen-base percentage allowed (20.0) and most run support per nine innings (5.6)

Angel Berroa

2004 Season

Last season, just about everything that could go wrong for Angel Berroa, did. The 2003 American League Rookie of the Year started out poorly, then got worse both at the plate and in the field. As the strikeouts and errors mounted, he was demoted to Double-A Wichita. When Berroa returned two weeks later, he'd regained his batting stroke, but the damage was done. It was a miserably disappointing season for Berroa, who led the majors in errors while also having one of the game's worst on-base percentages.

Hitting

Berroa crowds the plate in a hunched stance, and when he is on, he strides into the pitch and uses his strong, quick wrists to drive almost any offering with authority. However, he's an extremely impatient hitter prone to long stretches of overswinging and chasing bad pitches. He often becomes enamored of the longball and tries to hit everything out of the park. Berroa has surprising power for his lack of bulk, and he's at his best when staying back and using his line-drive stroke to take pitches to all fields. He's a good bunter who hits lots of grounders, using his foot speed to pressure infielders.

Baserunning & Defense

Berroa's defensive shortcomings are a classic case of letting small problems balloon into larger ones. When his footwork becomes flawed, he compensates by relying too much on his arm, resulting in errant throws. He has good range and a strong arm, but he needs to play shortstop at a more controlled pace to make the best use of his skills. A good baserunner, Berroa has above-average speed and has learned how to steal bases.

2005 Outlook

Veterans say baseball is a game of constant adjustment. To succeed for any length of time requires tinkering with your mechanics and modifying your approach. If Berroa can learn this lesson and make adjustments, he can limit the damage caused by his occasional slumps and return to his 2003 Rookie of the Year form.

Position: SS
Bats: R **Throws:** R
Ht: 6' 0" **Wt:** 175

Opening Day Age: 27
Born: 1/27/78 in Santo Domingo, DR
ML Seasons: 4

Overall Statistics

	G	AB	R	H	D	T	HR	RBI	SB	BB	SO	Avg	OBP	Slg
'04	134	512	72	134	27	6	8	43	14	23	87	.262	.308	.385
Car.	327	1207	180	330	64	14	25	125	40	62	207	.273	.323	.412

Where He Hits the Ball

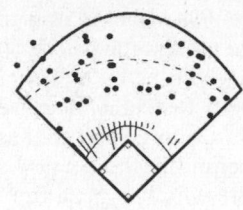 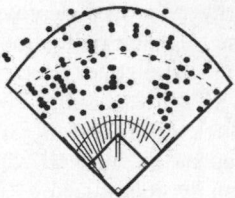

Vs. LHP   **Vs. RHP**

2004 Situational Stats

	AB	H	HR	RBI	Avg		AB	H	HR	RBI	Avg
Home	241	61	3	14	.253	LHP	139	36	2	12	.259
Road	271	73	5	29	.269	RHP	373	98	6	31	.263
First Half	280	67	5	28	.239	Sc Pos	109	29	3	36	.266
Scnd Half	232	67	3	15	.289	Clutch	67	16	1	7	.239

2004 Rankings (American League)

- 1st in errors at shortstop (28) and lowest fielding percentage at shortstop (.955)
- 3rd in lowest on-base percentage
- 6th in lowest slugging percentage
- 8th in highest groundball-flyball ratio (1.8) and lowest stolen-base percentage (63.6)
- 9th in lowest HR frequency (64.0 ABs per HR)
- 10th in hit by pitch (12)
- Led the Royals in at-bats, runs scored, triples, stolen bases, hit by pitch (12), plate appearances (554) and games played

John Buck

2004 Season

One of three players acquired from Houston and Oakland when the Royals traded Carlos Beltran in June, John Buck immediately became the club's everyday catcher. Expected to develop a rapport with the pitching staff while learning the ropes in the bigs, he hit poorly at first. However, by season's end Buck had become a useful hitter and a viable power source while also establishing himself behind the plate. Overall, it was a strong debut by the rookie backstop.

Hitting

Hitting from an upright stance, Buck is a first-pitch fastball hitter. He doesn't make good contact, tending instead to swing hard to generate power. Good plate coverage gives Buck power to the opposite field, though he prefers the ball up in the strike zone. He thrives when facing a pitcher who will challenge him with fastballs. Because Buck still is learning to adjust to offspeed pitches and hasn't hit well when behind in the count, he can be neutralized by hurlers who can get a first-pitch breaking ball over the plate.

Baserunning & Defense

Buck runs poorly, even for a catcher, and is overly tentative on the bases. Defense remains one of his strengths. He's comfortably in charge as a catcher, and pitchers have come to trust his ability to call a game. Buck moves well behind the plate but tends to take too long to finish his throws to the bases, even though he owns a strong, accurate arm.

2005 Outlook

Before he began to show his power stroke in the majors, Buck was already in the Royals' long-range plans. He's now entrenched enough that the club openly discussed making veteran Benito Santiago his understudy. Because Buck is inexperienced, the club is cautious in its expectations for 2005. Royals manager and former All-Star catcher Tony Pena has made Buck his special project, hoping to help Buck refine his catching skills and continue his growth as one of the league's better catching prospects.

Position: C
Bats: R **Throws:** R
Ht: 6' 3" **Wt:** 210

Opening Day Age: 24
Born: 7/7/80 in Kemmerer, WY
ML Seasons: 1

Overall Statistics

	G	AB	R	H	D	T	HR	RBI	SB	BB	SO	Avg	OBP	Slg
'04	71	238	36	56	9	0	12	30	1	15	79	.235	.280	.424
Car.	71	238	36	56	9	0	12	30	1	15	79	.235	.280	.424

Where He Hits the Ball

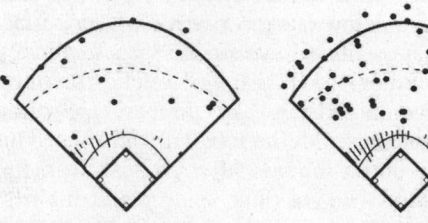

Vs. LHP   **Vs. RHP**

2004 Situational Stats

	AB	H	HR	RBI	Avg		AB	H	HR	RBI	Avg
Home	115	29	6	18	.252	LHP	72	16	3	10	.222
Road	123	27	6	12	.220	RHP	166	40	9	20	.241
First Half	37	7	0	0	.189	Sc Pos	51	11	4	19	.216
Scnd Half	201	49	12	30	.244	Clutch	30	5	1	2	.167

2004 Rankings (American League)

- 2nd in home runs among rookies
- 5th in RBI among rookies

David DeJesus

2004 Season

The Royals' center fielder of the future became the center fielder of the present when Carlos Beltran was traded to Houston at the end of June. David DeJesus showed noticeable improvement over his previous big league opportunities, growing into the leadoff role and refining his outfield play. After struggling with just one hit in his first 23 at-bats, DeJesus batted .303 after replacing Beltran. It was an encouraging debut by DeJesus, who placed among American League rookie hitting leaders.

Hitting

DeJesus has a fine batting eye and makes excellent contact. His batting style, speed and on-base ability make him a prototypical leadoff hitter. Possessing a compact swing that generates good bat speed, he waits well on pitches before punching them through the infield. His short stroke limits his power, but DeJesus can turn on a mistake and pull it for extra bases. He has shown a pronounced platoon differential and has trouble against lefties who alternate inside fastballs with outside breaking pitches.

Baserunning & Defense

While there's no doubt that DeJesus runs well, he was picked off numerous times in 2004 and often was caught stealing after getting a slow break from first. The baserunning problems were at least partially attributable to coaching, as the Royals admittedly were pushing DeJesus into defining his limits by overextending his lead off first. DeJesus has slightly above-average range in center and throws accurately, although his arm is relatively weak since undergoing Tommy John surgery in 2001.

2005 Outlook

DeJesus will bat leadoff and play center field for Kansas City in 2005. His biggest challenge will be making the necessary adjustments young hitters have to make the second time around the league. DeJesus also must show he's durable over the course of a full season, as his hard-charging style resulted in a variety of injuries during his short minor league career. A full season of steady production from the leadoff spot would be considered a successful campaign.

Position: CF
Bats: L **Throws:** L
Ht: 6' 0" **Wt:** 175

Opening Day Age: 25
Born: 12/20/79 in Brooklyn, NY
ML Seasons: 2

Overall Statistics

	G	AB	R	H	D	T	HR	RBI	SB	BB	SO	Avg	OBP	Slg
'04	96	363	58	104	15	3	7	39	8	33	53	.287	.360	.402
Car.	108	370	58	106	15	4	7	39	8	34	55	.286	.362	.405

Where He Hits the Ball

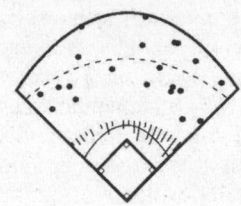

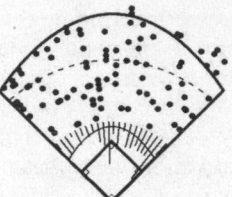

Vs. LHP   **Vs. RHP**

2004 Situational Stats

	AB	H	HR	RBI	Avg		AB	H	HR	RBI	Avg
Home	175	52	2	17	.297	LHP	98	22	0	8	.224
Road	188	52	5	22	.277	RHP	265	82	7	31	.309
First Half	67	11	0	4	.164	Sc Pos	72	21	0	30	.292
Scnd Half	296	93	7	35	.314	Clutch	44	9	0	2	.205

2004 Rankings (American League)

- 1st in batting average among rookies
- 3rd in lowest percentage of swings that missed (8.5) and RBI among rookies
- 5th in home runs among rookies
- 6th in caught stealing (11), on-base percentage for a leadoff hitter (.376) and errors in center field (4)
- Led the Royals in sacrifice bunts (8), caught stealing (11), bunts in play (20), lowest percentage of swings that missed (8.5), on-base percentage for a leadoff hitter (.376) and batting average at home

Jimmy Gobble

2004 Season

After pitching reasonably well through the first half, Jimmy Gobble saw his velocity dip slightly at midseason, resulting in a demotion to Triple-A Omaha to correct a flaw in his delivery. When Gobble returned a month later, he had regained velocity and had favorable results, going unbeaten in his last five starts. Despite the ups and downs, he finished the year among the club leaders in wins and innings—a good sophomore season overall.

Pitching

Gobble works off a low-90s, moving fastball to set up hitters for either his outstanding curveball or a well-disguised changeup. All three pitches are above average, but he sometimes falls into a rut of overusing one pitch. Gobble's delivery needs constant fine-tuning; he'll occasionally rush his delivery and stride too much, which takes velocity off his fastball and dulls the break on his curve. So far he hasn't been able to go deep into starts very often, and he's still developing stamina to go a full season without wearing down. Gobble is homer-prone for a pitcher who doesn't fan a lot of hitters, and mixing his pitches better would keep hitters more off-balance. His pitches have little lateral movement and thus far he's been hit well by both left- and righthanded hitters.

Defense

Gobble's motion to first base doesn't resemble his delivery to the plate, giving baserunners a tip off that a pickoff throw is coming. They've taken advantage of his lack of a good move and have stolen successfully against him. Gobble is a tentative fielder who moves quickly off the mound, but he isn't adept with the glove and does not throw well to the bases.

2005 Outlook

The Royals would like to see Gobble continue the learning curve and build on his successes from 2003 and 2004. They see him as a middle-rotation starter and a valuable part of their immediate future. The goals for Gobble in 2005 include maintaining a steady delivery, reducing the longballs he allows and building his stamina.

Position: SP
Bats: L **Throws:** L
Ht: 6' 3" **Wt:** 190

Opening Day Age: 23
Born: 7/19/81 in Bristol, TN
ML Seasons: 2

Overall Statistics

	W	L	Pct.	ERA	G	GS	Sv	IP	H	BB	SO	HR	Avg
'04	9	8	.529	5.35	25	24	0	148.0	157	43	49	24	.270
Car.	13	13	.500	5.16	34	33	0	200.2	213	58	80	32	.270

2004 Pitching Profile

	Jimmy Gobble	AL Average
Overall Strike %	62.3	62.3
1st Pitch Strike %	56.3	58.1
Ratio	1.35	1.42
Strikeouts per 9 IP	2.98	6.45
Walks per 9 IP	2.61	3.34
Home Runs per 9 IP	1.46	1.15
Strikeout/Walk Ratio	1.14	1.93
Groundball/Flyball Ratio	0.86	1.17

2004 Situational Stats

	W	L	ERA	Sv	IP		AB	H	HR	RBI	Avg
Home	3	5	4.98	0	68.2	LHB	145	46	7	20	.317
Road	6	3	5.67	0	79.1	RHB	436	111	17	64	.255
First Half	5	6	5.14	0	98.0	Sc Pos	130	44	6	57	.338
Scnd Half	4	2	5.76	0	50.0	Clutch	21	8	0	2	.381

2004 Rankings (American League)

- 5th in highest batting average allowed with runners in scoring position
- 10th in highest batting average allowed vs. lefthanded batters
- Led the Royals in wins, winning percentage and fewest pitches thrown per batter (3.58)

Zack Greinke

2004 Season

The future of Royals pitching arrived in May, when Zack Greinke was called up from Triple-A Omaha. He rewarded the club's patience with a string of strong starts to become the best pitcher on a weak staff. Greinke led AL rookie hurlers with at least 100 innings in ERA, while giving beleaguered Royals fans something to cheer about in an otherwise dismal season. His losing record was mostly a function of lack of run support, including being shut out four times.

Pitching

Greinke has outstanding command of a wide repertoire. Although he can hurl his four-seam fastball in the mid-90s, he prefers to take a little off to disrupt a hitter's timing, or induce movement by varying his grip. His two-seam fastball has great late sinking action and his slider breaks hard and late. However, Greinke's mid-60s curveball is the pitch that draws the most attention, as it freezes even the most seasoned hitters. Greinke varies speed and grip on each pitch such that he never throws the same pitch to the same batter in a game and will even try an occasional quick-pitch. In his rookie campaign, Greinke was kept on a strict pitch limit, never starting an inning after reaching the 100-pitch mark.

Defense

Baserunners also didn't know what to make of Greinke's varied deliveries. He disguises his pick-off move well and few baserunners tried to steal against him. Greinke's athleticism shows in his glove work; he moves quickly to field his position, handles bunts and grounders well, and covers first base quickly.

2005 Outlook

Since he obviously has the tools to succeed, the trick for Greinke will be to figure out which one to use in each situation. Instead of continuing to develop new pitches, he'll be pushed to refine his existing repertoire. Also on the Royals' agenda for their future ace is developing stamina. They will continue to protect Greinke's valuable arm with pitch-count limitations, but expand those limits a little to further his development.

Position: SP
Bats: R **Throws:** R
Ht: 6' 2" **Wt:** 200

Opening Day Age: 21
Born: 10/21/83 in Orlando, FL
ML Seasons: 1
Pronunciation: GRAIN-key

Overall Statistics

	W	L	Pct.	ERA	G	GS	Sv	IP	H	BB	SO	HR	Avg
'04	8	11	.421	3.97	24	24	0	145.0	143	26	100	26	.256
Car.	8	11	.421	3.97	24	24	0	145.0	143	26	100	26	.256

2004 Pitching Profile

	Zack Greinke	AL Average
Overall Strike %	65.7	62.3
1st Pitch Strike %	66.2	58.1
Ratio	1.17	1.42
Strikeouts per 9 IP	6.21	6.45
Walks per 9 IP	1.61	3.34
Home Runs per 9 IP	1.61	1.15
Strikeout/Walk Ratio	3.85	1.93
Groundball/Flyball Ratio	0.81	1.17

2004 Situational Stats

	W	L	ERA	Sv	IP		AB	H	HR	RBI	Avg
Home	6	6	3.31	0	84.1	LHB	311	78	9	22	.251
Road	2	5	4.90	0	60.2	RHB	248	65	17	39	.262
First Half	1	6	3.86	0	56.0	Sc Pos	97	22	7	37	.227
Scnd Half	7	5	4.04	0	89.0	Clutch	27	10	1	2	.370

2004 Rankings (American League)

- 1st in losses among rookies
- 2nd in wins among rookies
- 10th in lowest ERA at home
- Led the Royals in ERA, hit batsmen (8), highest strikeout-walk ratio (3.8), lowest batting average allowed (.256), lowest on-base percentage allowed (.297), lowest ERA at home, lowest ERA on the road and fewest walks per nine innings (1.6)

Ken Harvey

Position: 1B/DH
Bats: R **Throws:** R
Ht: 6' 2" **Wt:** 240

Opening Day Age: 27
Born: 3/1/78 in Los
Angeles, CA
ML Seasons: 3

2004 Season

Ken Harvey's second full big league season was much like the first—full of streaky hitting, strike-outs, clutch hits and bizarre collisions. After contending for the American League batting lead and making the All-Star team, Harvey almost disappeared in the second half, hitting .235 with just one home run the final two months of the season. It was a disappointing finish for Harvey, who improved his 2003 batting average by 21 points but failed to show development as a power hitter.

Hitting

For a big man with an uppercut swing, Harvey displays surprisingly little power. Part of the problem is his willingness to chase pitches out of the strike zone—especially outside pitches. He has a quick bat, but it is negated by his focus on pulling everything, and his aggressive approach keeps him from getting better pitches to hit. Harvey has failed to adjust as pitchers increasingly throw hard in on his hands. Leveling his swing and becoming more patient would help him make better contact and also help him better utilize the opposite field.

Baserunning & Defense

Although he's decent at scooping low throws, Harvey isn't a good first baseman. His footwork needs sharpening and he occasionally still is caught out of position on grounders to his right. Harvey also tends to become unaware of his surroundings and has repeatedly been involved in collisions with opponents or inanimate objects, resulting in serious injury to both Harvey and other players. He is a station-to-station baserunner who hasn't succeeded when taking chances on the bases.

2005 Outlook

Much is expected of Harvey as he enters what should be his most productive years. He's still considered an important element in the Royals' offense, but he must grow as a hitter in order to produce sufficiently as a first baseman or designated hitter. If Harvey can rein in his aggressive uppercut swing and make better contact, he could have a breakout season.

Overall Statistics

	G	AB	R	H	D	T	HR	RBI	SB	BB	SO	Avg	OBP	Slg
'04	120	456	47	131	20	1	13	55	1	28	89	.287	.338	.421
Car.	259	953	98	263	51	1	26	121	3	57	187	.276	.324	.413

Where He Hits the Ball

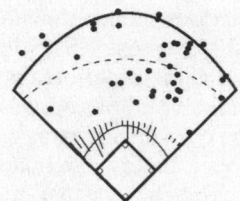

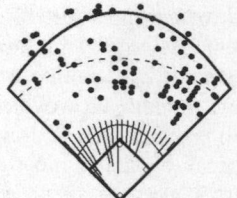

Vs. LHP   **Vs. RHP**

2004 Situational Stats

	AB	H	HR	RBI	Avg		AB	H	HR	RBI	Avg
Home	235	69	6	35	.294	LHP	128	35	3	17	.273
Road	221	62	7	20	.281	RHP	328	96	10	38	.293
First Half	292	89	10	34	.305	Sc Pos	123	34	2	40	.276
Scnd Half	164	42	3	21	.256	Clutch	53	19	1	5	.358

2004 Rankings (American League)

- 4th in batting average in the clutch
- 5th in lowest cleanup slugging percentage (.416)
- 10th in errors at first base (4)
- Led the Royals in batting average, highest groundball-flyball ratio (2.3), batting average in the clutch and batting average with two strikes (.236)

Darrell May

2004 Season

Coming off the best season of his career in 2003, Darrell May was expected to play an important role in the Royals' rotation in 2004. Instead, he struggled throughout the year, tying a club mark for losses and setting a new team mark for homers allowed. He also placed among the major's worst in numerous categories, including losses. May's spot in the rotation remained unchallenged only because the Royals had limited alternatives.

Pitching

May's upper-80s fastball lacks movement, so he relies more heavily on a cut fastball in the mid-80s that has better movement. He'll try to get hitters to chase sliders, thrown down and away (and rarely for strikes), before attempting to get them out with a changeup down in the strike zone. May doesn't walk a lot of hitters, but when his command is lacking he gets too much of the plate, resulting in home runs. He usually jumps ahead of hitters with a first-pitch strike but has trouble putting them away. Durability never has been an issue for May. He is able to take a regular turn in the rotation and does not tire quickly.

Defense

Although he pays a lot of attention to baserunners and will vary his delivery to limit their leads, May has trouble controlling the running game. He is a mediocre fielder who doesn't help himself with the glove. He is not especially quick off the mound, and is somewhat unsteady despite usually taking a conservative approach on throws to the bases.

2005 Outlook

May, whose future with the Royals looked shaky, gets a chance to turn things around after being dealt to the Padres in November in a four-player swap that also saw Ryan Bukvich go to San Diego in exchange for Terrence Long and Dennis Tankersley. Working for a contending team and in a pitchers' park to boot, he'll have a golden opportunity to show that his solid 2003 campaign was no fluke. Spacious Petco Park should help May, whose 38 home runs allowed tied for second in the American League last year.

Position: SP
Bats: L **Throws:** L
Ht: 6' 2" **Wt:** 185

Opening Day Age: 32
Born: 6/13/72 in San Bernardino, CA
ML Seasons: 6

Kansas City

Overall Statistics

	W	L	Pct.	ERA	G	GS	Sv	IP	H	BB	SO	HR	Avg
'04	9	19	.321	5.61	31	31	0	186.0	234	55	120	38	.306
Car.	25	39	.391	4.98	137	88	0	594.1	659	189	379	109	.279

2004 Pitching Profile

	Darrell May	AL Average
Overall Strike %	63.4	62.3
1st Pitch Strike %	64.1	58.1
Ratio	1.55	1.42
Strikeouts per 9 IP	5.81	6.45
Walks per 9 IP	2.66	3.34
Home Runs per 9 IP	1.84	1.15
Strikeout/Walk Ratio	2.18	1.93
Groundball/Flyball Ratio	0.80	1.17

2004 Situational Stats

	W	L	ERA	Sv	IP		AB	H	HR	RBI	Avg
Home	5	8	5.94	0	83.1	LHB	186	55	7	28	.296
Road	4	11	5.35	0	102.2	RHB	578	179	31	94	.310
First Half	6	9	5.24	0	103.0	Sc Pos	176	52	8	77	.295
Scnd Half	3	10	6.07	0	83.0	Clutch	10	2	0	1	.200

2004 Rankings (American League)

- 1st in losses, fielding percentage at pitcher (1.000) and highest slugging percentage allowed (.555)
- 2nd in home runs allowed, lowest winning percentage and most home runs allowed per nine innings (1.84)
- 3rd in highest ERA, highest batting average allowed (.306), lowest groundball-flyball ratio allowed (0.8) and highest ERA at home
- 5th in complete games (3)
- 7th in hits allowed and runners caught stealing (9)
- Led the Royals in wins, losses, games started, complete games (3), innings pitched, hits allowed, batters faced (832), home runs allowed, walks allowed, strikeouts, pitches thrown (3,008) and runners caught stealing (9)

Abraham Nunez

2004 Season

Acquired in a trading-deadline deal from Florida for Rudy Seanez, Abraham Nunez immediately became the Royals' everyday right fielder. He suffered from sparse use as a reserve outfielder with the Marlins, but the switch-hitter blossomed once given a full-time job in Kansas City. He made a quick impression as one of the club's best hitters in August before slumping, with just five extra-base hits in the final five weeks of the season. Still, his August showing positioned Nunez for full-time duty in the future.

Hitting

Nunez doesn't get cheated at the plate. Primarily a pull hitter, he looks to attack fastballs early in the count. At least once every at-bat he'll take a big rip. While Nunez will take a pitch, he's often fooled by offspeed offerings and must improve his pitch recognition, as pitchers are increasingly feeding him a steady diet of breaking balls. Equally mediocre from both sides of the plate, Nunez is a poor two-strike hitter whose focus on hitting fastballs often causes him to beat breaking pitches into the dirt.

Baserunning & Defense

The speedy Nunez' long legs help him fly around the bases, but he hasn't learned to read pitchers' moves and is a below-average basestealer at this point in his career. Nunez also owns a powerful arm that is less accurate than strong. He frequently misses cutoff men and will sometimes sail throws over the entire infield. Nunez' speed helps in the outfield, and though his range is above average, he doesn't get a good jump on the ball and doesn't read flyballs well.

2005 Outlook

Nunez likely will compete with newly acquired Terrence Long for the Royals' right-field job this spring. Opportunity is knocking for Nunez, as the Royals are in a rebuilding mode, looking to give young players a chance. But he has to turn his talent into useful skills on the baseball field, instead of merely showcasing his strong arm, speed and power.

Position: RF/LF
Bats: B **Throws:** R
Ht: 6' 3" **Wt:** 210

Opening Day Age: 28
Born: 2/5/77 in Haina, DR
ML Seasons: 2

Overall Statistics

	G	AB	R	H	D	T	HR	RBI	SB	BB	SO	Avg	OBP	Slg
'04	117	285	40	61	10	1	6	34	1	34	69	.214	.297	.319
Car.	136	302	42	63	10	1	6	35	1	34	74	.209	.288	.308

Where He Hits the Ball

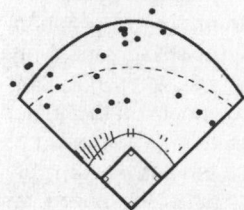 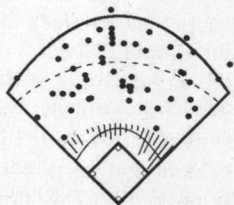

Vs. LHP   **Vs. RHP**

2004 Situational Stats

	AB	H	HR	RBI	Avg		AB	H	HR	RBI	Avg
Home	134	29	0	10	.216	LHP	86	19	4	17	.221
Road	151	32	6	24	.212	RHP	199	42	2	17	.211
First Half	55	10	1	4	.182	Sc Pos	79	20	2	28	.253
Scnd Half	230	51	5	30	.222	Clutch	48	10	2	5	.208

2004 Rankings (American League)

- Did not rank near the top or bottom in any category

Joe Randa

2004 Season

As he'd done in many previous seasons, Joe Randa gave the Royals steady play at the hot corner while displaying one of the club's most productive bats. Torn cartilage in his right knee put Randa on the disabled list for a month at midseason. The injury effected his mobility, but he was otherwise one of the few players the Royals counted on all season. He set or tied several club records in a memorable game at Detroit early in September, as he went 6-for-7 and scored six runs.

Hitting

Hitting from a relaxed stance, Randa makes good adjustments for situation and count, which helps him thrive in pressure situations. Although usually a patient contact hitter who uses the whole field, Randa will expand his strike zone and swing more aggressively in RBI situations. He can bunt or hit behind runners as the situation requires, but he's prone to chasing high fastballs when down in the count and his platoon differential gradually is becoming more pronounced. Randa rarely swings for the fences; he's at his best when hitting the ball where it's pitched.

Baserunning & Defense

Although he used to have at least average speed, Randa has seen age and nagging knee injuries erode his running game. He's a smart runner, though, who will take advantage of what the defense allows. Quick reflexes and an accurate arm have made Randa one of the game's steadiest defenders.

2005 Outlook

While Randa would like to stay in Kansas City, where he makes his offseason home, he'd also like to play for a winner, and the Royals appear to be implementing a youth movement that will supplant him at third base. A free agent who was not offered salary arbitration, Randa can be expected to join a team that needs solid third-base defense and an RBI bat in the lower part of its order. Wherever he goes, he will be a positive influence both on the field and in the clubhouse.

Position: 3B
Bats: R **Throws:** R
Ht: 5'11" **Wt:** 190

Opening Day Age: 35
Born: 12/18/69 in Milwaukee, WI
ML Seasons: 10
Nickname: The Joker

Overall Statistics

	G	AB	R	H	D	T	HR	RBI	SB	BB	SO	Avg	OBP	Slg
'04	128	485	65	139	31	2	8	56	0	40	77	.287	.343	.408
Car.	1283	4667	603	1335	271	34	102	643	42	369	631	.286	.341	.424

Where He Hits the Ball

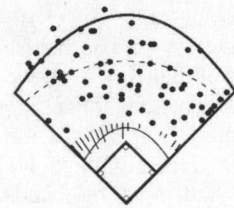 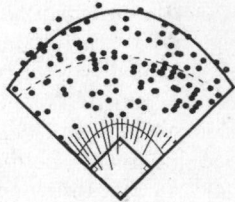

Vs. LHP   **Vs. RHP**

2004 Situational Stats

	AB	H	HR	RBI	Avg		AB	H	HR	RBI	Avg
Home	240	66	1	25	.275	LHP	144	43	3	16	.299
Road	245	73	7	31	.298	RHP	341	96	5	40	.282
First Half	248	70	2	24	.282	Sc Pos	105	29	0	43	.276
Scnd Half	237	69	6	32	.291	Clutch	64	19	0	6	.297

2004 Rankings (American League)

- 3rd in fielding percentage at third base (.967)
- 4th in sacrifice flies (8)
- Led the Royals in hits, singles, doubles, sacrifice flies (8), times on base (185), pitches seen (2,110), batting average vs. lefthanded pitchers and lowest percentage of swings on the first pitch (14.9)

Mike Sweeney

2004 Season

For the second straight year, Mike Sweeney missed a third of the season due to back problems. He struggled through a slow first half before regaining his batting stroke at midseason, only to go on the disabled list in late August with chronic back spasms and stiffness caused by a herniated disc. Although he was ready to come off the DL in September, Sweeney was shut down for the year by Royals management, who didn't want to risk further injury during an already lost season.

Hitting

Although persistent back problems have sapped his power by reducing his swing and preventing him from getting full extension, Sweeney remains a potent combination of contact and power hitting. His powerful line-drive stroke has natural loft, and he drives the ball to all fields with above-average punch. Sweeney is a patient hitter who reads pitches well and displays superior strike-zone judgment. Lefthanders recently have had some success throwing the ball in on his hands, but he still is a dangerous hitter with runners on base, equally likely to beat pitchers with a long-ball or a run-scoring single.

Baserunning & Defense

An aggressively smart baserunner, Sweeney takes the extra base and is effective as a basestealer because he reads pitchers' moves so well. He has a poor defensive reputation, but he has improved around the bag at first. Sweeney has decent range and mobility, but still has a great deal of trouble adjusting to errant throws.

2005 Outlook

Good health and a strong back are the top concerns for Sweeney in 2005. He's a much better hitter than he has shown the last two years, and he can be expected to prove it once again if he can have a complete and pain-free batting stroke. Few players bring as much emotion to the park as Sweeney, and the dismal 2004 season is sure to motivate him more than most to regain his status as one of the game's best hitters.

Position: 1B/DH
Bats: R **Throws:** R
Ht: 6' 3" **Wt:** 225

Opening Day Age: 31
Born: 7/22/73 in Orange, CA
ML Seasons: 10

Overall Statistics

	G	AB	R	H	D	T	HR	RBI	SB	BB	SO	Avg	OBP	Slg
'04	106	411	56	118	23	0	22	79	3	33	44	.287	.347	.504
Car.	1026	3717	588	1132	228	4	161	683	45	406	417	.305	.377	.498

Where He Hits the Ball

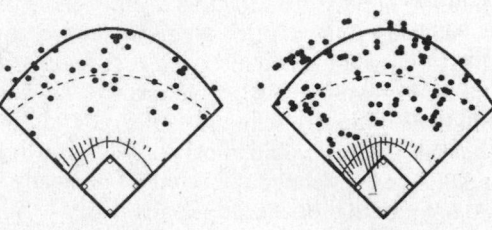

Vs. LHP   **Vs. RHP**

2004 Situational Stats

	AB	H	HR	RBI	Avg		AB	H	HR	RBI	Avg
Home	205	59	8	37	.288	LHP	113	25	4	8	.221
Road	206	59	14	42	.286	RHP	298	93	18	71	.312
First Half	294	82	16	57	.279	Sc Pos	118	39	7	60	.331
Scnd Half	117	36	6	22	.308	Clutch	48	12	1	9	.250

2004 Rankings (American League)

- 10th in errors at first base (4)
- Led the Royals in home runs, total bases (207), RBI, intentional walks (9), batting average with runners in scoring position and batting average vs. righthanded pitchers

Jaime Cerda

Position: RP
Bats: L **Throws:** L
Ht: 6' 0" **Wt:** 175

Opening Day Age: 26
Born: 10/26/78 in
Fresno, CA
ML Seasons: 3
Pronunciation:
SER-da

Overall Statistics

	W	L	Pct.	ERA	G	GS	Sv	IP	H	BB	SO	HR	Avg
'04	1	4	.200	3.15	53	0	2	45.2	41	30	33	1	.244
Car.	2	5	.286	3.82	112	0	2	103.2	95	64	73	5	.248

2004 Situational Stats

	W	L	ERA	Sv	IP		AB	H	HR	RBI	Avg
Home	0	3	3.32	0	21.2	LHB	65	12	0	6	.185
Road	1	1	3.00	2	24.0	RHB	103	29	1	11	.282
First Half	1	1	2.81	1	25.2	Sc Pos	61	12	0	16	.197
Scnd Half	0	3	3.60	1	20.0	Clutch	61	17	0	5	.279

2004 Season

Acquired in an offseason trade from the Mets in January 2004, Jaime Cerda made the most of his first opportunity to spend almost a full season in the major leagues. Cerda was a consistent setup man all year, and even earned the first two saves of his career while leading the Royals in ERA and games pitched.

Pitching & Defense

When he throws strikes, Cerda can be difficult to hit, especially for lefthanders. His funky delivery gives batters a difficult read and generates natural movement on his low-90s fastball. Few hitters get solid swings against Cerda, and he has succeeded in keeping the ball in the ballpark. He hasn't fared particularly well when used on consecutive days. Baserunners get a poor read on Cerda's pitching motion, reducing their jump off first. He's an awkward fielder who reacts slowly on bunts and grounders.

2005 Outlook

While control problems will prevent Cerda from becoming a closer, he can be a successful setup man, especially if used for situational work. Smoothing out his delivery in order to throw more strikes could turn Cerda into a lights-out setup man.

Chris George

Position: SP
Bats: L **Throws:** L
Ht: 6' 2" **Wt:** 200

Opening Day Age: 25
Born: 9/16/79 in
Houston, TX
ML Seasons: 4

Overall Statistics

	W	L	Pct.	ERA	G	GS	Sv	IP	H	BB	SO	HR	Avg
'04	1	2	.333	7.23	10	7	0	42.1	60	25	15	1	.331
Car.	14	20	.412	6.48	47	44	0	237.1	300	95	99	39	.309

2004 Situational Stats

	W	L	ERA	Sv	IP		AB	H	HR	RBI	Avg
Home	0	1	6.43	0	21.0	LHB	41	13	0	10	.317
Road	1	1	8.02	0	21.1	RHB	140	47	1	27	.336
First Half	1	1	5.20	0	27.2	Sc Pos	63	28	0	36	.444
Scnd Half	0	1	11.05	0	14.2	Clutch	3	2	0	0	.667

2004 Season

Long-time prospect Chris George opened the year with Triple-A Omaha and pitched well enough to warrant a June callup. After a pair of shellackings, he was returned to Omaha for a second time at the end of July. While there he made a mechanical adjustment and unexpectedly added five MPH to his fastball. Despite that, his results remained poor when he was recalled to KC in September.

Pitching & Defense

George works mostly with a low-90s fastball that has decent movement. He gets in trouble when he tries for strikeouts and leaves too many pitches up. George has had spotty command of his offspeed repertoire, although both his slider and changeup are effective pitches when kept down in the strike zone. He lacks a useful offspeed pitch against righthanders. He's a good fielder who holds baserunners well.

2005 Outlook

The key for George will be to keep his pitches down and out of the batter's hitting zone. Consistent command of one or more offspeed pitches will make his fastball more effective. Time may be running out for this much-heralded prospect, and 2005 may be George's last chance to establish himself as a big league starter.

Juan Gonzalez

Position: RF
Bats: R **Throws:** R
Ht: 6' 3" **Wt:** 220

Opening Day Age: 35
Born: 10/16/69 in Vega Baja, PR
ML Seasons: 16
Nickname: Igor

Overall Statistics

G	AB	R	H	D	T	HR	RBI	SB	BB	SO	Avg	OBP	Slg
33	127	17	35	4	1	5	17	0	9	19	.276	.326	.441
1688	6555	1061	1936	388	25	434	1404	26	457	1273	.295	.343	.561

2004 Situational Stats

	AB	H	HR	RBI	Avg		AB	H	HR	RBI	Avg
Home	56	16	1	5	.286	LHP	37	11	3	5	.297
Road	71	19	4	12	.268	RHP	90	24	2	12	.267
First Half	127	35	5	17	.276	Sc Pos	31	9	2	14	.290
Scnd Half	0	0	0	0	–	Clutch	19	5	1	3	.263

2004 Season

The Royals rolled the dice by chasing free-agent slugger Juan Gonzalez in the 2003-04 offseason. He always had hit well at home and, despite an extensive injury history, was seen to be healthy. However, Gonzalez played just 33 games before losing the rest of the season with a disc problem in his lower back. "The GM made a bad sign," said Royals GM Allard Baird after the season.

Hitting, Baserunning & Defense

Gonzalez has a naturally powerful swing to all fields and can reach almost any pitch with his long arms. He hits lefthanders especially well for both average and power. While he makes good contact, he's not selective and will chase breaking pitches out of the strike zone. He also doesn't adjust well once he's behind in the count. Gonzalez has decent foot speed, but often fails to take the extra base and has been excoriated for a lack of hustle in the outfield. Despite a superior arm, Gonzalez is a below-average outfielder.

2005 Outlook

The Royals declined an option on Gonzalez after the last game of the season. His power potential will induce another team to take a chance on him, and if he can stay in the lineup he'll reward that risk with a powerful bat.

Tony Graffanino

Position: 2B
Bats: R **Throws:** R
Ht: 6' 1" **Wt:** 190

Opening Day Age: 32
Born: 6/6/72 in Amityville, NY
ML Seasons: 9
Pronunciation: graf-a-NEEN-oh

Overall Statistics

	G	AB	R	H	D	T	HR	RBI	SB	BB	SO	Avg	OBP	Slg
'04	75	278	37	73	11	0	3	26	10	27	38	.263	.332	.335
Car.	649	1721	271	446	86	15	35	175	41	174	318	.259	.330	.388

2004 Situational Stats

	AB	H	HR	RBI	Avg		AB	H	HR	RBI	Avg
Home	148	41	0	13	.277	LHP	68	18	0	6	.265
Road	130	32	3	13	.246	RHP	210	55	3	20	.262
First Half	222	58	2	23	.261	Sc Pos	62	16	1	23	.258
Scnd Half	56	15	1	3	.268	Clutch	32	11	1	4	.344

2004 Season

Among the less-heralded free agents to join the Royals in the 2003 offseason, Tony Graffanino was expected to shore up second base and provide more bench options. A strong start was hampered by two separate trips to the disabled list, the latter due to a partial tear of his PCL in his left knee. He missed the last two months of the season.

Hitting, Baserunning & Defense

A patient hitter, Graffanino shows good strike-zone judgment and makes average contact. He has trouble with righthanded power pitchers. Still, Graffanino handles the bat well; he can bunt or be used on either end of a hit-and-run. Because he reads pitchers' moves well, Graffanino is a successful basestealer despite merely average speed. Although he lacks range to be a regular shortstop and his arm is mediocre for third base, he provides a steady glove anywhere around the infield.

2005 Outlook

In the second year of his two-year contract, Graffanino hopes to get a better chance to show what he can do. He'll usually start at second base while occasionally filling in elsewhere on the infield. Not a long-term solution, Graffanino will be pushed to the bench when a Royals prospect is ready to take over at the keystone.

Aaron Guiel

Position: LF
Bats: L **Throws:** R
Ht: 5'10" **Wt:** 200

Opening Day Age: 32
Born: 10/5/72 in
Vancouver, BC, Canada
ML Seasons: 3
Pronunciation:
GUY-el

Overall Statistics

	G	AB	R	H	D	T	HR	RBI	SB	BB	SO	Avg	OBP	Slg
'04	42	135	15	21	4	0	5	13	1	17	42	.156	.263	.296
Car.	211	729	108	175	47	0	24	103	5	63	166	.240	.314	.403

2004 Situational Stats

	AB	H	HR	RBI	Avg		AB	H	HR	RBI	Avg
Home	59	11	2	9	.186	LHP	41	7	1	8	.171
Road	76	10	3	4	.132	RHP	94	14	4	5	.149
First Half	75	13	4	10	.173	Sc Pos	38	5	0	7	.132
Scnd Half	60	8	1	3	.133	Clutch	25	7	1	5	.280

2004 Season

Coming off the best campaign of his career in 2003, Aaron Guiel had a lost season in 2004 as he suffered from blurred vision in his left eye. Two laser eye surgeries finally corrected the problem, but the recovery process kept him on the disabled list for much of the season.

Hitting, Baserunning & Defense

Powerfully-built, Guiel is a different hitter depending on the role he's given. As a leadoff man, he'll patiently wait for a pitch to slap into the outfield. With runners on base, however, he'll aggressively attack the first hittable pitch, trying to pull the ball for extra bases. Guiel crowds the plate and doesn't yield to inside pitches. He has trouble against lefties who pound the ball in on his hands. A hustling player who goes all-out in the field and on the bases, Guiel can steal bases but occasionally runs into outs. He has an adequate arm for a corner outfielder and improves his range by running intelligent routes on flyballs.

2005 Outlook

A free agent, Guiel signed a minor league deal to stay with the Royals. While he'd be overmatched playing every day, he can be a useful fourth outfielder who platoons in left or right field and provides a valuable bat off the bench.

Mike MacDougal

Position: RP
Bats: B **Throws:** R
Ht: 6' 4" **Wt:** 195

Opening Day Age: 28
Born: 3/5/77 in Las Vegas, NV
ML Seasons: 4

Overall Statistics

	W	L	Pct.	ERA	G	GS	Sv	IP	H	BB	SO	HR	Avg
'04	1	1	.500	5.56	13	0	1	11.1	16	9	14	2	.314
Car.	5	8	.385	4.42	90	3	28	99.2	103	52	88	8	.268

2004 Situational Stats

	W	L	ERA	Sv	IP		AB	H	HR	RBI	Avg
Home	0	0	1.80	1	5.0	LHB	23	7	1	4	.304
Road	1	1	8.53	0	6.1	RHB	28	9	1	4	.321
First Half	0	1	10.80	1	3.1	Sc Pos	19	3	1	6	.158
Scnd Half	1	0	3.38	0	8.0	Clutch	15	6	1	6	.400

2004 Season

Mike MacDougal was expected to be the Royals' bullpen ace last season. However, a stomach virus weakened him in spring training and kept him on the shelf the first month of the season. After walking too many hitters, MacDougal was sent to Triple-A Omaha in May, before returning with somewhat better control in September.

Pitching & Defense

MacDougal can reach 100 MPH with his rising, four-seam fastball, and his nasty slider is thrown very hard, too. Unfortunately, he often gets caught up in the excitement and tends to overthrow, causing his fastball to sail and his slider to bounce in the dirt. He even overthrows his changeup at times. Consistent deliveries are difficult for this flamethrower. MacDougal is so focused on the hitter that he sometimes completely forgets about baserunners, and his exaggerated delivery leaves him ill-prepared to field his position.

2005 Outlook

Although he certainly has a closer's mentality and hard stuff, MacDougal has to throw strikes with much more regularity before he can again be effective as a stopper. Big things are still expected of MacDougal, and he will be given a significant opportunity to seize the closer's role in 2005.

Desi Relaford

Position: 3B/2B/LF/SS
Bats: B **Throws:** R
Ht: 5' 9" **Wt:** 180

Opening Day Age: 31
Born: 9/16/73 in Valdosta, GA
ML Seasons: 9

Overall Statistics

	G	AB	R	H	D	T	HR	RBI	SB	BB	SO	Avg	OBP	Slg
'04	114	380	45	84	14	0	6	34	5	34	56	.221	.296	.305
Car.	852	2703	349	664	134	17	39	292	78	269	449	.246	.322	.351

2004 Situational Stats

	AB	H	HR	RBI	Avg		AB	H	HR	RBI	Avg
Home	174	39	2	16	.224	LHP	102	22	1	8	.216
Road	206	45	4	18	.218	RHP	278	62	5	26	.223
First Half	184	36	1	10	.196	Sc Pos	73	19	1	24	.260
Scnd Half	196	48	5	24	.245	Clutch	54	11	0	1	.204

2004 Season

It's a common thread—a productive and versatile super-sub wins a regular job, then suddenly can't produce. In Desi Relaford's case, he won the Royals' second-base job in spring training, then suffered a pulled left hamstring in his first at-bat of the season. When he returned from the disabled list, Relaford eventually was moved back to his accustomed bench role, with diminished success.

Hitting, Baserunning & Defense

Relaford is a mildly aggressive hitter who makes consistent contact. His usual approach is to spoil good fastballs while waiting for an offspeed pitch to drive. Relaford handles the bat well and can bunt or hit-and-run. A smart baserunner with good speed, he avoids unnecessary risks while often taking the extra base. Smooth with the glove, Relaford can play almost anywhere except catcher, although he's better suited to second or third base. His arm is exposed in the outfield and lack of range makes him a mediocre shortstop.

2005 Outlook

Wanting to play full-time again, Relaford became a free agent after the season. He will be changing teams, as the Royals didn't offer salary arbitration. If he hopes to secure a regular job, he'll have to be more productive at the plate.

Benito Santiago

Position: C
Bats: R **Throws:** R
Ht: 6' 1" **Wt:** 200

Opening Day Age: 40
Born: 3/9/65 in Ponce, PR
ML Seasons: 19
Pronunciation: sahn-tee-AH-go

Overall Statistics

	G	AB	R	H	D	T	HR	RBI	SB	BB	SO	Avg	OBP	Slg
'04	49	175	15	48	10	0	6	23	1	8	32	.274	.312	.434
Car.	1972	6928	754	1824	322	40	217	920	91	430	1267	.263	.307	.415

2004 Situational Stats

	AB	H	HR	RBI	Avg		AB	H	HR	RBI	Avg
Home	85	26	3	15	.306	LHP	44	11	1	5	.250
Road	90	22	3	8	.244	RHP	131	37	5	18	.282
First Half	175	48	6	23	.274	Sc Pos	42	12	1	17	.286
Scnd Half	0	0	0	0	–	Clutch	25	9	0	2	.360

2004 Season

As one of the Royals' important offseason acquisitions, Benito Santiago was expected to solidify a young pitching staff and provide on-field leadership. He gave the club an adequate mix of defense and power hitting before a broken left hand ended his season in June. Losing Santiago for the season hastened the Royals' acquisition of John Buck, and the catching torch was passed from Santiago.

Hitting, Baserunning & Defense

Santiago's hitting skills have eroded, but he still has moderate power. As his bat has slowed, he has become even more aggressive, looking for a fastball to pull for extra bases. He's easily fooled by pitchers who can throw offspeed stuff for strikes. Santiago no longer is the defensive stalwart he once was; his reactions have slowed and his arm is merely average. Santiago still has a bit of speed, but runs the bases too aggressively for his reduced mobility.

2005 Outlook

Although Santiago is under contract for another year and he'd like to start, the Royals already have announced Buck as their regular catcher for 2005. The club hopes to bring Santiago back in a reserve role, hoping he'll tutor Buck and provide a steadying influence on the young pitching staff.

Matt Stairs

Position: RF/1B/DH/LF
Bats: L **Throws:** R
Ht: 5' 9" **Wt:** 210

Opening Day Age: 37
Born: 2/27/68 in Saint John, NB, Canada
ML Seasons: 12

Overall Statistics

	G	AB	R	H	D	T	HR	RBI	SB	BB	SO	Avg	OBP	Slg
'04	126	439	48	117	21	3	18	66	1	49	92	.267	.345	.451
Car.	1172	3499	536	930	196	10	194	634	24	488	726	.266	.359	.494

2004 Situational Stats

	AB	H	HR	RBI	Avg			AB	H	HR	RBI	Avg
Home	206	59	6	27	.286	LHP	94	21	4	16	.223
Road	233	58	12	39	.249	RHP	345	96	14	50	.278
First Half	233	62	12	33	.266	Sc Pos	116	30	4	46	.259
Scnd Half	206	55	6	33	.267	Clutch	68	15	2	7	.221

2004 Season

Well-traveled Matt Stairs joined the Royals as a free agent in December 2003 and was expected to platoon against righthanded pitchers as a first baseman and designated hitter. Instead he became one of the club's steadiest hitters and an important power source in a suddenly weak lineup. Stairs was one of the Royals' few bright spots in 2004.

Hitting, Baserunning & Defense

Stairs is a guess hitter who is unafraid to swing for the fences. He has a well-refined batting eye and uses a compact stroke to make good contact. He'll fight off good breaking balls, looking for an inner-half fastball, then open up his swing and try to hit the ball out of the park. Stairs struggles against lefties. He's barely adequate as a first baseman and though he gets good reads on flyballs, he lacks the range or arm to impress as an outfielder. He's a slow but conservative baserunner who doesn't run into outs on the bases.

2005 Outlook

The Royals thought enough of Stairs' contribution last season to sign him to a contract extension before the 2004 campaign ended. Often over-looked as merely a platoon player, Stairs brings steady power hitting to any club, and his versatility in the field helps keep him in the lineup.

Scott Sullivan

Position: RP
Bats: R **Throws:** R
Ht: 6' 3" **Wt:** 210

Opening Day Age: 34
Born: 3/13/71 in Carrollton, AL
ML Seasons: 10

Overall Statistics

	W	L	Pct.	ERA	G	GS	Sv	IP	H	BB	SO	HR	Avg
'04	3	4	.429	4.77	49	0	0	60.1	73	24	45	8	.308
Car.	40	28	.588	3.98	558	0	9	737.1	671	281	622	89	.244

2004 Situational Stats

	W	L	ERA	Sv	IP			AB	H	HR	RBI	Avg
Home	2	1	3.38	0	34.2	LHB	93	33	6	18	.355
Road	1	3	6.66	0	25.2	RHB	144	40	2	27	.278
First Half	3	2	3.71	0	43.2	Sc Pos	79	21	1	35	.266
Scnd Half	0	2	7.56	0	16.2	Clutch	64	20	1	13	.313

2004 Season

For the first half of the 2004 season, Scott Sullivan was one of the Royals' few reliable relievers, pitching effectively in late-inning situations although he rarely had a lead to protect. Stiffness in his back began to take its toll later in the year, and he was put on the shelf for good at the end of August. Overall, it was not one of Sullivan's best seasons.

Pitching & Defense

Sullivan lives and dies with a low-90s sinker which he'll throw in almost any situation. He'll use a cutter and changeup to give hitters a different look, and will drop to a sidearm delivery against surprised righthanders to get called strikes. He's a durable pitcher, but he is best used situationally, as he has no reliable pitch against lefties. Sullivan is slow to react on grounders and throws inconsistently to the bases. His below-average pickoff move gives baserunners an edge.

2005 Outlook

As one of the more consistent setup men in the baseball, Sullivan has a few more years left in that role. He'll continue to pitch in the seventh and eighth innings as a bridge to the closer. However, Sullivan would be overmatched if used as a closer.

Kevin Appier (Pos: RHP, Age: 37)

W	L	Pct.	ERA	G	GS	Sv	IP	H	BB	SO	HR	Avg
0	1	.000	13.50	2	2	0	4.0	7	3	2	0	.368
169	137	.552	3.74	414	402	0	2595.1	2425	933	1994	232	.247

Appier made just two April starts before elbow discomfort started again. He went on the DL and never returned. He retired in July, but he signed a minor league deal with KC in December. 2005 Outlook: C

Brandon Berger (Pos: LF, Age: 30, Bats: R)

	G	AB	R	H	D	T	HR	RBI	SB	BB	SO	Avg	OBP	Slg
'04	11	35	5	7	2	0	0	2	1	0	7	.200	.200	.257
Car.	81	217	28	46	8	2	8	24	2	15	45	.212	.268	.378

Berger continues to show power in Triple-A ball, but hasn't done much with his major league opportunities. He signed a minor league deal with the Cardinals in December. 2005 Outlook: C

Adrian Brown (Pos: LF, Age: 31, Bats: B)

	G	AB	R	H	D	T	HR	RBI	SB	BB	SO	Avg	OBP	Slg
'04	5	11	0	3	0	0	0	0	0	0	2	.273	.273	.273
Car.	422	1098	160	286	43	8	11	84	44	107	152	.260	.328	.344

Brown's speed isn't of much value because he doesn't get on base regularly enough to capitalize on it. He was fairly productive as a part-time player for Pittsburgh in 1999 and 2000, but cups of coffee in each subsequent season haven't produced an on-base percentage higher than .284. 2005 Outlook: C

Dee Brown (Pos: LF, Age: 27, Bats: L)

	G	AB	R	H	D	T	HR	RBI	SB	BB	SO	Avg	OBP	Slg
'04	59	195	19	49	7	0	4	24	2	11	50	.251	.293	.349
Car.	263	811	86	190	37	1	14	89	8	50	205	.234	.281	.334

Brown looked like a promising hitter coming up in the late 1990s, but his success in the high minors never has translated well to the majors. He's a free agent who probably will move to another organization and Triple-A club. 2005 Outlook: C

Ryan Bukvich (Pos: RHP, Age: 26)

W	L	Pct.	ERA	G	GS	Sv	IP	H	BB	SO	HR	Avg
0	0	–	3.68	9	0	1	7.1	4	7	7	0	.182
2	0	1.000	6.54	44	0	1	42.2	42	35	35	4	.268

Bukvich looked like a potential closer, at least until he's struggled a bit at the Triple-A level the last two summers. In November, he and and starter Darrell May were dealt to San Diego for outfielder Terrence Long and pitcher Dennis Tankersley. 2005 Outlook: C

Shawn Camp (Pos: RHP, Age: 29)

W	L	Pct.	ERA	G	GS	Sv	IP	H	BB	SO	HR	Avg
'04	2	2	.500	3.92	42	0	2	66.2	74	16	51	10	.285
Car.	2	2	.500	3.92	42	0	2	66.2	74	16	51	10	.285

Camp hasn't been the most successful Triple-A pitcher the last two years, but he stuck with the Royals during the second half and gave them some solid innings. The Royals hope he can build on his 2004 campaign. 2005 Outlook: C

D.J. Carrasco (Pos: RHP, Age: 27)

	W	L	Pct.	ERA	G	GS	Sv	IP	H	BB	SO	HR	Avg
'04	2	2	.500	4.84	30	0	0	35.1	41	15	22	5	.287
Car.	8	7	.533	4.82	80	2	2	115.2	123	55	79	13	.276

Carrasco spent much of 2004 at Triple-A Omaha and pitched well enough to join the Royals for most of the second half. He'll try to establish himself in the majors this time around. 2005 Outlook: C

Alberto Castillo (Pos: C, Age: 35, Bats: R)

	G	AB	R	H	D	T	HR	RBI	SB	BB	SO	Avg	OBP	Slg
'04	29	89	12	24	6	0	1	11	0	14	10	.270	.365	.371
Car.	372	894	80	200	32	1	10	84	2	88	187	.224	.296	.295

Castillo has the catching skills to have floated in and out of the majors since 1995, despite career hitting percentages that stay south of .300. 2005 Outlook: C

Nate Field (Pos: RHP, Age: 29)

	W	L	Pct.	ERA	G	GS	Sv	IP	H	BB	SO	HR	Avg
'04	2	3	.400	4.26	43	0	3	44.1	40	19	30	5	.241
Car.	3	4	.429	4.56	67	0	3	71.0	67	36	52	10	.249

Field was less consistent after an impressive April in which he allowed just one earned run and fanned eight in eight innings as a reliever. He seemed to settle down in July, just before a torn oblique muscle near his left ribcage ended his season in August. 2005 Outlook: B

Byron Gettis (Pos: LF, Age: 25, Bats: R)

	G	AB	R	H	D	T	HR	RBI	SB	BB	SO	Avg	OBP	Slg
'04	21	39	7	7	1	1	0	1	0	8	14	.179	.327	.256
Car.	21	39	7	7	1	1	0	1	0	8	14	.179	.327	.256

An outfield prospect, Gettis took a long time to advance beyond Class-A ball, breaking out with a .302-16-103 season at Double-A Wichita in 2003. He wasn't as successful at Triple-A Omaha in 2004, but got a taste of the majors in June. The Tigers claimed him off waivers in October. 2005 Outlook: C

Alexis Gomez (Pos: LF, Age: 26, Bats: L)

	G	AB	R	H	D	T	HR	RBI	SB	BB	SO	Avg	OBP	Slg
'04	13	29	1	8	1	0	0	4	0	2	8	.276	.323	.310
Car.	18	39	1	10	1	0	0	4	0	2	10	.256	.293	.282

Gomez looked like the Royals' top outfield prospect, but he has stalled the last two seasons at Triple-A Omaha. Hamstring troubles hampered him in 2003, but he still struggled last summer. In October, Gomez was claimed off waivers by Detroit. 2005 Outook: C

Wilton Guerrero (Pos: 2B, Age: 30, Bats: B)

	G	AB	R	H	D	T	HR	RBI	SB	BB	SO	Avg	OBP	Slg
'04	24	32	7	7	0	1	0	1	1	0	4	.219	.219	.281
Car.	678	1678	197	473	53	30	11	127	42	64	249	.282	.308	.369

The MVP season belonged to brother Vladimir, not Wilton, though the older Guerrero had one of his best Triple-A seasons in 2004 and became familiar with the trip between Omaha and Kansas City. He was able to put the bat on the ball often enough through 2001, but seldom since. 2005 Outlook: C

Justin Huisman (Pos: RHP, Age: 25)

	W	L	Pct.	ERA	G	GS	Sv	IP	H	BB	SO	HR	Avg
'04	0	0	–	6.84	14	0	1	25.0	36	8	13	3	.336
Car.	0	0	–	6.84	14	0	1	25.0	36	8	13	3	.336

Huisman climbed quickly through the Colorado system, throwing strikes and inducing grounders, and he joined the Royals in a minor league trade last April. He wasn't quite as dependable at Triple-A Omaha in 2004, his first taste of the Triple-A level, but more time in KC is coming. 2005 Outlook: C

Damian Jackson (Pos: 2B, Age: 31, Bats: R)

	G	AB	R	H	D	T	HR	RBI	SB	BB	SO	Avg	OBP	Slg
'04	21	30	2	3	2	0	1	3	0	4	12	.100	.206	.267
Car.	642	1818	272	443	106	16	23	165	117	203	433	.244	.323	.358

Jackson didn't hit enough as a regular with the Padres in 2000-01, but he's hit even less since his at-bats have dropped below 200 a season the last three years. The Padres inked him to a minor league deal in November. 2005 Outlook: C

Matt Kinney (Pos: RHP, Age: 28)

	W	L	Pct.	ERA	G	GS	Sv	IP	H	BB	SO	HR	Avg
'04	3	5	.375	6.06	43	6	0	78.2	104	30	73	11	.315
Car.	17	27	.386	5.27	98	57	0	377.2	424	168	294	58	.284

Just once in four big league seasons has Kinney posted an ERA below 5.00, and he allowed far more hits per inning last summer than in any of his other seasons. He has spent little time in the minors since 2001, but that may be about to change. Kinney signed a minor league deal with the Giants in December. 2005 Outlook: C

Mendy Lopez (Pos: 2B, Age: 31, Bats: R)

	G	AB	R	H	D	T	HR	RBI	SB	BB	SO	Avg	OBP	Slg
'04	18	38	4	4	0	0	1	4	0	4	9	.105	.209	.184
Car.	190	422	45	102	18	5	6	40	7	27	106	.242	.292	.351

Lopez has generated some impressive Triple-A hitting percentages in recent seasons, but his success hasn't carried over in big league stints with the Royals, Marlins, Astros and Pirates. 2005 Outlook: C

Ruben Mateo (Pos: RF/LF, Age: 27, Bats: R)

	G	AB	R	H	D	T	HR	RBI	SB	BB	SO	Avg	OBP	Slg
'04	51	126	13	26	4	3	3	14	1	8	26	.206	.270	.357
Car.	295	876	106	219	44	6	21	89	11	49	189	.250	.303	.386

Mateo has split each of the last four seasons between the Triple-A level and the majors. He's hit better than .300 and shown power in Triple-A ball in each of the last three years, but the only hitting percentage better than .303 in the bigs has been his meager slugging mark. 2005 Outlook: C

Paul Phillips (Pos: C, Age: 27, Bats: R)

	G	AB	R	H	D	T	HR	RBI	SB	BB	SO	Avg	OBP	Slg
'04	4	5	2	1	0	0	0	0	0	0	1	.200	.333	.200
Car.	4	5	2	1	0	0	0	0	0	0	1	.200	.333	.200

Phillips is a catching prospect whose career has been sidetracked by injuries. In his first go-round at Triple-A Omaha in 2004, he hit .312 in 86 games and surfaced with the Royals in September. He isn't helped by KC's acquisition of catching prospects John Buck and Justin Huber. 2005 Outlook: C

Dennys Reyes (Pos: LHP, Age: 27)

	W	L	Pct.	ERA	G	GS	Sv	IP	H	BB	SO	HR	Avg
'04	4	8	.333	4.75	40	12	0	108.0	114	50	91	12	.273
Car.	19	29	.396	4.76	308	39	2	476.0	487	273	439	46	.268

Reyes bounces between roles, but he has a 4.10 career ERA as a reliever, with a much better H-IP ratio. He signed a minor league deal with San Diego at the end of November. 2005 Outlook: C

Jimmy Serrano (Pos: RHP, Age: 28)

	W	L	Pct.	ERA	G	GS	Sv	IP	H	BB	SO	HR	Avg
'04	1	2	.333	4.68	10	5	0	32.2	35	12	25	5	.280
Car.	1	2	.333	4.68	10	5	0	32.2	35	12	25	5	.280

A reliever for six minor league seasons, Serrano stumbled in five big league starts before doing well in the Royals' pen in September. He'll try to figure it out with the A's, who have signed him to a minor league deal. 2005 Outlook: C

Kelly Stinnett (Pos: C, Age: 35, Bats: R)

	G	AB	R	H	D	T	HR	RBI	SB	BB	SO	Avg	OBP	Slg
'04	20	59	10	18	0	0	3	7	0	5	16	.305	.379	.458
Car.	608	1731	200	412	81	4	57	204	10	174	480	.238	.321	.388

Stinnett hit well as a backup catcher, but Tommy John surgery in June ended his 2004 season. He doesn't have a future in KC, so he signed a minor league deal with Arizona in December. 2005 Outlook: C

Rich Thompson (Pos: RF, Age: 25, Bats: L)

	G	AB	R	H	D	T	HR	RBI	SB	BB	SO	Avg	OBP	Slg
'04	6	1	1	0	0	0	0	0	1	0	0	.000	.000	.000
Car.	6	1	1	0	0	0	0	0	1	0	0	.000	.000	.000

The outfield prospect showed more power in his first full Triple-A season. Thompson still needs to get on base more frequently or show more pop to have much of a big league career. 2005 Outlook: C

Mike Tonis (Pos: C, Age: 26, Bats: R)

	G	AB	R	H	D	T	HR	RBI	SB	BB	SO	Avg	OBP	Slg
'04	2	6	0	0	0	0	0	0	0	1	0	.000	.143	.000
Car.	2	6	0	0	0	0	0	0	0	1	0	.000	.143	.000

Tonis is a catching prospect with solid defensive skills. He falls back on the depth chart with KC's acquisition of catching prospects John Buck and Justin Huber. 2005 Outlook: C

Jorge Vasquez (Pos: RHP, Age: 26)

	W	L	Pct.	ERA	G	GS	Sv	IP	H	BB	SO	HR	Avg
'04	0	0	–	8.10	2	0	0	3.1	4	1	4	1	.267
Car.	0	0	–	8.10	2	0	0	3.1	4	1	4	1	.267

Vasquez has been working his way toward Kansas City on a slower pace. Some time at Triple-A Omaha may be in the cards before he is ready. 2005 Outlook: C

Eduardo Villacis (Pos: RHP, Age: 25)

	W	L	Pct.	ERA	G	GS	Sv	IP	H	BB	SO	HR	Avg
'04	0	1	.000	13.50	1	1	0	3.1	6	4	0	1	.375
Car.	0	1	.000	13.50	1	1	0	3.1	6	4	0	1	.375

Villacis enjoyed a solid Double-A debut in 2004, despite a move from the bullpen to the rotation. Most of his starting success came at Double-A Birmingham. 2005 Outlook: C

Kansas City Royals Minor League Prospects

Organization Overview:

Hopeful of another pennant push after their surprising run in 2003, the Royals stocked up on veterans, but the losses quickly mounted and the club traded centerpiece center fielder Carlos Beltran for a trio of nearly ready prospects, filling needs at catcher and third base. Zack Greinke starred on the mound while David DeJesus blossomed in center and many others got lengthy auditions after the All-Star break. The club also went to a six-man rotation down the stretch to showcase youngsters Jimmy Gobble, Denny Bautista and Chris George. The Royals' September face previewed their immediate future, as the club has made a complete commitment to a youth movement. Recent Royals drafts have focused heavily on college players deemed nearly ready for prime time in hopes of pushing them quickly to the bigs.

Denny Bautista

Position: P   **Opening Day Age:** 24
Bats: R **Throws:** R   **Born:** 8/23/80 in
Ht: 6' 5" **Wt:** 170   Sanchez, DR

Recent Statistics

	W	L	ERA	G	GS	Sv	IP	H	R	BB	SO	HR
2004 AA Bowie	3	5	4.74	14	13	0	62.2	58	37	33	72	5
2004 AA Wichita	4	3	2.53	12	12	0	81.2	68	32	32	73	3
2004 AL Baltimore	0	0	36.00	2	0	0	2.0	6	8	2	1	1
2004 AL Kansas City	0	4	6.51	5	5	0	27.2	38	20	11	18	2

Actually two years older than thought to be when signed by the Marlins in 2000, Bautista has a powerful fastball that reaches the upper 90s. He also has a good curveball and changeup, but inconsistent mechanics often cause the lanky Bautista to suddenly lose command. The Royals acquired him at midseason from the Orioles in exchange for Jason Grimsley. Bautista then pitched well enough at Double-A Wichita to earn a chance in the Royals' rotation in September. A Futures Game participant with high upside potential, he is one of several young hurlers who will be given a chance to earn a lower rotation spot with the parent club in 2005.

Andres Blanco

Position: SS   **Opening Day Age:** 20
Bats: B **Throws:** R   **Born:** 4/11/84 in
Ht: 5' 10" **Wt:** 155   Carabobo, VZ

Recent Statistics

	G	AB	R	H	D	T	HR	RBI	SB	BB	SO	Avg
2004 AA Wichita	93	324	34	80	10	2	0	21	7	18	44	.247
2004 AL Kansas City	19	60	9	19	2	2	0	5	1	5	6	.317

Blanco's defensive prowess has been compared to Omar Vizquel's. Both have strong, accurate arms and superb range. It is Blanco's glovework that got him to Kansas City for his major league debut in 2004, when

the Royals demoted Angel Berroa, largely due to Berroa's defensive struggles. Blanco easily can be overmatched by power pitchers and has virtually no power—he has never hit a home run as a professional. He uses a short stroke to punch at pitches, hoping to slap them through the infield. Blanco has reasonable strike-zone judgment and runs very well, so he can help his team on offense. But he'll have to make a lot of progress as a hitter to avoid a "good glove, no hit" tag.

Ruben Gotay

Position: 2B   **Opening Day Age:** 22
Bats: B **Throws:** R   **Born:** 12/25/82 in Rio
Ht: 5' 11" **Wt:** 160   Piedras, PR

Recent Statistics

	G	AB	R	H	D	T	HR	RBI	SB	BB	SO	Avg
2004 AA Wichita	106	404	71	117	22	6	9	68	9	51	60	.290
2004 AL Kansas City	44	152	17	41	7	3	1	16	0	9	36	.270

A late-round draft pick in 2000, Gotay has a mix of talent and few serious weaknesses. He's got good infield range and quick enough reflexes to play third base, although his relatively weak arm makes him better suited to second, where he twice has been named his league's best defensive second baseman in the last three years. The switch-hitting Gotay hits better from the left side, but he's an extremely patient batter who slashes line drives to all parts of the park and uses his above-average speed and gap power to pile up extra-base hits. The Royals' 2004 Minor League Player of the Year, Gotay will use his offensive skills to force his way into their big league lineup soon.

Chris Lubanski

Position: OF   **Opening Day Age:** 20
Bats: L **Throws:** L   **Born:** 3/24/85 in
Ht: 6' 3" **Wt:** 180   Lansdale, PA

Recent Statistics

	G	AB	R	H	D	T	HR	RBI	SB	BB	SO	Avg
2003 R Az Royals I	53	221	41	72	4	6	4	27	9	18	50	.326
2004 A Burlington	128	487	64	133	26	7	9	56	16	43	106	.273

Since his selection as the fifth player taken overall in the 2003 draft, Lubanski has continued to impress scouts. His strong showing in the Rookie-level Arizona League earned him honors as its top prospect in 2003, and he was chosen the club's best player at Class-A Burlington in 2004. Lubanski hits for both power and average. He has a smooth stroke and the ball jumps off his bat. He has struggled at times to make consistent contact, however, and is learning how to read pitches, but he projects as an important run producer. Strong, athletic and fast, Lubanski runs well enough to play center field, despite a below-average arm. Look for him to possibly earn a jump to Double-A.

Donnie Murphy

Position: 2B   **Opening Day Age:** 22
Bats: R **Throws:** R   **Born:** 3/10/83 in
Ht: 5' 10" **Wt:** 180   Lakewood, CA

Recent Statistics

	G	AB	R	H	D	T	HR	RBI	SB	BB	SO	Avg
2004 A Wilmington	129	485	67	124	32	5	10	75	1	52	96	.256
2004 AL Kansas City	7	27	1	5	3	0	0	3	1	0	7	.185

Another offense-oriented second baseman, Murphy uses a compact stroke to make consistent contact. He has exceptional strike-zone judgment and shows surprising power to all fields. The stockily built Murphy doesn't run well, and his range around the keystone is lacking, but he has enough of a throwing arm and power potential that he could end up at third base. Although his average dipped in a pitchers' park at high Class-A Wilmington in 2004, Murphy led the club in homers and RBI, earning a September callup to Kansas City. A hard-nosed player, he can produce with the bat, but at what position and how often he will play depend upon his progress with the glove.

Danny Tamayo

Position: P   **Opening Day Age:** 25
Bats: R **Throws:** R   **Born:** 6/3/79 in Miami,
Ht: 6' 1" **Wt:** 230   FL

Recent Statistics

	W	L	ERA	G	GS	Sv	IP	H	R	BB	SO	HR
2003 AA Wichita	11	14	4.56	27	26	0	154.0	159	84	56	95	16
2004 AA Wichita	12	7	3.92	25	25	0	142.1	165	66	36	123	15
2004 A Wilmington	0	1	9.53	3	3	0	11.1	16	12	5	10	1

In four minor league seasons, Tamayo has shown he needs a couple of years to master each level. In 2004, he succeeded at Double-A Wichita, placing among Texas League leaders in several categories. Although Tamayo's fastball only reaches the low 90s, he's unafraid to challenge hitters. He sets them up with the fastball and gets them out with an above-average changeup. He throws strikes, but his lack of a reliable breaking pitch may limit his advancement. After being named the club's Minor League Pitcher of the Year in 2004, Tamayo has an outside chance to make the big club in the spring. Most likely, he'll spend 2005 at Triple-A Omaha before a late-season callup to KC.

Mark Teahen

Position: 3B   **Opening Day Age:** 23
Bats: L **Throws:** R   **Born:** 9/6/81 in
Ht: 6' 3" **Wt:** 210   Redlands, CA

Recent Statistics

	G	AB	R	H	D	T	HR	RBI	SB	BB	SO	Avg
2003 A Modesto	121	453	68	128	27	4	3	71	4	66	113	.283
2004 AA Midland	53	197	31	66	15	4	6	36	0	29	44	.335
2004 AAA Sac'mento	20	69	9	19	8	0	0	10	0	11	22	.275
2004 AAA Omaha	66	246	33	69	15	1	8	31	0	21	69	.280

One of three prospects received when the Royals dealt Carlos Beltran in June, Teahen may have been the most coveted. He combines good plate discipline and outstanding power potential with superior defense to rate as one of the minor leagues' best third-base prospects. He has line-drive ability and can pull the ball for extra bases. Teahen's strong arm and solid glove make him a superior third sacker. He has struggled with making consistent contact at the plate, and hasn't yet made the most of his power potential, but he still has made rapid progress in the minors. Despite an outstanding Arizona Fall League showing, Teahen won't be rushed. Instead, he'll start the year at Triple-A and will be called up to Kansas City when he proves himself fully ready.

Mike Wood

Position: P   **Opening Day Age:** 24
Bats: R **Throws:** R   **Born:** 4/26/80 in West
Ht: 6' 3" **Wt:** 210   Palm Beach, FL

Recent Statistics

	W	L	ERA	G	GS	Sv	IP	H	R	BB	SO	HR
2004 AAA Sac'mento	11	3	2.80	15	15	0	90.0	83	42	24	66	8
2004 AL Kansas City	3	8	5.94	17	17	0	100.0	112	67	28	54	16

Despite possessing only a 90-MPH fastball, Wood succeeds because he changes speeds and works to the corners. He uses a seamless delivery that gives his pitches natural sink, and he's able to throw strikes consistently. He complements the heater with a sharp slider that drops away from righthanded hitters, and he also will work in splitters and changeups. Wood began his career as an infielder, so he has low mileage on his arm. He came to Kansas City in June as one of three prospects the club received in the Carlos Beltran trade. While Wood never will overpower big league hitters, his ability to consistently throw strikes will help him succeed as a durable, innings-eating starter or possibly as a long reliever.

Others to Watch

Righthander **Colt Griffin** (22) throws a four-seamer in the upper 90s, but his control is far too inconsistent to succeed as a starter, so the righthander shifted to short relief in 2004. He was slightly less wild in relief but still battled control problems for most of the year. . . A strong start at Class-A Burlington, including 34 stolen bases in 82 games, earned **Mitch Maier** (22) a midseason promotion to high Class-A Wilmington. Maier was expected to play a corner outfield spot, but instead stayed at third base. Because he has power and makes consistent contact, Maier will advance on the strength of his bat. . . There's no denying **Calvin Pickering**'s (28) power. He pounded out 35 homers in 89 games at Triple-A Omaha in 2004, earning a callup to Kansas City, where he continued to hit tape-measure homers until pitchers adjusted and stopped throwing him fastballs. Pickering is a defensive liability and tends to be an all-or-nothing kind of hitter. He can help a big league team as a lefty DH and pinch-hitter.

Hubert H. Humphrey Metrodome

Offense

The Metrodome belies its nickname, the "Homerdome." With a deep left field, a baggie in right that turns potential home runs into doubles, and a new, slow-moving turf installed in 2004, the Dome is overrated as an offensive ballpark. Part of the Metrodome's lack of production is due to the Twins' makeup—good pitching, good fielding, average hitting—but the park's reputation was forged in the late 1980s, when the Twins had a powerful lineup and little pitching depth.

Defense

After the Twins installed FieldTurf, they noticed a dramatic difference in the play of shortstops. Cristian Guzman, who seemed to lack range (especially to his right) on the old, hard turf, suddenly looked steadier on the new, soft stuff. Balls that scooted through for singles or got into the gaps for doubles were outs.

Who It Helps the Most

The Metrodome is a boon to lefthanded power hitters, and young Justin Morneau should become the first Twin since Harmon Killebrew to hit 40 homers in a season. With Jason Kubel and Joe Mauer also emerging, the Twins' power production soon should go through the Teflon roof. Now that the turf no longer helps speedy players as it once did, young power hitter Michael Cuddyer may settle into the infield, perhaps at second base, as the Twins hope he can emulate Jeff Kent.

Who It Hurts the Most

Righty power hitters find plenty of long drives dying on the left-field warning track. Slap hitters are finding that the new turf slows the ball down enough to turn more grounders into outs. Righty flyball pitchers can be hurt by the proximity of the baggie, while lefty flyball pitchers, like Kenny Rogers in 2003, benefit from the big left field and the Twins' excellent outfield defense.

Rookies & Newcomers

Strikeout artist Jesse Crain should benefit from the slow turf, excellent fielding behind him, and the deep left field. He could become one of the game's most dominant middle relievers.

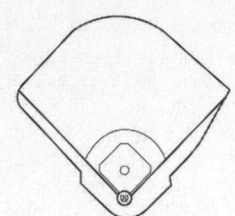

Dimensions: LF-343, LCF-385, CF-408, RCF-367, RF-327

Capacity: 45,423

Elevation: 815 feet

Surface: Turf

Foul Territory: Average

Park Factors

2004 Season

| | Home Games | | | Away Games | | | |
	Twins	Opp	Total	Twins	Opp	Total	Index
G	72	72	144	72	72	144	
Avg	.269	.268	.269	.264	.269	.266	101
AB	2449	2600	5049	2541	2461	5002	101
R	373	320	693	327	320	647	107
H	660	696	1356	671	661	1332	102
2B	137	106	243	137	116	253	95
3B	9	9	18	11	9	20	89
HR	83	74	157	89	74	163	95
BB	240	174	414	224	219	443	93
SO	420	537	957	432	445	877	108
E	46	41	87	44	51	95	92
E-Infield	41	36	77	38	42	80	96
LHB-Avg	.274	.258	.265	.252	.279	.265	100
LHB-HR	39	34	73	41	41	82	87
RHB-Avg	.266	.276	.271	.273	.260	.267	102
RHB-HR	44	40	84	48	33	81	104

2002-2003

| | Home Games | | | Away Games | | | |
	Twins	Opp	Total	Twins	Opp	Total	Index
G	144	144	288	143	143	286	
Avg	.276	.259	.268	.274	.269	.271	99
AB	4868	5145	10013	5100	4860	9960	100
R	710	628	1338	696	672	1368	97
H	1346	1333	2679	1397	1306	2703	98
2B	313	274	587	280	244	524	111
3B	46	30	76	25	21	46	164
HR	134	151	285	158	177	335	85
BB	462	373	835	414	375	789	105
SO	904	957	1861	949	806	1755	105
E	62	106	168	85	109	194	86
E-Infield	49	87	136	70	91	161	84
LHB-Avg	.287	.261	.274	.283	.276	.280	98
LHB-HR	64	78	142	79	80	.159	89
RHB-Avg	.265	.258	.261	.263	.263	.263	99
RHB-HR	70	73	143	79	97	176	81

2004 Rankings (American League)
- Second-highest strikeout factor
- Lowest walk factor

Ron Gardenhire

2004 Season

Ron Gardenhire won the division as a rookie manager with a talented bullpen, excellent fielding and a team motivated to prove it didn't deserve contraction. He won the division in his second year by again relying on, a strong bullpen and excellent fielding, and by helping an underachieving team rally in the second half. He won the division his third year by completely rebuilding the bullpen—always the strength of the team—and filling out the rotation with pitchers few contenders would have used as starters, Carlos Silva and Terry Mulholland. His next trick: winning a fourth straight title with loads of young talent.

Offense

Gardenhire would prefer to win games with sheer power, but uses the running game and small-ball strategies when he has a dominant pitcher on the mound or he feels his team needs an emotional jump start. Some of the Twins' fastest players aren't necessarily good basestealers. So Gardenhire sometimes takes risks to try to steal a run, and the risks aren't always rewarded. The good news is, the Twins have so many good young hitters blossoming right now.

Pitching & Defense

Gardenhire, like predecessor Tom Kelly, prides himself on working hard on fielding from the first day of spring training, and throughout the organization the focus is on fielding and fundamentals. It shows. Gardenhire will substitute an offensive player for a defensive player when he's desperate for runs—and usually regret it. He believes that once a young pitcher reaches 100 pitches, he's ready to depart. Gardenhire's greatest strength is his use of the bullpen and his ability to keep his key pitchers fresh all year.

2005 Outlook

In three years, Gardenhire has used two different closers, both of whom were unproven before doing the job successfully for the Twins. He's also used about a dozen cleanup hitters, almost as many leadoff batters, and myriad starters and middle relievers. The Twins' organizational depth, plus the coaching staff's ability to adapt, make the Twins the division favorite once again.

Born: 10/24/57 in Butzbach, West Germany

Playing Experience: 1981-1985, NYM

Managerial Experience: 3 seasons

Manager Statistics

Year	Team, Lg	W	L	Pct	GB	Finish
2004	Minnesota, AL	92	70	.568	–	1st Central
3 Seasons		276	209	.569	–	–

2004 Starting Pitchers by Days Rest

	<=3	4	5	6+
Twins Starts	1	93	50	10
Twins ERA	6.75	4.09	3.73	4.17
AL Avg Starts	2	82	47	21
AL ERA	5.36	4.87	4.65	4.93

2004 Situational Stats

	Ron Gardenhire	AL Average
Hit & Run Success %	23.5	36.8
Stolen Base Success %	71.6	68.6
Platoon Pct.	58.8	61.6
Defensive Subs	24	21
High-Pitch Outings	1	5
Quick/Slow Hooks	20/11	20/16
Sacrifice Attempts	68	53

2004 Rankings (American League)

- 1st in 2+ pitching changes in low-scoring games (35)
- 2nd in steals of third base (19) and pinch-hitters used (126)
- 3rd in stolen base attempts (162), steals of second base (97) and double steals (7)

Lew Ford

2004 Season

Lew Ford didn't even make the Twins out of spring training, yet he became one of their most valuable all-around players by midseason. He can hit, hit for occasional power, steal bases (22 steals in 24 attempts), run, throw and provide combative at-bats. His power tailed off late in the season, and he hit just one home run in August and another in September/October, probably the result of a young player dealing with a longer season than he had ever experienced before.

Hitting

The righthanded hitter has a quick bat and jumps all over inside pitches. Many of the hardest balls he hits are fouls down the third-base line, and most of his home runs are dead pulls. Because of his quick bat, he can foul off pitches and draw walks. Ford tends to take outside pitches up the middle when he's swinging well. A line-drive hitter who hits his doubles to left-center and down the left-field line, he should improve his home-run total as he learns to elevate the ball and becomes more familiar with American League pitchers.

Baserunning & Defense

The Twins feared that because of his eccentric personality, Ford might prove to be a poor baserunner, but he's aggressive in taking the extra base and is excellent on steal attempts because of his quick first step. Sometimes Ford takes awkward routes to flyballs, but he gets a quick jump. He has a strong arm that is maximized by his hustle, quick release and accuracy. He keeps a lot of runners from advancing by getting rid of the ball so quickly.

2005 Outlook

The biggest question is, where will Ford play in 2005? Last year, he spent time at all three outfield positions, then moved to DH when Shannon Stewart was healthy enough to man left field. Ford is a better left fielder than Stewart, but the Twins think Stewart is a better player when he plays the field. Ford may battle for playing time in right.

Position: LF/CF/DH/RF
Bats: R **Throws:** R
Ht: 6' 0" **Wt:** 195

Opening Day Age: 28
Born: 8/12/76 in Port Neches, TX
ML Seasons: 2

Overall Statistics

	G	AB	R	H	D	T	HR	RBI	SB	BB	SO	Avg	OBP	Slg
'04	154	569	89	170	31	4	15	72	20	67	75	.299	.381	.446
Car.	188	642	105	194	38	5	18	87	22	75	84	.302	.383	.461

Where He Hits the Ball

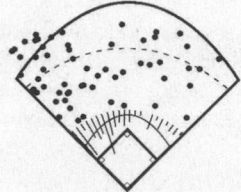
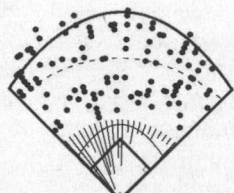

Vs. LHP   **Vs. RHP**

2004 Situational Stats

	AB	H	HR	RBI	Avg		AB	H	HR	RBI	Avg
Home	274	88	6	40	.321	LHP	174	51	8	24	.293
Road	295	82	9	32	.278	RHP	395	119	7	48	.301
First Half	313	96	9	42	.307	Sc Pos	139	44	4	56	.317
Scnd Half	256	74	6	30	.289	Clutch	84	21	1	11	.250

2004 Rankings (American League)

- 1st in stolen-base percentage (90.9)
- 6th in hit by pitch (13)
- 8th in lowest batting average with the bases loaded (.083)
- 10th in errors in center field (3)
- Led the Twins in runs scored, hits, singles, total bases (254), sacrifice flies (7), walks, hit by pitch (13), times on base (250), pitches seen (2,512), plate appearances (658), games played, on-base percentage, on-base percentage for a leadoff hitter (.392), and batting average at home

Cristian Guzman

Position: SS
Bats: B **Throws:** R
Ht: 6' 0" **Wt:** 205

Opening Day Age: 27
Born: 3/21/78 in Santo Domingo, DR
ML Seasons: 6
Pronunciation: GOOZ-mahn

2004 Season

In 2001, Cristian Guzman was one of baseball's most dynamic players. He became an All-Star by hitting for average, placing himself among the league leaders in triples, showing occasional home-run power and displaying excellent range and a strong throwing arm at shortstop. A shoulder injury that year has led to a decline in his skills, and inconsistent performance has made him a veteran shortstop who's more valuable as a fielder than a hitter.

Hitting

Guzman tends to take weak, choppy swings from the left side of the plate that belie his strength. Guzman is a strong man who displays excellent power in batting practice, but his lefthanded swing and his inability to work counts in his favor keep him from displaying that power regularly in games. He is capable of driving the ball from the right side of the plate when he abandons his slap-hitting approach. Guzman doesn't draw enough walks or hit enough homers to be a good offensive player, even when he elevates his average. He doesn't get as many infield hits as he once did, because he's a step slower than three years ago.

Baserunning & Defense

Guzman hasn't been the same baserunner or basestealer since injuring his shoulder in 2001, partly because he's lost speed, partly because he has never become adept at sliding feet-first. When he slid head-first, he was much more difficult to throw out; now he slows down as he approaches a base. Fielding has become his strength. He's not often spectacular, but has excellent hands and can throw from any angle.

2005 Outlook

While he never again will be mentioned among the game's elite shortstops, Guzman is a solid fielder who, when he gets hot, can hit for extra bases and use the whole field. He no longer is an everyday threat to take over a game, and he will need to continue working on his right shoulder and swing to maintain his competence. Those are the limitations he takes to Washington, as Guzman signed a four-year, $16.8 million deal in November to join the transplanted Expos.

Overall Statistics

	G	AB	R	H	D	T	HR	RBI	SB	BB	SO	Avg	OBP	Slg
'04	145	576	84	158	31	4	8	46	10	30	64	.274	.309	.384
Car.	841	3277	458	871	142	61	39	289	102	166	491	.266	.303	.382

Where He Hits the Ball

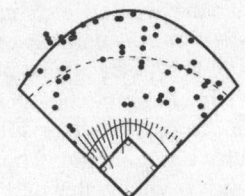

Vs. LHP

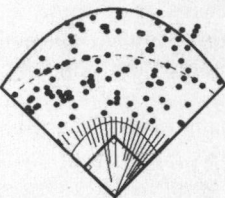

Vs. RHP

2004 Situational Stats

	AB	H	HR	RBI	Avg		AB	H	HR	RBI	Avg
Home	292	89	5	31	.305	LHP	184	60	3	11	.326
Road	284	69	3	15	.243	RHP	392	98	5	35	.250
First Half	344	98	5	28	.285	Sc Pos	123	36	2	40	.293
Scnd Half	232	60	3	18	.259	Clutch	92	24	1	7	.261

2004 Rankings (American League)

- 2nd in fielding percentage at shortstop (.983) and fewest pitches seen per plate appearance (3.36)
- 3rd in highest percentage of swings put into play (54.6)
- 4th in lowest on-base percentage
- 5th in sacrifice bunts (13), highest ground ball-flyball ratio (1.9) and lowest slugging percentage
- 6th in bunts in play (24) and lowest batting average vs. righthanded pitchers
- Led the Twins in at-bats, sacrifice bunts (13), highest groundball-flyball ratio (1.9), bunts in play (24), highest percentage of swings put into play (54.6), steals of third (5) and batting average vs. lefthanded pitchers

Torii Hunter

2004 Season

An early-season hamstring injury—and his career-long inability to get hot in the first half of the season—kept Torii Hunter from having the kind of breakthrough season the Twins have anticipated the last three years. Hunter had a 20-20 season for the second time in three seasons, and again was one of baseball's most dynamic, spectacular fielders. Few big leaguers combine his speed, power and fielding. Hunter has become the Twins' leader because of his buoyant personality and willingness to throw his body into outfield walls and opposing catchers.

Hitting

Early in his career, Hunter tried to adhere to the Twins' philosophy of using the whole field, but now seems to hit better when he concentrates on pulling the ball and hitting for power. He hits most of his home runs off breaking pitches that hang or find the middle of the plate. Hunter still gets himself out too often by swinging at pitches out of the strike zone. He has been a better hitter in big games, when he seems to raise his concentration level. He has performed well against the Yankees in each of the last two postseasons.

Baserunning & Defense

Either Hunter or Andruw Jones is the best center fielder in baseball. Jones may make even better breaks on the ball, but Hunter is more willing to sacrifice his body to make a catch. Hunter is a good baserunner who has learned to get great jumps on steal attempts, and the Twins' new, softer turf has been easier on his knees, allowing him to run more late in the season. He gets rid of the ball quickly with a strong and exceptionally accurate arm.

2005 Outlook

If he can stay healthy, Hunter could become a 30-30 player who drives in 100 runs and raises his average and on-base percentage. The key will be starting quickly and maintaining his legs, and with the Twins' outfield depth, manager Ron Gardenhire can afford to rest or DH him occasionally.

Position: CF/DH
Bats: R **Throws:** R
Ht: 6' 2" **Wt:** 211

Opening Day Age: 29
Born: 7/18/75 in Pine Bluff, AR
ML Seasons: 8

Overall Statistics

	G	AB	R	H	D	T	HR	RBI	SB	BB	SO	Avg	OBP	Slg
'04	138	520	79	141	37	0	23	81	21	40	101	.271	.330	.475
Car.	829	2963	429	791	169	22	119	450	73	200	596	.267	.319	.459

Where He Hits the Ball

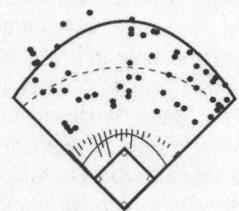 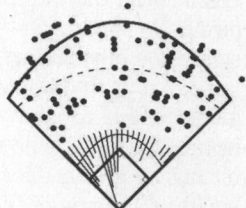

Vs. LHP   **Vs. RHP**

2004 Situational Stats

	AB	H	HR	RBI	Avg		AB	H	HR	RBI	Avg
Home	262	70	9	41	.267	LHP	157	40	8	27	.255
Road	258	71	14	40	.275	RHP	363	101	15	54	.278
First Half	267	74	11	42	.277	Sc Pos	130	37	4	58	.285
Scnd Half	253	67	12	39	.265	Clutch	87	19	3	12	.218

2004 Rankings (American League)

- 3rd in GDPs (23)
- 4th in fielding percentage in center field (.988)
- Led the Twins in doubles, RBI, stolen bases and GDPs (23)

Jacque Jones

2004 Season

Burdened by worries about his father's health and his status with the team, Jacque Jones never seemed comfortable and carefree in 2004. Still, he produced power, but lost points off his batting average and endured prolonged slumps at a point in his career when he was expected to improve his patience and consistency. He enjoyed a productive Division Series against New York in the days following his father's death.

Hitting

Jones has tremendous bat speed that can drive a fastball a long way. In late 2003 and last spring, he looked like he was increasing his patience and selectivity at the plate, but often looked overeager during the summer. When he slumps, Jones tends to swing at virtually anything near the dish early in the count. He will get himself in a hole and his at-bats will last a matter of seconds. As his salary increases, he will need to improve in these areas to remain an everyday player for a good team. Greater patience would generate a better on-base percentage, as well as better power numbers, because he'd be swinging at better pitches to hit.

Baserunning & Defense

A smart, aggressive baserunner, Jones isn't blindingly fast, but can steal the occasional base. He's one of the best-fielding corner outfielders in the game in terms of range, but continues to have trouble finding his release point on throws. One might fly to the backstop, and the next might roll to the cutoff man. His throws aren't consistent enough to play right field in many stadiums besides the Metrodome, which has a shallow right-field fence.

2005 Outlook

There's a lot of talent in Jones' body, and he has demonstrated the work ethic and attentiveness required to still improve. An emotional man, Jones could benefit from a more peaceful 2005. If he can combine his raw power and bat speed with a little more patience and a higher on-base percentage, he could become a borderline All-Star talent. If he doesn't progress, he could wind up platooning somewhere.

Position: RF
Bats: L **Throws:** L
Ht: 5'10" **Wt:** 195

Opening Day Age: 29
Born: 4/25/75 in San Diego, CA
ML Seasons: 6

Overall Statistics

	G	AB	R	H	D	T	HR	RBI	SB	BB	SO	Avg	OBP	Slg
'04	151	555	69	141	22	1	24	80	13	40	117	.254	.315	.427
Car.	834	2969	418	844	167	11	109	403	54	180	617	.284	.329	.458

Where He Hits the Ball

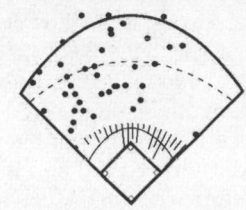
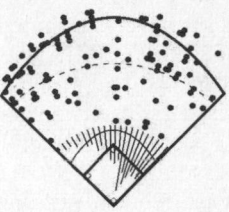

Vs. LHP   **Vs. RHP**

2004 Situational Stats

	AB	H	HR	RBI	Avg		AB	H	HR	RBI	Avg
Home	276	69	9	34	.250	LHP	155	38	2	18	.245
Road	279	72	15	46	.258	RHP	400	103	22	62	.258
First Half	311	81	14	49	.260	Sc Pos	136	37	10	63	.272
Scnd Half	244	60	10	31	.246	Clutch	84	26	6	20	.310

2004 Rankings (American League)

- 1st in fielding percentage in right field (.994) and lowest batting average with the bases loaded (.000)
- 2nd in lowest stolen-base percentage (56.5), highest percentage of swings that missed (28.7) and highest percentage of swings on the first pitch (40.6)
- 6th in highest groundball-flyball ratio (1.9) and lowest on-base percentage
- 8th in lowest percentage of pitches taken (48.2)
- 9th in caught stealing (10)
- Led the Twins in caught stealing (10) and strikeouts

Corey Koskie

2004 Season

One of baseball's best all-around third basemen—when nagging injuries haven't kept him off the field—Corey Koskie slumped from May through July. He batted .230 with just 29 RBI over those three months. An excellent if unconventional fielder, Koskie improved the accuracy of his throwing in 2004, and used his hockey-goalie background to knock down balls he couldn't field cleanly. He produced excellent power, considering his limited at-bats, but didn't hit for the kind of average that he usually generates.

Hitting

Koskie spent two-thirds of the season trying to make an unconventional batting stance work—and it never did. Late in the season, he looked at tapes from 2001, when he might have been the Twins' best all-around player, and realized he had raised his hands uncomfortably high. He lowered his hands and instantly looked like a different hitter, getting to the ball quicker to drive and pull it more frequently. A guess hitter who thinks constantly about mechanics, he still can look bad when he swings and misses.

Baserunning & Defense

Though not a natural or graceful baserunner, Koskie is aggressive and smart enough to take extra bases. When healthy, he is a threat to steal. In the field, he has good first-step quickness and hands. He gets rid of the ball quickly and has a strong arm. While he may not be in the class of Eric Chavez or Scott Rolen as a fielder, Koskie is as good as anyone else. Once known for making erratic throws, he seemed to concentrate and make more on-target tosses in 2004, knowing Gold Glover Doug Mientkiewicz no longer was there to save his mistakes.

2005 Outlook

The big question about Koskie entering the 2004 season was his health, and he enjoyed a reasonably healthy year. If the free-agent third baseman can maintain his stroke, he again could rank with the best all-around third basemen in the game, one capable of hitting 25 homers, stealing 20 bases, driving in 100 runs and scoring another 100.

Position: 3B
Bats: L **Throws:** R
Ht: 6' 3" **Wt:** 219

Opening Day Age: 31
Born: 6/28/73 in Anola, MB, Canada
ML Seasons: 7
Pronunciation: KOSS-key

Overall Statistics

	G	AB	R	H	D	T	HR	RBI	SB	BB	SO	Avg	OBP	Slg
'04	118	422	68	106	24	2	25	71	9	49	103	.251	.342	.495
Car.	816	2788	438	781	180	13	101	437	66	385	647	.280	.373	.463

Where He Hits the Ball

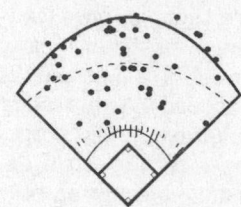 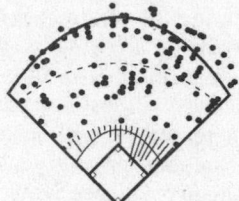

Vs. LHP   **Vs. RHP**

2004 Situational Stats

	AB	H	HR	RBI	Avg		AB	H	HR	RBI	Avg
Home	213	50	16	32	.235	LHP	133	31	5	19	.233
Road	209	56	9	39	.268	RHP	289	75	20	52	.260
First Half	237	58	13	37	.245	Sc Pos	102	25	1	37	.245
Scnd Half	185	48	12	34	.259	Clutch	75	18	3	11	.240

2004 Rankings (American League)

- 4th in lowest fielding percentage at third base (.963)
- Led the Twins in home runs and intentional walks (10)

Kyle Lohse

2004 Season

With Rick Reed gone in 2004, Kyle Lohse was supposed to step into the No. 3 starter role and show improvement as a key contributor to a contending team. He fell short. Plagued by a lack of command and a tendency to overthrow and lose his composure when he had a bad inning, Lohse failed to fulfill his promise in 2004. Twins executives refused to give up on him, believing his combination of size, strength, athleticism and three good pitches can make him a solid No. 2 or 3 starter.

Pitching

Too often in 2004, Lohse left his fastball over the middle of the plate, nibbled with his breaking pitches and fell behind, or issued hurtful walks. While he has good stuff, he can't overpower hitters with a 93-94 MPH fastball. He must locate the ball to succeed. Lohse has a good slider and curveball, but needs to consistently execute his changeup with the same arm speed as his fastball. When in trouble, he has bad mound presence, looking disgusted by umpires' calls and teammates' mistakes. Near the end of the season, he began handling himself better. To his credit, he always has been durable and willing to take the ball under any circumstances.

Defense

A good, agile athlete, Lohse shows quick reflexes as a fielder and good speed covering first base. He gets to lots of balls, usually fielding them cleanly, but sometimes makes mistakes trying to force the spectacular play. He has a decent move to first base, though he allowed a career-high 16 steals by opposing baserunners in 2004.

2005 Outlook

Lohse went 3-18 at Double-A New Britain in 2000. In 2001, he pitched well enough at New Britain and Triple-A Edmonton to get promoted to the majors. So, there's a precedent for a solid rebound in 2005. His ERA has risen each of the last three years, but he seems to be a mental adjustment away from being a dependable big league pitcher.

Position: SP
Bats: R **Throws:** R
Ht: 6' 2" **Wt:** 201

Opening Day Age: 26
Born: 10/4/78 in Chico, CA
ML Seasons: 4
Pronunciation: lowshe

Overall Statistics

	W	L	Pct.	ERA	G	GS	Sv	IP	H	BB	SO	HR	Avg
'04	9	13	.409	5.34	35	34	0	194.0	240	76	111	28	.305
Car.	40	39	.506	4.86	119	114	0	666.0	734	220	429	98	.279

2004 Pitching Profile

	Kyle Lohse	AL Average
Overall Strike %	61.4	62.3
1st Pitch Strike %	57.4	58.1
Ratio	1.63	1.42
Strikeouts per 9 IP	5.15	6.45
Walks per 9 IP	3.53	3.34
Home Runs per 9 IP	1.30	1.15
Strikeout/Walk Ratio	1.46	1.93
Groundball/Flyball Ratio	1.18	1.17

2004 Situational Stats

	W	L	ERA	Sv	IP		AB	H	HR	RBI	Avg
Home	6	6	4.33	0	89.1	LHB	448	130	17	65	.290
Road	3	7	6.19	0	104.2	RHB	339	110	11	45	.324
First Half	3	6	4.71	0	107.0	Sc Pos	193	51	7	78	.264
Scnd Half	6	7	6.10	0	87.0	Clutch	17	5	0	1	.294

2004 Rankings (American League)

- 1st in fielding percentage at pitcher (1.000) and highest on-base percentage allowed (.368)
- 2nd in highest ERA on the road
- 3rd in games started, lowest strikeout-walk ratio (1.5) and highest batting average allowed vs. righthanded batters
- 5th in highest batting average allowed (.305)
- 6th in losses and hits allowed
- 7th in highest ERA, highest slugging percentage allowed (.473) and highest walks per nine innings (3.5)
- 9th in runners caught stealing (8)
- 10th in walks allowed, stolen bases allowed (16) and lowest winning percentage
- Lcd thc Twins in losscs, gamcs startcd, home runs allowed, walks allowed, stolen bases allowed (16) and runners caught stealing (8)

Joe Mauer

2004 Season

Heralded rookie Joe Mauer displayed every skill needed to be an All-Star catcher for the next 10 years, except durability. In the spring, Mauer was everybody's pick to be the American League Rookie of the Year, but he was injured in the second game of the regular season and wound up with just 107 big league at-bats. This was a tremendous disappointment for an organization that traded away A.J. Pierzynski, based on the belief that Mauer would catch 120 games.

Hitting

When he was on the field, Mauer was a revelation. As a 21 year old, he had the best swing and approach to hitting on the team. In fact, he has one of the smoothest, most effortless swings in the game, as well as a Barry Bonds-like knowledge of the strike zone. Mauer can hit to all fields with power. His natural swing produces lots of singles up the middle, and he can go with the outside pitch or pull the inside pitch. He will get stronger and learn to sit on pitches, so his power numbers should increase dramatically early in his career.

Baserunning & Defense

Fast for a catcher, Mauer's speed probably will be affected by the knee injury that ruined his rookie year. While he is a good baserunner who is capable of turning gap hits into triples, Mauer is not much of a threat to steal. Defensively, he has an excellent arm and quick release, and already is adept at blocking pitches. Although he took quickly to handling major league pitchers, he will need to learn the league to call a better game.

2005 Outlook

If he's healthy and can get 550 at-bats, Mauer could be an All-Star. If the knee continues to bother Mauer, the Twins may have to switch him to first or third base. If he catches, he probably will get more days off and do some DH time instead. Mauer has a chance to be one of the best players of his era—health willing.

Position: C
Bats: L **Throws:** R
Ht: 6' 4" **Wt:** 220

Opening Day Age: 21
Born: 4/19/83 in St. Paul, MN
ML Seasons: 1

Overall Statistics

	G	AB	R	H	D	T	HR	RBI	SB	BB	SO	Avg	OBP	Slg
'04	35	107	18	33	8	1	6	17	1	11	14	.308	.369	.570
Car.	35	107	18	33	8	1	6	17	1	11	14	.308	.369	.570

Where He Hits the Ball

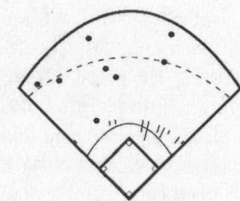 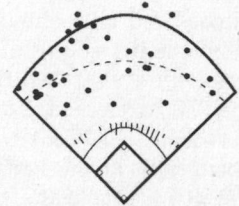

Vs. LHP   **Vs. RHP**

2004 Situational Stats

	AB	H	HR	RBI	Avg		AB	H	HR	RBI	Avg
Home	73	23	4	14	.315	LHP	33	6	0	4	.182
Road	34	10	2	3	.294	RHP	74	27	6	13	.365
First Half	106	33	6	17	.311	Sc Pos	22	6	2	13	.273
Scnd Half	1	0	0	0	.000	Clutch	18	4	1	4	.222

2004 Rankings (American League)

- Did not rank near the top or bottom in any category

Justin Morneau

2004 Season

At times in his rookie season, Justin Morneau showed himself to be the opposite of the quintessential Twins hitter who has been key to the franchise's resurgence. A young hitter with raw power, Morneau seemed willing to take big swings and absorb strikeouts for the occasional homer. He hit 19 homers in 280 at-bats, and should hit them more frequently once he learns pitchers and adjusts to how they work him. While he hits monstrous homers, Morneau sometimes will "miss" the ball and still hit it over the fence.

Hitting

Morneau often took a big cut last season, making him susceptible to breaking pitches. By the end of the year, though, he was better at fouling off pitches that fooled him, which should make him a combative hitter who can draw walks when pitchers try to work around him. Morneau has tremendous power when he pulls the ball, but he can hit for average as well, and seems to be at his best when he waits on the ball and drives it to left-center and right-center. He showed a late-season tendency to cut down his swing with two strikes and serve the ball to the outfield to drive in runs.

Baserunning & Defense

Morneau doesn't look natural as a baserunner or fielder. He looks awkward on the bases and hesitant to take the extra bag. His speed isn't an asset or a liability. He improved dramatically as a fielder as he adjusted to handling first base in the majors. Morneau became adept at scooping low and bouncing throws, and adequate on balls hit to him, but he needs work on deciding when to range to his right and when to let the second baseman have the ball. Comparisons to his predecessor, Gold Glove first baseman Doug Mientkiewicz, are unfair.

2005 Outlook

No Twin has hit 30 homers since 1987, and no one has hit 40 since Harmon Killebrew stroked 41 in 1970. Morneau will be the Twins' next Killebrew—a pure power hitter and run producer who will prove adequate in the field.

Position: 1B/DH
Bats: L **Throws:** R
Ht: 6' 4" **Wt:** 228

Opening Day Age: 23
Born: 5/15/81 in New Westminster, BC, Canada
ML Seasons: 2
Pronunciation: more-no

Minnesota

Overall Statistics

	G	AB	R	H	D	T	HR	RBI	SB	BB	SO	Avg	OBP	Slg
'04	74	280	39	76	17	0	19	58	0	28	54	.271	.340	.536
Car.	114	386	53	100	21	0	23	74	0	37	84	.259	.326	.492

Where He Hits the Ball

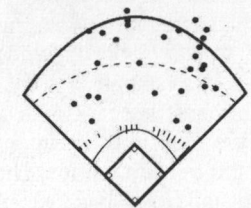

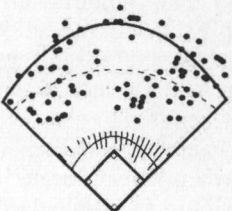

Vs. LHP **Vs. RHP**

2004 Situational Stats

	AB	H	HR	RBI	Avg		AB	H	HR	RBI	Avg
Home	129	35	9	29	.271	LHP	75	18	3	18	.240
Road	151	41	10	29	.272	RHP	205	58	16	40	.283
First Half	24	7	2	3	.292	Sc Pos	79	25	6	42	.316
Scnd Half	256	69	17	55	.270	Clutch	43	11	1	7	.256

2004 Rankings (American League)

- 9th in cleanup slugging percentage (.519)
- Led the Twins in slugging percentage, HR frequency (14.7 ABs per HR), cleanup slugging percentage (.519) and batting average with two strikes (.254)

Joe Nathan

2004 Season

Righthander Joe Nathan made a difficult and surprising transition from good setup man in the National League to dominant closer in the American League. He proved he could deal with the pressure and disappointments of the position, handling himself with great professionalism. The Twins' scouting report on him when they traded for him was that he usually was unimpressive in spring training, but gained arm strength as the season progressed. That proved true. He increased his velocity from 87 MPH in the spring to 98 MPH in some tense situations late in the summer.

Pitching

Nathan can throw his fastball up to 98 MPH, and his slider arrives at 88 MPH, giving him two dominant pitches and a way to vary speeds while remaining in power mode. His fastball is somewhat straight, so he has his best success with it when he gets hitters to chase it up in the zone, or when he can locate it on the outside corner. The slider is particularly devastating, because it approaches the velocity of a big league fastball before diving toward a lefthander's feet.

Defense

Like many closers, Nathan doesn't have a particularly good pickoff move, but he is quick and athletic enough to hold runners decently. He was drafted by the Giants as a shortstop, so he has good range and fielding instincts. In five big league seasons, he has yet to commit an error.

2005 Outlook

Nathan has shown he has the pitches and mentality to be an excellent closer for years to come. He proved durable in 2004, even though Twins manager Ron Gardenhire was willing to bring him in to get more than three outs, especially during the postseason. Because the Twins try to avoid making their closer warm up multiple times during a game, and are determined to give their relievers proper rest, Nathan should be able to stay healthy and strong in his new role.

Position: RP
Bats: R **Throws:** R
Ht: 6' 4" **Wt:** 205

Opening Day Age: 30
Born: 11/22/74 in Houston, TX
ML Seasons: 5

Overall Statistics

	W	L	Pct.	ERA	G	GS	Sv	IP	H	BB	SO	HR	Avg
'04	1	2	.333	1.62	73	0	44	72.1	48	23	89	3	.187
Car.	25	12	.676	3.59	194	29	45	338.2	273	165	289	39	.221

2004 Pitching Profile

	Joe Nathan	AL Average
Overall Strike %	63.3	62.3
1st Pitch Strike %	59.5	58.1
Ratio	0.98	1.42
Strikeouts per 9 IP	11.07	6.45
Walks per 9 IP	2.86	3.34
Home Runs per 9 IP	0.37	1.15
Strikeout/Walk Ratio	3.87	1.93
Groundball/Flyball Ratio	0.72	1.17

2004 Situational Stats

	W	L	ERA	Sv	IP		AB	H	HR	RBI	Avg
Home	1	1	1.75	18	36.0	LHB	132	28	2	10	.212
Road	0	1	1.49	26	36.1	RHB	125	20	1	4	.160
First Half	1	0	1.13	23	39.2	Sc Pos	58	10	0	10	.172
Scnd Half	0	2	2.20	21	32.2	Clutch	182	31	1	7	.170

2004 Rankings (American League)
- 1st in relief ERA (1.62)
- 2nd in save percentage (93.6), games finished (63) and fewest baserunners allowed per nine innings in relief (9.1)
- 3rd in saves
- 5th in lowest batting average allowed in relief (.187) and most strikeouts per nine innings in relief (11.1)
- 8th in first batter efficiency (.172)
- 9th in lowest batting average allowed vs. left handed batters
- 10th in games pitched
- Led the Twins in saves, games finished (63), lowest batting average allowed vs. righthanded batters, save percentage (93.6), relief ERA (1.62) and fewest baserunners allowed per nine innings in relief (9.1)

Brad Radke

2004 Season

Based purely on how he threw the ball, Brad Radke may have had his best season as a pro in 2004. Yet, a lack of run support and the Twins' strange propensity to lose close games that Radke started cost him an 18-20 win season. Usually, Radke suffers through a dead-arm period somewhere in the middle of the season, which damages his statistics and victory totals, but he remained strong and durable throughout 2004. His ability to pitch 219.2 innings was one reason the Twins' bullpen was so effective.

Pitching

Radke relies on a 90-MPH fastball that he locates precisely, but his best pitch is his changeup, which he throws with the same arm speed and motion as his fastball. It comes in at roughly 78 MPH. While Johan Santana's changeup causes hitters to swing and miss, Radke often gets popups and flyballs with his. He also throws a slider that plays well off his fastball, but he's at his best when he delivers well-located fastballs to get ahead in the count, then uses his changeup as an out pitch. His combination of control and determination to avoid walks means he gives up lots of home runs, but few big innings.

Defense

A good athlete with exceptional composure, Radke fields his position successfully and makes good decisions with the ball. That includes bunting situations, which aren't commonplace in the American League. Radke also holds runners well, which counters the advantage that runners get from his reliance on offspeed stuff.

2005 Outlook

Radke is the kind of pitcher for whom the quality-start statistic was invented. Even when he lacks his best stuff, he's capable of pitching seven innings and allowing just two or three runs. Although he has won more than 12 games only three times, he's the kind of smart, put-it-in-play pitcher who can win 18 to 20 games if he stays healthy and receives good fielding and run support from his team. He will stay in Minnesota after agreeing to a two-year, $18 million extension over the winter.

Position: SP
Bats: R **Throws:** R
Ht: 6' 2" **Wt:** 184

Opening Day Age: 32
Born: 10/27/72 in Eau Claire, WI
ML Seasons: 10
Pronunciation: RAD-key

Overall Statistics

W	L	Pct.	ERA	G	GS	Sv	IP	H	BB	SO	HR	Avg
11	8	.579	3.48	34	34	0	219.2	229	26	143	23	.267
127	118	.518	4.23	319	318	0	2088.0	2232	390	1267	269	.273

2004 Pitching Profile

	Brad Radke	AL Average
Overall Strike %	67.9	62.3
1st Pitch Strike %	66.9	58.1
Ratio	1.16	1.42
Strikeouts per 9 IP	5.86	6.45
Walks per 9 IP	1.07	3.34
Home Runs per 9 IP	0.94	1.15
Strikeout/Walk Ratio	5.50	1.93
Groundball/Flyball Ratio	1.13	1.17

2004 Situational Stats

	W	L	ERA	Sv	IP		AB	H	HR	RBI	Avg
Home	7	6	3.06	0	126.2	LHB	468	119	15	47	.254
Road	4	2	4.06	0	93.0	RHB	391	110	8	35	.281
First Half	5	5	3.47	0	124.1	Sc Pos	180	41	2	53	.228
Scnd Half	6	3	3.49	0	95.1	Clutch	68	20	2	9	.294

2004 Rankings (American League)

- 2nd in fewest walks per nine innings (1.1)
- 3rd in games started, highest strikeout-walk ratio (5.5) and lowest on-base percentage allowed (.291)
- 4th in ERA
- 5th in innings pitched and lowest ERA at home
- 9th in hits allowed, runners caught stealing (8), lowest slugging percentage allowed (.393), fewest home runs allowed per nine innings (.94) and least run support per nine innings (4.5)
- 10th in batters faced (901) and lowest batting average allowed with runners in scoring position
- Led the Twins in games started, batters faced (901), runners caught stealing (8), highest strikeout-walk ratio (5.5), fewest home runs allowed per nine innings (.94) and fewest walks per nine innings (1.1)

Johan Santana

2004 Season

Johan Santana was the American League's most dominant pitcher, overcoming early-season worries about his surgically repaired elbow to put together a four-month run that Sandy Koufax would have envied. Santana worked 21 straight quality starts, from June 9 until his final tuneup for the playoffs. He enjoyed a scoreless streak of 36.1 innings and set a team record with 13 consecutive victories. At season's end, he led the league in ERA, quality starts, opponent batting average and strikeouts while garnering his first AL Cy Young Award.

Pitching

Santana has three dominating pitches—a 94-MPH fastball, an 87-MPH slider and a 76-MPH changeup. The changeup is the most devastating, because it comes out of his hand looking just like his fastball. When it arrives 18 MPH slower than the heater, hitters swing and miss by embarrassing margins. The difference between 2003 and 2004 was his ability to locate his pitches, while in the past he relied more on changing speeds. Santana also learned to throw his slider with different breaks at different speeds, giving him a slurve-like alternative to his other pitches.

Defense

Santana grew up playing shortstop and center field, so he has plenty of athletic ability. He showed more composure in dealing with grounders, bunts and baserunners in 2004, but the lefthander still committed four errors and posted a fielding percentage below .900 for the fourth straight season. While he is not a pickoff artist, Santana varies his moves to first often enough to make stealing against him difficult.

2005 Outlook

Stamina wasn't a concern in 2004, as Santana has learned to condition and maintain himself as a starting pitcher. Getting over his worries about his elbow also was important. The lone drawback to his pitching style is that he throws a lot of pitches, making complete games a rarity. He collected his first last summer. It probably won't be his last, as Santana should be one of the game's best pitchers for years to come.

Position: SP
Bats: L **Throws:** L
Ht: 6' 0" **Wt:** 206

Opening Day Age: 26
Born: 3/13/79 in Tovar Merida, VZ
ML Seasons: 5

Overall Statistics

	W	L	Pct.	ERA	G	GS	Sv	IP	H	BB	SO	HR	Avg
'04	20	6	.769	2.61	34	34	0	228.0	156	54	265	24	.192
Car.	43	18	.705	3.47	151	75	1	624.1	519	220	663	65	.225

2004 Pitching Profile

	Johan Santana	AL Average
Overall Strike %	66.3	62.3
1st Pitch Strike %	64.0	58.1
Ratio	0.92	1.42
Strikeouts per 9 IP	10.46	6.45
Walks per 9 IP	2.13	3.34
Home Runs per 9 IP	0.95	1.15
Strikeout/Walk Ratio	4.91	1.93
Groundball/Flyball Ratio	0.93	1.17

2004 Situational Stats

	W	L	ERA	Sv	IP		AB	H	HR	RBI	Avg
Home	11	4	2.62	0	137.1	LHB	194	38	5	16	.196
Road	9	2	2.58	0	90.2	RHB	618	118	19	39	.191
First Half	7	6	3.78	0	123.2	Sc Pos	121	20	2	26	.165
Scnd Half	13	0	1.21	0	104.1	Clutch	44	11	1	4	.250

2004 Rankings (American League)

- 1st in ERA, strikeouts, lowest batting average allowed (.192), lowest slugging percentage allowed (.315), lowest on-base percentage allowed (.249), lowest ERA on the road, most strikeouts per nine innings (10.5), and lowest batting average allowed vs. righthanded batters
- 2nd in wins, innings pitched, winning percentage, lowest ERA at home and lowest batting average allowed with runners in scoring position
- 3rd in games started and lowest fielding percentage at pitcher (.892)
- 4th in highest strikeout-walk ratio (4.9)
- Led the Twins in wins, games started, innings pitched, hit batsmen (9), wild pitches (7), pitches thrown (3,426), pickoff throws (99), winning percentage, lowest ERA at home, lowest ERA on the road, most run support per nine innings (5.6)

Shannon Stewart

2004 Season

After signing a three-year, $18 million contract, Shannon Stewart missed much of the season with hamstring and foot injuries, with plantar fasciitis proving the biggest problem. He was effective when healthy, mimicking his career norms by hitting .304 with a .380 on-base percentage. Stewart has proved invaluable to the Twins when healthy, as his patient, intelligent approach at the plate contrasts with the overly aggressive manner of many Twins players.

Hitting

Other than in 2000, when he hit .319 with 21 homers for Toronto, Stewart's offensive career has followed a pattern—570 at-bats or more a year, a .300 average, occasional power, good on-base percentage. He hit 11 homers in just 378 at-bats last year, and had the best OBP of his big league career, so he has adapted well to playing in the Metrodome. Stewart likes pulling the ball, but will adjust and go with the pitch if worked away.

Baserunning & Defense

Although blessed with good speed, Stewart's history of leg injuries has kept him from being an aggressive basestealer. He had just six steals in nine attempts last year, and hasn't had more than 14 swipes since 2001, when he had 27. The Twins would rather have him healthy and on base than running wild. A decent fielder who puts his speed to good use, he is unable to throw with any strength because of an old football injury to his right shoulder. While opposing teams will take advantage, Stewart does hustle to the ball and gets rid of it quickly. On flyballs, he is capable of taking awkward routes, but also will make the occasional spectacular catch.

2005 Outlook

At this point in his career, Stewart is a known commodity—what's not known is whether he'll be able to stay on the field all year. Since Stewart arrived at the All Star break in 2003, the Twins' winning percentage when he's in the lineup is much higher than when he's out. Although his statistics aren't overwhelming, his value to the team has been confirmed during his tenure.

Position: LF/DH
Bats: R **Throws:** R
Ht: 5'11" **Wt:** 200

Opening Day Age: 31
Born: 2/25/74 in Cincinnati, OH
ML Seasons: 10

Minnesota

Overall Statistics

	G	AB	R	H	D	T	HR	RBI	SB	BB	SO	Avg	OBP	Slg
'04	92	378	46	115	17	2	11	47	6	47	44	.304	.380	.447
Car.	1012	4098	670	1242	257	34	90	441	172	387	514	.303	.370	.448

Where He Hits the Ball

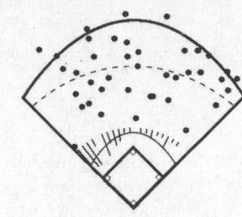 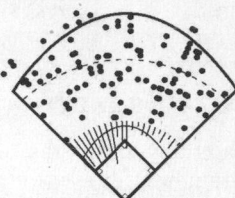

Vs. LHP   **Vs. RHP**

2004 Situational Stats

	AB	H	HR	RBI	Avg		AB	H	HR	RBI	Avg
Home	172	54	5	26	.314	LHP	113	29	3	10	.257
Road	206	61	6	21	.296	RHP	265	86	8	37	.325
First Half	129	37	3	17	.287	Sc Pos	92	33	2	38	.359
Scnd Half	249	78	8	30	.313	Clutch	63	19	2	8	.302

2004 Rankings (American League)

- 3rd in batting average with runners in scoring position
- 5th in on-base percentage for a leadoff hitter (.380)
- 6th in errors in left field (3)
- Led the Twins in batting average, most pitches seen per plate appearance (3.90), batting average with runners in scoring position, batting average vs. righthanded pitchers and batting average on the road

Grant Balfour

Position: RP
Bats: R **Throws:** R
Ht: 6' 2" **Wt:** 188

Opening Day Age: 27
Born: 12/30/77 in Sydney, Australia
ML Seasons: 3

Overall Statistics

	W	L	Pct.	ERA	G	GS	Sv	IP	H	BB	SO	HR	Avg
'04	4	1	.800	4.35	36	0	0	39.1	35	21	42	4	.238
Car.	5	1	.833	4.63	55	1	0	68.0	61	38	74	10	.240

2004 Situational Stats

	W	L	ERA	Sv	IP		AB	H	HR	RBI	Avg
Home	2	0	5.29	0	17.0	LHB	60	11	2	6	.183
Road	2	1	3.63	0	22.1	RHB	87	24	2	13	.276
First Half	3	0	4.12	0	19.2	Sc Pos	44	11	1	15	.250
Scnd Half	1	1	4.58	0	19.2	Clutch	54	14	1	4	.259

2004 Season

Shoulder problems hampered Grant Balfour throughout the season. When healthy, he was as dominant as any Twins pitcher, showing the ability to blow hitters away with a 95-MPH fastball. He stranded 23 of 30 inherited runners (76.7 percent), and first batters hit just .100 against him—both excellent numbers for any middle reliever.

Pitching & Defense

Like most young pitchers, Balfour tends to overthink or become tentative at times, which should never happen when you have his kind of stuff. Once a starter who tried to feature a variety of pitches, now Balfour can come into games in relief and rely on his fastball and slider. He can look mechanical on the mound or when making fielding plays, perhaps because he has a tight musculature, but he is athletic enough to make most of the plays.

2005 Outlook

With Joe Nathan at closer and Juan Rincon in the setup role, the Twins want Balfour to come in during the middle innings with men on base and blow hitters away, or pitch two innings at a time after a short start. If he's healthy, Balfour could become one of the game's most dominant middle relievers, and develop into a fine setup man.

Jesse Crain

Position: RP
Bats: R **Throws:** R
Ht: 6' 1" **Wt:** 205

Opening Day Age: 23
Born: 7/5/81 in Toronto, ON, Canada
ML Seasons: 1

Overall Statistics

	W	L	Pct.	ERA	G	GS	Sv	IP	H	BB	SO	HR	Avg
'04	3	0	1.000	2.00	22	0	0	27.0	17	12	14	2	.179
Car.	3	0	1.000	2.00	22	0	0	27.0	17	12	14	2	.179

2004 Situational Stats

	W	L	ERA	Sv	IP		AB	H	HR	RBI	Avg
Home	2	0	2.08	0	13.0	LHB	38	8	0	6	.211
Road	1	0	1.93	0	14.0	RHB	57	9	2	9	.158
First Half	0	0	–	0	0.0	Sc Pos	25	7	1	13	.280
Scnd Half	3	0	2.00	0	27.0	Clutch	30	5	1	5	.167

2004 Season

By the end of the 2004 season, the Twins had five relievers with closer-quality stuff—and that included Jesse Crain. After a dominant half-year at Triple-A Rochester, where he posted 19 saves and a 2.49 ERA, Crain was promoted and helped the Twins surge to the division title. He worked 10 straight games without allowing a run in early September, at a time when the Twins were hot.

Pitching & Defense

Crain is known to touch 100 MPH, but his fastball varied from 92-98 MPH when he shortened his stride late in the season to improve his command. Still, he had the stuff to get big league hitters out. Crain throws a big curve and a good slider, pitches the Twins believe will improve as he learns to relax on the mound. While he has a tendency to overthrow, he is nearly unhittable when his command is on. He is a decent fielder who needs to improve at holding baserunners, but he isn't likely to allow many as he matures.

2005 Outlook

For many teams, Crain would be ready to learn on the job as a closer. For the Twins, he'll pitch mostly in middle relief, and should be part of one of baseball's best bullpens.

Michael Cuddyer

Position: 2B/3B/1B
Bats: R **Throws:** R
Ht: 6' 2" **Wt:** 222

Opening Day Age: 26
Born: 3/27/79 in
Norfolk, VA
ML Seasons: 4
Pronunciation:
cuh-DIE-er

Overall Statistics

	G	AB	R	H	D	T	HR	RBI	SB	BB	SO	Avg	OBP	Slg
'04	115	339	49	89	22	1	12	45	5	37	74	.263	.339	.440
Car.	199	571	76	147	32	4	20	67	9	59	129	.257	.330	.433

2004 Situational Stats

	AB	H	HR	RBI	Avg		AB	H	HR	RBI	Avg
Home	161	47	8	29	.292	LHP	123	36	4	17	.293
Road	178	42	4	16	.236	RHP	216	53	8	28	.245
First Half	189	46	5	27	.243	Sc Pos	73	26	1	29	.356
Scnd Half	150	43	7	18	.287	Clutch	54	16	3	9	.296

2004 Season

Tabbed to be the Twins' right fielder in a disappointing 2003, Michael Cuddyer came to spring training with a handful of gloves and used them all. He played third base when Corey Koskie was hurt, second base when Luis Rivas was hurt or slumping, first base as a defensive replacement for Justin Morneau, and the outfield or DH when needed. While he might have produced more power, his hitting percentages were markedly better in the second half.

Hitting, Baserunning & Defense

The Twins expected Cuddyer to develop into a 25-homer guy, but injuries, slumps and other prospects have kept him from emerging as a regular. Strong enough to hit homers to any part of the park, Cuddyer excels at driving the ball to right-center. While he looks most out of place at second base, it might be his best position. He has such a strong arm he can play deep and still turn double plays. He looks less comfortable picking up the ball off the bat at third.

2005 Outlook

The Twins may give Cuddyer a position and see if he can be an everyday threat. He could provide an intriguing mix of power and affordability if the Twins can give him 500 at-bats.

Matthew LeCroy

Position: DH/C/1B
Bats: R **Throws:** R
Ht: 6' 2" **Wt:** 225

Opening Day Age: 29
Born: 12/13/75 in
Belton, SC
ML Seasons: 5
Pronunciation:
LEE-croy

Overall Statistics

	G	AB	R	H	D	T	HR	RBI	SB	BB	SO	Avg	OBP	Slg
'04	88	264	25	71	14	0	9	39	0	16	60	.269	.321	.424
Car.	329	997	107	263	59	1	41	159	0	71	226	.264	.318	.448

2004 Situational Stats

	AB	H	HR	RBI	Avg		AB	H	HR	RBI	Avg
Home	134	33	5	18	.246	LHP	90	29	4	13	.322
Road	130	38	4	21	.292	RHP	174	42	5	26	.241
First Half	153	41	6	24	.268	Sc Pos	66	15	3	29	.227
Scnd Half	111	30	3	15	.270	Clutch	46	12	2	7	.261

2004 Season

Every year, Matt LeCroy comes to spring training thinking he has a certain job, and every year his expectations go unmet. In 2004, he figured to be the Twins' primary designated hitter. Then outfielders Torii Hunter and Shannon Stewart suffered leg injuries that forced them into the DH role more often. During that time, Lew Ford established himself as a valuable bat, and he became the DH when the outfielders were healthy again.

Hitting, Baserunning & Defense

LeCroy has excellent power, but doesn't match up well against righthanded power pitchers. He needs at-bats to keep his stroke, making him slump-prone if he goes stretches without playing. A very slow runner, LeCroy hustles but has to play it safe on the bases. While he works at his fielding, a lack of throwing ability limits his innings at catcher, and he lacks range at first base.

2005 Outlook

Throughout his career, LeCroy has produced good power numbers in limited at-bats. At this point, he is viewed as a good bench player—a DH, pinch-hitter, backup first baseman and third-string catcher. But there are still those in the Twins' organization who believe he would produce good power numbers if given 500 at-bats.

Terry Mulholland

Position: RP/SP
Bats: R **Throws:** L
Ht: 6' 3" **Wt:** 220

Opening Day Age: 42
Born: 3/9/63 in Uniontown, PA
ML Seasons: 18
Pronunciation: mul-HOLL-and

Overall Statistics

W	L	Pct.	ERA	G	GS	Sv	IP	H	BB	SO	HR	Avg
5	9	.357	5.18	39	15	0	123.1	163	33	60	17	.327
124	140	.470	4.41	631	332	5	2513.2	2765	663	1306	286	.281

2004 Situational Stats

	W	L	ERA	Sv	IP		AB	H	HR	RBI	Avg
Home	1	4	5.60	0	54.2	LHB	141	40	5	21	.284
Road	4	5	4.85	0	68.2	RHB	358	123	12	42	.344
First Half	1	3	5.04	0	44.2	Sc Pos	104	29	4	40	.279
Scnd Half	4	6	5.26	0	78.2	Clutch	54	20	2	5	.370

2004 Season

Despite being 40-something, Terry Mulholland worked more innings than any year since 2000. He proved invaluable as a long reliever, then as a fifth starter. The southpaw saved the bullpen many times with his willingness to take the ball under any circumstance, and he was the starter for a few of the Twins' biggest wins.

Pitching & Defense

Smart and experienced, Mulholland survives without a dominant fastball, relying instead on sinkers, cutters, sliders and curves. He is most effective when he pitches inside, which sets up his soft stuff away. Mulholland prides himself on fielding his position well and holding runners close, aided by a deceptive move to first base. He also gets rid of the ball quickly, making him difficult to steal against.

2005 Outlook

In 2004, Mulholland went on an intriguing diet that made him leaner and stronger, and seemed to make him more durable and energetic. He shows no signs of slowing down. Although he's not the kind of pitcher teams want in their rotation in April, Mulholland can help a staff as a spot starter, long reliever and second lefty out of the bullpen. He also serves as a second pitching coach.

Nick Punto

Position: 2B/SS
Bats: B **Throws:** R
Ht: 5' 9" **Wt:** 176

Opening Day Age: 27
Born: 11/8/77 in San Diego, CA
ML Seasons: 4
Pronunciation: POON-toh

Overall Statistics

	G	AB	R	H	D	T	HR	RBI	SB	BB	SO	Avg	OBP	Slg
'04	38	91	17	23	0	0	2	12	6	12	19	.253	.340	.319
Car.	115	194	31	46	2	0	3	16	8	19	44	.237	.305	.294

2004 Situational Stats

	AB	H	HR	RBI	Avg		AB	H	HR	RBI	Avg
Home	44	14	2	11	.318	LHP	32	8	1	4	.250
Road	47	9	0	1	.191	RHP	59	15	1	8	.254
First Half	59	15	1	6	.254	Sc Pos	26	9	2	12	.346
Scnd Half	32	8	1	6	.250	Clutch	16	3	1	4	.188

2004 Season

Because of injuries to Twins second baseman Luis Rivas and shortstop Cristian Guzman, Nick Punto had opportunities to prove he can be a good, everyday player in an organization looking for affordable talent. Instead, Punto spent much of the season on the disabled list, out with an oblique strain during the first half and a season-ending fractured clavicle in late July.

Hitting, Baserunning & Defense

Punto displayed excellent speed and aggressiveness, the ability to handle the bat and bunt, and a knack for putting the ball in play—all qualities the Twins, a team willing to play small ball, value. He has good range in the field and a strong throwing arm, but it is his willingness to throw his body around that led to a broken collarbone late in the season, forcing the Twins to leave him off their postseason roster.

2005 Outlook

After Punto's injury-prone 2004, the Twins aren't likely to count on him to be a starter in 2005. He probably remains in a utility role, and he's well suited for that. He can play virtually anywhere on the field except catcher. If Punto can prove durable, he could develop into a starter at shortstop or second base.

Juan Rincon

Position: RP
Bats: R **Throws:** R
Ht: 5'11" **Wt:** 201

Opening Day Age: 26
Born: 1/23/79 in Maracaibo, VZ
ML Seasons: 4
Pronunciation: rin-CONE

Overall Statistics

	W	L	Pct.	ERA	G	GS	Sv	IP	H	BB	SO	HR	Avg
'04	11	6	.647	2.63	77	0	2	82.0	52	32	106	5	.181
Car.	16	14	.533	3.70	149	3	2	202.0	177	84	194	16	.234

2004 Situational Stats

	W	L	ERA	Sv	IP		AB	H	HR	RBI	Avg
Home	7	2	2.56	0	38.2	LHB	122	18	3	13	.148
Road	4	4	2.70	2	43.1	RHB	165	34	2	20	.206
First Half	8	3	1.84	2	44.0	Sc Pos	76	16	2	28	.211
Scnd Half	3	3	3.55	0	38.0	Clutch	173	29	3	26	.168

2004 Season

Juan Rincon made the transition from good middle reliever to excellent setup man, becoming one of the Twins' most important players. He tended to be either dominant or completely ineffective, but more often was dominant. Rincon pitched better when he was brought in to start the eighth inning than when runners already were on base. He often lost his composure on days he struggled, more because he took his job so seriously than because of immaturity.

Pitching & Defense

When he's at his best, Rincon will resemble Mariano Rivera, throwing a 94-MPH fastball that cuts into the hands of lefthanded batters. Rincon also has a good slider, but he might be best off relying almost solely on that cut fastball, as Rivera does. Rincon gave up a Ruben Sierra home run on a slider in Game 4 of the ALDS, when Sierra probably had no chance of catching up to Rincon's fastball. Rincon is an adequate fielder.

2005 Outlook

With more experience, Rincon could become one of baseball's best relievers. He must learn how to get out of innings when he lacks his best stuff. He also must learn to trust that cut fastball, instead of trying to trick hitters with breaking pitches.

Luis Rivas

Position: 2B
Bats: R **Throws:** R
Ht: 5'11" **Wt:** 186

Opening Day Age: 25
Born: 8/30/79 in La Guaira, VZ
ML Seasons: 5
Pronunciation: REE-vas

Overall Statistics

	G	AB	R	H	D	T	HR	RBI	SB	BB	SO	Avg	OBP	Slg
'04	109	336	44	86	19	5	10	34	15	13	53	.256	.283	.432
Car.	506	1748	237	458	83	25	29	165	74	104	272	.262	.307	.388

2004 Situational Stats

	AB	H	HR	RBI	Avg		AB	H	HR	RBI	Avg
Home	162	41	4	18	.253	LHP	103	30	4	14	.291
Road	174	45	6	16	.259	RHP	233	56	6	20	.240
First Half	199	53	5	18	.266	Sc Pos	82	17	2	24	.207
Scnd Half	137	33	5	16	.241	Clutch	40	10	2	3	.250

2004 Season

During the second half of the 2001 season, as the Twins were blowing a big lead to the Cleveland Indians, Luis Rivas emerged as one of their best all-around players. The Twins must wonder what happened to that player. Rivas lacks real power and a knack for getting on base. His primary attribute is his ability to turn the double play.

Hitting, Baserunning & Defense

Rivas is strong enough to drive the ball, but his aggressive approach often causes him to swing at bad pitches and fall behind in the count. He has the talent to be a useful hitter, but needs to overhaul his approach. He's an excellent basestealer who doesn't get on base often enough to make that skill pay off. Defensively, Rivas has very good range to his left, but struggles going to his right.

2005 Outlook

By failing to fulfill his potential, Rivas has called his future into question. He was a top shortstop prospect before the presence of Cristian Guzman forced his move to second base, and he no longer may have the range to play short. That would diminish his value as a utilityman. Twins officials say Rivas needs to improve his work ethic and attentiveness to regain his status as a rising young player.

J.C. Romero

Position: RP
Bats: B **Throws:** L
Ht: 5'11" **Wt:** 198

Opening Day Age: 28
Born: 6/4/76 in Rio Piedras, PR
ML Seasons: 6

Overall Statistics

	W	L	Pct.	ERA	G	GS	Sv	IP	H	BB	SO	HR	Avg
'04	7	4	.636	3.51	74	0	1	74.1	61	38	69	4	.224
Car.	21	17	.553	4.49	259	22	2	350.2	345	170	288	32	.259

2004 Situational Stats

	W	L	ERA	Sv	IP			AB	H	HR	RBI	Avg
Home	3	1	4.25	1	36.0	LHB		111	29	3	15	.261
Road	4	3	2.82	0	38.1	RHB		161	32	1	25	.199
First Half	4	1	4.71	1	36.1	Sc Pos		73	22	1	37	.301
Scnd Half	3	3	2.37	0	38.0	Clutch		161	37	2	31	.230

2004 Season

J.C. Romero endured a remarkably erratic 2004, pitching poorly enough to get demoted to the minors in June before returning to set a team record for consecutive scoreless innings. The streak of 36.2 innings ended in mid-September, and Romero fell apart while the Twins battled for home-field advantage for the first round of the playoffs. He hardly faced the Yankees. Even when he was setting the consecutive-innings record, he allowed plenty of inherited runners to score.

Pitching & Defense

Romero throws a 93-MPH fastball that sinks, a big-breaking slider and a changeup. He struggles when he tries to hit the corners with his pitches. The Twins have pleaded with him to throw toward the middle of the plate and let his natural movement produce grounders. Romero has proven stubborn and emotional, and his lack of composure helps turn small mistakes into big innings.

2005 Outlook

The lefthander has to prove he can control himself, not to mention his pitches. Despite Romero's talents, good stuff is irrelevant when you don't throw it over the plate. Romero could reassert himself as a dominant late-game reliever, or continue to tantalize with wasted talent.

Carlos Silva

Position: SP
Bats: R **Throws:** R
Ht: 6' 4" **Wt:** 240

Opening Day Age: 25
Born: 4/23/79 in Bolivar, VZ
ML Seasons: 3

Overall Statistics

	W	L	Pct.	ERA	G	GS	Sv	IP	H	BB	SO	HR	Avg
'04	14	8	.636	4.21	33	33	0	203.0	255	35	76	23	.310
Car.	22	9	.710	4.04	163	34	2	374.1	435	94	165	34	.297

2004 Situational Stats

	W	L	ERA	Sv	IP			AB	H	HR	RBI	Avg
Home	6	3	4.01	0	98.2	LHB		442	145	15	52	.328
Road	8	5	4.40	0	104.1	RHB		381	110	8	34	.289
First Half	8	7	4.51	0	111.2	Sc Pos		188	53	7	63	.282
Scnd Half	6	1	3.84	0	91.1	Clutch		35	16	1	6	.457

2004 Season

Carlos Silva may have been the most surprising pitcher on a staff full of surprises. Silva was an erratic pitcher for the Phillies in 2003; in 2004 he became a reliable No. 3 starter for a division winner. Big, strong, durable and coachable, he made dramatic progress in adapting to his new role. He proved to be a workhorse.

Pitching & Defense

Silva started the season with one reliable pitch—his sinking fastball. By the end of it, he had gained command of a good slider and had developed a changeup, largely with the help of Twins veteran Brad Radke. Silva allows so many balls to be put into play that he gives up a high opponent batting average, yet offsets that weakness with two dramatic strengths—a low walk rate and the ability to get double-play grounders. A big man, he's not a particularly good fielder, and he sometimes tries to execute hopeless plays.

2005 Outlook

Because he doesn't make hitters swing and miss often, Silva may plateau as a No. 3 starter, but he can be invaluable in that role because of his competitiveness and durability. He could become a quality-start type of pitcher who gives his team a chance to win nearly every trip to the mound.

Other Minnesota Twins

Joe Beimel (Pos: LHP, **Age**: 27)

	W	L	Pct.	ERA	G	GS	Sv	IP	H	BB	SO	HR	Avg
'04	0	0	—	43.20	3	0	0	1.2	8	2	2	1	.615
Car.	10	19	.345	5.24	167	23	0	264.2	296	129	155	29	.288

Beimel looked like a budding setup man with Pittsburgh a couple of seasons ago, but he was released late in spring training and signed by the Twins. He posted a 6.97 ERA and two saves at Triple-A Rochester before being roughed up by American League hitters in September. He signed a minor league deal with Tampa Bay after the season. 2005 Outlook: C

Henry Blanco (Pos: C, **Age**: 33, **Bats**: R)

	G	AB	R	H	D	T	HR	RBI	SB	BB	SO	Avg	OBP	Slg
'04	114	315	36	65	19	1	10	37	0	21	56	.206	.260	.368
Car.	538	1553	157	336	90	8	37	163	4	155	299	.216	.288	.356

Prized catching prospect Joe Mauer spent most of the 2004 season on the disabled list, opening the door to Blanco, a defensive specialist who got most of the playing time behind the plate. He reached career highs in at-bats, runs, homers and RBI, and the Cubs signed him as a free agent in December. 2005 Outlook: C

Pat Borders (Pos: C, **Age**: 41, **Bats**: R)

	G	AB	R	H	D	T	HR	RBI	SB	BB	SO	Avg	OBP	Slg
'04	38	95	9	22	6	0	1	10	3	1	22	.232	.247	.326
Car.	1060	3165	277	808	163	12	68	339	9	151	535	.255	.290	.379

The 41-year-old catcher split 2004 between Triple-A Tacoma in the Mariners' system, Seattle and Minnesota. He was most productive with the Twins in September/October, batting .286 with five RBI in 19 games. He signed a minor league deal with the Brewers in November. 2005 Outlook: C

Rob Bowen (Pos: C, **Age**: 24, **Bats**: B)

	G	AB	R	H	D	T	HR	RBI	SB	BB	SO	Avg	OBP	Slg
'04	17	27	1	3	0	0	1	2	0	4	10	.111	.226	.222
Car.	24	37	1	4	0	0	1	3	0	4	14	.108	.190	.189

Bowen spent a couple of months with Minnesota because of the knee injury to rookie catcher Joe Mauer. Despite the opportunity, Bowen struggled, batting just .197 in 77 games for Double-A New Britain and recording only three hits and 10 strikeouts with the Twins. 2005 Outlook: C

Aaron Fultz (Pos: LHP, **Age**: 31)

	W	L	Pct.	ERA	G	GS	Sv	IP	H	BB	SO	HR	Avg
'04	3	3	.500	5.04	55	0	1	50.0	50	23	37	5	.267
Car.	14	11	.560	4.85	286	0	3	299.0	309	118	250	35	.273

Fultz displayed a promising strikeout-walk ratio as a rookie with San Francisco in 2000, but last season he couldn't retire righthanded hitters, who batted .314 and slugged .500 against him. After the All-Star break, all hitters nicked him for a .300 average. 2005 Outlook: C

Seth Greisinger (Pos: RHP, **Age**: 29)

	W	L	Pct.	ERA	G	GS	Sv	IP	H	BB	SO	HR	Avg
'04	2	5	.286	6.18	12	9	0	51.0	68	15	36	12	.319
Car.	10	16	.385	5.56	41	38	0	218.2	256	76	116	33	.295

Once a top pitching prospect in the Tigers' system, Greisinger lost more than two years to elbow troubles. He's been a more hittable pitcher in the two seasons since his return, but he continues to battle for major league work with his 30th birthday just around the corner. 2005 Outlook: C

Matt Guerrier (Pos: RHP, **Age**: 26)

	W	L	Pct.	ERA	G	GS	Sv	IP	H	BB	SO	HR	Avg
'04	0	1	.000	5.68	9	2	0	19.0	22	6	11	5	.293
Car.	0	1	.000	5.68	9	2	0	19.0	22	6	11	5	.293

Guerrier enjoyed what arguably was his best Triple-A season in 2004, going 5-10 with a solid 3.19 ERA at Rochester, but the finesse pitcher wasn't as effective in his major league debut. The former White Sox prospect should get another look in the spring. 2005 Outlook: C

Jose Offerman (Pos: DH, **Age**: 36, **Bats**: B)

	G	AB	R	H	D	T	HR	RBI	SB	BB	SO	Avg	OBP	Slg
'04	77	172	22	44	14	2	2	22	1	29	31	.256	.363	.395
Car.	1565	5576	829	1527	249	71	55	524	172	761	897	.274	.361	.374

After sitting out all of 2003, Offerman got off to a 9-for-20 start in April before defensive troubles at second base and a May-June slump secured him more time on the bench. Still, he batted .414 (12-for-29) with three doubles as a pinch-hitter. 2005 Outlook: C

Augie Ojeda (Pos: 2B, **Age**: 30, **Bats**: B)

	G	AB	R	H	D	T	HR	RBI	SB	BB	SO	Avg	OBP	Slg
'04	30	59	16	20	1	0	2	7	1	10	3	.339	.429	.458
Car.	178	375	48	82	13	2	5	31	3	38	42	.219	.294	.304

The Twins recalled Ojeda in early August, when injuries decimated the infield, and he enjoyed his best stretch of hitting as a major leaguer. His .357 surge in September pushed his career average over the Mendoza line, and he also showed impressive patience at the plate. 2005 Outlook: C

Alex Prieto (Pos: 2B, **Age**: 28, **Bats**: R)

	G	AB	R	H	D	T	HR	RBI	SB	BB	SO	Avg	OBP	Slg
'04	16	32	4	8	1	0	1	4	0	3	9	.250	.306	.375
Car.	24	43	5	9	1	0	1	4	0	3	13	.209	.255	.302

Prieto's Triple-A hitting percentages have been on the slide since a decent 2001 season at Triple-A Omaha. Still, May injuries to Minnesota infielders opened the door to Prieto, who collected his first big league homer in 2004. 2005 Outlook: C

Carlos Pulido (**Pos**: LHP, **Age**: 33)

	W	L	Pct.	ERA	G	GS	Sv	IP	H	BB	SO	HR	Avg
'04	0	0	–	8.74	6	0	0	11.1	16	4	9	2	.333
Car.	3	8	.273	5.98	32	15	0	111.1	118	47	47	19	.277

Pulido's pro career started in the Minnesota system in 1989, and he performed well enough at Triple-A Rochester in 2003 to get his first cup of coffee in nine years. He wasn't as good last summer, with Rochester or Minnesota. 2005 Outlook: C

Joe Roa (**Pos**: RHP, **Age**: 33)

	W	L	Pct.	ERA	G	GS	Sv	IP	H	BB	SO	HR	Avg
'04	2	3	.400	4.50	48	0	0	70.0	84	24	47	9	.297
Car.	9	16	.360	4.94	120	19	0	266.0	330	72	154	39	.308

For the first time in 16 years of pro ball, Roa spent an entire season in the majors in 2004. He claimed the final bullpen spot in the spring and was at his best through April and May. Roa posted a 3.66 ERA before the All-Star break, a 5.58 mark after it. The Pirates signed him to a minor league deal in December. 2005 Outlook: C

Michael Ryan (**Pos**: DH, **Age**: 27, **Bats**: L)

	G	AB	R	H	D	T	HR	RBI	SB	BB	SO	Avg	OBP	Slg
'04	36	71	9	17	2	1	0	7	1	4	16	.239	.280	.296
Car.	70	143	25	42	9	1	5	20	3	10	30	.294	.338	.476

Ryan and Lew Ford were on the outside looking in with all of the outfield prospects in the Twins' system. Ford broke through in 2004, while Ryan struggled after dislocating a shoulder sliding into first base in June. He batted .211 at Triple-A Rochester and .239 for the Twins. 2005 Outlook: C

Brad Thomas (**Pos**: LHP, **Age**: 27)

	W	L	Pct.	ERA	G	GS	Sv	IP	H	BB	SO	HR	Avg
'04	0	0	–	16.88	3	0	0	2.2	7	1	0	0	.500
Car.	0	3	.000	9.89	11	5	0	23.2	33	18	8	7	.333

The Australian native made three appearances for the Twins in April before he was dealt to Boston for future considerations late that month. He was sidelined by elbow trouble just two days after the trade and worked just 4.1 innings for Boston's Triple-A affiliate in Pawtucket. 2005 Outlook: C

Minnesota Twins Minor League Prospects

Organization Overview:

Year after year, the Minnesota farm system fills holes on the major league roster, and the Twins keep winning. Nearly the entire roster is homegrown, and just in the last three seasons, Joe Mauer, Justin Morneau, Lew Ford, Michael Cuddyer, Jason Kubel, Juan Rincon, Grant Balfour and Jesse Crain have arrived. Players featured on these pages will arrive in 2005. Keep an eye on the early picks of the Twins' 2004 draft class, which included six pitchers chosen in the first three rounds, four out of high school. Farm director Jim Rantz says he's never seen such a crop of kids with the size and mound presence that the early-round draftees displayed last season.

Scott Baker

Position: P **Opening Day Age:** 23
Bats: R **Throws:** R **Born:** 9/19/81 in
Ht: 6' 4" **Wt:** 190 Shreveport, LA

Recent Statistics

	W	L	ERA	G	GS	Sv	IP	H	R	BB	SO	HR
2003 A Quad City	3	1	2.49	11	11	0	50.2	45	16	8	47	4
2004 A Ft. Myers	4	2	2.40	7	7	0	45.0	40	13	6	37	1
2004 AA New Britain	5	3	2.43	10	10	0	70.1	44	23	13	72	2
2004 AAA Rochester	1	3	4.97	9	9	0	54.1	65	31	15	36	3

A late second-round pick in 2003, Baker debuted at Class-A Quad City with four fairly polished pitches. He threw strikes and mixed all four offerings effectively in 2004, climbing from high Class-A Fort Myers to Triple-A Rochester. While Baker doesn't overpower hitters, his command of a low-90s sinker on both sides of the plate is hard on opponents. He pitched ahead in the count and didn't cough up walks last season, generating a 145-34 strikeout-walk ratio. Keeping the ball low in the zone consistently will be critical to succeeding at higher levels. He's a big, strong kid who could be an innings-eater. The fast-rising Baker could be in the Minnesota mix during the 2005 campaign.

Jason Bartlett

Position: SS **Opening Day Age:** 25
Bats: R **Throws:** R **Born:** 10/30/79 in
Ht: 6' 0" **Wt:** 180 Mountain View, CA

Recent Statistics

	G	AB	R	H	D	T	HR	RBI	SB	BB	SO	Avg
2004 AAA Rochester	67	269	54	89	15	7	3	29	7	33	37	.331
2004 R GC Twins	5	14	1	5	1	0	0	1	0	0	3	.357
2004 AL Minnesota	8	12	2	1	0	0	0	1	2	1	1	.083

Bartlett lacks a standout tool, but he's developed nicely since he was acquired from San Diego in 2002. Bartlett is a steady shortstop whose instincts and work ethic maximize what he has to offer. That's also true at the plate, as Bartlett refuses to throw away at-bats. He knows the strike zone and covers the plate well with his quick hands. He lost more than two months at Triple-A Rochester with a broken wrist, fractured by a pitch on May 8. A July callup due to injury, Bartlett's time in Minnesota showed his defensive footwork still needs some polish. Still, Bartlett could be the Twins' starting shortstop in 2005.

Boof Bonser

Position: P **Opening Day Age:** 23
Bats: R **Throws:** R **Born:** 10/14/81 in St.
Ht: 6' 4" **Wt:** 230 Petersburg, FL

Recent Statistics

	W	L	ERA	G	GS	Sv	IP	H	R	BB	SO	HR
2003 AA Norwich	7	10	4.00	24	24	0	135.0	122	80	67	103	11
2003 AAA Fresno	1	2	3.13	4	4	0	23.0	17	13	8	28	4
2004 AA New Britain	12	9	4.37	27	27	0	154.1	160	89	56	146	22
2004 AAA Rochester	1	0	1.29	1	1	0	7.0	5	1	1	7	1

The Twins like Bonser, acquired in the A.J. Pierzynski trade with the Giants, for his size and stuff. They believe his four pitches are major league offerings. In 2004, Bonser didn't excel at Double-A New Britain because of poor command of the strike zone. He also needed work on his game plan for attacking hitters. He was better on both counts in the second half, as he was changing speeds more effectively. Bonser won his last seven decisions at New Britain and finished with a quality start for Triple-A Rochester. Bonser has the build of an innings-eater, though the Twins want him to work on his conditioning to stay fit. He probably starts 2005 at Rochester.

J.D. Durbin

Position: P **Opening Day Age:** 23
Bats: R **Throws:** R **Born:** 2/24/82 in
Ht: 6' 0" **Wt:** 200 Portland, OR

Recent Statistics

	W	L	ERA	G	GS	Sv	IP	H	R	BB	SO	HR
2004 AA New Britain	4	1	2.52	13	13	0	64.1	62	21	22	53	4
2004 AAA Rochester	3	2	4.54	7	7	0	35.2	49	27	16	38	4
2004 AL Minnesota	0	1	7.36	4	1	0	7.1	12	6	6	6	0

A 2000 second-rounder, Durbin underwent minor surgery to repair a partially torn labrum in his throwing shoulder in May and missed six weeks of the Double-A season. A fastball-slider guy with sound mechanics but a maximum-effort delivery, the always-confident Durbin hardly skipped a beat. He returned with his mid-90s fastball intact and located his hard slider in four solid starts at New Britain before a promotion to Triple-A Rochester. He struck out a season-high 13 batters in his Triple-A debut. Durbin now buys into not throwing at maximum velocity and the value of a changeup. His command of it is good. While Durbin wasn't especially effective at Rochester, reaching the Triple-A level after shoulder surgery is noteworthy. Starting there in 2005 is likely.

Jason Kubel

Position: OF
Bats: L **Throws:** R
Ht: 5' 11" **Wt:** 200

Opening Day Age: 22
Born: 5/25/82 in Belle Fourche, SD

Recent Statistics

	G	AB	R	H	D	T	HR	RBI	SB	BB	SO	Avg
2004 AA New Britain	37	138	25	52	14	4	6	29	0	19	19	.377
2004 AAA Rochester	90	350	71	120	28	0	16	71	16	34	40	.343
2004 AL Minnesota	23	60	10	18	2	0	2	7	1	6	9	.300

A 12th-round pick in 2000, Kubel enjoyed a breakout year in 2004. He batted .377 in his first taste of Double-A ball, and won the league batting title at Triple-A Rochester. The Twins made room for Kubel on their playoff roster. He knows the strike zone, drives the ball to all fields with power and hangs in well against lefties. Kubel is a solid corner outfielder with good instincts and a strong right-field arm. While he needs to improve his jump on balls hit his way, he has enough speed to steal some bases. His dream season ended with extensive ligament damage in his left knee, suffered in the Arizona Fall League. He may miss all of 2005.

Francisco Liriano

Position: P
Bats: L **Throws:** L
Ht: 6' 2" **Wt:** 185

Opening Day Age: 21
Born: 10/26/83 in San Cristobal, DR

Recent Statistics

	W	L	ERA	G	GS	Sv	IP	H	R	BB	SO	HR
2003 A San Jose	0	1	54.00	1	1	0	0.2	5	4	2	0	0
2003 R Az Giants	0	1	4.32	4	4	0	8.1	5	4	6	9	1
2004 A Ft. Myers	6	7	4.00	21	21	0	117.0	118	56	43	125	6
2004 AA New Britain	3	2	3.18	7	7	0	39.2	45	14	17	49	4

Injuries compromised his previous two seasons, but Liriano escaped the bug in 2004, after he was acquired in the A.J. Pierzynski trade with the Giants. The left-hander had worked just 160 innings in three seasons in the Giants' system before throwing 156.2 innings at two stops in 2004. Liriano inspires comparisons to Twins ace Johan Santana, because of a similar build, comparable stuff and high ceiling. While Liriano clearly lacks Santana's command, he has a plus fastball with some late movement and a solid changeup. The lefthander can touch 94-95 MPH with the heater, and also mixes in a slider and curve, giving him a four-pitch arsenal.

Michael Restovich

Position: OF
Bats: R **Throws:** R
Ht: 6' 4" **Wt:** 257

Opening Day Age: 26
Born: 1/3/79 in Rochester, MN

Recent Statistics

	G	AB	R	H	D	T	HR	RBI	SB	BB	SO	Avg
2004 AAA Rochester	106	425	65	105	20	3	20	62	4	25	104	.247
2004 AL Minnesota	29	47	9	12	3	0	2	6	0	4	10	.255

An impressive athlete with loads of raw power, Restovich hasn't had that breakout year that could secure his place in the majors. His hitting percentages at the Triple-A level have slumped since reaching Edmonton in 2002, though that partially has to do with the Twins moving their Triple-A affiliation from the hitter-friendly Pacific Coast League. The inside fastball can give him trouble, and trying to make more consistent contact to counter his strikeouts compromises his power. While he lacks a quick first step in the outfield, the big man is an adequate defender and baserunner. Perhaps the lack of opportunity in Minnesota has affected his game, but with Jason Kubel out for 2005, Restovich gets one if the Twins cut loose Jacque Jones.

Terry Tiffee

Position: 3B
Bats: B **Throws:** R
Ht: 6' 3" **Wt:** 210

Opening Day Age: 25
Born: 4/21/79 in North Little Rock, AR

Recent Statistics

	G	AB	R	H	D	T	HR	RBI	SB	BB	SO	Avg
2004 AAA Rochester	82	316	42	97	26	3	12	68	0	21	26	.307
2004 AL Minnesota	17	44	7	12	4	0	2	8	0	3	3	.273

Tiffee has slipped through the cracks, perhaps by coming up with Joe Mauer and Justin Morneau as a 26th-round pick. A switch-hitter with some power, Tiffee is a better hitter from the left side. He enjoyed a solid first season at the Triple-A level, despite a back problem and a pulled hamstring in 2004. Then he reached Minnesota and won a few games with some key hits before a collision at home ended his season. He's not very quick around the third-base bag and doesn't run well, but his bat could be enough to stay at third with Minnesota. Perhaps in 2005 if Corey Koskie departs via free agency.

Others to Watch

Released by the Braves after three pro seasons, first baseman **Garrett Jones** (23) was signed before the 2002 campaign. In 2004, the lefthanded hitter exploded for 33 doubles, 30 homers and 92 RBI in 122 games at Double-A New Britain. His strikeout rate declined last summer en route to a career-high .311 average. . . With the 22nd overall pick in the 2004 draft, the Twins took University of Minnesota lefthander **Glen Perkins** (22), a Twin Cities native who was 15-0 against Big Ten opponents in two years with the Gophers. He pitched impressively in 12 pro starts, calling on a solid fastball and curve, and finished the year at Class-A Quad City. Perkins could be on the fast track. . . Two more 2004 picks who impressed in the rookie-level Gulf Coast League last summer were high school righthanders **Jay Rainville** (19) and **Anthony Swarzak** (19). Rainville, one of five first-round picks, impressed with a low-90s fastball and power curve, generating a 38-3 strikeout-walk ratio. Swarzak is less advanced, but led the rookie club with five wins and posted a 42-6 ratio. . . Another first-rounder last June was righthander **Kyle Waldrop** (19), who signed quickly and got a head start on his fellow hurlers. He featured a sound, fluid delivery and three pitches that he located expertly, including a 90-MPH fastball. Waldrop was 5-2 with a 2.14 ERA between two rookie-level clubs.

Yankee Stadium

Offense

Spacious Yankee Stadium is the ultimate dichotomy. Right field entices lefthanded hitters with its easily accessible short porch, while righthanded power hitters are frustrated by the asymmetrically deep left-field gaps. The differences in the outfield are counterbalanced by regularities on the infield. Uniformly long grass and extra room behind home plate transmute Yankee Stadium into a pitchers' park.

Defense

An infielder's arm is tested at Yankee Stadium. The thick infield grass slows everything down and makes for an increased amount of bang-bang plays. Properly navigating Death Valley in left-center can be tricky for outfielders. Center fielders try to help their counterpart to the right by playing deeper and by cheating a few steps to the shortstop side of second base.

Who It Helps the Most

New additions like Javier Vazquez and Miguel Cairo performed better in the Bronx. The deeper dimensions to left helped Vazquez keep a slight percentage more of his flyballs in the park and the heavy grass reduced would-be hits. Cairo sprayed the cavernous outfield with an array of singles and doubles.

Who It Hurts the Most

Yankee Stadium and Tony Clark is not a nice fit. His power is through the middle, and when he faced lefthanded pitchers his pop was all but nullified. For whatever reason Hideki Matsui has underachieved at home. In 2004, his on-base percentage was more than a hundred points higher outside of New York.

Rookies & Newcomers

Bubba Crosby did not live up to expectations last year, but he should benefit in Yankee Stadium with his gap power. Brad Halsey had a taste of the big time in 2004 and could be the next good left-handed starter for the Yankees. Dealing with the glare of the spotlight should be old hat for these two this season.

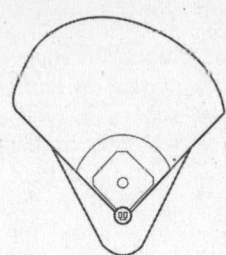

Dimensions: LF-318, LCF-399, CF-408, RCF-385, RF-314

Capacity: 57,478

Elevation: 55 feet

Surface: Grass

Foul Territory: Small

New York (AL)

Park Factors

2004 Season

	Home Games Yankees	Opp	Total	Away Games Yankees	Opp	Total	Index
G	72	72	144	70	70	140	
Avg	.271	.263	.267	.267	.279	.273	98
AB	2386	2558	4944	2460	2396	4856	99
R	394	329	723	393	375	768	92
H	647	672	1319	656	669	1325	97
2B	114	137	251	142	130	272	91
3B	7	9	16	9	18	27	58
HR	111	79	190	99	77	176	106
BB	284	195	479	301	201	502	94
SO	421	505	926	444	416	860	106
E	41	52	93	40	44	84	108
E-Infield	34	41	75	37	40	77	95
LHB-Avg	.259	.268	.264	.261	.279	.270	98
LHB-HR	49	45	94	44	41	85	113
RHB-Avg	.281	.257	.269	.272	.280	.276	98
RHB-HR	62	34	96	55	36	91	100

2002-2004

	Home Games Yankees	Opp	Total	Away Games Yankees	Opp	Total	Index
G	216	216	432	214	214	428	
Avg	.269	.258	.263	.273	.269	.271	97
AB	7203	7649	14852	7622	7384	15006	98
R	1129	963	2092	1230	989	2219	93
H	1940	1972	3912	2082	1989	4071	95
2B	359	402	761	434	434	868	89
3B	18	28	46	22	44	66	70
HR	300	211	511	310	190	500	103
BB	842	526	1368	910	563	1473	94
SO	1358	1564	2922	1454	1364	2818	105
E	145	157	302	149	123	272	110
E-Infield	124	120	244	128	105	233	104
LHB-Avg	.262	.259	.261	.270	.262	.267	98
LHB-HR	150	106	256	159	86	245	108
RHB-Avg	.276	.256	.266	.276	.275	.275	96
RHB-HR	150	105	255	151	104	255	99

2004 Rankings (American League)

- Third-highest strikeout factor
- Second-lowest walk factor
- Third-lowest run factor
- Third-lowest triple factor

Joe Torre

2004 Season

Any lingering doubts about the immediate managerial future of Joe Torre were erased in April 2004 when he agreed to a three-year, $19.2 million contract extension. The deal will keep him at the Yankees helm through 2007. With the exception of the historic collapse to Boston in the ALCS, the season was relatively uneventful for Torre. His club controlled the AL East for much of the year and unlike 2003, there were no major run-ins with the front office.

Offense

The 61 come-from-behind wins for the Yankees in 2004 were a major league record. Many of these games were determined by a late-inning rally where pinch-hitters were called to the plate. Torre, more than any other manager is baseball, puts his pinch-hitters in situations to succeed. He likes to exploit platoon advantages and prefers switch-hitting role players off the bench. Unless there is one out, Torre is recognizably station-to-station.

Pitching & Defense

Torre likes to go deep into games with his starters and favors a limited few arms out of the pen. He maintains well-defined roles for his relievers and goes almost exclusively with whom he trusts. Young pitchers occasionally will get a spot start from Torre, but their cup of coffee does not last long before they are whisked away back to the minors. Torre utilizes late-inning defensive substitutions and the pitchout more than most managers.

2005 Outlook

Torre will be without another one of his coaching confidants with the departure of Willie Randolph to the Mets. The coaching vanguard that was a part of the four championship teams has slowly eroded. Only pitching coach Mel Stottlemyre is left from those clubs. Despite this turnover, the Yankees have kept on winning. The bitter defeat at the hands of the Red Sox will not be forgotten as 2005 dawns. Expect the Yankees to play with a sense of urgency as they strive to regain baseball supremacy.

Born: 7/18/40 in Brooklyn, NY

Playing Experience: 1960-1977, Atl, StL, NYM

Managerial Experience: 23 seasons

Manager Statistics

Year	Team, Lg	W	L	Pct	GB	Finish
2004	New York, AL	101	61	.623	–	1st East
23 Seasons		1781	1570	.531	–	–

2004 Starting Pitchers by Days Rest

	<=3	4	5	6+
Yankees Starts	4	70	41	36
Yankees ERA	7.94	4.17	4.88	5.58
AL Avg Starts	2	82	47	21
AL ERA	5.36	4.87	4.65	4.93

2004 Situational Stats

	Joe Torre	AL Average
Hit & Run Success %	42.6	36.8
Stolen Base Success %	71.8	68.6
Platoon Pct.	64.9	61.6
Defensive Subs	36	21
High-Pitch Outings	3	5
Quick/Slow Hooks	17/13	20/16
Sacrifice Attempts	50	53

2004 Rankings (American League)

- 1st in steals of home plate (1)
- 2nd in pitchouts (35), defensive substitutions and starts on three days rest
- 3rd in fewest caught stealings of second base (25), double steals (7), pitchouts with a runner moving (6) and saves with over 1 inning pitched (10)

Kevin Brown

2004 Season

The trade that brought Kevin Brown to New York provided the Yankees with a proven starter with postseason experience, while at the same time sending the much-maligned Jeff Weaver to Los Angeles. Brown delivered immediate results, earning AL Pitcher of the Month honors for April with a 2.70 ERA. The honeymoon was short-lived, however, and by June a lower back strain put Brown on the disabled list for 44 days. Then in September, Brown broke the third and fifth metacarpal bones in his left hand assaulting a clubhouse wall. Pins were inserted to stabilize the hand, but a visibly rusty Brown never recovered, as his 8.68 postseason ERA indicates.

Pitching

All the injuries over the past few seasons may be catching up with Brown. A once dominant mid-90s bat-chomping fastball has been replaced by a high-80s fastball with far less sink and boring action. To compensate, Brown has become more reliant on his changeup and slider. His slider still can be devastating at times with its tight, hard tilt. When he's going well, Brown pounds the bottom of the strike zone, inducing a steady stream of groundballs. The large discrepancy from 2003 in his groundball-flyball ratio could be an ominous sign.

Defense

Brown will aggressively attack any ball in his vicinity, which helps compensate for the poor position in which his delivery leaves him. Back troubles have hindered his mobility. A high rate of pickoff attempts and a modified slide step are two methods he uses to keep the running game at bay. He's controlled it well over his career.

2005 Outlook

The clock is ticking on Brown as he enters the final year of his contract. Don't expect a repeat of 2003-type numbers, as Brown appears to be on the backside of an excellent career. The large drop in strikeouts per nine innings from 7.89 to 5.66 could be the clearest signal that his skills are diminishing. A middle-of-the-rotation guy good for 25 starts would be a bonus for the Yankees.

Position: SP
Bats: R **Throws:** R
Ht: 6' 4" **Wt:** 220

Opening Day Age: 40
Born: 3/14/65 in McIntyre, GA
ML Seasons: 18

Overall Statistics

W	L	Pct.	ERA	G	GS	Sv	IP	H	BB	SO	HR	Avg
10	6	.625	4.09	22	22	0	132.0	132	35	83	14	.262
207	137	.602	3.20	473	463	0	3183.0	2972	882	2347	203	.247

2004 Pitching Profile

	Kevin Brown	AL Average
Overall Strike %	63.1	62.3
1st Pitch Strike %	52.9	58.1
Ratio	1.27	1.42
Strikeouts per 9 IP	5.66	6.45
Walks per 9 IP	2.39	3.34
Home Runs per 9 IP	0.95	1.15
Strikeout/Walk Ratio	2.37	1.93
Groundball/Flyball Ratio	1.36	1.17

2004 Situational Stats

	W	L	ERA	Sv	IP		AB	H	HR	RBI	Avg
Home	6	2	3.65	0	69.0	LHB	280	73	9	26	.261
Road	4	4	4.57	0	63.0	RHB	224	59	5	31	.263
First Half	7	1	4.13	0	80.2	Sc Pos	121	30	6	48	.248
Scnd Half	3	5	4.03	0	51.1	Clutch	27	9	1	2	.333

2004 Rankings (American League)

- 5th in errors at pitcher (4)
- Led the Yankees in ERA, runners caught stealing (5), lowest slugging percentage allowed (.417), lowest on-base percentage allowed (.309), lowest ERA on the road and fewest home runs allowed per nine innings (.95)

Jason Giambi

2004 Season

The BALCO investigation, bursitis in his left hip, back spasms, sprained right ankle, intestinal parasite, respiratory infection, pulled left groin and benign tumor: this was 2004 for Jason Giambi. It is almost unfair to look at the numbers for anything other than an indication of how physically and emotionally draining 2004 must have been. That he was able to accrue 322 plate appearances through the myriad of injuries and doctor visits is amazing in itself.

Hitting

If you removed the price tag and erased health doubts, Giambi would be any general manager's dream. He's smart, patient and hits home runs. He habitually works counts in his favor and then looks one spot for a pitch to pound. If he doesn't get that pitch, he takes, oftentimes drawing a walk. He hits both righties and lefties well and is proficient at hitting with power to the opposite field. Due to recent ill health and injuries, Giambi's bat has been slow. He has looked overmatched on average 87-89 MPH fastballs. If he can get his strength and timing back, this will not continue.

Baserunning & Defense

Giambi is your usual base-clogging first baseman. Patellar tendinitis in his left knee has slowed him. Giambi serves the purposes of his infield position. He catches what is thrown his way and has shown some skill at picking low throws. Knee troubles have restricted his lateral mobility.

2005 Outlook

The manner in which Giambi and the Yankees kept details of the benign tumor private sparked wild speculation, but he denied steroid use all season. In early December, word broke that Giambi admitted to using steroids and human growth hormones in federal grand jury testimony a year earlier. The news explains Giambi's smaller body in the spring, when baseball began its first testing program, and raises questions about how productive he may be in upcoming seasons. On top of that, the Yankees are looking into voiding his big-dollar deal because of his use of performance-enhancing drugs.

Position: 1B/DH
Bats: L **Throws:** R
Ht: 6' 3" **Wt:** 230

Opening Day Age: 34
Born: 1/8/71 in West Covina, CA
ML Seasons: 10
Pronunciation: gee-OM-bee

Overall Statistics

	G	AB	R	H	D	T	HR	RBI	SB	BB	SO	Avg	OBP	Slg
'04	80	264	33	55	9	0	12	40	0	47	62	.208	.342	.379
Car.	1344	4757	851	1413	296	8	281	944	13	871	916	.297	.411	.540

Where He Hits the Ball

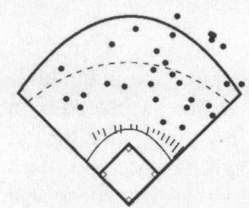 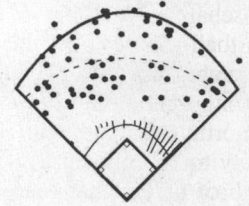

Vs. LHP   **Vs. RHP**

2004 Situational Stats

	AB	H	HR	RBI	Avg		AB	H	HR	RBI	Avg
Home	128	27	5	22	.211	LHP	80	21	6	17	.263
Road	136	28	7	18	.206	RHP	184	34	6	23	.185
First Half	212	51	11	35	.241	Sc Pos	65	17	4	30	.262
Scnd Half	52	4	1	5	.077	Clutch	37	12	2	3	.324

2004 Rankings (American League)

- 5th in lowest batting average with two strikes (.140)
- 10th in errors at first base (4)
- Led the Yankees in most pitches seen per plate appearance (4.08)

Orlando Hernandez

2004 Season

An insurance policy for the oft-injured Kevin Brown and recovering Jon Leiber, Orlando Hernandez himself began the season with more arm woes. Bursitis in his repaired shoulder pushed back his rehab schedule and delayed his return until the day before the break. His July arrival in New York could not have come at a better time. El Duque promptly took the reins and from mid-July through mid-September went 8-0 with a 2.49 ERA. Shoulder fatigue late in the year was a disappointing end to a good comeback season.

Pitching

Hernandez employs a five-pitch arsenal that might have the biggest velocity disparity in all of baseball. He will go from a 50-MPH eephus to a fastball that can touch 90 MPH. His changeup, curveball and slider fall somewhere in between. Along with the velocity differences come an assortment of arm angles that make him particularly tough on righthanded batters. Hernandez is one of those pitchers whose sum is greater than the parts. His willingness to pitch backwards, and his ability to throw strikes with any one of his five pitches, make El Duque a valuable asset to the composition of any staff.

Defense

Limberness and athleticism are two qualities that make Hernandez a dependable fifth infielder. Some might believe his exaggerated leg kick would translate into a high opponent stolen-base percentage, but the 69.2 percent in 2004 matched his career numbers and was only slightly above the overall AL success-rate of 68.9 percent from 1998-2004. Varying his times to the plate and looks to the bases has hindered potential basestealers.

2005 Outlook

It will be interesting to see if shoulder fatigue in September lingers into the 2005 season. If it does, we could be witnessing a repeat of 2003, when Hernandez continued to rehab a structurally damaged shoulder into May. El Duque proved he can still get it done in 2004. He is worth another one-year deal, but the Yankees would be taking a chance if they pencil him into their rotation.

Position: SP
Bats: R **Throws:** R
Ht: 6' 2" **Wt:** 220

Opening Day Age: 35
Born: 10/11/69 in Havana, Cuba
ML Seasons: 6
Pronunciation: her-NAN-dezz
Nickname: El Duque

Overall Statistics

	W	L	Pct.	ERA	G	GS	Sv	IP	H	BB	SO	HR	Avg
'04	8	2	.800	3.30	15	15	0	84.2	73	36	84	9	.230
Car.	61	40	.604	3.96	139	136	1	876.1	780	304	703	114	.236

2004 Pitching Profile

	Orlando Hernandez	AL Average
Overall Strike %	60.5	62.3
1st Pitch Strike %	56.9	58.1
Ratio	1.29	1.42
Strikeouts per 9 IP	8.93	6.45
Walks per 9 IP	3.83	3.34
Home Runs per 9 IP	0.96	1.15
Strikeout/Walk Ratio	2.33	1.93
Groundball/Flyball Ratio	0.85	1.17

2004 Situational Stats

	W	L	ERA	Sv	IP		AB	H	HR	RBI	Avg
Home	5	1	2.61	0	48.1	LHB	188	48	6	17	.255
Road	3	1	4.21	0	36.1	RHB	129	25	3	10	.194
First Half	1	0	3.60	0	5.0	Sc Pos	83	13	1	17	.157
Scnd Half	7	2	3.28	0	79.2	Clutch	17	3	0	2	.176

2004 Rankings (American League)

- Led the Yankees in winning percentage and lowest batting average allowed with runners in scoring position

Derek Jeter

2004 Season

The slow start for the Yankees coincided with an unusually slow start for Derek Jeter. He hit a paltry .168 through April and even was booed at Yankee Stadium during an 0-for-32 stretch, the worst such streak of his career. As the summer heated up, so did Jeter's bat. The nine homers he hit in June were the largest monthly total of his career. A broken fifth metacarpal bone in his right hand, courtesy of a Victor Zambrano fastball, forced him to miss two games in July, but he avoided any serious injury.

Hitting

Jeter aggressively attacks pitches early in the count. His ability to stay inside the ball and let it get deep is well documented. Early-season struggles were blamed on his hands prematurely leaking forward, not letting the ball travel enough before he swung. Jeter will use the whole field, but his power stroke is the opposite way. Pitchers habitually challenge him on the inner half, trying to expose holes, especially down and in. He effectively inside-outs many of these pitches and is capable of getting the bat head out front when needed.

Baserunning & Defense

If you trust the value of defensive metrics, 2004 marked a return to defensive respectability for Jeter. A jump in zone rating, range factor and fielding percentage resulted in his first Gold Glove. Jeter moves better to his right, where he is able to backhand balls in the six-hole before leaping to make his signature jump-throw across the diamond, but he still has a slow first step to his glove side. A running catch against Boston that propelled him into the stands and a 46-game errorless streak were the highlights of a steady season. Jeter is a plus runner who takes the extra base.

2005 Outlook

Jeter's final 2004 numbers can be a bit deceiving, considering he hit .329/.388/.538 after the month of May. Sustaining this level of productivity might be difficult over the course of an entire season, but expect Jeter to approach it in 2005.

Position: SS
Bats: R **Throws:** R
Ht: 6' 3" **Wt:** 195

Opening Day Age: 30
Born: 6/26/74 in Pequannock, NJ
ML Seasons: 10
Pronunciation: JEE-ter

Overall Statistics

G	AB	R	H	D	T	HR	RBI	SB	BB	SO	Avg	OBP	Slg
154	643	111	188	44	1	23	78	23	46	99	.292	.352	.471
1366	5513	1037	1734	283	42	150	693	201	559	972	.315	.385	.463

Where He Hits the Ball

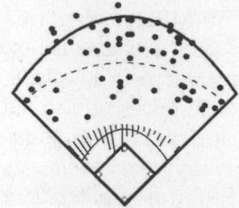 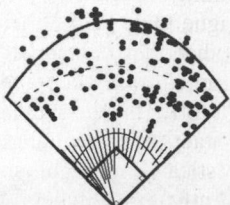

Vs. LHP   **Vs. RHP**

2004 Situational Stats

	AB	H	HR	RBI	Avg		AB	H	HR	RBI	Avg
Home	308	101	11	37	.328	LHP	156	49	6	17	.314
Road	335	87	12	41	.260	RHP	487	139	17	61	.285
First Half	350	97	13	48	.277	Sc Pos	146	41	5	57	.281
Scnd Half	293	91	10	30	.311	Clutch	81	23	3	15	.284

2004 Rankings (American League)

- 1st in steals of third (12)
- 2nd in sacrifice bunts (16)
- 3rd in highest percentage of swings on the first pitch (39.5)
- 4th in at-bats, doubles, hit by pitch (14), stolen-base percentage (85.2) and fielding percentage at shortstop (.981)
- 5th in plate appearances (721)
- 6th in runs scored, stolen bases and bunts in play (24)
- Led the Yankees in at-bats, hits, singles, doubles, sacrifice bunts (16), hit by pitch (14), plate appearances (721), bunts in play (24), steals of third (12), batting average at home and batting average with two strikes (.231)

Hideki Matsui

2004 Season

Hideki Matsui, a.k.a. "Groundzilla," as many in New York began to call him in 2003, proved last year why he was maybe the most feared hitter in Japan. A groundball-flyball ratio of 2.17:1 in 2003 was the impetus for the sarcastic moniker. "Godzilla" was back in 2004, however, bringing with him a few extra pounds of muscle and a growing familiarity with AL pitching that helped him punish opposing staffs. Matsui now has played 1,574 consecutive games dating back to his days in Japan.

Hitting

Matsui believed adjusting to the two-seam, or sinking, fastball was the toughest part of his big league indoctrination. Power numbers dropped as he had a difficult time lifting the ball. That changed in 2004, as he nearly doubled his home-run total from the previous year. Less focused on contact, Matsui drove the ball more for power, drastically lowering groundball rates and subsequently increasing his strikeout rate. Matsui again demonstrated a willingness to use the entire field, but prefers the ball middle-in, which he turns on with authority. He has a tendency to pull off the ball against lefties.

Baserunning & Defense

Matsui plays a serviceable left field, but any defensive accolades he receives usually are without warrant. He does not take great routes to the ball and his weak arm is no secret to AL third-base coaches. He actually performs better in center, but the acquisition of Kenny Lofton limited Matsui to only 15 innings there in 2004. Matsui does not take too many chances on the bases and is decidedly station-to-station at times.

2005 Outlook

Matsui enters the final year of the $21 million contract he signed with the Yankees. The huge improvement in offensive performance and the fact he is relatively young should compel New York management to offer him a new long-term deal. To not do this would be a mistake. In Matsui, the team has a guy who plays every game and is a staple in the middle of the lineup.

Position: LF
Bats: L **Throws:** R
Ht: 6' 2" **Wt:** 230

Opening Day Age: 30
Born: 6/12/74 in Kanazawa, Japan
ML Seasons: 2
Pronunciation: mat-soo-ee

Overall Statistics

	G	AB	R	H	D	T	HR	RBI	SB	BB	SO	Avg	OBP	Slg
'04	162	584	109	174	34	2	31	108	3	88	103	.298	.390	.522
Car.	325	1207	191	353	76	3	47	214	5	151	189	.292	.371	.477

Where He Hits the Ball

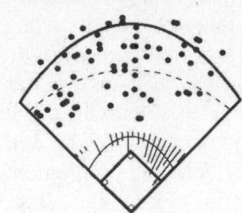 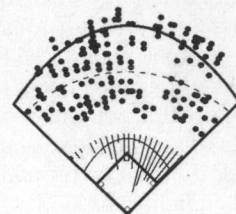

Vs. LHP   **Vs. RHP**

2004 Situational Stats

	AB	H	HR	RBI	Avg		AB	H	HR	RBI	Avg
Home	306	83	18	58	.271	LHP	189	50	6	30	.265
Road	278	91	13	50	.327	RHP	395	124	25	78	.314
First Half	316	93	17	58	.294	Sc Pos	154	45	7	75	.292
Scnd Half	268	81	14	50	.302	Clutch	82	31	7	19	.378

2004 Rankings (American League)

- 1st in games played
- 2nd in batting average in the clutch, errors in left field (7) and lowest fielding percentage in left field (.978)
- 3rd in walks and batting average on the road
- 5th in times on base (265)
- 8th in runs scored
- Led the Yankees in batting average, games played, batting average in the clutch, batting average vs. righthanded pitchers, cleanup slugging percentage (.621) and batting average on the road

Mike Mussina

2004 Season

Sometimes, won-lost record is overvalued. That was the case for Mike Mussina in 1996, when he won 19 games but posted a career-worst 4.81 ERA for Baltimore. Except for posting fewer wins, Mussina's 2004 season bears a remarkable similarity. Yet, in a subpar 2004, Mussina still took the ball every fifth day. Only a mild groin strain and right elbow inflammation kept him from an 11th season of 200+ innings. Mussina is an outstanding talent whose career has been marked by consistency, production and professionalism.

Pitching

Despite a drop in his 2004 numbers, Mussina still possesses the stuff to dominate at times, as when he held the potent Red Sox' lineup hitless through 6.1 innings in Game 1 of the ALCS. Mussina has impeccable command of a low-90s fastball. It has late life in the strike zone and occasionally he will sink it arm-side for added effect. To complement this pitch, Mussina mixes in a knuckle-curve, slider, changeup and splitter. With age, he has become adept at changing speeds with his breaking pitches and has experimented with different arm slots to disrupt the hitter. A workhorse his entire career, Mussina failed to reach the 200-inning plateau for the first time in a decade.

Defense

An excellent fielder, Mussina has enough Gold Gloves to fill a basement. Two errors this season matched the most he had ever made in a single campaign. Instincts and good positioning always have been his recipe for proficient fielding. The nearly 30-percent jump in successful stolen-base percentage probably was due to a tender right groin he nursed midseason.

2005 Outlook

As of right now, Mussina is the unquestioned ace of the Yankees' staff. It is not regular-season numbers alone that warrant this distinction. A postseason strikeout-walk ratio of 4.6:1 proves how well he has performed when it really counts. The 2005 season should be a better one for Mussina, and 200 strikeouts with 20 quality starts would not be a surprise.

Position: SP
Bats: L **Throws:** R
Ht: 6' 2" **Wt:** 185

Opening Day Age: 36
Born: 12/8/68 in Williamsport, PA
ML Seasons: 14
Pronunciation: myoo-SEE-nuh
Nickname: Moose

Overall Statistics

W	L	Pct.	ERA	G	GS	Sv	IP	H	BB	SO	HR	Avg
12	9	.571	4.59	27	27	0	164.2	178	40	132	22	.276
211	119	.639	3.59	413	413	0	2833.1	2675	637	2258	300	.249

2004 Pitching Profile

	Mike Mussina	AL Average
Overall Strike %	65.8	62.3
1st Pitch Strike %	62.2	58.1
Ratio	1.32	1.42
Strikeouts per 9 IP	7.21	6.45
Walks per 9 IP	2.19	3.34
Home Runs per 9 IP	1.20	1.15
Strikeout/Walk Ratio	3.30	1.93
Groundball/Flyball Ratio	1.23	1.17

2004 Situational Stats

	W	L	ERA	Sv	IP		AB	H	HR	RBI	Avg
Home	8	2	3.94	0	82.1	LHB	338	86	8	33	.254
Road	4	7	5.25	0	82.1	RHB	308	92	14	46	.299
First Half	9	6	5.20	0	107.1	Sc Pos	129	37	2	52	.287
Scnd Half	3	3	3.45	0	57.1	Clutch	27	6	1	2	.222

2004 Rankings (American League)

- 6th in highest strikeout-walk ratio (3.3)
- 8th in fewest walks per nine innings (2.2)
- 10th in highest stolen-base percentage allowed (76.9)
- Led the Yankees in most strikeouts per nine innings (7.2)

Jorge Posada

Position: C
Bats: B **Throws:** R
Ht: 6' 2" **Wt:** 205

Opening Day Age: 33
Born: 8/17/71 in Santurce, PR
ML Seasons: 10
Pronunciation: HOR-hay po-SAH-da

2004 Season

Jorge Posada put together another solid regular season following his spectacular showing in 2003. He reached base in 40 percent of his plate appearances and had only two less extra-base hits in 41 fewer plate appearances. But 2004 was much like the previous year in another regard. Once again Posada faltered during the postseason. His playoff line of .244/.352/.267 hamstrung part of the feared Yankees offense.

Hitting

Posada is a rarity as a switch-hitting catcher. He controls the strike zone with a more than functional plate discipline. Continually among the league leaders in walks, Posada is no easy out. From the right side he has more pop, a result of his pull conscious approach versus lefthanders. As a lefthanded hitter, he favors the ball just above the belt. Posada gets himself in trouble when he presses or attempts to do to much. This could help explain his postseason travails.

Baserunning & Defense

Posada has steadily improved his composite defense. He very seldom takes bad at-bats into the field anymore and by most accounts calls a good game. His rapport with the pitching staff is also noted, and this cannot be overlooked when assessing a catcher's defense. Defensive measures like passed balls or stolen-base percentage place him somewhere in the middle of the catching spectrum. His arm is sometimes short, but accurate. Posada is a bad baserunner and paid the price by having his nose broken when he didn't get out of the way of Angels shortstop Alfredo Amezaga's throw on the back end of a double play in May.

2005 Outlook

The future is bright for Posada, who has two years left on his contract. Because he didn't start catching until later in his career, it is probable that he won't break down at the same age as other backstops. He already has avoided some of the substantial injuries that have claimed other big-name catchers. Posada may be overshadowed by his teammates, but he is the oil that greases the wheels of the Yankees' machine.

Overall Statistics

	G	AB	R	H	D	T	HR	RBI	SB	BB	SO	Avg	OBP	Slg
'04	137	449	72	122	31	0	21	81	1	88	92	.272	.400	.481
Car.	1003	3369	521	910	212	5	156	607	10	562	850	.270	.379	.475

Where He Hits the Ball

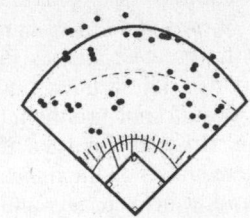
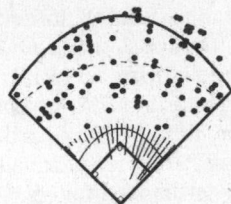

Vs. LHP	**Vs. RHP**

2004 Situational Stats

	AB	H	HR	RBI	Avg		AB	H	HR	RBI	Avg
Home	205	55	11	36	.268	LHP	142	39	8	28	.275
Road	244	67	10	45	.275	RHP	307	83	13	53	.270
First Half	236	65	11	40	.275	Sc Pos	129	32	5	60	.248
Scnd Half	213	57	10	41	.268	Clutch	62	21	3	11	.339

2004 Rankings (American League)

- 1st in GDPs (24)
- 2nd in errors at catcher (9) and highest percentage of runners caught stealing as a catcher (25.6)
- 3rd in walks
- 4th in on-base percentage
- Led the Yankees in GDPs (24), on-base percentage, highest groundball-flyball ratio (1.7) and batting average with the bases loaded (.471)

Mariano Rivera

2004 Season

In March 2004, Mariano Rivera signed a two-year, $21 million extension that will keep him in New York until at least 2006. The deal freed up Rivera to focus his efforts on pitching. A contented Rivera racked up a career-best 74 appearances and 53 saves in 2004, propelling the Yankees to their second straight 101-win season. The 53 saves were the most by any closer in either league. On May 28, he registered the 300th save of his career. One of the few remaining pieces from the 1990s championship teams, Rivera continues to be a dominant presence at the end of games.

Pitching

Everyone knows what is coming when Rivera readies himself to deliver: a mid-90s cutter that darts like a slider. One of the greatest pitches in baseball history, Rivera's cutter has stymied hitters for close to a decade, despite not producing an abundance of strikeouts. Instead, he runs it away from righthanded hitters and in on the hands of lefthanded hitters, generating broken bats and groundballs. When Rivera does throw something straight, it is usually a riding four-seamer that is intended to move the hitter's eye level upward.

Defense

Rivera needs to be ready after every pitch, as he often faces comebackers on the mound. His 4.69 total chances per nine innings in 2004 blew away all other pitchers who qualified. Rivera must take spring fielding sessions seriously because he made just one error in 2004. It is a good thing Rivera is a closer. He is slow to the plate and his pickoff move is wanting.

2005 Outlook

Did the regular-season demands placed on Rivera's right arm lead to the blown saves in Games 4 and 5 of the ALCS? Whatever you believe, it is hard to imagine Rivera reaching the 74-game plateau again in 2005. Judicious use and a little luck staying healthy should make the 500-save mark a realistic possibility several years from now.

Position: RP
Bats: R **Throws:** R
Ht: 6' 2" **Wt:** 170

Opening Day Age: 35
Born: 11/29/69 in Panama City, Panama
ML Seasons: 10

Overall Statistics

	W	L	Pct.	ERA	G	GS	Sv	IP	H	BB	SO	HR	Avg
'04	4	2	.667	1.94	74	0	53	78.2	65	20	66	3	.225
Car.	47	31	.603	2.43	586	10	336	728.1	580	197	648	40	.216

2004 Pitching Profile

	Mariano Rivera	AL Average
Overall Strike %	68.4	62.3
1st Pitch Strike %	64.0	58.1
Ratio	1.08	1.42
Strikeouts per 9 IP	7.55	6.45
Walks per 9 IP	2.29	3.34
Home Runs per 9 IP	0.34	1.15
Strikeout/Walk Ratio	3.30	1.93
Groundball/Flyball Ratio	2.13	1.17

2004 Situational Stats

	W	L	ERA	Sv	IP		AB	H	HR	RBI	Avg
Home	3	1	2.30	27	43.0	LHB	154	36	2	8	.234
Road	1	1	1.51	26	35.2	RHB	135	29	1	13	.215
First Half	0	0	0.99	32	45.1	Sc Pos	79	11	0	16	.139
Scnd Half	4	2	3.24	21	33.1	Clutch	227	54	2	19	.238

2004 Rankings (American League)

- 1st in saves and games finished (69)
- 3rd in save percentage (93.0) and relief ERA (1.94)
- 7th in games pitched and fewest baserunners allowed per nine innings in relief (10.3)
- Led the Yankees in saves, games finished (69), most GDPs induced per GDP situation (14.5%), save percentage (93.0) and relief ERA (1.94)

Alex Rodriguez

2004 Season

The offseason trade that sent Alex Rodriguez from Texas to New York secured the reigning American League MVP and arguably the best all-around player in baseball. He moved to third base and fit in nicely. No longer profiting from Ameriquest Field in Arlington, Rodriguez suffered a slight dip offensively. The percentage of his hits that went for extra bases dropped from 46 to 36 percent. His total bases were down and his slugging percentage dropped 88 points from 2003.

Hitting

Rodriguez' swing produces the treasured backspin that hitting coaches and physicists cite as essential to maximizing a baseball's travel. A-Rod hardly ever cuts himself short, his long arms allow for phenomenal extension, specifically on pitches middle-away. His truest power is to right-center, so opponents try to tie him up inside. Rodriguez has tried to shake the slider bat speed label by finding easier ways to get to these pitches. With a selective approach, he has shown exceptional skill hitting either lefties or righties.

Baserunning & Defense

The Yankees brought in ex-Yankee third baseman Graig Nettles before the season to help Rodriguez with footwork, positioning and proper reads at third. With the exception of a deflected ball to the face in spring training, his transition went off without a hitch. Rodriguez showed off his natural instincts and strong arm at third, moving well to both sides. He also displayed an uncanny knack for picking the right hop. His 28 steals were the most since his 40-40 year in 1998. Rodriguez is a shrewd baserunner who gets the most out of his speed.

2005 Outlook

The interference play in which Rodriguez slapped both ball and glove from Boston pitcher Bronson Arroyo during the ALCS did not endear him to fans on either side. The public image that A-Rod has worked to maintain took a small hit. Last October didn't have a happy ending for Rodriguez, who once again will pursue his first World Series ring in 2005.

Position: 3B
Bats: R **Throws:** R
Ht: 6' 3" **Wt:** 210

Opening Day Age: 29
Born: 7/27/75 in New York, NY
ML Seasons: 11
Pronunciation: rod-RI-guez
Nickname: A-Rod

New York (AL)

Overall Statistics

G	AB	R	H	D	T	HR	RBI	SB	BB	SO	Avg	OBP	Slg
155	601	112	172	24	2	36	106	28	80	131	.286	.375	.512
1430	5590	1121	1707	309	24	381	1096	205	639	1126	.305	.381	.574

Where He Hits the Ball

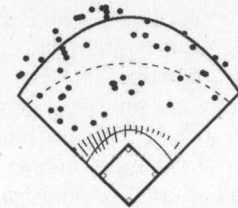

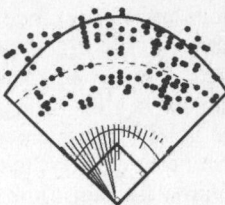

Vs. LHP   **Vs. RHP**

2004 Situational Stats

	AB	H	HR	RBI	Avg		AB	H	HR	RBI	Avg
Home	311	87	17	55	.280	LHP	132	41	14	28	.311
Road	290	85	19	51	.293	RHP	469	131	22	78	.279
First Half	337	91	22	58	.270	Sc Pos	157	39	8	66	.248
Scnd Half	264	81	14	48	.307	Clutch	80	22	2	13	.275

2004 Rankings (American League)

- 2nd in stolen-base percentage (87.5)
- 4th in fielding percentage at third base (.965)
- 5th in runs scored, stolen bases and pitches seen (2,747)
- 6th in home runs and errors at third base (13)
- Led the Yankees in home runs, total bases (308), stolen bases, strikeouts, pitches seen (2,747) and stolen-base percentage (87.5)
- Led AL third basemen in home runs and RBI

Gary Sheffield

2004 Season

Gary Sheffield finally filled the void in right field that dates back to Paul O'Neill's retirement in 2001. The free agent from Atlanta did not miss a beat and finished second place in the American League MVP vote. He put up terrific numbers while battling constant left-shoulder pain, first diagnosed as bursitis, but later changed to a slight separation of his trapezius muscle. A few cortisone shots and a Herculean pain tolerance made it possible for Sheffield to play in 154 games during the regular season.

Hitting

The strength of Sheffield's hands and wrists is second to none. To violently shake the bat as he does and still explode on good fastballs is no easy task. Sheffield also creates great torque with his hips, which help propel his tape-measure home runs. When his hands and hips are out of concert, he is still strong enough to muscle balls for hits. Pitchers usually take the hard-in, soft-away approach against him, with soft-away more regularly coming later in the sequence. Sheffield continues to be a selective hitter with good strike-zone understanding.

Baserunning & Defense

Sheffield easily possesses the strongest arm in the Yankees' outfield, and his 11 outfield assists led the club. When compared to fellow outfielders in New York, Sheffield's overall defense stands out. But when compared with other right fielders in baseball, his defensive prowess is marginal. The injured shoulder was a factor in 2004, forcing him to catch balls to the side because reaching his glove hand upward induced pain. His caution carried over to his baserunning. He stole just five bases.

2005 Outlook

Sheffield has not shown signs of slowing down as he enters his 18th big league season. It seems like he has been around forever, but Sheffield is just 36. If he can get the shoulder right, and arthroscopic surgery in November was expected to do that, anticipate another MVP-caliber year in 2005.

Position: RF/DH
Bats: R **Throws:** R
Ht: 6' 0" **Wt:** 205

Opening Day Age: 36
Born: 11/18/68 in Tampa, FL
ML Seasons: 17

Overall Statistics

G	AB	R	H	D	T	HR	RBI	SB	BB	SO	Avg	OBP	Slg
154	573	117	166	30	1	36	121	5	92	83	.290	.393	.534
2036	7302	1307	2175	386	24	415	1353	205	1202	879	.298	.400	.528

Where He Hits the Ball

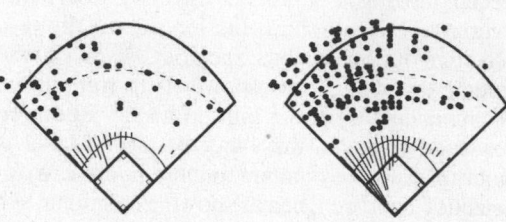

Vs. LHP   **Vs. RHP**

2004 Situational Stats

	AB	H	HR	RBI	Avg		AB	H	HR	RBI	Avg
Home	279	88	19	71	.315	LHP	140	44	8	30	.314
Road	294	78	17	50	.265	RHP	433	122	28	91	.282
First Half	301	91	16	59	.302	Sc Pos	169	55	8	83	.325
Scnd Half	272	75	20	62	.276	Clutch	78	26	6	20	.333

2004 Rankings (American League)

- 2nd in walks and times on base (269)
- 3rd in runs scored
- 4th in sacrifice flies (8), errors in right field (5) and lowest fielding percentage in right field (.983)
- 5th in RBI
- 6th in home runs
- Led the Yankees in home runs, runs scored, RBI, sacrifice flies (8), caught stealing (6), walks, intentional walks (7), times on base (269), slugging percentage, HR frequency (15.9 ABs per HR), batting average with runners in scoring position,and lowest percentage of swings on the first pitch (17.5)

Javier Vazquez

2004 Season

It was a tale of two halves for Javier Vazquez in his first year with the Yankees after coming over from Montreal. He was solid, if unspectacular, before the All-Star break, winning 10 games with an ERA of 3.56. Then came the miserable second half. A post-break 6.92 ERA and 4-5 record relegated him to a long relief role during most of the postseason.

Pitching

Vazquez has a repertoire that consists of a fastball, slider, changeup and curveball. His fastball can reach 94 MPH, but he has a proclivity to overthrow, negatively affecting his command. A deceptive changeup thrown with outstanding arm action all but neutralizes any lefthanded advantage and many scouts believe it to be his most effective pitch. His curveball is a quality third pitch, but problems with mechanics frequently leave Vazquez hanging it on the inner third. In light of early career overuse, it is imperative that Vazquez find an efficient, repeatable delivery.

Defense

Vazquez adroitly patrols the vicinity where he works. Nimble to the ball, he makes plays other pitchers would not. When it comes to stopping the running game, there are few righthanders who do it any better. His three pickoffs were more than the two stolen bases he gave up all season. When Torii Hunter stole second off him on August 17, it broke a streak of 239 innings and 34 games without giving up a stolen base.

2005 Outlook

There have been rumors the Yankees might look to trade Vazquez for someone more New York tested. Some even wondered if Vazquez was throwing with an injured shoulder. An MRI conducted in October showed no structural damage, and may have been a ploy by management to ease any health doubts for possible suitors. Vazquez is signed through 2007, and the Yankees would be wise to give him a little more time to figure things out. Understanding the need for better mechanics, without becoming the dreaded mechanical monster, is a tightrope Vazquez must walk.

Position: SP
Bats: R **Throws:** R
Ht: 6' 2" **Wt:** 205

Opening Day Age: 28
Born: 7/25/76 in Ponce, PR
ML Seasons: 7
Pronunciation: VAS-kez

Overall Statistics

	W	L	Pct.	ERA	G	GS	Sv	IP	H	BB	SO	HR	Avg
'04	14	10	.583	4.91	32	32	0	198.0	195	60	150	33	.255
Car.	78	78	.500	4.26	224	223	0	1427.1	1430	391	1226	188	.260

2004 Pitching Profile

	Javier Vazquez	AL Average
Overall Strike %	64.6	62.3
1st Pitch Strike %	63.1	58.1
Ratio	1.29	1.42
Strikeouts per 9 IP	6.82	6.45
Walks per 9 IP	2.73	3.34
Home Runs per 9 IP	1.50	1.15
Strikeout/Walk Ratio	2.50	1.93
Groundball/Flyball Ratio	0.85	1.17

2004 Situational Stats

	W	L	ERA	Sv	IP		AB	H	HR	RBI	Avg
Home	9	4	4.13	0	104.2	LHB	395	100	20	57	.253
Road	5	6	5.79	0	93.1	RHB	371	95	13	42	.256
First Half	10	5	3.56	0	118.2	Sc Pos	134	38	6	62	.284
Scnd Half	4	5	6.92	0	79.1	Clutch	52	10	1	5	.192

2004 Rankings (American League)

- 2nd in lowest stolen-base percentage allowed (28.6)
- 3rd in wild pitches (12)
- 4th in highest ERA on the road
- 5th in home runs allowed, balks (2) and lowest groundball-flyball ratio allowed (0.8)
- 8th in wins and most home runs allowed per nine innings (1.50)
- 9th in hit batsmen (11)
- Led the Yankees in wins, losses, games started, innings pitched, batters faced (849), home runs allowed, walks allowed, hit batsmen (11), strikeouts, wild pitches (12), balks (2), pitches thrown (3,209), pickoff throws (98), runners caught stealing (5), lowest batting average allowed (.255) and lowest stolen-base percentage allowed (28.6)

Bernie Williams

2004 Season

The 2004 season was supposed to be a rebound year for Bernie Williams after a frustrating 2003 campaign. Instead, Williams nearly repeated his previous performance. An appendectomy in February forced Williams to miss valuable parts of spring training and the season-opening trip to Japan. As a result, he got off to a slow start. Williams did collect his 2000th career hit, but his age is certainly showing.

Hitting

Decreasing bat speed is the likely culprit for much of Williams' recent struggles. Pitchers who expand upward with good fastballs give him trouble. Still, Williams is selective at the plate, producing impressive walk rates his entire career. He prefers the ball away, especially from the right side, where he can drive the ball with power to right field. He feasts off soft-tossing lefty types. From the left side he is gap-to-gap, taking advantage of the spacious left-center alley at Yankee Stadium.

Baserunning & Defense

For Williams, the biggest dropoff in production actually might have occurred on the defensive side. A four-time Gold Glove recipient, he now is seen as a liability in the middle of the diamond. Injuries and age have forced Williams to play an even deeper center field. Balls routinely drop in front of him and he rarely challenges an advancing baserunner because of his poor arm. Williams also knows his limitations on the bases, and no longer tries to stretch the double into a triple. Years of experience and plenty of guile still make Williams useful on the bases.

2005 Outlook

Using Williams as a designated hitter on a part-time basis played to mixed results. His production was noticeably less when used as a DH, but may have kept him healthier on the days he did play the outfield. A fairly productive final four months of the season, and the fact that Williams is signed only through 2005, could be the right combination to elicit a revival in his game.

Position: CF/DH
Bats: B **Throws:** R
Ht: 6' 2" **Wt:** 205

Opening Day Age: 36
Born: 9/13/68 in San Juan, PR
ML Seasons: 14

Overall Statistics

G	AB	R	H	D	T	HR	RBI	SB	BB	SO	Avg	OBP	Slg
148	561	105	147	29	1	22	70	1	85	96	.262	.360	.435
1804	6964	1248	2097	401	54	263	1132	144	983	1084	.301	.388	.488

Where He Hits the Ball

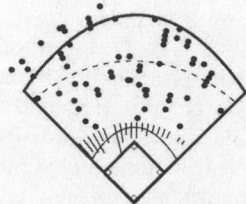 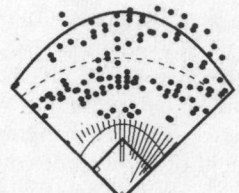

Vs. LHP   **Vs. RHP**

2004 Situational Stats

	AB	H	HR	RBI	Avg		AB	H	HR	RBI	Avg
Home	284	75	13	39	.264	LHP	166	44	9	26	.265
Road	277	72	9	31	.260	RHP	395	103	13	44	.261
First Half	300	78	11	30	.260	Sc Pos	131	32	3	45	.244
Scnd Half	261	69	11	40	.264	Clutch	74	15	4	11	.203

2004 Rankings (American League)

- 5th in highest percentage of pitches taken (62.2)
- 7th in walks and on-base percentage for a leadoff hitter (.371)
- 9th in GDPs (19)
- 10th in highest percentage of swings put into play (49.8)
- Led the Yankees in highest percentage of pitches taken (62.2) and on-base percentage for a leadoff hitter (.371)

Miguel Cairo

Position: 2B
Bats: R **Throws:** R
Ht: 6' 1" **Wt:** 208

Opening Day Age: 30
Born: 5/4/74 in Anaco, VZ
ML Seasons: 9
Pronunciation: KI-row

Overall Statistics

	G	AB	R	H	D	T	HR	RBI	SB	BB	SO	Avg	OBP	Slg
'04	122	360	48	105	17	5	6	42	11	18	49	.292	.346	.417
Car.	829	2372	313	647	111	22	25	231	87	143	274	.273	.322	.370

2004 Situational Stats

	AB	H	HR	RBI	Avg		AB	H	HR	RBI	Avg
Home	188	60	4	19	.319	LHP	128	43	1	15	.336
Road	172	45	2	23	.262	RHP	232	62	5	27	.267
First Half	163	50	3	21	.307	Sc Pos	81	19	2	37	.235
Scnd Half	197	55	3	21	.279	Clutch	50	16	0	1	.320

2004 Season

The versatility of Miguel Cairo has enhanced his overall appeal. Signed by New York in December 2003, his value increased when the Yankees dealt Alfonso Soriano to the Rangers. Cairo won the battle with Enrique Wilson for second base and did an adequate job.

Hitting, Baserunning & Defense

Cairo likes the straight stuff. A change in the starting position of the hands made September his best month. By beginning with his hands higher, he made the loading process easier. He will handle the ball up in the zone, and capitalizes on mistake pitches. Cairo has soft hands and works well around the second-base bag, hanging in to turn the double play. He has better-than-average speed but has not stolen many bases since his days in Tampa Bay. He now operates on the basepaths using his intelligence and good instincts.

2005 Outlook

Cairo wanted to return to New York, but he wasn't offered salary arbitration and the Yankees signed free agent Tony Womack to a two-year deal to take over at second base. Cairo will hook on somewhere, but he may have trouble finding a team that will offer the 400 plate appearances he got in New York last season.

Tony Clark

Position: 1B
Bats: B **Throws:** R
Ht: 6' 7" **Wt:** 245

Opening Day Age: 32
Born: 6/15/72 in Newton, KS
ML Seasons: 10

Overall Statistics

	G	AB	R	H	D	T	HR	RBI	SB	BB	SO	Avg	OBP	Slg
'04	106	253	37	56	12	0	16	49	0	26	92	.221	.297	.458
Car.	1093	3613	519	955	193	8	191	635	6	414	943	.264	.340	.481

2004 Situational Stats

	AB	H	HR	RBI	Avg		AB	H	HR	RBI	Avg
Home	112	22	5	17	.196	LHP	92	18	3	13	.196
Road	141	34	11	32	.241	RHP	161	38	13	36	.236
First Half	154	36	10	31	.234	Sc Pos	68	19	2	29	.279
Scnd Half	99	20	6	18	.202	Clutch	43	10	0	6	.233

2004 Season

Tony Clark probably did not anticipate making 99 appearances at first base in 2004, but that's just what he got. Jason Giambi and Travis Lee were ahead of him on the depth chart going into the spring, but health issues and injuries put Lee out indefinitely and limited Giambi's playing time. Clark struggled with the bat.

Hitting, Baserunning & Defense

After his 2003 season, it appeared Clark could be a useful right-handed platoon man, but he was nearly useless from the right side in '04. Clark's power from the left side is outstanding, and he provided three multi-homer games in 2004, including a trio of bombs in a late-August game against the Jays. Clark is notoriously streaky, however, and when he's not slugging the ball he's striking out at an alarming rate. He's a solid baserunner and an above-average defensive first basemen who can save an infield a few errors.

2005 Outlook

Clark could re-sign with the Yankees, though it's unlikely. His asking price these days is a little too high for what is received. If Clark lowers his price, a club looking for some lefthanded power, a decent glove at first and a veteran presence in the clubhouse could come calling.

Tom Gordon

Position: RP
Bats: R **Throws:** R
Ht: 5'10" **Wt:** 190

Opening Day Age: 37
Born: 11/18/67 in
Sebring, FL
ML Seasons: 16
Nickname: Flash

Overall Statistics

W	L	Pct.	ERA	G	GS	Sv	IP	H	BB	SO	HR	Avg
9	4	.692	2.21	80	0	4	89.2	56	23	96	5	.180
122	111	.524	3.99	671	203	114	1896.2	1703	893	1733	149	.239

2004 Situational Stats

	W	L	ERA	Sv	IP		AB	H	HR	RBI	Avg
Home	3	0	1.87	2	43.1	LHB	162	30	1	9	.185
Road	6	4	2.53	2	46.1	RHB	149	26	4	14	.174
First Half	2	3	1.78	2	50.2	Sc Pos	72	11	0	18	.153
Scnd Half	7	1	2.77	2	39.0	Clutch	214	36	4	17	.168

2004 Season

Tom Gordon looked right at home in his first season with the Yankees. Signed as a free agent, Gordon quickly established himself as the top setup man in baseball. His 36 holds paced the majors, and the .180 opponent batting average allowed led the Yankees. Gordon and Mariano Rivera are another addition to the Yankees' legacy of excellent setup-closer combinations.

Pitching & Defense

Gordon consistently challenges hitters with a mid-90s fastball, hard slider and devastating curveball. His arm strength has returned after elbow and shoulder injuries limited his action around the turn of the century. He's alleviated concerns about his durability the last two seasons—working 146 games—and he's followed a small few in making the transition from veteran starter to top-flight reliever. Gordon controls the running game and fields his position well.

2005 Outlook

Gordon has proven he is one of the best relievers around and could demand big money on the open market after this season. It is reasonable to anticipate a 2005 that approaches the 80-appearance level, an impressive ERA and more than a strikeout per inning.

Jon Lieber

Position: SP
Bats: L **Throws:** R
Ht: 6' 2" **Wt:** 230

Opening Day Age: 34
Born: 4/2/70 in Council
Bluffs, IA
ML Seasons: 10
Pronunciation:
LEE-ber

Overall Statistics

	W	L	Pct.	ERA	G	GS	Sv	IP	H	BB	SO	HR	Avg
'04	14	8	.636	4.33	27	27	0	176.2	216	18	102	20	.301
Car.	100	91	.524	4.20	299	252	2	1687.0	1819	329	1223	208	.274

2004 Situational Stats

	W	L	ERA	Sv	IP		AB	H	HR	RBI	Avg
Home	11	3	3.68	0	100.1	LHB	382	132	14	52	.346
Road	3	5	5.19	0	76.1	RHB	336	84	6	35	.250
First Half	7	5	4.77	0	83.0	Sc Pos	141	40	2	56	.284
Scnd Half	7	3	3.94	0	93.2	Clutch	36	9	2	5	.250

2004 Season

When Jon Lieber took the mound on May 1, it ended a 21-month layoff. Armed with a new tendon from his leg through Tommy John surgery, Lieber performed well. His 14 wins and 16 quality starts were team highs for New York.

Pitching & Defense

Playing behind Lieber must be a pleasure. He works quickly and throws strikes. Lieber can run it up there in the low 90s and offsets his fastball with both a slider and changeup away. Using his slider as an out pitch has made him notoriously tougher on righthanded batters, but against lefties he has to be more fine, opting instead to back-door the slider and fade the changeup. A drop in weight may have made him more agile in the field, but his four errors were the most he has ever had in a single year. A quick slide-step move keeps runners close.

2005 Outlook

Lieber's competitiveness shined through again in 2004, as he successfully recovered from Tommy John surgery. An $8 million option for 2005 was declined by the Yankees, and they were unable to sign him to a deal at a lower price. Instead, Lieber agreed to a three-year, $21 million deal to join a retooled Philadelphia rotation.

Esteban Loaiza

Position: SP
Bats: R **Throws:** R
Ht: 6' 3" **Wt:** 215

Opening Day Age: 33
Born: 12/31/71 in Tijuana, Mexico
ML Seasons: 10
Pronunciation:
s-TAY-bahn low-EYE-zah

Overall Statistics

	W	L	Pct.	ERA	G	GS	Sv	IP	H	BB	SO	HR	Avg
'04	10	7	.588	5.70	31	27	0	183.0	217	71	117	32	.296
Car.	100	89	.529	4.70	300	263	1	1663.0	1883	484	1082	210	.287

2004 Situational Stats

	W	L	ERA	Sv	IP		AB	H	HR	RBI	Avg
Home	7	3	6.39	0	93.0	LHB	409	122	15	54	.298
Road	3	4	5.00	0	90.0	RHB	324	95	17	58	.293
First Half	8	4	4.77	0	120.2	Sc Pos	177	52	6	78	.294
Scnd Half	2	3	7.51	0	62.1	Clutch	23	5	1	1	.217

2004 Season

The makeup wore off as Esteban Loaiza could not repeat the Cy Young-type performance of 2003 in 2004. He returned to pre-2003 form before being acquired from the White Sox on July 31. The trading-deadline deal proved to be fruitless for the Yankees, as Loaiza amassed just one win and an 8.50 ERA with New York.

Pitching & Defense

Loaiza is guilty of falling in love with his cut fastball. At times he relies almost exclusively on this 86-88 MPH pitch. This is regrettable because his 89-91 MPH fastball, slider and changeup comprise a workable repertoire. Loaiza is notably more vulnerable the second and third time through the order because of his reliance on the cutter. Loaiza's easy delivery leaves him in good fielding position and he controls the running game fairly well.

2005 Outlook

A free agent, Loaiza might not get many offers. He is drawing interest from Colorado and Tampa Bay, places that he would be under far less pressure to perform. It is unrealistic to ever expect a year like 2003 again from Loaiza.

Kenny Lofton

Traded To PHILLIES

Position: CF/RF
Bats: L **Throws:** L
Ht: 6' 0" **Wt:** 180

Opening Day Age: 37
Born: 5/31/67 in East Chicago, IN
ML Seasons: 14

Overall Statistics

	G	AB	R	H	D	T	HR	RBI	SB	BB	SO	Avg	OBP	Slg
'04	83	276	51	76	10	7	3	18	7	31	27	.275	.346	.395
Car.	1728	6794	1296	2019	328	93	118	666	545	812	882	.297	.372	.425

2004 Situational Stats

	AB	H	HR	RBI	Avg		AB	H	HR	RBI	Avg
Home	101	28	2	7	.277	LHP	26	8	0	2	.308
Road	175	48	1	11	.274	RHP	250	68	3	16	.272
First Half	118	35	1	7	.297	Sc Pos	51	10	0	14	.196
Scnd Half	158	41	2	11	.259	Clutch	44	11	1	2	.250

2004 Season

The well-traveled Kenny Lofton made his way to New York and endured a disappointing year, battling both injury troubles and dissatisfaction with his new role. Strains to his right quad and left hamstring, in April and June respectively, sidelined him. The two trips to the disabled list and inconsistent playing time never allowed the frustrated Lofton to get on an extended roll.

Hitting, Baserunning & Defense

Slapping the ball on the ground and beating out plays at first was what made Lofton such a threat in his younger years. Now less prone to hit the ball on the ground, Lofton tries to jerk more balls for power. He infrequently even attempts to bunt anymore. Lofton has lost a few steps in center field and plays the position cautiously, drawing the ire of the Yankee faithful in 2004. His arm is mediocre, which shows on relays from the gaps. The active career leader in stolen bases, Lofton is not the basestealing menace of years past.

2005 Outlook

Lofton will play out the second year of his $7.25 million deal in Philadelphia. On December 3, he was dealt to the Phillies for reliever Felix Rodriguez. Lofton should take over center field from Marlon Byrd and Jason Michaels.

New York (AL)

John Olerud

Position: 1B
Bats: L **Throws:** L
Ht: 6' 5" **Wt:** 225

Opening Day Age: 36
Born: 8/5/68 in Seattle, WA
ML Seasons: 16
Pronunciation: OLE-le-rude

Overall Statistics

G	AB	R	H	D	T	HR	RBI	SB	BB	SO	Avg	OBP	Slg
127	425	45	110	20	1	9	48	0	61	61	.259	.359	.374
2147	7419	1121	2189	493	13	248	1193	11	1259	996	.295	.399	.465

2004 Situational Stats

	AB	H	HR	RBI	Avg		AB	H	HR	RBI	Avg
Home	210	52	5	21	.248	LHP	92	23	2	8	.250
Road	215	58	4	27	.270	RHP	333	87	7	40	.261
First Half	261	64	5	22	.245	Sc Pos	101	27	1	37	.267
Scnd Half	164	46	4	26	.280	Clutch	83	19	1	8	.229

2004 Season

The considerable drop in power and the emerging play of Bucky Jacobsen led the Mariners to release John Olerud in July. He cleared waivers and signed with the Yankees on August 3. A veteran of six postseasons, Olerud was protection at first base for the Yankees, in light of Jason Giambi's uncertain health. Olerud hit .312 in a productive August for New York.

Hitting, Baserunning & Defense

With little wasted effort, Olerud's short, compact stroke is conducive to line drives to all parts of the field. He successfully directs anything middle-away into left field. A conspicuous loss of power since 2003 has turned him into a singles hitter. Olerud is smooth with the glove, skillfully digging errant throws in the dirt with uncommon ease. He is a slow but heady baserunner.

2005 Outlook

Olerud would be an asset off the Yankees' bench, but that's unlikely to happen after he wasn't offered salary arbitration. New York can't re-sign him until May 1. If he does not retire, Olerud may have few options because corner infielders without power are unattractive commodities for most clubs.

Paul Quantrill

Position: RP
Bats: L **Throws:** R
Ht: 6' 1" **Wt:** 198

Opening Day Age: 36
Born: 11/3/68 in London, ON, Canada
ML Seasons: 13
Pronunciation: KWAN-trill

Overall Statistics

	W	L	Pct.	ERA	G	GS	Sv	IP	H	BB	SO	HR	Avg
'04	7	3	.700	4.72	86	0	1	95.1	124	20	37	5	.316
Car.	66	76	.465	3.74	791	64	21	1186.2	1349	322	689	104	.290

2004 Situational Stats

	W	L	ERA	Sv	IP		AB	H	HR	RBI	Avg
Home	2	1	3.38	1	50.2	LHB	185	54	4	28	.292
Road	5	2	6.25	0	44.2	RHB	208	70	1	29	.337
First Half	5	2	3.05	0	56.0	Sc Pos	108	37	1	50	.343
Scnd Half	2	1	7.09	1	39.1	Clutch	156	53	1	16	.340

2004 Season

After leading the major leagues in appearances with Los Angeles the two previous seasons, Paul Quantrill could only find enough in him to lead the American League in 2004. Perhaps the heavy demands on his arm finally caught up with him. A case of "dead arm" made Quantrill ineffective after July. An 8.07 ERA over his last 29 games exemplified just how bad it got.

Pitching & Defense

Quantrill relies on a heavy sinker to get ground-balls. It usually sits in the high 80s with late sink, but a second-half drop in velocity made this pitch look more like batting practice. For Quantrill, the straightening out of his sinker is tantamount to disaster. His slider and changeup are more for show, neither being a strikeout pitch. Quantrill offsets his slow delivery by throwing over rather often to disrupt baserunners. His mobility off the mound is normally satisfactory, but a balky right knee, injured in Tokyo, hampered him all season.

2005 Outlook

The Yankees have already declined the 2006 option in Quantrill's contract, a byproduct of his second-half collapse in 2004. New York has added arms over the winter, which should reduce the workload and demands placed on Quantrill.

Ruben Sierra

Position: DH/RF
Bats: B **Throws:** R
Ht: 6' 1" **Wt:** 215

Opening Day Age: 39
Born: 10/6/65 in Rio Piedras, PR
ML Seasons: 18

Overall Statistics

	G	AB	R	H	D	T	HR	RBI	SB	BB	SO	Avg	OBP	Slg
	107	307	40	75	12	1	17	65	1	25	55	.244	.296	.456
	2111	7846	1067	2108	415	59	302	1289	142	597	1191	.269	.317	.452

2004 Situational Stats

	AB	H	HR	RBI	Avg		AB	H	HR	RBI	Avg
Home	169	37	8	30	.219	LHP	136	33	5	24	.243
Road	138	38	9	35	.275	RHP	171	42	12	41	.246
First Half	159	43	8	32	.270	Sc Pos	79	24	6	51	.304
Scnd Half	148	32	9	33	.216	Clutch	53	14	3	16	.264

2004 Season

The Yankees signed Ruben Sierra to a one-year, $1 million deal to have another lefthanded bat and emergency outfielder. He assembled a fairly typical Sierra-type year of low on-base percentage with the occasional blast. Sierra hit his 300th career home run and moved into sixth place on the all-time switch-hitting home-run list in 2004.

Hitting, Baserunning & Defense

Sierra has never shown an aptitude to get on base. The free swinger never has seen a fastball he didn't like. He tries to pull everything, making himself vulnerable to any change-of-pace pitch. On occasion he will run into a fastball, but Yankee fans are more accustomed to an exposed front-side flail. Historically a stronger hitter from the right side, he has trended better from the left side since 2002. In the field, Sierra possesses little arm strength and demonstrably less range than his earlier years.

2005 Outlook

It seemed unlikely Sierra would be back in New York, with Bubba Crosby in line to take over the role that Sierra filled in 2004. Yet, New York offered salary arbitration to Sierra, who once again could be providing pop off the Yankees' bench.

Enrique Wilson

Position: 2B/SS
Bats: B **Throws:** R
Ht: 5'11" **Wt:** 195

Opening Day Age: 31
Born: 7/27/73 in Santo Domingo, DR
ML Seasons: 8

Overall Statistics

	G	AB	R	H	D	T	HR	RBI	SB	BB	SO	Avg	OBP	Slg
'04	93	240	19	51	9	0	6	31	1	15	20	.213	.254	.325
Car.	540	1384	154	340	71	5	22	141	14	86	168	.246	.288	.352

2004 Situational Stats

	AB	H	HR	RBI	Avg		AB	H	HR	RBI	Avg
Home	92	14	2	5	.152	LHP	67	20	1	6	.299
Road	148	37	4	26	.250	RHP	173	31	5	25	.179
First Half	147	31	5	25	.211	Sc Pos	55	16	2	26	.291
Scnd Half	93	20	1	6	.215	Clutch	26	6	0	4	.231

2004 Season

Enrique Wilson was awarded the starting second-base job out of spring training, but it was short-lived after his .154 April showing. He did still manage to get 64 intermittent starts at the keystone, and his 240 at-bats represented the second-highest season total in his eight-year career.

Hitting, Baserunning & Defense

Wilson is your classic Punch-and-Judy switch-hitter. He sacrifices what little power he has in order to make contact. He rarely strikes out or draws walks, preferring to put the ball in play on the ground. He has much stronger at-bats from his natural right side. Wilson has good range to his left towards the four-hole and enough arm to make the throw on balls that are backhanded. His days on the left side of the infield should serve as a reminder that he possesses good arm strength. Light on his feet at second base, Wilson is much more deliberate as a baserunner.

2005 Outlook

There is little chance Wilson will be back in 2005, even if he is a favorite of manager Joe Torre. The Yankees need more production off the bench, especially in tough situations come playoff time. A young club without postseason aspirations probably is where Wilson will end up.

Homer Bush (Pos: 2B, Age: 32, Bats: R)

	G	AB	R	H	D	T	HR	RBI	SB	BB	SO	Avg	OBP	Slg
'04	9	7	2	0	0	0	0	0	1	0	2	.000	.125	.000
Car.	409	1274	176	363	50	5	11	115	65	57	238	.285	.324	.358

Bush returned to the Yankees' organization last season after chronically sore hips had forced him into early retirement in 2003. He hit .291/.327/.380 at Triple-A Columbus and appeared sparingly for the parent club. 2005 Outlook: C

Bubba Crosby (Pos: RF/LF/CF, Age: 28, Bats: L)

	G	AB	R	H	D	T	HR	RBI	SB	BB	SO	Avg	OBP	Slg
'04	55	53	8	8	2	0	2	7	2	2	13	.151	.196	.302
Car.	64	65	8	9	2	0	2	8	2	2	16	.138	.176	.262

Crosby wore out the path between Triple-A Columbus and New York in his first year with the Yankees. The reserve outfielder made four separate trips to New York, highlighted by a home run in his first official Yankee Stadium at-bat. 2005 Outlook: C

Jorge DePaula (Pos: RHP, Age: 26)

	W	L	Pct.	ERA	G	GS	Sv	IP	H	BB	SO	HR	Avg
'04	0	1	.000	5.00	3	1	0	9.0	9	4	2	2	.281
Car.	0	1	.000	2.66	7	2	0	20.1	12	5	9	3	.176

Trying to throw through lower back pain during spring training probably was not the best idea for the 26-year-old DePaula. Aiming to minimize irritation to one area may have resulted in an injury to DePaula's elbow. He underwent Tommy John surgery in April of 2004. 2005 Outlook: C

Felix Escalona (Pos: SS, Age: 26, Bats: R)

	G	AB	R	H	D	T	HR	RBI	SB	BB	SO	Avg	OBP	Slg
'04	5	8	1	0	0	0	0	0	0	0	2	.000	.111	.000
Car.	74	192	20	39	10	2	0	11	8	5	52	.203	.252	.276

It is hard to imagine many things worse than being a shortstop in the Yankees' system. It's a good thing for Escalona that he also has the ability to play second and third base. Hitting .308/.371/.431 at Triple-A Columbus, he has a moderate chance of securing a backup job this year. 2005 Outlook: C

John Flaherty (Pos: C, Age: 37, Bats: R)

	G	AB	R	H	D	T	HR	RBI	SB	BB	SO	Avg	OBP	Slg
'04	47	127	11	32	9	0	6	16	0	5	25	.252	.286	.465
Car.	1000	3245	309	828	171	3	78	384	10	169	488	.255	.293	.382

Only one other catcher has caught more games than Jorge Posada the last five years. This is why it is increasingly important to have a capable backup for Posada. Flaherty once again will be that guy in 2005. He has slugged .515 versus lefthanders as a Yankee. 2005 Outlook: B

Felix Heredia (Pos: LHP, Age: 29)

	W	L	Pct.	ERA	G	GS	Sv	IP	H	BB	SO	HR	Avg
'04	1	1	.500	6.28	47	0	0	38.2	44	20	25	5	.278
Car.	28	19	.596	4.44	508	2	6	455.2	447	231	349	45	.255

Heredia performed poorly en route to his worst ERA in nine big league seasons. A 9.00 ERA through mid-June destroyed Torre's confidence in the lefthander's ability to get people out. Heredia was limited to a total of 11 innings after the All-Star break. He's been dealt to the Mets. 2005 Outlook: B

Steve Karsay (Pos: RHP, Age: 33)

	W	L	Pct.	ERA	G	GS	Sv	IP	H	BB	SO	HR	Avg
'04	0	0	–	2.70	7	0	0	6.2	5	2	4	2	.217
Car.	31	38	.449	3.87	328	40	41	572.1	587	189	439	53	.266

The Yankees bullpen was dealt an early blow when Karsay's timetable to return was pushed back. A right rotator cuff surgery in May 2003 kept him off the field for the majority of a second straight year. He returned in September, but did not pitch in the playoffs. 2005 Outlook: B

Travis Lee (Pos: 1B, Age: 29, Bats: L)

	G	AB	R	H	D	T	HR	RBI	SB	BB	SO	Avg	OBP	Slg
'04	7	19	1	2	1	0	0	2	0	1	3	.105	.150	.158
Car.	856	2993	387	771	158	12	92	408	47	380	565	.258	.340	.411

Brought in to serve as Jason Giambi's counterpart at first base, Lee, like Giambi, battled injury. Lee appeared in just seven games for New York before undergoing season-ending shoulder surgery in May. The Yankees declined their 2005 contract option on Lee. 2005 Outlook: B

Sam Marsonek (Pos: RHP, Age: 26)

	W	L	Pct.	ERA	G	GS	Sv	IP	H	BB	SO	HR	Avg
'04	0	0	–	0.00	1	0	0	1.1	2	0	0	0	.333
Car.	0	0	–	0.00	1	0	0	1.1	2	0	0	0	.333

Marsonek's 2004 season was put on hold after he injured a knee slipping on a dock near his Florida home. The All-Star break incident happened at an inopportune time for Marsonek, in lieu of his recent major league callup. He returned to strike out 31 in 29 Arizona Fall League innings. 2005 Outlook: C

C.J. Nitkowski (Pos: LHP, Age: 32)

	W	L	Pct.	ERA	G	GS	Sv	IP	H	BB	SO	HR	Avg
'04	2	1	.667	5.73	41	0	0	33.0	40	16	26	4	.296
Car.	18	32	.360	5.35	329	44	3	475.2	514	261	345	57	.279

The Yankees enlisted the services of Nitkowski in a desperate attempt to find any lefthanded bullpen help. Nitkowski was not the answer, as evidenced by his 7.62 ERA and 18 hits allowed in 13 innings of work. 2005 Outlook: C

Donovan Osborne (Pos: LHP, Age: 35)

	W	L	Pct.	ERA	G	GS	Sv	IP	H	BB	SO	HR	Avg
'04	2	0	1.000	7.13	9	2	0	17.2	25	5	10	3	.347
Car.	49	46	.516	4.03	163	140	0	873.2	895	246	558	100	.266

Osborne resurfaced in 2004 after throwing just 16 innings the last four seasons combined. The storybook comeback turned into more of a horror story, as Osborne was released by the Yankees and Padres in the span of a month. 2005 Outlook: C

Bret Prinz (Pos: RHP, Age: 27)

	W	L	Pct.	ERA	G	GS	Sv	IP	H	BB	SO	HR	Avg
'04	1	0	1.000	5.08	26	0	0	28.1	28	14	22	5	.259
Car.	5	3	.625	4.83	95	0	9	85.2	91	47	62	11	.275

Prinz was sent to New York in the 2003 trade with Arizona involving Raul Mondesi. Healthy again, Prinz paid immediate dividends, throwing 9.2 scoreless innings in his initial seven games. Things turned sour from there, though, as he posted a 7.71 ERA the rest of the way. 2005 Outlook: C

Scott Proctor (Pos: RHP, Age: 28)

	W	L	Pct.	ERA	G	GS	Sv	IP	H	BB	SO	HR	Avg
'04	2	1	.667	5.40	26	0	0	25.0	29	14	21	5	.284
Car.	2	1	.667	5.40	26	0	0	25.0	29	14	21	5	.284

A former Florida State Seminole, Proctor made his major league debut in his seventh year of professional baseball this past season. The 28-year-old is not considered a front-line reliever, but will get a chance at solidifying the 10th or 11th spot on the upcoming staff. 2005 Outlook: C

Tanyon Sturtze (Pos: RHP, Age: 34)

	W	L	Pct.	ERA	G	GS	Sv	IP	H	BB	SO	HR	Avg
'04	6	2	.750	5.47	28	3	1	77.1	75	33	56	9	.254
Car.	35	41	.461	5.23	187	83	2	706.0	792	299	428	97	.287

Sturtze found a nice home with the Yankees after being traded by the Dodgers in May. By the end of the season, he was the third-most trusted member of the bullpen behind Mariano Rivera and Tom Gordon, earning him a little leverage in the offseason free agency market. 2005 Outlook: B

New York Yankees Minor League Prospects

Organization Overview:

Other teams re-build through the draft and by trading for prospects. The Yankees re-load by trading away prospects such as Nick Johnson, Brandon Claussen and Juan Rivera in exchange for established major leaguers, and by signing international free agents. The current major league starting lineup features three homegrown players, three All-Star players acquired by trade or free agency, and a star player signed from Japan. Instead of making room for good young players like Robinson Cano, Chien-Ming Wang and Brad Halsey, the Yankees underscored their preference for veterans by signing Tony Womack, Jaret Wright and others in December.

Robinson Cano

Position: 2B
Bats: L **Throws:** R
Ht: 6' 0" **Wt:** 172

Opening Day Age: 22
Born: 10/22/82 in San Pedro De Macoris, DR

Recent Statistics

	G	AB	R	H	D	T	HR	RBI	SB	BB	SO	Avg
2003 A Tampa	90	366	50	101	16	3	5	50	1	17	49	.276
2003 AA Trenton	46	164	21	46	9	1	1	13	0	9	16	.280
2004 AA Trenton	74	292	43	88	20	8	7	44	2	24	40	.301
2004 AAA Columbus	61	216	22	56	9	2	6	30	0	18	27	.259

Cano's name reportedly was on a list of players offered to the Rangers in the Alfonso Soriano for Alex Rodriguez trade, but Texas selected Joaquin Arias instead. Signed as a free agent in the Dominican Republic, Cano is the best minor leaguer at the team's weakest major league position, second base. In 2004, he hit for good power in the high minors at a young age. Cano is not a fast man for a middle infielder, but his throwing arm is strong and accurate. He's apt to put the ball in play, with relatively few strikeouts or walks. If he remains with the Yankees, he may get some time at second base for the big league club in 2005.

Eric Duncan

Position: 3B
Bats: L **Throws:** R
Ht: 6' 1" **Wt:** 205

Opening Day Age: 20
Born: 12/7/84 in Florham Park, NJ

Recent Statistics

	G	AB	R	H	D	T	HR	RBI	SB	BB	SO	Avg
2003 R GC Yankees	47	180	24	50	12	2	2	28	0	18	33	.278
2003 A Staten Isla	14	59	11	22	5	4	2	13	1	2	11	.373
2004 A Battle Creek	78	288	52	75	23	2	12	57	7	38	84	.260
2004 A Tampa	51	173	23	44	20	2	4	26	0	31	47	.254

Duncan is a third baseman in an organization whose major league third baseman happens to be Alex Rodriguez. Drafted out of high school in the first round in 2003, Duncan hit for excellent power in two levels of Class-A ball in 2004. He projects as a power-hitting lefthander, which for 80 years has been a recipe for

success in Yankee Stadium. He figures to start 2005 at Double-A Trenton, where he'll try to cut down on strikeouts. Even if he remains a Yankee, it's not clear that Duncan can be an adequate defensive third baseman. If he's not traded, he should arrive in the major leagues—probably as a DH or first baseman—no later than 2007.

Brad Halsey

Position: P
Bats: L **Throws:** L
Ht: 6' 1" **Wt:** 180

Opening Day Age: 24
Born: 2/14/81 in Houston, TX

Recent Statistics

	W	L	ERA	G	GS	Sv	IP	H	R	BB	SO	HR
2004 AAA Columbus	11	4	2.63	24	23	0	144.0	128	46	37	109	8
2004 AL New York	1	3	6.47	8	7	0	32.0	41	26	14	25	4

The Yankees drafted Halsey, of the 2002 College World Series champion Texas Longhorns, in the eighth round of that year's draft. Since then, the lefthander has posted 34 wins in the minor leagues, moving so quickly that manager Joe Torre reportedly said "we had no idea who he was" when Halsey was called up to start (and win) for the Yankees in a mid-June interleague game against the Dodgers. In 2004 at Triple-A Columbus, Halsey posted a strikeout-walk ratio of nearly 3:1 and yielded only eight home runs while facing 589 batters. On almost any other team, a 24-year-old lefthander with Halsey's record of accomplishment would go into spring training pegged as a third or fourth starter.

Dioner Navarro

Position: C
Bats: B **Throws:** R
Ht: 5' 10" **Wt:** 190

Opening Day Age: 21
Born: 2/9/84 in Caracas, VZ

Recent Statistics

	G	AB	R	H	D	T	HR	RBI	SB	BB	SO	Avg
2004 AA Trenton	70	255	32	69	14	1	3	29	1	33	44	.271
2004 AAA Columbus	40	136	18	34	8	2	1	16	1	14	17	.250
2004 AL New York	5	7	2	3	0	0	0	1	0	0	0	.429

Navarro is another undrafted international free agent signed by the Yankees. A native of Venezuela, the switch-hitting catcher joined the Yankees' organization at age 16, and moved rapidly through the minor leagues. Along the way, he made the transition from infielder to catcher. Returning to Double-A to start 2004, Navarro started off slowly, but recovered to earn a second-half promotion to Triple-A. He shows good strike-zone judgment and bat control. He has not yet hit for much power, but at his age most players are in Class-A ball or college. With Jorge Posada capably manning the position for the major league club, Navarro figures to hone his skills at Columbus. In five years, he'll probably be among baseball's elite catchers.

Andy Phillips

Position: 1B **Opening Day Age:** 27
Bats: R **Throws:** R **Born:** 4/6/77 in
Ht: 6' 0" **Wt:** 205 Tuscaloosa, AL

Recent Statistics

	G	AB	R	H	D	T	HR	RBI	SB	BB	SO	Avg
2004 AA Trenton	10	42	8	15	2	1	4	16	3	3	1	.357
2004 AAA Columbus	115	434	83	138	19	6	26	85	2	51	60	.318
2004 AL New York	5	8	1	2	0	0	1	2	0	0	1	.250

The Yankees drafted Phillips in the seventh round in 1999. He progressed rapidly through the minors, and reached Double-A Norwich in 2000. Through the end of 2002, he had 65 home runs and 271 RBI in 1,687 minor league at-bats. Then elbow surgery ended his 2003 season after only 17 games. But in 2004, Phillips showed that he had fully recovered, swatting a career-high 30 homers at first base for Double-A Trenton and Triple-A Columbus. In a September callup, he hit the first major league pitch he saw for a home run against the Red Sox. Phillips is ready for the big leagues now as a first baseman/DH.

Ramon Ramirez

Position: P **Opening Day Age:** 23
Bats: R **Throws:** R **Born:** 8/31/81 in
Ht: 5' 11" **Wt:** 170 Santiago, DR

Recent Statistics

	W	L	ERA	G	GS	Sv	IP	H	R	BB	SO	HR
2003 A Tampa	2	8	5.21	14	14	0	74.1	88	47	20	70	7
2003 AA Trenton	1	1	1.69	4	3	0	21.1	18	8	8	21	3
2003 AAA Columbus	0	1	4.50	2	1	0	6.0	5	5	1	5	1
2004 AAA Columbus	0	3	8.50	4	4	0	18.0	25	19	8	17	3
2004 AA Trenton	4	6	4.62	18	18	0	115.0	116	60	32	128	11

New York outbid other teams to buy the young but well-traveled righthander's contract from the Hiroshima Carp before the 2003 season. Ramirez originally was signed by the Rangers as an outfielder, but they released him, and he went to Japan. He features an excellent fastball and a hard, sharp curve. After spending most of 2003 in the high Class-A Florida State League, Ramirez pitched creditably for Double-A Trenton in 2004, averaging more than a strikeout per inning. A return to Trenton is likely for early 2005, but if all goes well Ramirez could find himself in New York to stay by the middle of 2006.

Bronson Sardinha

Position: OF **Opening Day Age:** 21
Bats: L **Throws:** R **Born:** 4/6/83 in Honolulu,
Ht: 6' 0" **Wt:** 190 HI

Recent Statistics

	G	AB	R	H	D	T	HR	RBI	SB	BB	SO	Avg
2003 A Tampa	59	212	23	41	8	2	1	17	8	24	57	.193
2003 A Battle Creek	71	269	54	74	16	0	8	41	5	40	40	.275
2004 A Tampa	63	248	37	78	12	2	2	33	9	29	39	.315
2004 AA Trenton	72	266	37	71	11	1	6	29	4	37	65	.267

In his first three minor league seasons, Sardinha saw time at shortstop and in the outfield. In late 2003, before they traded for Alex Rodriguez, the Yankees decided to move him to third. After committing 43 errors at the hot corner at two levels, a move back to the outfield seems likely. Sardinha is a good hitter with some speed, who also could develop considerable power. He was slated to play in the Arizona Fall League last fall, but broke a finger on his left hand just before the campaign started. He figures to be back at Double-A Trenton to start the 2005 season.

Chien-Ming Wang

Position: P **Opening Day Age:** 25
Bats: R **Throws:** R **Born:** 3/31/80 in Tainan,
Ht: 6' 2" **Wt:** 180 Taiwan

Recent Statistics

	W	L	ERA	G	GS	Sv	IP	H	R	BB	SO	HR
2003 R GC Yankees	0	0	0.00	1	1	0	3.0	2	0	0	2	0
2003 AA Trenton	7	6	4.65	21	21	0	122.0	143	71	32	84	7
2004 AA Trenton	6	5	4.05	18	18	0	109.0	112	53	26	90	6
2004 AAA Columbus	5	1	2.01	6	6	0	40.1	31	9	8	35	3

Wang is another quality international prospect signed by the Yankees. He has good command and a good delivery. His best pitch is his fastball, but he also features a split-finger pitch, slider and changeup. Signed for a large bonus a month after his 20th birthday, he pitched well in 2000 for short-season Staten Island but missed all of 2001 following shoulder surgery. A return performance at Staten Island was successful in 2002, after which he pitched creditably for Double-A Trenton. In 2004, Wang pitched very well for Trenton and Triple-A Columbus, and also played in the Olympics for his native Taiwan. If he stays healthy, he could join the Yankees' rotation at some point in 2005.

Others to Watch

Switch-hitting Dominican outfielder **Melky Cabrera** (20) signed as a free agent at age 17. A center fielder with a good arm, he hit for average and power in 2004, and probably will start 2005 at Double-A Trenton. . . Lefty **Alex Graman** (27) had a good year for Triple-A Columbus, compiling an 11-6 record with a 3.37 ERA. That would be good enough for a shot at most major league rotations, but probably not the Yankees'. . . Dominican outfielder **Rudy Guillen** (21) held his own as one of the younger players in the high Class-A Florida State League, but he made no progress in cutting down on strikeouts. He'll likely advance to Double-A Trenton at some point in 2005. . . High school righthander **Philip Hughes** (18) was the Yankees' selection as the 23rd overall choice in the 2004 draft. Hughes has an excellent fastball, and a good slider and changeup. He will start 2005 at Class-A Charleston. . . Baylor righthander **Steven White** (23) was the Yankees' fourth-round choice in 2003. He pitched very well in Class-A ball in 2004. White, who features a plus fastball and a plus curve, should be a part of the 2005 rotation at Double-A Trenton.

Network Associates Coliseum

Offense

Once again Oakland did very well at The Net, leading its division in home wins and finishing third in the American League in home winning percentage behind the Red Sox and Yankees. Oakland's improved hitters helped support the home effort, using the summer air to carry those flyballs deep and often out of the park.

Defense

Oakland's defense is very good at exploiting the well-manicured checkerboard grass and handling the long liners that bang off the walls. In the outfield, perhaps no one wields a more accurate arm than Mark Kotsay, and with Marco Scutaro and Bobby Crosby up the middle, along with Damian Miller behind the dish, hardly anyone was better up the middle. Playing at home just made it easier. The defense also knows how to play the shadows that haunt the right side during the dog days of summer.

Who It Helps the Most

Especially when the weather is dry, flyball hitters get that nice carry from Mother Nature that sparks extra-base hits. Conversely, flyball pitchers such as Barry Zito can be victimized. Groundball pitchers and teams with solid defense can take control of their own destiny playing in Oakland.

Who It Hurts the Most

Perhaps the irony of The Net is with Oakland hitters and their penchant for pitch selectivity and fighting off pitches. Pop one too many foul balls and suddenly a quality at-bat becomes a foul out. Flyball pitchers who must nibble may find their game compromised, especially in warmer weather.

Rookies & Newcomers

Veteran Jason Kendall will keep the Athletics strong up the middle, and prodigy Nick Swisher probably will join the mix. With Mark Redman traded, Joe Blanton may join one of the best rotations in the majors. He will have to get used to the conditions that often are dictated by temperature and humidity.

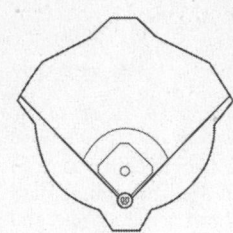

Dimensions: LF-330, LCF-362, CF-400, RCF-362, RF-330

Capacity: 43,662

Elevation: 25 feet

Surface: Grass

Foul Territory: Large

Park Factors

2004 Season

	Home Games			Away Games			
	Athletics	Opp	Total	Athletics	Opp	Total	Index
G	72	72	144	72	72	144	
Avg	.258	.254	.256	.269	.266	.267	96
AB	2446	2546	4992	2631	2451	5082	98
R	320	318	638	352	331	683	93
H	631	647	1278	708	651	1359	94
2B	124	141	265	165	116	281	96
3B	5	8	13	5	12	17	78
HR	84	70	154	82	71	153	102
BB	277	237	514	269	240	509	103
SO	438	464	902	499	456	955	96
E	39	50	89	43	38	81	110
E-Infield	31	38	69	37	30	67	103
LHB-Avg	.272	.267	.270	.283	.286	.284	95
LHB-HR	43	18	61	46	25	71	91
RHB-Avg	.244	.247	.246	.254	.253	.254	97
RHB-HR	41	52	93	36	46	82	112

2002-2004

	Home Games			Away Games			
	Athletics	Opp	Total	Athletics	Opp	Total	Index
G	216	216	432	216	216	432	
Avg	.259	.243	.251	.259	.261	.260	97
AB	7225	7461	14686	7696	7259	14955	98
R	1016	854	1870	1041	944	1985	94
H	1874	1811	3685	1991	1891	3882	95
2B	388	376	764	423	345	768	101
3B	28	24	52	29	38	67	79
HR	263	188	451	245	190	435	106
BB	791	647	1438	784	700	1484	99
SO	1252	1419	2671	1362	1317	2679	102
E	118	154	272	145	115	260	105
E-Infield	99	124	223	121	96	217	103
LHB-Avg	.271	.249	.261	.259	.264	.261	100
LHB-HR	138	58	196	136	75	211	97
RHB-Avg	.247	.239	.243	.258	.258	.258	94
RHB-HR	125	130	255	109	115	224	114

2004 Rankings (American League)

- Third-highest RHB home-run factor
- Second-lowest LHB batting-average factor
- Third-lowest batting-average factor

Ken Macha

2004 Season

With a stud rotation and four straight years of postseason play, Ken Macha and his Athletics faced high expectations. All Macha had to do was replace his MVP shortstop with a rookie, find a fill-in for his injured second sacker in late March, endure month-long injuries to Tim Hudson and Eric Chavez, adjust to the meltdown of closer Arthur Rhodes, and watch in wonder as two of his star pitchers struggled unexpectedly down the stretch behind the division-winning Angels. Perhaps Macha's 2004 managing job surpassed his division-winning performance in 2003.

Offense

With Dave Hudgens back as hitting coach for a full season, the offensive numbers improved despite the loss of Miguel Tejada. The team's batting average and on-base percentage were improved over 2003. Oakland banged 13 more homers and scored 25 more runs. Hudgens kept the hitters focused and coaxed banner years from Scott Hatteberg, Eric Byrnes, Erubiel Durazo and newcomer Mark Kotsay, not to mention the 2004 AL Rookie of the Year, Bobby Crosby.

Pitching & Defense

Under new pitching coach, former Athletics hurler Curt Young, the team ERA, hits and homers allowed all were up. Perhaps Oakland's starters—especially Barry Zito and Mark Mulder—missed former pitching coach Rick Peterson, or perhaps the league was learning how to adjust to the Big Three. Still, pitching definitely was the Athletics' Achilles heel in 2004. The Oakland defense, though, under brain-trust Ron Washington, excelled, leading the league in fielding as well as double plays.

2005 Outlook

Oakland certainly has the puzzle pieces to compete. Starting with arguably the deepest AL pitching staff, featuring four solid starters and a balanced pen, Oakland seems to have the goods on the hill. With the newest addition, Jason Kendall, set behind the plate, Mark Ellis back at second and both Byrnes and Crosby a year older, Oakland can look beyond Durazo and Chavez for offensive firepower in 2005.

Born: 9/29/50 in Wilkinsburg, Pennsylvania

Playing Experience: 1974-1981, Pit, Mon, Tor

Managerial Experience: 2 seasons

Manager Statistics

Year	Team, Lg	W	L	Pct	GB	Finish
2004	Oakland, AL	91	71	.562	1.0	2nd West
2 Seasons		187	137	.577	–	–

2004 Starting Pitchers by Days Rest

	<=3	4	5	6+
Athletics Starts	1	89	53	13
Athletics ERA	7.71	4.73	3.35	5.10
AL Avg Starts	2	82	47	21
AL ERA	5.36	4.87	4.65	4.93

2004 Situational Stats

	Ken Macha	AL Average
Hit & Run Success %	28.0	36.8
Stolen Base Success %	68.1	68.6
Platoon Pct.	59.8	61.6
Defensive Subs	6	21
High-Pitch Outings	9	5
Quick/Slow Hooks	12/19	20/16
Sacrifice Attempts	34	53

2004 Rankings (American League)

- 1st in intentional walks (42) and one-batter pitcher appearances (46)
- 2nd in fewest caught stealings of second base (20), fewest caught stealings of third base (2), starts with over 120 pitches (9) and 2+ pitching changes in low-scoring games (33)
- 3rd in pinch-hitters used (122)

Oakland

Eric Byrnes

2004 Season

It is not surprising that Eric Brynes, who does everything full-tilt boogie, drives a Corvette. The high-energy flychaser, whose production dipped markedly near the end of 2003, came into 2004 knowing he could play and that he had a job. Byrnes put in a full season's worth of work, setting new personal highs across the board, particularly in games, hits, homers, swipes, runs scored and RBI. He was an important cog, contributing mightily to the Oakland offense, often when it was least expected.

Hitting

Byrnes hits like he does everything: full tilt. While he still likes to jump on the first pitch, he is much more confident and patient with two strikes. Byrnes feasts off lefthanded pitchers, and delivers most of his damage when leading off an inning. He is a line-drive hitter with good gap power, but Byrnes also can turn on a pitch and send it flying.

Baserunning & Defense

Speed is an essential part of Byrnes' game, as he runs as hard as he fields, fields as hard as he hits, and hits as hard as he does everything else. He uses that speed on the bases, and in 2004, it brought him close to 100 runs scored. Byrnes is an excellent basestealer as well. With a glove, again, there is no stopping him. Byrnes delivers the frequent "web gem," in which he dives and flies through the air, parallel to the ground, nabbing the ball just before it hits the turf.

2005 Outlook

Expect a recharged Byrnes back, playing hard, employing what he learned during the 2004 season, and trying to improve upon very good numbers in 2005. The one thing no one can say about Byrnes is that he doesn't try, and his take-no-prisoners approach has made him a fan favorite.

Position: LF/CF/RF
Bats: R **Throws:** R
Ht: 6' 2" **Wt:** 210

Opening Day Age: 29
Born: 2/16/76 in Redwood City, CA
ML Seasons: 5
Pronunciation: burns

Overall Statistics

	G	AB	R	H	D	T	HR	RBI	SB	BB	SO	Avg	OBP	Slg
'04	143	569	91	161	39	3	20	73	17	46	111	.283	.347	.467
Car.	383	1125	193	305	71	14	38	140	33	96	206	.271	.336	.460

Where He Hits the Ball

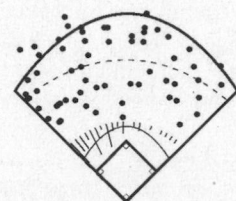
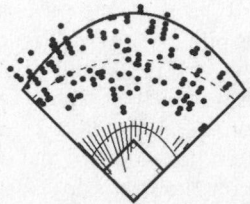

Vs. LHP   **Vs. RHP**

2004 Situational Stats

	AB	H	HR	RBI	Avg		AB	H	HR	RBI	Avg
Home	272	77	10	34	.283	LHP	157	54	7	23	.344
Road	297	84	10	39	.283	RHP	412	107	13	50	.260
First Half	287	80	11	33	.279	Sc Pos	142	38	4	48	.268
Scnd Half	282	81	9	40	.287	Clutch	94	21	2	10	.223

2004 Rankings (American League)

- 3rd in lowest groundball-flyball ratio (0.7)
- 4th in batting average vs. lefthanded pitchers and fielding percentage in left field (.989)
- Led the Athletics in runs scored, doubles, stolen bases, hit by pitch (12), stolen-base percentage (94.4), batting average vs. left handed pitchers and on-base percentage for a leadoff hitter (.368)

Eric Chavez

2004 Season

So many little things hurt Oakland's performance in 2004, and a major one was Eric Chavez breaking his hand, causing him to miss the entire month of June and a week of July. His mates certainly picked up most of the slack in Chavy's absence, but having its biggest bat present for the entire season was part of the Oakland road map to the postseason. As it was, Chavez matched his homer output of 2003, but in 113 fewer at-bats, suggesting there was more he would have provided if he had been healthy.

Hitting

As natural a hitter as one will find, Chavez has good reactions and ever-improving strike-zone judgment, as his quantum leap in on-base percentage in 2004 reflects. He hits to all fields. In a season of statistical quirks for Oakland, Chavez hit 49 points higher against southpaws than righthanders last summer, but slugged 30 points higher versus righties. Over his career, Chavez has been a better performer with runners aboard or in scoring position, and a .340 hitter with the bases loaded.

Baserunning & Defense

Chavez has excellent speed and is a smart baserunner. He can steal a base and easily move from first to third when circumstances permit. Defensively, Chavez can pick the hot corner with the best of them. Watching him on a short hop, or turning a 360, zeroing in on first base and gunning a throw to retire a runner can be nothing short of breath-taking.

2005 Outlook

Once again it looked like Chavez was going to put up that .300-30-100 season everyone has come to expect, but his 2004 season was cut short by injury. He did come back strong, though, and the skills set is still there. Chavez is primed with the experience and discipline necessary to deliver an MVP-type season. Watch for it in 2005.

Position: 3B
Bats: L **Throws:** R
Ht: 6' 1" **Wt:** 206

Opening Day Age: 27
Born: 12/7/77 in Los Angeles, CA
ML Seasons: 7
Pronunciation: shah-VEZ

Overall Statistics

	G	AB	R	H	D	T	HR	RBI	SB	BB	SO	Avg	OBP	Slg
'04	125	475	87	131	20	0	29	77	6	95	99	.276	.397	.501
Car.	869	3102	501	858	181	15	163	543	34	374	561	.277	.354	.502

Where He Hits the Ball

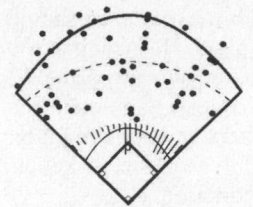 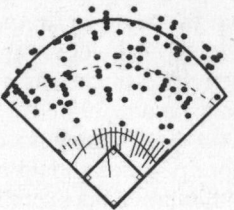

Vs. LHP	Vs. RHP

2004 Situational Stats

	AB	H	HR	RBI	Avg		AB	H	HR	RBI	Avg
Home	225	65	15	41	.289	LHP	183	56	9	28	.306
Road	250	66	14	36	.264	RHP	292	75	20	49	.257
First Half	199	52	13	37	.261	Sc Pos	123	34	8	52	.276
Scnd Half	276	79	16	40	.286	Clutch	85	24	4	10	.282

2004 Rankings (American League)

- 1st in walks
- 2nd in fielding percentage at third base (.968)
- 4th in highest percentage of pitches taken (62.3)
- 5th in on-base percentage and GDPs (21)
- 6th in errors at third base (13)
- 8th in intentional walks (10) and most pitches seen per plate appearance (4.05)
- Led the Athletics in home runs, walks, intentional walks (10), GDPs (21), on-base percentage and HR frequency (16.4 ABs per HR)

Oakland

Bobby Crosby

2004 Season

Enough is made of a player's rookie season to suggest how hard playing at the major league level is, so following in the footsteps of an American League MVP certainly doesn't make the task easier. Bobby Crosby, the 2003 Triple-A Pacific Coast League Rookie of the Year, was asked to do just that in taking over the shortstop duties from Miguel Tejada. He responded with a solid season at the plate and a brilliant one in the field. He was the AL Rookie of the Year for 2004, giving him back-to-back awards at two levels.

Hitting

Crosby, a good hitter with very good gap power, led AL rookies in homers. He is streaky and tends to press when he struggles, but experience should help him calm down at the plate. He swung at too many bad pitches as a rookie, but he posted 63 walks and a .395 OBP at Triple-A Sacramento in 2003. So, learning AL pitchers and showing a bit more patience should cut down on the strikeouts and improve his overall production.

Baserunning & Defense

Blessed with good speed, Crosby swiped 24 bases at Sacramento in 2003. Another sign of his decent wheels is his 70 runs scored, despite an anemic on-base percentage in his rookie year. His play sometimes borders on acrobatic with the glove. Crosby has excellent range and a very strong arm. He is capable of making those great plays deep in the hole, complete with the long throw across his body to first.

2005 Outlook

Crosby will get better, but it is worth remembering that he is beginning just his second big league season. It is unreasonable to expect that his propensity for slumps and streaks will come to an end so quickly. On the whole, however, Crosby's rookie season was comparable to that of his illustrious predecessor, Tejada. Be patient and he will get better.

Position: SS
Bats: R **Throws:** R
Ht: 6' 3" **Wt:** 195

Opening Day Age: 25
Born: 1/12/80 in Lakewood, CA
ML Seasons: 2

Overall Statistics

	G	AB	R	H	D	T	HR	RBI	SB	BB	SO	Avg	OBP	Slg
'04	151	545	70	130	34	1	22	64	7	58	141	.239	.319	.426
Car.	162	557	71	130	34	1	22	64	7	59	146	.233	.315	.417

Where He Hits the Ball

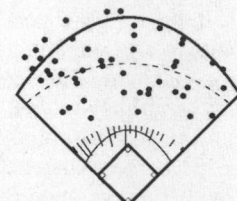 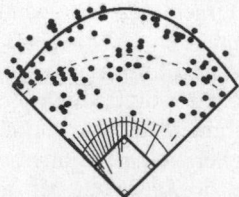

Vs. LHP   **Vs. RHP**

2004 Situational Stats

	AB	H	HR	RBI	Avg		AB	H	HR	RBI	Avg
Home	266	58	11	32	.218	LHP	139	27	6	13	.194
Road	279	72	11	32	.258	RHP	406	103	16	51	.254
First Half	290	77	11	35	.266	Sc Pos	141	29	3	40	.206
Scnd Half	255	53	11	29	.208	Clutch	93	26	3	13	.280

2004 Rankings (American League)

- 1st in home runs among rookies, RBI among rookies and lowest batting average at home
- 2nd in lowest batting average
- 3rd in most pitches seen per plate appearance (4.17), batting average among rookies and lowest batting average vs. lefthanded pitchers
- 4th in strikeouts and lowest batting average with runners in scoring position
- 5th in errors at shortstop (19) and fielding percentage at shortstop (.975)
- 7th in GDPs (20)
- Led the Athletics in sacrifice bunts (5), strikeouts and pitches seen (2,598)

Erubiel Durazo

2004 Season

Considering how slowly Erubiel Durazo got going in 2004, it is amazing that he generated the totals he did. It took until April 21 for Durazo to register his first RBI of the season, and he had just one home run until he homered twice on the last day of April in Tampa. Perhaps that offensive outburst was in response to the Tampa Bay spectator known as "The Heckler," a fan with a loud voice who always targets an opposing player. The Heckler picked on Durazo that day, but it may have lit a fire, as Durazo went on to produce career highs in just about every offensive category in 2004.

Hitting

Durazo is a disciplined hitter whose main strength is his power. What is surprising about his 2004 showing is that his walk total was nearly cut in half over 2003, yet his career-best hit total actually raised his on-base percentage. There is no doubt Durazo can hit, especially righthanders. After showing a tendency to hit better during day games early in his career, he was a much better night hitter in 2004. He also batted .364 with 21 RBI last season with the bags loaded.

Baserunning & Defense

Durazo put on his glove and took the field on four occasions in 2004, and in the process, committed a pair of errors and hit .182. Both Durazo and the Athletics are better off leaving the defensive duties to others. He is fairly fast for a 240-pounder, however, capable of stealing a bag and taking an extra base. Once all that muscle gets moving, it is hard to stop.

2005 Outlook

General manager Billy Beane knows there is an even better year in Durazo's future. Surely he is capable of banging 30 homers and knocking in 100 runs. He inched closer to those numbers last season. Perhaps a more-confident Durazo will see his walk totals return to normal, and with that should come a better season than his solid 2004 campaign.

Position: DH
Bats: L **Throws:** L
Ht: 6' 3" **Wt:** 210

Opening Day Age: 30
Born: 1/23/75 in Hermosillo, Mexico
ML Seasons: 6
Pronunciation: eh-ROO-bee-el du-RAH-zo

Overall Statistics

	G	AB	R	H	D	T	HR	RBI	SB	BB	SO	Avg	OBP	Slg
'04	142	511	80	164	35	1	22	88	3	56	104	.321	.396	.523
Car.	583	1796	318	511	102	5	90	314	6	293	404	.285	.387	.497

Where He Hits the Ball

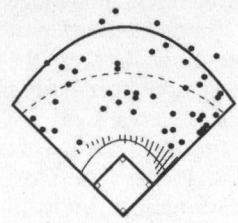

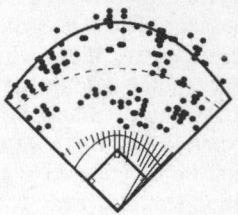

Vs. LHP **Vs. RHP**

2004 Situational Stats

	AB	H	HR	RBI	Avg		AB	H	HR	RBI	Avg
Home	246	78	12	41	.317	LHP	158	44	5	28	.278
Road	265	86	10	47	.325	RHP	353	120	17	60	.340
First Half	254	79	11	40	.311	Sc Pos	131	42	6	63	.321
Scnd Half	257	85	11	48	.331	Clutch	91	28	2	12	.308

2004 Rankings (American League)

- 4th in batting average vs. righthanded pitchers
- 5th in batting average and batting average on the road
- 7th in on-base percentage
- Led the Athletics in batting average, RBI, slugging percentage, fewest GDPs per GDP situation (5.8%), batting average in the clutch, batting average vs. righthanded pitchers and batting average on the road

Oakland

Jermaine Dye

2004 Season

Jermaine Dye's 2003 season was such an anomaly that a repeat in 2004 never was realistic. Just the same, Dye was watched with wariness in the spring, but he got off to a good start in 2004, delivering seven homers and 20 RBI in 23 April contests. For the most part, Dye finished the season with numbers that were true to form, despite an August dip that generated a .172 average for the month. A small thumb fracture was part of the problem, though Dye rebounded nicely in September.

Hitting

Dye swings from his heels to generate power, and he often can drive the ball. More often, though, he does not. The 128 strikeouts he posted last year were a career high, while the 49 walks were the lowest total among the five seasons that he has logged more than 130 games. In view of the wretched beating Dye took in 2003, last season must be considered a success. Perhaps the most telling stat, however, is that Dye hit just .240 with runners in scoring position.

Baserunning & Defense

Long-legged, Dye always has been blessed with very good speed, though knee injuries over the past couple of years have slowed him. The four bases he stole last year were more than the two previous seasons combined, and he also banged four triples, more than his total over the previous three seasons combined. So the afterburners can be accessed. Similarly, he does cover right field very well and has a terrific arm.

2005 Outlook

With a $14 million price tag attached, Oakland chose not to pick up its 2005 option on Dye. He wasn't going to score another contract like that heading into 2005, but he did come to terms on a two-year, $10.15 million contract to play right field for the Chicago White Sox. Now in his 30s, Dye may never approach the big payoff of his previous contract, unless he can display across-the-board improvement and a more consistent execution of his skills.

Position: RF
Bats: R **Throws:** R
Ht: 6' 5" **Wt:** 220

Opening Day Age: 31
Born: 1/28/74 in Vacaville, CA
ML Seasons: 9
Pronunciation: ger-MAIN

Overall Statistics

	G	AB	R	H	D	T	HR	RBI	SB	BB	SO	Avg	OBP	Slg
'04	137	532	87	141	29	4	23	80	4	49	128	.265	.329	.464
Car.	1039	3818	565	1037	213	17	161	611	23	346	772	.272	.334	.463

Where He Hits the Ball

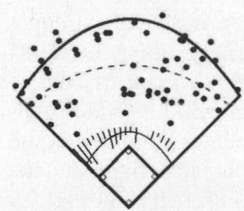 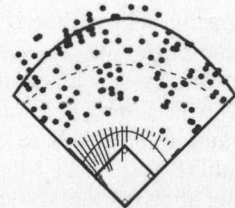

Vs. LHP   **Vs. RHP**

2004 Situational Stats

	AB	H	HR	RBI	Avg		AB	H	HR	RBI	Avg
Home	253	72	12	41	.285	LHP	161	45	8	30	.280
Road	279	69	11	39	.247	RHP	371	96	15	50	.259
First Half	333	95	16	54	.285	Sc Pos	146	35	3	47	.240
Scnd Half	199	46	7	26	.231	Clutch	91	20	1	11	.220

2004 Rankings (American League)

- 2nd in most pitches seen per plate appearance (4.25) and fielding percentage in right field (.992)
- 3rd in lowest percentage of swings on the first pitch (12.2)
- Led the Athletics in triples, most pitches seen per plate appearance (4.25), cleanup slugging percentage (.445) and lowest percentage of swings on the first pitch (12.2)

Rich Harden

2004 Season

On May 6, Rich Harden made his fifth start of the season with an 0-2 record and 4.37 ERA. Facing the Yankees, Harden allowed three walks in the first inning and five straight hits in the second, resulting in four runs. Then he found his slider and worked another 5.2 innings, allowing just one hit and striking out six to earn his first win. From that point, Harden stepped it up, going 10-5 (3.90 ERA) as Oakland's most dependable starter over the second half. He tied for second on Oakland's all-time single-season list of no-decisions with 13, and a stronger pen would have generated a better win total for Harden.

Pitching

As his name suggests, Harden throws hard. His fastball clocks near 94 MPH as the game begins, but he is one of those hurlers who gains velocity and later brings it at 97 MPH. With Harden mixing in a slider and a changeup, hitters find themselves overpowered, chasing the hard slider in the dirt or climbing the ladder for the fastball. The hitters who do make contact and fail are pretty well split between flyball outs and groundouts. He will need to work a little more on his control to reduce his walk total, but as a true power pitcher, Harden rounds out the Oakland rotation nicely.

Defense

Harden has a pretty good glove. He gets off the hill quickly and fields his position well. He still is getting the hang of holding runners, although would-be stealers were less successful in 2004 than they were in 2003. That will improve with experience.

2005 Outlook

The future seems bright for Harden. He should improve significantly, not just with another full season of starts under his belt, but also by having his hard repertoire mixed among the other Athletics starters. Opposing hitters should struggle to match the .242 batting average they posted against him last year.

Position: SP
Bats: L **Throws:** R
Ht: 6' 1" **Wt:** 180

Opening Day Age: 23
Born: 11/30/81 in Victoria, BC, Canada
ML Seasons: 2

Overall Statistics

	W	L	Pct.	ERA	G	GS	Sv	IP	H	BB	SO	HR	Avg
'04	11	7	.611	3.99	31	31	0	189.2	171	81	167	16	.242
Car.	16	11	.593	4.12	46	44	0	264.1	243	121	234	21	.246

2004 Pitching Profile

	Rich Harden	AL Average
Overall Strike %	62.7	62.3
1st Pitch Strike %	57.6	58.1
Ratio	1.33	1.42
Strikeouts per 9 IP	7.92	6.45
Walks per 9 IP	3.84	3.34
Home Runs per 9 IP	0.76	1.15
Strikeout/Walk Ratio	2.06	1.93
Groundball/Flyball Ratio	1.18	1.17

2004 Situational Stats

	W	L	ERA	Sv	IP		AB	H	HR	RBI	Avg
Home	6	3	3.02	0	95.1	LHB	382	97	8	40	.254
Road	5	4	4.96	0	94.1	RHB	326	74	8	37	.227
First Half	3	5	4.52	0	91.2	Sc Pos	139	37	3	55	.266
Scnd Half	8	2	3.49	0	98.0	Clutch	51	14	2	4	.275

2004 Rankings (American League)

- 2nd in lowest slugging percentage allowed (.366)
- 4th in lowest ERA at home and fewest home runs allowed per nine innings (.76)
- 5th in most pitches thrown per batter (3.93) and highest walks per nine innings (3.8)
- 6th in lowest batting average allowed (.242) and lowest batting average allowed vs. righthanded batters
- 7th in walks allowed
- 8th in strikeouts and most strikeouts per nine innings (7.9)
- Led the Athletics in strikeouts, lowest batting average allowed (.242), lowest slugging percentage allowed (.366) and most strikeouts per nine innings (7.9)

Scott Hatteberg

2004 Season

Scott Hatteberg assembled his best season ever in 2004, registering career highs in games, at-bats, runs, hits, RBI, average and total bases. His was among the key bats that helped push Oakland into first place in the American League West in late July. Hatteberg was a pivotal cog of an Oakland team that fell just short of a fifth straight postseason appearance.

Hitting

A disciplined hitter, Hatteberg is reaping the benefits of working the count in his favor. Calling on a quick bat, he is able to both use the gaps and drive pitches with occasional power. He hits lefthanded and righthanded pitchers equally well. The 72 walks to 48 strikeouts he generated last year is not only his largest differential between the two stats in a season, but it is nearly the inverse of the 70 strikeouts and 40 walks Hatteberg posted in 1997, his first full year in the majors. He hit .615-2-23 and slugged 1.231 over 13 at-bats when the bags were full last year.

Baserunning & Defense

While Hatteberg is a smart player, he is not fleet afoot on the bases. His one career swipe took place in 2001. In 2004, Hatteberg led AL first sackers in innings played and total chances. He was second among his peers with a role in 135 double plays. He committed just 10 errors, and considering 2004 was only Hatteberg's third season at the position, that is a significant accomplishment.

2005 Outlook

Whatever GM Billy Beane spotted in him that demonstrated potential, Hatteberg certainly has validated his signing, as he has been a solid producer. As a first sacker he might have more power, but his run production is fine, at least for now. Look for more of the same, although he is going into the final year of a contract. With Dan Johnson in the wings, a trade involving Hatteberg is not out of the question.

Position: 1B
Bats: L **Throws:** R
Ht: 6' 1" **Wt:** 210

Opening Day Age: 35
Born: 12/14/69 in Salem, OR
ML Seasons: 10
Pronunciation: HATT-eh-berg

Overall Statistics

	G	AB	R	H	D	T	HR	RBI	SB	BB	SO	Avg	OBP	Slg
'04	152	550	87	156	30	0	15	82	0	72	48	.284	.367	.420
Car.	889	2893	371	781	172	6	76	363	1	381	366	.270	.359	.412

Where He Hits the Ball

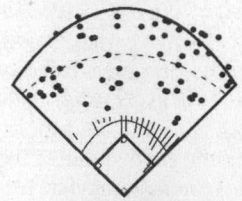 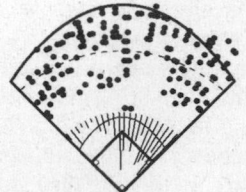

Vs. LHP　　　　**Vs. RHP**

2004 Situational Stats

	AB	H	HR	RBI	Avg		AB	H	HR	RBI	Avg
Home	272	77	8	45	.283	LHP	172	49	4	25	.285
Road	278	79	7	37	.284	RHP	378	107	11	57	.283
First Half	272	82	10	52	.301	Sc Pos	151	44	6	68	.291
Scnd Half	278	74	5	30	.266	Clutch	87	22	1	13	.253

2004 Rankings (American League)

- 1st in highest percentage of swings put into play (55.6) and errors at first base (10)
- 2nd in lowest percentage of swings that missed (8.0), highest percentage of pitches taken (63.9) and lowest fielding percentage at first base (.993)
- 3rd in batting average with the bases loaded (.615) and lowest cleanup slugging percentage (.390)
- 4th in sacrifice flies (8) and lowest percentage of swings on the first pitch (12.2)
- Led the Athletics in sacrifice flies (8), games played, highest percentage of pitches taken (63.9), lowest percentage of swings that missed (8.0) and batting average with the bases loaded (.615)

Tim Hudson

2004 Season

Even the grittiest of Oakland's players was not immune to down time, and in this instance, that means Tim Hudson. Just when teammate Eric Chavez returned from a lengthy stay on the disabled list, Hudson went down for the month of July with an oblique muscle strain. Despite missing the month, Hudson worked nearly 200 innings. He still had moments when he was on, such as his four-hit, 86-pitch gem versus Seattle on April 10. Although his performance took a dip over the second half, Hudson turned in the best all-around season among the Oakland rotation's vaunted "Big Three" in 2004.

Pitching

Hudson is a serious competitor when on the hill. He possesses a good low-90s fastball, along with an excellent changeup and slider. But it is a dirt-biting splitter, which tantalizes before the bottom falls out, that leaves hitters shaking their heads as they walk back to the dugout. Those who do make contact generally whack the ball into the ground, as Hudson secured twice as many groundouts as flyouts in 2004. That's a well-established ratio that works in Hudson's favor.

Defense

An excellent athlete, Hudson is solid on defense. He initiated three double plays while committing only one error during the 2004 season. He has learned to hold runners quite well during his Oakland tenure. He allowed 24 stolen bases in both 2000 and 2001, good for an 83-percent success rate by his opponents. Over the last two seasons, would-be basestealers were successful just 15 times, generating a success rate of 60 percent.

2005 Outlook

Just being healthy for 200-plus innings is all that Hudson wants at this point. All in all, his 2004 performance was pretty solid, except for a couple of his starts during the final weeks of the season. While he struggled in September, along with his highly regarded mates in the A's rotation, Barry Zito and Mark Mulder, don't expect it to happen again. With Hudson in the final year of his contract, he is the one among the trio who is generating the most offseason trade rumors.

Position: SP
Bats: R **Throws:** R
Ht: 6' 1" **Wt:** 164

Opening Day Age: 29
Born: 7/14/75 in Columbus, GA
ML Seasons: 6

Overall Statistics

	W	L	Pct.	ERA	G	GS	Sv	IP	H	BB	SO	HR	Avg
'04	12	6	.667	3.53	27	27	0	188.2	194	44	103	8	.267
Car.	92	39	.702	3.30	183	183	0	1240.2	1134	382	899	94	.244

2004 Pitching Profile

	Tim Hudson	AL Average
Overall Strike %	64.3	62.3
1st Pitch Strike %	59.6	58.1
Ratio	1.26	1.42
Strikeouts per 9 IP	4.91	6.45
Walks per 9 IP	2.10	3.34
Home Runs per 9 IP	0.38	1.15
Strikeout/Walk Ratio	2.34	1.93
Groundball/Flyball Ratio	2.53	1.17

2004 Situational Stats

	W	L	ERA	Sv	IP		AB	H	HR	RBI	Avg
Home	6	2	3.19	0	90.1	LHB	403	120	5	49	.298
Road	6	4	3.84	0	98.1	RHB	323	74	3	30	.229
First Half	7	3	2.98	0	108.2	Sc Pos	174	52	2	69	.299
Scnd Half	5	3	4.28	0	80.0	Clutch	85	22	2	10	.259

2004 Rankings (American League)

- 1st in shutouts (2) and fewest home runs allowed per nine innings (.38)
- 3rd in lowest slugging percentage allowed (.366) and highest groundball-flyball ratio allowed (2.5)
- 4th in winning percentage
- 5th in ERA and complete games (3)
- 6th in hit batsmen (12), fewest pitches thrown per batter (3.48) and fewest walks per nine innings (2.1)
- 7th in lowest ERA at home
- Led the Athletics in ERA, shutouts (2), hit batsmen (12), highest strikeout-walk ratio (2.3), lowest on-base percentage allowed (.318), highest groundball-flyball ratio allowed (2.5), fewest home runs allowed per nine innings (.38), and fewest walks per nine innings (2.1)

Mark Kotsay

2004 Season

At the age of 28, Mark Kotsay changed into an Oakland uniform and produced the season everyone knew he could. Kotsay set personal single-season highs in hits, doubles, batting average, slugging and on-base percentage. He played a brilliant center field and proved to be the spark needed atop the Athletics' batting order, something that had been missing for so many years. Kotsay had hitting streaks of 12 and 15 games, and bagged three four-hit games in 2004.

Hitting

Kotsay swings hard and stays on top of the ball, and the results are line drives all over the place. He has very good power to the gaps and can turn on a pitch. Kotsay also has shown good pitch selectivity, and after joining the Oakland system, he assembled his third-best single-season strikeout-walk ratio. That discipline helped him approach the 200-hit plateau. Kotsay proved to be very effective in 2004, both when hitting leadoff (.311-12-54 with a .366 OBP) and from the No. 3 slot (.367/.436/.592 in 55 plate appearances).

Baserunning & Defense

Good speed is a big part of Kotsay's game, both on the bases and in the field. He is a smart player and a good baserunner who can steal a base, though that is not a big part of the Oakland game. Defensively, he is among the best center fielders in the game, covering a large amount of real estate at The Net. In 2004, he tied his career high for total chances, and he scored double digits in assists for the third consecutive year with a strong and very accurate arm.

2005 Outlook

Going into what should be his peak production years, Kotsay is on the verge of quiet stardom. He is the kind of player who will hit .300 and get the 190 hits he generated in 2004 consistently, but his power numbers should bump to 20-plus homers and 40-plus doubles.

Position: CF
Bats: L **Throws:** L
Ht: 6' 0" **Wt:** 201

Opening Day Age: 29
Born: 12/2/75 in Whittier, CA
ML Seasons: 8
Pronunciation: KAH-tsay

Overall Statistics

	G	AB	R	H	D	T	HR	RBI	SB	BB	SO	Avg	OBP	Slg
'04	148	606	78	190	37	3	15	63	8	55	70	.314	.370	.459
Car.	1016	3727	512	1068	201	37	80	399	77	327	463	.287	.343	.425

Where He Hits the Ball

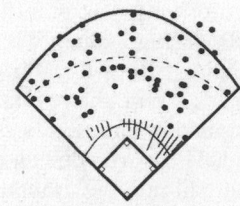 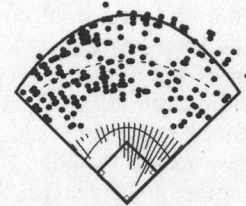

Vs. LHP   **Vs. RHP**

2004 Situational Stats

	AB	H	HR	RBI	Avg		AB	H	HR	RBI	Avg
Home	272	94	9	33	.346	LHP	152	51	4	21	.336
Road	334	96	6	30	.287	RHP	454	139	11	42	.306
First Half	302	96	4	33	.318	Sc Pos	114	32	1	44	.281
Scnd Half	304	94	11	30	.309	Clutch	103	24	1	7	.233

2004 Rankings (American League)

- 3rd in singles, errors in center field (6) and lowest fielding percentage in center field (.984)
- 5th in hits and batting average at home
- Led the Athletics in at-bats, hits, singles, total bases (278), sacrifice bunts (5), caught stealing (5), times on base (247), plate appearances (673), bunts in play (17), steals of third (3) and batting average at home
- Led AL center fielders in batting average

Mark Mulder

2004 Season

There must be some clever writer somewhere, thinking that Mark Mulder's 2004 was a Dickens-like "Tale of Two Seasons." There was the first half, when Mulder looked so dominant that it was obvious it was his turn for a Cy Young Award. Then, after the All-Star break, Mulder looked so very vulnerable and hittable. He was a horse, though, making 33 starts and lasting six innings or more in all but four outings, three of which were his final three starts of the season. Still, he had a year that most hurlers would be proud to call their own.

Pitching

Because Mulder works with a delivery that is so smooth, it must be alarming for opposing hitters to see a moving 93-MPH fastball come tearing out of all that poetry. Mulder also has a curve, slider and changeup. Add in his height and a deceptive delivery that keeps hitters guessing until the last minute, and the aggregate is success. While injuries have put him on the disabled list for two months over his career, he never has pitched less than 150 innings a season as a major leaguer, and has topped 200 innings three times.

Defense

Mulder is a groundball pitcher who is a terrific defender. In 2004, he handled an amazing 60 chances and registered 51 assists, both extraordinary totals. He did make three errors, but he also initiated three double plays. Needless to say, he covers a lot of ground around the hill. He also holds runners fairly well, limiting basestealers to a 50-percent success rate in recent seasons.

2005 Outlook

It is hard to think of a 17-win season as a disappointment, but Mulder and the A's front office are looking for a return to the form he displayed from 2001-03. Mulder certainly has the goods to prove he is a great pitcher, and at worst, 2004 seems like a bump in the road. And not a very big one at that.

Position: SP
Bats: L **Throws:** L
Ht: 6' 6" **Wt:** 208

Opening Day Age: 27
Born: 8/5/77 in South Holland, IL
ML Seasons: 5

Overall Statistics

	W	L	Pct.	ERA	G	GS	Sv	IP	H	BB	SO	HR	Avg
'04	17	8	.680	4.43	33	33	0	225.2	223	83	140	25	.264
Car.	81	42	.659	3.92	150	150	0	1003.0	990	298	668	99	.260

2004 Pitching Profile

	Mark Mulder	AL Average
Overall Strike %	61.1	62.3
1st Pitch Strike %	55.8	58.1
Ratio	1.36	1.42
Strikeouts per 9 IP	5.58	6.45
Walks per 9 IP	3.31	3.34
Home Runs per 9 IP	1.00	1.15
Strikeout/Walk Ratio	1.69	1.93
Groundball/Flyball Ratio	2.05	1.17

2004 Situational Stats

	W	L	ERA	Sv	IP		AB	H	HR	RBI	Avg
Home	9	4	4.62	0	124.2	LHB	167	45	3	21	.269
Road	8	4	4.19	0	101.0	RHB	677	178	22	87	.263
First Half	12	2	3.21	0	131.2	Sc Pos	195	52	8	85	.267
Scnd Half	5	6	6.13	0	94.0	Clutch	81	15	2	3	.185

2004 Rankings (American League)

- 1st in complete games (5), runners caught stealing (13) and GDPs induced (37)
- 3rd in batters faced (952), winning percentage and most GDPs induced per GDP situation (20.1%)
- 4th in innings pitched and fewest pitches thrown per batter (3.46)
- 5th in wins, pickoff throws (136) and highest groundball-flyball ratio allowed (2.1)
- 6th in walks allowed and hit batsmen (12)
- 7th in most run support per nine innings (6.5)
- 8th in games started and wild pitches (10)
- Led the Athletics in wins, complete games (5), innings pitched, hits allowed, batters faced (952), walks allowed, hit batsmen (12), wild pitches (10), runners caught stealing (13), GDPs induced (37), winning percentage, fewest pitches thrown per batter (3.46), most GDPs induced per GDP situation (20.1%) and most run support per nine innings (6.5)

Mark Redman

Traded To PIRATES

2004 Season

Oakland's addition of Mark Redman last offseason gave the A's rotation a front four that was as potentially dominant as any team's in the majors. Redman filled the fourth-starter spot well, though in nearly the same number of innings in 2004 as 2003, the southpaw allowed 46 more hits and 12 more home runs. Also, Redman's strikeout total took a significant dip over 2003. Redman was fairly steady down the stretch and composed a 5-3 record against Oakland's American League West rivals.

Pitching

For a big guy, Redman does not throw nearly as hard as one would think. His fastball is in the mid-80s, though he has a decent curve, split-finger and an excellent change. As a hurler who nibbles and doesn't dominate, perhaps Redman's better season with Florida in 2003 is more about being out of the American League. His 2004 numbers are similar to his years with Minnesota and Detroit. Redman is dependable, making 32 starts last season, but he lasted more than six innings only 14 times. Nine of those 14 times came in the second half, when Oakland needed quality starts.

Defense

Redman gets off the mound fairly well for a big man, and he has learned to field his position well. He has committed just two errors over the past two seasons, compared to the six he made with Detroit in 2002. Redman has a very good move to first and is tough to steal against, as eight of 13 would-be basestealers discovered last season.

2005 Outlook

Redman certainly gave the A's a reliable option, but they probably were hoping for more than they got in 2004. While he was better than nearly all other No. 5 starters in the majors, he was the trade bait the A's used with Joe Blanton in the wings. Redman and Arthur Rhodes were dealt to Pittsburgh in a November trade for catcher Jason Kendall. Redman looks like the No. 3 or 4 starter for the Pirates.

Position: SP
Bats: L **Throws:** L
Ht: 6' 5" **Wt:** 245

Opening Day Age: 31
Born: 1/5/74 in San Diego, CA
ML Seasons: 6

Overall Statistics

	W	L	Pct.	ERA	G	GS	Sv	IP	H	BB	SO	HR	Avg
'04	11	12	.478	4.71	32	32	0	191.0	218	68	102	28	.292
Car.	48	51	.485	4.37	139	127	0	806.2	854	255	523	91	.272

2004 Pitching Profile

	Mark Redman	AL Average
Overall Strike %	59.9	62.3
1st Pitch Strike %	57.7	58.1
Ratio	1.50	1.42
Strikeouts per 9 IP	4.81	6.45
Walks per 9 IP	3.20	3.34
Home Runs per 9 IP	1.32	1.15
Strikeout/Walk Ratio	1.50	1.93
Groundball/Flyball Ratio	1.00	1.17

2004 Situational Stats

	W	L	ERA	Sv	IP		AB	H	HR	RBI	Avg
Home	3	6	7.46	0	76.0	LHB	175	50	6	21	.286
Road	8	6	2.90	0	115.0	RHB	571	168	22	79	.294
First Half	6	6	4.84	0	100.1	Sc Pos	165	55	9	74	.333
Scnd Half	5	6	4.57	0	90.2	Clutch	51	14	3	6	.275

2004 Rankings (American League)

- 3rd in lowest ERA on the road
- 5th in lowest stolen-base percentage allowed (38.5) and highest slugging percentage allowed (.481)
- 6th in pickoff throws (130), lowest strikeout-walk ratio (1.5) and highest batting average allowed with runners in scoring position
- 7th in highest on-base percentage allowed (.353)
- 8th in complete games (2)
- 9th in runners caught stealing (8)
- 10th in highest batting average allowed (.292) and fewest strikeouts per nine innings (4.8)
- Led the Athletics in losses, home runs allowed, lowest stolen-base percentage allowed (38.5) and lowest ERA on the road

Barry Zito

2004 Season

What happened to the Barry Zito magic in 2004? Had the league simply figured him out? Were hitters sitting on his curve? Was he hurt? Was he tired? Did he miss former pitching coach Rick Peterson? There were no easy answers, as Zito struggled for most of the year. Although Zito was a bit better during the second half, 2004 has to be considered a disappointment for a pitcher who traditionally has been a dominant force after the All-Star break.

Pitching

It is no secret that Zito does not overpower anyone. His fastball, at best, clocks at 89 MPH, though he does have a solid change. But Zito lives and dies by his wicked 12-to-6 curve. Throwing it for strikes didn't come as easy in 2004, and Zito fell behind hitters more often and was hit a lot more. Near midseason, Zito added a two-seam fastball that fades from hitters, and that aided him during the second half.

Defense

Zito wields a good-enough glove, and he has handled between 36-45 total chances in each of the past four seasons. He did make a pair of errors last year. After allowing 23 steals in 2001, his first full season in the majors, Zito has been better at holding baserunners in check.

2005 Outlook

Heading into the 2005 season, more eyes will be focused on Zito than just about any other Oakland player. Looking back at 2004, perhaps Zito's biggest problem was that he is cerebral, and when he encountered problems, he probably did think too much. That was part of how Peterson helped Zito—and all Oakland pitchers—by keeping them in the moment, reminding them that "this pitch is the only one that matters." Ideally, Zito will remember that and leave his 2004 struggles behind him. That's the ticket to rediscovering his prior success.

Position: SP
Bats: L **Throws:** L
Ht: 6' 4" **Wt:** 215

Opening Day Age: 26
Born: 5/13/78 in Las Vegas, NV
ML Seasons: 5
Pronunciation: ZEE-toe

Overall Statistics

	W	L	Pct.	ERA	G	GS	Sv	IP	H	BB	SO	HR	Avg
'04	11	11	.500	4.48	34	34	0	213.0	216	81	163	28	.263
Car.	72	40	.643	3.41	153	153	0	981.0	832	372	774	95	.229

2004 Pitching Profile

	Barry Zito	AL Average
Overall Strike %	62.0	62.3
1st Pitch Strike %	57.4	58.1
Ratio	1.39	1.42
Strikeouts per 9 IP	6.89	6.45
Walks per 9 IP	3.42	3.34
Home Runs per 9 IP	1.18	1.15
Strikeout/Walk Ratio	2.01	1.93
Groundball/Flyball Ratio	0.85	1.17

2004 Situational Stats

	W	L	ERA	Sv	IP		AB	H	HR	RBI	Avg
Home	6	5	4.22	0	111.0	LHB	167	54	5	25	.323
Road	5	6	4.76	0	102.0	RHB	653	162	23	85	.248
First Half	4	7	4.62	0	111.0	Sc Pos	185	47	8	79	.254
Scnd Half	7	4	4.32	0	102.0	Clutch	52	13	1	7	.250

2004 Rankings (American League)

- 1st in most pitches thrown per batter (3.98)
- 2nd in pitches thrown (3,689) and pickoff throws (151)
- 3rd in games started
- 6th in batters faced (926) and lowest ground ball-flyball ratio allowed (0.8)
- 7th in walks allowed and highest batting average allowed vs. lefthanded batters
- 9th in runners caught stealing (8)
- 10th in strikeouts
- Led the Athletics in games started, home runs allowed, pitches thrown (3,689), pickoff throws (151) and stolen bases allowed (15)

Chad Bradford

Position: RP
Bats: R **Throws:** R
Ht: 6' 5" **Wt:** 203

Opening Day Age: 30
Born: 9/14/74 in
Jackson, MS
ML Seasons: 7

Overall Statistics

	W	L	Pct.	ERA	G	GS	Sv	IP	H	BB	SO	HR	Avg
'04	5	7	.417	4.42	68	0	1	59.0	51	24	34	5	.234
Car.	21	15	.583	3.47	294	0	7	296.0	281	87	206	21	.250

2004 Situational Stats

	W	L	ERA	Sv	IP		AB	H	HR	RBI	Avg
Home	4	2	2.65	0	34.0	LHB	57	17	2	5	.298
Road	1	5	6.84	1	25.0	RHB	161	34	3	22	.211
First Half	4	4	5.12	1	38.2	Sc Pos	55	15	0	20	.273
Scnd Half	1	3	3.10	0	20.1	Clutch	99	23	2	15	.232

2004 Season

Following two-plus solid years in a setup role, Chad Bradford hit a bump in 2004. He struggled at times, both with injuries and the consistency issues that impacted the entire Athletics pitching staff. Bradford was bothered by a sore back off and on, and his ERA and hits allowed per nine were way up, while his innings pitched dipped for the first time in three seasons.

Pitching & Defense

Relying heavily on his submarine delivery, Bradford delivers a fastball that tops out at 88-89 MPH. It is not uncommon for Bradford to scrape his knuckles on the mound during that delivery, and from that angle, pitches in the high 80s jump on hitters quickly. Bradford also has a change and a curve, but it is that combination of delivery and control that fuel his success. While Bradford is primarily a groundball pitcher, his glove work is not that solid in support of his pitching style. He does hold runners fairly well.

2005 Outlook

Odds are Bradford will be back in 2005, and both Bradford and Oakland management will be looking for a return to the form that made the righthander one of the more reliable setup men over the past couple of seasons.

Octavio Dotel

Position: RP
Bats: R **Throws:** R
Ht: 6' 0" **Wt:** 210

Opening Day Age: 31
Born: 11/25/73 in Santo Domingo, DR
ML Seasons: 6
Pronunciation:
OC-tay-vee-oh dough-TEL

Overall Statistics

	W	L	Pct.	ERA	G	GS	Sv	IP	H	BB	SO	HR	Avg
'04	6	6	.500	3.69	77	0	36	85.1	68	33	122	13	.217
Car.	36	29	.554	3.63	366	34	64	585.0	454	248	709	72	.213

2004 Situational Stats

	W	L	ERA	Sv	IP		AB	H	HR	RBI	Avg
Home	5	4	2.57	17	49.0	LHB	159	39	9	25	.245
Road	1	2	5.20	19	36.1	RHB	154	29	4	14	.188
First Half	1	5	4.30	16	46.0	Sc Pos	88	16	3	27	.182
Scnd Half	5	1	2.97	20	39.1	Clutch	232	50	9	33	.216

2004 Season

Every year, Oakland general manager Billy Beane fills a void on the roster to help push the Athletics into the postseason. In 2004, it was a three-team deal that netted Octavio Dotel in June. Dotel looked like the answer to Oakland's closer struggles, but he blew a save in his first A's appearance and then blew another five, despite putting together a fairly respectable season's worth of stats.

Pitching & Defense

Say what you will about Dotel: he throws very hard. Dotel's fastball can clock around 97 MPH, and he sets it up with a pretty good slider. When Dotel is on, his heater has some movement, but when it falls flat, it can be pounded. Experienced hitters who sit on his heater do take advantage. Dotel fields his position well, and he has improved at holding baserunners.

2005 Outlook

Dotel will be the stopper in Oakland when camp breaks. It would have been interesting to see how he would have handled the late-season pressure with Houston, which proved to have a longer run than Oakland. While he isn't always a sure thing, when he is on, Dotel is capable of being a dominant closer.

Justin Duchscherer

Position: RP
Bats: R **Throws:** R
Ht. 0' 3" **Wt:** 190

Opening Day Age: 27
Born: 11/19/77 in Aberdeen, SD
ML Seasons: 3
Pronunciation: DUKE-sher

Overall Statistics

	W	L	Pct.	ERA	G	GS	Sv	IP	H	BB	SO	HR	Avg
'04	7	6	.538	3.27	53	0	0	96.1	85	32	59	13	.241
Car.	9	8	.529	4.31	62	5	0	127.1	126	39	85	19	.259

2004 Situational Stats

	W	L	ERA	Sv	IP		AB	H	HR	RBI	Avg
Home	5	2	2.91	0	52.2	LHB	170	42	5	18	.247
Road	2	4	3.71	0	43.2	RHB	183	43	8	22	.235
First Half	4	1	3.27	0	52.1	Sc Pos	72	14	1	26	.194
Scnd Half	3	5	3.27	0	44.0	Clutch	126	28	3	13	.222

2004 Season

While the Oakland pen took its lumps in 2004, one pleasant surprise was Justin Duchscherer. A talented prospect who arrived via the Boston and Texas organizations, Duchscherer always had produced excellent minor league numbers, and he did the same in long relief in the bigs last year.

Pitching & Defense

Duchscherer has taken a while to get to the majors because his fastball tops out near 88 MPH. He lives and dies with his mid-80s cutter, which is a ligitimate out pitch. He has a changeup and has developed a curve that often has that good 12-to-6 drop. He has to be fine to be successful, but Duchscherer is good at mixing his pitches. He is surehanded at his position, having yet to commit a big league error. He was better at controlling the running game last year, after allowing seven steals in seven tries prior to 2004.

2005 Outlook

Duchscherer filled a valuable role for the team in 2004, spelling the starters nine times with stints of at least three innings. Since the Athletics' rotation is pretty tough to crack, he will have to settle for the same job in 2005. The A's will be happy with a repeat performance of his first full season in the majors.

Mark Ellis

Position: 2B
Bats: R **Throws:** R
Ht: 5'11" **Wt:** 180

Opening Day Age: 27
Born: 6/6/77 in Rapid City, SD
ML Seasons: 2

Overall Statistics

	G	AB	R	H	D	T	HR	RBI	SB	BB	SO	Avg	OBP	Slg
'04					Did Not Play									
Car.	252	898	136	231	47	9	15	87	10	92	148	.257	.331	.380

2004 Situational Stats

	AB	H	HR	RBI	Avg		AB	H	HR	RBI	Avg
Home	–	–	–	–	–	LHB	–	–	–	–	–
Road	–	–	–	–	–	RHB	–	–	–	–	–
First Half	–	–	–	–	–	Sc Pos	–	–	–	–	–
Scnd Half	–	–	–	–	–	Clutch	–	–	–	–	–

2004 Season

Mark Ellis wasn't as effective at the plate in 2003 after a promising rookie season a year earlier, but his bid to rebound in 2004 dissipated on March 25. A nasty collision resulted in a dislocated shoulder and season-ending surgery for a torn labrum.

Hitting, Baserunning & Defense

Ellis hits down on the ball hard and has good gap power. He shows a good eye, which produced excellent on-base percentages as a minor leaguer, and his doubles power in the minors suggests he can hit double-digit homers. Similarly, Ellis has good speed. He swiped 20 bags three times as a minor leaguer, and he has a success rate of 71 percent in 14 big league attempts. The converted shortstop made the adjustment to second base on the fly the last two years and has excellent range.

2005 Outlook

Great makeup puts Ellis in good standing with the Oakland front office. Drafted as a shortstop, he moved to second base without a whimper and went about learning the spot. His rapid climb through the A's system and his steady improvement at each level suggest Ellis may jump-start quickly this spring after missing an entire year.

Oakland

Chris Hammond

Position: RP
Bats: L **Throws:** L
Ht: 6' 1" **Wt:** 210

Opening Day Age: 39
Born: 1/21/66 in Atlanta, GA
ML Seasons: 12

Overall Statistics

	W	L	Pct.	ERA	G	GS	Sv	IP	H	BB	SO	HR	Avg
'04	4	1	.800	2.68	41	0	1	53.2	56	13	34	4	.277
Car.	60	60	.500	4.08	357	136	3	1036.1	1076	368	655	91	.271

2004 Situational Stats

	W	L	ERA	Sv	IP		AB	H	HR	RBI	Avg
Home	1	1	3.42	0	26.1	LHB	71	20	0	7	.282
Road	3	0	1.98	1	27.1	RHB	131	36	4	19	.275
First Half	2	1	4.61	1	27.1	Sc Pos	38	15	0	18	.395
Scnd Half	2	0	0.68	0	26.1	Clutch	59	22	1	8	.373

2004 Season

Coming off a brilliant 2002, Chris Hammond's totals returned to earth in '03 with New York, but they still were good enough for Oakland to grab him as a lefthanded setup pitcher to support new closer Arthur Rhodes. Hammond struggled during the first half, but after a month-long stint on the disabled list near midseason, he was terrific and finished with numbers in line with his 2003 totals.

Pitching & Defense

Hammond isn't close to overpowering, but he can sneak an upper-80s version of a fastball by hitters, and that gives him an effective changeup. He has good command and can throw a curve to mix it up, but generally Hammond's strength is being around the plate and pinpointing the changeup. He fields his spot very well, and only two runners have even tried to swipe a base off him over the last two seasons. One made it.

2005 Outlook

Oakland chose to not pick up its option on Hammond for 2005. Since Hammond isn't lights out against lefthanded batters, a situational spot isn't an ideal arrangement. Hammond will be 39 on Opening Day, so his career may be on the ropes if he doesn't find a team and a role that fits him next spring.

Jim Mecir

Position: RP
Bats: B **Throws:** R
Ht: 6' 1" **Wt:** 230

Opening Day Age: 34
Born: 5/16/70 in Queens, NY
ML Seasons: 10
Pronunciation: mah-SEAR

Overall Statistics

	W	L	Pct.	ERA	G	GS	Sv	IP	H	BB	SO	HR	Avg
'04	0	5	.000	3.59	65	0	2	47.2	45	19	49	5	.239
Car.	28	31	.475	3.83	422	0	12	483.2	443	208	416	39	.244

2004 Situational Stats

	W	L	ERA	Sv	IP		AB	H	HR	RBI	Avg
Home	0	1	1.73	1	26.0	LHB	89	21	3	11	.236
Road	0	4	5.82	1	21.2	RHB	99	24	2	8	.242
First Half	0	5	5.02	2	28.2	Sc Pos	41	10	1	15	.244
Scnd Half	0	0	1.42	0	19.0	Clutch	101	23	5	15	.228

2004 Season

In 2004, Jim Mecir provided a glimpse of the numbers Oakland had been looking for during his four-plus years with the team. His ERA was his lowest since 2001, as Mecir didn't allow a run from June 20 through September 11, a span of 30 appearances. Knee injuries limited his contribution for the third straight season, sparking talk of retirement. Still, he dropped his opponent batting average by 41 points from his 2003 mark.

Pitching & Defense

Mecir's fastball registers in the low 90s, but his "screwgie" is his big pitch. It is effective against hitters from either side of the plate. He also mixes in a slider. Primarily a groundball pitcher, Mecir can cop a strikeout. His defense is excellent. Mecir has committed only one error in 10 seasons. He is less effective controlling baserunners. Fifty of 63 would-be thieves have succeeded over his career.

2005 Outlook

Mecir is a free agent who isn't likely to stay with Oakland, considering his injury history with the team. Injured off and on throughout his tenure, he registered a 13-21 record and 3.91 ERA with the A's. Though he is nearly 35, Mecir should find a job if he doesn't retire.

Damian Miller Signed By BREWERS

Position: C
Bats: R **Throws:** R
Ht: 6' 3" **Wt:** 220

Opening Day Age: 35
Born: 10/13/69 in La Crosse, WI
ML Seasons: 8

Overall Statistics

	G	AB	R	H	D	T	HR	RBI	SB	BB	SO	Avg	OBP	Slg
'04	110	397	39	108	25	0	9	58	0	39	87	.272	.339	.403
Car.	716	2280	258	602	143	3	68	301	4	219	553	.264	.331	.419

2004 Situational Stats

	AB	H	HR	RBI	Avg		AB	H	HR	RBI	Avg
Home	201	53	5	31	.264	LHP	124	36	2	11	.290
Road	196	55	4	27	.281	RHP	273	72	7	47	.264
First Half	225	67	7	37	.298	Sc Pos	102	33	4	50	.324
Scnd Half	172	41	2	21	.238	Clutch	73	21	0	11	.288

2004 Season

Damian Miller was acquired from the Cubs by turning over Michael Barrett, and it was hoped the 35-year-old catcher would facilitate further development of the Athletics' great rotation. Miller's presence and defense did help the hurlers, but his bat also came up big. He collected 20 RBI in 19 June contests, including 16 in the five-game stretch of June 6-11. He continued to hit well in July (.324) and set career highs for hits and RBI in 2004.

Hitting, Baserunning & Defense

Miller covers the basics at the plate. He has occasional pop, very good gap power and the ability to bunt. He was brilliant in the clutch in 2004, hitting .324 with runners in scoring position and an amazing .412 with 17 RBI in 17 at-bats with the bags juiced. Defensively, Miller turned in a Gold Glove-like season, committing just a single error in 751 total chances. His arm is solid, if not spectacular.

2005 Outlook

The Athletics may have brought Miller back for one more year, but then they pulled off the Jason Kendall trade in late November. Two days later, Miller signed a three-year, $8.75 million deal to start for the Milwaukee Brewers. He should get at least 300 at-bats.

Arthur Rhodes Traded To INDIANS

Position: RP
Bats: L **Throws:** L
Ht: 6' 2" **Wt:** 212

Opening Day Age: 35
Born: 10/24/69 in Waco, TX
ML Seasons: 14

Overall Statistics

	W	L	Pct.	ERA	G	GS	Sv	IP	H	BB	SO	HR	Avg
'04	3	3	.500	5.12	37	0	9	38.2	46	21	34	9	.293
Car.	72	54	.571	4.36	551	61	26	922.0	816	409	902	107	.238

2004 Situational Stats

	W	L	ERA	Sv	IP		AB	H	HR	RBI	Avg
Home	3	1	3.60	5	20.0	LHB	51	16	2	10	.314
Road	0	2	6.75	4	18.2	RHB	106	30	7	15	.283
First Half	3	3	5.28	9	29.0	Sc Pos	56	12	1	17	.214
Scnd Half	0	0	4.66	0	9.2	Clutch	100	28	3	16	.280

2004 Season

2004 has to go down as the nadir of Arthur Rhodes' major league career. Signed to take the closer role, Rhodes once again was out of his element. He blew five of 14 save chances during the first months of the season, and that ineffectiveness, plus injuries, forced the acquisition of Octavio Dotel in June. Rhodes only pitched 9.2 innings over the second half, but the numbers suggest setup work is a better fit for Rhodes.

Pitching & Defense

Rhodes still can bring a heater at 90-plus MPH, but his location, and seemingly his confidence have been erratic since he injured his ankle in the middle of the 2003 season. Rhodes does have a decent curve and changeup, but his hard slider, combined with that fastball, is the key to his success. Rhodes holds baserunners very well, as only four of nine would-be thieves have been successful against him since 2000. His defense is even better, as Rhodes has not committed a fielding miscue since 1998.

2005 Outlook

Rhodes was dealt twice in two weeks after the season. He was shipped to Pittsburgh in the Jason Kendall trade and later moved to Cleveland for Matt Lawton. Rhodes should return to form in a setup role.

Ricardo Rincon

Position: RP
Bats: L **Throws:** L
Ht: 5' 9" **Wt:** 190

Opening Day Age: 34
Born: 4/13/70 in Veracruz, Mexico
ML Seasons: 8
Pronunciation: rin-CONE

Overall Statistics

	W	L	Pct.	ERA	G	GS	Sv	IP	H	BB	SO	HR	Avg
'04	1	1	.500	3.68	67	0	0	44.0	45	22	40	3	.256
Car.	20	23	.465	3.45	485	0	21	399.0	340	176	364	32	.230

2004 Situational Stats

	W	L	ERA	Sv	IP			AB	H	HR	RBI	Avg
Home	1	1	4.35	0	20.2	LHB		90	18	1	10	.200
Road	0	0	3.09	0	23.1	RHB		86	27	2	14	.314
First Half	0	0	4.84	0	22.1	Sc Pos		63	14	0	18	.222
Scnd Half	1	1	2.49	0	21.2	Clutch		85	23	0	17	.271

2004 Season

As with so many of Oakland's players, Ricardo Rincon assembled a nice portfolio of statistics in 2004, but that wasn't enough to get the team to the postseason. He filled the situational lefty role with some consistency, but over the past two years he has blown all seven save opportunities presented to him. In 2004, he often would get a critical strikeout to close an inning, only to allow a critical walk to start the next. It was that kind of year.

Pitching & Defense

Rincon should primarily face lefthanded hitters for a reason. Righthanded hitters batted .314 against him last season. But, he is deadly against lefties. With a heater than runs in the low 90s, Rincon can get that important strikeout. He also possesses a good slider, and he fields his position well enough. Twice last year baserunners tried to steal off Rincon, and both were successful.

2005 Outlook

Rincon probably will be back in Oakland for 2005, especially after Arthur Rhodes was dealt away. Once again Rincon should face mostly left-handed hitters while picking up at least 40 innings over roughly 60 appearances.

Nick Swisher

Position: LF
Bats: B **Throws:** L
Ht: 6' 0" **Wt:** 194

Opening Day Age: 24
Born: 11/25/80 in Parkersburg, WV
ML Seasons: 1

Overall Statistics

	G	AB	R	H	D	T	HR	RBI	SB	BB	SO	Avg	OBP	Slg
'04	20	60	11	15	4	0	2	8	0	8	11	.250	.352	.417
Car.	20	60	11	15	4	0	2	8	0	8	11	.250	.352	.417

2004 Situational Stats

	AB	H	HR	RBI	Avg			AB	H	HR	RBI	Avg
Home	45	11	1	4	.244	LHP		10	5	0	0	.500
Road	15	4	1	4	.267	RHP		50	10	2	8	.200
First Half	0	0	0	0	—	Sc Pos		15	3	0	5	.200
Scnd Half	60	15	2	8	.250	Clutch		12	5	1	3	.417

2004 Season

The controversial "Moneyball" player, a No. 1 pick in 2002, Nick Swisher jumped to Triple-A Sacramento in 2004. After turning in a strong rookie campaign at that level (.269-29-92 with a .406 OBP), he earned a September cup of coffee with Oakland. During that short stay, Swisher played steadily while Jermaine Dye nursed an injured finger, and the rookie showed an improving eye, some power and strong defense.

Hitting, Baserunning & Defense

Swisher has a very disciplined batting eye, though he will have to refine it as he adjusts to major league pitching. He showed a quick and explosive stick on several occasions in Oakland. While Swisher is not much of a stealing threat, he has good speed. Defensively, Swisher is akin to teammate Eric Byrnes, in that he is willing to get his uniform dirty to make the play. His arm is adequate.

2005 Outlook

With Oakland passing on bringing back Dye, the path seems clear for Swisher to make his mark in 2005. He'll take a few lumps as a rookie, but look for a swift learning curve from this smart young player. Swisher was a fan favorite in Sacramento, and with his talent, it's likely to be the same in Oakland.

Other Oakland Athletics

Ramon A. Castro (**Pos**: 3B, **Age**: 25, **Bats**: R)

	G	AB	R	H	D	T	HR	RBI	SB	BB	SO	Avg	OBP	Slg
'04	9	15	2	2	1	0	0	3	0	1	3	.133	.188	.200
Car.	9	15	2	2	1	0	0	3	0	1	3	.133	.188	.200

Castro showed an ability to coax a walk, but he hit just .236 at the Double-A and Triple-A levels with no power. He will have to hit more to stick with Washington, after signing a minor league deal with the Nationals in November. 2005 Outlook: C

Esteban German (**Pos**: 3B, **Age**: 27, **Bats**: R)

	G	AB	R	H	D	T	HR	RBI	SB	BB	SO	Avg	OBP	Slg
'04	31	60	9	15	1	1	0	7	0	4	13	.250	.297	.300
Car.	45	99	13	23	1	1	0	8	1	8	25	.232	.296	.263

German has hit .314 the last two summers at Triple-A, but he hasn't shown the same ability to reach base with Oakland. He signed a minor league deal with the Rangers in November. 2005 Outlook: C

Eric Karros (**Pos**: 1B, **Age**: 37, **Bats**: R)

	G	AB	R	H	D	T	HR	RBI	SB	BB	SO	Avg	OBP	Slg
	40	103	8	20	6	0	2	11	1	7	16	.194	.243	.311
	1755	6441	797	1724	324	11	284	1027	59	552	1167	.268	.325	.454

Karros produced solid numbers as a part-time player with the Cubs in 2003, but it didn't go well in Oakland last season. He struggled in April and May, and his opportunities dried up in June and July before his late-July release. 2005 Outlook: C

Bobby Kielty (**Pos**: LF/RF, **Age**: 28, **Bats**: B)

	G	AB	R	H	D	T	HR	RBI	SB	BB	SO	Avg	OBP	Slg
'04	83	238	29	51	14	1	7	31	1	35	47	.214	.321	.370
Car.	369	1058	157	265	62	5	34	148	16	166	230	.250	.357	.415

The switch-hitting Kielty hasn't fared nearly as well against righthanded pitching the last two years. His at-bats, hitting percentages and power dwindled to unanticipated lows in 2004. Jermaine Dye's departure provides some hope for him. 2005 Outlook: C

Justin Lehr (**Pos**: RHP, **Age**: 27)

	W	L	Pct.	ERA	G	GS	Sv	IP	H	BB	SO	HR	Avg
'04	1	1	.500	5.23	27	0	0	32.2	35	14	16	3	.280
Car.	1	1	.500	5.23	27	0	0	32.2	35	14	16	3	.280

Lehr enjoyed his best season as a reliever in his third summer in the pen, posting 13 saves, a 2.65 ERA and 40 strikeouts in 37.1 innings for Triple-A Sacramento. His big league initiation was rough, but he'll be back for more. 2005 Outlook: C

Mark McLemore (**Pos**: 2B/3B, **Age**: 40, **Bats**: B)

	G	AB	R	H	D	T	HR	RBI	SB	BB	SO	Avg	OBP	Slg
'04	77	250	29	62	14	0	2	21	0	41	33	.248	.355	.320
Car.	1832	6192	943	1602	255	47	53	615	272	875	983	.259	.349	.341

Near the end of the season, McLemore said he expected to retire, and he did so in December. His ability to draw a walk in 2004 suggested he still had some value, though he's hit .240 the last two years. 2005 Outlook: D

Billy McMillon (**Pos**: LF, **Age**: 33, **Bats**: L)

	G	AB	R	H	D	T	HR	RBI	SB	BB	SO	Avg	OBP	Slg
'04	52	92	10	17	4	0	3	11	0	8	22	.185	.255	.326
Car.	269	601	66	149	35	3	16	93	4	64	140	.248	.322	.396

McMillon has hit better than .300 his last five Triple-A seasons, with an OBP near .400 and good doubles power. Bothered by a back injury, he wasn't as good in Oakland in 2004 as he was in 2003, when he posted decent hitting percentages of .268/.354/.458 in 66 games. 2005 Outlook: C

Adam Melhuse (**Pos**: C, **Age**: 33, **Bats**: B)

	G	AB	R	H	D	T	HR	RBI	SB	BB	SO	Avg	OBP	Slg
'04	69	214	23	55	11	0	11	31	0	16	47	.257	.309	.463
Car.	173	386	44	95	20	1	17	57	1	34	90	.246	.306	.435

Melhuse spent the entire 2004 season in the majors, a first for the 33-year-old catcher. Despite showing good pop with the A's the last two seasons, he won't be the 2005 starter. The A's traded two big league hurlers to acquire catcher Jason Kendall from Pittsburgh. 2005 Outlook: C

Mike Rose (**Pos**: C, **Age**: 28, **Bats**: B)

	G	AB	R	H	D	T	HR	RBI	SB	BB	SO	Avg	OBP	Slg
'04	2	2	1	0	0	0	0	0	0	0	2	.000	.000	.000
Car.	2	2	1	0	0	0	0	0	0	0	2	.000	.000	.000

A minor league catcher, Rose has hit for a decent average with a high walk total and an impressive OBP at Oakland's Triple-A Sacramento the last two summers. While he's too old to be a prospect, he signed a minor league deal and will battle for a backup role with the Dodgers. 2005 Outlook: C

Kirk Saarloos (**Pos**: RHP, **Age**: 25)

	W	L	Pct.	ERA	G	GS	Sv	IP	H	BB	SO	HR	Avg
'04	2	1	.667	4.44	6	5	0	24.1	27	12	10	4	.284
Car.	10	9	.526	5.43	59	26	0	159.0	182	56	107	20	.292

Saarloos was a promising prospect in the Houston system after going 17-1 at Double-A Round Rock and Triple-A New Orleans in 2002-03. Not as effective with Houston, he was dealt to Oakland in April. A bone spur was found in his elbow in August, and now he may face Tommy John surgery. 2005 Outlook: C

Marco Scutaro (**Pos**: 2B/SS, **Age**: 29, **Bats**: R)

	G	AB	R	H	D	T	HR	RBI	SB	BB	SO	Avg	OBP	Slg
'04	137	455	50	124	32	1	7	43	0	16	58	.273	.297	.393
Car.	212	566	62	148	36	2	10	55	2	29	83	.261	.297	.385

Scutaro took over most of the second-base chores when Mark Ellis suffered a season-ending injury late in spring training. Scutaro was solid at second and hit enough to not force the A's into acquiring a replacement. Despite his 32 doubles, he is better suited to a utility role. 2005 Outlook: C

Oakland Athletics Minor League Prospects

Organization Overview:

Under GM Billy Beane, the Oakland philosophy, "be selective," has evolved into a mantra. Beane has shrewdly learned to use the compensation picks he gets when losing Oakland stars to get players as close to "selective" major league ready as he can. For example, Oakland got a total of four first-round picks in the 2004 draft, and he restocked his hitting corps with players who already are adept at taking a pitch. Beane also likes pitchers who can avoid the free pass, like his fourth and final first-round pick last season, Huston Street, who nailed 197 collegiate hitters while walking just 37 at Texas. While skeptics still may question "Sabrmetrics," four straight postseason appearances followed by a near miss in 2004 speak for themselves.

John Baker

Position: C
Bats: L **Throws:** R
Ht: 6' 1" **Wt:** 220

Opening Day Age: 24
Born: 1/20/81 in Alameda, CA

Recent Statistics

	G	AB	R	H	D	T	HR	RBI	SB	BB	SO	Avg
2003 A Kane County	82	304	42	94	23	2	6	49	1	47	77	.309
2003 AA Midland	43	150	16	36	3	0	1	21	0	14	46	.240
2004 AA Midland	117	440	67	123	32	5	15	78	1	37	95	.280
2004 AAA Sac'mento	14	49	11	17	3	0	0	10	0	6	23	.347

Scouted by Oakland locally at the University of California, Baker was chosen in the fourth round of the 2002 draft. He started strong as a pro until hitting Double-A Midland halfway through the 2003 campaign, noticeably taking a hit to his on-base percentage, which dropped to .316. Baker rebounded in 2004, and hit with gap power at Double- and Triple-A, earning a trip to the Arizona Fall League in the process. Plodding would be a way to describe both Baker's speed and his defense, although he can run the bases and make the plays. Baker is the minor league catcher most likely to succeed in the Athletics' organization heading into 2005.

Joe Blanton

Position: P
Bats: R **Throws:** R
Ht: 6' 3" **Wt:** 225

Opening Day Age: 24
Born: 12/11/80 in Bowling Green, KY

Recent Statistics

	W	L	ERA	G	GS	Sv	IP	H	R	BB	SO	HR
2004 AAA Sac'mento	11	8	4.19	28	26	0	176.1	199	101	34	143	13
2004 AL Oakland	0	0	5.63	3	0	0	8.0	6	5	2	6	1

An Oakland first-round pick in 2002—another year they copped multiples—Blanton was selected from the University of Kentucky. With a fastball in the low 90s and a good slider, he had been a dominant force, whipping his way up to Triple-A in 2004 by posting two-year totals of 12-10 (2.52), 195 strikeouts over 189

innings, while allowing just 150 hits and 34 walks. That spelled a .214 batting average and last year's ticket to Sacramento, where his numbers jumped a bit, but still were very solid considering the speed of Blanton's ascent. He was similarly impressive during a September callup. With the trade of Mark Redman, Blanton has a strong chance of making the A's rotation coming out of spring training.

Freddie Bynum

Position: 2B
Bats: L **Throws:** R
Ht: 6' 1" **Wt:** 175

Opening Day Age: 25
Born: 2/15/80 in Wilson, NC

Recent Statistics

	G	AB	R	H	D	T	HR	RBI	SB	BB	SO	Avg
2003 AA Midland	132	510	84	134	18	9	5	58	22	56	135	.263
2004 AA Midland	65	265	38	71	13	4	1	22	18	24	56	.268
2004 AAA Sac'mento	66	258	42	73	11	2	2	26	21	19	61	.283

A speedy second-round pick in 2000, Bynum still has been slow at getting the hang of professional pitching at the higher levels. His on-base totals took a big hit to .344, down 41 points, when he advanced to Double-A Midland in 2003. As a result, Bynum returned to Double-A to start 2004, and though he did advance to the Triple-A Pacific Coast League, his strikeout-walk ratio and power totals are just not that attractive. Bynum is solid defensively, capable of playing both middle spots, but his game is just not strong enough to speculate on more than a major league utility role, if that.

Jairo Garcia

Position: P
Bats: R **Throws:** R
Ht: 6' 0" **Wt:** 164

Opening Day Age: 22
Born: 3/7/83 in Nizao, DR

Recent Statistics

	W	L	ERA	G	GS	Sv	IP	H	R	BB	SO	HR
2004 A Kane County	1	0	0.30	25	0	16	30.0	16	2	6	49	0
2004 AA Midland	2	0	1.50	13	0	2	18.0	10	3	15	32	0
2004 AAA Sac'mento	1	2	3.95	11	0	1	13.2	10	6	9	21	1
2004 AL Oakland	0	0	12.71	4	0	0	5.2	5	8	9	5	3

A lanky Dominican in the mold of Pedro Martinez, Garcia heads into his fifth professional season. He throws a good 90-MPH fastball, slider and change. He began as a starter while spending a couple of years with the Athletics' rookie team before moving to short-season Vancouver to finish 2002. He spent all of 2003 at Class-A Kane County, where he began the conversion from starter to reliever to closer. In 2004, Garcia was ready to step up, and he did, converting 16 of 16 save opportunities before advancing to Double-A, then Triple-A and eventually the Net. With a good spring, Garcia is a strong bet to make the team's relief corps.

Dan Johnson

Position: 1B
Bats: L **Throws:** R
Ht: 6' 2" **Wt:** 220

Opening Day Age: 25
Born: 8/10/79 in Coon Rapids, MN

Recent Statistics

	G	AB	R	H	D	T	HR	RBI	SB	BB	SO	Avg
2003 AA Midland	139	538	90	156	26	4	27	114	7	68	82	.290
2003 AAA Sac'mento	1	4	0	1	1	0	0	0	0	0	0	.250
2004 AAA Sac'mento	142	536	95	160	29	5	29	111	0	89	93	.299

Nick Swisher may have received the most ink of any Oakland prospect over the past few seasons, but no Athletics player has generated a buzz during that same period within the Oakland baseball community like Johnson has. A prototype power-hitting first baseman with a terrific eye, he is a little shorter than Jim Thome, but Johnson's corresponding skill set compares favorably to the ex-Indian. He has advanced and mastered each level one year at a time. A look at his '04 totals at Triple-A suggest Johnson is ready for a shot at the majors, but with Erubiel Durazo and Scott Hatteberg already in tow, someone will have to give.

Adam Morrissey

Position: 3B
Bats: R **Throws:** R
Ht: 5' 11" **Wt:** 185

Opening Day Age: 23
Born: 6/8/81 in Gosford, Australia

Recent Statistics

	G	AB	R	H	D	T	HR	RBI	SB	BB	SO	Avg
2003 AA Midland	125	469	66	125	27	2	5	65	9	50	99	.267
2004 AAA Sac'mento	109	392	61	114	26	1	9	56	1	40	89	.291

Oakland acquired Morrissey from the Cubs in exchange for Mark Bellhorn in the fall of 2001, and Morrissey hit well at high Class-A Modesto (.291-3-26), before hitting a bit of a wall at Double-A Midland (.235-2-22) to finish 2002. In 2003, he conquered Double-A, and though his on-base totals went up, his power numbers fell. He also shifted from second base to third, and to keep the guy off balance with his promotion to Triple-A in 2004, Morrissey primarily was a second sacker again. He does have good speed and is capable of double digits in steals. He has good power to the gaps, so the potential to be a solid big league middle infielder is there.

Omar Quintanilla

Position: SS
Bats: L **Throws:** R
Ht: 5' 9" **Wt:** 185

Opening Day Age: 23
Born: 10/24/81 in El Paso, TX

Recent Statistics

	G	AB	R	H	D	T	HR	RBI	3B	BB	SO	Avg
2003 A Vancouver	32	129	22	44	5	4	0	14	7	12	20	.341
2003 A Modesto	8	36	9	15	3	0	2	6	0	3	6	.417
2004 A Modesto	108	452	75	142	32	5	11	72	1	37	54	.314
2004 AA Midland	23	94	20	33	10	0	2	20	2	10	9	.351

Oakland's first-rounder in 2003 is a fireplug of a guy with a quick bat and some serious pop potential. Quintanilla, who starred at the University of Texas, has a solid bat and a good eye. He has advanced through the ranks as a shortstop. At that spot, Quintanilla has good enough range, but with incumbents Bobby Crosby and Mark Ellis—who is coming back from a major shoulder injury—the better option for Quintanilla may be second base. The realized potential of an infield consisting of Dan Johnson, Quintanilla, Bobby Crosby and Eric Chavez could validate the "Moneyball" philosophy as much as anything.

Mike Rouse

Position: SS
Bats: L **Throws:** R
Ht: 6' 0" **Wt:** 185

Opening Day Age: 24
Born: 4/25/80 in San Jose, CA

Recent Statistics

	G	AB	R	H	D	T	HR	RBI	SB	BB	SO	Avg
2003 AA Midland	129	457	75	137	33	3	3	53	7	63	83	.300
2003 AAA Sac'mento	2	7	2	3	0	0	0	1	0	0	0	.429
2004 AAA Sac'mento	99	323	53	89	11	2	10	40	0	50	68	.276

A fifth-round selection of the Blue Jays in 2001, Oakland scooped up Rouse, along with hurler Chris Mowday, in exchange for Cory Lidle after the 2002 season. Rouse is a scrappy kind of infielder with a very good eye and a terrific ability to make contact. His 33 doubles at Double-A Midland in 2003 are much more suggestive of power potential than the three homers he produced over the same time frame. Rouse has good speed and is a capable basestealer and runner. Though his niche has been at short, if he has a future in Oakland, he will have to make it elsewhere. In fact, a conversion to the outfield is not out of the question.

Others to Watch

Perhaps southpaw **Steven Bondurant** (25), a 15th-round pick in 2003, can officially be dubbed a sleeper. At least after looking at his first full season at Class-A Kane County, where Bondurant went 14-5 (2.08), 132 whiffs over 125.2 innings. It could be that Bonderant just had an age and experience advantage, but those numbers certainly suggest he will be followed closely. . . Righthander **Steve Obenchain** (23) is yet another of the first-rounders that Oakland collected in 2002. Obenchain is big—6-foot-5, 220 pounds—and yet he is not as much of a power pitcher as one would think. He needs to add a little velocity or a couple of new pitches, but just being a first-rounder makes him worth tracking for now. . . 2004 first-round pick **Landon Powell** (23) was a compensation pick for Oakland after losing Keith Foulke. A switch-hitter, Powell hit just .237-3-19 at short-season Vancouver, but he walked 26 times while whiffing just 22 times. . . One of two first-rounders in 2004, righty **Huston Street** (21) is a potential closer with a 95-MPH heater. After signing, Street ripped through Class-A Kane County, Double-A Midland and then Triple-A Sacramento for a couple of innings, earning eight saves and striking out 30 in just 26 innings along the way. He has some serious stuff.

Offense

Make no mistake, Safeco Field is not a hitters' park. The Mariners, who didn't have much of a productive lineup no matter where they played, hit just .255 at home despite having a handful of hitters who are suited for the stadium. The ball doesn't travel well to left field, especially early in the season when the air is cool and heavy. The stadium favors lefthanded pull and gap hitters.

Defense

Safeco's spacious surroundings make it the perfect stadium for groundball pitchers. Last season, the Mariners had a 4.30 ERA at home compared to 5.26 on the road. Pitchers can get away with more balls up in the strike zone, even though there's a jet stream that will carry the ball out to left. If you're a righthanded power hitter, this isn't the place to play.

Who It Helps the Most

Joel Pineiro won five of his six decisions at Safeco in 2004. Ryan Franklin posted a 3.92 ERA at home, but was hammered (5.62) on the road. Ichiro Suzuki hit well at home, though he also hit well just about anywhere else.

Who It Hurts the Most

Pretty much every righthanded hitter on the M's roster struggled at home. Bret Boone, who in the past has had success driving the ball the other way, slumped at home last season. Pitcher Jamie Moyer allowed 20 home runs at home and had a 5.00 ERA.

Rookies & Newcomers

Top pitching prospects Clint Nageotte and Travis Blackley were rushed to the big leagues before they were ready. Blackley's game—he changes speeds, hits corners, much like Jamie Moyer does—is better suited for Safeco Field than Nageotte, who is more of a power pitcher. Center fielder Jeremy Reed was impressive during his September callup. He's a spray hitter who can cover a lot of ground.

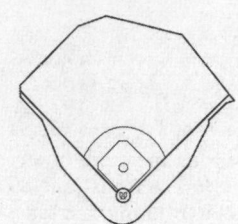

Dimensions: LF-331, LCF-390, CF-405, RCF-387, RF-327

Capacity: 47,447

Elevation: -2 feet

Surface: Grass

Foul Territory: Average

Park Factors

2004 Season

| | Home Games | | | Away Games | | | |
	Mariners	Opp	Total	Mariners	Opp	Total	Index
G	73	73	146	71	71	142	
Avg	.253	.256	.255	.292	.284	.288	88
AB	2473	2623	5096	2673	2456	5129	97
R	286	372	658	359	395	754	85
H	626	672	1298	781	697	1478	85
2B	119	167	286	132	126	258	112
3B	6	5	11	12	15	27	41
HR	65	105	170	59	92	151	113
BB	227	261	488	208	250	458	107
SO	493	509	1002	442	412	854	118
E	53	51	104	43	49	92	110
E-Infield	48	47	95	36	39	75	123
LHB-Avg	.286	.243	.264	.321	.278	.300	88
LHB-HR	24	50	74	21	31	52	146
RHB-Avg	.229	.266	.248	.270	.288	.279	89
RHB-HR	41	55	96	38	61	99	96

2002-2004

| | Home Games | | | Away Games | | | |
	Mariners	Opp	Total	Mariners	Opp	Total	Index
G	217	217	434	215	215	430	
Avg	.263	.249	.256	.285	.271	.279	92
AB	7251	7571	14822	7797	7302	15099	97
R	983	949	1932	1117	1058	2175	88
H	1905	1886	3791	2225	1982	4207	89
2B	333	377	710	430	377	807	90
3B	39	18	57	37	30	67	87
HR	184	259	443	203	261	464	97
BB	813	686	1499	710	649	1359	112
SO	1357	1470	2827	1350	1275	2625	110
E	118	152	270	117	134	251	107
E-Infield	99	135	234	97	111	208	111
LHB-Avg	.276	.251	.263	.302	.277	.290	91
LHB-HR	71	141	212	77	115	192	113
RHB-Avg	.252	.247	.249	.272	.266	.269	93
RHB-HR	113	118	231	126	146	272	86

2004 Rankings (American League)

- Highest strikeout factor
- Highest LHB home-run factor
- Lowest batting-average factor
- Lowest run factor
- Lowest hit factor
- Lowest triple factor
- Lowest LHB batting-average factor
- Second-lowest RHB batting-average factor

Mike Hargrove

2004 Season

Mike Hargrove spent the 2004 season as a special assistant to Cleveland GM Mark Shapiro. Hargrove was fired in 2003 after the last of four consecutive losing seasons in Baltimore. He said the season away from managing was enough to rekindle his love for running a team. He gets that chance in 2005, managing a Seattle club that lost 99 games just three seasons removed from winning 116 games.

Offense

Hargrove said during his hiring press conference in October that he prefers a lineup with three or four thumpers and a handful of players who can run. He wouldn't have liked the 2004 Seattle lineup, which lacked much in the way of power. Hargrove sometimes has been tough to figure as a manager. Occasionally he'll go by the book, but sometimes he'll hit-and-run, steal and squeeze in unconventional situations. Hargrove is a big proponent of walks and on-base percentage.

Pitching & Defense

Hargrove hasn't always been active in the pitching game, but that's mostly because he had his good friend and pitching coach, Mark Wiley, with him in Cleveland and then in Baltimore. Hargrove's first decision was to retain pitching coach Bryan Price, who is well-liked by the Mariners' brass. Price knows the Seattle staff, as well as a handful of young pitchers who figure prominently in the team's plans in 2005.

2005 Outlook

After firing Bob Melvin following the 2004 season, Seattle general manager Bill Bavasi went in search of a manager with: 1. Experience. 2. Fire. He's got both in Hargrove, who went through a similar rebuilding project during his early years in Cleveland. The result: he took two Indians teams to the World Series. Hargrove gives Seattle some presence and personality. That was one of the knocks on Melvin, who had never managed in the major leagues before.

Born: 10/26/49 in Perryton, TX

Playing Experience: 1974-1985, Tex, Cle, SD

Managerial Experience: 13 seasons

Manager Statistics

Year	Team, Lg	W	L	Pct	GB	Finish
2003	Baltimore, AL	71	91	.438	30.0	4th East
13 Seasons		996	963	.508	–	–

2004 Starting Pitchers by Days Rest

	<=3	4	5	6+
Mariners Starts	2	73	61	15
Mariners ERA	7.36	4.82	4.57	5.91
AL Avg Starts	2	82	47	21
AL ERA	5.36	4.87	4.65	4.93

2004 Situational Stats

	Bob Melvin	AL Average
Hit & Run Success %	40.6	36.8
Stolen Base Success %	72.4	68.6
Platoon Pct.	58.8	61.6
Defensive Subs	16	21
High-Pitch Outings	12	5
Quick/Slow Hooks	16/17	20/16
Sacrifice Attempts	59	53

2004 Rankings — Bob Melvin (American League)

- 1st in double steals (8), starting lineups used (151) and starts with over 120 pitches (12)
- 2nd in sacrifice-bunt percentage (86.4%), hit-and-run attempts (96) and one-batter pitcher appearances (45)
- 3rd in stolen-base percentage and first-batter platoon percentage

Seattle

Bret Boone

2004 Season

Bret Boone got off to a slow start at the plate in 2004 and never recovered. He hit .195 in May and .213 in June as the Mariners continued their freefall in the American League West Division. Boone's .251 batting average with 24 homers and 83 RBI were, by far, the worst offensive numbers he's posted in Seattle. Part of Boone's struggles in 2004 might have been attributed to nagging back problems. While Boone struggled offensively in 2004, he's still regarded as one of the top defensive second basemen in baseball and won his fourth Gold Glove (third straight).

Hitting

Whereas Boone feasted on righthanded pitching in 2003, he hit only .249 with 16 home runs against righthanders in 2004. He wasn't as quick in turning on balls inside. Boone always has been at his best when driving the ball to the opposite field. In 2004, he often tried to muscle-up and pull the ball, which hurt him. Boone had offseason laser surgery on his eyes, which he is hoping will rectify his ability to pick up the spin on the breaking ball.

Baserunning & Defense

Boone's solid footwork allows him to get to balls headed into right field. A very strong throwing arm helps as well. He has excellent hands and tremendous instincts, and makes playing second base look easy. Despite having average speed, Boone is an aggressive baserunner capable of reaching double digits in stolen bases (he had 10 in 2004).

2005 Outlook

By reaching 500 plate appearances in 2004, Boone triggered a $9 million option for the 2005 season. There was speculation last season that Seattle might be interested in trading Boone. However, after a down year and the fact that Boone will be almost 36 on Opening Day, he might not attract the kind of attention he once did. If the Mariners are to rebound in 2005, they'll need Boone to revert to his old form at the plate.

Position: 2B
Bats: R **Throws:** R
Ht: 5'10" **Wt:** 190

Opening Day Age: 35
Born: 4/6/69 in El Cajon, CA
ML Seasons: 13

Overall Statistics

G	AB	R	H	D	T	HR	RBI	SB	BB	SO	Avg	OBP	Slg
148	593	74	149	30	0	24	83	10	56	135	.251	.317	.423
1692	6357	894	1703	351	25	245	984	90	524	1230	.268	.327	.447

Where He Hits the Ball

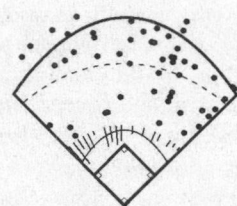 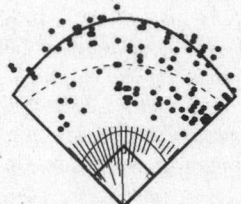

Vs. LHP   **Vs. RHP**

2004 Situational Stats

	AB	H	HR	RBI	Avg		AB	H	HR	RBI	Avg
Home	309	75	12	43	.243	LHP	148	38	8	24	.257
Road	284	74	12	40	.261	RHP	445	111	16	59	.249
First Half	305	72	11	36	.236	Sc Pos	183	42	5	56	.230
Scnd Half	288	77	13	47	.267	Clutch	105	19	3	16	.181

2004 Rankings (American League)

- 2nd in errors at second base (14) and lowest fielding percentage at second base (.978)
- 5th in lowest batting average vs. righthanded pitchers
- 6th in highest percentage of swings that missed (27.1)
- 7th in strikeouts
- 8th in lowest batting average, lowest on-base percentage, lowest batting average in the clutch and lowest batting average at home
- Led the Mariners in home runs, RBI, strikeouts, GDPs (18), HR frequency (24.7 ABs per HR) and cleanup slugging percentage (.478)

Ryan Franklin

2004 Season

After being a pleasant surprise in 2003, Ryan Franklin flopped in 2004. A victim of poor run support for two years running, Franklin was hit much harder in '04 than he was the previous campaign, as he had more trouble keeping the ball down in the strike zone and coughed up 33 home runs. He was a disaster on the road, going 1-10 with a 5.62 ERA, and he didn't win a game in July and August and had an 11-game losing streak. To put it bluntly, Franklin was a bad pitcher on a bad team.

Pitching

Franklin has a diverse arsenal—fastball, curveball, slider, changeup and split-finger—though none are considered plus pitches. For a pitcher with average velocity, he got in big trouble in 2004 when he tried to challenge too many hitters with fastballs. He has good command, which is vital for a flyball pitcher. For the second straight year, he walked just 61 batters despite working more than 200 innings. Franklin had success against righthanded batters in 2003, but was hit hard last year.

Defense

Opposing teams didn't run on Franklin too much in 2004, and he yielded just seven stolen bases. Part of that was because of a quick pickoff move that Franklin wasn't afraid to showcase. A compact and quick delivery to the plate also helped him immensely. Franklin fields his position well, and is quick to get off the mound to cover a bunt or first base.

2005 Outlook

Some think Franklin is better suited for a long-reliever role, though he'll likely be given another chance to earn a rotation spot in spring training. He'll need to show Seattle something better in 2005, as he's entering the second year of a $4.3 million, two-year contract. One start he gets bombed, the next he tosses a complete-game shutout, as he did against Anaheim in September. You never know what you're getting with Franklin, which was vexing to the Mariners.

Position: SP
Bats: R **Throws:** R
Ht: 6' 3" **Wt:** 180

Opening Day Age: 32
Born: 3/5/73 in Fort Smith, AR
ML Seasons: 5

Overall Statistics

	W	L	Pct.	ERA	G	GS	Sv	IP	H	BB	SO	HR	Avg
'04	4	16	.200	4.90	32	32	0	200.1	224	61	104	33	.285
Car.	27	35	.435	4.10	149	76	0	620.2	626	176	334	96	.263

2004 Pitching Profile

	Ryan Franklin	AL Average
Overall Strike %	63.4	62.3
1st Pitch Strike %	62.8	58.1
Ratio	1.42	1.42
Strikeouts per 9 IP	4.67	6.45
Walks per 9 IP	2.74	3.34
Home Runs per 9 IP	1.48	1.15
Strikeout/Walk Ratio	1.70	1.93
Groundball/Flyball Ratio	0.78	1.17

2004 Situational Stats

	W	L	ERA	Sv	IP		AB	H	HR	RBI	Avg
Home	3	6	3.92	0	85.0	LHB	433	119	13	49	.275
Road	1	10	5.62	0	115.1	RHB	353	105	20	56	.297
First Half	3	7	5.28	0	104.0	Sc Pos	189	50	8	72	.265
Scnd Half	1	9	4.48	0	96.1	Clutch	62	14	3	7	.226

2004 Rankings (American League)

- 1st in pickoff throws (219), lowest winning percentage and least run support per nine innings (3.1)
- 2nd in losses, balks (3) and lowest ground ball-flyball ratio allowed (0.8)
- 4th in highest slugging percentage allowed (.490)
- 5th in home runs allowed
- 6th in highest ERA on the road and fewest strikeouts per nine innings (4.7)
- 7th in runners caught stealing (9) and lowest stolen-base percentage allowed (43.8)
- 8th in complete games (2)
- 9th in most home runs allowed per nine innings (1.48) and lowest fielding percentage at pitcher (.921)
- Led the Mariners in losses, complete games (2), hits allowed, balks (3), pickoff throws (219), runners caught stealing (9) and GDPs induced (15)

Seattle

Eddie Guardado

2004 Season

Eddie Guardado, a free-agent signee after the 2003 campaign, was having a good season for a terrible team when he went on the disabled list at the beginning of August after reporting soreness in his left shoulder. Guardado initially was told he had a torn rotator cuff, though a second examination showed he didn't have a tear. Guardado also had surgery on his left knee to repair a torn meniscus. The Mariners are hopeful he'll be ready by the start of spring training.

Pitching

Guts. That's what makes Guardado a success. One scout said he has "the biggest guts in the game." Guardado has an average fastball and curveball and a slightly better-than-average slider. So how is he successful? He hides the ball as good as anyone in the game. Hitters always have had trouble picking up what he's throwing. And Guardado isn't afraid to throw any pitch in any situation or bust hitters inside.

Defense

Guardado isn't what you would call a natural athlete, though he fields his position well. He had trouble at times in 2004 getting off the mound, though most of his mobility can be pinned on a bum left knee that bothered him since spring training. Guardado has a history of holding runners well, and did not yield a single stolen base last year. His quick delivery makes it tough to run on him.

2005 Outlook

The Mariners declined to pick up the 2005 option on Guardado, but since the contract included a two-way option, Guardado choose to pick up his end of the agreement and will return to Seattle in 2005. Considering Guardado's health concerns (shoulder, knee), the Mariners are no doubt holding their breath that he'll be ready for the start of the '05 campaign. In short, the Mariners need Guardado to be healthy, as no one else was able to fill the closer role in 2004 and no one else currently is waiting in the wings.

Position: RP
Bats: R **Throws:** L
Ht: 6' 0" **Wt:** 205

Opening Day Age: 34
Born: 10/2/70 in Stockton, CA
ML Seasons: 12
Pronunciation: gwar-DAH-doe

Overall Statistics

	W	L	Pct.	ERA	G	GS	Sv	IP	H	BB	SO	HR	Avg
'04	2	2	.500	2.78	41	0	18	45.1	31	14	45	8	.194
Car.	38	49	.437	4.40	680	25	134	743.0	693	282	650	107	.248

2004 Pitching Profile

	Eddie Guardado	AL Average
Overall Strike %	67.9	62.3
1st Pitch Strike %	67.6	58.1
Ratio	0.99	1.42
Strikeouts per 9 IP	8.93	6.45
Walks per 9 IP	2.78	3.34
Home Runs per 9 IP	1.59	1.15
Strikeout/Walk Ratio	3.21	1.93
Groundball/Flyball Ratio	0.49	1.17

2004 Situational Stats

	W	L	ERA	Sv	IP		AB	H	HR	RBI	Avg
Home	1	0	1.66	10	21.2	LHB	46	5	1	5	.109
Road	1	2	3.80	8	23.2	RHB	114	26	7	12	.228
First Half	2	1	2.06	15	39.1	Sc Pos	25	6	1	8	.240
Scnd Half	0	1	7.50	3	6.0	Clutch	114	24	6	15	.211

2004 Rankings (American League)

- 1st in lowest save percentage (72.0)
- 3rd in blown saves (7)
- Led the Mariners in saves, games finished (35), save percentage (72.0) and blown saves (7)

Raul Ibanez

2004 Season

Raul Ibanez was one of the few Mariners who got off to a good start in 2004 at the plate. He was hitting .266 with a team-high 10 home runs and 27 RBI heading into June when he severely strained his right hamstring. He missed a month of action and it took all of July for him to get his swing back. Ibanez did hit .340 in August and .352 in September. He matched a club record by reaching base 11 consecutive times, including a six-hit game.

Hitting

Ibanez has a compact line-drive swing, though a slight uppercut allows for him to hit for power on occasion. In the past, Ibanez typically had trouble against lefthanded pitchers. But he hit .295 against southpaws in 2004, driving the ball the other way better and showing improved patience at the plate. Some scouts think that Ibanez' short stroke is the perfect fit for gaps at Safeco Field. He was also one of Seattle's top two-strike hitters, and he didn't loose much when he had to shorten his swing.

Baserunning & Defense

Originally drafted as a catcher, Ibanez spent most of the season playing left field. He took much better routes for flyballs than he did in the past in Kansas City. He doesn't have a plus arm. Ibanez has adequate speed, though he didn't run much after straining his hamstring in June. He moved to first base later in the season and struggled there at times.

2005 Outlook

Many feel Ibanez is perfectly suited to replace now-retired Edgar Martinez as the Mariners' full-time DH. Ibanez' hamstring injury limited him to just 481 at-bats in 2004, and the Mariners would like to see how his bat plays out for a full year, especially at Safeco Field. Ibanez has two years left on a three-year, $13 million deal. Moving him to first base would allow Randy Winn to move from center field to left. But that will happen only if rookie Jeremy Reed claims the center-field job in spring training.

Position: LF/1B
Bats: L **Throws:** R
Ht: 6' 2" **Wt:** 200

Opening Day Age: 32
Born: 6/2/72 in Manhattan, NY
ML Seasons: 9
Pronunciation: ee-BON-yez

Overall Statistics

	G	AB	R	H	D	T	HR	RBI	SB	BB	SO	Avg	OBP	Slg
'04	123	481	67	146	31	1	16	62	1	36	72	.304	.353	.472
Car.	752	2343	335	664	134	19	85	367	21	193	366	.283	.338	.466

Where He Hits the Ball

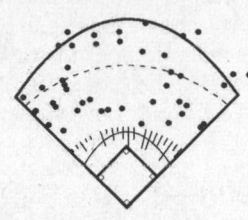
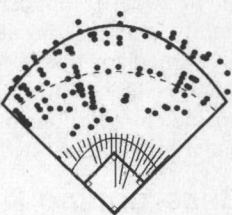

Vs. LHP   **Vs. RHP**

2004 Situational Stats

	AB	H	HR	RBI	Avg		AB	H	HR	RBI	Avg
Home	226	68	9	26	.301	LHP	146	43	4	16	.295
Road	255	78	7	36	.306	RHP	335	103	12	46	.307
First Half	202	53	11	28	.262	Sc Pos	122	33	2	42	.270
Scnd Half	279	93	5	34	.333	Clutch	92	25	4	13	.272

2004 Rankings (American League)

- 4th in lowest fielding percentage in left field (.983)
- 5th in errors in left field (4)
- Led the Mariners in slugging percentage

Jose Lopez

2004 Season

Jose Lopez didn't figure on making it to Seattle in 2004, but the Mariners' struggles combined with his advanced skills saw the then-20-year-old make his major league debut on July 31. Considered the top position prospect in the organization, Lopez got more than just a trial stint with Seattle. Some feel he might need more seasoning at Triple-A, where he hit .295 with 13 home runs in 74 games. Some think he's ready now.

Hitting

Many scouts feel Lopez will become a hitter capable of producing 25 home runs in a few years. Already a good contact hitter, he was exposed a bit in 2004 by opposing pitchers who fed him a steady diet of breaking pitches. That partly accounted for his 31 strikeouts. He doesn't walk much, either. But all agree that he has a lot of upside. In addition to his five home runs, Lopez had 13 doubles.

Baserunning & Defense

The burning question for the Mariners is what to do with Lopez in the field. A shortstop by trade, he has good instincts on how to play the position, as well as a plus arm. But Lopez, who made 10 errors in 57 games with Seattle, might be better suited for second or third base. Some scouts feel he'll outgrow shortstop because his bigger legs might cut down on his range. Lopez posted double-digit totals for stolen bases in the minors. He gets good jumps and is aggressive.

2005 Outlook

Lopez' skills are advanced for a player his age. With time, he could become one of the top shortstops in the game. He showed in his stay in Seattle that he's undaunted by facing older and more experienced pitchers. And no one is questioning his instincts for the game. It's just a matter of time for Lopez, and, as some feel, a matter of where he'll end up playing.

Position: SS
Bats: R **Throws:** R
Ht: 6' 2" **Wt:** 170

Opening Day Age: 21
Born: 11/24/83 in Anzoategui, VZ
ML Seasons: 1

Overall Statistics

	G	AB	R	H	D	T	HR	RBI	SB	BB	SO	Avg	OBP	Slg
'04	57	207	28	48	13	0	5	22	0	8	31	.232	.263	.367
Car.	57	207	28	48	13	0	5	22	0	8	31	.232	.263	.367

Where He Hits the Ball

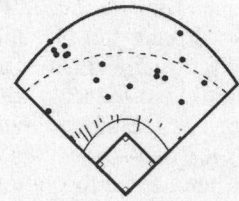 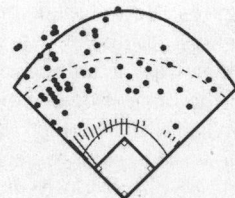

Vs. LHP   **Vs. RHP**

2004 Situational Stats

	AB	H	HR	RBI	Avg		AB	H	HR	RBI	Avg
Home	97	22	4	11	.227	LHP	56	12	0	3	.214
Road	110	26	1	11	.236	RHP	151	36	5	19	.238
First Half	0	0	0	0	–	Sc Pos	56	16	2	17	.286
Scnd Half	207	48	5	22	.232	Clutch	37	7	0	2	.189

2004 Rankings (American League)

- Led the Mariners in fewest GDPs per GDP situation (2.9%)

Bobby Madritsch

2004 Season

Two years removed from pitching for Winnipeg of the independent Northern League, Bobby Madritsch got his break when he was promoted from Triple-A to Seattle just after the All-Star break. A strong showing—he was 6-3 with a 3.27 ERA—all but earned Madritsch a job in Seattle's starting rotation in 2005. In September, he tossed 16 consecutive scoreless innings in defeating Anaheim and Boston.

Pitching

Madritsch is as aggressive as they come. One scout said he "has no fear, and will challenge anyone." He has a plus 90-95 MPH fastball that he'll bust inside on hitters. It's hard to tell if his ball will cut or tail. He's also armed with a plus changeup that's difficult to get an early read on. Madritsch is especially tough on lefthanded batters, who often have trouble picking up the ball from his arm angle. He would help himself by developing more of a breaking ball.

Defense

For a lefthanded pitcher, Madritsch doesn't have much in the way of a pickoff move. This is something the Mariners hope he'll work on prior to the start of the 2005 season. Teams were able to run on Madritsch at times in 2004. But because he is a good athlete, he's able to field his position well. That's of utmost importance, considering that he often allows the ball to be put in play.

2005 Outlook

A strong showing in 2004 means Madritsch likely will open the season as the Mariners' No. 3 or 4 starting pitcher. He threw a combined 150.1 innings between Triple-A Tacoma and Seattle last year, yet was still going strong at the end of the season. Seattle likes Madritsch's makeup and aggressive approach to pitching. He'll be 29 on Opening Day, but there's something to be said for late bloomers.

Position: SP
Bats: L **Throws:** L
Ht: 6' 2" **Wt:** 190

Opening Day Age: 29
Born: 2/28/76 in Oak Lawn, IL
ML Seasons: 1

Overall Statistics

	W	L	Pct.	ERA	G	GS	Sv	IP	H	BB	SO	HR	Avg
'04	6	3	.667	3.27	15	11	0	88.0	74	33	60	3	.232
Car.	6	3	.667	3.27	15	11	0	88.0	74	33	60	3	.232

2004 Pitching Profile

	Bobby Madritsch	AL Average
Overall Strike %	65.7	62.3
1st Pitch Strike %	62.2	58.1
Ratio	1.22	1.42
Strikeouts per 9 IP	6.14	6.45
Walks per 9 IP	3.38	3.34
Home Runs per 9 IP	0.31	1.15
Strikeout/Walk Ratio	1.82	1.93
Groundball/Flyball Ratio	1.02	1.17

2004 Situational Stats

	W	L	ERA	Sv	IP		AB	H	HR	RBI	Avg
Home	3	2	3.10	0	49.1	LHB	91	20	1	10	.220
Road	3	1	3.49	0	38.2	RHB	228	54	2	17	.237
First Half	0	0	—	0	0.0	Sc Pos	77	19	1	21	.247
Scnd Half	6	3	3.27	0	88.0	Clutch	58	13	0	1	.224

2004 Rankings (American League)

- 4th in wins among rookies
- Led the Mariners in winning percentage and lowest batting average allowed vs. righthanded batters

Gil Meche

2004 Season

Simply put, Gil Meche had a strange season. After stumbling to a 1-5 start with a 7.06 ERA and 29 walks in 43.1 innings, he was sent to Triple-A Tacoma at the beginning of June. After a mechanical flaw was detected in his delivery, Meche came back to the parent club and finished strong, posting a 6-2 record and a 3.79 ERA in his last 12 starts. Better yet, Meche—who spent most of the 2000-02 seasons battling shoulder injuries—was healthy the entire 2004 campaign.

Pitching

Meche was a mess early on in 2004. He lacked confidence and, even worse, command. While he was at Tacoma last season, roving pitching instructor Cal McLish saw that Meche was trying to hard to nip corners, pitching more like a sinker-slider pitcher. McLish encouraged Meche to trust his stuff and go after hitters. Meche did, and regained his confidence, which led to his strong finish with Seattle. He prefers to use a two- and four-seam fastball frequently, and both have plenty of pop. Meche's slider also is a plus pitch that he's developed more confidence in. He also will mix in a nice curveball and changeup.

Defense

Meche is regarded as an average fielder. However, he doesn't have much of a pickoff move, though he will throw over to first base in an attempt to keep runners close. That said, Meche is capable of shortening his delivery, which will help thwart the running game. Opposing basestealers are under 50 percent against him in his big league career.

2005 Outlook

Many scouts feel Meche has some of the best stuff in the American League, and all that he lacked was confidence. He seems to have regained his edge late in 2004 after returning from the minors. Some feel Meche has a chance to win 15-20 games and become the dominant arm on the Mariners' staff. He'll get that chance in 2005.

Position: SP
Bats: R **Throws:** R
Ht: 6' 3" **Wt:** 200

Opening Day Age: 26
Born: 9/8/78 in Lafayette, LA
ML Seasons: 4
Pronunciation: MESH

Overall Statistics

	W	L	Pct.	ERA	G	GS	Sv	IP	H	BB	SO	HR	Avg
'04	7	7	.500	5.01	23	23	0	127.2	139	47	99	21	.273
Car.	34	28	.548	4.58	86	85	0	485.1	474	207	336	67	.257

2004 Pitching Profile

	Gil Meche	AL Average
Overall Strike %	61.1	62.3
1st Pitch Strike %	50.4	58.1
Ratio	1.46	1.42
Strikeouts per 9 IP	6.98	6.45
Walks per 9 IP	3.31	3.34
Home Runs per 9 IP	1.48	1.15
Strikeout/Walk Ratio	2.11	1.93
Groundball/Flyball Ratio	0.83	1.17

2004 Situational Stats

	W	L	ERA	Sv	IP		AB	H	HR	RBI	Avg
Home	3	5	4.40	0	71.2	LHB	297	80	14	42	.269
Road	4	2	5.79	0	56.0	RHB	212	59	7	26	.278
First Half	1	5	7.06	0	43.1	Sc Pos	128	35	3	43	.273
Scnd Half	6	2	3.95	0	84.1	Clutch	21	5	0	1	.238

2004 Rankings (American League)

- Led the Mariners in lowest stolen-base percentage allowed (37.5)

Jamie Moyer

2004 Season

Jamie Moyer suffered through his worst season as a professional since 1988, going 7-13 with a 5.21 ERA in 34 games. He was bad on the road and struggled even at spacious Safeco Field, where he was 4-8 with a 5.00 ERA. He allowed 44 home runs, which far exceeded his total of 19 from 2003, when he was 21-7 with a 3.27 ERA. A sign of an aging pitcher or just bad location? It was hard to tell with Moyer, who won one game after June 18.

Pitching

It's not as if Moyer suffered from a lack of velocity in 2004. He never had much in the way of a fastball (mid-80s) to begin with. Moyer's problems had everything to do with location. Whereas in previous seasons he did a good job of hitting corners and getting hitters to chase pitches out of the strike zone, Moyer didn't fool anyone in 2004. His changeup—which is a plus pitch for him—was as good as it's been, but he didn't have anything else for hitters to think about. Righthanded batters, who Moyer has typically done well against, hit him well in 2004.

Defense

Moyer has a quick pickoff move and has never been afraid to use it. Opposing baserunners stole just nine bases off him in 2004. For a pitcher who will be 42 when the 2005 season starts, Moyer is quick to get off the mound to field bunts or to cover first base on balls hit to the right side. A very capable fielder.

2005 Outlook

The Mariners desperately need Moyer to regain his command in 2005 if they're to climb out of the basement of the American League West. There is talk that Moyer, who many thought cheated time for so long, might be done, and that his 2004 season is a harbinger of things to come. A competitor, Moyer likely won't go that quietly.

Position: SP
Bats: L **Throws:** L
Ht: 6' 0" **Wt:** 175

Opening Day Age: 42
Born: 11/18/62 in Sellersville, PA
ML Seasons: 18

Overall Statistics

W	L	Pct.	ERA	G	GS	Sv	IP	H	BB	SO	HR	Avg
7	13	.350	5.21	34	33	0	202.0	217	63	125	44	.272
192	145	.570	4.15	506	453	0	2939.2	3002	843	1782	358	.264

2004 Pitching Profile

	Jamie Moyer	AL Average
Overall Strike %	61.7	62.3
1st Pitch Strike %	58.9	58.1
Ratio	1.39	1.42
Strikeouts per 9 IP	5.57	6.45
Walks per 9 IP	2.81	3.34
Home Runs per 9 IP	1.96	1.15
Strikeout/Walk Ratio	1.98	1.93
Groundball/Flyball Ratio	0.91	1.17

2004 Situational Stats

	W	L	ERA	Sv	IP		AB	H	HR	RBI	Avg
Home	4	8	5.00	0	104.1	LHB	229	67	9	30	.293
Road	3	5	5.44	0	97.2	RHB	570	150	35	90	.263
First Half	6	6	4.26	0	112.0	Sc Pos	147	49	11	75	.333
Scnd Half	1	7	6.40	0	90.0	Clutch	58	11	1	4	.190

2004 Rankings (American League)

- 1st in home runs allowed, fielding percentage at pitcher (1.000) and most home runs allowed per nine innings (1.96)
- 5th in lowest winning percentage
- 6th in losses, highest slugging percentage allowed (.481) and highest batting average allowed with runners in scoring position
- 7th in pitches thrown (3,414)
- 8th in games started and least run support per nine innings (4.5)
- 9th in hit batsmen (11), highest ERA and highest ERA on the road
- 10th in pickoff throws (119), lowest ground ball-flyball ratio allowed (0.9) and most pitches thrown per batter (3.84)
- Led the Mariners in games started, innings pitched, batters faced (888), home runs allowed, strikeouts and pitches thrown (3,414)

Miguel Olivo

2004 Season

Miguel Olivo was obtained in June from the Chicago White Sox as part of the trade that sent pitcher Freddy Garcia to the Windy City. Olivo, for all of his upside, wasn't exactly a hit in his half season in Seattle. In fact, he didn't hit much at all. He batted .200 with the Mariners and suffered through a 0-for-31 slump late in the season. Olivo didn't shine on defense, either, where he had trouble with passed balls and blocking balls in the dirt.

Hitting

Olivo is a bit of a free swinger, a trait that started to manifest itself even before he came to Seattle. During his aforementioned slump, he appeared to be overmatched at the plate, especially by pitchers with power arms. He also was prone to chasing balls out of the strike zone, especially during his slump. But scouts feel that Olivo will develop into a 20-homer man. He showed some pop in 2004 with gap power, which should play well at spacious Safeco Field.

Baserunning & Defense

Olivo is blessed with a strong and accurate arm. His quick release makes it tough to steal on him. His problems come with blocking balls in the dirt. He had nine passed balls in just 49 games with Seattle. Scouts felt he wasn't moving his feet fast enough and that he got away from what he was doing in Chicago. Some have questioned his pitch-calling abilities, as well. Olivo is a good athlete and an aggressive baserunner.

2005 Outlook

In trading away Freddy Garcia, the Mariners felt they were getting a frontline catcher to replace Dan Wilson. They still feel that way, even after Olivo slumped in the field and at the plate during his half season with Seattle. The Mariners contend he's an All-Star in the making, one who will supplant Wilson this season. He's 26 and coming into his prime, but he still needs to show improvement in several areas, both at and behind the plate.

Position: C
Bats: R **Throws:** R
Ht: 6' 0" **Wt:** 215

Opening Day Age: 26
Born: 7/15/78 in Villa Vasquez, DR
ML Seasons: 3

Overall Statistics

	G	AB	R	H	D	T	HR	RBI	SB	BB	SO	Avg	OBP	Slg
'04	96	301	46	70	15	4	13	40	7	20	84	.233	.286	.439
Car.	216	637	85	149	35	5	20	72	13	41	169	.234	.286	.399

Where He Hits the Ball

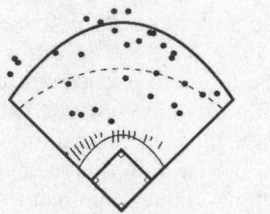
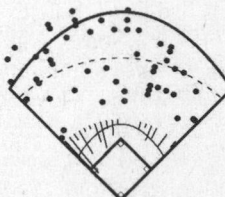

Vs. LHP　　　　**Vs. RHP**

2004 Situational Stats

	AB	H	HR	RBI	Avg		AB	H	HR	RBI	Avg
Home	159	39	8	22	.245	LHP	87	28	6	23	.322
Road	142	31	5	18	.218	RHP	214	42	7	17	.196
First Half	144	38	7	26	.264	Sc Pos	66	13	3	27	.197
Scnd Half	157	32	6	14	.204	Clutch	45	10	1	3	.222

2004 Rankings (American League)

- 6th in lowest fielding percentage at catcher (.991)
- 8th in errors at catcher (5)

Joel Pineiro

2004 Season

As was the case with so many of his teammates, Joel Pineiro got off to a miserable start in 2004, going 1-3 with a 8.26 ERA in April as the Mariners stumbled out of the gate and quickly fell out of contention in the American League West. But instead of getting better, things just got worse. Pineiro didn't win his second game until June and then went on the disabled list for good in July with a strained flexor bundle. Much as he has throughout his career in Seattle, Pineiro showed flashes of dominance. But he also showed a susceptibility to getting hit hard.

Pitching

Pineiro was faced with a vexing dilemma at the start of the 2004 season. He was getting hit hard despite having, what he and the Mariners felt, was very good stuff. Pineiro likes to use his fastball, which runs in the low 90s. He's had success with his two-seamer, though he got away from it at times last season. Pineiro also has a plus slider and curveball and a good changeup. He's at his best when he can keep his slider down in the zone. Scouts like his aggressiveness.

Defense

Pineiro is regarded as an above-average defensive player. He's made just two errors over the past two seasons. Pineiro has had trouble in the past with holding baserunners on and slowing the running game. Part of that can be attributed to a high leg kick. He showed an improved pickoff move from the 2003 season, but 11 of 14 basestealers were successful against him last season.

2005 Outlook

The Mariners are anxious to see how Pineiro's right elbow responds after he missed most of the second half of the season. When healthy, he has good enough stuff to be a No. 2 starter on any staff. A workhorse who can top 200 innings, Pineiro needs to bounce back to his form of 2003, when he won 16 games and had a 3.78 ERA.

Position: SP
Bats: R **Throws:** R
Ht: 6' 1" **Wt:** 200

Opening Day Age: 26
Born: 9/25/78 in Rio Padres, PR
ML Seasons: 5

Overall Statistics

	W	L	Pct.	ERA	G	GS	Sv	IP	H	BB	SO	HR	Avg
'04	6	11	.353	4.67	21	21	0	140.2	144	43	111	21	.265
Car.	43	31	.581	3.66	115	93	0	641.1	600	207	464	69	.248

2004 Pitching Profile

	Joel Pineiro	AL Average
Overall Strike %	62.7	62.3
1st Pitch Strike %	57.0	58.1
Ratio	1.33	1.42
Strikeouts per 9 IP	7.10	6.45
Walks per 9 IP	2.75	3.34
Home Runs per 9 IP	1.34	1.15
Strikeout/Walk Ratio	2.58	1.93
Groundball/Flyball Ratio	1.18	1.17

2004 Situational Stats

	W	L	ERA	Sv	IP		AB	H	HR	RBI	Avg
Home	5	5	4.03	0	73.2	LHB	258	54	7	28	.209
Road	1	6	5.37	0	67.0	RHB	285	90	14	45	.316
First Half	4	10	4.69	0	121.0	Sc Pos	121	34	7	55	.281
Scnd Half	2	1	4.58	0	19.2	Clutch	37	5	0	1	.135

2004 Rankings (American League)

- 6th in lowest winning percentage
- 7th in highest batting average allowed vs. righthanded batters
- 8th in lowest batting average allowed vs. lefthanded batters
- Led the Mariners in stolen bases allowed (11), highest strikeout-walk ratio (2.6), highest groundball-flyball ratio allowed (1.2) and most strikeouts per nine innings (7.1)

Ichiro Suzuki

2004 Season

In a dismal season in Seattle that saw the Mariners fall a single defeat shy of 100 losses, Ichiro Suzuki's pursuit of the single-season hit record was about the only thing worth watching in 2004. Ichiro surpassed George Sisler's 84-year-old record of 257 hits with a late push at the plate. Ichiro finished the season with 262 hits. He also won the American League batting crown with a .372 batting average, this after a slow start that saw him hit .255 in April and .274 in June. To top it all off, he pocketed his fourth straight Gold Glove.

Hitting

Scouts rave about Ichiro's bat control and how he can essentially do what he wants with any pitch. He walked more in 2004 and struck out less—a sign that he's still getting better. Ichiro flicks the bat through the strike zone with ease, and he'll drive a ball the other way just as easy as pulling it. A lot of his hits last season were ones that never left the infield because he gets out of the box so quickly. He didn't drive the ball as much in 2004 as he had in the past, but he looked more locked in at the plate.

Baserunning & Defense

Ichiro has the speed and range to cover a lot of ground. He would be an ideal center fielder, expect that he has one of the strongest arms in baseball, which makes him a valuable commodity in right. Simply put, there's no taking an extra base on Ichiro. He gets good jumps and steals third base more so than most other players. He's great at reading a pitcher's move.

2005 Outlook

After Ichiro slumped late in the 2003 season, some wondered if his best days weren't behind him. But he showed his skeptics that he's still on top of his game with his record-setting performance. Ichiro signed a four-year, $44 million extension in December 2003, so he'll be at the top of the Seattle lineup at least through the 2007 campaign.

Position: RF
Bats: L **Throws:** R
Ht: 5' 9" **Wt:** 172

Opening Day Age: 31
Born: 10/22/73 in Kasugai, Japan
ML Seasons: 4
Pronunciation: ee-chee-row

Overall Statistics

	G	AB	R	H	D	T	HR	RBI	SB	BB	SO	Avg	OBP	Slg
'04	161	704	101	262	24	5	8	60	36	49	63	.372	.414	.455
Car.	634	2722	450	924	114	29	37	242	157	183	247	.339	.384	.443

Where He Hits the Ball

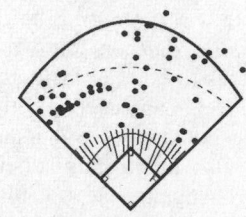 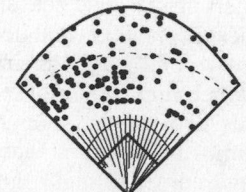

Vs. LHP   **Vs. RHP**

2004 Situational Stats

	AB	H	HR	RBI	Avg		AB	H	HR	RBI	Avg
Home	346	117	4	19	.338	LHP	208	84	5	21	.404
Road	358	145	4	41	.405	RHP	496	178	3	39	.359
First Half	371	119	3	31	.321	Sc Pos	121	45	0	52	.372
Scnd Half	333	143	5	29	.429	Clutch	122	48	1	15	.393

2004 Rankings (American League)

- 1st in batting average, at-bats, hits, singles, intentional walks (19), times on base (315), plate appearances (762), highest groundball-flyball ratio (3.3), batting average with runners in scoring position, batting average in the clutch, batting average vs. lefthanded pitchers, batting average vs. righthanded pitchers, on-base percentage for a leadoff hitter (.418) and batting average on the road
- 2nd in stolen bases, on-base percentage and batting average with two strikes (.284)
- 3rd in games played and fielding percentage in right field (.992)
- 4th in lowest HR frequency (88.0 ABs per HR)
- Led AL right fielders in batting average

Randy Winn

2004 Season

Much like the rest of his teammates in 2004, Randy Winn got off to a slow start as the Mariners fell out of contention quickly in the American League West. But it was the second consecutive season Winn got off to a slow start. He has long been rumored to be the odd-man out in trade talks, but Seattle didn't make a move, leaving him as the answer in center field. By the end of the season, Winn again had made up some ground and his final statistics were nearly identical to 2003, though his average took a dip.

Hitting

Winn has evolved from purely a slap hitter in his early years into someone who can spray the ball to all fields and drive a ball on the inside third of the plate. Scouts feel he should hit the ball on the ground more like leadoff hitter Ichiro Suzuki to take advantage of his speed. Winn can handle the bat well, but he lacks the patience to be a top-of-the-order hitter. He generally is better off hitting lower in the order, where he sees better pitches.

Baserunning & Defense

Winn is a good athlete, having been a basketball player at Santa Clara. But he's proven to be a bad fit in center field. His arm is average at best, but where he really runs into problems is tracking fly-balls. He takes bad routes, though he's sometimes able to overcome that because of his speed. He was moved to left field when rookie Jeremy Reed joined the team in September. Winn fared better there.

2005 Outlook

Scouts regard Winn as a good fourth outfielder on a good team. A notorious slow starter, his final piece of work doesn't look bad on paper. But if Jeremy Reed wins the center-field job in spring training, Winn looks like an average option in left field. The Mariners need a consistent bat with power, and Winn will never be that guy.

Position: CF/LF
Bats: B **Throws:** R
Ht: 6' 2" **Wt:** 197

Opening Day Age: 30
Born: 6/9/74 in Los Angeles, CA
ML Seasons: 7

Overall Statistics

	G	AB	R	H	D	T	HR	RBI	SB	BB	SO	Avg	OBP	Slg
'04	157	626	84	179	34	6	14	81	21	53	98	.286	.346	.427
Car.	833	3062	451	869	165	38	49	338	124	259	553	.284	.344	.411

Where He Hits the Ball

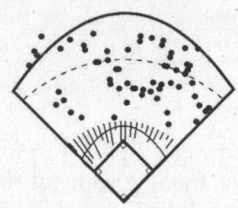 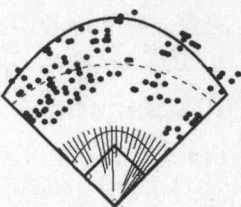

Vs. LHP		**Vs. RHP**	

2004 Situational Stats

	AB	H	HR	RBI	Avg		AB	H	HR	RBI	Avg
Home	304	78	6	36	.257	LHP	191	49	3	17	.257
Road	322	101	8	45	.314	RHP	435	130	11	64	.299
First Half	320	89	8	36	.278	Sc Pos	156	48	3	60	.308
Scnd Half	306	90	6	45	.294	Clutch	121	42	6	30	.347

2004 Rankings (American League)

- 3rd in fielding percentage in center field (.989)
- 4th in steals of third (8)
- 5th in batting average in the clutch
- 6th in at-bats and errors in center field (4)
- Led the Mariners in doubles, triples, sacrifice bunts (9), sacrifice flies (7), hit by pitch (8), bunts in play (18) and steals of third (8)

Seattle

Jolbert Cabrera

Position:
3B/1B/LF/2B/SS
Bats: R **Throws:** R
Ht: 6' 1" **Wt:** 195

Opening Day Age: 32
Born: 12/8/72 in
Cartagena, Colombia
ML Seasons: 7
Pronunciation:
HOLE-bert kah-brair-RAH

Overall Statistics

	G	AB	R	H	D	T	HR	RBI	SB	BB	SO	Avg	OBP	Slg
'04	113	359	38	97	19	2	6	47	10	16	70	.270	.312	.384
Car.	561	1291	172	333	73	8	15	145	36	65	212	.258	.305	.362

2004 Situational Stats

	AB	H	HR	RBI	Avg		AB	H	HR	RBI	Avg
Home	162	41	2	16	.253	LHP	126	36	2	17	.286
Road	197	56	4	31	.284	RHP	233	61	4	30	.262
First Half	192	55	3	26	.286	Sc Pos	95	32	2	41	.337
Scnd Half	167	42	3	21	.251	Clutch	70	15	1	9	.214

2004 Season

When Seattle third baseman Scott Spiezio went on the DL at the end of spring training with a sore back, the Mariners traded for Jolbert Cabrera. And though the M's struggled in 2004, Cabrera gave Seattle just what it wanted—versatility. The guy played everywhere. Better yet, he hit well enough to earn a career-best 359 at-bats.

Hitting, Baserunning & Defense

Cabrera doesn't walk much, and always has had an aggressive mindset at the plate. This serves him well against lefthanded pitching, though his big swing occasionally has gotten him in trouble against righthanders. The Mariners didn't run much, though Cabrera, who has a good first step, did manage to tie his career-high with 10 stolen bases. Defensively, Cabrera did everything but pitch and catch. He made only six errors in 2004.

2005 Outlook

The Mariners feel that Cabrera is a better option as an utilityman than Willie Bloomquist, mostly because of his bat. Seattle is a good fit for Cabrera because he'd be hard-pressed to get as many at-bats with another team. Having him play every day and bat fifth—as he sometimes did last season—just isn't a good idea, even on a bad team. But as a role player, Cabrera is a valuable asset.

Shigetoshi Hasegawa

Position: RP
Bats: R **Throws:** R
Ht: 5'11" **Wt:** 180

Opening Day Age: 36
Born: 8/1/68 in Kobe,
Japan
ML Seasons: 8
Pronunciation:
shig-eh-toe-shi hoss-eh-gawa

Overall Statistics

	W	L	Pct.	ERA	G	GS	Sv	IP	H	BB	SO	HR	Avg
'04	4	6	.400	5.16	68	0	0	68.0	67	31	46	5	.260
Car.	44	40	.524	3.65	471	8	33	653.2	625	249	417	72	.256

2004 Situational Stats

	W	L	ERA	Sv	IP		AB	H	HR	RBI	Avg
Home	3	2	2.95	0	39.2	LHB	113	30	2	20	.265
Road	1	4	8.26	0	28.1	RHB	145	37	3	18	.255
First Half	2	3	5.50	0	37.2	Sc Pos	81	21	0	32	.259
Scnd Half	2	3	4.75	0	30.1	Clutch	104	29	5	17	.279

2004 Season

Disaster. That one word best describes Shigetoshi Hasegawa's season in 2004. The veteran righthander went from having the lowest ERA of any reliever in the American League in 2003 to getting hammered by opposing hitters in 2004. In a year in which Seattle needed quality innings from Hasegawa, he simply failed to deliver.

Pitching & Defense

Whereas in 2003 Hasegawa was good at keeping the ball down, his pitches were flat and up in the strike zone far too often in 2004. That's a problem when you're stuff isn't overpowering by any means. Hasegawa's forkball and slider—pitches that hitters often pound into the ground—weren't nearly as effective. He frequently fell behind hitters. He also walked 31 batters. Hasegawa is regarded as a capable fielder with a quick, compact delivery that stifles the running game.

2005 Outlook

The Mariners owe Hasegawa $2.975 million in 2005, and there's a $325,000 buyout of his 2006 option. The Mariners need Hasegawa to revert back to his form of 2003. Hasegawa is 36, and though he has a good track record as a setup pitcher, the Mariners are concerned that his best days might be behind him.

Bucky Jacobsen

Position: 1B/DH
Bats: R **Throws:** R
Ht: 6' 4" **Wt:** 220

Opening Day Age: 29
Born: 8/30/75 in
Riverton, WY
ML Seasons: 1

Overall Statistics

	G	AB	R	H	D	T	HR	RBI	SB	BB	SO	Avg	OBP	Slg
'04	42	160	17	44	9	0	9	28	0	14	47	.275	.335	.500
Car.	42	160	17	44	9	0	9	28	0	14	47	.275	.335	.500

2004 Situational Stats

	AB	H	HR	RBI	Avg		AB	H	HR	RBI	Avg
Home	78	18	7	18	.231	LHP	50	17	4	12	.340
Road	82	26	2	10	.317	RHP	110	27	5	16	.245
First Half	0	0	0	0	–	Sc Pos	49	12	2	18	.245
Scnd Half	160	44	9	28	.275	Clutch	36	11	2	6	.306

2004 Season

A career minor leaguer, Bucky Jacobsen became a fan favorite after being called up from Triple-A Tacoma in July. He showed legitimate power with Seattle—something the team needed desperately—before being shut down in September with a knee injury.

Hitting, Baserunning & Defense

Jacobsen has raw power, which served him well early in his debut with the Mariners last season. However, many feel his big swing won't play well at Safeco. There's questions as to how much Jacobsen will be exposed to balls above the waist and sliders away. After some early success in 2004, opposing pitchers started feeding him more breaking balls. Jacobsen doesn't run well and is an average first baseman, though he's likely better suited as a designated hitter.

2005 Outlook

Jacobsen has plenty of pop. There's no doubting that. He turned himself from a career minor leaguer into someone who might fit in Seattle's future plans. However, the jury still is out as to whether he's a full-time player. Depending on his performance in the spring, Jacobsen could make the roster as a DH or a first baseman. If he hits, he'll play somewhere for Seattle in 2005.

Justin Leone

Position: 3B
Bats: R **Throws:** R
Ht: 6' 1" **Wt:** 190

Opening Day Age: 27
Born: 7/9/77 in Las
Vegas, NV
ML Seasons: 1

Overall Statistics

	G	AB	R	H	D	T	HR	RBI	SB	BB	SO	Avg	OBP	Slg
'04	31	102	15	22	5	0	6	13	1	9	32	.216	.298	.441
Car.	31	102	15	22	5	0	6	13	1	9	32	.216	.298	.441

2004 Situational Stats

	AB	H	HR	RBI	Avg		AB	H	HR	RBI	Avg
Home	40	8	2	6	.200	LHP	27	6	3	6	.222
Road	62	14	4	7	.226	RHP	75	16	3	7	.213
First Half	12	4	0	0	.333	Sc Pos	18	3	1	5	.167
Scnd Half	90	18	6	13	.200	Clutch	25	4	2	4	.160

2004 Season

Justin Leone was called up from Triple-A at the beginning of July, and he struggled at the plate and in the field during a 102 at-bat trial run late in the summer. Despite striking out a lot, Leone showed he has good pop in his bat. His season ended in August after he fractured a bone in his left hand.

Hitting, Baserunning & Defense

Leone showed better patience in dealing with breaking balls, which had plagued him during his first five seasons in the organization. Some feel that he takes too many pitches, looking for a ball in the middle of the plate. Leone's a low-ball hitter who doesn't like the ball elevated on him. Defensively, he had throwing problems in Seattle, though he's regarded as a very good third baseman. He has decent speed, especially for a corner infielder.

2005 Outlook

Unless Scott Spiezio bounces back quickly from a terrible season, third base in Seattle is wide open. Leone and another rookie, Greg Dobbs, will be given every chance to win the job. The Mariners know Leone has good power, but they'd like to see him cut down on his strikeouts. That he also can play second base and shortstop might help his cause.

J.J. Putz

Position: RP
Bats: R **Throws:** R
Ht: 6' 5" **Wt:** 220

Opening Day Age: 28
Born: 2/22/77 in
Trenton, MI
ML Seasons: 2

Overall Statistics

	W	L	Pct.	ERA	G	GS	Sv	IP	H	BB	SO	HR	Avg
'04	0	3	.000	4.71	54	0	9	63.0	66	24	47	10	.274
Car.	0	3	.000	4.73	57	0	9	66.2	70	27	50	10	.273

2004 Situational Stats

	W	L	ERA	Sv	IP		AB	H	HR	RBI	Avg
Home	0	1	4.50	5	28.0	LHB	111	26	8	19	.234
Road	0	2	4.89	4	35.0	RHB	130	40	2	25	.308
First Half	0	2	4.84	0	35.1	Sc Pos	84	23	2	33	.274
Scnd Half	0	1	4.55	9	27.2	Clutch	98	27	4	15	.276

2004 Season

J.J. Putz had been a full-time starter in the minors before the Mariners converted him into a reliever in 2003. He didn't make the team out of spring training but was called up in April. Putz pitched in a variety of roles and fared well at times. He pitched strong at the end of the season, converting his last nine save opportunities.

Pitching & Defense

While Putz got a chance to close with Seattle in 2004, he's much better suited for middle relief. He has a resilient arm and can go short or long. Putz has a plus fastball and a curveball with late bite that's improved vastly in the last two seasons. He got into trouble when he got his pitches too far up in the strike zone. Putz has good footwork and can field his position well, but his pickoff move is average.

2005 Outlook

Putz stands a good chance of making the M's Opening Day roster, mostly because of his versatility. Seattle needs guys who can eat innings, and Putz can do just that. There are still some concerns with his command, but if he throws strikes, the Mariners will find a spot for him in 2005.

Jeremy Reed

Position: CF
Bats: L **Throws:** L
Ht: 6' 0" **Wt:** 185

Opening Day Age: 23
Born: 6/15/81 in San Dimas, CA
ML Seasons: 1

Overall Statistics

	G	AB	R	H	D	T	HR	RBI	SB	BB	SO	Avg	OBP	Slg
'04	18	58	11	23	4	0	0	5	3	7	4	.397	.470	.466
Car.	18	58	11	23	4	0	0	5	3	7	4	.397	.470	.466

2004 Situational Stats

	AB	H	HR	RBI	Avg		AB	H	HR	RBI	Avg
Home	22	6	0	1	.273	LHP	5	1	0	2	.200
Road	36	17	0	4	.472	RHP	53	22	0	3	.415
First Half	0	0	0	0	–	Sc Pos	13	4	0	5	.308
Scnd Half	58	23	0	5	.397	Clutch	7	2	0	0	.286

2004 Season

After a breakthrough 2003 season in which he led the minors with a .373 average and .453 OBP, Jeremy Reed started well with the White Sox' Triple-A affiliate before he was dealt to Seattle in last June's Freddy Garcia trade. Reed combined to hit .289 at two Triple-A stops, and he was even better with the Mariners in September. The left-handed hitter mostly played center field, moving Randy Winn to left and Raul Ibanez to first base.

Hitting, Baserunning & Defense

Reed makes contact easily with a line-drive stroke that sprays balls to all fields. He has good gap power, hits lefties successfully and consistently totals more walks than strikeouts. Reed is a good outfielder with a solid arm, and he may have enough speed to play center. That still isn't certain, as Safeco Field has a big outfield, but Reed has tremendous instincts, which may make up for his lack of pure speed. He still needs to fine-tune his jumps and angles on balls hit his way.

2005 Outlook

While he may be better defensively suited to a corner, where more power is preferred, Reed may be the best all-around center fielder on the 40-man roster heading into spring training. He will battle for the starting job.

George Sherrill

Position: RP
Bats: L **Throws:** L
Ht: 6' 0" **Wt:** 210

Opening Day Age: 27
Born: 4/19/77 in Memphis, TN
ML Seasons: 1

Overall Statistics

	W	L	Pct.	ERA	G	GS	Sv	IP	H	BB	SO	HR	Avg
'04	2	1	.667	3.80	21	0	0	23.2	24	9	16	3	.258
Car.	2	1	.667	3.80	21	0	0	23.2	24	9	16	3	.258

2004 Situational Stats

	W	L	ERA	Sv	IP			AB	H	HR	RBI	Avg
Home	2	0	3.95	0	13.2	LHB		46	11	2	11	.239
Road	0	1	3.60	0	10.0	RHB		47	13	1	6	.277
First Half	0	0	–	0	0.0	Sc Pos		31	9	0	14	.290
Scnd Half	2	1	3.80	0	23.2	Clutch		62	15	2	11	.242

2004 Season

George Sherrill, like fellow pitcher Bobby Madritsch, was one of a few pleasant surprises for the Mariners in 2004. Like Madritsch, Sherrill was a former Independent League pitcher who was noticed by scout Charley Kerfeld. A left-hander, Sherrill performed well after a July callup from Triple-A. He was 2-1 with a 3.80 ERA and showed that he can get lefthanded batters out.

Pitching & Defense

Sherrill is a short-arm pitcher with a breaking ball that ranks as a little above average. He hides his fastball well and throws it out of his earhole, much like a catcher. His fastball is sneaky and gets on you quickly. He was shut down in mid-September because of fatigue, but he has been durable during his short career. He's a plus defender with a good pickoff move.

2005 Outlook

With Seattle's bullpen looking wide open, Sherrill figures to land a spot on the roster. He showed that he's not just a situational lefthander, and the Mariners were impressed with how he went after righthanded hitters. As a former independent leaguer, Sherrill has had to fight for everything. Seattle likes that toughness trait in him.

Scott Spiezio

Position: 3B/1B
Bats: B **Throws:** R
Ht: 6' 2" **Wt:** 220

Opening Day Age: 32
Born: 9/21/72 in Joliet, IL
ML Seasons: 9
Pronunciation: SPEE-zio

Overall Statistics

	G	AB	R	H	D	T	HR	RBI	SB	BB	SO	Avg	OBP	Slg
'04	112	367	38	79	12	3	10	41	4	36	60	.215	.288	.346
Car.	1044	3353	440	858	195	23	101	465	32	344	470	.256	.327	.418

2004 Situational Stats

	AB	H	HR	RBI	Avg		AB	H	HR	RBI	Avg
Home	169	37	5	16	.219	LHP	74	15	1	8	.203
Road	198	42	5	25	.212	RHP	293	64	9	33	.218
First Half	248	54	9	33	.218	Sc Pos	97	16	1	27	.165
Scnd Half	119	25	1	8	.210	Clutch	78	16	5	10	.205

2004 Season

The Mariners, in their eternal search for an every-day third baseman, inked Scott Spiezio to a three-year contract in December 2003. Three months into the 2004 season, they saw the error of their ways in trying to make a utility player into an everyday player. A nagging back injury all season didn't help Spiezio's cause.

Hitting, Baserunning & Defense

Spiezio is considered an average hitter who occasionally will show some pop. He's much better from the lefthand side of the plate, where he looks to spray the ball to all fields. That said, Spiezio can turn on a ball well on the inside third of the plate. Defensively, he is an average third baseman but a better defender at first. He's capable of stealing up to 10 bases because he gets good jumps.

2005 Outlook

The Mariners would like to see more of a return on the three-year deal they gave Spiezio, as he's still owed $5.6 million. The team will use him in a number of spots in 2005—at third base, first base, DH and as a pinch-hitter. GM Bill Bavasi hinted late in the 2004 season that Spiezio would see more time at first. He'll have to hit to stay there, though.

Ron Villone

Position: RP/SP
Bats: L **Throws:** L
Ht: 6' 3" **Wt:** 230

Opening Day Age: 35
Born: 1/16/70 in Englewood, NJ
ML Seasons: 10
Pronunciation: vill-OWN

Overall Statistics

	W	L	Pct.	ERA	G	GS	Sv	IP	H	BB	SO	HR	Avg
'04	8	6	.571	4.08	56	10	0	117.0	102	64	86	12	.232
Car.	47	49	.490	4.80	394	93	5	882.2	848	467	675	108	.255

2004 Situational Stats

	W	L	ERA	Sv	IP		AB	H	HR	RBI	Avg
Home	5	1	4.05	0	60.0	LHB	143	29	3	20	.203
Road	3	5	4.11	0	57.0	RHB	296	73	9	39	.247
First Half	3	2	2.87	0	53.1	Sc Pos	114	28	4	45	.246
Scnd Half	5	4	5.09	0	63.2	Clutch	75	11	2	6	.147

2004 Season

The Mariners signed Ron Villone, who actually was Seattle's first-round pick in 1992, to be a left-handed setup man for new closer Eddie Guardado. But roster changes and injuries forced Villone into the rotation during the middle of the season. That wasn't his strong suit, but when the year was over, Villone might have been the team's pitching MVP.

Pitching & Defense

Villone's stuff is considered average, though his cut fastball gave lefthanded batters a lot of trouble in 2004. Villone also uses a changeup and a hard slider. The Mariners liked Villone's fearless approach to pitching. He goes after people and isn't afraid to go inside, even to righthanders, which also can get him in trouble. He's an average fielder who does a good job of controlling the running game. He has three pickoffs in each of the past two years.

2005 Outlook

Having Villone in the starting rotation isn't the ideal for a good team. He's regarded as a three-inning pitcher. Anything past that, and he'll often get in trouble. That said, Villone did everything Seattle asked of him in 2004. The best-case scenario for 2005 is that he settles back into a long-relief or a setup role.

Dan Wilson

Position: C
Bats: R **Throws:** R
Ht: 6' 3" **Wt:** 215

Opening Day Age: 36
Born: 3/25/69 in Barrington, IL
ML Seasons: 13

Overall Statistics

	G	AB	R	H	D	T	HR	RBI	SB	BB	SO	Avg	OBP	Slg
'04	103	319	23	80	13	0	2	33	0	26	57	.251	.305	.310
Car.	1288	4159	439	1092	211	13	88	517	23	280	753	.263	.310	.383

2004 Situational Stats

	AB	H	HR	RBI	Avg		AB	H	HR	RBI	Avg
Home	149	34	1	13	.228	LHP	79	16	2	12	.203
Road	170	46	1	20	.271	RHP	240	64	0	21	.267
First Half	207	55	2	24	.266	Sc Pos	86	21	1	32	.244
Scnd Half	112	25	0	9	.223	Clutch	72	18	0	4	.250

2004 Season

The 2004 season was going to be the year Ben Davis finally supplanted Dan Wilson as Seattle's catcher. That didn't happen, as Davis flopped and was traded to the White Sox in the Freddy Garcia deal. Wilson hit .251 in 2004, with a career-low two home runs. He's clearly on the downside of his career, though still a valuable commodity as a backup.

Hitting, Baserunning & Defense

Wilson had a poor second half and played sporadically after catcher Miguel Olivo was obtained from Chicago. Normally solid against lefties, Wilson batted only .203 against southpaws. Wilson has a short, quick stroke, but in 2004, his bat dragged through the strike zone at times. Wilson is good for a young staff. His arm isn't as strong as it once was, though he blocks balls as well as anyone. He runs better than most catchers.

2005 Outlook

The Mariners wanted Wilson back in 2005 for two reasons: to work with a young pitching staff and to mentor Olivo. If Wilson gets more than 300 at-bats, then he's likely playing too much. He has been through the good and bad times with Seattle. A fan favorite, this might be Wilson's last season as a player.

Other Seattle Mariners

Scott Atchison (**Pos**: RHP, **Age**: 29)

	W	L	Pct.	ERA	G	GS	Sv	IP	H	BB	SO	HR	Avg
'04	2	3	.400	3.52	25	0	0	30.2	29	14	36	4	.250
Car.	2	3	.400	3.52	25	0	0	30.2	29	14	36	4	.250

Atchison replaced George Sherrill as Triple-A Tacoma's closer in July. Atchison's gradual move to the pen over the past three years has produced better numbers, and he posted a 1.88 ERA over his final 14 games with the M's. 2005 Outlook: C

Willie Bloomquist (**Pos**: 3B/1B/SS, **Age**: 27, **Bats**: R)

	G	AB	R	H	D	T	HR	RBI	SB	BB	SO	Avg	OBP	Slg
'04	93	188	27	46	10	0	2	18	13	10	48	.245	.283	.330
Car.	194	417	68	110	21	2	3	39	20	34	89	.264	.319	.345

Bloomquist once again played all four infield positions and in the outfield, but hitting percentages have been heading in the wrong direction. He isn't a defensive stud and makes his share of errors. 2005 Outlook: C

Hiram Bocachica (**Pos**: CF/RF, **Age**: 29, **Bats**: R)

	G	AB	R	H	D	T	HR	RBI	SB	BB	SO	Avg	OBP	Slg
'04	50	90	9	22	5	0	3	6	5	12	27	.244	.337	.400
Car.	222	423	53	94	24	1	13	32	12	31	110	.222	.278	.376

A trade to Detroit late in 2002 was an opportunity, but a 1-for-22 April in 2003 ended his Tigers tenure. A strong first half at Triple-A Tacoma in 2004 led to a stint with Seattle. Oakland signed him to a minor league deal in November. 2005 Outlook: C

Masao Kida (**Pos**: RHP, **Age**: 36)

	W	L	Pct.	ERA	G	GS	Sv	IP	H	BB	SO	HR	Avg
'04	0	0	—	5.65	10	0	0	14.1	19	6	10	1	.328
Car.	1	1	.500	5.86	64	2	1	93.2	112	39	68	8	.299

Kida was called up by the Dodgers in August and made three scoreless appearances. When they tried to send him down, Seattle claimed him off waivers. He posted an 8.38 ERA in seven games, but the Mariners re-signed him to a minor league deal. 2005 Outlook: C

Mickey Lopez (**Pos**: 2B, **Age**: 31, **Bats**: B)

	G	AB	R	H	D	T	HR	RBI	SB	BB	SO	Avg	OBP	Slg
'04	6	4	1	1	0	0	0	0	0	1	0	.250	.500	.250
Car.	6	4	1	1	0	0	0	0	0	1	0	.250	.500	.250

Lopez enjoyed one of his better seasons since reaching the Triple-A level in 1998. He earned a September callup, and if he never makes it back, he can say he got a hit in the bigs. A ninth-inning infield single on the final day of the season did the trick. 2005 Outlook: C

Edgar Martinez (**Pos**: DH, **Age**: 42, **Bats**: R)

	G	AB	R	H	D	T	HR	RBI	SB	BB	SO	Avg	OBP	Slg
'04	141	486	45	128	23	0	12	63	1	58	107	.263	.342	.385
	2055	7213	1219	2247	514	15	309	1261	49	1283	1202	.312	.418	.515

Martinez didn't become a regular until he was 27, but he collected 2,247 hits, 309 home runs and career hitting percentages of .312/.418/.515. Injuries limited him to DH duties for much of his career, but what a sweet career it was. 2005 Outlook: D

Julio Mateo (**Pos**: RHP, **Age**: 27)

	W	L	Pct.	ERA	G	GS	Sv	IP	H	BB	SO	HR	Avg
'04	1	2	.333	4.68	45	0	1	57.2	56	16	43	11	.251
Car.	5	2	.714	3.83	107	0	2	164.1	145	41	129	27	.235

Mateo enjoyed a surprising rookie year in 2003, allowing just 69 hits and 13 walks in 85.2 frames. He was as erratic as most of his bullpen mates in 2004, getting roughed up in May and July before elbow tendinitis became an issue in late July. 2005 Outlook: B

Rene Rivera (**Pos**: C, **Age**: 21, **Bats**: R)

	G	AB	R	H	D	T	HR	RBI	SB	BB	SO	Avg	OBP	Slg
'04	2	3	0	0	0	0	0	0	0	0	1	.000	.000	.000
Car.	2	3	0	0	0	0	0	0	0	0	1	.000	.000	.000

A second-round pick in 2001, Rivera spent 2004 in the high Class-A California League and didn't show much at the plate. He's a solid catch-and-throw guy behind the plate, and Seattle's need for a third catcher in September prompted a surprise callup. 2005 Outlook: C

Ramon Santiago (**Pos**: SS, **Age**: 25, **Bats**: B)

	G	AB	R	H	D	T	HR	RBI	SB	BB	SO	Avg	OBP	Slg
'04	19	39	8	7	1	0	0	2	0	3	3	.179	.256	.205
Car.	225	705	82	161	24	6	6	51	18	49	117	.228	.295	.305

Santiago was an impressive defensive prospect coming up in the Detroit system, but a weak bat has kept him from emerging as a starter. He was below the Mendoza line at both Triple-A Tacoma and Seattle in 2004, and a reserve role looks like his calling. 2005 Outlook: C

Rafael Soriano (**Pos**: RHP, **Age**: 25)

	W	L	Pct.	ERA	G	GS	Sv	IP	H	BB	SO	HR	Avg
'04	0	3	.000	13.50	6	0	0	3.1	9	3	3	0	.450
Car.	3	6	.333	3.30	56	8	2	103.2	84	31	103	10	.215

Soriano has a mid-90s heater and hard slider that generated a 1.53 ERA and 68 strikeouts as a 2003 rookie. An oblique injury in spring training was followed by a tender elbow in May, and Soriano had Tommy John surgery in August. He's probably out all season. 2005 Outlook: D

Matt Thornton (**Pos**: LHP, **Age**: 28)

	W	L	Pct.	ERA	G	GS	Sv	IP	H	BB	SO	HR	Avg
'04	1	2	.333	4.13	19	1	0	32.2	30	25	30	2	.250
Car.	1	2	.333	4.13	19	1	0	32.2	30	25	30	2	.250

With a low-90s fastball and nasty slider, Thornton surprised and nearly made the Mariners in the spring of 2002. By that June, he needed Tommy John surgery. A herniated disc limited him to eight starts in 2003, and he's still trying to regain his form. 2005 Outlook: C

Randy Williams (**Pos**: LHP, **Age**: 29)

	W	L	Pct.	ERA	G	GS	Sv	IP	H	BB	SO	HR	Avg
'04	0	0	—	5.79	6	0	0	4.2	3	6	4	0	.188
Car.	0	0	—	5.79	6	0	0	4.2	3	6	4	0	.188

Williams was recalled for the first time on September 11 because of injuries. He had a few decent outings, and in November he was traded to San Diego for Class-A infielder Billy Hogan. 2005 Outlook: C

Seattle Mariners Minor League Prospects

Organization Overview:

The Mariners crashed and burned in 2004, losing 99 games and setting the stage for a younger Seattle club in 2005. The Triple-A rotation at Tacoma featured five impressive arms, all blocked by veterans in Seattle. By early August, all five—Cha Seung Baek, Travis Blackley, Bobby Madritsch, Clint Nageotte and Matt Thornton—had spent time in the majors. They will battle for larger roles in 2005, and many players featured on these pages could get a look. The Mariners are close to getting a payoff on their spree of international signings in recent years. Five players highlighted below were signed out of Australia, South Korea and Venezuela.

Cha Seung Baek

Position: P
Bats: R **Throws:** R
Ht: 6' 4" **Wt:** 190
Opening Day Age: 24
Born: 5/29/80 in Pusan, South Korea

Recent Statistics

	W	L	ERA	G	GS	Sv	IP	H	R	BB	SO	HR
2004 AA San Antonio	0	0	0.00	1	1	0	5.0	2	0	0	5	0
2004 R Az Mariners	0	0	1.29	2	2	0	7.0	3	2	1	5	0
2004 AAA Tacoma	5	4	4.21	14	14	0	72.2	85	41	24	56	7
2004 AL Seattle	2	4	5.52	7	5	0	31.0	35	23	11	20	5

Signed in 1998, Baek endured Tommy John surgery in 2001 and missed most of two seasons. He returned in 2003 and reestablished the command and feel for pitching that made him a prospect. After a midseason bump to Double-A San Antonio, he dominated hitters down the stretch for the Texas League champs. Triple-A Tacoma presented a stiffer challenge, as Baek needed to command both sides of the plate better. Still, he reached Seattle, debuted with two scoreless relief outings and blanked Texas for eight innings in his final 2004 start. Baek mixes four pitches well. He has good sink on his 89-93 MPH fastball and works his curveball at various speeds. He needs to be more aggressive inside.

Travis Blackley

Position: P
Bats: L **Throws:** L
Ht: 6' 3" **Wt:** 190
Opening Day Age: 22
Born: 11/4/82 in Melbourne, Australia

Recent Statistics

	W	L	ERA	G	GS	Sv	IP	H	R	BB	SO	HR
2004 AAA Tacoma	8	6	3.83	19	18	0	110.1	100	49	47	80	14
2004 AL Seattle	1	3	10.04	6	6	0	26.0	35	31	22	16	9

Signed in 2000, Blackley was diagnosed with a small elbow fracture during instructional league in 2001, requiring the insertion of a pin. He made a remarkable recovery and excelled in 2002, fanning 152 in 121.1 innings as the high Class-A California League's youngest pitcher. He was even better at Double-A San Antonio in 2003, going 17-3 (2.61) to lead the minors

in wins. He calls on a high-80s fastball, an excellent curveball, a changeup that is his best pitch, and a cut fastball that he threw naturally after returning from elbow surgery. He struggled with command and confidence early on at Triple-A Tacoma in 2004, but pitched extremely well there near midseason. He joined Seattle, where he repeated his earlier struggles, as Blackley nibbled and didn't attack hitters.

Shin-Soo Choo

Position: OF
Bats: L **Throws:** L
Ht: 5' 11" **Wt:** 178
Opening Day Age: 22
Born: 7/13/82 in Pusan, South Korea

Recent Statistics

	G	AB	R	H	D	T	HR	RBI	SB	BB	SO	Avg
2003 A Inland Empi	110	412	62	118	18	13	9	55	18	44	84	.286
2004 AA San Antonio	132	517	89	163	17	7	15	84	40	56	97	.315

A late-2000 signing, Choo led the Rookie-level Arizona League in walks, triples and runs in 2001. He jumped to full-season Class-A ball and played in the Futures Game in 2002. Only in 2003 did Choo fail to hit .300 over a season, but he still displayed his quick, line-drive stroke and the advanced plate discipline that has generated a career .395 OBP in the minors. He ranked among Double-A Texas League leaders in several offensive categories in a breakout 2004. Choo adjusted better to breaking stuff, though low offerings in the dirt still give him trouble. His 15 homers suggest the power anticipated by the Mariners is emerging. He's nearly a complete player, with impressive defensive skills and instincts, a strong arm and good speed as an outfielder.

Greg Dobbs

Position: 3B
Bats: L **Throws:** R
Ht: 6' 1" **Wt:** 205
Opening Day Age: 26
Born: 7/2/78 in Los Angeles, CA

Recent Statistics

	G	AB	R	H	D	T	HR	RBI	SB	BB	SO	Avg
2004 AA San Antonio	51	203	25	66	14	4	5	34	5	11	23	.325
2004 AAA Tacoma	67	255	28	69	9	2	8	31	4	5	36	.271
2004 AL Seattle	18	53	4	12	1	0	1	9	0	1	14	.226

Dobbs, signed as a nondrafted free agent in May 2001, used his classic lefthanded stroke to bat .324 at two Class-A stops that summer. He ruptured his left Achilles tendon in the second game of the Double-A Texas League campaign in 2003, and missed the rest of the season. Yet, he made a successful return in 2004, batting .295-13-65 in the high minors. He wasn't as effective with the Mariners in September, though he hit .333 (5-for-15) with runners in scoring position. Dobbs was a better defender in 2004, but needs more work on his fielding. If he doesn't make the Seattle roster as a starter, he probably goes to Tacoma to play every day.

Felix Hernandez

Position: P
Bats: R **Throws:** R
Ht: 6' 3" **Wt:** 170

Opening Day Age: 18
Born: 4/8/86 in Valencia, VZ

Recent Statistics

	W	L	ERA	G	GS	Sv	IP	H	R	BB	SO	HR
2003 A Everett	7	2	2.29	11	7	0	55.0	43	17	24	73	2
2003 A Wisconsin	0	0	1.93	2	2	0	14.0	9	4	3	18	1
2004 A Inland Empi	9	3	2.74	16	15	0	92.0	85	31	26	114	5
2004 AA San Antonio	5	1	3.30	10	10	0	57.1	47	23	21	58	3

Signed in July 2002, Hernandez dominated against older college talent in the Rookie-level Northwest League in 2003. He turned 18 the day before his 2004 debut at high Class-A Inland Empire, and he celebrated with a stellar season that involved a strong showing in the Futures Game and ended at Double-A San Antonio. He locates his mid- to high-90s fastball expertly, and his power curve may be an even better pitch. He also called on a promising changeup that he used more as the season progressed. His exceptional body control and mechanics make for an effortless motion. Hernandez may be the best pitching prospect in the game.

Clint Nageotte

Position: P
Bats: R **Throws:** R
Ht: 6' 3" **Wt:** 200

Opening Day Age: 24
Born: 10/25/80 in Parma, OH

Recent Statistics

	W	L	ERA	G	GS	Sv	IP	H	R	BB	SO	HR
2004 AAA Tacoma	6	6	4.46	14	14	0	80.2	78	42	35	63	9
2004 AL Seattle	1	6	7.36	12	5	0	36.2	48	31	27	24	3

A 1999 fifth-round pick, Nageotte has piled up strike-outs with his combo of low-90s fastball and paralyzing slider. He led the minor leagues in whiffs in 2002, before going 11-7 (3.10) for the Double-A Texas League champs in 2003. His two primary pitches are closer material, though Seattle would like him to rely less on his hard-breaking slider. At times in 2004, his changeup was very good and he used it more often. The importance of fastball command hit home with Nageotte at the major league level. It could elevate his game. He may be a better fit for the bullpen, but his progress on his changeup may keep him a starter.

Chris Snelling

Position: OF
Bats: L **Throws:** L
Ht: 5' 10" **Wt:** 165

Opening Day Age: 23
Born: 12/3/81 in North Miami, FL

Recent Statistics

	G	AB	R	H	D	T	HR	RBI	SB	BB	SO	Avg
2003 AA San Antonio	47	180	24	02	12	2	3	25	1	8	30	.333
2003 AAA Tacoma	18	67	11	18	2	0	3	10	1	5	12	.269
2004 R Az Mariners	10	32	8	10	4	1	0	9	1	7	3	.313

Injuries have sidetracked Snelling since he was signed in 1999. He claimed a high Class-A California League batting title in 2001 with a stress fracture in his right ankle. In fact, he's hit .300 in six minor league seasons, despite breaking a thumb in spring training in 2002 and tearing the ACL in his left knee that summer, eight games after joining Seattle. His 2003 season ended with torn meniscus in the same knee, and he accrued just 32 at-bats last summer after spring surgery for a wrist injury. When healthy, Snelling has the skills and instincts to hit for average, show some pop, draw walks and handle any outfield position with a right-field arm.

Jamal Strong

Position: OF
Bats: R **Throws:** R
Ht: 5' 10" **Wt:** 180

Opening Day Age: 26
Born: 8/5/78 in Pasadena, CA

Recent Statistics

	G	AB	R	H	D	T	HR	RBI	SB	BB	SO	Avg
2003 R Az Mariners	2	7	5	5	0	1	0	4	3	3	1	.714
2003 AAA Tacoma	56	210	38	64	6	1	2	19	26	25	38	.305
2003 AL Seattle	12	2	2	0	0	0	0	0	0	0	0	.000
2004 AAA Tacoma	64	238	46	77	11	2	3	24	19	38	28	.324

Drafted in 2000, Strong excels on the strength of little-ball skills and speed. He has a career .408 OBP and 45 steals in 120 games at Triple-A Tacoma the last two seasons. In 2003, he separated a shoulder sliding in spring training and was limited to 70 games. Yet, he batted .305 with a .390 OBP at Tacoma. A knee injury limited Strong to 64 games last summer. While he has kept his little-ball game on track through injuries, Strong can be busted inside and will have to show he can handle the inner half of the plate against big league pitching. His routes in center field still need work, but his speed compensates for his defensive shortcomings.

Others to Watch

Showing impressive power to all fields, outfielder **Wladimir Balentien** (20) set a Rookie-level Arizona League record with 16 homers in 2003, and he totaled 33 extra-base hits in just 187 at-bats. Then he hit 17 more homers in two Class-A stops in 2004. . . A 2001 pick, **Bobby Livingston** (22) was working close to 90 MPH and hitting his spots in 2004, en route to a 12-6 (3.57) season at high Class-A Inland Empire. He gets good sink on his fastball, his secondary pitches were solid, and he added a cutter that runs in on righthanded hitters. . . Righthander **Aaron Taylor** (27) is 6-foot-8 with a mid-90s fastball. He can be intimidating when he has his split-finger pitch and slider working. Shoulder surgery late in 2003 limited him to 42.1 innings last summer, but his arm strength should be better in 2005. His power arm could figure in Seattle's pen. . . The Mariners' first pick of the 2004 draft, shortstop **Matt Tuiasosopo** (18) chose baseball over a football career at the University of Washington. He didn't follow in his father's or brother's NFL footsteps. Matt is very athletic and strong with an impressive bat. He hit a homer in his first pro at-bat in the Rookie-level Arizona League. He was promoted to short season Everett after batting .412 with 11 extra-base hits in 20 rookie ball games.

Tropicana Field

Offense

Tropicana Field has not turned out to be much of a home-run hitters' park. The park has ranked in the middle third of AL stadiums in runs and the bottom third in home runs and batting average. The deep gaps, assymetrical design and oddly angled walls do produce an extraordinary high number of triples.

Defense

The Rays figured out that the best way to cover the spacious outfield is with fast and athletic defenders. But there still can be issues caused by the unusual configuration, along with the problematic catwalks and white-colored roof. Infield play at the Trop can be a bit tricky because of the unusual combination of a synthetic FieldTurf infield with all-dirt basepaths.

Who It Helps the Most

Dewon Brazelton finds the spacious park to his liking, posting spectacularly different numbers there. Carl Crawford has adapted his game the most, hitting 59 points better at home by slashing the ball into the deep gaps and down the lines, and taking advantage of cautious infielders by hitting the ball on the ground and beating out their throws.

Who It Hurts the Most

Righthanded hitters tend to have problems, especially those swinging for the fences, and that was the case with Julio Lugo and Rocco Baldelli. Among pitchers, relievers Trever Miller and Lance Carter had problems, though seemingly not for any particular reasons.

Rookies & Newcomers

With Baldelli likely out until the All-Star break due to a knee injury, speedy outfielder Joey Gathright may get a chance to play regularly. He had problems in several short 2004 stints, but it tends to take new outfielders a while to get comfortable in the surroundings. Infielder B.J. Upton has had problems fielding in the minors, so he too may need an extended adjustment period to the Trop turf.

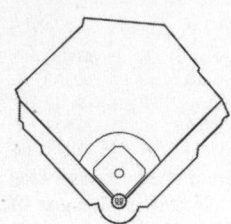

Dimensions: LF-315, LCF-370, CF-404, RCF-370, RF-322

Capacity: 43,969

Elevation: 15 feet

Surface: Turf

Foul Territory: Average

Park Factors

2004 Season

	Home Games			Away Games			
	Devil Rays	Opp	Total	Devil Rays	Opp	Total	Index
G	69	69	138	72	72	144	
Avg	.253	.249	.251	.259	.282	.270	93
AB	2299	2416	4715	2501	2403	4904	100
R	302	323	625	308	438	746	87
H	581	602	1183	648	678	1326	93
2B	110	129	239	129	156	285	87
3B	22	10	32	13	12	25	133
HR	64	84	148	64	91	155	99
BB	203	231	434	197	278	475	95
SO	388	422	810	448	388	836	101
E	49	44	93	62	43	105	92
E-Infield	43	39	82	47	37	84	102
LHB-Avg	.266	.256	.261	.245	.279	.260	100
LHB-HR	41	46	87	40	38	78	111
RHB-Avg	.239	.244	.242	.273	.285	.279	87
RHB-HR	23	38	61	24	53	77	86

2002-2004

	Home Games			Away Games			
	Devil Rays	Opp	Total	Devil Rays	Opp	Total	Index
G	213	213	426	215	215	430	
Avg	.262	.259	.261	.255	.283	.269	97
AB	7277	7534	14811	7516	7177	14693	102
R	929	1099	2028	926	1250	2176	94
H	1909	1951	3860	1917	2032	3949	99
2B	368	413	781	383	453	836	93
3B	55	37	92	41	32	73	125
HR	171	258	429	203	289	492	87
BB	604	794	1398	563	837	1400	99
SO	1326	1297	2623	1401	1116	2517	103
E	149	140	289	163	129	292	100
E-Infield	128	129	257	128	113	241	108
LHB-Avg	.272	.267	.270	.259	.285	.271	100
LHB-HR	111	131	242	109	132	241	98
RHB-Avg	.253	.252	.253	.251	.282	.267	95
RHB-HR	60	127	187	94	157	251	75

2004 Rankings (American League)

- Lowest RHB batting-average factor
- Second-lowest batting-average factor
- Second-lowest run factor
- Second-lowest hit factor
- Second-lowest double factor

Lou Piniella

2004 Season

Lou Piniella didn't have to think hard to say the 2004 season was the toughest he had had as a major league manager. He knew the Rays weren't as bad as they played in a 10-28 start, knew they weren't as good as they looked in a 30-10 run and pleaded with ownership for improvements so they could sustain the momentum they built. Piniella grew increasingly frustrated as the Rays struggled through the second half, then finally found some measure of satisfaction in meeting his preseason prediction of getting out of last place for the first time and winning a team-record 70 games.

Offense

Piniella likes to keep things moving, and the Rays did that by ranking second in the league in stolen bases while hitting into the second-fewest double plays. He tried numerous lineups to get the most out of a roster that was heavy on speed but light on power. Piniella likes to alternate right- and lefthanded hitters throughout the lineup, but would occasionally get away from that to try different combinations. Despite his best efforts, the Rays were last in the league in average, and second-to-last in runs and home runs.

Pitching & Defense

Chuck Hernandez did an admirable job in his first year as pitching coach, given the inexperience of the staff and the expectations Piniella had for it. The Rays had one of the more successful bullpens in the league, but the ineffectiveness of the starters forced Piniella to go to the pen for a major league-high 549.1 innings. Piniella likes to put strong defensive teams on the field, and was particularly perturbed with the sloppy play that dogged the Rays in the second half.

2005 Outlook

Piniella clearly expected the Rays to be better than they have been, and admitted the process has been humbling. He seems resigned to the team making only marginal improvements this winter, and probably again next winter, which means he is likely to finish his contract in 2006 and then move on.

Born: 8/28/43 in Tampa, FL

Playing Experience: 1964-1984, Bal, Cle, KC, NYY

Managerial Experience: 18 seasons

Manager Statistics

Year	Team, Lg	W	L	Pct	GB	Finish
2004	Tampa Bay, AL	70	91	.435	30.5	4th East
18 Seasons		1452	1325	.523	–	–

2004 Starting Pitchers by Days Rest

	<=3	4	5	6+
Devil Rays Starts	0	77	35	35
Devil Rays ERA	–	5.09	6.18	5.60
AL Avg Starts	2	82	47	21
AL ERA	5.36	4.87	4.65	4.93

2004 Situational Stats

	Lou Piniella	AL Average
Hit & Run Success %	37.7	36.8
Stolen Base Success %	75.9	68.6
Platoon Pct.	62.5	61.6
Defensive Subs	25	21
High-Pitch Outings	8	5
Quick/Slow Hooks	21/13	20/16
Sacrifice Attempts	46	53

2004 Rankings (American League)

- 1st in stolen-base percentage, steals of third base (21), steals of home plate (1) and saves with over 1 inning pitched (15)
- 2nd in stolen base attempts (174), steals of second base (110), mid-inning pitching changes (207) and first-batter platoon percentage
- 3rd in pitchouts with a runner moving (6) and starts with over 120 pitches (8)

Danys Baez

2004 Season

The Devil Rays signed Danys Baez to be their closer, and he couldn't have done a much better job. He was sixth in the AL with 30 saves, fourth with a 90.9 save percentage and fourth with saves in 43 percent of his team's victories. After blowing opportunities in consecutive mid-June outings, he ran off a streak of 18 straight saves, one shy of Roberto Hernandez' team record. He held hitters to a .198 average with men on base, and allowed only one hit in 11 bases-loaded at-bats.

Pitching

Baez struggled when the Indians bounced him between the bullpen and the rotation, but he excelled when the Rays told him to concentrate solely on closing. Baez throws hard, with a fastball regularly in the mid- to upper 90s, and he has proved to be strong and durable. In Cleveland, he had trouble controlling his emotions and tended to overthrow, but that was not an issue in Tampa Bay. The Rays worked with him on throwing more first-pitch strikes, which allows him to later expand the strike zone, and he needs to cut down on his walks.

Defense

Baez is strong, competitive and a decent athlete, and as a result tends to do a pretty good job defensively. He has been known to rush a throw or two to first base. He could do a better job of holding on runners, and is working on it.

2005 Outlook

The Rays couldn't have been more pleased with the job Baez did and will be happy with more of the same, as they hope to have even more games that need to be saved. Baez evolved into something of a leader among the Rays' younger relievers, and team officials would like the mentoring to continue. If Jesus Colome shows the potential to be a reliable closer, Baez could be available in a trade as the season goes on, since he makes $3.5 million in 2005 and the Rays hold a $4 million option for 2006.

Position: RP
Bats: R **Throws:** R
Ht: 6' 3" **Wt:** 225

Opening Day Age: 27
Born: 9/10/77 in Pinar del Rio, Cuba
ML Seasons: 4
Pronunciation: DAN-ees BUY-ez

Overall Statistics

	W	L	Pct.	ERA	G	GS	Sv	IP	H	BB	SO	HR	Avg
'04	4	4	.500	3.57	62	0	30	68.0	60	29	52	6	.237
Car.	21	27	.438	3.86	217	26	61	359.1	319	154	300	34	.238

2004 Pitching Profile

	Danys Baez	AL Average
Overall Strike %	63.0	62.3
1st Pitch Strike %	57.6	58.1
Ratio	1.31	1.42
Strikeouts per 9 IP	6.88	6.45
Walks per 9 IP	3.84	3.34
Home Runs per 9 IP	0.79	1.15
Strikeout/Walk Ratio	1.79	1.93
Groundball/Flyball Ratio	1.05	1.17

2004 Situational Stats

	W	L	ERA	Sv	IP		AB	H	HR	RBI	Avg
Home	4	2	2.76	18	42.1	LHB	123	31	3	18	.252
Road	0	2	4.91	12	25.2	RHB	130	29	3	11	.223
First Half	3	1	3.26	17	38.2	Sc Pos	90	18	3	25	.200
Scnd Half	1	3	3.99	13	29.1	Clutch	160	39	3	22	.244

2004 Rankings (American League)

- 4th in save percentage (90.9)
- 5th in games finished (59)
- 6th in saves
- Led the Devil Rays in games pitched, saves, games finished (59), save percentage (90.9), blown saves (3) and relief losses (4)

Rocco Baldelli

2004 Season

Rocco Baldelli's 2004 season wasn't nearly as disappointing as some made it out to be. The real bummer was the serious knee injury he sustained in late October that could keep him out for half the 2005 campaign. Baldelli started 2004 slow after adding muscle in hopes of staying stronger, and battled a series of injuries, including leg problems that landed him on the DL in August. While his average and extra-base hits were down, he did hit more homers, struck out less and played solid defense.

Hitting

Baldelli has been balancing the somewhat conflicting directives of trying to accelerate the development of his power while also learning to be more disciplined at the plate. He tends to be too aggressive at times, and the Rays are preaching a happy medium as he becomes more comfortable with hitting breaking balls. His average figures to increase as he better learns the strike zone. Baldelli also has tremendous speed, which makes bunting and infield hits a key part of his game, though the knee injury could change that.

Baserunning & Defense

Baldelli had been considered one of the fastest righthanded hitters in the majors, though that probably won't be the case, at least initially, as he recovers from the November surgery to repair the ACL tear in his left knee. He is an instinctive and smart player who runs the bases well. His defense improved as he got more comfortable playing inside Tropicana Field, and his athleticism makes him an exciting defender. His arm is above-average.

2005 Outlook

It still seems unlikely that Baldelli will be back in the Rays' lineup much before the All-Star break, and possibly not until after. The Rays had toyed with the idea of moving him to right field, and that talk may resurface depending on how he recovers. Before the injury, the Rays were hoping to bolster their lineup enough to get Baldelli out of the middle, and either hit him second or drop him to sixth or so.

Position: CF/DH
Bats: R **Throws:** R
Ht: 6' 4" **Wt:** 187

Opening Day Age: 23
Born: 9/25/81 in Woonsocket, RI
ML Seasons: 2

Overall Statistics

	G	AB	R	H	D	T	HR	RBI	SB	BB	SO	Avg	OBP	Slg
'04	136	518	79	145	27	3	16	74	17	30	88	.280	.326	.436
Car.	292	1155	168	329	59	11	27	152	44	60	216	.285	.326	.425

Where He Hits the Ball

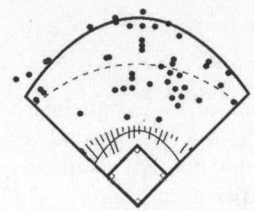 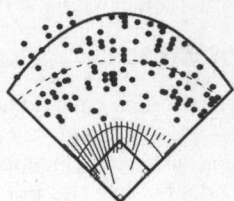

Vs. LHP   **Vs. RHP**

2004 Situational Stats

	AB	H	HR	RBI	Avg		AB	H	HR	RBI	Avg
Home	238	65	6	29	.273	LHP	124	41	6	19	.331
Road	280	80	10	45	.286	RHP	394	104	10	55	.264
First Half	308	89	7	36	.289	Sc Pos	149	41	5	57	.275
Scnd Half	210	56	9	38	.267	Clutch	60	16	2	9	.267

2004 Rankings (American League)

- 1st in lowest fielding percentage in center field (.978)
- 2nd in errors in center field (8)
- 5th in stolen-base percentage (81.0)
- Led the Devil Rays in stolen-base percentage (81.0), batting average vs. lefthanded pitchers and cleanup slugging percentage (.495)

Dewon Brazelton

2004 Season

Dewon Brazelton came into the 2004 season looking like a different pitcher than the Rays had seen, going back to the delivery he used in college and showing the benefits of working hard to get into better shape. The result was a better pitcher, but one who still has room for considerable improvement. There were times, such as a June 25 start against Florida, when he took a no-hitter into the eighth inning, when he looked to be every bit the frontline starter the Rays expected to get. But there were also times, such as the way he finished 0-4, 8.17 in his last seven starts, that he looked every bit the young, tentative, inconsistent starter. He also has to overcome a mental block about pitching on the road—in 15 career starts away from Tropicana, he is 0-11.

Pitching

Brazelton has two quality major league pitches, a fastball that usually is in the low 90s with movement and a changeup that can just absolutely handcuff even the most experienced hitters. The Rays have been working with him for years on refining his slider as his third pitch and, even more difficult, convincing him it is good enough to be used in tough situations.

Defense

He may be pitching like the Brazelton of old, but when it comes to fielding and running, he just looks like an old Brazelton. Even with an extensive offseason workout program, Brazelton is not going to be mistaken for any of the team's top athletes. Previous knee problems are a bit of an issue when he comes off the mound.

2005 Outlook

Brazelton will be entering his fourth pro season, still looking to spend a whole year in the big leagues. The Rays hope to acquire a couple of veteran starters to allow younger pitchers such as Brazelton, Scott Kazmir and Doug Waechter to work in the less pressurized 3-4-5 spots. If so, they would like to see what Brazelton can do over 30-plus starts.

Position: SP
Bats: R **Throws:** R
Ht: 6' 4" **Wt:** 214

Opening Day Age: 24
Born: 6/16/80 in Tullahoma, TN
ML Seasons: 3
Pronunciation:
de-wan bra-zel-ton

Overall Statistics

	W	L	Pct.	ERA	G	GS	Sv	IP	H	BB	SO	HR	Avg
'04	6	8	.429	4.77	22	21	0	120.2	121	53	64	12	.260
Car.	7	15	.318	5.34	34	33	0	182.0	190	82	93	24	.270

2004 Pitching Profile

	Dewon Brazelton	AL Average
Overall Strike %	61.1	62.3
1st Pitch Strike %	54.5	58.1
Ratio	1.44	1.42
Strikeouts per 9 IP	4.77	6.45
Walks per 9 IP	3.95	3.34
Home Runs per 9 IP	0.90	1.15
Strikeout/Walk Ratio	1.21	1.93
Groundball/Flyball Ratio	0.78	1.17

2004 Situational Stats

	W	L	ERA	Sv	IP		AB	H	HR	RBI	Avg
Home	6	3	2.90	0	87.0	LHB	257	65	5	27	.253
Road	0	5	9.62	0	33.2	RHB	208	56	7	30	.269
First Half	2	2	3.20	0	39.1	Sc Pos	112	33	5	45	.295
Scnd Half	4	6	5.53	0	81.1	Clutch	26	6	0	2	.231

2004 Rankings (American League)

- 3rd in lowest ERA at home
- 9th in hit batsmen (11)
- Led the Devil Rays in pickoff throws (81), lowest ERA at home and fewest home runs allowed per nine innings (.90)

Carl Crawford

2004 Season

Carl Crawford made his first All-Star team, won Devil Rays MVP honors, just missed his first Gold Glove and led the majors in triples and the American League in stolen bases. He has recored at least 175 hits and 50 steals in each of the past two seasons, and is only the 11th American League player (done 18 times) to total 50 extra-base hits, 50 steals and 100 runs in a single campaign.

Hitting

Crawford continued to benefit in 2004 from two big changes he made to his game the year before—he opened his stance midway through the 2003 season at the urging of hitting coach Lee Elia and has been a .300 hitter since, and he has committed himself to working tirelessly to get better. Crawford is a spectacular athlete with sprinters' speed. He is evolving from a slap hitter to a burgeoning power hitter who drives the ball into the gaps and legs out doubles and triples.

Baserunning & Defense

Crawford still is working on being a polished baserunner, and he likely will get bolder when he learns the pitchers better. He is known for his running and hitting, which makes his defensive contributions underrated. His speed and athleticism allow him to cover vast amounts of turf and put himself in position to attempt plays others would have no chance on. He has a decent arm, and can make it look better with good positioning and a quick release.

2005 Outlook

With Rocco Baldelli likely out until after the All-Star break because of a knee injury, Crawford moves from left to center field, at least for the first half of the season. And if Crawford's power continues to develop, it may not be long until he moves down in the order, dropping from leadoff to second or third. If he continues to improve, he may add a batting title and a Gold Glove to the stolen-base titles he is likely to keep winning for years.

Position: LF/CF
Bats: L **Throws:** L
Ht: 6' 2" **Wt:** 210

Opening Day Age: 23
Born: 8/5/81 in Houston, TX
ML Seasons: 3

Overall Statistics

	G	AB	R	H	D	T	HR	RBI	SB	BB	SO	Avg	OBP	Slg
'04	152	626	104	185	26	19	11	55	59	35	81	.296	.331	.450
Car.	366	1515	207	429	55	34	18	139	123	70	224	.283	.315	.400

Where He Hits the Ball

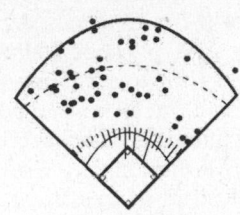

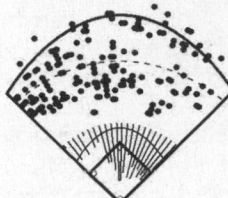

Vs. LHP   **Vs. RHP**

2004 Situational Stats

	AB	H	HR	RBI	Avg		AB	H	HR	RBI	Avg
Home	304	99	6	33	.326	LHP	146	43	1	11	.295
Road	322	86	5	22	.267	RHP	480	142	10	44	.296
First Half	362	110	4	34	.304	Sc Pos	116	34	3	44	.293
Scnd Half	264	75	7	21	.284	Clutch	86	23	1	9	.267

2004 Rankings (American League)

- 1st in triples, stolen bases and caught stealing (15)
- 2nd in fielding percentage in left field (.996)
- 3rd in steals of third (9)
- 4th in singles and fewest GDPs per GDP situation (2.2%)
- Led the Devil Rays in at-bats, runs scored, hits, singles, triples, stolen bases, caught stealing (15), plate appearances (672), steals of third (9), fewest GDPs per GDP situation (2.2%), batting average with the bases loaded (.500), batting average vs. righthanded pitchers, on-base percentage for a leadoff hitter (.337), batting average at home and batting average with two strikes (.245)

Tampa Bay

Jose Cruz Jr.

2004 Season

The Devil Rays signed Jose Cruz Jr. thinking he would hit around .300, total close to 30 homers with 100 RBI, deliver some clutch hits, steal bases and play excellent defense. They missed on all fronts. Instead they got a player who had a few hot streaks but was consistently inconsistent at the plate, seemed to lose interest as the season wore on, failed to deliver in the clutch, took few chances on the bases and made a whopping 10 errors, the second highest total among all major league outfielders.

Hitting

Cruz started out the year hitting just about anything that was thrown at him, but after two weeks he went into a career-worst 0-for-37 streak. AL pitchers soon figured out what NL pitchers did the year before, that they can get Cruz to get himself out. After a decent May and June, he started swinging at just about everything and had only 21 extra-base hits after the All-Star break. Cruz ranked among the league leaders in free passes through mid-August, then drew only six more over the final six weeks and finished with 76.

Baserunning & Defense

Manager Lou Piniella hoped Cruz would regain the form and aggressiveness that made him a 30-30 man for Toronto in 2001. Cruz didn't do it at the plate or on the bases, stealing only 11 times in 17 attempts. As disappointing as his offense was, his poor defense was mindboggling. Cruz won a Gold Glove in 2003 and had made only 10 errors total in his four previous seasons. He seemed hesitant and unsure when playing at Tropicana Field.

2005 Outlook

Cruz' career is starting to take on a pattern. He gets off to a decent start and struggles as the year goes on. The Rays have him under contract for 2005. Until Rocco Baldelli's offseason knee injury, the Rays were looking to trade Cruz before or during the season, knowing super-prospect Delmon Young is getting close to taking over in right field. Perhaps Cruz will be moved near the trade deadline during the second half.

Position: RF
Bats: B **Throws:** R
Ht: 6' 0" **Wt:** 210

Opening Day Age: 30
Born: 4/19/74 in Arroyo, PR
ML Seasons: 8

Overall Statistics

	G	AB	R	H	D	T	HR	RBI	SB	BB	SO	Avg	OBP	Slg
'04	153	545	76	132	25	8	21	78	11	76	117	.242	.333	.433
Car.	1058	3826	590	956	199	30	175	535	102	507	918	.250	.336	.455

Where He Hits the Ball

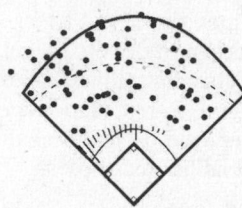 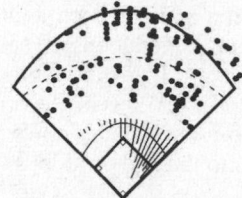

Vs. LHP   **Vs. RHP**

2004 Situational Stats

	AB	H	HR	RBI	Avg		AB	H	HR	RBI	Avg
Home	276	71	13	43	.257	LHP	159	42	6	22	.264
Road	269	61	8	35	.227	RHP	386	90	15	56	.233
First Half	275	66	14	45	.240	Sc Pos	142	34	8	59	.239
Scnd Half	270	66	7	33	.244	Clutch	71	19	5	12	.268

2004 Rankings (American League)

- 1st in errors in right field (10), lowest batting average vs. righthanded pitchers and lowest fielding percentage in right field (.970)
- 3rd in lowest batting average on the road
- 4th in sacrifice flies (8)
- 5th in lowest batting average and highest percentage of swings on the first pitch (37.9)
- 6th in triples
- 8th in lowest groundball-flyball ratio (0.8)
- Led the Devil Rays in sacrifice flies (8), walks and strikeouts

Toby Hall

2004 Season

Toby Hall did a better job calling pitches in his second full season in the big leagues, but the rest of his game didn't improve. Hall drove in more runs than he had before, but he hit with less power and his average again hovered around the .250 mark after a late-season slump. He went backward in throwing out runners, his percentage plummeting from 41.3 percent in 2003 to 27.9 percent.

Hitting

Hall does a good job putting the ball in play, striking out only once every 10.8 plate appearances. The problem is that the Rays need their catcher to be more than a singles hitter. Hall is so protective of the strike zone that he often doesn't hit the ball hard enough to get extra-base hits. The Rays would prefer he take some more aggressive and explosive swings, even if it means striking out a few more times. He also falls into an occasional rut of chasing breaking balls outside the zone.

Baserunning & Defense

Hall's drop-off in thwarting potential basestealers wasn't totally his fault, since the Rays had several young pitchers who weren't good at holding on runners. He has a tremendous arm but sometimes his mechanics go awry, and he has to work on them constantly to stay sharp. His other work behind the plate has improved, which is important because of the demands manager Lou Piniella places on his catcher. He could get better at blocking pitches by being more mobile. As a baserunner, Hall is your typically slow catcher.

2005 Outlook

It doesn't appear as though Hall is going to develop into the heavy-hitting, middle-of-the-lineup slugger the Rays were hoping for. Since he is eligible for arbitration for the first time, Tampa is going to consider other options. Most likely the team will bring him back and hope to get him to hit with more power, improving at least into the 15-20 homer range.

Position: C
Bats: R **Throws:** R
Ht: 6' 3" **Wt:** 240

Opening Day Age: 29
Born: 10/21/75 in Tacoma, WA
ML Seasons: 5

Overall Statistics

	G	AB	R	H	D	T	HR	RBI	SB	BB	SO	Avg	OBP	Slg
'04	119	404	35	103	21	0	8	60	0	24	41	.255	.300	.366
Car.	387	1397	151	363	79	1	31	180	2	69	124	.260	.299	.384

Where He Hits the Ball

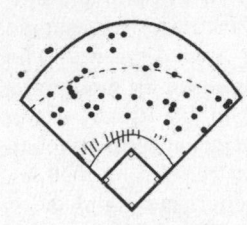
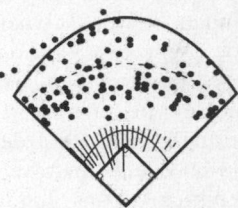

Vs. LHP   **Vs. RHP**

2004 Situational Stats

	AB	H	HR	RBI	Avg		AB	H	HR	RBI	Avg
Home	192	52	6	31	.271	LHP	102	30	3	14	.294
Road	212	51	2	29	.241	RHP	302	73	5	46	.242
First Half	209	60	5	34	.287	Sc Pos	115	32	3	51	.278
Scnd Half	195	43	3	26	.221	Clutch	55	11	3	11	.200

2004 Rankings (American League)

- 1st in most GDPs per GDP situation (26.7%)
- 2nd in lowest percentage of pitches taken (45.7)
- 6th in errors at catcher (6)
- 7th in fielding percentage at catcher (.992) and GDPs (20)
- Led the Devil Rays in GDPs (20)

Mark Hendrickson

2004 Season

The Devil Rays were hoping for big things when they acquired Mark Hendrickson from Toronto, though they weren't expecting him to be their big winner. Despite a rough start, a brutal finish and two brief demotions from the rotation, Hendrickson won a team-high 10 games and led the Rays with 30 starts and 183.1 innings. He had stretches when he was very, very good. But he also had times when he was very bad, such as an 0-5, 10.41 August as part of an eight-game winless streak.

Pitching

Hendrickson often is measured against Randy Johnson because they are both tall, thin and left-handed, but that is where the comparisons should stop. Whereas Johnson is a hard-thrower who racks up strikeouts, Hendrickson is more of a finesse type, mixing a fastball that usually sits in the high 80s with a decent changeup, curveball and a cutter that he can run in on batters. Hendrickson has gotten better, but righthanded batters still give him trouble. Hendrickson sometimes gets too concerned about throwing strikes, and in an effort to get ahead in the count gets hit hard on first pitches. The Rays have tried, with mixed results, to get him to be more aggressive outside the strike zone and move the ball around.

Defense

The former NBA forward is a relatively good athlete and fields his position better than one would expect for someone his size. He is agile and has good hands, though he occasionally leaves himself in awkward fielding positions. Hendrickson is working on getting better control of the running game, reducing the number of bases stolen against him from 20 in 2003 to 11.

2005 Outlook

Hendrickson turned 30 last summer, but the Rays consider him to have a relatively young arm since he spent four years in the NBA and has pitched only two full seasons in the big leagues. While he is not going to dominate like, say, Johnson, Hendrickson could develop into a dependable middle-of-the-rotation starter.

Position: SP
Bats: L **Throws:** L
Ht: 6' 9" **Wt:** 230

Opening Day Age: 30
Born: 6/23/74 in Mount Vernon, WA
ML Seasons: 3

Overall Statistics

	W	L	Pct.	ERA	G	GS	Sv	IP	H	BB	SO	HR	Avg
'04	10	15	.400	4.81	32	30	0	183.1	211	46	87	21	.285
Car.	22	24	.478	4.88	78	64	0	378.1	443	98	184	46	.292

2004 Pitching Profile

	Mark Hendrickson	AL Average
Overall Strike %	61.2	62.3
1st Pitch Strike %	55.2	58.1
Ratio	1.40	1.42
Strikeouts per 9 IP	4.27	6.45
Walks per 9 IP	2.26	3.34
Home Runs per 9 IP	1.03	1.15
Strikeout/Walk Ratio	1.89	1.93
Groundball/Flyball Ratio	1.34	1.17

2004 Situational Stats

	W	L	ERA	Sv	IP		AB	H	HR	RBI	Avg
Home	6	7	4.56	0	106.2	LHB	169	42	5	27	.249
Road	4	8	5.17	0	76.2	RHB	572	169	16	73	.295
First Half	6	7	4.59	0	102.0	Sc Pos	184	66	3	79	.359
Scnd Half	4	8	5.09	0	81.1	Clutch	34	13	0	2	.382

2004 Rankings (American League)

- 1st in fielding percentage at pitcher (1.000) and highest batting average allowed with runners in scoring position
- 3rd in losses
- 4th in fewest strikeouts per nine innings (4.3)
- 5th in balks (2) and least run support per nine innings (4.2)
- 6th in highest stolen-base percentage allowed (84.6)
- 8th in complete games (2), fewest pitches thrown per batter (3.59) and lowest winning percentage
- 9th in fewest walks per nine innings (2.3)
- Led the Devil Rays in wins, losses, games started, complete games (2), innings pitched, hits allowed, batters faced (803), home runs allowed, balks (2), pitches thrown (2,881), stolen bases allowed (11) and GDPs induced (17)

Aubrey Huff

2004 Season

Aubrey Huff got off to such a poor start that he was not disappointed to finish just shy of a second straight season of hitting .300 with 30 homers. Once Huff got going, he stayed in a groove most of the season, hitting .319 with 26 homers and 95 RBI over his final 129 games. He did so despite changing positions again by moving back to third base, and battling a sore back that ended his consecutive games played streak at 398.

Hitting

Huff often is described as a professional hitter, as much for what he does and how easy he makes it look, with good mechanics that produce a natural sweet swing. He has done an excellent job learning to hit lefties and to stop chasing pitches off the plate. Huff knows he can hit just about any fastball and occasionally will sit and wait for one. The Rays want him to look more frequently for breaking balls and changeups and hit them too.

Baserunning & Defense

When Huff was moved to right field after struggling defensively at third base to open the 2003 season, it seemed his days at the hot corner were over. But when manager Lou Piniella unexpectedly moved him back there a week into the 2004 season, he did fine. Huff is neither acrobatic nor extremely athletic, but he makes most of the routine plays, much as he does when playing first. In the outfield, he is a little more limited but can hold his own. Huff is not especially fleet but is a solid baserunner.

2005 Outlook

The Rays headed into the offseason with Huff's position unsettled by design, considering him, in the words of manager Lou Piniella, "a floater." Most likely Huff will be the starter at first base, but depending on what other moves the Rays make, he could end up at third, in right or left field, or at DH. The club might want to think twice about that since he hit only .236 as a DH in 2004.

Position: 3B/1B/DH
Bats: L **Throws:** R
Ht: 6' 4" **Wt:** 231

Opening Day Age: 28
Born: 12/20/76 in Marion, OH
ML Seasons: 5

Overall Statistics

	G	AB	R	H	D	T	HR	RBI	SB	BB	SO	Avg	OBP	Slg
'04	157	600	92	178	27	2	29	104	5	56	74	.297	.360	.493
Car.	582	2223	304	655	131	6	98	329	12	174	299	.295	.348	.491

Where He Hits the Ball

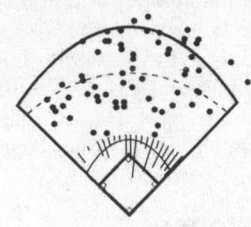
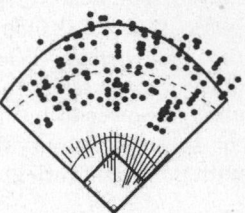

Vs. LHP   **Vs. RHP**

2004 Situational Stats

	AB	H	HR	RBI	Avg		AB	H	HR	RBI	Avg
Home	303	88	16	57	.290	LHP	184	56	8	39	.304
Road	297	90	13	47	.303	RHP	416	122	21	65	.293
First Half	334	90	13	52	.269	Sc Pos	159	43	7	74	.270
Scnd Half	266	88	16	52	.331	Clutch	81	24	5	16	.296

2004 Rankings (American League)

- 1st in lowest batting average with the bases loaded (.000)
- 6th in highest percentage of swings put into play (50.9)
- 7th in games played
- 8th in errors at third base (12)
- Led the Devil Rays in batting average, home runs, total bases (296), RBI, times on base (240), games played and slugging percentage

Julio Lugo

2004 Season

Julio Lugo established himself as a starting player with a solid 2004 season, though it isn't clear where he will be starting. The Rays briefly moved him to second base, then quickly moved him back to shortstop. Lugo seemed to tire as the season wore on, but he still put up solid numbers. He led the Rays in hitting with runners in scoring position at .309, but his 25 errors were the second most by any major league shortstop.

Hitting

One of Lugo's biggest problems is trying too hard to come up with big hits, often jumping at pitches and swinging for the fences. He made strides to correct that, nearly tripling his number of doubles while hitting less than half as many home runs as the year before. When Lugo stays within his game, he can spray the ball around the field with enough power to hit it into the gaps. He also has the speed and ability to scratch his way onto base with bunts and infield hits.

Baserunning & Defense

With above-average speed, Lugo can be a force on the bases, and should be able to match or surpass the 21 steals he logged last year. His natural aggressiveness makes him a constant threat to take an extra base. His defense is unsteady, but he is one of those players who will make several spectacular plays in a row, then boot a routine play. Most of his troubles come from erratic throws that usually are caused by fundamental mistakes.

2005 Outlook

Tampa Bay officials debate whether they should pay Lugo his arbitration-inflated salary or trade him, and whether they should keep him at shortstop or move him to second to make room for top prospect B.J. Upton. At the same time, manager Lou Piniella said he expected Lugo to be at shortstop and went so far as to call him the heart and soul of the team. Eventually, Upton will get his chance at short, but Lugo may keep him waiting.

Position: SS
Bats: R **Throws:** R
Ht: 6' 1" **Wt:** 170

Opening Day Age: 29
Born: 11/16/75 in Barahona, DR
ML Seasons: 5
Pronunciation: lou-GO

Overall Statistics

	G	AB	R	H	D	T	HR	RBI	SB	BB	SO	Avg	OBP	Slg
'04	157	581	83	160	41	4	7	75	21	54	106	.275	.338	.396
Car.	640	2334	363	633	114	17	50	242	76	209	489	.271	.334	.399

Where He Hits the Ball

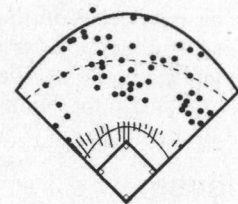 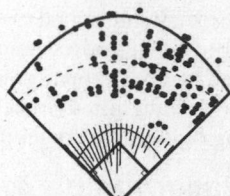

Vs. LHP   **Vs. RHP**

2004 Situational Stats

	AB	H	HR	RBI	Avg		AB	H	HR	RBI	Avg
Home	282	66	3	37	.234	LHP	150	45	0	19	.300
Road	299	94	4	38	.314	RHP	431	115	7	56	.267
First Half	315	90	6	50	.286	Sc Pos	152	47	2	65	.309
Scnd Half	266	70	1	25	.263	Clutch	85	27	1	10	.318

2004 Rankings (American League)

- 2nd in errors at shortstop (25) and lowest fielding percentage at shortstop (.963)
- 3rd in lowest batting average at home
- 4th in sacrifice flies (8)
- 5th in steals of third (7) and lowest HR frequency (83.0 ABs per HR)
- 6th in doubles and stolen-base percentage (80.8)
- 7th in games played
- Led the Devil Rays in doubles, sacrifice bunts (7), sacrifice flies (8), pitches seen (2,490), games played, bunts in play (20), batting average with runners in scoring position, batting average in the clutch, and batting average on the road

Tino Martinez

2004 Season

While the Cardinals may have felt (correctly it turns out) they were better off in 2004 without Tino Martinez, the Devil Rays definitely felt they were better with him, especially with St. Louis paying $7 million of his $7.5 million salary. Martinez had a relatively happy homecoming playing in his native Tampa Bay area, re-establishing himself offensively despite his fewest at-bats in a decade.

Hitting

Martinez' bat speed has naturally slowed with age, and the deterioration can leave him vulnerable to high fastballs, but he can make up for it with his smarts at the plate. He struggled against lefthanders during two years in the NL, but hit a respectable .246 with nine homers against them in 2004. One thing he brought to the Rays was the trademark patience he developed during his glory days with the Yankees.

Baserunning & Defense

Martinez is one of the slowest runners in the game, but at least he knows it and makes smart decisions on the bases. He did have a triple and three stolen bases during the season. While Martinez' range has diminished some, his hands are soft and his experience helps him be in the right position for most plays. He ranked second in the AL with a .997 fielding percentage, the fourth straight year, and seventh overall, he was first or second in his league.

2005 Outlook

The "bad guy" whispers that followed Martinez out of St. Louis couldn't have seemed more wrong, as he was a tremendous team leader and solid veteran presence in Tampa Bay. While the Rays declined his $8 million option, they have interest in bringing him back but may want to see what other holes they can fill first. Martinez, meanwhile, has some interest in coming back but wants to see if the team is improved. He probably would be more effective batting lower in the order on a better team than hitting fourth for the Rays.

Position: 1B/DH
Bats: L **Throws:** R
Ht: 6' 2" **Wt:** 230

Opening Day Age: 37
Born: 12/7/67 in Tampa, FL
ML Seasons: 15

Overall Statistics

G	AB	R	H	D	T	HR	RBI	SB	BB	SO	Avg	OBP	Slg
138	458	63	120	20	1	23	76	3	66	72	.262	.362	.461
1892	6808	965	1852	356	21	322	1222	25	742	1015	.272	.345	.472

Where He Hits the Ball

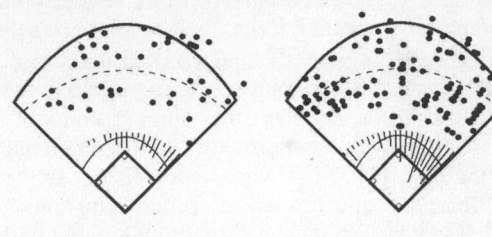

Vs. LHP   **Vs. RHP**

2004 Situational Stats

	AB	H	HR	RBI	Avg		AB	H	HR	RBI	Avg
Home	233	59	9	33	.253	LHP	126	31	9	29	.246
Road	225	61	14	43	.271	RHP	332	89	14	47	.268
First Half	237	64	13	44	.270	Sc Pos	119	29	8	54	.244
Scnd Half	221	56	10	32	.253	Clutch	61	12	2	7	.197

2004 Rankings (American League)

- 2nd in fielding percentage at first base (.997)
- 4th in lowest cleanup slugging percentage (.392)
- Led the Devil Rays in intentional walks (9), hit by pitch (9), on-base percentage, HR frequency (19.9 ABs per HR), most pitches seen per plate appearance (3.88), highest percentage of pitches taken (59.4) and lowest percentage of swings on the first pitch (19.3)

Tampa Bay

B.J. Upton

2004 Season

The Devil Rays decided by August that B.J. Upton was ready and made him the youngest player in the majors at age 19. The second overall pick in 2002, he hit the ball well and, at times, with power; showcased tremendous athletic skills, especially an extraordinary arm and excellent speed; and made plenty of seemingly careless defensive mistakes. In 41 starts, Upton didn't go more than two games without a hit. But he made seven errors in 16 games at shortstop, prompting a move to third base.

Hitting

Upton's talent is extraordinary and his strength surprising, given his relatively small frame. With good hands and quick wrists, he has an extremely live bat, and impressed enough that manager Lou Piniella was making open references to the young Alex Rodriguez. But there are things Upton needs to do better, such as improving against righthanded pitching, using his whole body in his swing, and learning how to adjust to the adjustments pitchers make to him, such as getting him out with breaking balls away.

Baserunning & Defense

Upton is known as a five-tool player, and his foot speed should not be underrated as a tremendous weapon. Defense is the big area of concern, as evidenced by the 91 errors he made in 228 minor league games at shortstop. Upton has the ability to make spectacular plays. His problem has been occasional lapses on what seem to be routine plays. Of particular concern have been his throws when he fails to set himself properly.

2005 Outlook

The Rays have to make several decisions about Upton, but the biggest one is whether they think his bat advanced enough to help them now while he continues to work on his shortstop defense. If so, he could make the team as the starting third baseman or in the outfield as the Rays patch the hole left by Rocco Baldelli's knee injury. If not, they will send Upton back to Triple-A, at least for a few months.

Position: SS/3B/DH
Bats: R **Throws:** R
Ht: 6' 3" **Wt:** 180

Opening Day Age: 20
Born: 8/21/84 in Norfolk, VA
ML Seasons: 1

Overall Statistics

	G	AB	R	H	D	T	HR	RBI	SB	BB	SO	Avg	OBP	Slg
'04	45	159	19	41	8	2	4	12	4	15	46	.258	.324	.409
Car.	45	159	19	41	8	2	4	12	4	15	46	.258	.324	.409

Where He Hits the Ball

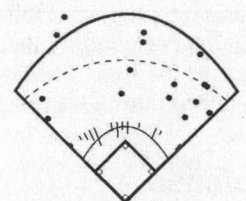 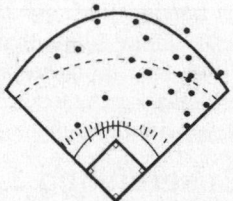

Vs. LHP   **Vs. RHP**

2004 Situational Stats

	AB	H	HR	RBI	Avg		AB	H	HR	RBI	Avg
Home	74	16	2	5	.216	LHP	61	25	1	3	.410
Road	85	25	2	7	.294	RHP	98	16	3	9	.163
First Half	0	0	0	0	–	Sc Pos	38	11	1	8	.289
Scnd Half	159	41	4	12	.258	Clutch	21	5	0	1	.238

2004 Rankings (American League)

- Did not rank near the top or bottom in any category

Doug Waechter

2004 Season

Doug Waechter's 2004 season won't provide many fond memories. After Waechter's impressive month-long preview at the end of the 2003 season, the Devil Rays expected big things from him. But he didn't pitch well in the spring, was sent to the minors to open the season, missed two weeks due to a blister and pitched inconsistently after being recalled in late April. Waechter went on the disabled list in June due to a strained finger tendon and was out for nearly three months, then pitched poorly after being activated on September 6.

Pitching

As bad as the results were, the Devil Rays were not discouraged because they feel a few mechanical adjustments can get Waechter straightened out. The problem came in having him make the adjustments as he was trying to get back on the mound after the injury. When Waechter is right, he has smooth mechanics that produce a sneaky low-90s fastball, and a plus slider and changeup as complementary weapons. What is also impressive about Waechter is his attitude. He has a toughness, determination and competitiveness that will help him develop into a frontline starter.

Defense

Waechter is a tremendous athlete—good enough to turn down a scholarship offer to be the quarterback at the University of South Florida—and will do whatever necessary to make a play. He fields the position well and lacks only experience in making the right plays. Like many young pitchers, he could use some work in holding runners, and will continue to smooth out his slide-step delivery.

2005 Outlook

The Rays would like to think Waechter can pick up where he left off in 2003, though with the benefit of his good 2004 outings, such as when he took a no-hitter into the sixth inning at Minnesota on June 2. Eventually, the Rays hope he will be a front-of-the-rotation starter. For now, they would be happy if he can pitch an entire season at the back end of the rotation.

Position: SP
Bats: R **Throws:** R
Ht: 6' 4" **Wt:** 209

Opening Day Age: 24
Born: 1/28/81 in St. Petersburg, FL
ML Seasons: 2
Nickname: WECK-ter

Overall Statistics

	W	L	Pct.	ERA	G	GS	Sv	IP	H	BB	SO	HR	Avg
'04	5	7	.417	6.01	14	14	0	70.1	68	33	36	20	.252
Car.	8	9	.471	5.11	20	19	0	105.2	97	48	65	24	.243

2004 Pitching Profile

	Doug Waechter	AL Average
Overall Strike %	58.8	62.3
1st Pitch Strike %	49.5	58.1
Ratio	1.44	1.42
Strikeouts per 9 IP	4.61	6.45
Walks per 9 IP	4.22	3.34
Home Runs per 9 IP	2.56	1.15
Strikeout/Walk Ratio	1.09	1.93
Groundball/Flyball Ratio	0.53	1.17

2004 Situational Stats

	W	L	ERA	Sv	IP		AB	H	HR	RBI	Avg
Home	2	4	7.36	0	33.0	LHB	154	43	17	33	.279
Road	3	3	4.82	0	37.1	RHB	116	25	3	14	.216
First Half	3	6	4.97	0	50.2	Sc Pos	44	10	1	18	.227
Scnd Half	2	1	8.69	0	19.2	Clutch	11	3	2	3	.273

2004 Rankings (American League)

- 5th in losses among rookies

Rob Bell

Position: SP
Bats: R **Throws:** R
Ht: 6' 5" **Wt:** 225

Opening Day Age: 28
Born: 1/17/77 in
Newburgh, NY
ML Seasons: 5

Overall Statistics

	W	L	Pct.	ERA	G	GS	Sv	IP	H	BB	SO	HR	Avg
'04	8	8	.500	4.46	24	19	0	123.0	121	41	57	16	.253
Car.	29	33	.468	5.58	113	105	0	608.0	643	252	380	111	.271

2004 Situational Stats

	W	L	ERA	Sv	IP		AB	H	HR	RBI	Avg
Home	2	4	4.89	0	57.0	LHB	229	64	7	34	.279
Road	6	4	4.09	0	66.0	RHB	250	57	9	28	.228
First Half	3	3	4.50	0	50.0	Sc Pos	119	34	5	47	.286
Scnd Half	5	5	4.44	0	73.0	Clutch	13	2	0	0	.154

2004 Season

Rob Bell ranked third on the team with eight wins and 123 innings pitched despite spending the first six weeks in the minors and never really being given a regular job in the rotation. While he was impressive at times, his stats show a revealing split—he was 7-2 with a 3.24 ERA against teams that were below .500 and 1-6, 6.55 against teams with winning records.

Pitching & Defense

Bell does not have dynamic stuff, but in the last couple years he has learned to use what he has. He mixes his pitches, sprinkling in curves, changeups and an occasional splitter to prevent hitters from sitting on his average fastball. He is not much of a strikeout pitcher, and he still puts too many runners on base to win consistently. Bell is an excellent athlete and does a good job fielding his position.

2005 Outlook

Bell feels he could be on the verge of a breakthrough if given consistent work, and the Rays are in the market for some innings-eating starters, though they are looking to upgrade. They have moved Bell on and off the roster the last two years, and he probably won't stick around if he doesn't get a major league deal.

Geoff Blum

Position: 3B/2B
Bats: B **Throws:** R
Ht: 6' 3" **Wt:** 200

Opening Day Age: 31
Born: 4/26/73 in
Redwood City, CA
ML Seasons: 6
Pronunciation:
bluhm

Overall Statistics

	G	AB	R	H	D	T	HR	RBI	SB	BB	SO	Avg	OBP	Slg
'04	112	339	38	73	21	0	8	35	2	24	58	.215	.266	.348
Car.	682	2056	252	523	112	8	56	252	15	179	357	.254	.316	.398

2004 Situational Stats

	AB	H	HR	RBI	Avg		AB	H	HR	RBI	Avg
Home	149	29	2	13	.195	LHP	80	23	3	15	.288
Road	190	44	6	22	.232	RHP	259	50	5	20	.193
First Half	196	40	4	13	.204	Sc Pos	82	19	1	26	.232
Scnd Half	143	33	4	22	.231	Clutch	53	8	1	3	.151

2004 Season

The Devil Rays acquired Geoff Blum from Houston thinking that he was a utility infielder who was only an opportunity away from becoming an everyday third baseman. Instead, he struggled from the start of spring training, never made the adjustment to the AL, and went on to have the worst season of his pro career.

Hitting, Baserunning & Defense

Blum's strength had been consistency. But he was so lost at the left side of the plate and his mechanics were so off that he actually hit much better righthanded in 2004. The more he struggled, the more frustrated he got and the more often he got himself out chasing bad pitches. Blum has smooth hands and moves well enough for a big guy that he can still be an asset defensively, though he looks more comfortable at third than second, shortstop or in the outfield. While Blum isn't fast, he is a solid baserunner.

2005 Outlook

The Rays weren't going to pay Blum in excess of $1 million to be a backup again, so he headed back to the National League by signing a one-year deal with San Diego. He will assume the role of a versatile and valuable utilityman.

Jorge Cantu

Position: 2B/3B
Bats: R **Throws:** R
Ht: 6' 1" **Wt:** 184

Opening Day Age: 23
Born: 1/30/82 in
Reynosa, Mexico
ML Seasons: 1

Overall Statistics

	G	AB	R	H	D	T	HR	RBI	SB	BB	SO	Avg	OBP	Slg
'04	50	173	25	52	20	1	2	17	0	9	44	.301	.341	.462
Car.	50	173	25	52	20	1	2	17	0	9	44	.301	.341	.462

2004 Situational Stats

	AB	H	HR	RBI	Avg		AB	H	HR	RBI	Avg
Home	74	24	0	9	.324	LHP	51	19	0	2	.373
Road	99	28	2	8	.283	RHP	122	33	2	15	.270
First Half	0	0	0	0	–	Sc Pos	45	11	1	14	.244
Scnd Half	173	52	2	17	.301	Clutch	25	8	0	4	.320

2004 Season

Jorge Cantu was so far off the Rays' radar that he wasn't invited to spring training 2004. Now he is so much a part of their plans that he may go to spring training 2005 as the starting second baseman. After a stunning breakout performance at Triple-A, Cantu earned a brief late-July promotion, then came back for good in mid-August. He was named the team's Outstanding Rookie.

Hitting, Baserunning & Defense

In 95 games at Durham, Cantu said that everything he had been taught finally clicked. He is a free swinger who is quick to the inside pitch, but needs to learn the strike zone better and stop chasing balls away. He is quick and nimble enough to play shortstop, but the Rays project him as a second baseman. He doesn't steal many bases but is fast enough to be considered a plus baserunner.

2005 Outlook

At worst, Cantu is expected to be the team's top utility infielder. But unless Tampa Bay lands a veteran second baseman with a big bat, Cantu may get the chance to go into spring training as the starter. The Rays feel that with some adjustments he will be able to cut down his strikeouts and increase his power.

Lance Carter

Position: RP
Bats: R **Throws:** R
Ht: 6' 1" **Wt:** 190

Opening Day Age: 30
Born: 12/18/74 in
Bradenton, FL
ML Seasons: 4

Overall Statistics

	W	L	Pct.	ERA	G	GS	Sv	IP	H	BB	SO	HR	Avg
'04	3	3	.500	3.47	56	0	0	80.1	77	23	36	12	.252
Car.	12	9	.571	3.65	132	0	28	185.0	167	50	100	28	.240

2004 Situational Stats

	W	L	ERA	Sv	IP		AB	H	HR	RBI	Avg
Home	1	2	4.42	0	36.2	LHB	159	43	7	27	.270
Road	2	1	2.68	0	43.2	RHB	147	34	5	12	.231
First Half	2	2	3.48	0	41.1	Sc Pos	76	15	2	27	.197
Scnd Half	1	1	3.46	0	39.0	Clutch	62	14	4	8	.226

2004 Season

An All-Star closer in 2003, Lance Carter lost his job with the signing of Danys Baez, but still had a valuable role as a late-inning setup man and had a good season. He made 56 appearances and led Rays relievers with 80.1 innings. Carter stranded 22 of the 34 runners he inherited, but was on the mound for two walkoff losses.

Pitching & Defense

By moving into the setup role, Carter actually was more valuable because he often was used to pitch more than one inning. Unlike the prototypical hard-throwing closer, Carter gets by with control and finesse. He uses an average fastball to set up an excellent changeup and will mix in the occasional breaking ball to keep hitters even more off-balance. Carter keeps his cool on the mound, fields his position well and is known for doing all the little things.

2005 Outlook

Carter is likely to have a similar role in 2005, though he may be used as more of a sixth- and seventh-inning reliever to serve as a bridge to setup man Jesus Colome and then Baez. Carter was a starter in the minors as recently as 2002, but the Rays are leery of taxing him since he has had two Tommy John surgeries.

Jesus Colome

Position: RP
Bats: R **Throws:** R
Ht: 6' 4" **Wt:** 205

Opening Day Age: 27
Born: 12/23/77 in San Pedro de Macoris, DR
ML Seasons: 4
Pronunciation: hay-soos cal-um-ay

Overall Statistics

	W	L	Pct.	ERA	G	GS	Sv	IP	H	BB	SO	HR	Avg
'04	2	2	.500	3.27	33	0	3	41.1	28	18	40	4	.193
Car.	9	19	.321	4.73	149	0	5	205.1	190	122	173	27	.248

2004 Situational Stats

	W	L	ERA	Sv	IP		AB	H	HR	RBI	Avg
Home	1	0	2.70	2	23.1	LHB	53	13	3	9	.245
Road	1	2	4.00	1	18.0	RHB	92	15	1	9	.163
First Half	2	2	1.77	2	20.1	Sc Pos	39	9	1	14	.231
Scnd Half	0	0	4.71	1	21.0	Clutch	70	13	2	13	.186

2004 Season

After a poor spring landed him in Triple-A for two months, Jesus Colome developed into a reliable and occasionally dominating setup man for the Devil Rays until being sidelined in mid-September with a sore shoulder. Colome allowed only a .193 average, averaged nearly a strikeout an inning and allowed only five of 25 inherited runners to score.

Pitching & Defense

Colome throws his fastball regularly in the 97-100 MPH range. What has made him more effective is the ability to throw his slider and changeup and, just as importantly, convincing him to trust the offspeed pitches in key situations. He also has experimented with some different arm slots. Colome still can get a bit excited on the field, but he has become considerably more mature and does a better job of making the necessary plays.

2005 Outlook

Colome was told by Dr. James Andrews that his shoulder needed only rest and that he should be 100 percent by the start of spring training. The Rays are hoping so because they are counting on him to be the primary setup man, with the idea that with further experience he eventually can take over as the closer, perhaps even by the end of '05.

John Halama

Position: RP/SP
Bats: L **Throws:** L
Ht: 6' 5" **Wt:** 215

Opening Day Age: 33
Born: 2/22/72 in Brooklyn, NY
ML Seasons: 7
Pronunciation: ha-LA-ma

Overall Statistics

	W	L	Pct.	ERA	G	GS	Sv	IP	H	BB	SO	HR	Avg
'04	7	6	.538	4.70	34	14	0	118.2	134	27	59	17	.284
Car.	52	43	.547	4.52	205	114	0	816.2	931	247	443	101	.288

2004 Situational Stats

	W	L	ERA	Sv	IP		AB	H	HR	RBI	Avg
Home	3	4	3.70	0	58.1	LHB	139	37	2	16	.266
Road	4	2	5.67	0	60.1	RHB	333	97	15	47	.291
First Half	4	3	4.09	0	55.0	Sc Pos	90	26	1	40	.289
Scnd Half	3	3	5.23	0	63.2	Clutch	26	3	1	1	.115

2004 Season

The early offseason signing of John Halama didn't get much attention, but he turned out to be one of the Devil Rays' most valuable additions. While Halama didn't pitch all that well, he provided depth to a staff left bare by injuries and inconsistent performances. Halama was much better as a reliever (2-1, 2.45) than as a starter (5-5, 6.03), but that didn't stop the Rays from moving him into the rotation when they needed a hand.

Pitching & Defense

Halama is not an overpowering pitcher, relying on a fastball that usually is in the high 80s and needing good control of his assortment of breaking balls and offspeed pitches. His problems as a starter come when he tries to get through the lineup a second and third time, as he tends to tire after about 60 pitches. He's got a good move to first, and was errorless in 16 total chances last season.

2005 Outlook

Halama started the last game of the season for the Rays and said he expected to be with another team in 2005. He probably is right, after the Rays didn't offer him arbitration. They have a fairly deep bullpen and are making it a priority to upgrade the rotation.

Travis Harper

Position: RP
Bats: L **Throws:** R
Ht: 6' 4" **Wt:** 192

Opening Day Age: 28
Born: 5/21/76 in
Harrisonburg, VA
ML Seasons: 5

Overall Statistics

	W	L	Pct.	ERA	G	GS	Sv	IP	H	BB	SO	HR	Avg
'04	6	2	.750	3.89	52	0	0	78.2	69	23	59	8	.234
Car.	16	23	.410	4.49	158	14	2	296.1	301	99	199	41	.264

2004 Situational Stats

	W	L	ERA	Sv	IP		AB	H	HR	RBI	Avg
Home	4	1	4.70	0	38.1	LHB	117	27	4	21	.231
Road	2	1	3.12	0	40.1	RHB	178	42	4	21	.236
First Half	2	0	4.62	0	37.0	Sc Pos	78	16	1	27	.205
Scnd Half	4	2	3.24	0	41.2	Clutch	80	16	1	7	.200

2004 Season

Travis Harper continued to be a versatile and valuable member of the Tampa Bay bullpen, giving manager Lou Piniella the option of using him long or short while knowing he probably is going to get groundballs for key outs. Despite spending the first three weeks of the season at Triple-A, Harper was second on the team with 78.2 relief innings and picked up a career-high six wins.

Pitching & Defense

Harper doesn't wow hitters with overpowering stuff, but he uses a full repertoire, including a heavy sinking fastball usually clocked in the low 90s that is his best pitch, a sharp-breaking curve and a changeup. His biggest improvement has been his ability to deal with pressure situations, holding hitters to a .205 average with runners in scoring position. Harper gets a lot of groundballs and usually fields his position well, and he does a decent job of holding on runners.

2005 Outlook

Harper has proven himself as a dependable major league-quality reliever, but the Rays are deep in the bullpen. Finances could be a factor since Harper will be arbitration eligible for the first time. Otherwise, he should be a regular contributor in middle relief.

Trever Miller

Position: RP
Bats: R **Throws:** L
Ht: 6' 3" **Wt:** 200

Opening Day Age: 31
Born: 5/29/73 in
Louisville, KY
ML Seasons: 6

Overall Statistics

	W	L	Pct.	ERA	G	GS	Sv	IP	H	BB	SO	HR	Avg
'04	1	1	.500	3.12	60	0	1	49.0	48	15	43	3	.257
Car.	8	9	.471	4.77	244	5	6	237.2	264	113	173	26	.281

2004 Situational Stats

	W	L	ERA	Sv	IP		AB	H	HR	RBI	Avg
Home	1	0	4.84	1	22.1	LHB	98	21	2	17	.214
Road	0	1	1.69	0	26.2	RHB	89	27	1	14	.303
First Half	1	1	2.96	0	27.1	Sc Pos	73	21	2	30	.288
Scnd Half	0	0	3.32	1	21.2	Clutch	58	18	2	13	.310

2004 Season

Lefthanded reliever Trever Miller got off to a rough start with the Devil Rays, allowing two grand slams within a week in early May. But once he got comfortable in his role and once manager Lou Piniella got comfortable using him, he turned out to be a relatively effective specialist. For the season, Miller pitched in 60 games, second-most on the team.

Pitching & Defense

Miller doesn't blow hitters away, usually mixing a biting slider with a few well-placed fastballs. He can throw the slider from a couple of different angles, making it look more like a slurve to left-handers but giving it a hard break against righthanders. Miller did a good job in 2003 against righthanders but struggled a bit in 2004. Having bounced around the minors for several years, Miller established himself as a reliable big league pitcher with a second straight successful season. He's got a decent move to first.

2005 Outlook

Piniella likes versatility and variety in his bullpen, and Miller was able to provide some of both after signing a one-year deal with the Rays. Though a free agent, he is expected back again to fill the role as the primary lefthanded specialist.

Rey Sanchez

Position: 2B
Bats: R **Throws:** R
Ht: 5' 9" **Wt:** 170

Opening Day Age: 37
Born: 10/5/67 in Rio Piedras, PR
ML Seasons: 14
Pronunciation: RAY SAN-chezz

Overall Statistics

	G	AB	R	H	D	T	HR	RBI	SB	BB	SO	Avg	OBP	Slg
'04	91	285	23	70	14	3	2	26	0	12	28	.246	.281	.337
Car.	1467	4807	542	1305	192	32	15	387	55	227	505	.271	.308	.334

2004 Situational Stats

	AB	H	HR	RBI	Avg		AB	H	HR	RBI	Avg
Home	139	35	2	11	.252	LHP	83	24	0	10	.289
Road	146	35	0	15	.240	RHP	202	46	2	16	.228
First Half	188	50	2	15	.266	Sc Pos	68	19	1	23	.279
Scnd Half	97	20	0	11	.206	Clutch	44	13	1	3	.295

2004 Season

The Rays signed slick-fielding Rey Sanchez to take over as the everyday shortstop, but manager Lou Piniella decided in spring training to keep Julio Lugo at short and play Sanchez regularly at second. That arrangement didn't last long, as Sanchez got off to such a slow start offensively that he was reduced to part-time play.

Hitting, Baserunning & Defense

Sanchez never has been known for his offense. He is a singles hitter who can help a team at the bottom of the order by hitting behind runners and getting an occasional bunt down. He would help more if he had better plate discipline and drew more walks. Sanchez is not much of a basestealer, and age has pretty much taken that out of his game completely. What Sanchez still does very well is field. He needs an occasional day off, but he can play second base, and, with extra rest, shortstop, with the best of them.

2005 Outlook

Sanchez has been with six teams over the last four years, and he probably is going to be on the move again. He still could help a team looking for either a stopgap starter or a quality utility infielder, and should end up with a one-year deal somewhere.

Jorge Sosa

Position: RP
Bats: B **Throws:** R
Ht: 6' 2" **Wt:** 170

Opening Day Age: 27
Born: 4/28/77 in Santo Domingo, DR
ML Seasons: 3
Pronunciation: hor-hey

Overall Statistics

	W	L	Pct.	ERA	G	GS	Sv	IP	H	BB	SO	HR	Avg
'04	4	7	.364	5.53	43	8	1	99.1	100	54	94	17	.259
Car.	11	26	.297	5.17	103	41	1	327.1	325	168	214	47	.260

2004 Situational Stats

	W	L	ERA	Sv	IP		AB	H	HR	RBI	Avg
Home	3	4	5.80	1	49.2	LHB	192	55	14	44	.286
Road	1	3	5.26	0	49.2	RHB	194	45	3	14	.232
First Half	2	0	6.05	1	38.2	Sc Pos	106	25	5	42	.236
Scnd Half	2	7	5.19	0	60.2	Clutch	68	15	1	4	.221

2004 Season

Having completed the successful conversion of Jorge Sosa from outfielder to pitcher, the Devil Rays still can't seem to decide what type of pitcher he is. For a third straight year, he was bounced between the majors and minors, and between the rotation and the bullpen. And for a third straight season, he hasn't distinguished himself.

Pitching & Defense

What Sosa does well is throw hard. Very hard. He can work regularly in the high 90s with his fastball, and knows it, which is not necessarily a good thing since he gets too concerned about velocity. The Rays have been working with him to develop his slider, and a split-finger fastball that looks a bit like a changeup. He needs all three pitches to be a starter. Even with his position player background, Sosa is not smooth defensively, looking very stiff and uncomfortable on the mound.

2005 Outlook

Sosa probably is headed back for another season of middle relief. He has yet to show the Rays that he can be consistently successful as a starter and struggled in a tryout as a late-inning setup man. Depending on what else the Rays do during the winter, there could be openings in the rotation.

Other Tampa Bay Devil Rays

Midre Cummings (Pos: DH, Age: 33, Bats: L)

	G	AB	R	H	D	T	HR	RBI	SB	BB	SO	Avg	OBP	Slg
'04	22	54	10	15	4	0	2	7	1	5	12	.278	.361	.463
Car.	458	1111	136	286	60	8	22	124	9	94	199	.257	.319	.385

Cummings looked like a budding star when he won the Class-A Midwest League batting title at age 19 in 1991, but poor plate discipline has kept him from approaching his career .301 average in the minors over 994 games. His hitting percentages were solid in a short stint with the Rays. 2005 Outlook: C

Brook Fordyce (Pos: C, Age: 34, Bats: R)

	G	AB	R	H	D	T	HR	RBI	SB	BB	SO	Avg	OBP	Slg
'04	54	151	14	31	6	0	2	9	0	9	34	.205	.259	.285
Car.	623	1807	172	467	103	4	41	188	8	119	295	.258	.309	.388

Except for solid offensive seasons in 1999 and 2000, Fordyce hasn't excelled at the plate or defensively, but he's forged a fairly lengthy career. He may never see 300 at-bats again, but he'll probably hook on somewhere. He worked well with Rays pitchers, so he may be back. 2005 Outlook: C

Charles Gipson (Pos: SS, Age: 32, Bats: R)

	G	AB	R	H	D	T	HR	RBI	SB	BB	SO	Avg	OBP	Slg
'04	5	4	1	2	0	0	0	0	1	0	1	.500	.500	.500
Car.	354	310	76	74	14	7	0	29	15	29	68	.239	.313	.329

Gipson had one of his best Triple-A seasons in 2004, batting .296 with a .381 OBP in 96 games with Durham. He passed through waivers twice en route to Triple-A, and he never reappeared in Tampa after June 5. His major league stays are getting shorter as he gets older. 2005 Outlook: C

Dicky Gonzalez (Pos: RHP, Age: 26)

	W	L	Pct.	ERA	G	GS	Sv	IP	H	BB	SO	HR	Avg
'04	0	0	–	6.14	4	0	0	7.1	9	2	7	1	.310
Car.	3	2	.600	5.02	20	7	0	66.1	81	19	38	5	.307

After almost a decade in the minors, Gonzalez still posts some impressive strikeout-walk ratios, and the overall results have been pretty good, but his second stop in the majors last May ended after just two weeks. He joined Yakult in Japan, posted a 1.90 ERA and re-signed. 2005 Outlook: D

Jeremi Gonzalez (Pos: RHP, Age: 30)

	W	L	Pct.	ERA	G	GS	Sv	IP	H	BB	SO	HR	Avg
'04	0	5	.000	6.97	11	8	0	50.1	72	20	22	9	.346
Car.	24	32	.429	4.60	70	76	0	460.2	453	199	282	56	.258

Gonzalez was a promising Cubs prospect in the mid-1990s. Elbow woes that began in 1998 sidetracked his career, but he reemerged with a promising 2003 for the Rays. In 2004, he wasn't nearly as effective and bounced between the minors and Tampa all season before his November release. 2005 Outlook: C

Fred McGriff (Pos: DH, Age: 41, Bats: L)

	G	AB	R	H	D	T	HR	RBI	SB	BB	SO	Avg	OBP	Slg
'04	27	72	7	13	3	0	2	7	0	9	19	.181	.272	.306
Car.	2460	8757	1349	2490	441	24	493	1550	72	1305	1882	.284	.377	.509

McGriff didn't make the Rays out of spring training, but went to Triple-A Durham in May. In search of some offensive spark, the Rays recalled him later that month, and he got a chance to shoot for his 500th home run. He was released eight weeks later, still seven homers short. 2005 Outlook: C

Damian Moss (Pos: LHP, Age: 28)

	W	L	Pct.	ERA	G	GS	Sv	IP	H	BB	SO	HR	Avg
'04	0	1	.000	16.88	5	2	0	8.0	13	5	6	2	.351
Car.	22	19	.537	4.50	74	61	0	361.2	340	195	204	47	.252

Moss annually battles to post more whiffs than walks, whether in the high minors or the majors. The lefty made the Rays out of spring training, but apparently found too much of the strike zone this time around. Sent down on April 30, Moss wasn't much better at the Triple-A level. 2005 Outlook: C

Eduardo Perez (Pos: 1B, Age: 35, Bats: R)

	G	AB	R	H	D	T	HR	RBI	SB	BB	SO	Avg	OBP	Slg
'04	13	38	2	8	2	0	1	7	0	4	9	.211	.286	.342
Car.	597	1453	193	357	72	3	59	233	19	150	330	.246	.321	.421

Perez had an opportunity for playing time in Tampa, with third base unsettled and the Rays looking for righthanded pop. But the only pop from Perez, sadly, was his left Achilles, which he tore in early May. He immediately underwent successful surgery that ended his season. 2005 Outlook: C

Todd Ritchie (Pos: RHP, Age: 33)

	W	L	Pct.	ERA	G	GS	Sv	IP	H	BB	SO	HR	Avg
'04	0	2	.000	9.00	4	2	0	8.0	12	6	4	4	.343
Car.	43	54	.443	4.71	184	120	0	835.1	929	262	516	104	.281

A first-round pick of the Twins in 1990, Ritchie finally seemed to be coming around when he went 15-9 (3.50) with Pittsburgh in 1999. He's gone 26-42 (5.06) since then, and last summer he was coming back from shoulder surgery in 2003. He wasn't so hot at Triple-A Durham, either. 2005 Outlook: C

Damian Rolls (Pos: 3B/LF, Age: 27, Bats: R)

	G	AB	R	H	D	T	HR	RBI	SB	BB	SO	Avg	OBP	Slg
'04	53	117	12	19	5	0	0	9	2	10	36	.162	.231	.205
Car.	266	819	103	203	42	2	9	73	27	42	184	.248	.291	.337

Second base, third base and shortstop have been wide-open slots for much of Rolls' tenure in the Rays' system, and he's been given numerous chances to take one of those jobs. But he hasn't been able to nail down regular duty in Tampa, and he was released in November. 2005 Outlook: C

Tampa Bay

Bobby Seay (Pos: LHP, Age: 26)

	W	L	Pct.	ERA	G	GS	Sv	IP	H	BB	SO	HR	Avg
'04	0	0	–	2.38	21	0	0	22.2	21	5	17	2	.239
Car.	1	1	.500	3.63	45	0	0	44.2	41	16	34	5	.243

Seay was a top prospect, signed in 1996, but injuries and a slow trek up the developmental ladder have kept the lefty in the minors. After two impressive Triple-A seasons, he was recalled in early July and pitched well for the Rays. He finally may be in their big league plans. 2005 Outlook: B

Randall Simon (Pos: 1B, Age: 29, Bats: L)

	G	AB	R	H	D	T	HR	RBI	SB	BB	SO	Avg	OBP	Slg
'04	69	192	16	36	6	0	3	14	0	18	19	.188	.266	.266
Car.	514	1588	172	450	71	3	49	235	2	80	142	.283	.320	.424

Forever fearful of walking, the free-swinging Simon has made a career of getting wood on baseball. After hitting .300 or better for three seasons ending in 2002, Simon had trouble lining up wood with cowhide in 2004. That's his only skill. 2005 Outlook: C

Jason Standridge (Pos: RHP, Age: 26)

	W	L	Pct.	ERA	G	GS	Sv	IP	H	BB	SO	HR	Avg
'04	0	0	–	9.00	3	1	0	10.0	14	4	7	5	.326
Car.	0	5	.000	6.38	21	9	0	67.2	78	38	37	18	.291

One of Tampa's best pitching prospects a few years ago, Standridge hasn't been able to put it all together. After eight years in the system, he has signed a minor league deal with a Texas team in need of pitching, and he'll see if he can avoid the annual move between Triple-A clubs. 2005 Outlook: C

John Webb (Pos: RHP, Age: 25)

	W	L	Pct.	ERA	G	GS	Sv	IP	H	BB	SO	HR	Avg
'04	0	0	–	7.00	4	0	0	9.0	12	7	9	2	.324
Car.	0	0	–	7.00	4	0	0	9.0	12	7	9	2	.324

Webb was a Cubs prospect making his way back from Tommy John surgery in 2001. After fracturing his right fibula during the offseason a year ago, the Rays claimed him off waivers in February 2004. He was 3-4 (3.64) in Double- and Triple-A ball and reached Tampa. The pen always needs help. 2005 Outlook: C

Tampa Bay Devil Rays Minor League Prospects

Organization Overview:

After years of getting little from a farm system that was loaded with toolsy players and short on skills, the future is brighter heading into the 2005 season. Aubrey Huff is a 100-RBI man who hits .300, Carl Crawford and Rocco Baldelli are fixed in the outfield, and B.J. Upton has arrived. On top of that, the Rays had potential stars Delmon Young and Scott Kazmir debut in the system in 2004. Southpaw Kazmir is one of the top pitching prospects in the game, a welcome addition to a farm system that has been teased by its young arms, but has had few rock-solid starters emerge. Dewon Brazelton and Doug Waechter are still candidates to succeed in the majors, and plenty of young pitchers could get a chance to establish themselves in 2005.

Wes Bankston

Position: 1B **Opening Day Age:** 21
Bats: R **Throws:** R **Born:** 11/27/83 in Dallas, TX
Ht: 6' 3" **Wt:** 205

Recent Statistics

	G	AB	R	H	D	T	HR	RBI	SB	BB	SO	Avg
2003 A Chrlstn (SC)	103	375	46	96	18	1	12	60	2	53	94	.256
2004 A Chrlstn (SC)	127	470	82	136	30	3	23	101	9	73	104	.289

After a promising 2002 debut at Rookie-level Princeton, where he claimed home-run and RBI crowns, Bankston had his 2003 season at Class-A Charleston compromised by a wrist injury. He returned there in 2004 and turned on the power. His overall game was better in his second go-round in the South Atlantic League, with improved selectivity at the plate keying a better offensive season. While his swing can get a bit long, his power potential remains an intriguing tool. With a crowded outfield picture in Tampa, Bankston moved to first base last summer. He handled the move well, aided by the big man's athleticism and mobility.

Joey Gathright

Position: OF **Opening Day Age:** 23
Bats: L **Throws:** R **Born:** 4/27/81 in Hattiesburg, MS
Ht: 5' 10" **Wt:** 170

Recent Statistics

	G	AB	R	H	D	T	HR	RBI	SB	BB	SO	Avg
2004 AA Montgomery	32	126	23	43	5	1	0	8	10	11	30	.341
2004 AAA Durham	60	236	34	77	9	1	0	8	33	19	46	.326
2004 AL Tampa Bay	19	52	11	13	0	0	0	1	6	2	14	.250

A 32nd-rounder in 2001, Gathright debuted in 2002 and climbed through the system in three seasons. While Gathright has learned to slap the ball around and use his speed to beat out hits, he's not as refined at working counts to draw walks or get better pitches to hit. He is one of the fastest guys in the game, which gives him great range in center field. His arm is not an asset, however, and his stolen-base percentage suffers because he steals bases on pure speed. Cracking into the Rays' young outfield will be difficult, but Rocco Baldelli's offseason knee surgery opens a door. Gathright hit .365 with 15 steals in 15 games in the Arizona Fall League before a minor shoulder ailment ended his season.

Chad Gaudin

Position: P **Opening Day Age:** 22
Bats: R **Throws:** R **Born:** 3/24/83 in New Orleans, LA
Ht: 5' 11" **Wt:** 165

Recent Statistics

	W	L	ERA	G	GS	Sv	IP	H	R	BB	SO	HR
2004 AAA Durham	1	3	4.72	17	7	2	47.2	48	26	17	52	8
2004 AL Tampa Bay	1	2	4.85	26	4	0	42.2	59	27	16	30	4

As a 5-foot-11 righthander who was a 34th-round pick, Gaudin isn't your typical top pitching prospect. Yet, he's climbed through the Rays' system in a little more than two years, locating the ball successfully with a 90-MPH fastball that he can bump up or take a little off, a late-biting slider and a changeup. He enjoyed a dominant 2003 at high Class-A Bakersfield and Double-A Orlando, followed by a promising debut with the Rays, mostly in relief. He began 2004 pitching well out of the Rays' pen, but struggled in a move to the rotation in June. After a demotion to Triple-A Durham, Gaudin developed a sore shoulder in July and struggled there and with Tampa the rest of the year. He was dealt to Toronto for catcher Kevin Cash as this edition went to press.

Jonny Gomes

Position: OF **Opening Day Age:** 24
Bats: R **Throws:** R **Born:** 11/22/80 in San Francisco, CA
Ht: 6' 1" **Wt:** 205

Recent Statistics

	G	AB	R	H	D	T	HR	RBI	SB	BB	SO	Avg
2004 AAA Durham	114	390	73	100	27	1	26	78	8	51	136	.256
2004 AL Tampa Bay	5	14	0	1	0	0	0	1	0	1	6	.071

A 2001 pick, Gomes is a power prospect who generates plenty of homers and a boatload of strikeouts. Aggressive at the plate, the righthanded hitter can power the ball to most parts of the park. While he produced 54 extra-base hits in 114 games for Triple-A Durham in 2004, his 136 whiffs dwarfed his 100 hits on the season. His strikeouts easily have outpaced his hits in each of his pro seasons, and he's been unable to refine his approach enough to make more consistent contact. Gomes runs well on the bases and in the field, but he isn't likely to land a job in the talent-rich Tampa Bay outfield. A groin injury he suffered at Durham bothered him during his stay with the Rays in May.

Scott Kazmir

Position: P   **Opening Day Age:** 21
Bats: L **Throws:** L   **Born:** 1/24/84 in
Ht: 6' 0" **Wt:** 170   Houston, TX

Recent Statistics

	W	L	ERA	G	GS	Sv	IP	H	R	BB	SO	HR
2004 A St. Lucie	1	2	3.42	11	11	0	50.0	49	20	22	51	3
2004 AA Binghamton	2	1	1.73	4	4	0	26.0	16	6	9	29	0
2004 AA Montgomery	1	2	1.44	4	4	0	25.0	14	7	11	24	0
2004 AL Tampa Bay	2	3	5.67	8	7	0	33.1	33	22	21	41	4

It's hard to believe the Mets dealt Kazmir, their 2002 first-rounder, near last July's trade deadline. Southpaws with his combination of mid-90s fastball and blistering slider are rare, and he had both offerings on track after overcoming mechanical issues and an abdominal strain early in 2004. He has the stuff to be a big league closer, but a much-improved changeup last summer makes for a top rotation prospect. Kazmir showed that stuff with five scoreless innings against Seattle in his big league debut on August 23, and he threw three-hit ball and fanned nine in six scoreless frames at Fenway Park to outduel Pedro Martinez on September 14. Kazmir has yet to work more than 135 innings in a season.

Seth McClung

Position: P   **Opening Day Age:** 24
Bats: B **Throws:** R   **Born:** 2/7/81 in
Ht: 6' 6" **Wt:** 235   Lewisburg, WV

Recent Statistics

	W	L	ERA	G	GS	Sv	IP	H	R	BB	SO	HR
2003 AL Tampa Bay	4	1	5.35	12	5	0	38.2	33	23	25	25	6
2004 A Chrlstn (SC)	0	0	0.00	3	3	0	9.1	5	0	4	10	0
2004 AA Montgomery	1	1	4.73	3	3	0	13.1	10	7	4	8	3
2004 AAA Durham	2	1	3.29	11	0	0	13.2	10	5	7	12	0

A 1999 pick, McClung finished the 2002 season in the Double-A Orlando rotation and made the Rays out of spring training as a reliever in 2003. He moved into the rotation late that April and turned in three quality starts in five outings before elbow trouble led to Tommy John surgery that June. He returned last July and regained his mid-90s velocity by season's end. He also has a sharp-breaking curve and an aggressive demeanor that were assets in the Triple-A Durham pen. Remaining a starter will require a consistent changeup and better control.

Chad Orvella

Position: P   **Opening Day Age:** 24
Bats: R **Throws:** R   **Born:** 10/1/80 in Renton,
Ht: 5' 11" **Wt:** 180   WA

Recent Statistics

	W	L	ERA	G	GS	Sv	IP	H	R	BB	SO	HR
2003 A Hudson Val	0	0	0.00	10	0	8	12.1	6	0	1	15	0
2004 A Chrlstn (SC)	1	0	1.33	22	0	4	47.1	28	9	5	76	4
2004 A Bakersfield	0	1	3.06	15	0	4	17.2	13	7	4	24	2
2004 AA Montgomery	0	0	0.00	6	0	4	7.0	0	0	0	14	0
2004 AAA Durham	0	0	5.40	2	0	0	1.2	1	1	1	2	1

This college shortstop was a 13th-round pick in 2003, but the Rays drafted him after seeing him work as a reliever at North Carolina State. The righthander worked 12.1 scoreless innings and fanned 15 in his pro debut at short-season Hudson Valley. Then he climbed to Triple-A Durham in his first full pro season in 2004, pinpointing a mid-90s fastball that can touch 96 MPH. In 73.2 innings last season, he fanned 116 and walked just 10. Orvella also has a solid changeup and slider, and he commands both pitches well. The break of his slider lacks consistency, but it didn't stop his rapid rise in 2004. He's been a full-time pitcher for less than two years, yet he looks like a potential big league closer.

Delmon Young

Position: OF   **Opening Day Age:** 19
Bats: R **Throws:** R   **Born:** 9/14/85 in
Ht: 6' 3" **Wt:** 205   Montgomery, AL

Recent Statistics

	G	AB	R	H	D	T	HR	RBI	SB	BB	SO	Avg
2004 A Chrlstn (SC)	131	513	95	165	26	5	25	116	21	53	120	.322

A run of April strikeouts had to spark some self-doubt in Young, who predicted he'd reach the majors in 2004, soon after signing as the first overall pick in 2003. While he didn't light up the Class-A South Atlantic League early on, despite an Opening Day home run, Young hit for average with good power in his pro debut. His quick bat and baseball instincts sparked adjustments at the plate, and the teenager made them all season long to lead the league in hits and RBI. He has big-time power to all fields, as well as a strong arm that recorded 14 assists in his debut season. Young, who spent the entire summer at Charleston, could be a fast climber.

Others to Watch

Shortstop **Reid Brignac** (19) displayed terrific bat speed and advanced plate discipline for Rookie-level Princeton, with a .361 average in 97 at-bats before advancing to Class-A Charleston. His defensive game was just as impressive. . . Outfielder **Matt Diaz** (27) hit .354 in the high minors in 2003, and he had a .332-21-93 season with Triple-A Durham in 2004. His defensive game isn't an asset, so he may not find a regular job in the Rays' young outfield. . . Outfielder **Elijah Dukes** (20) is extremely athletic, a five-tool talent with good instincts. He has the power and speed to be an impact player, but his plate patience is a concern, as is his makeup. He finished his second pro season at high Class-A Bakersfield. . .A 2002 pick, **Jason Hammel** (22) emerged with a dominating second half at high Class-A Bakersfield in 2004. The righthander was 6-2 (1.89) there, and allowed just one earned run over his final five starts. His best pitch was a low-90s fastball, and his 12-to-6 curve broke sharply when at its best. . . Signed as a free agent after six pro seasons, **Franklin Nunez** (28) was a much-improved pitcher in 2004, combining to go 4-3 (2.47) with 89 strikeouts in 62 innings for Double-A Montgomery and Triple-A Durham. Recalled in the second half, he should compete for work in the Rays' pen in 2005.

Ameriquest Field in Arlington

Offense

Front office frustration with Ameriquest Field's reputation as an offensive park sparked general manager John Hart to refer to it as "this airport we play in." It's great for building offense, but not pitching. The short right-field porch invites left-handed hitters to dump flyballs into the stands for homers. The big power alleys attract lots of doubles. The lack of foul ground gives hitters extra outs. It is the American League's most hitter-friendly park.

Defense

The sharp grounds crew made several changes to the field to help improve defense. The area in front of home plate, which tended to dry out quickly, is now soaked with water to prevent high-chop infield hits. The infield grass is a hair longer and grown closer to the lines. The idea is to keep the ball in the infield and give one of the AL's best infields a chance for essential outs.

Who It Helps the Most

The park was built with Rafael Palmeiro's swing in mind. A lefthanded hitter who can get the ball into the air will thrive here. The dimensions and wind currents favor lefties. Lefthanded hitting Hank Blalock hit 72 points higher at home than on the road in 2004, and David Delluci hit 44 points higher at home.

Who It Hurts the Most

This place remains a nightmare for flyball pitchers and guys who lack above-average command. It's why Chan Ho Park has been such a bad fit with the Rangers. The Rangers have made progress by turning to more groundball-oriented pitchers.

Rookies & Newcomers

The Rangers have struggled to develop their own pitchers because young pitchers often struggle with command, which sets the tone for bad things at Ameriquest. When they see a good pitch hit for a homer, they tend to lose conviction in throwing the same pitch again. Righthanders Nick Regilio, Kameron Loe and Erik Thompson may take the Ameriquest test in 2005.

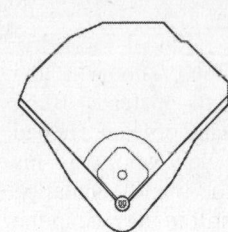

Dimensions: LF-332, LCF-390, CF-400, RCF-381, RF-325

Capacity: 49,115

Elevation: 551 feet

Surface: Grass

Foul Territory: Small

Park Factors

2004 Season

	Home Games Rangers	Opp	Total	Away Games Rangers	Opp	Total	Index
G	72	72	144	72	72	144	
Avg	.287	.273	.280	.245	.276	.260	108
AB	2470	2585	5055	2494	2405	4899	103
R	439	365	804	308	332	640	126
H	708	706	1414	610	664	1274	111
2B	154	136	290	144	122	266	106
3B	20	17	37	12	10	22	163
HR	102	87	189	89	79	168	109
BB	238	244	482	212	251	463	101
SO	445	447	892	517	426	943	92
E	52	39	91	48	38	86	106
E-Infield	48	32	80	44	32	76	105
LHB-Avg	.282	.252	.266	.229	.264	.248	107
LHB-HR	51	40	91	40	33	73	118
RHB-Avg	.290	.291	.290	.254	.287	.269	108
RHB-HR	51	47	98	49	46	95	102

2002-2004

	Home Games Rangers	Opp	Total	Away Games Rangers	Opp	Total	Index
G	216	216	432	216	216	432	
Avg	.285	.279	.282	.247	.275	.261	108
AB	7375	7755	15130	7613	7261	14874	102
R	1303	1225	2528	931	1106	2037	124
H	2104	2167	4271	1881	1998	3879	110
2B	420	471	891	395	405	800	109
3B	55	54	109	34	45	79	136
HR	354	278	632	261	240	501	124
BB	719	792	1511	644	837	1481	100
SO	1324	1413	2737	1485	1282	2767	97
E	130	132	262	146	130	276	95
E-Infield	108	107	215	126	108	234	92
LHB-Avg	.285	.270	.276	.241	.274	.259	107
LHB-HR	156	127	283	104	114	218	124
RHB-Avg	.286	.288	.287	.251	.276	.262	109
RHB-HR	198	151	349	157	126	283	124

2004 Rankings (American League)

- Highest run factor
- Second-highest batting-average factor
- Second-highest hit factor
- Second-highest triple factor
- Second-highest LHB batting-average factor
- Second-highest RHB batting-average factor
- Third-highest LHB home-run factor
- Second-lowest strikeout factor

Buck Showalter

2004 Season

After losing Alex Rodriguez, Rafael Palmeiro, Juan Gonzalez and starter John Thomson, the Rangers were left for dead. Instead, Buck Showalter ended up with his kind of team. He had a bunch of scrappy "dirt" players who, with his help, forged an us-against-the-world mentality. The Rangers somehow were still in the race in the final week of the season, finishing with an 18-win improvement over 2003. It will likely go down as the best job of Showalter's nine-year managing career.

Offense

Showalter likes to keep all of his players involved in the lineup. He made significant changes to the top half of the order when things stagnated in July. He likes to be able to be aggressive, and his reconstituted team better suited those purposes. Stolenbase attempts went up and sacrifice flies jumped from 42 in 2003 to 57 last summer.

Pitching & Defense

Of all the balls he had to juggle in 2004, none was handled better by Showalter than the pitching staff. Only one starting pitcher on the Opening Day roster (Kenny Rogers) was with the team all season. With some help from pitching coach Orel Hershiser, who got the pitchers to believe in a groundball-first philosophy, the Rangers somehow wound up with the lowest staff ERA (4.53) in their 11 seasons at Ameriquest Field. Showalter quickly identified his bullpen as an asset and got the most out of it.

2005 Outlook

After all the progress of 2004, the Rangers will have to deal with expectations in 2005. Showalter also will have to morph with his players. In the past, his controlling style ended up costing him teams in New York and Arizona. Both teams went on to win the World Series a year after he departed. These Rangers could be headed for a similar destination in a year or two. Showalter's personal growth will determine if he eventually goes with them.

Born: 5/23/56 in DeFuniak Springs, FL

Playing Experience: No major league playing experience

Managerial Experience: 9 seasons

Manager Statistics

Year	Team, Lg	W	L	Pct	GB	Finish
2004	Texas, AL	89	73	.549	3.0	3rd West
9 Seasons		723	668	.520	–	–

2004 Starting Pitchers by Days Rest

	<=3	4	5	6+
Rangers Starts	3	91	23	29
Rangers ERA	2.95	5.41	6.14	4.50
AL Avg Starts	2	82	47	21
AL ERA	5.36	4.87	4.65	4.93

2004 Situational Stats

	Buck Showalter	AL Average
Hit & Run Success %	43.6	36.8
Stolen Base Success %	65.7	68.6
Platoon Pct.	64.1	61.6
Defensive Subs	17	21
High-Pitch Outings	3	5
Quick/Slow Hooks	30/11	20/16
Sacrifice Attempts	32	53

2004 Rankings (American League)

- 1st in quick hooks, mid-inning pitching changes (241) and first-batter platoon percentage
- 2nd in hit-and-run success percentage and relief appearances (468)
- 3rd in saves with over 1 inning pitched (10)

Rod Barajas

2004 Season

Not guaranteed of a spot until spring's final days, Rod Barajas ended up becoming the Rangers' primary starter at catcher when Gerald Laird went down with a torn left thumb ligament in May. Barajas went on to have a breakout year of sorts. Despite a .249 average, he had some of the team's biggest hits, including a walkoff homer against the Yankees in May. He showed himself to be a smart catcher, willing to invest lots of time into making his pitchers better. That was evidenced by the Rangers' 4.50 ERA with him behind the plate.

Hitting

Barajas showed good power, more than doubling his best single-season home-run total, and his 26 doubles in 358 at-bats shouldn't be overlooked. The problems are fatigue, overexposure and, surprisingly, an unwillingness to walk. He took over as the regular catcher in mid-May, but hit .189 over July and August. After getting some rest (in the form of a platoon in August), he surged again in September. He must walk more, a fact supported by his anemic .265 career on-base percentage.

Baserunning & Defense

Barajas is such a slow runner, it is sometimes painful to watch him, but he isn't paid to run the bases. He is paid to catch. On the defensive side, he moves well behind the plate for a big guy, but he never will be a strong thrower. Last year, 42 of 58 runners (72.4 percent) were successful against him. For his career, it's a 72.8-percent success rate.

2005 Outlook

Though arbitration eligible, Barajas will be back. There is no question about that. Even though the Rangers have a catching prospect who is nearly ready in Laird, they signed Sandy Alomar Jr. in order to give Laird more time at Triple-A Oklahoma. Although Barajas wore down when he played every day for more than a month, he will be the primary catcher at the start of the 2005 campaign.

Position: C
Bats: R **Throws:** R
Ht: 6' 2" **Wt:** 220

Opening Day Age: 29
Born: 9/5/75 in Ontario, CA
ML Seasons: 6
Pronunciation: bar-AH-hoss

Overall Statistics

	G	AB	R	H	D	T	HR	RBI	SB	BB	SO	Avg	OBP	Slg
'04	108	358	50	89	26	1	15	58	0	13	63	.249	.276	.453
Car.	319	867	94	197	55	1	26	124	1	42	162	.227	.265	.383

Where He Hits the Ball

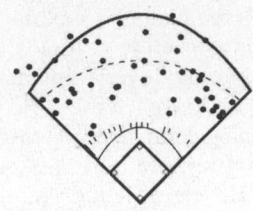
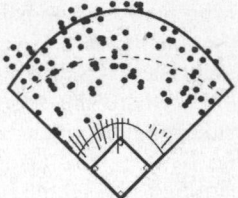

Vs. LHP   **Vs. RHP**

2004 Situational Stats

	AB	H	HR	RBI	Avg		AB	H	HR	RBI	Avg
Home	186	51	8	29	.274	LHP	101	25	4	19	.248
Road	172	38	7	29	.221	RHP	257	64	11	39	.249
First Half	185	50	12	35	.270	Sc Pos	91	24	3	42	.264
Scnd Half	173	39	3	23	.225	Clutch	55	9	4	13	.164

2004 Rankings (American League)

- 3rd in lowest fielding percentage at catcher (.990)
- 4th in errors at catcher (7)
- 5th in lowest batting average in the clutch
- 9th in fewest GDPs per GDP situation (4.2%)
- Led the Rangers in sacrifice bunts (8) and batting average with the bases loaded (.500)

Hank Blalock

2004 Season

At midseason, Hank Blalock was on top of the baseball world. He was an All-Star for the second straight year, was in the home-run derby and was among the American League leaders in homers. It turned sour for him in the second half, as he got away from being a line-drive hitter and started to swing for home runs. Pitchers started taking advantage of his willingness to swing at almost everything. Nonetheless, he still finished with the first 30-homer, 100-RBI season of his career. He finally did make adjustments in the final two weeks of the season.

Hitting

When Blalock makes contact, his lashing, violent swing punishes the ball—to the tune of 73 extra-base hits in 2004. He can hit the ball to all fields, though he has started trying to pull everything at home, where the short porch favors lefties. He made the adjustment to facing lefthanded pitching, batting .282 against lefties. His next task: learning to hit on the road. His career home average (.315) is ridiculously higher than his road average (.242).

Baserunning & Defense

Blalock's defense often gets overlooked because he is such a talented hitter, but he has an above-average arm and reacts well to the ball. He may go behind the bag as well as anybody in the league. As a baserunner, he is average, maybe a tick below, but he's heady and willing to take advantage of any opportunity to move up.

2005 Outlook

If Blalock is to continue to merit comparisons to George Brett, Tony Gwynn and the great line-drive hitters of the last generation, he'll have to stop swinging for the fences. He also will have to learn how to restrain some of his aggressiveness. The thing about him is, he is an intelligent player who learned from mistakes in 2002 to come back with a big 2003. He's liable to make the necessary adjustments again in '05.

Position: 3B
Bats: L **Throws:** R
Ht: 6' 1" **Wt:** 200

Opening Day Age: 24
Born: 11/21/80 in San Diego, CA
ML Seasons: 3
Pronunciation: BLAY-lock

Overall Statistics

	G	AB	R	H	D	T	HR	RBI	SB	BB	SO	Avg	OBP	Slg
'04	159	624	107	172	38	3	32	110	2	75	149	.276	.355	.500
Car.	351	1338	212	373	79	6	64	217	4	139	289	.279	.347	.490

Where He Hits the Ball

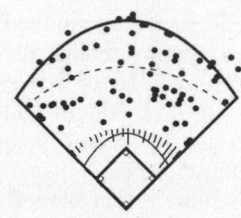
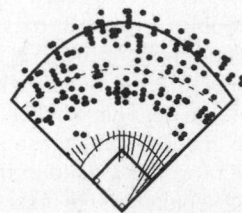

Vs. LHP **Vs. RHP**

2004 Situational Stats

	AB	H	HR	RBI	Avg		AB	H	HR	RBI	Avg
Home	315	98	16	63	.311	LHP	195	55	5	29	.282
Road	309	74	16	47	.239	RHP	429	117	27	81	.273
First Half	353	107	23	68	.303	Sc Pos	143	49	10	75	.343
Scnd Half	271	65	9	42	.240	Clutch	86	26	7	11	.302

2004 Rankings (American League)

- 2nd in strikeouts
- 3rd in errors at third base (17) and lowest fielding percentage at third base (.957)
- 4th in sacrifice flies (8), pitches seen (2,807) and lowest groundball-flyball ratio (0.7)
- 5th in games played
- 6th in plate appearances (713) and lowest batting average on the road
- 7th in total bases (312) and batting average with runners in scoring position
- Led the Rangers in doubles, sacrifice flies (8), walks, strikeouts, GDPs (13), pitches seen (2,807) and batting average with runners in scoring position
- Led AL third basemen in RBI

Francisco Cordero

2004 Season

The single biggest reason for the Rangers' 2004 success was the ascent of the bullpen. And the single biggest reason for the success of the bullpen was the surety that Francisco Cordero provided in his first full year as closer. He fell just shy of recording the 11th 50-save season in history. He came within a week of becoming the first American League pitcher since 1981 to go a full season of at least 60 innings without allowing a home run. This is what then-GM Doug Melvin had in mind when he made Cordero the key acquisition in sending Juan Gonzalez to Detroit after the 1999 season.

Pitching

Cordero's fastball, which jets up to 98 MPH, is what always has made him a scout's favorite. What's made him a dominant big league pitcher, though, is his evolving command of a tight slider. He made huge strides with it in 2003, and it looked simply unhittable for most of 2004. He could throw it in any count, and that kept hitters from picking up any significant trends. Because of it, he's averaged better than a strikeout per inning over the last two years.

Defense

As Cordero has grown in virtually every aspect of being a pitcher, so has he grown as a fielder. Though his delivery to the plate is fairly deliberate, he's become much more aware of runners. He's picked off a pair of baserunners in each of the past two seasons. He's developed into somewhat of a groundball pitcher and has the ability to start a double play on a comebacker.

2005 Outlook

Cordero has signed a multiyear extension with the Rangers, and providing he's healthy, he'll be the closer for the foreseeable future. And that's as it should be. In less than two full seasons as the Rangers' closer, he's evolved into one of the top two or three closers in the AL.

Position: RP
Bats: R **Throws:** R
Ht: 6' 2" **Wt:** 235

Opening Day Age: 29
Born: 5/11/75 in Santo Domingo, DR
ML Seasons: 6
Pronunciation: cor-DAIR-oh
Nickname: Coco

Texas

Overall Statistics

	W	L	Pct.	ERA	G	GS	Sv	IP	H	BB	SO	HR	Avg
'04	3	4	.429	2.13	67	0	49	71.2	60	32	79	1	.226
Car.	13	17	.433	3.23	258	0	74	298.1	272	151	279	20	.244

2004 Pitching Profile

	Francisco Cordero	AL Average
Overall Strike %	64.4	62.3
1st Pitch Strike %	62.5	58.1
Ratio	1.28	1.42
Strikeouts per 9 IP	9.92	6.45
Walks per 9 IP	4.02	3.34
Home Runs per 9 IP	0.13	1.15
Strikeout/Walk Ratio	2.47	1.93
Groundball/Flyball Ratio	1.03	1.17

2004 Situational Stats

	W	L	ERA	Sv	IP		AB	H	HR	RBI	Avg
Home	3	2	2.21	24	36.2	LHB	149	35	0	19	.235
Road	0	2	2.06	25	35.0	RHB	116	25	1	8	.216
First Half	2	0	2.08	27	39.0	Sc Pos	89	19	0	24	.213
Scnd Half	1	4	2.20	22	32.2	Clutch	220	49	1	27	.223

2004 Rankings (American League)

- 2nd in saves and games finished (63)
- 4th in relief ERA (2.13)
- 5th in balks (2) and save percentage (90.7)
- Led the Rangers in games pitched, saves, games finished (63), balks (2), save percentage (90.7), lowest batting average allowed with runners in scoring position, blown saves (5), relief losses (4) and relief ERA (2.13)

David Dellucci

2004 Season

The Rangers signed David Dellucci last winter as much for what he could do in the clubhouse as on the field. He is the model of the kind of player Buck Showalter craves, constantly hustling and completely selfless. Dellucci clearly squeezes the most from his talent. He gave the Rangers that and more, netting career highs in homers (17) and RBI (61). His walkoff double against Oakland on September 23 brought the Rangers within two games of first place with 10 to play, and perhaps was the franchise's most dramatic win in the last 10 years.

Hitting

Dellucci's inability to hit lefties keeps him from being anything more than a fourth outfielder. He is 17-for-119 (.143) against lefties over the last five seasons. The more he plays, the more pitchers are able to pitch to him. He hit .330 through 100 at-bats in the first two months of the season, then hit .203 over the final four months, when he played more frequently because of injuries.

Baserunning & Defense

As an outfielder, Dellucci is limited to left field because of a below-average arm. He played center in an occasional pinch, but he doesn't have the range for the position or the arm for right field. Still, without fear, he'll go into the walls or dive into the gaps to make a catch. While he has just average speed, Dellucci grasps Showalter's desire to be aggressive and make things happen on the basepaths. He has the instincts to push the envelope for occasional extra bases.

2005 Outlook

As long as Buck Showalter has a job, it seems Dellucci will have a home in Texas if he chooses to return, even though his limitations make it necessary for the Rangers' other backup outfielder to be extremely versatile. Dellucci rewards Showalter's loyalty with exceptional professionalism and the occasional big hit. He simply must be monitored closely for fatigue and falling into bad habits at the plate.

Position: LF
Bats: L **Throws:** L
Ht: 5'11" **Wt:** 190

Opening Day Age: 31
Born: 10/31/73 in Baton Rouge, LA
ML Seasons: 8
Pronunciation: duh-LOO-chee

Overall Statistics

	G	AB	R	H	D	T	HR	RBI	SB	BB	SO	Avg	OBP	Slg
'04	107	331	59	80	13	1	17	61	9	47	88	.242	.342	.441
Car.	648	1595	222	417	76	21	44	224	30	172	396	.261	.339	.418

Where He Hits the Ball

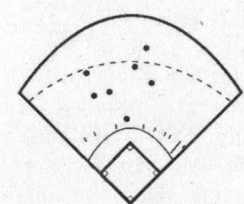 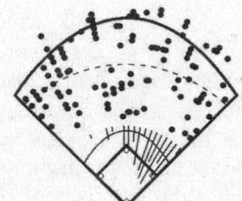

Vs. LHP   **Vs. RHP**

2004 Situational Stats

	AB	H	HR	RBI	Avg		AB	H	HR	RBI	Avg
Home	192	50	9	41	.260	LHP	28	3	0	2	.107
Road	139	30	8	20	.216	RHP	303	77	17	59	.254
First Half	176	48	9	38	.273	Sc Pos	82	24	4	44	.293
Scnd Half	155	32	8	23	.206	Clutch	45	15	4	13	.333

2004 Rankings (American League)

- 5th in highest percentage of swings that missed (27.5)
- 8th in lowest batting average with two strikes (.148)
- 9th in batting average in the clutch
- Led the Rangers in most pitches seen per plate appearance (4.11) and batting average in the clutch

Ryan Drese

2004 Season

The Rangers are pointing every pitcher in their system towards becoming more like Ryan Drese. Why not? He showed that a pitcher can learn to be successful in Arlington. He did it by finally abandoning his dream of being a power pitcher and embracing the sinker preached by pitching coach Orel Hershiser. The results spoke for themselves: a 14-win season and 200-plus innings. He also spent the majority of the season in the thick of the American League ERA race. A poor September, perhaps due to fatigue from approaching the 200-inning barrier for the first time in his career, pushed his ERA above four.

Pitching

The Rangers believe that through the sinker, all things are possible. The sinker allowed Drese to compete, even when he had just one pitch. His willingness to throw it early in the count and his ability to command it made him among the American League's most efficient pitchers (he averaged 14.9 pitches per inning). Getting ahead in the count made hitters swing at the sinker and induced groundballs, 2.2 for every flyball in 2004.

Defense

A groundball pitcher must be adept at fielding his position. Drese has made progress in this area, but still has room to grow. He gets to first base very well to take feeds and double-play relays. Drese was involved in the second-highest number of double plays (five) by a pitcher in the AL. He made two errors, one of them on a bad pickoff throw, but otherwise was quite good at holding runners.

2005 Outlook

Drese will be counted on heavily in 2005. He went into the offseason no worse than the No. 2 starter in the rotation and may surpass the 40-year-old Kenny Rogers. You can bet hitters will be better prepared for the sinker in 2005, so Drese is going to have to make some adjustments.

Position: SP
Bats: R **Throws:** R
Ht: 6' 3" **Wt:** 235

Opening Day Age: 28
Born: 4/5/76 in San Francisco, CA
ML Seasons: 4
Pronunciation: drees

Overall Statistics

	W	L	Pct.	ERA	G	GS	Sv	IP	H	BB	SO	HR	Avg
'04	14	10	.583	4.20	34	33	0	207.2	233	58	98	16	.285
Car.	27	25	.519	5.18	80	71	0	427.2	502	159	250	41	.296

2004 Pitching Profile

	Ryan Drese	AL Average
Overall Strike %	61.8	62.3
1st Pitch Strike %	57.1	58.1
Ratio	1.40	1.42
Strikeouts per 9 IP	4.25	6.45
Walks per 9 IP	2.51	3.34
Home Runs per 9 IP	0.69	1.15
Strikeout/Walk Ratio	1.69	1.93
Groundball/Flyball Ratio	2.20	1.17

2004 Situational Stats

	W	L	ERA	Sv	IP		AB	H	HR	RBI	Avg
Home	10	4	3.26	0	107.2	LHB	452	126	13	53	.279
Road	4	6	5.22	0	100.0	RHB	365	107	3	34	.293
First Half	4	5	3.78	0	114.1	Sc Pos	200	50	1	69	.250
Scnd Half	10	5	4.73	0	93.1	Clutch	42	16	1	6	.381

2004 Rankings (American League)

- 2nd in fewest home runs allowed per nine innings (.69)
- 3rd in fewest pitches thrown per batter (3.46) and fewest strikeouts per nine innings (4.2)
- 4th in highest groundball-flyball ratio allowed (2.2)
- 8th in wins, games started, complete games (2) and hits allowed
- 9th in hit batsmen (11), GDPs induced (26) and lowest ERA at home
- 10th in lowest strikeout-walk ratio (1.7)
- Led the Rangers in ERA, losses, complete games (2), GDPs induced (26), lowest slugging percentage allowed (.409), highest groundball-flyball ratio allowed (2.2), fewest pitches thrown per batter (3.46), lowest ERA at home, fewest home runs allowed per nine innings (.69) and fewest walks per nine innings (2.5)

Kevin Mench

2004 Season

Fun-loving Kevin Mench moved from the Rangers' doghouse into their long-range plans by staying healthy for most of the year and, more importantly, proving he could be serious about his approach to hitting. Nervous he'd be traded at the July 31 deadline, Mench batted .297 with 12 homers and 30 RBI from August 1 on. He led the Rangers with 29 extra-base hits in the final two months. Only Carlos Delgado and Manny Ramirez had more in the American League.

Hitting

The keys to Mench's big second half were both about maturity. He learned to "feel" his swing better and was better at working his way out of bad habits quickly. He also was more willing to accept walks. Mench made a weight shift that allowed him to stay back on the ball better. In turn, it allowed him to see the ball longer and better recognize pitches. It made Mench more dangerous because he started using the gap in right center more often. It also minimized his habit of diving over the plate and getting drilled with pitches.

Baserunning & Defense

Mench's nickname is Shrek, because he's got a giant-sized melon, but he's not a lumbering monster. He split time between left and right, which are two vastly different positions in Arlington. He's got just enough range to handle the big left field. He's got a plus arm for right. Though he didn't steal a base in 2004, he moves a lot faster than he looks. He is not necessarily just a station-to-station runner.

2005 Outlook

Despite his 2004 progress, Mench still found his way to the disabled list for a three-week stay, which did nothing to diminish concerns about his durability. That said, he will continue to be coveted by other teams, but he seems to have finally cemented his place in the Rangers' plans. Mench is likely to spend most of 2005 in left field after Texas signed strong-armed right fielder Richard Hidalgo to a one-year contract in December.

Position: RF/LF/DH
Bats: R **Throws:** R
Ht: 6' 0" **Wt:** 225

Opening Day Age: 27
Born: 1/7/78 in Wilmington, DE
ML Seasons: 3

Overall Statistics

	G	AB	R	H	D	T	HR	RBI	SB	BB	SO	Avg	OBP	Slg
'04	125	438	69	122	30	3	26	71	0	33	63	.279	.335	.539
Car.	273	929	136	257	62	5	43	142	2	74	163	.277	.338	.493

Where He Hits the Ball

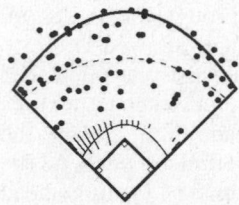 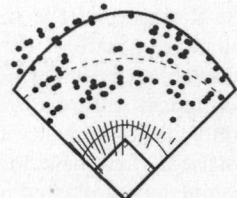

Vs. LHP   **Vs. RHP**

2004 Situational Stats

	AB	H	HR	RBI	Avg		AB	H	HR	RBI	Avg
Home	231	69	14	33	.299	LHP	144	46	10	28	.319
Road	207	53	12	38	.256	RHP	294	76	16	43	.259
First Half	221	61	13	37	.276	Sc Pos	110	26	4	40	.236
Scnd Half	217	61	13	34	.281	Clutch	58	8	0	4	.138

2004 Rankings (American League)

- 2nd in lowest batting average in the clutch
- 9th in batting average with two strikes (.262)
- 10th in lowest batting average with the bases loaded (.100)
- Led the Rangers in lowest percentage of swings on the first pitch (15.5)

Laynce Nix

2004 Season

Laynce Nix was the 10th different Opening Day center fielder in the 11 seasons the Rangers have called Ameriquest Field home. The team was hoping he'd be the last for quite some time. The experiment went well for the first half of the season, but a sprained right shoulder, a big second-half offensive drop and several balls that escaped him had the Rangers going into the winter unsure if he was better suited for center or a corner.

Hitting

Nix' productivity dropped as the season progressed, which was the biggest reason for the Rangers' concern. Teams look for young players to get a better grasp of pitching as they gain experience. Nix went 142 at-bats between mid-August and the last day of the season without a homer. His average dropped almost 80 points in the second half compared to the first half. In limited exposure, he showed no ability to hit lefthanded pitching, which could relegate him to being a platoon player for the time being.

Baserunning & Defense

The conundrum on Nix is this: as a corner outfielder, he's a plus defender. He's got better-than-average range and a better-than-average arm. As a center fielder, it's stretching his limits to the max to be average. He'll have the arm to play the position; the bigger issue is whether he has enough range. Ameriquest requires a center fielder who can play shallow, then close on balls quickly in the left-center gap. It's hard to improve range. On the basepaths, he fits the club's ideal of being aggressive without necessarily stealing many bases.

2005 Outlook

Nix has too much talent not to be in the mix in 2005. Where depends on how the Rangers allocate their free-agent dollars and who they may acquire via a trade. But the winter of 2004 was important for Nix. He needs to come to camp able to make the adjustments at the plate that he was unable to make in 2004. Otherwise, he could start to fall from the picture.

Position: CF
Bats: L **Throws:** L
Ht: 6' 0" **Wt:** 200

Opening Day Age: 24
Born: 10/30/80 in Houston, TX
ML Seasons: 2
Pronunciation: nicks

Overall Statistics

	G	AB	R	H	D	T	HR	RBI	SB	BB	SO	Avg	OBP	Slg
'04	115	371	58	92	20	4	14	46	1	23	113	.248	.293	.437
Car.	168	555	83	139	30	4	22	76	4	32	166	.250	.292	.438

Where He Hits the Ball

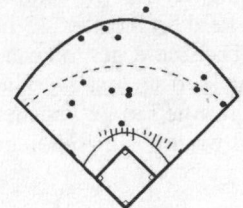 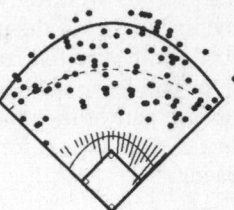

Vs. LHP	**Vs. RHP**

2004 Situational Stats

	AB	H	HR	RBI	Avg		AB	H	HR	RBI	Avg
Home	195	50	9	30	.256	LHP	74	13	1	7	.176
Road	176	42	5	16	.239	RHP	297	79	13	39	.266
First Half	151	44	9	23	.291	Sc Pos	94	17	4	28	.181
Scnd Half	220	48	5	23	.218	Clutch	56	12	0	6	.214

2004 Rankings (American League)

- 1st in highest percentage of swings that missed (30.0)
- 2nd in fielding percentage in center field (.996) and lowest batting average with runners in scoring position
- 4th in lowest percentage of swings put into play (33.4)

Chan Ho Park

2004 Season

Year 3 of the Chan Ho Park mega-contract produced the same old results. He struggled with command. He got lit up by opponents. He spent significant time on the disabled list. And in the end, he was more of a liability to the Rangers than an asset to their pitching staff. He topped it off by throwing several pitches at Anaheim players in a key late-season game that cost him the respect of several teammates.

Pitching

Park has struggled to get anybody out since his velocity took a downward turn in 2002. He got some of the velocity back, but had no command. The results were ugly. When he tried to control the inside part of the plate, he'd hit a batter (13 in 95.2 innings last season). Then he'd get too cautious and leave his middling stuff up and over the middle part of the plate. It resulted in 22 homers. In a 200-inning season, that would be a 46-homer pace.

Defense

Perhaps out of desire to prove himself, Park gets too excitable in key situations and makes bad fielding decisions. He's made three errors in 28 chances over the last two years. His delivery is slow, too. Since Park came to Texas, 14 of the 20 runners who have tried to steal against him have been successful. That just reinforces the notion that Park is a pitcher in rapid decline.

2005 Outlook

There are two more years left on Park's unwieldy contract, which, for all intents and purposes, make him unmovable. The Rangers long ago gave up hope that Park would be a staff ace. They'd simply settle for a 30-start, 200-inning season in which he regularly gave them a chance to compete. Even asking that, however, may be wishful thinking, given Park's track record in Texas and his five trips to the DL over the last three years.

Position: SP
Bats: R **Throws:** R
Ht: 6' 2" **Wt:** 210

Opening Day Age: 31
Born: 6/30/73 in Kong Ju City, South Korea
ML Seasons: 11

Overall Statistics

	W	L	Pct.	ERA	G	GS	Sv	IP	H	BB	SO	HR	Avg
'04	4	7	.364	5.46	16	16	0	95.2	105	33	63	22	.281
Car.	94	72	.566	4.18	269	224	0	1454.2	1294	696	1298	171	.240

2004 Pitching Profile

	Chan Ho Park	AL Average
Overall Strike %	61.5	62.3
1st Pitch Strike %	56.2	58.1
Ratio	1.44	1.42
Strikeouts per 9 IP	5.93	6.45
Walks per 9 IP	3.10	3.34
Home Runs per 9 IP	2.07	1.15
Strikeout/Walk Ratio	1.91	1.93
Groundball/Flyball Ratio	1.18	1.17

2004 Situational Stats

	W	L	ERA	Sv	IP		AB	H	HR	RBI	Avg
Home	1	4	6.60	0	45.0	LHB	184	51	11	27	.277
Road	3	3	4.44	0	50.2	RHB	190	54	11	29	.284
First Half	2	4	5.80	0	49.2	Sc Pos	81	22	3	30	.272
Scnd Half	2	3	5.09	0	46.0	Clutch	20	8	1	3	.400

2004 Rankings (American League)

- 5th in hit batsmen (13)
- Led the Rangers in hit batsmen (13) and lowest ERA on the road

Kenny Rogers

2004 Season

Just 16 years in, Kenny Rogers had the most complete season of his career. The Rangers wanted him to provide an example of professionalism for a relatively inexperienced staff. He ended up as the ace of a contending staff. He was named to the All-Star Game for the first time since 1995. His 18 wins were a personal best. Rogers did tire some in the second half, but still wound up with a career-high 35 starts and his most innings pitched since 2000.

Pitching

Ever since he had a rib removed to improve circulation in 2001, Rogers has seen improved velocity. He's not a power pitcher by any means, but he still can get a fastball up to 90 MPH when he needs to. He's got a nice little curve and uses the changeup, and he'll throw them just about anywhere, though he likes to stay away with the change. Rogers never gives in to hitters and isn't afraid to go into deep counts. Hitters used that against him in the second half, though, pushing his pitch count high and tiring him out earlier.

Defense

As a groundball pitcher, Rogers helps himself with quick reactions, good hands and impeccable instincts. He won his third Gold Glove in the last five years in 2004. During that period, he's handled more total chances than any pitcher in the American League. He has an outstanding pickoff move and can vary his times to first base. The only drawback is an occasional preoccupation with the baserunner, which can affect his concentration on the hitter.

2005 Outlook

Can Rogers be the next Jamie Moyer, reaching the heights of his career after his 40th birthday? Like Moyer, Rogers has come to understand the art of pitching. While age seemed to finally catch up with Moyer in 2004, Rogers, who is two years younger, excelled. What the Rangers must be aware of, though, is the decline could come at any time. Seattle learned that painfully with Moyer last year.

Position: SP
Bats: L **Throws:** L
Ht: 6' 1" **Wt:** 211

Opening Day Age: 40
Born: 11/10/64 in Savannah, GA
ML Seasons: 16
Nickname: The Gambler

Texas

Overall Statistics

W	L	Pct.	ERA	G	GS	Sv	IP	H	BB	SO	HR	Avg
18	9	.667	4.76	35	35	0	211.2	248	66	126	24	.292
176	123	.589	4.27	657	370	28	2666.2	2780	964	1664	271	.269

2004 Pitching Profile

	Kenny Rogers	AL Average
Overall Strike %	61.1	62.3
1st Pitch Strike %	57.0	58.1
Ratio	1.48	1.42
Strikeouts per 9 IP	5.36	6.45
Walks per 9 IP	2.81	3.34
Home Runs per 9 IP	1.02	1.15
Strikeout/Walk Ratio	1.91	1.93
Groundball/Flyball Ratio	1.26	1.17

2004 Situational Stats

	W	L	ERA	Sv	IP		AB	H	HR	RBI	Avg
Home	10	3	4.24	0	108.1	LHB	194	57	3	15	.294
Road	8	6	5.31	0	103.1	RHB	654	191	21	96	.292
First Half	12	3	4.21	0	117.2	Sc Pos	201	59	4	79	.294
Scnd Half	6	6	5.46	0	94.0	Clutch	34	9	1	5	.265

2004 Rankings (American League)

- 1st in games started
- 2nd in lowest stolen-base percentage allowed (28.6)
- 3rd in wins and pitches thrown (3,506)
- 4th in hits allowed, batters faced (935), pickoff throws (141), winning percentage and most run support per nine innings (6.8)
- 8th in complete games (2)
- 9th in highest batting average allowed (.292)
- 10th in highest slugging percentage allowed (.466) and highest on-base percentage allowed (.348)
- Led the Rangers in wins, games started, complete games (2), innings pitched, hits allowed, batters faced (935), home runs allowed, walks allowed, strikeouts, pitches thrown (3,506), pickoff throws (141), runners caught stealing (5), lowest stolen-base percentage allowed (28.6) and most run support per nine innings (6.8)

2004 Season

While Alex Rodriguez' arrival in New York last February was treated as something of a coronation, little attention was paid to the man traded for him: Alfonso Soriano. Going from a contender to expected cellar-dweller, Soriano could have sulked. He didn't. He put together a season that has been typical of his four-year career. He is far more productive than any second baseman in the league, but he slumped again in the second half, which keeps him from being an elite player.

Hitting

For the fourth straight season, Soriano struck out at least 120 times and failed to draw 40 walks. He will swing at anything. When he's in a groove, he can hit almost anything, but he is prone to long slumps. He will start to lunge at pitches and gets off balance. Then the strikeouts come in bunches.

Baserunning & Defense

When Soriano arrived in Texas, he made it clear he intended to stay at second base, because, he said, he was a two-time All-Star at the position. It certainly wasn't based on defense. For the fourth consecutive year, he led all second basemen in errors. Most of those errors are "lazy" errors that seem to come when Soriano gets tired. As he wore down, the errors started piling up. Soriano's stolen-base total dropped off in 2004, but that was more because he spent most of 2004 in the No. 3 hole. In the three previous seasons, he averaged 40 steals a year.

2005 Outlook

At midseason 2003, Soriano was the American League's Most Valuable Player. By the end of 2004, his future was up in the air. He is a liability at second base. He lacks the discipline to hit No. 1 or No. 3. In addition, his health was up in the air at season's end. He missed the final two weeks with a torn tendon at the bottom of his hamstring and opted not to have it surgically repaired.

Position: 2B
Bats: R **Throws:** R
Ht: 6' 1" **Wt:** 180

Opening Day Age: 29
Born: 1/7/76 in San Pedro de Macoris, DR
ML Seasons: 6
Pronunciation: soar-ee-ah-no

Overall Statistics

	G	AB	R	H	D	T	HR	RBI	SB	BB	SO	Avg	OBP	Slg
'04	145	608	77	170	32	4	28	91	18	33	121	.280	.324	.484
Car.	646	2618	403	741	156	14	126	361	139	124	551	.283	.323	.498

Where He Hits the Ball

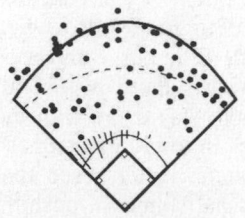 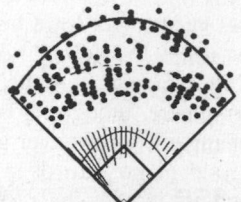

Vs. LHP **Vs. RHP**

2004 Situational Stats

	AB	H	HR	RBI	Avg		AB	H	HR	RBI	Avg
Home	293	93	12	47	.317	LHP	158	42	9	31	.266
Road	315	77	16	44	.244	RHP	450	128	19	60	.284
First Half	367	106	17	55	.289	Sc Pos	146	37	4	58	.253
Scnd Half	241	64	11	36	.266	Clutch	83	22	3	9	.265

2004 Rankings (American League)

- 1st in errors at second base (23) and lowest fielding percentage at second base (.969)
- 4th in lowest percentage of pitches taken (46.1)
- 7th in lowest groundball-flyball ratio (0.7)
- 8th in stolen-base percentage (78.3)
- Led the Rangers in stolen bases, hit by pitch (10) and steals of third (2)
- Led AL second basemen in home runs and RBI

Mark Teixeira

2004 Season

Bothered by a strained neck ligament in spring training and a pulled left oblique muscle in April, Mark Teixeira didn't really get into a rhythm until June. When he did, though, he was as good as any power hitter in the American League. Teixeira led the AL in homers after June 1, and was second to Miguel Tejada in RBI over that span.

Hitting

The switch-hitter is still significantly better against lefthanded pitchers, but Teixeira did improve his average from the left side by 25 points in 2004. He also seemed to better tailor his lefthanded swing for Ameriquest Field, lifting balls into the air to right and taking advantage of the short right-field wall. An impressive trend: Teixeira's strikeouts went down slightly and his walks jumped significantly in virtually the same number of at-bats as in 2003. That's the sign of a maturing hitter.

Baserunning & Defense

Sometimes it's hard to remember that Teixeira was drafted as a third baseman, because he's made the move to first look quite easy. In just two seasons at the position, he's developing into a solid fielding first basemen. He has plus range and isn't afraid to make a throw when necessary. He does still have an occasional problem with a scoop, but he appears to be dedicated to learning the position. Though he's just an average runner, he certainly doesn't clog the basepaths.

2005 Outlook

It's possible the Rangers could ask Teixeira to change positions again. A move to the outfield would make room for Adrian Gonzalez at first. It's also uncertain whether he'll end up hitting fifth, where the club would like him to stay for a year or two, or take over as the cleanup hitter for good. The one thing that is clear is Teixeira will be in the Rangers' plans for the foreseeable future.

Position: 1B
Bats: B **Throws:** R
Ht: 6' 3" **Wt:** 220

Opening Day Age: 24
Born: 4/11/80 in Annapolis, MD
ML Seasons: 2
Pronunciation: tuh-SHARE-uh

Texas

Overall Statistics

	G	AB	R	H	D	T	HR	RBI	SB	BB	SO	Avg	OBP	Slg
'04	145	545	101	153	34	2	38	112	4	68	117	.281	.370	.560
Car.	291	1074	167	290	63	7	64	196	5	112	237	.270	.351	.520

Where He Hits the Ball

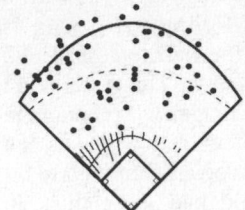
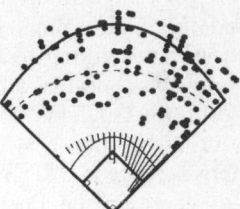

Vs. LHP   **Vs. RHP**

2004 Situational Stats

	AB	H	HR	RBI	Avg		AB	H	HR	RBI	Avg
Home	265	79	18	64	.298	LHP	163	51	10	34	.313
Road	280	74	20	48	.264	RHP	382	102	28	78	.267
First Half	258	71	18	48	.275	Sc Pos	137	43	16	84	.314
Scnd Half	287	82	20	64	.286	Clutch	75	19	6	17	.253

2004 Rankings (American League)

- 1st in errors at first base (10) and lowest fielding percentage at first base (.992)
- 5th in home runs, intentional walks (12) and HR frequency (14.3 ABs per HR)
- 6th in slugging percentage
- 7th in RBI and cleanup slugging percentage (.530)
- Led the Rangers in home runs, RBI, intentional walks (12), hit by pitch (10), slugging percentage, HR frequency (14.3 ABs per HR) and cleanup slugging percentage (.530)
- Led AL first basemen in home runs and RBI

2004 Season

Michael Young set the tone for the Rangers by walking into manager Buck Showalter's office in the first week of spring training. Without prompting, Young said he'd move from second to short to replace Alex Rodriguez and accommodate the acquisition of Alfonso Soriano. Young established the team-first attitude and quickly became the team leader. He backed it up on the field, reaching the All-Star Game for the first time and hitting .300 with at least 200 hits and 100 runs scored for the second straight season.

Hitting

Young may be developing into a latter-day version of Pudge Rodriguez at the plate, but with a tad more discipline. Like Rodriguez, Young is more than willing to take the ball to right field. Young is confident and fearless. Those traits are best reflected in his 2004 averages with runners in scoring position (.342) and with two strikes (an above-average .227). He is versatile enough to hit anywhere in the lineup and had more than 30 starts in each of the top three spots.

Baserunning & Defense

When middle infielders switch positions, it's usually from short to second, not the other way around. Young was perhaps the best defensive second baseman in the league in 2003 before making the move. He proved more than adequate as a shortstop. He had plenty of arm for the position and had no trouble reading the ball after the move. He turns the double play as well as any shortstop in the league. He is a smart, heady, above-average baserunner who has an uncanny knack for grabbing extra bases.

2005 Outlook

Young has developed into one of the most respected players in the clubhouse. He now is in the middle of a four-year contract and is entrenched in the Rangers' infield. Young's defensive abilities give the Rangers options if they decide not to bring back Alfonso Soriano. Young could stay at short or move back to second. Either way, he is expected to remain an asset both offensively and defensively.

Position: SS
Bats: R **Throws:** R
Ht: 6' 1" **Wt:** 190

Opening Day Age: 28
Born: 10/19/76 in Covina, CA
ML Seasons: 5

Overall Statistics

	G	AB	R	H	D	T	HR	RBI	SB	BB	SO	Avg	OBP	Slg
'04	160	690	114	216	33	9	22	99	12	44	89	.313	.353	.483
Car.	584	2317	354	666	110	30	56	282	34	147	396	.287	.328	.433

Where He Hits the Ball

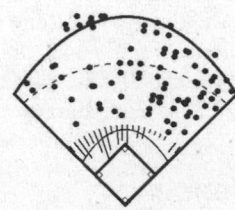 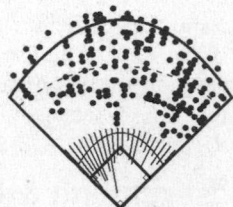

Vs. LHP	Vs. RHP

2004 Situational Stats

	AB	H	HR	RBI	Avg		AB	H	HR	RBI	Avg
Home	344	119	9	57	.346	LHP	188	62	7	29	.330
Road	346	97	13	42	.280	RHP	502	154	15	70	.307
First Half	382	127	12	53	.332	Sc Pos	161	55	5	70	.342
Scnd Half	308	89	10	46	.289	Clutch	91	27	1	12	.297

2004 Rankings (American League)

- 2nd in at-bats, hits, singles and plate appearances (739)
- 4th in runs scored, triples, games played and batting average at home
- 5th in total bases (333), errors at shortstop (19) and lowest fielding percentage at shortstop (.972)
- 6th in pitches seen (2,724)
- Led the Rangers in batting average, at-bats, runs scored, hits, singles, triples, total bases (333), times on base (261), plate appearances (739), games played, stolen-base percentage (80.0), batting average vs. lefthanded pitchers, batting average vs. righthanded pitchers, on-base percentage for a leadoff hitter (.368) and batting average at home

Carlos Almanzar

Position: RP
Bats: R **Throws:** R
Ht: 6' 2" **Wt:** 190

Opening Day Age: 31
Born: 11/6/73 in
Santiago, DR
ML Seasons: 7
Pronunciation:
al-MAN-sar

Overall Statistics

	W	L	Pct.	ERA	G	GS	Sv	IP	H	BB	SO	HR	Avg
'04	7	3	.700	3.72	67	0	0	72.2	66	19	44	8	.244
Car.	13	13	.500	4.62	204	1	0	234.0	242	75	167	33	.267

2004 Situational Stats

	W	L	ERA	Sv	IP		AB	H	HR	RBI	Avg
Home	5	1	3.69	0	39.0	LHB	115	26	2	14	.226
Road	2	2	3.74	0	33.2	RHB	155	40	6	19	.258
First Half	6	1	3.63	0	44.2	Sc Pos	63	12	1	24	.190
Scnd Half	1	2	3.86	0	28.0	Clutch	115	27	2	19	.235

2004 Season

During the first half, Carlos Almanzar threw strikes, got groundball outs and was the major span in the bridge to closer Francisco Cordero. But in the midst of working a career-high 72.2 innings, Almanzar weakened. He was 7-2 (3.47 ERA) with just four homers and 10 walks allowed in 49.1 innings on August 1. He went 0-1 (4.24 ERA) with four homers and nine walks in 23.1 innings during the final two months.

Pitching & Defense

Almanzar lives primarily on a two-seam fastball that runs away from righthanded hitters more than it sinks. He always has commanded it well. His breaking ball is erratic, though, and it spins and hovers in the hitting zone when it's not right. He has not made an error in his last 33 chances dating to the 1999 season. Prior to last season, basestealers were successful on 13 of 14 attempts, but Almanzar allowed just one steal in 2004.

2005 Outlook

Almanzar established himself as a capable late-inning reliever in 2004, but he also sparked questions. His late-season struggles and a forearm injury raise concerns about how much he can be used. He is eligible for arbitration, which raises an entirely different set of issues about how he fits.

Joaquin Benoit

Position: SP/RP
Bats: R **Throws:** R
Ht: 6' 0" **Wt:** 220

Opening Day Age: 27
Born: 7/26/77 in
Santiago, DR
ML Seasons: 4
Pronunciation:
ben-WUH

Overall Statistics

	W	L	Pct.	ERA	G	GS	Sv	IP	H	BB	SO	HR	Avg
'04	3	5	.375	5.68	28	15	0	103.0	113	31	95	19	.279
Car.	15	15	.500	5.59	71	46	1	297.2	311	143	245	51	.267

2004 Situational Stats

	W	L	ERA	Sv	IP		AB	H	HR	RBI	Avg
Home	2	1	5.77	0	57.2	LHB	209	52	7	29	.249
Road	1	4	5.56	0	45.1	RHB	196	61	12	34	.311
First Half	3	4	6.18	0	71.1	Sc Pos	98	21	4	43	.214
Scnd Half	0	1	4.55	0	31.2	Clutch	0	0	0	0	–

2004 Season

Still perplexing after all these years, Joaquin Benoit took himself out of the Rangers' starting rotation once and for all in 2004 with more control issues. His troubles have made him quite susceptible to the home run. He allowed 1.8 per nine innings as a starter in 2004. Texas management often expressed exasperation with his unpredictability.

Pitching & Defense

Benoit has the prototypical live arm, which is why the Rangers protected him throughout 2004, even though he was out of options. His fastball runs so much, Benoit has trouble reining it in and commanding the strike zone. When he tries to work the corners, walks abound. When his command fails, a home-run festival breaks out. He needs to cut down on his pitches per inning (18.3 for his career) to have a long-term career of any type. He is a marginal fielder who regressed at holding runners on base last year.

2005 Outlook

Benoit may have exhausted his chances with the Rangers. There are other, younger pitchers waiting in line. Wherever he ends up, he seems much better suited to be a middle reliever/swing starter. He is 3-0 with a 3.95 ERA in 25 career relief appearances that total 68.1 innings.

Doug Brocail

Position: RP
Bats: L **Throws:** R
Ht: 6' 5" **Wt:** 235

Opening Day Age: 37
Born: 5/16/67 in
Clearfield, PA
ML Seasons: 10
Pronunciation:
broh-KALE

Overall Statistics

	W	L	Pct.	ERA	G	GS	Sv	IP	H	BB	SO	HR	Avg
'04	4	1	.800	4.13	43	0	1	52.1	54	20	43	2	.269
Car.	32	37	.464	3.89	381	42	6	615.1	618	210	446	62	.263

2004 Situational Stats

	W	L	ERA	Sv	IP		AB	H	HR	RBI	Avg
Home	3	0	4.91	1	33.0	LHB	79	15	1	12	.190
Road	1	1	2.79	0	19.1	RHB	122	39	1	16	.320
First Half	0	1	7.45	0	19.1	Sc Pos	75	19	0	25	.253
Scnd Half	4	0	2.18	1	33.0	Clutch	35	10	0	1	.286

2004 Season

Doug Brocail was quite a comeback story. He missed the previous three seasons with a variety of arm problems and was a last-minute sign by the Rangers. He went to the minors to continue his rehab and pitched in the majors only four times before June 1. Yet, by midseason, he had regained his velocity and more. Over the second half, he was as good as any reliever in the Texas bullpen.

Pitching & Defense

While it didn't take long for Brocail to start throwing in the mid-90s again, it was finding the touch on his curveball that turned his season around. He could be counted on to stop rallies, allowing only five of 33 inherited runners to score. He made one error in 17 chances, but was quick to react to balls and willing to do whatever necessary to get an out.

2005 Outlook

Missing three years of wear and tear may make Brocail a "young" 37-year-old. He still has plenty of velocity and seems to have regained his touch. His ability to throw more than an inning also makes him attractive to the Rangers, who re-signed him to a one-year deal soon after the 2004 playoffs.

R.A. Dickey

Position: SP/RP
Bats: R **Throws:** R
Ht: 6' 3" **Wt:** 220

Opening Day Age: 30
Born: 10/29/74 in
Nashville, TN
ML Seasons: 3

Overall Statistics

	W	L	Pct.	ERA	G	GS	Sv	IP	H	BB	SO	HR	Avg
'04	6	7	.462	5.61	25	15	1	104.1	136	33	57	17	.311
Car.	15	16	.484	5.41	67	28	2	233.0	284	78	155	36	.300

2004 Situational Stats

	W	L	ERA	Sv	IP		AB	H	HR	RBI	Avg
Home	3	4	6.46	1	61.1	LHB	221	62	11	40	.281
Road	3	3	4.40	0	43.0	RHB	216	74	6	32	.343
First Half	5	6	5.90	0	76.1	Sc Pos	106	40	10	62	.377
Scnd Half	1	1	4.82	1	28.0	Clutch	25	5	0	2	.200

2004 Season

R.A. Dickey continues to overachieve simply by pitching in the majors. He has transformed himself from a medical freak of nature (born without a right elbow ligament) to a major league pitcher. Though it wasn't really the right role for him, Dickey took the ball as a starter and gave it everything he had. He was exceptional for a month, then cratered. After some back problems, he had some late-season success as a long reliever.

Pitching & Defense

Perhaps because of the lack of a ligament, Dickey has never had a great fastball, but he does approach 90 MPH. His best pitch, though, is a splitter called "The Thing." At times he falls in love with it and uses it too much. When he mixes the two pitches, he's good for a turn through the lineup. A groundball pitcher, he will help himself with his fielding. He's unafraid to risk injury to make a play.

2005 Outlook

Dickey may have marginal major league skills, but he's a Hall of Famer when it comes to desire and work ethic. Every spring, he may have to win a long reliever job. But with his approach and his team-first attitude, he'll always win a close battle.

Frank Francisco

Position: RP
Bats: R **Throws:** R
Ht: 6' 2" **Wt:** 180

Opening Day Age: 25
Born: 9/11/79 in Santo Domingo, DR
ML Seasons: 1

Overall Statistics

	W	L	Pct.	ERA	G	GS	Sv	IP	H	BB	SO	HR	Avg
'04	5	1	.833	3.33	45	0	0	51.1	36	28	60	4	.198
Car.	5	1	.833	3.33	45	0	0	51.1	36	28	60	4	.198

2004 Situational Stats

	W	L	ERA	Sv	IP		AB	H	HR	RBI	Avg
Home	3	0	1.42	0	25.1	LHB	73	18	2	7	.247
Road	2	1	5.19	0	26.0	RHB	109	18	2	9	.165
First Half	1	1	4.63	0	23.1	Sc Pos	48	8	0	11	.167
Scnd Half	4	0	2.25	0	28.0	Clutch	91	20	3	9	.220

2004 Season

Until mid-September, Frank Francisco had an outside shot at AL Rookie of the Year honors. He arrived in mid-May and simply overpowered hitters. But he was at the center of the Rangers' brawl with Oakland fans on September 13 and hurled a chair into the stands, hitting a fan. He was suspended for the final 15 games of the season.

Pitching & Defense

The Rangers acquired Francisco in the 2003 deal that sent Carl Everett to the Chicago White Sox. After learning the value of throwing strikes at Double-A Frisco, he showed off his power arm in the majors. He reared back and fired fastballs that approached the high 90s and supplemented them with a good splitter. It's a devastating combination, especially when he's throwing the first pitch for a strike. He wasn't tested much defensively as a rookie.

2005 Outlook

The fallout from Francisco's chair-throwing incident clouds his future. Will he be affected by constant booing wherever he goes? Will there be legal ramifications? How will a sure-to-be-filed civil suit impact him? He's got a great arm. If he can deal with the outside problems, he'll be a key figure in the Rangers' bullpen.

Brian Jordan

Position: RF/DH
Bats: R **Throws:** R
Ht: 6' 1" **Wt:** 225

Opening Day Age: 38
Born: 3/29/67 in Baltimore, MD
ML Seasons: 13

Overall Statistics

	G	AB	R	H	D	T	HR	RBI	SB	BB	SO	Avg	OBP	Slg
'04	61	212	27	47	13	1	5	23	2	16	35	.222	.275	.363
Car.	1332	4838	719	1376	257	35	178	787	117	332	773	.284	.336	.462

2004 Situational Stats

	AB	H	HR	RBI	Avg		AB	H	HR	RBI	Avg
Home	124	30	4	17	.242	LHP	85	22	3	13	.259
Road	88	17	1	6	.193	RHP	127	25	2	10	.197
First Half	49	5	0	3	.102	Sc Pos	60	10	0	16	.167
Scnd Half	163	42	5	20	.258	Clutch	34	7	1	4	.206

2004 Season

Continuing knee problems, the result of three years in the NFL and 13 in the majors, plagued Brian Jordan in 2004. He missed most of the first half and really wasn't effective until September. Jordan was able to help the young Rangers learn about professionalism and leadership, but what the team needed even more was a big middle-of-the-order bat. That may be more than is possible to ask from him any longer.

Hitting, Baserunning & Defense

Jordan had surgery to repair a tendon in his left knee in July 2003, and the recovery was slow. The balky knee makes it difficult to generate any power. He may be better suited to part-time duty facing only lefthanded pitching, against whom he has hit .310 the last three years. When healthy, Jordan is a plus defender with a great arm, and a better-than-average baserunner. He just hasn't been healthy for a long time.

2005 Outlook

Jordan hasn't been able to contribute on a steady basis for two years. His career success will get him a chance to win a job, but he may be relegated to DH duties. And he may have to go to spring camp as a non-roster player.

Ron Mahay

Position: RP
Bats: L **Throws:** L
Ht: 6' 2" **Wt:** 185

Opening Day Age: 33
Born: 6/28/71 in Crestwood, IL
ML Seasons: 9

Overall Statistics

	W	L	Pct.	ERA	G	GS	Sv	IP	H	BB	SO	HR	Avg
'04	3	0	1.000	2.55	60	0	0	67.0	60	29	54	5	.235
Car.	15	5	.750	3.78	209	3	2	259.1	230	126	213	35	.235

2004 Situational Stats

	W	L	ERA	Sv	IP		AB	H	HR	RBI	Avg
Home	1	0	2.27	0	35.2	LHB	110	25	2	13	.227
Road	2	0	2.87	0	31.1	RHB	145	35	3	22	.241
First Half	2	0	3.06	0	35.1	Sc Pos	73	17	2	29	.233
Scnd Half	1	0	1.99	0	31.2	Clutch	87	16	1	7	.184

2004 Season

Over the past two years, Ron Mahay has developed into a solid, if not essential, piece of a successful bullpen. After a late-season collapse under the weight of a career-high innings count in 2003, Mahay came back stronger and more durable in 2004. The Rangers responded by using him at almost any point in the game (other than the ninth), and in any situation ranging from one batter to three innings.

Pitching & Defense

Mahay is refining a three-pitch arsenal. He primarily pitches off his 89-92 MPH two-seam sinking fastball. He mixes in a slider that runs away from lefties and a splitter that he uses against righties. Mahay was converted from the outfield, so he's a good athlete with good instincts and excellent reactions. In the past, those athletic skills have worked against him because he tries to do too much. He seemed to learn from that lesson in '04.

2005 Outlook

A lefty who also is effective against righties and can pitch more than an inning at a time is an extremely valuable commodity. The Rangers realize this. At the end of 2004, they rewarded Mahay with a two-year deal, and he'll be a versatile key figure for 2005.

Gary Matthews Jr.

Position: RF/CF
Bats: B **Throws:** R
Ht: 6' 3" **Wt:** 225

Opening Day Age: 30
Born: 8/25/74 in San Francisco, CA
ML Seasons: 6

Overall Statistics

	G	AB	R	H	D	T	HR	RBI	SB	BB	SO	Avg	OBP	Slg
'04	87	280	37	77	17	1	11	36	5	33	64	.275	.350	.461
Car.	597	1692	253	418	89	10	42	181	45	203	365	.247	.328	.386

2004 Situational Stats

	AB	H	HR	RBI	Avg		AB	H	HR	RBI	Avg
Home	123	36	7	21	.293	LHP	90	22	4	10	.244
Road	157	41	4	15	.261	RHP	190	55	7	26	.289
First Half	125	35	5	18	.280	Sc Pos	61	16	4	27	.262
Scnd Half	155	42	6	18	.271	Clutch	46	12	2	5	.261

2004 Season

Released by Atlanta on March 31, Gary Matthews Jr. was a valuable pickup by the Rangers. He ended up playing center field against lefthanded starters and filling in in right for the injured Brian Jordan. He did everything asked of him until a September right calf strain ended his season. That seemed to raise questions about his durability.

Hitting, Baserunning & Defense

Matthews never had done much against righthanded pitching until hooking up with Rangers hitting instructor Rudy Jaramillo. Matthews grasped Jaramillo's simple tenets of separating the parts of a swing and saw his average jump from the left side after hitting .240 that way in his first five seasons. Matthews has the special talents necessary to patrol Arlington's huge center field. He also has the arm strength to play right. He is slightly above average as a runner.

2005 Outlook

Because the Rangers usually carry a 12th pitcher, the bench players must be as versatile as possible. Being a switch-hitting outfielder who can acquit himself well at all three positions would seem to make Matthews a great fit. Yet, he's played for six different teams in the last six years, so another change is possible.

Brian Shouse

Position: RP
Bats: L **Throws:** L
Ht: 5'11" **Wt:** 190

Opening Day Age: 36
Born: 9/26/68 in Effingham, IL
ML Seasons: 5

Overall Statistics

	W	L	Pct.	ERA	G	GS	Sv	IP	H	BB	SO	HR	Avg
'04	2	0	1.000	2.23	53	0	0	44.1	36	18	34	3	.224
Car.	2	2	.500	3.48	151	0	1	132.0	129	47	93	10	.257

2004 Situational Stats

	W	L	ERA	Sv	IP		AB	H	HR	RBI	Avg
Home	1	0	1.23	0	22.0	LHB	96	18	2	11	.188
Road	1	0	3.22	0	22.1	RHB	65	18	1	4	.277
First Half	2	0	2.65	0	17.0	Sc Pos	52	7	0	9	.135
Scnd Half	0	0	1.98	0	27.1	Clutch	46	8	1	5	.174

2004 Season

Though he began the year on the DL with an inflamed left rotator cuff, Brian Shouse enjoyed a breakout year in 2004. On June 24, after 11 years and 111 major league appearances, he recorded his first career win. He improved his effectiveness against righthanders just enough so that Buck Showalter could use him for more than one batter when needed.

Pitching & Defense

Shouse's stuff is just average, but his effectiveness lies in his delivery. He throws from a very low-side arm angle, and the funkiness just bedevils lefties. Necessary for long-term success in Arlington, the delivery produces groundballs. He averaged 2.8 per flyball in 2004. An excellent athlete, Shouse helps himself defensively. He has not made an error in 53 total chances in his career. And he's handled at least 20 chances in each of the last two seasons.

2005 Outlook

Shouse remains a bargain for the Rangers as a one-batter specialist. With Ron Mahay handling longer assignments and Shouse available as a second bullet against the toughest lefties, the Rangers should be well-situated from the left-hand side.

Eric Young

Position: LF/DH/2B
Bats: R **Throws:** R
Ht: 5' 8" **Wt:** 186

Opening Day Age: 37
Born: 5/18/67 in New Brunswick, NJ
ML Seasons: 13
Nickname: E.Y.

Overall Statistics

	G	AB	R	H	D	T	HR	RBI	SB	BB	SO	Avg	OBP	Slg
'04	104	344	55	99	25	2	1	27	14	43	28	.288	.377	.381
Car.	1614	5839	954	1664	312	45	74	516	450	628	433	.285	.361	.392

2004 Situational Stats

	AB	H	HR	RBI	Avg		AB	H	HR	RBI	Avg
Home	140	36	1	13	.257	LHP	164	54	1	15	.329
Road	204	63	0	14	.309	RHP	180	45	0	12	.250
First Half	161	53	0	9	.329	Sc Pos	76	23	1	25	.303
Scnd Half	183	46	1	18	.251	Clutch	49	10	0	3	.204

2004 Season

Thrust into the unfamiliar role of part-time utilityman, Eric Young thrived for the Rangers. He started at six different positions (including DH) and hit .300 for most of the year. At 37, he proved to be more productive in a slightly less-demanding role. His 344 at-bats were his fewest in 10 years, but only once in the last eight years did he hit better than his 2004 mark of .288.

Hitting, Baserunning & Defense

Young played surprisingly well in the outfield, but infield defense is becoming more of a challenge. Young played regularly at second late last season and made five errors in his final eight starts there. Young reached 450 career steals in 2004 and remains a threat on the bases, but he must better utilize his declining speed. He was caught nine times in 23 steal attempts.

2005 Outlook

By playing other positions, Young has found a way to extend his career. Think of a poor man's Tony Phillips who could play three times a week in left field or at second base. While he is unable to fill in as a shortstop, Young found a taker in the San Diego Padres, who signed him to a one-year, $1 million deal.

Manny Alexander (**Pos**: 2B, **Age**: 34, **Bats**: R)

	G	AB	R	H	D	T	HR	RBI	SB	BB	SO	Avg	OBP	Slg
'04	21	21	3	5	2	0	0	3	0	1	7	.238	.273	.333
Car.	562	1219	164	285	48	11	15	111	37	82	266	.234	.285	.328

During the course of a decent Triple-A season at Oklahoma, Alexander made his first appearance in a big league uniform since 2000. He hit close to his career hitting percentages in 21 games with Texas, and he signed his third straight minor league deal with the club in November. 2005 Outlook: C

Chad Allen (**Pos**: LF, **Age**: 30, **Bats**: R)

	G	AB	R	H	D	T	HR	RBI	SB	BB	SO	Avg	OBP	Slg
'04	20	58	4	14	4	1	0	6	0	2	13	.241	.262	.345
Car.	246	798	97	214	43	7	14	79	15	61	160	.268	.321	.392

Allen has been a .342 hitter with good doubles power at the Triple-A level over the last two seasons, but he's 19-for-82 (.232) with just seven extra-base hits in the majors over that span. He's been with five different Triple-A affiliates in five years, and the trend may continue. 2005 Outlook: C

Danny Ardoin (**Pos**: C, **Age**: 30, **Bats**: R)

	G	AB	R	H	D	T	HR	RBI	SB	BB	SO	Avg	OBP	Slg
'04	6	8	1	1	0	0	0	1	0	3	2	.125	.364	.125
Car.	21	40	5	5	1	0	1	6	0	11	12	.125	.314	.225

Ardoin arguably did his best hitting as a pro in 2004, batting .308 with a .422 OBP, 12 doubles, 10 homers and 44 RBI in 68 games at Triple-A Oklahoma. He spent his 30th birthday in Texas during a three-week stay in July. He'll try to come back for more. 2005 Outlook: C

Mike Bacsik (**Pos**: LHP, **Age**: 27)

	W	L	Pct.	ERA	G	GS	Sv	IP	H	BB	SO	HR	Avg
'04	1	1	.500	4.60	3	3	0	15.2	16	1	6	2	.267
Car.	5	5	.500	5.88	22	15	0	98.0	120	31	52	15	.305

Bacsik went from Cleveland to the Mets in the 2001 Robbie Alomar deal, following a solid year at Triple-A Buffalo. The numbers suggest his performance has dropped off in each subsequent Triple-A season, but he blanked Detroit for seven frames in one of three big league starts in '04. He signed a minor league deal with the Phillies in December. 2005 Outlook: C

Nick Bierbrodt (**Pos**: LHP, **Age**: 26)

	W	L	Pct.	ERA	G	GS	Sv	IP	H	BB	SO	HR	Avg
'04	1	1	.500	5.82	4	4	0	17.0	14	19	10	4	.246
Car.	6	9	.400	6.66	38	25	0	144.2	178	85	112	30	.304

Once a promising southpaw, Bierbrodt survived a driveby shooting in South Carolina in 2002. His control was an issue before his misfortune, but it's been worse since the shooting. Over the last two seasons, he's walked 97 in 137 innings at the Triple-A and major league levels. 2005 Outlook: C

Mickey Callaway (**Pos**: RHP, **Age**: 29)

	W	L	Pct.	ERA	G	GS	Sv	IP	H	BB	SO	HR	Avg
'04	0	1	.000	7.94	4	3	0	11.1	18	7	9	2	.367
Car.	4	11	.267	6.27	40	20	0	130.2	166	58	86	17	.311

Elbow trouble sidelined Callaway for most of the first half, and his throwing shoulder shut him down in August. When he was OK, he made two scoreless Double-A starts and failed to work five innings in his three big league starts. Solid Triple-A seasons in 2001 and 2002 are old news. 2005 Outlook: C

Jason Conti (**Pos**: CF, **Age**: 30, **Bats**: L)

	G	AB	R	H	D	T	HR	RBI	SB	BB	SO	Avg	OBP	Slg
'04	22	55	6	10	3	0	0	4	0	5	19	.182	.250	.236
Car.	182	420	47	100	24	5	6	47	7	33	124	.238	.296	.362

For the third time in his last four Triple-A seasons, Conti has batted better than .300. He hit .328 with a .381 OBP for Triple-A Oklahoma in 2004, but couldn't stay above the Mendoza line with Texas. He signed another minor league deal with the Rangers in November. 2005 Outlook: C

Scott Erickson (**Pos**: RHP, **Age**: 37)

W	L	Pct.	ERA	G	GS	Sv	IP	H	BB	SO	HR	Avg
1	4	.200	6.67	6	6	0	27.0	38	20	9	3	.336
141	132	.516	4.54	361	356	0	2294.0	2511	833	1235	214	.282

Erickson had Tommy John surgery in August 2000, and shoulder surgery to repair a torn labrum and frayed rotator cuff in March 2003. It was a long road back, and then a hamstring injury just before his first 2004 start put him out three months. His last solid season was 1997. 2005 Outlook: C

Andy Fox (**Pos**: 2B, **Age**: 34, **Bats**: L)

	G	AB	R	H	D	T	HR	RBI	SB	BB	SO	Avg	OBP	Slg
'04	46	55	4	5	0	0	1	1	0	1	19	.091	.107	.145
Car.	776	1925	248	461	65	17	30	168	74	197	407	.239	.324	.338

Fox enjoyed a couple of decent seasons with Arizona at the end of the 1990s, including one as a starter, but he's a .160 hitter (26-for-163) the last two years with Florida, Montreal and Texas. Defensively, he can play a boatload of positions. 2005 Outlook: C

Brad Fullmer (**Pos**: DH, **Age**: 30, **Bats**: L)

	G	AB	R	H	D	T	HR	RBI	SB	BB	SO	Avg	OBP	Slg
'04	76	258	41	60	19	1	11	33	1	27	30	.233	.310	.442
Car.	807	2789	395	778	203	16	114	442	32	216	373	.279	.336	.486

Fullmer became a big league regular at age 23 and has shown he can hit righthanded pitching successfully. Knee surgery in the middle of the 2003 season, followed by more discomfort in the knee and a back ailment in 2004, has sidetracked his bat the last two summers. 2005 Outlook: C

Rosman Garcia (Pos: RHP, Age: 26)

	W	L	Pct.	ERA	G	GS	Sv	IP	H	BB	SO	HR	Avg
'04	0	0	—	5.40	4	0	0	6.2	9	5	5	1	.310
Car.	1	2	.333	5.94	50	0	0	53.0	72	28	30	5	.319

Garcia made good progress in the minors in 2002 and 2003, but he wasn't very effective in the Triple-A bullpen last summer. The righthander has to keep making adjustments to better hitters at higher levels if he is going to be of help in Texas. 2005 Outlook: C

Travis Hughes (Pos: RHP, Age: 26)

	W	L	Pct.	ERA	G	GS	Sv	IP	H	BB	SO	HR	Avg
'04	0	0	—	13.50	2	0	0	1.1	4	2	4	0	.500
Car.	0	0	—	13.50	2	0	0	1.1	4	2	4	0	.500

Hughes became a full-time reliever in 2004. While he didn't have a dominating season in the high minors, he averaged a strikeout per inning and reached Texas in September. His 5.40 ERA in Triple-A the last two seasons suggests he needs more seasoning. 2005 Outlook: C

Colby Lewis (Pos: RHP, Age: 25)

	W	L	Pct.	ERA	G	GS	Sv	IP	H	BB	SO	HR	Avg
'04	1	1	.500	4.11	3	3	0	15.1	13	13	11	1	.228
Car.	12	13	.480	6.83	44	33	0	176.2	218	109	127	28	.307

After a difficult season in 2003, Lewis made three starts in April before shoulder woes led to rotator cuff surgery in May. He'll try to recapture his moving mid-90s fastball before returning near the All-Star break. He'll come back with Detroit after an October waiver claim. 2005 Outlook: C

Sam Narron (Pos: LHP, Age: 23)

	W	L	Pct.	ERA	G	GS	Sv	IP	H	BB	SO	HR	Avg
'04	0	0	—	13.50	1	1	0	2.2	5	4	1	3	.385
Car.	0	0	—	13.50	1	1	0	2.2	5	4	1	3	.385

Narron doesn't get attention as a prospect or light up radar guns, but he's climbed through the Texas system in two-plus years on the strength of his curve and changeup. He could surprise. 2005 Outlook: C

Jeff Nelson (Pos: RHP, Age: 38)

	W	L	Pct.	ERA	G	GS	Sv	IP	H	BB	SO	HR	Avg
'04	1	2	.333	5.32	29	0	1	23.2	17	19	22	3	.207
Car.	47	41	.534	3.38	743	0	32	745.1	598	401	793	51	.223

Nelson's numbers have been in decline the last few years, but his 2004 performance was compromised by knee and elbow injuries. Knee surgery and a cleanup of his throwing elbow early in the first half put him out until August, and he struggled in September. He still could be useful. 2005 Outlook: B

Ramon Nivar (Pos: CF, Age: 25, Bats: R)

	G	AB	R	H	D	T	HR	RBI	SB	BB	SO	Avg	OBP	Slg
'04	7	18	3	4	0	0	0	4	1	0	7	.222	.211	.222
Car.	35	108	12	23	1	2	0	11	5	4	17	.213	.246	.259

In 2003, Nivar batted .345 at the top two stops in the Texas system, but his defensive game wasn't ready for the Texas outfield last summer after a move from second base to center field. His bat was off the mark in 2004, and the speedster now seems to be lost in the shuffle. 2005 Outlook: C

Herbert Perry (Pos: DH/1B, Age: 35, Bats: R)

	G	AB	R	H	D	T	HR	RBI	SB	BB	SO	Avg	OBP	Slg
'04	49	134	13	30	2	1	5	17	0	14	19	.224	.307	.366
Car.	529	1696	241	461	102	6	55	246	12	128	291	.272	.335	.436

Perry always has been able to hit, but injuries have plagued him throughout his career. Shoulder, calf and knee ailments limited him to 49 games in 2004. Now his age starts working against him. 2005 Outlook: C

Jay Powell (Pos: RHP, Age: 33)

	W	L	Pct.	ERA	G	GS	Sv	IP	H	BB	SO	HR	Avg
'04	1	1	.500	3.38	23	0	0	24.0	24	11	17	3	.267
Car.	36	23	.610	4.19	507	0	22	539.0	542	268	422	42	.262

Powell was expected to be a key figure in the Rangers' pen when he signed a three-year deal before the 2002 campaign. He tore a tendon in his pitching hand in his first season with Texas, and elbow troubles in 2004 led to Tommy John surgery last July. 2005 Outlook: C

Nick Regilio (Pos: RHP, Age: 26)

	W	L	Pct.	ERA	G	GS	Sv	IP	H	BB	SO	HR	Avg
'04	0	4	.000	6.05	6	4	0	19.1	20	15	12	3	.278
Car.	0	4	.000	6.05	6	4	0	19.1	20	15	12	3	.278

Regilio has a history of injuries, from a ribcage injury in 2001 and biceps tendinitis in 2002 to season-ending rotator cuff surgery in the spring of 2003. He regained his low-90s heat in 2004 and fared OK in his first taste of Triple-A ball. If healthy, he could put it together. 2005 Outlook: C

Ryan Snare (Pos: LHP, Age: 26)

	W	L	Pct.	ERA	G	GS	Sv	IP	H	BB	SO	HR	Avg
'04	0	0	—	10.80	1	0	0	3.1	5	2	0	3	.333
Car.	0	0	—	10.80	1	0	0	3.1	5	2	0	3	.333

Snare had shown good command of three pitches prior to 2004, but he was much too hittable en route to an 11-6 record at Triple-A Oklahoma. He can't dominate hitters in the high minors, so his command must be excellent to stick in the majors. 2005 Outlook: C

Michael Tejera (Pos: LHP, Age: 28)

	W	L	Pct.	ERA	G	GS	Sv	IP	H	BB	SO	HR	Avg
'04	0	1	.000	13.50	8	2	0	9.1	15	9	10	1	.366
Car.	11	13	.458	5.06	108	27	3	236.1	251	110	170	25	.276

Tejera couldn't get big league hitters out in 2004, especially lefties, and he was claimed off waivers by Texas in September. He unveiled a nearly sidearm delivery to get lefties out late in the season. 2005 Outlook: C

John Wasdin (Pos: RHP, Age: 32)

	W	L	Pct.	ERA	G	GS	Sv	IP	H	BB	SO	HR	Avg
'04	2	4	.333	6.78	15	10	0	65.0	83	23	36	18	.305
Car.	33	34	.493	5.38	276	54	3	668.0	732	211	457	119	.278

Wasdin has been surfacing in the majors since 1995, his first Triple-A season. Over the last two years, he's gone 17-6 (3.42 ERA) and thrown a perfect game at the Triple-A level, but he's 2-5 (7.97 ERA) in the majors during that span. The contending Rangers were hoping for better, but they re-signed him to a minor league deal in November. 2005 Outlook: C

Texas Rangers Minor League Prospects

Organization Overview:

The Rangers seemed to be making significant progress in the minor league system over the last three seasons with assistant GM Grady Fuson running the show, but a midseason power struggle left Fuson out of the organization. And at the end of the year, Texas was shifting all kinds of duties within the system. What is consistent, however, is the attention the Rangers have spent to developing pitching. They had two first-round picks in 2004 and both were pitchers: Thomas Diamond and Eric Hurley. There appears to be a longer list of potential pitching prospects to choose from than the organization has had in some time. Several trades also have helped restock the system. Among those acquired: pitchers Frank Francisco, Josh Rupe, Chris Young, first baseman Adrian Gonzalez and shortstop Joaquin Arias.

Juan Dominguez

Position: P   **Opening Day Age:** 24
Bats: R **Throws:** R   **Born:** 5/18/80 in
Ht: 6' 2" **Wt:** 195   Ensanchez Ramirez, DR

Recent Statistics

	W	L	ERA	G	GS	Sv	IP	H	R	BB	SO	HR
2004 AAA Oklahoma	5	1	3.13	9	9	0	54.2	41	20	19	41	3
2004 AA Frisco	0	0	1.08	3	2	0	8.1	4	1	1	11	0
2004 AL Texas	1	2	3.91	4	4	0	23.0	25	11	5	14	2

Due to a number of injuries within the rotation, the Rangers were prepared to give Dominguez, their 2003 Minor League Pitcher of the Year, an extended look. All he did was perplex them. He's got a great fastball and a Pedro-like change, but to this point Dominguez does nothing more than tantalize. He made a great start at Yankee Stadium for his first big league win and had another fine outing at Oakland in the midst of the pennant race. The problem? They were three months apart due to his longer-than-expected recovery from a back strain. He complicated matters by pulling himself out of a late-season start with flu-like symptoms. The Rangers responded by putting him on the 60-day DL, a move meant as much for punishment as anything else.

Adrian Gonzalez

Position: 1B   **Opening Day Age:** 22
Bats: L **Throws:** L   **Born:** 5/8/82 in San
Ht: 6' 2" **Wt:** 220   Diego, CA

Recent Statistics

	G	AB	R	H	D	T	HR	RBI	SB	BB	SO	Avg
2004 AAA Oklahoma	123	457	61	139	28	3	12	88	1	39	73	.304
2004 AL Texas	16	42	7	10	3	0	1	7	0	2	6	.238

Depending on where the Rangers go in free agency, Gonzalez either could be this team's starting first baseman in 2005 or traded to another team to address a more important need. He is a slick fielder who could be a .300 hitter in the majors, but questions still abound as to whether he will develop enough power to hold down a corner-infield spot. Think Mark Grace. If the Rangers don't add a big bat, they may move Mark Teixeira to the outfield and give Gonzalez a chance at first base. At this stage, Gonzalez may be of more value to the Rangers as a trade commodity than anything else.

John Hudgins

Position: P   **Opening Day Age:** 23
Bats: R **Throws:** R   **Born:** 8/31/81 in
Ht: 6' 2" **Wt:** 195   Oklahoma City, OK

Recent Statistics

	W	L	ERA	G	GS	Sv	IP	H	R	BB	SO	HR
2003 A Clinton	0	0	0.00	1	0	0	2.0	1	0	0	4	0
2004 A Stockton	3	1	2.35	15	11	2	65.0	49	19	18	73	4
2004 AA Frisco	5	3	3.13	12	12	0	69.0	57	29	18	64	12
2004 AAA Oklahoma	0	1	7.50	3	2	0	12.0	19	10	5	8	1

The Rangers' third-round choice in 2003, Hudgins lasted only one appearance in his first pro stint before arm troubles due to a heavy workload at Stanford sidelined him. He came back strong in 2004, pitching at three different levels and showing perhaps more maturity than any prospect in the Rangers' system. In fact, he's pushing for placement on the 40-man roster, even though the Rangers could go another year before protecting him. He's not an overpowering pitcher, but does seem to have the advanced understanding of pitching that other Stanford grads such as Mike Mussina and Rick Helling have shown. He won't start 2005 in the majors, but he could show up there before the campaign is through.

Gerald Laird

Position: C   **Opening Day Age:** 25
Bats: R **Throws:** R   **Born:** 11/13/79 in
Ht: 6' 2" **Wt:** 220   Westminster, CA

Recent Statistics

	G	AB	R	H	D	T	HR	RBI	SB	BB	SO	Avg
2004 AAA Oklahoma	6	22	2	4	2	0	0	2	1	2	8	.182
2004 AL Texas	49	147	20	33	6	0	1	16	0	12	35	.224

Laird forced his way onto the roster—and forced the Rangers to trade Einar Diaz—with a strong spring. As the club's starting catcher, he was in the thick of the early 2004 American League Rookie of the Year race when he tore the ligament in his left thumb on a play at the plate in mid-May. Laird underwent surgery, but made it back by late-July. He wasn't the same player. It was clear the thumb was still bothering him, and it affected his ability to catch balls and do anything offensively. Now its uncertain if he'll have the position for 2005. While his offense remains a mystery, it is clear he throws fairly well and seems to have a grasp of calling games.

Kameron Loe

Position: P **Opening Day Age:** 23
Bats: R **Throws:** R **Born:** 9/10/81 in Simi
Ht: 6' 8" **Wt:** 225 Valley, CA

Recent Statistics

	W	L	ERA	G	GS	Sv	IP	H	R	BB	SO	HR
2004 AA Frisco	7	7	3.12	19	19	0	112.2	122	42	29	97	5
2004 AAA Oklahoma	5	2	3.27	8	8	0	52.1	52	20	13	42	6
2004 AL Texas	0	0	5.40	2	1	0	6.2	6	5	6	3	0

The Rangers really haven't drafted and developed a starting pitcher whose had any kind of long-term success with the club since Rick Helling in 1992—and he was briefly traded away after reaching the majors. They hope Loe can break the streak. Though tall and imposing on the mound, he's not overpowering. His fastball is really just 86-88 MPH, but he does throw strikes, which is essential to success in Arlington. The team didn't have to put him on the 40-man roster until after the season, but was curious enough to add him in September and take a brief look. His six walks in 6.2 innings were probably just enough to let Loe know the strike zone is different in the majors.

Erasmo Ramirez

Position: P **Opening Day Age:** 28
Bats: L **Throws:** L **Born:** 4/29/76 in Santa
Ht: 6' 0" **Wt:** 190 Ana, CA

Recent Statistics

	W	L	ERA	G	GS	Sv	IP	H	R	BB	SO	HR
2004 AAA Oklahoma	1	0	7.20	14	0	0	20.0	25	16	6	10	2
2004 AL Texas	5	3	4.29	34	0	0	35.2	34	19	7	21	5

Like Brian Shouse, Ramirez is another beguiling sidearming lefty. While he won't blow anybody away with his 83-85 MPH fastball, he gets the necessary speed differential to fool hitters with a sometimes painfully slow change. He can throw it at several speeds, the lowest of which will occasionally dip below 70 MPH. Lefties seemed to figure him out last year, but he's been surprisingly good against righthanders. In parts of two seasons, they've hit just .240, which makes him more than just a one-batter option. Ramirez had a minor league option left last year, so he was the odd man out as the Rangers continually manipulated their roster to have additional fresh arms in the bullpen.

Ricardo Rodriguez

Position: P **Opening Day Age:** 26
Bats: R **Throws:** R **Born:** 5/21/78 in Manga,
Ht: 6' 3" **Wt:** 190 DR

Recent Statistics

	W	L	ERA	G	GS	Sv	IP	H	R	BB	SO	HR
2004 AAA Oklahoma	2	2	5.11	6	6	0	37.0	42	23	12	18	5
2004 AL Texas	3	1	2.03	5	4	0	26.2	28	10	12	15	1

Since joining the Rangers' organization, Rodriguez has turned into just the latest in Texas' long legacy of star-crossed pitching prospects. He didn't pitch after being acquired in 2003 because of a hip injury, then lost out on a rotation spot at the start of 2004 because he had minor league options remaining. When the Rangers did call him up in June, their initial reports on him seemed to be reaffirmed: good hard sinker and unafraid to throw strikes. And then his right elbow was shattered by a line drive. It required surgery (and a pin) to put the joint back together. There is no guarantee that it will heal in proper alignment. If healthy, however, he could be a real contender for a rotation spot.

Chris Young

Position: P **Opening Day Age:** 25
Bats: R **Throws:** R **Born:** 5/25/79 in Dallas,
Ht: 6' 10" **Wt:** 250 TX

Recent Statistics

	W	L	ERA	G	GS	Sv	IP	H	R	BB	SO	HR
2004 AA Frisco	6	5	4.48	18	18	0	88.1	94	48	31	75	9
2004 AAA Oklahoma	3	0	1.48	5	5	0	30.1	20	7	9	34	2
2004 AL Texas	3	2	4.71	7	7	0	36.1	36	21	10	27	7

The Rangers picked up Young on the last day of spring in the deal that sent Einar Diaz to Montreal. Joining his hometown organization seemed to spark the former Princeton basketball center, especially after a midseason promotion to Triple-A. Desperate for starters, the Rangers called him up in late August. He showed a better-than-expected fastball (92-95 MPH), and his over-the-top delivery, especially delivered from his height, gave batters pause. Perhaps because he grew up with Ameriquest as his home park, he showed no fear of the place. He's going to have to improve his stamina, but he's got a chance to be a part of the '05 rotation.

Others to Watch

Jason Botts (24) has played some first and some outfield. He had 24 homers at Double-A, then tore up the Arizona Fall League. If the Rangers don't land a big bat in free agency, he could get a shot as the team's DH. . . Look for righthander **Thomas Diamond** (21), the Rangers' top pick in 2004, to zoom through the system. He had 68 strikeouts and a 2.15 ERA at two minor league stops after signing last June. . . The Rangers are absolutely in love with two shortstop prospects, which could mean the eventual return of Michael Young to second base. **Ian Kinsler** (22) had a breakout year, hitting .402 at Class-A before a promotion to Double-A, where he "slumped" to .300. **Joaquin Arias** (20), acquired from the Yankees in the Alex Rodriguez trade, caught fire as the season progressed at high Class-A Stockton. By the time Arias went to the instructional league, the Rangers were wondering if he could be ready by 2006. . . Righthanders **Josh Rupe** (22) and **Matt Lorenzo** (22) are still a year away from reaching the majors, but both give the Rangers hope they can develop their own pitchers. Rupe was 6-2 with a 2.82 ERA at three different levels in 2004, while Lorenzo had a very impressive Arizona Fall League after going just 5-10 with a 4.10 ERA at two Class-A affiliates.

SkyDome

Offense

Balls carry to right-center field when SkyDome's roof is open, but there are fewer 'true' ballparks in the game when the roof is closed. The team is expected to purchase a new artificial surface in time for this season. Whatever surface is chosen, it will, like the current surface, heat up dramatically when the roof is open during the summer, leading to more high bounces over the heads of outfielders.

Defense

Once the Blue Jays assume ownership of SkyDome, it wouldn't be a surprise to see the club add some quirky angles to the outfield wall to give the cookie-cutter field some personality. Interestingly, some visiting outfielders claim that there has been a change in the trajectory of fly-balls ever since a series of high-rise condominiums have been constructed around SkyDome.

Who It Helps the Most

Line-drive hitters and contact hitters can take advantage of the alleys and the artificial turf, so it's no surprise that Reed Johnson hit 60 points higher at home and Vernon Wells 50 points more. Roy Halladay has been a more effective pitcher in SkyDome during his career while reliever Justin Speier's home ERA was half of what it was on the road.

Who It Hurts the Most

Eric Hinske's numbers were better away from SkyDome, as were Orlando Hudson's. Starter Josh Towers' home ERA is 6.22 compared to 3.95 on the road, and it's not because of a drastic split in walks or home runs. The Blue Jays' team slugging percentage was 40 points higher at home.

Rookies & Newcomers

Starter David Bush was 4-0 at SkyDome, where he recorded his first complete game. Utility infielder Frank Menechino was a monster there, hitting .369 and slugging .639, while the hitting percentages of 2004 rookies Alexis Rios and Gabe Gross showed little tilt home or away. Rookie shortstop Russ Adams should take advantage of the artificial surface and alleys at SkyDome.

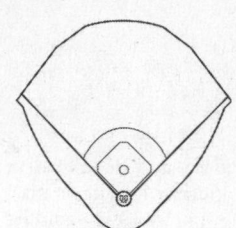

Dimensions: LF-328, LCF-375, CF-400, RCF-375, RF-328

Capacity: 50,598

Elevation: 300 feet

Surface: Turf

Foul Territory: Large

Park Factors

2004 Season

| | Home Games | | | Away Games | | | |
	Blue Jays	Opp	Total	Blue Jays	Opp	Total	Index
G	72	72	144	71	71	142	
Avg	.263	.284	.273	.257	.267	.262	105
AB	2406	2557	4963	2514	2357	4871	100
R	343	396	739	303	358	661	110
H	632	725	1357	645	629	1274	105
2B	129	141	270	127	122	249	106
3B	20	12	32	11	12	23	137
HR	71	84	155	61	85	146	104
BB	249	285	534	216	263	479	109
SO	463	454	917	509	396	905	99
E	44	56	100	35	50	85	116
E-Infield	41	50	91	29	42	71	126
LHB-Avg	.248	.290	.271	.260	.278	.269	101
LHB-HR	36	46	82	34	50	84	94
RHB-Avg	.274	.277	.275	.254	.257	.255	108
RHB-HR	35	38	73	27	35	62	118

2002-2004

| | Home Games | | | Away Games | | | |
	Blue Jays	Opp	Total	Blue Jays	Opp	Total	Index
G	216	216	432	215	215	430	
Avg	.272	.278	.275	.262	.268	.265	104
AB	7309	7698	15007	7635	7230	14865	100
R	1119	1174	2293	1061	1057	2118	108
H	1988	2137	4125	1999	1941	3940	104
2B	462	452	914	404	363	767	118
3B	53	38	91	40	46	86	105
HR	239	261	500	217	233	450	110
BB	730	766	1496	682	741	1423	104
SO	1407	1395	2802	1574	1215	2789	100
E	135	153	288	142	133	275	104
E-Infield	123	128	251	123	111	234	107
LHB-Avg	.268	.281	.275	.264	.272	.268	103
LHB-HR	120	129	249	108	118	226	110
RHB-Avg	.275	.275	.275	.260	.265	.263	105
RHB-HR	119	132	251	109	115	224	110

2004 Rankings (American League)
- Highest RHB batting-average factor
- Second-highest walk factor
- Second-highest infield-error factor
- Second-highest RHB home-run factor
- Third-highest run factor

John Gibbons

2004 Season

The Blue Jays fired Carlos Tosca as manager on August 8 and replaced him with first-base coach John Gibbons, who was 482-420 (.534) as a minor league manager in the Mets' organization before joining Toronto in 2002. The Blue Jays were in fifth place in the American League East at the time of Tosca's firing, 24.5 games back, and went 20-30 under Gibbons.

Offense

The Blue Jays seldom had their Opening Day lineup in place. As a result, after a season in which they ranked near the top of the AL in most offensive categories, Toronto had one of the circuit's least-effective offenses. The team took few strides toward becoming the high on-base, big-hit club upon which GM J.P. Ricciardi has predicated his building plan. Outwardly, Gibbons exudes a more aggressive personality than Tosca, and he says he would like to see the team be more active on the basepaths.

Pitching & Defense

The Blue Jays did a much better job of catching the ball, thanks to dramatic improvements by third baseman Eric Hinske and second baseman Orlando Hudson and the arrival of strong-armed right fielder Alexis Rios. Cy Young Award winner Roy Halladay was largely ineffective after developing tendinitis in his right shoulder, and the organization once again was unable to address its myriad bullpen concerns. The bullpen converted just 37 of 53 save opportunities, but Ricciardi liked what he saw of Gibbons' creativity in the use of his relievers. Gibbons gave his catchers free rein, letting them call pitchouts.

2005 Outlook

Team owner Rogers Communications planned to hold the line on salaries, giving Ricciardi a $3 million increase from last year's total of $50 million. Gibbons had the "interim" tag removed from his name as soon as the regular season ended. He will work this year on a one-year contract and will have a new pitching coach, Brad Arnsberg, and a new bench coach, Ernie Whitt, a local favorite as a player who managed Canada's Olympic team.

Born: 6/08/62 in Great Falls, Montana

Playing Experience: 1984-1986, NYM

Managerial Experience: 1 season

Manager Statistics

Year	Team, Lg	W	L	Pct	GB	Finish
2004	Toronto, AL	20	30	.400	33.5	5th East
1 Season		20	30	.400	–	–

2004 Starting Pitchers by Days Rest

	<=3	4	5	6+
Blue Jays Starts	1	17	22	8
Blue Jays ERA	3.38	5.23	4.71	6.13
AL Avg Starts	2	82	47	21
AL ERA	5.36	4.87	4.65	4.93

2004 Situational Stats

	John Gibbons	AL Average
Hit & Run Success %	31.3	36.8
Stolen Base Success %	64.7	68.6
Platoon Pct.	67.8	61.6
Defensive Subs	1	21
High-Pitch Outings	2	5
Quick/Slow Hooks	9/3	20/16
Sacrifice Attempts	2	53

2004 Rankings (American League)

- Did not rank near the top in any category

Miguel Batista

2004 Season

Miguel Batista signed a three-year, $13.1 million contract to become the Blue Jays' No. 2 starter behind ace Roy Halladay. But he fought his command all season long and was moved into the closer's role in mid-September, after a span of six losses in eight starts. Batista was 10-12 (4.88) as a starter before his move to the bullpen and finished 5-for-5 in save opportunities. His strikeout-walk ratio fell to 1.08 from 2.37 in 2003.

Pitching

No pitcher shook off Blue Jays catchers more than Batista, who throughout his career has alternated between falling too much in love with his fastball and cut fastball and not using them enough. Batista can hit 95 MPH with his four-seam fastball and has a wide repertoire, but his sinking fastball and cutter should be his bread and butter. Ultimately, his success as a closer will depend on his ability to decide which offspeed pitch he best throws and then sticking with it.

Defense

Batista is a good athlete who is quick off the mound and seems more self-confident and less prone to brain cramps than earlier in his career. He uses a slide step with men on base and continued to improve markedly in that phase of the game, allowing just nine of 20 opposing baserunners to steal successfully in 2004.

2005 Outlook

General manager J.P. Ricciardi said that the Blue Jays wouldn't know whether Batista would be in the bullpen or the rotation until some time in January. Batista accepted the 2004 move to the bullpen without complaint and appeared energized by the possibility. If he does find himself back in the starting rotation, it's clear now that he doesn't have the stuff to be a No. 2 starter, and it's safe to say that expectations will be lower for him this season.

Position: SP
Bats: R **Throws:** R
Ht: 6' 1" **Wt:** 197

Opening Day Age: 34
Born: 2/19/71 in Santo Domingo, DR
ML Seasons: 10
Pronunciation: bah-TEESE-tah

Overall Statistics

	W	L	Pct.	ERA	G	GS	Sv	IP	H	BB	SO	HR	Avg
'04	10	13	.435	4.80	38	31	5	198.2	206	96	104	22	.273
Car.	52	63	.452	4.46	292	152	6	1100.2	1109	480	706	106	.265

2004 Pitching Profile

	Miguel Batista	AL Average
Overall Strike %	58.8	62.3
1st Pitch Strike %	52.7	58.1
Ratio	1.52	1.42
Strikeouts per 9 IP	4.71	6.45
Walks per 9 IP	4.35	3.34
Home Runs per 9 IP	1.00	1.15
Strikeout/Walk Ratio	1.08	1.93
Groundball/Flyball Ratio	1.79	1.17

2004 Situational Stats

	W	L	ERA	Sv	IP		AB	H	HR	RBI	Avg
Home	8	6	4.98	2	119.1	LHB	432	114	11	56	.264
Road	2	7	4.54	3	79.1	RHB	323	92	11	50	.285
First Half	8	6	4.02	0	123.0	Sc Pos	181	56	6	84	.309
Scnd Half	2	7	6.07	5	75.2	Clutch	66	17	0	10	.258

2004 Rankings (American League)

- 1st in walks allowed and lowest strikeout walk ratio (1.1)
- 2nd in runners caught stealing (11) and highest walks per nine innings (4.3)
- 3rd in wild pitches (12)
- 6th in losses, highest groundball-flyball ratio allowed (1.8) and highest on-base percentage allowed (.355)
- 8th in complete games (2) and fewest strike outs per nine innings (4.7)
- 9th in lowest stolen-base percentage allowed (45.0)
- Led the Blue Jays in losses, complete games (2), innings pitched, hits allowed, batters faced (867), walks allowed, wild pitches (12), runners caught stealing (11), GDPs induced (22) and lowest stolen-base percentage allowed (45.0)

Dave Bush

2004 Season

Drafted as a reliever, Dave Bush arrived in the major leagues in only his second full season as a starter and showed a maturity that belied his experience, flirting with a no-hitter on July 20 against Oakland. He held up well while pitching farther into a season than he had ever been asked to do before, and finished off the campaign on October 1 with a complete-game, two-hit shutout in a 7-0 win over a depleted New York Yankees lineup.

Pitching

Bush is a stylish pitcher who has a low-90s fastball and a good curveball. But lefthanded batters roasted him in his rookie season, and the Blue Jays will spend much of spring training helping him refine an already quality changeup. While he is eager and willing to throw the change to righthanders even when he is behind in the count, against lefties he was essentially a two-pitch pitcher. The Blue Jays were pleased with the fact that Bush was able to self-correct some mechanical difficulties during games, yet another sign of his poise.

Defense

Bush is a smart player and good athlete who does everything well, and that includes fielding his position. He has a slide-step delivery that he can use with men on base, but the Blue Jays didn't force the issue last season. They can be expected to ask more of him this season.

2005 Outlook

It will be a disappointment if Bush does not solidify his place in the Jays' rotation this spring. While he doesn't have the stuff to be a front-of-the-rotation pitcher, he certainly is a No. 3 or No. 4 starter and seems to have enough moxie to ensure a long major league career. Mastering the changeup will go a long way toward setting the tone for this season and beyond.

Position: SP
Bats: R **Throws:** R
Ht: 6' 2" **Wt:** 212

Opening Day Age: 25
Born: 11/9/79 in Pittsburgh, PA
ML Seasons: 1

Overall Statistics

	W	L	Pct.	ERA	G	GS	Sv	IP	H	BB	SO	HR	Avg
'04	5	4	.556	3.69	16	16	0	97.2	95	25	64	11	.255
Car.	5	4	.556	3.69	16	16	0	97.2	95	25	64	11	.255

2004 Pitching Profile

	David Bush	AL Average
Overall Strike %	65.4	62.3
1st Pitch Strike %	61.2	58.1
Ratio	1.23	1.42
Strikeouts per 9 IP	5.90	6.45
Walks per 9 IP	2.30	3.34
Home Runs per 9 IP	1.01	1.15
Strikeout/Walk Ratio	2.56	1.93
Groundball/Flyball Ratio	1.00	1.17

2004 Situational Stats

	W	L	ERA	Sv	IP		AB	H	HR	RBI	Avg
Home	4	0	2.77	0	52.0	LHB	218	63	9	26	.289
Road	1	4	4.73	0	45.2	RHB	155	32	2	19	.206
First Half	0	1	3.86	0	11.2	Sc Pos	80	24	2	32	.300
Scnd Half	5	3	3.66	0	86.0	Clutch	21	4	0	1	.190

2004 Rankings (American League)

- Led the Blue Jays in ERA, winning percentage, highest strikeout-walk ratio (2.6), lowest on-base percentage allowed (.309), lowest ERA at home and lowest batting average allowed vs. righthanded batters

Frank Catalanotto

2004 Season

Despite a season marred by a groin injury that proved difficult to diagnose, Frank Catalanotto still was rewarded with a two-year contract extension worth $5.4 million in September. He kicked his season into gear by victimizing four White Sox hurlers for a six-hit game on May 1, and he was batting .426 for the month when he went on the disabled list for the first time on May 20. After two more stints on the DL, a Montreal doctor diagnosed the injury as a strain more common to hockey players, and it necessitated season-ending surgery in August.

Hitting

A studious hitter who spends at least an hour per day all season long analyzing videotape, Catalanotto is a gap hitter who is productive in the No. 2 spot because of his intelligence and bat control, skills that set him apart from numerous Blue Jays regulars. He is particularly effective hitting early in the count and with men on base. The Blue Jays may test that productivity in 2005 by batting him in the middle of the lineup.

Baserunning & Defense

Catalanotto doesn't run much, but he has shown a knack for taking the extra base and makes good decisions on the basepaths. His throwing arm is average at best, and designated hitter remains his best position. Yet, Catalanotto is a versatile defender, capable of playing both corner outfield positions as well as second and first base. He is a smart defensive player, and his arm is less of a liability in left field.

2005 Outlook

Though his relationship with the club sometimes seemed strained because of indecisiveness about his injury, Catalanotto has become a fixture with Toronto and will be asked to assume a bigger role if the club loses Carlos Delgado. Catalanotto will be counted on to be in the lineup every day in 2005, though his position will be determined by whatever offseason moves the team makes. He could find himself in an outfield platoon or even at first base.

Position: LF/DH
Bats: L **Throws:** R
Ht: 5'11" **Wt:** 195

Opening Day Age: 30
Born: 4/27/74 in Smithtown, NY
ML Seasons: 8
Pronunciation: ca-tal-a-NAH-tow

Overall Statistics

	G	AB	R	H	D	T	HR	RBI	SB	BB	SO	Avg	OBP	Slg
'04	75	249	27	73	19	1	1	26	1	17	33	.293	.344	.390
Car.	714	2220	350	658	147	22	55	267	39	179	308	.296	.358	.457

Where He Hits the Ball

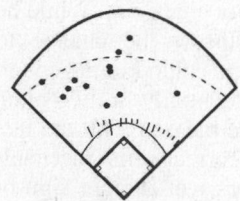 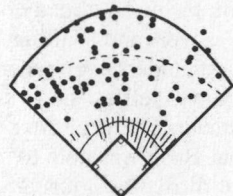

Vs. LHP   **Vs. RHP**

2004 Situational Stats

	AB	H	HR	RBI	Avg		AB	H	HR	RBI	Avg
Home	122	30	1	15	.246	LHP	44	10	0	4	.227
Road	127	43	0	11	.339	RHP	205	63	1	22	.307
First Half	165	54	1	23	.327	Sc Pos	57	17	0	23	.298
Scnd Half	84	19	0	3	.226	Clutch	41	11	0	4	.268

2004 Rankings (American League)
- Led the Blue Jays in batting average vs. righthanded pitchers

Carlos Delgado

2004 Season

After missing five weeks with a strained muscle near his rib cage, Carlos Delgado finished with a flourish, compiling a 1.033 OPS after the All-Star break. It was a turbulent season for Delgado, the Blue Jays' all-time leader in home runs and RBI, who was in the final year of a four-year contract and exercised a no-trade clause to prevent the team from trading him in at the trade deadline. Yet Delgado still reached the 30-homer mark for his eighth consecutive season, the 14th major leaguer to accomplish the feat.

Hitting

Two years ago, Delgado changed his stance to leave himself more erect in the batter's box and give his bat a better path through the strike zone. The results were immediate, as Delgado was more effective against lefthanded pitching. Last season proved more difficult because of adjustments necessitated by his rib injury and nagging soreness in his knees. At times he seemed more inclined to give in to frustration and hit the ball into the pronounced defensive shift teams put on him. But by September he was his old self, handling the high, inside pitch as well as the low-and-outside breaking pitch.

Baserunning & Defense

Delgado understands his limitations on the basepaths and usually errs on the side of caution. He has worked diligently on his defense in recent years, but sometimes wears down because of soreness in the knees, no doubt exacerbated by the artificial surface at SkyDome. The Blue Jays' infield defense improved dramatically in 2004, and Delgado did his part.

2005 Outlook

Delgado's affinity for the city of Toronto figured to be tested by free agency, since the team initially said it was unwilling to pay him more than 50 percent of what he made in 2004, when he chewed up more than a third of the payroll. But Delgado's finishing kick showed that he is still an offensive force. He will find a home in the middle of a new team's lineup, as the Jays didn't offer him salary arbitration.

Position: 1B
Bats: L **Throws:** R
Ht: 6' 3" **Wt:** 230

Opening Day Age: 32
Born: 6/25/72 in Aguadilla, PR
ML Seasons: 12
Pronunciation: del-GAH-doh

Toronto

Overall Statistics

G	AB	R	H	D	T	HR	RBI	SB	BB	SO	Avg	OBP	Slg
128	458	74	123	26	0	32	99	0	69	115	.269	.372	.535
1423	5008	889	1413	343	11	336	1058	9	827	1242	.282	.392	.556

Where He Hits the Ball

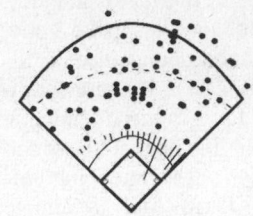 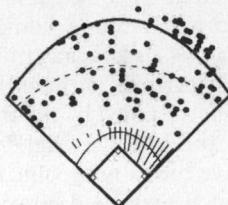

Vs. LHP   **Vs. RHP**

2004 Situational Stats

	AB	H	HR	RBI	Avg		AB	H	HR	RBI	Avg
Home	235	63	18	55	.268	LHP	177	48	9	37	.271
Road	223	60	14	44	.269	RHP	281	75	23	62	.267
First Half	202	45	10	36	.223	Sc Pos	129	34	9	63	.264
Scnd Half	256	78	22	63	.305	Clutch	70	20	6	17	.286

2004 Rankings (American League)

- 2nd in sacrifice flies (11)
- 4th in HR frequency (14.3 ABs per HR) and fielding percentage at first base (.996)
- 5th in intentional walks (12) and lowest percentage of swings put into play (35.3)
- 6th in hit by pitch (13) and cleanup slugging percentage (.535)
- 7th in highest percentage of swings that missed (27.0) and highest percentage of swings on the first pitch (36.3)
- Led the Blue Jays in home runs, RBI, sacrifice flies (11), walks, intentional walks (12), hit by pitch (13), times on base (205), strikeouts, slugging percentage, on-base percentage, HR frequency (14.3 ABs per HR), and cleanup slugging percentage (.535)

Gabe Gross

2004 Season

Rushed up to the major leagues from Triple-A Syracuse, Gabe Gross saw limited duty against lefthanded pitching and struggled against most righthanded pitching, too. Formerly a starting quarterback for Auburn and the 15th player chosen in the 2001 draft, Gross hit a grand slam off the Oakland A's Justin Duchsherer on September 5 and had five outfield assists. The latter figure removed any concern the team had about lingering effects from a strained elbow that threatened to cut into Gross' playing time in the minors.

Hitting

Gross has a chance to hit his share of home runs once he establishes himself in the major leagues. He has a sound knowledge of the strike zone, making significant strides in that area since deciding to focus on baseball in 2001. If there was a concern noted by the Blue Jays, it was a tendency to break down slightly on his back leg, which gave him a noticeable upper-cut swing. That tendency prevented him from taking full advantage of his strength and instead of driving the ball into the gap he often was hitting weak, flyball outs.

Baserunning & Defense

Gross is a gifted athlete with good agility for a player of his size, and he has become a better judge of flyballs simply through an accumulation of playing time. He pleasantly surprised the Blue Jays with both the accuracy and strength of his throws, and showed good awareness in developing situations. He is a sound fundamental player, capable of playing both corner outfield positions.

2005 Outlook

Depending on the moves the club makes this winter, Gross could elbow his way into the lineup with a strong spring training. But in a perfect world, the Jays would let him start out in Triple-A and work on his consistency. Still, it's safe to say that Gross impressed the team with his instincts for the game and that he removed any lingering questions about his ability to defend like a major leaguer.

Position: LF
Bats: L **Throws:** R
Ht: 6' 3" **Wt:** 209

Opening Day Age: 25
Born: 10/21/79 in Baltimore, MD
ML Seasons: 1

Overall Statistics

	G	AB	R	H	D	T	HR	RBI	SB	BB	SO	Avg	OBP	Slg
'04	44	129	18	27	4	0	3	16	2	19	31	.209	.311	.310
Car.	44	129	18	27	4	0	3	16	2	19	31	.209	.311	.310

Where He Hits the Ball

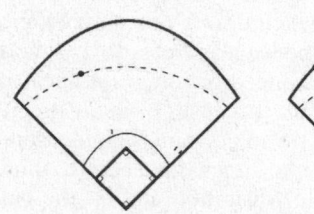
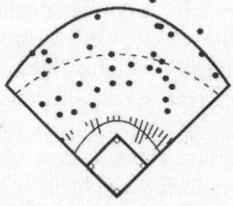

Vs. LHP   **Vs. RHP**

2004 Situational Stats

	AB	H	HR	RBI	Avg		AB	H	HR	RBI	Avg
Home	63	13	2	13	.206	LHP	11	1	0	0	.091
Road	66	14	1	3	.212	RHP	118	26	3	16	.220
First Half	0	0	0	0	–	Sc Pos	33	8	1	13	.242
Scnd Half	129	27	3	16	.209	Clutch	17	3	0	2	.176

2004 Rankings (American League)

- Did not rank near the top or bottom in any category

Roy Halladay

2004 Season

After winning the American League Cy Young Award in 2003 and signing a four-year, $42 million contract, Roy Halladay had every reason to believe he was on the cusp of big things in 2004. Unfortunately, shoulder tendinitis sparked two trips to the disabled list, including one from July 17-September 21. Halladay started the year 5-4 (3.58) before going 2-3 (5.85) in seven starts between DL stints, and at one point it was feared that he had a tear in the shoulder. In Halladay's eight losses, the Blue Jays combined to score just 15 runs. His strikeout-walk ratio fell from 6.38 in 2003 to 2.44.

Pitching

Halladay felt the fatigue in his shoulder affected his arm angle and arm speed before he went on the DL, which allowed opposing batters to tear into his cut fastball and a curve that starts at a righthander's shoulders and ends up at the knees over the outside black. The break on his curveball was nowhere near as sharp as in 2003, most likey a result of his shoulder woes. When healthy, Halladay throws a four-seam fastball that has late life and reaches the high 90s. In spring training, he experimented with a changeup that he can put in the back of the hitter's mind and possibly get a one-pitch out. He may add it to his arsenal, but for now, the Blue Jays simply want him to show that he's healthy.

Defense

Halladay's height is his biggest strength defensively, and also the biggest hindrance to his pick-off move. He can be slow to the plate with runners on base, and throughout his career he has been easy pickings for basestealers.

2005 Outlook

Halladay follows a Clemens-esque workout regimen that he planned on refining after last year's shoulder problems. Considering the thought he puts into his preparation, and the memories of being sent down to the minors in 2001 to rebuild his delivery and mental approach, Halladay can be expected to rebound in 2005.

Position: SP
Bats: R **Throws:** R
Ht: 6' 6" **Wt:** 230

Opening Day Age: 27
Born: 5/14/77 in Denver, CO
ML Seasons: 7
Pronunciation: HAL-luh-day

Toronto

Overall Statistics

	W	L	Pct.	ERA	G	GS	Sv	IP	H	BB	SO	HR	Avg
'04	8	8	.500	4.20	21	21	0	133.0	140	39	95	13	.272
Car.	67	39	.632	3.89	165	140	1	974.2	985	281	702	87	.260

2004 Pitching Profile

	Roy Halladay	AL Average
Overall Strike %	64.3	62.3
1st Pitch Strike %	60.9	58.1
Ratio	1.35	1.42
Strikeouts per 9 IP	6.43	6.45
Walks per 9 IP	2.64	3.34
Home Runs per 9 IP	0.88	1.15
Strikeout/Walk Ratio	2.44	1.93
Groundball/Flyball Ratio	2.27	1.17

2004 Situational Stats

	W	L	ERA	Sv	IP		AB	H	HR	RBI	Avg
Home	5	3	3.19	0	62.0	LHB	281	80	8	29	.285
Road	3	5	5.07	0	71.0	RHB	233	60	5	30	.258
First Half	7	6	4.03	0	114.0	Sc Pos	117	32	2	44	.274
Scnd Half	1	2	5.21	0	19.0	Clutch	27	7	1	4	.259

2004 Rankings (American League)

- 5th in balks (2)
- Led the Blue Jays in lowest slugging percentage allowed (.381), highest groundball-flyball ratio allowed (2.3), most run support per nine innings (5.7) and fewest home runs allowed per nine innings (.88)

Eric Hinske

2004 Season

Two years later, Eric Hinske still wasn't the same hitter he was in 2002, when he was the American League's Rookie of the Year. But he is a much better fielder. One year removed from surgery to repair a broken hook of the hamate bone, Hinske was a non-factor offensively for most of 2004 despite a strong spring training. He rescued his 2003 season by hitting 45 doubles, but last year he managed just 23 and was unable to shoulder an added offensive burden in a season in which Vernon Wells and Carlos Delgado missed significant playing time.

Hitting

Hinske has said he prefers batting second, but he has been ticketed for the middle of the order. Tough on low fastballs middle-away but susceptible to the high fastball, he went through periods last year where he seemed incapable of driving the ball, especially on offspeed pitches when he was behind in the count. Hinske had problems with his mechanics for much of the season, despite several stints of videotape work. He seemed to leave his hands out of position far too often—usually not bringing them back far enough.

Baserunning & Defense

Once considered to be a ham-handed fielder, Hinske took huge steps towards becoming a solid if not Gold Glove-caliber defensive player. He led all American League third baseman in fielding percentage in 2004. That's not a complete surprise, since Hinske is a good athlete for a big man and now has three seasons of experience in the field. Hinske stole 25 bases in his first two years and was caught just three times, though last season he was successful on just 12 of 20 attempts.

2005 Outlook

Hinske is in the third year of a five-year contract and due a significant raise from $900,000 to $3 million. All talk of moving him across the diamond to first base is dead, but the Blue Jays need more production from third base than Hinske has given them in the last two years.

Position: 3B
Bats: L **Throws:** R
Ht: 6' 2" **Wt:** 235

Opening Day Age: 27
Born: 8/5/77 in Menasha, WI
ML Seasons: 3
Pronunciation: hin-SKEE

Overall Statistics

	G	AB	R	H	D	T	HR	RBI	SB	BB	SO	Avg	OBP	Slg
'04	155	570	66	140	23	3	15	69	12	54	109	.246	.312	.375
Car.	430	1585	239	407	106	8	51	216	37	190	351	.257	.336	.430

Where He Hits the Ball

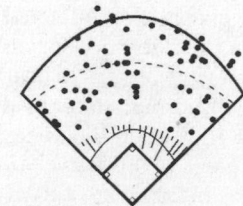 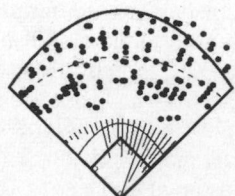

Vs. LHP   **Vs. RHP**

2004 Situational Stats

	AB	H	HR	RBI	Avg		AB	H	HR	RBI	Avg
Home	270	61	6	29	.226	LHP	168	45	4	26	.268
Road	300	79	9	40	.263	RHP	402	95	11	43	.236
First Half	310	85	8	40	.274	Sc Pos	145	31	3	52	.214
Scnd Half	260	55	7	29	.212	Clutch	75	15	1	4	.200

2004 Rankings (American League)

- 1st in fielding percentage at third base (.978)
- 2nd in lowest slugging percentage, lowest batting average vs. righthanded pitchers and lowest batting average at home
- 4th in lowest stolen-base percentage (60.0)
- 5th in lowest on-base percentage
- 7th in lowest batting average and lowest batting average with runners in scoring position
- Led the Blue Jays in at-bats, caught stealing (8), pitches seen (2,413), plate appearances (634) and games played

Orlando Hudson

2004 Season

At one point in his career, there was a concern that Orlando Hudson and Blue Jays GM J.P. Ricciardi couldn't co-exist. Yet there was Ricciardi last year, plugging Hudson for a Gold Glove, and with good reason: few players at his position showed the range on shallow flyballs of Hudson. But it was at the plate that Hudson made the biggest strides, becoming a much more integral part of the Blue Jays' offense.

Hitting

Hudson is a line-drive hitter who feasts on low balls, likes to use the whole field and last year showed surprising power from the right side. The Blue Jays managed to get him to lower his hands from the right side (shortening his swing) and keep his upper body more erect. Harder-throwing lefties still present a major problem for Hudson, and his swing lengthens noticeably against them, but he does a better job of staying in for the fight than he did earlier in his career. He has a tendency to rush himself at the plate, and that throws off his upper body.

Baserunning & Defense

The Blue Jays would like Hudson to show more aggressiveness on the basepaths and take advantage of his speed and athleticism. Hudson was a third baseman in his minor league career, and that arm strength serves him well at second, as well as on balls hit into the hole. He has quick feet and has become fearless on the double play. His development was one of the reasons that the Blue Jays put together the second-highest fielding percentage in the AL after tying for 11th in 2003.

2005 Outlook

Hudson never will produce the on-base percentages necessary for a leadoff hitter, but he is ticketed to be the everyday No. 2 hitter in the Blue Jays' lineup, especially now that he has upgraded his work from the right side of the plate. It's a sign of his growing reputation that he is a favorite trade target of other teams.

Position: 2B
Bats: B **Throws:** R
Ht: 6' 0" **Wt:** 185

Opening Day Age: 27
Born: 12/12/77 in Darlington, SC
ML Seasons: 3

Toronto

Overall Statistics

	G	AB	R	H	D	T	HR	RBI	SB	BB	SO	Avg	OBP	Slg
'04	135	489	73	132	32	7	12	58	7	51	98	.270	.341	.438
Car.	331	1155	147	312	63	18	25	138	12	101	212	.270	.332	.421

Where He Hits the Ball

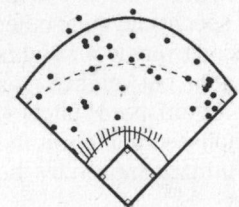 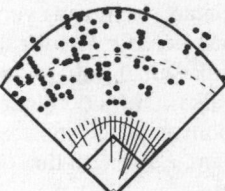

Vs. LHP   **Vs. RHP**

2004 Situational Stats

	AB	H	HR	RBI	Avg		AB	H	HR	RBI	Avg
Home	239	58	5	26	.243	LHP	122	32	4	19	.262
Road	250	74	7	32	.296	RHP	367	100	8	39	.272
First Half	230	60	7	34	.261	Sc Pos	113	30	4	45	.265
Scnd Half	259	72	5	24	.278	Clutch	59	13	2	8	.220

2004 Rankings (American League)

- 4th in errors at second base (12)
- 5th in fielding percentage at second base (.984)
- Led the Blue Jays in triples, sacrifice bunts (3) and batting average on the road

Reed Johnson

2004 Season

The closest thing the Blue Jays have had to a bona fide leadoff hitter for two years, Reed Johnson set a career high with 61 ribbies and had nine three-hit games. Johnson moved to left field when rookie right fielder Alexis Rios was called up, and for the second year in a row tailed off noticeably in the second half, hitting a weak .212 in September/October.

Hitting

Johnson shows occasional power, but he's at his best using the outfield gaps. When he gets in a prolonged funk, it's usually because the timing of his front foot is off, which prevents him from squaring up on balls. Johnson needs to make more contact to earn an everyday spot by anything other than default, and for the second year in a row his strikeout totals significantly outweighed his walks. He is vulnerable to offspeed pitches. Johnson is the most accomplished bunter on the team, a strength that is not utilized enough by the Jays.

Baserunning & Defense

On any other team, Johnson would be given a greater opportunity to show his considerable potential as a basestealer. As it is, he is one of the quickest Blue Jays and also one of the headiest at taking the extra base. Johnson covers a lot of territory in the outfield and willingly sacrifices his body, and his arm strength is better than he is sometimes given credit. He had nine outfield assists, second on the team.

2005 Outlook

Johnson has an old, grainy, framed picture in his locker of Ty Cobb sliding in spikes high. As long as Johnson continues to play aggressively, he will have a job, but his days of being anything other than a platoon player are limited, especially with prospects Rios and Gabe Gross closing in on regular employment with the parent club.

Position: LF/RF/CF
Bats: R **Throws:** R
Ht: 5'10" **Wt:** 180

Opening Day Age: 28
Born: 12/8/76 in Riverside, CA
ML Seasons: 2

Overall Statistics

	G	AB	R	H	D	T	HR	RBI	SB	BB	SO	Avg	OBP	Slg
'04	141	537	68	145	25	2	10	61	6	28	98	.270	.320	.380
Car.	255	949	147	266	46	4	20	113	11	48	165	.280	.334	.400

Where He Hits the Ball

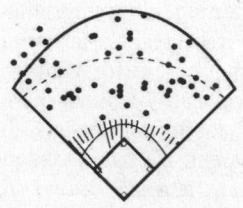 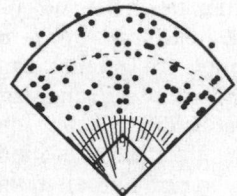

Vs. LHP   **Vs. RHP**

2004 Situational Stats

	AB	H	HR	RBI	Avg		AB	H	HR	RBI	Avg
Home	270	81	8	37	.300	LHP	173	52	5	21	.301
Road	267	64	2	24	.240	RHP	364	93	5	40	.255
First Half	325	90	7	46	.277	Sc Pos	127	39	1	51	.307
Scnd Half	212	55	3	15	.259	Clutch	77	18	0	7	.234

2004 Rankings (American League)

- 2nd in highest groundball-flyball ratio (2.1)
- 3rd in lowest on-base percentage for a leadoff hitter (.317)
- 4th in lowest slugging percentage
- 6th in bunts in play (24)
- 7th in lowest batting average on the road
- 8th in most GDPs per GDP situation (18.5%)
- 10th in hit by pitch (12), lowest on-base percentage and lowest batting average vs. righthanded pitchers
- Led the Blue Jays in singles, sacrifice bunts (3), GDPs (17), bunts in play (24) and lowest percentage of swings on the first pitch (17.9)

Ted Lilly

Position: SP
Bats: L **Throws:** L
Ht: 6' 1" **Wt:** 190

Opening Day Age: 29
Born: 1/4/76 in Lomita, CA
ML Seasons: 6
Pronunciation: LILL-ee

2004 Season

In his first season with the Blue Jays, Ted Lilly overcame a strained left wrist that cut into his spring training to earn his first All-Star berth. He held opponents to a .230 batting average that was second-lowest in the league. Lilly's record should have been better. He was done in at times by his run support, such as in July, when he was 0-3 in five starts despite holding opponents to a .195 average. With ace Roy Halladay hurt, Lilly was the closest thing the Blue Jays had to a dependable starter for the entire season.

Pitching

Lilly added a couple of miles per hour to his fastball. Still, he struggled at times trying to find a balance between the pitch and a very good curveball and changeup. He also continued a habit of sometimes not throwing his pitches with enough conviction, causing him to be too erect in his delivery. With Lilly susceptible to the home-run ball, the Blue Jays felt he was tipping his pitches by fanning his glove on his changeup and worked with him to curtail the habit. Lilly's curveball is a textbook 12-to-6 offering that comes in on the same plane as his fastball. Lilly has faced nagging questions about his focus throughout his career, and the Blue Jays shared those concerns at times.

Defense

Opponents stole successfully seven of eight times against Lilly, who still needs work on his move to first base. As a flyball pitcher, Lilly's defensive skills often aren't a factor, but when called upon, he fields his position adequately.

2005 Outlook

Lilly is in the final year of a two-year contract, and the Blue Jays have him under control for one more year after that before he becomes a free agent. In an organization with a higher payroll, he would be negotiating a contract extension, but the Blue Jays can be expected to wait until the end of the 2005 season to work out a deal with him.

Overall Statistics

	W	L	Pct.	ERA	G	GS	Sv	IP	H	BB	SO	HR	Avg
'04	12	10	.545	4.06	32	32	0	197.1	171	89	168	26	.230
Car.	34	34	.500	4.49	128	103	0	628.0	594	243	543	93	.245

2004 Pitching Profile

	Ted Lilly	AL Average
Overall Strike %	62.7	62.3
1st Pitch Strike %	57.1	58.1
Ratio	1.32	1.42
Strikeouts per 9 IP	7.66	6.45
Walks per 9 IP	4.06	3.34
Home Runs per 9 IP	1.19	1.15
Strikeout/Walk Ratio	1.89	1.93
Groundball/Flyball Ratio	0.80	1.17

2004 Situational Stats

	W	L	ERA	Sv	IP		AB	H	HR	RBI	Avg
Home	5	6	4.23	0	87.1	LHB	148	29	4	14	.196
Road	7	4	3.93	0	110.0	RHB	596	142	22	69	.238
First Half	7	6	4.27	0	105.1	Sc Pos	164	38	6	57	.232
Scnd Half	5	4	3.82	0	92.0	Clutch	35	11	1	3	.314

2004 Rankings (American League)

- 1st in balks (4)
- 2nd in lowest batting average allowed (.230) and highest stolen-base percentage allowed (87.5)
- 3rd in walks allowed
- 4th in lowest groundball-flyball ratio allowed (0.8) and highest walks per nine innings (4.1)
- 6th in strikeouts, lowest batting average allowed vs. lefthanded batters and most pitches thrown per batter (3.91)
- 7th in least run support per nine innings (4.5)
- Led the Blue Jays in wins, games started, complete games (2), home runs allowed, strikeouts, balks (4), pitches thrown (3,305), pickoff throws (78), lowest batting average allowed (.230), lowest ERA on the road, lowest batting average allowed vs. lefthanded batters, lowest batting average allowed with runners in scoring position and most strikeouts per nine innings (7.7)

Alexis Rios

2004 Season

Rushed up from Triple-A Syracuse because of injuries to several regulars, Alexis Rios led all American League rookies in multi-hit games, triples, stolen bases and outfield assists. Rios became the Blue Jays' everyday right fielder and had a four-hit game on July 18 against the Rangers, part of a month in which he went 34-for-99 (.343) and hit in 21 of 25 games, including a streak of four two-hit games.

Hitting

Forget the lack of power numbers. Blue Jays hitting coach Mike Barnett draws parallels between Rios and another young slugger he coached as a minor leaguer in the White Sox' organization, Magglio Ordonez. Rios was content in his rookie season to drive pitches to the opposite field. Once his wiry, athletic body fills out, the home runs will come mostly to center and right-center, particularly if he pays more attention to the transfer of weight while he's swinging. Rios is a work in progress, but he has a quick, short stroke and showed an ability to make adjustments.

Baserunning & Defense

Rios' arm strength came as advertised—above average—and so, too, did his baserunning prowess, as he was successful on 15 of 18 attempts. Rios showed an ability to separate his offense from his defense and not take a poor at-bat into the field with him. Rios throws from a three-quarters arm slot instead of over the top (catcher Gregg Zaun referred to it as a "power-sinker from right field") and as a result, he sometimes flies open when he rushes a throw.

2005 Outlook

Rios will be batting either fifth or sixth for the Blue Jays this season and starting every day in right field. Part of the club's offseason personnel decisions involved adding some pop to the middle of the lineup to remove any extra pressure from Rios, who will be asked to continue working to the opposite field while patiently waiting for the power to arrive.

Position: RF
Bats: R **Throws:** R
Ht: 6' 5" **Wt:** 194

Opening Day Age: 24
Born: 2/18/81 in Coffee, AL
ML Seasons: 1

Overall Statistics

	G	AB	R	H	D	T	HR	RBI	SB	BB	SO	Avg	OBP	Slg
'04	111	426	55	122	24	7	1	28	15	31	84	.286	.338	.383
Car.	111	426	55	122	24	7	1	28	15	31	84	.286	.338	.383

Where He Hits the Ball

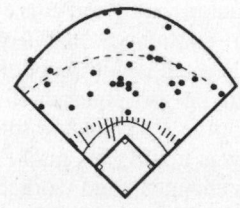
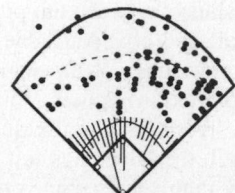

Vs. LHP **Vs. RHP**

2004 Situational Stats

	AB	H	HR	RBI	Avg		AB	H	HR	RBI	Avg
Home	214	62	0	16	.290	LHP	101	29	0	6	.287
Road	212	60	1	12	.283	RHP	325	93	1	22	.286
First Half	153	42	0	10	.275	Sc Pos	101	24	0	25	.238
Scnd Half	273	80	1	18	.293	Clutch	61	19	0	4	.311

2004 Rankings (American League)

- 2nd in batting average among rookies
- 4th in fielding percentage in right field (.991)
- Led the Blue Jays in batting average, triples, stolen bases, highest groundball-flyball ratio (2.4) and stolen-base percentage (83.3)

Vernon Wells

2004 Season

Vernon Wells fought his way out of a gruesome 7-for-45 hitting funk at the end of April and was extremely productive in May and June before going on the disabled list on June 16. Literally just an inch away from suffering a torn Achilles tendon, Wells missed 24 games with a strained calf muscle. He didn't hit his stride offensively again until September, hitting .291 with seven home runs and 18 RBI.

Hitting

Wells is a prototypical line-drive gap hitter who feeds off low fastballs and mistake breaking pitches. He also has spurts of impatience at the plate. The Blue Jays stress working the pitcher and on-base percentage, but many in the organization believe Wells would be a less-effective hitter if he cuts down on his natural aggressiveness. Mechanically, the Blue Jays have noticed that Wells opens up with his front foot at times, which causes him to pull off the ball and drag his bat through the strike zone. Wells is a smart player all-around, and that translates to his approach to hitting, as he studies opposing pitchers' routines.

Baserunning & Defense

Wells could steal more bases, but that's not part of the Blue Jays' modus operandi. When healthy, he is aggressive and quick to take the extra base. Wells' first Gold Glove in 2004 solidified his reputation among baseball people as a premier defender. Quick enough to make up for mistakes and fearless at the wall, Wells' first step is almost always the right one. He has improved his physical fitness markedly since deciding before the 2003 season to spend some offseason time at a Scottsdale-based fitness facility used by professional athletes.

2005 Outlook

Wells and ace Roy Halladay are the closest things the Blue Jays have to untouchables. With Carlos Delgado leaving as a free agent, Wells could land in the cleanup spot after spending most of his career batting third. Wells is in the third year of a five-year, $14.5-million contract that will pay him $2.9 million in 2005.

Position: CF
Bats: R **Throws:** R
Ht: 6' 1" **Wt:** 225

Opening Day Age: 26
Born: 12/8/78 in Shreveport, LA
ML Seasons: 6

Toronto

Overall Statistics

	G	AB	R	H	D	T	HR	RBI	SB	BB	SO	Avg	OBP	Slg
'04	134	536	82	146	34	2	23	67	9	51	83	.272	.337	.472
Car.	511	2008	309	581	130	11	81	298	28	129	281	.289	.333	.486

Where He Hits the Ball

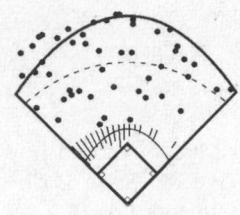

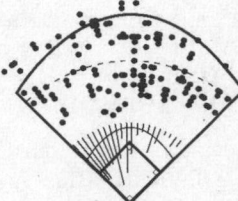

Vs. LHP   **Vs. RHP**

2004 Situational Stats

	AB	H	HR	RBI	Avg		AB	H	HR	RBI	Avg
Home	255	76	14	37	.298	LHP	150	43	10	24	.287
Road	281	70	9	30	.249	RHP	386	103	13	43	.267
First Half	260	78	9	30	.300	Sc Pos	139	32	6	44	.230
Scnd Half	276	68	14	37	.246	Clutch	76	14	1	7	.184

2004 Rankings (American League)

- 1st in fielding percentage in center field (.997)
- 4th in fewest pitches seen per plate appearance (3.44)
- 6th in highest percentage of swings on the first pitch (37.8)
- 7th in steals of third (5)
- Led the Blue Jays in runs scored, hits, doubles, total bases (253), GDPs (17) and steals of third (5)
- Led AL center fielders in home runs

Kevin Cash

Position: C
Bats: R **Throws:** R
Ht: 6' 0" **Wt:** 185

Opening Day Age: 27
Born: 12/6/77 in Tampa, FL
ML Seasons: 3

Overall Statistics

	G	AB	R	H	D	T	HR	RBI	SB	BB	SO	Avg	OBP	Slg
'04	60	181	18	35	9	0	4	21	0	10	59	.193	.249	.309
Car.	101	301	29	52	12	0	5	29	0	15	85	.173	.222	.262

2004 Situational Stats

	AB	H	HR	RBI	Avg		AB	H	HR	RBI	Avg
Home	82	16	2	7	.195	LHP	75	16	2	11	.213
Road	99	19	2	14	.192	RHP	106	19	2	10	.179
First Half	136	28	3	16	.206	Sc Pos	54	9	0	13	.167
Scnd Half	45	7	1	5	.156	Clutch	29	8	0	9	.276

2004 Season

The injury to veteran Greg Myers exposed how little faith the Blue Jays have in Kevin Cash's ability to be in the regular lineup. Gregg Zaun came in and became the team's No. 1 catcher, while Cash suffered a strained rib cage that put him on the DL. Cash hit .266 in April and managed just 117 at-bats the rest of the year.

Hitting, Baserunning & Defense

Cash has quick hands, but he too often rushes his swing and body. He is capable of executing the hit-and-run, but since the Jays don't play small ball, he gets lost in the shuffle. Cash is a smart handler of pitchers and he threw out more than 40 percent of opposing baserunners, but the team was concerned that he tended to shy away from contact at the plate. Cash is quick to the point of being skittish, and he sometimes leaves himself out of position to receive throws.

2005 Outlook

With prospect Guillermo Quiroz knocking at the door as a much better offensive player, Cash wasn't viewed as the long-term solution in Toronto. During the winter meetings, the Jays dealt him to Tampa Bay, where the defensive specialist will battle Toby Hall for playing time.

Vinnie Chulk

Position: RP
Bats: R **Throws:** R
Ht: 6' 2" **Wt:** 195

Opening Day Age: 26
Born: 12/19/78 in Miami, FL
ML Seasons: 2

Overall Statistics

	W	L	Pct.	ERA	G	GS	Sv	IP	H	BB	SO	HR	Avg
'04	1	3	.250	4.66	47	0	2	56.0	59	27	44	6	.271
Car.	1	3	.250	4.70	50	0	2	61.1	65	30	46	6	.271

2004 Situational Stats

	W	L	ERA	Sv	IP		AB	H	HR	RBI	Avg
Home	1	1	4.73	1	26.2	LHB	118	36	5	21	.305
Road	0	2	4.60	1	29.1	RHB	100	23	1	9	.230
First Half	0	0	2.16	2	25.0	Sc Pos	60	15	2	25	.250
Scnd Half	1	3	6.68	0	31.0	Clutch	84	24	4	23	.286

2004 Season

The Blue Jays' bullpen has been a mess for the past three seasons, but for much of last year Vinnie Chulk was the team's most trusted setup man. Pitching with a swagger, he had a 1.59 ERA in June and was given a responsible bullpen role. But his ERA was 6.32 the rest of the season, and he was scored on in seven of his last 10 outings.

Pitching & Defense

Chulk added three MPH to his fastball in spring training, and when the Blue Jays moved him to the first-base side of the pitching rubber at the end of the spring, the transformation was complete. The move allowed Chulk to hit the outside corner, and also gave him the option of throwing a backdoor slider to lefties. Chulk has a basic pitcher's arsenal—fastball, slider, changeup and curveball—and he experiments with different arm angles, sometimes to his detriment.

2005 Outlook

Chulk's stuff appeared short at crucial times. It will not be a good sign for the Blue Jays if he comes out of spring training still being relied on as a primary setup man, but he showed enough last year to figure in the organization's plans at some point in 2005.

Jason Frasor

Position: RP
Bats: R **Throws:** R
Ht: 5'10" **Wt:** 170

Opening Day Age: 27
Born: 8/9/77 in Chicago, IL
ML Seasons: 1

Overall Statistics

	W	L	Pct.	ERA	G	GS	Sv	IP	H	BB	SO	HR	Avg
'04	4	6	.400	4.08	63	0	17	68.1	64	36	54	4	.251
Car.	4	6	.400	4.08	63	0	17	68.1	64	36	54	4	.251

2004 Situational Stats

	W	L	ERA	Sv	IP		AB	H	HR	RBI	Avg
Home	4	4	4.85	9	39.0	LHB	142	33	4	19	.232
Road	0	2	3.07	8	29.1	RHB	113	31	0	12	.274
First Half	3	2	2.17	9	37.1	Sc Pos	73	17	0	25	.233
Scnd Half	1	4	6.39	8	31.0	Clutch	166	42	1	20	.253

2004 Season

Jason Frasor spent most of the season as the Blue Jays' closer until tiring in August. A survivor of two separate Tommy John surgeries who hadn't pitched above Double-A until last season, Frasor had a 20-inning scoreless streak during one stretch of the year and didn't allow a run in 13 of his first 14 appearances.

Pitching & Defense

Diminutive in stature, Frasor throws a mid-90s fastball and a nasty curve without using maximum effort. The Blue Jays taught him a changeup, but Frasor was hesitant to use the pitch in game situations until later in the season. Frasor still needs refining with runners on base and at times would forget to look over at them, but the Blue Jays believe that was a product of inexperience and focusing on his pitching.

2005 Outlook

Frasor's pitches did not have the same life as the season wore on. But the Blue Jays have tried to convince him that he can be as effective as another tiny reliever, Tom Gordon. The team is not ready to say that Frasor is the long-term answer as a closer, but as long as he works cheap, the Blue Jays will try to find a spot for him at the back of the bullpen.

Chris Gomez

Position: SS/1B
Bats: R **Throws:** R
Ht: 6' 1" **Wt:** 188

Opening Day Age: 33
Born: 6/16/71 in Los Angeles, CA
ML Seasons: 12

Overall Statistics

	G	AB	R	H	D	T	HR	RBI	SB	BB	SO	Avg	OBP	Slg
'04	109	341	41	96	11	1	3	37	3	28	41	.282	.337	.346
Car.	1189	3848	429	984	196	17	55	411	31	351	666	.256	.322	.358

2004 Situational Stats

	AB	H	HR	RBI	Avg		AB	H	HR	RBI	Avg
Home	189	53	1	26	.280	LHP	100	30	2	15	.300
Road	152	43	2	11	.283	RHP	241	66	1	22	.274
First Half	212	60	2	22	.283	Sc Pos	88	28	2	35	.318
Scnd Half	129	36	1	15	.279	Clutch	54	20	3	14	.370

2004 Season

No longer considered anybody's shortstop of the future, Chris Gomez was acquired to fill the same role that Mike Bordick filled in 2003—as a combination insurance policy and security blanket for Chris Woodward. As was the case with Bordick, Gomez ended up becoming the closest thing the Blue Jays had to a regular shortstop, appearing in 109 games.

Hitting, Baserunning & Defense

While Gomez wasn't asked to do a great deal offensively, he did hit .300 against lefties and didn't mail in any at-bats. Knee surgeries earlier in his career have robbed Gomez of much of his speed and some of his range, but he showed himself to be a savvy baserunner and defender. Gomez' biggest asset was his professionalism and consistency of approach.

2005 Outlook

With prospect Russ Adams penciled in as the everyday shortstop, Gomez would be no more than a mentor and security blanket for Adams if he stayed with Toronto. Soon after the Jays acquired utilityman John McDonald from Cleveland in early December, Gomez signed a minor league deal with Baltimore and was claimed by Philadelphia in the Triple-A Rule 5 draft.

Frank Menechino

Position: 2B/DH/SS
Bats: R **Throws:** R
Ht: 5' 8" **Wt:** 198

Opening Day Age: 34
Born: 1/7/71 in Staten Island, NY
ML Seasons: 6
Pronunciation: men-a-keen-o

Overall Statistics

	G	AB	R	H	D	T	HR	RBI	SB	BB	SO	Avg	OBP	Slg
'04	84	269	40	74	13	4	9	26	0	37	52	.275	.371	.454
Car.	380	1109	185	270	51	7	32	136	3	175	246	.243	.358	.389

2004 Situational Stats

	AB	H	HR	RBI	Avg		AB	H	HR	RBI	Avg
Home	139	45	6	18	.324	LHP	108	34	6	15	.315
Road	130	29	3	8	.223	RHP	161	40	3	11	.248
First Half	169	47	5	17	.278	Sc Pos	64	17	0	16	.266
Scnd Half	100	27	4	9	.270	Clutch	34	6	1	5	.176

2004 Season

The Blue Jays acquired Frank Menechino in May in a trade with Oakland, after Menechino opened the season on the 15-day disabled list with a strained right calf and was then optioned to Triple-A Sacramento. He became Toronto's most valuable reserve infielder—twice flirting with a cycle—and was used up and down the batting order. He hit seven home runs out of the leadoff spot.

Hitting, Baserunning & Defense

The stocky Menechino hits from gap to gap with surprising power. With his plate patience, he was a sparkplug at times out of the leadoff spot. Coming to Toronto re-united Menechino with Mike Barnett, the Blue Jays' hitting coach who was with him in the White Sox' system. Menechino gets in trouble when pitchers start pounding him inside because he becomes over-anxious. He is a useful defender at second base, third and shortstop. On a team that is often laconic, he brought a notable amount of energy.

2005 Outlook

Menechino revived his career with Toronto, and the club re-signed him. Orlando Hudson is solid at second base and prospect Russ Adams is ticketed for shortstop, but it's a safe bet that Menechino will get his at-bats as a valuable reserve off the bench.

Justin Miller

Position: SP
Bats: R **Throws:** R
Ht: 6' 2" **Wt:** 209

Opening Day Age: 27
Born: 8/27/77 in Torrance, CA
ML Seasons: 2

Overall Statistics

	W	L	Pct.	ERA	G	GS	Sv	IP	H	BB	SO	HR	Avg
'04	3	4	.429	6.06	19	15	0	81.2	101	42	47	14	.316
Car.	12	9	.571	5.77	44	33	0	184.0	204	108	115	26	.289

2004 Situational Stats

	W	L	ERA	Sv	IP		AB	H	HR	RBI	Avg
Home	1	3	6.97	0	50.1	LHB	166	61	10	34	.367
Road	2	1	4.60	0	31.1	RHB	154	40	4	25	.260
First Half	1	1	4.20	0	40.2	Sc Pos	83	27	2	44	.325
Scnd Half	2	3	7.90	0	41.0	Clutch	8	3	0	1	.375

2004 Season

After sitting out the 2003 season because of shoulder surgery to repair damage caused by weightlifting, Justin Miller pitched his way on and off the major league staff at various times during the season. He tantalized the Blue Jays by pitching eight innings of two-hit ball against the Angels in September, but he finished the year in the bullpen.

Pitching & Defense

Miller's two-seam fastball is effective with its late movement, and when he is healthy he uses it to induce pitch-saving groundball outs. But he has yet to develop an offspeed pitch for lefthanded hitters, and is a sinker-slider pitcher who is better suited to the bullpen. Miller sometimes throws his mechanics off by letting his front leg be his work leg. He fields his position adequately, although when his mechanics are messed up he often is too much off balance to make a proper play on the ball.

2005 Outlook

The Blue Jays love Miller's stuff and his demeanor, and he spent much of last season lobbying for a bullpen role. But first-pitch swingers hit .455 off him last season and he had difficulty when behind in the count, so he is a work in progress even in a relief capacity.

Justin Speier

Position: RP
Bats: R **Throws:** R
Ht: 6' 4" **Wt:** 205

Opening Day Age: 31
Born: 11/6/73 in Walnut Creek, CA
ML Seasons: 7
Pronunciation: SPY-er

Overall Statistics

	W	L	Pct.	ERA	G	GS	Sv	IP	H	BB	SO	HR	Avg
'04	3	8	.273	3.91	62	0	7	69.0	61	25	52	8	.239
Car.	22	18	.550	4.40	336	0	17	399.0	368	141	335	65	.244

2004 Situational Stats

	W	L	ERA	Sv	IP		AB	H	HR	RBI	Avg
Home	2	1	2.12	4	34.0	LHB	133	35	7	22	.263
Road	1	7	5.66	3	35.0	RHB	122	26	1	13	.213
First Half	2	5	5.29	1	32.1	Sc Pos	79	22	3	27	.278
Scnd Half	1	3	2.70	6	36.2	Clutch	132	38	5	24	.288

2004 Season

The Blue Jays thought they were getting a dependable setup man when they traded for Justin Speier last December. Instead, they found themselves with just one more maddeningly inconsistent reliever. Speier, after some elbow woes in the first half, saved his season with a strong August in which he recorded a 1.80 ERA and experienced a dramatic jump in velocity.

Pitching & Defense

Inconsistency has plagued Speier throughout his career. While he can hit the mid-90s with a sinking fastball, his hard slider will flatten out when he gets sloppy with his arm angle. Speier calls on a split-finger pitch to get groundball outs with runners on base, and he was better when he stopped overthrowing the splitter and got a better tilt on his slider in August. He is an average fielder, and his quirky delivery sometimes makes him easy to run on.

2005 Outlook

In three seasons with Colorado, Speier allowed only 17 of 92 inherited runners to score. The Blue Jays believe that statistic is a more accurate reflection of his abilities than the 10 of 26 he allowed to score last year. He will be given every chance to rebound this season and secure a key bullpen role.

Josh Towers

Position: SP
Bats: R **Throws:** R
Ht: 6' 1" **Wt:** 188

Opening Day Age: 28
Born: 2/26/77 in Port Hueneme, CA
ML Seasons: 4

Overall Statistics

	W	L	Pct.	ERA	G	GS	Sv	IP	H	BB	SO	HR	Avg
'04	9	9	.500	5.11	21	21	0	116.1	148	26	51	16	.310
Car.	25	23	.521	4.96	64	52	1	348.1	422	54	164	63	.301

2004 Situational Stats

	W	L	ERA	Sv	IP		AB	H	HR	RBI	Avg
Home	4	5	6.22	0	59.1	LHB	276	86	8	27	.312
Road	5	4	3.95	0	57.0	RHB	201	62	8	34	.308
First Half	3	3	5.40	0	43.1	Sc Pos	114	34	5	46	.298
Scnd Half	6	6	4.93	0	73.0	Clutch	25	5	1	1	.200

2004 Season

After wondering whether he had a place in the organization in April, Josh Towers came back from the minor leagues and filled in at the back end of the rotation, and he may have pitched himself into the picture for 2005. Former Blue Jays manager Carlos Tosca felt that Towers could be immature at times on the mound and his season was briefly interrupted by a strained muscle in his right shoulder. Towers lost his last five decisions, but his six wins after the All-Star break were a team high.

Pitching & Defense

Towers throws four pitches, all of them around the strike zone and none of them very hard. But he is a competitor who isn't afraid to push batters off the plate. Towers relies on fastball location and getting outs early in the count. As a finesse pitcher, he gets into trouble with his curveball when he doesn't finish off his delivery. He made a pair of errors last year in 24 chances.

2005 Outlook

Towers is at best a back-of-the-rotation starter, and his place in the rotation will be an indication of the effectiveness of the Blue Jays' offseason rebuilding plans. He is 17-10 with one save in his Blue Jays career.

Chris Woodward

Position: SS
Bats: R **Throws:** R
Ht: 6' 0" **Wt:** 185

Opening Day Age: 28
Born: 6/27/76 in Covina, CA
ML Seasons: 6
Nickname: Woody

Overall Statistics

	G	AB	R	H	D	T	HR	RBI	SB	BB	SO	Avg	OBP	Slg
'04	69	213	21	50	13	4	1	24	1	14	46	.235	.283	.347
Car.	351	1067	144	264	59	12	26	135	6	81	238	.247	.300	.398

2004 Situational Stats

	AB	H	HR	RBI	Avg		AB	H	HR	RBI	Avg
Home	91	14	0	7	.154	LHP	59	15	0	6	.254
Road	122	36	1	17	.295	RHP	154	35	1	18	.227
First Half	125	32	0	11	.256	Sc Pos	50	15	1	22	.300
Scnd Half	88	18	1	13	.205	Clutch	33	6	0	1	.182

2004 Season

Chris Woodward showed himself to be physically and emotionally incapable of handling the rigors of being an everyday position player, this time missing 24 games with a strained hamstring. Given one last chance by manager John Gibbons, who remembered Woodward from their days together in the Arizona Fall League, he quickly found himself on the bench once Russ Adams was called up from Triple-A Syracuse in September.

Hitting, Baserunning & Defense

Woodward has quick hands and a wiry, athletic body that allowed him to show some pop in the past. Last season, however, he was an offensive as well as defensive liability who was easily overmatched, particularly by a high fastball. His bat speed dropped noticeably and he stopped making contact. Woodward has some quickness but lacks range in the field, and he makes far too many errors on routine plays. Woodward can steal a base, but he appears tentative at times.

2005 Outlook

One of the Jays' first moves at the end of the season was to outright Woodward, who declined a minor league assignment and became a free agent. He is enough of an athlete that he should catch on with some team as a reserve infielder.

Gregg Zaun

Position: C
Bats: B **Throws:** R
Ht: 5'10" **Wt:** 190

Opening Day Age: 33
Born: 4/14/71 in Glendale, CA
ML Seasons: 10
Pronunciation: ZAHN

Overall Statistics

	G	AB	R	H	D	T	HR	RBI	SB	BB	SO	Avg	OBP	Slg
'04	107	338	46	91	24	0	6	36	0	47	61	.269	.367	.393
Car.	686	1825	220	457	97	7	39	222	19	234	279	.250	.339	.375

2004 Situational Stats

	AB	H	HR	RBI	Avg		AB	H	HR	RBI	Avg
Home	173	44	2	19	.254	LHP	81	22	0	6	.272
Road	165	47	4	17	.285	RHP	257	69	6	30	.268
First Half	174	53	2	18	.305	Sc Pos	79	23	0	27	.291
Scnd Half	164	38	4	18	.232	Clutch	48	14	1	5	.292

2004 Season

Let go by the Montreal Expos after spending spring training as a non-roster invitee, Gregg Zaun became the de facto No. 1 catcher for the Blue Jays after an early-season injury to Greg Myers. Zaun impressed the organization with his ability to handle the steady stream of journeymen and unproven youngsters the team ran out of its bullpen, and became a valued clubhouse presence.

Hitting, Baserunning & Defense

Zaun is a front-foot hitter with a great deal of movement in his swing. He made the best of his playing time from both sides of the plate and had spurts where he showed an uncharacteristic patience. A hard-nosed presence on the field, Zaun aggressively blocked the plate and took charge of the team's sometimes-uncertain defense, though throwing out just under 26 percent of opposing baserunners. Zaun's fitness has improved in part, he says, because he has become more careful with some of the lifestyle choices he was making.

2005 Outlook

No longer happy to be a backup catcher, Zaun resurrected his career with the Blue Jays in 2004 and went into the winter looking for a team that would give him significant playing time. Toronto would like to re-sign him.

Other Toronto Blue Jays

Dave Berg (**Pos**: LF, **Age**: 34, **Bats**: R)

	G	AB	R	H	D	T	HR	RBI	SB	BB	SO	Avg	OBP	Slg
'04	58	154	13	39	4	0	3	23	0	4	27	.253	.278	.338
Car.	682	1600	190	430	91	6	21	163	8	133	308	.269	.328	.373

Except for missing most of July with extreme fatigue, for which doctors couldn't find a medical explanation, Berg had a pretty typical year as a utilityman. One difference is that Berg's walk rate has been on a noteworthy decline in recent years, which diminishes his value. 2005 Outlook: C

Howie Clark (**Pos**: 1B/RF, **Age**: 31, **Bats**: L)

	G	AB	R	H	D	T	HR	RBI	SB	BB	SO	Avg	OBP	Slg
'04	40	115	17	25	6	0	3	12	0	13	15	.217	.292	.348
Car.	92	238	29	66	14	1	3	23	0	19	27	.277	.338	.382

Clark enjoyed one of his best Triple-A stints with Syracuse in 2004, posting hitting percentages of .313/.407/.453 in 72 games. He got his longest look in the majors at age 30, but failed to approach the .333 average he had recorded in the big leagues prior to 2004. The Pirates signed him to a minor league deal in November. 2005 Outlook: C

Eric Crozier (**Pos**: DH, **Age**: 26, **Bats**: L)

	G	AB	R	H	D	T	HR	RBI	SB	BB	SO	Avg	OBP	Slg
'04	14	33	5	5	2	0	2	4	0	6	19	.152	.282	.394
Car.	14	33	5	5	2	0	2	4	0	6	19	.152	.282	.394

Having a breakout year the summer you turn 26 is better than no breakout year at all, but Crozier must build on his .292-21-69 season in 109 games at two Triple-A stops in 2004. Acquired from Cleveland for Josh Phelps in August, he will compete for time at first base with the Jays. 2005 Outlook: C

Valerio de los Santos (**Pos**: LHP, **Age**: 32)

	W	L	Pct.	ERA	G	GS	Sv	IP	H	BB	SO	HR	Avg
'04	0	0	–	6.17	17	0	0	11.2	11	10	10	0	.250
Car.	8	10	.444	4.38	206	2	1	226.0	194	104	181	32	.235

De Los Santos tantalized with an impressive debut in 1998, showing so much promise over the final six weeks of the season. Only for brief stretches since then has the lefthander been effective. Shoulder woes have been part of the problem, and they sidelined him for the second half. 2005 Outlook: C

Sean Douglass (**Pos**: RHP, **Age**: 25)

	W	L	Pct.	ERA	G	GS	Sv	IP	H	BB	SO	HR	Avg
'04	0	2	.000	6.28	14	3	0	38.2	37	28	36	6	.252
Car.	2	8	.200	6.51	38	15	0	120.1	130	80	100	21	.277

With a decent fastball and changeup, and a strong sense of how to work hitters, Douglass climbed steadily through the Orioles' system in the late 1990s before stalling in Triple-A ball. He now has four Triple-A years in, and he couldn't get over the hump with Toronto in 2004, either. He'll try again, this time with Detroit after signing a minor league deal in November. 2005 Outlook: C

Bobby Estalella (**Pos**: C, **Age**: 30, **Bats**: R)

	G	AB	R	H	D	T	HR	RBI	SB	BB	SO	Avg	OBP	Slg
'04	12	27	3	5	0	0	2	4	0	3	11	.185	.290	.407
Car.	310	904	126	195	49	5	48	147	6	130	290	.216	.315	.440

Estalella missed the second half with an ankle injury, but he passed through Arizona and Toronto before the break. The backup catcher lifts a few homers in a limited number of at-bats, but he's had trouble hitting north of the Mendoza line in recent seasons. He's in search of a job. 2005 Outlook: C

Bob File (**Pos**: RHP, **Age**: 28)

	W	L	Pct.	ERA	G	GS	Sv	IP	H	BB	SO	HR	Avg
'04	1	0	1.000	4.81	24	0	0	33.2	45	12	15	4	.331
Car.	6	4	.600	4.20	89	0	0	111.1	110	43	55	10	.267

After a fairly quick climb through the minors, File enjoyed a solid major league debut in 2001. But an oblique strain early in 2002 and shoulder surgery late that year kept him from establishing himself in Toronto. He was back in 2004 and will try to find a place in the Jays' pen. 2005 Outlook: C

Kevin Frederick (**Pos**: RHP, **Age**: 28)

	W	L	Pct.	ERA	G	GS	Sv	IP	H	BB	SO	HR	Avg
'04	0	2	.000	6.59	22	0	0	28.2	32	16	22	4	.283
Car.	0	2	.000	7.59	30	0	0	40.1	45	26	27	7	.283

Frederick enjoyed a dominating season at Double-A New Haven and Triple-A Syracuse, allowing just 33 hits in 48.2 innings, while posting a 1.11 ERA and 52 strikeouts. He was recalled in late July and didn't generate similar results in his first big league stint since September 2002. 2005 Outlook: C

Ryan Glynn (**Pos**: RHP, **Age**: 30)

	W	L	Pct.	ERA	G	GS	Sv	IP	H	BB	SO	HR	Avg
'04	1	0	1.000	4.05	6	2	0	20.0	19	8	14	4	.250
Car.	9	16	.360	6.19	47	37	0	209.1	256	110	101	36	.299

Toronto was Glynn's fourth organization since the former Texas prospect left the Rangers' system at the end of 2001. After going 7-2 with a 3.40 ERA as a starter with Triple-A Syracuse last summer, Glynn surfaced in Toronto and did his best big league pitching. Hope springs eternal. 2005 Outlook: C

Pat Hentgen (**Pos**: RHP, **Age**: 36)

	W	L	Pct.	ERA	G	GS	Sv	IP	H	BB	SO	HR	Avg
	2	9	.182	6.95	18	16	0	80.1	90	42	33	16	.283
	131	112	.539	4.32	344	306	1	2075.1	2111	775	1290	269	.264

Hentgen lacked the arm speed and velocity to get people out last year, and in July, the 13-year veteran retired. He left the door open for 2005 by filing for free agency, but Hentgen is likely to depart with a 131-112 mark and 4.32 ERA, pitching for Toronto, Baltimore and St. Louis. 2005 Outlook: C

Chad Hermansen (Pos: LF, Age: 27, Bats: R)

	G	AB	R	H	D	T	HR	RBI	SB	BB	SO	Avg	OBP	Slg
'04	4	7	0	0	0	0	0	0	0	0	3	.000	.000	.000
Car.	189	492	49	96	23	2	13	34	9	38	168	.195	.255	.329

Hermansen was one of Toronto's last cuts last spring, but joined the Jays in April. After a one-week stay, he returned to Triple-A Syracuse, lost a big chunk of 2004 to injury and didn't hit well in 42 games. He hasn't had much Triple-A or big league success in recent years. 2005 Outlook: C

Jason Kershner (Pos: LHP, Age: 28)

	W	L	Pct.	ERA	G	GS	Sv	IP	H	BB	SO	HR	Avg
'04	0	1	.000	6.04	24	2	0	22.1	30	8	15	3	.316
Car.	3	5	.375	4.22	89	2	1	100.1	93	37	65	11	.242

After an excellent stint at Triple-A Syracuse to open the 2003 season, Kershner enjoyed a solid second half in Toronto as a rookie. The lefty couldn't match his performance at the start of 2004, and in June he was back in Syracuse. He signed a minor league deal with the Red Sox in December. 2005 Outlook: C

Kerry Ligtenberg (Pos: RHP, Age: 33)

	W	L	Pct.	ERA	G	GS	Sv	IP	H	BB	SO	HR	Avg
'04	1	6	.143	6.38	57	0	3	55.0	73	25	49	6	.313
Car.	17	20	.459	3.57	379	0	48	381.0	341	154	352	42	.237

Ligtenberg hadn't posted an ERA worse than 3.61 in six big league seasons, and he had a chance to assume a ninth-inning role in his first season with the Jays. But a hip injury and poor outings plagued him for much of 2004, and he was shut down in mid-September. 2005 Outlook: B

Aquilino Lopez (Pos: RHP, Age: 29)

	W	L	Pct.	ERA	G	GS	Sv	IP	H	BB	SO	HR	Avg
'04	1	1	.500	6.00	18	0	0	21.0	21	13	13	5	.266
Car.	2	4	.333	3.99	90	0	14	94.2	79	47	77	10	.224

In December 2002, Lopez was a Rule 5 pick by the Jays and had a solid spring. He became the closer when Cliff Politte went down and saved 14 games. Last spring, he pitched poorly in camp and it carried into the season and to Syracuse, where he had a 7.17 ERA. What a difference a year makes. 2005 Outlook: C

Dave Maurer (Pos: LHP, Age: 30)

	W	L	Pct.	ERA	G	GS	Sv	IP	H	BB	SO	HR	Avg
'04	0	0	—	54.00	3	0	0	1.1	6	5	1	1	.600
Car.	1	1	.500	8.87	22	0	0	22.1	32	14	18	5	.330

Maurer pitched effectively at Triple-A Syracuse all season to earn his first callup since 2002 in late August. After a couple of brutal outings over a one-week stay, the Jays outrighted him back to Syracuse on September 1, the day young players usually arrive in the majors. 2005 Outlook: C

Greg Myers (Pos: C, Age: 38, Bats: L)

	G	AB	R	H	D	T	HR	RBI	SB	BB	SO	Avg	OBP	Slg
'04	8	18	0	4	2	0	0	1	0	2	4	.222	.300	.333
Car.	1102	3030	333	775	150	7	87	395	3	267	538	.256	.314	.396

After his best major league season in 2003 at age 37, Myers severely sprained his left ankle last April and never returned. The healing process was slow and frustrating, but he signed a new minor league deal with the Jays in November. There can't be many years left in those legs. 2005 Outlook: C

Mike Nakamura (Pos: RHP, Age: 28)

	W	L	Pct.	ERA	G	GS	Sv	IP	H	BB	SO	HR	Avg
'04	0	3	.000	7.36	19	0	0	25.2	27	7	24	7	.262
Car.	0	3	.000	7.51	31	0	1	38.1	47	9	38	11	.290

Nakamura has been impressive at the Triple-A level the last two seasons, posting a 3.04 ERA and 171 whiffs in 133.1 innings of mostly relief. The longball has kept the Japanese-born and Australian-bred righty from succeeding in the majors. He will be playing in Japan this season with Nippon. 2005 Outlook: C

Adam Peterson (Pos: RHP, Age: 25)

	W	L	Pct.	ERA	G	GS	Sv	IP	H	BB	SO	HR	Avg
'04	0	0	—	16.88	3	0	0	2.2	7	3	2	1	.467
Car.	0	0	—	16.88	3	0	0	2.2	7	3	2	1	.467

A fourth-round pick in 2002, Peterson was enjoying a dominating season at Double-A New Haven when he was recalled last June, barely two years after being drafted. His baptism with the Jays wasn't pretty, but he should be back. He needs some Triple-A time after struggling there, too. 2005 Outlook: C

Simon Pond (Pos: LF, Age: 28, Bats: L)

	G	AB	R	H	D	T	HR	RBI	SB	BB	SO	Avg	OBP	Slg
'04	16	49	4	8	2	0	1	6	0	5	12	.163	.250	.265
Car.	16	49	4	8	2	0	1	6	0	5	12	.163	.250	.265

A native of British Columbia, Pond was drafted by the Expos in 1994 and finally surfaced in the majors by making the Jays' Opening Day roster. Most of his playing time came in May, though he did little with his chances. He's shown enough bat in the high minors to warrant a 2005 look. 2005 Outlook: C

Toronto Blue Jays Minor League Prospects

Organization Overview:

Toronto received an infusion of homegrown talent in 2004, with Alexis Rios taking over in right field, Dave Bush securing a rotation spot and Vinnie Chulk slipping into the Jays' bullpen. By September, Gabe Gross was in the majors, Guillermo Quiroz got a first look and Russ Adams made an impressive debut. The same can be said for fifth-starter candidate Gustavo Chacin and reliever Brandon League in brief auditions. The minor league system was on the upswing, posting a .572 winning percentage that ranked second in baseball. There was an interesting collection of talent at high Class-A Dunedin, which included regulars Vito Chiaravalotti, Miguel Negron and Raul Tablado, as well as pitchers Josh Banks, Shaun Marcum, Ismael Ramirez, Francisco Rosario and Jamie Vermilyea.

Russ Adams

Position: SS **Opening Day Age:** 24
Bats: L **Throws:** R **Born:** 8/30/80 in
Ht: 6' 1" **Wt:** 180 Laurinburg, NC

Recent Statistics

	G	AB	R	H	D	T	HR	RBI	SB	BB	SO	Avg
2004 AAA Syracuse	122	483	58	139	37	3	6	45	6	45	62	.288
2004 AL Toronto	22	72	10	22	2	1	4	10	1	5	5	.306

Drafted 14th overall in 2002, the athletic Adams reached Double-A New Haven in his first full season as a pro in 2003, and assumed the starting shortstop job in Toronto last September. He's a hard worker with a good batting eye, posting decent OBPs in the minors and drawing more walks than strikeouts. His extra-base totals have been lean prior to 2004, when he delivered 37 doubles at Triple-A Syracuse and hit four big league homers in 22 games. Adams' defensive game improved in 2004. The majors will be a test for his below-average arm, but a combination of range, instincts and good hands has allowed him to handle short in the minors. The Jays may hand him leadoff duties in 2005.

Gustavo Chacin

Position: P **Opening Day Age:** 24
Bats: L **Throws:** L **Born:** 12/4/80 in
Ht: 5' 11" **Wt:** 193 Maracaibo, VZ

Recent Statistics

	W	L	ERA	G	GS	Sv	IP	H	R	BB	SO	HR
2004 AAA Syracuse	2	0	2.31	2	2	0	11.2	16	4	3	14	0
2004 AA New Hamp	16	2	2.86	25	25	0	141.2	113	53	49	109	15
2004 AL Toronto	1	1	2.57	2	2	0	14.0	8	4	3	6	0

Signed in 1998, Chacin reached Double-A ball late in 2000 as a teenager, but has stalled there. He threw more strikes in 2004, developed a cut fastball that elevated his game and went 16-2 for New Hampshire. He also posted two wins in two outings at Triple-A Syracuse—

making him the winningest pitcher in the minors—and two quality starts in the majors. In his big league debut, Chacin beat the Yankees with seven strong innings on September 20, and he closed with seven one-run innings against the Orioles. A fastball-changeup pitcher with a less-developed curve, Chacin's cutter thwarted righthanded hitters, as he changed speeds with it effectively. He needs to refine an out pitch against lefties. Chacin is the favorite to be the Jays' fifth starter in 2005.

Aaron Hill

Position: SS **Opening Day Age:** 23
Bats: R **Throws:** R **Born:** 3/21/82 in Visalia,
Ht: 5' 11" **Wt:** 195 CA

Recent Statistics

	G	AB	R	H	D	T	HR	RBI	SB	BB	SO	Avg
2003 A Auburn	33	122	22	44	4	0	4	34	1	16	20	.361
2003 A Dunedin	32	119	26	34	7	0	0	11	1	11	10	.286
2004 AA New Hamp	135	480	78	134	26	2	11	80	3	63	61	.279

A top-flight player at LSU, Hill was Toronto's first-round pick in 2003. The tools-rich Hill reached high Class-A Dunedin before his first pro season was over, and the young shortstop made a smooth transition to Double-A ball in 2004. He confidently worked counts and showed some pop, driving the ball to all fields. He's a smart player at the plate and in the field. Hill has the arm strength to play short, but he needs to show more range. He reads the ball off the bat effectively and is learning to better position himself against hitters. He made 24 errors in 2004, but improved defensively during the season. He'll get the chance to show he can stick at short at Triple-A Syracuse.

Brandon League

Position: P **Opening Day Age:** 22
Bats: R **Throws:** R **Born:** 3/16/83 in
Ht: 6' 3" **Wt:** 192 Honolulu, HI

Recent Statistics

	W	L	ERA	G	GS	Sv	IP	H	R	BB	SO	HR
2004 AA New Hamp	6	4	3.38	41	10	2	104.0	92	44	41	90	3
2004 AL Toronto	1	0	0.00	3	0	0	4.2	3	0	1	2	0

A second-rounder in 2001, League began 2004 in the bullpen, preparing for an eventual relief role. He finished the minor league season pitching effectively as a starter, before working three solid relief outings for the Jays in September. League has a terrific arm and the stuff to start. He throws a mid-90s fastball that has good sink when he stays on top of it. His slider is an effective pitch and his changeup has promise. He uses a three-quarters arm motion, which produces flat pitches and inconsistent control if his arm angle drops too low. He may start 2005 in the Toronto pen, and he could emerge as a setup man. The Jays like that he can get strikeouts, something their relievers have struggled to do in recent years.

Dustin McGowan

Position: P
Bats: R **Throws:** R
Ht: 6' 3" **Wt:** 220

Opening Day Age: 23
Born: 3/24/82 in Savannah, GA

Recent Statistics

	W	L	ERA	G	GS	Sv	IP	H	R	BB	SO	HR
2003 A Dunedin	5	6	2.85	14	14	0	75.2	62	29	25	66	1
2003 AA New Haven	7	0	3.17	14	14	0	76.2	78	28	19	72	1
2004 AA New Hamp	2	0	4.06	6	6	0	31.0	24	14	15	29	4

After a terrific 2003 in which McGowan was 12-6 (3.01) at high Class-A Dunedin and Double-A New Haven, the 2000 first-rounder quickly earned a promotion to Triple-A Syracuse in 2004. He didn't make a start there, as McGowan underwent Tommy John surgery that will sideline him until May or June. When healthy, McGowan works with a moving mid-90s fastball and a changeup that comes at hitters with the same arm speed as the heater. He mixes in a curve and slider, an out pitch for him in 2003, and his stuff looked good enough to someday front a rotation before he went under the knife. McGowan could be working off a mound by February, but the Jays won't rush him.

Guillermo Quiroz

Position: C
Bats: R **Throws:** R
Ht: 6' 1" **Wt:** 202

Opening Day Age: 23
Born: 11/29/81 in Maracaibo, VZ

Recent Statistics

	G	AB	R	H	D	T	HR	RBI	SB	BB	SO	Avg
2004 AAA Syracuse	76	255	32	58	19	1	8	32	0	28	54	.227
2004 AL Toronto	17	52	2	11	2	0	0	6	1	2	8	.212

Signed in 1998, Quiroz is athletic and agile behind the plate, with solid receiving skills and a strong arm. He speaks fluent English and works well with pitchers. He enjoyed his best pro season at Double-A New Haven in 2003. He batted .282 with 27 doubles, 20 homers and 79 RBI in 108 games. Quiroz broke a bone in his left hand early in 2004, missed nearly two months and struggled upon returning. Most likely the injury factored into his final numbers, as it takes time to regain hand strength. Still, he singled twice in his big league debut against Oakland on September 4. Quiroz should start at Triple-A Syracuse in 2005.

Francisco Rosario

Position: P
Bats: R **Throws:** R
Ht: 6' 0" **Wt:** 160

Opening Day Age: 24
Born: 9/28/80 in San Rafael Del Yuma, DR

Recent Statistics

	W	L	ERA	G	GS	Sv	IP	H	R	BB	SO	HR
2004 A Dunedin	1	1	4.67	6	6	0	17.1	16	12	11	16	2
2004 AA New Hamp	2	4	4.31	12	12	0	48.0	48	25	16	45	6

Signed in 1999, Rosario emerged as a prospect in 2002, going 9-4 (1.94) between two Class-A stops. At the close of the 2002 season, Rosario blew out his elbow in the Arizona Fall League. He missed all of 2003 after Tommy John surgery, but returned last April. Rosario was working in the mid-90s by the end of 2004. All four of his pitches—fastball, curve, slider and changeup—can be major league offerings, but his stuff and mechanics were inconsistent until late in the season. He pitched some big games for Double-A New Hampshire, working the regular-season clincher and claiming two playoff wins for the Eastern League champs. Rosario needs to throw more strikes, but he should be more consistent another year removed from surgery.

Jamie Vermilyea

Position: P
Bats: R **Throws:** R
Ht: 6' 4" **Wt:** 195

Opening Day Age: 23
Born: 2/10/82 in Tucson, AZ

Recent Statistics

	W	L	ERA	G	GS	Sv	IP	H	R	BB	SO	HR
2003 A Auburn	5	1	2.37	9	2	0	30.1	22	10	5	53	0
2003 A Dunedin	0	2	2.49	9	0	2	21.2	21	6	2	25	1
2004 A Dunedin	5	1	3.09	18	6	0	55.1	54	22	13	37	4
2004 AA New Hamp	3	2	2.51	20	6	5	57.1	43	20	12	39	2

A ninth-round pick in 2003, Vermilyea dominated at two Class-A levels in his debut season. He wasn't as dominant as a swingman in 2004. Still, Vermilyea threw a seven-inning perfect game to close out a June 28 doubleheader and finished 8-3 (2.80) for the season. He sets a good tempo and throws, trying to get ahead of hitters, which opens his options with his five-pitch arsenal. He's mostly a sinker-slider guy who will turn to his splitter. His low-90s fastball has late sink and his changeup fades nicely from fastball-like arm speed. Vermilyea is thought of as a relief option in the long term, but he'll start as long as he is successful at it.

Others to Watch

A 2003 second-round pick, **Josh Banks** (22) dominated high Class-A hitters in the Florida State League. After going 7-1 with a 1.80 ERA, 60 strikeouts and just eight walks in 11 starts, Banks moved to Double-A New Hampshire with a five-pitch arsenal and command of a low-90s fastball. . . Acquired from Boston in July, switch-hitting third baseman **John Hattig** (25) combined to hit .296 and slug .532 at two Double-A stops in 2004. He also drew walks and posted a .391 OBP. It was a breakout year in terms of power for Hattig, a native of Guam. His bat is ahead of his glove. . . After sparking Southwest Missouri State to the College World Series in 2003 as a shortstop and closer, **Shaun Marcum** (23) is a starting pitcher as a pro. He was 10-6 (3.16) for two Class-A clubs in 2004, pitching to a location successfully with four pitches, including a 90-MPH fastball and plus slider. He walked four and fanned 72 at high Class-A Dunedin. . . Righthander **Ismael Ramirez** (24) throws a four-seam fastball that he can bump to 94-95 MPH. Yet, he excels at working hitters and keeping them off balance with a four-pitch arsenal he can throw for strikes. He led the high Class-A Florida State League with 15 wins, going 15-6 with a 2.72 ERA.

National League Players

Bank One Ballpark

Offense

It goes unnoticed by many, but Phoenix has the second-highest elevation in the majors, making Bank One Ballpark a hitters' park. Flyballs travel well, especially when the roof is open and the air is warmer. The roof usually is closed from mid-June through late September. Center field is deep and plays fair, but home runs are easier from gap to foul line. The park has a good hitting background.

Defense

There are tricky corners in the outfield. The overhangs in left- and right-center field can cause caroms or confuse center fielders on flyballs. Drives into the corners can rattle around. Late in the season, the grass can get loose and cause large divots. The infield usually plays true.

Who It Helps the Most

The park doesn't help Brandon Webb as much as not hurt him compared to other pitchers, since he keeps the ball out of the air. Rookie closer Greg Aquino posted a 1.58 groundball-flyball ratio last season, and his ERA at home was 2.42 compared to 4.15 on the road. Luis Gonzalez, a dead-pull flyball hitter, is well-suited to BOB, but so are line-drive hitters like Chad Tracy and Shea Hillenbrand, whose shots can carry into the gaps or out of the park.

Who It Hurts the Most

Flyball pitchers, such as Casey Fossum and Jose Valverde, have trouble at home. Several other young pitchers—Andrew Good, Casey Daigle, Lance Cormier and Edgar Gonzalez—were homer-prone at BOB and posted ERAs beyond 5.00 in 2004.

Rookies & Newcomers

Russ Ortiz is 4-3 with a 4.81 ERA in eight career starts at BOB. Lefty Mike Gosling had a 3.55 ERA in his three home outings in 2004, compared to a 5.68 mark on the road. Rookie catcher Koyie Hill enjoyed his first taste of home cooking, going 8-for-21 (.381) with a double and homer, while fellow rookie backstop Chris Snyder hit much better on the road during his September callup.

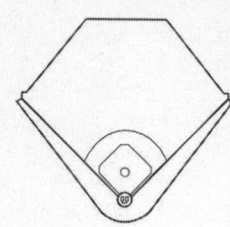

Dimensions: LF-330, LCF-374, CF-407, RCF-374, RF-334

Capacity: 49,033

Elevation: 1090 feet

Surface: Grass

Foul Territory: Average

Park Factors

2004 Season

| | Home Games | | | Away Games | | | |
	Dbacks	Opp	Total	Dbacks	Opp	Total	Index
G	72	72	144	72	72	144	
Avg	.265	.261	.263	.241	.272	.256	103
AB	2436	2537	4973	2492	2405	4897	102
R	303	396	699	241	407	648	108
H	645	663	1308	601	653	1254	104
2B	140	139	279	121	122	243	113
3B	16	17	33	15	16	31	105
HR	72	98	170	52	77	129	130
BB	206	302	508	195	303	498	100
SO	420	551	971	496	489	985	97
E	56	39	95	64	29	93	102
E-Infield	48	33	81	53	21	74	109
LHB-Avg	.286	.265	.276	.244	.306	.272	101
LHB-HR	41	39	80	20	32	52	150
RHB-Avg	.248	.259	.254	.239	.250	.245	104
RHB-HR	31	59	90	32	45	77	116

2002-2004

| | Home Games | | | Away Games | | | |
	Dbacks	Opp	Total	Dbacks	Opp	Total	Index
G	219	219	438	216	216	432	
Avg	.274	.254	.264	.245	.254	.250	106
AB	7370	7694	15064	7491	7149	14640	101
R	1083	1058	2141	824	971	1795	118
H	2020	1954	3974	1838	1819	3657	107
2B	421	410	831	350	323	673	120
3B	68	54	122	45	31	76	156
HR	224	250	474	191	213	404	114
BB	813	738	1551	667	721	1388	109
SO	1300	1779	3079	1461	1608	3069	98
E	143	125	268	153	132	285	93
E-Infield	120	107	227	128	108	236	95
LHB-Avg	.284	.273	.279	.254	.270	.261	107
LHB-HR	118	102	220	101	89	190	114
RHB-Avg	.263	.243	.252	.236	.245	.241	104
RHB-HR	106	148	254	90	124	214	114

2004 Rankings (National League)

- Highest LHB home-run factor
- Second-highest home-run factor

Bob Melvin

2004 Season

Bob Melvin was not Arizona's first choice; the Diamondbacks originally hired Wally Backman for their opening. But four days after that announcement, they withdrew the offer to Backman because of concerns about off-field issues in his private life and turned to Melvin. A former Diamondbacks bench coach, Melvin was fired by Seattle after just two seasons as manager. The Mariners picked up his 2005 option in May to try to quell speculation about his status, but after the team went 63-99, Melvin was let go.

Offense

Melvin will be aggressive on the bases, but seems reluctant to steal or hit-and-run when trailing. While the hit-and-run might be a useful tool for an offense that was anemic in 2004, Melvin may not have much speed to work with this season. He will shuffle his batting order to try to get the offense going, a problem that the Diamondbacks endured often under Bob Brenly. Lineup changes should not be an issue with a younger roster.

Pitching & Defense

Pitching coach Mark Davis is more familiar with Arizona's young pitchers, and Melvin may defer to him as he did with Seattle pitching coach Bryan Price. Not overusing the youngsters probably will be stressed by management after all the injuries last year. Defensively, no National League club committed more errors than the Diamondbacks, who ranked last in the circuit in fielding percentage. Rookies committed a large chunk of the miscues.

2005 Outlook

Melvin seems realistic about how much a 51-111 team can improve. The front office and ownership are comfortable with him, in part because of their familiarity with him as Arizona's bench coach in 2001 and 2002. Melvin has a two-year contract with team options for 2007 and 2008. He was criticized in Seattle for being passive, but by getting out from the shadow of Lou Piniella, he could show more personality in his new job. Communicating with players, a skill he nurtured and utilized as bench coach, will be important.

Born: 10/28/61 in Palo Alto, California

Playing Experience: 1985-1994, Det, SF, Bal, KC, Bos, CWS, NYY

Managerial Experience: 2 seasons

Manager Statistics

Year	Team, Lg	W	L	Pct	GB	Finish
2004	Seattle, AL	63	99	.389	29.0	4th West
2 Seasons		156	168	.481	–	–

2004 Starting Pitchers by Days Rest

	<=3	4	5	6+
Mariners Starts	2	73	61	15
Mariners ERA	7.36	4.82	4.57	5.91
AL Avg Starts	2	82	47	21
AL ERA	5.36	4.87	4.65	4.93

2004 Situational Stats

	Bob Melvin	AL Average
Hit & Run Success %	40.6	36.8
Stolen Base Success %	72.4	68.6
Platoon Pct.	58.8	61.6
Defensive Subs	16	21
High-Pitch Outings	12	5
Quick/Slow Hooks	16/17	20/16
Sacrifice Attempts	59	53

2004 Rankings (American League)

- 1st in double steals (8), starting lineups used (151) and starts with over 120 pitches (12)
- 2nd in sacrifice-bunt percentage (86.4%), hit-and-run attempts (96) and one-batter pitcher appearances (45)
- 3rd in stolen-base percentage and first-batter platoon percentage

Danny Bautista

2004 Season

Danny Bautista had a career season in 2004, setting personal highs in games, at-bats, runs, hits, doubles, RBI and walks. He also matched his bests in home runs and stolen bases. By the final two months of the season, with Steve Finley traded and Luis Gonzalez and Richie Sexson injured, Bautista usually was Arizona's No. 3 hitter. After a fast start, with April and June his most productive months, he faded in the No. 3 spot in August and September.

Hitting

Bautista has a solid approach, hitting inside-out and using all fields when he isn't swinging too hard. Trying to pull the ball or hit home runs gets him into trouble. He is more of a gap hitter. He has enough strength, but with a downward swing, he hits balls with backspin more often than elevating them. He is a free swinger who doesn't walk much. He collected just 35 walks in 582 plate appearances in 2004.

Baserunning & Defense

Bautista is a good athlete with speed, which makes him capable of covering all three outfield spots. Still, he often makes mistakes in the field and on the bases. Over-aggressiveness usually is the culprit. He can misread balls in the outfield and sometimes gets poor jumps. Although he has a very strong arm, it is not always accurate and he doesn't always hit the cutoff man.

2005 Outlook

Bautista was a free agent after the season. Coming off his best year, he may have wanted a raise from the $4 million he made in 2004. But after his fade when he assumed a bigger role down the stretch, producing just 13 extra-base hits and one homer following the All-Star break, a bigger contract does not fit into Arizona's plans. On a good team, Bautista is a fourth outfielder or a lower-in-the-order hitter.

Position: RF
Bats: R **Throws:** R
Ht: 5'11" **Wt:** 225

Opening Day Age: 32
Born: 5/24/72 in Santo Domingo, DR
ML Seasons: 12
Pronunciation: BAUGH-tees-ta

Overall Statistics

	G	AB	R	H	D	T	HR	RBI	SB	BB	SO	Avg	OBP	Slg
'04	141	539	64	154	27	1	11	65	6	35	66	.286	.332	.401
Car.	895	2517	317	685	121	19	62	319	37	149	409	.272	.315	.409

Where He Hits the Ball

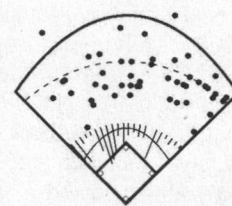
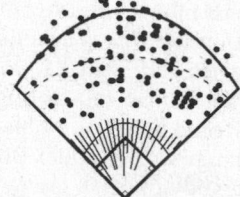

Vs. LHP　　　**Vs. RHP**

2004 Situational Stats

	AB	H	HR	RBI	Avg		AB	H	HR	RBI	Avg
Home	268	79	4	29	.295	LHP	154	43	1	14	.279
Road	271	75	7	36	.277	RHP	385	111	10	51	.288
First Half	301	95	10	48	.316	Sc Pos	122	38	3	49	.311
Scnd Half	238	59	1	17	.248	Clutch	88	34	4	21	.386

2004 Rankings (National League)

- 2nd in batting average in the clutch and fielding percentage in right field (.986)
- 6th in errors in right field (4)
- 7th in fewest pitches seen per plate appearance (3.38)
- Led the Diamondbacks in GDPs (20), highest groundball-flyball ratio (1.9), batting average with runners in scoring position, batting average in the clutch, batting average with the bases loaded (.375) and batting average on the road

Alex Cintron

2004 Season

After a strong 2003 season in which he showed surprising power, Alex Cintron opened the 2004 campaign as Arizona's starting shortstop and No. 5 hitter. But his production dropped off after a decent April, and after a time in the No. 2 spot, he was demoted to the bottom third of the Arizona batting order. In September, with Jerry Gil called up and Cintron's defense still shaky, he split his time between shortstop and second base.

Hitting

Cintron has a long, uppercut swing from both sides, which helped generate 45 extra-base hits in 117 games in 2003. But he is more of a contact hitter who, when not overswinging, usually puts the ball in play successfully. Cintron has more power as a righthanded hitter, but his swing wasn't as quick in 2004. He may attempt to get rid of the high leg kick he has used as a timing device, which should help him get by with his slower bat speed.

Baserunning & Defense

Cintron lacks the quick first step and range to be a good shortstop, partly because he plays too upright. He has good arm strength but sometimes throws off the wrong foot. He can play third base but is better at second. Cintron has speed to steal bases on occasion, but his basestealing technique needs work if he is ever to reach double digits in steals.

2005 Outlook

While Cintron is young enough to rebound and show he can play every day, the Diamondbacks may sign a free-agent shortstop, leaving Cintron to compete for a job at second base. He could wind up a utility player if he cannot beat out Matt Kata or Scott Hairston for the starting position at second. How Cintron does in 2005 will go a long way in determining if he has a future in Arizona's rebuilding plans.

Position: SS/2B
Bats: B **Throws:** R
Ht: 6' 2" **Wt:** 199

Opening Day Age: 26
Born: 12/17/78 in Humacao, PR
ML Seasons: 4
Pronunciation: sin-TRONE

Overall Statistics

	G	AB	R	H	D	T	HR	RBI	SB	BB	SO	Avg	OBP	Slg
'04	154	564	56	148	31	7	4	49	3	31	59	.262	.301	.363
Car.	317	1094	137	308	63	14	17	104	5	72	105	.282	.326	.411

Where He Hits the Ball

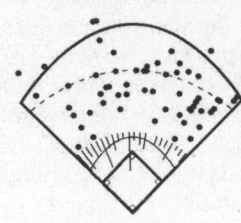 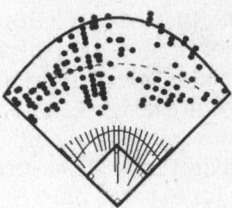

Vs. LHP   **Vs. RHP**

2004 Situational Stats

	AB	H	HR	RBI	Avg		AB	H	HR	RBI	Avg
Home	265	69	1	21	.260	LHP	156	46	1	11	.295
Road	299	79	3	28	.264	RHP	408	102	3	38	.250
First Half	314	76	3	28	.242	Sc Pos	141	40	1	43	.284
Scnd Half	250	72	1	21	.288	Clutch	87	17	0	9	.195

2004 Rankings (National League)

- 3rd in lowest slugging percentage
- 4th in lowest percentage of pitches taken (46.9) and lowest fielding percentage at shortstop (.972)
- 5th in lowest on-base percentage
- 6th in errors at shortstop (15)
- Led the Diamondbacks in at-bats, triples, sacrifice bunts (12), plate appearances (613), games played and bunts in play (18)

Arizona

2004 Season

Casey Fossum came from Boston in November 2003, in the blockbuster deal that moved Curt Schilling to the Red Sox. Fossum opened the 2004 season on the disabled list, as he recovered from shoulder surgery the previous October. After five minor league rehab starts, Fossum entered the rotation on May 14 and never missed a turn the rest of the way. The results weren't pretty, as the lefthander was quite hittable in his first full season as a big league starter.

Pitching

Fossum throws a fastball is the 88-92 MPH range, but his best pitches are two overhand curveballs—one with tight rotation, one that comes in slower—that he can throw for strikes. Fossum also throws a cut fastball and a decent changeup. His three-quarters arm slot can be tough on hitters, but not in 2004, when he coughed up 31 homers and allowed opposing hitters to bat .302 and slug .515 against him. His fastball tends to be flat and often leads to home runs. He has trouble pitching down to righthanded hitters, who touched him for even higher hitting percentages.

Defense & Hitting

A good athlete, Fossum handles the bat OK and runs well. He fields his position fine, and he has yet to commit an error in 102 big league games. He has a good pickoff move and has been tough to run on. Last season, however, baserunners were more effective against him, stealing successfully on 15 of 23 attempts.

2005 Outlook

Fossum, who is eligible for arbitration, appears slated for a second season in Arizona's rotation. Stamina has been a concern for the slight left-hander. While many baseball people think he is better suited for relief, perhaps as a lefty special-ist, Arizona's need is for starters. Look for more on-the-job training for a young pitcher based in a park that plays much more favorably for hitters.

Position: SP
Bats: L **Throws:** L
Ht: 6' 1" **Wt:** 160

Opening Day Age: 27
Born: 1/9/78 in Cherry Hill, NJ
ML Seasons: 4

Overall Statistics

	W	L	Pct.	ERA	G	GS	Sv	IP	H	BB	SO	HR	Avg
'04	4	15	.211	6.65	27	27	0	142.0	171	63	117	31	.302
Car.	18	26	.409	5.27	102	60	2	372.0	410	147	307	56	.280

2004 Pitching Profile

	Casey Fossum	NL Average
Overall Strike %	62.3	62.5
1st Pitch Strike %	58.8	58.5
Ratio	1.65	1.39
Strikeouts per 9 IP	7.42	6.74
Walks per 9 IP	3.99	3.38
Home Runs per 9 IP	1.96	1.11
Strikeout/Walk Ratio	1.86	1.99
Groundball/Flyball Ratio	1.16	1.25

2004 Situational Stats

	W	L	ERA	Sv	IP		AB	H	HR	RBI	Avg
Home	2	6	7.03	0	65.1	LHB	136	35	4	15	.257
Road	2	9	6.34	0	76.2	RHB	431	136	27	81	.316
First Half	2	8	6.27	0	60.1	Sc Pos	125	40	7	62	.320
Scnd Half	2	7	6.94	0	81.2	Clutch	13	4	2	4	.308

2004 Rankings (National League)

- 1st in lowest winning percentage
- 2nd in losses, balks (2), highest batting average allowed vs. righthanded batters and highest batting average allowed with runners in scoring position
- 6th in home runs allowed
- 7th in runners caught stealing (8)
- Led the Diamondbacks in home runs allowed and balks (2)

Luis Gonzalez

2004 Season

An MRI exam of Luis Gonzalez' right elbow, taken after the 2003 season, showed a 50 percent tear in his ulnar collateral ligament. But with the Diamondbacks expecting to contend in 2004, he opted against surgery. When it became clear the team was not in the National League West or wild-card race, Gonzalez underwent Tommy John surgery on August 2, and the procedure revealed that he had a fully torn ligament.

Hitting

With his elbow hurting last year, Gonzalez did not pull the ball quite as much as in the past, and his power came in the form of doubles more than homers. Whether he returns to his pre-surgery form—when he would jump all over a mistake pitch and show good power to left-center field—remains to be seen. He has an exaggerated open stance that he closes as the pitch is delivered. Gonzalez has good pitch recognition. He also has a good eye for the strike zone and will draw his share of walks.

Baserunning & Defense

Gonzalez is a smart baserunner but not much of a basestealer. He plays a deep left field, so he gets to more balls at the wall than in front of him. He never had much of a throwing arm even when healthy, and even if his elbow is fine, runners will be able to take extra bases on him.

2005 Outlook

By choosing to have surgery when he did, Gonzalez should be ready for the start of the regular season. The reconstructed elbow should allow him to throw better and even may restore some power to his swing. He is signed for two more seasons with $21.5 million heading his way. If Gonzalez rebounds well, the Diamondbacks would have the option of dealing him. Only Steve Finley hit more homers in an Arizona uniform in 2004, so he may be critical to an offense that ranked last in all of baseball in runs and homers last summer.

Position: LF
Bats: L **Throws:** R
Ht: 6' 2" **Wt:** 200

Opening Day Age: 37
Born: 9/3/67 in Tampa, FL
ML Seasons: 15

Overall Statistics

G	AB	R	H	D	T	HR	RBI	SB	BB	SO	Avg	OBP	Slg
105	379	69	98	28	5	17	48	2	68	58	.259	.373	.493
2008	7187	1129	2057	458	63	292	1172	117	911	971	.286	.370	.489

Where He Hits the Ball

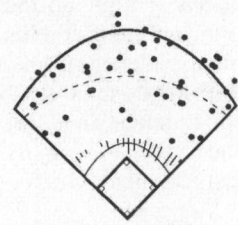 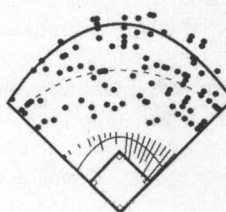

Vs. LHP   **Vs. RHP**

2004 Situational Stats

	AB	H	HR	RBI	Avg		AB	H	HR	RBI	Avg
Home	187	56	10	28	.299	LHP	127	31	9	21	.244
Road	192	42	7	20	.219	RHP	252	67	8	27	.266
First Half	319	86	15	43	.270	Sc Pos	58	14	3	23	.241
Scnd Half	60	12	2	5	.200	Clutch	50	8	1	5	.160

2004 Rankings (National League)

- 3rd in lowest cleanup slugging percentage (.446)
- 4th in lowest batting average in the clutch
- 5th in errors in left field (6)
- 8th in intentional walks (11)
- Led the Diamondbacks in runs scored, walks, intentional walks (11), slugging percentage, on-base percentage, most pitches seen per plate appearance (4.07) and highest percentage of pitches taken (59.7)

2004 Season

Scott Hairston got a look as a utility player in spring training and got a four-day callup in early May. He came back up May 17 to split time with Matt Kata, and when Kata suffered a season-ending shoulder injury on May 29, Hairston became the full-time starter. By September he was sharing time with Alex Cintron, who was being tested at second base in addition to playing shortstop. Hairston batted .280 and homered five times in August, arguably his most productive month, but he slumped and hit just .140 from September 1 through the close of the season.

Hitting

With a quick bat, Hairston has a high upside offensively. He could be an impact hitter with his advanced pitch recognition and plate discipline. He hits the ball hard when he makes contact, driving the ball into the gaps and for home runs. But he can overswing at times and didn't draw many walks in his Arizona debut last summer.

Baserunning & Defense

Hairston has shown little aptitude for second base. He is mechanical and tentative in his play, unable to throw from multiple angles and slow on the pivot. He has no instincts for the position, often going to the wrong spot on cutoff plays. While he has above-average speed, Hairston also makes mistakes on the bases. He's never turned his speed into stolen bases as a minor leaguer, so he isn't likely to become a threat to steal in the majors.

2005 Outlook

Hairston could battle Matt Kata and Alex Cintron for the job at second base. Or the Diamondbacks could decide Hairston never will become an adequate second baseman and move him to the outfield. A switch to the outfield, where he played three games during his stay with the Diamondbacks in 2004, probably would require his starting the new season in the minors.

Position: 2B
Bats: R **Throws:** R
Ht: 6' 0" **Wt:** 188

Opening Day Age: 24
Born: 5/25/80 in Fort Worth, TX
ML Seasons: 1

Overall Statistics

	G	AB	R	H	D	T	HR	RBI	SB	BB	SO	Avg	OBP	Slg
'04	101	339	39	84	15	6	13	29	3	21	88	.248	.293	.442
Car.	101	339	39	84	15	6	13	29	3	21	88	.248	.293	.442

Where He Hits the Ball

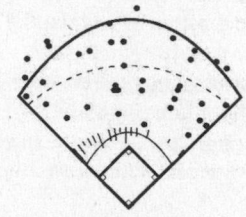

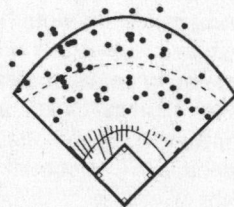

Vs. LHP   **Vs. RHP**

2004 Situational Stats

	AB	H	HR	RBI	Avg		AB	H	HR	RBI	Avg
Home	167	42	6	10	.251	LHP	101	31	6	9	.307
Road	172	42	7	19	.244	RHP	238	53	7	20	.223
First Half	163	42	4	11	.258	Sc Pos	68	12	1	16	.176
Scnd Half	176	42	9	18	.239	Clutch	59	18	3	7	.305

2004 Rankings (National League)

- 3rd in lowest on-base percentage for a leadoff hitter (.287)
- 4th in errors at second base (11)
- Led the Diamondbacks in strikeouts and fewest GDPs per GDP situation (8.2%)

Shea Hillenbrand

2004 Season

Shea Hillenbrand opened the season as Arizona's starting third baseman, but he got off to a slow start and lost his job to Chad Tracy in mid-April. When Richie Sexson suffered a shoulder injury at the end of April, Hillenbrand took over at first base and played there the remainder of the season. After batting just .184 during the opening month, he was Arizona's most consistent hitter, leading the team in average, doubles and RBI.

Hitting

Hillenbrand has good plate coverage and makes contact well with a short, level swing. He is a line-drive hitter who can reach double-digit homers, but he is more of a doubles hitter. There are few more aggressive hitters in the game and his pitch recognition can be lacking, so hardly anyone draws as few walks as Hillenbrand does. He had just 24 free passes in 604 plate appearances in 2004. He was struck by 12 pitches, so he was almost as likely to take one for the team as draw a walk.

Baserunning & Defense

Over the second half of last year, Hillenbrand became a capable first baseman. He can scoop balls in the dirt and start double plays. But at third base, Hillenbrand has below-average hands and range. First base is a better option if he can show enough pop to justify playing there. While he has below-average speed and is not a threat to steal, Hillenbrand makes few mistakes on the bases.

2005 Outlook

Hillenbrand is eligible for arbitration for the second time and could earn about $4 million. He now looks like the odd man out at the infield corners, however, after the Diamondbacks signed third baseman Troy Glaus to a four-year contract in December. Reportedly Chad Tracy has been told he will stay in the Arizona lineup at first base, meaning Hillenbrand could be dealt or not offered a contract by the December deadline, which would make him a free agent. Either way, Hillenbrand could be on the move again after a season and a half in Arizona.

Position: 1B/3B
Bats: R **Throws:** R
Ht: 6' 1" **Wt:** 211

Opening Day Age: 29
Born: 7/27/75 in Mesa, AZ
ML Seasons: 4
Pronunciation: SHAY

Overall Statistics

	G	AB	R	H	D	T	HR	RBI	SB	BB	SO	Avg	OBP	Slg
'04	148	562	68	174	36	3	15	80	2	24	49	.310	.348	.464
Car.	577	2179	274	627	134	10	65	309	10	86	275	.288	.322	.448

Where He Hits the Ball

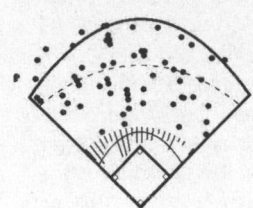 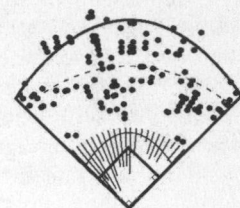

Vs. LHP   **Vs. RHP**

2004 Situational Stats

	AB	H	HR	RBI	Avg		AB	H	HR	RBI	Avg
Home	265	92	9	48	.347	LHP	158	51	6	27	.323
Road	297	82	6	32	.276	RHP	404	123	9	53	.304
First Half	295	92	8	42	.312	Sc Pos	143	44	4	58	.308
Scnd Half	267	82	7	38	.307	Clutch	92	18	1	5	.196

2004 Rankings (National League)

- 1st in errors at first base (13), batting average with two strikes (.302) and lowest fielding percentage at first base (.989)
- 3rd in batting average at home
- 7th in highest percentage of swings put into play (54.0) and lowest batting average with the bases loaded (.111)
- 8th in hit by pitch (12)
- Led the Diamondbacks in batting average, hits, singles, doubles, total bases (261), RBI, sacrifice flies (6), hit by pitch (12), times on base (210), lowest percentage of swings that missed (10.4), highest percentage of swings put into play (54.0), batting average vs. left handed pitchers, batting average at home and batting average with two strikes (.302)

Arizona

2004 Season

Motivated by rumblings he may have been on the downside of his career after an injury-plagued 2003, Randy Johnson was as good as ever in 2004. Because the Diamondbacks scored two runs or fewer in 17 of his 35 starts, Johnson's 16-14 record was no indication of how he pitched, as he was second in the league in ERA and first in strikeouts and lowest opponent batting average. His strikeout-walk ratio was the best of his career. His right knee, which ruined his 2003 season, was fine.

Pitching

Johnson no longer regularly cranks it up to 99 MPH. He may hit 98 on a good night, but pitches at 90-96 MPH and regularly works inside. His slider doesn't have quite the wicked break of the past, but he has better command of both pitches. Sometimes he will even throw back-door sliders to the outside corner against righthanded hitters, as well as one that breaks toward their shoes. Johnson also throws a split-finger pitch that acts as a changeup and a two-seam fastball that can get him a groundball.

Defense & Hitting

Johnson's hitting continues to improve, as he puts the ball in play more often and can occasionally drive it. His bunting is below average and he is not a good baserunner. Johnson's pickoff move is nothing special. He is a below-average fielder and often is late covering first base on grounders to the right side.

2005 Outlook

Johnson is signed for $16 million for 2005, and Arizona went into the offseason willing to listen to trade offers—as it did in July—yet still interested in signing Johnson to an extension. As the business of baseball moved into December, it seemed more likely that he would be changing addresses. Although Johnson will turn 42 in September, there is no reason to believe he cannot continue as an elite pitcher.

Position: SP
Bats: R **Throws:** L
Ht: 6'10" **Wt:** 231

Opening Day Age: 41
Born: 9/10/63 in Walnut Creek, CA
ML Seasons: 17
Nickname: Big Unit

Overall Statistics

W	L	Pct.	ERA	G	GS	Sv	IP	H	BB	SO	HR	Avg
16	14	.533	2.60	35	35	0	245.2	177	44	290	18	.197
246	128	.658	3.07	489	479	2	3368.0	2612	1302	4161	301	.213

2004 Pitching Profile

	Randy Johnson	NL Average
Overall Strike %	69.1	62.5
1st Pitch Strike %	63.8	58.5
Ratio	0.90	1.39
Strikeouts per 9 IP	10.62	6.74
Walks per 9 IP	1.61	3.38
Home Runs per 9 IP	0.66	1.11
Strikeout/Walk Ratio	6.59	1.99
Groundball/Flyball Ratio	1.17	1.25

2004 Situational Stats

	W	L	ERA	Sv	IP		AB	H	HR	RBI	Avg
Home	8	7	2.47	0	135.0	LHB	147	24	2	9	.163
Road	8	7	2.77	0	110.2	RHB	751	153	16	64	.204
First Half	10	7	2.99	0	129.1	Sc Pos	172	34	4	52	.198
Scnd Half	6	7	2.17	0	116.1	Clutch	102	29	7	17	.284

2004 Rankings (National League)

- 1st in games started, strikeouts, lowest batting average allowed (.197), lowest slugging percentage allowed (.315), lowest on-base percentage allowed (.241) and fielding percentage at pitcher (1.000)
- 2nd in ERA, innings pitched, pitches thrown (3,633), runners caught stealing (10), highest strikeout-walk ratio (6.6), lowest ERA on the road, most strikeouts per nine innings (10.6) and lowest batting average allowed vs. righthanded batters
- 3rd in shutouts (2), batters faced (964) and lowest batting average allowed vs. lefthanded batters
- 4th in losses, complete games (4), lowest ERA at home and fewest walks per nine innings (1.6)
- Led the Diamondbacks in wins, complete games (4), shutouts (2), and fewest home runs allowed per nine innings (.66)

2004 Season

In need of offensive punch, the Diamondbacks traded six players to Milwaukee for Richie Sexson and two others in December 2003. Sexson quickly delivered, slamming nine homers and driving in 22 runs in his first 19 games. But on April 28, he suffered a dislocated left shoulder on a checked swing. He returned in three weeks, but re-injured the shoulder on another checked swing in his second game back on May 22. Sexson had season-ending surgery in the early days of June.

Hitting

With his tall frame and long arms, Sexson looks for extension on his swing. That extension generates well above-average power to all fields. He can be tied up at times inside, especially when looking for something in the middle or away. Pitchers have to be precise in going inside, however, because Sexson can adjust and turn on a pitch. Sexson's plate discipline has improved a bit in recent years. His walks have been on the rise, peaking with 98 in 2003, and his strikeouts have tailed off a bit from a career-high 178 in 2001.

Baserunning & Defense

Despite his size, Sexson is athletic and almost graceful. He is a good first baseman with range, thanks in part to a long wingspan, and he is able to start the double play. He runs the bases well, although he is not fast and does not steal often.

2005 Outlook

A free agent heading into the offseason, Sexson is likely to get a large contract despite his shoulder problems last year. At the start of December, he rejected what reportedly was Arizona's final contract offer, so he seems destined to change addresses before spring training. Shoulder injuries have a tendency to linger, as was the case with Shawn Green. If Sexson is completely recovered—he was swinging a bat by the end of October—he again will be a major power threat.

Position: 1B
Bats: R **Throws:** R
Ht: 6' 8" **Wt:** 237

Opening Day Age: 30
Born: 12/29/74 in Portland, OR
ML Seasons: 8
Pronunciation: SECKS-un

Overall Statistics

	G	AB	R	H	D	T	HR	RBI	SB	BB	SO	Avg	OBP	Slg
'04	23	90	20	21	4	0	9	23	0	14	21	.233	.337	.578
Car.	836	3065	487	832	154	16	200	616	10	341	806	.271	.349	.528

Where He Hits the Ball

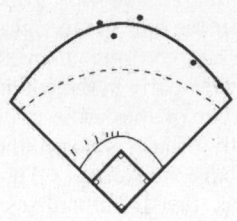
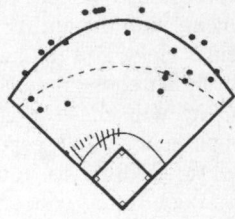

Vs. LHP   **Vs. RHP**

2004 Situational Stats

	AB	H	HR	RBI	Avg		AB	H	HR	RBI	Avg
Home	45	11	6	13	.244	LHP	18	4	0	1	.222
Road	45	10	3	10	.222	RHP	72	17	9	22	.236
First Half	90	21	9	23	.233	Sc Pos	28	7	4	14	.250
Scnd Half	0	0	0	0	–	Clutch	16	5	2	8	.313

2004 Rankings (National League)

• Led the Diamondbacks in cleanup slugging percentage (.578)

Arizona

Luls Terrero

2004 Season

Luis Terrero served two Pacific Coast League suspensions during the first half of the 2004 season. The first one was for 36 games for getting in an on-field altercation and throwing a ball into the stands. As part of his suspension, he underwent anger-management counseling. The other was for one game for kissing home plate after homering. When Steve Finley was traded to Los Angeles on July 31, Terrero became Arizona's regular center fielder. He showed flashes of brilliance at the plate, on the bases and in the outfield, but also moments of sloppiness.

Hitting

Terrero has five-tool potential. He has very good power, with the ability to hit the ball out to right-center field. But his swing can get long at times. He shows some plate discipline early in the count, but he will chase pitches out of the strike zone when he's behind, especially offerings down and away, leading to too many strikeouts. That approach is a concern, as the Diamondbacks would like to use him at or near the top of the batting order.

Baserunning & Defense

Terrero is a legitimate center fielder with a very strong throwing arm, but he can get sloppy and careless at times. He is aggressive in the field and on the bases. Although Terrero has good speed, he still needs to refine his basestealing technique, and his baserunning instincts are questionable.

2005 Outlook

Terrero could open the season as Arizona's center fielder, if the Diamondbacks do not sign a free-agent center fielder. He probably won't be found at the top of the order, however, after striking out 78 times in 229 at-bats, while posting only one-fourth as many walks. As long as he maintains the good attitude he showed in the second half of 2004, and erases the questions about his makeup that surfaced in the minors, he has a chance to blossom into an exciting player. Developing a better approach that includes more patience at the plate would elevate his game.

Position: CF
Bats: R **Throws:** R
Ht: 6' 2" **Wt:** 206

Opening Day Age: 24
Born: 5/18/80 in Barahona, DR
ML Seasons: 2
Pronunciation:
LOU-eese tur-RARE-oh

Overall Statistics

	G	AB	R	H	D	T	HR	RBI	SB	BB	SO	Avg	OBP	Slg
'04	62	229	21	56	14	0	4	14	10	20	78	.245	.319	.358
Car.	67	233	21	57	14	0	4	14	10	20	79	.245	.320	.356

Where He Hits the Ball

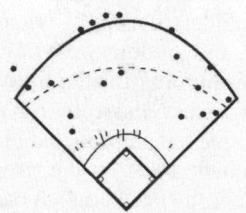
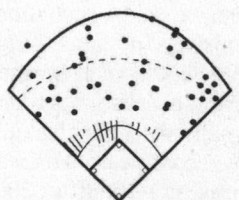

Vs. LHP　　　　**Vs. RHP**

2004 Situational Stats

	AB	H	HR	RBI	Avg		AB	H	HR	RBI	Avg
Home	118	25	2	8	.212	LHP	56	15	3	7	.268
Road	111	31	2	6	.279	RHP	173	41	1	7	.237
First Half	9	2	0	0	.222	Sc Pos	39	12	0	10	.308
Scnd Half	220	54	4	14	.245	Clutch	41	10	0	1	.244

2004 Rankings (National League)

- 2nd in errors in center field (6)
- 9th in steals of third (4)
- Led the Diamondbacks in stolen bases, stolen-base percentage (83.3) and steals of third (4)

Chad Tracy

2004 Season

Chad Tracy was the last player cut in spring training, since Donnie Sadler's versatility was deemed more useful. But Tracy was called up April 21 after Roberto Alomar suffered a broken hand, and the rookie was inserted at third base to give the offense a boost. Tracy kept the job all year, as Shea Hillenbrand moved to first base after Richie Sexson's injury. After needing time to adjust to big league pitching, Tracy batted .293 with a .351 on-base percentage from July 1 through the end of the season.

Hitting

A .335 hitter in four minor league seasons, Tracy has a flat swing and keeps his hands inside the ball well, often going to left field. He stays balanced and has a quick stroke, allowing him to be a good contact hitter. He recognizes pitches well, drawing a decent number of walks, but does not generate much home-run power with his swing. The longball wasn't part of his minor league repertoire either, though he powered 70 doubles in the high minors in 2002 and 2003.

Baserunning & Defense

A first baseman until his last year in college, Tracy lacks range at third base. His reactions are slow and his footwork clumsy at times. He goes through periods where he struggles with his throws, often because of poor footwork. But Tracy has a strong work ethic and should improve defensively.

2005 Outlook

Arizona is committed to playing Tracy, considering he will be inexpensive as a second-year player. The only thing that has changed since the end of last season is where Tracy will play. With the signing of third baseman Troy Glaus, the Diamondbacks are planning to try Tracy at first base in 2005. He made steady progress and reached Triple-A Tucson over just three minor league seasons prior to 2004, so he could take another step forward in the new year. If his defense improves or he develops power, he could become a solid everyday player.

Position: 3B/1B
Bats: L **Throws:** R
Ht: 6' 2" **Wt:** 200

Opening Day Age: 24
Born: 5/22/80 in Charlotte, NC
ML Seasons: 1

Arizona

Overall Statistics

	G	AB	R	H	D	T	HR	RBI	SB	BB	SO	Avg	OBP	Slg
'04	143	481	45	137	29	3	8	53	2	45	60	.285	.343	.407
Car.	143	481	45	137	29	3	8	53	2	45	60	.285	.343	.407

Where He Hits the Ball

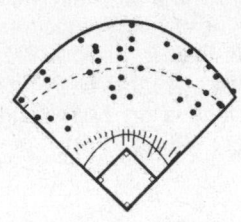
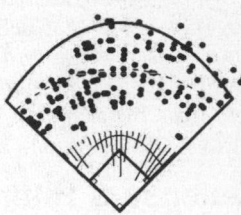

Vs. LHP	Vs. RHP

2004 Situational Stats

	AB	H	HR	RBI	Avg		AB	H	HR	RBI	Avg
Home	230	69	6	32	.300	LHP	107	23	1	10	.215
Road	251	68	2	21	.271	RHP	374	114	7	43	.305
First Half	252	70	5	32	.278	Sc Pos	122	36	3	46	.295
Scnd Half	229	67	3	21	.293	Clutch	76	19	1	7	.250

2004 Rankings (National League)

- 1st in errors at third base (25) and lowest fielding percentage at third base (.935)
- 3rd in lowest percentage of swings on the first pitch (9.6)
- 4th in batting average among rookies
- 5th in RBI among rookies
- Led the Diamondbacks in pitches seen (2,098), batting average vs. righthanded pitchers and lowest percentage of swings on the first pitch (9.6)

Jose Valverde

2004 Season

While Jose Valverde began the season as the setup man in front of closer Matt Mantei, the righthander took over ninth-inning duties when Mantei endured a rough start. Velverde blew two of his first five save chances. Then he converted five straight opportunities before going on the disabled list in mid-June. What was first diagnosed as tendinitis eventually turned out to be a torn labrum, and he didn't pitch again after June 13. He posted a 1.69 ERA and nine strikeouts in his final six appearances.

Pitching

With a short-arm delivery, with his elbow practically in front of his hand, Valverde is funky and deceptive. Yet that delivery also raises concerns about possible injury. His fastball is 92-95 MPH, and he has a good split-finger pitch that fools hitters from his arm slot. When he is aggressive and throws strikes, he can be very effective.

Defense & Hitting

While Valverde is not very athletic and has little experience with the bat, he has a double in his only major league plate appearance. He doesn't see much action defensively on the mound, either, with only 12 chances in parts of two seasons, but he made his first two big league errors in 2004. Baserunners were a problem in his rookie season, when all six basestealing attempts against him were successful. He didn't face a single attempt in his 29 appearances last year.

2005 Outlook

Valverde should be recovered from surgery in time to be ready for spring training. He could regain the closer's role, or he could wind up in the setup mix with Arizona's other righthanded relievers—Mike Koplove, Oscar Villarreal and Brian Bruney. Valverde's short-arm delivery and his low to mid-90s heat can make the ball tough for hitters to pick up, but his unorthodox mechanics also make him prone to injury.

Position: RP
Bats: R **Throws:** R
Ht: 6' 4" **Wt:** 254

Opening Day Age: 25
Born: 7/24/79 in San Pedro de Macoris, DR
ML Seasons: 2
Pronunciation: val-VAIR-day

Overall Statistics

	W	L	Pct.	ERA	G	GS	Sv	IP	H	BB	SO	HR	Avg
'04	1	2	.333	4.25	29	0	8	29.2	23	17	38	7	.213
Car.	3	3	.500	2.93	83	0	18	80.0	47	43	109	11	.166

2004 Pitching Profile

	Jose Valverde	NL Average
Overall Strike %	61.6	62.5
1st Pitch Strike %	58.0	58.5
Ratio	1.35	1.39
Strikeouts per 9 IP	11.53	6.74
Walks per 9 IP	5.16	3.38
Home Runs per 9 IP	2.12	1.11
Strikeout/Walk Ratio	2.24	1.99
Groundball/Flyball Ratio	0.78	1.25

2004 Situational Stats

	W	L	ERA	Sv	IP		AB	H	HR	RBI	Avg
Home	1	1	5.40	2	11.2	LHB	46	7	1	4	.152
Road	0	1	3.50	6	18.0	RHB	62	16	6	18	.258
First Half	1	2	4.25	8	29.2	Sc Pos	30	8	2	16	.267
Scnd Half	0	0	—	0	0.0	Clutch	62	11	3	12	.177

2004 Rankings (National League)

- Did not rank near the top or bottom in any category

Brandon Webb

2004 Season

The trade of Curt Schilling to Boston thrust Brandon Webb into the No. 2 spot in the rotation as a second-year player. He pitched better than his record indicated, though he did have trouble with control, setting a team record for walks in a season. Like Randy Johnson, Webb suffered from poor run support, with three or fewer runs scored in 17 of his 35 starts. Over his final 10 starts in 2004, Webb was 3-2 with a 2.59 ERA.

Pitching

Webb's signature pitch is a devastating sinker, and it's one of the best in the game. At 86-90 MPH, it's a pitch that is very difficult for hitters to elevate or lay off, even when it starts at their thighs and drops out of the strike zone. Webb drives the ball down well from a high arm angle. He also has a very good changeup and a curve that he delivers from the same arm slot. With a long delivery, Webb can get out of synch at times, leading to walks. Sometimes he betrays himself with bad body language.

Defense & Hitting

Webb is not a good fielder, often struggling simply to pick up the ball. He needs to improve his defense, since his sinker leads to a significant number of balls up the middle. He has trouble making contact at the plate, though he is better at getting a bunt down. Still, his bunting could improve.

2005 Outlook

If Webb can overcome his problems from last year—walks and the inability to recover from errors behind him, leading to unearned runs—he should be an effective pitcher. He could benefit from better infield defense behind him, since a lack of range all over the field hurt him in 2004. Better run support from the Arizona lineup would help, as well.

Position: SP
Bats: R **Throws:** R
Ht: 6' 2" **Wt:** 228

Opening Day Age: 25
Born: 5/9/79 in Ashland, KY
ML Seasons: 2

Arizona

Overall Statistics

	W	L	Pct.	ERA	G	GS	Sv	IP	H	BB	SO	HR	Avg
'04	7	16	.304	3.59	35	35	0	208.0	194	119	164	17	.248
Car.	17	25	.405	3.24	64	63	0	388.2	334	187	336	29	.232

2004 Pitching Profile

	Brandon Webb	NL Average
Overall Strike %	59.1	62.5
1st Pitch Strike %	56.4	58.5
Ratio	1.50	1.39
Strikeouts per 9 IP	7.10	6.74
Walks per 9 IP	5.15	3.38
Home Runs per 9 IP	0.74	1.11
Strikeout/Walk Ratio	1.38	1.99
Groundball/Flyball Ratio	3.55	1.25

2004 Situational Stats

	W	L	ERA	Sv	IP		AB	H	HR	RBI	Avg
Home	6	7	2.90	0	105.2	LHB	429	115	11	58	.268
Road	1	9	4.31	0	102.1	RHB	354	79	6	32	.223
First Half	3	9	3.81	0	113.1	Sc Pos	221	43	5	73	.195
Scnd Half	4	7	3.33	0	94.2	Clutch	25	8	0	2	.320

2004 Rankings (National League)

- 1st in losses, games started, walks allowed, wild pitches (17), stolen bases allowed (31), highest groundball-flyball ratio allowed (3.5), errors at pitcher (5) and highest walks per nine innings (5.1)
- 2nd in runners caught stealing (10)
- 3rd in highest on-base percentage allowed (.353) and lowest fielding percentage at pitcher (.915)
- 4th in lowest winning percentage
- Led the Diamondbacks in losses, games started, hits allowed, walks allowed, hit batsmen (11), wild pitches (17), pickoff throws (136), stolen bases allowed (31), runners caught stealing (10), GDPs induced (24), highest groundball-flyball ratio allowed (3.5), most run support per nine innings (4.2) and lowest batting average allowed with runners in scoring position

Greg Aquino

Position: RP
Bats: R **Throws:** R
Ht: 6' 1" **Wt:** 188

Opening Day Age: 27
Born: 1/11/78 in Palenque, DR
ML Seasons: 1
Pronunciation: uh-KEE-no

Overall Statistics

	W	L	Pct.	ERA	G	GS	Sv	IP	H	BB	SO	HR	Avg
'04	0	2	.000	3.06	34	0	16	35.1	24	17	26	4	.194
Car.	0	2	.000	3.06	34	0	16	35.1	24	17	26	4	.194

2004 Situational Stats

	W	L	ERA	Sv	IP		AB	H	HR	RBI	Avg
Home	0	1	2.42	9	22.1	LHB	66	11	1	6	.167
Road	0	1	4.15	7	13.0	RHB	58	13	3	10	.224
First Half	0	0	4.50	0	6.0	Sc Pos	34	6	0	11	.176
Scnd Half	0	2	2.76	16	29.1	Clutch	65	11	1	8	.169

2004 Season

Greg Aquino nearly made the team out of spring training. A former minor league shortstop who began pitching in 1999, he was converted to relief at Triple-A Tucson in 2004. By late July, with Matt Mantei and Jose Valverde injured, Aquino was Arizona's closer. He converted his first 10 saves chances and wound up 16-for-19 with solid numbers in his major league debut, after posting a 6.37 ERA at Tucson as he adjusted to relief work.

Pitching, Defense & Hitting

Aquino throws 90-96 MPH, but his out pitch is a slider he throws to both lefthanded and righthanded hitters. The tilt on the slider makes it effective against lefties. At times he struggles with command of the pitch. He has a fluid delivery and a loose arm, and thus should be able to stay healthy. Aquino, who was a solid defensive shortstop in the minors, is a good fielder and can handle the bat.

2005 Outlook

Aquino should open the season either as Arizona's closer or as the setup man for Jose Valverde. If Aquino has the poise he showed in spurts as a rookie and continues to progress, he could be an above-average closer.

Brian Bruney

Position: RP
Bats: R **Throws:** R
Ht: 6' 3" **Wt:** 226

Opening Day Age: 23
Born: 2/17/82 in Astoria, OR
ML Seasons: 1
Pronunciation: BREW-nee

Overall Statistics

	W	L	Pct.	ERA	G	GS	Sv	IP	H	BB	SO	HR	Avg
'04	3	4	.429	4.31	30	0	0	31.1	20	27	34	2	.189
Car.	3	4	.429	4.31	30	0	0	31.1	20	27	34	2	.189

2004 Situational Stats

	W	L	ERA	Sv	IP		AB	H	HR	RBI	Avg
Home	1	2	4.05	0	13.1	LHB	42	9	2	8	.214
Road	2	2	4.50	0	18.0	RHB	64	11	0	4	.172
First Half	2	2	2.70	0	13.1	Sc Pos	26	5	1	10	.192
Scnd Half	1	2	5.50	0	18.0	Clutch	48	8	2	8	.167

2004 Season

Brian Bruney had three stints with the Diamondbacks interrupted by a stint on the disabled list in June and a demotion back to Triple-A Tucson in late July, when he was told to work on his offspeed pitches. He was back for the final six weeks and finished by allowing only one run in his final 11.2 innings.

Pitching, Defense & Hitting

Because of Bruney's short-arm delivery, he can have trouble throwing quality breaking balls. His fastball is 90-94 MPH, but at times he is too reliant on it. He has a changeup but still does not seem to have a feel for the pitch. His slider has only a small break and he has a tendency to spin it at times. He often pitches around the edges of the strike zone, leading to a high number of walks. He has yet to bat in the majors, and made one error in six chances last year.

2005 Outlook

Bruney projects as a setup man or middle-inning pitcher in a crowded group of righthanded relievers. It should be noted that since he has pitched out of the bullpen almost exclusively since being drafted, he has only 272 innings of pro experience, and thus could get better with time.

Edgar Gonzalez

Position: SP
Bats: R **Throws:** R
Ht: 6' 0" **Wt:** 215

Opening Day Age: 22
Born: 2/23/83 in Monterrey, Mexico
ML Seasons: 2

Overall Statistics

	W	L	Pct.	ERA	G	GS	Sv	IP	H	BB	SO	HR	Avg
'04	0	9	.000	9.32	10	10	0	46.1	72	18	31	15	.362
Car.	2	10	.167	8.07	19	12	0	64.2	100	25	45	18	.364

2004 Situational Stats

	W	L	ERA	Sv	IP			AB	H	HR	RBI	Avg
Home	0	3	9.20	0	14.2	LHB		94	39	10	30	.415
Road	0	6	9.38	0	31.2	RHB		105	33	5	17	.314
First Half	0	1	13.50	0	4.0	Sc Pos		52	20	5	30	.385
Scnd Half	0	8	8.93	0	42.1	Clutch		5	3	1	2	.600

2004 Season

One of the most promising pitching prospects in the Arizona system, Edgar Gonzalez was called up for a spot start June 5 and returned to the minors. Then he came back up to stay on July 22. But when his record reached 0-9 with a 9.32 ERA after 10 starts, he was taken out of the rotation. A split fingernail kept him from pitching over the final three-plus weeks of the season.

Pitching, Defense & Hitting

All of Gonzalez' pitches—fastball, slider, change-up and curve—are major league average. He can vary the speed on his fastball, which is clocked at 87-91 MPH. With his smooth delivery, Gonzalez may be able to develop above-average command. Lacking a dominant pitch, he needs to be aggressive and smart to be successful. Gonzalez handles the bat decently.

2005 Outlook

After being one of the youngest pitchers to start in the majors the last two seasons, Gonzalez could make a bid for the back end of Arizona's rotation in the spring. He could enhance his chances by pitching well in winter ball, but he still probably needs more time in the minors. The Diamondbacks also would like to see a better work ethic.

Robby Hammock

Position: C/LF
Bats: R **Throws:** R
Ht: 5'10" **Wt:** 187

Opening Day Age: 27
Born: 5/13/77 in Macon, GA
ML Seasons: 2
Pronunciation: HAM-mick

Overall Statistics

	G	AB	R	H	D	T	HR	RBI	SB	BB	SO	Avg	OBP	Slg
'04	62	195	22	47	16	2	4	18	3	13	39	.241	.287	.405
Car.	127	390	52	102	26	4	12	46	6	30	83	.262	.315	.441

2004 Situational Stats

	AB	H	HR	RBI	Avg		AB	H	HR	RBI	Avg
Home	96	25	1	10	.260	LHP	79	20	3	8	.253
Road	99	22	3	8	.222	RHP	116	27	1	10	.233
First Half	155	33	2	15	.213	Sc Pos	49	11	0	13	.224
Scnd Half	40	14	2	3	.350	Clutch	36	10	0	2	.278

2004 Season

In the days leading up to spring training, Robby Hammock required left knee surgery on February 13, which caused him to open the 2004 season on the disabled list. He was the team's primary catcher for nearly three months, but he went back on the DL in mid-July through early September. Hammock seemed healthy in September, although he played the outfield only and didn't catch any games.

Hitting, Baserunning & Defense

A good athlete, Hammock is a capable hitter for average who goes to right field well. He gets in trouble trying to hit for power. But his bat isn't quite enough to make him a regular corner infielder or outfielder, and his body frame is not suitable for regular catching duty. Since he is an accomplished catcher and also can play third base and the outfield fine, he is a good utility player. He also has good speed.

2005 Outlook

The Diamondbacks have admitted Hammock is not suited to everyday catching duty. He is a useful reserve, however, and likely will serve as a third catcher who sees time at third base or the corner outfield spots.

Koyie Hill

Position: C
Bats: B **Throws:** R
Ht: 6' 0" **Wt:** 190

Opening Day Age: 26
Born: 3/9/79 in Tulsa, OK
ML Seasons: 2
Pronunciation: koy

Overall Statistics

	G	AB	R	H	D	T	HR	RBI	SB	BB	SO	Avg	OBP	Slg
'04	13	36	3	9	1	0	1	6	1	2	6	.250	.289	.361
Car.	16	39	3	10	2	0	1	6	1	2	8	.256	.293	.385

2004 Situational Stats

	AB	H	HR	RBI	Avg		AB	H	HR	RBI	Avg
Home	21	8	1	5	.381	LHP	7	2	0	1	.286
Road	15	1	0	1	.067	RHP	29	7	1	5	.241
First Half	0	0	0	0	–	Sc Pos	9	3	1	6	.333
Scnd Half	36	9	1	6	.250	Clutch	7	2	1	4	.286

2004 Season

Koyie Hill was the key player, or at least the most advanced, in the trade-deadline deal that sent center fielder Steve Finley and catcher Brent Mayne to the Los Angeles Dodgers. Hill was installed immediately as Arizona's No. 1 catcher, but he suffered a broken right ankle August 17 in a home-plate collision with Pittsburgh's Ty Wigginton. That ended Hill's season.

Hitting, Baserunning & Defense

Hill has a smooth, level stroke from both sides of the plate. He is a solid line-drive, gap hitter who makes good contact. A college third baseman, he is raw in the field, though with decent arm strength and some aptitude for calling a game. He still needs work on his receiving and ball-blocking skills. While he's not a burner on the bases, he runs well for a catcher.

2005 Outlook

Hill should be recovered from his ankle injury by spring training. His rise through the Dodgers' organization was fairly rapid, and often he's adjusted quickly to a new level. So, he's expected to enter this season as Arizona's No. 1 catcher and hold his own.

Matt Kata

Position: 2B
Bats: B **Throws:** R
Ht: 6' 1" **Wt:** 185

Opening Day Age: 27
Born: 3/14/78 in Fairview Park, OH
ML Seasons: 2
Pronunciation: KAY-ta

Overall Statistics

	G	AB	R	H	D	T	HR	RBI	SB	BB	SO	Avg	OBP	Slg
'04	42	162	17	40	9	2	2	13	4	13	29	.247	.301	.364
Car.	120	450	59	114	25	7	9	42	7	38	82	.253	.310	.400

2004 Situational Stats

	AB	H	HR	RBI	Avg		AB	H	HR	RBI	Avg
Home	74	18	1	9	.243	LHP	53	10	1	2	.189
Road	88	22	1	4	.250	RHP	109	30	1	11	.275
First Half	162	40	2	13	.247	Sc Pos	25	9	0	11	.360
Scnd Half	0	0	0	0	–	Clutch	26	9	1	3	.346

2004 Season

The signing of Roberto Alomar in January relegated Matt Kata to the bench. Alomar suffered a broken hand on April 20, making Kata the team's regular second baseman. Kata's season ended on May 29, however, when he made a diving stop of a grounder and suffered a torn left labrum.

Hitting, Baserunning & Defense

Kata has somewhat of a gliding swing, making it hard for him to adjust to offspeed pitches. He does have some power. Kata has above-average speed and is an intelligent baserunner. He is a very good second baseman, with above-average range. Kata has experience playing shortstop and third base, although his arm is not really suited to much action on the left side of the diamond.

2005 Outlook

Kata's shoulder should be fine by spring training. He will compete for the second-base job against Scott Hairston and, if the team signs a free-agent shortstop, Alex Cintron. Hairston's bat should be in the lineup, but his defensive struggles may leave Kata and Cintron to battle for second-base duties. If he is not a starter, Kata should be a capable infield backup.

Mike Koplove

Position: RP
Bats: R **Throws:** R
Ht: 5'10" **Wt:** 178

Opening Day Age: 28
Born: 8/30/76 in
Philadelphia, PA
ML Seasons: 4
Pronunciation:
COP-luv

Overall Statistics

	W	L	Pct.	ERA	G	GS	Sv	IP	H	BB	SO	HR	Avg
'04	4	4	.500	4.05	76	0	2	86.2	86	37	55	7	.269
Car.	13	6	.684	3.44	171	0	2	196.0	172	79	142	13	.240

2004 Situational Stats

	W	L	ERA	Sv	IP		AB	H	HR	RBI	Avg
Home	3	0	3.67	2	41.2	LHB	144	45	4	25	.313
Road	1	4	4.40	0	45.0	RHB	176	41	3	15	.233
First Half	2	2	4.89	2	46.0	Sc Pos	93	25	1	30	.269
Scnd Half	2	2	3.10	0	40.2	Clutch	173	47	4	26	.272

2004 Season

Mike Koplove recovered from 2003 shoulder surgery to lead the team with 76 appearances last year. He even served as the closer for a brief time while Matt Mantei and Jose Valverde were out, and before Greg Aquino had the job. Koplove was the primary setup man for most of the year. Over his final 27 appearances, he had a 2.21 ERA.

Pitching, Defense & Hitting

Koplove pitches with guts. Despite a fastball of just 86-90 MPH, he goes after hitters and uses its sink to get grounders. With his sidearm delivery, he gives lefthanded hitters a good look at the ball. He also has a good changeup and a breaking ball—something between a slider and curve—that he can use against righthanders. Koplove has a history of being effective with men on base. A former college shortstop, he is a very good fielder.

2005 Outlook

Koplove, who is eligible for arbitration, will be part of the righthanded setup mix in Arizona's bullpen. He is a useful guy to have around, since he can work multiple innings, but his workload needs to be monitored closely to keep him from breaking down.

Matt Mantei

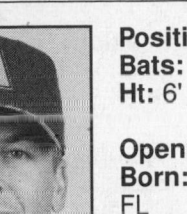

Position: RP
Bats: R **Throws:** R
Ht: 6' 1" **Wt:** 198

Opening Day Age: 31
Born: 7/7/73 in Tampa, FL
ML Seasons: 9
Pronunciation:
MAN-tie

Overall Statistics

	W	L	Pct.	ERA	G	GS	Sv	IP	H	BB	SO	HR	Avg
'04	0	3	.000	11.81	12	0	4	10.2	17	6	13	5	.354
Car.	13	18	.419	3.86	281	0	93	296.1	226	176	374	29	.210

2004 Situational Stats

	W	L	ERA	Sv	IP		AB	H	HR	RBI	Avg
Home	0	2	5.06	2	5.1	LHB	19	5	3	8	.263
Road	0	1	18.56	2	5.1	RHB	29	12	2	8	.414
First Half	0	3	11.81	4	10.2	Sc Pos	15	7	2	11	.467
Scnd Half	0	0	—	0	0.0	Clutch	32	11	5	12	.344

2004 Season

Matt Mantei opened the season as Arizona's closer, but lost the role after a disastrous first month that included five ninth-inning home runs in 8.1 innings, an 11.88 ERA and three blown saves in seven chances. Soon after that he went on the disabled list with inflammation in his throwing shoulder, and he eventually required season-ending surgery for bone spurs that were irritating his rotator cuff.

Pitching, Defense & Hitting

When healthy, Mantei has superb stuff: a fastball in the 96-99 MPH range with life, and a curve and slider with large breaks that he has been able to throw for strikes in recent years. At times he slows his delivery to the plate to improve his command. He also has a tendency to overthrow and fly open in his delivery. But he has the classic closer's mentality of being able to put failure behind him quickly.

2005 Outlook

With his history of injuries, Mantei had to take a low-base, incentive-laden contract as a free agent. Boston signed him to a $750,000 deal for 2005, and he will work a setup role for the Red Sox. If he can stay healthy, Mantei could be a bullpen bargain.

Arizona

Stephen Randolph

Position: RP
Bats: L **Throws:** L
Ht: 6' 3" **Wt:** 202

Opening Day Age: 30
Born: 5/1/74 in
Okinawa, Japan
ML Seasons: 2

Overall Statistics

	W	L	Pct.	ERA	G	GS	Sv	IP	H	BB	SO	HR	Avg
'04	2	5	.286	5.51	45	6	0	81.2	73	76	62	11	.235
Car.	10	6	.625	4.89	95	6	0	141.2	123	119	112	18	.232

2004 Situational Stats

	W	L	ERA	Sv	IP		AB	H	HR	RBI	Avg
Home	2	4	5.63	0	46.1	LHB	103	25	2	16	.243
Road	0	1	5.35	0	35.1	RHB	207	48	9	40	.232
First Half	2	2	4.12	0	39.1	Sc Pos	83	28	4	46	.337
Scnd Half	0	3	6.80	0	42.1	Clutch	30	6	2	7	.200

2004 Season

As he did in 2003, Stephen Randolph opened the season as the second lefthander in Arizona's bullpen. In mid-August, with the team looking for starters, it gave Randolph a chance to return to the role he had in the minor leagues. In six starts, Randolph went 0-3 with a 7.76 ERA and 21 walks in 26.2 innings.

Pitching, Defense & Hitting

Randolph is a puzzle, since he has above-average pitches—an 88-92 MPH fastball with movement, a slider that is tough on lefthanded hitters and a changeup—but no command of them. Part of the problem is that his head does not remain still through his delivery. He simply walks too many people to be consistently effective. A college first baseman, Randolph is a very good hitter for a pitcher and runs well.

2005 Outlook

The Diamondbacks have decisions to make on Randolph. Is he a starter or a reliever? Will they have room for him on the 2005 roster? Despite his command problems, Randolph's pure stuff will make him attractive to a number of teams, if not Arizona.

Oscar Villarreal

Position: RP
Bats: L **Throws:** R
Ht: 6' 0" **Wt:** 205

Opening Day Age: 23
Born: 11/22/81 in Nuevo
Leon, Mexico
ML Seasons: 2
Pronunciation:
VEE-yuh-ree-al

Overall Statistics

	W	L	Pct.	ERA	G	GS	Sv	IP	H	BB	SO	HR	Avg
'04	0	2	.000	7.00	17	0	0	18.0	25	7	17	3	.342
Car.	10	9	.526	3.26	103	1	0	116.0	105	53	97	9	.242

2004 Situational Stats

	W	L	ERA	Sv	IP		AB	H	HR	RBI	Avg
Home	0	1	6.00	0	9.0	LHB	28	7	0	6	.250
Road	0	1	8.00	0	9.0	RHB	45	18	3	15	.400
First Half	0	2	7.00	0	18.0	Sc Pos	28	11	3	20	.393
Scnd Half	0	0	—	0	0.0	Clutch	34	9	0	5	.265

2004 Season

Oscar Villarreal set a franchise record in 2003 with 86 appearances, but the workload seemed to catch up to him last year. He missed most of spring training with a sore elbow and opened the season on the active roster despite just three Cactus League outings. By mid-May, he was on the disabled list for good, eventually requiring surgery in August to transpose a nerve in his elbow.

Pitching, Defense & Hitting

With a fastball that arrives at 88-93 MPH, Villarreal also gets good movement, making the pitch cut or sink. He will throw his slider to lefthanded or righthanded hitters and vary the break and bite on it. His command is not always on, but he is aggressive with his pitches. Villarreal's defense is below average and he does not have much experience as a hitter.

2005 Outlook

Villarreal should be healthy for spring training. With some depth in righthanded relief, Arizona may consider using him as a starter, the role he had throughout his minor league career. If Villarreal remains in the Diamondbacks' bullpen, the team can be encouraged in knowing that his walk rate was much lower in the second half of his rookie season in 2003.

Other Arizona Diamondbacks

Carlos Baerga (Pos: 1B, Age: 36, Bats: B)

	G	AB	R	H	D	T	HR	RBI	SB	BB	SO	Avg	OBP	Slg
'04	79	85	6	20	2	0	2	11	0	6	12	.235	.309	.329
Car.	1337	5281	713	1543	272	17	132	755	59	284	563	.292	.332	.425

After a solid 2003 season in which he hit .343, Baerga was not nearly as productive last year. He missed a month with a strained left calf and only played six games in the field. The beginning of the his coaching career seems imminent. 2005 Outlook: D

Juan Brito (Pos: C, Age: 27, Bats: R)

	G	AB	R	H	D	T	HR	RBI	SB	BB	SO	Avg	OBP	Slg
'04	54	171	17	35	7	0	3	12	1	9	41	.205	.246	.298
Car.	63	194	18	42	9	0	3	13	1	9	44	.216	.252	.309

Brito hit .314 in just over 100 AB at Triple-A Tucson, which earned him a promotion to the big club. He has bounced around the minors since 1997 and he signed back with Arizona after the season, so he'll continue to hang around as a third catcher. 2005 Outlook: C

Randy Choate (Pos: LHP, Age: 29)

	W	L	Pct.	ERA	G	GS	Sv	IP	H	BB	SO	HR	Avg
'04	2	4	.333	4.62	74	0	0	50.2	52	28	49	1	.267
Car.	5	6	.455	4.50	156	0	0	142.0	125	79	113	5	.238

Choate was acquired late in the spring from Montreal and struggled from the get-go. After spending much of August in the minors, he posted a 1.54 ERA upon returning in September. He has held opposing lefties to a .223 average over his career. 2005 Outlook: C

Greg Colbrunn (Pos: 1B, Age: 35, Bats: R)

	G	AB	R	H	D	T	HR	RBI	SB	BB	SO	Avg	OBP	Slg
'04	20	27	1	3	0	0	0	1	0	1	5	.111	.143	.111
Car.	992	2769	337	801	155	12	98	422	29	170	444	.289	.338	.460

Since 2001, Colbrunn has been on the DL no less than eight times. He has collected just 85 AB over the last two seasons due to an injury to his right wrist. He could always hit, but time will tell if he will be sound enough to swing the bat. 2005 Outlook: C

Casey Daigle (Pos: RHP, Age: 23)

	W	L	Pct.	ERA	G	GS	Sv	IP	H	BB	SO	HR	Avg
'04	2	3	.400	7.16	10	10	0	49.0	63	27	17	9	.320
Car.	2	3	.400	7.16	10	10	0	49.0	63	27	17	9	.320

A strong spring performance catapulted Daigle into the starting rotation before reality struck and he got hammered. He was sent to Triple-A on June 1 and posted a 6.88 ERA there. How bad can life be when one can play catch with Jennie Finch? 2005 Outlook: C

Doug DeVore (Pos: LF/RF, Age: 27, Bats: L)

	G	AB	R	H	D	T	HR	RBI	SB	BB	SO	Avg	OBP	Slg
'04	50	107	5	24	3	2	3	13	1	7	31	.224	.272	.374
Car.	50	107	5	24	3	2	3	13	1	7	31	.224	.272	.374

DeVore did not make the Opening Day roster for the D-backs, but he was called up no less than four different times over the course of the year. He has either 14 or 15 home runs in each of his five full minor league seasons and could make the club as a fifth outfielder. 2005 Outlook: C

Chad Durbin (Pos: RHP, Age: 27)

	W	L	Pct.	ERA	G	GS	Sv	IP	H	BB	SO	HR	Avg
'04	6	7	.462	6.97	24	8	0	60.2	72	35	48	11	.291
Car.	17	30	.362	6.22	75	56	0	331.1	396	144	196	56	.297

Durbin served as a swingman for the Indians for most of the season before they waived him and the Diamondbacks picked him up. He has a lifetime ERA of 4.04 in nine seasons in the minors, though he has not been nearly as effective in the bigs. 2005 Outlook: C

Mike Fetters (Pos: RHP, Age: 40)

	W	L	Pct.	ERA	G	GS	Sv	IP	H	BB	SO	HR	Avg
'04	0	1	.000	8.68	23	0	1	18.2	23	14	14	2	.299
Car.	31	41	.431	3.86	620	6	100	716.2	699	351	518	62	.259

Fetters began last season without a club before the D-backs signed him in mid-June. After a month in the minors, they brought him up. The club was kind enough to bring him in to record his 100th major league save in his final appearance. 2005 Outlook: D

Andrew Good (Pos: RHP, Age: 25)

	W	L	Pct.	ERA	G	GS	Sv	IP	H	BB	SO	HR	Avg
'04	1	2	.333	5.31	17	2	0	40.2	43	13	26	8	.272
Car.	5	4	.556	5.30	33	12	0	107.0	117	29	68	23	.278

Good was up-and-down between the majors and minors last season, missing a month in the middle with soreness in the elbow on which he had Tommy John surgery in 2000. He has a lifetime K/W ratio of 3.7:1 in six minor league seasons, but he is not overpowering. He was released in December. 2005 Outlook: C

Andy Green (Pos: 3B/2B, Age: 27, Bats: R)

	G	AB	R	H	D	T	HR	RBI	SB	BB	SO	Avg	OBP	Slg
'04	46	109	13	22	2	1	1	4	1	5	17	.202	.241	.266
Car.	46	109	13	22	2	1	1	4	1	5	17	.202	.241	.266

Green made himself useful as a utility player for Arizona last year, playing three positions. He hit .312 in his last two minor league seasons, but without much pop. He hopes to win a bench role in the spring. 2005 Outlook: C

Quinton McCracken (Pos: LF, Age: 34, Bats: B)

	G	AB	R	H	D	T	HR	RBI	SB	BB	SO	Avg	OBP	Slg
'04	74	176	26	48	11	1	2	13	3	15	27	.273	.328	.381
Car.	820	2194	331	613	113	28	19	229	83	202	401	.279	.340	.382

Released by the Mariners in June, McCracken picked up quite a bit of playing time in August in his second stint in Arizona. He can play all three OF spots and hit .313 as a pinch-hitter last year. The 34-year-old re-signed with the D-backs in December. 2005 Outlook: C

Shane Nance (Pos: LHP, Age: 27)

	W	L	Pct.	ERA	G	GS	Sv	IP	H	BB	SO	HR	Avg
'04	1	1	.500	5.84	19	0	0	12.1	19	12	9	2	.352
Car.	1	3	.250	5.02	49	0	0	43.0	57	26	39	8	.315

After coming to the D-backs as part of the Richie Sexson deal, Nance spent the first month of the season on the DL with inflammation in his elbow. Upon his return, he split his time between Triple-A Tucson and the big club, and was ineffective at both levels. 2005 Outlook: C

Tim Olson (Pos: 3B/SS, Age: 26, Bats: R)

	G	AB	R	H	D	T	HR	RBI	SB	BB	SO	Avg	OBP	Slg
'04	48	97	8	18	7	0	2	5	1	16	18	.186	.301	.320
Car.	48	97	8	18	7	0	2	5	1	16	18	.186	.301	.320

Olson spent most of the summer with the Diamondbacks and played five different positions for them. He hit .299 and posted a .517 slugging percentage in his half-season with Triple-A Tucson. He refused a minor league assignment in December and is a free agent. Outlook: C

Shane Reynolds (Pos: RHP, Age: 37)

	W	L	Pct.	ERA	G	GS	Sv	IP	H	BB	SO	HR	Avg
'04	0	1	.000	4.50	1	1	0	2.0	6	2	0	0	.500
Car.	114	96	.543	4.09	305	278	0	1791.2	1935	419	1403	191	.275

Reynolds began the year on the DL with right shoulder inflammation, then went 2-2 with a 5.34 ERA in seven rehab starts in the minors. He lasted just two innings in his lone major league outing before torn cartilage in his right knee ended his season. 2005 Outlook: D

Donnie Sadler (Pos: SS, Age: 29, Bats: R)

	G	AB	R	H	D	T	HR	RBI	SB	BB	SO	Avg	OBP	Slg
'04	18	23	1	3	2	0	0	0	0	1	7	.130	.167	.217
Car.	417	767	125	155	29	8	6	46	25	55	163	.202	.262	.284

After rotting on Arizona's bench for the first two months of the season, the D-backs released him and the White Sox picked him up. The lifetime .202 hitter collected just seven at-bats at Triple-A Charlotte. He may have trouble finding work this season. 2005 Outlook: D

Scott Service (Pos: RHP, Age: 38)

	W	L	Pct.	ERA	G	GS	Sv	IP	H	BB	SO	HR	Avg
'04	1	1	.500	7.08	21	0	0	20.1	24	10	17	5	.286
Car.	20	22	.476	4.99	338	1	16	416.1	435	182	413	56	.272

Service went 5-0 with nine saves for Triple-A Tucson, so the Rattlers called him up to bolster their bullpen. He was unable to duplicate his success and then spent two months on the DL with a lower back strain. 2005 will be his 20th season as a pro. 2005 Outlook: C

Steve Sparks (Pos: RHP, Age: 39)

	W	L	Pct.	ERA	G	GS	Sv	IP	H	BB	SO	HR	Avg
'04	3	7	.300	6.04	29	18	0	120.2	139	45	57	18	.287
Car.	59	76	.437	4.88	270	182	3	1319.2	1451	520	658	154	.280

After serving as a reliever for two clubs in 2003, Sparks made 18 starts for Arizona and went 2-7 with a 6.00 ERA in those outings. The knuckler has posted a sub-4.00 ERA just once in his big league career and will have to scramble to find a major league job. 2005 Outlook: D

Brandon Villafuerte (Pos: RHP, Age: 29)

	W	L	Pct.	ERA	G	GS	Sv	IP	H	BB	SO	HR	Avg
'04	0	3	.000	4.05	20	0	0	20.0	25	14	13	2	.313
Car.	1	7	.125	4.12	91	0	3	102.2	109	60	77	14	.275

In 23 games for Triple-A Tucson, Villafuerte went 2-2 with a 2.64 ERA and four saves, which earned him a promotion to the big leagues. After a mediocre month in the majors, Arizona tried to send him back down, but he refused the assignment and became a free agent. 2005 Outlook: D

Alan Zinter (Pos: 1B, Age: 36, Bats: B)

	G	AB	R	H	D	T	HR	RBI	SB	BB	SO	Avg	OBP	Slg
'04	28	34	2	7	2	0	1	6	0	5	15	.206	.300	.353
Car.	67	78	7	13	4	0	3	9	0	5	34	.167	.214	.333

Zinter hit .335 with a .945 OPS for Triple-A Tuscon over the first couple of months, and was called up in early June. Two weeks later, he tore his left plantar fascia and went on the 60-day DL. He has some pop and could help a club off the bench. 2005 Outlook: C

Arizona Diamondbacks Minor League Prospects

Organization Overview:

Arizona has a number of hitting prospects, but the organization seems to be lacking up the middle. Sergio Santos, the Diamondbacks' No. 1 pick in 2002, has played shortstop but projects as a third baseman. The trade for Koyie Hill and Chris Snyder's performance in a late-season callup alleviated some concern at catcher. Pitching is another concern. If Ramon Pena (formerly known as Adriano Rosario) has no visa issues as a result of having used a false name and birth date, he gives the Diamondbacks a possible top-of-the-rotation prospect. Otherwise, the pitching crop is relievers or back-end types. The two first-round picks from 2003, outfielders Conor Jackson and Carlos Quentin, are on the fast track, having successfully jumped from high Class-A to Double-A last year. Jackson could wind up at first base.

Jason Bulger

Position: P **Opening Day Age:** 26
Bats: R **Throws:** R **Born:** 12/6/78 in
Ht: 6' 4" **Wt:** 205 Snellville, GA

Recent Statistics

	W	L	ERA	G	GS	Sv	IP	H	R	BB	SO	HR
2003 A Lancaster	2	1	6.75	4	4	0	17.1	23	13	5	20	3
2004 A Lancaster	0	1	1.52	21	0	11	23.2	14	4	10	31	0
2004 AA El Paso	0	3	3.91	24	0	8	25.1	24	12	19	25	0

Bulger still is a bit of a work in progress. When Arizona drafted him in the first round (22nd overall) in 2001, Bulger had hardly pitched—he was a college third baseman who added closer duties as a junior. Then reconstructive elbow surgery in 2003 set him back. He was converted to relief last season, and worked in 45 games at two different levels. Bulger has a pitcher's body and had touched 97 MPH at times (usually pitching at 94-95 MPH), but his fastball is relatively straight. He throws a hard curve and has a changeup he uses against lefthanded hitters. He has a good work ethic and is expected to open this season as the closer at Triple-A Tucson.

Jerry Gil

Position: SS **Opening Day Age:** 22
Bats: R **Throws:** R **Born:** 10/14/82 in San
Ht: 6' 3" **Wt:** 183 Pedro de Macoris, DR

Recent Statistics

	G	AB	R	H	D	T	HR	RBI	SB	BB	SO	Avg
2004 AAA Tucson	114	421	53	117	31	8	11	58	12	12	94	.270
2004 NL Arizona	29	86	3	15	2	1	0	8	2	0	33	.174

Whether Gil will hit enough to be a useful major leaguer remains in doubt. He does have the wiry strength to hit for some power but has never shown much strike-zone judgment. He has struck out 90 or more times in three different minor league seasons, and his walk totals remain paltry. He is a smooth fielding shortstop with a very strong arm, but in a late-August callup last year, he was overmatched at the plate. Gil was jumped from Class-A South Bend in 2003 to Triple-A Tucson in 2004, so he definitely needs more seasoning. If he can become a moderately decent hitter, his glove will earn him playing time with the parent club.

Mike Gosling

Position: P **Opening Day Age:** 24
Bats: L **Throws:** L **Born:** 9/23/80 in
Ht: 6' 0" **Wt:** 210 Madison, WI

Recent Statistics

	W	L	ERA	G	GS	Sv	IP	H	R	BB	SO	HR
2004 AAA Tucson	9	5	5.82	24	21	0	128.1	160	101	53	67	16
2004 NL Arizona	1	1	4.62	6	4	0	25.1	26	13	13	14	5

Shoulder surgery in September 2003 got Gosling off to a late start last year, but his velocity recovered to 89-91 MPH. A second-round selection in the 2001 draft out of Stanford, the lefthander's best pitch is his changeup, and his strength is knowing how to pitch (not unlike other well-known Stanford products). He uses movement, changes speeds and is not afraid to work inside. Gosling impressed the Diamondbacks in a late-season callup last year, working at least five innings in each of his four starts with the parent club. He has a good shot at making the back end of the 2005 rotation.

Conor Jackson

Position: OF **Opening Day Age:** 22
Bats: R **Throws:** R **Born:** 5/7/82 in Austin,
Ht: 6' 3" **Wt:** 210 TX

Recent Statistics

	G	AB	R	H	D	T	HR	RBI	SB	BB	SO	Avg
2003 A Yakima	68	257	44	82	35	1	6	60	3	36	41	.319
2004 A Lancaster	67	258	64	89	19	2	11	54	4	45	36	.345
2004 AA El Paso	60	226	33	68	13	2	6	37	3	24	36	.301

With a quick bat and excellent pitch recognition, Jackson should be an impact offensive player. He was the Diamondbacks' first-round selection in the 2003 draft out of Cal, where he hit .388 with 14 doubles as a senior. He makes consistent solid contact and has learned to hit for power with backspin. He has hit better than .300 at three minor league levels, and his strike-zone judgment allows him to post impressive on-base figures. Jackson may turn out to be an adequate left fielder, but his arm is below average. He played the corner infield positions in college and may wind up at third base or hit enough to warrant a move to first.

Carlos Quentin

Position: OF   **Opening Day Age:** 22
Bats: R **Throws:** R **Born:** 8/28/82 in
Ht: 6' 2" **Wt:** 220 Bellflower, CA

Recent Statistics

	G	AB	R	H	D	T	HR	RBI	SB	BB	SO	Avg
2004 A Lancaster	65	242	64	75	14	1	15	51	5	25	33	.310
2004 AA El Paso	60	210	39	75	19	0	6	38	0	18	23	.357

Arizona's second first-round pick in 2003, Quentin did not make his pro debut until last year because he required Tommy John surgery soon after signing. Quentin has a quick but violent swing and tends to dive over the plate. He has learned how to be hit by a pitch, having set a minor league record with 43 plunkings at two different levels combined last year. There is some question whether that hitting style will make him susceptible to inside pitches at the major league level. He is a good right fielder, with instincts and a strong arm. Quentin could contend for a roster spot this year if Arizona does not sign a free-agent outfielder.

Sergio Santos

Position: SS   **Opening Day Age:** 21
Bats: R **Throws:** R **Born:** 7/4/83 in
Ht: 6' 3" **Wt:** 190 Bellflower, CA

Recent Statistics

	G	AB	R	H	D	T	HR	RBI	SB	BB	SO	Avg
2003 A Lancaster	93	341	55	98	13	2	8	49	5	41	64	.287
2003 AA El Paso	37	137	13	35	7	1	2	16	0	8	25	.255
2004 AA El Paso	89	347	53	98	19	5	11	52	3	24	89	.282

Santos projects as a third baseman in the majors, but he could be an impact player. The 2002 first-round draft choice (27th overall), he has drawn comparisons to Troy Glaus with his above-average power, a strong arm and a good first step, but he does not have the range to play shortstop. He tends to tinker with his batting stance, and he needs to develop a better sense of the strike zone. Santos missed the end of last season with a left shoulder injury, which might be a long-term concern. He probably needs a full season at Triple-A, and there's no urgency to get him to Arizona after the Diamondbacks signed third basemen Troy Glaus during the offseason.

Chris Snyder

Position: C   **Opening Day Age:** 24
Bats: R **Throws:** R **Born:** 2/12/81 in
Ht: 6' 3" **Wt:** 220 Houston, TX

Recent Statistics

	G	AB	R	H	D	T	HR	RBI	SB	BB	SO	Avg
2004 AA El Paso	99	346	66	104	31	0	15	57	3	46	57	.301
2004 NL Arizona	29	96	10	23	6	0	5	15	0	13	25	.240

When Koyie Hill suffered a season-ending ankle injury in mid-August, Arizona promoted Snyder directly from Double-A El Paso, and he held his own for the most part. A 2002 second-round pick out of the University of Houston, he has a big frame and shows very good power, including to right-center field. His swing is long, so he may not hit for a high average. Snyder is an excellent receiver, fairly athletic for his size, and has the aptitude for calling a game. He has good arm strength but needs to work on a more explosive release to nail more basestealers if he hopes to have all-around value behind the plate in the majors.

Jon Zeringue

Position: OF   **Opening Day Age:** 22
Bats: R **Throws:** R **Born:** 3/29/83 in
Ht: 6' 2" **Wt:** 215 Thibodaux, LA

Recent Statistics

	G	AB	R	H	D	T	HR	RBI	SB	BB	SO	Avg
2004 A Lancaster	56	230	36	77	14	3	10	41	9	14	53	.335

Arizona's second-round pick last year out of Louisiana State, Zeringue is a potential five-tool player who had no problems adjusting to hitting with wood and could come quick. He has a short, compact swing that generates power, with plate discipline that enables him to draw walks. He pounded out 27 extra-base hits at high Class-A Lancaster in just 230 at-bats, while producing an OPS (on-base plus slugging percentage) of better than .900. He is a prototype right fielder, with a strong arm and good speed for his size. Double-A El Paso is his next stop, with a cup of coffee not far off.

Others to Watch

Reggie Abercrombie (23), who also came over in the Steve Finley trade, is a good athlete and true center fielder. He needs to cut down on his strikeouts. . . Righthander **Lance Cormier** (24) showed a good feel for pitching in the minors, but was not as aggressive nor willing to use his changeup while in the majors. His stuff is average but he may be able to succeed with it. . . **Jamie D'Antona** (22) has 28 homers in his first 157 pro games, and he reached Double-A El Paso in his second pro season. He has impressive power but may not be able to handle third base long-term. . . Righthander **Enrique Gonzalez** (22) throws hard despite his size (5-foot-10, 196 pounds) and had success last year after moving into the rotation at high Class-A Lancaster. . . Outfielder **Josh Kroeger** (22) has a slow bat and struggled in his callup last year after a .331-29-87 season between Double-A El Paso and Triple-A Tucson. He needs to improve his work ethic and may wind up an extra outfielder at best. . . Acquired in the Steve Finley trade from Los Angeles—which had just got him from Florida in the Paul Lo Duca deal—**Bill Murphy** (23) projects as a bottom-of-the rotation starter. His best pitch is a changeup, and he also throws a curve, but he tends to leave pitches up. He has a soft body but above-average mental makeup and pitches with no fear.

Offense

Turner Field gained an early reputation as a pitchers' park upon opening eight years ago, but in recent seasons the facility has been relatively neutral in terms of scoring and batting average. Doubles and triples are a little lower than the norm. The hardest place to go deep is the right-center field power alley, which is a stout 390 feet.

Defense

The Braves have the ideal center fielder for Turner Field in Andruw Jones, as the relatively deep power alleys require a defender capable of covering lots of territory. Right field requires a strong arm, and the presence of Gary Sheffield in 2003 and J.D. Drew in 2004 were perfect fits. Players rate the infield grass as one of the smoothest surfaces in the NL. Foul territory is about normal for a new ballpark.

Who It Helps the Most

Righthander Jaret Wright took advantage of the large dimensions at Turner Field, posting a 2.56 ERA at home versus a 4.04 ERA on the road. Lefthander Mike Hampton had similar success (3.65 home/4.95 road). Turner Field may as well be the fountain of youth for first baseman Julio Franco, who hit .337 at home compared to a .276 norm on the road.

Who It Hurts the Most

It did not take lefthanded hitter Adam LaRoche long to discover how difficult it can be to pull pitches for home runs at Turner Field. After having considerable success in Atlanta in 2003, Russ Ortiz' ERA was nearly a run higher (4.57 versus 3.53) at home.

Rookies & Newcomers

The Braves had an influx of young newcomers in 2004 and could see a similar scenario in 2005. Outfielder Ryan Langerhans is out of options and will be a strong candidate to serve in a reserve role. Atlanta is expected to shop for pitchers in the free-agent market, but pitching prospects Dan Meyer and Kyle Davies could see activity at Turner Field at some point this season.

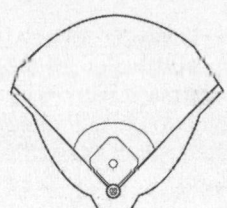

Dimensions: LF-335, LCF-380, CF-401, RCF-390, RF-330

Capacity: 50,091

Elevation: 1050 feet

Surface: Grass

Foul Territory: Average

Park Factors

2004 Season

| | Home Games | | | Away Games | | | |
	Braves	Opp	Total	Braves	Opp	Total	Index
G	72	72	144	69	69	138	
Avg	.268	.258	.263	.273	.264	.269	98
AB	2418	2507	4925	2426	2299	4725	100
R	361	291	652	340	277	617	101
H	648	647	1295	663	607	1270	98
2B	125	106	231	131	98	229	97
3B	17	5	22	18	11	29	73
HR	81	75	156	72	59	131	114
BB	273	236	509	253	223	476	103
SO	529	498	1027	480	395	875	113
E	52	39	91	46	44	90	97
E-Infield	49	29	78	44	38	82	91
LHB-Avg	.270	.272	.271	.292	.270	.282	96
LHB-HR	40	34	74	37	22	59	118
RHB-Avg	.267	.247	.257	.258	.260	.259	99
RHB-HR	41	41	82	35	37	72	111

2002-2004

| | Home Games | | | Away Games | | | |
	Braves	Opp	Total	Braves	Opp	Total	Index
G	219	219	438	209	209	418	
Avg	.272	.250	.261	.270	.260	.265	98
AB	7309	7573	14882	7439	7006	14445	98
R	1074	888	1962	1044	871	1915	98
H	1988	1893	3881	2011	1819	3830	97
2B	381	347	728	406	343	749	94
3B	45	28	73	41	37	78	91
HR	256	197	453	244	186	430	102
BB	770	736	1506	729	722	1451	101
SO	1375	1391	2766	1397	1296	2693	100
E	162	145	307	149	135	284	103
E-Infield	141	116	257	135	110	245	100
LHB-Avg	.276	.257	.266	.276	.252	.265	100
LHB-HR	87	69	156	69	63	132	113
RHB-Avg	.270	.246	.258	.267	.264	.265	97
RHB-HR	169	128	297	175	123	298	98

2004 Rankings (National League)

- Highest strikeout factor
- Third-lowest LHB batting-average factor

Atlanta

Bobby Cox

2004 Season

Bobby Cox added to his legacy last year when he became only the ninth manager in major league history to reach the 2,000-win mark. Cox may have done his best managing job to date, guiding the Braves to 96 wins despite losing such All-Stars as Gary Sheffield, Javy Lopez, Greg Maddux and Vinny Castilla to free agency and Marcus Giles and Horacio Ramirez to prolonged injuries.

Offense

The changes in offensive personnel caused Cox to alter his approach last year. Normally content to wait for the big hit, the skipper saw his team manufacture more runs in 2004, ranking fifth in the National League in runs scored despite placing 10th in home runs. Although he continues to platoon as much as any manager since Casey Stengel, Cox has become more open to employing rookies in starting roles. His adjustments enabled the Braves to get solid offensive years from such unproven hitters as Johnny Estrada, Adam LaRoche and Charles Thomas.

Pitching & Defense

Butterfingers became an uncharacteristic trait of the Braves last year, with Atlanta committing 116 errors. Cox was able to overcome an occasionally shaky infield by employing the game's best defensive outfield in the second half in Thomas, Andruw Jones and J.D. Drew. Pitching was once again a calling card for the Braves, who led the NL in ERA and ranked second in shutouts. Cox is a big believer in using relievers for as little as one batter, all with the hope of getting the most ideal matchups.

2005 Outlook

The last 14 teams that Cox has managed from the season's onset have won division titles, including 13 in Atlanta. Considered old-school by many observers, Cox maintains respect in the clubhouse because of his consistency and refusal to blame his players publicly. He will overtake Leo Durocher and Walter Alston in the all-time victory column this year, and is only 123 wins shy of tying for fifth place with Joe McCarthy.

Born: 5/21/41 in Tulsa, OK

Playing Experience: 1968-1969, NYY

Managerial Experience: 23 seasons

Manager Statistics

Year	Team, Lg	W	L	Pct	GB	Finish
2004	Atlanta, NL	96	66	.593	–	1st East
23 Seasons		2002	1531	.567	–	–

2004 Starting Pitchers by Days Rest

	<=3	4	5	6+
Braves Starts	3	81	57	13
Braves ERA	11.45	4.17	3.43	2.80
NL Avg Starts	2	82	46	23
NL ERA	4.58	4.35	4.28	4.73

2004 Situational Stats

	Bobby Cox	NL Average
Hit & Run Success %	32.7	38.0
Stolen Base Success %	72.9	71.7
Platoon Pct.	65.9	55.2
Defensive Subs	11	18
High-Pitch Outings	4	6
Quick/Slow Hooks	15/12	21/12
Sacrifice Attempts	105	99

2004 Rankings (National League)

- 1st in saves with over 1 inning pitched (16)
- 2nd in 2+ pitching changes in low-scoring games (40)
- 3rd in relief appearances (483)

2004 Season

Considered a potential standout if he could just stay healthy, J.D. Drew accomplished both feats in his first season with the Braves. The outfielder was the team's most consistent offensive force throughout the campaign, as evidenced by his reaching base safely via a hit, walk or hit by pitch in 133 of the 145 games he played, including 41 straight from June 10 to July 27. He also put together hitting streaks of 22 and 16 games, while posting career highs in home runs, RBI, runs, walks and games played.

Hitting

Despite having Chipper Jones bat third for most of the past decade, Atlanta manager Bobby Cox deemed Drew as "the perfect No. 3 hitter." He provided above-average power in the top third of the lineup while stroking line drives to all fields with his superior bat speed. One sign that Drew matured into a complete hitter is his performance against lefties. Southpaws limited Drew to a .218 norm in 2003, but he bounced back to hit .287 against them last year. Even though he struck out a career-high 116 times, Drew displayed better strike-zone judgment and was able to coax 118 walks, nearly double his previous best.

Baserunning & Defense

As productive as he was at the plate, Drew was even better in right field, putting together a Gold Glove-caliber performance. He showed above-average range and one of the league's stronger arms to give Atlanta a dominating presence in the garden. Drew also is one of the NL's best baserunners, a trait he has not shown with consistency in the past due to nagging injuries with his legs.

2005 Outlook

Drew entered the offseason as a free agent. The Braves wanted to keep him, as some observers describe Drew as having the best all-around natural ability of any Atlanta player since Hank Aaron. Yet, money was an issue. In December, the Braves chose not to offer Drew arbitration. He will change addresses and the Braves won't get a draft pick for a player who was the key to a 2003 trade that cost them three pitchers.

Position: RF
Bats: L **Throws:** R
Ht: 6' 1" **Wt:** 200

Opening Day Age: 29
Born: 11/20/75 in Valdosta, GA
ML Seasons: 7

Overall Statistics

	G	AB	R	H	D	T	HR	RBI	SB	BB	SO	Avg	OBP	Slg
'04	145	518	118	158	28	8	31	93	12	118	116	.305	.436	.569
Car.	742	2415	473	693	114	26	127	373	71	389	529	.287	.391	.513

Where He Hits the Ball

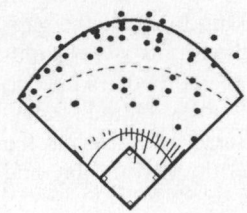 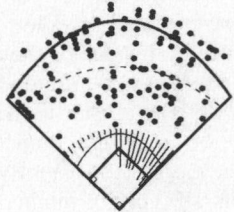

Vs. LHP   **Vs. RHP**

2004 Situational Stats

	AB	H	HR	RBI	Avg		AB	H	HR	RBI	Avg
Home	244	73	14	43	.299	LHP	167	48	6	31	.287
Road	274	85	17	50	.310	RHP	351	110	25	62	.313
First Half	282	88	21	55	.312	Sc Pos	145	43	6	61	.297
Scnd Half	236	70	10	38	.297	Clutch	74	19	5	13	.257

2004 Rankings (National League)

- 1st in fielding percentage in right field (.990)
- 4th in runs scored and on-base percentage
- 5th in triples and walks
- 6th in times on base (281)
- Led the Braves in home runs, runs scored, hits, triples, total bases (295), walks, times on base (281), pitches seen (2,565), slugging percentage, on-base percentage, most pitches seen per plate appearance (3.98), and highest percentage of pitches taken (59.3)
- Led NL right fielders in batting average

Johnny Estrada

2004 Season

The departure of free agent Javy Lopez allowed the Braves to showcase the talents of Johnny Estrada. Acquired from Philadelphia in a controversial trade for pitcher Kevin Millwood prior to the 2003 campaign, Estrada batted .338 with runners in scoring position and joined Ted Simmons as the only switch-hitting catchers since 1923 to post a .300 batting average. Estrada also paced the team with 45 two-out RBI. He had three or more hits in 15 games, including a pair of 4-for-4 performances and a five-hit, five-RBI outing against Milwaukee on May 15.

Hitting

Not unlike Lopez, Estrada is known as an offensive-oriented receiver, stroking hits into the gaps from both sides of the plate with his sweet, compact swings. Although he has good pop in his bat, producing a team-high 36 doubles, Estrada focuses on making contact instead of clearing the fences. He consistently puts the ball in play and hits all types of pitchers.

Baserunning & Defense

Estrada's overall defense was better than advertised. He works well with pitchers, calls a good game, and moves much better behind the dish than Lopez did. Estrada has a decent arm, but the accuracy of his throws can leave something to be desired. He made nine errors last year, most of them coming on poor throws, and retired a hair under 19 percent of basestealers. Estrada has only average speed and is not a threat to steal a base, but he uses his intelligence well on the basepaths.

2005 Outlook

Surprisingly, Estrada was the Braves' lone representative at the All-Star Game in Houston last July. He was steady thoughout the season, leaving few opportunities for veteran backup Eddie Perez. Estrada will be challenged by the possible addition of new members to the starting rotation, yet the 28-year-old receiver should fare well both this year and for the foreseeable future.

Position: C
Bats: B **Throws:** R
Ht: 5'11" **Wt:** 209

Opening Day Age: 28
Born: 6/27/76 in Hayward, CA
ML Seasons: 4

Overall Statistics

	G	AB	R	H	D	T	HR	RBI	SB	BB	SO	Avg	OBP	Slg
'04	134	462	56	145	36	0	9	76	0	39	66	.314	.378	.450
Car.	249	813	84	226	52	0	17	117	0	57	103	.278	.336	.405

Where He Hits the Ball

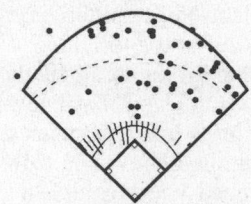 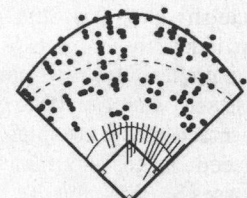

Vs. LHP	**Vs. RHP**

2004 Situational Stats

	AB	H	HR	RBI	Avg		AB	H	HR	RBI	Avg
Home	223	61	4	39	.274	LHP	125	34	3	14	.272
Road	239	84	5	37	.351	RHP	337	111	6	62	.329
First Half	262	87	4	47	.332	Sc Pos	139	47	4	64	.338
Scnd Half	200	58	5	29	.290	Clutch	63	20	1	8	.317

2004 Rankings (National League)

- 2nd in errors at catcher (9), lowest percentage of pitches taken (44.0) and lowest percentage of runners caught stealing as a catcher (17.6)
- 3rd in batting average on the road and highest percentage of swings on the first pitch (42.3)
- Led the Braves in batting average, doubles, hit by pitch (11), batting average vs. righthanded pitchers and batting average on the road

Rafael Furcal

2004 Season

Rafael Furcal overcame a disappointing first two months to give the Braves their usual solid production at the top of the lineup. Along with battling an early back ailment, the shortstop missed 19 games in May after jamming his right ring finger. Furcal rebounded to lead the team with 43 multi-hit games, and owned a .409 on-base percentage in August to help the team secure the National League East crown. Furcal was arrested for driving while impaired for the second time in four years during September and reported to prison for three weeks on October 12.

Hitting

Although Furcal clubbed 14 home runs last year, one shy of the career high he established in 2003, he is best when employing a leadoff mentality at the plate. The switch-hitter shortened his swing in the second half in order to focus more on making contact instead of hitting for power, and used his speed to get on base. Still, the lean Furcal possesses surprising pop. He has improved his overall approach by reducing his strikeouts the past two seasons.

Baserunning & Defense

Furcal possesses as much range as any shortstop in the game. The trouble comes when he tries to use the cannon attached to his right shoulder to make impossible plays. Wild throws have led to poor fielding percentages and 24 errors last season. Furcal is one of the fastest baserunners in the game. He has learned the art of stealing bases, succeeding on 29 of his 35 attempts last year.

2005 Outlook

The Braves hope Furcal has learned his lesson regarding his early morning carousing. He is well liked in the clubhouse and continues to mature both on the field and off. If he can maintain his focus on the diamond and smooth out some rough edges, Furcal has the package to be one of the NL's premier shortstops and leadoff hitters.

Position: SS
Bats: B **Throws:** R
Ht: 5'10" **Wt:** 165

Opening Day Age: 26
Born: 8/24/78 in Loma de Cabrera, DR
ML Seasons: 5
Pronunciation: fur-CALL

Overall Statistics

	G	AB	R	H	D	T	HR	RBI	SB	BB	SO	Avg	OBP	Slg
'04	143	563	103	157	24	5	14	59	29	58	71	.279	.344	.414
Car.	663	2642	454	749	129	27	45	234	143	258	397	.283	.347	.404

Where He Hits the Ball

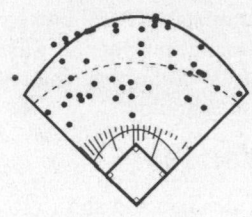
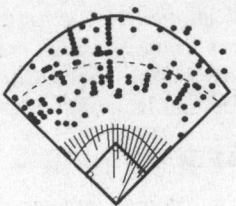

Vs. LHP　　　**Vs. RHP**

2004 Situational Stats

	AB	H	HR	RBI	Avg		AB	H	HR	RBI	Avg
Home	260	76	5	24	.292	LHP	163	45	6	18	.276
Road	303	81	9	35	.267	RHP	400	112	8	41	.280
First Half	265	73	10	29	.275	Sc Pos	117	31	3	45	.265
Scnd Half	298	84	4	30	.282	Clutch	73	27	1	11	.370

2004 Rankings (National League)

- 1st in errors at shortstop (24)
- 2nd in lowest fielding percentage at shortstop (.962)
- 6th in bunts in play (35)
- 7th in batting average in the clutch
- 8th in stolen-base percentage (82.9)
- 9th in stolen bases
- Led the Braves in singles, stolen bases, caught stealing (6), stolen-base percentage (82.9), bunts in play (35), lowest percentage of swings that missed (11.8), highest percentage of swings put into play (48.0), batting average in the clutch, on-base percentage for a leadoff hitter (.343) and lowest percentage of swings on the first pitch (19.7)

Atlanta

353

Marcus Giles

2004 Season

Marcus Giles had another productive season despite a May 15 collision with Andruw Jones at Milwaukee which resulted in a fractured right clavicle. He returned to action on July 15 after missing 52 games and got in rhythm toward the end of the slate, hitting at a .380 clip with five doubles and three home runs in his last 20 games.

Hitting

A power hitter in the minors, Giles continues to emerge as one of the most consistent No. 2 hitters in the major leagues. His bat has good pop and he makes decent contact with his short stroke and good strike-zone discipline. He is adept at hitting the ball to the opposite field and is developing into an above-average hit-and-run batter. Giles' power was limited and his extra-base hit production was down upon his return from the collarbone injury due to a lack of strength in the shoulder.

Baserunning & Defense

Some scouts wondered if Giles had the ability to play second base in the major leagues, but he has proven his skeptics wrong. He has good quickness and decent if not soft hands, he turns the double play very well, and he has developed a solid relationship with shortstop Rafael Furcal. His arm is solid for the keystone sack, and Giles rarely makes mental errors. An aggressive runner with slightly above-average speed, Giles is not afraid to stretch a single into a double. He also does an excellent job of reading pitchers, enabling him to steal 17 bases in 21 opportunities last season.

2005 Outlook

The Braves are a little concerned that Giles has become injury prone after suffering a pair of concussions over the past two seasons. Part of that can be attributed to his hard-nosed approach, which is a trait the Braves love about the second baseman. An All-Star in 2003, Giles should compete for the honor again this year if he can remain on the field.

Position: 2B
Bats: R **Throws:** R
Ht: 5' 8" **Wt:** 180

Opening Day Age: 26
Born: 5/18/78 in San Diego, CA
ML Seasons: 4
Pronunciation: JYLES

Overall Statistics

	G	AB	R	H	D	T	HR	RBI	SB	BB	SO	Avg	OBP	Slg
'04	102	379	61	118	22	2	8	48	17	36	70	.311	.378	.443
Car.	383	1387	225	405	91	7	46	171	34	148	228	.292	.366	.467

Where He Hits the Ball

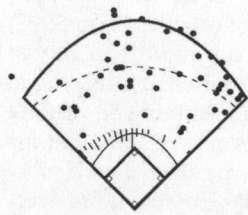 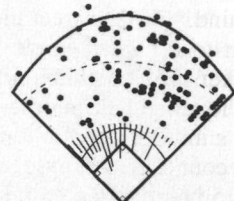

Vs. LHP **Vs. RHP**

2004 Situational Stats

	AB	H	HR	RBI	Avg		AB	H	HR	RBI	Avg
Home	176	56	6	28	.318	LHP	92	37	5	18	.402
Road	203	62	2	20	.305	RHP	287	81	3	30	.282
First Half	118	40	3	18	.339	Sc Pos	97	31	2	38	.320
Scnd Half	261	78	5	30	.299	Clutch	52	10	1	8	.192

2004 Rankings (National League)

- 3rd in errors at second base (12)
- 8th in lowest percentage of pitches taken (48.2)
- 10th in stolen-base percentage (81.0)
- Led the Braves in sacrifice flies (7) and batting average with two strikes (.253)

Mike Hampton

2004 Season

Inconsistent for much of the first half, Mike Hampton did not win his first game until May 23 and failed to pick up his second victory until June 24. By altering his pitch selection, Hampton caught fire with a 5-0 record and a 2.62 ERA in July, and went 12-2 during his last 16 outings. The lefthander suffered a torn meniscus in his left knee on Septempber 11 and pitched just twice after that.

Pitching

In order for Hampton to have success, he must get ahead in the count. His four-seam, low-90s fastball is his main weapon, but he gets into trouble when he has to throw that pitch after falling behind. With the count in his favor, Hampton will turn to an above-average changeup and a nasty sinker, which helped him rank among the National League leaders in percentage of groundballs induced (66.8). When Hampton is behind in the count, hitters sit on his four-seamer, which led to 15 home runs allowed last year. Hampton gets stronger as the game progresses. He surrendered 29 percent of his runs in the first inning, when opponents batted .331 against him.

Defense & Hitting

Despite his aching knees, Hampton maintains his athleticism and moves well off the mound to field his position. He does an excellent job of holding runners, mixing a variety of quick pickoff moves and a short slide step that limited opponents to six stolen bases last season. Many everyday players are envious of Hampton's hitting prowess. His 14 career home runs lead all active pitchers.

2005 Outlook

Hampton is not the dominating pitcher he was while with the Mets and Astros, but he has reemerged as an effective, albeit inconsistent lefthander in his two seasons with the Braves. He eclipsed 2,000 career innings in his final regular-season start, and shows no sign of tailing off in the near future.

Position: SP
Bats: R **Throws:** L
Ht: 5'10" **Wt:** 195

Opening Day Age: 32
Born: 9/9/72 in Brooksville, FL
ML Seasons: 12

Overall Statistics

W	L	Pct.	ERA	G	GS	Sv	IP	H	BB	SO	HR	Avg
13	9	.591	4.28	29	29	0	172.1	198	65	87	15	.290
133	98	.576	3.99	363	309	1	2004.2	2082	808	1245	172	.271

2004 Pitching Profile

	Mike Hampton	NL Average
Overall Strike %	61.7	62.5
1st Pitch Strike %	56.5	58.5
Ratio	1.53	1.39
Strikeouts per 9 IP	4.54	6.74
Walks per 9 IP	3.39	3.38
Home Runs per 9 IP	0.78	1.11
Strikeout/Walk Ratio	1.34	1.99
Groundball/Flyball Ratio	2.01	1.25

2004 Situational Stats

	W	L	ERA	Sv	IP		AB	H	HR	RBI	Avg
Home	7	5	3.65	0	88.2	LHB	146	37	3	15	.253
Road	6	4	4.95	0	83.2	RHB	537	161	12	57	.300
First Half	4	8	5.11	0	100.1	Sc Pos	169	38	3	56	.225
Scnd Half	9	1	3.13	0	72.0	Clutch	30	10	0	1	.333

2004 Rankings (National League)

- 2nd in balks (2)
- 3rd in highest groundball-flyball ratio allowed (2.0)
- 4th in fewest strikeouts per nine innings (4.5)
- 5th in highest batting average allowed (.290)
- 6th in lowest stolen-base percentage allowed (54.5), highest on-base percentage allowed (.351) and highest batting average allowed vs. righthanded batters
- 8th in lowest strikeout-walk ratio (1.3)
- 10th in highest ERA on the road
- Led the Braves in losses, balks (2), highest groundball-flyball ratio allowed (2.0) and lowest stolen-base percentage allowed (54.5)

Andruw Jones

2004 Season

Last year was another roller-coaster ride for Andruw Jones. A hot streak during July and August, when he hit a combined .287 with 10 home runs and 34 RBI, coincided with Atlanta's run to the top of the National League East standings. Jones reached the 90-RBI plateau for the sixth time in seven campaigns and fell one shy of hitting 30 home runs for the fifth straight season.

Hitting

Jones can turn on a fastball. The ball makes a different sound jumping off his bat, and his strength can produce prodigious longballs. Yet as productive as his numbers can be, Jones frustrates the Braves with his inability to take his game to the next level. A streaky hitter, he struck out a career-high 147 times last year and owned an .833 OPS (on-base plus slugging percentage), which ranked just 17th among NL outfielders. Despite spending eight-plus seasons in the major leagues, Jones continues to be fooled by breaking balls down and away.

Baserunning & Defense

Jones remains a premier center fielder. He committed just three errors for the third straight year last season and continued to cover significant ground from gap to gap. He gets as good a jump on balls as any outfielder in the game. That said, Jones' increase in size over the last few seasons has reduced his range, especially on short flyballs. His speed on the basepaths has decreased, due in part to back spasms last season and aching knees that have bothered him occasionally since his teenage years.

2005 Outlook

Jones' name has been mentioned in trade talks, but the fact that he is owed $39 million through the 2007 campaign will make him tough to move. He has been a cornerstone in the Atlanta lineup since hitting two home runs in his first two World Series at-bats in 1996, and at age 27, he should continue to be an impact player for at least the next half-dozen years.

Position: CF
Bats: R **Throws:** R
Ht: 6' 1" **Wt:** 210

Opening Day Age: 27
Born: 4/23/77 in Willemstad, Curacao
ML Seasons: 9

Overall Statistics

G	AB	R	H	D	T	HR	RBI	SB	BB	SO	Avg	OBP	Slg
154	570	85	149	34	4	29	91	6	71	147	.261	.345	.488
1291	4685	760	1254	250	29	250	766	124	501	1017	.268	.342	.493

Where He Hits the Ball

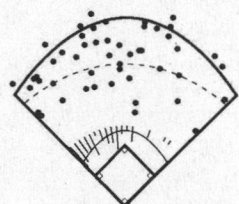 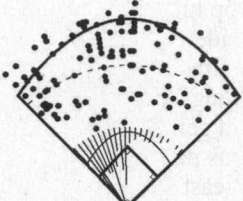

Vs. LHP   **Vs. RHP**

2004 Situational Stats

	AB	H	HR	RBI	Avg		AB	H	HR	RBI	Avg
Home	275	75	13	41	.273	LHP	151	40	7	24	.265
Road	295	74	16	50	.251	RHP	419	109	22	67	.260
First Half	316	79	15	51	.250	Sc Pos	171	39	7	61	.228
Scnd Half	254	70	14	40	.276	Clutch	80	23	5	12	.288

2004 Rankings (National League)

- 3rd in GDPs (24)
- 4th in fielding percentage in center field (.993) and highest percentage of swings that missed (31.0)
- 8th in strikeouts
- Led the Braves in at-bats, caught stealing (6), intentional walks (9), strikeouts, GDPs (24), plate appearances (646) and games played

Chipper Jones

2004 Season

A wrist sprain and a strained right hamstring caused Chipper Jones to miss 25 games and led to a miserable first half, but a blazing August in which he hit .337 with a team-high 11 home runs and 29 RBI enabled the Braves' fixture to post another solid season. Jones' torrid second-half RBI pace helped him finish just four shy of the century mark, marking the first time he had failed to drive in 100 runs in a season since 1995.

Hitting

Much of the switch-hitter's problems last year stemmed from the left side, where Jones batted just .238. The hamstring injury caused him to drop his hands, making it difficult for him to stay inside on pitches against righthanders. Once his health improved, Jones again displayed the strong, quick hands from both sides of the plate that generate above-average power. He also maintains patience and a keen batting eye, resulting in at least 80 walks in each of the last seven seasons.

Baserunning & Defense

Improved health was not the only reason Jones attributed to his improved play in the second half. He returned to third base at midseason after manning left field for the past few years and played the position as well as he ever has. Jones' throws had more accuracy than in the past and his range at the hot corner was above average. Although his speed rates only a hair above average, Jones remains a smart and aggressive baserunner who rarely makes mistakes on the basepaths.

2005 Outlook

Jones will celebrate his 33rd birthday in April, yet he has shown no indication of decline in his overall game. Barring injuries, his batting average should rebound to the .300 level this year. He also should make further dents in the record book, where he currently ranks sixth in Braves franchise history in hits and fifth in major league annals for home runs by a switch-hitter.

Position: 3B/LF
Bats: B **Throws:** R
Ht: 6' 4" **Wt:** 210

Opening Day Age: 32
Born: 4/24/72 in DeLand, FL
ML Seasons: 11

Overall Statistics

G	AB	R	H	D	T	HR	RBI	SB	BB	SO	Avg	OBP	Slg
137	472	69	117	20	1	30	96	2	84	96	.248	.362	.485
1542	5616	1035	1705	325	27	310	1039	118	937	877	.304	.401	.537

Where He Hits the Ball

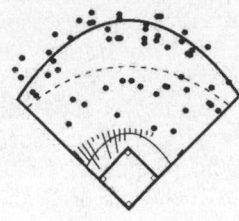 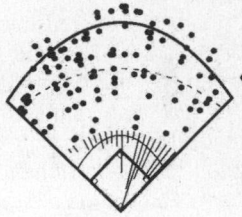

Vs. LHP   **Vs. RHP**

2004 Situational Stats

	AB	H	HR	RBI	Avg		AB	H	HR	RBI	Avg
Home	247	58	19	52	.235	LHP	149	40	12	35	.268
Road	225	59	11	44	.262	RHP	323	77	18	61	.238
First Half	220	47	12	34	.214	Sc Pos	131	35	10	66	.267
Scnd Half	252	70	18	62	.278	Clutch	66	13	3	12	.197

2004 Rankings (National League)

- 4th in lowest batting average vs. righthanded pitchers
- 5th in lowest batting average at home
- 9th in lowest batting average, lowest batting average with the bases loaded (.118) and lowest cleanup slugging percentage (.490)
- Led the Braves in RBI, sacrifice flies (7), HR frequency (15.7 ABs per HR) and cleanup slugging percentage (.490)

Atlanta

357

Adam LaRoche

2004 Season

Adam LaRoche proved to be one of the top rookies in the National League during the season's second half. The son of former major league pitcher Dave LaRoche missed 31 games after separating his left shoulder on May 28 in a home-plate collision with Philadelphia's Mike Lieberthal. He recovered and finished the season on a tear, hitting .354 with a .684 slugging average in his last 27 games. LaRoche tied a major league mark with four doubles in a game, a feat he accomplished on May 15 at Milwaukee.

Hitting

Scouted as a pitcher, LaRoche wanted to hit and only the Braves were willing to let him follow his dream. He proved his point as his rookie season progressed. LaRoche struggled early in the year when he tried to pull most pitches. Opposing pitchers also pounded him inside, yet LaRoche made the adjustment by showing more patience and taking pitches to the opposite field. Possessing a pure stroke, LaRoche can drive the ball to all fields and is capable of reaching the left-field stands at Turner Field when he keeps his weight back.

Baserunning & Defense

LaRoche is a Gold Glove-caliber defender and has even attracted comparisons to a young J.T. Snow. LaRoche moves well around the base and has excellent range. He also is capable of making excellent relay throws, a skill that comes from his years on the mound. LaRoche has benefited from the tutelage of veteran Julio Franco. LaRoche is an average runner but is not a slug on the basepaths.

2005 Outlook

LaRoche learned how to hit for power as the season progressed. He homered in consecutive games for the first time on September 28-29, then clubbed his first pinch-hit homer on the final day of the campaign. After going through several players at first over the past few years, the Braves appear to have found a fixture in LaRoche.

Position: 1B
Bats: L **Throws:** L
Ht: 6' 3" **Wt:** 180

Opening Day Age: 25
Born: 11/6/79 in Orange County, CA
ML Seasons: 1

Overall Statistics

	G	AB	R	H	D	T	HR	RBI	SB	BB	SO	Avg	OBP	Slg
'04	110	324	45	90	27	1	13	45	0	27	78	.278	.333	.488
Car.	110	324	45	90	27	1	13	45	0	27	78	.278	.333	.488

Where He Hits the Ball

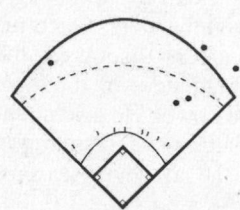
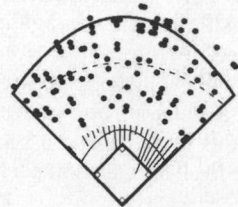

Vs. LHP   **Vs. RHP**

2004 Situational Stats

	AB	H	HR	RBI	Avg		AB	H	HR	RBI	Avg
Home	148	36	7	21	.243	LHP	20	5	1	2	.250
Road	176	54	6	24	.307	RHP	304	85	12	43	.280
First Half	152	38	3	15	.250	Sc Pos	75	19	0	26	.253
Scnd Half	172	52	10	30	.302	Clutch	48	9	0	5	.188

2004 Rankings (National League)

- 6th in lowest batting average with two strikes (.139)

Russ Ortiz

2004 Season

In his second season with the Braves, Russ Ortiz overcame an inconsistent start to the season to win National League Pitcher of the Month honors for July after posting a 5-0 record and a 1.67 ERA in six starts. However, Ortiz struggled with his control down the stretch while surrendering 14 home runs over a seven-start period, from August 14-September 14.

Pitching

Though somewhat of an enigma, the durable Ortiz eats innings and is one of the true workhorses in the major leagues. Ortiz has one of the best changeups in the game and does an outstanding job of changing speeds and altering the batter's eye level. He throws a heavy fastball in the low 90s along with a hard, sharp curveball. He adds and subtracts from his pitches and refuses to give in to hitters, sometimes to his disadvantage. That philosophy is a major reason why he ranked second in the major leagues in walks and was among the leaders in pitches per game.

Defense & Hitting

Ortiz is a good fielder with soft hands and quick reflexes. He is not shy about trying to nail a lead runner and does a good job of covering first base. He throws over to first base frequently while trying to hold runners close, but his pickoff move is only average for a righthander. Ortiz is one of the game's better hitters among moundsmen. His six career home runs are tied for third among all active pitchers.

2005 Outlook

The Braves floated Ortiz' name on the trade market around the All-Star break and passed on bringing the free agent back in 2005. In December, the righthander signed a four-year, $33 million contract to join the Arizona Diamondbacks. Ortiz was in demand during the free-agent bidding, as his 77 victories since the 2000 All-Star break are the most in the NL during that period. Too inconsistent to be deemed an ace, Ortiz is an excellent No. 2 or 3 starter who can rest a weary bullpen.

Position: SP
Bats: R **Throws:** R
Ht: 6' 1" **Wt:** 208

Opening Day Age: 30
Born: 6/5/74 in Encino, CA
ML Seasons: 7
Pronunciation: OR-teez

Overall Statistics

	W	L	Pct.	ERA	G	GS	Sv	IP	H	BB	SO	HR	Avg
'04	15	9	.625	4.13	34	34	0	204.2	197	112	143	23	.258
Car.	103	60	.632	4.00	222	212	0	1341.2	1223	682	1004	131	.245

2004 Pitching Profile

	Russ Ortiz	NL Average
Overall Strike %	59.7	62.5
1st Pitch Strike %	51.9	58.5
Ratio	1.51	1.39
Strikeouts per 9 IP	6.29	6.74
Walks per 9 IP	4.93	3.38
Home Runs per 9 IP	1.01	1.11
Strikeout/Walk Ratio	1.28	1.99
Groundball/Flyball Ratio	1.10	1.25

2004 Situational Stats

	W	L	ERA	Sv	IP		AB	H	HR	RBI	Avg
Home	7	6	4.57	0	112.1	LHB	378	97	11	42	.257
Road	8	3	3.61	0	92.1	RHB	386	100	12	42	.259
First Half	10	6	3.58	0	115.2	Sc Pos	192	42	3	56	.219
Scnd Half	5	3	4.85	0	89.0	Clutch	55	16	2	3	.291

2004 Rankings (National League)

- 1st in fielding percentage at pitcher (1.000)
- 2nd in walks allowed
- 3rd in pickoff throws (161)
- 4th in highest on-base percentage allowed (.352) and highest walks per nine innings (4.9)
- 5th in games started
- 6th in pitches thrown (3,471), lowest strike out-walk ratio (1.3) and highest ERA at home
- 7th in complete games (2) and stolen bases allowed (18)
- 9th in wins and most pitches thrown per batter (3.87)
- 10th in GDPs induced (21)
- Led the Braves in sacrifice bunts (10), wins, losses, games started, complete games (2), innings pitched, batters faced (896), home runs allowed, pitches thrown (3,471), pickoff throws (161), stolen bases allowed (18), and runners caught stealing (7)

Atlanta

John Smoltz

2004 Season

After winning 143 games in the 1990s and the Cy Young Award in 1996 as a starter, John Smoltz continued his Eckersley-esque career by becoming only the sixth pitcher in major league history to post three straight 40-save seasons. His performance was all the more impressive considering that Smoltz underwent elbow surgery to clean up some scar tissue over the winter.

Pitching

Smoltz' days as a starter are obvious, thanks to his deep repertoire for a reliever. His 88-90 MPH slider is second only to Randy Johnson's in the NL, and his fastball continues to reside in the mid-90s with excellent movement. His curveball has a nice, tight spin, and his changeup is effective because of his judicious use of the offering. The variety of pitches keeps hitters guessing, and his pure power enables Smoltz to get away with pitching up in the strike zone. His command is as good as any pitcher's in the game, with Smoltz walking only one batter during the first three months of last season. The righthander has issued a combined 21 base on balls over the past two years.

Defense & Hitting

An accomplished basketball player in his youth, the competitive Smoltz maintains excellent athleticism, which enables him to field his position well with his soft hands and quick reflexes. He has a good pickoff move, and his power repertoire keeps the running game in check. Smoltz rarely gets to bat nowadays, but as a starter he was one of the best with the bat among pitchers.

2005 Outlook

Smoltz tells anyone willing to listen how he longs to return to a starting role. His wish becomes reality in 2005, as the Braves allowed Russ Ortiz and Jaret Wright to depart as free agents and traded for closer Dan Kolb during the offseason. After developing into one of the game's premier closers over the last four seasons, Smoltz will require some time to stretch out his arm and adjust to the extra workload at age 37.

Position: RP
Bats: R **Throws:** R
Ht: 6' 3" **Wt:** 220

Opening Day Age: 37
Born: 5/15/67 in Warren, MI
ML Seasons: 16

Overall Statistics

W	L	Pct.	ERA	G	GS	Sv	IP	H	BB	SO	HR	Avg
0	1	.000	2.76	73	0	44	81.2	75	13	85	8	.245
163	121	.574	3.27	602	361	154	2699.2	2327	829	2398	216	.232

2004 Pitching Profile

	John Smoltz	NL Average
Overall Strike %	69.6	62.5
1st Pitch Strike %	70.0	58.5
Ratio	1.08	1.39
Strikeouts per 9 IP	9.37	6.74
Walks per 9 IP	1.43	3.38
Home Runs per 9 IP	0.88	1.11
Strikeout/Walk Ratio	6.54	1.99
Groundball/Flyball Ratio	1.35	1.25

2004 Situational Stats

	W	L	ERA	Sv	IP		AB	H	HR	RBI	Avg
Home	0	1	3.19	24	42.1	LHB	145	37	5	20	.255
Road	0	0	2.29	20	39.1	RHB	161	38	3	7	.236
First Half	0	0	2.41	16	41.0	Sc Pos	76	19	3	21	.250
Scnd Half	0	1	3.10	28	40.2	Clutch	222	51	5	20	.230

2004 Rankings (National League)

- 3rd in games finished (61)
- 4th in saves and save percentage (89.8)
- 7th in most strikeouts per nine innings in relief (9.4)
- 9th in most GDPs induced per GDP situation (20.0%) and fewest baserunners allowed per nine innings in relief (9.7)
- Led the Braves in saves, games finished (61), wild pitches (6), most GDPs induced per GDP situation (20.0%), save percentage (89.8), first batter efficiency (.200), relief innings (81.2), most strikeouts per nine innings in relief (9.4), and fewest baserunners allowed per nine innings in relief (9.7)

John Thomson

2004 Season

Pitching for his fourth major league team in three seasons, John Thomson put together his best showing at the game's top level by posting a career-high 14 victories. He was at his best in the second half, going 8-1 in 15 starts and allowing two earned runs or less in 12 of those outings. The righthander ended the season with a five-game winning streak and went 4-0 with a 1.36 ERA during September.

Pitching

Thomson's performance has improved the past two years by learning from the masters. At Texas in 2003, Rangers pitching coach Orel Hershiser worked with Thomson on his changeup and tight curveball, which he uses as his offspeed pitch. Last year, Atlanta pitching coach Leo Mazzone convinced Thomson to use both sides of the plate for the first time in his career. The righthander continued to jam hitters with his fastball, but his sinker was particularly effective when he started working it down and away, especially against righthanded hitters. Thomson also has the best command of any Atlanta starter not named Byrd.

Defense & Hitting

By trying to coax hitters into putting the ball on the ground, Thomson has had plenty of practice as a fielder. He can hold his own with the leather, and shows decent athleticism around the mound and in covering first base. His pickoff move is not effective, and his methodical delivery means only Russ Ortiz surrendered more stolen bases than the 14 the Braves gave up with Thomson on the mound. At bat, Thomson recorded 10 sacrifice bunts and 13 hits, two more than Mike Hampton, who has the reputation as the game's best hitting pitcher.

2005 Outlook

Thomson is putting things together and pitching as well as he ever has in the major leagues. He is a more polished pitcher than he was two years ago and has the ability to be a 15-game winner for the next several seasons.

Position: SP
Bats: R **Throws:** R
Ht: 6' 3" **Wt:** 220

Opening Day Age: 31
Born: 10/1/73 in Vicksburg, MS
ML Seasons: 7
Nickname: Red

Overall Statistics

	W	L	Pct.	ERA	G	GS	Sv	IP	H	BB	SO	HR	Avg
'04	14	8	.636	3.72	33	33	0	198.1	210	52	133	20	.276
Car.	56	71	.441	4.71	179	178	0	1080.2	1181	306	690	137	.280

2004 Pitching Profile

	John Thomson	NL Average
Overall Strike %	65.1	62.5
1st Pitch Strike %	63.4	58.5
Ratio	1.32	1.39
Strikeouts per 9 IP	6.04	6.74
Walks per 9 IP	2.36	3.38
Home Runs per 9 IP	0.91	1.11
Strikeout/Walk Ratio	2.56	1.99
Groundball/Flyball Ratio	1.36	1.25

2004 Situational Stats

	W	L	ERA	Sv	IP		AB	H	HR	RBI	Avg
Home	7	4	4.03	0	91.2	LHB	339	93	9	38	.274
Road	7	4	3.46	0	106.2	RHB	422	117	11	50	.277
First Half	6	7	4.82	0	106.1	Sc Pos	184	50	4	61	.272
Scnd Half	8	1	2.45	0	92.0	Clutch	29	8	2	3	.276

2004 Rankings (National League)

- 6th in GDPs induced (24)
- 7th in fewest pitches thrown per batter (3.52)
- 8th in pickoff throws (115)
- 9th in highest batting average allowed (.276)
- 10th in most run support per nine innings (5.9)
- Led the Braves in sacrifice bunts (10), hits allowed, hit batsmen (6), GDPs induced (24), lowest ERA on the road and most run support per nine innings (5.9)

Atlanta

Jaret Wright

2004 Season

After recording only nine wins in the major leagues over the previous four seasons, Jaret Wright proved to be the game's top rags-to-riches story in 2004. The righthander won a career-high 15 games while leading the Atlanta rotation in ERA and strikeouts. He posted a nine-game winning streak at midseason, and limited opponents to a .242 batting average, good for 10th in the National League. A bruised foot suffered in his final regular-season start limited Wright's effectiveness against the Astros in the playoffs.

Pitching

Shoulder problems had hindered Wright since he enjoyed a promising start with the Indians in 1997. Improved health last year enabled him to get the necessary extension on his delivery, resulting in as much as 6-8 inches of additional movement on his pitches. He also started throwing his sinker again after ditching the pitch because of his ailing shoulder, and he made impressive progress with his command by focusing on location instead of chucking every pitch with maximum effort. Wright hits the outside corner with his mid-90s fastball against righties, while his running heater comes back over the inside part of the plate against lefties. He has improved his strikeout-walk ratio by doing a better job of commanding his changeup and breaking ball.

Defense & Hitting

Wright does a decent job of fielding his position. His pickoff move is nothing special, but he is capable of holding baserunners reasonably close with a quick delivery to home plate. He is no better than an average hitter, posting a half-dozen hits and the same number of sacrifice bunts.

2005 Outlook

Wright was not at the top of the list among Atlanta rotation candidates when spring training opened last year, but he concluded the campaign as the Braves' ace. Although Wright entered the offseason as a free agent, Atlanta was expected to be aggressive in retaining the righthander's services because of the 29-year-old's considerable potential.

Position: SP
Bats: R **Throws:** R
Ht: 6' 2" **Wt:** 230

Opening Day Age: 29
Born: 12/29/75 in Anaheim, CA
ML Seasons: 8

Overall Statistics

	W	L	Pct.	ERA	G	GS	Sv	IP	H	BB	SO	HR	Avg
'04	15	8	.652	3.28	32	32	0	186.1	168	70	159	11	.242
Car.	52	45	.536	5.09	180	128	2	758.1	796	369	569	80	.272

2004 Pitching Profile

	Jaret Wright	NL Average
Overall Strike %	60.7	62.5
1st Pitch Strike %	57.4	58.5
Ratio	1.28	1.39
Strikeouts per 9 IP	7.68	6.74
Walks per 9 IP	3.38	3.38
Home Runs per 9 IP	0.53	1.11
Strikeout/Walk Ratio	2.27	1.99
Groundball/Flyball Ratio	1.28	1.25

2004 Situational Stats

	W	L	ERA	Sv	IP		AB	H	HR	RBI	Avg
Home	6	3	2.56	0	95.0	LHB	347	90	8	40	.259
Road	9	5	4.04	0	91.1	RHB	347	78	3	26	.225
First Half	6	5	3.58	0	98.0	Sc Pos	159	36	2	52	.226
Scnd Half	9	3	2.95	0	88.1	Clutch	17	4	1	1	.235

2004 Rankings (National League)

- 1st in fewest home runs allowed per nine innings (.53)
- 4th in lowest slugging percentage allowed (.337)
- 5th in highest stolen-base percentage allowed (86.7)
- 6th in lowest ERA at home
- 9th in wins
- 10th in lowest batting average allowed (.242) and most strikeouts per nine innings (7.7)
- Led the Braves in ERA, wins, strikeouts, winning percentage, lowest batting average allowed (.242), lowest slugging percentage allowed (.337), lowest ERA at home, fewest home runs allowed per nine innings (.53), and most strikeouts per nine innings (7.7)

Antonio Alfonseca

Signed By MARLINS

Position: RP
Bats: R **Throws:** R
Ht: 6' 5" **Wt:** 250

Opening Day Age: 32
Born: 4/16/72 in La Romana, DR
ML Seasons: 8
Pronunciation: al-fon-SAY-kah

Overall Statistics

	W	L	Pct.	ERA	G	GS	Sv	IP	H	BB	SO	HR	Avg
'04	6	4	.600	2.57	79	0	0	73.2	71	28	45	5	.255
Car.	29	34	.460	3.89	479	0	121	520.0	560	202	355	47	.278

2004 Situational Stats

	W	L	ERA	Sv	IP		AB	H	HR	RBI	Avg
Home	4	1	1.30	0	41.2	LHB	117	29	3	9	.248
Road	2	3	4.22	0	32.0	RHB	161	42	2	16	.261
First Half	5	3	3.32	0	40.2	Sc Pos	90	19	0	19	.211
Scnd Half	1	1	1.64	0	33.0	Clutch	113	28	2	10	.248

2004 Season

Signed in the offseason to help fill the Braves' barren bullpen, Antonio Alfonseca posted a career-low 2.57 ERA in a career-high 79 appearances. Alfonseca was the team's best reliever from August 17 through the end of the season, surrendering just three earned runs over his last 25 outings.

Pitching, Defense & Hitting

Alfonseca has re-established himself as one of the National League's better setup men. His attack is centered on his above-average sinker. If that pitch is working, Alfonseca is hard to beat. If not, he usually finds himself in trouble, particularly with his overall command. At the behest of Atlanta pitching coach Leo Mazzone, Alfonseca added a changeup during spring training, yet rarely used the pitch when his sinker failed. The righthander has good quickness for a big man and is an average fielder, but he's vulnerable to basestealers. Alfonseca struck out his lone trip to the plate last year.

2005 Outlook

Although he had success as a closer with the Marlins a few years ago, Alfonseca's makeup appears better suited for the seventh and eighth innings. His performance in 2004 guaranteed him a decent contract, and Alfonseca agreed to a two-year deal to return to Florida.

Paul Byrd

Position: SP
Bats: R **Throws:** R
Ht: 6' 1" **Wt:** 190

Opening Day Age: 34
Born: 12/3/70 in Louisville, KY
ML Seasons: 9

Overall Statistics

	W	L	Pct.	ERA	G	GS	Sv	IP	H	BB	SO	HR	Avg
'04	8	7	.533	3.94	19	19	0	114.1	123	19	79	18	.270
Car.	60	53	.531	4.33	215	127	0	907.1	919	262	552	137	.262

2004 Situational Stats

	W	L	ERA	Sv	IP		AB	H	HR	RBI	Avg
Home	3	5	3.79	0	57.0	LHB	213	70	7	22	.329
Road	5	2	4.08	0	57.1	RHB	242	53	11	27	.219
First Half	2	1	2.82	0	22.1	Sc Pos	94	20	2	26	.213
Scnd Half	6	6	4.21	0	92.0	Clutch	17	8	0	1	.471

2004 Season

After undergoing ligament replacement surgery on his right elbow on July 1, 2003, Paul Byrd returned to the Atlanta rotation last June and allowed three earned runs or less in 15 of his 19 starts. His eight victories represented the third-highest total in his major league career.

Pitching, Defense & Hitting

Byrd showed surprising arm strength for his first year back from surgery. He continued to be tough on righthanders with his old-fashioned, over-the-head delivery, mixing his low-90s fastball with a sharp slider and solid changeup. When lefties began touching him, Byrd proved his arm felt fine by throwing a sinkerball. His sinker breaks away from lefthanded hitters and induces groundball outs. Byrd is an excellent fielder but will surrender stolen bases with his slow delivery. Byrd is a good hitter who makes consistent contact.

2005 Outlook

Byrd entered the offseason as a free agent, but he appreciates the patience the Braves showed during his recovery and has let those close to him know he wants to return to Atlanta. If his arm continues to gain strength the way most pitchers do in their second year removed from surgery, Byrd could flirt with a 15-win campaign.

Atlanta

Juan Cruz

Position: RP
Bats: R **Throws:** R
Ht: 6' 2" **Wt:** 165

Opening Day Age: 26
Born: 10/15/78 in
Bonao, DR
ML Seasons: 4

Overall Statistics

	W	L	Pct.	ERA	G	GS	Sv	IP	H	BB	SO	HR	Avg
'04	6	2	.750	2.75	50	0	0	72.0	59	30	70	7	.224
Car.	14	21	.400	3.99	128	23	1	275.0	249	134	255	29	.245

2004 Situational Stats

	W	L	ERA	Sv	IP		AB	H	HR	RBI	Avg
Home	3	0	1.50	0	42.0	LHB	109	26	3	11	.239
Road	3	2	4.50	0	30.0	RHB	154	33	4	15	.214
First Half	2	0	3.41	0	37.0	Sc Pos	63	10	1	16	.159
Scnd Half	4	2	2.06	0	35.0	Clutch	58	14	1	4	.241

2004 Season

The Braves obtained one of the better young arms in the game in Juan Cruz on March 25, 2004, acquiring the righthander from the Cubs in exchange for two minor leaguers. Cruz owned the second-best strikeouts-per-nine innings ratio among Atlanta relievers at 8.75 and the second-best bullpen ERA as well (2.75).

Pitching, Defense & Hitting

Cruz was a starter in the minors, but stamina was a question, which may translate into a permanent role as a reliever. He can make hitters' lives difficult with his sinking mid-90s fastball and a good changeup that features both fade and depth. He challenges hitters and can be nasty against righties. Lack of consistent command sometimes causes him to be too fine, which leads to gopher balls. Cruz is not a good fielder but continues to show improvement in controlling the running game. He was a decent hitter in the minors.

2005 Outlook

Deemed one of the Cubs' top prospects while in the minors, Cruz has yet to achieve his full potential. His arm strength and overall stuff are undeniable, which could lead to bigger things in the near future. In the meantime, Cruz will be a key component in the Atlanta bullpen again this year.

Mark DeRosa

Position: 3B/SS
Bats: R **Throws:** R
Ht: 6' 1" **Wt:** 205

Opening Day Age: 30
Born: 2/26/75 in
Passaic, NJ
ML Seasons: 7

Overall Statistics

	G	AB	R	H	D	T	HR	RBI	SB	BB	SO	Avg	OBP	Slg
'04	118	309	33	74	16	0	3	31	1	23	53	.239	.293	.320
Car.	393	975	135	259	48	2	17	99	6	65	149	.266	.318	.371

2004 Situational Stats

	AB	H	HR	RBI	Avg		AB	H	HR	RBI	Avg
Home	140	29	0	5	.207	LHP	86	20	1	6	.233
Road	169	45	3	26	.266	RHP	223	54	2	25	.242
First Half	249	58	3	26	.233	Sc Pos	75	14	0	24	.187
Scnd Half	60	16	0	5	.267	Clutch	52	12	0	5	.231

2004 Season

Deemed the starting third baseman after the Braves lost Vinny Castilla to free agency, Mark DeRosa lost his job in June when Chipper Jones was shifted back to third base from left field. A .178 batting average in May and an Atlanta record-tying four errors in one game on May 2 contributed to DeRosa's downfall. DeRosa rebounded to hit safely in 16 of his last 23 starts before suffering a tear of his right ACL on September 25.

Hitting, Baserunning & Defense

The versatile DeRosa is capable of playing average defense at all four infield positions and left field, and will not hurt a team at shortstop for short stretches. His hands are soft, his range is good and his arm is strong enough for third, but not ideal to make the throw from the hole at short. DeRosa is an aggressive hitter with average power. He hurt himself last year by swinging at bad pitches and getting behind in the count. DeRosa has average speed but runs the bases well.

2005 Outlook

In all likelihood, last year was DeRosa's final chance to became a starter in Atlanta. His roster spot, however, remains secure under manager Bobby Cox, provided DeRosa accepts his role as a pinch-hitter and versatile reserve.

Julio Franco

Position: 1B
Bats: R **Throws:** R
Ht: 6' 1" **Wt:** 188

Opening Day Age: 46
Born: 8/23/58 in San Pedro de Macoris, DR
ML Seasons: 20

Overall Statistics

G	AB	R	H	D	T	HR	RBI	SB	BB	SO	Avg	OBP	Slg
125	320	37	99	18	3	6	57	4	36	68	.309	.378	.441
2269	8189	1233	2457	382	53	161	1110	269	863	1212	.300	.366	.419

2004 Situational Stats

	AB	H	HR	RBI	Avg		AB	H	HR	RBI	Avg
Home	175	59	5	36	.337	LHP	134	41	2	20	.306
Road	145	40	1	21	.276	RHP	186	58	4	37	.312
First Half	174	48	6	30	.276	Sc Pos	95	33	4	53	.347
Scnd Half	146	51	0	27	.349	Clutch	55	18	1	12	.327

2004 Season

Julio Franco must have discovered the fountain of youth. The first baseman added to his legacy last year while celebrating his 46th birthday. His .309 batting average was the highest since 1900 for a player who opened a campaign at age 43 or older. Franco also led the Braves with 15 pinch-hits and 16 pinch-hit RBI.

Hitting, Baserunning & Defense

With the bat wrapped around his head and his knees nearly knocking, Franco employs an unorthodox, yet effective swing. He batted over .300 against both righties and lefties last year, and he can drive the ball to all parts of the field. He maintains decent speed and runs the bases well, enabling him to steal four bases in six attempts last year. Franco also continues to man first base extremely well. A former middle infielder, he has soft hands and quick feet around the base.

2005 Outlook

Based on the way the chiseled infielder has played the last three seasons with the Braves, Franco is destined to establish a few more records before his playing days conclude. Although he entered the offseason as a free agent, Franco was re-signed and should be a significant part of the Atlanta bench.

Kevin Gryboski

Position: RP
Bats: R **Throws:** R
Ht: 6' 5" **Wt:** 225

Opening Day Age: 31
Born: 11/15/73 in Wilkes-Barre, PA
ML Seasons: 3
Pronunciation: gri-BOS-ski

Overall Statistics

	W	L	Pct.	ERA	G	GS	Sv	IP	H	BB	SO	HR	Avg
'04	3	2	.600	2.84	69	0	2	50.2	54	23	24	2	.280
Car.	11	7	.611	3.38	190	0	2	146.2	148	83	89	11	.269

2004 Situational Stats

	W	L	ERA	Sv	IP		AB	H	HR	RBI	Avg
Home	2	0	4.03	1	29.0	LHB	68	21	1	14	.309
Road	1	2	1.25	1	21.2	RHB	125	33	1	20	.264
First Half	1	1	3.04	1	26.2	Sc Pos	80	24	0	31	.300
Scnd Half	2	1	2.63	1	24.0	Clutch	76	19	1	14	.250

2004 Season

In his third season as a prominent member of the Atlanta bullpen, Kevin Gryboski attained career-bests with 69 appearances and a 2.84 ERA. He gave up only two home runs all season.

Pitching, Defense & Hitting

Gryboski had a good ERA last year, but he lived dangerously for much of the campaign. He struggled with his control, leading to an average of more than four walks per nine innings. His heavy, sinking fastball in the low 90s was effective against righthanders, but lefties teed off on him when he had difficulty placing his heater low and inside. Gryboski's strength is his ability to induce groundball outs. The righthander possesses supreme confidence in his ability. His fielding is adequate, but his relatively slow delivery prevents him from holding runners on base.

2005 Outlook

Gryboski is a favorite of Atlanta manager Bobby Cox, if for no other reason than his intense competitiveness and guile. Cox saw potential where others did not, as Gryboski toiled in the minors for more than seven years before the Braves gave him a shot at the big league level. The righthander will have a significant role in the Atlanta bullpen again this year.

Eli Marrero

Position: LF/RF
Bats: R **Throws:** R
Ht: 6' 1" **Wt:** 180

Opening Day Age: 31
Born: 11/17/73 in Havana, Cuba
ML Seasons: 8
Pronunciation: muh-RARE-ro

Overall Statistics

	G	AB	R	H	D	T	HR	RBI	SB	BB	SO	Avg	OBP	Slg
'04	90	250	37	80	18	1	10	40	4	23	50	.320	.374	.520
Car.	615	1675	232	419	88	10	53	227	50	142	303	.250	.307	.410

2004 Situational Stats

	AB	H	HR	RBI	Avg			AB	H	HR	RBI	Avg
Home	112	35	6	21	.313		LHP	106	44	5	21	.415
Road	138	45	4	19	.326		RHP	144	36	5	19	.250
First Half	115	39	5	20	.339		Sc Pos	60	21	4	31	.350
Scnd Half	135	41	5	20	.304		Clutch	48	11	0	6	.229

2004 Season

Acquired from St. Louis during the 2003 winter meetings, Eli Marrero missed the first seven games with a strained abdominal muscle and 30 games in late April and May with an upper respiratory infection. Finally healthy, Marrero batted at a .342 clip after coming off the disabled list on May 29.

Hitting, Baserunning & Defense

Fully regaining his strength at midseason, Marrero hit for both power and average while batting everywhere in the lineup except leadoff and cleanup. Marrero appeared to be more confident at the plate than in the past and used the entire field instead of trying to pull most pitches, as he had with the Cardinals. Marrero was just as versatile defensively, seeing action at all three outfield positions. Possessing slightly above-average speed, he has good range in the garden and is an excellent baserunner. His arm is strong enough to return to catcher if the need should arise.

2005 Outlook

Marrero was everything he was advertised to be and more for the Braves last year. He will resume his role as a fourth outfielder and pinch-hitter in 2005, and should accumulate 250-300 at-bats in 100 or so appearances.

Horacio Ramirez

Position: SP
Bats: L **Throws:** L
Ht: 6' 1" **Wt:** 219

Opening Day Age: 25
Born: 11/24/79 in Carson, CA
ML Seasons: 2

Overall Statistics

	W	L	Pct.	ERA	G	GS	Sv	IP	H	BB	SO	HR	Avg
'04	2	4	.333	2.39	10	9	0	60.1	51	30	31	7	.226
Car.	14	8	.636	3.60	39	38	0	242.2	232	102	131	28	.254

2004 Situational Stats

	W	L	ERA	Sv	IP			AB	H	HR	RBI	Avg
Home	1	0	1.93	0	23.1		LHB	50	11	2	5	.220
Road	1	4	2.68	0	37.0		RHB	176	40	5	16	.227
First Half	2	4	2.28	0	59.1		Sc Pos	52	10	0	13	.192
Scnd Half	0	0	9.00	0	1.0		Clutch	14	3	1	1	.214

2004 Season

Lefthander Horacio Ramirez got off to a strong start last season before tendinitis in his left shoulder caused him to miss four months. After making his final start on May 25, Ramirez ranked fifth in the National League with a 2.28 ERA. He pitched in relief in one game, on September 26, and concluded the campaign limiting opposing hitters to a paltry .226 batting average.

Pitching, Defense & Hitting

Ramirez has attracted comparisons to a young Tom Glavine with the way he is able to work the corners and keep his pitches down in the strike zone. He mixes a four-seam fastball in the low 90s with a cutter that has a sharp break, resembling a slider. His changeup adds a foot to his fastball because of the contrast in speeds. A decent fielder, Ramirez' pickoff move rates among the best in the NL. He is not accomplished with the lumber.

2005 Outlook

Even though Ramirez regained much of the strength in his shoulder by the end of the season, the Braves had no desire to remove the resurgent Paul Byrd from the rotation. With Atlanta losing a few starting pitchers to free agency, a healthy Ramirez will be needed in order for the team to compete in the NL East.

Chris Reitsma

Position: RP
Bats: R **Throws:** R
Ht: 6' 5" **Wt:** 235

Opening Day Age: 27
Born: 12/31/77 in Minneapolis, MN
ML Seasons: 4
Pronunciation: REETS-muh

Overall Statistics

	W	L	Pct.	ERA	G	GS	Sv	IP	H	BB	SO	HR	Avg
'04	6	4	.600	4.07	84	0	2	79.2	89	20	60	9	.284
Car.	28	36	.438	4.44	209	53	14	484.0	534	133	293	63	.280

2004 Situational Stats

	W	L	ERA	Sv	IP		AB	H	HR	RBI	Avg
Home	2	2	3.92	1	39.0	LHB	145	45	4	19	.310
Road	4	2	4.20	1	40.2	RHB	168	44	5	15	.262
First Half	3	2	3.78	0	47.2	Sc Pos	73	13	3	25	.178
Scnd Half	3	2	4.50	2	32.0	Clutch	186	59	6	26	.317

2004 Season

Acquired from the Reds on March 26, 2004, in exchange for pitchers Jung Bong and Bubba Nelson, Chris Reitsma appeared in a franchise-record 84 games out of the Atlanta bullpen. The righthander tied for second in the NL with 31 holds and allowed just three of 20 inherited runners to score (all in the same game, on June 22 at Florida).

Pitching, Defense & Hitting

Reitsma's bread-and-butter pitch is a mid-90s sinker that produces numerous groundballs. He also throws a decent changeup and a four-seam fastball, a pitch he employs mostly against left-handed hitters. The extended workload last year caused his fastball to flatten out, and he also struggled during the middle portion of the campaign when he lost the feel of his changeup. Reitsma fields his position well and does a good job of holding runners with a slide step and a quickened delivery to the plate. His hitting is not a factor.

2005 Outlook

Reitsma's season came to a raw end when he gave up four runs in the seventh inning of Game 5 in the National League Division Series. Only 27, he gives the Braves a much-needed young presence in the bullpen and should become a mainstay with a repeat performance of his 2004 slate.

Charles Thomas

Position: LF
Bats: L **Throws:** L
Ht: 6' 0" **Wt:** 190

Opening Day Age: 26
Born: 12/26/78 in Fairfield, CA
ML Seasons: 1

Overall Statistics

	G	AB	R	H	D	T	HR	RBI	SB	BB	SO	Avg	OBP	Slg
'04	83	236	35	68	8	4	7	31	3	21	45	.288	.368	.445
Car.	83	236	35	68	8	4	7	31	3	21	45	.288	.368	.445

2004 Situational Stats

	AB	H	HR	RBI	Avg		AB	H	HR	RBI	Avg
Home	123	36	2	15	.293	LHP	32	9	1	8	.281
Road	113	32	5	16	.283	RHP	204	59	6	23	.289
First Half	46	16	3	9	.348	Sc Pos	66	17	1	21	.258
Scnd Half	190	52	4	22	.274	Clutch	33	5	0	0	.152

2004 Season

Charles Thomas went from being a relative unknown in the organization last season to Atlanta's starting left fielder. He was leading the International League in hitting in June when he received an unexpected promotion after Dewayne Wise succumbed to an injury. Thomas made the most of the opportunity by hitting .400 in his first 19 games while energizing the club.

Hitting, Baserunning & Defense

Thomas was struggling in Class-A ball midway through the 2003 season before he received an injury-related promotion to Double-A Greenville. He began driving the ball to the gaps, and continued to hit to all fields last year. Thomas is best when he keeps the ball on the ground and uses his plus speed. He also can steal bases, but his greatest strength is his heady, opportunistic baserunning. Thomas has excellent range in the outfield and an above-average arm with good accuracy.

2005 Outlook

Thomas attracted rave reviews last season, but he showed late in the campaign that he will need to make adjustments in order to remain an impact player. If he proves this spring that he is not a one-year wonder, Thomas will serve as the Braves' starting left fielder or fourth outfielder.

Atlanta

Armando Almanza (Pos: LHP, Age: 32)

	W	L	Pct.	ERA	G	GS	Sv	IP	H	BB	SO	HR	Avg
'04	1	1	.500	6.17	13	0	0	11.2	9	7	13	3	.200
Car.	14	13	.519	4.87	248	0	2	210.2	184	133	230	33	.238

Almanza failed to find his form in his first year back since elbow surgery. He was demoted to Triple-A Richmond after posting a lofty 6.17 ERA in Atlanta. He signed a minor league deal with the Giants in December. 2005 Outlook: B

Will Cunnane (Pos: RHP, Age: 30)

	W	L	Pct.	ERA	G	GS	Sv	IP	H	BB	SO	HR	Avg
'04	1	1	.500	7.30	9	0	0	12.1	18	4	11	3	.346
Car.	13	12	.520	5.26	184	12	3	274.0	312	128	234	38	.289

Cunnane made the final roster spot out of spring training but missed an opportunity to solidify a bullpen role after struggling out of the gate. He was once again victimized by the longball, and by May found himself back in Richmond. 2005 Outlook: C

Tim Drew (Pos: RHP, Age: 26)

	W	L	Pct.	ERA	G	GS	Sv	IP	H	BB	SO	HR	Avg
'04	0	0	–	4.50	11	0	0	16.0	21	5	7	2	.318
Car.	2	4	.333	7.02	35	11	2	84.2	113	39	40	16	.322

Drew impressed during brief stints in Atlanta. One bad outing against the Padres inflated his overall line, but a 1.42 ERA in his other 10 appearances will give him an outside chance of making someone's bullpen in 2005. 2005 Outlook: C

Jesse Garcia (Pos: SS/2B, Age: 31, Bats: R)

	G	AB	R	H	D	T	HR	RBI	SB	BB	SO	Avg	OBP	Slg
'04	50	115	14	29	4	1	1	10	1	16	.252	.265	.330
Car.	155	237	37	53	5	2	3	19	7	5	37	.224	.243	.300

The Braves' organization did not need another backup infielder, so Garcia was released in September. He signed a minor league deal with the Padres in the hope that they are looking for someone with a little speed and a steady glove to fill a utility role. 2005 Outlook: C

Nick Green (Pos: 2B, Age: 26, Bats: R)

	G	AB	R	H	D	T	HR	RBI	SB	BB	SO	Avg	OBP	Slg
'04	95	264	40	72	15	3	3	26	1	12	63	.273	.312	.386
Car.	95	264	40	72	15	3	3	26	1	12	63	.273	.312	.386

Green filled in admirably at second base when Marcus Giles went down with a broken clavicle. Green got off to a quick start with Atlanta, reaching base in nearly 40 percent of his at-bats through his first 17 games, but cooled down as the season progressed. 2005 Outlook: C

Mike Hessman (Pos: 1B, Age: 27, Bats: R)

	G	AB	R	H	D	T	HR	RBI	SB	BB	SO	Avg	OBP	Slg
'04	29	69	8	9	3	0	2	5	0	1	24	.130	.155	.261
Car.	48	90	10	15	5	0	4	8	0	6	30	.167	.227	.356

Hessman has been wholly unproductive in his cameos with Atlanta. He's looked completely overmatched by big league righthanders, as they have dominated him to the tune of .137/.185/.294. 2005 Outlook: C

Damon Hollins (Pos: LF, Age: 30, Bats: R)

	G	AB	R	H	D	T	HR	RBI	SB	BB	SO	Avg	OBP	Slg
'04	7	22	3	8	2	0	0	5	0	0	4	.364	.364	.455
Car.	15	37	4	11	2	0	0	7	0	0	7	.297	.297	.351

Hollins appeared to be following in the long line of prospects-turned-suspects. To everyone's astonishment, he hit 20 homers and slugged .553 at Triple-A Richmond. Tampa Bay signed him to a minor league deal in November. 2005 Outlook: C

Tom Martin (Pos: LHP, Age: 34)

	W	L	Pct.	ERA	G	GS	Sv	IP	H	BB	SO	HR	Avg
'04	0	2	.000	3.97	76	0	1	45.1	49	19	30	7	.283
Car.	9	9	.500	4.73	278	0	3	228.1	239	107	168	27	.272

While in Los Angeles, Martin began to emulate his teammate's ferocity and focus, going so far as to wear Gagne-like eyewear. The adjustments turned Martin into one of the better lefthanded relievers in the league. 2005 Outlook: A

Sam McConnell (Pos: LHP, Age: 29)

	W	L	Pct.	ERA	G	GS	Sv	IP	H	BB	SO	HR	Avg
'04	1	0	1.000	3.86	10	0	0	9.1	11	4	4	0	.289
Car.	1	0	1.000	3.86	10	0	0	9.1	11	4	4	0	.289

McConnell finally cracked through the Triple-A level and picked up his first major league win. He possesses an above-average change and has what scouts call pitchability. His command and know-how could place him at the back of the Braves' rotation. 2005 Outlook: B

Eddie Perez (Pos: C, Age: 36, Bats: R)

	G	AB	R	H	D	T	HR	RBI	SB	BB	SO	Avg	OBP	Slg
'04	74	170	14	39	12	0	3	13	0	11	29	.229	.286	.353
Car.	548	1487	134	378	83	2	38	166	1	83	229	.254	.298	.389

Who could have envisioned a scenario where Greg Maddux would be leaving Atlanta while Perez was coming back? Defensively solid and career savvy, Perez has made a nice living as the most famous "personal catcher" of this generation. 2005 Outlook: C

Travis Smith (Pos: RHP, Age: 32)

	W	L	Pct.	ERA	G	GS	Sv	IP	H	BB	SO	HR	Avg
'04	2	3	.400	6.20	16	4	0	40.2	48	12	26	12	.293
Car.	6	5	.545	6.61	29	14	0	96.2	118	32	59	22	.306

With a minor league resume of more than 1,000 innings pitched, an 82-45 record and a 3.62 ERA, it is hard to imagine why Smith has not gotten any extended looks. He signed a minor league deal with the Marlins shortly after the season ended. 2005 Outlook: C

Dewayne Wise (Pos: LF/RF, Age: 27, Bats: L)

	G	AB	R	H	D	T	HR	RBI	SB	BB	SO	Avg	OBP	Slg
'04	77	162	24	37	9	4	6	17	6	9	28	.228	.272	.444
Car.	147	296	41	60	13	5	9	30	12	14	48	.203	.243	.372

Wise was one of three non-roster invitees to make the Opening Day roster. A pulled left hamstring and strained left elbow limited his effectiveness, and he was claimed off waivers by Detroit in October. 2005 Outlook: C

Atlanta Braves Minor League Prospects

Organization Overview:

The Braves are riding an unfathomable wave of 13 straight division titles because of the constant production emitting from the farm system. In 2004, first baseman Adam LaRoche's arrival gave Atlanta a homegrown infield. The team also received significant contributions from rookies Nick Green and Charles Thomas, unheralded prospects who made the most of their opportunities. The Braves may have more depth in their organization than at any time in the past dozen years. Atlanta features a plethora of lefthanded hitting outfielders, several premier shortstops and three potential major league catchers in Brian McCann, Jarrod Saltalamacchia and Brayan Pena. Pitching, which is always a team strength, is deep at every level.

Wilson Betemit

Position: 3B
Bats: B **Throws:** R
Ht: 6' 3" **Wt:** 190

Opening Day Age: 24
Born: 7/28/80 in Santo Domingo, DR

Recent Statistics

	G	AB	R	H	D	T	HR	RBI	SB	BB	SO	Avg
2004 AAA Richmond	105	356	48	99	24	2	13	59	3	32	99	.278
2004 NL Atlanta	22	47	2	8	0	0	0	3	0	4	16	.170

Betemit received considerable attention following the 2001 season, when he climbed from high Class-A Myrtle Beach to Atlanta. Since then he has been unable to produce consistently, thereby reducing the expectations for a player once deemed a potential superstar. Nevertheless, the switch-hitting Betemit is expected to spend 2005 with the Braves. He sprays line drives to all fields and continues to add power to his game. He also has good hands and decent range, and his arm strength ranks among the best among infielders in the Atlanta farm system. If he can continue to make strides with his consistency at the plate, particularly from the right side, Betemit still could emerge as significant contributor at the big league level.

Kyle Davies

Position: P
Bats: R **Throws:** R
Ht: 6' 3" **Wt:** 195

Opening Day Age: 21
Born: 9/9/83 in Decatur, GA

Recent Statistics

	W	L	ERA	G	GS	Sv	IP	H	R	BB	SO	HR
2003 A Rome	8	8	2.89	27	27	0	146.1	128	52	53	148	9
2004 A Myrtle Beach	9	2	2.63	14	14	0	75.1	55	24	32	95	3
2004 AAA Richmond	0	1	9.00	1	1	0	5.0	5	5	3	5	0
2004 AA Greenville	4	0	2.32	11	10	0	62.0	40	18	22	73	9

After doing things his way during his first two years in the Atlanta farm system, Davies decided to take the Braves' advice and alter the mechanics of his delivery prior to the 2003 slate. He overcame some initial awkwardness to put together a solid showing before dominating at every step during the 2004 campaign. Davies is one of the fiercest competitors in the minors. His changeup rates as the best in the Atlanta system, and his hard fastball, which has increased in velocity from 86-87 MPH to 92-93 MPH since revamping his mechanics, can be overpowering. Davies' command has made significant strides of late, and the consistency of his slider will determine how soon he is pitching in Atlanta.

Jeff Francoeur

Position: OF
Bats: R **Throws:** R
Ht: 6' 4" **Wt:** 205

Opening Day Age: 21
Born: 1/8/84 in Atlanta, GA

Recent Statistics

	G	AB	R	H	D	T	HR	RBI	SB	BB	SO	Avg
2003 A Rome	134	524	78	147	26	9	14	68	14	30	68	.281
2004 A Myrtle Beach	88	334	56	98	26	0	15	52	10	22	70	.293
2004 AA Greenville	18	76	8	15	2	0	3	9	1	0	14	.197

Atlanta's first-round draft pick in 2002, Francoeur showed his desire and toughness last season when he suffered a broken cheekbone upon fouling a bunt attempt in July. Expected to miss the rest of the year after undergoing surgery, he returned a month later and earned a promotion to Double-A. An aggressive hitter with a line-drive stroke, Francoeur has plus power and is expected to hit for a high average in the majors. He possesses exceptional speed and is an intelligent baserunner. He has the speed and range to play center field and the arm to man right, with his ultimate destination to be determined by the needs of the parent club.

Kelly Johnson

Position: OF
Bats: L **Throws:** R
Ht: 6' 1" **Wt:** 180

Opening Day Age: 23
Born: 2/22/82 in Austin, TX

Recent Statistics

	G	AB	R	H	D	T	HR	RBI	SB	BB	SO	Avg
2003 R GC Braves	6	26	10	10	1	1	1	3	1	3	4	.385
2003 AA Greenville	98	334	46	92	22	5	6	45	10	35	81	.275
2004 AA Greenville	135	479	70	135	35	3	16	50	9	49	102	.282

A shortstop since he was drafted with the 38th overall pick in 2000, Johnson made a seamless move to the outfield last year at Double-A and proved capable of manning all three positions. He showed excellent range and got good jumps on balls while displaying above-average arm strength. Offensively, Johnson has made significant strides in his plate coverage by spreading his stance. He can drive the ball to all fields and should develop more power as his body matures. The Braves say the key to his development centers on his confidence. Once he turns that corner, he has the package to be an everyday player in the major leagues.

Ryan Langerhans

Position: OF
Bats: L **Throws:** L
Ht: 6' 3" **Wt:** 195

Opening Day Age: 25
Born: 2/20/80 in San Antonio, TX

Recent Statistics

	G	AB	R	H	D	T	HR	RBI	SB	BB	SO	Avg
2003 AA Greenville	94	336	42	85	23	2	6	38	10	46	85	.253
2003 AAA Richmond	38	132	13	37	10	2	4	11	2	11	29	.280
2003 NL Atlanta	16	15	2	4	0	0	0	0	0	0	6	.267
2004 AAA Richmond	135	456	103	136	34	3	20	72	5	70	113	.298

The Braves have been patient with Langerhans, ever since the team drafted him in the third round in 1998. That patience is about to reap rewards after he made all the adjustments at the plate and emerged as a solid hitter who has the potential to hit for power and average. Still, Langerhans' strength is his defense. He can play all three outfield positions with aplomb, and owns one of the strongest arms among outfielders in the Atlanta system. He not only covers a large amount of ground in the garden, but also is a smart and aggressive baserunner. He should be a fourth outfielder with the Braves in 2005, and could emerge as a starter.

Andy Marte

Position: 3B
Bats: R **Throws:** R
Ht: 6' 1" **Wt:** 185

Opening Day Age: 21
Born: 10/21/83 in Villa Tapia, DR

Recent Statistics

	G	AB	R	H	D	T	HR	RBI	SB	BB	SO	Avg
2003 A Myrtle Beach	130	463	69	132	35	1	16	63	5	67	109	.285
2004 R GC Braves	3	15	4	7	4	0	1	6	0	2	2	.467
2004 AA Greenville	107	387	52	104	28	1	23	68	1	58	105	.269

Chipper Jones returned to his old home at the hot corner in 2004 and never looked better with the leather. Marte, meanwhile, continued his rapid ascent through the Atlanta organization by ranking as the top prospect in the Double-A Southern League, despite missing nearly a month with a sprained ankle. Balls jump off his bat, and he is capable of clearing walls in any part of the ballpark. Defensively, Marte has steady hands, a strong arm and good range at the hot corner. Most impressive, according to Atlanta officials, is his unwavering, even demeanor on the diamond, a trait that serves as yet another indicator of how mature Marte is at 21 years old.

Brian McCann

Position: C
Bats: L **Throws:** R
Ht: 6' 3" **Wt:** 190

Opening Day Age: 21
Born: 2/20/84 in Athens, GA

Recent Statistics

	G	AB	R	H	D	T	HR	RBI	SB	BB	SO	Avg
2003 A Rome	115	424	40	123	31	3	12	71	7	24	73	.290
2004 A Myrtle Beach	111	385	45	107	35	0	16	66	2	31	54	.278

Some scouts wondered if McCann had the tools necessary to remain behind the plate as a professional when the Braves selected him in the second round of the 2002 draft. Those questions are no longer asked, for McCann is considered by many observers to be the top all-around receiver in the minors. He has a sweet swing from the left side of the plate that produces line drives to all fields. He works well with pitchers and his strong arm retired 30 percent of basestealers last year. He is also a fiery leader. Some seasoning at the Double-A level may be all McCann needs before receiving his first taste of the majors.

Dan Meyer

Position: P
Bats: R **Throws:** L
Ht: 6' 3" **Wt:** 210

Opening Day Age: 23
Born: 7/3/81 in Woodbury, NJ

Recent Statistics

	W	L	ERA	G	GS	Sv	IP	H	R	BB	SO	HR
2004 AA Greenville	6	3	2.22	14	13	0	65.0	50	17	12	86	1
2004 AAA Richmond	3	3	2.79	12	11	0	61.1	62	23	25	60	6
2004 NL Atlanta	0	0	0.00	2	0	0	2.0	2	0	1	1	0

Meyer split the 2004 season between the Double- and Triple-A ranks, and performed better at the higher level during the second half of the campaign. Meyer displays confidence and fearlessness on the mound. He has good stuff and throws strikes consistently with all three of his offerings. His fastball resides in the low 90s and his changeup is an above-average pitch. His slider has a chance to be a nasty toss, and will be once he maintains the feel of it from start to start. The Braves love the way the lefty challenges hitters by working all parts of the plate, which should enable him to develop into at least a middle-of-the-rotation starter in the majors.

Others to Watch

Roman Colon (25) was a starter through his first six seasons before getting a brief taste of relief during the 2003 slate. The righthander moved to the bullpen on a full-time basis last year and saw his velocity increase substantially to the mid-90s, while his split-finger fastball and slider improved. . . There are scouts and coaches who believe **Luis Hernandez** (20) is one of the premier shortstops in the minors. The Venezuelan product has been a slick and consistent fielder throughout his brief pro career, yet began hitting for average from both sides of the plate last year. He drives the ball to all fields. . . **Anthony Lerew** (22) can throw three pitches for strikes, but his increase in velocity last year has taken his game to another level. The righthander improved the speed of his fastball from the low 90s to 95-96 MPH, while topping out at 97. If he maintains velocity while continuing to display impressive command, Lerew will have a chance to move quickly. . . Outfielder **Bill McCarthy** (25) has blazed through the system. Promoted from Double-A in 2004, he proved to be one of Triple-A Richmond's catalysts during the postseason. McCarthy has good pop in his bat and drives the ball to all fields. He is also a smart baserunner with good range and a steady glove in the outfield. His future probably will come in left field.

Wrigley Field

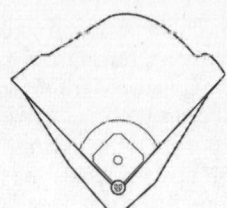

Dimensions: LF-355, LCF-368, CF-400, RCF-368, RF-353

Capacity: 39,345

Elevation: 595 feet

Surface: Grass

Foul Territory: Small

Offense

The wind affects play and determines the out comes of games—at Wrigley Field perhaps more than any other park in the big leagues. When the wind blows in, Wrigley is a park for pitchers, who also love the tall, thick grass in the infield. When it blows out, the ballpark is tailor-made for a power-hitting team like the Cubs. Not surprisingly, the Cubs were 26-13 in 2004 when the wind was blowing out at game time.

Defense

Over the last several years, the Cubs have had infielders who've possessed very little range. That doesn't hurt them at home because the grass eats up and slows down groundballs, enabling even slow-footed fielders to reach them. There is little foul territory at Wrigley, and that decreased with the addition of three rows of premium box seats behind home plate.

Who It Helps the Most

Righthanded power hitters and sinkerball pitchers love Wrigley Field. Moises Alou cleaned up at Wrigley Field, slugging .714 there as opposed to .400 on the road. Aramis Ramirez took to day games, and Derrek Lee used the short power alleys, just as the Cubs hoped he would. Pitcher Carlos Zambrano was nearly untouchable at home, and Greg Maddux and Matt Clement had ERAs about a run better at Wrigley than on the road.

Who It Hurts the Most

Interestingly, Todd Walker tore it up at Fenway Park with the Red Sox in 2003, but he batted just .236 at Wrigley Field with the Cubs in 2004. Another gap hitter, Michael Barrett, fared better away from home.

Rookies & Newcomers

Nomar Garciaparra, who joined the Cubs in mid-season, did not fare all that well at Wrigley. He should be better there in 2005. Rookie outfielder Jason Dubois, who hit 31 home runs for Triple-A Iowa in 2004, could find left-center field to his liking. If the Cubs don't sign a veteran to replace Moises Alou, Dubois could compete for a starting job.

Park Factors

2004 Season

| | Home Games | | | Away Games | | | |
	Cubs	Opp	Total	Cubs	Opp	Total	Index
G	76	76	152	74	74	148	
Avg	.273	.250	.261	.263	.243	.253	103
AB	2622	2671	5293	2597	2440	5037	102
R	404	339	743	331	281	612	118
H	715	668	1383	682	593	1275	106
2B	138	121	259	151	107	258	96
3B	12	14	26	13	14	27	92
HR	131	94	225	89	66	155	138
BB	234	255	489	220	257	477	98
SO	469	632	1101	537	604	1141	92
E	43	63	106	37	45	82	126
E-Infield	36	49	85	32	35	67	124
LHB-Avg	.270	.249	.258	.255	.273	.265	97
LHB-HR	27	49	76	22	41	63	113
RHB-Avg	.274	.251	.263	.266	.221	.246	107
RHB-HR	104	45	149	67	25	92	155

2002-2004

| | Home Games | | | Away Games | | | |
	Cubs	Opp	Total	Cubs	Opp	Total	Index
G	223	223	446	218	218	436	98
Avg	.255	.243	.249	.259	.250	.254	98
AB	7481	7703	15184	7620	7174	14794	100
R	1015	986	2001	1000	924	1924	102
H	1908	1872	3780	1971	1790	3761	98
2B	371	352	723	416	341	757	93
3B	33	33	66	40	41	81	79
HR	298	247	545	257	186	443	120
BB	761	803	1564	677	787	1464	104
SO	1609	1976	3585	1606	1730	3336	105
E	152	157	309	134	143	277	109
E-Infield	128	124	252	113	118	231	107
LHB-Avg	.247	.245	.246	.255	.265	.260	95
LHB-HR	79	107	186	87	98	185	98
RHB-Avg	.259	.241	.251	.261	.239	.251	100
RHB-HR	219	140	359	170	88	258	135

2004 Rankings (National League)

- Highest home-run factor
- Highest RHB home-run factor
- Second-highest run factor
- Third-highest batting-average factor
- Third-highest hit factor
- Third-highest error factor
- Third-highest infield-error factor
- Second-lowest strikeout factor

Chicago (NL)

Dusty Baker

2004 Season

After a magical ride in 2003, Dusty Baker found distraction and controversy at every turn in 2004. It started with injuries to pitching aces Mark Prior and Kerry Wood, and it continued as Mark Grudzielanek, Sammy Sosa, Todd Hollandsworth and closer Joe Borowski came up lame at various points of the season. A more critical Chicago media and fan base openly questioned Baker's offensive strategy, his handling of pitchers and the leadership tactics of a players' manager when his players misbehaved. The year ended with a sour taste as Sosa publicly ripped Baker for allegedly blaming Sosa for the Cubs' failures.

Offense

Baker drew ridicule for his spring-training remark that "walks are overrated unless you can run." He backed off those comments a bit, but Baker is a manager who likes his hitters to be aggressive on both first pitches and 3-0 counts. Although he professes to prefer a set batting order, Baker was not shy about juggling his lineup. The Cubs had little speed, so Baker didn't utilize the hit-and-run or steal much. He's by-the-book in sacrifice situations.

Pitching & Defense

Long criticized for letting his starting pitchers work deep into games, Baker took it easier on Wood and Prior after they came back from injuries. He did allow emerging ace Carlos Zambrano to throw almost 112 pitches per start, and Zambrano did not seem to be adversely affected down the stretch. Baker is fond of saying, "If you can't play defense, you can't play for me." Overall, Baker's Cubs have been average on defense, with a lack of range masking some problems. Cubs pitchers must do much better at holding runners.

2005 Outlook

Entering the third year of a four-year contract, Baker will feel the heat to get the Cubs back to the postseason and demonstrate he's in charge in the clubhouse. With aggressive GM Jim Hendry having talked the Tribune Co. into spending more for players, all eyes will be on Baker to deliver.

Born: 6/15/49 in Riverside, CA

Playing Experience: 1968-1986, Atl, LA, SF, Oak

Managerial Experience: 12 seasons

Manager Statistics

Year	Team, Lg	W	L	Pct	GB	Finish
2004	Chicago, NL	89	73	.549	16.0	3rd Central
12 Seasons		1017	862	.541	–	–

2004 Starting Pitchers by Days Rest

	<=3	4	5	6+
Cubs Starts	1	74	59	21
Cubs ERA	5.40	3.71	3.81	3.51
NL Avg Starts	2	82	46	23
NL ERA	4.58	4.35	4.28	4.73

2004 Situational Stats

	Dusty Baker	NL Average
Hit & Run Success %	33.3	38.0
Stolen Base Success %	70.2	71.7
Platoon Pct.	44.0	55.2
Defensive Subs	6	18
High-Pitch Outings	13	6
Quick/Slow Hooks	14/7	21/12
Sacrifice Attempts	110	99

2004 Rankings (National League)

- 1st in pitchouts (68), pitchouts with a runner moving (13) and starts with over 120 pitches (13)
- 3rd in sacrifice bunt attempts

Moises Alou

2004 Season

After a miserable June (.192 BA), Moises Alou performed like an old warhorse and wound up with a career-best 39 home runs. He also was able to shake off nagging back and calf injuries to play in 155 games, second-most in his career. In a clubhouse lacking vocal leaders, Alou did his best to prod his teammates, but his comments in July complaining about the team broadcasters being negative may have been misguided. Umpires grew weary of Alou slamming his equipment to the ground and complaining after calls went against him.

Hitting

One thing is certain about Alou—if he gets his pitch, he's going to swing at it no matter the count. The super-aggressive Alou led National League hitters in swinging at the first pitch, going after it 46.4 percent of the time and leading the majors with 14 first-pitch home runs. Nevertheless, Alou drew 68 bases on balls, his highest total since 1998. He has a short, quick stroke and great power to all fields.

Baserunning & Defense

Much was made of Alou getting doubled off base on flyballs three times in a one-month period. For that, he made no apologies, saying he was being aggressive and trying to get his teammates RBI. Those examples stood out because they happened in a concentrated period, but overall, Alou is at least an average baserunner. He made a career-high eight errors, but he's adequate in left field, and it helps to have the speedy Corey Patterson in center field. His arm is on the weak side.

2005 Outlook

Alou talked hopefully of returning to the Cubs in 2005, but the club did not pick up his option, making him a free agent. Although he will be 39 in July, he is coming off two productive seasons in which he played 150-plus games. If he stays healthy, he may have at least one good year left.

Position: LF
Bats: R **Throws:** R
Ht: 6' 3" **Wt:** 220

Opening Day Age: 38
Born: 7/3/66 in Atlanta, GA
ML Seasons: 13
Pronunciation: MOY-zes ah-LOO

Overall Statistics

G	AB	R	H	D	T	HR	RBI	SB	BB	SO	Avg	OBP	Slg
155	601	106	176	36	3	39	106	3	68	80	.293	.361	.557
1619	5888	935	1764	354	34	278	1092	95	624	786	.300	.367	.513

Where He Hits the Ball

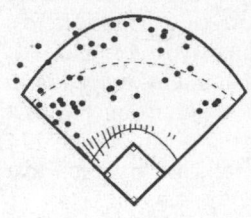 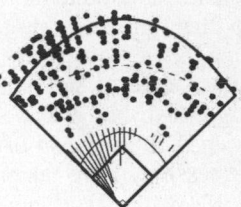

Vs. LHP	Vs. RHP

2004 Situational Stats

	AB	H	HR	RBI	Avg		AB	H	HR	RBI	Avg
Home	301	102	29	67	.339	LHP	114	34	4	10	.298
Road	300	74	10	39	.247	RHP	487	142	35	96	.292
First Half	330	91	19	49	.276	Sc Pos	145	44	9	63	.303
Scnd Half	271	85	20	57	.314	Clutch	106	28	6	14	.264

2004 Rankings (National League)

- 1st in highest percentage of swings on the first pitch (46.3)
- 2nd in errors in left field (8) and lowest fielding percentage in left field (.969)
- 3rd in cleanup slugging percentage (.612)
- 4th in total bases (335) and batting average at home
- Led the Cubs in home runs, runs scored, hits, total bases (335), RBI, walks, times on base (244) and batting average at home
- Led NL left fielders in RBI

Chicago (NL)

Michael Barrett

2004 Season

Cubs GM Jim Hendry coveted Michael Barrett for several years, and Hendry finally was able to obtain him in a trade with Oakland last year. Despite some rough edges on defense, Barrett more than justified Hendry's faith in him, with a career best 16 home runs and his best overall numbers since 1999. It helped that Barrett stayed healthy, something he was unable to do with the Expos in 2003.

Hitting

Assured of a job and not having an up-and-coming catching prospect breathing down his neck, Barrett was able to relax at the plate and let his considerable athletic ability work for him. More so than in years past, Barrett used all fields, though his power came primarily in left and left-center. Like several of his teammates, Barrett is an aggressive hitter who likes to jump on the first pitch. The workload of playing a career-high 134 games may have taken its toll, as he batted just .230 over the final month of the season.

Baserunning & Defense

Barrett showed surprising speed for a catcher, with 32 doubles and six triples, but overall, he remained a station-to-station baserunner. Barrett may have been overly critical of his own play behind the plate, beginning with spring training. Back then, Barrett acknowledged he was having trouble catching the Cubs staff, which features power pitchers with good movement. The talk died down as the season went on, but Mark Prior joined Greg Maddux late in the season in using backup Paul Bako as his catcher over Barrett. With a staff that's slow to deliver the ball, Barrett threw out 18 of 90 basestealers.

2005 Outlook

Having shaken the doubts about his offensive game, Barrett should arrive at spring training 2005 much more relaxed. A year's experience should help Barrett find a comfort zone behind the plate. If that happens, the Cubs may want to lock him up for several years.

Position: C
Bats: R **Throws:** R
Ht: 6' 3" **Wt:** 210

Opening Day Age: 28
Born: 10/22/76 in Atlanta, GA
ML Seasons: 7

Overall Statistics

	G	AB	R	H	D	T	HR	RBI	SB	BB	SO	Avg	OBP	Slg
'04	134	456	55	131	32	6	16	65	1	33	64	.287	.337	.489
Car.	676	2257	255	587	143	15	54	258	9	177	300	.260	.316	.409

Where He Hits the Ball

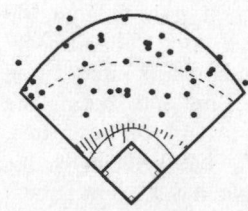 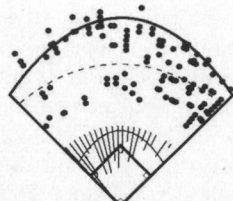

Vs. LHP   **Vs. RHP**

2004 Situational Stats

	AB	H	HR	RBI	Avg		AB	H	HR	RBI	Avg
Home	244	63	9	32	.258	LHP	105	26	3	12	.248
Road	212	68	7	33	.321	RHP	351	105	13	53	.299
First Half	254	74	10	43	.291	Sc Pos	118	36	3	45	.305
Scnd Half	202	57	6	22	.282	Clutch	92	22	3	14	.239

2004 Rankings (National League)

- 3rd in lowest percentage of runners caught stealing as a catcher (20.0)
- 5th in errors at catcher (6)
- Led the Cubs in triples, sacrifice flies (8), highest groundball-flyball ratio (1.5) and batting average on the road

Matt Clement

2004 Season

Matt Clement went from one of the Cubs' two most dependable starters in the first half of the season to persona non grata by the end. Once again the victim of poor run support, Clement had a 7-8 record with a nice 2.91 ERA at the All-Star break. Upper-shoulder and neck pain limited his effectiveness in the second half, and after a poor start at Florida in mid-September, manager Dusty Baker declined to use him again the rest of the way, opting instead for lefty Glendon Rusch. That appeared to baffle Clement, who bit his tongue, saying, "It's not about me."

Pitching

Clement's bread and butter pitch is a good hard slider that breaks sharply down and away from righthanded batters and in on the hands or at the shins of lefties. He also has a good four-seam fastball with a lot of life and a two-seamer he uses as a deadly sinker. Clement is somewhat of a fussbudget on the mound, and he slows the game down considerably with men on base. He is prone to occasional wildness, usually ranking among the league leaders in wild pitches.

Defense & Hitting

Clement is only an adequate fielder who has had trouble throwing the ball to bases on grounders. Part of the reason he slows down his pace with men on base is that he's more content to step off and look runners back to first instead of making pickoff throws. On a staff of good-hitting pitchers, Clement was fifth- or sixth-best among Cubs starters, but he was average overall. His sacrifice bunts fell from eight in 2003 to four in 2004.

2005 Outlook

With the Cubs being deep in starting pitching, they appeared to have little interest in re-signing free agent Clement by the end of the 2004 season. With his live arm and good repertoire, he'll have no trouble catching on with another team as a No. 3 or 4 starter.

Position: SP
Bats: R **Throws:** R
Ht: 6' 3" **Wt:** 210

Opening Day Age: 30
Born: 8/12/74 in Butler, PA
ML Seasons: 7
Pronunciation: klah-MENT

Overall Statistics

	W	L	Pct.	ERA	G	GS	Sv	IP	H	BB	SO	HR	Avg
'04	9	13	.409	3.68	30	30	0	181.0	155	77	190	23	.229
Car.	69	75	.479	4.34	194	192	0	1156.1	1057	544	1028	118	.243

2004 Pitching Profile

	Matt Clement	NL Average
Overall Strike %	62.3	62.5
1st Pitch Strike %	56.8	58.5
Ratio	1.28	1.39
Strikeouts per 9 IP	9.45	6.74
Walks per 9 IP	3.83	3.38
Home Runs per 9 IP	1.14	1.11
Strikeout/Walk Ratio	2.47	1.99
Groundball/Flyball Ratio	1.60	1.25

2004 Situational Stats

	W	L	ERA	Sv	IP		AB	H	HR	RBI	Avg
Home	7	6	3.19	0	113.0	LHB	329	77	13	42	.234
Road	2	7	4.50	0	68.0	RHB	348	78	10	34	.224
First Half	7	8	2.91	0	117.1	Sc Pos	155	37	4	48	.239
Scnd Half	2	5	5.09	0	63.2	Clutch	45	11	1	3	.244

2004 Rankings (National League)

- 2nd in wild pitches (14)
- 3rd in errors at pitcher (3)
- 4th in highest stolen-base percentage allowed (88.9) and lowest fielding percentage at pitcher (.925)
- 5th in hit batsmen (12) and most strikeouts per nine innings (9.4)
- 6th in least run support per nine innings (4.0)
- 7th in strikeouts and highest walks per nine innings (3.8)
- 8th in lowest batting average allowed (.229)
- 9th in losses
- 10th in stolen bases allowed (16) and lowest winning percentage
- Led the Cubs in losses, strikeouts and wild pitches (14)

Nomar Garciaparra

2004 Season

Nomar Garciaparra began the 2004 season on Boston's disabled list with an Achilles tendon problem. In addition to his body being hurt, his feelings were bruised after the Red Sox made him a multi-year contract offer he deemed too low, then failed in a well-publicized attempt to trade for All-Star shortstop Alex Rodriguez. Garciaparra returned to Boston's lineup in June, then was dealt to the Cubs at the July 31 trading deadline. The Achilles and a nagging groin injury were issues down the stretch for Garciaparra, who also suffered a wrist injury after coming to the Cubs. However, his improved mental outlook enabled him to help the Cubs down the stretch.

Hitting

Despite the injuries, Garciaparra continued to hit the ball hard after changing leagues. However, he was lacking his usual home-run power. An aggressive hitter like most of the Cubs, he swung at the first pitch nearly 50 percent of the time. The high grass and tough winds at Wrigley Field held down Garciaparra's batting average there.

Baserunning & Defense

The injuries did not seem to hinder Garciaparra appreciably with the glove. The tall grass at Wrigley only helped him. Garciaparra goes to the hole well, and his strong arm helped him there. On balls up the middle he makes a full turn similar to a pirouette, and his arm strength enables him to throw out runners handily. Garciaparra is a good baserunner, but the injuries took a giant toll on his stolen-base numbers.

2005 Outlook

Garciaparra's desire and enthusiasm for the game seemed to find new life with the Cubs. The Chicago media left him alone for the most part, too. As a free agent, he surprised a few people in December by signing a one-year, $8 million contract with incentives to stay with the Cubs. Both the Cubs and Garciaparra hope that a return to health will result in a return to his old form. That might be needed to convince people he is worth a lucrative long-term deal. The extra year in Chicago may convince him to stick around.

Position: SS
Bats: R **Throws:** R
Ht: 6' 0" **Wt:** 190

Opening Day Age: 31
Born: 7/23/73 in Whittier, CA
ML Seasons: 9
Pronunciation: no-mar GARCIA-par-uh

Overall Statistics

	G	AB	R	H	D	T	HR	RBI	SB	BB	SO	Avg	OBP	Slg
'04	81	321	52	99	21	3	9	41	4	24	30	.308	.365	.477
Car.	1009	4133	737	1330	293	50	182	710	86	295	420	.322	.370	.549

Where He Hits the Ball

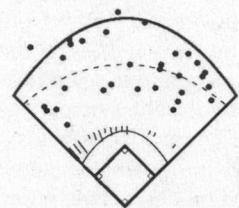

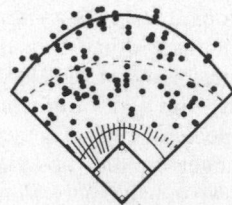

Vs. LHP   **Vs. RHP**

2004 Situational Stats

	AB	H	HR	RBI	Avg		AB	H	HR	RBI	Avg
Home	178	52	6	29	.292	LHP	75	18	2	9	.240
Road	143	47	3	12	.329	RHP	246	81	7	32	.329
First Half	107	35	4	16	.327	Sc Pos	82	26	3	33	.317
Scnd Half	214	64	5	25	.299	Clutch	44	18	1	3	.409

2004 Rankings (National League)

- Did not rank near the top or bottom in any category

Derrek Lee

Position: 1B
Bats: R **Throws:** R
Ht: 6' 5" **Wt:** 245

Opening Day Age: 29
Born: 9/6/75 in Sacramento, CA
ML Seasons: 8

2004 Season

During the early part of last season, Cubs fans openly wondered why the team had traded youngster Hee Seop Choi to the Florida Marlins for Derrek Lee. But after hitting only four home runs in his first 46 games, Lee caught fire in June, eventually reaching career bests in doubles, home runs and RBI. Lee was also an iron man at first base, playing 161 games. The workload may have caught up with him down the stretch, as he batted just .217 over the final month.

Hitting

Lee is a slashing, line drive hitter who hits the ball to all fields but was able to take advantage of Wrigley Field's cozy left-center field power alley. He likes to get his arms extended, and he can be tied up inside and with high pitches. Manager Dusty Baker was able to use Lee as high as the No. 2 spot in the order because of his intelligent approach at the plate.

Baserunning & Defense

Lee, who won the first Gold Glove of his career in 2003 with the Marlins, lived up to his reputation after joining the Cubs. Baker nicknamed him "Rodan" for his wide wingspan. Agile around first base and strong to both his right and left, he's also very adept at digging balls out of the dirt. Lee has good speed on the bases, but with the Cubs relying primarily on the home run to score runs, he wound up with 12 stolen bases, down from his 2003 total of 21.

2005 Outlook

Though Lee is still a young man at 29, the Cubs would like to get him a breather now and then in 2005. The season-ending injury suffered by Todd Hollandsworth in June and the lack of another true first baseman kept Lee in the lineup more than Baker would have liked. Playing in Wrigley Field for at least the next two years, Lee could approach the 40-homer mark more than once.

Overall Statistics

	G	AB	R	H	D	T	HR	RBI	SB	BB	SO	Avg	OBP	Slg
'04	161	605	90	168	39	1	32	98	12	68	128	.278	.356	.504
Car.	1027	3489	521	928	201	19	162	519	63	440	886	.266	.353	.474

Where He Hits the Ball

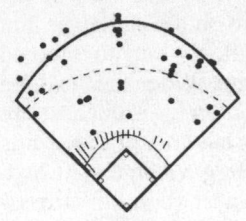
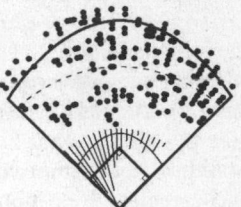

Vs. LHP   **Vs. RHP**

2004 Situational Stats

	AB	H	HR	RBI	Avg		AB	H	HR	RBI	Avg
Home	305	86	18	55	.282	LHP	111	34	9	23	.306
Road	300	82	14	43	.273	RHP	494	134	23	75	.271
First Half	316	96	12	49	.304	Sc Pos	145	40	8	65	.276
Scnd Half	289	72	20	49	.249	Clutch	100	27	5	13	.270

2004 Rankings (National League)

- 2nd in fielding percentage at first base (.996)
- 3rd in games played
- 9th in errors at first base (6)
- Led the Cubs in doubles, walks, hit by pitch (8), times on base (244), pitches seen (2,712), plate appearances (688), games played, steals of third (2) and batting average vs. lefthanded pitchers

Greg Maddux

2004 Season

Bringing back Greg Maddux after 11 years in Atlanta was supposed to be icing on the cake for a Cubs team which already had a good and deep pitching staff. By year's end, Maddux wound up tied with Carlos Zambrano for the team lead in victories with 16, extending his unprecedented run of consecutive seasons with at least 15 victories to 17. On August 7 at San Francisco, he notched the 300th victory of his career.

Pitching

Maddux' mantra is what it always has been: locate the fastball and change speeds. Never overpowering, Maddux relies on putting the fastball where he wants to put it and on changing speeds. His expert use of finger pressure on the ball gives him movement and sink and allows him to succeed without being overpowering. When he walks a batter, particularly with men on base, chances are he's pitching around him. One area of concern is Maddux' home run total. He gave up a staff-high and career-high 35 homers last year, far surpassing the 24 he yielded with the Braves in 2003 (his previous career high).

Defense & Hitting

By far the best fielding pitcher on the Cubs, Maddux won his 14th Gold Glove in 2004. Not only does he field the ball well, he never seems to make a bad decision on where to throw the ball. The only shortcoming in Maddux' defensive work is that he has trouble holding baserunners. He is an excellent bunter and a decent hitter.

2005 Outlook

If Maddux pitches 187.1 innings this year, his option for 2006 automatically will kick in. Even with Maddux turning 39 in April, there's no reason to believe he can't reach that incentive. He keeps himself in good shape, and with manager Dusty Baker keeping a close eye on Maddux' pitch counts (he averaged 88.6 pitches per game in 2004), the Cubs figure to benefit from his amazing consistency for two more years.

Position: SP
Bats: R **Throws:** R
Ht: 6' 0" **Wt:** 185

Opening Day Age: 38
Born: 4/14/66 in San Angelo, TX
ML Seasons: 19
Pronunciation: MADD-ucks

Overall Statistics

W	L	Pct.	ERA	G	GS	Sv	IP	H	BB	SO	HR	Avg
16	11	.593	4.02	33	33	0	212.2	218	33	151	35	.269
305	174	.637	2.95	608	604	0	4181.1	3843	871	2916	269	.245

2004 Pitching Profile

	Greg Maddux	NL Average
Overall Strike %	66.5	62.5
1st Pitch Strike %	63.3	58.5
Ratio	1.18	1.39
Strikeouts per 9 IP	6.39	6.74
Walks per 9 IP	1.40	3.38
Home Runs per 9 IP	1.48	1.11
Strikeout/Walk Ratio	4.58	1.99
Groundball/Flyball Ratio	1.78	1.25

2004 Situational Stats

	W	L	ERA	Sv	IP		AB	H	HR	RBI	Avg
Home	8	5	3.56	0	113.2	LHB	362	98	22	52	.271
Road	8	6	4.55	0	99.0	RHB	447	120	13	41	.268
First Half	7	7	4.51	0	111.2	Sc Pos	145	33	6	52	.228
Scnd Half	9	4	3.48	0	101.0	Clutch	55	16	0	2	.291

2004 Rankings (National League)

- 1st in runners caught stealing (12) and fewest pitches thrown per batter (3.36)
- 2nd in home runs allowed
- 3rd in stolen bases allowed (26) and fewest walks per nine innings (1.4)
- 4th in highest strikeout-walk ratio (4.6)
- 5th in wins
- 6th in highest groundball-flyball ratio allowed (1.8) and most home runs allowed per nine innings (1.48)
- 7th in complete games (2)
- Led the Cubs in sacrifice bunts (9), wins, games started, complete games (2), innings pitched, hits allowed, home runs allowed, pickoff throws (97), runners caught stealing (12), highest strikeout-walk ratio (4.6), lowest on-base percentage allowed (.303), highest groundball-flyball ratio allowed (1.8), and fewest walks per nine innings (1.4)

Corey Patterson

2004 Season

After undergoing knee surgery in July of 2003, Corey Patterson worked hard in the offseason and looked as if he hadn't lost a step of speed in center field or running the bases. He began the year as the Cubs' No. 2 hitter, but manager Dusty Baker made a bold move on August 1, putting the free-swinging Patterson in the leadoff spot. For a month, Patterson tore things up, but he cooled considerably in September.

Hitting

There's nothing Patterson can't do as a hitter. He can hit line drives, bunt for base hits and hit for power. He just needs to do it all more consistently. His main problems are a lack of patience, poor command of the strike zone and a stubborn streak that can serve him well or hold him back. Patterson is a free swinger who will jump on anything that looks good to him early in the count. He's susceptible to high fastballs out of the zone, especially with two strikes. He has improved markedly against lefthanded pitchers, hitting 31 points higher vs. southpaws last season than he did against righties.

Baserunning & Defense

Though not yet in the category of Andruw Jones or Jim Edmonds as a defensive center fielder, Patterson isn't far behind. He has great speed, something he has needed with Moises Alou and Sammy Sosa flanking him. Patterson's throwing arm is a good one. He led the Cubs with a career-best 32 stolen bases, and he's getting better every day at reading pitchers' moves.

2005 Outlook

GM Jim Hendry, who drafted Patterson in 1998, says he believes Patterson is capable of batting anywhere in the order and succeeding. If the Cubs can obtain a better leadoff man, it's possible Patterson could move to the No. 3 spot, a place manager Dusty Baker said he eventually envisions Patterson. If Patterson can become more selective at the plate, he is a potential 30-30 man and an All-Star.

Position: CF
Bats: L **Throws:** R
Ht: 5' 9" **Wt:** 180

Opening Day Age: 25
Born: 8/13/79 in Atlanta, GA
ML Seasons: 5

Overall Statistics

	G	AB	R	H	D	T	HR	RBI	SB	BB	SO	Avg	OBP	Slg
'04	157	631	91	168	33	6	24	72	32	45	168	.266	.320	.452
Car.	463	1725	246	452	84	18	57	197	71	88	434	.262	.303	.431

Where He Hits the Ball

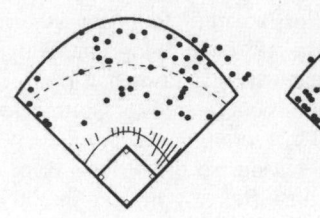

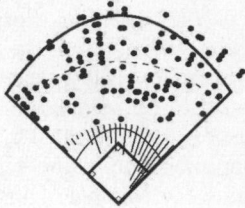

Vs. LHP   **Vs. RHP**

2004 Situational Stats

	AB	H	HR	RBI	Avg		AB	H	HR	RBI	Avg
Home	316	87	14	42	.275	LHP	173	50	8	26	.289
Road	315	81	10	30	.257	RHP	458	118	16	46	.258
First Half	325	89	10	35	.274	Sc Pos	129	31	7	47	.240
Scnd Half	306	79	14	37	.258	Clutch	104	33	6	13	.317

2004 Rankings (National League)

- 1st in fielding percentage in center field (.997)
- 3rd in strikeouts
- 4th in bunts in play (36)
- 6th in stolen bases, caught stealing (9) and lowest percentage of pitches taken (48.0)
- 7th in at-bats
- 9th in lowest on-base percentage for a leadoff hitter (.317)
- 10th in lowest stolen-base percentage (78.0) and highest percentage of swings on the first pitch (36.7)
- Led the Cubs in at-bats, singles, triples, stolen bases, caught stealing (9), strikeouts, stolen-base percentage (78.0) and bunts in play (36)

Mark Prior

2004 Season

Last season was supposed to be the one that firmly established Mark Prior as the finest young pitcher in the game. But coming off an 18-win season in 2003, Prior was beset from the start of spring training with a recurring Achilles tendon problem. As he recovered, he overdid it and strained his right elbow. That cost Prior the first two months of the season, and the delay cost him command and effectiveness. Seemingly healthy by the end of the season, Prior looked like his old self, fueling hopes for 2005.

Pitching

When he's on, Prior is that rare breed of power pitcher who has exquisite command. He has a fastball that clocks in the mid- to upper 90s, a good curveball and a still-developing changeup. The problem last year was that Prior had trouble with the command of his curve, allowing hitters to sit on his fastball. Once command on his curve returned late in the season, so did Prior's effectiveness. Manager Dusty Baker, criticized in 2003 for running up Prior's pitch counts, took it easy from the get-go last year before gradually building the workload back up. Through all the frustration, Prior did a good job of keeping his poise on and off the mound.

Defense & Hitting

Prior didn't fare as well at the plate as he did in 2003, but he's a good all-around athlete who should help himself for years to come. He handles the bat well and is capable of generating power. He's an adept bunter. Prior fields his position well and has a good move to first.

2005 Outlook

An offseason of healthy rest should make all the difference for Prior in 2005. With no lingering injuries to favor, his mechanics should be OK from the start. Last season proved to be a tough learning experience for Prior. Fortunately for the Cubs, he's smart enough to learn from those experiences and physically able to put them to use.

Position: SP
Bats: R **Throws:** R
Ht: 6' 5" **Wt:** 230

Opening Day Age: 24
Born: 9/7/80 in San Diego, CA
ML Seasons: 3

Overall Statistics

	W	L	Pct.	ERA	G	GS	Sv	IP	H	BB	SO	HR	Avg
'04	6	4	.600	4.02	21	21	0	118.2	112	48	139	14	.251
Car.	30	16	.652	3.08	70	70	0	446.2	393	136	531	43	.235

2004 Pitching Profile

	Mark Prior	NL Average
Overall Strike %	63.7	62.5
1st Pitch Strike %	58.8	58.5
Ratio	1.35	1.39
Strikeouts per 9 IP	10.54	6.74
Walks per 9 IP	3.64	3.38
Home Runs per 9 IP	1.06	1.11
Strikeout/Walk Ratio	2.90	1.99
Groundball/Flyball Ratio	0.87	1.25

2004 Situational Stats

	W	L	ERA	Sv	IP		AB	H	HR	RBI	Avg
Home	2	2	5.23	0	65.1	LHB	194	50	7	15	.258
Road	4	2	2.53	0	53.1	RHB	253	62	7	30	.245
First Half	2	2	4.00	0	36.0	Sc Pos	89	23	4	35	.258
Scnd Half	4	2	4.03	0	82.2	Clutch	17	2	1	1	.118

2004 Rankings (National League)

- Led the Cubs in lowest ERA on the road and most strikeouts per nine innings (10.5)

Aramis Ramirez

Position: 3B
Bats: R **Throws:** R
Ht: 6' 1" **Wt:** 215

Opening Day Age: 26
Born: 6/25/78 in Santo Domingo, DR
ML Seasons: 7
Pronunciation: ah-RAH-mis

2004 Season

In his first full season with the Cubs after coming over in a July 2003 trade with the Pirates, Aramis Ramirez was undoubtedly the Cubs' MVP. No longer was he expected to be "the man," as he was in Pittsburgh, Ramirez was able to relax and put together his best season since 2001, when he batted .300 with 34 homers and 112 RBI for the Pirates. The only thing that slowed Ramirez was a groin injury he suffered running the bases in June. It bothered him from then on, and manager Dusty Baker needed to rest him in spots.

Hitting

Better discipline at the plate and a more relaxed approach made Ramirez a much more dangerous hitter last year. He is an aggressive hitter but not a wild swinger: he drew a career-high 49 walks in 2004, while reducing his strikeouts from 99 to 62, a very low total for a home-run hitter. He hits the ball to all fields, but generates his best power to left and left-center.

Baserunning & Defense

For years, Ramirez was criticized for sloppy and indifferent play at third base. He improved markedly last year, however, cutting his error total from 33 to 10. From the time he joined the Cubs in 2003, Ramirez began taking groundball after groundball with coaches Wendell Kim and Sonny Jackson. As a result he improved his footwork, enabling him to make more accurate throws to first base. Ramirez' main drawback on defense is that his range isn't very good. He's a slow runner.

2005 Outlook

Ramirez isn't in the class of St. Louis' Scott Rolen as an all-around third baseman, but he opened a lot of eyes in 2004. He's heading into his final year of eligibility for salary arbitration. The Cubs will look to sign him to a long-term deal, giving them stability and production they haven't enjoyed at third base since the days of Ron Santo.

Overall Statistics

	G	AB	R	H	D	T	HR	RBI	SB	BB	SO	Avg	OBP	Slg
'04	145	547	99	174	32	1	36	103	0	49	62	.318	.373	.578
Car.	767	2840	352	776	156	7	127	458	9	194	473	.273	.324	.467

Where He Hits the Ball

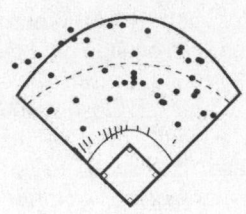
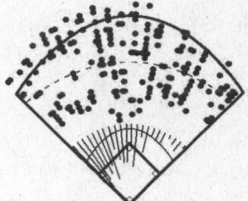

Vs. LHP	Vs. RHP

2004 Situational Stats

	AB	H	HR	RBI	Avg		AB	H	HR	RBI	Avg
Home	257	81	22	57	.315	LHP	90	24	6	14	.267
Road	290	93	14	46	.321	RHP	457	150	30	89	.328
First Half	307	100	15	56	.326	Sc Pos	122	41	8	67	.336
Scnd Half	240	74	21	47	.308	Clutch	98	31	5	16	.316

2004 Rankings (National League)

- 2nd in GDPs (25)
- 4th in most GDPs per GDP situation (21.7%)
- 5th in fielding percentage at third base (.969)
- 7th in total bases (316)
- 8th in slugging percentage
- Led the Cubs in batting average, singles, GDPs (25), slugging percentage, on-base percentage, batting average with runners in scoring position, batting average with the bases loaded (.455), batting average vs. righthanded pitchers, cleanup slugging percentage (.631) and batting average with two strikes (.256)

2004 Season

It all started with a sneeze. Sammy Sosa threw out his back with a violent sneeze before a game at San Diego last May. The "gesundheit" period lasted a month, the time he spent on the disabled list. From there, Sosa showed flashes of his still-awesome power, but his offensive numbers declined for the third straight season. His 2004 season ended on a sour and controversial note, when he left the ballpark early without permission on the final day of the season and then told a reporter he was tired of being blamed for the Cubs' failures by manager Dusty Baker.

Hitting

The back injury and a later hip injury seemed to have a profound effect on Sosa at the plate. Where once his strength was driving low, outside pitches hard to the opposite field, he found himself flailing away and coming up empty at those same pitches in 2004. Partly as a result, most of his power shifted from center and right-center to left and left-center. Sosa still is an aggressive hitter, but pitchers got away with more mistakes against him in 2004 than they did in several years.

Baserunning & Defense

Sosa's defense continued to decline in 2004, and at times, it was painful watching him try to throw the ball toward third base or home plate. A nagging biceps injury didn't help, but Sosa's defensive game has been going downhill for several years. Sosa still hustles on the bases and is capable of taking the extra bag on balls hit to the outfield. He's no longer a basestealing threat.

2005 Outlook

Who knows the reason for Sosa's strange behavior and verbal outburst at the end of 2004? The Cubs considered trading him after the season, but his hefty salary made that difficult. Wherever he plays, he's still capable of more than one 30-plus homer season, although his best spot might be as a DH in the American League.

Position: RF
Bats: R **Throws:** R
Ht: 6' 0" **Wt:** 220

Opening Day Age: 36
Born: 11/12/68 in San Pedro de Macoris, DR
ML Seasons: 16

Overall Statistics

G	AB	R	H	D	T	HR	RBI	SB	BB	SO	Avg	OBP	Slg
126	478	69	121	21	0	35	80	0	56	133	.253	.332	.517
2138	8021	1383	2220	340	43	574	1530	233	856	2110	.277	.348	.545

Where He Hits the Ball

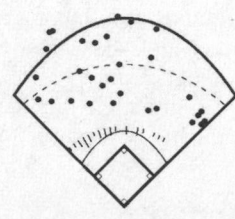
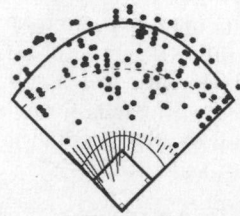

Vs. LHP **Vs. RHP**

2004 Situational Stats

	AB	H	HR	RBI	Avg		AB	H	HR	RBI	Avg
Home	231	64	18	39	.277	LHP	95	24	4	12	.253
Road	247	57	17	41	.231	RHP	383	97	31	68	.253
First Half	208	58	16	39	.279	Sc Pos	125	28	9	50	.224
Scnd Half	270	63	19	41	.233	Clutch	72	15	5	8	.208

2004 Rankings (National League)

- 2nd in highest percentage of swings that missed (32.1)
- 3rd in fielding percentage in right field (.984)
- 5th in lowest batting average on the road
- 6th in errors in right field (4)
- Led the Cubs in HR frequency (13.7 ABs per HR) and most pitches seen per plate appearance (4.00)
- Led NL right fielders in home runs

Kerry Wood

2004 Season

After exceeding the 30-start mark in each of the previous two seasons, Kerry Wood missed two months of the 2004 season with a strained right triceps. The injury allowed him to pitch only 140.1 innings, his lowest output since 2000, when he was coming back from reconstructive elbow surgery. Wood also finished below .500 for the first time in his career. Inconsistency plagued Wood down the stretch, when he won just one of his last eight starts.

Pitching

Although his repertoire has broadened and Wood has become more of a pitcher than a thrower, he's still a power guy. His best pitch, and the one that sets up everything else, is a fastball that consistently registers in the mid- to upper 90s. Wood's curveball also is among the best. It's over-the-top with a sharp downward break. Wood also has brought the slider back into the mix, with good results. Wood has a well-earned reputation as a pitcher who will come inside, but most of his hit batters come on a still-developing changeup. Wood is still prone to suffering that one bad inning that can wreck a start. He tends to be emotional on the mound, and is still learning to get hold of himself when things go bad.

Defense & Hitting

Wood helps himself as much as anybody on a good-hitting Cubs pitching staff. He homered once in 2004, bringing his career total to seven. He also is a competent bunter. Wood has developed a good move to first base and is a solid fielder.

2005 Outlook

Nobody has to tell Wood he had a subpar 2004. He's his own worst critic, and he's not afraid to say he's failed when it's true. The Cubs locked up Wood with a two-year contract extension last spring. His offseason conditioning has gotten better each year. Reaching 200 innings is a point of pride with Wood. No doubt he'll come to camp driven to reach that goal.

Position: SP
Bats: R **Throws:** R
Ht: 6' 5" **Wt:** 225

Opening Day Age: 27
Born: 6/16/77 in Irving, TX
ML Seasons: 6

Overall Statistics

	W	L	Pct.	ERA	G	GS	Sv	IP	H	BB	SO	HR	Avg
'04	8	9	.471	3.72	22	22	0	140.1	127	51	144	16	.244
Car.	67	50	.573	3.63	164	164	0	1043.0	804	512	1209	109	.214

2004 Pitching Profile

	Kerry Wood	NL Average
Overall Strike %	64.3	62.5
1st Pitch Strike %	55.8	58.5
Ratio	1.27	1.39
Strikeouts per 9 IP	9.24	6.74
Walks per 9 IP	3.27	3.38
Home Runs per 9 IP	1.03	1.11
Strikeout/Walk Ratio	2.82	1.99
Groundball/Flyball Ratio	1.20	1.25

2004 Situational Stats

	W	L	ERA	Sv	IP		AB	H	HR	RBI	Avg
Home	2	5	3.83	0	54.0	LHB	248	65	10	32	.262
Road	6	4	3.65	0	86.1	RHB	273	62	6	28	.227
First Half	4	3	2.72	0	49.2	Sc Pos	132	27	2	41	.205
Scnd Half	4	6	4.27	0	90.2	Clutch	56	13	2	5	.232

2004 Rankings (National League)

- 6th in hit batsmen (11)

2004 Season

While all eyes were on Kerry Wood and Mark Prior, Carlos Zambrano emerged in 2004 as the true ace of the Cubs' pitching staff. The big bull of a righthander seemed to enjoy being the go-to guy. Critics of manager Dusty Baker warned that Zambrano would fade down the stretch because of a heavy workload. All Zambrano did was win pitcher-of-the-month honors for September with his 4-0 record and 1.01 ERA.

Pitching

When he's on, Zambrano has the best stuff on the talented Cubs staff, and he's the hardest of their pitchers to hit. It all starts with hard, moving two-seam and four-seam fastballs that regularly check in at the mid-90s. He also has a cannonball of a sinker that he throws with a split grip. The "heavy" pitch often gets beaten into the ground. It's little wonder Zambrano loves pitching at Wrigley Field, with its tall, thick grass. He was 10-2 at Wrigley, compared with 6-6 on the road. Zambrano admittedly is an emotional pitcher on the mound. This is a double-edged sword because at times he can lose control of himself, show up teammates and infuriate opponents. A workhorse, he averaged almost 112 pitches per game in 2004.

Defense & Hitting

The switch-hitting Zambrano loves to come to the plate. He is capable of hitting the ball out of the park, and he's a good baserunner for a pitcher. He holds runners well and made strides as a fielder, taking more care throwing the ball after fielding grounders. He still needs to avoid trying to field bouncers with his bare hand.

2005 Outlook

Zambrano will be only 24 on his next birthday, and of all of the Cubs' young pitchers, he seems to have gotten his stuff together the fastest and has remained the healthiest. He cut his walks and upped his strikeouts in 2004. If all these trends keep up and he continues to mature, Zambrano will be a serious Cy Young candidate.

Position: SP
Bats: B **Throws:** R
Ht: 6' 5" **Wt:** 255

Opening Day Age: 23
Born: 6/1/81 in Puerto Cabello, VZ
ML Seasons: 4
Pronunciation: zam-BRAH-no

Overall Statistics

	W	L	Pct.	ERA	G	GS	Sv	IP	H	BB	SO	HR	Avg
'04	16	8	.667	2.75	31	31	0	209.2	174	81	188	14	.225
Car.	34	29	.540	3.25	101	80	0	539.2	467	246	453	34	.235

2004 Pitching Profile

	Carlos Zambrano	NL Average
Overall Strike %	62.1	62.5
1st Pitch Strike %	56.0	58.5
Ratio	1.22	1.39
Strikeouts per 9 IP	8.07	6.74
Walks per 9 IP	3.48	3.38
Home Runs per 9 IP	0.60	1.11
Strikeout/Walk Ratio	2.32	1.99
Groundball/Flyball Ratio	1.63	1.25

2004 Situational Stats

	W	L	ERA	Sv	IP		AB	H	HR	RBI	Avg
Home	10	2	2.38	0	106.0	LHB	370	86	7	31	.232
Road	6	6	3.13	0	103.2	RHB	403	88	7	35	.218
First Half	9	4	2.61	0	114.0	Sc Pos	195	35	4	49	.179
Scnd Half	7	4	2.92	0	95.2	Clutch	28	4	2	3	.143

2004 Rankings (National League)

- 1st in hit batsmen (20)
- 2nd in balks (2), fewest home runs allowed per nine innings (.60) and lowest batting average allowed with runners in scoring position
- 3rd in lowest ERA at home
- 4th in ERA
- 5th in wins, lowest slugging percentage allowed (.338) and most pitches thrown per batter (3.91)
- Led the Cubs in ERA, wins, batters faced (887), walks allowed, hit batsmen (20), balks (2), pitches thrown (3,468), GDPs induced (17), winning percentage, lowest batting average allowed (.225), lowest ERA at home, lowest batting average allowed vs. righthanded batters, most run support per nine innings (6.1), lowest batting average allowed with runners in scoring position and fewest home runs allowed per nine innings (.60)

Joe Borowski

Position: RP
Bats: R **Throws:** R
Ht: 6' 2" **Wt:** 225

Opening Day Age: 33
Born: 5/4/71 in
Bayonne, NJ
ML Seasons: 8
Pronunciation:
bor-OW-ski

Overall Statistics

	W	L	Pct.	ERA	G	GS	Sv	IP	H	BB	SO	HR	Avg
'04	2	4	.333	8.02	22	0	9	21.1	27	15	17	3	.303
Car.	13	18	.419	3.80	221	1	44	256.0	248	107	214	25	.255

2004 Situational Stats

	W	L	ERA	Sv	IP		AB	H	HR	RBI	Avg
Home	2	3	8.18	4	11.0	LHB	32	11	3	11	.344
Road	0	1	7.84	5	10.1	RHB	57	16	0	7	.281
First Half	2	4	8.02	9	21.1	Sc Pos	34	11	1	15	.324
Scnd Half	0	0	—	0	0.0	Clutch	52	15	3	12	.288

2004 Season

The trouble signs were there in spring training, when management let it be known that the velocity on closer Joe Borowski's fastball was in the mid- to upper-80s rather than the upper-80s to lower-90s, where it had been the previous year, when this journeyman broke through with 33 saves in 37 chances. Borowski at first denied anything was wrong, but after saving nine games, he finally admitted in early June that his right shoulder wasn't healthy. Tests revealed a partial tear in the right rotator cuff. Borowski chose to strengthen the area around the tear instead of opting for surgery. He missed the rest of the season.

Pitching, Defense & Hitting

Borowski has never been overpowering, but when he's on, he's able to spot his fastball and set up his out pitch, a good slider that's effective against both right- and lefthanded batters. He also has a decent changeup. Borowski is a good fielder with an average move. He's not a factor at the plate.

2005 Outlook

The Cubs hope the year of rehab and rest gives Borowski the strength he'll need to pitch effectively again in 2005. Because of the questions about his health, Borowski is most likely to be a setup man again.

Kyle Farnsworth

Position: RP
Bats: R **Throws:** R
Ht: 6' 4" **Wt:** 240

Opening Day Age: 28
Born: 4/14/76 in
Wichita, KS
ML Seasons: 6

Overall Statistics

	W	L	Pct.	ERA	G	GS	Sv	IP	H	BB	SO	HR	Avg
'04	4	5	.444	4.73	72	0	0	66.2	67	33	78	10	.260
Car.	22	37	.373	4.78	343	26	4	478.2	468	224	467	75	.254

2004 Situational Stats

	W	L	ERA	Sv	IP		AB	H	HR	RBI	Avg
Home	1	3	5.25	0	36.0	LHB	105	28	3	19	.267
Road	3	2	4.11	0	30.2	RHB	153	39	7	19	.255
First Half	3	3	3.35	0	40.1	Sc Pos	73	20	3	28	.274
Scnd Half	1	2	6.84	0	26.1	Clutch	155	41	4	19	.265

2004 Season

With the closer's job open after Joe Borowski went down with a season-ending shoulder injury, Kyle Farnsworth had a golden opportunity last year. But his maddening inconsistency made manager Dusty Baker skittish about using him in that role. After a tough outing in late August, Farnsworth kicked a fan on his way back to the clubhouse, putting him on the DL with a bruised knee. He then finished the year strongly, raising hopes once again.

Pitching, Defense & Hitting

Farnsworth's overpowering fastball sometimes reaches the 100-MPH mark. However, he had no other effective weapon until late last season, when he developed a late-breaking slider that came in at around 92 MPH. It's a pitch that can help Farnsworth turn the corner in his career. Farnsworth is an adequate fielder at best. A shorter leg kick he developed late in the year should help him hold runners better. He's not a factor at the plate.

2005 Outlook

Cubs GM Jim Hendry indicated he wouldn't actively shop Farnsworth. The risk in trading him is that he will develop into a dominating reliever and possibly a premier closer elsewhere. The late-season improvements provide the Cubs with hope, but it's hope they've had for several years.

Chicago (NL)

Mark Grudzielanek

Position: 2B
Bats: R **Throws:** R
Ht: 6' 1" **Wt:** 190

Opening Day Age: 34
Born: 6/30/70 in Milwaukee, WI
ML Seasons: 10
Pronunciation: grud-zuh-LAN-nick

Overall Statistics

	G	AB	R	H	D	T	HR	RBI	SB	BB	SO	Avg	OBP	Slg
'04	81	257	32	79	12	1	6	23	1	15	32	.307	.347	.432
Car.	1299	5082	681	1456	273	26	66	443	117	260	693	.287	.330	.389

2004 Situational Stats

	AB	H	HR	RBI	Avg		AB	H	HR	RBI	Avg
Home	135	44	3	13	.326	LHP	82	18	0	4	.220
Road	122	35	3	10	.287	RHP	175	61	6	19	.349
First Half	70	20	1	5	.286	Sc Pos	44	13	2	18	.295
Scnd Half	187	59	5	18	.316	Clutch	46	21	0	5	.457

2004 Season

For the second time in his two-year stint with the Cubs, Mark Grudzielanek missed significant time because of injury. In 2004, a lingering right Achilles' tendon strain put Grudzielanek on the disabled list for two months right after Opening Day. The injury, plus a job-sharing situation at second base with Todd Walker, limited Grudzielanek to 81 games, but he had another solid year, all things considered.

Hitting, Baserunning & Defense

A line-drive hitter who uses the whole field, Grudzielanek served as a stopgap leadoff man before he got hurt. An aggressive hitter who doesn't take a lot of pitches, he performed better when used lower in the batting order. The Cubs seemed to like Grudzielanek's defense more than they did Walker's. Grudzielanek turns the double play well and has a strong throwing arm. The Achilles' tendon injury made He is a non-factor as a basestealer, though he has good speed when healthy.

2005 Outlook

The Cubs did not exercise their 2005 contract option on Grudzielanek, making him a free agent. Grudzielanek admitted the Achilles tendon situation could affect him the rest of his career. He still is a capable starter or platoon player at second.

LaTroy Hawkins

Position: RP
Bats: R **Throws:** R
Ht: 6' 5" **Wt:** 215

Opening Day Age: 32
Born: 12/21/72 in Gary, IN
ML Seasons: 10

Overall Statistics

	W	L	Pct.	ERA	G	GS	Sv	IP	H	BB	SO	HR	Avg
'04	5	4	.556	2.63	77	0	25	82.0	72	14	69	10	.233
Car.	49	61	.445	4.83	443	98	69	900.0	1028	304	601	115	.288

2004 Situational Stats

	W	L	ERA	Sv	IP		AB	H	HR	RBI	Avg
Home	2	2	1.99	9	40.2	LHB	135	31	5	12	.230
Road	3	2	3.27	16	41.1	RHB	174	41	5	18	.236
First Half	2	1	2.47	11	47.1	Sc Pos	77	15	2	19	.195
Scnd Half	3	3	2.86	14	34.2	Clutch	201	50	7	22	.249

2004 Season

LaTroy Hawkins was pressed into duty as the Cubs' closer in early June after Joe Borowski went down with a season-ending shoulder injury. Hawkins pitched well in stretches but also suffered some disasters. He gave up a three-run, game-tying homer to the Mets' Victor Diaz on the second-to-last Saturday of the season, helping to send the Cubs into a tailspin that took them out of the wild-card lead and sent them home early.

Pitching, Defense & Hitting

Hawkins has a good, live arm with a fastball that tops out in the 95-98 MPH range. Pitching coach Larry Rothschild also helped Hawkins to improve his slider, which he used to keep hitters off-balance at get strikeouts. Hawkins also will mix in an occasional splitter or change. Hawkins is a good fielder who holds runners well and uses a slide step to quicken his delivery to the plate.

2005 Outlook

The Cubs were more than happy with Hawkins' performance as an eighth-inning setup man. With Borowski's uncertain status and Hawkins' inconsistency as a closer, they went into the winter eyeing the free-agent market for a new closer. That should allow Hawkins once again to move comfortably into a setup role.

Jon Leicester

Position: RP
Bats: R **Throws:** R
Ht: 6' 2" **Wt:** 220

Opening Day Age: 26
Born: 2/7/79 in
Mariposa, CA
ML Seasons: 1
Pronunciation:
lester

Overall Statistics

	W	L	Pct.	ERA	G	GS	Sv	IP	H	BB	SO	HR	Avg
'04	5	1	.833	3.89	32	0	0	41.2	40	15	35	7	.256
Car.	5	1	.833	3.89	32	0	0	41.2	40	15	35	7	.256

2004 Situational Stats

	W	L	ERA	Sv	IP		AB	H	HR	RBI	Avg
Home	2	1	6.50	0	18.0	LHB	51	19	4	9	.373
Road	3	0	1.90	0	23.2	RHB	105	21	3	9	.200
First Half	2	0	2.63	0	13.2	Sc Pos	26	7	0	8	.269
Scnd Half	3	1	4.50	0	28.0	Clutch	39	9	2	5	.231

2004 Season

For a good chunk of his minor league career, Jon Leicester was a starting pitcher. The Cubs moved him to the bullpen exclusively in 2004, and something seemed to click. Until he faded a bit toward the end, Leicester was one of the Cubs' more dependable relievers. He showed the Cubs he could work early, middle or late in games.

Pitching, Defense & Hitting

Leicester's velocity always had been good during his minor-league days, and he may have picked up a tick or two in 2004, bringing his fastball to the 93-94 MPH range. The biggest reasons for the rise in Leicester's stock were improved command, particularly with his slider, and learning how to change speeds more effectively. Leicester batted only once in 2004. He's a decent athlete who fields well and holds runners adequately.

2005 Outlook

The Cubs are searching for bullpen help, and in Leicester, they have someone in house who might be a good, low-cost alternative. His good showing in 2004 will give him an inside track toward winning an Opening Day roster spot in 2005. His experience as a minor league starter could make him a valuable swing man.

Ramon Martinez

Position: SS/3B
Bats: R **Throws:** R
Ht: 6' 1" **Wt:** 190

Opening Day Age: 32
Born: 10/10/72 in
Philadelphia, PA
ML Seasons: 7

Overall Statistics

	G	AB	R	H	D	T	HR	RBI	SB	BB	SO	Avg	OBP	Slg
'04	102	260	22	64	15	1	3	30	1	26	40	.246	.313	.346
Car.	578	1477	181	396	79	9	26	170	8	135	209	.268	.330	.387

2004 Situational Stats

	AB	H	HR	RBI	Avg		AB	H	HR	RBI	Avg
Home	131	29	1	13	.221	LHP	70	17	0	4	.243
Road	129	35	2	17	.271	RHP	190	47	3	26	.247
First Half	199	52	2	23	.261	Sc Pos	74	20	0	26	.270
Scnd Half	61	12	1	7	.197	Clutch	45	12	0	4	.267

2004 Season

A favorite player of manager Dusty Baker from their days together in San Francisco, utility man Ramon Martinez had another serviceable year for the Cubs. Martinez logged most of his time at shortstop, seeing time at third base and second base as well.

Hitting, Baserunning & Defense

There is nothing flashy about Martinez in any aspect of his game. But he manages to get the job done, especially in the field. Martinez has decent range and a strong enough arm to play short. With teammate Aramis Ramirez suffering with a groin injury for much of 2004, Martinez was an adequate backup at third base. At the plate, he is a line-drive hitter with little power. Occasionally, he'll put a charge into one, but most of his big hits are doubles. He has average speed.

2005 Outlook

While Martinez has been with Baker since 1998, he lost his utility role late last year to Neifi Perez, and had the Cubs made the postseason, Martinez would have been the odd-man out. Because of his versatility and his ability in the field, Martinez likely will find a job in 2005. As usual, most of his work will come as a super-sub or as a late-inning defensive replacement.

Kent Mercker

Position: RP
Bats: L **Throws:** L
Ht: 6' 2" **Wt:** 205

Opening Day Age: 37
Born: 2/1/68 in
Indianapolis, IN
ML Seasons: 15

Overall Statistics

	W	L	Pct.	ERA	G	GS	Sv	IP	H	BB	SO	HR	Avg
'04	3	1	.750	2.55	71	0	0	53.0	39	27	51	4	.205
Car.	69	65	.515	4.19	562	150	20	1221.2	1202	569	849	139	.259

2004 Situational Stats

	W	L	ERA	Sv	IP		AB	H	HR	RBI	Avg
Home	1	0	3.12	0	26.0	LHB	96	23	3	11	.240
Road	2	1	2.00	0	27.0	RHB	94	16	1	9	.170
First Half	1	0	2.45	0	25.2	Sc Pos	54	8	1	15	.148
Scnd Half	2	1	2.63	0	27.1	Clutch	70	16	3	11	.229

2004 Season

Recurring lower-back problems limited Kent Mercker's effectiveness at times in 2004, but he pitched through the pain while working a career-high 71 games. However, Mercker gave up a game-winning homer to the Mets' Craig Brazell on September 25, sending the Cubs on a tailspin from which they never recovered. Mercker also got himself suspended late in the year for berating an umpire, and found himself in a couple of nasty imbroglios with the team's TV announcers.

Pitching, Defense & Hitting

Despite the back problems, Mercker enjoyed a good season overall. He features a fastball around 90 MPH that he can cut and sink. He also has a curve and change, and he is effective against both lefties and righties. He is a so-so fielder and vulnerable to opposing basestealers.

2005 Outlook

Mercker's left arm seems sound. The big question is how his back will hold up as he turns 37 in February. The Cubs seemed lukewarm to having him back in 2005, especially after his alleged outbursts against Cub broadcasters Chip Caray and Steve Stone became talk-show fodder. With left-handed relievers always in need, Mercker should not have much trouble finding work.

Mike Remlinger

Position: RP
Bats: L **Throws:** L
Ht: 6' 1" **Wt:** 215

Opening Day Age: 39
Born: 3/23/66 in
Middletown, NY
ML Seasons: 12
Pronunciation:
REM-lin-jurr

Overall Statistics

	W	L	Pct.	ERA	G	GS	Sv	IP	H	BB	SO	HR	Avg
'04	1	2	.333	3.44	48	0	2	36.2	33	16	35	3	.246
Car.	51	48	.515	3.77	560	59	18	817.0	711	404	800	94	.235

2004 Situational Stats

	W	L	ERA	Sv	IP		AB	H	HR	RBI	Avg
Home	0	1	5.79	1	18.2	LHB	66	20	3	18	.303
Road	1	1	1.00	1	18.0	RHB	68	13	0	8	.191
First Half	0	1	5.19	0	8.2	Sc Pos	36	13	2	24	.361
Scnd Half	1	1	2.89	2	28.0	Clutch	87	20	1	12	.230

2004 Season

A slow recovery from offseason shoulder surgery cost Mike Remlinger the first two months of the season, and a flare-up put him on the disabled list for two weeks in late June and early July. It took time for Remlinger to feel comfortable on the mound, and as a result, inconsistency bugged him throughout the year. He pitched best when given a couple of days off between assignments, a less than ideal trait for a relief pitcher.

Pitching, Defense & Hitting

Perhaps because he has such a straight-on delivery, Remlinger is much more effective against righthanded batters. In other words, he's not your typical situational lefty who comes in to get one left-handed batter out. When healthy, Remlinger has a 90-MPH fastball, a slider and change. He has a decent move to first base, making it tough to run on him. He's not a factor at the plate.

2005 Outlook

Remlinger is entering the final season of a three-year deal. He came to Chicago with the shoulder bothering him, and as a result, his stay has been somewhat of a disappointment. Remlinger is a vocal presence in the clubhouse. An offseason of rest may help him find the form that made him one of the game's most dependable setup men.

Glendon Rusch

Position: SP/RP
Bats: L **Throws:** L
Ht: 6' 1" **Wt:** 220

Opening Day Age: 30
Born: 11/7/74 in
Seattle, WA
ML Seasons: 8
Pronunciation:
RUSH

Overall Statistics

	W	L	Pct.	ERA	G	GS	Sv	IP	H	BB	SO	HR	Avg
'04	6	2	.750	3.47	32	16	2	129.2	127	33	90	10	.256
Car.	48	78	.381	4.93	225	183	4	1163.1	1342	346	850	143	.291

2004 Situational Stats

	W	L	ERA	Sv	IP		AB	H	HR	RBI	Avg
Home	3	2	3.58	1	70.1	LHB	120	27	1	12	.225
Road	3	0	3.34	1	59.1	RHB	377	100	9	42	.265
First Half	4	1	4.06	0	71.0	Sc Pos	111	34	4	45	.306
Scnd Half	2	1	2.76	2	58.2	Clutch	53	15	0	6	.283

2004 Season

Glendon Rusch showed up in the Cubs camp at the end of spring training after being let go by the Texas Rangers. After a month with their Triple-A Iowa club, Rusch was promoted to Chicago and wound up being one of the Cubs' most dependable pitchers. He had most of his success as a starting pitcher, but he took the ball enthusiastically in all roles and performed well, going from a 1-12 mark with Milwaukee in 2003 to 6-2 in 2004.

Pitching, Defense & Hitting

Rusch is hardly overpowering, but he helped himself in 2004 by working quickly and gaining better command of his curveball and by spotting his fastball well. Against lefthanded batters, Rusch often dropped down to or just below three-quarters, and this proved to be effective. Rusch is an excellent fielder who holds runners well. He showed he was more than adept with the bat, hitting a pair of homers. He's also a good bunter.

2005 Outlook

The Cubs were interested in bringing Rusch back, and the two sides agreed to a two-year deal. The club has been without a consistently good lefthanded starter for many years, and Rusch could fill the bill while the Cubs wait for more youngsters to develop in their system.

Todd Walker

Position: 2B
Bats: L **Throws:** R
Ht: 6' 0" **Wt:** 185

Opening Day Age: 31
Born: 5/25/73 in
Bakersfield, CA
ML Seasons: 9

Overall Statistics

	G	AB	R	H	D	T	HR	RBI	SB	BB	SO	Avg	OBP	Slg
'04	129	372	60	102	19	4	15	50	0	43	52	.274	.352	.468
Car.	1022	3667	536	1059	236	25	86	448	63	333	489	.289	.347	.437

2004 Situational Stats

	AB	H	HR	RBI	Avg		AB	H	HR	RBI	Avg
Home	191	45	6	20	.236	LHP	41	11	0	2	.268
Road	181	57	9	30	.315	RHP	331	91	15	48	.275
First Half	244	69	11	29	.283	Sc Pos	78	24	1	32	.308
Scnd Half	128	33	4	21	.258	Clutch	63	10	1	6	.159

2004 Season

Todd Walker played the good soldier all season long for the Cubs, but he wanted to make one thing perfectly clear: he feels he's an everyday player. Walker signed with the Cubs as a free agent, bypassing bigger money for his stated goal of playing for a winner. With Mark Grudzielanek injured for stretches, Walker got more playing time than originally expected and made the most of it. He also emerged as someone not afraid to speak his mind in the clubhouse.

Hitting, Baserunning & Defense

Walker is an aggressive hitter who can use the entire field. He has good power, especially against righties, and is able to turn on fastballs and drive them. Against lefties he is more of a slap hitter. Much maligned as a defensive player, Walker more than held his own at second base. The lingering doubt the Cubs have about his play at second base is his ability to turn the double play. Walker is a good baserunner with fair speed. He was 0-for-3 in stolen-base attempts.

2005 Outlook

The Cubs liked Walker's lefthanded bat at the top of their order, and they signed him to a one-year, $2.5 million deal with an option for 2006. He should see more action this season.

Other Chicago Cubs

Paul Bako (Pos: C, Age: 32, Bats: L)

	G	AB	R	H	D	T	HR	RBI	SB	BB	SO	Avg	OBP	Slg
'04	49	138	13	28	8	0	1	10	1	15	29	.203	.288	.283
Car.	517	1438	132	343	75	8	14	129	4	153	359	.239	.312	.331

Bako's primary duty in 2004 was serving as Greg Maddux' personal catcher, a role he filled while the two were teammates in Atlanta. He is solid defensively, but leaves something to be desired on offense, batting just .239 with 14 home runs in 517 career games. 2005 Outlook: C

Ryan Dempster (Pos: RHP, Age: 27)

	W	L	Pct.	ERA	G	GS	Sv	IP	H	BB	SO	HR	Avg
'04	1	1	.500	3.92	23	0	2	20.2	16	13	18	1	.208
Car.	51	56	.477	4.99	184	156	2	984.2	1024	516	796	121	.271

The Cubs signed Dempster prior to the 2004 season, hoping he could bounce back from major elbow surgery. He joined the club in August and posted a respectable ERA in 23 appearances. Fifth starter is possible this year, but long relief is more likely. 2005 Outlook: A

Mike DiFelice (Pos: C, Age: 35, Bats: R)

	G	AB	R	H	D	T	HR	RBI	SB	BB	SO	Avg	OBP	Slg
'04	17	25	3	3	0	1	0	2	0	3	4	.120	.214	.200
Car.	501	1456	140	348	79	8	28	157	3	91	306	.239	.289	.362

DiFelice has seen playing time with six different major league clubs over the last nine seasons, including two in 2004. At 35, he could land a job as a second or third catcher going into this season, but another year spent primarily in the minors should be expected. 2005 Outlook: C

Tom Goodwin (Pos: LF, Age: 36, Bats: L)

	G	AB	R	H	D	T	HR	RBI	SB	BB	SO	Avg	OBP	Slg
'04	77	105	11	21	8	0	0	3	5	8	22	.200	.254	.276
Car.	1288	3846	636	1029	125	39	24	284	369	365	660	.268	.332	.339

Goodwin has served as a role player for the Cubs the past two years, seeing most of his time as a pinch-hitter/pinch-runner. However, after stealing 19 bases in 2003, the veteran outfielder swiped just five last season. His days as an everyday outfielder are well behind him. 2004 Outlook: C

Ben Grieve (Pos: RF, Age: 28, Bats: L)

	G	AB	R	H	D	T	HR	RBI	SB	BB	SO	Avg	OBP	Slg
'04	123	250	30	65	17	0	8	35	0	39	70	.260	.361	.424
Car.	953	3195	470	859	192	5	118	491	24	461	777	.269	.367	.443

Grieve enjoyed three impressive seasons with the A's, which included winning the 1998 AL Rookie of the Year Award, but then floundered in Tampa, batting .254 with 34 homers in 345 games. He could be a productive everyday outfielder in the right situation. 2005 Outlook: C

Todd Hollandsworth (Pos: RF, Age: 31, Bats: L)

	G	AB	R	H	D	T	HR	RBI	SB	BB	SO	Avg	OBP	Slg
'04	57	148	28	47	6	2	8	22	1	17	26	.318	.392	.547
Car.	897	2664	398	742	157	19	85	330	71	229	583	.279	.336	.447

Hollandsworth provided the Cubs with some clutch hitting and late-inning heroics early in the 2004 season, batting .318 with eight homers. But he fouled a ball off his right shin in late June, coincidentally in the same place where he suffered nerve damage in 2001, ending his season. 2005 Outlook: B

David Kelton (Pos: LF, Age: 25, Bats: R)

	G	AB	R	H	D	T	HR	RBI	SB	BB	SO	Avg	OBP	Slg
'04	8	10	1	1	1	0	0	0	0	0	3	.100	.100	.200
Car.	18	22	2	3	2	0	0	1	0	0	8	.136	.136	.227

Kelton was slated to become the Cubs' third baseman of the future, but when the team acquired Aramis Ramirez in 2003, his focus turned to the outfield. He spent the bulk of last season at Triple-A Iowa, batting .245 with 19 home runs, but posted a dismal .303 on-base percentage. 2005 Outlook: C

Jose Macias (Pos: 3B/2B/RF, Age: 33, Bats: B)

	G	AB	R	H	D	T	HR	RBI	SB	BB	SO	Avg	OBP	Slg
'04	98	194	23	52	6	3	3	22	4	5	38	.268	.292	.376
Car.	547	1469	186	377	69	17	25	160	39	87	219	.257	.301	.378

Macias matched his career high, hitting .268 in 194 at-bats in 2004. The utilityman played five different positions for the Cubs last season and committed just one error in 94 chances. His versatility should land him a job on a major league bench again this year. 2005 Outlook: C

Sergio Mitre (Pos: RHP, Age: 24)

	W	L	Pct.	ERA	G	GS	Sv	IP	H	BB	SO	HR	Avg
'04	2	4	.333	6.62	12	9	0	51.2	71	20	37	6	.327
Car.	2	5	.286	6.86	15	11	0	60.1	86	24	40	7	.337

Due to injuries, Mitre was asked to fill a hole in the Cubs' rotation early last season and went 2-4 with a 6.51 ERA in nine starts. The rest of the year was spent in Triple-A, where he was 6-3 with a 2.98 ERA. With the rotation stocked with proven talent, there's no room for Mitre. 2005 Outlook: C

Calvin Murray (Pos: CF, Age: 33, Bats: R)

	G	AB	R	H	D	T	HR	RBI	SB	BB	SO	Avg	OBP	Slg
'04	11	5	2	1	0	0	0	1	0	1	0	.200	.333	.200
Car.	288	633	108	146	33	4	8	54	22	71	111	.231	.315	.333

Murray turned 33 midway through the 2004 campaign and posted one of the best minor league seasons in his pro career. The light-hitting outfielder appeared in 130 games with Triple-A Iowa, batting .311 with seven home runs and 54 RBI. He was second on the club with 25 stolen bases. 2005 Outlook: C

Rey Ordonez (**Pos**: SS, **Age**: 34, **Bats**: R)

	G	AB	R	H	D	T	HR	RBI	SB	BB	SO	Avg	OBP	Slg
'04	23	61	2	10	3	0	1	5	0	2	14	.164	.190	.262
Car.	973	3115	291	767	129	17	12	287	28	191	339	.246	.289	.310

A three-time Gold Glove winner with the Mets, Ordonez has seen his playing time decrease dramatically of late, appearing in just 57 major league games over the past two seasons combined. He batted just .164 and posted the worst fielding percentage of his career (.959) in 2004. 2005 Outlook: C

Neifi Perez (**Pos**: SS/2B, **Age**: 31, **Bats**: B)

	G	AB	R	H	D	T	HR	RBI	SB	BB	SO	Avg	OBP	Slg
'04	126	381	40	97	17	1	4	39	1	24	41	.255	.296	.336
Car.	1108	4190	545	1129	188	59	52	400	48	201	423	.269	.301	.380

Perez joined the Cubs after being cut by the Giants last season and batted .371 in 23 games. The Cubs were so impressed with his play, they re-signed him for 2005. He'll back up Nomar Garciaparra. 2005 Outlook: C

Andy Pratt (**Pos**: LHP, **Age**: 25)

	W	L	Pct.	ERA	G	GS	Sv	IP	H	BB	SO	HR	Avg
'04	0	1	.000	21.60	4	0	0	1.2	0	7	1	0	.000
Car.	0	1	.000	15.00	5	0	0	3.0	1	11	2	0	.100

Although he didn't allow a hit, Pratt gave up four runs on seven walks in just 1.2 innings with the Cubs last season before being demoted. He pitched at every level of the minors, but saw no improvement in his control, and eventually was traded to the Milwaukee Brewers. 2005 Outlook: C

Todd Wellemeyer (**Pos**: RHP, **Age**: 26)

	W	L	Pct.	ERA	G	GS	Sv	IP	H	BB	SO	HR	Avg
'04	2	1	.667	5.92	20	0	0	24.1	27	20	30	1	.287
Car.	3	2	.600	6.23	35	0	1	52.0	52	39	60	6	.265

Wellemeyer pitched well in his first nine appearances last season, recording a 2.08 ERA. But after missing nearly two months with a strained muscle in his pitching shoulder, he posted a gaudy 10.32 ERA in 11 outings. He should claim a spot in the Cubs' bullpen this year. 2005 Outlook: B

Michael Wuertz (**Pos**: RHP, **Age**: 26)

	W	L	Pct.	ERA	G	GS	Sv	IP	H	BB	SO	HR	Avg
'04	1	0	1.000	4.34	31	0	1	29.0	22	17	30	4	.218
Car.	1	0	1.000	4.34	31	0	1	29.0	22	17	30	4	.218

Wuertz was nearly unhittable after the All-Star break last season, going 1-0 with a 0.77 ERA and striking out 18 in 11.2 innings for Chicago. In 37 relief appearances with Triple-A Iowa, the righthander was 1-1 with a 2.42 ERA and led the minor league club with 19 saves. 2005 Outlook: C

Chicago Cubs Minor League Prospects

Organization Overview:

As the Cubs stumbled through the homestretch last fall, it seemed that there was little help from the farm system, but that may not have been necessarily the case. Dealing with a wealth of pitching riches, GM Jim Hendry was able to orchestrate a sequence of trades that brought Nomar Garciaparra to the Cubs in return for a package that included prospects Francis Beltran, Brendan Harris and Justin Jones. While that did not ultimately send the Cubbies to a second consecutive postseason berth, it did illustrate the strength of the organization. The Cubs' system is deep in strong young arms. On their heels are some heavy hitters, including a logjam at first base. In all, the Cubs' farm could count three 2004 league MVPs and two league championships.

Bobby Brownlie

Position: P
Bats: R **Throws:** R
Ht: 6' 0" **Wt:** 210

Opening Day Age: 24
Born: 10/5/80 in Edison, NJ

Recent Statistics

	W	L	ERA	G	GS	Sv	IP	H	R	BB	SO	HR
2003 A Daytona	5	4	3.00	13	13	0	66.0	48	26	24	59	2
2004 AA West Tenn	9	9	3.36	26	26	0	147.1	127	62	36	114	15

The Cubs are waiting for Brownlie to make the next leap forward in his progression to the big leagues, and the front office has been patient to that end. He signed late after the Cubs made him their first choice in the 2002 draft, and was shut down early in 2003 after pitching the previous winter. The rest must have done him some good, as he racked up 147.1 innings at Double-A. His strikeout-walk ratio was better than 3-to-1 with a low-90s fastball and a curve that drops 12-to-6. If Matt Clement takes the free-agent route to other climes, Brownlie could conceivably be in the running to fill the vacant rotation slot before 2005 is over.

Brian Dopirak

Position: 1B
Bats: R **Throws:** R
Ht: 6' 4" **Wt:** 225

Opening Day Age: 21
Born: 12/20/83 in Tampa, FL

Recent Statistics

	G	AB	R	H	D	T	HR	RBI	SB	BB	SO	Avg
2003 A Boise	52	192	25	46	4	0	13	37	0	24	58	.240
2003 A Lansing	19	78	8	21	3	0	2	10	0	2	22	.269
2004 A Lansing	137	541	94	166	38	0	39	120	4	48	123	.307

Dopirak was snagged in the second round of the 2002 draft from Dunedin High School in Florida. Dopirak came out of the draft with the label of having the most power potential of any high school hitter, but with the caveat that lack of consistent contact could impede his growth. Last year in Class-A he put a lot of those doubts to rest. Dopirak simply terrorized opposing pitchers,

leading the league in home runs, doubles and hits, while finishing runnerup in runs, RBI and slugging percentage. His consistency was epitomized by a 27-game hitting streak that he strung together in midseason. All of this culminated in league MVP honors, a testament to Dopirak's improvement on controlling the strike zone.

Jason Dubois

Position: OF
Bats: R **Throws:** R
Ht: 6' 5" **Wt:** 220

Opening Day Age: 26
Born: 3/26/79 in Virginia Beach, VA

Recent Statistics

	G	AB	R	H	D	T	HR	RBI	SB	BB	SO	Avg
2004 AAA Iowa	109	386	76	122	26	1	31	99	2	41	97	.316
2004 NL Chicago	20	23	2	5	0	1	1	5	0	1	7	.217

The Cubs nearly lost Dubois a couple winters ago when they left him unprotected for the Rule 5 draft and Toronto snapped him up. But he could not stick on the 25-man roster, and Dubois returned to the Cubs. After spending 2003 at Double-A West Tenn, the 25-year-old turned it up a notch at Iowa last year. Dubois feasted on Triple-A pitching, clubbing 31 homers in just 386 at-bats. He returned to Wrigley for the September push and topped off his season somewhat notoriously as Sammy Sosa's replacement in right field on the final day of the season. Dubois may not make enough contact to hold down a steady job in the majors, though he may get a chance at one in 2005. Otherwise, his bat could earn him a role as a platoon outfielder/first baseman.

Angel Guzman

Position: P
Bats: R **Throws:** R
Ht: 6' 3" **Wt:** 190

Opening Day Age: 23
Born: 12/14/81 in Caracas, VZ

Recent Statistics

	W	L	ERA	G	GS	Sv	IP	H	R	BB	SO	HR
2003 AA West Tenn	3	3	2.81	15	15	0	89.2	83	30	26	87	8
2004 A Daytona	3	1	4.20	7	7	0	30.0	27	15	0	40	2
2004 AA West Tenn	0	3	5.60	4	4	0	17.2	20	11	4	13	2

While experts are excited about Guzman's potential, there has to be some questions about his stamina. His promising 2003 season was curtailed by a minor tear in his labrum, repaired with arthroscopic surgery that July. He began last year in Daytona before moving up to Double-A, but worked only 47.2 innings all told before the Cubs shut him down for the year as a precautionary move when he felt some shoulder discomfort. At full strength, he displays a heavy, sinking fastball that touches the mid-90s and an overhand curve that has batters burning worms, and an excellent change of pace. Guzman is a candidate to battle for a rotation slot with the Cubs, or be a bullpen option.

Richard Lewis

Position: 2B **Opening Day Age:** 24
Bats: R **Throws:** R **Born:** 6/29/80 in
Ht: 6' 1" **Wt:** 185 Marietta, GA

Recent Statistics

	G	AB	R	H	D	T	HR	RBI	SB	BB	SO	Avg
2003 AA Greenville	129	460	59	110	23	3	6	47	19	44	101	.239
2004 AA West Tenn	99	380	68	125	27	10	10	59	7	37	94	.329
2004 AAA Iowa	31	117	13	28	8	1	3	11	4	4	21	.239

The Cubs obtained Lewis in the preseason Juan Cruz deal that also saw Chicago receive Andy Pratt. For now at least, it looks like another coup for GM Jim Hendry, after Lewis copped MVP honors in the Double-A Southern League, where he hit .329 with some decent line-drive pop before getting a promotion to Triple-A. He won't be a big threat to steal, but he runs the bases well, and he was selected the Southern League's best second baseman after committing just two errors. He was bumped up to Triple-A, where his season ended in the year's final game when Lewis broke his right leg sliding. With a full recovery, he could end up with the Cubs before 2005 is over.

Sean Marshall

Position: P **Opening Day Age:** 22
Bats: L **Throws:** L **Born:** 8/30/82 in
Ht: 6' 6" **Wt:** 195 Richmond, VA

Recent Statistics

	W	L	ERA	G	GS	Sv	IP	H	R	BB	SO	HR
2003 A Boise	5	6	2.57	14	14	0	73.2	66	31	23	88	1
2003 A Lansing	1	0	0.00	1	1	0	7.0	5	1	0	11	0
2004 A Lansing	2	0	1.11	7	7	0	48.2	29	7	4	51	1
2004 AA West Tenn	2	2	5.90	6	6	0	29.0	36	20	12	23	2

Marshall was selected in the sixth round of the 2003 draft, and he started off 2004 like a house afire at Class-A Lansing, dominating the Midwest League with a 1.11 ERA in 48.2 innings. That earned him a quick jump to Double-A West Tennessee, where he fared less well, going 2-2, 5.90 before shutting down for the year with an injured finger tendon on his pitching hand. The Cubs expect him to be back for the start of 2005, when he'll likely pick up where he left off in West Tenn. The lanky lefthander throws a low-90s heater, along with a curve and change, all with good command and location, and has allowed just four home runs in his 158.1 pro innings.

Felix Pie

Position: OF **Opening Day Age:** 20
Bats: L **Throws:** L **Born:** 2/8/85 in La
Ht: 6' 2" **Wt:** 165 Romana, DR

Recent Statistics

	G	AB	R	H	D	T	HR	RBI	SB	BB	SO	Avg
2003 A Lansing	124	505	72	144	22	9	4	47	19	41	98	.285
2004 A Daytona	110	431	79	128	18	10	8	47	32	39	116	.297

Of all the prospects that Cubs followers have kept tabs on, perhaps Pie tickles them the most. To be sure, he is still raw—he needs to cut down on strikeouts drastically and boost his walk rate in order to be the leadoff hitter the Cubs envision. Pie is still learning the fine art of basestealing, but who can argue with his success at the high Class-A level last year? He stole 32 bases and is a sight in center field, playing shallow and chasing down drives in the alleys, while sporting a strong and accurate arm. The Double-A Southern League will be the next venue for the Pie tour, and a successful year could even result in a late-season callup to the bigs.

Renyel Pinto

Position: P **Opening Day Age:** 22
Bats: L **Throws:** L **Born:** 7/8/82 in Cupira,
Ht: 6' 5" **Wt:** 195 VZ

Recent Statistics

	W	L	ERA	G	GS	Sv	IP	H	R	BB	SO	HR
2003 A Daytona	3	8	3.22	20	19	0	114.2	91	47	45	104	4
2004 AA West Tenn	11	8	2.92	25	25	0	141.2	107	50	72	179	10
2004 AAA Iowa	1	1	7.71	2	2	0	9.1	9	9	8	9	2

Another Venezuelan find for the Cubs' scouting crew, Pinto exploded on the scene in his first taste of Double-A ball last year. Named the Southern League's top left-hander, he topped the circuit in ERA and strikeouts. Pinto can bring the heat in the low to mid-90s, and also sports an effective curve and change. At this point, the only complaint is a relative lack of control. He walked 80 in a total of 151 innings in 2004, which included a couple of late-season starts at Triple-A Iowa. On the other hand, some observers claim that he is just wild enough to be effective. He could claim a lefty role in the Cubs' pen before all is said and done this year.

Others to Watch

Along with Brian Dopirak, **Kevin Collins** (23) provided a dangerous one-two punch at Class-A Lansing last year. Even after missing several weeks with a separated shoulder after a close encounter with the outfield wall, Collins led the Midwest League in slugging at .615 and finished second with 33 home runs. . . . Lefty **Jon Connolly** (21) joined the Cubs from the Tigers' organization, where he was named their 2003 Pitcher of the Year, and proceeded to lead the high Class-A Florida State League in ERA last summer. . . Outfielder **Adam Greenberg** (24) aspires to be the Cubs' leadoff man of the future, and posted a .381 OBP at Daytona. Two years ago, he hit for the cycle in the first four innings of a game. . . 2003 No. 1 choice **Ryan Harvey** (20) took short-season Northwest League MVP honors in both the All-Star game and the Championship Series, where the outfielder clubbed four homers with six RBI and hit .556 in a three-game sweep. . . First baseman **Brandon Sing** (24) was named the high Class-A Florida State League MVP after leading the circuit in home runs (32), RBI (94), runs (86), OBP (.399) and slugging (.571). He will play more games in the outfield in 2005 with Brian Dopirak coming on strong behind him.

Chicago (NL)

Great American Ball Park

Offense

National League pitchers consider Great American Ball Park too much of a home-run haven. The ball flies to all fields and a lot of what look like routine flyballs carry to the walls and beyond. The infield plays fast but true.

Defense

There are not extreme gaps in the outfield, so ground can be covered by most outfielders. The infield also plays very fairly. There is some decent foul ground to aid pitchers who are not yet shell-shocked by watching flyballs get boosted into the outfield stands.

Who It Helps the Most

Several Reds have their power numbers aided by playing at home, including Wily Mo Pena. However, hitters like Pena and Adam Dunn can hit balls out of any park. Many Reds pitchers learned to pitch at their new home, and it was not the liability one would think it would be. Sinkerballers like Danny Graves and Paul Wilson had better ERAs at home than on the road.

Who It Hurts the Most

Flyball pitchers like Jose Acevedo are hurt by having to pitch in Great American. However, the park also hurts hitters who fall in love with trying to lift the ball to the friendly fences and hurt themselves as a result. One particular offender was Jason LaRue, who hit nearly 80 points better on the road, where he more often just tried to make contact.

Rookies & Newcomers

Dustin Moseley, one of the Reds' top pitching prospects, depends on outstanding command to succeed. It will have to be superb if Moseley is to succeed at Great American. Otherwise, with largely the same mix of players likely to return, the key for Cincinnati will be to keep its stars healthy. If they can play on a regular basis—with a succession of bombers like Dunn, Pena, Austin Kearns, Ken Griffey Jr. and Sean Casey—the Reds will put up some huge numbers at home and be an exciting team for the great Cincinnati fan base to follow.

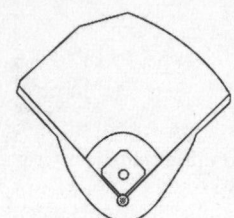

Dimensions: LF-328, LCF-379, CF-404, RCF-370, RF-325

Capacity: 42,271

Elevation: 550 feet

Surface: Grass

Foul Territory: Average

Park Factors

2004 Season

	Home Games			Away Games			
	Reds	Opp	Total	Reds	Opp	Total	Index
G	75	75	150	75	75	150	
Avg	.238	.264	.251	.257	.291	.274	92
AB	2448	2658	5106	2646	2590	5236	98
R	308	393	701	379	418	797	88
H	582	702	1284	681	754	1435	89
2B	119	160	279	142	174	316	91
3B	11	9	20	17	22	39	53
HR	88	116	204	94	97	191	110
BB	259	246	505	283	271	554	93
SO	586	491	1077	656	431	1087	102
E	49	36	85	55	41	96	89
E-Infield	38	31	69	45	30	75	92
LHB-Avg	.258	.256	.257	.275	.291	.282	91
LHB-HR	58	47	105	57	41	98	111
RHB-Avg	.220	.270	.248	.241	.291	.268	92
RHB-HR	30	69	99	37	56	93	108

2003-2004

	Home Games			Away Games			
	Reds	Opp	Total	Reds	Opp	Total	Index
G	150	150	300	147	147	294	
Avg	.243	.268	.256	.250	.290	.270	95
AB	4953	5333	10286	5150	5071	10221	99
R	630	798	1428	690	821	1511	93
H	1204	1427	2631	1288	1470	2758	93
2B	236	314	550	247	325	572	96
3B	16	15	31	32	49	81	38
HR	176	226	402	163	181	344	116
BB	500	501	1001	523	543	1066	93
SO	1172	940	2112	1268	817	2085	101
E	121	88	209	112	90	202	101
E-Infield	97	78	175	92	75	167	103
LHB-Avg	.256	.260	.258	.263	.287	.274	94
LHB-HR	97	86	183	89	76	165	113
RHB-Avg	.233	.272	.254	.240	.292	.267	95
RHB-HR	79	140	219	74	105	179	120

2004 Rankings (National League)

- Lowest batting-average factor
- Lowest LHB batting-average factor
- Second-lowest run factor
- Second-lowest hit factor
- Second-lowest triple factor
- Third-lowest RHB batting-average factor

Dave Miley

2004 Season

The Reds looked terrible in Dave Miley's first spring training as manager. However, Miley got the team going early and for the first two months of the regular season, Cincinnati was one of baseball's biggest surprises. Injuries and the reality of talent eventually caught up with the standings, but Miley kept the Reds playing hard all the way. He and his excellent coaching staff were able to do some valuable talent evaluation as the season progressed, which should serve them well this year.

Offense

It seems to be Miley's nature to want to press the action. However, with a lineup that was riddled with injuries, loaded with inexperience and plagued by strikeouts, he usually had to rein in his instincts and try to pick his spots to put runners in motion. If Miley has all his pieces in place, he will play for big innings because of the power potential of the Reds' projected regular lineup.

Pitching & Defense

Miley may have been guilty of overworking closer Danny Graves in the first few months of the season, though it was understandable that he sought to win every game he could with the Reds so hot. Miley does not have a starting rotation that is likely to eat innings, so saving wear and tear on his bullpen is a problem. He is smart enough to lean heavily on his excellent pitching coach Don Gullett. Miley and his coaches also had to work constantly with their young infield and outfield to position batters correctly.

2005 Outlook

In his first full season, Miley got very positive reviews from the players and those around the club. And though Miley was inherited by new GM Dan O'Brien, the Reds' brass rewarded the manager with a contract extension through 2006. Miley has a strong but open personality that seems to wear well on his club. If he can get a break with injuries and field a regular lineup, he has a chance to more fully establish himself as a manager to watch.

Born: 4/03/62 in Tampa, Florida

Playing Experience: No major league playing experience

Managerial Experience: 2 seasons

Manager Statistics

Year	Team, Lg	W	L	Pct	GB	Finish
2004	Cincinnati, NL	76	86	.469	29.0	4th Central
2 Seasons		98	121	.447	–	–

2004 Starting Pitchers by Days Rest

	<=3	4	5	6+
Reds Starts	0	68	58	25
Reds ERA	–	5.18	4.75	6.37
NL Avg Starts	2	82	46	23
NL ERA	4.58	4.35	4.28	4.73

2004 Situational Stats

	Dave Miley	NL Average
Hit & Run Success %	37.0	38.0
Stolen Base Success %	75.5	71.7
Platoon Pct.	57.2	55.2
Defensive Subs	25	18
High-Pitch Outings	2	6
Quick/Slow Hooks	20/20	21/12
Sacrifice Attempts	80	99

2004 Rankings (National League)

- 1st in steals of home plate (1) and fewest caught stealings of third base (2)
- 2nd in slow hooks and relief appearances (497)
- 3rd in pitchouts with a runner moving (5), starting lineups used (132) and mid-inning pitching changes (156)

Jose Acevedo

2004 Season

Jose Acevedo produced, at best, mixed results as a regular member of the Reds' starting rotation. Acevedo was competitive through the first two months but mirroring the rest of the Reds, he collapsed in June and July, when he was 1-7 with an ERA of 8.83. Acevedo became more of a spot starter during the second half. And he was a pleasant surprise in limited work out of the bullpen, allowing zero earned runs in his 17 relief innings.

Pitching

With average velocity and lack of one overpowering pitch, Acevedo has to compete by changing speeds and hitting spots with his cutter and an assortment of offspeed pitches. He has excellent control but often gets too much of the strike zone, which makes him far too easy to hit. Opponents usually don't swing and miss against Acevedo, and he is prone to allowing the longball. Acevedo has worked to add a sinker, and in relief, he seemed much more aggressive about going after hitters, instead of nibbling as he did as a starter.

Defense & Hitting

Acevedo does a fair job of holding runners, though he does not have an exceptional pickoff move. He fields his position well overall. He was largely helpless in his first full season of hitting, managing only two hits and a handful of successful sacrifice bunts.

2005 Outlook

By the end of last season, the Reds felt better about the depth of their starting pitcher options. Acevedo's stuff is not good enough to hold up as a starter, when he must face hitters two or three times a game. However, the Reds liked what they saw out of Acevedo as a reliever. His feel for pitching and control could make him a good change of pace coming out of the bullpen, and Cincinnati will enter spring training projecting him as one of its main setup men.

Position: SP/RP
Bats: R **Throws:** R
Ht: 6' 0" **Wt:** 185

Opening Day Age: 27
Born: 12/18/77 in Santo Domingo, DR
ML Seasons: 4
Pronunciation: AH-ceh-vedo

Overall Statistics

	W	L	Pct.	ERA	G	GS	Sv	IP	H	BB	SO	HR	Avg
'04	5	12	.294	5.94	39	27	0	157.2	188	45	117	30	.292
Car.	16	21	.432	5.59	68	54	0	304.1	334	97	222	58	.277

2004 Pitching Profile

	Jose Acevedo	NL Average
Overall Strike %	66.0	62.5
1st Pitch Strike %	63.5	58.5
Ratio	1.48	1.39
Strikeouts per 9 IP	6.68	6.74
Walks per 9 IP	2.57	3.38
Home Runs per 9 IP	1.71	1.11
Strikeout/Walk Ratio	2.60	1.99
Groundball/Flyball Ratio	0.85	1.25

2004 Situational Stats

	W	L	ERA	Sv	IP		AB	H	HR	RBI	Avg
Home	4	4	5.11	0	79.1	LHB	278	95	13	42	.342
Road	1	8	6.78	0	78.1	RHB	366	93	17	57	.254
First Half	4	7	5.38	0	103.2	Sc Pos	150	45	8	69	.300
Scnd Half	1	5	7.00	0	54.0	Clutch	40	9	2	7	.225

2004 Rankings (National League)

- 3rd in lowest winning percentage and highest batting average allowed with runners in scoring position
- 5th in highest batting average allowed vs. lefthanded batters
- 8th in home runs allowed
- Led the Reds in losses, home runs allowed, GDPs induced (10), highest strikeout-walk ratio (2.6) and lowest batting average allowed vs. righthanded batters

Sean Casey

2004 Season

Re-asserting himself as a top-echelon player, Sean Casey had his best all-around season in five years, highlighted by his third selection to the All-Star team. At the break, Casey was challenging for a batting title before his production steadily dropped back to earth the rest of the way. However, he still matched his career best in runs batted in and was one home run short of matching his best longball total, all while hitting for the second-best average in his career.

Hitting

Casey came to spring training last year with added muscle, and the new strength was evident. He became quicker on inside pitches and was able to pull balls much more frequently for extra bases. At the same time, he retained his ability to take outside pitches to the opposite field with extra-base authority. Casey is one of baseball's toughest men to strike out, with an exceptional knack for fighting off pitches. He hangs in well against left-handed pitching, and though often aggressive early in the count, he has steadily improved in his ability to work himself into hitters' counts.

Baserunning & Defense

Hardly a burner, Casey is an aggressive baserunner who usually shows good judgment and occasionally can surprise with a stolen base. His defensive skills remain average with subpar range and so-so hands, a combination that last year produced eight errors at first base. He does do a good job of picking low throws out of the dirt.

2005 Outlook

When the Reds got off to a strong 2004 start, Casey showed what he could do with a contender, ranking early on among the league leaders in most offensive categories. He has matured physically and many teams would be happy with the numbers he put up last season, numbers that should be matched or bettered in coming years. Beyond that, Casey is recognized as one of the game's good guys. An asset to the organization both on and off the field, he is under contract for two more seasons.

Position: 1B
Bats: L **Throws:** R
Ht: 6' 4" **Wt:** 225

Opening Day Age: 30
Born: 7/2/74 in Willingboro, NJ
ML Seasons: 8
Pronunciation: KAY-see

Overall Statistics

	G	AB	R	H	D	T	HR	RBI	SB	BB	SO	Avg	OBP	Slg
'04	146	571	101	185	44	2	24	99	2	46	36	.324	.381	.534
Car.	944	3488	514	1060	224	11	109	547	13	340	419	.304	.370	.468

Where He Hits the Ball

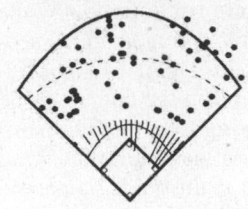 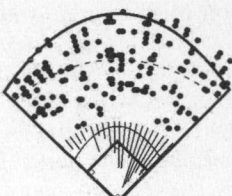

Vs. LHP   **Vs. RHP**

2004 Situational Stats

	AB	H	HR	RBI	Avg		AB	H	HR	RBI	Avg
Home	286	82	9	40	.287	LHP	183	56	10	35	.306
Road	285	103	15	59	.361	RHP	388	129	14	64	.332
First Half	287	101	15	54	.352	Sc Pos	138	42	6	69	.304
Scnd Half	284	84	9	45	.296	Clutch	80	23	4	16	.288

2004 Rankings (National League)

- 2nd in batting average on the road and fewest pitches seen per plate appearance (3.22)
- 5th in batting average vs. righthanded pitchers
- 6th in highest percentage of swings put into play (54.6), errors at first base (8) and fielding percentage at first base (.994)
- Led the Reds in batting average, at-bats, hits, singles, doubles, sacrifice flies (6), GDPs (16), highest percentage of swings put into play (54.6), batting average with the bases loaded (.444), batting average vs. lefthanded pitchers, batting average vs. righthanded pitchers, batting average on the road and batting average with two strikes (.230)

Cincinnati

Adam Dunn

2004 Season

Adam Dunn overcame an all-time record for strike-outs and an awful month of May to finally have the breakthrough power season long predicted for him. If not for the poor showing in May, Dunn might have passed the magical 50-home run plateau. Despite falling short of that mark, his much-bally-hooed, 535-foot homer on August 10 off Jose Lima that eventually settled on a piece of driftwood at the edge of the Ohio River solidified his spot among the game's most prodigious power hitters.

Hitting

Obviously, a hitter who strikes out nearly 200 times needs to cut down on his whiffs. At the same time, Dunn showed much better pitch selection in getting his walks into triple figures while also hitting for a career-high average and his second-best on-base percentage. Dunn will not cut down his swing when behind in the count and he can be too selective in waiting for a pitch to hammer out of the park. He is vulnerable to breaking pitches low and away, and teams have had some success pounding him inside. However, he has become quicker on inside pitches and when he can get his arms extended, Dunn can hit balls where few other men can.

Baserunning & Defense

No one wants to mess with Dunn when he is trying to break up a double play or bearing down on home plate. He makes good decisions on the bases and cannot be ignored as a basestealing possibility. Dunn has worked hard on his outfield skills, and he has become a very serviceable outfielder with passable range. He has average throwing strength but has improved the quickness of his release.

2005 Outlook

Dunn is capable of stringing together several seasons of 40-plus home runs. At some point, the Reds would like to see him at least limit his strikeouts somewhat because he is too talented to settle into a one-dimensional, Dave Kingman-like career. He is just entering what should be his prime years, and he can be one of the game's great power hitters for years to come.

Position: LF/1B
Bats: L **Throws:** R
Ht: 6' 6" **Wt:** 240

Opening Day Age: 25
Born: 11/9/79 in Houston, TX
ML Seasons: 4

Overall Statistics

	G	AB	R	H	D	T	HR	RBI	SB	BB	SO	Avg	OBP	Slg
'04	161	568	105	151	34	0	46	102	6	108	195	.266	.388	.569
Car.	501	1728	313	430	92	4	118	273	37	348	565	.249	.382	.512

Where He Hits the Ball

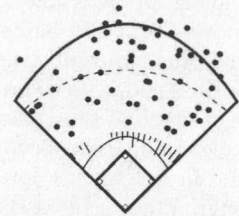 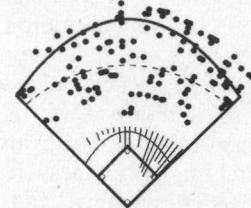

Vs. LHP   **Vs. RHP**

2004 Situational Stats

	AB	H	HR	RBI	Avg		AB	H	HR	RBI	Avg
Home	275	73	25	44	.265	LHP	180	46	10	21	.256
Road	293	78	21	58	.266	RHP	388	105	36	81	.271
First Half	297	78	25	53	.263	Sc Pos	142	34	9	56	.239
Scnd Half	271	73	21	49	.269	Clutch	93	30	11	22	.323

2004 Rankings (National League)

- 1st in strikeouts
- 2nd in home runs, errors in left field (8) and lowest percentage of swings put into play (33.0)
- 3rd in pitches seen (2,888), games played, most pitches seen per plate appearance (4.24) and lowest fielding percentage in left field (.970)
- 4th in HR frequency (12.3 ABs per HR) and lowest groundball-flyball ratio (0.7)
- Led the Reds in runs scored, total bases (323), RBI, walks, intentional walks (11), times on base (264), plate appearances (681), games played, slugging percentage, on-base percentage, and cleanup slugging percentage (.563)
- Led NL left fielders in home runs

Danny Graves

2004 Season

After an ill conceived trial as a starting pitcher, Danny Graves was back in his customary role as closer. And for a while, he was as hot as any closer in history. Graves had 24 saves by the end of May and was on a pace to shatter all records. However, the Reds stopped getting leads and Graves also tired late, managing only eight of his eventual career-high 41 total saves after the All-Star break, when he also had some lower back spasms.

Pitching

Back in the bullpen where he belonged, Graves relied again on his good sinking fastball, with which he regained his aggressiveness. Graves only throws in the low 90s at best, but in closing situations, he can take advantage of batters' anxiousness by going almost exclusively with the sinker. That was something he could not do as a starter, when his lack of offspeed and quality breaking pitches was exposed. Graves has the personality for being a closer, and is willing to challenge inside and go right after hitters. He also is able to put a bad outing behind him and be ready to pitch the next day.

Defense & Hitting

Graves does only a fair job of holding runners, something that did not have as much importance after returning to bullpen work. He fields his position well with good athletic skills. As a reliever, he does not have to hit, which is a good thing since he shows little ability with a bat in his hands.

2005 Outlook

There is no question anymore about Graves' role. He has demonstrated once and for all that his ability is only suited to being a reliever. The Reds rode him hard during last year's first several weeks, and the excessive workload caught up with him in the second half. However, if his outings are a little better monitored, he should be counted on to be a solid 30-plus save closer for the Reds, who have him signed for two more years.

Position: RP
Bats: R **Throws:** R
Ht: 6' 0" **Wt:** 185

Opening Day Age: 31
Born: 8/7/73 in Saigon, Vietnam
ML Seasons: 9

Overall Statistics

	W	L	Pct.	ERA	G	GS	Sv	IP	H	BB	SO	HR	Avg
'04	1	6	.143	3.95	68	0	41	68.1	77	13	40	12	.282
Car.	40	42	.488	3.89	465	30	172	755.2	780	246	406	84	.269

2004 Pitching Profile

	Danny Graves	NL Average
Overall Strike %	64.8	62.5
1st Pitch Strike %	60.7	58.5
Ratio	1.32	1.39
Strikeouts per 9 IP	5.27	6.74
Walks per 9 IP	1.71	3.38
Home Runs per 9 IP	1.58	1.11
Strikeout/Walk Ratio	3.08	1.99
Groundball/Flyball Ratio	1.69	1.25

2004 Situational Stats

	W	L	ERA	Sv	IP		AB	H	HR	RBI	Avg
Home	1	3	2.97	20	39.1	LHB	116	31	5	20	.267
Road	0	3	5.28	21	29.0	RHB	157	46	7	23	.293
First Half	1	3	2.72	33	49.2	Sc Pos	73	19	2	32	.260
Scnd Half	0	3	7.23	8	18.2	Clutch	198	53	8	35	.268

2004 Rankings (National League)

- 1st in blown saves (9)
- 5th in lowest save percentage (82.0)
- 6th in saves and games finished (59)
- 7th in worst first batter efficiency (.359)
- 8th in fewest strikeouts per nine innings in relief (5.3)
- 10th in relief losses (6)
- Led the Reds in saves, games finished (59), most GDPs induced per GDP situation (17.6%), save percentage (82.0), blown saves (9) and relief losses (6)

Ken Griffey Jr.

2004 Season

Yet another frustrating season unfolded for Ken Griffey Jr., who once again had a campaign cut short by injury. This time, it was a torn hamstring that required surgery and rendered Griffey unavailable for virtually the entire second half of the season. He ended up with 300 at-bats in which he had begun to show flashes of his former superstar form, managing 20 home runs for the first time since 2001. He also became a member of the 500-homer club, crushing the fateful blow on June 20 at St. Louis off hurler Matt Morris.

Hitting

The Griffey who was an exciting blend of power and average has become a distant memory. He is now more of an upper-cut hitter, as he apparently has tried to compensate for a weaker lower body and declining bat speed. Griffey has all but abandoned his formerly prodigious ability to slash balls to all fields with extra-base power and now seems intent on trying to pull the ball with every swing. He rolls over far too many pitches to produce weak grounders. He also falls off too many pitches, which results in less contact and more strikeouts.

Baserunning & Defense

Various injuries to his ankle, quadriceps and hamstrings have made Griffey a tentative baserunner with average speed and someone who is reluctant to bust it down the line. The same absence of explosiveness extends to the outfield, where his range has gone backward. He still gets great jumps, and Griffey's arm strength has come back well after recent shoulder troubles.

2005 Outlook

The question no longer is whether Griffey will ever return to his former heights. The Reds would just like to see him stick in the lineup and collect the 35 or so home runs and 100 RBI a full complement of at-bats could produce. In an effort to keep Griffey healthier, the Reds likely will shift him to right field and hope that he can avoid the disabled list and maintain a semi-regular presence in their lineup.

Position: CF
Bats: L **Throws:** L
Ht: 6' 3" **Wt:** 205

Opening Day Age: 35
Born: 11/21/69 in Donora, PA
ML Seasons: 16
Nickname: Junior

Overall Statistics

	G	AB	R	H	D	T	HR	RBI	SB	BB	SO	Avg	OBP	Slg
	83	300	49	76	18	0	20	60	1	44	67	.253	.351	.513
	1997	7379	1320	2156	400	36	501	1444	178	984	1323	.292	.377	.560

Where He Hits the Ball

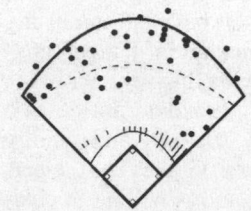 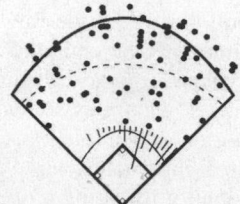

Vs. LHP   **Vs. RHP**

2004 Situational Stats

	AB	H	HR	RBI	Avg		AB	H	HR	RBI	Avg
Home	119	32	11	31	.269	LHP	111	22	5	13	.198
Road	181	44	9	29	.243	RHP	189	54	15	47	.286
First Half	295	74	20	60	.251	Sc Pos	73	24	6	39	.329
Scnd Half	5	2	0	0	.400	Clutch	53	13	2	10	.245

2004 Rankings (National League)

- 9th in lowest batting average with two strikes (.143)
- Led the Reds in batting average with runners in scoring position

Aaron Harang

2004 Season

There were some bumps along the road, but Aaron Harang overall had a solid first full season as a member of the Reds' rotation. He had most of his June taken away by a stint on the disabled list with a strained right elbow ligament, and he had some rough starts in the second half when his ERA was over a full run higher. But Harang finished second on the club in wins, and he pitched one of the two Reds' complete-game shutouts of the season.

Pitching

With velocity that just touches 90 MPH, Harang is not going to make many batters miss. He can be effective when he stays down in the strike zone and hits spots with a decent slider and much-improved change, with which he gets many of his strikeouts. He has been working on adding a two-seam fastball. However, he leaves too many fastballs up in the strike zone and can get roughed up with longballs. Harang has decent control, though he is prone to nibbling with men on base. He has become more capable of holding his stuff deeper into games, as he has matured physically and can be depended on to get through at least 6-7 innings.

Defense & Hitting

Harang needs to continue to work on holding runners, as he can be vulnerable to steals and slow to the plate. Still, opposing basestealers were just 7-for-12 with him on the mound last year. He managed four hits in his first full season of being required to bat, and showed improving ability to handle sacrifice-bunt situations.

2005 Outlook

No one expects Harang to blossom into being an ace-caliber pitcher. However, he is a serviceable arm who can give Cincinnati some needed innings in a rotation that for too long has been a revolving door. With what should be a good offense supporting him, Harang can win 12-14 games.

Position: SP
Bats: R **Throws:** R
Ht: 6' 7" **Wt:** 240

Opening Day Age: 26
Born: 5/9/78 in San Diego, CA
ML Seasons: 3
Pronunciation: ha-RANG

Overall Statistics

	W	L	Pct.	ERA	G	GS	Sv	IP	H	BB	SO	HR	Avg
'04	10	9	.526	4.86	28	28	0	161.0	177	53	125	26	.280
Car.	20	19	.513	4.96	60	58	0	315.2	344	117	231	44	.279

2004 Pitching Profile

	Aaron Harang	NL Average
Overall Strike %	64.4	62.5
1st Pitch Strike %	60.4	58.5
Ratio	1.43	1.39
Strikeouts per 9 IP	6.99	6.74
Walks per 9 IP	2.96	3.38
Home Runs per 9 IP	1.45	1.11
Strikeout/Walk Ratio	2.36	1.99
Groundball/Flyball Ratio	1.05	1.25

2004 Situational Stats

	W	L	ERA	Sv	IP		AB	H	HR	RBI	Avg
Home	4	4	4.73	0	80.0	LHB	267	70	10	26	.262
Road	6	5	5.00	0	81.0	RHB	366	107	16	51	.292
First Half	5	2	4.25	0	78.1	Sc Pos	164	41	6	50	.250
Scnd Half	5	7	5.44	0	82.2	Clutch	18	3	0	0	.167

2004 Rankings (National League)

- 9th in highest ERA on the road
- Led the Reds in strikeouts, lowest ERA on the road and most strikeouts per nine innings (7.0)

D'Angelo Jimenez

2004 Season

After a career of injuries and bouncing among different teams, D'Angelo Jimenez established himself as member of the Reds' nucleus. He had a solid offensive season, setting a career high in RBI and on-base percentage, while nearly matching his best home-run and hit totals. He improved his eye at the plate, and Jimenez also continued a career pattern of being a more productive hitter in the second half.

Hitting

All of Jimenez' home runs last year came batting from the left side, where he hit 37 points higher than from the right. The disparity has caused some consideration for him to give up switch-hitting. He sometimes will think longball too much early in the count and often overswings, which is a big reason for a too-high strikeout total. However, Jimenez has extra-base pop to all fields and can pull a fastball low in the strike zone for power. In addition to adding muscle, Jimenez' knowledge of the strike zone also has improved, as reflected in a walk total that was second only to Adam Dunn on the Reds.

Baserunning & Defense

With above-average speed and quick acceleration, Jimenez has become a genuine basestealing threat. He at times can be overly aggressive and will make some mistakes on the bases. He came a long way defensively last year at second base, showing good range and a much-improved ability to turn the double play. He has a strong, accurate arm and good hands.

2005 Outlook

At an age when he is just entering his playing prime, Jimenez has quieted many doubters of his attitude and consistency to be a legitimate major league second baseman. His salary is starting to escalate, and that could be a factor in the Reds' thinking down the road. However, for now, they feel very comfortable about the keystone position being in Jimenez' hands.

Position: 2B
Bats: B **Throws:** R
Ht: 6' 0" **Wt:** 195

Opening Day Age: 27
Born: 12/21/77 in Santo Domingo, DR
ML Seasons: 5
Pronunciation: he-MEN-ez

Overall Statistics

	G	AB	R	H	D	T	HR	RBI	SB	BB	SO	Avg	OBP	Slg
'04	152	563	76	152	28	3	12	67	13	82	99	.270	.364	.394
Car.	505	1881	254	506	88	17	33	205	32	240	333	.269	.352	.386

Where He Hits the Ball

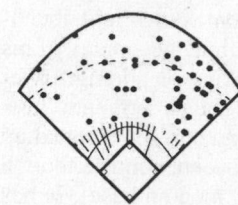
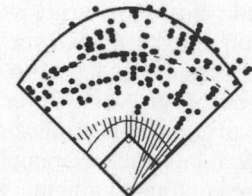

Vs. LHP   **Vs. RHP**

2004 Situational Stats

	AB	H	HR	RBI	Avg		AB	H	HR	RBI	Avg
Home	268	69	6	36	.257	LHP	154	37	0	11	.240
Road	295	83	6	31	.281	RHP	409	115	12	56	.281
First Half	297	77	6	27	.259	Sc Pos	130	41	3	54	.315
Scnd Half	266	75	6	40	.282	Clutch	86	18	1	9	.209

2004 Rankings (National League)

- 2nd in lowest percentage of swings on the first pitch (8.7)
- 3rd in fielding percentage at second base (.990), highest percentage of pitches taken (65.1) and lowest stolen-base percentage (65.0)
- 6th in lowest on-base percentage for a leadoff hitter (.310)
- 7th in most pitches seen per plate appearance (4.16)
- Led the Reds in highest percentage of pitches taken (65.1), lowest percentage of swings that missed (10.1) and lowest percentage of swings on the first pitch (8.7)

Austin Kearns

2004 Season

The wait for Austin Kearns' ascent into stardom continues after his 2004 season was washed out by forearm and thumb injuries that cost him nearly two-thirds of the year. Kearns never got going, opening the campaign with a terrible April in which he hit only .137. He was injured in late April when an errant pitch broke his forearm, and he did not return until mid-May. Thumb surgery then kept him on the shelf for most of June, July and August. Kearns ended up with barely more than 200 at-bats.

Hitting

Kearns has yet to play a full major league season, and his lost at-bats could be retarding his progress. He can be easily jammed, and after his forearm injury last year, Kearns seemed to be more tentative about attacking inside pitches. His plate coverage also suffered because he was less willing to go after pitches away. He has excellent bat speed and the power to hit to all fields. However, he has a tendency to try and pull too many pitches and gives away too many at-bats.

Baserunning & Defense

Kearns has decent speed and is capable of an occasional steal. He is a good baserunner, with the ability and judgment to take extra bases. He has the range and arm strength to play any of the three outfield positions. However, to maximize its personnel, Cincinnati intends to try to convert Kearns to third base, where he should have the athletic skills to be serviceable at the new position.

2005 Outlook

Much is made of Ken Griffey's lost time to injuries, but for the Reds, it might be even more important to keep Kearns healthy. Kearns has lost valuable time to injuries over the last four years, and as a result, his considerable promise is on hold. He can be a cornerstone player, and he can become especially valuable if he can successfully make the switch to third, thus filling what has been a huge hole for Cincinnati. The Reds have reason to believe that if he can get a full season worth of at-bats, Kearns can be a 100-RBI threat in the middle of their lineup.

Position: RF
Bats: R **Throws:** R
Ht: 6' 3" **Wt:** 220

Opening Day Age: 24
Born: 5/20/80 in Lexington, KY
ML Seasons: 3

Overall Statistics

	G	AB	R	H	D	T	HR	RBI	SB	BB	SO	Avg	OBP	Slg
'04	64	217	28	50	10	2	9	32	2	28	71	.230	.321	.419
Car.	253	881	133	244	45	5	37	146	13	123	220	.277	.372	.465

Where He Hits the Ball

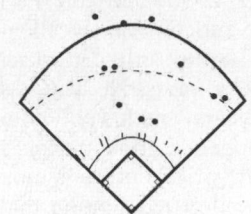
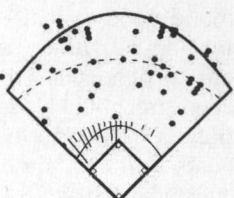

Vs. LHP   **Vs. RHP**

2004 Situational Stats

	AB	H	HR	RBI	Avg		AB	H	HR	RBI	Avg
Home	129	27	3	15	.209	LHP	47	10	2	7	.213
Road	88	23	6	17	.261	RHP	170	40	7	25	.235
First Half	87	17	3	13	.195	Sc Pos	44	10	1	20	.227
Scnd Half	130	33	6	19	.254	Clutch	32	7	3	8	.219

2004 Rankings (National League)

- Did not rank near the top or bottom in any category

Barry Larkin

2004 Season

In what was his final season in Cincinnati, Barry Larkin ended on a sour note, as he was relegated to the bench over the season's final two months. After a solid first half in which he hit nearly .300 and had an assortment of big hits, Larkin had problems with a strained oblique muscle and then was largely benched after returning to health. After July, he had only 53 at-bats, many of them cameo appearances late in games.

Hitting

There's still life in Larkin's bat, and last year he returned in the spring in excellent condition and seemingly stronger than in recent years. He is quick through the hitting zone and can turn around good fastballs. He remains an excellent breaking-ball hitter, and Larkin still can slash balls to right-center for extra bases. He also has added strength in his later years, and his ability to go deep cannot be overlooked. Larkin manages counts well and is tough to strike out, regaining some of the patience and pitch recognition that made him a .300 hitter for most of his career.

Baserunning & Defense

Numerous leg injuries have all but eliminated Larkin's ability to be a serious basestealing threat, but he can still take a base in the right situation and retains his excellent judgment on the basepaths. His range at shortstop has gone backward, as has his throwing ability, but he can make the routine plays and is a stabilizing presence for young infielders. Larkin also has shown a recent willingness to practice at other positions to enhance his versatility.

2005 Outlook

Though it won't be with the Reds, Larkin remains interested in continuing his career for another year. He would be an attractive option in different ways, perhaps as a veteran shortstop who could bring leadership to a young club or as a proven winner, willing to be a utility player on a contending club. Wherever he goes, Larkin brings class and savvy, as well as the ability to still make contributions on the field.

Position: SS
Bats: R **Throws:** R
Ht: 6' 0" **Wt:** 185

Opening Day Age: 40
Born: 4/28/64 in Cincinnati, OH
ML Seasons: 19

Overall Statistics

G	AB	R	H	D	T	HR	RBI	SB	BB	SO	Avg	OBP	Slg
111	346	55	100	15	3	8	44	2	34	39	.289	.352	.419
2180	7937	1329	2340	441	76	198	960	379	939	817	.295	.371	.444

Where He Hits the Ball

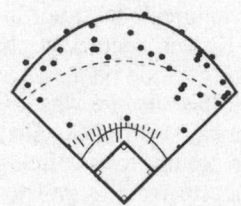 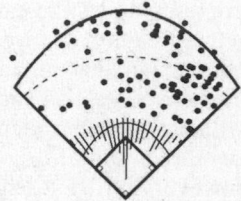

Vs. LHP **Vs. RHP**

2004 Situational Stats

	AB	H	HR	RBI	Avg		AB	H	HR	RBI	Avg
Home	184	55	5	24	.299	LHP	92	19	4	14	.207
Road	162	45	3	20	.278	RHP	254	81	4	30	.319
First Half	258	76	4	33	.295	Sc Pos	78	20	2	32	.256
Scnd Half	88	24	4	11	.273	Clutch	57	14	0	5	.246

2004 Rankings (National League)

- 2nd in most GDPs per GDP situation (22.9%)
- Led the Reds in GDPs (16), highest ground ball-flyball ratio (1.8) and batting average at home

Jason LaRue

2004 Season

Jason LaRue had maybe his best all-around season, batting over .250 for the first time and setting a career high in RBI. LaRue was in double figures in home runs for a fourth straight season as well. He came on strong in the latter part of the season, batting .280 after the All-Star break.

Hitting

LaRue, who worked hard with batting coach Chris Chambliss, finally started cutting down his swing and put more balls in play as last season progressed, and the result was a much more productive batting average. He is going to strike out a lot because he is too willing to take a big rip at high fastballs and because he will chase too many breaking balls. He also puts himself behind in too many counts by being overly aggressive on first pitches. However, LaRue has big-time power when he gets his arms extended on low fastballs, and he has begun hitting more balls to the opposite field after being pull-happy for most of his young career.

Baserunning & Defense

Though lacking exceptional speed, LaRue is not wholly a typical catcher and occasionally will try to steal a base. He also is aggressive and usually successful when he tries for the extra base. He remains a catcher who needs to work at his craft. He has a strong arm and threw out a respectable 29.6 percent of opposing basestealers. However, he can be erratic and often has trouble with balls in the dirt. Last year LaRue was charged with 15 passed balls, tied for most in the majors.

2005 Outlook

The Reds know that LaRue strikes out too much and can have his share of trouble behind the plate. However, he has become an increasingly dependable receiver, and he brings the added dimension of power with his bat. The Reds think that if LaRue can carry his second-half improvement into this season, he can take his play to another plateau and perhaps reach 20 homers and 70 or so RBI, which would be a huge bonus for the Cincinnati lineup.

Position: C
Bats: R **Throws:** R
Ht: 5'11" **Wt:** 200

Opening Day Age: 31
Born: 3/19/74 in Houston, TX
ML Seasons: 6
Pronunciation: la-ROO

Overall Statistics

	G	AB	R	H	D	T	HR	RBI	SB	BB	SO	Avg	OBP	Slg
'04	114	390	46	98	24	2	14	55	0	26	108	.251	.334	.431
Car.	533	1674	203	401	95	6	62	222	11	129	493	.240	.319	.415

Where He Hits the Ball

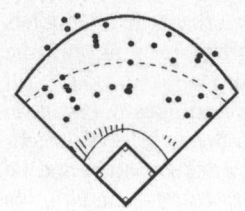 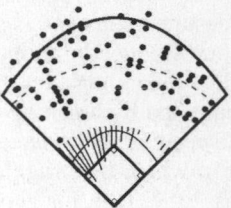

Vs. LHP   **Vs. RHP**

2004 Situational Stats

	AB	H	HR	RBI	Avg		AB	H	HR	RBI	Avg
Home	193	41	3	15	.212	LHP	95	26	4	11	.274
Road	197	57	11	40	.289	RHP	295	72	10	44	.244
First Half	215	49	8	29	.228	Sc Pos	103	25	7	44	.243
Scnd Half	175	49	6	26	.280	Clutch	73	19	2	8	.260

2004 Rankings (National League)

- 2nd in hit by pitch (24) and lowest fielding percentage at catcher (.989)
- 3rd in errors at catcher (8) and lowest percentage of swings put into play (33.4)
- 4th in lowest batting average with two strikes (.136)
- 6th in highest percentage of swings that missed (30.7)
- Led the Reds in hit by pitch (24)

Wily Mo Pena

2004 Season

There was no more positive development last year for Cincinnati than the emergence of Wily Mo Pena. Long considered an exceptional talent, Pena finally got a chance to play every day and he took advantage of the opportunity. He was second on the Reds in home runs and fourth in RBI, all produced in barely more than 300 at-bats (of which a third amazingly resulted in strikeouts). He also impressed the Reds by recovering from a slump following his hot first six weeks as a starter and rebounded to have a strong September.

Hitting

Pena doesn't have to take a backseat to anyone's power. He can turn around fastballs with tape-measure results and is able to reach inside pitches more frequently after slightly backing off the plate. Pena, however, remains a raw product still bedeviled by breaking balls and does not wait on offspeed pitches. He can go through long stretches in which he struggles to make contact and he has little feel for working counts, though his patience improved as his exposure to major league pitching increased. He has also shown the ability to kill lefthanded pitching.

Baserunning & Defense

Despite his good size, Pena has above-average speed and should be able to steal in double figures as he gains more experience. He has excellent range and a cannon for a throwing arm, and the Reds think his tools could allow him to play center field, though his experience largely has been in the corner outfield positions.

2005 Outlook

Among Pena's many attributes is a strong work ethic that has impressed the Reds' coaches. He improved significantly in all areas last year, and Pena likely will come to spring training with the Reds' center-field job. His breakthrough season was not a fluke, and if he continues just normal development, he has the ability to be another 40-homer giant in the middle of the Cincinnati lineup.

Position: RF/CF
Bats: R **Throws:** R
Ht: 6' 3" **Wt:** 215

Opening Day Age: 23
Born: 1/23/82 in Laguna Salada, DR
ML Seasons: 3
Pronunciation: will-ee moe PAIN-ya

Overall Statistics

	G	AB	R	H	D	T	HR	RBI	SB	BB	SO	Avg	OBP	Slg
'04	110	336	45	87	10	1	26	66	5	22	108	.259	.316	.527
Car.	203	519	66	127	16	2	32	83	8	34	172	.245	.302	.468

Where He Hits the Ball

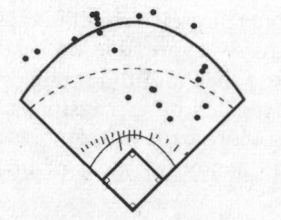
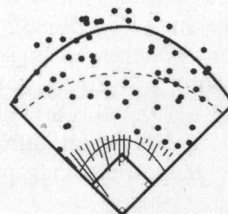

Vs. LHP   **Vs. RHP**

2004 Situational Stats

	AB	H	HR	RBI	Avg		AB	H	HR	RBI	Avg
Home	174	48	13	37	.276	LHP	86	26	9	22	.302
Road	162	39	13	29	.241	RHP	250	61	17	44	.244
First Half	159	43	10	28	.270	Sc Pos	85	25	5	37	.294
Scnd Half	177	44	16	38	.249	Clutch	52	9	3	11	.173

2004 Rankings (National League)

- 3rd in lowest batting average with two strikes (.121)
- 6th in errors in right field (4)
- 8th in lowest batting average in the clutch

Paul Wilson

Position: SP
Bats: R **Throws:** R
Ht: 6' 5" **Wt:** 215

Opening Day Age: 32
Born: 3/28/73 in
Orlando, FL
ML Seasons: 6

2004 Season

At the end of May, the Reds were challenging for first place and Paul Wilson was challenging for the Cy Young Award with a 7-0 record. Reality, alas, returned to Cincinnati, with the Reds falling out of contention and Wilson managing only four wins the rest of the season, part of which was missed with soreness in his lower back. However, Wilson for a second straight year led all Cincinnati starters in wins and innings pitched.

Pitching

His many arm problems have robbed Wilson of some of the stuff that had caused the Mets to make him the first player drafted in 1994. However, he has made himself into a very competitive pitcher by refining his changeup and using the movement of a good cutter and sinker to keep batters off balance. He will at times be aggressive inside with his fastball, which just touches 90 MPH, but Wilson will nibble when in trouble. He is not afraid of pitching around hitters to get to someone he has a better feel for retiring. He has also averaged nearly seven innings a start, giving the Reds some needed stability in an otherwise rag-tag rotation.

Defense & Hitting

Wilson has added a slide step to his array of ways to hold runners, something with which he's improved. He fields his position well and was error-free in 2004. He struggles to make contact at the plate and is not much of a hitting factor.

2005 Outlook

The Reds went into the offseason hoping to re-sign Wilson, and they accomplished their goal by agreeing to terms on a two-year, $7.35 million pact with an option for 2007. For many clubs, Wilson was viewed as a solid option for the middle or back end of the rotation, but for the Reds, he is as close to an ace as the club has and a solid leader in the clubhouse. If the lineup stays healthy behind him, Wilson is good enough to approach 15 wins.

Overall Statistics

	W	L	Pct.	ERA	G	GS	Sv	IP	H	BB	SO	HR	Avg
'04	11	6	.647	4.36	29	29	0	183.2	192	63	117	26	.271
Car.	39	53	.424	4.71	161	144	0	895.1	961	319	589	116	.275

2004 Pitching Profile

	Paul Wilson	NL Average
Overall Strike %	62.9	62.5
1st Pitch Strike %	62.5	58.5
Ratio	1.39	1.39
Strikeouts per 9 IP	5.73	6.74
Walks per 9 IP	3.09	3.38
Home Runs per 9 IP	1.27	1.11
Strikeout/Walk Ratio	1.86	1.99
Groundball/Flyball Ratio	1.11	1.25

2004 Situational Stats

	W	L	ERA	Sv	IP		AB	H	HR	RBI	Avg
Home	6	3	3.32	0	105.2	LHB	301	85	11	41	.282
Road	5	3	5.77	0	78.0	RHB	408	107	15	47	.262
First Half	9	2	3.66	0	108.1	Sc Pos	159	41	5	58	.258
Scnd Half	2	4	5.38	0	75.1	Clutch	44	8	1	2	.182

2004 Rankings (National League)

- 1st in fielding percentage at pitcher (1.000)
- 4th in lowest stolen-base percentage allowed (50.0)
- 5th in pickoff throws (144)
- 8th in most home runs allowed per nine innings (1.27)
- Led the Reds in ERA, wins, games started, innings pitched, hits allowed, batters faced (798), walks allowed, hit batsmen (8), pitches thrown (2,876), pickoff throws (144), GDPs induced (10), lowest batting average allowed (.271), lowest slugging percentage allowed (.441), lowest on-base percentage allowed (.334), lowest stolen-base percentage allowed (50.0), lowest ERA at home, most run support per nine innings (5.7) and fewest home runs allowed per nine innings (1.27)

Cincinnati

Juan Castro

Position: 3B/SS/2B
Bats: R **Throws:** R
Ht: 5'11" **Wt:** 195

Opening Day Age: 32
Born: 6/20/72 in Los Mochis, Mexico
ML Seasons: 10
Pronunciation: KASS-tro

Overall Statistics

	G	AB	R	H	D	T	HR	RBI	SB	BB	SO	Avg	OBP	Slg
'04	111	299	36	73	21	2	5	26	1	14	51	.244	.277	.378
Car.	668	1599	160	361	75	9	25	129	4	99	296	.226	.269	.331

2004 Situational Stats

	AB	H	HR	RBI	Avg		AB	H	HR	RBI	Avg
Home	150	38	3	11	.253	LHP	80	19	1	9	.238
Road	149	35	2	15	.235	RHP	219	54	4	17	.247
First Half	142	38	1	10	.268	Sc Pos	69	17	1	22	.246
Scnd Half	157	35	4	16	.223	Clutch	57	14	1	7	.246

2004 Season

Juan Castro showed his versatility by starting at all four infield positions. Most of his action came at third base, an area that was a year-long problem for the Reds. Castro struggled when required to play every day for extended periods, hitting .125 in 72 at-bats in July, after which his playing time gradually shrunk.

Hitting, Baserunning & Defense

Castro occasionally can show surprising power, but he is more consistent when he is not over-swinging and trying to take balls where they're pitched. He often guesses on first-pitch fastballs, though he did hit .347 when putting the first pitch into play last season. Castro has just average speed and is not a basestealing threat. He has the skills to play anywhere in the infield, though his range and arm seem best suited at second base.

2005 Outlook

The small-market Twins inked Castro to a two-year, $2.05 million deal in late November. He really is not suited to be an everyday option, but the Twins will give him a chance to compete for the starting job at shortstop. If he doesn't win the position outright, he still should see plenty of time as a backup to youngster Jason Bartlett and as a versatile option around the infield.

Brandon Claussen

Position: SP
Bats: R **Throws:** L
Ht: 6' 1" **Wt:** 200

Opening Day Age: 25
Born: 5/1/79 in Rapid City, SD
ML Seasons: 2
Pronunciation: CLAW-sin

Overall Statistics

	W	L	Pct.	ERA	G	GS	Sv	IP	H	BB	SO	HR	Avg
'04	2	8	.200	6.14	14	14	0	66.0	80	35	45	9	.299
Car.	3	8	.273	5.72	15	15	0	72.1	88	36	50	10	.298

2004 Situational Stats

	W	L	ERA	Sv	IP		AB	H	HR	RBI	Avg
Home	1	4	3.96	0	36.1	LHB	56	21	3	13	.375
Road	1	4	8.80	0	29.2	RHB	212	59	6	29	.278
First Half	0	0	—	0	0.0	Sc Pos	81	24	3	33	.296
Scnd Half	2	8	6.14	0	66.0	Clutch	4	2	0	0	.500

2004 Season

Brandon Claussen joined the Reds' rotation on July 20 and was an immediate hit with a strong seven-inning outing that earned him a victory in his first start. However, he would end up winning only once more in his next 13 starts. Claussen at times had tough luck, coming up empty seven times despite allowing three runs or fewer.

Pitching, Defense & Hitting

Claussen's velocity is not eye-popping, and he needs to compete by changing speeds and using a very good slider, with which he gets the majority of his strikeouts. He is a good competitor, and now nearly three years removed from major elbow surgery, he has a chance to mature physically. Claussen has only an average pickoff move. He showed ability to at least make contact in his first year as a hitter.

2005 Outlook

There were mixed reports on Claussen when he came from the Yankees in a 2003 trade. He is not ace material, but the ability and the heart is there for him to be a useful starting pitcher. He will get a chance this spring to be part of the Reds' rotation, and they hope he can be a 10-12 game winner in his first full season in the majors.

Ryan Freel

Position:
3B/RF/CF/2B/LF
Bats: R **Throws:** R
Ht: 5'10" **Wt:** 180

Opening Day Age: 29
Born: 3/8/76 in
Jacksonville, FL
ML Seasons: 3

Overall Statistics

	G	AB	R	H	D	T	HR	RBI	SB	BB	SO	Avg	OBP	Slg
'04	143	505	74	140	21	8	3	28	37	67	88	.277	.375	.368
Car.	195	664	98	185	28	9	7	43	48	77	105	.279	.368	.380

2004 Situational Stats

	AB	H	HR	RBI	Avg		AB	H	HR	RBI	Avg
Home	249	65	1	15	.261	LHP	115	27	1	5	.235
Road	256	75	2	13	.293	RHP	390	113	2	23	.290
First Half	267	75	1	16	.281	Sc Pos	106	27	0	23	.255
Scnd Half	238	65	2	12	.273	Clutch	74	24	0	7	.324

2004 Season

Injuries throughout the Cincinnati roster gave Ryan Freel the chance to be an everyday player for the first time, and he saw action at third base, center field and right field. Freel became a favorite of the Reds' fans with his hustling style of play that included 37 stolen bases and eight triples to place him among the league leaders in both categories.

Hitting, Baserunning & Defense

Freel largely is a slap hitter without much power, and he is at his best when he simply tries to put the ball in play. He has trouble with breaking stuff, but he has surprisingly good patience overall and is a good fastball hitter. He is a quick-starting baserunner who will take risks on the basepaths, and he steals for a high percentage. Freel is more than adequate at third, though he is best suited to the outfield, where his range is excellent.

2005 Outlook

The Reds got more than they could have expected last year out of Freel. However, for manager Dave Miley, the ideal situation would be a healthy club on which Freel is employed as a utility option. His versatility and hustle can make him a very important bench player.

Josh Hancock

Position: SP
Bats: R **Throws:** R
Ht: 6' 3" **Wt:** 205

Opening Day Age: 26
Born: 4/11/78 in
Cleveland, MS
ML Seasons: 3

Overall Statistics

	W	L	Pct.	ERA	G	GS	Sv	IP	H	BB	SO	HR	Avg
'04	5	2	.714	5.09	16	11	0	63.2	73	28	36	17	.282
Car.	5	3	.625	4.86	21	12	0	74.0	80	30	46	18	.271

2004 Situational Stats

	W	L	ERA	Sv	IP		AB	H	HR	RBI	Avg
Home	2	0	3.63	0	34.2	LHB	132	35	7	18	.265
Road	3	2	6.83	0	29.0	RHB	127	38	10	20	.299
First Half	0	1	11.57	0	7.0	Sc Pos	56	14	3	22	.250
Scnd Half	5	1	4.29	0	56.2	Clutch	9	0	0	0	.000

2004 Season

Acquired from Philadelphia in mid-summer along with shortstop Anderson Machado for pitcher Todd Jones, Josh Hancock made nine starts for the Reds in mid-August and September. Hancock pitched well, lasting into at least the sixth inning on seven occasions and winning three of his four decisions in the Cincinnati rotation. In his final outing of the season, he gave up two earned runs in eight innings in a win over the Cubs.

Pitching, Defense & Hitting

Hancock does not have exceptional velocity, but he gets good movement on his fastball and has developed a good slider. He also has a useful change, though all his stuff is of fine-line quality that results in a lot of homers when it is left over the plate. He holds runners fairly well but proved to be a bit of a liability with the glove. Hancock is not yet a factor as a hitter.

2005 Outlook

Cincinnati over the last couple of years has acquired some serviceable young arms, one of which is Hancock, who will get a chance to earn a spot in the rotation. He doesn't blow anyone away with his stuff, but his feel for pitching can make him useful both as a starter or in middle relief.

Cincinnati

Luke Hudson

Position: SP
Bats: R **Throws:** R
Ht: 6' 3" **Wt:** 195

Opening Day Age: 27
Born: 5/2/77 in Fountain Valley, CA
ML Seasons: 2

Overall Statistics

	W	L	Pct.	ERA	G	GS	Sv	IP	H	BB	SO	HR	Avg
'04	4	2	.667	2.42	9	9	0	48.1	36	25	38	3	.208
Car.	4	2	.667	2.65	12	9	0	54.1	41	31	45	4	.210

2004 Situational Stats

	W	L	ERA	Sv	IP		AB	H	HR	RBI	Avg
Home	1	2	4.26	0	25.1	LHB	81	13	2	2	.160
Road	3	0	0.39	0	23.0	RHB	92	23	1	9	.250
First Half	0	0	–	0	0.0	Sc Pos	39	5	0	7	.128
Scnd Half	4	2	2.42	0	48.1	Clutch	0	0	0	0	–

2004 Season

Another one of the young Reds' pitchers given late-season auditions, Luke Hudson was impressive in his nine big league starts. Only once did he allow more than three earned runs, and four times he did not allow any earned runs. This after making 19 combined starts at the Double- and Triple-A levels in 2004.

Pitching, Defense & Hitting

With a history of arm troubles, the Reds were careful with Hudson's innings. However, he has big-time potential with a fastball that touches the 95-97 MPH range and a devastating power curve. He has started showing a changeup. His control needs work, though his walk rates in the minors last year improved. He is slow delivering home, and will need to work on his glove around the mound. Hudson shows the ability to become a factor at the plate, and he drove in a pair of runs on two hits with the parent club last season.

2005 Outlook

Hudson has the best stuff of any of the Reds' starters, and he comes to camp with high expectations. If Hudson continues to mature and his command improves, the Reds think that down the road he can be at least a 15-game winner.

Felipe Lopez

Position: SS/3B
Bats: B **Throws:** R
Ht: 6' 1" **Wt:** 185

Opening Day Age: 24
Born: 5/12/80 in Bayamon, PR
ML Seasons: 4

Overall Statistics

	G	AB	R	H	D	T	HR	RBI	SB	BB	SO	Avg	OBP	Slg
'04	79	264	35	64	18	2	7	31	1	25	81	.242	.314	.405
Car.	272	920	119	216	45	11	22	101	18	88	269	.235	.304	.379

2004 Situational Stats

	AB	H	HR	RBI	Avg		AB	H	HR	RBI	Avg
Home	124	28	3	9	.226	LHP	65	19	2	12	.292
Road	140	36	4	22	.257	RHP	199	45	5	19	.226
First Half	46	7	0	5	.152	Sc Pos	60	16	1	24	.267
Scnd Half	218	57	7	26	.261	Clutch	45	10	1	1	.222

2004 Season

The jury remains out on Felipe Lopez after he produced mixed results during a two-month, late-season trial as the Reds' everyday shortstop. Lopez showed flashes of his power with 27 extra-base hits in just 264 at-bats, but his erratic play in the field and his inability to consistently make contact were continuing liabilities.

Hitting, Baserunning & Defense

Lopez remains a raw hitter who too often goes out of the strike zone and cannot handle breaking pitches. He has good bat speed and can drive the ball when he makes contact, something he does much better swinging from the right side. He has above-average speed but lacks good baserunning instincts. Lopez has a powerful arm and good infield range, but his hands are not good and he has accuracy problems at both short and third. He had 15 errors in 292 total chances last season.

2005 Outlook

It is too early for the Reds to give up on Lopez. He has solid tools and is just entering his physical prime. While Lopez will have to prove he has started to mature and developed some consistency, the shortstop job is open with Barry Larkin's departure, and Lopez is in line to start.

John Riedling

Position: RP
Bats: R **Throws:** R
Ht: 5'11" **Wt:** 190

Opening Day Age: 29
Born: 8/29/75 in Fort Lauderdale, FL
ML Seasons: 5
Pronunciation: READ-ling

Overall Statistics

	W	L	Pct.	ERA	G	GS	Sv	IP	H	BB	SO	HR	Avg
'04	5	3	.625	5.10	70	0	0	77.2	90	40	46	10	.286
Car.	13	12	.520	4.13	200	8	3	274.1	269	135	182	21	.256

2004 Situational Stats

	W	L	ERA	Sv	IP		AB	H	HR	RBI	Avg
Home	2	1	4.85	0	39.0	LHB	117	34	6	22	.291
Road	3	2	5.35	0	38.2	RHB	198	56	4	38	.283
First Half	4	2	3.80	0	47.1	Sc Pos	100	32	6	52	.320
Scnd Half	1	1	7.12	0	30.1	Clutch	115	32	4	19	.278

2004 Season

Over the season's first three months, John Riedling was as solid as any setup man in baseball. He had a 4-1 record with 12 holds by the end of June. However, his numbers badly deteriorated as the season wore on. He also failed in his chances to close games, going 0-for-7 in save tries.

Pitching, Defense & Hitting

Riedling has the stuff to be effective. His fastball can touch the 95-MPH range, and he also throws a splitter that can produce strikeouts. However, he struggles with his command and his stuff is thrown at all the same speed, making him too easy for hitters to read. He simply gives up too many base hits. He fields his position well but does little to slow down opposing basestealers, who were 10-for-10 on his watch in 2004. He is not anything to worry about as a hitter.

2005 Outlook

Cincinnati always has liked Riedling's aggressive makeup, but his second-half struggles last year and inability to help out in save situations raised some alarms. He likely will come to camp with a setup job, but with younger arms on the way, he is also the kind of veteran the Reds could look to shop.

Todd Van Poppel

Position: RP/SP
Bats: R **Throws:** R
Ht: 6' 5" **Wt:** 235

Opening Day Age: 33
Born: 12/9/71 in Hinsdale, IL
ML Seasons: 11
Pronunciation: VAN-pop-pell

Overall Statistics

	W	L	Pct.	ERA	G	GS	Sv	IP	H	BB	SO	HR	Avg
'04	4	6	.400	6.09	48	11	0	115.1	136	32	72	22	.298
Car.	40	52	.435	5.58	359	98	4	907.0	944	461	711	143	.269

2004 Situational Stats

	W	L	ERA	Sv	IP		AB	H	HR	RBI	Avg
Home	2	3	6.85	0	67.0	LHB	193	60	11	33	.311
Road	2	3	5.03	0	48.1	RHB	264	76	11	46	.288
First Half	3	3	5.79	0	70.0	Sc Pos	126	40	8	60	.317
Scnd Half	1	3	6.55	0	45.1	Clutch	41	13	3	7	.317

2004 Season

Todd Van Poppel had only limited success in both starting and relief outings in 2004. He won only two of his 11 starts, all but one coming in late May and June. He also struggled in relief, where he was used in long and middle roles. On the positive side, he did manage to top the 100-inning mark for the first time since 1995.

Pitching, Defense & Hitting

Over the last two years, Van Poppel has been trying to re-work his delivery to be tougher on righthanded hitters and also get more sink on the ball. However, though he still can throw the ball by people for strikeouts, his inconsistent command makes him too hittable. He is fairly easy to run on because of his slow delivery. He is not an automatic out when he gets a chance to bat, posting three hits in 17 at-bats last year. He generally is a clean fielder.

2005 Outlook

The Reds declined to offer arbitration to Van Poppel. At this stage of his career, he likely is forced to accept a non-guaranteed invitation to spring training and try to hang on at the back end of someone's bullpen.

Cincinnati

Ryan Wagner

Position: RP
Bats: R **Throws:** R
Ht: 6' 4" **Wt:** 210

Opening Day Age: 22
Born: 7/15/82 in
Yoakum, TX
ML Seasons: 2

Overall Statistics

	W	L	Pct.	ERA	G	GS	Sv	IP	H	BB	SO	HR	Avg
'04	3	2	.600	4.70	49	0	0	51.2	59	27	37	7	.284
Car.	5	2	.714	3.80	66	0	0	73.1	72	39	62	9	.254

2004 Situational Stats

	W	L	ERA	Sv	IP		AB	H	HR	RBI	Avg
Home	2	1	1.80	0	30.0	LHB	58	13	1	5	.224
Road	1	1	8.72	0	21.2	RHB	150	46	6	36	.307
First Half	2	1	5.94	0	16.2	Sc Pos	63	19	4	37	.302
Scnd Half	1	1	4.11	0	35.0	Clutch	49	10	2	11	.204

2004 Season

The Reds were careful with Ryan Wagner in his first full year in the bullpen, limiting his appearances at times to guard against arm problems. Wagner was mostly used in middle relief after he struggled early in late-game situations. He finished the year with eight holds, but he blew all three of his save chances.

Pitching, Defense & Hitting

Cincinnati pitching coach Don Gullett has worked with Wagner on trusting his 90-plus MPH fastball more. Wagner falls in love with his slider, a quality pitch but one that major league hitters learned to lay off as it dived out of the strike zone. He struck out just 10 more batters than he walked in 2004, a ratio he certainly will need to improve upon going forward. Wagner does not hold runners well and has had trouble with routine fielding plays (two errors last season). He will rarely, if ever, hit.

2005 Outlook

The Reds consider Wagner to be part of their bullpen mix. However, the organization no longer is viewing him as a certain closer of the future, and with other young arms challenging him for work, Wagner has something to prove this spring.

Gabe White

Position: RP
Bats: L **Throws:** L
Ht: 6' 2" **Wt:** 205

Opening Day Age: 33
Born: 11/20/71 in
Sebring, FL
ML Seasons: 10

Overall Statistics

	W	L	Pct.	ERA	G	GS	Sv	IP	H	BB	SO	HR	Avg
'04	1	3	.250	6.94	64	0	1	59.2	72	12	41	14	.294
Car.	34	26	.567	4.55	466	15	17	562.1	542	140	453	95	.252

2004 Situational Stats

	W	L	ERA	Sv	IP		AB	H	HR	RBI	Avg
Home	1	2	9.00	0	31.0	LHB	104	30	6	20	.288
Road	0	1	4.71	1	28.2	RHB	141	42	8	30	.298
First Half	0	2	6.68	0	32.1	Sc Pos	62	22	3	35	.355
Scnd Half	1	1	7.24	1	27.1	Clutch	66	17	5	12	.258

2004 Season

The Reds re-acquired Gabe White from the Yankees in early June and the lefthander pitched well for Cincinnati much of the time. However, he also was prone to the occasional meltdown, allowing three or more runs in less than two innings on six different occasions throughout the season. Those tough outings added up to a 6.23 ERA for the Reds last year, which was a marked improvement on the 8.27 mark he posted with the Yankees.

Pitching, Defense & Hitting

White is aggressive, sometimes to a fault. He trusts his fastball too much and when he doesn't spot it well, he can get hit hard. He does not have a reliable breaking ball, so batters can sit on his fastball or change and do damage. He fields his position well and has a quick delivery to the plate. He has yielded just three steals in 106.1 innings over the past two seasons. He did not come to the plate once this year, and hasn't had a hit since 2000.

2005 Outlook

Cincinnati allowed White to become a free agent, as the Reds did not offer him arbitration. However, veteran lefthanders always seem to find work, and White still can be a useful part of someone's bullpen.

Other Cincinnati Reds

Jung Keun Bong (Pos: LHP, **Age**: 24)

	W	L	Pct.	ERA	G	GS	Sv	IP	H	BB	SO	HR	Avg
'04	1	1	.500	4.70	3	3	0	15.1	17	10	11	3	.270
Car.	7	4	.636	5.17	48	4	1	78.1	81	43	62	11	.272

Bong was acquired from the Braves just days before the 2004 season began. Cincinnati immediately proceeded to convert him back into a starter, feeling it was the best way to fully utilize his above-average changeup. His season was cut short by a frayed labrum. 2005 Outlook: C

Darren Bragg (Pos: CF/RF, **Age**: 35, **Bats**: L)

	G	AB	R	H	D	T	HR	RBI	SB	BB	SO	Avg	OBP	Slg
'04	47	101	13	19	3	1	4	9	1	10	31	.188	.261	.356
Car.	916	2461	341	627	145	14	46	260	56	304	570	.255	.340	.381

Bragg began last year with the Yankees Triple-A Columbus affiliate, hitting .282 with a .836 OPS in 70 games, before being released in July. A brief stint in San Diego was followed by an August signing with Cincinnati. He made 18 outfield starts with the Reds. 2005 Outlook: C

Jermaine Clark (Pos: RF, **Age**: 28, **Bats**: L)

	G	AB	R	H	D	T	HR	RBI	SB	BB	SO	Avg	OBP	Slg
'04	14	30	4	4	1	0	0	2	1	1	8	.133	.212	.167
Car.	42	78	7	12	3	0	0	9	3	7	13	.154	.236	.192

The Athletics secured the services of Clark by offering him a minor league contract in November. He is the type of player Oakland likes, minus the power numbers. He has a career .384 OBP in the minors and the 10 home runs he hit at Louisville in 2004 were a career high. 2005 Outlook: C

Jacob Cruz (Pos: RF, **Age**: 32, **Bats**: L)

	G	AB	R	H	D	T	HR	RBI	SB	BB	SO	Avg	OBP	Slg
'04	96	147	22	33	8	0	3	28	0	16	43	.224	.317	.340
Car.	299	602	83	146	28	2	15	87	4	69	161	.243	.332	.370

Cruz breaks the mold as a lefthanded hitter who handles lefthanded pitching better. He credits a high school coach for the sound approach against lefties that has produced a big league lefty/righty split of .382/.486/.509 versus .229/.315/.356. 2005 Outlook: C

Jimmy Haynes (Pos: RHP, **Age**: 32)

	W	L	Pct.	ERA	G	GS	Sv	IP	H	BB	SO	HR	Avg
'04	0	3	.000	9.60	5	4	0	15.0	26	7	8	3	.388
Car.	63	89	.414	5.37	227	203	1	1200.2	1358	601	762	148	.290

The Reds made the decision to sign Haynes to a two-year, $5 million deal after his 15-win 2002 season. Wrong move. Haynes could neither throw strikes nor stay healthy the past two years, which resulted in the Reds placing him on waivers in May. The Devil Rays signed him to a minor league deal in December. 2005 Outlook: C

Tim Hummel (Pos: 3B/1B, **Age**: 26, **Bats**: R)

	G	AB	R	H	D	T	HR	RBI	SB	BB	SO	Avg	OBP	Slg
'04	56	110	10	24	4	0	1	7	1	8	17	.218	.281	.282
Car.	82	194	19	43	9	0	3	17	1	16	30	.222	.285	.314

Stuck behind D'Angelo Jimenez at second base, Hummel looked elsewhere for playing time in 2004, including trying his hand at first base. His versatility in the field, however, did not make up for less than pedestrian plate production. 2005 Outlook: C

Brandon Larson (Pos: 3B, **Age**: 28, **Bats**: R)

	G	AB	R	H	D	T	HR	RBI	SB	BB	SO	Avg	OBP	Slg
'04	40	118	13	25	6	0	3	14	1	14	35	.212	.304	.339
Car.	109	291	29	52	11	0	8	37	4	35	86	.179	.271	.299

Times have been tough for Larson since a breakout 2002 Triple-A campaign vaulted him into management's favor. Once destined as the future at third base, Larson has seen his star shrink. Injuries and a two-year .164/.264/.256 line are likely reasons. 2005 Outlook: C

Anderson Machado (Pos: SS, **Age**: 24, **Bats**: B)

	G	AB	R	H	D	T	HR	RBI	SB	BB	SO	Avg	OBP	Slg
'04	17	56	6	15	5	1	0	4	3	10	26	.268	.379	.393
Car.	18	56	6	15	5	1	0	4	4	10	26	.268	.379	.393

The 24-year-old Machado is noted for his speed and plate discipline. In fact, he led the Double-A Eastern League with 49 stolen bases and 108 walks in 2003. The problem for Machado has been high strikeout rates and low batting averages. His .268 Reds average was a welcome sight. 2005 Outlook: C

Mike Matthews (Pos: LHP, **Age**: 31)

	W	L	Pct.	ERA	G	GS	Sv	IP	H	BB	SO	HR	Avg
'04	2	1	.667	6.30	35	0	0	30.0	31	16	15	7	.265
Car.	13	10	.565	4.41	224	10	1	238.2	228	117	173	29	.255

Bothered by left elbow bone chips, Matthews posted his highest earned run average since 2000. A June outing in which he gave up eight earned runs on nine hits in less than an inning did not help the situation. Matthews filed for free agency in October. 2005 Outlook: C

Corky Miller (Pos: C, **Age**: 29, **Bats**: R)

	G	AB	R	H	D	T	HR	RBI	SB	BB	SO	Avg	OBP	Slg
'04	13	39	2	1	0	0	0	3	0	6	12	.026	.204	.026
Car.	83	232	20	47	12	0	6	26	1	24	55	.203	.301	.332

Miller yo-yoed for short stretches between Cincinnati and Triple-A Louisville in his seventh year as a professional. An 0-for-29 start with the Reds, the worst such streak of his career, effectively ended most catching duties. Minnesota claimed Miller off waivers after the season. 2005 Outlook: C

Aaron Myette (Pos: RHP, Age: 27)

	W	L	Pct.	ERA	G	GS	Sv	IP	H	BB	SO	HR	Avg
'04	0	0	–	8.31	5	0	0	4.1	3	8	6	0	.188
Car.	6	12	.333	8.16	47	30	0	154.1	185	106	134	26	.298

Myette registered a solid 2.89 ERA in 41 games at Louisville. His 45 hits allowed and 58 strikeouts in 62.1 innings were sufficient enough to warrant a minor league contract with the Phillies. 2005 Outlook: C

Phil Norton (Pos: LHP, Age: 29)

	W	L	Pct.	ERA	G	GS	Sv	IP	H	BB	SO	HR	Avg
'04	2	5	.286	5.07	69	0	0	65.2	71	38	48	5	.284
Car.	2	6	.250	5.07	92	2	0	92.1	94	54	61	10	.270

Norton was second on the team in appearances, but shoddy command away from Great American Ball Park hindered his overall effectiveness. His .331/.440/.484 averages against, and 25 walks in 31.0 innings on the road, made success nearly impossible. 2005 Outlook: C

Ray Olmedo (Pos: SS, Age: 23, Bats: B)

	G	AB	R	H	D	T	HR	RBI	SB	BB	SO	Avg	OBP	Slg
'04	8	1	0	0	0	0	0	0	0	1	0	.000	.500	.000
Car.	87	231	24	55	6	1	0	17	1	14	46	.238	.282	.273

A torn ulnar collateral ligament, sustained while playing in the Venezuelan Winter League, will keep Olmedo on the DL to begin 2005. Any chance of him assuming the Reds' vacant shortstop job appears to have all but disappeared. 2005 Outlook: C

Juan Padilla (Pos: RHP, Age: 28)

	W	L	Pct.	ERA	G	GS	Sv	IP	H	BB	SO	HR	Avg
'04	1	0	1.000	7.71	18	0	0	25.2	39	12	17	7	.355
Car.	1	0	1.000	7.71	18	0	0	25.2	39	12	17	7	.355

What will a 2.02 Triple-A ERA and strikeout-walk ratio of 52:6 at the Yankees' Columbus affiliate get you? For Padilla in 2004, not very much. The Reds claimed him off waivers in September, only to let him go a month later. He signed a minor league deal with the Mets. 2005 Outlook: C

Brian Reith (Pos: RHP, Age: 27)

	W	L	Pct.	ERA	G	GS	Sv	IP	H	BB	SO	HR	Avg
'04	2	2	.500	7.27	22	0	0	26.0	30	19	24	5	.288
Car.	4	12	.250	5.92	73	9	1	127.2	147	71	85	26	.292

No one can say Reith didn't get a shot. After compiling a 2-10 record and 5.58 ERA with Cincinnati from 2001-03, the Reds afforded him another opportunity in 2004. The outcome was no different, forcing Cincinnati to cut ties. He was picked up by Pittsburgh. 2005 Outlook: C

Jason Romano (Pos: RF, Age: 25, Bats: R)

	G	AB	R	H	D	T	HR	RBI	SB	BB	SO	Avg	OBP	Slg
'04	26	34	3	5	0	0	1	4	0	2	12	.147	.194	.235
Car.	110	161	23	31	4	1	1	9	8	10	44	.193	.238	.248

Traded three times, and a member of five different clubs, Romano has seen his fair share of cities since 2002. Still only 25, he has been slowed by leg troubles, including a torn right hamstring in 2004. The crowded Reds' outfield is not the best fit for someone who needs at-bats. 2005 Outlook: C

Jesus Sanchez (Pos: LHP, Age: 30)

	W	L	Pct.	ERA	G	GS	Sv	IP	H	BB	SO	HR	Avg
'04	0	2	.000	7.53	3	3	0	14.1	18	9	8	4	.305
Car.	23	34	.404	5.32	162	83	0	524.2	564	281	384	82	.280

A regular on the Marlins' staff from 1998-2000, Sanchez has amassed less than 100 innings and a total of eight decisions since that period. Acquired by Toronto in July, the 30-year-old still could be a valuable asset as a situational lefty. 2005 Outlook: C

Javier Valentin (Pos: C, Age: 29, Bats: B)

	G	AB	R	H	D	T	HR	RBI	SB	BB	SO	Avg	OBP	Slg
'04	82	202	18	47	10	1	6	20	0	17	36	.233	.293	.381
Car.	272	728	65	167	36	4	17	81	0	55	139	.229	.283	.360

Cincinnati gave Valentin a vote of confidence by re-signing him to a one-year, $450,000 contract this off-season. With Corky Miller gone, Valentin will be assured of backup duties for a second year. The LaRue/Valentin combo makes up one of the best defensive catching duos in baseball. 2005 Outlook: B

Joe Valentine (Pos: RHP, Age: 25)

	W	L	Pct.	ERA	G	GS	Sv	IP	H	BB	SO	HR	Avg
'04	2	3	.400	5.22	24	1	4	29.1	23	25	29	4	.211
Car.	2	3	.400	6.03	26	1	4	31.1	28	26	30	5	.233

Valentine looked good filling in for closer Danny Graves near the end of 2004. He converted all four save opportunities with a fastball running into the mid-90s. The velocity that was missing to begin 2004 seems to have returned with the move back to the bullpen. 2005 Outlook: C

John Vander Wal (Pos: RF, Age: 38, Bats: L)

	G	AB	R	H	D	T	HR	RBI	SB	BB	SO	Avg	OBP	Slg
'04	42	51	2	6	2	0	2	4	0	4	20	.118	.182	.275
Car.	1372	2751	374	717	170	18	97	430	38	385	698	.261	.351	.441

Vander Wal couldn't get much going for Cincinnati, as his surgically repaired right knee limited him to mostly pinch-hitting duty. With the exception of 2004, he has hit a solid .274/.368/.480 since 1999. 2005 Outlook: C

Cincinnati Reds Minor League Prospects

Organization Overview:

After pumping out high-powered offensive performers like Adam Dunn, Austin Kearns and Wily Mo Pena in recent years, the next wave of Cincinnati prospects may be pitchers. And an arms infusion may be just what the doctor ordered. Trades netted Aaron Harang and Brandon Claussen in 2003, while Ryan Wagner made his major league debut shortly after getting drafted that June. They remain key components of Cincinnati's staff. And now starters Dustin Moseley and Richie Gardner appear on the horizon, while relievers Todd Coffey and Brian Shackelford could vie for bullpen slots in 2005. Others, such as Thomas Pauly, may be right behind the first group. The young hurlers offer reason to hope the Reds soon can post their first winning season since 2000.

Will Bergolla

Position: 2B **Opening Day Age:** 22
Bats: R **Throws:** R **Born:** 2/4/83 in
Ht: 6' 0" **Wt:** 150 Carabobo, VZ

Recent Statistics

	G	AB	R	H	D	T	HR	RBI	SB	BB	SO	Avg
2003 A Potomac	128	523	77	142	25	3	2	31	52.	29	59	.272
2004 AA Chattanooga	116	466	79	132	26	1	4	38	36	40	63	.283

Bergolla signed with the Reds at age 16 in 1999. He's an athletic, polished Venezuelan who shows good instincts on the diamond and is an offensive-minded player. He can be an asset at the top of the batting order when he's able to reach base, because of his speed and ability to steal bases. However, his walk rate hasn't been impressive above Rookie-level, though he did show improvement at Double-A last season. He's a solid defender at second base and also can play shortstop. With Barry Larkin's tenure in Cincinnati coming to an end, it may be worth giving Bergolla an extended trial at the position. He's expected to move up another level in 2005.

Todd Coffey

Position: P **Opening Day Age:** 24
Bats: R **Throws:** R **Born:** 9/9/80 in Shelby,
Ht: 6' 5" **Wt:** 245 NC

Recent Statistics

	W	L	ERA	G	GS	Sv	IP	H	R	BB	SO	HR
2003 A Dayton	3	3	2.25	39	0	9	56.0	61	20	14	53	1
2003 A Potomac	0	2	1.96	11	0	2	23.0	16	6	3	21	0
2004 AA Chattanooga	4	1	2.38	40	0	20	45.1	36	13	4	53	3
2004 AAA Louisville	1	0	5.27	15	0	4	13.2	15	8	2	11	1

Coffey wasn't particularly highly regarded coming out of high school, when he waited until the 41st round before the Reds chose him in 1998. He missed a year due to injury in 2000, but has really come into his own

the past couple years. Check out his outstanding strike-out-walk ratios last season. Pitchers with those kind of numbers almost have to enjoy success. Coffey throws hard, with a fastball that can reach 96 MPH. He also has a slider, but it's the split-finger pitch he's developed that has put him on the prospect map. He followed last year's strong performance with a nice showing in the Arizona Fall League. He has a chance to be the Reds' closer in the near future.

Edwin Encarnacion

Position: 3B **Opening Day Age:** 22
Bats: R **Throws:** R **Born:** 1/7/83 in La
Ht: 6' 1" **Wt:** 195 Romana, DR

Recent Statistics

	G	AB	R	H	D	T	HR	RBI	SB	BB	SO	Avg
2003 A Potomac	58	215	40	69	15	1	6	29	7	24	32	.321
2003 AA Chattanooga	67	254	40	69	13	1	5	36	8	22	44	.272
2004 AA Chattanooga	120	469	73	132	35	1	13	76	17	53	79	.281

Encarnacion has played above his age throughout his professional career, continuing to show the skills that make him possibly the best position prospect in the system. Shortstop agile, he is a plus defender at third base, with an arm that draws raves. But it's his bat that could make him an impact player. The doubles he delivers with regularity have a chance of turning into homers as he matures. He also has the speed to steal bases and the Reds think he could be a .300 hitter. Third base has been unsettled for the Reds since Aaron Boone was traded. While they're talking about trying Austin Kearns at the position, it could be a short-term solution if Encarnacion continues to emerge.

Richie Gardner

Position: P **Opening Day Age:** 23
Bats: R **Throws:** R **Born:** 2/1/82 in Santa
Ht: 6' 3" **Wt:** 185 Rosa, CA

Recent Statistics

	W	L	ERA	G	GS	Sv	IP	H	R	BB	SO	HR
2004 A Potomac	8	3	2.50	18	12	1	86.1	77	31	13	80	3
2004 AA Chattanooga	5	2	2.56	11	11	0	70.1	68	24	13	59	7

The 2003 draft may wind up being a boon to the Reds' pitching staff. Ryan Wagner and Thomas Pauly were taken in the first two rounds that June, while Gardner was plucked in Round 6. A product of the University of Arizona, Gardner didn't make his pro debut until 2004 but then moved quickly. He made a smooth transition to the minors, pitching very impressively at two levels and climbing to Double-A. He possesses great command and a plus slider, and does the little things well, such as holding runners and fielding his position. If he continues to demonstrate the polish he exhibited last season, Gardner soon could be pushing for a major league job.

Dustin Moseley

Position: P
Bats: R **Throws:** R
Ht: 6' 3" **Wt:** 190

Opening Day Age: 23
Born: 12/26/81 in Texarkana, AR

Recent Statistics

	W	L	ERA	G	GS	Sv	IP	H	R	BB	SO	HR
2003 AA Chattanooga	5	6	3.83	18	18	0	112.2	116	55	28	73	10
2003 AAA Louisville	2	3	2.70	8	8	0	50.0	46	19	14	27	5
2004 AA Chattanooga	3	2	2.66	8	8	0	47.1	33	16	10	40	4
2004 AAA Louisville	2	4	4.65	12	12	0	71.2	78	38	34	48	7

Moseley has been one of the Reds' top pitching prospects since getting taken with a supplemental first-round pick in the 2000 draft. Although he seemed to stall a bit in 2004, it's understandable considering the back problems and death in his family that he endured last season. Moseley isn't overpowering, with a fastball that tops out at 91 MPH and usually resides in the upper 80s. But he features plus command and pitchability. He also throws a cutter, changeup and curveball. He had a good Arizona Fall League, and could have a shot at making the major league staff in spring training.

Thomas Pauly

Position: P
Bats: R **Throws:** R
Ht: 6' 1" **Wt:** 195

Opening Day Age: 23
Born: 7/28/81 in Jacksonville, FL

Recent Statistics

	W	L	ERA	G	GS	Sv	IP	H	R	BB	SO	HR
2003 A Dayton	2	5	4.02	12	12	0	47.0	45	26	10	36	5
2004 A Potomac	8	7	2.97	28	19	0	121.1	96	47	26	135	12

Pauly is an extremely bright kid, which you'd probably expect from a guy who attended Princeton. His pitching ability emerged in college, as he led the Ivy League in ERA in both 2002 and 2003. The Reds were impressed enough to choose him in the second round of the '03 draft, one round after they had grabbed Ryan Wagner. Pauly is strong and durable, with a power fastball that ranges between 90-95 MPH. He also has a decent slider, but it's his changeup that ultimately may be his best pitch. He led the high Class-A Carolina League in strikeouts last season, and figures to open 2005 at Double-A.

Stephen Smitherman

Position: OF
Bats: R **Throws:** R
Ht: 6' 4" **Wt:** 235

Opening Day Age: 26
Born: 9/1/78 in McAlester, OK

Recent Statistics

	G	AB	R	H	D	T	HR	RBI	SB	BB	SO	Avg
2003 AAA Louisville	17	63	1	8	0	0	0	5	0	4	19	.127
2003 AA Chattanooga	105	365	60	113	21	2	19	73	11	54	95	.310
2003 NL Cincinnati	21	44	3	7	2	0	1	6	1	3	9	.159
2004 AAA Louisville	129	452	55	123	35	1	10	52	5	42	107	.272

Through the first half of 2003, Smitherman had been a .300 hitter with respectable power at nearly every stop since signing with the Reds as a 23rd-round pick in 2000. But he failed to hit in a major league trial late that season, and then got off to a slow start last year. To his credit, he made adjustments and wound up with respectable numbers. Smitherman is a big, strong guy who runs well for his size. He has been a doubles-hitting machine in the minors, and it's possible he could seize a big league job if given another opportunity. But at age 26, he may be running out of chances to be anything more than a fourth outfielder.

Joey Votto

Position: 1B
Bats: L **Throws:** R
Ht: 6' 3" **Wt:** 205

Opening Day Age: 21
Born: 9/10/83 in Toronto, Ontario

Recent Statistics

	G	AB	R	H	D	T	HR	RBI	SB	BB	SO	Avg
2003 A Dayton	60	195	19	45	8	0	1	20	2	34	64	.231
2003 R Billings	70	240	47	76	17	3	6	37	4	56	80	.317
2004 A Dayton	111	391	60	118	26	2	14	72	9	79	110	.302
2004 A Potomac	24	84	11	25	7	0	5	20	1	11	21	.298

The Reds selected Votto in the second round of the 2002 draft out of a Toronto high school. Canadian springs can limit playing time, and Votto now is blossoming as a pro. He's described as a natural, gifted, pure hitter whose power will come. While he more than doubled his previous career high in home runs between two stops last year, his most impressive skills right now almost certainly are his patience and management of the strike zone. He figures to coax 100 walks per season with regularity in the future. He has settled into first base and quietly improved. The package of his defense, lefthanded bat, emerging power and high on-base percentage has drawn comparisons to John Olerud.

Others to Watch

Outfielder **Tony Blanco** (23) has made great strides in plate discipline and pitch recognition, which may help explain the 29 homers he clubbed last season en route to Double-A. The ball makes a different sound when it comes off his bat. Selected by Washington in the Rule 5 draft, he could spend 2005 in the majors. . . **Jesse Gutierrez** (26) has caught a bit in the past but played first base exclusively in Double-A last season. He's hit at every level he's played and is a run producer with decent power. . . **Javon Moran** (22) was acquired from the Phillies' organization last August. He plays a dynamite center field and can fly, stealing 50 bases at two Class-A stops in 2004. . . Righthander **Elizardo Ramirez** (22) also was part of the trade that sent Cory Lidle to the Phillies. He has posted some terrific strikeout-walk ratios in the past, and reached Double-A last season. . . Lefthander **Brian Shackelford** (28) is a compelling story. He hit 20 home runs at Double-A as recently as 2001. But he's now a pitcher with a lively fastball and good cutter that makes him tough on righthanded batters. Don't be surprised if he winds up in the lefthanded mix in the Reds' bullpen in 2005.

Coors Field

Offense

Coors Field has a well-deserved reputation as a hitters' haven. With the altitude, a quality hitter can drive the ball out of the ballpark to any field. However, what causes more headaches for the pitchers is the size of the outfield. Lazy flyballs often fall in because outfielders tend to play too deep. Additionally, the infield is one of the fastest in the major leagues.

Defense

There is a premium on quality defensive players to minimize the impact of Coors Field on pitchers. The best outfield would be one with three outfielders capable of playing center field. It's important to have outfielders who have confidence in their ability to go back on the ball, allowing them to play shallow and catch popups.

Who It Helps the Most

Most hitters get a big offensive boost playing at Coors. Todd Helton has a lifetime .377 average in his home park. Rookie Luis Gonzalez batted .373 at Coors last year. Tough-minded, competitive pitchers find the challenge at Coors Field invigorating. In 2004, Shawn Estes was 8-2 at Coors Field, and Joe Kennedy was 6-1 with a 3.59 ERA. Jason Jennings is 23-13 at Coors in his career.

Who It Hurts the Most

Pitchers who nibble have no chance to survive Coors Field. Coors is a big inning waiting to happen, and if pitchers don't throw strikes they are feeding the eventual outburst.

Rookies & Newcomers

The Rockies are in the midst of a youth movement. Jeff Francis claimed a spot in the rotation with a quality September. Chin-hui Tsao is being counted on to handle late-inning relief duties. The Rockies will give a look in the spring at an all-rookie left side of the infield with Clint Barmes at shortstop and Garrett Atkins at third. J.D. Closser has been given the job at catcher.

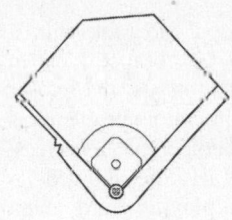

Dimensions: LF-347, LCF-390, CF-415, RCF-375, RF-350

Capacity: 50,449

Elevation: 5280 feet

Surface: Grass

Foul Territory: Average

Park Factors

2004 Season

| | Home Games | | | Away Games | | | |
	Rockies	Opp	Total	Rockies	Opp	Total	Index
G	72	72	144	72	72	144	
Avg	.302	.307	.304	.245	.267	.256	119
AB	2490	2611	5101	2460	2367	4827	106
R	435	477	912	295	334	629	145
H	751	801	1552	602	633	1235	126
2B	166	163	329	127	127	254	123
3B	18	20	38	12	13	25	144
HR	106	100	206	82	77	159	123
BB	272	329	601	229	285	514	111
SO	467	425	892	576	421	997	85
E	44	66	110	31	31	62	177
E-Infield	29	52	81	24	25	49	165
LHB-Avg	.319	.307	.313	.261	.265	.263	119
LHB-HR	56	39	95	33	28	61	144
RHB-Avg	.289	.306	.298	.233	.269	.252	119
RHB-HR	50	61	111	49	49	98	109

2002-2004

| | Home Games | | | Away Games | | | |
	Rockies	Opp	Total	Rockies	Opp	Total	Index
G	216	216	432	219	219	438	
Avg	.302	.291	.296	.239	.275	.256	116
AB	7382	7754	15136	7465	7257	14722	104
R	1328	1293	2621	859	1100	1959	136
H	2228	2259	4487	1782	1994	3776	120
2B	476	447	923	372	398	770	117
3B	67	58	125	29	43	72	169
HR	287	324	611	207	234	441	135
BB	795	790	1585	710	840	1550	99
SO	1309	1265	2574	1725	1162	2887	87
E	141	171	312	132	124	256	124
E-Infield	110	132	242	110	103	213	115
LHB-Avg	.328	.298	.312	.259	.289	.274	114
LHB-HR	127	131	258	85	85	170	147
RHB-Avg	.286	.287	.287	.227	.266	.246	117
RHB-HR	160	193	353	122	149	271	127

2004 Rankings (National League)

- Highest batting-average factor
- Highest run factor
- Highest hit factor
- Highest double factor
- Highest error factor
- Highest LHB batting-average factor
- Highest RHB batting-average factor
- Lowest strikeout factor

Clint Hurdle

2004 Season

The Rockies' bullpen imploded and took with it any chance the club had to be competitive. An experiment with Shawn Chacon as the closer didn't work, but that wasn't the whole problem, as the relievers other than Chacon blew 25 saves. Through the struggles, Clint Hurdle showed an ability to keep the Rockies playing hard, even when there was nothing to play for, an attribute that becomes more important as the team gets younger.

Offense

The constant with the Rockies is Todd Helton hitting in the No. 3 spot and battling for a batting title. With cleanup hitter Vinny Castilla gone, the Rockies are going to count on 2003 NL RBI leader Preston Wilson bouncing back from two surgeries on his left knee in 2004 and reasserting himself as a run producer. Aaron Miles stepped in and filled the need for a leadoff hitter. Typically the Rockies scramble to score runs away from Coors Field, but Hurdle shows his fondness for the sacrifice bunt even at Coors.

Pitching & Defense

The rotation is young and promising. Joe Kennedy arrived from Tampa Bay and had a quality season in 2004, ignoring concerns about Coors Field. He gets strong support with righthanders Jason Jennings and Aaron Cook, and rookie lefthander Jeff Francis. Hurdle needs to let the starters stretch out and save the wear on his bullpen. The defense will suffer with the free-agent losses of Castilla and shortstop Royce Clayton.

2005 Outlook

The Rockies are an unknown heading into 2005. A key will be how a rebuilt bullpen holds up. The Rockies set a major league record with 34 blown saves last year. With young arms and a new closer, the Rockies will be looking to finish off those games, which could provide an emotional lift for what promises to be a young lineup with more potential than proven ability.

Born: 7/30/57 in Big Rapids, Michigan

Playing Experience: 1977-1987, KC, Cin, NYM, StL

Managerial Experience: 3 seasons

Manager Statistics

Year	Team, Lg	W	L	Pct	GB	Finish
2004	Colorado, NL	68	94	.420	25.0	4th West
3 Seasons		209	255	.450	–	–

2004 Starting Pitchers by Days Rest

	<=3	4	5	6+
Rockies Starts	4	78	52	16
Rockies ERA	5.14	5.52	5.26	4.65
NL Avg Starts	2	82	46	23
NL ERA	4.58	4.35	4.28	4.73

2004 Situational Stats

	Clint Hurdle	NL Average
Hit & Run Success %	35.3	38.0
Stolen Base Success %	57.1	71.7
Platoon Pct.	55.5	55.2
Defensive Subs	22	18
High-Pitch Outings	3	6
Quick/Slow Hooks	23/22	21/12
Sacrifice Attempts	133	99

2004 Rankings (National League)

- 1st in fewest caught stealings of third base (2), sacrifice bunt attempts, intentional walks (65) and slow hooks
- 2nd in pinch-hitters used (288)
- 3rd in starts on three days rest and first-batter platoon percentage

Jeromy Burnitz

Position: RF/CF/LF
Bats: L **Throws:** R
Ht: 6' 0" **Wt:** 213

Opening Day Age: 35
Born: 4/15/69 in
Westminster, CA
ML Seasons: 12
Pronunciation:
ber-NITS

2004 Season

Jeromy Burnitz was able to re-establish himself as a run-producing power hitter in 2004, while adding the dimension of hitting for average. Burnitz hit a career-best .283 despite his eighth 100-plus strikeout season. He also reached the 30-homer plateau for the sixth time in seven years and returned to the 100-RBI level for the first time in three years. Burnitz did enjoy the benefits of Coors Field, but most of all he showed consistency, particularly in terms of run production.

Hitting

There's a reason Burnitz strikes out in triple figures. He lets it all go when he swings and doesn't make adjustments in a two-strike situation. Burnitz tends to experiment too much and gets out of sync, but in 2004, reunited with his original pro manager, Clint Hurdle, he was able to focus on a basic hitting approach, which paid off with rare consistency for him. He sits on a fastball early in the count, and can be fooled with offspeed pitches, particularly away because he's trying to yank everything.

Baserunning & Defense

Burnitz has a step above average speed, but it's not an asset. He plays the game out of control at times and doesn't have the natural feel for stealing bases. He can take an extra base but will hustle himself into trouble. Burnitz split his time among all three outfield positions with Colorado last year, and actually played a stronger center field than any other. However, his size and all-out play wore him down in the final weeks of the season. He has the arm strength to play right field.

2005 Outlook

The Rockies declined a $3 million mutual option to keep Burnitz in Colorado for the 2005 campaign. He reaffirmed the fact that he can play every day, and will get that opportunity. He is a first-rate clubhouse presence, who showed his unselfishness with the Rockies by never complaining about being moved around in the field.

Overall Statistics

G	AB	R	H	D	T	HR	RBI	SB	BB	SO	Avg	OBP	Slg
150	540	94	153	30	4	37	110	5	58	124	.283	.356	.559
1423	4792	798	1219	255	27	275	845	68	660	1193	.254	.351	.491

Where He Hits the Ball

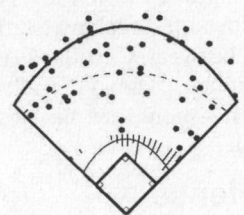
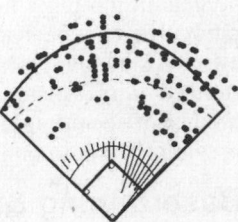

Vs. LHP   **Vs. RHP**

2004 Situational Stats

	AB	H	HR	RBI	Avg		AB	H	HR	RBI	Avg
Home	270	87	24	68	.322	LHP	136	38	10	28	.279
Road	270	66	13	42	.244	RHP	404	115	27	82	.285
First Half	303	87	18	57	.287	Sc Pos	157	45	4	66	.287
Scnd Half	237	66	19	53	.278	Clutch	97	27	7	24	.278

2004 Rankings (National League)

- 7th in RBI, highest percentage of swings that missed (30.4) and highest percentage of swings on the first pitch (38.8)
- 8th in home runs and HR frequency (14.6 ABs per HR)
- 9th in batting average at home
- 10th in lowest percentage of swings put into play (35.8)
- Led the Rockies in home runs, triples and HR frequency (14.6 ABs per HR)

Vinny Castilla

2004 Season

After a four-year absence, Vinny Castilla returned to Colorado in 2004 and regained his old Rockies magic. He led the National League with 131 RBI. Castilla took advantage of Coors Field when it came to hitting for average, but had 21 of his 35 home runs on the road.

Hitting

At the age of 37, Castilla regained the bat speed that made him one of the most feared fastball hitters in baseball. When Castilla is hitting well, he sits on pitches, looking to drive them up the middle with the strength to go out of the ballpark the other way. When he gets into a slump it's because he gets in too big a hurry and tries to jerk every pitch. He can be had with soft breaking stuff away. Asked to hit cleanup last year, Castilla even showed some plate discipline. The 51 walks might not seem huge, but it's more than his two previous seasons combined.

Baserunning & Defense

Easily the most impressive aspect of Castilla's game is his defense. He cut his errors from 19 in 2003 to six last year, showing the soft hands, extremely accurate arm and good first-step reaction that was his trademark as a younger player. He is exceptionally strong at making the play charging in and throwing off balance. Castilla is not blessed with speed, and realizes that. He might get an extra base occasionally, but he's not a basestealing threat.

2005 Outlook

After declining the Rockies' option for 2005, Castilla signed a two-year, $6.2 million deal with Washington, where he is expected to provide a run-producing, middle-of-the-lineup bat and big-time leadership for the young Hispanic players on the team. But will he enjoy life outside of Coors Field? The last time Castilla left the Rockies, he suffered through such a bad time that the Devil Rays released him with almost a full year remaining on his contract.

Position: 3B
Bats: R **Throws:** R
Ht: 6' 1" **Wt:** 205

Opening Day Age: 37
Born: 7/4/67 in Oaxaca, Mexico
ML Seasons: 14
Pronunciation: cas-TEE-yah

Overall Statistics

G	AB	R	H	D	T	HR	RBI	SB	BB	SO	Avg	OBP	Slg
148	583	93	158	43	3	35	131	0	51	113	.271	.332	.535
1625	6053	823	1696	303	27	303	1012	29	371	938	.280	.324	.489

Where He Hits the Ball

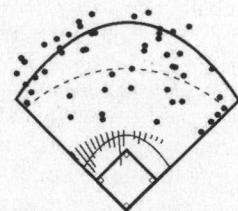 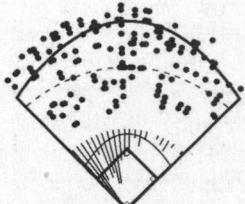

Vs. LHP **Vs. RHP**

2004 Situational Stats

	AB	H	HR	RBI	Avg		AB	H	HR	RBI	Avg
Home	299	96	14	80	.321	LHP	161	43	9	29	.267
Road	284	62	21	51	.218	RHP	422	115	26	102	.273
First Half	309	84	16	71	.272	Sc Pos	203	52	7	86	.256
Scnd Half	274	74	19	60	.270	Clutch	100	29	5	28	.290

2004 Rankings (National League)

- 1st in RBI and fielding percentage at third base (.987)
- 2nd in lowest batting average on the road
- 5th in GDPs (22)
- 7th in sacrifice flies (8) and cleanup slugging percentage (.553)
- 8th in total bases (312)
- 9th in doubles
- Led the Rockies in at-bats, RBI, sacrifice flies (8), hit by pitch (6), GDPs (22) and cleanup slugging percentage (.553)
- Led NL third basemen in RBI

Shawn Chacon

2004 Season

The Rockies took a gamble and moved Shawn Chacon into the closer's role in 2004, even though he'd never pitched relief. Things didn't go well. Chacon finished with 35 saves, the second most in franchise history, but that's the only number he could be proud of. He allowed 128 base runners in 63.1 innings, and walked as many batters (52) as he struck out. He blew nine save opportunities and gave up 12 home runs.

Pitching

Chacon is a competitor, which was a reason the Rockies tried him in relief. However, he has to channel that competitiveness and not try to overthrow, particularly his curveball. The hard curve, his big pitch, isn't bothered by the Colorado altitude, but he needs to be ahead in the count so that hitters can't lay off it. As a starting pitcher, Chacon has shown a fastball that is consistent from 92-94 MPH, but as a reliever he'd have games he wouldn't hit 90 MPH. He has a solid changeup, but the pitch was missing in action when he was in relief and he was reluctant to use his full assortment. He also has a cutter which he now uses instead of a slider against lefthanded hitters.

Defense & Hitting

A football quarterback and basketball player in high school, Chacon moves around the mound well and can field his position. He has an exceptional pickoff move that is a boost for catchers because it makes baserunners more cautious. He was a horrible hitter as a rookie but worked hard to become an offensive contributor.

2005 Outlook

Chacon is headed back to the rotation in 2005, and it's a wise idea. He now admits he'd rather start, and he has the arsenal of pitches to handle the role. The question is whether he has the physical stamina. A part of the decision to try Chacon out of the bullpen was the fact he has yet to win a game after August 1.

Position: RP
Bats: R **Throws:** R
Ht: 6' 3" **Wt:** 212

Opening Day Age: 27
Born: 12/23/77 in Anchorage, AK
ML Seasons: 4
Pronunciation: chah-CONE

Overall Statistics

	W	L	Pct.	ERA	G	GS	Sv	IP	H	BB	SO	HR	Avg
'04	1	9	.100	7.11	66	0	35	63.1	71	52	52	12	.282
Car.	23	38	.377	5.37	137	71	35	479.2	474	257	346	75	.259

2004 Pitching Profile

	Shawn Chacon	NL Average
Overall Strike %	58.2	62.5
1st Pitch Strike %	51.7	58.5
Ratio	1.94	1.39
Strikeouts per 9 IP	7.39	6.74
Walks per 9 IP	7.39	3.38
Home Runs per 9 IP	1.71	1.11
Strikeout/Walk Ratio	1.00	1.99
Groundball/Flyball Ratio	0.70	1.25

2004 Situational Stats

	W	L	ERA	Sv	IP		AB	H	HR	RBI	Avg
Home	1	5	8.04	18	31.1	LHB	123	29	6	25	.236
Road	0	4	6.19	17	32.0	RHB	129	42	6	20	.326
First Half	1	5	6.81	20	38.1	Sc Pos	90	19	3	33	.211
Scnd Half	0	4	7.56	15	25.0	Clutch	159	43	10	33	.270

2004 Rankings (National League)

- 1st in blown saves (9), highest relief ERA (7.11) and most baserunners allowed per nine innings in relief (18.2)
- 2nd in relief losses (9)
- 4th in games finished (60) and lowest save percentage (79.5)
- 6th in wild pitches (9)
- 9th in saves
- Led the Rockies in games pitched, saves, games finished (60), wild pitches (9), save percentage (79.5), blown saves (9), relief losses (9) and most strikeouts per nine innings in relief (7.4)

2004 Season

At the age of 34 and with no market for his services after back-to-back subpar years with the Chicago White Sox and Milwaukee, Royce Clayton became a stop-gap for the Rockies and played well enough that instead of dealing him in July, the Rockies kept him. He led National League shortstops in fielding percentage, was a steady No. 2 hitter in the lineup, and became a vital clubhouse force, particularly in terms of helping young players.

Hitting

Clayton was a perfect fit in the No. 2 slot. He led the majors with a club-record 24 sacrifice bunts, the most in the big leagues since 1993, and also had 15 bunt singles. He can be overpowered (career-high 125 strikeouts in 2004), but he handled the breaking ball better last year because of his focus on hitting the ball to right field, which kept him on the ball longer. Clayton is not a power threat, but he can surprise if a pitch is on the inner half of the plate.

Baserunning & Defense

Clayton's glove is the reason he has been a regular shortstop in the big leagues for nearly 13 full seasons. He has soft hands, reacts quickly and shows good range because of his ability to read hitters in situations. He doesn't have that overpowering arm, but he has a quick release and his throws are on line. He does not make mental mistakes, either in the field or on the bases. Clayton is only a step better than average as a runner, but he is aware of situations and will take extra bases on a routine basis.

2005 Outlook

Clayton will be with his fifth team in six years. The Rockies let it be known that they would have liked to have Clayton back, but it would have been in a backup role and they knew that wasn't going to work for Clayton. He is still in great shape and has a desire to play every day.

Position: SS
Bats: R **Throws:** R
Ht: 6' 0" **Wt:** 185

Opening Day Age: 35
Born: 1/2/70 in Burbank, CA
ML Seasons: 14

Overall Statistics

G	AB	R	H	D	T	HR	RBI	SB	BB	SO	Avg	OBP	Slg
146	574	95	160	36	4	8	54	10	48	125	.279	.338	.397
1751	6208	803	1598	291	50	105	627	202	483	1172	.257	.313	.371

Where He Hits the Ball

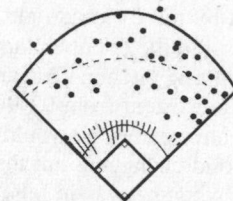 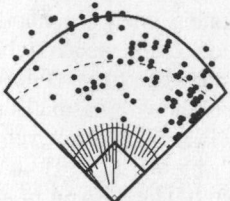

Vs. LHP   **Vs. RHP**

2004 Situational Stats

	AB	H	HR	RBI	Avg		AB	H	HR	RBI	Avg
Home	284	85	6	33	.299	LHP	146	42	1	11	.288
Road	290	75	2	21	.259	RHP	428	118	7	43	.276
First Half	322	96	6	36	.298	Sc Pos	123	31	1	39	.252
Scnd Half	252	64	2	18	.254	Clutch	84	22	1	5	.262

2004 Rankings (National League)

- 1st in sacrifice bunts (24) and fielding percentage at shortstop (.986)
- 2nd in bunts in play (52)
- 3rd in highest groundball-flyball ratio (2.3)
- Led the Rockies in triples, sacrifice bunts (24), strikeouts, highest groundball-flyball ratio (2.3), stolen-base percentage (66.7), bunts in play (52) and steals of third (2)

Aaron Cook

2004 Season

Aaron Cook's solid 2004 season was brought to a sudden end when he was forced to leave an August 7 start because of dizziness, and doctors discovered blood clots in both lungs. He later underwent surgery to remove his upper right rib. Doctors felt the rib was creating a compression that created the clots.

Pitching

Cook has the type of sinker that allows him to win with only one pitch. He will start out a game in the low 90s, but by the end of the game he will hit in the upper 90s. Cook doesn't have much of an off-speed pitch, but he doesn't need it. The key for him is to throw his slider a few times early in a game and put it in the mind of hitters. The biggest obstacle Cook has faced is self-confidence, and all signs were that Cook finally clicked in the middle of last season. He was 3-1 with a 1.96 ERA in a five-start stretch before the injury.

Defense & Hitting

Cook has the athletic ability to be an asset defensively. He moves around the mound well, coming off quickly in bunt situations. However, he needs to become more consistent with his throws. He does hold runners well and gets the ball to the plate quickly. He should be a better hitter, but so far he has been a liability.

2005 Outlook

Cook is ready to explode. It's a matter of how quickly he fully recovers from the surgery. He probably won't be ready for Opening Day, but he should be set to go by May. With the way Cook finished up last year, and the type of raw stuff he possesses, the Rockies are looking for him to establish himself as an ace for their rotation. His sinker, which has more sink and similar velocity to Kevin Brown's, is the type of pitch that gives hope that Cook will be able to cope with Coors Field.

Position: SP
Bats: R **Throws:** R
Ht: 6' 3" **Wt:** 205

Opening Day Age: 26
Born: 2/8/79 in Ft. Campbell, KY
ML Seasons: 3

Overall Statistics

	W	L	Pct.	ERA	G	GS	Sv	IP	H	BB	SO	HR	Avg
'04	6	4	.600	4.28	16	16	0	96.2	112	39	40	7	.294
Car.	12	11	.522	5.16	68	37	0	256.1	313	109	97	19	.306

2004 Pitching Profile

	Aaron Cook	NL Average
Overall Strike %	60.3	62.5
1st Pitch Strike %	57.3	58.5
Ratio	1.56	1.39
Strikeouts per 9 IP	3.72	6.74
Walks per 9 IP	3.63	3.38
Home Runs per 9 IP	0.65	1.11
Strikeout/Walk Ratio	1.03	1.99
Groundball/Flyball Ratio	2.32	1.25

2004 Situational Stats

	W	L	ERA	Sv	IP		AB	H	HR	RBI	Avg
Home	2	4	5.30	0	52.2	LHB	202	54	4	23	.267
Road	4	0	3.07	0	44.0	RHB	179	58	3	18	.324
First Half	4	3	5.20	0	64.0	Sc Pos	90	22	1	31	.244
Scnd Half	2	1	2.48	0	32.2	Clutch	13	4	0	0	.308

2004 Rankings (National League)

- Did not rank near the top or bottom in any category

Shawn Estes

2004 Season

Shawn Estes faced a make-or-break season in 2004 and made it. After spending time with four organizations the three previous years and going 13-23 in 2002-03, he led the Rockies with 15 victories, a franchise record for a lefthanded pitcher. More importantly, Estes, the first non-roster invitee to be start on Opening Day for the Rockies, showed he had the mental toughness to survive Coors Field (8-2).

Pitching

Estes has four pitches, and he will mix all four. His fastball will touch 90 MPH on a consistent basis and has sinking action. He led National League pitchers by getting 34 GDPs last year. Estes also has a cut fastball that has become an important pitch for him against righthanded hitters. He'll run the ball in on their hands. His changeup is a quality pitch that he could benefit from using more. He has a tendency to be too fine, and won't give in when he gets behind in the count, which is why he has a high walk ratio.

Defense & Hitting

Estes helped his stamina and flexibility with a strenuous offseason program prior to 2004, which was apparent in the way he moved around the mound. He has limited his reliance in recent years on a slide step, but will vary his delivery time to the plate, which combined with a plus pickoff move keeps baserunners honest. He can help himself with the bat.

2005 Outlook

After having to sign with Colorado because nobody else would even give him an invitation to spring training in 2004, Estes has reaffirmed his value to a team as a starting pitcher. He wanted to return to the Rockies, but with a tight budget and youth movement in place, the Rockies had to pass on the multiyear hopes Estes harbored. However, he is only 32, healthy and a pitcher who has won 15 games twice and 19 games once in the big leagues. And don't forget, he is lefthanded.

Position: SP
Bats: R **Throws:** L
Ht: 6' 2" **Wt:** 200

Opening Day Age: 32
Born: 2/18/73 in San Bernardino, CA
ML Seasons: 10
Pronunciation: ES-tus
Nickname: Buck

Overall Statistics

	W	L	Pct.	ERA	G	GS	Sv	IP	H	BB	SO	HR	Avg
'04	15	8	.652	5.84	34	34	0	202.0	223	105	117	30	.291
Car.	92	81	.532	4.71	252	251	0	1505.0	1521	792	1124	137	.268

2004 Pitching Profile

	Shawn Estes	NL Average
Overall Strike %	57.5	62.5
1st Pitch Strike %	53.3	58.5
Ratio	1.62	1.39
Strikeouts per 9 IP	5.21	6.74
Walks per 9 IP	4.68	3.38
Home Runs per 9 IP	1.34	1.11
Strikeout/Walk Ratio	1.11	1.99
Groundball/Flyball Ratio	1.73	1.25

2004 Situational Stats

	W	L	ERA	Sv	IP		AB	H	HR	RBI	Avg
Home	8	2	6.22	0	89.2	LHB	168	47	6	30	.280
Road	7	6	5.53	0	112.1	RHB	599	176	24	91	.294
First Half	8	4	5.87	0	110.1	Sc Pos	181	53	8	91	.293
Scnd Half	7	4	5.79	0	91.2	Clutch	31	9	2	2	.290

2004 Rankings (National League)

- 1st in GDPs induced (34), highest ERA and highest ERA at home
- 2nd in balks (2), most run support per nine innings (6.5) and highest on-base percentage allowed (.380)
- 3rd in walks allowed, lowest strikeout-walk ratio (1.1) and highest ERA on the road
- 4th in highest batting average allowed (.291) and highest slugging percentage allowed (.481)
- Led the Rockies in wins, games started, innings pitched, home runs allowed, walks allowed, hit batsmen (11), balks (2), pitches thrown (3,372), pickoff throws (108), GDPs induced (34), winning percentage, highest groundball-flyball ratio allowed (1.7), lowest stolen-base percentage allowed (61.1), most GDPs induced per GDP situation (21.1%) and most run support per nine innings (6.5)

Todd Helton

Position: 1B
Bats: L **Throws:** L
Ht: 6' 2" **Wt:** 204

Opening Day Age: 31
Born: 8/20/73 in Knoxville, TN
ML Seasons: 8

Colorado

2004 Season

Todd Helton continued to rank among the elite players in the game last year, earning his fifth All-Star invitation and finishing second in the National League batting race for the second year in a row. He remained the constant in a Rockies lineup that suffered with the injuries to Preston Wilson and Larry Walker, who was eventually traded in August.

Hitting

Helton is a bona fide No. 3 hitter who could move to the cleanup spot because he has the ability to expand his strike zone when it comes time to drive in runs. He has the hand-eye coordination to handle all types of pitching, and when he is swinging the bat properly he is especially strong driving the ball to left and left-center field. He has taught himself to anticipate situations and turn on the inside pitch. He is a good contact man for a run producer, and an excellent two-strike hitter who does not make concessions with his swing.

Baserunning & Defense

After some problems in the field in 2003, Helton made winning a third Gold Glove his primary goal last year. He got it. He has good range, and the former quarterback comes out when he fields a ball and has a chance to throw a runner out. He also can scoop the ball out of the dirt, saving the rest of the infield countless errors. Helton is a below-average runner, but he runs the bases well and will force the situation.

2005 Outlook

Helton has accepted the fact that the organization is looking for him to emerge as the clubhouse leader, and this is a year for him to assert himself. He could be moved to fourth in the lineup, as he is the Rockies' only lefthanded power threat. But he's such a good No. 3 hitter, with the discipline to get pitches he can drive, that it would be a shame to drop him down in the order.

Overall Statistics

	G	AB	R	H	D	T	HR	RBI	SB	BB	SO	Avg	OBP	Slg
'04	154	547	115	190	49	2	32	96	3	127	72	.347	.469	.620
Car.	1135	4051	832	1372	328	22	251	836	30	667	542	.339	.432	.616

Where He Hits the Ball

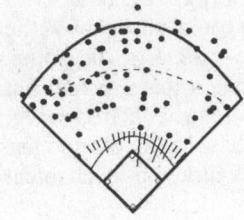

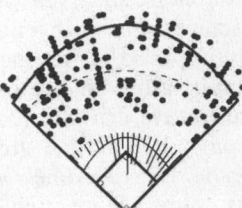

Vs. LHP	**Vs. RHP**

2004 Situational Stats

	AB	H	HR	RBI	Avg		AB	H	HR	RBI	Avg
Home	277	102	21	60	.368	LHP	172	55	7	27	.320
Road	270	88	11	36	.326	RHP	375	135	25	69	.360
First Half	293	102	17	57	.348	Sc Pos	127	40	2	54	.315
Scnd Half	254	88	15	39	.346	Clutch	76	25	4	12	.329

2004 Rankings (National League)

- 1st in fielding percentage at first base (.997)
- 2nd in batting average, walks, times on base (320), on-base percentage, batting average vs. righthanded pitchers and batting average at home
- 3rd in doubles, total bases (339) and intentional walks (19)
- Led the Rockies in runs scored, hits, pitches seen (2,749), plate appearances (683), games played, slugging percentage, most pitches seen per plate appearance (4.02), highest percentage of pitches taken (58.2), batting average in the clutch, batting average on the road, and batting average with two strikes (.266)
- Led NL first basemen in batting average

Matt Holliday

2004 Season

Former high school All-America quarterback Matt Holliday has finally begun to repay the Rockies for the confidence they showed in 1998 when they convinced him to make baseball his career. Given an early callup last year because of injuries, Holliday was a solid third or fourth outfielder most of the season, getting a chance at everyday duty when Larry Walker was out of the lineup and then later when Walker was traded to St. Louis in August.

Hitting

It is very obvious in batting practice that Holliday has raw power. He has an uncanny strike zone awareness, and even when struggling, he doesn't become a free swinger. As a rookie, he showed the ability to adjust during the course of the game, getting a big hit late on a pitch that got him out earlier. He can get a little long with his swing, though he has the strength to fight off pitches inside. He sometimes gets a little too mechanical instead of just reacting.

Baserunning & Defense

It's obvious Holliday wasn't an option quarterback. He is a tad below average as a runner, and don't expect to see him steal bases. However, he shows good instincts on the bases that allow him to get extra bases. He's also unafraid of contact. Holliday signed as a third baseman, but former Rockies manager Buddy Bell mandated a move to the outfield. He still has some uncertain moments, but with help from coach Dave Collins last season made big enough strides. He has a plus arm for a left fielder, but is a bit below average in right field.

2005 Outlook

With the trade of Walker and then the decision in the offseason to not re-sign Jeromy Burnitz, Holliday is slated to hold down a regular outfield spot this year. He might be best served at first if he could stay down in the lineup, like the No. 7 slot, but the Rockies might not have that luxury. He could explode into a home-run threat.

Position: LF
Bats: R **Throws:** R
Ht: 6' 4" **Wt:** 235

Opening Day Age: 25
Born: 1/15/80 in Stillwater, OK
ML Seasons: 1

Overall Statistics

	G	AB	R	H	D	T	HR	RBI	SB	BB	SO	Avg	OBP	Slg
'04	121	400	65	116	31	3	14	57	3	31	86	.290	.349	.488
Car.	121	400	65	116	31	3	14	57	3	31	86	.290	.349	.488

Where He Hits the Ball

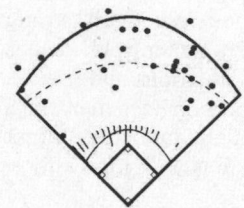 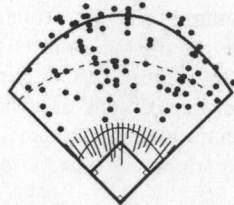

Vs. LHP   **Vs. RHP**

2004 Situational Stats

	AB	H	HR	RBI	Avg		AB	H	HR	RBI	Avg
Home	204	69	10	36	.338	LHP	97	23	2	10	.237
Road	196	47	4	21	.240	RHP	303	93	12	47	.307
First Half	245	71	9	37	.290	Sc Pos	103	27	4	40	.262
Scnd Half	155	45	5	20	.290	Clutch	57	16	0	5	.281

2004 Rankings (National League)

- 1st in lowest fielding percentage in left field (.963)
- 3rd in batting average among rookies
- 4th in home runs among rookies, RBI among rookies and errors in left field (7)
- Led the Rockies in hit by pitch (6)

Jason Jennings

2004 Season

In slightly more than three years, Jason Jennings has moved into second place on the Rockies' all time win list with 43. He had 11 wins in 2004, but also had five leads that the Rockies middle relievers let slip away. Jennings continued to show durability, making 33 starts and reaching the 200-inning level for the first time. However, his walks increased for the third year in a row.

Pitching

Jennings has three quality pitches. His strength is a hard sinker that will sit between 90-93 MPH. He also has a solid average changeup. He gets in trouble, however, because he has a fascination with his slider. He can get into such a predictable pattern with the slider that hitters have no fear about sitting on the pitch. Jennings also gets caught up in trying to overthink. He has to be more aggressive, busting righthanded batters inside and changing speeds on lefthanded hitters. With his sinker, he just needs to let it fly.

Defense & Hitting

Don't be deceived by the bulky body. Jennings is a modern-day Rick Reuschel, from the hard sinker to the amazing agility in the field to the ability to be a legitimate threat in the lineup. He has an excellent pickoff move and is quick to the plate, limiting basestealing opportunities. He also is a superb fielder who can pick up an extra out or two a game with his glove. At the plate, he's an extra-base threat.

2005 Outlook

Jennings will continue to be a workhorse in the Colorado rotation. He's the perfect Rockies pitcher. He's not a male model by any means, but he competes, and Coors Field doesn't phase him—he is 23-13 lifetime at Coors. A key for Jennings is that the Rockies are getting into a position with their arms where he can start to slip back into the No. 3 slot in the rotation, which is where he can be a key factor.

Position: SP
Bats: L **Throws:** R
Ht: 6' 2" **Wt:** 245

Opening Day Age: 26
Born: 7/17/78 in Dallas, TX
ML Seasons: 4

Overall Statistics

	W	L	Pct.	ERA	G	GS	Sv	IP	H	BB	SO	HR	Avg
'04	11	12	.478	5.51	33	33	0	201.0	241	101	133	27	.299
Car.	43	34	.558	5.03	104	104	0	607.0	696	278	405	75	.292

2004 Pitching Profile

	Jason Jennings	NL Average
Overall Strike %	58.7	62.5
1st Pitch Strike %	55.9	58.5
Ratio	1.70	1.39
Strikeouts per 9 IP	5.96	6.74
Walks per 9 IP	4.52	3.38
Home Runs per 9 IP	1.21	1.11
Strikeout/Walk Ratio	1.32	1.99
Groundball/Flyball Ratio	1.54	1.25

2004 Situational Stats

	W	L	ERA	Sv	IP		AB	H	HR	RBI	Avg
Home	6	7	6.15	0	101.0	LHB	391	133	15	66	.340
Road	5	5	4.86	0	100.0	RHB	414	108	12	50	.261
First Half	8	7	6.19	0	104.2	Sc Pos	225	62	5	77	.276
Scnd Half	3	5	4.76	0	96.1	Clutch	37	8	0	4	.216

2004 Rankings (National League)

- 1st in hits allowed, highest batting average allowed (.299) and highest on-base percentage allowed (.381)
- 2nd in highest ERA at home
- 3rd in highest ERA
- 4th in walks allowed
- 5th in highest slugging percentage allowed (.478)
- 6th in highest batting average allowed vs. lefthanded batters and highest walks per nine innings (4.5)
- 7th in batters faced (925), runners caught stealing (8) and lowest strikeout-walk ratio (1.3)
- 10th in most home runs allowed per nine innings (1.21)
- Led the Rockies in losses, hits allowed, batters faced (925), strikeouts, stolen bases allowed (14) and runners caught stealing (8)

Joe Kennedy

2004 Season

Joe Kennedy blossomed in his Rockies debut in 2004. He recorded the lowest ERA by a starting pitcher in franchise history at 3.66, going 6-1 with a 3.59 ERA in 14 Coors Field starts en route to the first winning record of his career. He did miss a month with left shoulder inflammation.

Pitching

Kennedy has a plus fastball with plenty of life. He started to trust the pitch more in 2004, and it showed in the results. He cut the fastball to run in on the hands of righthanded hitters. With his cross-body mechanics the ball is extremely hard to pick up, particularly for lefthanded hitters, who hit just .183 off him. However, there is concern that the cross-body mechanics will not only affect his health, but keep him from becoming real consistent in his approach. Kennedy has shown the makings of a quality 12-to-6 curveball, but seemed hesitant to use it at Coors Field. He does have a quality offspeed pitch that is vital for survival at Coors.

Defense & Hitting

Kennedy needs to concentrate better in the field. He will get to balls but make debatable plays because of a lack of thought process. He also has to control his body better to allow him to make better throws. He worked on his move to first, and caught five runners last year. Kennedy wasn't required to hit until last year, and it showed. He needs to work on bunting, if nothing else.

2005 Outlook

Kennedy could be ready to emerge as a top-quality lefthander. He showed signs in Tampa Bay, and was the Devil Rays' Opening Day starter in 2003, but never blossomed. Given a change of scenery, he took a step in that direction, despite Coors Field. The Rockies will give him every opportunity to move into a top-of-the-rotation spot in 2005, most likely fitting between righthanders Aaron Cook and Jason Jennings.

Position: SP
Bats: R **Throws:** L
Ht: 6' 4" **Wt:** 237

Opening Day Age: 25
Born: 5/24/79 in La Mesa, CA
ML Seasons: 4

Overall Statistics

	W	L	Pct.	ERA	G	GS	Sv	IP	H	BB	SO	HR	Avg
'04	9	7	.563	3.66	27	27	0	162.1	163	67	117	17	.265
Car.	27	38	.415	4.63	109	99	1	610.1	656	203	381	75	.276

2004 Pitching Profile

	Joe Kennedy	NL Average
Overall Strike %	62.0	62.5
1st Pitch Strike %	56.6	58.5
Ratio	1.42	1.39
Strikeouts per 9 IP	6.49	6.74
Walks per 9 IP	3.71	3.38
Home Runs per 9 IP	0.94	1.11
Strikeout/Walk Ratio	1.75	1.99
Groundball/Flyball Ratio	1.51	1.25

2004 Situational Stats

	W	L	ERA	Sv	IP		AB	H	HR	RBI	Avg
Home	6	1	3.59	0	82.2	LHB	142	26	4	13	.183
Road	3	6	3.73	0	79.2	RHB	473	137	13	50	.290
First Half	5	4	3.95	0	100.1	Sc Pos	157	31	5	43	.197
Scnd Half	4	3	3.19	0	62.0	Clutch	29	12	2	6	.414

2004 Rankings (National League)

- 2nd in errors at pitcher (4) and lowest fielding percentage at pitcher (.913)
- 5th in lowest batting average allowed vs. left handed batters
- 8th in fewest pitches thrown per batter (3.56) and lowest batting average allowed with runners in scoring position
- 9th in highest walks per nine innings (3.7)
- 10th in highest on-base percentage allowed (.342)
- Led the Rockies in ERA, stolen bases allowed (14), highest strikeout-walk ratio (1.7), lowest batting average allowed (.265), lowest on-base percentage allowed (.342), lowest ERA at home, lowest batting average allowed vs. lefthanded batters, lowest batting average allowed with runners in scoring position and most strikeouts per nine innings (6.5)

Aaron Miles

2004 Season

After nine years in the minor leagues, Aaron Miles finally got a chance in the big leagues. He took great advantage of it. While Miles needed a two-week refresher course at Triple-A Colorado Springs in late May, he eventually settled in as the Rockies' leadoff hitter and starting second baseman. He led major league rookies with 153 hits and 75 runs scored, and led National League rookies with a .293 average.

Hitting

The switch-hitting Miles does a solid job from both sides of the plate. His hitting style is to go the opposite way, dumping singles into the open areas. He showed he can hold his own away from Coors Field (.277 road BA). Miles probably is better suited in the long run to hit second because he doesn't have the speed or patience you'd like from the top guy in the lineup. Even in the minor leagues, the most walks he's ever drawn are 40.

Baserunning & Defense

Miles is a step above average on the bases, but far from a burner. He was only 12-for-19 in steals as a rookie, and had only 135 stolen bases—with 87 caught stealings—in his nine minor league seasons. He is aggressive and will take the extra base when he gets a chance. Miles showed he is a solid average defensive player, with the toughness to hang in on double-play pivots. He has a strong arm for a second baseman, but needs quicker feet to expand his range.

2005 Outlook

Despite a bum right knee that required offseason surgery, Miles played himself into a job as the Rockies' leadoff hitter and second baseman, at least for the time being. The projected second baseman of the future, Jayson Nix, has struggled the last 12 months at both the Double-A level and in the Arizona Fall League, which means Miles isn't going to have much pressure from within, other than from last year's super sub, Luis Gonzalez.

Position: 2B
Bats: B **Throws:** R
Ht: 5' 7" **Wt:** 180

Opening Day Age: 28
Born: 12/15/76 in Pittsburg, CA
ML Seasons: 2

Overall Statistics

	G	AB	R	H	D	T	HR	RBI	SB	BB	SO	Avg	OBP	Slg
'04	134	522	75	153	15	3	6	47	12	29	53	.293	.329	.368
Car.	142	534	78	157	18	3	6	49	12	29	53	.294	.329	.373

Where He Hits the Ball

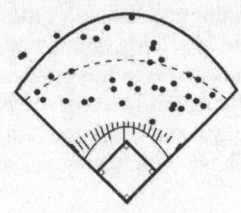 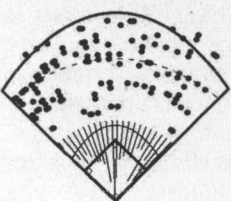

Vs. LHP   **Vs. RHP**

2004 Situational Stats

	AB	H	HR	RBI	Avg		AB	H	HR	RBI	Avg
Home	266	82	4	30	.308	LHP	120	32	2	13	.267
Road	256	71	2	17	.277	RHP	402	121	4	34	.301
First Half	253	81	3	25	.320	Sc Pos	116	38	3	44	.328
Scnd Half	269	72	3	22	.268	Clutch	74	24	1	10	.324

2004 Rankings (National League)

- 1st in batting average among rookies
- 4th in lowest fielding percentage at second base (.984)
- 6th in lowest percentage of swings that missed (8.6)
- 7th in highest groundball-flyball ratio (1.9) and errors at second base (10)
- Led the Rockies in singles, stolen bases, caught stealing (7), lowest percentage of swings that missed (8.6), highest percentage of swings put into play (49.3), steals of third (2), batting average with runners in scoring position, batting average with the bases loaded (.600), on-base percentage for a lead off hitter (.328) and lowest percentage of swings on the first pitch (18.5)

Preston Wilson

2004 Season

After leading the National League in RBI in 2003, Preston Wilson hit the skids in 2004. A gimpy left knee that he hurt during winter workouts bothered Wilson all season. He underwent surgery in April to repair a torn meniscus, and was out until mid-June. He was back on the disabled list in late August, and in September, he underwent a microfracture procedure to enhance cartilage growth.

Hitting

Forget about what went on in 2004. Wilson can handle a fastball. But to be successful, he needs to show patience. He has a big swing and he is going to strike out, but the key for him is to swing at strikes. Wilson is strong enough and has a quick enough bat to have power to all fields, and Coors Field has given him quick rewards for having that type of approach. By looking to go the other way he improves his plate coverage and limits his vulnerability to breaking pitches, which remains a major problem.

Baserunning & Defense

The knee injury has slowed Wilson down. His days of 20-plus stolen bases are behind him, but then with his power that's not a major issue. He does take an extra base, and runs hard. Time will tell if Wilson can re-establish himself in center field. He has played the position with no reluctance to make the big play. He has a plus arm in terms of strength and accuracy for a center fielder.

2005 Outlook

The Rockies would like to see Wilson reclaim his cleanup spot in the lineup and his center-field spot on defense. The decision hinges on how well Wilson's left knee responds to offseason rehab. He is a skilled athlete who has enough power that he could be moved to right field to eliminate some of the physical demands involved in playing center field. That won't happen until the Rockies and Wilson are convinced that he can't handle the grind in center.

Position: CF
Bats: R **Throws:** R
Ht: 6' 2" **Wt:** 213

Opening Day Age: 30
Born: 7/19/74 in Bamberg, SC
ML Seasons: 7

Overall Statistics

	G	AB	R	H	D	T	HR	RBI	SB	BB	SO	Avg	OBP	Slg
'04	58	202	24	50	11	0	6	29	2	17	49	.248	.315	.391
Car.	809	2918	436	774	164	12	146	501	104	272	799	.265	.334	.480

Where He Hits the Ball

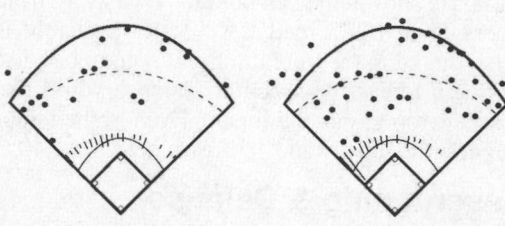

Vs. LHP   Vs. RHP

2004 Situational Stats

	AB	H	HR	RBI	Avg		AB	H	HR	RBI	Avg
Home	102	26	3	17	.255	LHP	69	20	2	13	.290
Road	100	24	3	12	.240	RHP	133	30	4	16	.226
First Half	95	21	2	15	.221	Sc Pos	72	16	1	22	.222
Scnd Half	107	29	4	14	.271	Clutch	34	8	2	5	.235

2004 Rankings (National League)

- 2nd in errors in center field (6)

Scott Dohmann

Position: RP
Bats: R **Throws:** R
Ht: 6' 1" **Wt:** 181

Opening Day Age: 27
Born: 2/13/78 in New Orleans, LA
ML Seasons: 1

Overall Statistics

	W	L	Pct.	ERA	G	GS	Sv	IP	H	BB	SO	HR	Avg
'04	0	3	.000	4.11	41	0	0	46.0	41	19	49	8	.236
Car.	0	3	.000	4.11	41	0	0	46.0	41	19	49	8	.236

2004 Situational Stats

	W	L	ERA	Sv	IP		AB	H	HR	RBI	Avg
Home	0	1	4.30	0	29.1	LHB	76	16	3	7	.211
Road	0	2	3.78	0	16.2	RHB	98	25	5	25	.255
First Half	0	0	3.44	0	18.1	Sc Pos	55	15	3	24	.273
Scnd Half	0	3	4.55	0	27.2	Clutch	32	8	3	9	.250

2004 Season

With the Colorado bullpen a mess, righthander Scott Dohmann was prematurely called to the big leagues on May 15 and handled himself well. He showed the ability to get a strikeout, and was particularly effective against lefthanded hitters. He did have a bit of a problem with the home-run ball, allowing eight in 46 innings.

Pitching, Defense & Hitting

Dohmann was converted to a reliever at Double-A Tulsa in 2003, and added a couple miles per hour to his fastball, which is now a solid 92-94 MPH. The key pitch for him, however, is a hard slider which he can run in on lefthanded hitters effectively. He still needs to work on consistency, especially learning to miss down if he's going to miss. Dohmann is a good athlete with a compact delivery to the plate. He is a non-factor offensively.

2005 Outlook

Dohmann will be asked to fill a late-inning bullpen role this season. The Rockies know they need strikeout pitchers, particularly in the later innings at hitter-friendly Coors Field. Dohmann's stamina will get a major test. His 59 appearances between Triple-A and the big leagues last year marked the first time he had ever appeared in more than 50 games in a season.

Jeff Fassero

Position: RP/SP
Bats: L **Throws:** L
Ht: 6' 1" **Wt:** 200

Opening Day Age: 42
Born: 1/5/63 in Springfield, IL
ML Seasons: 14
Pronunciation: fuh-SAIR-oh

Overall Statistics

	W	L	Pct.	ERA	G	GS	Sv	IP	H	BB	SO	HR	Avg
'04	3	8	.273	5.46	41	12	0	112.0	136	44	60	9	.304
Car.	116	116	.500	4.09	662	235	25	1927.2	1968	685	1576	203	.263

2004 Situational Stats

	W	L	ERA	Sv	IP		AB	H	HR	RBI	Avg
Home	1	5	8.17	0	50.2	LHB	148	49	3	23	.331
Road	2	3	3.23	0	61.1	RHB	300	87	6	43	.290
First Half	1	6	5.43	0	63.0	Sc Pos	117	31	3	54	.265
Scnd Half	2	2	5.51	0	49.0	Clutch	59	22	0	8	.373

2004 Season

Jeff Fassero signed with Colorado in 2004 because he wanted an opportunity to start. He wound up as a Mr. Fix It on the pitching staff, bouncing between the rotation and bullpen, and didn't like it. When he demanded a bonus to make a final start in the last week of the season, the Rockies finally had enough of his whining and released him.

Pitching, Defense & Hitting

Fassero's major asset is that he is lefthanded, but the problem is he can't get lefthanders out. He doesn't have a pitch to keep them honest, and won't use his offspeed stuff against them. He fits nicely as a long reliever because teams will turn to righthanded hitters and he can get the average righthanded hitter out, using his changeup and a slider that he runs in on their hands. Fassero is athletic, moving quickly off the mound and handling bunts impressively. He doesn't pay much attention to baserunners and is not an asset with the bat.

2005 Outlook

If Fassero is willing to accept a bullpen role, he will be allowed to hang around. However, he can wear out his welcome because of his negative attitude when things are not going the way he wants, a surprising situation for a pitcher with Fassero's lengthy track record.

Brian Fuentes

Position: RP
Bats: L **Throws:** L
Ht: 6' 4" **Wt:** 220

Opening Day Age: 29
Born: 8/9/75 in Merced, CA
ML Seasons: 4
Pronunciation: foo-WHEN-tayz

Overall Statistics

	W	L	Pct.	ERA	G	GS	Sv	IP	H	BB	SO	HR	Avg
'04	2	4	.333	5.64	47	0	0	44.2	46	19	48	5	.269
Car.	8	8	.500	4.04	163	0	4	158.1	141	74	178	18	.242

2004 Situational Stats

	W	L	ERA	Sv	IP		AB	H	HR	RBI	Avg
Home	1	1	8.10	0	23.1	LHB	61	13	1	10	.213
Road	1	3	2.95	0	21.1	RHB	110	33	4	16	.300
First Half	1	2	4.18	0	23.2	Sc Pos	46	15	2	21	.326
Scnd Half	1	2	7.29	0	21.0	Clutch	101	21	1	8	.208

2004 Season

Brian Fuentes has been the Rockies' most consistent reliever the last three years, and his absence for 62 games with a strained back muscle during the 2004 season was considered a major reason for the club's bullpen implosion. When healthy, Fuentes had three stretches of at least six consecutive scoreless appearances.

Pitching, Defense & Hitting

Fuentes has a funky sidearm motion that he compares to the mechanics of throwing a Frisbee. He can intimidate lefthanded hitters because of his arm angle, which is emphasized because of his height. He can hit 90 MPH with his fastball, which is above normal for a sidearmer, and he also has a hard slider that he will run in on the hands of righthanders. His mechanics make it a struggle for him to hold baserunners, because he leans so far over when he gets ready to drive toward the plate that he can't regroup.

2005 Outlook

Fuentes will be the Rockies' primary eighth-inning reliever this year, with the idea that he can at least occasionally fill in as the closer. Depending on how the bullpen shakes down, he either could be a co-closer or even be allowed to try and handle the closing role on his own.

Luis Gonzalez

Position: 2B/LF/3B/RF/SS
Bats: R **Throws:** R
Ht: 5'11" **Wt:** 170

Opening Day Age: 25
Born: 6/26/79 in Maracay, VZ
ML Seasons: 1

Overall Statistics

	G	AB	R	H	D	T	HR	RBI	SB	BB	SO	Avg	OBP	Slg
'04	102	322	42	94	17	2	12	40	1	15	67	.292	.330	.469
Car.	102	322	42	94	17	2	12	40	1	15	67	.292	.330	.469

2004 Situational Stats

	AB	H	HR	RBI	Avg		AB	H	HR	RBI	Avg
Home	153	57	4	20	.373	LHP	97	26	3	9	.268
Road	169	37	8	20	.219	RHP	225	68	9	31	.302
First Half	204	51	7	21	.250	Sc Pos	67	17	4	28	.254
Scnd Half	118	43	5	19	.364	Clutch	47	9	1	3	.191

2004 Season

A Rule 5 selection from the Cleveland Indians, Luis Gonzalez made an impressive jump from Double-A to the big leagues in 2004. He was the ultimate utility player, starting games at second base, left field, third base, shortstop, right field and DH. Though his numbers were helped considerably by Coors Field, he ranked among the top 10 major league rookies in most offensive stats.

Hitting, Baserunning & Defense

Gonzalez can handle the bat, and he has shown the ability to hit with some power. He has an aggressive approach at the plate, and can hit anybody's fastball. Breaking balls can be a problem for him when he gets overeager. He is a step below average as a runner, and not a basestealer. Gonzalez acquitted himself well at all the defensive positions last year, but his best spot is third base. He has range limitations at shortstop and second, and is still adjusting to the outfield.

2005 Outlook

Gonzalez will battle with Garrett Atkins in spring training for the third-base job. Even if Atkins winds up with the bulk of the playing time, Gonzalez figures to get plenty of at-bats backing up shortstop Clint Barmes, a rookie, and second baseman Aaron Miles.

Todd Greene

Position: C
Bats: R **Throws:** R
Ht: 5'10" **Wt:** 208

Opening Day Age: 33
Born: 5/8/71 in Augusta, GA
ML Seasons: 9

Overall Statistics

	G	AB	R	H	D	T	HR	RBI	SB	BB	SO	Avg	OBP	Slg
'04	75	195	23	55	14	0	10	35	0	13	38	.282	.325	.508
Car.	437	1288	155	319	66	1	62	177	5	50	266	.248	.279	.445

2004 Situational Stats

	AB	H	HR	RBI	Avg		AB	H	HR	RBI	Avg
Home	107	32	6	23	.299	LHP	71	26	7	20	.366
Road	88	23	4	12	.261	RHP	124	29	3	15	.234
First Half	118	32	5	21	.271	Sc Pos	62	17	5	29	.274
Scnd Half	77	23	5	14	.299	Clutch	28	5	1	2	.179

2004 Season

Todd Greene put together a solid season as the Rockies' No. 2 catcher, initially behind Charles Johnson and then behind rookie J.D. Closser. He provided righthanded power and a solid influence on the Rockies' young starters. Aaron Cook and Jason Jennings, in particular, responded to Greene's game-calling.

Hitting, Baserunning & Defense

Greene has power and can turn on a fastball. However, he has to guard against overexposure; once pitchers start working counts on him, Greene can get off balance. He's a step below average as a runner, attempting only nine stolen bases in 437 big league games. Defensively, he moves well behind the plate and calls a good game. However, Greene isn't going to stop a running game. He threw out only a pair of 31 baserunners attempting to steal on him last year.

2005 Outlook

Greene is a quality No. 2 catcher who provides a team with a threat off the bench. He is very good at helping a young pitcher through a game, which makes him invaluable in a part-time role because he also can teach a young catcher the tricks of the trade. As important as anything is the fact that he has accepted that role.

Tim Harikkala

Position: RP
Bats: R **Throws:** R
Ht: 6' 2" **Wt:** 185

Opening Day Age: 33
Born: 7/15/71 in West Palm Beach, FL
ML Seasons: 4

Overall Statistics

	W	L	Pct.	ERA	G	GS	Sv	IP	H	BB	SO	HR	Avg
'04	6	6	.500	4.74	55	0	0	62.2	55	23	30	10	.235
Car.	7	8	.467	5.83	64	1	0	83.1	81	32	39	12	.256

2004 Situational Stats

	W	L	ERA	Sv	IP		AB	H	HR	RBI	Avg
Home	3	2	4.79	0	35.2	LHB	103	25	7	21	.243
Road	3	4	4.67	0	27.0	RHB	131	30	3	19	.229
First Half	3	1	2.83	0	35.0	Sc Pos	58	14	1	26	.241
Scnd Half	3	5	7.16	0	27.2	Clutch	139	41	9	29	.295

2004 Season

For a guy who had only nine games in the big leagues the first 12 years of his pro career and who hadn't even been in spring training at the minor league level the two previous years, Tim Harikkala put a solid 2004 season together until a final-month meltdown.

Pitching, Defense & Hitting

Harikkala doesn't have anything special, but he does have exquisite command. His fastball is average, 90-91 MPH with little movement. He also has a nickel slider that he can run in on lefthanded hitters. What he does best is work fast and throw strikes, not giving hitters a chance to get comfortable. Harikkala moves around the mound well, and has such a simple delivery that he can hold runners. He has a tendency to rush things and can get in trouble with errant throws to the bases. He seldom gets to bat.

2005 Outlook

Harikkala was a waiver claim by Oakland, which wants him to provide a veteran presence to the bullpen. Harikkala can handle that job if he takes a deep breath. He was fine with the Rockies in 2004 when he felt he was playing on house money, but when it got to late August and he started to think about 2005, he was noticeably different.

Charles Johnson

Position: C
Bats: R **Throws:** R
Ht: 6' 3" **Wt:** 225

Opening Day Age: 33
Born: 7/20/71 in Fort Pierce, FL
ML Seasons: 11

Overall Statistics

	G	AB	R	H	D	T	HR	RBI	SB	BB	SO	Avg	OBP	Slg
'04	109	305	42	72	20	0	13	47	2	49	91	.236	.350	.430
Car.	1169	3790	460	931	207	4	167	565	6	466	986	.246	.330	.435

2004 Situational Stats

	AB	H	HR	RBI	Avg		AB	H	HR	RBI	Avg
Home	152	35	7	26	.230	LHP	73	17	5	10	.233
Road	153	37	6	21	.242	RHP	232	55	8	37	.237
First Half	208	55	11	37	.264	Sc Pos	71	18	2	29	.254
Scnd Half	97	17	2	10	.175	Clutch	52	10	2	9	.192

2004 Season

Reality hit hard for Charles Johnson in 2004. After killing a trade to Los Angeles at the trading deadline, Johnson made only nine starts in the final seven weeks of the season, and just three in September. His 305 at-bats were the second fewest of his big league career.

Hitting, Baserunning & Defense

Johnson has never made adjustments with the bat. He can be overpowered inside and will chase the pitch low and away, but he has power if he gets an average fastball up in the zone. He is among the slowest players in the game. Defensively, the four-time Gold Glove winner has become a liability. He throws decently, but he snaps at pitches, stealing strikes from his pitchers, and doesn't move behind the plate, a problem in Colorado because of the young pitchers with hard sinkers.

2005 Outlook

Johnson is getting close to the end. The Rockies decided they were better off with a true backup to help bring along rookie J.D. Closser, and were willing to eat the bulk of Johnson's $9 million salary for 2005. His reputation will still find him work, but it won't be on a regular basis. He physically can't handle the daily demands behind the plate anymore.

Steve Reed

Position: RP
Bats: R **Throws:** R
Ht: 6' 2" **Wt:** 212

Opening Day Age: 40
Born: 3/11/65 in Los Angeles, CA
ML Seasons: 13

Overall Statistics

	W	L	Pct.	ERA	G	GS	Sv	IP	H	BB	SO	HR	Avg
'04	3	8	.273	3.68	65	0	0	66.0	72	17	38	7	.281
Car.	48	42	.533	3.51	803	0	18	838.0	770	274	615	102	.247

2004 Situational Stats

	W	L	ERA	Sv	IP		AB	H	HR	RBI	Avg
Home	1	4	5.06	0	32.0	LHB	103	29	2	11	.282
Road	2	4	2.38	0	34.0	RHB	153	43	5	22	.281
First Half	1	2	2.48	0	40.0	Sc Pos	71	17	1	24	.239
Scnd Half	2	6	5.54	0	26.0	Clutch	121	37	6	21	.306

2004 Season

Age doesn't catch up with Steve Reed. In 2004, at the age of 39, he equaled Lee Smith's record with his 12th consecutive season of at least 50 appearances. Reed led Rockies relievers with a 3.68 ERA, leaving him with a 3.51 ERA in 179 career appearances at Coors Field.

Pitching, Defense & Hitting

Reed can pitch often, but a manager has to be careful how long to leave him in a game, as he is not going to get past the legit lefthanded bats. Lefthanded hitters have a career .288 average against him, 65 points higher than righthanders. He has a sinker-slider mix with a submarine delivery that can puzzle righthanded hitters. His pitches go down and in to lefthanded hitters, which is their hot zone. Reed moves around the mound well and has a quick move to first, which is important. He has to keep runners close because he has a slow delivery to the plate.

2005 Outlook

Reed can help a contending team, but in a seventh/eighth-inning role. He has not shown an ability to close out games at the big league level. However, he isn't afraid of coming into a mid-inning jam and will throw strikes. He's a luxury on a non-contender because of the limited role.

Mark Sweeney

Position: RF/1B
Bats: L **Throws:** L
Ht: 6' 1" **Wt:** 215

Opening Day Age: 35
Born: 10/26/69 in
Framingham, MA
ML Seasons: 10

Overall Statistics

	G	AB	R	H	D	T	HR	RBI	SB	BB	SO	Avg	OBP	Slg
'04	122	177	25	47	12	2	9	40	1	32	51	.266	.377	.508
Car.	765	1135	135	290	62	6	27	155	10	162	260	.256	.349	.392

2004 Situational Stats

	AB	H	HR	RBI	Avg		AB	H	HR	RBI	Avg
Home	80	26	6	26	.325	LHP	9	5	1	3	.556
Road	97	21	3	14	.216	RHP	168	42	8	37	.250
First Half	119	32	4	25	.269	Sc Pos	54	15	2	28	.278
Scnd Half	58	15	5	15	.259	Clutch	50	11	3	17	.220

2004 Season

Mark Sweeney reaffirmed his status as one of the game's ultimate lefthanded pinch-hitters in 2004. Benefiting from manager Clint Hurdle's effort to keep Sweeney fresh by getting him regular at-bats, even in blowouts, Sweeney led all pinch-hitters with five homers and 23 RBI, the second highest total since 1980.

Hitting, Baserunning & Defense

Sweeney can hit. He looks for a fastball and he has the bat speed to drive it. Righthanders can't get inside against him. He may have been able to hit lefthanders at one point, but he hasn't had enough opportunity in the big leagues (79 at-bats in 10 years) to maintain any type of an edge. Sweeney can handle the corner outfield spots and first base decently, but he lacks the power to claim a regular job at those positions. He is a solid average runner who can take the extra base.

2005 Outlook

Sweeney has earned his keep in the big leagues because of his willingness to accept a bench role. He not only provides a legitimate threat off the bench, but also is a strong clubhouse asset. He takes time with younger players to help them acclimate, which gives him another edge in hanging on to a job as an extra player.

Jamey Wright

Position: SP
Bats: R **Throws:** R
Ht: 6' 6" **Wt:** 235

Opening Day Age: 30
Born: 12/24/74 in
Oklahoma City, OK
ML Seasons: 9

Overall Statistics

	W	L	Pct.	ERA	G	GS	Sv	IP	H	BB	SO	HR	Avg
'04	2	3	.400	4.12	14	14	0	78.2	82	45	41	8	.266
Car.	53	72	.424	5.08	192	189	0	1134.1	1241	578	601	125	.286

2004 Situational Stats

	W	L	ERA	Sv	IP		AB	H	HR	RBI	Avg
Home	0	0	3.98	0	40.2	LHB	162	41	4	15	.253
Road	2	3	4.26	0	38.0	RHB	146	41	4	21	.281
First Half	0	0	—	0	0.0	Sc Pos	111	22	2	30	.198
Scnd Half	2	3	4.12	0	78.2	Clutch	10	3	0	1	.300

2004 Season

After spending the first four months of 2004 with Kansas City's Triple-A Omaha affiliate, Jamey Wright got his release and rejoined the club which originally drafted him, the Rockies. He was only 2-3 in 14 starts, but allowed two or fewer runs in nine of them. He left four games with a lead the bullpen couldn't hold.

Pitching, Defense & Hitting

Wright has a hard sinker with good action. He also can throw a slider that he will run in on lefthanded hitters. He has never gotten comfortable with changing speeds, which is why he has yet to claim a solid spot in a rotation. He allowed only a .219 average with runners on base last year, .198 when they were in scoring position. Wright can get a little out of focus defensively, but he has a wonderful move to first and second. He had four pickoffs in his brief big league time last year. He can bunt decently but doesn't make contact often when he swings.

2005 Outlook

Wright is adamant about getting a chance to start and be in the big leagues in 2005. He has the potential that scouts can't walk away from. He's a quality guy on a team, making it easier for a manager to overlook the inconsistencies.

Other Colorado Rockies

Adam Bernero (Pos: RHP, Age: 28)

	W	L	Pct.	ERA	G	GS	Sv	IP	H	BB	SO	HR	Avg
'04	1	1	.500	5.57	16	2	0	32.1	36	17	21	7	.283
Car.	6	23	.207	5.82	110	34	0	314.0	347	119	198	50	.283

Bernero missed almost all of the first half of the season with impingement in his right shoulder, but posted a 3.17 ERA at Triple-A Colorado Springs. He refused a minor league assignment after the season and is a free agent. The big righthander could help somebody as a middle reliever. 2005 Outlook: C

Travis Driskill (Pos: RHP, Age: 33)

	W	L	Pct.	ERA	G	GS	Sv	IP	H	BB	SO	HR	Avg
'04	0	0	–	6.48	5	0	0	8.1	13	3	6	0	.361
Car.	11	13	.458	5.29	54	19	1	189.0	225	60	117	29	.294

Driskill spent most of the season as a swingman at Triple-A Colorado Springs, where he allowed 141 hits in 111.2 IP. Though he has been pitching professionally since 1993, he has yet to hurl 200 innings in the bigs. He signed a minor league deal with the Astros. 2005 Outlook: C

Chris Gissell (Pos: RHP, Age: 27)

	W	L	Pct.	ERA	G	GS	Sv	IP	H	BB	SO	HR	Avg
'04	0	1	.000	14.54	5	1	0	8.2	20	3	11	4	.465
Car.	0	1	.000	14.54	5	1	0	8.2	20	3	11	4	.465

Gissell has been pitching at Double-A or higher since 1998, but had his first sip of big league coffee last year. After giving up runs in each of his five appearances, it may be his last. He will try to hook up with yet another organization this year. 2005 Outlook: C

Denny Hocking (Pos: LF/SS, Age: 34, Bats: B)

	G	AB	R	H	D	T	HR	RBI	SB	BB	SO	Avg	OBP	Slg
'04	55	94	7	19	2	0	0	4	0	7	20	.202	.257	.223
Car.	931	2298	280	575	111	17	25	219	36	195	432	.250	.308	.346

After an 11-year career in Minnesota, Hocking signed with the Rockies last year. He played very little and was eventually released, and the Cubs picked him up. He is a useful utilityman, as he has played everywhere but pitcher and catcher in his career. 2005 Outlook: C

Kevin Jarvis (Pos: RHP, Age: 35)

	W	L	Pct.	ERA	G	GS	Sv	IP	H	BB	SO	HR	Avg
'04	1	0	1.000	10.80	10	0	0	15.0	26	9	7	5	.382
Car.	34	46	.425	5.93	174	114	1	749.1	894	248	438	145	.296

Since winning 12 games for the Padres in 2001, Jarvis has been losing an ongoing battle with his elbow. He ended the year in the Pirates' organization, which is the eighth of his 14-year professional career. In 2004, he gave up 137 hits in 103 minor league innings. 2005 Outlook: C

Marc Kroon (Pos: RHP, Age: 31)

	W	L	Pct.	ERA	G	GS	Sv	IP	H	BB	SO	HR	Avg
'04	0	0	–	6.00	6	0	0	6.0	7	10	3	1	.350
Car.	0	2	.000	7.76	26	0	0	26.2	29	26	23	3	.282

Kroon recorded 20 saves at Colorado Springs last year, but was ineffective in his major league stint. The former second-round draft pick missed both the 2001 and 2002 seasons while recovering from two different surgeries on his elbow. 2005 Outlook: C

Javier Lopez (Pos: LHP, Age: 27)

	W	L	Pct.	ERA	G	GS	Sv	IP	H	BB	SO	HR	Avg
'04	1	2	.333	7.52	64	0	0	40.2	45	26	20	1	.287
Car.	5	3	.625	5.27	139	0	1	99.0	103	58	60	6	.270

A nearly month-long stint in the minors straightened Lopez out last year. Before the demotion, his ERA was 9.93; afterwards it was a sparkling 1.54. He looks to be destined for situational relief, as righthanders hit .350 against him, while he held lefties to a .221 average. 2005 Outlook: C

Vladimir Nunez (Pos: RHP, Age: 30)

	W	L	Pct.	ERA	G	GS	Sv	IP	H	BB	SO	HR	Avg
'04	3	3	.500	7.01	22	0	0	25.2	26	14	22	6	.280
Car.	20	32	.385	4.83	230	27	21	408.1	396	178	302	53	.259

Since saving 20 games for the 2002 Marlins, Nunez' career has gone downhill fast. He posted an ERA of 1.69 last April, but in May it ballooned to 10.80 and he was sent down. He has had enough of Colorado and signed a minor league deal with Texas in November. 2005 Outlook: C

Kit Pellow (Pos: RF/LF, Age: 31, Bats: R)

	G	AB	R	H	D	T	HR	RBI	SB	BB	SO	Avg	OBP	Slg
'04	59	121	15	29	5	1	2	10	1	8	43	.240	.308	.347
Car.	99	202	27	52	9	2	4	19	2	17	68	.257	.335	.381

Pellow shuttled back and forth between Triple-A and the big club last season, and became a free agent after the season. He has hit as many as 35 homers in a season in the minors, and can play all four corners and even catch in a pinch, so he could help the Mariners, who signed him to a minor league deal in November. 2005 Outlook: C

Jorge Piedra (Pos: CF/LF, Age: 25, Bats: L)

	G	AB	R	H	D	T	HR	RBI	SB	BB	SO	Avg	OBP	Slg
'04	38	91	15	27	8	0	3	10	0	5	19	.297	.340	.484
Car.	38	91	15	27	8	0	3	10	0	5	19	.297	.340	.484

After hitting .334 with 15 homers in his first taste of Triple-A last season, Piedra did not embarass himself in the bigs. By playing all three outfield positions, he looks to have the inside track at the fourth-outfielder spot, or even as half of a platoon. 2005 Outlook: B

Rene Reyes (Pos: CF, Age: 27, Bats: B)

	G	AB	R	H	D	T	HR	RBI	SB	BB	SO	Avg	OBP	Slg
'04	28	61	5	9	2	0	0	1	0	5	17	.148	.212	.180
Car.	81	177	18	39	9	1	2	8	2	10	36	.220	.261	.316

Reyes has a career batting average of .330 in six minor league seasons, but he never got much of a shot with the Rockies. The Cubs signed him to a minor league contract, and he could get some playing time as a backup. 2005 Outlook: C

Denny Stark (Pos: RHP, Age: 30)

	W	L	Pct.	ERA	G	GS	Sv	IP	H	BB	SO	HR	Avg
'04	0	5	.000	11.42	6	6	0	26.0	53	18	10	9	.427
Car.	15	13	.536	5.78	64	42	0	254.0	290	123	120	51	.286

Stark went 11-4 for the Rockies in 2002, but it has been all downhill for him since. He has been plagued by injuries throughout his career, and lost the last two months of the 2004 season with a severe groin pull. The 30-year-old will try to get a fresh start with a new club. 2005 Outlook: C

Andy Tracy (Pos: 3B, Age: 31, Bats: L)

	G	AB	R	H	D	T	HR	RBI	SB	BB	SO	Avg	OBP	Slg
'04	15	16	1	3	1	0	0	1	0	1	8	.188	.235	.250
Car.	136	263	34	59	10	1	13	41	1	29	95	.224	.302	.418

Tracy put up some big numbers at Triple-A Colorado Springs last season, hitting .315 with 33 homers and 120 RBI. The Rockies re-signed him to a minor league deal in November, but the chances of him getting any significant playing time with the parent club are slim. 2005 Outlook: C

Turk Wendell (Pos: RHP, Age: 37)

	W	L	Pct.	ERA	G	GS	Sv	IP	H	BB	SO	HR	Avg
'04	0	0	–	7.02	12	0	0	16.2	21	12	11	4	.328
Car.	36	33	.522	3.93	552	6	33	645.2	583	324	515	73	.242

Wendell went on the DL with a stiff shoulder in the middle of May and that was the end of the season. He already missed an entire season in 2002, and to the dismay of licorice-makers everywhere, it appears that his career may be over. 2005 Outlook: D

Jason Young (Pos: RHP, Age: 25)

	W	L	Pct.	ERA	G	GS	Sv	IP	H	BB	SO	HR	Avg
'04	0	1	.000	12.96	2	2	0	8.1	15	5	7	3	.385
Car.	0	3	.000	9.71	10	5	0	29.2	49	14	25	11	.363

After seven Triple-A starts, Young was brought up to the big club, but a fractured rib ended his season in just his second outing. The former second-round draft pick should make the 2005 rotation, and he has the makings of a good one. 2005 Outlook: B

Colorado Rockies Minor League Prospects

Organization Overview:

In 1998, Rockies ownership told the scouting department to worry more about physical ability and less about signability. Six years later, the results of that more aggressive approach are starting to be felt throughout the organization. Last year, three rookies had an impact—left fielder Matt Holliday, super sub Luis Gonzalez and second baseman Aaron Miles. They each represented different types of scouting: Holliday was a draft choice, signed out of high school; Gonzalez was a Rule 5 draftee, uncovered by the professional scouting department; and Miles came in a trade. The Rockies now are focusing on developing a homegrown pitching staff. The core of the 2005 rotation projects to be Aaron Cook, a second-round draft choice in 1997, Jason Jennings, a No. 1 draft pick in 1997, and Jeff Francis, the team's top draft pick in 2002.

Garrett Atkins

Position: 3B   **Opening Day Age:** 25
Bats: R **Throws:** R   **Born:** 12/12/79 in
Ht: 6' 3" **Wt:** 210   Orange, CA

Recent Statistics

	G	AB	R	H	D	T	HR	RBI	SB	BB	SO	Avg
2004 AAA Col Spngs	122	445	88	163	43	3	15	94	0	57	45	.366
2004 NL Colorado	15	28	3	10	2	0	1	8	0	4	3	.357

Atkins struggled in his big league debut in 2003, but re-affirmed his prospect status in 2004 by returning to Triple-A Colorado Springs and winning the Pacific Coast League batting title. The concern with Atkins is his defense. He is a converted first baseman who has had trouble making adjustments to the hot corner. During the winter, he addressed some concerns by getting involved in a sports enhancement facility where the focus was on foot speed and agility. There's little question about his ability to hit. He is not going to be a 30-plus homer guy, but he does drive the ball in the gaps and shows run-production abilities. Atkins gets a chance this spring to win the everyday third-base job.

Clint Barmes

Position: SS   **Opening Day Age:** 26
Bats: R **Throws:** R   **Born:** 3/6/79 in
Ht: 6' 0" **Wt:** 175   Vincennes, IN

Recent Statistics

	G	AB	R	H	D	T	HR	RBI	SB	BB	SO	Avg
2004 AAA Col Spngs	125	533	104	175	42	2	16	51	20	28	61	.328
2004 NL Colorado	20	71	14	20	3	1	2	10	0	3	10	.282

Barmes was given a second year at Triple-A Colorado Springs in 2004, and now he's being given the big league shortstop job in 2005. A 10th-round draft choice out of Indiana State in 2000, Barmes originally was considered a potential utility infielder. He is one of those players who doesn't open eyes at first, but the more he plays the more of an impression he makes. He doesn't do anything exceptionally well—except hustle and compete. He has shown enough feel for shortstop in the last two years that he should be able to play himself into having the arm and necessary range to adequately man the position. He fits well into the No. 2 slot, showing the ability to drive the ball into gaps.

J.D. Closser

Position: C   **Opening Day Age:** 25
Bats: B **Throws:** R   **Born:** 1/15/80 in Beech
Ht: 5' 10" **Wt:** 176   Grove, IN

Recent Statistics

	G	AB	R	H	D	T	HR	RBI	SB	BB	SO	Avg
2004 AAA Col Spngs	83	298	53	89	19	1	7	54	0	41	47	.299
2004 NL Colorado	36	113	5	36	6	0	1	10	0	6	22	.319

Closser was acquired prior to the 2002 season from Arizona, along with Jack Cust for lefthanded reliever Mike Myers. He has an energy that has been missing from Colorado backstops in recent seasons. He has good arm strength, but the mechanics get out of whack and he can have trouble throwing out baserunners. He still needs to move better behind the plate, as too many balls get by him. He has decent power and is a capable switch-hitter from both sides of the plate. He also can hit for average if he doesn't become pull conscious. Closser has become the Rockies' prime catching prospect, and he has been given the big league job for 2005.

Jeff Francis

Position: P   **Opening Day Age:** 24
Bats: L **Throws:** L   **Born:** 1/8/81 in
Ht: 6' 5" **Wt:** 200   Vancouver, Canada

Recent Statistics

	W	L	ERA	G	GS	Sv	IP	H	R	BB	SO	HR
2004 AA Tulsa	13	1	1.98	17	17	0	113.2	73	26	22	147	9
2004 AAA Col Spngs	3	2	2.85	7	7	0	41.0	35	16	7	49	3
2004 NL Colorado	3	2	5.15	7	7	0	36.2	42	22	13	32	8

Francis was the Rockies' first-round pick in 2002, and he made a rapid rise during the 2004 season. After opening the season at Double-A Tulsa, where he pitched enough innings to qualify for the Texas League ERA title, he was promoted to Triple-A Colorado Springs before finishing the season in the Rockies' rotation. Francis isn't going to overpower hitters. His fastball is a solid 90-92 MPH, but he also has a slider, curve and changeup, and the physics major in college has a feel for how to mix his pitches. Most importantly, he has excellent command within the strike zone and a funky enough delivery that hitters don't seem to get a good look at the ball out of his hand.

Choo Freeman

Position: OF   **Opening Day Age:** 25
Bats: R **Throws:** R **Born:** 10/20/79 in Pine
Ht: 6' 2" **Wt:** 200   Bluff, AR

Recent Statistics

	G	AB	R	H	D	T	HR	RBI	SB	BB	SO	Avg
2004 AAA Col Spngs	100	380	58	107	21	7	10	50	7	28	84	.297
2004 NL Colorado	45	90	15	17	3	2	1	11	1	14	21	.189

Freeman has been the Rockies' center field hope-for-the-future ever since he was drafted as a sandwich pick after the first round in 1998. It hasn't come quickly for him, but then it took his cousin, Torii Hunter, seven years to make it with Minnesota. Freeman hasn't made the strides offensively that scouts have projected, but he does play a quality center field, has a decent arm and runs well above average. He still is a bit too mechanical in his hitting approach, trying to make sure he does things correctly instead of merely reacting to the situation. But he is an athlete, wants to learn and works his tail off. Freeman should get a chance to at least be a fourth outfielder with Colorado in 2005.

Brad Hawpe

Position: OF   **Opening Day Age:** 25
Bats: L **Throws:** L **Born:** 6/22/79 in Fort
Ht: 6' 3" **Wt:** 200   Worth, TX

Recent Statistics

	G	AB	R	H	D	T	HR	RBI	SB	BB	SO	Avg
2004 AAA Col Spngs	92	345	62	111	19	1	31	86	3	36	91	.322
2004 NL Colorado	42	105	12	26	3	2	3	9	1	11	34	.248

Hawpe has legitimate lefthanded, middle-of-the-lineup power. The question he has to answer is whether he can make consistent enough contact to hit up in the middle, or will he be left to hit in the sixth or seventh spot. Signed as a first baseman, he was converted to the outfield because of Todd Helton, and Hawpe has worked hard to become average in right. He has the arm strength for the position and has improved his lateral movement. The bat, however, is what's going to make or break him. He can hit the ball out of all parts of the ballpark, and has to go to the plate with that in mind instead of thinking too much about pulling the ball.

Allan Simpson

Position: P   **Opening Day Age:** 27
Bats: R **Throws:** R **Born:** 8/26/77 in
Ht: 6' 4" **Wt:** 185   Springfield, IL

Recent Statistics

	W	L	ERA	G	GS	Sv	IP	H	R	BB	SO	HR
2004 AAA Col Spngs	2	1	2.80	27	0	4	35.1	30	14	10	43	1
2004 NL Colorado	2	1	5.08	32	0	0	39.0	44	26	20	44	4

Simpson was acquired from Seattle in a December 2003 trade of minor league pitchers. He worked his way into the Rockies' bullpen plans last summer, showing the ability to get strikeouts in late-inning situations. He has that nasty kind of movement that allows him to get hitters to swing at non-strikes. Simpson has a fastball that is solidly in the 92-plus MPH range. The big pitch for him is a hard split-finger fastball, which neutralizes lefthanded bats. He does need to be more consistent in the strike zone. Simpson's commitment to getting better was apparent when, despite getting a decent cup of coffee in 2004, he decided to pitch winter ball for Obregon and was dominating in the Mexican Pacific League.

Chin-hui Tsao

Position: P   **Opening Day Age:** 23
Bats: R **Throws:** R **Born:** 6/2/81 in Hua-
Ht: 6' 2" **Wt:** 177   Lien, Taiwan

Recent Statistics

	W	L	ERA	G	GS	Sv	IP	H	R	BB	SO	HR
2004 A Asheville	1	0	1.80	2	2	0	10.0	8	2	1	14	1
2004 AA Tulsa	1	1	2.77	2	2	0	13.0	12	4	2	10	1
2004 AAA Col Spngs	1	1	8.53	4	4	0	12.2	22	12	5	14	5
2004 NL Colorado	0	0	3.86	10	0	1	9.1	7	4	1	11	2

Colorado's first major international sign, Tsao got a taste of working in relief when he pitched for his native Taiwan in the 2004 Olympics. He has had various physical problems, including a recurring blister situation, which the Rockies feel they might be able to control better by using him for short bursts instead of trying to stretch him out. His fastball will sit in the 94-96 MPH range. He also has a hard slider with a sharp break, and his changeup has come along well since he underwent reconstructive right elbow surgery in 2001. Tsao is going to get a shot at late-inning bullpen work in 2005, with the idea that he could become the homegrown closer the Rockies are looking to develop.

Others to Watch

Third baseman **Jeff Baker** (23) battles a recurring wrist problem that limited him to only three games in the Arizona Fall League. He has a definite power bat and shows the athletic ability that has the Rockies pondering possible moves to second base or right field. . . Righthanded starter **Ubaldo Jimenez** (21) was on the fast track until being sidelined in May last year by the initial stages of a stress fracture in his right shoulder. He calls on a fastball in the mid-90s with a quality curveball and a changeup. . . Second baseman **Jayson Nix** (22) hit a bump in the road in 2004, struggling in his debut at the Double-A level. He has become a quality defensive player, and has some pop in the bat. . . Center fielder **Jeff Salazar** (24) could be in the big leagues by midseason. He has the defense right now to be among the game's elite, and has the potential of a live bat that would make him a plus run-producer for a center fielder. . . Third baseman **Ian Stewart** (19) is a franchise-type player, referred to as a lefthanded-hitting Scott Rolen. The Rockies' first-round draft pick in 2003, Stewart has tremendous power, a desire to be one of the best to ever play the game and has made the necessary adjustments defensively.

Pro Player Stadium

Offense

After spending significant effort over the previous two years trying to build a lineup that would thrive at home, the Marlins saw their hitters struggle at Pro Player Stadium in 2004. Speed is at a premium here, and the Marlins ranked only seventh in the NL in stolen bases last year. The park continues to be a tough place to score a run in, and especially tough on home-run hitters.

Defense

Pro Player's Teal Tower causes headaches in left center. The 28-foot-high out of town scoreboard is good for at least one disappointed slugger most nights, and it causes all sorts of strange caroms that can handcuff the uninitiated. The infield and outfield grass is among the fastest in the league, causing trouble at times for converted outfielder Miguel Cabrera.

Who It Helps the Most

Shortstop Alex Gonzalez hit 35 points higher at home, where he hit 13 of his 23 homers. Second baseman Luis Castillo hit 21 points higher at home. Center fielder Juan Pierre hit 24 points higher at home. Among pitchers, Josh Beckett's ERA was considerably lower at home. A.J. Burnett's home ERA was almost half of the mark he posted on the road.

Who It Hurts the Most

Backup catcher Mike Redmond hit 69 points higher on the road. Utilityman Damion Easley also hit much better on the road. Left fielder Miguel Cabrera hit 19 points higher on the road. Reliever Nate Bump, a groundball specialist, had a home ERA that was nearly a run and a half higher than on the road.

Rookies & Newcomers

In a limited sample, noted flyball pitcher Ismael Valdez enjoyed the spacious expanse of Pro Player Stadium. Another 2004 midseason acquisition, Paul Lo Duca, batted only .239 at Pro Player last year. Lefthander Al Leiter, a former Marlin signed over the winter, is 22-9 (2.77) in 38 starts there.

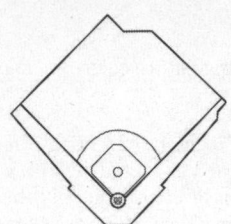

Dimensions: LF-330, LCF-385, CF-404, RCF-385, RF-345

Capacity: 36,331

Elevation: 10 feet

Surface: Grass

Foul Territory: Average

Park Factors

2004 Season

| | Home Games | | | Away Games | | | |
	Marlins	Opp	Total	Marlins	Opp	Total	Index
G	69	69	138	72	72	144	
Avg	.264	.246	.255	.267	.269	.268	95
AB	2253	2364	4617	2507	2386	4893	98
R	293	279	572	339	339	678	88
H	594	582	1176	669	643	1312	94
2B	122	108	230	121	137	258	94
3B	13	15	28	14	17	31	96
HR	58	72	130	64	79	143	96
BB	214	239	453	220	212	432	111
SO	408	522	930	447	434	881	112
E	28	53	81	48	55	103	82
E-Infield	23	43	66	37	42	79	87
LHB-Avg	.280	.252	.263	.293	.269	.279	94
LHB-HR	9	35	44	6	33	39	108
RHB-Avg	.257	.242	.250	.257	.270	.263	95
RHB-HR	49	37	86	58	46	104	92

2002-2004

| | Home Games | | | Away Games | | | |
	Marlins	Opp	Total	Marlins	Opp	Total	Index
G	213	213	426	216	216	432	
Avg	.269	.247	.258	.259	.270	.265	97
AB	7054	7387	14441	7474	7157	14631	100
R	975	865	1840	925	1038	1963	95
H	1897	1825	3722	1937	1935	3872	97
2B	365	363	728	383	412	795	93
3B	58	56	114	38	43	81	143
HR	185	175	360	205	226	431	85
BB	748	767	1515	665	726	1391	110
SO	1330	1649	2979	1415	1322	2737	110
E	104	146	250	138	167	305	83
E-Infield	82	119	201	117	141	258	79
LHB-Avg	.282	.246	.261	.270	.280	.276	95
LHB-HR	24	71	95	21	89	110	82
RHB-Avg	.264	.248	.256	.255	.264	.259	99
RHB-HR	161	104	265	184	137	321	86

2004 Rankings (National League)
- Second-highest strikeout factor

Jack McKeon

2004 Season

Still glowing from his first World Series title, Jack McKeon was determined to enjoy his follow-up campaign. The reconstituted Marlins held or shared the NL East lead for much of the first three months before going through a seven-week slump. A furious push that began in late August ran out of steam in the season's final two weeks. McKeon managed to keep things fairly upbeat throughout, even in the face of multiple hurricanes that forced the Marlins to give up three home games and finish with 30 games in 27 days.

Offense

Runs again were at a premium for the Marlins, who finished 11th in the league in runs and 12th in home runs. They were just seventh in sacrifice bunts, which ran counter to their reputation as small-ball purveyors. After leading the majors in stolen bases the previous two seasons, they sank to seventh in the league. Just one NL team was caught stealing more than the Marlins. McKeon stuck with a set lineup for the most part, only occasionally flip-flopping Juan Pierre and Luis Castillo at the top of the order or Miguel Cabrera and Mike Lowell in the middle.

Pitching & Defense

McKeon continues to view relievers as interchangeable commodities. The Marlins burned through 25 pitchers, 19 of whom made relief appearances, in a revolving-door season. The season-ending elbow injury that sidelined setup man Chad Fox blew a hole in the bullpen that forced McKeon to mix and match until Guillermo Mota arrived via a July 30 trade.

2005 Outlook

McKeon's tenures typically turn contentious with each passing year as players bray under his motivational tactics. There were signs of that last year with the young Marlins, but winning the 2003 World Series should head off all but the most persistent of clubhouse lawyers. McKeon, who turned 74 in November, needs to manage into the 2006 season to supplant Casey Stengel as the second-oldest manager in major league history.

Born: 11/23/30 in South Amboy, NJ

Playing Experience: No major league playing experience

Managerial Experience: 14 seasons

Manager Statistics

Year	Team, Lg	W	L	Pct	GB	Finish
2004	Florida, NL	83	79	.512	13.0	3rd East
14 Seasons		928	861	.519	–	–

2004 Starting Pitchers by Days Rest

	<=3	4	5	6+
Marlins Starts	5	79	44	22
Marlins ERA	2.70	4.54	3.67	3.53
NL Avg Starts	2	82	46	23
NL ERA	4.58	4.35	4.28	4.73

2004 Situational Stats

	Jack McKeon	NL Average
Hit & Run Success %	38.9	38.0
Stolen Base Success %	69.1	71.7
Platoon Pct.	47.1	55.2
Defensive Subs	18	18
High-Pitch Outings	2	6
Quick/Slow Hooks	18/7	21/12
Sacrifice Attempts	107	99

2004 Rankings (National League)

- 1st in steals of home plate (1), fewest caught stealings of third base (2) and double steals (3)
- 2nd in starts on three days rest
- 3rd in steals of third base (14) and pitchouts with a runner moving (5)

Josh Beckett

2004 Season

Coming off a dazzling October that included World Series MVP honors, Josh Beckett was expected to blossom into a year-long ace. Instead he made three more trips to the disabled list, twice with blister-related problems on his right middle finger and once with a pulled muscle in his side. That gave him seven DL stints in the past three seasons and left him thoroughly frustrated with his inability to stay active. Beckett remains just a .500 pitcher for his career, a statistic that confounds logic when the total package is considered.

Pitching

When he's healthy and on, Beckett still can chew up hitters like nobody's business. His four-seam fastball tops out at 97 MPH and he gets good movement on his sinker at 92-94 MPH. He has a plus 12-to-6 curveball that is the equal of Kerry Wood's, but his changeup isn't as consistent as it should be at this stage in his development. Lefties hit 89 points higher against Beckett than righties last year, in large part because of this deficiency. Beckett has tinkered with a splitter but has yet to develop the confidence to throw it regularly in tight spots. His biggest problem remains his bursts of anger when things go wrong on the mound. He still struggles to put bad pitches and bad calls behind him and tends to brood, sometimes for days, after disappointing outings.

Defense & Hitting

Beckett will run into a fastball from time to time at the plate, but he's a poor hitter and just a fair bunter. He's a good athlete who fields his position well and pays close attention to baserunners.

2005 Outlook

Eligible for salary arbitration for the first time, Beckett should see his pay double from $1.5 million. He remains, at least in theory, a bargain for a small-revenue team like the Marlins, but another disjointed year and a few more trips to the DL could lead to the once unthinkable: an early-career trade.

Position: SP
Bats: R **Throws:** R
Ht: 6' 5" **Wt:** 222

Opening Day Age: 24
Born: 5/15/80 in Spring, TX
ML Seasons: 4

Overall Statistics

	W	L	Pct.	ERA	G	GS	Sv	IP	H	BB	SO	HR	Avg
'04	9	9	.500	3.79	26	26	0	156.2	137	54	152	16	.235
Car.	26	26	.500	3.49	77	74	0	430.1	376	165	441	41	.234

2004 Pitching Profile

	Josh Beckett	NL Average
Overall Strike %	65.5	62.5
1st Pitch Strike %	63.4	58.5
Ratio	1.22	1.39
Strikeouts per 9 IP	8.73	6.74
Walks per 9 IP	3.10	3.38
Home Runs per 9 IP	0.92	1.11
Strikeout/Walk Ratio	2.81	1.99
Groundball/Flyball Ratio	1.25	1.25

2004 Situational Stats

	W	L	ERA	Sv	IP		AB	H	HR	RBI	Avg
Home	4	5	3.45	0	91.1	LHB	285	80	10	41	.281
Road	5	4	4.27	0	65.1	RHB	297	57	6	26	.192
First Half	4	5	3.89	0	76.1	Sc Pos	142	34	4	47	.239
Scnd Half	5	4	3.70	0	80.1	Clutch	27	4	1	1	.148

2004 Rankings (National League)

- 1st in lowest batting average allowed vs. righthanded batters
- Led the Marlins in strikeouts, lowest stolen-base percentage allowed (50.0) and most strikeouts per nine innings (8.7)

Armando Benitez

2004 Season

After getting traded twice and finishing out the 2003 season as a setup man in Seattle, Armando Benitez found diminished interest in his services last winter. He signed a one-year, $3.5 million deal with the Marlins and proceeded to enjoy the best season of his uneven career. Clearly enjoying the more relaxed atmosphere in South Florida, he made the All-Star team for the second straight year and set a club record for saves.

Pitching

Last year Benitez regained the confidence in his 95-97 MPH fastball, which is down a tick from its peak a few years ago. He dominated both righties and lefties, using a tight slider to put away the former and an occasional splitter to extinguish the latter. He has long had the ability to get four or more outs at the end of games, but even that ruggedness was tested with the way manager Jack McKeon used him during the first half. The loss of Chad Fox to another elbow injury in April forced more of a burden on Benitez, who responded ably to the challenge. He did spend three weeks on the disabled list in late July and early August with a tender elbow, but Benitez came back throwing gas for the final seven and a half weeks.

Defense & Hitting

Benitez has put on a few power shows in batting practice but received just one plate appearance all year. His thick midsection makes it tough for him to field bunts, and opposing basestealers were successful in all nine of their attempts against him. The lack of baserunners against Benitez largely negated that weakness.

2005 Outlook

The Marlins would have loved to re-sign Benitez, but the free agent's asking price was beyond their tight budget. In November, he signed a three-year, $21 million contract with the Giants, who have been searching for a reliable closer since Robb Nen broke down with injuries. In Benitez, they might have their man.

Position: RP
Bats: R **Throws:** R
Ht: 6' 4" **Wt:** 229

Opening Day Age: 32
Born: 11/3/72 in Ramon Santana, DR
ML Seasons: 11
Pronunciation: buh-NEE-tezz

Florida

Overall Statistics

	W	L	Pct.	ERA	G	GS	Sv	IP	H	BB	SO	HR	Avg
'04	2	2	.500	1.29	64	0	47	69.2	36	21	62	6	.152
Car.	32	33	.492	2.85	628	0	244	654.0	428	335	826	73	.185

2004 Pitching Profile

	Armando Benitez	NL Average
Overall Strike %	67.6	62.5
1st Pitch Strike %	63.5	58.5
Ratio	0.82	1.39
Strikeouts per 9 IP	8.01	6.74
Walks per 9 IP	2.71	3.38
Home Runs per 9 IP	0.78	1.11
Strikeout/Walk Ratio	2.95	1.99
Groundball/Flyball Ratio	0.54	1.25

2004 Situational Stats

	W	L	ERA	Sv	IP		AB	H	HR	RBI	Avg
Home	2	1	1.53	23	35.1	LHB	101	17	3	7	.168
Road	0	1	1.05	24	34.1	RHB	136	19	3	12	.140
First Half	2	0	0.98	30	46.0	Sc Pos	55	9	2	15	.164
Scnd Half	0	2	1.90	17	23.2	Clutch	178	30	5	18	.169

2004 Rankings (National League)

- 1st in saves, relief ERA (1.29), lowest batting average allowed in relief (.152) and fewest baserunners allowed per nine innings in relief (7.4)
- 2nd in save percentage (92.2)
- 6th in games finished (59)
- 7th in first batter efficiency (.143)
- Led the Marlins in saves, games finished (59), lowest batting average allowed vs. left handed batters, lowest batting average allowed vs. righthanded batters, save percentage (92.2), first batter efficiency (.143), blown saves (4), relief innings (69.2), relief ERA (1.29), lowest batting average allowed in relief (.152), most strikeouts per nine innings in relief (8.0) and fewest baserunners allowed per nine innings in relief (7.4)

A.J. Burnett

2004 Season

The unquestioned ace of the Marlins' staff before he blew out his elbow in April of 2003, A.J. Burnett made a triumphant return from reconstructive elbow surgery. He made it back a little over 13 months after the operation, and after some early spottiness became the club's second-most reliable starter after Carl Pavano. Burnett was shut down with some minor inflammation in his elbow following an 11-strikeout win over the Cubs on September 12. He might have made another start or two, but with the playoffs out of reach, caution was exercised and he made just one relief outing.

Pitching

There were times when Burnett's command deserted him, as often happens in the first year after Tommy John surgery, but for the most part he was extremely good in every way. Held to a strict pitch count early in his return, he stuck mainly to his 94-96 MPH fastball and humpbacked curve in order to conserve bullets. His fastball, which had been clocked several times at 100 MPH in 2002, returned to that level post-surgery. When he gets on a roll, Burnett stalks the mound like a panther, making hitters dance amid an array of effectively wild hard stuff. Surgery did nothing to interrupt the maturation in his thought process on the mound.

Defense & Hitting

Burnett, with two career homers, doesn't get cheated at the plate. He is a solid bunter as well. A lanky athlete, he fields his position well but needs to do a better job minding baserunners. He allowed 14 stolen bases in 19 attempts.

2005 Outlook

Due a substantial raise from $2.5 million through salary arbitration, Burnett could be the highest-paid pitcher on the staff if Pavano leaves via free agency. Regardless, Burnett will be counted on to be a 200-inning horse who regularly gives the Marlins 120 pitches per start. He still has the stuff to contend for a Cy Young someday soon.

Position: SP
Bats: R **Throws:** R
Ht: 6' 4" **Wt:** 230

Opening Day Age: 28
Born: 1/3/77 in North Little Rock, AR
ML Seasons: 6

Overall Statistics

	W	L	Pct.	ERA	G	GS	Sv	IP	H	BB	SO	HR	Avg
'04	7	6	.538	3.68	20	19	0	120.0	102	38	113	9	.231
Car.	37	38	.493	3.83	102	99	0	644.2	535	298	555	54	.228

2004 Pitching Profile

	A.J. Burnett	NL Average
Overall Strike %	62.5	62.5
1st Pitch Strike %	61.2	58.5
Ratio	1.17	1.39
Strikeouts per 9 IP	8.48	6.74
Walks per 9 IP	2.85	3.38
Home Runs per 9 IP	0.68	1.11
Strikeout/Walk Ratio	2.97	1.99
Groundball/Flyball Ratio	1.49	1.25

2004 Situational Stats

	W	L	ERA	Sv	IP		AB	H	HR	RBI	Avg
Home	6	0	2.80	0	74.0	LHB	243	60	4	25	.247
Road	1	6	5.09	0	46.0	RHB	199	42	5	19	.211
First Half	1	3	4.40	0	45.0	Sc Pos	92	24	2	33	.261
Scnd Half	6	3	3.24	0	75.0	Clutch	19	4	2	3	.211

2004 Rankings (National League)

- 5th in lowest batting average allowed vs. righthanded batters
- Led the Marlins in wild pitches (7), highest strikeout-walk ratio (3.0), lowest batting average allowed (.231), lowest slugging percentage allowed (.344), lowest on-base percentage allowed (.296), highest groundball-flyball ratio allowed (1.5), lowest ERA at home and most run support per nine innings (5.3)

Miguel Cabrera

Position: RF/LF
Bats: R **Throws:** R
Ht: 6' 2" **Wt:** 210

Opening Day Age: 21
Born: 4/18/83 in
Maracay, VZ
ML Seasons: 2

2004 Season

In his first full season in the majors, Miguel Cabrera added to his growing resume with his first All-Star Game appearance at age 21. He moved to right field in the spring, then bounced back to left after a July 30 trade brought Juan Encarnacion back from the Dodgers to play right. Cabrera just missed joining a select list of hitters to bat .300 with 30 homers and 100 RBI at 21 or younger. Those who have: Mel Ott, Alex Rodriguez, Albert Pujols, Ted Williams, Eddie Mathews, Hal Trosky and Jimmie Foxx.

Hitting

Most impressive last year, perhaps, was Cabrera's lack of any sort of lengthy slump. He rarely appeared frustrated, although his average against lefties dropped more than 100 points off his rookie season. More patient in year No. 2, Cabrera increased his walk rate, but his overall strikeouts rose significantly as well. He has the power to hit to all fields but sometimes looks to go the other way too much for the Marlins' liking. He can be vulnerable to hard stuff inside and will chase high fastballs and quality breaking balls away.

Baserunning & Defense

Cabrera struggled to make the transition to Pro Player Stadium's spacious right field over the first four months, looking much more comfortable upon his return to left. Cabrera got plenty of chances to show off his plus arm, which got more accurate in his first full season in the outfield. However, he still makes too many careless mistakes in the field as his concentration sometimes wanders. Cabrera has just five stolen bases in his two big league seasons and is only an average baserunner.

2005 Outlook

Cabrera won't be eligible for salary arbitration for another two seasons, so he will remain one of the top bargains in the game. His versatility enables him to play all four corner spots, but he's most likely to remain in left for now. Should Jeff Conine leave after 2005, Cabrera likely would return to the infield.

Overall Statistics

	G	AB	R	H	D	T	HR	RBI	SB	BB	SO	Avg	OBP	Slg
'04	160	603	101	177	31	1	33	112	5	68	148	.294	.366	.512
Car.	247	917	140	261	52	4	45	174	5	93	232	.285	.352	.497

Where He Hits the Ball

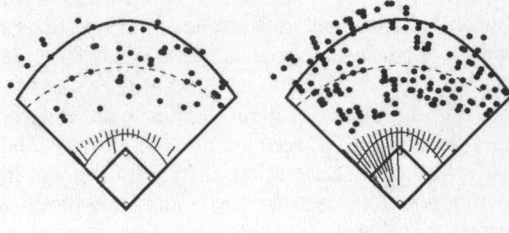

Vs. LHP **Vs. RHP**

2004 Situational Stats

	AB	H	HR	RBI	Avg		AB	H	HR	RBI	Avg
Home	296	84	14	50	.284	LHP	126	33	7	27	.262
Road	307	93	19	62	.303	RHP	477	144	26	85	.302
First Half	332	98	20	59	.295	Sc Pos	202	48	7	75	.238
Scnd Half	271	79	13	53	.292	Clutch	85	30	5	17	.353

2004 Rankings (National League)

- 1st in errors in right field (7)
- 5th in RBI and games played
- 7th in sacrifice flies (8) and strikeouts
- 9th in pitches seen (2,722), batting average with the bases loaded (.462) and GDPs (20)
- 10th in total bases (309)
- Led the Marlins in home runs, runs scored, total bases (309), RBI, sacrifice flies (8), strikeouts, GDPs (20), pitches seen (2,722), slugging percentage, HR frequency (18.3 ABs per HR) and batting average in the clutch

Florida

2004 Season

After signing the first multiyear contract of his career—a three-year, $15.5 million deal with a vesting option for 2007—Luis Castillo was under the microscope more than ever. He responded well, posting a sound if unspectacular season.

Hitting

A natural righthanded hitter, Castillo continues to improve from the left side. As a righty, he becomes more pull conscious and swings for the fences too much at times. As a result, he can struggle with good changeups. From the left side, he has started to turn on more inside pitches, but his hallmark still is the slap-and-dash game. One of the keys hitting coach Bill Robinson looks for is when Castillo fouls off pitches with line drives over the third-base dugout. Castillo is comfortable working deep counts and is a good two-strike hitter. He's also an excellent bunter who usually ranks among the league leaders in infield hits. Castillo used to struggle mightily with runners in scoring position, putting too much pressure on himself, but that's no longer a problem.

Baserunning & Defense

After winning his first Gold Glove in 2003, Castillo made it two in a row in 2004. Owner of one of the game's strongest arms at second base, he again teamed with shortstop Alex Gonzalez for numerous highlights in the middle infield. Castillo hasn't been the same threat on the bases since having surgery after the 2002 season to repair a torn labrum in his left hip. However, when the situation calls for a key stolen base, Castillo still knows how to swipe one. He still is prone to vapor-locking on the bases, sometimes running into needless outs.

2005 Outlook

Castillo is signed through 2006 with a vesting option for 2007. He moved down as low as seventh in the batting order last year, but even with the addition of Paul Lo Duca, a capable No. 2 hitter, Castillo figures to remain behind leadoff man Juan Pierre.

Position: 2B
Bats: B **Throws:** R
Ht: 5'11" **Wt:** 190

Opening Day Age: 29
Born: 9/12/75 in San Pedro de Macoris, DR
ML Seasons: 9
Pronunciation: ca-STEE-yo

Overall Statistics

	G	AB	R	H	D	T	HR	RBI	SB	BB	SO	Avg	OBP	Slg
'04	150	564	91	164	12	7	2	47	21	75	68	.291	.373	.348
Car.	1006	3908	603	1141	118	38	16	241	271	468	597	.292	.368	.354

Where He Hits the Ball

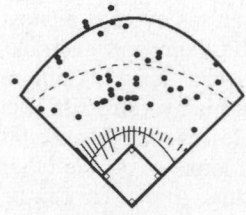
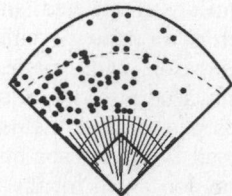

Vs. LHP　　　　**Vs. RHP**

2004 Situational Stats

	AB	H	HR	RBI	Avg		AB	H	HR	RBI	Avg
Home	282	85	1	22	.301	LHP	143	44	1	9	.308
Road	282	79	1	25	.280	RHP	421	120	1	38	.285
First Half	326	92	2	28	.282	Sc Pos	130	39	1	45	.300
Scnd Half	238	72	0	19	.303	Clutch	85	26	0	7	.306

2004 Rankings (National League)

- 1st in highest groundball-flyball ratio (3.6) and lowest HR frequency (282.0 ABs per HR)
- 2nd in fielding percentage at second base (.991) and lowest slugging percentage
- 4th in singles
- 6th in stolen-base percentage (84.0) and highest percentage of pitches taken (64.0)
- 8th in lowest percentage of swings that missed (9.0)
- Led the Marlins in walks, highest groundball-flyball ratio (3.6), stolen-base percentage (84.0), most pitches seen per plate appearance (4.08), highest percentage of pitches taken (64.0) and on-base percentage for a leadoff hitter (.389)

Juan Encarnacion

2004 Season

After helping the Marlins win the 2003 World Series, Juan Encarnacion was dealt to the Dodgers in a salary dump. He struggled from the outset, in part because of a torn labrum in his left shoulder that required surgery after the season. After four months of poor production in Los Angeles, he was dealt back to the Marlins in the six-player block-buster at the July trading deadline. Back among friends, he still played below average for his position and salary level.

Hitting

Encarnacion never has been one to draw many walks, which made him a strong trade candidate in Los Angeles from the minute Paul De Podesta took over as general manager. His numbers suffered across the board because of the shoulder problem, and he finished the year in the bottom 10 in the majors in on-base percentage. Encarnacion has power to all fields and doesn't mind hitting with two strikes, but he still prefers to put the first pitch in play. A classic mistake hitter, he will deposit hanging breaking balls in the seats with the best of them. However, his overeager approach leaves him susceptible to quality off-speed pitches on the outer half.

Baserunning & Defense

Encarnacion has good speed, but his basestealing totals have declined noticeably. He has above-average ability in right field and has been known to make the diving catch, but he still makes too many mistakes on routes and throws. He sometimes airmails the cutoff man, in part because he throws with just one finger.

2005 Outlook

Encarnacion is still due $4.4 million in the final year of a two-year contract, which makes him a prime candidate for another trade as the Marlins try to make budget. If he stays, he'll remain in right field and try to prove he's healthy as he heads into his first crack at free agency next winter. He no longer is considered a middle-of-the-order hitter, however.

Position: RF
Bats: R **Throws:** R
Ht: 6' 3" **Wt:** 215

Opening Day Age: 29
Born: 3/8/76 in Las Matas de Farfan, DR
ML Seasons: 8
Pronunciation: en-car-NAH-see-own

Overall Statistics

	G	AB	R	H	D	T	HR	RBI	SB	BB	SO	Avg	OBP	Slg
'04	135	484	63	114	30	2	16	62	5	38	86	.236	.299	.405
Car.	887	3339	442	884	173	37	112	465	113	199	620	.265	.311	.439

Where He Hits the Ball

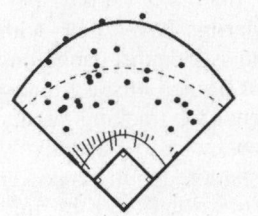
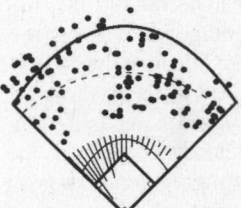

Vs. LHP   **Vs. RHP**

2004 Situational Stats

	AB	H	HR	RBI	Avg		AB	H	HR	RBI	Avg
Home	235	58	8	33	.247	LHP	115	25	1	7	.217
Road	249	56	8	29	.225	RHP	369	89	15	55	.241
First Half	283	68	12	41	.240	Sc Pos	117	32	2	42	.274
Scnd Half	201	46	4	21	.229	Clutch	72	18	2	9	.250

2004 Rankings (National League)

- 1st in lowest fielding percentage in right field (.977)
- 3rd in errors in right field (6), lowest batting average (.236), lowest on-base percentage (.299) and lowest batting average vs. lefthanded pitchers (.217)
- 4th in lowest batting average on the road (.225)
- 5th in lowest batting average vs. righthanded pitchers (.241)

Alex Gonzalez

2004 Season

Despite a miserable slump that carried through the 2003 postseason, the Marlins rewarded Alex Gonzalez with a two-year, $6.2 million contract. He opened 2004 extremely slowly at the plate and sat out several nights in favor of utilityman Damion Easley. But Gonzalez got rolling in late May and eventually set career highs in homers and RBI. He did this despite battling bone chips and scar tissue in his throwing elbow, which required surgical removal at season's end.

Hitting

On the negative side, Gonzalez still never has drawn more than 33 walks in a season, and last year he ranked last in the majors in on-base percentage. However, the Marlins have stuck with him because they view him as the most dangerous No. 8 hitter in the game. A trained mistake hitter, Gonzalez needs to do a better job tracking quality breaking balls on the outer half. Deceptively strong, he tends to grow enamored with his power stroke at the expense of situational hitting. Righthanders ate him up by preying on his unwillingness to take balls off the plate. Lacking the speed to leg out hits, he is prone to long slumps.

Baserunning & Defense

For a middle infielder, Gonzalez never has been much of a basestealer, and his baserunning is just decent. His defense has been Gold Glove quality for the past few years, but the rest of the league is still figuring that out. He has a cannon arm and has thrown runners out from his knees from deep in the hole on several occasions. He cut down on the sloppy errors that had plagued him in the past and tied a career-low with just 16 miscues.

2005 Outlook

The Marlins will pay Gonzalez $3.4 million this season and then re-assess their options at the end of the year. Gonzalez fits well with an organization openly committed to pitching and defense. Pitchers love having him behind them and are willing to overlook his flaws at the plate.

Position: SS
Bats: R **Throws:** R
Ht: 6' 0" **Wt:** 202

Opening Day Age: 28
Born: 2/15/77 in Cagua, VZ
ML Seasons: 7

Overall Statistics

	G	AB	R	H	D	T	HR	RBI	SB	BB	SO	Avg	OBP	Slg
'04	159	561	67	130	30	3	23	79	3	27	126	.232	.270	.419
Car.	766	2786	318	673	153	23	76	330	18	139	591	.242	.287	.395

Where He Hits the Ball

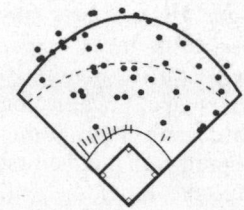

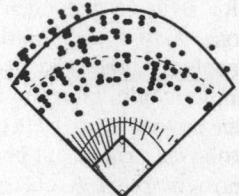

Vs. LHP   **Vs. RHP**

2004 Situational Stats

	AB	H	HR	RBI	Avg		AB	H	HR	RBI	Avg
Home	281	70	13	42	.249	LHP	115	32	5	21	.278
Road	280	60	10	37	.214	RHP	446	98	18	58	.220
First Half	300	75	12	40	.250	Sc Pos	155	38	9	61	.245
Scnd Half	261	55	11	39	.211	Clutch	86	16	3	11	.186

2004 Rankings (National League)

- 1st in lowest on-base percentage, lowest batting average vs. righthanded pitchers and lowest batting average on the road
- 2nd in lowest batting average
- 3rd in lowest percentage of pitches taken (45.5)
- 5th in errors at shortstop (16) and lowest fielding percentage at shortstop (.976)
- 6th in lowest groundball-flyball ratio (0.7)
- Led the Marlins in intentional walks (9)
- Led NL shortstops in home runs and RBI

Paul Lo Duca

2004 Season

Paul Lo Duca helped carry the Dodgers into first place with a strong first four months, then was shocked to the point of tears when he was traded to the Marlins on July 30. He delivered a pinch-hit homer in his first plate appearance with Florida and quickly became a strong clubhouse presence. Viewed by some as a reasonable knockoff of Pudge Rodriguez, Lo Duca's strong contributions down the stretch couldn't lift the Marlins into the playoffs.

Hitting

Your classic pesky hitter, Lo Duca doesn't have much power but makes up for it with a gap stroke. He is tough to strike out and hits well to the opposite field. With the Dodgers, Lo Duca was known for second-half fadeouts, but he hit .337 in August for the Marlins. In part, that was because he was energized by his new challenge, but it also was due to extra work with Marlins hitting coach Bill Robinson, who got Lo Duca to employ his hands more during his swing. He may have worn down in the August heat, causing him to slump at the start of September. When he got tired, he began to overswing and chase pitches up in the zone.

Baserunning & Defense

Lo Duca has worked hard to improve his receiving and throwing skills, but he threw out only 25 percent of opposing basestealers after joining the Marlins, and he still has a problem with passed balls. His game-calling is sound and he works well with pitchers, both on and off the field. For a catcher, Lo Duca is fairly quick but not much of a basestealer, not that it keeps him from trying.

2005 Outlook

As a fifth-year arbitration eligible, Lo Duca could see his salary climb past $6.5 million. The Marlins are expected to pony up, but if their determination to retain free-agent pitcher Carl Pavano grows to an obsession, Lo Duca could be a roster casualty.

Position: C
Bats: R **Throws:** R
Ht: 5'10" **Wt:** 185

Opening Day Age: 32
Born: 4/12/72 in Brooklyn, NY
ML Seasons: 7
Pronunciation: lah-duke-uh

Overall Statistics

	G	AB	R	H	D	T	HR	RBI	SB	BB	SO	Avg	OBP	Slg
'04	143	535	68	153	29	2	13	80	4	36	49	.286	.338	.421
Car.	640	2317	296	660	133	5	60	306	10	169	182	.285	.340	.424

Where He Hits the Ball

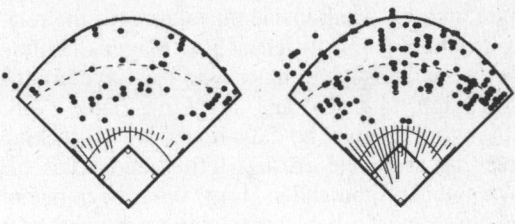

Vs. LHP   **Vs. RHP**

2004 Situational Stats

	AB	H	HR	RBI	Avg		AB	H	HR	RBI	Avg
Home	246	75	8	36	.305	LHP	137	43	2	15	.314
Road	289	78	5	44	.270	RHP	398	110	11	65	.276
First Half	304	95	9	43	.313	Sc Pos	127	41	4	64	.323
Scnd Half	231	58	4	37	.251	Clutch	72	22	1	13	.306

2004 Rankings (National League)

- 2nd in batting average with the bases loaded (.563)
- 3rd in highest percentage of runners caught stealing as a catcher (23.8)
- 5th in GDPs (22)
- Led the Marlins in batting average with runners in scoring position (.333) and batting average with the bases loaded (.625)
- Led NL catchers in RBI (76)

2004 Season

After signing a four-year, $32 million extension that was conditional on the Marlins landing a new stadium, Mike Lowell continued making himself the face of the franchise. He had another big first half and made his third straight All-Star appearance. However, his second-half fade may have cost his team a shot at the playoffs.

Hitting

Lowell always had been a dead-pull hitter, but he made a concerted effort last year to hit more balls to right-center, where he has enough power to take pitchers out of the park. He showed better pitch selection and built his walk total to a career best. He still likes the ball middle-in and thigh high, and will yank inside mistakes over the relatively short porch in left at Pro Player Stadium. He's a marked flyball hitter who can have trouble with high fastballs and breaking balls away, although in general he did a better job of tracking breaking stuff. He crushes lefties and holds his own against righthanders. Lowell has been one of the club's most reliable clutch hitters, but last year only nine of his 27 homers came with men on base.

Baserunning & Defense

Lowell regularly makes jokes about his lack of running speed, but he is a smart baserunner who usually scores when expected. His defense keeps getting better. Last year, Lowell cut his errors to just seven, a career low for a full season. He makes all the routine plays, has a solid and accurate arm and makes the barehand charge as well as anybody.

2005 Outlook

Lowell's original contract allowed him to opt for free agency if a new stadium deal wasn't announced by November 1. The Marlins chose to drop the stadium clause and guarantee the last three years of the deal at a combined $25.5 million. Lowell still doesn't have a no-trade provision, however, as the club no longer grants them.

Position: 3B
Bats: R **Throws:** R
Ht: 6' 3" **Wt:** 210

Opening Day Age: 31
Born: 2/24/74 in San Juan, PR
ML Seasons: 7

Overall Statistics

	G	AB	R	H	D	T	HR	RBI	SB	BB	SO	Avg	OBP	Slg
'04	158	598	87	175	44	1	27	85	5	64	77	.293	.365	.505
Car.	839	3069	422	851	205	2	135	520	17	308	471	.277	.346	.477

Where He Hits the Ball

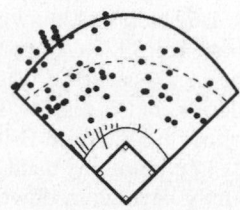 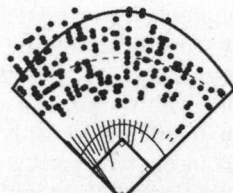

Vs. LHP   **Vs. RHP**

2004 Situational Stats

	AB	H	HR	RBI	Avg		AB	H	HR	RBI	Avg
Home	280	83	14	42	.296	LHP	128	44	11	29	.344
Road	318	92	13	43	.289	RHP	470	131	16	56	.279
First Half	331	101	20	55	.305	Sc Pos	167	45	4	56	.269
Scnd Half	267	74	7	30	.277	Clutch	87	28	7	16	.322

2004 Rankings (National League)

- 2nd in fielding percentage at third base (.982) and lowest groundball-flyball ratio (0.6)
- 4th in batting average vs. lefthanded pitchers
- 7th in doubles and batting average with two strikes (.267)
- 8th in cleanup slugging percentage (.541)
- Led the Marlins in doubles, batting average vs. lefthanded pitchers and cleanup slugging percentage (.541)

Carl Pavano

2004 Season

After years of injuries and bad breaks that kept him from putting everything together, Carl Pavano finally lived up to the potential that made him a key figure in a deal for Pedro Martinez. Building on the gains of a solid 2003 season which included two strong postseason starts, Pavano set a Marlins franchise mark for victories. He also posted his second straight 200-inning season and contributed quality starts nearly 75 percent of the time. That he did all of this in his final year before free agency was a stroke of rare good luck for the formerly star-crossed pitcher.

Pitching

Velocity no longer is the thing with Pavano, who is far wiser after several surgeries on his throwing arm. He features a 91-94 MPH fastball that he can locate to all four quadrants of the strike zone. He complements the fastball with a tight slider and has a split and a change to keep lefties honest. Pavano's biggest strength is his ability to throw any of those four pitches for strikes in any count. Surprisingly, considering the false starts of his early career, Pavano has become one of the more durable and reliable pitchers in the game.

Defense & Hitting

Pavano isn't the most graceful hitter, but he did count two homers and three doubles among his career-high 13 hits last season. He also led the staff in sacrifice bunts. A lumbering sort with deliberate actions, he is just an average fielder who doesn't do the best job against the running game.

2005 Outlook

The Marlins would love to retain Pavano but realize the free-agent market could get away from them. A long list of suitors is expected to line up for the steady righthander, with his original organization in Boston among them. However, Pavano has made it clear that he values comfort and loyalty, and just might take less money and years to stay with the Marlins.

Position: SP
Bats: R **Throws:** R
Ht: 6' 5" **Wt:** 241

Opening Day Age: 29
Born: 1/8/76 in New Britain, CT
ML Seasons: 7
Pronunciation: pa-VAH-no

Overall Statistics

	W	L	Pct.	ERA	G	GS	Sv	IP	H	BB	SO	HR	Avg
'04	18	8	.692	3.00	31	31	0	222.1	212	49	139	16	.253
Car.	57	58	.496	4.21	167	149	0	937.2	985	271	617	95	.271

2004 Pitching Profile

	Carl Pavano	NL Average
Overall Strike %	65.3	62.5
1st Pitch Strike %	64.4	58.5
Ratio	1.17	1.39
Strikeouts per 9 IP	5.63	6.74
Walks per 9 IP	1.98	3.38
Home Runs per 9 IP	0.65	1.11
Strikeout/Walk Ratio	2.84	1.99
Groundball/Flyball Ratio	1.43	1.25

2004 Situational Stats

	W	L	ERA	Sv	IP		AB	H	HR	RBI	Avg
Home	6	6	3.20	0	101.1	LHB	393	105	11	40	.267
Road	12	2	2.83	0	121.0	RHB	445	107	5	32	.240
First Half	9	4	2.85	0	123.0	Sc Pos	182	39	4	53	.214
Scnd Half	9	4	3.17	0	99.1	Clutch	72	20	2	9	.278

2004 Rankings (National League)

- 1st in balks (3) and fielding percentage at pitcher (1.000)
- 2nd in wins
- 3rd in shutouts (2)
- 4th in fewest pitches thrown per batter (3.47) and lowest ERA on the road
- 6th in innings pitched, hit batsmen (11) and fewest home runs allowed per nine innings (.65)
- Led the Marlins in ERA, wins, complete games (2), shutouts (2), innings pitched, hits allowed, batters faced (909), hit batsmen (11), balks (3), pitches thrown (3,155), pickoff throws (114), stolen bases allowed (16), GDPs induced (18), winning percentage, fewest pitches thrown per batter (3.47), lowest ERA on the road, fewest home runs allowed per nine innings (.65) and fewest walks per nine innings (2.0)

Juan Pierre (Great Speed)

2004 Season

Coming off an eye-opening season as the fire-starter for the World Series champs, Juan Pierre was paid more attention than ever, both at the plate and on the basepaths. He slumped badly in June, but all in all Pierre managed to turn in another strong season. His consecutive-games streak stands at 335 games and counting.

Hitting

For the third time in the past four years, Pierre banged out 200 hits. It's no accident. Though he could show more patience for a leadoff hitter, his remarkable hand-eye coordination allows him to put almost any ball in play. He is fearless against lefties and doesn't give in against anybody, Randy Johnson included. He saw more hard stuff on the inner half last year, putting a crimp in his slap-and-dash ways. So Pierre eventually adjusted and started pulling more pitches between the first and second basemen. Always thinking, he's not afraid to be innovative at the plate. He didn't bunt as much in the first half, but started to reclaim that part of his repertoire after the break.

Baserunning & Defense

Largely due to the adjustments by opposing pitchers, Pierre didn't come close to defending his first NL stolen-base crown. He was caught a career-high 24 times in 69 attempts and saw his success rate drop from 76 to 65 percent. His defense remains a huge plus at spacious Pro Player Stadium. His range allowed the Marlins to get by with Miguel Cabrera and Jeff Conine flanking him for the first four months. Pierre's arm probably precludes him from Gold Glove consideration, but he never gives up on balls in the gap and makes his share of highlight catches. His resemblance to a young Mickey Rivers remains eerie.

2005 Outlook

Pierre is due $3.6 million in the final year of his contract, after which he will be a fifth-year eligible for salary arbitration. He could yet grow too pricey for the budget-conscious Marlins, but for now he remains their heart and soul.

Position: CF
Bats: L **Throws:** L
Ht: 6' 0" **Wt:** 180

Opening Day Age: 27
Born: 8/14/77 in Mobile, AL
ML Seasons: 5
Pronunciation: pee-AIR

Overall Statistics

	G	AB	R	H	D	T	HR	RBI	SB	BB	SO	Avg	OBP	Slg
'04	162	678	100	221	22	12	3	49	45	45	35	.326	.374	.407
Car.	683	2755	424	859	98	35	7	200	210	185	166	.312	.361	.380

Where He Hits the Ball

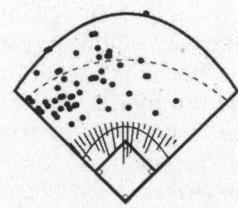 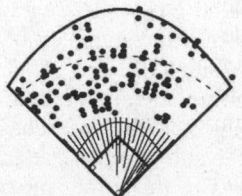

Vs. LHP   Vs. RHP

2004 Situational Stats

	AB	H	HR	RBI	Avg		AB	H	HR	RBI	Avg
Home	325	110	1	24	.338	LHP	187	57	0	9	.305
Road	353	111	2	25	.314	RHP	491	164	3	40	.334
First Half	363	108	2	27	.298	Sc Pos	116	32	1	43	.276
Scnd Half	315	113	1	22	.359	Clutch	83	24	0	4	.289

2004 Rankings (National League)

- 1st in at-bats, hits, singles, triples, caught stealing (24), plate appearances (748), games played, bunts in play (66), lowest percentage of swings that missed (5.5) and highest percentage of swings put into play (59.0)
- 2nd in stolen bases, highest groundball-flyball ratio (2.3) and fielding percentage in center field (.995)
- 3rd in sacrifice bunts (15), on-base percentage for a leadoff hitter (.382) and steals of third (8)
- 4th in batting average vs. righthanded pitchers, batting average with two strikes (.280), lowest HR frequency (226.0 ABs per HR) and lowest stolen-base percentage (65.2)
- 5th in batting average at home
- Led NL center fielders in batting average

Dontrelle Willis

2004 Season

There was no sophomore jinx for the reigning National League Rookie of the Year, but Dontrelle Willis definitely found the rest of the league more prepared for him the second time around. Willis stayed healthy and made all his starts, but was unable to string together three quality starts all season, and failed to go beyond five innings in nine of his 32 outings.

Pitching

Many predicted it would be easier to hit Willis with each successive turn through the league, and that proved to be at least somewhat true. He began the year seeking to smooth out his herky-jerky delivery, but eventually realized that the added deception of his impossibly high leg kick was something he simply could not sacrifice. Willis still dominated lefties, but righthanders fared almost 40 points better against him in his second season. Part of the problem was Willis' difficulties in improving his average changeup. He still relied almost exclusively on an 89-92 MPH fastball that he must locate to have success. His slider is a plus pitch, but he must get to two strikes for it to be most effective. He rarely throws the slider for strikes.

Defense & Hitting

Willis is such a good hitter that Marlins manager Jack McKeon used him as a pinch-hitter nine times in 2004. He generates surprising bat speed and managed four extra-base hits with his take-no-prisoners plate approach. Willis has a decent pickoff move but could stand improvement in that area. Very athletic, he made numerous leaping plays on the mound and pounces on sacrifice bunts quickly enough to gun down lead runners.

2005 Outlook

Like fellow 2003 rookie sensation Miguel Cabrera, Willis figures to remain under Marlins control through the 2006 season. Only then will he get the arbitration-fed salary bump many felt he deserved after his dazzling rookie campaign, when he regularly packed the park, home and away. That buzz has calmed down significantly, but Willis remains a solid middle-of-the-rotation piece for the Marlins.

Position: SP
Bats: L **Throws:** L
Ht: 6' 4" **Wt:** 239

Opening Day Age: 23
Born: 1/12/82 in Oakland, CA
ML Seasons: 2
Nickname: D-Train

Overall Statistics

	W	L	Pct.	ERA	G	GS	Sv	IP	H	BB	SO	HR	Avg
'04	10	11	.476	4.02	32	32	0	197.0	210	61	139	20	.273
Car.	24	17	.585	3.70	59	59	0	357.2	358	119	281	33	.261

2004 Pitching Profile

	Dontrelle Willis	NL Average
Overall Strike %	64.8	62.5
1st Pitch Strike %	62.9	58.5
Ratio	1.38	1.39
Strikeouts per 9 IP	6.35	6.74
Walks per 9 IP	2.79	3.38
Home Runs per 9 IP	0.91	1.11
Strikeout/Walk Ratio	2.28	1.99
Groundball/Flyball Ratio	1.28	1.25

2004 Situational Stats

	W	L	ERA	Sv	IP		AB	H	HR	RBI	Avg
Home	5	7	3.82	0	99.0	LHB	128	26	1	13	.203
Road	5	4	4.22	0	98.0	RHB	640	184	19	75	.288
First Half	7	5	3.99	0	103.2	Sc Pos	179	48	5	67	.268
Scnd Half	3	6	4.05	0	93.1	Clutch	37	8	0	2	.216

2004 Rankings (National League)

- 7th in complete games (2)
- 10th in lowest batting average allowed vs. lefthanded batters
- Led the Marlins in losses, games started, complete games (2), home runs allowed, walks allowed and runners caught stealing (7)

Nate Bump

Position: RP
Bats: L **Throws:** R
Ht: 6' 2" **Wt:** 196

Opening Day Age: 28
Born: 7/24/76 in Towanda, PA
ML Seasons: 2

Overall Statistics

	W	L	Pct.	ERA	G	GS	Sv	IP	H	BB	SO	HR	Avg
'04	2	4	.333	5.01	50	2	1	73.2	86	32	44	7	.297
Car.	6	4	.600	4.91	82	2	1	110.0	120	52	61	10	.281

2004 Situational Stats

	W	L	ERA	Sv	IP			AB	H	HR	RBI	Avg
Home	1	3	5.68	1	38.0	LHB		117	33	3	13	.282
Road	1	1	4.29	0	35.2	RHB		173	53	4	35	.306
First Half	2	3	4.31	0	39.2	Sc Pos		98	30	2	38	.306
Scnd Half	0	1	5.82	1	34.0	Clutch		65	17	1	14	.262

2004 Season

Groomed as a starter in the minor leagues, Nate Bump has made just two starts in his first 82 big league showings. Neither went well, as he was gone by the fourth inning both times. He held down a long-relief role all year in a low-budget Marlins bullpen, even getting a brief look in a setup role after the season-ending elbow injury to Chad Fox. His ERA was 5.01 overall, but 3.57 in relief.

Pitching, Defense & Hitting

Bump is the classic sinkerballer who produced 2.24 groundballs for every flyball last season. He relies on a 90-92 MPH fastball for outs. He has a solid average curveball and a decent changeup that actually helped him hold lefties 24 points lower than righties. A good athlete, Bump is quick off the mound and does a decent job of limiting the running game. He has just five at-bats in the majors and still is looking for his first hit.

2005 Outlook

Low-revenue teams like the Marlins must cut costs somewhere, and the bullpen and bench are prime areas. That alone makes Bump a solid candidate to return in a long-relief role. Depending on what happens with free agency, Bump could get a look at the back end of the rotation.

Jeff Conine

Position: LF/1B
Bats: R **Throws:** R
Ht: 6' 1" **Wt:** 220

Opening Day Age: 38
Born: 6/27/66 in Tacoma, WA
ML Seasons: 14
Pronunciation: COH-nine

Overall Statistics

G	AB	R	H	D	T	HR	RBI	SB	BB	SO	Avg	OBP	Slg
140	521	55	146	35	1	14	83	5	48	78	.280	.340	.432
1650	5877	749	1684	326	29	195	935	45	566	1009	.287	.348	.451

2004 Situational Stats

	AB	H	HR	RBI	Avg		AB	H	HR	RBI	Avg
Home	244	68	9	41	.279	LHP	109	30	5	21	.275
Road	277	78	5	42	.282	RHP	412	116	9	62	.282
First Half	266	68	6	33	.256	Sc Pos	136	41	7	70	.301
Scnd Half	255	78	8	50	.306	Clutch	74	17	0	8	.230

2004 Season

After rejoining the Marlins late in 2003, Jeff Conine's first full season with the club since 1997 was marred by perhaps the worst first half of his career. There were rampant trade rumors in July as the Marlins considered replacing him with Steve Finley, Larry Walker or someone else. In the end, they dealt Hee Seop Choi instead and moved Conine to first, where he thrived.

Hitting, Baserunning & Defense

Conine missed time with back spasms on at least two occasions and had to take three cortisone shots in his ailing throwing shoulder over the course of the summer. The shoulder problem left him experimenting too much at the plate, but Conine turned it on down the stretch. He was fine in left field, though runners occasionally took advantage of his arm. He was better at first base, where he showed a penchant for blowing up sacrifice bunts by gunning down the lead baserunner. He might be the club's smartest baserunner.

2005 Outlook

Due to make $3 million in the final year of a restructured deal, Conine should be a fixture at first base and in the middle of the order. His veteran leadership is valued highly, and he easily could wind up finishing his career in South Florida.

Damion Easley

Position: 2B/1B/SS
Bats: R **Throws:** R
Ht: 5'11" **Wt:** 190

Opening Day Age: 35
Born: 11/11/69 in New York, NY
ML Seasons: 13

Overall Statistics

	G	AB	R	H	D	T	HR	RBI	SB	BB	SO	Avg	OBP	Slg
'04	98	223	26	53	20	1	9	43	4	24	36	.238	.331	.457
Car.	1325	4519	617	1139	246	23	129	556	109	425	785	.252	.329	.402

2004 Situational Stats

	AB	H	HR	RBI	Avg		AB	H	HR	RBI	Avg
Home	103	21	5	17	.204	LHP	87	13	2	10	.149
Road	120	32	4	26	.267	RHP	136	40	7	33	.294
First Half	107	28	5	20	.262	Sc Pos	70	18	2	33	.257
Scnd Half	116	25	4	23	.216	Clutch	47	11	3	12	.234

2004 Season

Out of baseball after the lowly Devil Rays released him at midseason in 2003, Damion Easley came back with a renewed attitude and was one of the Marlins' most pleasant surprises. Easley filled a utility role and saw action at six different positions. He never complained and quickly earned the respect of his new teammates.

Hitting, Baserunning & Defense

As productive as Easley was in spot starts, he struggled mightily as a pinch-hitter. Not even discussions with career pinch-hit king Lenny Harris, a Marlins teammate, could help Easley master the role. Easley has excellent bat speed but sometimes gets too quick for his own good. He uses all fields and stays on top of the ball as well as anyone on the team. He has good instincts on the bases but isn't much of a basestealer. His range at second base isn't much to talk about, but he usually handles the balls he gets to.

2005 Outlook

Easley was a free agent after the season, but re-signed a one-year contract. While Easley might have had a chance to get more playing time with another team, his agent, Paul Cohen, put it succinctly: "Basically, he loves Florida." Easley figures to hold down the same utility role this year.

Ben Howard

Position: RP
Bats: R **Throws:** R
Ht: 6' 0" **Wt:** 221

Opening Day Age: 26
Born: 1/15/79 in Danville, IL
ML Seasons: 3

Overall Statistics

	W	L	Pct.	ERA	G	GS	Sv	IP	H	BB	SO	HR	Avg
'04	1	1	.500	5.50	31	0	0	37.2	37	21	33	6	.261
Car.	2	5	.286	5.20	40	8	0	83.0	81	50	67	20	.256

2004 Situational Stats

	W	L	ERA	Sv	IP		AB	H	HR	RBI	Avg
Home	0	1	6.08	0	13:1	LHB	64	16	4	13	.250
Road	1	0	5.18	0	24.1	RHB	78	21	2	11	.269
First Half	0	1	5.89	0	18.1	Sc Pos	43	10	2	19	.233
Scnd Half	1	0	5.12	0	19.1	Clutch	19	5	2	4	.263

2004 Season

Acquired from the Padres for reliever Blaine Neal late in spring training, Ben Howard opened the year at Triple-A. A starter for all but 21 of his 161 appearances in the Padres' system (majors and minors), Howard eventually settled into a middle-relief role with the Marlins. He was among many who auditioned to replace the injured Chad Fox in a setup role. However, Howard didn't get many shots at pitching with a lead after the mid-June acquisition of veteran Billy Koch.

Pitching, Defense & Hitting

Howard's fastball sits at 92-94 MPH and has good life. He also has a plus slider and a changeup that helped him hold lefties to an average 19 points lower than righthanders. He runs into problems when his mechanics get out of whack and he starts rushing his delivery. Howard had three at-bats all season and is an average fielder. He needs to do a better job holding baserunners, who swiped six bases in seven tries against him.

2005 Outlook

Howard still makes close to the minimum, which at the least makes him a strong candidate for another middle-relief spot in the Marlins' bullpen. If free agents Carl Pavano and/or Ismael Valdez leave, Howard could get a serious crack at the rotation.

Florida

Billy Koch

Guillermo Mota

Position: RP
Bats: R **Throws:** R
Ht: 6' 3" **Wt:** 220

Opening Day Age: 30
Born: 12/14/74 in Rockville Center, NY
ML Seasons: 6
Pronunciation: COTCH

Position: RP
Bats: R **Throws:** R
Ht: 6' 4" **Wt:** 205

Opening Day Age: 31
Born: 7/25/73 in San Pedro de Macoris, DR
ML Seasons: 6
Pronunciation: mo-TAH

Overall Statistics

	W	L	Pct.	ERA	G	GS	Sv	IP	H	BB	SO	HR	Avg
'04	2	3	.400	4.41	47	0	8	49.0	45	36	50	6	.241
Car.	29	25	.537	3.89	379	0	163	407.1	379	191	357	41	.247

Overall Statistics

	W	L	Pct.	ERA	G	GS	Sv	IP	H	BB	SO	HR	Avg
'04	9	8	.529	3.07	78	0	4	96.2	75	37	85	8	.218
Car.	20	22	.476	3.42	330	0	5	397.1	330	145	315	36	.227

2004 Situational Stats

	W	L	ERA	Sv	IP		AB	H	HR	RBI	Avg
Home	2	1	3.00	3	30.0	LHB	89	21	4	13	.236
Road	0	2	6.63	5	19.0	RHB	98	24	2	14	.245
First Half	1	2	4.86	8	37.0	Sc Pos	53	14	0	19	.264
Scnd Half	1	1	3.00	0	12.0	Clutch	76	24	4	16	.316

2004 Situational Stats

	W	L	ERA	Sv	IP		AB	H	HR	RBI	Avg
Home	5	2	2.56	1	45.2	LHB	153	30	3	13	.196
Road	4	6	3.53	3	51.0	RHB	191	45	5	21	.236
First Half	6	3	1.65	1	54.2	Sc Pos	89	17	1	25	.191
Scnd Half	3	5	4.93	3	42.0	Clutch	212	53	6	30	.250

2004 Season

The year started badly for former ace closer Billy Koch and just kept getting worse, even after a June 17 trade that sent him from the White Sox to the Marlins. The Marlins gave him six weeks and many chances to turn things around and become a viable setup man for Armando Benitez. Finally they gave up and acquired Guillermo Mota and Rudy Seanez in separate trades. Koch took the ball just six more times before leaving the club for personal reasons in mid-September. He was released in October.

2004 Season

After forming a devastating late-game combination with Eric Gagne in the Dodgers' bullpen for the third straight year, Guillermo Mota was dealt to Florida on July 30, shaking up the bullpens of both clubs. Mota handled closing duties for more than two weeks while Armando Benitez was on the DL, then settled back into his familiar setup role. He finished the year poorly, posting a 10.66 ERA in his last 11 appearances.

Pitching, Defense & Hitting

The triple-digit fastball is long gone, and so is Koch's intimidating aura. His fastball now sits at 92-94 MPH, but it's arrow straight and he struggles to locate it. He tried without luck to integrate a curveball and a cut fastball. He held both righties and lefties below .250, but his utter lack of command kept the bases busy, and the bullpen too. Koch is an awkward fielder who lets runners get big leads behind him.

Pitching, Defense & Hitting

Mota has all the pitches to be a top-rate closer, though he is still mostly untested in the role. He features a 94-96 MPH fastball, a plus change he learned from Gagne and a slider he doesn't throw as much as he should. For someone with such velocity, Mota has a strange tendency to lean too heavily on his change. He was beaten for home runs on the pitch several times in September. Mota is a good fielder but has had major problems controlling the running game.

2005 Outlook

After making $6.375 million last year, Koch probably will have to take a $500,000 make-good deal and hope he can make back some of the difference through incentives. His profile has fallen that far.

2005 Outlook

With Benitez signing with the Giants as a free agent, Mota should become the Marlins' closer. His salary could double to close to $3 million through arbitration, and under regular ninth-inning pressure for the first time, he'll have to earn it.

Matt Perisho

Position: RP
Bats: L **Throws:** L
Ht: 6' 0" **Wt:** 200

Opening Day Age: 29
Born: 6/8/75 in
Burlington, IA
ML Seasons: 7
Pronunciation:
PAIR-ih-show

Overall Statistics

	W	L	Pct.	ERA	G	GS	Sv	IP	H	BB	SO	HR	Avg
'04	5	3	.625	4.40	66	0	0	47.0	45	26	42	6	.247
Car.	9	17	.346	6.60	152	28	0	262.0	333	151	192	41	.311

2004 Situational Stats

	W	L	ERA	Sv	IP		AB	H	HR	RBI	Avg
Home	3	0	4.32	0	25.0	LHB	87	18	4	12	.207
Road	2	3	4.50	0	22.0	RHB	95	27	2	15	.284
First Half	4	2	4.00	0	27.0	Sc Pos	63	15	3	20	.238
Scnd Half	1	1	4.95	0	20.0	Clutch	73	23	4	17	.315

2004 Season

After spending all but five appearances of 2002-03 in the minor leagues, Matt Perisho went to Venezuela and pitched well enough to earn a non-roster invitation to Marlins camp. He won the role as the only situational lefty in the bullpen and quickly earned manager Jack McKeon's trust in those situations. He missed three weeks in the second half with a minor arm ailment, but was back on the horse for the stretch run.

Pitching, Defense & Hitting

Though his fastball sits in the 88-90 MPH range, Perisho has a herky-jerky motion and good deception. He dominated lefties early in the year with a plus slider, and he used a changeup on occasion to keep righthanded batters honest. He was one of the more effective Marlins pitchers against lefthanded batters last season. His thick lower half makes him only an average defender who can be susceptible to bunts. He is just average at holding runners, but as a lefty reliever he doesn't have to worry about that too much.

2005 Outlook

Arbitration eligible, Perisho figures to get a decent raise over the minimum salary he made last year. The Marlins figure to bring him back as their primary lefthanded specialist.

Mike Redmond

Position: C
Bats: R **Throws:** R
Ht: 5'11" **Wt:** 200

Opening Day Age: 33
Born: 5/5/71 in Seattle, WA
ML Seasons: 7

Overall Statistics

	G	AB	R	H	D	T	HR	RBI	SB	BB	SO	Avg	OBP	Slg
'04	81	246	19	63	15	0	2	25	1	14	28	.256	.315	.341
Car.	485	1338	118	380	67	2	11	132	1	99	160	.284	.348	.362

2004 Situational Stats

	AB	H	HR	RBI	Avg		AB	H	HR	RBI	Avg
Home	114	25	0	6	.219	LHP	56	10	1	2	.179
Road	132	38	2	19	.288	RHP	190	53	1	23	.279
First Half	171	45	1	21	.263	Sc Pos	48	15	0	21	.313
Scnd Half	75	18	1	4	.240	Clutch	36	7	0	4	.194

2004 Season

Expected to split time behind the plate with Ramon Castro, Mike Redmond's playing time expanded when Castro flopped. The respected backup wound up logging 171 at-bats by the All-Star break, and after a solid start, his hitting began to suffer. Redmond returned to a reserve role with the acquisition of Paul Lo Duca on July 30.

Hitting, Baserunning & Defense

As Redmond wore down, his swing got longer and pitchers took advantage of him. Even his career-long dominance of lefties disappeared, and not because they necessarily pitched him any differently than before. During the first half he tried to pull more pitches and got in some trouble that way. Revered by Marlins pitchers for his game-calling and receiving skills, Redmond uncharacteristically struggled with his throwing. He hustles on the basepaths but has a typical catcher's speed.

2005 Outlook

Redmond got his first crack at free agency after the season and signed a two-year, $1.8 million contract with the Twins in November. He figures to serve as the top backup to promising second-year catcher Joe Mauer, with his playing time somewhat dependent on how well Mauer has recovered from 2004 knee surgery.

Florida

Rudy Seanez

Position: RP
Bats: R **Throws:** R
Ht: 5'11" **Wt:** 200

Opening Day Age: 36
Born: 10/20/68 in Brawley, CA
ML Seasons: 13
Pronunciation: see-AHN-ez

Overall Statistics

	W	L	Pct.	ERA	G	GS	Sv	IP	H	BB	SO	HR	Avg
'04	3	2	.600	3.33	39	0	0	46.0	39	19	46	3	.228
Car.	20	19	.513	4.37	323	0	11	333.1	292	179	333	34	.234

2004 Situational Stats

	W	L	ERA	Sv	IP		AB	H	HR	RBI	Avg
Home	1	2	3.47	0	23.1	LHB	83	21	0	10	.253
Road	2	0	3.18	0	22.2	RHB	88	18	3	19	.205
First Half	0	1	5.68	0	12.2	Sc Pos	64	17	1	25	.266
Scnd Half	3	1	2.43	0	33.1	Clutch	48	13	2	16	.271

2004 Season

Rudy Seanez found himself pitching in the middle of a pennant race with the Marlins following a July 31 trade. But first he had to pitch his way back to health at Triple-A Omaha and with the bottom-feeding Royals. The progression was nothing new to the oft-injured Seanez, who has made at least one minor league outing in all but two of his 19 professional seasons.

Pitching, Defense & Hitting

Seanez still can run the fastball up there at 96 MPH, down a tick from his best of a few years ago but still formidable. Strangely, though, Seanez often pitches backwards, trying to trick hitters with his slider and change instead of going right at them. Still, he dominates righties and holds his own against lefties. He does a better job than most short relievers at controlling the running game. He's a decent fielder, despite a history of back problems.

2005 Outlook

The Marlins appreciated Seanez' work, but in November the free agent signed a one-year, $550,000 contract with the Padres, a club he had previously pitched for in 1993 and 2001. If healthy, he figures to help the San Diego bullpen in middle relief.

Ismael Valdez

Position: SP
Bats: R **Throws:** R
Ht: 6' 4" **Wt:** 230

Opening Day Age: 31
Born: 8/21/73 in Ciudad Victoria, Mexico
ML Seasons: 11
Pronunciation: ees-mah-ALE val-DEZ

Overall Statistics

	W	L	Pct.	ERA	G	GS	Sv	IP	H	BB	SO	HR	Avg
'04	14	9	.609	5.19	34	31	0	170.0	202	49	67	33	.294
Car.	102	103	.498	4.05	311	281	1	1776.2	1808	501	1146	228	.263

2004 Situational Stats

	W	L	ERA	Sv	IP		AB	H	HR	RBI	Avg
Home	9	3	2.55	0	95.1	LHB	352	103	18	50	.293
Road	5	6	8.56	0	74.2	RHB	334	99	15	45	.296
First Half	8	5	4.82	0	99.0	Sc Pos	151	35	5	52	.232
Scnd Half	6	4	5.70	0	71.0	Clutch	14	5	0	1	.357

2004 Season

After changing the spelling of his last name following some offseason genealogical research, Ismael Valdez signed a one-year contract with San Diego. He was terrible away from spacious Petco Park, but got enough run support at home to win nine games for the Padres before a July 31 trade to Florida. Valdez gave the Marlins a dependable alternative at the back of their rotation.

Pitching, Defense & Hitting

Valdez' fastball, which once reached the mid-90s, rarely leaves the high 80s anymore. But he uses his smarts and guile to outthink hitters and keep them off balance. He is a six-inning pitcher at this stage of his career, mixing a solid curveball, slider and changeup into his repertoire. A flyball pitcher, he needs to work in a large park to be successful. Valdez has a decent pickoff move and rebounded from a poor year afield in 2003.

2005 Outlook

Valdez has said he would like to return to South Florida, where he can take advantage of another spacious park. Despite his impressive win total, he isn't likely to receive any multiyear offers or anything all that lucrative. He could be a good fit for the Marlins, who offered him arbitration.

Other Florida Marlins

Chris Aguila (Pos: RF, Age: 26, Bats: R)

	G	AB	R	H	D	T	HR	RBI	SB	BB	SO	Avg	OBP	Slg
'04	29	45	10	10	2	1	3	5	0	2	12	.222	.255	.511
Car.	29	45	10	10	2	1	3	5	0	2	12	.222	.255	.511

Aguila benefited from the thin Albuquerque air en route to a .312/.380/.494 showing for the Triple-A Isotopes. Increased power numbers will give him a shot at making the club this spring. 2005 Outlook: C

Toby Borland (Pos: RHP, Age: 35)

	W	L	Pct.	ERA	G	GS	Sv	IP	H	BB	SO	HR	Avg
'04	1	1	.500	5.40	18	0	0	18.1	18	12	18	3	.254
Car.	11	9	.550	4.17	207	0	8	269.2	263	146	211	23	.254

He may be from Quitman, Louisiana, but quitting is about the last thing that crosses 35-year-old Toby Borland's mind. His 3.25 career minor league ERA, dating back to 1988, has only been good enough to secure him a big league job in two seasons, yet Borland has never stopped trying. He signed a minor league deal with St. Louis in December. 2005 Outlook: C

Ramon Castro (Pos: C, Age: 29, Bats: R)

	G	AB	R	H	D	T	HR	RBI	SB	BB	SO	Avg	OBP	Slg
'04	32	96	9	13	3	0	3	8	0	11	30	.135	.231	.260
Car.	207	466	40	99	17	0	18	53	0	56	116	.212	.296	.365

Castro was not even a factor for the Marlins in his 32 games. An inflamed toe that required surgery and his impending trial for sexual assault seemed to preoccupy Castro all season. He was declared a free agent in October, and might be wearing a different pinstripe this year. 2005 Outlook: C

Wil Cordero (Pos: 1B, Age: 33, Bats: R)

	G	AB	R	H	D	T	HR	RBI	SB	BB	SO	Avg	OBP	Slg
'04	27	66	6	13	3	0	1	6	1	3	19	.197	.250	.288
Car.	1218	4260	585	1172	259	19	122	564	49	322	761	.275	.332	.431

Cordero missed almost the entire 2004 season with knee troubles. Arthroscopic surgery on both knees put him on the disabled list from May to September. The 33-year-old signed a minor league deal with Washington in December. 2005 Outlook: C

Chad Fox (Pos: RHP, Age: 34)

	W	L	Pct.	ERA	G	GS	Sv	IP	H	BB	SO	HR	Avg
'04	0	1	.000	6.75	12	0	0	10.2	9	8	17	1	.225
Car.	10	11	.476	3.45	203	0	5	216.1	185	120	250	19	.229

Diagnosed with ulnar neuritis in his right elbow, Fox only appeared in a handful of games before being shut down in late April. He rested and rehabbed the elbow the remainder of the season, doing anything to avoid a potential third Tommy John surgery. 2005 Outlook: C

Franklyn Gracesqui (Pos: LHP, Age: 25)

	W	L	Pct.	ERA	G	GS	Sv	IP	H	BB	SO	HR	Avg
'04	0	1	.000	11.25	7	0	1	4.0	6	3	1	0	.333
Car.	0	1	.000	11.25	7	0	1	4.0	6	3	1	0	.333

Gracesqui has the stuff to be a star, but faulty control has consistently plagued his professional career. After registering a save in his major league debut, he could only find the plate on 10 of his next 27 pitches over the course of two outings. 2005 Outlook: C

Lenny Harris (Pos: LF, Age: 40, Bats: L)

	G	AB	R	H	D	T	HR	RBI	SB	BB	SO	Avg	OBP	Slg
'04	79	95	7	20	5	0	1	6	1	0	3	8	.211	.232	.295
Car.	1820	3854	455	1033	157	21	36	356	131	272	326	.268	.317	.348

Harris has turned into an albatross off the bench the last two seasons. He has hovered around the Mendoza line as a pinch-hitter, batting a paltry .211/.272/.284 in that capacity. The diminished pinch-hitting prowess means Harris probably is more valuable as a coach than as a player. 2005 Outlook: C

Logan Kensing (Pos: RHP, Age: 22)

	W	L	Pct.	ERA	G	GS	Sv	IP	H	BB	SO	HR	Avg
'04	0	3	.000	9.88	5	3	0	13.2	19	9	7	5	.345
Car.	0	3	.000	9.88	5	3	0	13.2	19	9	7	5	.345

Kensing made the jump from the high Class-A Florida State League to the major leagues in September, filling in for an injured A.J. Burnett. The former second-rounder out of Texas A&M was overmatched by big league hitters, and most likely will start 2005 at Double-A. 2005 Outlook: C

Josias Manzanillo (Pos: RHP, Age: 37)

	W	L	Pct.	ERA	G	GS	Sv	IP	H	BB	SO	HR	Avg
'04	3	3	.500	6.12	26	0	1	32.1	38	15	27	6	.292
Car.	13	15	.464	4.71	267	1	6	342.0	330	153	300	46	.255

An amazing 22-year veteran of professional action, Manzanillo has seen his share of minor league motels. He brings an animated flare to the mound, but his repertoire consists mostly of smoke and mirrors these days. 2005 Outlook: C

Mike Mordecai (Pos: 3B, Age: 37, Bats: R)

	G	AB	R	H	D	T	HR	RBI	SB	BB	SO	Avg	OBP	Slg
'04	69	84	7	19	3	0	1	5	0	6	18	.226	.278	.298
Car.	791	1360	157	333	75	7	24	132	13	112	260	.245	.303	.363

Mordecai parlayed his 2003 National League Championship Series heroics into another one-year deal with the Marlins for 2004. A poor performance this past season, however, almost certainly will facilitate the end of Mordecai's days in South Florida. 2005 Outlook: C

Mike Neu (**Pos**: RHP, **Age**: 27)

	W	L	Pct.	ERA	G	GS	Sv	IP	H	BB	SO	HR	Avg
'04	0	0	–	4.50	1	0	0	4.0	5	2	2	1	.313
Car.	0	0	–	3.72	33	0	1	46.0	48	28	22	3	.265

Neu spent all of 2003 in the Oakland bullpen after being snagged via the Rule 5 draft from Cincinnati. He was traded to Florida for Mark Redman before the 2004 season, but threw in just one game for the Marlins. Questions about durability and lack of size still abound. 2005 Outlook: C

Tommy Phelps (**Pos**: LHP, **Age**: 31)

	W	L	Pct.	ERA	G	GS	Sv	IP	H	BB	SO	HR	Avg
'04	1	1	.500	4.76	19	4	0	34.0	34	12	28	6	.268
Car.	4	3	.571	4.27	46	11	0	97.0	104	35	71	9	.277

The lefthanded Phelps was off to a good start in his first 15 games, posting a 2.05 ERA and .218 batting average against, before elbow troubles took their toll. A mid-season surgery to remove bone spurs prematurely ended his year. 2005 Outlook: B

Aaron Small (**Pos**: RHP, **Age**: 33)

	W	L	Pct.	ERA	G	GS	Sv	IP	H	BB	SO	HR	Avg
'04	0	0	–	8.27	7	0	0	16.1	24	7	8	5	.343
Car.	15	10	.600	5.49	146	3	4	218.0	267	101	121	24	.306

Small has logged almost 1,600 minor league innings in his 16 years of professional service. At 33, he opted to become a free agent in October, and still has a tiny window of opportunity to solidify a big league job. 2005 Outlook: C

Larry Sutton (**Pos**: 1B, **Age**: 34, **Bats**: L)

	G	AB	R	H	D	T	HR	RBI	SB	BB	SO	Avg	OBP	Slg
'04	8	5	0	1	0	0	0	1	0	1	2	.200	.333	.200
Car.	252	572	63	135	23	2	12	78	4	55	102	.236	.302	.346

Hitter-friendly Isotopes Park in Albuquerque sits at an elevation similar to Denver's Coors Field. This helps explain the other-worldly production of Sutton in 308 Triple-A at-bats. His 21 home runs and .373/.475/.692 look like they were torn from Todd Helton's stat line. 2005 Outlook: C

Matt Treanor (**Pos**: C, **Age**: 29, **Bats**: R)

	G	AB	R	H	D	T	HR	RBI	SB	BB	SO	Avg	OBP	Slg
'04	29	55	7	13	2	0	0	1	0	4	13	.236	.311	.273
Car.	29	55	7	13	2	0	0	1	0	4	13	.236	.311	.273

It may have taken him 10 years to reach the major leagues, but Treanor made the most of his first official big league at-bat, singling to left field off of Cincinnati's Cory Lidle. Treanor made 14 starts at catcher for the banged up Marlins in 2004. 2005 Outlook: C

Justin Wayne (**Pos**: RHP, **Age**: 25)

	W	L	Pct.	ERA	G	GS	Sv	IP	H	BB	SO	HR	Avg
'04	3	3	.500	5.79	19	1	0	32.2	35	18	20	6	.282
Car.	5	8	.385	6.13	26	8	0	61.2	66	36	37	10	.277

Wayne, a consensus All-American and first-round draft pick out of Stanford, has not lived up to expectations since being selected in 2000. Working out of the bullpen for the first time in his career, he struggled to get outs and was sent to Albuquerque by June. 2005 Outlook: C

David Weathers (**Pos**: RHP, **Age**: 35)

	W	L	Pct.	ERA	G	GS	Sv	IP	H	BB	SO	HR	Avg
'04	7	7	.500	4.15	66	2	0	82.1	85	35	61	12	.274
Car.	52	62	.456	4.46	614	69	14	1016.0	1104	456	734	94	.282

Weathers journeyed through New York, Houston and Florida last season. Since 2000, he has proven to be a valuable righty reliever, able to bridge the gap between starter and closer. His 3.12 ERA and surprising effectiveness against lefthanded hitters will land him a job in 2005. 2005 Outlook: B

Florida Marlins Minor League Prospects

Organization Overview:

En route to the 2003 World Series title, the Marlins dipped liberally into their farm system for help. Opportunities weren't as plentiful in 2004, when the Marlins faded late. On the plus side, Florida didn't have to raid its system as readily for trade bait. The organization did deal off slick-fielding Triple-A shortstop Wilson Valdez to get setup man Billy Koch from the White Sox in June, and the Marlins put Double-A left-hander Bill Murphy in the six-player blockbuster with the Dodgers on July 30. The system went a combined 62 games under .500, although 39 of those came courtesy of the overmatched Greensboro Bats, who went 50-89 in the South Atlantic League. Of the top five affiliates, only Double-A Carolina (73-66) had a winning record.

Yorman Bazardo

Position: P **Opening Day Age:** 20
Bats: R **Throws:** R **Born:** 7/11/84 in
Ht: 6' 2" **Wt:** 170 Maracay, VZ

Recent Statistics

	W	L	ERA	G	GS	Sv	IP	H	R	BB	SO	HR
2003 A Greensboro	9	8	3.12	21	21	0	130.0	132	56	26	70	8
2004 A Jupiter	5	9	3.27	25	25	0	154.1	161	78	30	95	3

Bazardo might have the best overall arm in the system. After Bazardo was a starter in the Venezuelan Summer League, the Marlins stuck him in the bullpen, using him mostly in two-inning stints. He has started the past two seasons, and his profile has skyrocketed. Part of a highly talented pitching staff at high Class-A Jupiter, Bazardo distinguished himself. He was considered one of four untouchables in the system at the July trade deadline. Tall and long-limbed, Bazardo pitches at 92-94 MPH and has touched 98 as late as the eighth inning. He has a plus changeup and a developing slider. He is aggressive and has good action on his sinker. He is around the strike zone and gets lots of quick outs.

Jeremy Hermida

Position: OF **Opening Day Age:** 21
Bats: L **Throws:** R **Born:** 1/30/84 in
Ht: 6' 4" **Wt:** 200 Marietta, GA

Recent Statistics

	G	AB	R	H	D	T	HR	RBI	SB	BB	SO	Avg
2003 A Greensboro	133	468	73	133	23	5	6	49	28	80	100	.284
2003 AAA Albuquerque	1	3	0	0	0	0	0	0	0	0	3	.000
2004 A Jupiter	91	340	53	101	17	1	10	50	10	42	73	.297

Hermida has a smooth, quick stroke, good plate discipline for his level, a strong work ethic and good make-up. He is comfortable working deep in counts and projects to have good power to all fields. He's a little better than an average runner and has good instincts on the bases. Hermida has come a long way defensively, but he still needs to improve his throwing as well as his jumps and routes. His arm is erratic and average, and has struggled with minor injuries (ankle, heel, hamstring) each of his first three seasons. After a solid showing in the Arizona Fall League, where he was one of the youngest players invited, Hermida should start out at Double-A Carolina.

Scott Olsen

Position: P **Opening Day Age:** 21
Bats: L **Throws:** L **Born:** 1/12/84 in
Ht: 6' 4" **Wt:** 190 Kalamazoo, MI

Recent Statistics

	W	L	ERA	G	GS	Sv	IP	H	R	BB	SO	HR
2003 A Greensboro	7	9	2.81	25	24	0	128.1	101	51	59	129	4
2004 A Jupiter	7	6	2.97	25	25	0	136.1	127	57	53	158	8

Virtually unknown in high school, Olsen has blossomed since signing for $160,000 as a tall, projectable lefty with a loose arm and an easy delivery. Olsen added another tick in velocity last year, pitching at 91-93 MPH and topping out at 96 MPH. His fastball has late life and he has tightened his slider to give it more depth. He is aggressive and competitive with a bit of a mean streak. He is learning to use the slider as an out pitch. Olsen has a slight frame that could use another 15-20 pounds of muscle, but for the second straight year, he finished strong. He was as dominant as any pitcher in the high Class-A Florida State League over his last month or so.

Eric Reed

Position: OF **Opening Day Age:** 24
Bats: L **Throws:** L **Born:** 12/2/80 in Little
Ht: 5' 10" **Wt:** 170 Rock, AR

Recent Statistics

	G	AB	R	H	D	T	HR	RBI	SB	BB	SO	Avg
2003 A Jupiter	134	514	86	154	15	8	0	25	53	52	83	.300
2004 AA Carolina	55	222	32	68	9	6	3	14	24	14	55	.306

Despite a wiry frame, Reed is a former high school powerlifting champion who squatted 450 pounds in college. He signed for $85,000 and was named the organization's Minor League Player of the Year in his first full season in 2003. Reed has tremendous speed to first and in the outfield. He is regularly timed at 3.8 seconds to first base. Often compared to Marlins center fielder Juan Pierre, Reed may be faster and a better defender. After missing the last three months of the 2004 season with a broken wrist suffered in a bar fight, Reed was placed on the Arizona Fall League taxi squad. He figures to start at Double-A Carolina, where he will continue to prepare himself as Pierre's eventual replacement.

Jason Stokes

Position: 1B
Bats: R **Throws:** R
Ht: 6' 4" **Wt:** 225

Opening Day Age: 23
Born: 1/23/82 in Irving, TX

Recent Statistics

	G	AB	R	H	D	T	HR	RBI	SB	BB	SO	Avg
2003 A Jupiter	121	462	67	119	31	3	17	89	6	36	135	.258
2004 R Gcmarlins	3	8	1	2	1	0	1	0	1	0	3	.250
2004 AA Carolina	106	394	66	107	26	0	23	78	5	42	121	.272

Stokes' greatest tool remains his powerful bat. He takes a big swing and rarely cuts back, even with two strikes, but does show power to all fields. He runs well for a big man and has decent hands. Injuries continue to plague Stokes, particularly in his troublesome left wrist. The joint flared up again in 2004, causing Stokes to miss time at the end of the year. The condition limited his extra work throughout the second half. He was considering a second wrist surgery in two years. Some scouts view him as a one-dimensional player who must hit for power to have real value. His high strikeout totals have inspired some doubts, and his defense remains average at best due to poor lateral movement.

Taylor Tankersley

Position: P
Bats: L **Throws:** L
Ht: 6' 1" **Wt:** 220

Opening Day Age: 22
Born: 3/7/83 in Vicksburg, MS

Recent Statistics

	W	L	ERA	G	GS	Sv	IP	H	R	BB	SO	HR
2004 A Jamestown	1	1	3.38	6	6	0	26.2	21	14	8	32	2

Tankersley received a $1.3 million signing bonus after going 27th overall last June. He has great versatility after starting and relieving at Alabama. He shows a bulldog mentality, has a little mean streak and throws from a low three-quarters arm slot, which makes him particularly tough on lefties. Tankersley shows a plus slider, strong work ethic and baseball-rat tendencies. He pitches at 88-91 MPH and tops out at 93. His emotions sometimes get the best of him, and his changeup needs refinement. With his college background and maturity level, both physical and mental, he should move quickly through the system. After some impressive work in the short-season New York-Penn League, he should start 2005 at Class-A Greensboro.

Jason Vargas

Position: P
Bats: L **Throws:** L
Ht: 6' 0" **Wt:** 215

Opening Day Age: 22
Born: 2/2/83 in Apple Valley, CA

Recent Statistics

	W	L	ERA	G	GS	Sv	IP	H	R	BB	SO	HR
2004 A Jamestown	3	1	1.96	8	8	0	41.1	35	17	13	41	2
2004 A Greensboro	2	1	2.37	3	3	0	19.0	9	5	2	17	1

Initially a two-way player, Vargas attended three different colleges before the Marlins took him in the second round last June from Long Beach State. Nephew of former major league infielder Randy Velarde, Vargas was overshadowed on a staff that included the bally-hooed righthander Jered Weaver. Vargas pitches at 90-92 MPH and tops out at 95. His tight slider is a putaway pitch to lefties, while his changeup is average but has good downward action at times. His makeup is excellent and he has a strong mound presence, working quickly and going right after hitters. He has a strong work ethic, but tired near the end of last year after a late promotion to the Class-A South Atlantic League.

Josh Willingham

Position: C
Bats: R **Throws:** R
Ht: 6' 1" **Wt:** 200

Opening Day Age: 26
Born: 2/17/79 in Florence, AL

Recent Statistics

	G	AB	R	H	D	T	HR	RBI	SB	BB	SO	Avg
2004 AA Carolina	112	338	81	95	24	0	24	76	6	91	87	.281
2004 NL Florida	12	25	2	5	0	0	1	1	0	4	8	.200

Willingham made a surprising jump from Double-A to the majors last July, making three starts behind the plate and getting a chance to handle a top pitching staff. He has made himself into perhaps the best pure hitter in the system. He has a short swing, power to all fields and a willingness to work counts and take walks. He is instinctive, knowledgeable and has great makeup and work ethic. Willingham has made great strides as a catcher since converting to the position in the fall of 2002. He has average arm strength and works hard at calling a game. At best he could wind up like a Craig Wilson, bouncing from first to the outfield.

Others to Watch

Righthander **Trevor Hutchinson** (25) throws a heavy sinker at 89-91 MPH. He also has a slider and change-up, both of which are average. He is a strike-thrower who produces lots of groundballs. Health is a concern after a minor elbow problem that kept him out three-plus weeks at midseason. An MRI was negative. An MRI on his shoulder in November also came back negative. . . **Josh Johnson** (21) has added velocity since signing for $300,000 out of high school. That's due in part to mechanical changes and also to physical maturation. The righty pitches at 91-93 MPH and tops out at 96 MPH. His changeup and slider showed progress. . . Righthander **Randy Messenger** (23) consistently disappointed over his first five pro seasons, when he posted a combined 27-25, 4.80 mark. He returned to Double-A Carolina and reinvented himself as a short reliever and started blowing hitters away with a 93-96 MPH fastball. His breaking ball still needs work. . . **Josh Wilson** (24) showed more patience at the plate last season, used the whole field and did a better job of staying on top of the ball. The shortstop projects as a solid No. 2 hitter in the mold of Pirates shortstop Jack Wilson (no relation), although Josh is more patient.

Minute Maid Park

Offense

Known as a hitters' park since its inception, Minute Maid is slowly starting to lose its mystique. After hitting a club-record 135 homers in its opening season, the Astros haven't hit as many as 110 in any year since, settling for 96 last season. The quirky dimensions, with seats jutting out close to the left-field line and the outfield lines curving around the two bullpens, make for adventurous outings for fielders.

Defense

One of the big complaints about the outfield has been Tal's Hill in center field, the 30-degree slope that is the brainchild of team president Tal Smith. Many center fielders have found it intimidating, but Carlos Beltran proved it's really no mystery, negotiating it both running backwards and forwards. Good pitchers through the years also have proven that the short porch in left field can be overcome with judicious pitches.

Who It Helps the Most

Righthanded hitters still like the Crawford Boxes, only 315 feet away. Jeff Bagwell especially likes them and hit 18 of his 27 homers at home last year. Lance Berkman hit a solid .321 at Minute Maid.

Who It Hurts the Most

Roy Oswalt gave up 10 of his 17 home runs at home and Roger Clemens nine of his 15. Carlos Beltran had only seven of his 23 Astros homers at home, and some thought his problems stemmed from being a pull hitter who became too conscious of that short left-field wall.

Rookies & Newcomers

Anyone new to the field must learn that grounders hit down the left-field line can bounce off the seating that comes just a few feet from the foul line, or disappear into the corner and bounce around wildly. Also, the hand-operated league scoreboard on the left-field wall makes for all kinds of unusual plays.

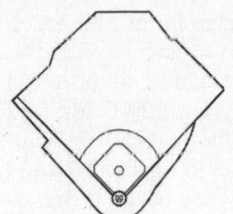

Dimensions: LF-315, LCF-362, CF-435, RCF-373, RF-326

Capacity: 40,950

Elevation: 22 feet

Surface: Grass

Foul Territory: Average

Park Factors

2004 Season

	Home Games Astros	Opp	Total	Away Games Astros	Opp	Total	Index
G	75	75	150	75	75	150	
Avg	.278	.246	.262	.262	.267	.264	99
AB	2474	2564	5038	2602	2522	5124	98
R	373	309	682	385	335	720	95
H	687	631	1318	681	674	1355	97
2B	128	123	251	146	140	286	89
3B	21	19	40	14	12	26	156
HR	90	78	168	89	79	168	102
BB	272	214	486	272	271	543	91
SO	430	643	1073	498	550	1048	104
E	47	50	97	47	42	89	109
E-Infield	39	40	79	37	36	73	108
LHB-Avg	.284	.258	.266	.288	.286	.287	93
LHB-HR	19	29	48	43	38	81	60
RHB-Avg	.276	.236	.259	.252	.253	.252	103
RHB-HR	71	49	120	46	41	87	141

2002-2004

	Home Games Astros	Opp	Total	Away Games Astros	Opp	Total	Index
G	222	222	444	222	222	444	
Avg	.276	.249	.262	.251	.260	.255	103
AB	7386	7592	14978	7720	7368	15088	99
R	1118	922	2040	1034	948	1982	103
H	2039	1889	3928	1936	1918	3854	102
2B	401	369	770	415	406	821	94
3B	57	47	104	33	41	74	142
HR	255	217	472	244	217	461	103
BB	812	654	1466	773	819	1592	93
SO	1335	1725	3060	1540	1589	3129	99
E	128	144	272	124	139	263	103
E-Infield	110	115	225	100	118	218	103
LHB-Avg	.283	.261	.269	.264	.276	.271	99
LHB-HR	77	75	152	85	96	181	84
RHB-Avg	.273	.240	.258	.245	.250	.247	105
RHB-HR	178	142	320	159	121	280	116

2004 Rankings (National League)

- Highest triple factor
- Second-highest RHB home-run factor
- Lowest LHB home-run factor
- Second-lowest double factor
- Second-lowest walk factor
- Second-lowest LHB batting-average factor

Phil Garner

2004 Season

Phil Garner came into a quagmire at midseason and at first didn't seem to have much impact. The richly talented Astros were floundering at 44-44 when he arrived and they went 12-16 his first month as manager. But then they caught fire, winning 36 of their final 46 games to finish 92-70 and take the NL wild-card spot. They beat the Braves in the NLDS, Houston's first-ever postseason series victory, then took the Cardinals to seven games in the NLCS. Garner finished fourth in the NL Manager of the Year voting and won a two-year contract with an option year.

Offense

Garner said from the start he likes to run more and make things happen, and the team did both. A large part of that was Carlos Beltran, whose perfect 28-for-28 in stolen bases made this team much more dangerous on the basepaths. With or without Beltran, look for Garner to have the team running, hitting behind the runners and taking more chances in 2005.

Pitching & Defense

Unlike his predecessor, Garner was more likely to leave a pitcher in late in the game. He also showed an inclination for the unconventional pitcher substitution, such as bringing closer Brad Lidge in for two or even three innings and even using Roy Oswalt in an occasional relief role. Those moves were made largely out of desperation late in the season, but Garner at least showed flexibility and creativity when using the bullpen. Defensively, he also could be creative, using Orlando Palmeiro, Jason Lane and Willy Taveras in late-inning outfield shifts.

2005 Outlook

Garner promoted a more relaxed clubhouse, something that fits well with a veteran team with such self-motivating players like Jeff Bagwell and Craig Biggio. The Astros seemed much more comfortable and more focused on what they had to do late in the season. That should carry over into this season, but much of what Garner can or can't do will be told in free agency.

Born: 4/30/49 in Jefferson City, TN

Playing Experience: 1973-1988, Oak, Pit, Hou, LA, SF

Managerial Experience: 12 seasons

Manager Statistics

Year	Team, Lg	W	L	Pct	GB	Finish
2004	Houston, NL	48	26	.649	13.0	2nd Central
12 Seasons		756	828	.477	–	–

2004 Starting Pitchers by Days Rest

	<=3	4	5	6+
Astros Starts	0	48	13	11
Astros ERA	–	3.97	4.90	3.40
NL Avg Starts	2	82	46	23
NL ERA	4.58	4.35	4.28	4.73

2004 Situational Stats

	Phil Garner	NL Average
Hit & Run Success %	39.5	38.0
Stolen Base Success %	82.1	71.7
Platoon Pct.	52.9	55.2
Defensive Subs	13	18
High-Pitch Outings	3	6
Quick/Slow Hooks	20/4	21/12
Sacrifice Attempts	45	99

2004 Rankings (National League)

- Did not rank near the top in any category.

Jeff Bagwell

2004 Season

Jeff Bagwell always has had early- and midseason slumps. But this year's started in June and lasted much longer than the previous ones, haunting him all the way through August. He began to come out of it in September and was instrumental in the team's late-season surge, tying Jeff Kent for most September RBI on the team with 22 apiece. He also shook his history of poor playoffs by hitting .286 with a pair of homers and eight RBI.

Hitting

The torn labrum Bagwell had surgery on in 2001 still bothers him greatly, and he knows it always will. He admitted this year for the first time that it not only was affecting his throwing but also his hitting, causing a "hitch" in his swing at times. Bagwell's unorthodox crouch and powerful inside-out swing had to be adjusted some because of it. He realized late in the season that he would have to pick up the ball slightly sooner and try to come up out of the crouch more quickly than he was comfortable doing in order to get on top of the ball.

Baserunning & Defense

Bagwell's six stolen bases and four caught stealing were a sign he no longer is a basestealing threat. But he remains a smart baserunner who knows when to go for the extra base. Defensively, he also is far from the Gold Glove first baseman he once was, but he made only six errors last season, fewest of his career. That was because he plays within his limitations and consistently makes the smart play. The shoulder keeps him from making long or hard throws.

2005 Outlook

Bagwell no longer is the player he once was, but he doesn't need to be to help this team. His quiet intensity and professional approach have a settling effect on the younger players. And if he can continue to adjust his swing to the shoulder problems, he can help the team at the plate. Only time will tell how quickly his skills will continue to deteriorate.

Position: 1B
Bats: R **Throws:** R
Ht: 6' 0" **Wt:** 215

Opening Day Age: 36
Born: 5/27/68 in Boston, MA
ML Seasons: 14
Pronunciation: BAG-well

Overall Statistics

G	AB	R	H	D	T	HR	RBI	SB	BB	SO	Avg	OBP	Slg
156	572	104	152	29	2	27	89	6	96	131	.266	.377	.465
2111	7697	1506	2289	484	32	446	1510	202	1383	1537	.297	.408	.542

Where He Hits the Ball

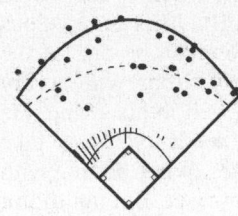 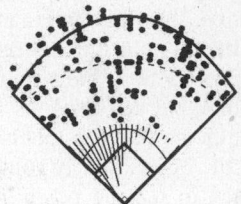

Vs. LHP   **Vs. RHP**

2004 Situational Stats

	AB	H	HR	RBI	Avg		AB	H	HR	RBI	Avg
Home	280	83	18	49	.296	LHP	101	15	4	10	.149
Road	292	69	9	40	.236	RHP	471	137	23	79	.291
First Half	310	83	11	40	.268	Sc Pos	159	48	11	65	.302
Scnd Half	262	69	16	49	.263	Clutch	81	20	1	7	.247

2004 Rankings (National League)

- 1st in lowest batting average vs. lefthanded pitchers
- 3rd in fielding percentage at first base (.995)
- 5th in pitches seen (2,819)
- 8th in most pitches seen per plate appearance (4.15) and lowest batting average on the road
- 9th in errors at first base (6)
- Led the Astros in runs scored, strikeouts, pitches seen (2,819) and most pitches seen per plate appearance (4.15)

Houston

2004 Season

One of the game's blossoming superstars, Carlos Beltran had an extraordinary season followed by a even more phenomenal postseason. He hit .267 with 104 RBI while splitting the year between Kansas City and Houston. He fell just two home runs shy of becoming only the fourth player ever to register a 40-40 campaign. Then in the playoffs, he hit .435 with a playoff record-tying eight home runs and 14 RBI, all while making a couple of spectacular plays in the outfield and stealing 6 of 6 bases.

Hitting

Beltran got into trouble in the National League trying to pull too many outside pitches and batted only .258 while in Houston. But he is a marvelous hitter whom the Astros know can be one of the league's best. He's extremely strong with a very quick bat and uses his legs well in his swing. He pulls the ball too much and needs to learn to take it the opposite way sometimes. When batting with men in scoring position, however, Beltran didn't show enough patience and often swung at bad pitches.

Baserunning & Defense

Beltran's highlight film could be an instructional video on what a five-tool player is. He runs like a gazelle and easily can turn what appears to be a double into a standup triple. The National League still hasn't caught him stealing in 34 tries (including playoffs). He studies pitchers well and has such explosion when he runs that catchers rarely have a chance. Though Beltran often plays somewhat shallow, no one can hit balls over his head. He covers a huge amount of ground and makes the acrobatic catch. He also has a plus arm.

2005 Outlook

Beltran is poised to be one of the game's best players wherever he goes. He is a 40-40 man looking for a place to happen, and he now has shown that he's at his best in the playoffs, which he had never had a chance to do before last season. Any contending team will get a huge boost from his multiple talents.

Position: CF
Bats: B **Throws:** R
Ht: 6' 1" **Wt:** 190

Opening Day Age: 27
Born: 4/24/77 in Manati, PR
ML Seasons: 7
Pronunciation: BELL-tron

Overall Statistics

	G	AB	R	H	D	T	HR	RBI	SB	BB	SO	Avg	OBP	Slg
'04	159	599	121	160	36	9	38	104	42	92	101	.267	.367	.548
Car.	885	3467	616	985	173	52	146	569	192	371	641	.284	.353	.490

Where He Hits the Ball

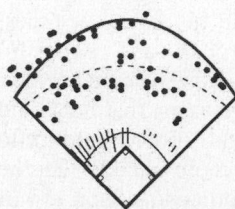 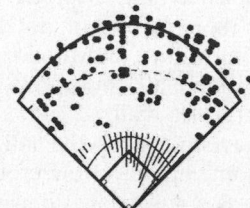

Vs. LHP   **Vs. RHP**

2004 Situational Stats

	AB	H	HR	RBI	Avg		AB	H	HR	RBI	Avg
Home	284	64	15	41	.225	LHP	174	48	11	33	.276
Road	315	96	23	63	.305	RHP	425	112	27	71	.264
First Half	323	89	21	63	.276	Sc Pos	136	36	8	63	.265
Scnd Half	276	71	17	41	.257	Clutch	83	22	7	26	.265

2004 Rankings (National League)

- 1st in steals of third (11)
- 4th in errors in center field (5)
- 9th in triples (7)
- 10th in stolen bases (28)
- Led the Astros in stolen bases (28), HR frequency (14.5 ABs per HR), steals of third (11), fewest GDPs per GDP situation (5.7%) and lowest percentage of swings on the first pitch (23.1)

Lance Berkman

2004 Season

Lance Berkman returned to All-Star form after a so-so 2003 season. He led the team in batting average, on-base percentage, walks and homers, and was second in RBI. He split time in the outfield, playing left field, then switching to right after the Carlos Beltran trade. Berkman struggled in June, but came back steadily and hit .352 in September/October. Though Beltran got the most notice, Berkman also had a tremendous postseason, hitting .348 with four homers and 12 RBI.

Hitting

Berkman probably has the most raw power on the team and can swat home runs with a flick of his wrist. He also has exceptional hand-eye coordination, though it is much better lefthanded. He has a solid approach to hitting and usually doesn't overthink it. He drives the ball to all fields well, hitting it the opposite way if you pitch him outside and cutting down on his swing if you pitch him inside. His weakness is hitting righthanded, and some wonder if he should stick strictly to lefthanded hitting.

Baserunning & Defense

Berkman's baserunning instincts aren't very good and he sometimes runs himself into trouble or gets picked off embarrassingly. Club officials think he just needs to study pitchers and situations more because he has the natural speed to be more of a baserunning threat. Defensively, he is a first baseman playing the outfield. He is athletic and runs well enough to make some good plays, but also misses some he should make. His arm is average to a tick above average.

2005 Outlook

Less than a month after the 2004 season ended, Berkman injured his right knee playing flag football at a church event. He had to undergo surgery to repair cartilage and the ACL in early November. Club officials publicly remained optimistic, and Berkman swore his rehab would be shorter than most. But privately, officials know that such injuries can affect a player for a good year, even if he does return in April or May as expected.

Position: RF/LF
Bats: B **Throws:** L
Ht: 6' 1" **Wt:** 220

Opening Day Age: 29
Born: 2/10/76 in Waco, TX
ML Seasons: 6

Overall Statistics

	G	AB	R	H	D	T	HR	RBI	SB	BB	SO	Avg	OBP	Slg
'04	160	544	104	172	40	3	30	106	9	127	101	.316	.450	.566
Car.	775	2683	516	814	195	17	156	535	40	501	542	.303	.416	.563

Where He Hits the Ball

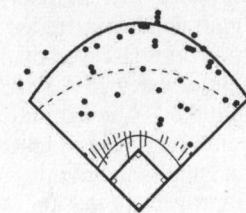

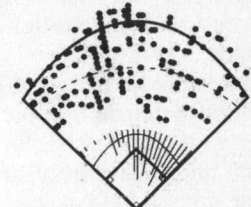

Vs. LHP	Vs. RHP

2004 Situational Stats

	AB	H	HR	RBI	Avg		AB	H	HR	RBI	Avg
Home	268	86	8	44	.321	LHP	125	34	4	21	.272
Road	276	86	22	62	.312	RHP	419	138	26	85	.329
First Half	284	85	16	59	.299	Sc Pos	154	47	7	75	.305
Scnd Half	260	87	14	47	.335	Clutch	78	27	3	22	.346

2004 Rankings (National League)

- 2nd in walks
- 3rd in times on base (309) and on-base percentage
- 4th in intentional walks (14)
- 5th in games played
- 7th in batting average vs. righthanded pitchers
- Led the Astros in batting average, home runs, runs scored, total bases (308), caught stealing (7), walks, times on base (309), slugging percentage, on-base percentage, highest percentage of pitches taken (60.8), batting average vs. righthanded pitchers, cleanup slugging percentage (.529) and batting average on the road

Houston

Craig Biggio

2004 Season

Craig Biggio had a solid season at the plate, although he stumbled badly in the field. For the second straight season, he was asked to work at a new defensive position, moving from center to left field after the acquisition of Carlos Beltran. Left proved to be a mystery to him much of the time. At the plate, he hit a career-high 24 home runs with a team-high 47 doubles. But he also was a bust as a leadoff hitter, walking only 40 times and striking out 91.

Hitting

Biggio is the classic righthanded pull hitter, especially when he hits with power. He has hit more singles to all fields, but doubles and homers almost always go to left. Biggio junked his trademark foot-lift before each swing last season, something he had used his entire career. He said he felt it helped him pick up the ball quicker and get to it more easily. Some club officials thought that might have been more mental than anything but were so glad to see his improvement that they didn't argue.

Baserunning & Defense

Biggio was once a real baserunning threat, but time and his knee surgery in 2000 have robbed him of most of that. Defensively, he has become a liability whether in center or left field. He doesn't have the arm for either position and isn't fast enough to cover much ground. Opposing teams constantly took advantage of his lack of arm when he was in center. An infielder most of his career, he has never had to cover such great amounts of ground.

2005 Outlook

Without hesitation, the Astros picked up Biggio's option for 2005 last October. From a PR standpoint, the club hardly could afford not to after the team icon had such a good year at the plate. But some wonder if he will be in the club's plans as much this year. Depending on free-agent signings, Biggio might be relegated to a backup position. There's also the question of his batting leadoff if he does return full time to the lineup.

Position: LF/CF
Bats: R **Throws:** R
Ht: 5'11" **Wt:** 185

Opening Day Age: 39
Born: 12/14/65 in Smithtown, NY
ML Seasons: 17
Pronunciation: BIDG-ee-oh

Overall Statistics

G	AB	R	H	D	T	HR	RBI	SB	BB	SO	Avg	OBP	Slg
156	633	100	178	47	0	24	63	7	40	94	.281	.337	.469
2409	9221	1603	2639	564	51	234	994	396	1060	1467	.286	.373	.435

Where He Hits the Ball

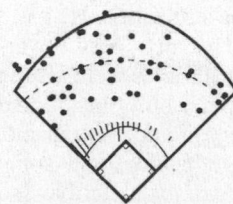 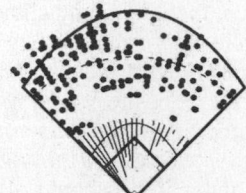

Vs. LHP   **Vs. RHP**

2004 Situational Stats

	AB	H	HR	RBI	Avg		AB	H	HR	RBI	Avg
Home	326	95	13	34	.291	LHP	119	36	6	12	.303
Road	307	83	11	29	.270	RHP	514	142	18	51	.276
First Half	356	107	13	36	.301	Sc Pos	118	27	1	36	.229
Scnd Half	277	71	11	27	.256	Clutch	80	14	3	10	.175

2004 Rankings (National League)

- 1st in errors in left field (9)
- 3rd in fewest pitches seen per plate appearance (3.33)
- 4th in doubles
- 5th in hit by pitch (15)
- 6th in at-bats
- 7th in lowest percentage of pitches taken (48.0)
- 9th in plate appearances (700) and lowest batting average in the clutch
- Led the Astros in at-bats, hits, singles, doubles, hit by pitch (15), plate appearances (700) and on-base percentage for a leadoff hitter (.338)

2004 Season

What more could Roger Clemens have done? The now seven-time Cy Young Award winner showed age has no affect on his brilliant abilities. He answered the bell 33 times and his 2.98 ERA and 218 strikeouts were his best since 1998 when he was with Toronto. Clemens also pitched many of the Astros' biggest games, including seven strong innings to beat Atlanta in the Division Series opener and topping St. Louis in Game 3 of the NLCS after the team had lost the first two games.

Pitching

Though Clemens doesn't consistently throw in the upper 90s now, he still can hit 94-96 MPH with ease, and stays in the 91-92 range. He moves around the two-seamer, four-seamer and slider to both sides of the plate and changes speeds on them. But his split-finger has become his most devastating pitch, and possibly the best splitter in the business. It runs in at 88-89 MPH and looks like a fastball until the bottom drops out at the last instant. He probably has a better plan for each game than any pitcher in baseball and is unshakeable under pressure.

Defense & Hitting

Clemens is not particularly fast off the mound, but his competitiveness spurs him to handle bunts and make plays at first effectively. He's a reasonably good fielder who did not make an error last season for the sixth time in his career. He never has had a dangerous pickoff move, and basestealers have been successful two out of every three attempts against him in his career. In the NL for the first time, he worked considerably on his hitting and became decent with the bat, actually leading the pitching staff with seven RBI.

2005 Outlook

If he returns, Clemens will again give the Astros a potent 1-2 punch along with Roy Oswalt. The only question is how long can Clemens maintain the fire he needs to stay competitive. When he has it, he is as good as he has ever been and seems capable of going two or three more years at minimum.

Position: SP
Bats: R **Throws:** R
Ht: 6' 4" **Wt:** 235

Opening Day Age: 42
Born: 8/4/62 in Dayton, OH
ML Seasons: 21
Nickname: Rocket

Houston

Overall Statistics

W	L	Pct.	ERA	G	GS	Sv	IP	H	BB	SO	HR	Avg
18	4	.818	2.98	33	33	0	214.1	169	79	218	15	.217
328	164	.667	3.18	640	639	0	4493.0	3846	1458	4317	336	.230

2004 Pitching Profile

	Roger Clemens	NL Average
Overall Strike %	63.6	62.5
1st Pitch Strike %	63.0	58.5
Ratio	1.16	1.39
Strikeouts per 9 IP	9.15	6.74
Walks per 9 IP	3.32	3.38
Home Runs per 9 IP	0.63	1.11
Strikeout/Walk Ratio	2.76	1.99
Groundball/Flyball Ratio	1.47	1.25

2004 Situational Stats

	W	L	ERA	Sv	IP		AB	H	HR	RBI	Avg
Home	12	3	2.71	0	133.0	LHB	395	86	5	29	.218
Road	6	1	3.43	0	81.1	RHB	383	83	10	38	.217
First Half	10	3	2.62	0	116.2	Sc Pos	181	35	3	50	.193
Scnd Half	8	1	3.41	0	97.2	Clutch	54	14	0	6	.259

2004 Rankings (National League)

- 1st in winning percentage and fielding percentage at pitcher (1.000)
- 2nd in wins and runners caught stealing (10)
- 3rd in lowest slugging percentage allowed (.329)
- 4th in pickoff throws (160), stolen bases allowed (23), lowest batting average allowed (.217) and fewest home runs allowed per nine innings (.63)
- 5th in ERA and strikeouts
- Led the Astros in ERA, walks allowed, strikeouts, wild pitches (5), pickoff throws (160), stolen bases allowed (23), winning percentage, lowest batting average allowed (.217), lowest slugging percentage allowed (.329),lowest on-base percentage allowed (.292), lowest ERA at home, lowest ERA on the road, fewest home runs allowed per nine innings (.63) and most strikeouts per nine innings (9.2)

Morgan Ensberg

2004 Season

Morgan Ensberg fell off his 2003 numbers and completely baffled the Astros brass, mostly with his lack of power. In 2003, he had hit 25 home runs, tying the club record for homers by a third baseman. Then last season, he was placed in the starting lineup and went three months without going deep. His first came July 2 and by that time, he was sharing time with Mike Lamb. Then in late August, Ensberg started experiencing back spasms and missed most of the next three weeks. He came back to play most of the postseason because the team needed his glove.

Hitting

Ensberg is considered a very good contact hitter with excellent hand-eye coordination. He has a picture-perfect swing, usually keeps his approach simple and will hit singles to all fields. He is very good with the game on the line, when he seems to intensify his concentration and frequently come up with big hits. Ensberg's problem is that he tends to over-think situations and tries to be too perfect. When he just goes to the plate and swings away, he has much more success.

Baserunning & Defense

Ensberg is a fairly good fielder with a strong arm to first. He goes to both sides equally well though he doesn't have great range. A sore elbow probably contributed to his slightly elevated number of errors (13) last season. He's undoubtedly the best defensive third baseman the Astros have. His baserunning is average and he gets caught stealing nearly as often as he is successful. But he has decent speed and goes all out in sliding and breaking up double plays.

2005 Outlook

The Astros think Ensberg's lack of home runs early last season caused him to change his swing for a while and that compounded the problems. They still believe he can be a power hitter who hits for average and is very reliable in the clutch. The Astros expect him to settle in and eventually nail down the third-base job for years to come.

Position: 3B
Bats: R **Throws:** R
Ht: 6' 2" **Wt:** 210

Opening Day Age: 29
Born: 8/26/75 in Hermosa Beach, CA
ML Seasons: 4

Overall Statistics

	G	AB	R	H	D	T	HR	RBI	SB	BB	SO	Avg	OBP	Slg
'04	131	411	51	113	20	3	10	66	6	36	46	.275	.330	.411
Car.	311	935	134	259	42	6	38	145	15	102	132	.277	.352	.457

Where He Hits the Ball

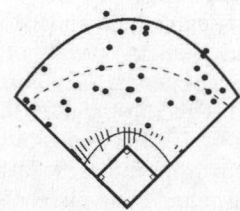 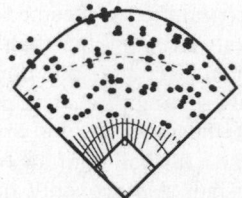

Vs. LHP   **Vs. RHP**

2004 Situational Stats

	AB	H	HR	RBI	Avg		AB	H	HR	RBI	Avg
Home	210	60	9	45	.286	LHP	103	29	1	13	.282
Road	201	53	1	21	.264	RHP	308	84	9	53	.273
First Half	237	61	3	35	.257	Sc Pos	128	41	2	55	.320
Scnd Half	174	52	7	31	.299	Clutch	60	23	2	15	.383

2004 Rankings (National League)

- 3rd in batting average in the clutch
- 4th in lowest fielding percentage at third base (.949)
- 7th in errors at third base (13)
- 8th in highest percentage of swings put into play (53.0) and most GDPs per GDP situation (18.7%)
- Led the Astros in highest percentage of swings put into play (53.0), batting average with runners in scoring position and batting average in the clutch

Adam Everett

Position: SS
Bats: R **Throws:** R
Ht: 6' 0" **Wt:** 170

Opening Day Age: 28
Born: 2/5/77 in Austell, GA
ML Seasons: 4

2004 Season

Adam Everett finally became the hitter the Astros had said for years he could become. He had a career-high 11-game hitting streak in July and ended up hitting .273, which was 15 points better than his career minor league average. He also started to display the superb fielding ability he has long been noted for. Then he got hit on his left wrist on August 6, breaking the ulna bone, and missed most of the rest of the season. He tried to return late but only made five cursory appearances in the playoffs (0 starts).

Hitting

Everett finally started hitting to his strengths last season. He is a very good bunter, ranking second in the majors with 22 sacrifice bunts last year, and a good contact hitter. The Astros tried to get him to relax and be more selective in the strike zone. They wanted him to forget about hitting to all fields and be smart at the plate. When he did that, he was very effective hitting to the middle and pulling the ball.

Baserunning & Defense

Defense is Everett's calling card. With wide range, a fluid movement to the ball, superb glove skills and a steady arm, he is predicted for defensive stardom. He showed that more last season than he had in parts of two previous years, often wowing crowds with spectacular plays. Astros pitchers said they figured he saved them one to two runs a week minimum. He's also a superb baserunner with exceptional speed who can stretch singles to doubles.

2005 Outlook

Everett was anxious to return last season, but his broken wrist bone wasn't strong enough when he did. After an offseason of rehab work by Everett, the Astros expect him to be an elite shortstop. He's not projected to be a huge hitter, but he can do the job while becoming one of the game's best fielders. He might get more of a look at the lead-off role if he can learn to be more selective.

Overall Statistics

	G	AB	R	H	D	T	HR	RBI	SB	BB	SO	Avg	OBP	Slg
'04	104	384	66	105	15	2	8	31	13	17	56	.273	.317	.385
Car.	281	862	129	221	36	5	16	86	25	57	142	.256	.315	.365

Where He Hits the Ball

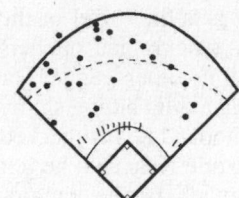
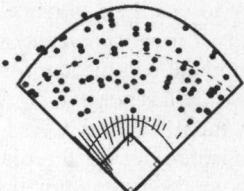

Vs. LHP **Vs. RHP**

2004 Situational Stats

	AB	H	HR	RBI	Avg		AB	H	HR	RBI	Avg
Home	183	59	5	13	.322	LHP	68	16	2	9	.235
Road	201	46	3	18	.229	RHP	316	89	6	22	.282
First Half	300	77	4	17	.257	Sc Pos	74	21	1	22	.284
Scnd Half	84	28	4	14	.333	Clutch	58	14	0	5	.241

2004 Rankings (National League)

- 2nd in sacrifice bunts (22)
- 3rd in bunts in play (43)
- 9th in errors at shortstop (10)
- Led the Astros in sacrifice bunts (22), bunts in play (43), fewest GDPs per GDP situation (5.7%) and batting average at home

2004 Season

Jeff Kent did everything the Astros could have hoped he would do at the plate, leading the team in RBI, triples and sacrifice flies as he made his fourth All-Star team. Still one of baseball's best-ever slugging second basemen, Kent became baseball's all-time leader in home runs by a second sacker (278). He slipped in the playoffs, hitting only .234, although he did produce a dramatic walkoff homer in Game 5 of the NLCS.

Hitting

Club officials say Kent is just a hitting machine and say it's no accident he has been so consistent over the years. He has an extremely short, compact swing which is something hitting instructors try to teach all players. He gets the barrel of the bat to the strike zone very quickly and pitchers know he can hit any fastball in either league. For a while last season, he was in a mild hitting slump in June and July. Coaches noticed he had backed considerably off the plate while Kent said he felt he was getting jammed too much. But he compromised and came back to hit .295 in September-October.

Baserunning & Defense

Kent is a below average baserunner and when the Astros were losing at mid-season, some thought he became disillusioned and at times wasn't trying on the bases. He trotted to first base on some hits, made some baserunning blunders that cost the team a run or two and there were grumblings in the clubhouse. But in the winning streak late in the season, he seemed rejuvenated and those problems disappeared. He is an ordinary fielder who will occasionally make the surprising play and sometimes miss the average grounder.

2005 Outlook

Club officials dearly wanted Kent back if they could get him at a more budget-friendly price. They failed in their negotiating efforts and decided not to offer arbitration to him. In December, Kent agreed to a two-year, $17 million deal to join the Los Angeles Dodgers. Depending on the Dodgers' offseason moves, Kent could play first or second base.

Position: 2B
Bats: R   **Throws:** R
Ht: 6' 1"   **Wt:** 210

Opening Day Age: 37
Born: 3/7/68 in Bellflower, CA
ML Seasons: 13

Overall Statistics

G	AB	R	H	D	T	HR	RBI	SB	BB	SO	Avg	OBP	Slg
145	540	96	156	34	8	27	107	7	49	96	.289	.348	.531
1777	6604	1039	1910	438	42	302	1207	86	592	1255	.289	.352	.505

Where He Hits the Ball

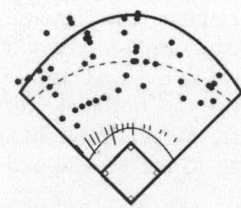
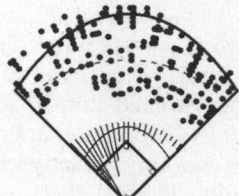

Vs. LHP   **Vs. RHP**

2004 Situational Stats

	AB	H	HR	RBI	Avg		AB	H	HR	RBI	Avg
Home	274	84	14	58	.307	LHP	109	31	7	19	.284
Road	266	72	13	49	.271	RHP	431	125	20	88	.290
First Half	281	80	10	52	.285	Sc Pos	177	51	8	82	.288
Scnd Half	259	76	17	55	.293	Clutch	64	15	2	9	.234

2004 Rankings (National League)

- 2nd in sacrifice flies (11)
- 4th in fielding percentage at second base (.989) and GDPs (23)
- 5th in triples
- Led the Astros in triples, RBI, sacrifice flies (11) and GDPs (23)
- Led NL second basemen in home runs and RBI

Brad Lidge

2004 Season

Brad Lidge became a bona fide star when the Astros needed him the most last season. After Billy Wagner and Octavio Dotel were traded, the team desperately needed Lidge to take over the closer role. He did so in spectacular fashion, converting 29 of 33 saves and setting a National League record for strikeouts by a reliever with 157 in the process. At times, he seemed to be the only legitimate option in the bullpen. In the play-offs, Lidge was dominant, appearing seven times and striking out 20 in 12.1 innings.

Pitching

Lidge is a fastball-slider pitcher who relies on his slider as his primary pitch. He throws 96-97 MPH and tops out at 99 with his fastball, and can overwhelm some hitters with it. But he has developed the slider into such a devastating pitch, he can throw it at will. He disguises it, making it look like a fastball upon delivery, but it breaks late, leaving many hitters looking silly. He also throws it in and out of the strike zone and generally baffles hitters with it. He has been known to throw several sliders in a row and hitters still can't touch it when they know it's coming.

Defense & Hitting

Lidge comes off the mound well, is athletic and can cover first easily. He reacts well to balls batted up the middle. He has a fair move to first but had to use it rarely since he allowed few baserunners. He's virtually a non-hitter.

2005 Outlook

Lidge proved he is one of the best in the game at closing after Dotel was dealt in late June, and the Astros think he only will get better and better. Lidge never once complained of having to throw two and sometimes three innings, but the reality is that he had a history of arm problems in the minors. If he's overused, that problem might pop up again.

Position: RP
Bats: R **Throws:** R
Ht: 6' 5" **Wt:** 210

Opening Day Age: 28
Born: 12/23/76 in Sacramento, CA
ML Seasons: 3

Overall Statistics

	W	L	Pct.	ERA	G	GS	Sv	IP	H	BB	SO	HR	Avg
'04	6	5	.545	1.90	80	0	29	94.2	57	30	157	8	.174
Car.	13	8	.619	2.87	164	1	30	188.1	129	81	266	14	.195

2004 Pitching Profile

	Brad Lidge	NL Average
Overall Strike %	67.0	62.5
1st Pitch Strike %	61.9	58.5
Ratio	0.92	1.39
Strikeouts per 9 IP	14.93	6.74
Walks per 9 IP	2.85	3.38
Home Runs per 9 IP	0.76	1.11
Strikeout/Walk Ratio	5.23	1.99
Groundball/Flyball Ratio	0.71	1.25

2004 Situational Stats

	W	L	ERA	Sv	IP		AB	H	HR	RBI	Avg
Home	2	2	1.69	19	48.0	LHB	173	33	3	9	.191
Road	4	3	2.12	10	46.2	RHB	155	24	5	14	.155
First Half	2	4	2.34	7	50.0	Sc Pos	79	8	1	12	.101
Scnd Half	4	1	1.41	22	44.2	Clutch	238	43	5	19	.181

2004 Rankings (National League)

- 1st in lowest percentage of inherited runners scored (6.7) and most strikeouts per nine innings in relief (14.9)
- 2nd in relief innings (94.2) and lowest batting average allowed in relief (.174)
- 3rd in first batter efficiency (.113)
- 4th in fewest baserunners allowed per nine innings in relief (8.8)
- Led the Astros in games pitched, saves, games finished (44), lowest batting average allowed vs. lefthanded batters, lowest batting average allowed vs. righthanded batters, save percentage (87.9), first batter efficiency (.113), lowest batting average allowed with runners in scoring position, relief wins (6), relief innings (94.2), relief ERA (1.90), lowest batting average allowed in relief (.174), most strikeouts per nine innings in relief (14.9),and fewest baserunners allowed per nine innings in relief (8.8)

Wade Miller

2004 Season

It was an extremely frustrating season for Wade Miller, who was expected to be one of a quartet of strong starters for the team. He made 15 starts and had a 7-7 record with a 3.35 ERA before going on the disabled list June 26 with a shoulder problem that was later described as a frayed labrum. Surgery was ruled out at the time, and he rehabbed it extensively but could never return last season.

Pitching

Miller has a complicated delivery that has to be just right for him to be effective. When he's right, Miller has as much stuff as practically anyone on the staff, throwing his fastball in the mid-90s and his slider around 90 MPH. The slightest deviation, however, and he not only has troubles pitching, but can be prone to injury. In mid-May, he was having problems and came out of a game with a strained neck, which was similar to a problem he had in the past. He seemed to be back on track in June before the shoulder began to bother him too much. An ironman who had pitched an average of 188 innings per year since 2000, Miller never was his former self last year.

Defense & Hitting

Miller has a quick pickoff move to first and usually manages to keep baserunners reasonably close. He's a fair fielder who has made only five errors in his career. As a hitter, he has worked hard at improving and it began to show last season. He hit .259 and had eight sacrifice bunts, though he's still looking for his first home run.

2005 Outlook

Miller continued to rehab his shoulder without surgery over the offseason, and the uncertainty of his situation had the Astros thinking about not tendering him a contract by the December deadline. The truth is the Astros badly need Miller to return to his 2001-03 form, when he had three straight years of double-figure wins. He can be a strong No. 4 or good No. 3 starter, and team officials still think if he puts it all together one year, he'll win 20. This season, however, they will be happy if he can report on time and stay healthy for the season.

Position: SP
Bats: R **Throws:** R
Ht: 6' 2" **Wt:** 220

Opening Day Age: 28
Born: 9/13/76 in Reading, PA
ML Seasons: 6

Overall Statistics

	W	L	Pct.	ERA	G	GS	Sv	IP	H	BB	SO	HR	Avg
'04	7	7	.500	3.35	15	15	0	88.2	76	44	74	11	.228
Car.	58	39	.598	3.87	127	123	0	768.0	699	306	659	91	.244

2004 Pitching Profile

	Wade Miller	NL Average
Overall Strike %	58.1	62.5
1st Pitch Strike %	49.0	58.5
Ratio	1.35	1.39
Strikeouts per 9 IP	7.51	6.74
Walks per 9 IP	4.47	3.38
Home Runs per 9 IP	1.12	1.11
Strikeout/Walk Ratio	1.68	1.99
Groundball/Flyball Ratio	0.79	1.25

2004 Situational Stats

	W	L	ERA	Sv	IP		AB	H	HR	RBI	Avg
Home	3	3	3.40	0	42.1	LHB	151	32	3	10	.212
Road	4	4	3.30	0	46.1	RHB	182	44	8	16	.242
First Half	7	7	3.35	0	88.2	Sc Pos	76	12	1	11	.158
Scnd Half	0	0	—	0	0.0	Clutch	9	2	0	0	.222

2004 Rankings (National League)

- Did not rank near the top or bottom in any category

Roy Oswalt

2004 Season

The righthander with the unusual delivery had what arguably was his finest season, leading the National League in wins and finishing third in the Cy Young Award voting. The team's Opening Day starter for the second straight year, Roy Oswalt topped the staff in innings pitched and starts. In the playoffs, he wasn't at his best, though he went 1-0 in three starts. He gamely tried to come back to pitch in relief of Roger Clemens in the final game of the NLCS, but it was too little too late.

Pitching

With the amazing speed differential of his fastball and curve, Oswalt has long been expected to be among baseball's best pitchers. Last season, he seemed to put it all together, although a painful ribcage injury dogged him much of the year. Oswalt took cortisone and pain shots for the problem, never missed a start and won 12 of his last 14 decisions. He throws his imposing fastball at 96-97 MPH, then comes in with a curve in the 70s to strike hitters out, often making them look bad in the process. He also went to throwing his curve at different speeds last year, further confounding hitters. He improved his slider and used it more last season, and is developing a sneaky changeup.

Defense & Hitting

Because of his unusual open pitching delivery, Oswalt has a sneaky slide-step move and is good at holding runners. He's also good at coming off the mound to field bunts, is fairly quick at reacting to hits up the middle and also covers first well. Oswalt led the pitchers and was second on the team overall in sacrifice bunts with 13.

2005 Outlook

The sky's the limit with this guy. The Astros believe if Oswalt can go a season injury-free, he will become a dominant pitcher and project himself even more squarely into the Cy Young Award race. They think as he continues to mature, he could become the acknowledged best pitcher in the league.

Position: SP
Bats: R **Throws:** R
Ht: 6' 0" **Wt:** 185

Opening Day Age: 27
Born: 8/29/77 in Weir, MS
ML Seasons: 4
Pronunciation: OWES-walt

Houston

Overall Statistics

	W	L	Pct.	ERA	G	GS	Sv	IP	H	BB	SO	HR	Avg
'04	20	10	.667	3.49	36	35	0	237.0	233	62	206	17	.260
Car.	63	27	.700	3.11	120	110	0	739.0	690	177	666	62	.249

2004 Pitching Profile

	Roy Oswalt	NL Average
Overall Strike %	66.1	62.5
1st Pitch Strike %	62.5	58.5
Ratio	1.24	1.39
Strikeouts per 9 IP	7.82	6.74
Walks per 9 IP	2.35	3.38
Home Runs per 9 IP	0.65	1.11
Strikeout/Walk Ratio	3.32	1.99
Groundball/Flyball Ratio	1.19	1.25

2004 Situational Stats

	W	L	ERA	Sv	IP		AB	H	HR	RBI	Avg
Home	11	4	3.09	0	119.1	LHB	460	118	7	44	.257
Road	9	6	3.90	0	117.2	RHB	435	115	10	49	.264
First Half	8	7	3.65	0	130.2	Sc Pos	199	56	7	75	.281
Scnd Half	12	3	3.30	0	106.1	Clutch	71	16	2	11	.225

2004 Rankings (National League)

- 1st in wins and games started
- 2nd in batters faced (983)
- 3rd in shutouts (2), innings pitched, hits allowed and errors at pitcher (3)
- 4th in pitches thrown (3,590)
- 5th in fewest home runs allowed per nine innings (.65) and lowest fielding percentage at pitcher (.939)
- 6th in sacrifice bunts (13), hit batsmen (11), strikeouts, highest strikeout-walk ratio (3.3) and lowest stolen-base percentage allowed (54.5)
- Led the Astros in wins, losses, games started, complete games (2), shutouts (2), innings pitched, hits allowed, home runs allowed, hit batsmen (11), wild pitches (5), GDPs induced (21),highest strikeout walk ratio (3.3), lowest stolen-base percentage allowed (54.5), fewest pitches thrown per batter (3.65) and most run support per nine innings (6.0)

Andy Pettitte

2004 Season

Last year was one of Andy Pettitte's most disappointing in baseball, and he managed only 15 starts, many of them under severe duress. He first went on the disabled list with a strained elbow in April, then went back on the DL in late May with a strained forearm. He gamely came back to make five starts in July, but was pitching with pain most of the time. Finally, in mid-August he succumbed to the elbow injury and eventually had surgery to repair a torn flexor tendon.

Pitching

Pettitte throws a fastball and a cutter that is probably his best pitch. He throws the cutter to both sides of the plate and also has a good curve and a changeup, and he moves all of his pitches in and out at varying speeds. Pettitte can throw in the low 90s but rarely had his normal velocity most of last season. He depended much of the time on moving the ball in and out and trying to coax hitters into swinging at bad pitches. The Astros admired his toughness and willingness to fight through the pain.

Defense & Hitting

Pettitte has a very good pickoff move to first base. He also covers first well and can field bunts. He has never been much of a hitter and suffered his first injury, a strained elbow, on a checked swing in his first game of the season. He did have three sacrifice bunts and a pair of RBI last season.

2005 Outlook

Pettitte began throwing off a flat surface in December and should be fit by spring training. The team is looking for that magnificent quartet of starters it anticipated last season with Roy Oswalt, Roger Clemens, Pettitte and Wade Miller. Team officials noted Pettitte's surgery was the same operation Billy Wagner had in 2000, and Wagner came back to save 39 games the following year. If Pettitte returns that strong, he will be a superb No. 2 or 3 starter.

Position: SP
Bats: L **Throws:** L
Ht: 6' 5" **Wt:** 225

Opening Day Age: 32
Born: 6/15/72 in Baton Rouge, LA
ML Seasons: 10
Pronunciation: pet-it

Overall Statistics

	W	L	Pct.	ERA	G	GS	Sv	IP	H	BB	SO	HR	Avg
'04	6	4	.600	3.90	15	15	0	83.0	71	31	79	8	.226
Car.	155	82	.654	3.94	298	291	0	1875.2	1972	610	1354	151	.271

2004 Pitching Profile

	Andy Pettitte	NL Average
Overall Strike %	63.4	62.5
1st Pitch Strike %	57.8	58.5
Ratio	1.23	1.39
Strikeouts per 9 IP	8.57	6.74
Walks per 9 IP	3.36	3.38
Home Runs per 9 IP	0.87	1.11
Strikeout/Walk Ratio	2.55	1.99
Groundball/Flyball Ratio	1.88	1.25

2004 Situational Stats

	W	L	ERA	Sv	IP		AB	H	HR	RBI	Avg
Home	2	4	5.80	0	40.1	LHB	69	20	3	8	.290
Road	4	0	2.11	0	42.2	RHB	245	51	5	27	.208
First Half	5	2	4.14	0	54.1	Sc Pos	74	18	3	27	.243
Scnd Half	1	2	3.45	0	28.2	Clutch	9	1	1	2	.111

2004 Rankings (National League)

- 4th in lowest batting average allowed vs. righthanded batters

Brad Ausmus

Position: C
Bats: R **Throws:** R
Ht: 5'11" **Wt:** 190

Opening Day Age: 35
Born: 4/14/69 in New Haven, CT
ML Seasons: 12
Pronunciation: AHHS-muss

Overall Statistics

	G	AB	R	H	D	T	HR	RBI	SB	BB	SO	Avg	OBP	Slg
'04	129	403	38	100	14	1	5	31	2	33	56	.248	.306	.325
Car.	1443	4730	580	1207	205	30	68	461	87	464	764	.255	.326	.354

2004 Situational Stats

	AB	H	HR	RBI	Avg		AB	H	HR	RBI	Avg
Home	197	42	2	9	.213	LHP	78	24	2	12	.308
Road	206	58	3	22	.282	RHP	325	76	3	19	.234
First Half	245	58	3	18	.237	Sc Pos	97	20	1	24	.206
Scnd Half	158	42	2	13	.266	Clutch	53	16	0	5	.302

2004 Season

Brad Ausmus had another bad season at the plate, and at times it was dismal. Under new hitting coach Gary Gaetti, he seemed to rejuvenate in August. But he fell back to .233 in September/October when he spent more time on the bench as manager Phil Garner let Raul Chavez start more games.

Hitting, Baserunning & Defense

Ausmus seemed less aggressive at the plate last season and didn't consistently get on top of the ball most of the time. He still has a good eye and is strong enough but rarely gets good elevation on the ball. The Astros feel he needs to work on turning his hips more and cut down on sliding his foot forward as he swings. Defensively, he does not have the Gold Glove arm of old. His fielding was comparable to the past, however, and he is very good on not letting the ball get by him. He's a slow baserunner.

2005 Outlook

With John Buck, the once heir apparent, lost in the Carlos Beltran trade, the team needs Ausmus to help the young catchers and pitchers mature. But if he continues to struggle at the plate, expect him to see less time behind it.

Brandon Backe

Position: RP
Bats: R **Throws:** R
Ht: 6' 0" **Wt:** 180

Opening Day Age: 26
Born: 4/5/78 in Galveston, TX
ML Seasons: 3
Pronunciation: BACK-ee

Overall Statistics

	W	L	Pct.	ERA	G	GS	Sv	IP	H	BB	SO	HR	Avg
'04	5	3	.625	4.30	33	9	0	67.0	75	27	54	10	.290
Car.	6	4	.600	4.98	70	9	0	124.2	130	59	96	19	.275

2004 Situational Stats

	W	L	ERA	Sv	IP		AB	H	HR	RBI	Avg
Home	4	1	2.61	0	38.0	LHB	101	35	4	10	.347
Road	1	2	6.52	0	29.0	RHB	158	40	6	18	.253
First Half	1	1	5.32	0	22.0	Sc Pos	59	15	2	18	.254
Scnd Half	4	2	3.80	0	45.0	Clutch	9	2	1	1	.222

2004 Season

Brandon Backe was the pitching sensation of last season, a find no one expected at the beginning of the year. He started out in New Orleans, then came up in mid-April and May to pitch some out of the bullpen. In September and August, he was more than anyone could have hoped for as he went 4-2 as a starter and pitched a couple of spectacular games in the playoffs.

Pitching, Defense & Hitting

Backe has four legitimate major league pitches in a fastball, cutter, slider and changeup. He tops out at 94 MPH, but normally sits around 91. He uses a four- and a two-seam fastball, and changes speeds on them. The team was especially impressed with his aggressiveness and his ability to be undaunted under pressure. Backe started in the Tampa Bay organization as a position player and is a plus fielder with a good bat.

2005 Outlook

The Astros believe Backe can be no worse than No. 4 or 5 in the rotation, and down the road perhaps even better than that. Since he has pitched extensively for only the last two seasons, his arm has little wear and tear and the team believes his future is bright.

Carlos Hernandez

Position: SP
Bats: B **Throws:** L
Ht: 5'10" **Wt:** 200

Opening Day Age: 24
Born: 4/22/80 in Guacara, VZ
ML Seasons: 3

Overall Statistics

	W	L	Pct.	ERA	G	GS	Sv	IP	H	BB	SO	HR	Avg
'04	1	3	.250	6.43	9	9	0	42.0	50	23	26	11	.303
Car.	9	8	.529	4.54	35	33	0	170.2	173	91	136	23	.264

2004 Situational Stats

	W	L	ERA	Sv	IP		AB	H	HR	RBI	Avg
Home	0	0	5.40	0	10.0	LHB	37	12	4	9	.324
Road	1	3	6.75	0	32.0	RHB	128	38	7	20	.297
First Half	0	0	–	0	0.0	Sc Pos	41	9	2	17	.220
Scnd Half	1	3	6.43	0	42.0	Clutch	2	0	0	0	.000

2004 Season

Carlos Hernandez had poor major league results in his return from rotator cuff surgery in 2003. He stayed at Triple-A much of the season as he couldn't crank his fastball over 88 MPH most of the time. In August, he was called up and had a couple of fairly good starts. But the team needed him badly in the stretch run and he quickly proved he didn't have it.

Pitching, Defense & Hitting

Hernandez once was one of the Astros' brightest pitching prospects, with a lively fastball and a curve that dropped off the table. But shoulder surgery knocked him out of 2003 and he was very slow to come back last year. Club officials thought that might have helped start him down the road to being a better overall pitcher, since he had to learn to pitch more than just be a power thrower. He's an average fielder and not much of a hitter.

2005 Outlook

The extensive surgery Hernandez had usually doesn't allow a player to return to full strength until the second season. If Hernandez can get his fastball up to pre-surgery velocity in the mid-90s, club officials still think he can be an effective major league pitcher once again.

Mike Lamb

Position: 3B/1B
Bats: L **Throws:** R
Ht: 6' 1" **Wt:** 190

Opening Day Age: 29
Born: 8/9/75 in West Covina, CA
ML Seasons: 5

Overall Statistics

	G	AB	R	H	D	T	HR	RBI	SB	BB	SO	Avg	OBP	Slg
'04	112	278	38	80	14	3	14	58	1	31	63	.288	.356	.511
Car.	469	1407	202	398	70	5	33	175	4	114	205	.283	.340	.410

2004 Situational Stats

	AB	H	HR	RBI	Avg		AB	H	HR	RBI	Avg
Home	125	44	8	36	.352	LHP	43	15	2	13	.349
Road	153	36	6	22	.235	RHP	235	65	12	45	.277
First Half	117	36	6	27	.308	Sc Pos	89	28	4	42	.315
Scnd Half	161	44	8	31	.273	Clutch	46	14	1	9	.304

2004 Season

Though he wasn't a full-time player, Mike Lamb set career highs in home runs and RBI, and his .288 average was his best for any full season. He also showed his versatility by starting at first, second and third.

Hitting, Baserunning & Defense

Lamb's hitting was one of the team's brightest surprises last season. In April, he drove in a career-high six runs in one game. Then he stepped in when Morgan Ensberg was sidelined by back spasms in late August and hit .293 with five homers and 17 RBI as the club went on a 17-4 tear. He was an excellent pinch-hitter and his 10 pinch-hit RBI were seventh in the majors. But Lamb's defensive shortcomings became a glaring problem. Though he started only 65 games, 53 of them at third, he led the team in errors with 14 and at times seemed lost at third base. He also was slow on the bases.

2005 Outlook

Team officials like Lamb's clubhouse presence and upbeat attitude. They hope he can settle into being a utility player and a top-notch pinch-hitter. If they have to resort to him playing third base on a daily basis for any reason, they know they're in trouble.

Jason Lane

Position: LF/RF/CF
Bats: R **Throws:** L
Ht: 6' 2" **Wt:** 220

Opening Day Age: 28
Born: 12/22/76 in Santa Rosa, CA
ML Seasons: 3

Overall Statistics

	G	AB	R	H	D	T	HR	RBI	SB	BB	SO	Avg	OBP	Slg
'04	107	136	21	37	10	2	4	19	1	16	33	.272	.348	.463
Car.	169	232	38	65	15	3	12	39	2	26	47	.280	.351	.526

2004 Situational Stats

	AB	H	HR	RBI	Avg		AB	H	HR	RBI	Avg
Home	76	21	4	11	.276	LHP	50	14	2	7	.280
Road	60	16	0	8	.267	RHP	86	23	2	12	.267
First Half	90	20	2	8	.222	Sc Pos	39	13	1	16	.333
Scnd Half	46	17	2	11	.370	Clutch	20	8	1	6	.400

2004 Season

Jason Lane has long been compared to Lance Berkman by the Astros organization. Though most observers agree he is ready for a starting job, the team hasn't had a spot for him in the outfield, so his promise has been on hold. He saw most of his playing time as a pinch-hitter or late-inning defensive replacement last season.

Hitting, Baserunning & Defense

Lane has natural power, good speed and is one of the team's best competitors. Last season, he struggled early with some mechanics in his swing and some in the organization began to wonder if he could hit. Basically, he had to unlearn some bad habits. But he showed later in the season that he still has the raw power and exceptional hand-eye coordination. He's a plus outfielder who can chase down most hits and has a strong arm. He's not threat to steal.

2005 Outlook

Officials in the organization love Lane's competitiveness and still think he is destined for stardom. They say he has "stupid" power and can crush the ball when his swing is right. He's the type who might turn out to be the team's best power hitter, one they believe can hit 40-50 home runs a season.

Dan Miceli

Position: RP
Bats: R **Throws:** R
Ht: 6' 0" **Wt:** 215

Opening Day Age: 34
Born: 9/9/70 in Newark, NJ
ML Seasons: 12
Pronunciation: muh-SELL-ee

Overall Statistics

	W	L	Pct.	ERA	G	GS	Sv	IP	H	BB	SO	HR	Avg
'04	6	6	.500	3.59	74	0	2	77.2	74	27	83	10	.247
Car.	41	48	.461	4.47	579	9	35	650.1	640	277	595	88	.257

2004 Situational Stats

	W	L	ERA	Sv	IP		AB	H	HR	RBI	Avg
Home	2	3	4.97	1	38.0	LHB	150	46	7	22	.307
Road	4	3	2.27	1	39.2	RHB	149	28	3	14	.188
First Half	3	4	3.81	1	49.2	Sc Pos	88	18	1	26	.205
Scnd Half	3	2	3.21	1	28.0	Clutch	175	43	5	20	.246

2004 Season

The Astros leaned on Dan Miceli and his experienced arm much of the season. He ended up with a career-high 74 appearances, but Miceli seemed overworked late in the season. Then he came down with conjunctivitis (pink eye) in both eyes, a highly unusual condition that was so severe he went on the disabled list. Still, in September he was at his best, not allowing an earned run in any of his 11 appearances.

Pitching, Defense & Hitting

Miceli is a competitive pitcher who relies on a fastball in the 90-91 MPH range, a slider and changeup. The Astros felt very good when he faced righthanders, who hit only .188 against him. He is slow to come off the mound for bunts, has difficulty covering first on grounders to the right side and has an ordinary move to first. His hitting, like most relievers, is a non-factor. He's 2-for-22 in his career, although one of those hits came in his two at-bats last season.

2005 Outlook

The Astros liked Miceli's work, but couldn't come to a quick agreement with him and decided not to offer arbitration. He's a 10-year veteran who could add stability to some team's bullpen.

Pete Munro

Position: SP
Bats: R **Throws:** R
Ht: 6' 3" **Wt:** 210

Opening Day Age: 29
Born: 6/14/75 in Flushing, NY
ML Seasons: 5
Pronunciation: mun-ROW

Overall Statistics

	W	L	Pct.	ERA	G	GS	Sv	IP	H	BB	SO	HR	Avg
'04	4	7	.364	5.15	21	19	0	99.2	120	26	63	12	.302
Car.	13	19	.406	4.88	120	40	0	315.1	380	114	189	31	.304

2004 Situational Stats

	W	L	ERA	Sv	IP		AB	H	HR	RBI	Avg
Home	3	3	5.02	0	52.0	LHB	184	62	8	24	.337
Road	1	4	5.29	0	47.2	RHB	213	58	4	23	.272
First Half	1	2	4.45	0	30.1	Sc Pos	108	24	1	32	.222
Scnd Half	3	5	5.45	0	69.1	Clutch	2	2	0	0	1.000

2004 Season

The journeyman righthander was signed by Houston June 3 after the Twins had released him, and after injuries decimated the starting rotation, Pete Munro ended up being the No. 4 man through sheer necessity. The team tried to work around him in the playoffs, but he did start two games, pitching well in Game 2 of the NLCS but getting shelled in Game 6.

Pitching, Defense & Hitting

Munro is a grinder who can be effective when his sinker is dropping. He throws a two-seamer in the 87-90 MPH range and also has a cutter, curve and changeup. He has to have absolute control of his pitches or he will get hit hard. The Astros like his savvy, his competitiveness and his matter-of-fact approach. He pitched mostly out of the bullpen in 2003 and could return there in the future. He is a little slow coming off the mound and has never mastered hitting.

2005 Outlook

Munro might have a shot at making the team's bullpen as a long reliever, but he does not figure in the starting rotation unless numerous injuries again hit the team. He will be a long shot to return if everyone's healthy and the bullpen is improved.

Tim Redding

Position: SP/RP
Bats: R **Throws:** R
Ht: 6' 0" **Wt:** 200

Opening Day Age: 27
Born: 2/12/78 in Rochester, NY
ML Seasons: 4

Overall Statistics

	W	L	Pct.	ERA	G	GS	Sv	IP	H	BB	SO	HR	Avg
'04	5	7	.417	5.72	27	17	0	100.2	125	43	56	15	.309
Car.	21	28	.429	4.75	91	72	0	405.2	444	167	290	52	.279

2004 Situational Stats

	W	L	ERA	Sv	IP		AB	H	HR	RBI	Avg
Home	2	4	5.82	0	51.0	LHB	171	59	8	38	.345
Road	3	3	5.62	0	49.2	RHB	233	66	7	24	.283
First Half	3	6	6.07	0	75.2	Sc Pos	98	33	5	47	.337
Scnd Half	2	1	4.68	0	25.0	Clutch	8	4	1	3	.500

2004 Season

Tim Redding had a disappointing season, both for himself and the organization. He was expected to be a solid No. 5 starter, if not better. But he stumbled out of the gate, and eventually was sent to Triple-A before coming back up in September and spending most of his time in the bullpen.

Pitching, Defense & Hitting

Redding might be the team's biggest pitching enigma. During an impressive rise through the minors, he was expected to one day be one of the team's best pitchers, with a two- and four-seam fastball, hard-breaking curve and slider. But he also had a reputation for blowing up when things went badly. He had command problems all last year and team officials aren't sure why. Redding is a fair hitter who laid down the sacrifice bunt well in 2003, and an ordinary fielder. Basestealers pretty much have their way with him.

2005 Outlook

Redding will be given another chance to make the big league roster, but no one is laying bets on him. Astros officials still believe he has great stuff and can be a strong No. 4 or 5 pitcher. But he must learn to control his emotions and get command of his pitches.

Jose Vizcaino

Position: SS/2B/3B
Bats: B **Throws:** R
Ht: 6' 1" **Wt:** 190

Opening Day Age: 37
Born: 3/26/68 in San Cristobal, DR
ML Seasons: 16
Pronunciation: vis-kie-ee-no

Overall Statistics

	G	AB	R	H	D	T	HR	RBI	SB	BB	SO	Avg	OBP	Slg
'04	138	358	34	98	21	3	3	33	1	20	39	.274	.311	.374
Car.	1642	5050	599	1374	188	45	33	449	72	346	675	.272	.319	.347

2004 Situational Stats

	AB	H	HR	RBI	Avg		AB	H	HR	RBI	Avg
Home	165	45	1	15	.273	LHP	68	17	1	8	.250
Road	193	53	2	18	.275	RHP	290	81	2	25	.279
First Half	157	47	2	12	.299	Sc Pos	78	22	0	25	.282
Scnd Half	201	51	1	21	.254	Clutch	61	16	0	6	.262

2004 Season

The versatile Jose Vizcaino once again saved the Astros when he stepped in for injured shortstop Adam Everett in August and started most of the rest of the season. Oddly, Everett broke the same ulna bone Vizcaino had broken the year before. Vizcaino started slowly in his return from the injury last year, hovering around .200 much of the first three months of the season. But he finished strong, hitting .297 in August, but hit only .191 in the playoffs.

Hitting, Baserunning & Defense

Vizcaino is a good contact hitter who shoots singles all over the field. He also had his best season since 1997 in producing extra-base hits with 27. As a utility infielder, Vizcaino is very valuable to the team starting at every infield position last season. He's no Adam Everett in the field, but he's adequate at short and probably best at second base. Vizcaino has average speed and is no threat to steal, but he is a smart baserunner.

2005 Outlook

Needing insurance for injuries and rookie second baseman Chris Burke, the Astros re-signed Vizcaino to a one-year contract in December. He proved valuable in 2004, and he could see as much playing time in 2005.

Dan Wheeler

Position: RP
Bats: R **Throws:** R
Ht: 6' 3" **Wt:** 222

Opening Day Age: 27
Born: 12/10/77 in Providence, RI
ML Seasons: 5

Overall Statistics

	W	L	Pct.	ERA	G	GS	Sv	IP	H	BB	SO	HR	Avg
'04	3	1	.750	4.29	46	1	0	65.0	76	20	55	10	.289
Car.	6	9	.400	4.95	111	9	2	187.1	219	66	151	28	.290

2004 Situational Stats

	W	L	ERA	Sv	IP		AB	H	HR	RBI	Avg
Home	1	0	3.43	0	21.0	LHB	108	41	7	22	.380
Road	2	1	4.70	0	44.0	RHB	155	35	3	20	.226
First Half	3	0	4.42	0	38.2	Sc Pos	77	23	2	30	.299
Scnd Half	0	1	4.10	0	26.1	Clutch	43	12	0	3	.279

2004 Season

Dan Wheeler was a late-season pickup in a trade with the Mets and was an instant surprise. After he had recorded a so-so 4.80 ERA in 32 relief appearances with New York, he came to Houston and didn't allow a run in 12 of his 14 appearances and was a factor in the team's stretch run.

Pitching, Defense & Hitting

Wheeler throws a fastball, slider and split-finger pitch, but he doesn't overpower anyone. He impressed the Astros with his calm, self-assured approach to pitching. He throws the fastball at 89-90 MPH and tries mostly to move it around the strike zone. He kept his fastball down in the zone much of the time with Houston, and that made him very effective. He is aggressive and frequently gets ahead of hitters because of it. His defense is average and he has only one major league hit in his seven at-bats.

2005 Outlook

Unless the team brings in a lot of new blood in the bullpen, Wheeler probably has a shot at making the roster this season if he can continue to throw the way he did late last year. He's far from a lock, but the Astros like his demeanor and competitiveness.

Jason Alfaro (Pos: SS, Age: 27, Bats: R)

	G	AB	R	H	D	T	HR	RBI	SB	BB	SO	Avg	OBP	Slg
'04	7	11	1	2	0	0	0	0	0	0	5	.182	.182	.182
Car.	7	11	1	2	0	0	0	0	0	0	5	.182	.182	.182

Alfaro had an excellent year at Triple-A New Orleans last year. His .325 batting average was good for ninth place in the Pacific Coast League, a solid feat considering New Orleans is a PCL pitchers' park. The Blue Jays signed him in November. 2005 Outlook: C

Eric Bruntlett (Pos: SS, Age: 27, Bats: R)

	G	AB	R	H	D	T	HR	RBI	SB	BB	SO	Avg	OBP	Slg
'04	45	52	14	13	2	0	4	8	4	7	13	.250	.328	.519
Car.	76	106	17	27	5	0	5	12	4	7	23	.255	.293	.443

Carried as the seventh infielder out of spring training, Bruntlett surprisingly displayed a modicum of pop at the major league level. He homered every 13 at-bats, compared to every 55 at Triple-A New Orleans. Don't be fooled by the small sample size, Bruntlett is no Jeff Kent. 2005 Outlook: C

Kirk Bullinger (Pos: RHP, Age: 35)

	W	L	Pct.	ERA	G	GS	Sv	IP	H	BB	SO	HR	Avg
'04	1	0	1.000	6.16	27	0	1	30.2	36	10	11	5	.286
Car.	2	0	1.000	6.53	49	0	1	51.0	63	13	22	8	.296

Bullinger more than doubled his career output in almost every pitching category in 2004. The 13-year minor league veteran actually was offered a legitimate bullpen spot, rather than the usual cup of coffee. The results left much to be desired. 2005 Outlook: C

Raul Chavez (Pos: C, Age: 32, Bats: R)

	G	AB	R	H	D	T	HR	RBI	SB	BB	SO	Avg	OBP	Slg
'04	64	162	9	34	8	0	0	23	0	10	38	.210	.256	.259
Car.	117	278	19	64	12	1	2	34	2	16	56	.230	.273	.302

Chavez spent the whole season in the big leagues for the first time in his career last season. His hitting was anemic, especially against lefthanders, who owned him to the tune of .139/.184/.167. Chavez does have his pluses defensively, and will backup Brad Ausmus again this year. 2005 Outlook: C

Brandon Duckworth (Pos: RHP, Age: 29)

	W	L	Pct.	ERA	G	GS	Sv	IP	H	BB	SO	HR	Avg
'04	1	2	.333	6.86	19	6	0	39.1	55	13	23	11	.337
Car.	16	20	.444	5.09	84	64	0	364.1	377	155	298	51	.268

Traded to the Astros in the Billy Wagner deal, Duckworth is not a good fit for Minute Maid Park. His proclivity to give up the longball was exhibited last season by his colossal 2.52 HR/9 rate. For Duckworth to have success, he must return to the groundball pitcher of old. 2005 Outlook: C

Jared Fernandez (Pos: RHP, Age: 33)

	W	L	Pct.	ERA	G	GS	Sv	IP	H	BB	SO	HR	Avg
'04	0	0	—	54.00	2	1	0	1.0	6	5	0	0	.750
Car.	4	7	.364	4.75	33	17	0	102.1	115	47	60	8	.287

For every Tim Wakefield, there's probably eight or nine Jared Fernandez'. Fernandez, a knuckleballer, has had a tough time convincing organizations that his specialty pitch is not merely a gimmick. His 87 minor league wins and 4.37 ERA have not swayed hardened opinions. 2005 Outlook: D

Mike Gallo (Pos: LHP, Age: 27)

	W	L	Pct.	ERA	G	GS	Sv	IP	H	BB	SO	HR	Avg
'04	2	0	1.000	4.74	69	0	0	49.1	55	20	34	12	.284
Car.	3	0	1.000	4.08	101	0	0	79.1	83	30	50	15	.278

Gallo was the only lefthanded arm in the Astros' bullpen for much of 2004. He averaged far less than an inning per appearance because of Phil Garner's penchant for using him for only one batter. Gallo will occupy the same role this year. 2005 Outlook: B

Jeremy Griffiths (Pos: RHP, Age: 27)

	W	L	Pct.	ERA	G	GS	Sv	IP	H	BB	SO	HR	Avg
'04	0	0	—	10.38	1	1	0	4.1	4	3	5	1	.235
Car.	1	4	.200	7.35	10	7	0	45.1	61	22	30	6	.319

Griffiths was part of the June trade that sent Richard Hidalgo to the Mets. Griffiths reminds some of Jeff Juden because of his physically imposing stature, but he lacks the dominant fastball that oftentimes accompanies men of his size. He most likely will begin this season in Triple-A. 2005 Outlook: C

Chad Harville (Pos: RHP, Age: 28)

	W	L	Pct.	ERA	G	GS	Sv	IP	H	BB	SO	HR	Avg
'04	3	2	.600	4.69	59	0	0	55.2	56	27	46	8	.257
Car.	4	4	.500	5.13	98	0	1	94.2	101	54	81	13	.272

The revolving door that was the 2004 Houston bullpen had one permanent fixture in Harville. He was fourth on the Astros' team in appearances and a viable righthanded setup option for Phil Garner. 2005 Outlook: B

Darren Oliver (Pos: LHP, Age: 34)

	W	L	Pct.	ERA	G	GS	Sv	IP	H	BB	SO	HR	Avg
'04	3	3	.500	5.94	27	10	0	72.2	87	21	46	14	.305
Car.	87	79	.524	5.07	306	228	2	1407.0	1591	582	834	172	.288

Picked up near the trading deadline as insurance for the ailing Andy Pettitte, Oliver was supposed to provide the Astros with lefthanded depth. Instead, he only added to the rotation of injured pitchers looking for the next e-stim treatment. A balky shoulder was the culprit. 2005 Outlook: C

Orlando Palmeiro (Pos: LF/RF, Age: 36, Bats: L)

	G	AB	R	H	D	T	HR	RBI	SB	BB	SO	Avg	OBP	Slg
'04	102	133	19	32	5	0	3	12	2	18	19	.241	.344	.346
Car.	888	1909	260	528	87	11	9	183	34	228	182	.277	.356	.348

Palmeiro has made a solid career for himself as one of the superior pinch-hitter/defensive-replacement guys out there. He's not going to hit for much power, but he makes consistent contact and can be counted on in a pinch. His 12.2 PA/K and .350 pinch-hit OBP prove this. He re-signed with the Astros in December. 2005 Outlook: B

Chad Qualls (Pos: RHP, Age: 26)

	W	L	Pct.	ERA	G	GS	Sv	IP	H	BB	SO	HR	Avg
'04	4	0	1.000	3.55	25	0	1	33.0	34	8	24	3	.266
Car.	4	0	1.000	3.55	25	0	1	33.0	34	8	24	3	.266

The Astros have pushed Qualls quickly through their system. In 2002, he led the Double-A Texas League with 142 strikeouts, less than a year removed from the Class-A affiliate. Qualls also responded well to a 2004 midseason move to the bullpen. He should be a factor in 2005. 2005 Outlook: B

Russ Springer (Pos: RHP, Age: 36)

	W	L	Pct.	ERA	G	GS	Sv	IP	H	BB	SO	HR	Avg
'04	0	1	.000	2.63	16	0	0	13.2	15	6	9	1	.278
Car.	20	34	.370	5.12	384	27	8	562.2	579	258	505	86	.264

Roger Clemens was not the only pitcher to come out of retirement to join the Astros for the 2004 season. Springer, who also retired after 2003 to spend more time with his family, came out of retirement in June, and by August was helping in Houston's playoff push. 2005 Outlook: C

Chris Tremie (Pos: C, Age: 35, Bats: R)

	G	AB	R	H	D	T	HR	RBI	SB	BB	SO	Avg	OBP	Slg
'04	1	0	0	0	0	0	0	0	0	0	0	–	–	–
Car.	22	41	3	6	1	0	0	1	0	4	7	.146	.222	.171

Tremie has toiled away for 13 years in the minors, hitting .221/.295/.299 over his career. Born in Houston, he is a sentimental favorite with the hometown crowd. He was one of two former University of Houston catchers to appear in a major league game last year. 2005 Outlook: D

Houston

Organization Overview:

In many ways, the Astros are in a similar position as the Cardinals, the team Houston met in the NLCS last season. While both organizations excelled on the major league level, their minor league systems haven't exactly been highly regarded the past couple years. In a division that includes the Cubs, a club with a fertile farm system, the lack of prospects eventually may catch up to last year's playoff teams. Houston has been able to graduate a number of righthanded pitchers in recent years, and it did produce a catcher (John Buck) who helped land Carlos Beltran. The Astros have drafted a lot of pitchers and restored some depth, and have upgraded the up-the-middle positions. But the organization still would like more pure power, lefthanded bats and southpaw pitching.

Matt Albers

Position: P
Bats: L **Throws:** R
Ht: 6' 0" **Wt:** 195
Opening Day Age: 22
Born: 1/20/83 in Houston, TX

Recent Statistics

	W	L	ERA	G	GS	Sv	IP	H	R	BB	SO	HR
2003 A Tri-City	5	4	2.92	15	14	0	86.1	69	37	25	94	1
2004 A Lexington	8	3	3.31	22	21	0	111.1	95	51	57	140	3

Like Roy Oswalt and Tim Redding, Albers is a relatively short righthanded pitcher who the Astros haven't been reluctant to develop. All three are around 6-feet, though Albers is a burly guy who has had a tendency to gain weight in the past. Nevertheless, he's surprisingly athletic for his build and boasts perhaps the best pure arm strength in the system. His active fastball sits comfortably at 94 MPH, and he's developed a feel for his breaking pitch. Since signing as a draft-and-follow in 2002, Albers has averaged nearly 11 strikeouts per nine innings, and he's rarely been hurt by the longball. If he continues to put things together, he has a chance to be a frontline starter in the big leagues.

Ezequiel Astacio

Position: P
Bats: R **Throws:** R
Ht: 6' 3" **Wt:** 156
Opening Day Age: 25
Born: 11/4/79 in Hato Mayor, DR

Recent Statistics

	W	L	ERA	G	GS	Sv	IP	H	R	BB	SO	HR
2003 A Clearwater	15	5	3.29	25	22	0	147.2	140	60	29	83	9
2004 AA Round Rock	13	10	3.89	28	28	0	176.0	155	89	56	185	12

Along with Brandon Duckworth and Taylor Buchholz, Astacio was part of the bounty the Astros received from the Phillies for Billy Wagner. And Astacio may turn out to be the biggest payoff for Houston. A year after leading the high Class-A Florida State League in wins in 2003, Astacio moved up to Double-A and paced the Texas League in strikeouts. He's a power pitcher who can cross-seam opposing hitters up the ladder. He features two- and four-seam fastballs that possess movement and late life, as well as a hard curve with bite. He has added a split-finger pitch, which he took to quickly, and that's now a strikeout pitch. At age 25, he's certainly ready for Triple-A, and possibly more.

Taylor Buchholz

Position: P
Bats: R **Throws:** R
Ht: 6' 3" **Wt:** 220
Opening Day Age: 23
Born: 10/13/81 in Lower Merion, PA

Recent Statistics

	W	L	ERA	G	GS	Sv	IP	H	R	BB	SO	HR
2003 AA Reading	9	11	3.55	25	24	0	144.2	146	62	33	114	14
2004 AAA New Orl'ns	6	7	5.23	20	17	0	98.0	107	60	29	74	16

Another part of the package acquired in the Billy Wagner trade, Buchholz has tended to pitch a league over his age. He often has been a slow starter, and 2004 was not an exception. However, he didn't pack it in, and despite a fatigued shoulder at the end of the season, he showed positive signs in his first season at Triple-A. Buchholz is a high-fastball pitcher who's working on a two-seamer. He has a good feel for a hard curveball, can change speeds off it, and it's a strikeout pitch. His changeup has a ways to go, and he needs to work on his approach to lefthanded batters. Still, Buchholz' ceiling remains high, and he's close to challenging for a major league job.

Chris Burke

Position: 2B
Bats: R **Throws:** R
Ht: 5' 11" **Wt:** 180
Opening Day Age: 25
Born: 3/11/80 in Louisville, KY

Recent Statistics

	G	AB	R	H	D	T	HR	RBI	SB	BB	SO	Avg
2004 AAA New Orl'ns	123	483	93	152	33	6	16	52	37	55	76	.315
2004 NL Houston	17	17	2	1	0	0	0	.0	0	3	3	.059

Burke didn't miss a beat after moving up to Triple-A last year, setting career highs in nearly every offensive category. His 16 homers nearly doubled his previous career total in three professional seasons. Then again, Burke had shared the SEC lead with 20 homers in 2001, just before the Astros chose him with the 10th overall pick of that year's draft. Selected as a shortstop, he's now made the transition to second base, where he may not show much flair but does possess nice instincts. Burke prepares well and offers good leadership skills. He profiles as a No. 2 hitter—he can steal a base, lay down a bunt and exhibits enough power to be dangerous. With Jeff Kent off to Los Angeles, Burke could take over at second base for Houston in 2005.

Raymar Diaz

Position: P
Bats: R **Throws:** R
Ht: 6' 8" **Wt:** 195

Opening Day Age: 21
Born: 11/13/83 in San
Lurce, PR

Recent Statistics

	W	L	ERA	G	GS	Sv	IP	H	R	BB	SO	HR
2003 R Martinsville	4	0	0.90	19	0	5	30.0	17	4	13	29	1
2004 A Lexington	1	3	4.43	24	1	2	42.2	31	21	26	37	3
2004 A Tri-City	6	5	3.19	15	15	0	79.0	70	36	31	70	9

Diaz was selected in the 47th round of the 2002 draft out of a junior college in Texas, but he didn't sign with Houston until the following spring. He's a very tall, loose kid who's still going through the development process. Despite his size, he's athletic and can repeat his delivery. His heat is nothing special right now, with a fastball in the 89-92 MPH range. But he can change speeds off his curveball, has added a slider and has developed a split-finger pitch on his own. He seemed to lose velocity as a starter, so it's possible that working in relief may be his best role. He also might add some miles to his fastball as he fills out.

Hector Gimenez

Position: C
Bats: B **Throws:** R
Ht: 5' 10" **Wt:** 180

Opening Day Age: 22
Born: 9/28/82 in
Varacuy, VZ

Recent Statistics

	G	AB	R	H	D	T	HR	RBI	SB	BB	SO	Avg
2003 A Salem	109	381	41	94	17	1	7	54	2	29	75	.247
2004 AA Round Rock	97	331	38	81	16	3	6	45	2	18	64	.245

Whatever pain the Astros may have suffered when losing John Buck in the Carlos Beltran deal was lessened by the presence of Gimenez. Gimenez played at Double-A at age 21 in 2004, and showed why he's considered the best defensive catcher in Houston's system. He has good hands and his arm strength is a plus. Gimenez is a switch-hitter with some power potential. Control of the strike zone is an issue, as he's prone to chase bad pitches. Ironically, he'll also take some good pitches, waiting for the perfect offering, and the Astros would like him to be more aggressive. With Buck out of the way, it appears Gimenez is the catching heir apparent in Houston.

Fernando Nieve

Position: P
Bats: R **Throws:** R
Ht: 6' 0" **Wt:** 170

Opening Day Age: 22
Born: 7/15/82 in Puerto
Cabello, VZ

Recent Statistics

	W	L	ERA	G	GS	Sv	IP	H	R	BB	SO	HR
2003 A Lexington	14	9	3.65	28	28	0	150.1	133	69	65	144	10
2004 A Salem	10	6	2.96	24	24	0	149.0	136	52	40	117	3
2004 AA Round Rock	2	0	1.56	3	3	0	17.1	12	4	8	17	0

Not only is Nieve yet another Astros prospect signed out of Venezuela, but he's also another relatively short righthanded pitcher in their system. But his dynamic arm would get noticed regardless of his background or stature. Nieve throws four pitches, highlighted by a fastball that can reach 97 MPH and sits comfortably in the 93-94 range. The curveball, slider and changeup are his other offerings, with one question involving which breaking ball he'll eventually settle on. He tends to overthrow when ineffective, and often will have a power mentality in which he tries to strike out everyone. Pitching in the Venezuelan winter league seemed to put him over the hump in 2004, when Nieve eventually rose to Double-A and excelled in three starts there.

Willy Taveras

Position: OF
Bats: R **Throws:** R
Ht: 6' 0" **Wt:** 160

Opening Day Age: 23
Born: 12/25/81 in
Tenares, DR

Recent Statistics

	G	AB	R	H	D	T	HR	RBI	SB	BB	SO	Avg
2004 AA Round Rock	103	409	76	137	13	1	2	27	55	38	76	.335
2004 NL Houston	10	1	2	0	0	0	0	0	1	0	1	.000

Taveras signed with Cleveland as a 17-year-old in 1999. He got caught up in a backload of center-field prospects in the Indians' system, and the Astros plucked him in the Rule 5 major league draft following the 2003 season. Speed clearly is his best asset. His wheels make him an above-average defender with outstanding range, and he's stolen at least 50 bases each of the past three years. Although he's gotten stronger, Taveras doesn't try to hit the ball out of the park. He's a disciplined kid offensively, and his top-of-the-order speed and ability to get on base make him an effective weapon. At worst, he projects as a quality backup.

Others to Watch

Outfielder **Josh Anderson** (22) may be a victim of his own aggression at times, but he has the ability to become a good basestealer. His speed also comes in handy as a lefthanded hitter who can bunt and reach the gaps. . . Outfielder **Mitch Einertson** (18) knocked the stuffing out of the ball in the Rookie-level Appalachian League, where he tied a league record with 24 home runs. He's not a real big guy, but the ball comes off his bat hard and he's a legitimate home-run threat. He was an outfielder in his first pro season, and the Astros may explore infield options with him. . . Righthander **Juan Gutierrez** (21) features three quality pitches, including a 92-94 MPH fastball and hard slider. With a good feel for changing speeds, he challenges hitters and has a chance to be a top-of-the-rotation starter. . . At 6-foot-8 and 250 pounds, righthander **Jason Hirsh** (23) is a horse on the mound. He isn't afraid to work inside and his late-breaking curve has sharp downward action. But his low-90s fastball loses velocity after a few innings. . . **D.J. Houlton** (25) has no margin of error with his 88-90 MPH fastball, and he must work the edges of the plate. But he has the ability to pitch inside and his curveball can retire major leaguers. He was picked up by the Dodgers in the Rule 5 draft in December.

Dodger Stadium

Offense

Few parks suppress scoring more than Dodger Stadium. Though the dimensions are fairly standard down the lines and to center field, the gaps are deep. Also, the park is just 15 miles from the ocean, so the night air is heavy. Balls tend to travel farther in the daytime. And there is a lot of foul territory behind home plate and in front of the dugouts, though the club is putting in more luxury seats this season, thus cutting back on the foul ground.

Defense

The rubberized warning track that circled the field is being replaced by a conventional dirt-and-gravel track this season. Though most of the outfield plays true, the corners can be a little tricky, as balls can take superball-like bounces off the concrete base. By late summer, the hot desert sun has baked the infield, so there can be some tricky bounces.

Who It Helps the Most

Any and all pitchers love to work in Chavez Ravine. Jose Lima's revival was greatly aided by his home park, where he fashioned an ERA of 3.08. Jeff Weaver also regained his confidence thanks to some longballs falling short of the wall.

Who It Hurts the Most

Flyball hitters like Steve Finley are negatively affected by the park. Adrian Beltre also was hurt slightly by playing there, which is what made his 2004 season all the more spectacular.

Rookies & Newcomers

Jeff Kent won't find Dodger Stadium as friendly to righthanded hitters as Minute Maid Park. On the other hand, Brad Penny should enjoy his new digs, though he has been pitching in the equally pitcher-friendly confines of Pro Player Stadium. Hee Seop Choi came from Florida in the same trade as Penny, and some of the moonshots that his uppercut stroke produces will fall harmlessly into outfielders' gloves. If and when young pitchers such as Edwin Jackson and Greg Miller come up to stay, they should take advantage of their home park.

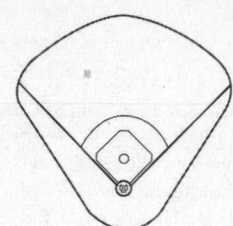

Dimensions: LF-330, LCF-385, CF-395, RCF-385, RF-330

Capacity: 56,000

Elevation: 340 feet

Surface: Grass

Foul Territory: Large

Park Factors

2004 Season

	Home Games Dodgers	Opp	Total	Away Games Dodgers	Opp	Total	Index
G	72	72	144	72	72	144	
Avg	.259	.246	.252	.265	.263	.264	95
AB	2393	2467	4860	2551	2391	4942	98
R	320	280	600	358	322	680	88
H	619	607	1226	677	630	1307	94
2B	88	95	183	113	132	245	76
3B	10	8	18	19	15	34	54
HR	90	79	169	91	79	170	101
BB	226	213	439	260	258	518	86
SO	467	498	965	513	461	974	101
E	36	45	81	33	53	86	94
E-Infield	27	37	64	21	44	65	98
LHB-Avg	.248	.278	.261	.251	.272	.259	101
LHB-HR	39	33	72	39	32	71	98
RHB-Avg	.271	.224	.244	.281	.259	.269	91
RHB-HR	51	46	97	52	47	99	104

2002-2004

	Home Games Dodgers	Opp	Total	Away Games Dodgers	Opp	Total	Index
G	216	216	432	216	216	432	
Avg	.250	.234	.242	.266	.253	.260	93
AB	7081	7303	14384	7699	7134	14833	97
R	833	767	1600	1000	903	1903	84
H	1772	1707	3479	2045	1805	3850	90
2B	305	267	572	386	370	756	78
3B	29	15	44	48	50	98	46
HR	209	216	425	222	196	418	105
BB	598	694	1292	648	768	1416	94
SO	1292	1635	2927	1411	1483	2894	104
E	137	148	285	117	161	278	103
E-Infield	111	130	241	89	126	215	112
LHB-Avg	.246	.240	.243	.253	.254	.254	96
LHB-HR	84	73	157	94	70	164	98
RHB-Avg	.254	.230	.241	.277	.252	.264	91
RHB-HR	125	143	268	128	126	254	110

2004 Rankings (National League)

- Lowest double factor
- Lowest walk factor
- Second-lowest RHB batting-average factor
- Third-lowest batting-average factor
- Third-lowest run factor
- Third-lowest hit factor
- Third-lowest triple factor

Jim Tracy

2004 Season

Jim Tracy will never publicly criticize one of his troops, and he puts his players in situations in which they can succeed. He tends to give his veterans a long leash, a perfect example being Hideo Nomo last season. But he also is open to young players winning him over, as both Jayson Werth and Yhency Brazoban earned more prominent roles.

Offense

Once Tracy decides to platoon at a position, such as Alex Cora and Jose Hernandez at second base, he sticks to it. While he always is looking to add some pop to his lineup, Tracy is quite willing to use a more speedy, aggressive bunch. He likes to move runners and has become less predictable in picking his spots. Late-inning situations are a chess match for Tracy, who tries to force opposing pitching changes.

Pitching & Defense

While Tracy keeps a close eye on pitch counts, he also lets a workhorse like Jeff Weaver go an extra frame or two. Once the skipper gets into the bullpen, the roles are strictly defined, and he had to scramble a bit after the trade of setup man Guillermo Mota. After a tough August loss in which the bullpen blew an eighth-inning lead, Tracy started bringing Eric Gagne in a bit earlier, and he has been known to ride a hot reliever to the point of exhaustion. When he gets a late lead, Tracy occasionally will go to his bench for a defensive replacement.

2005 Outlook

Tracy has gained the confidence of the new regime and will be working with a new multiyear contract. He has wrung out extra wins in each of his four seasons, and last year he led the team to its first postseason win since 1988. If Tracy and GM Paul DePodesta—who is not afraid to make dramatic changes if he feels that the club can be improved—can get and stay on the same page, the franchise has a shot at returning to greatness.

Born: 12/31/55 in Hamilton, OH

Playing Experience: 1980-1981, ChC

Managerial Experience: 4 seasons

Manager Statistics

Year	Team, Lg	W	L	Pct	GB	Finish
2004	Los Angeles, NL	93	69	.574	–	1st West
4 Seasons		356	292	.549	–	–

2004 Starting Pitchers by Days Rest

	<=3	4	5	6+
Dodgers Starts	0	90	40	25
Dodgers ERA	–	4.58	4.29	5.10
NL Avg Starts	2	82	46	23
NL ERA	4.58	4.35	4.28	4.73

2004 Situational Stats

	Jim Tracy	NL Average
Hit & Run Success %	36.2	38.0
Stolen Base Success %	71.3	71.7
Platoon Pct.	67.6	55.2
Defensive Subs	9	18
High-Pitch Outings	4	6
Quick/Slow Hooks	20/10	21/12
Sacrifice Attempts	90	99

2004 Rankings (National League)

- 1st in steals of home plate (1), squeeze plays (10), pinch-hitters used (295) and saves with over 1 inning pitched (16)
- 3rd in one-batter pitcher appearances (46)

Adrian Beltre

2004 Season

Despite finishing second in the voting to Barry Bonds, Adrian Beltre had an MVP-worthy season in 2004, posting career highs in almost every offensive category. A slow starter in 2003, Beltre hit .353 in April last season, with seven homers and 20 RBI. His 26 homers after the All-Star break led all major leaguers, and he ended up with as many homers as any third baseman has ever hit in one season.

Hitting

Responding well to new hitting coach Tim Wallach's tutelage in the spring, Beltre was a much more patient hitter last year, cutting his strikeouts and raising his walks. In 2004, Beltre used the entire field, and he has the power to leave any part of the park. Pitchers can get him to chase fastballs up and breaking stuff down and away, but he jumps on mistakes. He hit .347 versus righties last season and actually has fared better against them over his career than when facing southpaws.

Baserunning & Defense

Beltre played almost the entire 2004 season with bone spurs in his left ankle, an injury that most affected his baserunning. He ran with a noticeable limp. When healthy, he has above-average speed and is fairly aggressive on the basepaths, yet will very seldom run himself into an out. Beltre is a fantastic third baseman. He charges softly-hit grounders and bunts as well as anybody, and he has tremendous range to his left. He also has a strong arm and has made great strides with his accuracy.

2005 Outlook

After years of failing to reach his potential, the light came on for Beltre last year. The 25-year-old rode the perfect storm of a newfound focus to one of the greatest seasons ever seen in Los Angeles. Whether he remains with the Dodgers was their biggest question mark entering the offseason. They may be helped by the fact that few if any of the other mega-buck clubs have an opening at the hot corner.

Position: 3B
Bats: R **Throws:** R
Ht: 5'11" **Wt:** 220

Opening Day Age: 25
Born: 4/7/79 in Santo Domingo, DR
ML Seasons: 7
Pronunciation: BELL-tray

Overall Statistics

	G	AB	R	H	D	T	HR	RBI	SB	BB	SO	Avg	OBP	Slg
'04	156	598	104	200	32	0	48	121	7	53	87	.334	.388	.629
Car.	966	3462	456	949	176	18	147	510	62	286	590	.274	.332	.463

Where He Hits the Ball

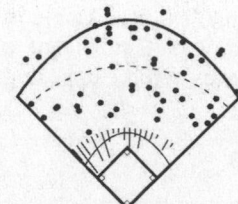 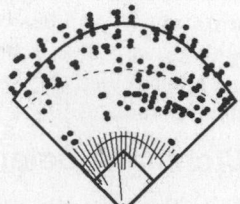

Vs. LHP   **Vs. RHP**

2004 Situational Stats

	AB	H	HR	RBI	Avg		AB	H	HR	RBI	Avg
Home	288	94	23	61	.326	LHP	134	39	6	17	.291
Road	310	106	25	60	.342	RHP	464	161	42	104	.347
First Half	314	99	22	56	.315	Sc Pos	157	46	12	75	.293
Scnd Half	284	101	26	65	.356	Clutch	101	37	11	26	.366

2004 Rankings (National League)

- 1st in home runs
- 2nd in total bases (376) and cleanup slugging percentage (.657)
- 3rd in batting average vs. righthanded pitchers and fielding percentage at third base (.978)
- 4th in batting average, hits, RBI and slugging percentage
- Led the Dodgers in runs scored, hits, doubles, times on base (255), on-base percentage, HR frequency (12.5 ABs per HR), batting average in the clutch, batting average at home, batting average on the road and batting average with two strikes (.231)
- Led NL third basemen in batting average and home runs

Milton Bradley

2004 Season

The Dodgers snagged Milton Bradley off of the Indians' hands just before the season started. He came as advertised, talented as well as troubled. In two different incidents, Bradley threw baseballs all over Dodger Stadium and a plastic bottle at the feet of some bleacher bums. He also displayed a combination of patience, speed and power that is rather rare in today's game. He did wear down, however, hitting just .241 over the season's final two months.

Hitting

Since Bradley is not afraid to go deep into the count, he probably is best suited for one of the top two spots in the order. Though he has plenty of pop, he is a line-drive hitter who uses the entire field. He is a fine situational hitter as well, and will give himself up for a productive out. Bradley has a tendency to lose focus and he will give too many at-bats away, however. He is a fine bunter, able to lay down a sacrifice in any direction or drag one for a hit.

Baserunning & Defense

Bradley has above-average speed and gets around the bases very well. He takes the art of basestealing as a personal challenge, and his gritted teeth and extended leads sometimes tip his hand. Bradley can and did play all three outfield spots for the Dodgers last season, and he was more than adequate at each spot. He gets great jumps and moves well in all directions. Combine his center-field range with his right-field arm, and it makes a total defensive package.

2005 Outlook

With Steve Finley moving on, Bradley will slide back over to center and the team will lose nothing defensively. The volatile young man sought out anger management counseling over the winter, yet he had another encounter with police in Ohio in November. Only time will tell if the rage that so clearly burns inside him is exactly what propels him to excellence. Bradley grew up in Southern California, so if he cannot calm down and succeed in Los Angeles, where can he prosper?

Position: CF/RF/LF
Bats: B **Throws:** R
Ht: 6' 0" **Wt:** 205

Opening Day Age: 26
Born: 4/15/78 in Harbor City, CA
ML Seasons: 5

Overall Statistics

	G	AB	R	H	D	T	HR	RBI	SB	BB	SO	Avg	OBP	Slg
'04	141	516	72	138	24	0	19	67	15	71	123	.267	.362	.424
Car.	459	1610	223	427	101	9	41	195	48	202	351	.265	.350	.416

Where He Hits the Ball

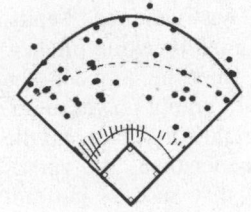

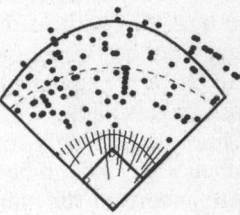

Vs. LHP	Vs. RHP

2004 Situational Stats

	AB	H	HR	RBI	Avg		AB	H	HR	RBI	Avg
Home	225	56	8	22	.249	LHP	146	43	4	21	.295
Road	291	82	11	45	.282	RHP	370	95	15	46	.257
First Half	268	76	9	35	.284	Sc Pos	140	33	2	43	.236
Scnd Half	248	62	10	32	.250	Clutch	74	24	4	14	.324

2004 Rankings (National League)

- 1st in lowest stolen-base percentage (57.7)
- 3rd in caught stealing (11)
- 6th in errors in right field (4)
- 7th in errors in center field (4)
- Led the Dodgers in caught stealing (11), walks and strikeouts

Los Angeles

Hee Seop Choi

2004 Season

No doubt looking to impress his new teammates in Florida, Hee Seop Choi came out like gangbusters last season. He hit .295 in April with nine homers and 18 RBI, only to hit a total of six longballs with 28 RBI the rest of the year. Acquired at the trade deadline by the Dodgers, Choi was a complete washout in Los Angeles. Stepping into the middle of a pennant race, the Korean looked overmatched and seldom stepped off the bench in September.

Hitting

Choi has a superb eye and only when badly fooled does the big guy swing at a bad pitch. That said, he has a lot of holes in his swing. Opponents like to bust him with hard stuff just under the hands, and Choi has trouble with most breaking pitches. He has a big uppercut, so when he connects the ball travels a long way. For a young power hitter, Choi is surprisingly comfortable driving a ball the other way. Though he hit better than .300 versus lefthanders in the minors, that success has not translated to the bigs.

Baserunning & Defense

Choi moves well for a man his size. That said, he is not going to be stealing many bags over the course of his career. On defense, he has all the tools to be a Gold Glove winner some day. His hands are soft and his footwork around the first-base bag is excellent. The lefthander makes the lead throw on the double play with strength and accuracy, and he looks like he has been playing first base at the major league level for years.

2005 Outlook

While the Dodgers were extremely disappointed by Choi's inability to produce, they have high hopes that a solid spring will straighten him out. The club wants to shorten his swing without hindering his natural power. If he can regain his confidence, Los Angeles (and its sizable Korean community) would appear to be a good fit for the personable young slugger.

Position: 1B
Bats: L **Throws:** L
Ht: 6' 5" **Wt:** 240

Opening Day Age: 26
Born: 3/16/79 in Chun-Nam, South Korea
ML Seasons: 3
Pronunciation: hee sop choy

Overall Statistics

	G	AB	R	H	D	T	HR	RBI	SB	BB	SO	Avg	OBP	Slg
'04	126	343	53	86	21	1	15	46	1	63	96	.251	.370	.449
Car.	230	595	90	139	39	1	25	78	2	107	182	.234	.356	.429

Where He Hits the Ball

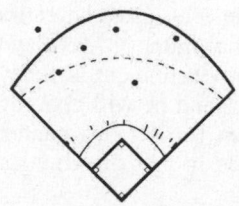

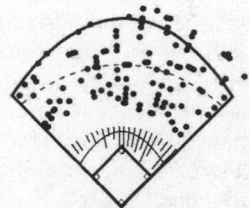

Vs. LHP   **Vs. RHP**

2004 Situational Stats

	AB	H	HR	RBI	Avg		AB	H	HR	RBI	Avg
Home	168	41	8	25	.244	LHP	36	6	1	4	.167
Road	175	45	7	21	.257	RHP	307	80	14	42	.261
First Half	240	66	14	35	.275	Sc Pos	81	18	5	32	.222
Scnd Half	103	20	1	11	.194	Clutch	53	14	2	7	.264

2004 Rankings (National League)

- 3rd in lowest fielding percentage at first base (.990)
- 5th in errors at first base (9)

Steve Finley

Position: CF
Bats: L **Throws:** L
Ht: 6' 2" **Wt:** 194

Opening Day Age: 40
Born: 3/12/65 in Union City, TN
ML Seasons: 16

2004 Season

Acquired at the trade deadline from the Diamondbacks, Steve Finley produced almost exactly the same numbers as he had generated over the first four months of the campaign. He is a streaky hitter, however, as evidenced by three monthly averages of .333 or higher and two others below the .200 mark. His walkoff grand slam to clinch the pennant for the Dodgers will forever live in club lore regardless of what transpired afterwards.

Hitting

Early in the count, Finley looks for a certain pitch that he knows he can handle and tries to yank it out, and no one this side of Barry Bonds turns faster on pitches on the inner half. That guesswork is even more necessary against lefthanders, against whom Finley has a bit of trouble. Though he has evolved into a slugger, Finley remains an excellent situational hitter and will sacrifice an at-bat to move a runner along.

Baserunning & Defense

The 40-year-old took up a new training regimen several years back and has the body of a much younger athlete. Though no longer the guy who stole 44 bags back in 1992, he still can move around the bases very well. Finley positions himself well in center field and gets great jumps on balls hit to either gap, so he still shows very good range. The 2004 Gold Glove winner also has a better throwing arm than most center fielders—it is both strong and accurate.

2005 Outlook

Finley became a free agent when the season ended. As he lives and trains race horses in Southern California, it was difficult to imagine him straying too far from the West Coast. As things turned out, Finley simply will head south down I-5 to Anaheim, agreeing to a two-year, $14 million deal to play center field for the Angels. His arrival will allow Garret Anderson to move back to left field, and the outfield tandem of Anderson, Finley and American League MVP Vladimir Guerrero will be one of the most potent in the league.

Overall Statistics

G	AB	R	H	D	T	HR	RBI	SB	BB	SO	Avg	OBP	Slg
162	628	92	170	28	1	36	94	9	61	82	.271	.333	.490
2289	8471	1327	2336	405	109	285	1071	305	764	1169	.276	.337	.450

Where He Hits the Ball

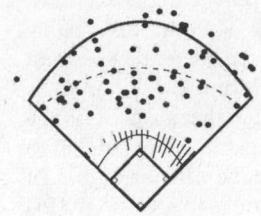 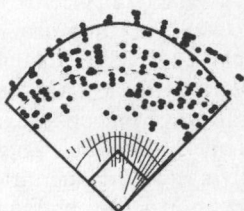

Vs. LHP	**Vs. RHP**

2004 Situational Stats

	AB	H	HR	RBI	Avg		AB	H	HR	RBI	Avg
Home	307	87	23	50	.283	LHP	192	47	11	29	.245
Road	321	83	13	44	.259	RHP	436	123	25	65	.282
First Half	345	99	21	45	.287	Sc Pos	140	34	8	61	.243
Scnd Half	283	71	15	49	.251	Clutch	105	36	10	29	.343

2004 Rankings (National League)

- 1st in games played (162)
- 5th in fielding percentage in center field (.992)
- Led the Dodgers in batting average with the bases loaded (.625)

Los Angeles

2004 Season

Eric Gagne finally showed signs of mortality last season when his streak of 84 consecutive saves was broken on July 5. Ironically, he struggled a bit at home, where he had an ERA over 3.00 and suffered both of his blown saves. After Gagne had a fairly light workload in the first half of the season, manager Jim Tracy rode his closer pretty hard down the stretch. Gagne worked at least 17 innings in each of the final two months, but after a rough August (4.24 ERA), he rebounded in September to help lead his team to the postseason.

Pitching

Gagne generates a lot of heat with very little movement thanks to his powerful lower body. Always pitching from the stretch, his fastball reaches 98 MPH, though the velocity heads southward by the end of the season. The killer is the vulcan changeup—so named because of the v-shaped grip—that comes in at 87-MPH before diving towards the dirt. Gagne also has a big ol' traditional curveball that barely touches 70 MPH. He dominates because he hits the corners with his two principal pitches and gets the breaker over enough to keep hitters honest.

Defense & Hitting

Though his follow-through leaves him in a bit of a vulnerable spot, Gagne's reactions are quick and he is fundamentally sound afield. Basestealers generally had their way with him when he was a starter, but with his compact motion and quick delivery, no one tried to steal on him last year. When the occasional hitter reaches base, Gagne pays little attention to them. He has fanned on all four of his plate appearances since becoming the closer.

2005 Outlook

Gagne has one last arbitration year before entering free agency, so it will be intriguing to see if the Dodgers can lock him up for a few extra seasons. While the 29-year-old has shown some signs of wear and tear, he has converted an amazing 96 percent of his save chances (152/158) over the last three campaigns.

Position: RP
Bats: R **Throws:** R
Ht: 6' 2" **Wt:** 234

Opening Day Age: 29
Born: 1/7/76 in Montreal, PQ, Canada
ML Seasons: 6
Pronunciation: gahn-yay

Overall Statistics

	W	L	Pct.	ERA	G	GS	Sv	IP	H	BB	SO	HR	Avg
'04	7	3	.700	2.19	70	0	45	82.1	53	22	114	5	.181
Car.	24	21	.533	3.29	282	48	152	530.0	413	179	604	60	.214

2004 Pitching Profile

	Eric Gagne	NL Average
Overall Strike %	68.6	62.5
1st Pitch Strike %	64.5	58.5
Ratio	0.91	1.39
Strikeouts per 9 IP	12.46	6.74
Walks per 9 IP	2.40	3.38
Home Runs per 9 IP	0.55	1.11
Strikeout/Walk Ratio	5.18	1.99
Groundball/Flyball Ratio	1.09	1.25

2004 Situational Stats

	W	L	ERA	Sv	IP		AB	H	HR	RBI	Avg
Home	4	3	3.10	22	40.2	LHB	146	34	2	15	.233
Road	3	0	1.30	23	41.2	RHB	147	19	3	8	.129
First Half	2	0	1.85	23	39.0	Sc Pos	65	13	0	16	.200
Scnd Half	5	3	2.49	22	43.1	Clutch	230	39	4	19	.170

2004 Rankings (National League)

- 1st in save percentage (95.7)
- 2nd in most strikeouts per nine innings in relief (12.5)
- 3rd in saves, lowest batting average allowed in relief (.181) and fewest baserunners allowed per nine innings in relief (8.7)
- 4th in relief wins (7)
- 5th in first batter efficiency (.123)
- 6th in games finished (59)
- Led the Dodgers in games pitched, saves, games finished (59), lowest batting average allowed vs. righthanded batters, save percentage (95.7), lowest percentage of inherited runners scored (0.0), first batter efficiency (.123), relief innings (82.1), lowest batting average allowed in relief (.181), most strikeouts per nine innings in relief (12.5) and fewest baserunners allowed per nine innings in relief (8.7)

Shawn Green

2004 Season

Whether it was the position change to first base or his surgically repaired right shoulder, Shawn Green's power stroke was missing throughout the first half of last season. As spring turned to summer, the lanky lefty's pop started to return, and he had a slugging percentage of .529 after the All-Star break. His inability to come through in the clutch continued throughout the campaign, however, as Green hit just .199 with runners in scoring position.

Hitting

Green's approach at the plate is a bit different depending on who is on the hill. Against righthanders, he is more aggressive and looks for something he can drive. He has upper-deck power from just left of dead-center to the right-field foul pole. When facing a southpaw, Green takes a more defensive stance and is willing to poke singles the opposite way. Green has a long and complicated swing that can lead to long slumps in which he rolls a lot of grounders to the right side.

Baserunning & Defense

Age has sapped him of his basestealing abilities, but Green still is an excellent baserunner and can move pretty well once he gets going. The lifelong outfielder's move to first base could not be called seamless by any stretch of the imagination, but he also did not embarrass himself. He is somewhat mechanical in the field, and that hurts him in the infield, where quicker decisions are necessary. His outfield arm is above average in both strength and accuracy.

2005 Outlook

Dodgers GM Paul DePodesta's offseason moves will determine where Green will play in the field in 2005, that is, if he remains in LA. With Green owed $16 million in the final year of his deal, it would be a surprise for another club to deal for him, but there were trade rumors floating around early in the offseason. Green will be hitting somewhere in the middle of someone's lineup this season, and when he gets hot, he can carry a club for a month or longer.

Position: 1B/RF
Bats: L **Throws:** L
Ht: 6' 4" **Wt:** 200

Opening Day Age: 32
Born: 11/10/72 in Des Plaines, IL
ML Seasons: 12

Overall Statistics

G	AB	R	H	D	T	HR	RBI	SB	BB	SO	Avg	OBP	Slg
157	590	92	157	28	1	28	86	5	71	114	.266	.352	.459
1514	5525	907	1560	347	27	281	885	139	600	1076	.282	.357	.508

Where He Hits the Ball

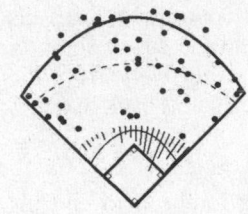 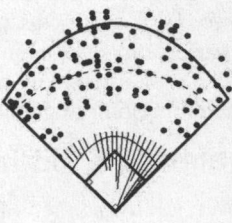

Vs. LHP   **Vs. RHP**

2004 Situational Stats

	AB	H	HR	RBI	Avg		AB	H	HR	RBI	Avg
Home	297	83	16	45	.279	LHP	181	42	8	31	.232
Road	293	74	12	41	.253	RHP	409	115	20	55	.281
First Half	316	80	10	41	.253	Sc Pos	166	33	6	55	.199
Scnd Half	274	77	18	45	.281	Clutch	86	23	6	13	.267

2004 Rankings (National League)

- 1st in lowest cleanup slugging percentage (.437)
- 3rd in lowest batting average with runners in scoring position
- 4th in fielding percentage at first base (.995)
- 7th in lowest batting average vs. lefthanded pitchers
- 8th in highest groundball-flyball ratio (1.9)
- Led the Dodgers in walks, GDPs (17), pitches seen (2,595) and highest groundball-flyball ratio (1.9)

Los Angeles

Kazuhisa Ishii

2004 Season

It was a tale of two seasons for Kaz Ishii. Through his first 18 starts, he went 11-4 with a 3.94 ERA. From the middle of July on, however, he won just two more games and compiled an ERA just under 6.00. Overall, Ishii gathered 13 wins largely because he enjoyed the best run support in the NL.

Pitching

While he is not overpowering, Ishii's 88-MPH fastball gets on hitters quicker than they expect because it comes out from behind his right knee. Ishii also will cut the fastball to jam lefthanders, and he has a fine changeup to confound righties. A big sweeping curveball completes the repertoire. Ishii's nemesis is his control; he loses his release point and cannot find the strike zone. In fact, Ishii often will pitch exclusively from the stretch in order to get his mechanics back in order.

Defense & Hitting

After taking a liner off the forehead to end his 2002 season, Ishii can be excused for being a bit gun-shy on balls hit back through the box. That said, he is compact and gets off the mound in good shape, especially when covering first on grounders hit to the right side. Ishii is not much of a hitter and his lifetime average is under .100. He laid down six sacrifices in 2004, but it always is a dicey proposition as to whether he is going to put the ball on the ground.

2005 Outlook

Ishii has one more year on his contract, and while he has been a source of frequent frustration for the club, he is reasonably priced. The Dodgers are not exactly loaded with starting pitchers, so it would be no surprise to see Ishii filling out the back end of the rotation in April. That is not to say that he will finish the season there. Over the course of his career, Ishii is 29-12 with a 3.50 ERA before the All-Star break. Afterwards, he is 7-13 with a 5.77 ERA.

Position: SP
Bats: L **Throws:** L
Ht: 6' 0" **Wt:** 200

Opening Day Age: 31
Born: 9/9/73 in Chiba, Japan
ML Seasons: 3
Pronunciation: kaz-u-heesa ee-shee-ee

Overall Statistics

	W	L	Pct.	ERA	G	GS	Sv	IP	H	BB	SO	HR	Avg
'04	13	8	.619	4.71	31	31	0	172.0	155	98	99	21	.246
Car.	36	25	.590	4.30	86	86	0	473.0	421	305	382	57	.242

2004 Pitching Profile

	Kazuhisa Ishii	NL Average
Overall Strike %	59.4	62.5
1st Pitch Strike %	53.7	58.5
Ratio	1.47	1.39
Strikeouts per 9 IP	5.18	6.74
Walks per 9 IP	5.13	3.38
Home Runs per 9 IP	1.10	1.11
Strikeout/Walk Ratio	1.01	1.99
Groundball/Flyball Ratio	0.64	1.25

2004 Situational Stats

	W	L	ERA	Sv	IP		AB	H	HR	RBI	Avg
Home	6	3	4.16	0	75.2	LHB	164	43	6	24	.262
Road	7	5	5.14	0	96.1	RHB	466	112	15	63	.240
First Half	10	4	4.00	0	101.1	Sc Pos	153	44	0	59	.288
Scnd Half	3	4	5.73	0	70.2	Clutch	5	1	0	0	.200

2004 Rankings (National League)

- 1st in most run support per nine innings (6.7) and fielding percentage at pitcher (1.000)
- 2nd in lowest strikeout-walk ratio (1.0), lowest groundball-flyball ratio allowed (0.6) and highest walks per nine innings (5.1)
- 3rd in shutouts (2)
- 5th in walks allowed, runners caught stealing (9) and highest ERA on the road
- 7th in complete games (2)
- 8th in highest on-base percentage allowed (.348)
- 9th in lowest stolen-base percentage allowed (57.1), highest ERA and fewest strikeouts per nine innings (5.2)
- Led the Dodgers in wins, complete games (2), shutouts (2), walks allowed, runners caught stealing (9) and most run support per nine innings (6.7)

Cesar Izturis

2004 Season

What a difference a year made for Cesar Izturis. After bouncing back and forth between the top two spots in the batting order, he became the full-time leadoff guy when Dave Roberts went to Boston at the trade deadline. Izturis embraced the patience preached by hitting coach Tim Wallach. While the young shortstop's strikeouts remained exactly the same as the year before (70), he increased his walk total from 25 to 43.

Hitting

After hitting just .195 against righthanders in 2002, Izturis almost gave up switch-hitting. Last year, he hit .295 against righties. The key to his success is that he does not try to do too much at the plate. Realizing that speed is his game, he hits the ball where it is pitched and keeps it on the ground. He occasionally will turn on a low inside fastball, especially from the left side, and drive it into the right-field gap.

Baserunning & Defense

Not only does Izturis' blazing speed help him at the plate, but the increased opportunities on the bases made him a more savvy thief. He also is a smart baserunner who very rarely runs into an out. Of course, the best part of Izturis' game is his magnificient defense, where he has almost no weaknesses. He has great range to either side and gets to more balls up the middle than perhaps any shortstop in baseball. Izturis also has plenty of arm to throw from the hole, and his footwork is magical around the second-base bag.

2005 Outlook

It took the breakout year with the stick for Izturis to finally get on the radar screen of the Gold Glove voters, and he won the first of what should be many. He makes the entire infield better and is so good defensively that anything he can contribute offensively can be considered a bonus. The young Venezuelan is evolving into a player who the Dodgers will build around.

Position: SS
Bats: B **Throws:** R
Ht: 5' 9" **Wt:** 175

Opening Day Age: 25
Born: 2/10/80 in Barquisimeto, VZ
ML Seasons: 4
Pronunciation: IS-tur-is

Overall Statistics

	G	AB	R	H	D	T	HR	RBI	SB	BB	SO	Avg	OBP	Slg
'04	159	670	90	193	32	9	4	62	25	43	70	.288	.330	.381
Car.	498	1801	199	471	83	19	8	142	50	84	194	.262	.293	.342

Where He Hits the Ball

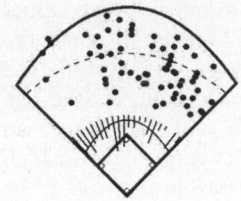
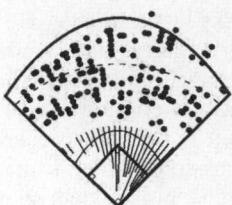

Vs. LHP   **Vs. RHP**

2004 Situational Stats

	AB	H	HR	RBI	Avg		AB	H	HR	RBI	Avg
Home	330	89	1	25	.270	LHP	182	49	1	12	.269
Road	340	104	3	37	.306	RHP	488	144	3	50	.295
First Half	343	100	2	30	.292	Sc Pos	148	49	2	55	.331
Scnd Half	327	93	2	32	.284	Clutch	100	25	0	10	.250

2004 Rankings (National League)

- 1st in lowest batting average with the bases loaded (.000)
- 2nd in at-bats, singles and plate appearances (728)
- 3rd in fielding percentage at shortstop (.985)
- 4th in triples
- 6th in hits and caught stealing (9)
- 7th in lowest HR frequency (167.5 ABs per HR) and lowest stolen-base percentage (73.5)
- 8th in games played
- 9th in sacrifice bunts (12) and errors at shortstop (10)
- Led the Dodgers in at-bats, singles, doubles, triples, sacrifice bunts (12), plate appearances (728), games played and batting average with runners in scoring position

Los Angeles

2004 Season

Signed as minor league free agent before last season, Jose Lima was an insurance policy that paid off big time for the Dodgers. He served as a swingman over the first couple of months of the season, then became a full-time member of the rotation in early June. Lima thrived in the midst of the pennant pressure. In his last six starts, he went 3-1 with a 2.95 ERA, climaxed by a complete-game five-hitter against the Cardinals when facing elimination in the Division Series.

Pitching

Lima has a little more giddyup on his fastball than one might think, as he can bump it up to 90-MPH in a pinch, though it has more movement at a few ticks less than that. He has to have enough velocity to keep batters honest, as it is all about the changeup for Lima. The change looks just like the fastball coming out of Lima's hand, and he can spot it on both corners. He will also mix in an occasional slider. Lima works very quickly, which keeps his fielders alert. They are going to be active with him on the mound, as he fanned fewer than five batters per nine innings last season.

Defense & Hitting

Lima does whatever it takes to hold runners close, including back-to-back pickoff throws as well as the slide step, but opposing basestealers are 15-for-15 over the last two seasons. He is an agile defender and is fundamentally sound on the defensive side. While he takes some ugly cuts at the plate, Lima hit a respectable .188 last year.

2005 Outlook

The free agent may have earned himself a multi-year deal with his clutch performance down the stretch. Whether that contract is with the Dodgers is up in the air. Lima's constant cheerleading from the top step of the dugout is fine so long as he is pitching well, but potential employers should take a close look at his road numbers. In 2004, Lima went 4-4 with a 5.56 ERA away from pitcher-friendly Chavez Ravine.

Position: SP/RP
Bats: R **Throws:** R
Ht: 6' 2" **Wt:** 205

Opening Day Age: 32
Born: 9/30/72 in Santiago, DR
ML Seasons: 11
Pronunciation: LEE-mah

Overall Statistics

	W	L	Pct.	ERA	G	GS	Sv	IP	H	BB	SO	HR	Avg
'04	13	5	.722	4.07	36	24	0	170.1	178	34	93	33	.271
Car.	84	82	.506	5.00	312	199	5	1381.2	1539	322	888	233	.282

2004 Pitching Profile

	Jose Lima	NL Average
Overall Strike %	66.4	62.5
1st Pitch Strike %	63.7	58.5
Ratio	1.24	1.39
Strikeouts per 9 IP	4.91	6.74
Walks per 9 IP	1.80	3.38
Home Runs per 9 IP	1.74	1.11
Strikeout/Walk Ratio	2.74	1.99
Groundball/Flyball Ratio	1.24	1.25

2004 Situational Stats

	W	L	ERA	Sv	IP		AB	H	HR	RBI	Avg
Home	9	1	3.08	0	102.1	LHB	324	90	16	36	.278
Road	4	4	5.56	0	68.0	RHB	333	88	17	38	.264
First Half	8	3	4.32	0	83.1	Sc Pos	129	28	3	36	.217
Scnd Half	5	2	3.83	0	87.0	Clutch	37	9	1	3	.243

2004 Rankings (National League)

- 1st in fielding percentage at pitcher (1.000)
- 2nd in fewest pitches thrown per batter (3.44)
- 3rd in winning percentage and most home runs allowed per nine innings (1.74)
- 4th in home runs allowed
- 5th in fewest walks per nine innings (1.8)
- 6th in highest slugging percentage allowed (.470)
- 7th in fewest strikeouts per nine innings (4.9)
- 10th in GDPs induced (21) and least run support per nine innings (4.4)
- Led the Dodgers in wins, home runs allowed, winning percentage, fewest pitches thrown per batter (3.44), lowest ERA at home, lowest batting average allowed with runners in scoring position and fewest walks per nine innings (1.8)

Brad Penny

2004 Season

Acquired from the Marlins in a big six-player deadline deal, Brad Penny's first start in Los Angeles was an eight-inning, two-hit shutout that showed why the club had snagged him. He never made it through the first inning in his next outing, however, as he grabbed his upper arm in writhing pain and ran off the mound. He tried to return in late September, but the strained right biceps was not yet healed, and he was shut down for the season.

Pitching

Penny is pure power, relying mostly on a four-seam fastball that registers regularly in the mid-90s. He also throws a sinking two-seamer in the 92-MPH range and a power curveball that buckles knees. A changeup was rumored, but it never appeared in Chavez Ravine. His command has improved as he has matured, and when Penny is painting the black with his fastball, opposing hitters are in for a long day. He does not appear to be in the best of shape, however, so he can wear down as his pitch count rises.

Defense & Hitting

Penny does not get off the mound very well and can get a bit flustered on the tougher plays. His move is poor, and he takes a while to unleash the pitch. After banging out four extra-base hits for Florida the previous season, Penny went just 3-for-51 last year, but he looks relatively comfortable with a bat in his hands. However, he laid down just one successful sacrifice all year.

2005 Outlook

Penny's injury is rather unusual, so it is difficult to tell whether it is a simple strain or a sign that something else is wrong. There have been past rumors of shoulder problems—the Reds turned down a trade for Penny a few years back after looking at medical reports—but Penny insists that they were unfounded. Arm problems or not, he posted a career-low 3.15 ERA last year, building on his strong World Series performance, which capped off the previous postseason.

Position: SP
Bats: R **Throws:** R
Ht: 6' 4" **Wt:** 250

Opening Day Age: 26
Born: 5/24/78 in Broken Arrow, OK
ML Seasons: 5

Overall Statistics

	W	L	Pct.	ERA	G	GS	Sv	IP	H	BB	SO	HR	Avg
'04	9	10	.474	3.15	24	24	0	143.0	130	45	111	12	.243
Car.	49	44	.527	4.03	134	133	0	793.1	776	265	576	79	.258

2004 Pitching Profile

	Brad Penny	NL Average
Overall Strike %	63.8	62.5
1st Pitch Strike %	60.4	58.5
Ratio	1.22	1.39
Strikeouts per 9 IP	6.99	6.74
Walks per 9 IP	2.83	3.38
Home Runs per 9 IP	0.76	1.11
Strikeout/Walk Ratio	2.47	1.99
Groundball/Flyball Ratio	1.10	1.25

2004 Situational Stats

	W	L	ERA	Sv	IP		AB	H	HR	RBI	Avg
Home	6	4	3.06	0	70.2	LHB	273	66	7	19	.242
Road	3	6	3.24	0	72.1	RHB	263	64	5	29	.243
First Half	8	7	3.20	0	115.1	Sc Pos	119	24	2	27	.202
Scnd Half	1	3	2.93	0	27.2	Clutch	24	10	0	4	.417

2004 Rankings (National League)
- Did not rank near the top or bottom in any category

Odalis Perez

2004 Season

After complaining in 2003 that his teammates did not supply him offensive help, Odalis Perez' was rewarded last year with the worst run support in the National League. Perez sat out almost a month with an inflamed rotator cuff, and his left shoulder bothered him most of the season, but the talented lefty still managed to toss almost 200 innings. He ended up with only seven wins, however, with 18 no-decisions.

Pitching

Though by no means a flamethrower, Perez routinely throws in the upper 80s and can reach back to hit 92 MPH on occasion. The fastball's natural action is to bear in on righthanders, and he complements it with a fine changeup that drops down and away from righties. Over the course of his career, Perez has actually been slightly more effective against righthanded hitters than versus lefties. He uses a decent curveball to keep lefties off-balance, but it is clearly his third-best pitch. He is not the most durable pitcher, however. He already has had elbow surgery, and the rotator-cuff soreness last year raises a red flag for the future.

Defense & Hitting

Perez is a solid defensive player. He is quick on balls back through the box and gets off the hill in good shape. His move to first is just mediocre, and Perez must throw over quite often, as he is a bit slow to the plate. He generally makes contact at the plate, but with little authority, and usually can get the bunt down.

2005 Outlook

The volatile lefty became a free agent when the 2004 season ended, and he may have bought his ticket out of town with two abysmal starts in the NLDS. Perez never has been overly popular with his teammates, especially when his displeasure shows up in the press before it is expressed in the clubhouse. When and if he is healthy, however, Perez is a valued commodity as a 27-year-old left-handed pitcher who posted ERAs under 3.00 in three different months last year.

Position: SP
Bats: L **Throws:** L
Ht: 6' 0" **Wt:** 150

Opening Day Age: 27
Born: 6/7/77 in Las Matas de Farfan, DR
ML Seasons: 6
Pronunciation: oh-DALL-iss

Overall Statistics

	W	L	Pct.	ERA	G	GS	Sv	IP	H	BB	SO	HR	Avg
'04	7	6	.538	3.25	31	31	0	196.1	180	44	128	26	.250
Car.	45	43	.511	4.00	145	126	0	803.0	771	224	582	95	.255

2004 Pitching Profile

	Odalis Perez	NL Average
Overall Strike %	65.2	62.5
1st Pitch Strike %	60.7	58.5
Ratio	1.14	1.39
Strikeouts per 9 IP	5.87	6.74
Walks per 9 IP	2.02	3.38
Home Runs per 9 IP	1.19	1.11
Strikeout/Walk Ratio	2.91	1.99
Groundball/Flyball Ratio	1.62	1.25

2004 Situational Stats

	W	L	ERA	Sv	IP		AB	H	HR	RBI	Avg
Home	3	3	3.31	0	89.2	LHB	178	48	8	23	.270
Road	4	3	3.21	0	106.2	RHB	543	132	18	49	.243
First Half	4	3	2.96	0	106.1	Sc Pos	154	34	6	47	.221
Scnd Half	3	3	3.60	0	90.0	Clutch	54	11	3	3	.204

2004 Rankings (National League)

- 1st in least run support per nine innings (3.3)
- 2nd in balks (2)
- 4th in GDPs induced (25)
- 7th in lowest on-base percentage allowed (.294) and most GDPs induced per GDP situation (21.0%)
- 8th in lowest ERA on the road and fewest walks per nine innings (2.0)
- 10th in ERA, highest groundball-flyball ratio allowed (1.6) and fewest pitches thrown per batter (3.59)
- Led the Dodgers in ERA, balks (2), GDPs induced (25), lowest on-base percentage allowed (.294), highest groundball-flyball ratio allowed (1.6), most GDPs induced per GDP situation (21.0%) and lowest ERA on the road

Jeff Weaver

2004 Season

Snagged off the Yankee scrapheap before last season, Jeff Weaver returned home to Southern California and resuscitated his career. He took a while to settle in, going 1-4 with a 5.40 ERA in his first six starts, but over the next four months, Weaver went 11-6 with a 3.14 ERA. He ran out of gas down the stretch, winning just one of his last seven starts, including a bad outing in the NLDS versus St. Louis.

Pitching

Weaver brings a full arsenal out to the mound, and he expands it by altering his release point at times. The lanky righthander throws a fastball in the low 90s that bores in on righthanders. His slider is hard and tight, and Weaver will mix in a sweeping breaking ball. When he gets ahead in the count against some righthanded hitters, he will drop down to a sidearm delivery and try to catch them off guard. In fact, the tendency to think too much can get in the way of his naturally great stuff. Weaver is an emotional roller-coaster on the hill who often lets one bad call or a miscue throw him off his game.

Defense & Hitting

Weaver fielded his position flawlessly last year and he is not afraid to stick any of his long limbs out to knock balls down. He has a very quick move over to first and gets the pitch to the plate pretty quickly as well. For a guy who just came over to the National League, Weaver looked quite good at the plate, with three of his 15 hits going for extra bases.

2005 Outlook

The Dodgers look to be building their rotation around Weaver this season. The guy is durable—he has never been on the disabled list—and at 28 years old, he should be just entering his peak. If pitching coach Jim Colborn can just get the righty to settle down and trust his superb stuff, Weaver easily could be a 15-game winner in 2005.

Position: SP
Bats: R **Throws:** R
Ht: 6' 5" **Wt:** 200

Opening Day Age: 28
Born: 8/22/76 in Northridge, CA
ML Seasons: 6

Overall Statistics

	W	L	Pct.	ERA	G	GS	Sv	IP	H	BB	SO	HR	Avg
'04	13	13	.500	4.01	34	34	0	220.0	219	67	153	19	.260
Car.	64	76	.457	4.48	192	175	2	1172.0	1239	338	780	123	.272

2004 Pitching Profile

	Jeff Weaver	NL Average
Overall Strike %	64.5	62.5
1st Pitch Strike %	61.4	58.5
Ratio	1.30	1.39
Strikeouts per 9 IP	6.26	6.74
Walks per 9 IP	2.74	3.38
Home Runs per 9 IP	0.78	1.11
Strikeout/Walk Ratio	2.28	1.99
Groundball/Flyball Ratio	1.06	1.25

2004 Situational Stats

	W	L	ERA	Sv	IP		AB	H	HR	RBI	Avg
Home	4	8	3.55	0	109.0	LHB	405	118	13	57	.291
Road	9	5	4.46	0	111.0	RHB	437	101	6	36	.231
First Half	6	9	4.22	0	113.0	Sc Pos	185	49	7	72	.265
Scnd Half	7	4	3.79	0	107.0	Clutch	28	8	0	4	.286

2004 Rankings (National League)

- 1st in fielding percentage at pitcher (1.000)
- 3rd in hit batsmen (14)
- 5th in games started and batters faced (935)
- 6th in wild pitches (9)
- 7th in innings pitched
- 8th in hits allowed and lowest groundball-fly ball ratio allowed (1.1)
- 9th in losses
- 10th in pickoff throws (111)
- Led the Dodgers in wins, losses, games started, innings pitched, hits allowed, batters faced (935), hit batsmen (14), strikeouts, wild pitches (9), pitches thrown (3,429), pickoff throws (111) and fewest home runs allowed per nine innings (.78)

Los Angeles

Wilson Alvarez

Position: RP/SP
Bats: L **Throws:** L
Ht: 6' 1" **Wt:** 255

Opening Day Age: 35
Born: 3/24/70 in Maracaibo, VZ
ML Seasons: 13

Overall Statistics

	W	L	Pct.	ERA	G	GS	Sv	IP	H	BB	SO	HR	Avg
'04	7	6	.538	4.03	40	15	1	120.2	109	31	102	12	.244
Car.	101	88	.534	3.94	334	261	4	1723.2	1593	798	1314	183	.247

2004 Situational Stats

	W	L	ERA	Sv	IP		AB	H	HR	RBI	Avg
Home	4	3	3.20	1	70.1	LHB	114	35	6	22	.307
Road	3	3	5.19	0	50.1	RHB	333	74	6	29	.222
First Half	3	3	3.56	1	65.2	Sc Pos	94	25	1	34	.266
Scnd Half	4	3	4.58	0	55.0	Clutch	31	6	0	0	.194

2004 Season

For the second year in a row, Wilson Alvarez shuttled back and forth between the bullpen and the starting rotation for the Dodgers. A chronically sore hip eventually limited the veteran to shorter stints, and he thrived in the long relief role, posting a 2.44 ERA out of the pen.

Pitching, Defense & Hitting

No longer the flamethrower of his youth, Alvarez remains sneaky fast, as he hides the ball throughout a rocking-chair windup. Alvarez is not afraid of backing hitters off the plate with his 88-MPH fastball, then follows it with a 12-to-6 curveball and a fine changeup. The veteran lefty holds runners extremely well; over the course of his career, opposing basestealers have a sub-.500 success rate. As he has gotten older and heavier, Alvarez has more trouble fielding his position. He takes a pretty healthy cut at the plate and can get the bunt down when asked to sacrifice.

2005 Outlook

It would behoove Alvarez to develop an offseason training regimen, as the extra pounds have no doubt contributed to some of his nagging injuries. That said, he has been a very effective swingman for the Dodgers, but he's a free agent who may have a new address in 2005.

Yhency Brazoban

Position: RP
Bats: R **Throws:** R
Ht: 6' 1" **Wt:** 170

Opening Day Age: 24
Born: 6/11/80 in Santo Domingo, DR
ML Seasons: 1

Overall Statistics

	W	L	Pct.	ERA	G	GS	Sv	IP	H	BB	SO	HR	Avg
'04	6	2	.750	2.48	31	0	0	32.2	25	15	27	2	.219
Car.	6	2	.750	2.48	31	0	0	32.2	25	15	27	2	.219

2004 Situational Stats

	W	L	ERA	Sv	IP		AB	H	HR	RBI	Avg
Home	3	1	1.84	0	14.2	LHB	49	11	0	2	.224
Road	3	1	3.00	0	18.0	RHB	65	14	2	7	.215
First Half	0	0	—	0	0.0	Sc Pos	34	6	1	8	.176
Scnd Half	6	2	2.48	0	32.2	Clutch	55	15	1	6	.273

2004 Season

Yhency Brazoban progressed so quickly that GM Paul DePodesta felt that he had the depth to include valuable setup man Guillermo Mota in the Brad Penny trade with the Marlins. Brazoban's ERA after the deal was 2.48, while Mota's was 4.81.

Pitching, Defense & Hitting

Brazoban was converted from the outfield because his fastball routinely hits 95 MPH. He backs that up with a hard slider in the mid- to upper 80s. Though he sometimes struggles with his command, Brazoban ended up with a strikeout-walk ratio of almost 3:1 over three levels last season. While he still has a lot to learn with regard to holding runners, Brazoban should have no trouble fielding his position. As a reliever, he will seldom be asked to handle a bat, but the big guy looks like he could do some damage if he ever gets ahold of one.

2005 Outlook

The biggest challenge that the Dodgers face with Brazoban is limiting the young flamethrower's innings. He pitched 96 frames last year and then went home to pitch some more in the Dominican Winter League. Brazoban should be Eric Gagne's principal setup man this season, and if the closer ever teaches the young man the Vulcan change—as he did with Mota—look out.

Giovanni Carrara

Position: RP
Bats: R **Throws:** R
Ht: 6' 2" **Wt:** 230

Opening Day Age: 37
Born: 3/4/68 in Anzoategui, VZ
ML Seasons: 8
Pronunciation: ka-rah-rah

Overall Statistics

	W	L	Pct.	ERA	G	GS	Sv	IP	H	BB	SO	HR	Avg
'04	5	2	.714	2.18	42	0	2	53.2	46	20	48	1	.228
Car.	22	13	.629	4.85	216	18	3	369.0	395	157	257	63	.274

2004 Situational Stats

	W	L	ERA	Sv	IP		AB	H	HR	RBI	Avg
Home	3	0	0.92	1	29.1	LHB	77	14	0	2	.182
Road	2	2	3.70	1	24.1	RHB	125	32	1	13	.256
First Half	1	0	0.00	0	5.2	Sc Pos	55	10	1	14	.182
Scnd Half	4	2	2.44	2	48.0	Clutch	59	12	0	2	.203

2004 Season

The Dodgers signed Giovanni Carrara to a minor league contract after he toiled the first two months of the season in the Cubs' organization. He came up to the big club at the start of July and had an immediate impact in the bullpen. After the Guillermo Mota deal, Carrara became one of the principal setup men and even closed a couple of games.

Pitching, Defense & Hitting

Carrara does not overwhelm anyone with his stuff, but he brings a full arsenal to the mound. He throws a couple of fastballs, a two-seamer in the mid- to upper 80s and four-seamer that occasionally hits 90 MPH. He uses a changeup that runs away from lefties and a 70-MPH loopy curveball to mess up righthanders' timing. Carrara fields his position well and has never committed an error in his eight-year career. He gets rid of the ball quickly, and no one stole a base on him last year.

2005 Outlook

A journeyman like Carrara always will be looking over his shoulder, but he has earned a return trip to Dodger Stadium, where he has a lifetime ERA of 2.43. He has a rubber arm and can start or fill any role in the pen.

Alex Cora

Position: 2B
Bats: L **Throws:** R
Ht: 6' 0" **Wt:** 180

Opening Day Age: 29
Born: 10/18/75 in Caguas, PR
ML Seasons: 7

Overall Statistics

	G	AB	R	H	D	T	HR	RBI	SB	BB	SO	Avg	OBP	Slg
'04	138	405	47	107	9	4	10	47	3	47	41	.264	.364	.380
Car.	684	1961	203	482	84	21	27	173	18	148	261	.246	.314	.351

2004 Situational Stats

	AB	H	HR	RBI	Avg		AB	H	HR	RBI	Avg
Home	195	55	4	24	.282	LHP	46	11	2	8	.239
Road	210	52	6	23	.248	RHP	359	96	8	39	.267
First Half	210	62	6	23	.295	Sc Pos	85	25	4	38	.294
Scnd Half	195	45	4	24	.231	Clutch	65	18	1	4	.277

2004 Season

The highlight of last season for Alex Cora was an epic 18-pitch at-bat versus Matt Clement on May 12 that culminated in a dramatic two-run homer. Cora proceeded to hit .357 in the months of May and June. He eventually returned to his norm, as he hit just .212 from July 25 on.

Hitting, Baserunning & Defense

New hitting coach Tim Wallach preached patience to the Dodgers, and his message got through to Cora, who walked more than he struck out for the first time in his career. The lefty sprays singles from foul line to foul line, but he can golf balls on the inner half over the right-field wall. Cora has average speed and occasionally will run himself into an out. He is like a second shortstop in the infield, as he has good range to both sides and a strong arm.

2005 Outlook

The Dodgers control Cora's services for one more season before he is eligible for free agency. While Cora and Cesar Izturis perform magic on a nightly basis defensively, the club may decide at some point that it needs to upgrade the offensive production up the middle. Jeff Kent was signed for two years, and he could be used at first or second base.

Darren Dreifort

Position: RP
Bats: R **Throws:** R
Ht: 6' 2" **Wt:** 211

Opening Day Age: 32
Born: 5/3/72 in Wichita, KS
ML Seasons: 9
Pronunciation: DRY-fort

Overall Statistics

	W	L	Pct.	ERA	G	GS	Sv	IP	H	BB	SO	HR	Avg
'04	1	4	.200	4.44	60	0	1	50.2	43	36	63	5	.232
Car.	48	60	.444	4.36	274	113	11	872.2	826	389	802	90	.251

2004 Situational Stats

	W	L	ERA	Sv	IP			AB	H	HR	RBI	Avg
Home	1	1	3.09	0	23.1	LHB		67	14	4	11	.209
Road	0	3	5.60	1	27.1	RHB		118	29	1	17	.246
First Half	1	1	3.76	0	38.1	Sc Pos		57	12	1	22	.211
Scnd Half	0	3	6.57	1	12.1	Clutch		95	21	2	15	.221

2004 Season

Less than three weeks after being promoted to the setup role when Guillermo Mota was dealt to Florida, Darren Dreifort went down with yet another injury. This time, it was a torn ACL in his right knee. When healthy, Dreifort was somewhat effective, especially at home.

Pitching, Defense & Hitting

Dreifort relies on just two pitches, a heavy sinking fastball in the low to mid-90s and a hard slider that tops out in the upper 80s. Both balls move so much that he can aim for the middle of the plate and he will end up with a strike on the black. Dreifort throws everything from the stretch, and has a quick-enough release to either the plate or first base that he keeps potential basestealers honest. A fine athlete, Dreifort fields his position well and can get off the mound in a hurry.

2005 Outlook

Dreifort is entering the final segment of a five-year, $55 million deal, and so far the Dodgers have little to show for their investment. After undergoing reconstructive surgeries on both his knee and hip, Dreifort will *not* be ready to go at the start of the season. The club will just have to pay up and hope they get something out of him in 2005.

Jose Hernandez

Position: 2B/SS/3B
Bats: R **Throws:** R
Ht: 6' 1" **Wt:** 190

Opening Day Age: 35
Born: 7/14/69 in Vega Alta, PR
ML Seasons: 13
Pronunciation: her-NAN-dezz

Overall Statistics

G	AB	R	H	D	T	HR	RBI	SB	BB	SO	Avg	OBP	Slg
95	211	32	61	12	1	13	29	3	26	61	.289	.370	.540
1418	4232	583	1072	182	32	159	553	40	358	1291	.253	.313	.424

2004 Situational Stats

	AB	H	HR	RBI	Avg		AB	H	HR	RBI	Avg
Home	99	25	5	11	.253	LHP	126	39	11	20	.310
Road	112	36	8	18	.321	RHP	85	22	2	9	.259
First Half	108	31	5	10	.287	Sc Pos	51	11	1	15	.216
Scnd Half	103	30	8	19	.291	Clutch	39	8	1	6	.205

2004 Season

The Dodgers became Jose Hernandez' eighth major league team (and fifth in the last three seasons) last year, and they could not have been happier with the results. Playing mostly second base when the club faced a lefty, Hernandez posted a career-high .289 batting average and matched his home-run total from 2003 despite compiling 300 fewer at-bats.

Hitting, Baserunning & Defense

Hernandez takes a huge cut and was in fact benched late in the 2002 campaign so as to avoid breaking the single-season strikeout mark. When he connects, however, he has enough pop to leave any part of the yard. He hammers lefthanders, but when righthanders put a wrinkle on it, Hernandez has more trouble making contact. He played five different positions last year and looked perfectly comfortable at every spot. He runs the bases well.

2005 Outlook

Hernandez is better suited for a utility role than as a regular, as the holes in his swing can be exposed with too much playing time. That said, he would be a valuable insurance policy for any contender. Whether that club is the Dodgers remains to be seen, as they have young and talented Antonio Perez ready to step into a bench role.

Edwin Jackson

Position: SP
Bats: R **Throws:** R
Ht: 6' 3" **Wt:** 190

Opening Day Age: 21
Born: 9/9/83 in Neu-Ulm, West Germany
ML Seasons: 2

Overall Statistics

	W	L	Pct.	ERA	G	GS	Sv	IP	H	BB	SO	HR	Avg
'04	2	1	.667	7.30	8	5	0	24.2	31	11	16	7	.307
Car.	4	2	.667	5.01	12	8	0	46.2	48	22	35	9	.270

2004 Situational Stats

	W	L	ERA	Sv	IP		AB	H	HR	RBI	Avg
Home	2	1	6.38	0	18.1	LHB	52	16	3	6	.308
Road	0	0	9.95	0	6.1	RHB	49	15	4	10	.306
First Half	2	0	3.86	0	11.2	Sc Pos	22	3	0	5	.136
Scnd Half	0	1	10.38	0	13.0	Clutch	0	0	0	0	–

2004 Season

Edwin Jackson was recalled for one start in June, then two more in July before a strained right forearm sent him to the DL. Jackson spent the last month of the season with LA and made a couple of starts, but he clearly was not the same pitcher that had showed so much promise in '03.

Pitching, Defense & Hitting

Jackson's velocity was down several ticks last season, topping out in the low 90s. He gets good movement on his slider, but getting it over for a strike is another matter. Jackson continues to work on his changeup, and the mastery of the offspeed pitch will be key. Though he has a nice compact delivery to the plate, his pickoff move is only fair. Jackson is an excellent athlete who handles the glove and the bat with skill.

2005 Outlook

Jackson will get another shot at a starting slot, but he will have to clearly earn it this time. As talented as he is, it must be remembered that the 21-year-old has just over 400 professional innings under his belt. Jackson still needs to hone his skills, which could mean another half-season at Triple-A Las Vegas or work as a long man in the Dodger bullpen.

Hideo Nomo

Position: SP
Bats: R **Throws:** R
Ht: 6' 2" **Wt:** 210

Opening Day Age: 36
Born: 8/31/68 in Osaka, Japan
ML Seasons: 10
Pronunciation: hih-DAY-oh NO-mo

Overall Statistics

	W	L	Pct.	ERA	G	GS	Sv	IP	H	BB	SO	HR	Avg
'04	4	11	.267	8.25	18	18	0	84.0	105	42	54	19	.312
Car.	118	101	.539	4.05	301	299	0	1871.1	1631	853	1856	232	.235

2004 Situational Stats

	W	L	ERA	Sv	IP		AB	H	HR	RBI	Avg
Home	2	6	8.26	0	44.2	LHB	139	47	7	26	.338
Road	2	5	8.24	0	39.1	RHB	198	58	12	43	.293
First Half	3	10	8.06	0	67.0	Sc Pos	105	34	4	51	.324
Scnd Half	1	1	9.00	0	17.0	Clutch	0	0	0	0	–

2004 Season

After undergoing shoulder surgery the previous winter, Hideo Nomo opened the campaign in the majors but clearly was not himself. He went to the DL twice for a total of almost three months, and he struggled mightily when he *was* able to take the ball.

Pitching, Defense & Hitting

When he is right, Nomo tops out in the upper 80s with his fastball. But he must have enough velocity on the heater so hitters cannot sit on his devastating split-finger pitch. When he gets ahead in the count, Nomo starts the splitter about waist-high and by the time it reaches the plate, the batter is flailing at the air as the ball hits the dirt. Nomo pitched exclusively from the stretch at the tail end of 2004, but opposing basestealers still were 15-for-19 against him. He is gawky with both the bat and the glove.

2005 Outlook

Nomo ended up with the highest ERA of any pitcher who ever recorded 15 or more decisions in a season, and his career could be done. That said, he was written off after the 1998 campaign and has won almost 70 games since then. Someone will give Nomo a shot, and no one should be surprised if he makes 30 decent starts this year.

Los Angeles

David Ross

Position: C
Bats: R Throws: R
Ht: 6' 2" Wt: 205

Opening Day Age: 28
Born: 3/19/77 in Bainbridge, GA
ML Seasons: 3

Overall Statistics

	G	AB	R	H	D	T	HR	RBI	SB	BB	SO	Avg	OBP	Slg
'04	70	165	13	28	3	1	5	15	0	15	62	.170	.253	.291
Car.	118	299	34	62	11	1	16	35	0	30	108	.207	.292	.411

2004 Situational Stats

	AB	H	HR	RBI	Avg		AB	H	HR	RBI	Avg
Home	76	15	2	7	.197	LHP	64	8	1	1	.125
Road	89	13	3	8	.146	RHP	101	20	4	14	.198
First Half	70	12	2	5	.171	Sc Pos	31	5	0	8	.161
Scnd Half	95	16	3	10	.168	Clutch	20	3	1	2	.150

2004 Season

After David Ross banged out 10 homers in only 124 at-bats in 2003, the Dodgers had high hopes that he could provide similar pop over a full season. How wrong they were. Not only did Ross hit half as many longballs in more at-bats, but he failed to make contact almost one-third of the time. Even after Paul Lo Duca was traded to the Marlins, Ross remained buried on the bench.

Hitting, Baserunning & Defense

Ross can turn on mistakes on the inner half, but that's about the extent of his batting prowess. He cannot catch up with above-average heat and has little chance against anything with a wrinkle. Ross went to an 0-2 count in more than 20 percent of his plate appearances last season. On the basepaths, he runs like a catcher, and his hands and feet are not that quick behind the plate. While Ross has adequate arm strength, his throws are often offline.

2005 Outlook

No longer a kid, Ross proved last year that he does not have the talent to play in the major leagues. The Dodgers will be upgrading at the position this season, and Ross will return to Triple-A Las Vegas, only coming up should an injury strike one of the frontliners.

Jayson Werth

Position: LF/RF
Bats: R Throws: R
Ht: 6' 5" Wt: 215

Opening Day Age: 25
Born: 5/20/79 in Springfield, IL
ML Seasons: 3

Overall Statistics

	G	AB	R	H	D	T	HR	RBI	SB	BB	SO	Avg	OBP	Slg
'04	89	290	56	76	11	3	16	47	4	30	85	.262	.338	.486
Car.	130	384	67	98	17	4	18	63	6	39	118	.255	.329	.461

2004 Situational Stats

	AB	H	HR	RBI	Avg		AB	H	HR	RBI	Avg
Home	149	41	11	31	.275	LHP	93	27	8	19	.290
Road	141	35	5	16	.248	RHP	197	49	8	28	.249
First Half	66	21	6	14	.318	Sc Pos	75	17	3	25	.227
Scnd Half	224	55	10	33	.246	Clutch	53	13	1	8	.245

2004 Season

Jayson Werth was acquired from Toronto just before Opening Day last season, and then he went on the DL for two months with a strained oblique muscle. After platooning in left field for a month upon his return, Werth was a full-timer by season's end.

Hitting, Baserunning & Defense

Werth can hit the ball a long way and to any part of the yard. Though his swing is rather long, he has a good sense of the strike zone. As his playing time increased and the scouting reports made their rounds, opponents were able to beat him with the classic up-and-in, down-and-away approach. He runs quite well and can steal a base on occasion. A converted catcher, Werth played all three outfield positions last season. While his range is decent, his inexperience showed on hard-hit balls right at him. His arm is strong and accurate.

2005 Outlook

Werth ended the season with a slight ligamnet tear in his right elbow. If the elbow heals properly, he is slated to be the full-time left fielder this year. While he may have earned that opportunity, several question marks remain. One is durability, and the other is whether he can make enough contact.

Other Los Angeles Dodgers

Chin-Feng Chen (**Pos**: LF, **Age**: 27, **Bats**: R)

	G	AB	R	H	D	T	HR	RBI	SB	BB	SO	Avg	OBP	Slg
'04	8	8	1	0	0	0	0	0	0	2		3 .000	.200	.000
Car.	12	14	2	0	0	0	0	0	0	3		6 .000	.176	.000

Chen was called up three different times last season, but seldom left the bench. He has played for Triple-A Las Vegas in each of the last three years, hitting in the .280s with 20-plus homers each time, but he never has gotten a shot in the bigs. 2005 Outlook: C

Elmer Dessens (**Pos**: RHP, **Age**: 34)

	W	L	Pct.	ERA	G	GS	Sv	IP	H	BB	SO	HR	Avg
'04	2	6	.250	4.46	50	10	2	105.0	123	31	73	15	.287
Car.	40	49	.449	4.46	249	128	3	914.0	1031	265	550	115	.287

Dessens began the season in Arizona's rotation, but was sent to the bullpen after going 1-4 with a 7.56 ERA in his first seven starts. The Dodgers accquired him in a post-deadline waiver deal, and re-signed him in December. 2005 Outlook: C

Brian Falkenborg (**Pos**: RHP, **Age**: 27)

	W	L	Pct.	ERA	G	GS	Sv	IP	H	BB	SO	HR	Avg
'04	1	0	1.000	7.53	6	0	0	14.1	19	9	11	2	.322
Car.	1	0	1.000	6.23	8	0	0	17.1	21	11	12	2	.304

Falkenbourg started the season on the DL with a strained right knee, then served as a long man in the Dodger pen for a month. Sent back to Triple-A Las Vegas, where he was mostly a starter, he went 4-6 with a 6.17 ERA, though he fanned 87 in 89 innings. 2005 Outlook: C

Jose Flores (**Pos**: 2B, **Age**: 31, **Bats**: R)

	G	AB	R	H	D	T	HR	RBI	SB	BB	SO	Avg	OBP	Slg
'04	9	4	0	1	0	0	0	0	0	1		2 .250	.400	.250
Car.	16	7	2	1	0	0	0	0	1	2		2 .143	.400	.143

After getting snagged from the A's system by GM Paul DePodesta in the spring, Flores hit .313 with a .407 OBP at Triple-A Las Vegas. He has played 11 seasons in the minors, but has a total of just seven big league at-bats. 2005 Outlook: C

Jason Grabowski (**Pos**: LF, **Age**: 28, **Bats**: L)

	G	AB	R	H	D	T	HR	RBI	SB	BB	SO	Avg	OBP	Slg
'04	113	173	18	38	7	0	7	20	0	19	50	.220	.297	.382
Car.	125	189	21	41	8	1	7	21	0	23	56	.217	.302	.381

Rescued from the A's minor league system just before the season began, Grabowski was one of the main left-handed bats off the Dodger bench all season long. He hit just .133 from August 1 on, but he has a .290 lifetime average in seven minor league seasons. 2005 Outlook: C

Brent Mayne (**Pos**: C, **Age**: 36, **Bats**: L)

	G	AB	R	H	D	T	HR	RBI	SB	BB	SO	Avg	OBP	Slg
'04	83	190	14	42	6	1	0	15	1	27	41	.221	.314	.263
Car.	1279	3614	359	951	178	8	38	403	18	370	580	.263	.332	.348

Mayne did not receive much playing time with Arizona and missed more than a month with a strained lower back. After coming over to LA at the trade deadline, the 36-year-old did most of the catching down the stretch. Dodger pitchers had a 3.78 ERA with Mayne behind the plate. 2005 Outlook: C

Rodney Myers (**Pos**: RHP, **Age**: 35)

	W	L	Pct.	ERA	G	GS	Sv	IP	H	BB	SO	HR	Avg
'04	0	0	–	0.00	1	0	0	2.0	1	0	1	0	.167
Car.	7	5	.583	5.07	167	1	1	239.2	265	110	161	28	.285

Myers spent a total of three days in the majors last season, though he pitched two shutout innings in his only appearance, and ended the year in the Mets' system. After totaling 81.2 IP since 2000, he will be scrambling for a job once again this year. 2005 Outlook: C

Olmedo Saenz (**Pos**: 1B, **Age**: 34, **Bats**: R)

	G	AB	R	H	D	T	HR	RBI	SB	BB	SO	Avg	OBP	Slg
'04	77	111	17	31	1	0	8	22	0	12	33	.279	.352	.505
Car.	429	1055	148	280	62	5	43	146	3	91	220	.265	.345	.456

Saenz proved to be a valuable bench player for the Dodgers last year, finishing with a .313 batting average as a pinch-hitter. He could earn more playing time in a platoon at first base this season, as Saenz pounds left-ies; he hit .338 versus southpaws with a 1.058 OPS. 2005 Outlook: C

Duaner Sanchez (**Pos**: RHP, **Age**: 25)

	W	L	Pct.	ERA	G	GS	Sv	IP	H	BB	SO	HR	Avg
'04	3	1	.750	3.38	67	0	0	80.0	81	27	44	9	.266
Car.	4	1	.800	4.60	82	0	0	92.0	102	35	53	13	.285

Sanchez was a valuable component in the Dodger bullpen last year, pitching more than one inning in 24 of his appearances. He posted a 1.69 ERA in September, and throws a fastball in the mid-90s. The 25-year-old could evolve into a closer some day. 2005 Outlook: C

Scott Stewart (**Pos**: LHP, **Age**: 29)

	W	L	Pct.	ERA	G	GS	Sv	IP	H	BB	SO	HR	Avg
'04	1	2	.333	6.58	34	0	0	26.0	43	12	26	5	.377
Car.	11	6	.647	3.99	214	0	20	180.2	187	60	161	19	.268

Stewart spent the first couple of months with the Indians before they sent him down to Triple-A Buffalo. Desperate for lefthanded bullpen help, the Dodgers acquired him in a post-deadline deal. Lefthanders hit .411 against him last year. 2005 Outlook: C

Joe Thurston (Pos: 2B, Age: 25, Bats: L)

	G	AB	R	H	D	T	HR	RBI	SB	BB	SO	Avg	OBP	Slg
'04	17	17	1	3	1	1	0	1	0	0	5	.176	.167	.353
Car.	37	40	4	11	2	1	0	2	0	1	7	.275	.279	.375

Thurston's window of opportunity came in 2003 when he tanked a spring training audition for the starting job. He has a lifetime average of .296 in six minor league seasons, but he may need to move on to a new organization to get another shot at the bigs. 2005 Outlook: C

Mike Venafro (Pos: LHP, Age: 31)

	W	L	Pct.	ERA	G	GS	Sv	IP	H	BB	SO	HR	Avg
'04	0	0	–	4.00	17	0	0	9.0	11	3	6	1	.306
Car.	14	10	.583	4.11	300	0	5	249.2	261	91	129	15	.274

After pitching for the Royals' Triple-A club in Omaha for most of the season, Venafro was signed by the Dodgers in August. The "Moneyball" cast member probably earned himself a spring training invite by holding opposing lefties to a .200 average. 2005 Outlook: C

Robin Ventura (Pos: 1B/3B, Age: 37, Bats: L)

	G	AB	R	H	D	T	HR	RBI	SB	BB	SO	Avg	OBP	Slg
'04	102	152	19	37	3	0	5	28	0	22	31	.243	.337	.362
Car.	2079	7064	1006	1885	338	14	294	1182	24	1075	1179	.267	.362	.444

Ventura capped off a fine 16-year career by hitting two more grand slams last year, moving him into a tie with Willie McCovey for third on the all-time list with 18. He has retired, though it would not be a surprise to see him stay in the game in another capacity. 2005 Outlook: D

Tom Wilson (Pos: C, Age: 34, Bats: R)

	G	AB	R	H	D	T	HR	RBI	SB	BB	SO	Avg	OBP	Slg
'04	13	12	1	2	0	0	0	0	0	1	5	.167	.231	.167
Car.	214	554	75	140	29	0	15	76	0	58	169	.253	.327	.386

Wilson spent time with three different Triple-A clubs last season and ended the year in a pennant race with the Dodgers. He has been playing professionally since 1991 and has hit 20-plus homers in two different minor league seasons. 2005 Outlook: C

Los Angeles Dodgers Minor League Prospects

Organization Overview:

Since GM Paul DePodesta inherited a resurgent minor league system, he has seen no need for a big overhaul. Director of Scouting Logan White was retained and has now orchestrated three superb drafts in a row, so the lower levels are loaded with up-and-comers. With few prospects ready to provide immediate offensive help, DePodesta made a series of minor deals to bring in some bats. Somewhat surprisingly, the Dodger system has not become "Moneyball South." Rather, the principles of power and patience simply are being integrated and perhaps emphasized a bit more. Several pitchers appear to be about ready to help the big club, but all have struggled with injury problems over the last couple of seasons.

Willy Aybar

Position: 2B
Bats: B **Throws:** R
Ht: 6' 0" **Wt:** 175
Opening Day Age: 22
Born: 3/9/83 in Bani, DR

Recent Statistics

	G	AB	R	H	D	T	HR	RBI	SB	BB	SO	Avg
2003 A Vero Beach	119	445	47	122	29	3	11	74	9	41	70	.274
2004 AA Jacksonville	126	482	56	133	27	0	15	77	8	50	77	.276

Though he already has played five seasons in the minors, Aybar is just 22 years old. The switch-hitter has a patient approach at the slab and he tends to make contact. While predominantly a line-drive hitter, his power is starting to emerge as he fills out, and he has hit 10-plus homers in each of the last three campaigns. After playing a fine third base in his first four seasons, Aybar was moved over to second last year. He has the hands and agility to handle the keystone, and now just needs some experience at making the turn. The young Dominican will start the 2005 season at Triple-A Las Vegas and should be knocking on the big league door in 2006.

Chad Billingsley

Position: P
Bats: R **Throws:** R
Ht: 6' 2" **Wt:** 195
Opening Day Age: 20
Born: 7/29/84 in Defiance, OH

Recent Statistics

	W	L	ERA	G	GS	Sv	IP	H	R	BB	SO	HR
2003 R Ogden	5	4	2.83	11	11	0	54.0	49	24	15	62	0
2004 A Vero Beach	7	4	2.35	18	18	0	92.0	68	32	49	111	6
2004 AA Jacksonville	4	0	2.98	8	8	0	42.1	32	16	22	47	1

Billingsley has dominated opposing hitters since the Dodgers selected him in the first round of the 2003 draft. The burly righthander's arm action is nice and loose, and he routinely hits 95 MPH with his fastball. Billingsley has two breaking pitches, an action slider in the mid-80s and a solid curveball, and he already has

confidence in his changeup as well. In three different minor league levels, he has allowed just seven homers while collecting 220 strikeouts in 188.1 innings. The 20-year-old will try to pick up where he left off in Double-A Jacksonville, where he has yet to lose in eight starts.

Joel Guzman

Position: SS
Bats: R **Throws:** R
Ht: 6' 6" **Wt:** 198
Opening Day Age: 20
Born: 11/24/84 in Quisqueya, DR

Recent Statistics

	G	AB	R	H	D	T	HR	RBI	SB	BB	SO	Avg
2003 A S Georgia	58	217	33	51	13	0	8	29	4	9	62	.235
2003 A Vero Beach	62	240	30	59	13	1	5	24	0	11	60	.246
2004 A Vero Beach	87	329	52	101	22	8	14	51	8	21	78	.307
2004 AA Jacksonville	46	182	25	51	11	3	9	35	1	13	44	.280

The light may have turned on for Guzman last season. The Dodgers sent him back for another try at Class-A Vero Beach, and he exhibited all the tools for which they invested more than $2 million several years earlier. Guzman always has been able to pound fastballs, but he is now learning to sit back on breaking pitches and offspeed stuff. Though Director of Player Development Terry Collins is keeping the 20-year-old at shortstop for now, it is probably a matter of time before the 6-foot-6 Guzman moves to another spot on the diamond. After seeing Guzman hold his own in Double-A Jacksonville, as well as in the Dominican Winter League, the parent club may soon have to find a lineup.

Joel Hanrahan

Position: P
Bats: R **Throws:** R
Ht: 6' 3" **Wt:** 215
Opening Day Age: 23
Born: 10/6/81 in Des Moines, IA

Recent Statistics

	W	L	ERA	G	GS	Sv	IP	H	R	BB	SO	HR
2003 AA Jacksonville	10	4	2.43	23	23	0	133.1	117	44	53	130	5
2003 AAA Las Vegas	1	2	10.08	5	5	0	25.0	36	28	20	13	2
2004 AAA Las Vegas	7	7	5.05	25	22	0	119.1	128	78	75	97	22

Hanrahan's 2004 campaign got off to a bad start when his shoulder began to bother him in the spring. Though he eventually was able to make 22 starts for Triple-A Las Vegas, he lacked his usual command. When healthy, Hanrahan has a nice sinker-slider combo, the former registering 92-94 MPH and the breaking pitch in the mid-80s. He also will mix in a changeup, though it still needs work to become major league quality. Throughout his five-year pro career, the 23-year-old has struggled upon his callup to a higher level, so he may need more time at Triple-A, but he should be making an appearance in Los Angeles before the 2005 season is out.

James Loney

Position: 1B **Opening Day Age:** 20
Bats: L **Throws:** L **Born:** 5/7/84 in Houston,
Ht: 6' 3" **Wt:** 205 TX

Recent Statistics

	G	AB	R	H	D	T	HR	RBI	SB	BB	SO	Avg
2003 A Vero Beach	125	468	64	129	31	3	7	46	9	43	80	.276
2004 AA Jacksnville	104	395	39	94	19	2	4	35	5	42	75	.238

After impressing everyone while playing with the big club in spring training, Loney had a disappointing season at Double-A Jacksonville, where his average dipped all the way down to .238. He has struggled with injuries throughout his pro career and last year was no different, as he missed four weeks with a severely infected finger. Loney has a beautiful lefthanded stroke and naturally drives balls on the outer half into the left-center field gap, and no one doubts that the power will come as he fills out. Defensively, he could play in the majors today, and could be a future Gold Glover. After a fine campaign in the Arizona Fall League, Loney should move up another level this season. Now if he can just stay healthy...

Greg Miller

Position: P **Opening Day Age:** 20
Bats: L **Throws:** L **Born:** 11/3/84 in Orange,
Ht: 6' 5" **Wt:** 190 CA

Recent Statistics

	W	L	ERA	G	GS	Sv	IP	H	R	BB	SO	HR
2003 AA Jacksnville	1	1	1.01	4	4	0	26.2	15	5	7	40	1
2003 A Vero Beach	11	4	2.49	21	21	0	115.2	103	40	41	111	5

Miller did not throw a single pitch in a game this season, yet he remains one of the top pitching prospects in baseball. After feeling pain in his shoulder in the spring, surgeons removed a bursa sac. He was throwing well before the season was out, but the Dodgers decided to remain on the safe side and held him out. Before the procedure, Miller threw a four-seamer in the 91-93 MPH range and backed it up with a superb curveball and a workable change. A cutter/slider might have been the pitch that was straining his shoulder and if so, it could be dropped. The 20-year-old picked up 25 pounds while rehabbing and should be stronger when he returns to Double-A Jacksonville this year.

Antonio Perez

Position: 2B **Opening Day Age:** 25
Bats: R **Throws:** R **Born:** 1/26/80 in Bani,
Ht: 5' 11" **Wt:** 170 DR

Recent Statistics

	G	AB	R	H	D	T	HR	RBI	SB	BB	SO	Avg
2004 AAA Las Vegas	125	476	92	141	24	6	22	88	22	61	87	.296
2004 NL Los Angeles	13	13	5	3	1	0	0	0	1	0	5	.231

Though the deal did not include the high-profile names of his previous two trades (Ken Griffey Jr. and Lou Piniella), Perez was picked up from the Devil Rays right before Opening Day. He is a fine offensive player, especially for a middle infielder, and fits the "Moneyball" profile perfectly. He waits for his pitch, generally makes good contact and has good power to all fields. Perez can handle the duties both at shortstop and second base. He should make the Dodger ballclub this season, perhaps taking Jose Hernandez' spot as Alex Cora's platoon mate at second while filling in at other positions.

Cody Ross

Position: OF **Opening Day Age:** 24
Bats: R **Throws:** L **Born:** 12/23/80 in
Ht: 5' 11" **Wt:** 180 Portales, NM

Recent Statistics

	G	AB	R	H	D	T	HR	RBI	SB	BB	SO	Avg
2003 AAA Toledo	124	470	74	135	35	6	20	61	15	32	86	.287
2003 AL Detroit	6	19	1	4	1	0	1	5	0	1	3	.211
2004 AAA Las Vegas	60	238	44	65	17	2	14	49	2	18	43	.273

Ross is another guy who Los Angeles general manager Paul DePodesta plucked off another club's roster at the end of spring training, this time from the Tigers. Unfortunately, wrist and knee problems limited Ross' playing time, but the scrappy throwback player still managed to send 14 balls out of the yard for Triple-A Las Vegas in just 60 games. Though he strikes out a fair amount of the time, Ross also will take a walk and he has above-average speed. The 24-year-old can play anywhere in the outfield and could make the major league club if he has a good spring.

Others to Watch

Jonathan Broxton (20) brings serious heat (95-96 MPH), and he struck out 144 in 128.1 IP at high Class-A Vero Beach last season. After battling the scale the previous campaign, the 20-year-old righthander lost 35-40 pounds last year. . . The Dodgers converted **Russell Martin** (22) from third base to catcher a few seasons back, and he has evolved into an excellent catch-and-throw guy. He had 40 extra-base hits for high Class-A Vero Beach last year, and drew 71 walks to just 54 strikeouts. . . Bert Blyleven's nephew, **Brian Pilkington** (22), missed the entire 2004 campaign and has battled shoulder problems since he was a second-round pick in the 2001 draft. When healthy, the righty has posted a 5.6-1 strikeout-walk ratio. . . Several teams mentioned **Chuck Tiffany** (20) when the Dodgers were looking for help down the stretch. Though he had a balky shoulder, the 20-year-old southpaw tossed a perfect game as well as a combined no-hitter at Class-A Columbus last season. His curveball and circle change are already big league quality. . . **Delwyn Young** (22) has a lifetime average of .301 in his three pro seasons and hit 22 homers in high Class-A Vero Beach last season. The switch-hitter needs to cut down on his strikeouts and improve his defense at second base, but he is moving quickly up the ladder.

Miller Park

Offense

Miller Park is a fairly average park for offense and pitching in the National League. It's almost symmetrical, with the foul pole and power alley in right field ever-so-slightly longer than in left. Last summer was notable for a lack of heat and humidity in Milwaukee, so the ball did not carry as well as in previous seasons. Also, the Brewers had less power, and their staff featured more groundball pitchers than in 2002 and 2003. The result was that scoring at Miller Park was down about seven percent. When the roof and window panels are closed, the ball doesn't carry.

Defense

Foul territory extends only about 200 feet down either line, so hardly any foul popups are caught by outfielders. Balls hit sharply past first or third base are likely to bounce off the grandstand fence and back toward the infield. There are no sharp angles in the outfield fence, as in some other new parks. The infield is well maintained, and there are very few bad hops in Milwaukee.

Who It Helps the Most

Hitters whose strength is to the alleys will benefit. In 2004, Russell Branyan hit more than two-thirds of his home runs at Miller Park. Pitchers who can keep the ball on the ground fare better. Corner outfielders with modest speed can cheat toward the alleys because they don't have to worry about running down long foul balls.

Who It Hurts the Most

Because Miller favors power hitters, not singles hitters, the team it has hurt the most is the power-deficient Brewers. Scott Podsednik was better on the road the last two years, and Brady Clark was markedly better away from Miller Park in 2004. The park also hurts flyball pitchers.

Rookies & Newcomers

Carlos Lee is well suited to hit for power in Miller Park. Slap hitters Damian Miller and David Krynzel may have trouble. Ben Hendrickson posted a lofty groundout-flyout ratio for the 2004 club and may do well there. Jose Capellan must keep the ball down to have success.

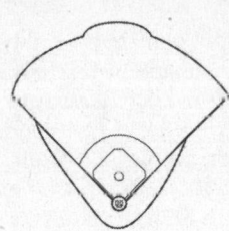

Dimensions: LF-344, LCF-371, CF-400, RCF-374, RF-345

Capacity: 41,900

Elevation: 635 feet

Surface: Grass

Foul Territory: Small

Park Factors

2004 Season

	Home Games Brewers	Opp	Total	Away Games Brewers	Opp	Total	Index
G	75	75	150	71	71	142	
Avg	.247	.253	.250	.243	.271	.257	97
AB	2541	2672	5213	2409	2380	4789	103
R	315	358	673	251	355	606	105
H	627	675	1302	585	645	1230	100
2B	152	163	315	117	137	254	114
3B	17	17	34	13	14	27	116
HR	59	76	135	63	78	141	88
BB	284	223	507	209	215	424	110
SO	627	557	1184	555	453	1008	108
E	51	63	114	58	46	104	104
E-Infield	47	55	102	48	37	85	114
LHB-Avg	.261	.246	.254	.250	.279	.262	97
LHB-HR	32	27	59	38	27	65	84
RHB-Avg	.231	.257	.246	.234	.266	.253	97
RHB-HR	27	49	76	25	51	76	91

2002-2004

	Home Games Brewers	Opp	Total	Away Games Brewers	Opp	Total	Index
G	225	225	450	221	221	442	
Avg	.251	.260	.256	.249	.278	.263	97
AB	7489	7992	15481	7574	7399	14973	102
R	910	1138	2048	885	1130	2015	100
H	1876	2080	3956	1885	2055	3940	99
2B	394	448	842	369	405	774	105
3B	37	51	88	40	47	87	98
HR	217	281	498	216	253	469	103
BB	786	789	1575	704	809	1513	101
SO	1657	1573	3230	1688	1345	3033	103
E	155	141	296	160	150	310	94
E-Infield	140	123	263	133	125	258	100
LHB-Avg	.263	.265	.264	.255	.274	.264	100
LHB-HR	82	115	197	83	92	175	106
RHB-Avg	.242	.257	.250	.244	.280	.263	95
RHB-HR	135	166	301	133	161	294	101

2004 Rankings (National League)

- Third-highest double factor
- Third-highest walk factor
- Third-highest strikeout factor

Milwaukee

2004 Season

Ned Yost's second season as manager of the Brewers extended the progress made in his first. The Richie Sexson trade late in 2003 gave him more tools to employ, bringing Lyle Overbay, Junior Spivey, Chad Moeller, Craig Counsell, Chris Capuano and Jorge de la Rosa. The pitching was solid throughout the year, with four starters, a closer and three setup men with clearly defined roles. Yost will have to rebuild the bullpen after trades made at the winter meetings.

Offense

Yost used the wisdom gained from years coaching for Bobby Cox to get as much production as any-one could from his team's talent on offense, lim-ited, as it was, by a major league-low $27.5 mil-lion payroll. The loss of Junior Spivey near mid-season hurt the offense, but enabled Yost to find at least 385 at-bats each for second-year infielders Keith Ginter and Bill Hall. While Yost prefers a set lineup, except for his catcher platoon, he will platoon for one-sided hitters like Russell Branyan. He'll use sacrifices, stolen bases, hit-and-run plays—anything to produce runs.

Pitching & Defense

With the exception of Chris Capuano's injuries, Brewers pitchers managed to stay healthy in 2004, resulting in a much-improved staff ERA. With two light-hitting catchers, Yost devised a platoon in which Chad Moeller and Gary Bennett both saw plenty of action behind the plate. The Brewers ranked near the bottom of the National League in fielding percentage last season. Second and third base were key trouble spots, and both are up for grabs in 2005.

2005 Outlook

The task for 2005 is to sustain for a full season the level of success attained in the first half of 2004. That will require building up an offense suffering from a lack of power. That's Yost's problem, but not his fault. He has the team pointed in the right direction and has the respect and confidence of his players. It's beyond his control whether resources will be available to make the improvements nec-essary to win.

Born: 8/19/54 in Eureka, California

Playing Experience: 1980-1985, Mil, Tex, Mon

Managerial Experience: 2 seasons

Manager Statistics

Year	Team, Lg	W	L	Pct	GB	Finish
2004	Milwaukee, NL	67	94	.416	37.5	6th Central
2 Seasons		135	188	.418	–	–

2004 Starting Pitchers by Days Rest

	<=3	4	5	6+
Brewers Starts	1	91	25	32
Brewers ERA	–	4.01	3.51	5.59
NL Avg Starts	2	82	46	23
NL ERA	4.58	4.35	4.28	4.73

2004 Situational Stats

	Ned Yost	NL Average
Hit & Run Success %	38.2	38.0
Stolen Base Success %	77.5	71.7
Platoon Pct.	56.2	55.2
Defensive Subs	13	18
High-Pitch Outings	9	6
Quick/Slow Hooks	19/8	21/12
Sacrifice Attempts	84	99

2004 Rankings (National League)

- 1st in stolen base attempts (178), steals of second base (124) and fewest caught stealings of third base (2)
- 3rd in stolen-base percentage, steals of third base (14), squeeze plays (9), starting lineups used (132) and pinch-hitters used (283)

Russell Branyan

2004 Season

Miller Park is built for a guy like Russell Branyan, and he didn't disappoint the home folks, especially when facing righthanded pitchers. The Brewers acquired Branyan from the Indians in late July. He rewarded them with an OPS that was .051 higher than $8 million man Geoff Jenkins. On a team desperate for power in the second half, Branyan took playing time at third base from Wes Helms, Keith Ginter and Bill Hall.

Hitting

Branyan has a well-established level of play. He'll hit under .250 with some power, but because he can't lay off breaking balls and high fastballs, he strikes out at an alarming rate. He whiffed 43 percent of the time in 2004. When he does make contact, however, he usually hits the ball in the air, and he usually hits it hard. Nearly two-thirds of his hits went for extra bases in 2004, and he homered once in every 14.4 at-bats. At that rate, Branyan could hit about 30 home runs if given 450 at-bats. It's by no means clear that the Brewers have better options for the fifth and sixth slots in their batting order.

Baserunning & Defense

Although he often played left field for the Reds and Indians, Branyan's defensive innings for the Brewers came almost exclusively at third base. He is a below-average defensive third baseman, but not disastrously so. He has worked to improve his defense and throws reasonably well. Because so few of his hits are singles, Branyan does not clog the bases ahead of Keith Ginter or Bill Hall. He rarely steals a base.

2005 Outlook

If the Brewers don't add enough power at other positions, Branyan may be their best bet to hit behind Geoff Jenkins against righthanded pitchers in 2005. His power comes at a cost, in batting average, defense and speed. And Branyan doesn't hit lefthanders at all. If he can't make it in Milwaukee, it's unlikely he'll land a starting job elsewhere in 2005, at least until injuries thin the available talent at third base.

Position: 3B
Bats: L **Throws:** R
Ht: 6' 3" **Wt:** 195

Opening Day Age: 29
Born: 12/19/75 in Warner Robins, GA
ML Seasons: 7
Pronunciation: BRAN-yen

Overall Statistics

	G	AB	R	H	D	T	HR	RBI	SB	BB	SO	Avg	OBP	Slg
'04	51	158	21	37	11	1	11	27	1	20	68	.234	.324	.525
Car.	451	1262	177	288	61	6	81	207	6	161	517	.228	.319	.479

Where He Hits the Ball

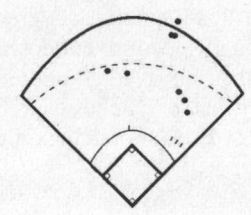 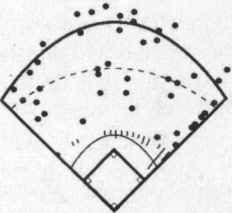

Vs. LHP **Vs. RHP**

2004 Situational Stats

	AB	H	HR	RBI	Avg		AB	H	HR	RBI	Avg
Home	90	26	8	23	.289	LHP	30	5	1	3	.167
Road	68	11	3	4	.162	RHP	128	32	10	24	.250
First Half	0	0	0	0	–	Sc Pos	38	6	2	14	.158
Scnd Half	158	37	11	27	.234	Clutch	28	6	2	4	.214

2004 Rankings (National League)

- Led the Brewers in fewest GDPs per GDP situation (2.6%)

Milwaukee

Chris Capuano

2004 Season

Chris Capuano was the more advanced prospect of the two pitchers acquired by Milwaukee in the Richie Sexson trade, and manager New Yost wasted no time inserting him into the rotation. Capuano was an adequate fourth starter for the Brewers last summer, though he lost time to back and quadriceps injuries. In his first full major league season, he worked well with catcher Chad Moeller. Four of Capuano's eight quality starts came in July and early August, before elbow problems ended his season in late August.

Pitching

Capuano gets such good movement on his fastball, slider and changeup that he's sometimes difficult to catch. And he's smart, as his Economics degree from Duke will attest. Capuano needs to cut down on the longballs and lengthen his average outing. In 2004, he averaged fewer than 87 pitches and 16 outs per start. As with most Brewers pitchers, he received very little run support.

Defense & Hitting

Despite making 17 starts, Capuano had only 30 at-bats. He handled them pretty well, with six hits and two doubles, but he did not have a sacrifice bunt all year. Defensively, he's sound, fielding well and covering first base while handling 19 chances flawlessly. He has a great pickoff move that completely neutralizes basestealing; he allowed only one stolen base while facing 385 batters.

2005 Outlook

Capuano's elbow problem was diagnosed as tendinitis by Dr. James Andrews, and no surgery was required. He is expected to be ready for the start of spring training. It wouldn't be necessary to rush him back if he isn't ready to go, as the Brewers' rotation is more settled now than at the start of the 2004 season. Since No. 2 starter Doug Davis also is a lefty, Capuano, if healthy, probably would pitch in the fourth or fifth slot. Eventually he projects as a No. 2 guy himself.

Position: SP
Bats: L **Throws:** L
Ht: 6' 3" **Wt:** 210

Opening Day Age: 26
Born: 8/19/78 in Springfield, MA
ML Seasons: 2
Pronunciation: cap-u-ON-o

Overall Statistics

	W	L	Pct.	ERA	G	GS	Sv	IP	H	BB	SO	HR	Avg
'04	6	8	.429	4.99	17	17	0	88.1	91	37	80	18	.269
Car.	8	12	.400	4.90	26	22	0	121.1	118	48	103	21	.260

2004 Pitching Profile

	Chris Capuano	NL Average
Overall Strike %	61.2	62.5
1st Pitch Strike %	55.6	58.5
Ratio	1.45	1.39
Strikeouts per 9 IP	8.15	6.74
Walks per 9 IP	3.77	3.38
Home Runs per 9 IP	1.83	1.11
Strikeout/Walk Ratio	2.16	1.99
Groundball/Flyball Ratio	0.92	1.25

2004 Situational Stats

	W	L	ERA	Sv	IP		AB	H	HR	RBI	Avg
Home	2	4	4.96	0	45.1	LHB	58	12	0	4	.207
Road	4	4	5.02	0	43.0	RHB	280	79	18	48	.282
First Half	3	5	3.69	0	53.2	Sc Pos	75	23	7	40	.307
Scnd Half	3	3	7.01	0	34.2	Clutch	0	0	0	0	–

2004 Rankings (National League)
- 2nd in losses among rookies
- 4th in wins among rookies

Doug Davis

2004 Season

Brewers general manager Doug Melvin had Doug Davis and Danny Kolb in his previous job as the Rangers' GM, and their success played a major role in the Brewers' much-improved 2004 pitching. Davis was released twice during the 2003 season, but was very effective as a Milwaukee starter over the final quarter of 2003 after Melvin signed him. In 2004, Davis built on that success, serving as the club's No. 2 starter, missing only one start and posting a 2.49 ERA over the final two months.

Pitching

Davis is a prototypical crafty lefthander, changing speeds and location to keep hitters off balance. His best pitches are a cut fastball and a slow curve. In Ned Yost's catcher platoon, Davis always pitched to Chad Moeller when Moeller was healthy. The result was an ERA nearly two-thirds of a point better than any previous season, with a marked improvement in his strikeouts per inning. Most important, he was consistent, with only one rough patch right after the All-Star break.

Defense & Hitting

Davis' failings at the plate hurt his chances to post wins in 2004. He frequently was taken down for a pinch-hitter because the Brewers had a weak offense, and because he can't hit a lick. Davis is that rare player who throws left and bats right, but he went 0-for-42 to start the season. He did manage to put down six sacrifice bunts in 2004. Davis fields his position well, and though lacking a very good move to first base, still manages to hold basestealing to an acceptable level.

2005 Outlook

Like Ben Sheets, Davis pitched well enough in 2004 to win 15-17 games if given adequate offensive support. He has had his two best years in Milwaukee, and as a groundball pitcher, he has an advantage pitching at Miller Park. The Brewers gladly will take a repeat of Davis' 2004 performance this year, and hope that an improved offense can get him the wins he deserves.

Position: SP
Bats: R **Throws:** L
Ht: 6' 4" **Wt:** 213

Opening Day Age: 29
Born: 9/21/75 in Sacramento, CA
ML Seasons: 6

Overall Statistics

	W	L	Pct.	ERA	G	GS	Sv	IP	H	BB	SO	HR	Avg
'04	12	12	.500	3.39	34	34	0	207.1	192	79	166	14	.247
Car.	40	41	.494	4.35	127	107	0	663.2	723	279	440	68	.280

2004 Pitching Profile

	Doug Davis	NL Average
Overall Strike %	63.0	62.5
1st Pitch Strike %	60.2	58.5
Ratio	1.31	1.39
Strikeouts per 9 IP	7.21	6.74
Walks per 9 IP	3.43	3.38
Home Runs per 9 IP	0.61	1.11
Strikeout/Walk Ratio	2.10	1.99
Groundball/Flyball Ratio	1.42	1.25

2004 Situational Stats

	W	L	ERA	Sv	IP		AB	H	HR	RBI	Avg
Home	6	4	2.59	0	107.2	LHB	143	37	2	15	.259
Road	6	8	4.24	0	99.2	RHB	635	155	12	54	.244
First Half	9	6	3.46	0	117.0	Sc Pos	184	44	3	54	.239
Scnd Half	3	6	3.29	0	90.1	Clutch	33	7	1	4	.212

2004 Rankings (National League)

- 3rd in fewest home runs allowed per nine innings (.61)
- 5th in games started
- 8th in lowest ERA at home and most pitches thrown per batter (3.88)
- 9th in lowest slugging percentage allowed (.361)
- Led the Brewers in wins, games started, walks allowed, hit batsmen (7), pickoff throws (100), stolen bases allowed (15), runners caught stealing (6), GDPs induced (18), winning percentage, lowest slugging percentage allowed (.361), lowest stolen-base percentage allowed (71.4) and fewest home runs allowed per nine innings (.61)

2004 Season

In 2003, Keith Ginter led all National League rookies with 14 home runs and appeared to have the inside track to be the Brewers' everyday second baseman in 2004. The acquisition of Junior Spivey changed those plans for the first half, but manager Ned Yost called on Ginter to replace the slumping Wes Helms at third base. When Spivey went down and Russell Branyan took over the third-base job, Ginter got most of the playing time at second base, although he missed nearly all of August with a strained left wrist.

Hitting

While Ginter received fewer than 400 at-bats, only Geoff Jenkins had more home runs for Milwaukee. A guess hitter who will look for his pitch, Ginter starts his hands in the hitting position, making him very quick to the ball, and he picks up his foot without striding. He's a first-ball fastball hitter who can hit for power to all fields. Ginter has trouble hitting the slider, however.

Baserunning & Defense

As a second baseman, Ginter does not have great range, and he managed to turn only 19 double plays in 54 games there. Bill Hall has greater range and is better at turning the double play, but committed a few more errors. At third base, Ginter was charged with just three errors in 47 games last season. His speed is no better than average for a middle infielder, but he was successful in eight of nine attempts to steal.

2005 Outlook

With Lyle Overbay at first base, it would be helpful for the Brewers to get some pop from a middle infielder. On their current roster, Ginter is the most likely source. With the Brewers unlikely to contend in 2005, they should give Ginter the job and see what he can do. In a year, super-prospect Rickie Weeks may be ready to claim the job, and Ginter may be looking for another position.

Position: 2B/3B
Bats: R **Throws:** R
Ht: 5'10" **Wt:** 195

Opening Day Age: 28
Born: 5/5/76 in Norwalk, CA
ML Seasons: 5
Pronunciation: GHIN-ter

Overall Statistics

	G	AB	R	H	D	T	HR	RBI	SB	BB	SO	Avg	OBP	Slg
'04	113	386	47	101	23	2	19	60	8	37	100	.262	.333	.479
Car.	274	834	108	214	47	4	35	115	9	92	205	.257	.344	.448

Where He Hits the Ball

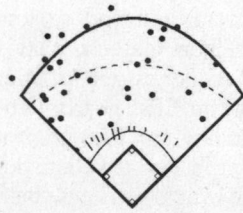
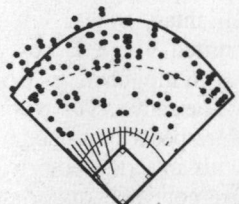

Vs. LHP   **Vs. RHP**

2004 Situational Stats

	AB	H	HR	RBI	Avg		AB	H	HR	RBI	Avg
Home	174	47	9	31	.270	LHP	80	26	6	13	.325
Road	212	54	10	29	.255	RHP	306	75	13	47	.245
First Half	245	63	10	34	.257	Sc Pos	109	29	6	46	.266
Scnd Half	141	38	9	26	.270	Clutch	64	16	1	6	.250

2004 Rankings (National League)

- Led the Brewers in slugging percentage, HR frequency (20.3 ABs per HR), most pitches seen per plate appearance (4.13) and batting average vs. lefthanded pitchers

Bill Hall

2004 Season

The Richie Sexson trade brought Craig Counsell and Junior Spivey to Milwaukee, and there was speculation that Bill Hall might return to the minors in 2004. As it turned out, Hall spent all of 2004 with the major league club, playing semi-regularly after Spivey's season-ending injury in June. Manager Ned Yost used Hall in more than 30 games each at second base and shortstop, and another 11 at third base. Unfortunately, the ball often found him.

Hitting

With his combination of home runs, RBI and stolen bases from a middle-infield position, Hall is the prototype of a player who is more valuable in fantasy baseball than in real life. The Brewers drafted him out of high school and gave him 1,806 minor league at-bats before promoting him to the majors at the end of 2002. But in virtually all aspects of his game, Hall at age 25 is still a work in progress. He needs to make more consistent contact and show more discipline at the plate. Although he bats righthanded, Hall was terrible against lefthanded pitchers for a second consecutive year.

Baserunning & Defense

Although he's fast and possesses obvious athletic ability, neither baserunning nor defense are an asset at this point in Hall's career. Playing less than 800 innings, he still finished among the top 10 National League infielders in errors committed, with 19. He was successful only two-thirds of the time attempting to steal, a percentage that essentially reduces his speed to a non-asset.

2005 Outlook

The question with Hall is can he improve his defense or hitting enough to justify making him the starting second baseman ahead of Keith Ginter. If not, and with top prospect Rickie Weeks likely to take over the job in Milwaukee before the end of next year, Hall might profit by a move to the outfield.

Position: 2B/SS/3B
Bats: R **Throws:** R
Ht: 6' 0" **Wt:** 195

Opening Day Age: 25
Born: 12/28/79 in Nettleton, MS
ML Seasons: 3

Overall Statistics

	G	AB	R	H	D	T	HR	RBI	SB	BB	SO	Avg	OBP	Slg
'04	126	390	43	93	20	3	9	53	12	20	119	.238	.276	.374
Car.	197	568	69	137	30	6	15	78	13	30	160	.241	.280	.394

Where He Hits the Ball

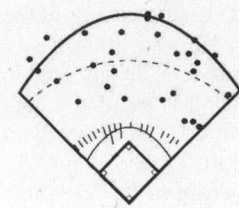
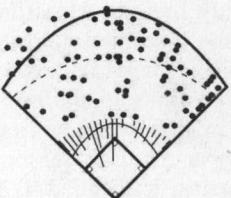

Vs. LHP   **Vs. RHP**

2004 Situational Stats

	AB	H	HR	RBI	Avg		AB	H	HR	RBI	Avg
Home	218	53	5	31	.243	LHP	105	20	3	17	.190
Road	172	40	4	22	.233	RHP	285	73	6	36	.256
First Half	165	41	5	29	.248	Sc Pos	95	22	4	39	.232
Scnd Half	225	52	4	24	.231	Clutch	72	16	2	11	.222

2004 Rankings (National League)

- 5th in highest percentage of swings that missed (30.9)
- 9th in errors at second base (9)
- Led the Brewers in batting average with the bases loaded (.385)

2004 Season

With last December's departure of Richie Sexson, Geoff Jenkins became the Brewers' only major power source in 2004. Injuries ended his season in 2002 and 2003, but he stayed healthy for all of 2004, posting homer and RBI totals very close to those of 2003, when he played 124 games. Perhaps the Brewers' biggest offensive problem in 2004 was the inability to drive in runners, and with runners in scoring position, Jenkins hit just .247.

Hitting

The Brewers look to Jenkins for power. He's an aggressive hitter: although he was the only Brewer with more than 19 homers, he walked only 46 times. He strikes out about a quarter of the time, and his total of 152 whiffs in 2004 was a career high. Like many lefthanders, he has trouble on pitches up and in. His swing is more compact now than when he first came up, and he tends to upper-cut. Last season, Jenkins's batting average against lefthanded pitchers dropped by 55 points from his 2003 level.

Baserunning & Defense

Jenkins is a good defensive left fielder, but with only average speed. He throws well, notching 10 assists and only one error (a missed shoestring catch) in 2004, after recording 11 assists in 2003. He's not a threat to steal, but his power still enabled him to lead the team in runs.

2005 Outlook

Jenkins turned 30 in the summer of 2004. Injuries in 2002 and 2003 left the Brewers wondering what he could do in 600 at-bats, but the results were not encouraging to those who thought he might emerge as an All-Star caliber left fielder in the National League. Jenkins is signed through 2006 at $8 million per year, so if the Brewers fall out of contention in 2005, it would not be surprising to see him traded.

Position: LF
Bats: L **Throws:** R
Ht: 6' 1" **Wt:** 212

Opening Day Age: 30
Born: 7/21/74 in Olympia, WA
ML Seasons: 7

Overall Statistics

	G	AB	R	H	D	T	HR	RBI	SB	BB	SO	Avg	OBP	Slg
'04	157	617	88	163	36	6	27	93	3	46	152	.264	.325	.473
Car.	807	2965	467	826	195	18	149	484	25	250	735	.279	.344	.507

Where He Hits the Ball

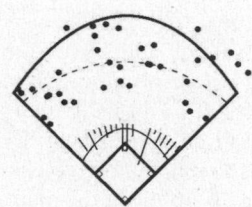
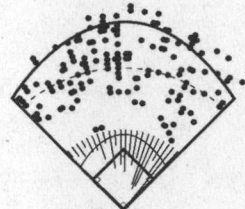

Vs. LHP   **Vs. RHP**

2004 Situational Stats

	AB	H	HR	RBI	Avg		AB	H	HR	RBI	Avg
Home	313	86	13	48	.275	LHP	158	34	6	24	.215
Road	304	77	14	45	.253	RHP	459	129	21	69	.281
First Half	350	88	12	48	.251	Sc Pos	174	43	4	65	.247
Scnd Half	267	75	15	45	.281	Clutch	99	20	3	7	.202

2004 Rankings (National League)

- 1st in fielding percentage in left field (.996)
- 2nd in lowest batting average vs. lefthanded pitchers
- 4th in strikeouts
- 7th in lowest cleanup slugging percentage (.480)
- Led the Brewers in home runs, runs scored, total bases (292), RBI, sacrifice flies (6), intentional walks (10), hit by pitch (12), strikeouts and GDPs (19)

Dan Kolb

Position: RP
Bats: R **Throws:** R
Ht: 6' 4" **Wt:** 240

Opening Day Age: 30
Born: 3/29/75 in
Sterling, IL
ML Seasons: 6

2004 Season

Brewers general manager Doug Melvin remembered Danny Kolb from his days as GM of the Texas Rangers, and signed Kolb as a free agent when he was released by the Rangers in 2003. In his first full major league season in 2004, Kolb established himself among the National League's premier closers, and broke Bob Wickman's single-season club record for saves, with 39. At the All-Star Game, he was pressed into early service as a guy who could warm up quickly, pitching the second inning after Roger Clemens got shelled.

Pitching

Now fully recovered from rotator cuff surgery in 2002, Kolb relies on a heavy, sinking fastball that he throws in the mid-90s. He occasionally complements it with a slider. With a better-than-expected supporting cast, Kolb rarely had to pitch more than one inning. He usually started the ninth inning and very rarely appeared in non-save situations. The results are a tribute to Kolb, Melvin, manager Ned Yost and pitching coach Mike Maddux. Inheriting only 11 baserunners during the 2004 season, Kolb stranded all but three. He's nearly as effective against lefthanders as righties. For a 40-save man, however, Kolb notched remarkably few strikeouts.

Defense & Hitting

Kolb is a good fielder who does an outstanding job of limiting opponents' baserunning, chiefly by limiting their baserunners. Just one opponent stole a base in 2004 when Kolb was on the mound. Given his role as a one-inning pitcher, Kolb never gets to the plate as a hitter, and never runs the bases.

2005 Outlook

On December 11, Kolb was traded to Atlanta for Jose Capellan and a player to be named. The deal allows the Braves to return John Smoltz to their starting rotation. After serious arm problems in 2000, 2001 and 2002, Kolb has now posted back-to-back healthy seasons. He has not been overworked. As he turns 30, Kolb can look back on a career that seemed very nearly ended just two years ago, and forward to his status as a premier big league closer for the next several years.

Overall Statistics

	W	L	Pct.	ERA	G	GS	Sv	IP	H	BB	SO	HR	Avg
'04	0	4	.000	2.98	64	0	39	57.1	50	15	21	3	.234
Car.	6	13	.316	3.65	169	0	61	177.2	164	83	110	10	.243

2004 Pitching Profile

	Dan Kolb	NL Average
Overall Strike %	66.8	62.5
1st Pitch Strike %	60.3	58.5
Ratio	1.13	1.39
Strikeouts per 9 IP	3.30	6.74
Walks per 9 IP	2.35	3.38
Home Runs per 9 IP	0.47	1.11
Strikeout/Walk Ratio	1.40	1.99
Groundball/Flyball Ratio	3.49	1.25

2004 Situational Stats

	W	L	ERA	Sv	IP		AB	H	HR	RBI	Avg
Home	0	3	3.58	19	32.2	LHB	90	23	0	5	.256
Road	0	1	2.19	20	24.2	RHB	124	27	3	15	.218
First Half	0	1	1.62	26	33.1	Sc Pos	50	16	1	17	.320
Scnd Half	0	3	4.88	13	24.0	Clutch	169	40	2	18	.237

2004 Rankings (National League)

- 1st in fewest strikeouts per nine innings in relief (3.3)
- 6th in save percentage (88.6)
- 8th in saves
- Led the Brewers in saves, games finished (48), lowest batting average allowed vs. righthanded batters, save percentage (88.6), blown saves (5), relief ERA (2.98) and fewest baserunners allowed per nine innings in relief (10.7)

Milwaukee

Lyle Overbay

2004 Season

Lyle Overbay was the key position player obtained by the Brewers in the Richie Sexson trade with Arizona before the season. While Sexson suffered an early season-ending injury, Overbay emerged as a very pleasant surprise. Beginning in late April, he amassed an 18-game hitting streak in which he batted .471, and he was hitting .330 with 21 doubles in 49 games by the end of May. When he finished his first full big league season, Overbay led the majors and broke Robin Yount's franchise record with 53 doubles.

Hitting

Overbay is a first baseman in the tradition of Mark Grace and Sean Casey—not a power hitter, but a man who can hit .305 with 45 doubles, while driving in and scoring 90 runs. In the absence of any available candidate who could hit for power, manager Ned Yost plugged him into the No. 4 slot early in 2004. Overbay responded with a big first half before coming back to earth after the All-Star break.

Baserunning & Defense

Defense is an important part of Overbay's game. In an infield that saw more than its share of shuffling last season, Overbay provided some stability. No Brewer second baseman had more than 41 double plays, but Overbay recorded 110. Possessed of average speed, he attempted only three stolen bases, but Overbay ran well enough to set the Brewers' team record for doubles.

2005 Outlook

Teams can win championships with guys like Overbay at first base, if they have power from their catcher, center fielder, right fielder or shortstop. For 2005 and beyond, he should remain a valuable and productive player. But because the Brewers are short on power, and top prospect Prince Fielder really can play only first base, it's unlikely that Overbay still will be at that position for Milwaukee in 2006.

Position: 1B
Bats: L **Throws:** L
Ht: 6' 2" **Wt:** 227

Opening Day Age: 28
Born: 1/28/77 in Centralia, WA
ML Seasons: 4

Overall Statistics

	G	AB	R	H	D	T	HR	RBI	SB	BB	SO	Avg	OBP	Slg
'04	159	579	83	174	53	1	16	87	2	81	128	.301	.385	.478
Car.	257	845	106	246	73	1	20	116	3	116	201	.291	.376	.451

Where He Hits the Ball

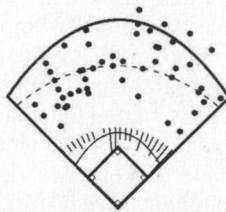
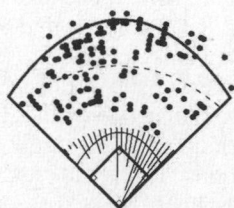

Vs. LHP   **Vs. RHP**

2004 Situational Stats

	AB	H	HR	RBI	Avg		AB	H	HR	RBI	Avg
Home	283	91	6	47	.322	LHP	151	45	5	20	.298
Road	296	83	10	40	.280	RHP	428	129	11	67	.301
First Half	326	112	10	62	.344	Sc Pos	141	38	3	64	.270
Scnd Half	253	62	6	25	.245	Clutch	99	28	2	12	.283

2004 Rankings (National League)

- 1st in doubles
- 3rd in errors at first base (11)
- 4th in lowest fielding percentage at first base (.992)
- 8th in games played
- Led the Brewers in batting average, hits, doubles, sacrifice flies (6), walks, times on base (257), games played, batting average vs. righthanded pitchers, cleanup slugging percentage (.533) and batting average at home

Scott Podsednik

2004 Season

As a free agent signed after the 2002 season, Scott Podsednik in 2003 played the role of center fielder/leadoff man to perfection, hitting .314, stealing 43 bases and scoring 100 runs. In 2004, he set a new Brewers single-season record with 70 stolen bases. But his batting average and slugging mark each dropped by 70 points from his breakthrough 2003 levels. A cold streak in July, when he batted .239, carried into August (.232), and he batted .218 from September 1 through the end of the season.

Hitting

Podsednik needs to hit more balls on the ground and fewer in the air. Although he hit only 12 home runs, Podsednik led the team by a wide margin with 141 flyball outs, 25 more than runnerup Geoff Jenkins. On the rare occasions Podsednik came to bat with a man in scoring position, he hit .209 in 2004. That was down 172 points from 2003, when he also was a better two-strike hitter than last summer.

Baserunning & Defense

Speed is Podsednik's game—he's among the fastest guys in baseball. He's a reliable, and sometimes spectacular, center fielder, covering the considerable gap between Jenkins in left and the team's 2004 right-field combo of Brady Clark and Ben Grieve. Podsednik also throws well. He's an outstanding baserunner who reached scoring position through his own efforts more than 100 times in 2004. His 84.3-percent success rate at stealing bases suggests that he could steal more and score more runs, if he can get his on-base percentage back to his 2003 level.

2005 Outlook

Podesdnik was traded to the White Sox along with Luis Vizcaino and a player to be named for Carlos Lee in December. With his speed, Podsednik can be a useful major league center fielder while hitting only .250. He'll enter 2005 as a starter for the White Sox in either center or left field, but the dropoff in his hitting percentages from his impressive first full season in 2003 raises a warning flag.

Position: CF
Bats: L **Throws:** L
Ht: 6' 0" **Wt:** 188

Opening Day Age: 29
Born: 3/18/76 in West, TX
ML Seasons: 4
Pronunciation: puh-SED-nik

Overall Statistics

	G	AB	R	H	D	T	HR	RBI	SB	BB	SO	Avg	OBP	Slg
'04	154	640	85	156	27	7	12	39	70	58	105	.244	.313	.364
Car.	327	1224	188	336	56	16	22	105	113	118	203	.275	.343	.400

Where He Hits the Ball

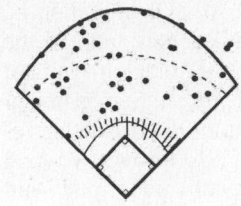
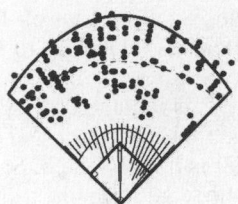

Vs. LHP   **Vs. RHP**

2004 Situational Stats

	AB	H	HR	RBI	Avg		AB	H	HR	RBI	Avg
Home	319	68	3	14	.213	LHP	147	33	3	14	.224
Road	321	88	9	25	.274	RHP	493	123	9	25	.249
First Half	352	89	9	26	.253	Sc Pos	115	24	3	27	.209
Scnd Half	288	67	3	13	.233	Clutch	99	25	3	14	.253

2004 Rankings (National League)

- 1st in stolen bases and lowest batting average at home
- 2nd in caught stealing (13) and steals of third (10)
- 4th in pitches seen (2,837), plate appearances (713), lowest slugging percentage and lowest batting average vs. lefthanded pitchers
- 5th in at-bats, stolen-base percentage (84.3) and lowest percentage of swings on the first pitch (11.9)
- Led the Brewers in singles, triples, bunts in play (33), highest percentage of pitches taken (63.3), lowest percentage of swings that missed (12.5), highest percentage of swings put into play (52.0), and on-base percentage for a leadoff hitter (.315)

Milwaukee

Victor Santos

2004 Season

Yet another pitcher plucked from the Texas system, Victor Santos has spent the last four seasons with four different clubs, working mostly as a reliever. He joined the Brewers' bullpen in April and moved into the rotation in May. After getting his bearings, he won six of seven decisions and allowed just two longballs in eight starts from June 1 through the All-Star break. He emerged as a reliable third starter over the middle three months of the season. After starting 8-3, he visibly weakened in August, when he had trouble keeping the ball down.

Pitching

Santos is a finesse pitcher with good mechanics and excellent control. Like Wes Obermueller, he pitched exclusively to Gary Bennett and had the best season of his career. The matchup worked well, as Bennett usually calls for a curve on one of the first two pitches, and Santos' overhand curveball is his best pitch. Santos also throws two- and four-seam fastballs, a slider, split-finger pitch and changeup. In most games, he will use the changeup or the splitter, but not both. Lefthanded hitters tend to hit the ball in the air, while his outs from righthanders come about equally on groundballs and flyballs.

Defense & Hitting

As you can tell from his hitting, Santos has spent most of his major league career in the American League. In 2004, he went 2-for-39 with six sacrifice bunts. He's no bargain on defense, either, committing three errors in only 20 chances. Opposing baserunners were successful in 15 of 18 steal attempts.

2005 Outlook

Although his ERA was on the high side, Santos was a solid starter for the Brewers in 2004. Barring trade or injury, he'll enter the 2005 season in the Brewers' rotation. His task will be to recapture the success he enjoyed in the first half of 2004, and extend it over a full season. To do so, he will need to work on his defense and cut down on his delivery time out of the stretch.

Position: SP
Bats: R **Throws:** R
Ht: 6' 3" **Wt:** 190

Opening Day Age: 28
Born: 10/2/76 in San Pedro de Macoris, DR
ML Seasons: 4

Overall Statistics

	W	L	Pct.	ERA	G	GS	Sv	IP	H	BB	SO	HR	Avg
'04	11	12	.478	4.97	31	28	0	154.0	169	57	115	18	.278
Car.	13	20	.394	5.20	96	41	0	282.0	301	144	207	35	.274

2004 Pitching Profile

	Victor Santos	NL Average
Overall Strike %	61.0	62.5
1st Pitch Strike %	53.5	58.5
Ratio	1.47	1.39
Strikeouts per 9 IP	6.72	6.74
Walks per 9 IP	3.33	3.38
Home Runs per 9 IP	1.05	1.11
Strikeout/Walk Ratio	2.02	1.99
Groundball/Flyball Ratio	0.96	1.25

2004 Situational Stats

	W	L	ERA	Sv	IP		AB	H	HR	RBI	Avg
Home	4	8	5.09	0	92.0	LHB	250	61	6	34	.244
Road	7	4	4.79	0	62.0	RHB	357	108	12	48	.303
First Half	8	3	4.08	0	81.2	Sc Pos	159	42	3	59	.264
Scnd Half	3	9	5.97	0	72.1	Clutch	25	8	1	3	.320

2004 Rankings (National League)

- 3rd in errors at pitcher (3) and highest ERA at home
- 4th in highest batting average allowed vs. righthanded batters
- Led the Brewers in hit batsmen (7) and stolen bases allowed (15)

Ben Sheets

2004 Season

This was the year Ben Sheets came into his own as one of the premier starting pitchers in the National League. As he pitched in the All-Star Game, he was 9-5 with a major league-best 2.26 ERA. But his run support of 3.28 runs per nine innings was worst in the NL through the end of August, and in the second half he managed only three wins, despite a respectable ERA and a 1.53 mark in his final seven starts. He easily surpassed Teddy Higuera's franchise record for strikeouts in a season.

Pitching

At age 26, Sheets has the talent, poise and mental toughness to be a dominant pitcher in the NL for the foreseeable future. Pitching almost exclusively to Chad Moeller, Sheets cut down on the mistakes and inconsistency that marked his first three major league seasons. He throws strikes with three solid pitches—a fastball that can reach 95 MPH, hard curve and changeup. He showed exceptional control in 2004, posting a strikeout-walk ratio of 8.25:1. He also fared much better against lefthanded hitters. Lefties had torched him to the tune of a .320 average and .538 slugging mark his first two seasons in 2001 and 2002.

Defense & Hitting

One thing Sheets knows about pitching is that he can't hit it, though he had nine sacrifice bunts last season. He fields well and does a good job of limiting the running game. Like Davis and Santos, he gave up 15 stolen bases last season, an acceptable level when spread over 34 starts.

2005 Outlook

Sheets had a microscopic lumbar discectomy to repair a herniated disc in October, but should begin his offseason throwing program on schedule in January. With the Brewers' offense and infield defense, it's unlikely that Sheets can approach 20 wins in 2005, but he should post his share of wins and strikeouts with a decent ERA. Sheets is emerging as a team leader, but with the franchise's uncertain financial situation, a trade is always a possibility as he accumulates service time.

Position: SP
Bats: R   **Throws:** R
Ht: 6' 1"   **Wt:** 218

Opening Day Age: 26
Born: 7/18/78 in Baton Rouge, LA
ML Seasons: 4

Overall Statistics

	W	L	Pct.	ERA	G	GS	Sv	IP	H	BB	SO	HR	Avg
'04	12	14	.462	2.70	34	34	0	237.0	201	32	264	25	.226
Car.	45	53	.459	3.92	127	127	0	825.2	836	193	685	98	.262

2004 Pitching Profile

	Ben Sheets	NL Average
Overall Strike %	68.2	62.5
1st Pitch Strike %	66.3	58.5
Ratio	0.98	1.39
Strikeouts per 9 IP	10.03	6.74
Walks per 9 IP	1.22	3.38
Home Runs per 9 IP	0.95	1.11
Strikeout/Walk Ratio	8.25	1.99
Groundball/Flyball Ratio	1.19	1.25

2004 Situational Stats

	W	L	ERA	Sv	IP		AB	H	HR	RBI	Avg
Home	8	6	2.59	0	121.2	LHB	427	99	15	39	.232
Road	4	8	2.81	0	115.1	RHB	464	102	10	41	.220
First Half	9	5	2.26	0	123.1	Sc Pos	184	41	2	48	.223
Scnd Half	3	9	3.17	0	113.2	Clutch	45	11	3	7	.244

2004 Rankings (National League)

- 1st in highest strikeout-walk ratio (8.3)
- 2nd in complete games (5), strikeouts, lowest on-base percentage allowed (.255), fewest walks per nine innings (1.2) and least run support per nine innings (3.5)
- 3rd in ERA, innings pitched and lowest ERA on the road
- 4th in losses, batters faced (937) and most strikeouts per nine innings (10.0)
- 5th in games started and pitches thrown (3,586)
- Led the Brewers in ERA, sacrifice bunts (9), wins, losses, games started, innings pitched, hits allowed, batters faced (937), home runs allowed, pitches thrown (3,586), stolen bases allowed (15), highest strikeout-walk ratio (8.3), lowest batting average allowed (.226), lowest ERA at home, lowest ERA on the road, most strikeouts per nine innings (10.0) and fewest walks per nine innings (1.2)

2004 Season

Injuries hampered Junior Spivey's development with the Diamondbacks, making them willing to include him in the Richie Sexson trade in December 2003. At the time, there was widespread speculation that the Brewers would trade him to a contender at midseason, but injury struck again when left shoulder surgery ended his year in early July. Spivey batted close to .300 and showed power in both April and June, but he slumped in May while battling a hamstring injury that put him on the shelf for almost three weeks.

Hitting

Spivey's approach to hitting is that of a power hitter. Whether that's the most appropriate use of his talent is open to question. Over the course of his career, he has averaged a home run every 31.5 at-bats, but a strikeout every 4.5. His career strike-outs nearly double his walks. Spivey's power is to left field. He has lost major portions of the last two seasons to injuries, an ankle in 2003, the left shoulder in 2004. If he could stay healthy for a full season, he might hit 15-20 home runs and steal 15-20 bases while driving in 65 runs.

Baserunning & Defense

Possessed of speed and agility, Spivey has excellent defensive range for a second baseman. He handles popups very well, turns the double play pretty well, and gets to more than his share of groundballs. The result is a range factor better than 5.00 at second base, more than a half-play per game better than Bill Hall or Keith Ginter. But he has not been able to use his speed to his advantage as a basestealer.

2005 Outlook

Spivey is a arbitration eligible this winter. He has indicated interest in returning to the Brewers, but with Ginter and Hall available and Rickie Weeks perhaps a year and a half away, it's questionable whether the Brewers will pursue him. It's unlikely that they would commit to more than a one-year contract. Spivey should land a starting job somewhere.

Position: 2B
Bats: R **Throws:** R
Ht: 6' 0" **Wt:** 201

Opening Day Age: 30
Born: 1/28/75 in Oklahoma City, OK
ML Seasons: 4
Pronunciation: spy-VEE

Overall Statistics

	G	AB	R	H	D	T	HR	RBI	SB	BB	SO	Avg	OBP	Slg
'04	59	228	33	62	13	0	7	28	5	25	48	.272	.359	.421
Car.	380	1294	221	359	75	11	41	177	23	146	290	.277	.362	.447

Where He Hits the Ball

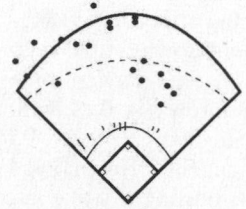 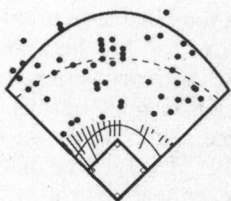

Vs. LHP   **Vs. RHP**

2004 Situational Stats

	AB	H	HR	RBI	Avg		AB	H	HR	RBI	Avg
Home	113	39	4	14	.345	LHP	43	12	3	5	.279
Road	115	23	3	14	.200	RHP	185	50	4	23	.270
First Half	228	62	7	28	.272	Sc Pos	66	16	0	18	.242
Scnd Half	0	0	0	0	–	Clutch	38	6	0	4	.158

2004 Rankings (National League)

• 4th in errors at second base (11)

Mike Adams

Position: RP
Bats: R **Throws:** R
Ht: 6' 5" **Wt:** 190

Opening Day Age: 26
Born: 7/29/78 in Corpus Christi, TX
ML Seasons: 1

Overall Statistics

	W	L	Pct.	ERA	G	GS	Sv	IP	H	BB	SO	HR	Avg
'04	2	3	.400	3.40	46	0	0	53.0	50	14	39	5	.248
Car.	2	3	.400	3.40	46	0	0	53.0	50	14	39	5	.248

2004 Situational Stats

	W	L	ERA	Sv	IP		AB	H	HR	RBI	Avg
Home	0	2	5.47	0	26.1	LHB	87	21	2	10	.241
Road	2	1	1.35	0	26.2	RHB	115	29	3	15	.252
First Half	1	0	1.85	0	24.1	Sc Pos	66	15	2	21	.227
Scnd Half	1	3	4.71	0	28.2	Clutch	108	26	3	16	.241

2004 Season

Mike Adams blew through the minor leagues in less than three years and became a valuable cog in the Brewers' much-improved bullpen during the first half of 2004. He worked nine straight scoreless outings to start the season, but his performance after the All-Star break was down, though still acceptable.

Pitching, Defense & Hitting

A lanky Texan, Adams usually appeared on the frequent occasions when the Brewers needed a reliever for the seventh inning to set up the eighth inning for Luis Vizcaino. Adams proved very effective in that role. He relies on a mid-90s fastball and a hard slider. He handled five fielding chances without an error or a putout in 2004. Adams did not come to the plate as a hitter. Only 26, he's eventually projectable as a closer, if he gets the opportunity and stays healthy.

2005 Outlook

That opportunity may have come. The December trades of Dan Kolb and Luis Vizcaino left Adams and Jeff Bennett as the only reliable relievers returning to the Brewers. Adams is in a position to move into the closer job, or become the principal setup man if the team acquires an established closer before Opening Day.

Gary Bennett

Signed By NATIONALS

Position: C
Bats: R **Throws:** R
Ht: 6' 0" **Wt:** 208

Opening Day Age: 32
Born: 4/17/72 in Waukegan, IL
ML Seasons: 9

Overall Statistics

	G	AB	R	H	D	T	HR	RBI	SB	BB	SO	Avg	OBP	Slg
'04	75	219	18	49	14	0	3	20	1	22	32	.224	.297	.329
Car.	390	1158	104	286	54	3	14	128	5	97	187	.247	.310	.335

2004 Situational Stats

	AB	H	HR	RBI	Avg		AB	H	HR	RBI	Avg
Home	107	25	3	14	.234	LHP	39	10	1	5	.256
Road	112	24	0	6	.214	RHP	180	39	2	15	.217
First Half	121	22	1	9	.182	Sc Pos	60	9	1	17	.150
Scnd Half	98	27	2	11	.276	Clutch	27	5	0	1	.185

2004 Season

Gary Bennett shared playing time behind the plate with Chad Moeller in Ned Yost's catching platoon, catching righthanded starters Wes Obermueller and Victor Santos. Santos had a career-best season, continuing the success Bennett had at San Diego catching Brian Lawrence, Jake Peavy and Adam Eaton in 2003.

Hitting, Baserunning & Defense

Neither Bennett nor Moeller did much at the plate in 2004. Bennett was slightly better, recovering from a sub-.200 first-half batting average to bring his season-ending average up to .224. Bennett also was better at putting the ball in play and posted a better slugging percentage. He likes to call for a curveball on the first or second pitch of each at-bat. Like Moeller, he threw out roughly 20 percent of baserunners attempting to steal in 2004.

2005 Outlook

Needing space on the 40 man roster, the Brewers outrighted Bennett to their Triple-A club in October, and he opted for free agency. The veteran backup later agreed to a one-year, $750,000 contract to join the Washington Nationals. He fulfills the Nats' needs for a backup to starting catcher Brian Schneider.

Milwaukee

Jeff Bennett

Position: RP
Bats: R **Throws:** R
Ht: 6' 3" **Wt:** 206

Opening Day Age: 24
Born: 6/10/80 in Donelson, TN
ML Seasons: 1

Overall Statistics

	W	L	Pct.	ERA	G	GS	Sv	IP	H	BB	SO	HR	Avg
'04	1	5	.167	4.79	60	0	0	71.1	78	26	45	12	.278
Car.	1	5	.167	4.79	60	0	0	71.1	78	26	45	12	.278

2004 Situational Stats

	W	L	ERA	Sv	IP		AB	H	HR	RBI	Avg
Home	1	2	4.82	0	37.1	LHB	117	34	6	21	.291
Road	0	3	4.76	0	34.0	RHB	164	44	6	26	.268
First Half	1	4	4.32	0	41.2	Sc Pos	91	23	1	34	.253
Scnd Half	0	1	5.46	0	29.2	Clutch	72	20	3	12	.278

2004 Season

The Brewers selected Jeff Bennett from the Pittsburgh Pirates in the 2003 Rule 5 draft, and were obliged to keep him on the major league roster all year or offer him back to the Pirates. He rewarded the Brewers with a solid season as a reliever.

Pitching, Defense & Hitting

Bennett became one of the rare Rule 5 players who actually spent the full season on the major league roster and played. Featuring a 95-MPH fastball, he was an important contributor in the Brewers' bullpen. Bennett also calls on a good slider, but has trouble throwing it for strikes. For some reason, he was more effective in day games than at night. While he was successful at limiting stolen bases, he had some difficulty keeping the ball in the park. At bat, he struck out in his only two plate appearances.

2005 Outlook

Now that Bennett has spent the 2004 season on the major league roster, the Brewers are free to send him to the minors. Bennett was both a starter and a reliever in the minor leagues, but with a bullpen that has been dismantled by trades, the Brewers may want to keep him in the pen for 2005.

Brady Clark

Position: RF
Bats: R **Throws:** R
Ht: 6' 2" **Wt:** 202

Opening Day Age: 31
Born: 4/18/73 in Portland, OR
ML Seasons: 5

Overall Statistics

	G	AB	R	H	D	T	HR	RBI	SB	BB	SO	Avg	OBP	Slg
'04	138	353	41	99	18	1	7	46	15	53	48	.280	.385	.397
Car.	427	886	106	237	47	2	19	116	33	103	117	.267	.353	.389

2004 Situational Stats

	AB	H	HR	RBI	Avg		AB	H	HR	RBI	Avg
Home	183	42	1	16	.230	LHP	92	23	1	12	.250
Road	170	57	6	30	.335	RHP	261	76	6	34	.291
First Half	167	42	4	23	.251	Sc Pos	92	26	1	35	.283
Scnd Half	186	57	3	23	.306	Clutch	61	14	1	5	.230

2004 Season

Brady Clark didn't play a professional game until age 24, and didn't reach the majors until he was 27. At age 31 last summer, he posted career highs in games and at-bats. With Ben Grieve successively ineffective, injured and traded, Clark emerged as the Brewers' everyday right fielder in the second half. He hit .310 with a .404 OBP through June and July, slumped in August, but rebounded to hit .368 and slug .574 in September.

Hitting, Baserunning & Defense

Manager Ned Yost used Clark in several slots in the batting order, sometimes using him to break up the lefthanded core at the top of the lineup. He has good strike-zone judgment and posted more walks than strikeouts. No area of his game is above average, but he hits for a little power and steals some bases. Defensively, Clark is an adequate right fielder. He recorded five assists in the equivalent of 96 full games last season.

2005 Outlook

The Brewers traded center fielder Scott Podsednik in December, which opens the door to playing time to rookie Dave Krynzel and Clark, a journeyman corner outfielder. Leadoff duties also are up for grabs, but Clark is not the kind of player helped by Miller Park, which favors power hitters.

Craig Counsell

Position: SS
Bats: L **Throws:** R
Ht: 6' 0" **Wt:** 184

Opening Day Age: 34
Born: 8/21/70 in South Bend, IN
ML Seasons: 9
Nickname: Rudy

Overall Statistics

	G	AB	R	H	D	T	HR	RBI	SB	BB	SO	Avg	OBP	Slg
'04	140	473	59	114	19	5	2	23	17	59	88	.241	.330	.315
Car.	798	2496	348	653	112	20	18	211	49	310	354	.262	.345	.344

2004 Situational Stats

	AB	H	HR	RBI	Avg		AB	H	HR	RBI	Avg
Home	222	50	1	11	.225	LHP	87	16	0	4	.184
Road	251	64	1	12	.255	RHP	386	98	2	19	.254
First Half	255	66	2	15	.259	Sc Pos	105	21	0	18	.200
Scnd Half	218	48	0	8	.220	Clutch	63	14	0	2	.222

2004 Season

The Brewers' 2003 shortstop, Royce Clayton, left as a free agent. With no real alternative, manager Ned Yost used Mequon resident Craig Counsell, acquired in the Richie Sexson trade, as the everyday shortstop in 2004. Counsell did what could have been expected, delivering solid if rarely spectacular defense, but making little contribution to the Brewers' anemic offense.

Hitting, Baserunning & Defense

With his front leg cocked and his bat stretched as high as possible behind his head, Counsell is instantly recognizable at the plate. It doesn't look like he can get to the ball, and much of the time he can't, at least not with much authority. Two Brewers pitchers, Wes Obermueller and Brooks Kieschnick, posted better OPS than Counsell in 2004. Defensivly, he is surehanded with a below-average arm. He is a decent baserunner.

2005 Outlook

The Brewers declined Counsell's 2005 option at the end of the season. There probably is not another team in baseball that would give him 300 at-bats, let alone 473, though he has value as a back-up shortstop. The Brewers are likely to search for an upgrade from the pool of free agents and non-tendered players.

Wes Helms

Position: 3B/1B
Bats: R **Throws:** R
Ht: 6' 4" **Wt:** 231

Opening Day Age: 28
Born: 5/12/76 in Gastonia, NC
ML Seasons: 6

Overall Statistics

	G	AB	R	H	D	T	HR	RBI	SB	BB	SO	Avg	OBP	Slg
'04	92	274	24	72	13	1	4	28	0	24	60	.263	.331	.361
Car.	424	1194	130	300	61	4	44	155	2	99	310	.251	.315	.420

2004 Situational Stats

	AB	H	HR	RBI	Avg		AB	H	HR	RBI	Avg
Home	140	31	3	17	.221	LHP	72	22	1	6	.306
Road	134	41	1	11	.306	RHP	202	50	3	22	.248
First Half	159	41	2	17	.258	Sc Pos	81	17	4	26	.210
Scnd Half	115	31	2	11	.270	Clutch	41	12	2	9	.293

2004 Season

In December 2002, the Brewers acquired Wes Helms from the Braves and handed him the third-base job. He repaid them with 23 homers and 67 RBI in 476 at-bats. But 2004 was a disaster, as Helms managed just 18 extra-base hits and went 136 at-bats without a homer from May 12 through September 2. He lost six weeks to a torn meniscus in his right knee during the first half. Eventually, he lost his starting job to Russell Branyan.

Hitting, Baserunning & Defense

Helms' game is hitting for power, and that power has evaporated. After Branyan's acquisition in July, Helms' playing time was reduced against lefthanded pitchers, but he improved his batting average in the second half. He has not stolen a base over the past two years, and although he has a strong throwing arm, his fielding average at third base was an atrocious .904 in 2004.

2005 Outlook

The task for Helms is simply to survive at the major league level. The Brewers may try to acquire a power-hitting third baseman in the off-season. On top of that, Branyan clearly has moved ahead of him for playing time at third, and manager Ned Yost indicated at season's end that Helms is not guaranteed a roster spot for 2005.

Milwaukee

525

Brooks Kieschnick

Position: RP
Bats: L **Throws:** R
Ht: 6' 4" **Wt:** 251

Opening Day Age: 32
Born: 6/6/72 in Robstown, TX
ML Seasons: 6
Pronunciation: KEESH-nick

Overall Statistics

	W	L	Pct.	ERA	G	GS	Sv	IP	H	BB	SO	HR	Avg
'04	1	1	.500	3.77	32	0	0	43.0	44	13	28	6	.262
Car.	2	2	.500	4.59	74	0	0	96.0	110	26	67	11	.283

2004 Situational Stats

	W	L	ERA	Sv	IP		AB	H	HR	RBI	Avg
Home	1	0	1.99	0	22.2	LHB	80	22	3	8	.275
Road	0	1	5.75	0	20.1	RHB	88	22	3	17	.250
First Half	1	0	3.82	0	30.2	Sc Pos	43	12	2	18	.279
Scnd Half	0	1	3.65	0	12.1	Clutch	39	11	1	5	.282

2004 Season

In 2004, Brooks Kieschnick continued in his understandably unusual role as a long-relief pitcher who also is his team's best lefthanded power threat off the bench. This has something to do with the Brewers' $27.5 million payroll. He contributed nothing of any real value in either role. Shoulder problems severely limited his pitching in the second half.

Pitching, Defense & Hitting

Kieschnick was the Cubs' left fielder of the future in the mid-1990s. Then-general manager Larry Himes took him in the first round of the 1993 draft, but Himes' South Side magic (drafting Robin Ventura, Alex Fernandez, Frank Thomas and Jack McDowell with first-round choices in the late 1980s) got lost in the move uptown. When hitting for a living didn't work out, Kieschnick moved to the mound. He hits well for a pitcher, and pitches well for a pinch-hitter.

2005 Outlook

If his shoulder is healthy, Kieschnick will compete for a slot on the Brewers' roster as a reliever/pinch-hitter. Last year he had a radio program on the side, and he figures to stick around the game as a broadcaster when his playing days are over.

Chad Moeller

Position: C
Bats: R **Throws:** R
Ht: 6' 3" **Wt:** 210

Opening Day Age: 30
Born: 2/18/75 in Upland, CA
ML Seasons: 5
Pronunciation: MOE-ler

Overall Statistics

	G	AB	R	H	D	T	HR	RBI	SB	BB	SO	Avg	OBP	Slg
'04	101	317	25	66	13	1	5	27	0	21	74	.208	.265	.303
Car.	289	845	85	200	44	5	16	83	2	76	201	.237	.303	.357

2004 Situational Stats

	AB	H	HR	RBI	Avg		AB	H	HR	RBI	Avg
Home	166	35	3	15	.211	LHP	62	15	2	8	.242
Road	151	31	2	12	.205	RHP	255	51	3	19	.200
First Half	180	43	4	22	.239	Sc Pos	96	14	1	20	.146
Scnd Half	137	23	1	5	.168	Clutch	52	12	1	2	.231

2004 Season

Acquired from the Diamondbacks in the Richie Sexson trade, Chad Moeller was behind the plate for 2004 starts by Ben Sheets, Doug Davis and Chris Capuano. With Arizona in 2003, he hit seven home runs, scored 29 runs and knocked in 29 in 239 at-bats, but failed to attain even those modest levels last summer. His hitting got worse as the season progressed.

Hitting, Baserunning & Defense

Although his reputation with Arizona was as an offensive catcher, he proved the weaker offensive half of manager Ned Yost's catching platoon in 2004. Moeller is in the major leagues because of his skills as a catcher. He calls a good game, does a good job of blocking pitches in the dirt, and doesn't let opposing baserunners run wild. Speed is not part of his game—he's stolen just two bases in 289 career games.

2005 Outlook

In November, the Brewers signed Damian Miller to be their everyday catcher. Gary Bennett has departed for Washington, so Moeller will see his at-bats drop off markedly as Milwaukee's second catcher. Since the Brewers don't have pinch-hitters better than Miller, Moeller may not see much action as a late-inning replacement.

Wes Obermueller

Position: SP
Bats: R **Throws:** R
Ht: 6' 2" **Wt:** 209

Opening Day Age: 28
Born: 12/22/76 in
Cedar Rapids, IA
ML Seasons: 3

Overall Statistics

	W	L	Pct.	ERA	G	GS	Sv	IP	H	BB	SO	HR	Avg
'04	6	8	.429	5.80	25	20	0	118.0	138	42	59	15	.291
Car.	8	15	.348	5.79	39	33	0	191.1	233	69	98	28	.298

2004 Situational Stats

	W	L	ERA	Sv	IP		AB	H	HR	RBI	Avg
Home	5	3	4.78	0	69.2	LHB	218	62	6	24	.284
Road	1	5	7.26	0	48.1	RHB	257	76	9	40	.296
First Half	3	5	6.69	0	72.2	Sc Pos	111	31	4	48	.279
Scnd Half	3	3	4.37	0	45.1	Clutch	3	2	0	0	.667

2004 Season

Acquired from the Royals in July 2003, Wes Obermueller was the Brewers' fifth starter for the first half of 2004. He was demoted to Triple-A Indianapolis at the All-Star break after four rough starts in which he had trouble working beyond the fourth or fifth inning. He returned to the Milwaukee rotation in August and shut out the red-hot Astros on six hits on September 25.

Pitching, Defense & Hitting

Obermueller's progress in the minors was slowed by injuries, but he stayed healthy in 2004. Although he shows good movement at times, he lacks a dominant pitch and will need to master location to stick in the majors. He allows way too many baserunners and home runs. A former shortstop and center fielder at the University of Iowa, Obermueller was a force at the plate in 2004. It's been suggested that he could emulate Brooks Kieschnick's role as a pitcher/pinch-hitter.

2005 Outlook

Obermueller pitched better after his return to the Brewers, putting himself back in contention for a spot in the 2005 rotation. If everyone's healthy, he'll compete against Victor Santos and Ben Hendrickson for the opportunity. He could start 2005 at Triple-A Nashville.

Luis Vizcaino

Traded To WHITE SOX

Position: RP
Bats: R **Throws:** R
Ht: 5'11" **Wt:** 184

Opening Day Age: 30
Born: 8/6/74 in Bani, DR
ML Seasons: 6
Pronunciation:
vis-ki-ee-no

Overall Statistics

	W	L	Pct.	ERA	G	GS	Sv	IP	H	BB	SO	HR	Avg
'04	4	4	.500	3.75	73	0	1	72.0	61	24	63	12	.228
Car.	15	12	.556	4.52	273	0	7	274.2	246	105	254	45	.238

2004 Situational Stats

	W	L	ERA	Sv	IP		AB	H	HR	RBI	Avg
Home	2	3	4.10	0	37.1	LHB	129	21	6	21	.163
Road	2	1	3.38	1	34.2	RHB	138	40	6	20	.290
First Half	2	2	2.88	0	40.2	Sc Pos	80	17	5	33	.213
Scnd Half	2	2	4.88	1	31.1	Clutch	178	38	7	24	.213

2004 Season

After a miserable first half in 2003, Luis Vizcaino righted the ship after the All-Star break. In 2004, he re-established himself as a valuable relief pitcher, appearing in nearly half the Brewers' games while spending the whole season as Dan Kolb's primary setup man. Reversing his 2003 pattern, Vizcaino's effectiveness declined a bit after the break last summer.

Pitching, Defense & Hitting

Vizcaino is not afraid to throw his fastball up in the strike zone, but last year, 12 of them didn't come back. Also working with a good split-finger pitch, Vizcaino has been especially effective against lefthanded hitters. He always works out of the stretch, and his quick delivery was effective in limiting opponents to four stolen bases in 2004. Because he very rarely works more than one inning, Vizcaino did not have an at-bat in 2004.

2005 Outlook

In December, Vizcaino was traded to the Chicago White Sox along with Scott Podsednik and a player to be named for Carlos Lee. Vizcaino is expected to assume the role of primary setup man, working the eighth inning, and perhaps freeing Dustin Hermanson to join the Chicago rotation.

Milwaukee

Jorge de la Rosa (**Pos**: LHP, **Age**: 23)

	W	L	Pct.	ERA	G	GS	Sv	IP	H	BB	SO	HR	Avg
'04	0	3	.000	6.35	5	5	0	22.2	29	14	5	1	.309
Car.	0	3	.000	6.35	5	5	0	22.2	29	14	5	1	.309

De la Rosa came over from Arizona in the Richie Sexson deal. He made 20 starts at Indianapolis, registering a 4.52 ERA. His 86 strikeouts in 85.2 innings was an encouraging sign considering it was his first full year at Triple-A. The five starts he made for Milwaukee were ugly. 2005 Outlook: C

Trent Durrington (**Pos**: 3B, **Age**: 29, **Bats**: R)

	G	AB	R	H	D	T	HR	RBI	SB	BB	SO	Avg	OBP	Slg
'04	53	82	13	19	2	3	2	4	4	4	23	.232	.267	.402
Car.	112	221	32	43	4	3	2	7	9	16	51	.195	.249	.267

This Australian product has not fared well in his brief forays into the major league realm. Durrington's nack for getting on base in the minors has not carried over to the big leagues. His .249 career OBP and .203 slugging percentage versus righthanders just aren't getting it done. 2005 Outlook: C

Matt Erickson (**Pos**: 2B, **Age**: 29, **Bats**: L)

	G	AB	R	H	D	T	HR	RBI	SB	BB	SO	Avg	OBP	Slg
'04	4	6	0	1	0	0	0	0	0	0	1	.167	.167	.167
Car.	4	6	0	1	0	0	0	0	0	0	1	.167	.167	.167

Erickson, a Wisconsin native, lived out a childhood dream by playing for the Brewers this past season. He knows how to handle the game and is versatile enough to play a number of different positions. He is also a selective hitter, demonstrated by a .399 career minor league OBP. 2005 Outlook: C

Ben Ford (**Pos**: RHP, **Age**: 29)

	W	L	Pct.	ERA	G	GS	Sv	IP	H	BB	SO	HR	Avg
'04	1	1	.500	6.38	19	0	0	24.0	25	10	13	4	.269
Car.	1	2	.333	7.80	31	2	0	45.0	52	20	23	7	.291

Ford brought a 7.20 ERA and 1.8 home runs per nine innings with him to the disabled list in May. The trip to the DL was caused by shoulder irritation, later to be diagnosed as tendinitis. It was a frustrating year for Ford, despite career highs in both innings and appearances. 2005 Outlook: C

Gary Glover (**Pos**: RHP, **Age**: 28)

	W	L	Pct.	ERA	G	GS	Sv	IP	H	BB	SO	HR	Avg
'04	2	1	.667	3.50	4	3	0	18.0	18	8	8	2	.265
Car.	16	14	.533	4.92	134	36	1	320.1	329	115	178	45	.264

Indianapolis was the final stop on the 2004 Gary Glover Triple-A tour. Previous destinations included Rochester of the International League, and Des Moines, home to the Iowa Cubs of the PCL. Milwaukee wants him to stay put for now though, signing him to a one-year deal in October. 2005 Outlook: C

Adrian Hernandez (**Pos**: RHP, **Age**: 30)

	W	L	Pct.	ERA	G	GS	Sv	IP	H	BB	SO	HR	Avg
'04	0	2	.000	8.44	6	1	0	16.0	20	14	14	1	.294
Car.	0	6	.000	6.55	14	5	0	44.0	45	30	33	10	.257

Hernandez, no relation to Orlando and Livan, used doctored documents to escape Cuba, signing with the Yankees in the summer of 2000. "El Duquecito," or little El Duque as he is known, has not enjoyed the success of other fellow defectors. High walk rates have rendered him ineffective. 2005 Outlook: C

Mark Johnson (**Pos**: C, **Age**: 29, **Bats**: L)

	G	AB	R	H	D	T	HR	RBI	SB	BB	SO	Avg	OBP	Slg
'04	7	11	1	1	0	0	0	2	0	3	2	.091	.267	.091
Car.	322	917	114	199	37	4	16	81	8	123	195	.217	.313	.318

The Brewers re-signed Johnson in November to a minor league deal that guarantees him an invitation to spring training. However, Milwaukee signed Damian Miller to be their everyday catcher, so Johnson may again see very little time in the bigs this year. 2005 Outlook: C

Jeff Liefer (**Pos**: RF, **Age**: 30, **Bats**: L)

	G	AB	R	H	D	T	HR	RBI	SB	BB	SO	Avg	OBP	Slg
'04	16	28	2	6	2	0	1	5	0	2	8	.214	.258	.393
Car.	269	723	84	168	34	1	30	105	2	55	208	.232	.286	.407

Liefer has floundered since his 2001 breakout season with the Chicago White Sox, which saw him hit 18 home runs and slug a solid .520 in only 254 at-bats. The three subsequent years have been plagued with minor league demotions and a miserable .212/.267/.357 big league stat line. He signed a minor league deal with the Indians in November. 2005 Outlook: C

Pedro Liriano (**Pos**: RHP, **Age**: 24)

	W	L	Pct.	ERA	G	GS	Sv	IP	H	BB	SO	HR	Avg
'04	0	0	–	4.02	11	0	0	15.2	15	3	10	3	.238
Car.	0	0	–	4.02	11	0	0	15.2	15	3	10	3	.238

The consensus among scouts is that Liriano's services would best be utilized out of the bullpen. Indianapolis manager Cecil Cooper thought the same thing, sending him to the pen late in the season. Liriano needs to refine his command and will be in the Triple-A pen to begin 2005. 2005 Outlook: C

Chris Magruder (**Pos**: RF, **Age**: 27, **Bats**: B)

	G	AB	R	H	D	T	HR	RBI	SB	BB	SO	Avg	OBP	Slg
'04	56	89	11	21	6	1	2	10	0	8	21	.236	.310	.393
Car.	169	402	51	91	23	3	9	43	2	27	87	.226	.281	.366

The switch-hitting Magruder played in 56 games following a midseason callup. Nearly a third of his at-bats came as a situational pinch-hitter, with a .172 mark in that role. His struggles mirrored those of the entire Milwaukee team over the course of the second half. 2005 Outlook: C

Travis Phelps (Pos: RHP, Age: 27)

	W	L	Pct.	ERA	G	GS	Sv	IP	H	BB	SO	HR	Avg
'04	0	1	.000	10.50	4	0	0	6.0	8	3	3	2	.286
Car.	3	5	.375	4.34	79	0	5	105.2	91	54	93	15	.229

Phelps, a former 89th-round draft pick, threw well for Triple-A Richmond as a member of the Braves' organization in 2003. Signed as a free agent by Milwaukee last season, he spent his second straight year in the International League. He became a free agent again in October. 2005 Outlook: C

Chris Saenz (Pos: RHP, Age: 23)

	W	L	Pct.	ERA	G	GS	Sv	IP	H	BB	SO	HR	Avg
'04	1	0	1.000	0.00	1	1	0	6.0	2	3	7	0	.100
Car.	1	0	1.000	0.00	1	1	0	6.0	2	3	7	0	.100

The Milwaukee organization is not noted for developing many promising arms, but in April the 22-year-old Saenz hinted at what might be to come. His dominating performance against the Cardinals was short-lived however, when management announced that he had September elbow surgery. 2005 Outlook: D

Matt Wise (Pos: RHP, Age: 29)

	W	L	Pct.	ERA	G	GS	Sv	IP	H	BB	SO	HR	Avg
'04	1	2	.333	4.44	30	3	0	52.2	51	15	30	3	.252
Car.	5	9	.357	4.63	56	18	0	147.2	145	47	106	21	.256

Wise had right elbow ligament replacement surgery in March 2003 and bounced back to have an excellent 2004 campaign. He was like an all-purpose cleaner, able to be applied to any kind of mess or situation. A deceptive changeup was the ingredient that made it all work. 2005 Outlook: B

Milwaukee Brewers Minor League Prospects

Organization Overview:

In 2003, the Brewers' biggest problem was pitching, and there seemed little prospect of improvement from within. In 2004 the pitching improved, but the offense became a major problem and the farm system was not yet in a position to provide help. No rookie position player got more than 41 at-bats with the parent club last year. But the premier player prospects were mostly in the high minors in 2004, and the big league club can look forward to an infusion of potential impact players such as Rickie Weeks and Prince Fielder in the next couple of years. Scouting director Jack Zduriencik and farm director Reid Nichols get credit for drafting and developing players who earned Milwaukee a rating by *Baseball America* as the best farm system in baseball.

Jose Capellan

Position: P   **Opening Day Age:** 24
Bats: R **Throws:** R   **Born:** 1/13/81 in Cotui,
Ht: 6' 4" **Wt:** 235   DR

Recent Statistics

	W	L	ERA	G	GS	Sv	IP	H	R	BB	SO	HR
2004 A Myrtle Beach	5	1	1.94	8	8	0	46.1	27	11	11	62	0
2004 AA Greenville	5	1	2.50	9	8	0	50.1	53	15	19	53	1
2004 AAA Richmond	4	2	2.51	7	7	0	43.0	33	13	15	37	0
2004 NL Atlanta	0	1	11.25	3	2	0	8.0	14	10	5	4	2

Capellan blazed his way through the Atlanta system last year, moving nearly as fast as his hard fastball, which has been clocked as high as 100 MPH. He went a combined 14-4 in 2004 before concluding the campaign in Atlanta, and opened eyes by dominating during his one inning in the Futures Game. Capellan complements his fastball with a good curveball that lacks only consistency. His changeup has improved and can be unhittable when he mixes it correctly with his heater. Capellan has developed an effortless delivery. The continued development of his breaking ball and changeup will determine whether he remains a starter or moves to the bullpen at the big league level. Milwaukee will try him as a starter after acquiring him in December's Dan Kolb trade with Atlanta.

Prince Fielder

Position: 1B   **Opening Day Age:** 20
Bats: L **Throws:** R   **Born:** 5/9/84 in Ontario,
Ht: 6' 0" **Wt:** 260   CA

Recent Statistics

	G	AB	R	H	D	T	HR	RBI	SB	BB	SO	Avg
2003 A Beloit	137	502	81	157	22	2	27	112	2	71	80	.313
2004 AA Huntsville	135	497	70	135	29	1	23	78	11	65	93	.272

In 2004, Fielder became the latest in a string of top prospects the Brewers have promoted to Double-A before they turned 21. After a slow start, he adjusted well, and although he is not a fast man, he added steals to his repertoire. He has good plate discipline. The Brewers selected Fielder with the seventh overall pick in 2002, and he's been hitting for power ever since, with 63 homers in 1,257 pro at-bats. The son of Cecil Fielder, Prince was the starting first baseman for the U.S. team in the 2004 Futures Game. He also improved on defense in 2004, cutting his errors to 15, and could emerge as the Brewers' first baseman by mid-2006.

J.J. Hardy

Position: SS   **Opening Day Age:** 22
Bats: R **Throws:** R   **Born:** 8/19/82 in Tucson,
Ht: 6' 2" **Wt:** 180   AZ

Recent Statistics

	G	AB	R	H	D	T	HR	RBI	SB	BB	SO	Avg
2003 AA Huntsville	114	416	67	116	26	0	12	62	6	58	54	.279
2004 AAA Indianapols	26	101	17	28	10	0	4	20	0	9	8	.277

Hardy is seen as the Brewers' shortstop of the future, but a separated left shoulder and torn labrum ended his 2004 campaign after only 101 at-bats for Triple-A Indianapolis. A second-round choice in the 2001 draft, Hardy followed the organization's pattern of promotion to Double-A before age 21 in 2002, and in 2003 added some pop and a big improvement in plate discipline to his solid defensive skills. He does not run much, but Hardy's defense is good enough for the majors now. After Hardy missed nearly all of 2004, the Brewers probably would prefer to have him start the season at Triple-A Nashville, but with the departure of Craig Counsell, Hardy could be the starting shortstop on Opening Day.

Corey Hart

Position: 3B   **Opening Day Age:** 23
Bats: R **Throws:** R   **Born:** 3/24/82 in Bowling
Ht: 6' 6" **Wt:** 200   Green, KY

Recent Statistics

	G	AB	R	H	D	T	HR	RBI	SB	BB	SO	Avg
2004 AAA Indianapols	121	441	68	124	29	8	15	67	17	41	92	.281
2004 NL Milwaukee	1	0	0	0	0	0	0	0	0	0	1	.000

Hart led the Double-A Southern League in hits, doubles and RBI, and was named the league MVP at age 21 in 2003. He earned that distinction with the bat, but was a poor defensive third baseman, and in 2004 made the switch to right field at Triple-A Indianapolis. He continued to hit until a shoulder injury ended his season, thus preventing a September promotion to the major league club. With the Brewers' need for power, Hart was in position to compete for the right-field job in spring training, until Carlos Lee was acquired in December. Hart probably goes to Triple-A Nashville to work on his plate discipline. Once established in the majors, he has the potential to be a 20 homer/20 steal guy.

Ben Hendrickson

Position: P
Bats: R **Throws:** R
Ht: 6' 4" **Wt:** 190

Opening Day Age: 24
Born: 2/4/81 in St. Cloud, MN

Recent Statistics

	W	L	ERA	G	GS	Sv	IP	H	R	BB	SO	HR
2004 AAA Indianapls	11	3	2.02	21	21	0	125.0	114	32	26	93	6
2004 NL Milwaukee	1	8	6.22	10	9	0	46.1	58	33	20	29	6

Hendrickson re-emerged as a top prospect in 2004, winning Pitcher of the Year honors in the Triple-A International League. Drafted in 1999, the last year Sal Bando was the Brewers' GM, Hendrickson posted ERAs under 3.00 at three levels in 2001 and 2002 while averaging nearly a strikeout per inning. But an inflamed elbow limited him to 17 games in 2003. Hendrickson features a sharp overhand curve and excellent control. In his brief big league experience, he was among the Brewers' leaders in the ratio of groundouts to flyouts, which should be a ticket to success in Miller Park. He figures to compete for a rotation spot this spring, and it wouldn't be surprising to see him emerge as a quality No. 3 starter by season's end.

Dave Krynzel

Position: OF
Bats: L **Throws:** L
Ht: 6' 1" **Wt:** 180

Opening Day Age: 23
Born: 11/7/81 in Dayton, OH

Recent Statistics

	G	AB	R	H	D	T	HR	RBI	SB	BB	SO	Avg
2004 R Az Brewers	5	16	8	8	1	1	0	0	2	3	2	.500
2004 AAA Indianapols	69	257	36	71	10	4	6	27	10	20	65	.276
2004 NL Milwaukee	16	41	6	9	1	0	0	3	0	3	15	.220

Selected 11th overall 2000, Krynzel is an excellent defensive center fielder who also strikes out in more than a quarter of his at-bats. He missed half of 2004 at Triple-A Indianapolis with a broken foot before getting his first taste of the major leagues in September. Krynzel has very good speed, but was successful in only 10 of 18 stolen-base attempts for Indianapolis. He does not hit enough to be a major league corner outfielder, but the center-field job is open with the departure of Scott Podsednik. Krynzel and Brady Clark will contend for the opening, and the rookie could start 2005 back in Triple-A if he isn't going to play every day with Milwaukee.

Brad Nelson

Position: OF
Bats: L **Throws:** R
Ht: 6' 2" **Wt:** 220

Opening Day Age: 22
Born: 12/23/82 in Algona, IA

Recent Statistics

	G	AB	R	H	D	T	HR	RBI	SB	BB	SO	Avg
2003 A High Desert	41	167	23	52	9	1	1	18	2	12	22	.311
2003 AA Huntsville	39	143	15	30	12	0	1	14	2	11	34	.210
2004 AA Huntsville	137	500	61	127	31	1	19	77	11	47	146	.254

A teenage idol in 2002, Nelson didn't mess around, leading all minor leaguers with 49 doubles and 116 RBI while swatting 20 homers. Highly regarded for his potential as a power hitter, the Algona, Iowa native suffered a broken hamate bone in 2003, which cost him two months on the DL. He recovered nicely at Double-A Huntsville in 2004, rediscovering his power swing and re-establishing his status as a top prospect. Since Prince Fielder clearly is the Brewers' first baseman of the future, Nelson was moved to left field in 2004, where he showed limited range. He runs a lot, but not successfully. With a 3-1 strikeout-walk ratio in 2004, Nelson needs to cut down on his whiffs.

Rickie Weeks

Position: 2B
Bats: R **Throws:** R
Ht: 6' 0" **Wt:** 195

Opening Day Age: 22
Born: 9/13/82 in Daytona Beach, FL

Recent Statistics

	G	AB	R	H	D	T	HR	RBI	SB	BB	SO	Avg
2003 R Az Brewers	1	4	0	2	0	0	0	4	1	0	2	.500
2003 A Beloit	20	63	13	22	8	1	1	16	2	15	9	.349
2003 NL Milwaukee	7	12	1	2	1	0	0	0	0	1	6	.167
2004 AA Huntsville	133	479	67	124	35	6	8	42	11	55	107	.259

The Brewers used the second pick in the 2003 draft to select Weeks, who set an NCAA record by hitting .473 for Southern University. Weeks played well for Class-A Beloit in '03, and last year jumped to Double-A Huntsville. After having played center field and shortstop for much of his college career, he has made the transition to second, and should become a good major league second baseman. Weeks has yet to develop the basestealing skills that would make his outstanding speed a major asset. His presence on the horizon could persuade Milwaukee to go with Bill Hall at the keystone to start the year, but a strong first half could land Weeks in Milwaukee by the break.

Others to Watch

Milwaukee hasn't produced a quality big league catcher in over a decade, but **Lou Palmisano** (22) could break the streak. A 2003 third-rounder, he was the MVP in the Rookie-level Pioneer League that year and hit .293 at Class-A Beloit in 2004. . . After two years in the Dominican Summer League, second baseman **Hernan Iribarren** (20) ripped up the Rookie-level Arizona League and earned a promotion to Class-A Beloit. His cumulative 2004 stats were .422 (108-for-256) with five homers, 46 RBI and 16 stolen bases. . . Lefty **Manny Parra** (22), signed as a draft-and-follow for $1.55 million in 2002, pitched well for high Class-A High Desert, going 5-2 with a 3.48 ERA and striking out 64 in 67.1 innings. But questions persist about the status of his left shoulder. . . With the fifth pick in the 2004 draft, the Brewers selected righthanded pitcher **Mark Rogers** (19) from Orr's Island, Maine. He features a fastball in the mid-90s, a good curveball and changeup. Rogers signed in time to appear in nine games in the Rookie-level Arizona League.

Offense

Shea Stadium helps pitchers keep most of their offerings inside the fences. The unenclosed, symmetrical ballpark features one of the deepest center fields in the game at 410 feet, and the strong winds off Flushing Bay, particularly during the spring and fall, can keep hard-hit balls from carrying. The lone part of the ballpark that features occasional carry is right-center, where the huge scoreboard can block the winds and give left-handed power hitters a fair shot at going deep.

Defense

Shea's natural grass infield remains one of the slowest and most uneven surfaces in the game. Outfielders can play more shallow than in other parks since the ball does not carry well. Bloop doubles are frequent at Shea.

Who It Helps the Most

It is no mistake that Mets pitchers surrendered the third-fewest home runs in the NL in 2004. No one made better use of Shea Stadium than Steve Trachsel and Al Leiter. The flyball pitchers take full advantage of the ballpark's generous dimensions. Mike Piazza continues to hit well in the comforts of home, batting 100 points higher (.319 to .219) at Shea.

Who It Hurts the Most

Mike Cameron discovered just how difficult Shea can be for righthanded power hitters. Even though Cameron failed to hit for average anywhere, 19 of his 30 home runs came on the road. Fellow newcomer Eric Valent had difficulty at home as well, batting .233 at Shea versus .298 on the road.

Rookies & Newcomers

The arrival of David Wright and Jose Reyes in the past two years and the trade that sent Scott Kazmir to Tampa Bay have depleted the top of the Mets' farm system. The leading contenders to contribute in 2005, first baseman Craig Brazell and infielder/outfielder Victor Diaz, excelled at Shea during cups of coffee last year.

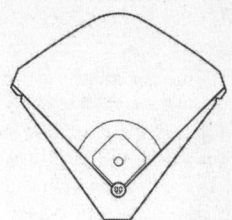

Dimensions: LF-338, LCF-378, CF-410, RCF-378, RF-338

Capacity: 57,405

Elevation: 20 feet

Surface: Grass

Foul Territory: Average

Park Factors

2004 Season

	Home Games Mets	Opp	Total	Away Games Mets	Opp	Total	Index
G	72	72	144	69	69	138	
Avg	.251	.260	.255	.247	.267	.256	100
AB	2423	2550	4973	2385	2302	4687	102
R	288	321	609	300	326	626	93
H	608	662	1270	588	614	1202	101
2B	128	125	253	125	129	254	94
3B	7	5	12	11	17	28	40
HR	71	62	133	90	77	167	75
BB	223	266	489	215	262	477	97
SO	494	453	947	515	387	902	99
E	64	44	108	50	31	81	128
E-Infield	54	40	94	39	24	63	143
LHB-Avg	.262	.267	.265	.238	.264	.252	105
LHB-HR	18	27	45	19	29	48	91
RHB-Avg	.247	.255	.251	.250	.268	.259	97
RHB-HR	53	35	88	71	48	119	69

2002-2004

	Home Games Mets	Opp	Total	Away Games Mets	Opp	Total	Index
G	218	218	436	208	208	416	
Avg	.250	.260	.255	.251	.267	.259	99
AB	7230	7669	14899	7160	6898	14058	101
R	869	968	1837	902	947	1849	95
H	1809	1993	3802	1798	1843	3641	100
2B	352	384	736	351	371	722	96
3B	27	32	59	33	59	92	61
HR	191	207	398	213	215	428	88
BB	674	762	1436	656	737	1393	97
SO	1400	1426	2826	1454	1200	2654	100
E	191	140	331	153	135	288	110
E-Infield	160	127	287	127	110	237	116
LHB-Avg	.262	.261	.261	.252	.253	.253	103
LHB-HR	81	80	161	69	64	133	114
RHB-Avg	.243	.259	.251	.250	.275	.263	96
RHB-HR	110	127	237	144	151	295	76

2004 Rankings (National League)

- Second-highest error factor
- Second-highest infield-error factor
- Third-highest LHB batting-average factor
- Lowest triple factor
- Second-lowest home-run factor
- Second-lowest RHB home-run factor

Willie Randolph

2004 Season

While Willie Randolph served as bench coach in the Bronx last year, Art Howe was made the scapegoat for another disappointing season in Flushing. Criticized for his perceived lack of intensity, Howe's patient, positive approach and ability to relate to a variety of personalities was deemed weak and failed to energize the New York faithful. Howe, however, never had a healthy lineup. Murphy's Law was working full throttle and did not stop until the team's front office bungled the firing of Howe with two weeks left in the season.

Offense

The frequent injuries caused the Mets to struggle to score runs last year. With Jose Reyes and Kaz Matsui hitting one-two in the lineup, the Mets have above-average speed at the top, and Randolph is expected to make the most of their talent. Although the team did not run much during the first half of the 2004 campaign, the Mets led the major leagues in stolen-base percentage (82.3).

Pitching & Defense

The Mets ranked 28th in the major leagues in fielding, ahead of only Arizona and Detroit. Expect that scenario to change with Randolph at the helm. The infield should be much improved with Randolph helping Reyes and Matsui change positions up the middle and third baseman David Wright adjust to a full season. The rotation is aging at the top and needs the likes of Victor Zambrano and Aaron Heilman to fulfill their potential. The bullpen could use some younger and more powerful arms in 2005.

2005 Outlook

Not unlike Howe, Randolph is expected to produce a positive environment, only without the country club atmosphere that defined the Mets' clubhouse last year. The former second baseman was hired to provide a harder edge to the team's makeup and help mold a young and impressionable infield. With new general manager Omar Minaya at the controls, Randolph is expected to guide a roster that features multiple changes. If nothing else, life should be more exciting at Shea Stadium than in the recent past.

Born: 7/06/54 in Holly Hill, South Carolina

Playing Experience: 1975-1992, Pit, NYY, LA, Oak, Mil, NYM

Managerial Experience: No major league managerial experience

Manager Statistics (Art Howe)

Year	Team, Lg	W	L	Pct	GB	Finish
2004	New York, NL	71	91	.438	25.0	4th East
14 Seasons		1129	1137	.498	–	–

2004 Starting Pitchers by Days Rest

	<=3	4	5	6+
Mets Starts	1	85	39	27
Mets ERA	8.53	3.90	4.15	4.50
NL Avg Starts	2	82	46	23
NL ERA	4.58	4.35	4.28	4.73

2004 Situational Stats

	Art Howe	NL Average
Hit & Run Success %	36.5	38.0
Stolen Base Success %	82.3	71.7
Platoon Pct.	49.7	55.2
Defensive Subs	22	18
High-Pitch Outings	8	6
Quick/Slow Hooks	25/10	21/12
Sacrifice Attempts	95	99

2004 Rankings — Art Howe (National League)

- 1st in stolen-base percentage, fewest caught stealings of second base (19) and 2+ pitching changes in low-scoring games (43)
- 2nd in pitchouts with a runner moving (8), starting lineups used (136) and quick hooks
- 3rd in steals of second base (95), pitchouts (26) and intentional walks (55)

Kris Benson

2004 Season

The Mets acquired Kris Benson's services from the Pirates on July 30 along with infielder Jeff Keppinger in exchange for infielder Ty Wigginton, pitcher Matt Peterson and infielder Jose Bautista. After posting a 3.01 ERA in his final 10 starts with Pittsburgh, Benson pitched well with the Mets, including a career-best shutout streak of 18.1 innings from September 9-19.

Pitching

Benson had success last year by finding consistency with his mechanics. The righthander employs a three-quarters arm slot and creates good deception in his windup. He throws a four-seam fastball in the low 90s that can hit 94 MPH, and a two-seamer that drives in on the hands of righthanded hitters and sits in the 89-91 MPH range. Benson also does a good job of changing speeds by mixing in a cut fastball, slider, overhand curveball and changeup, the last of which needs improvement. He is at his best when he moves the ball around in the lower part of the strike zone, but gets in trouble when he falls behind in the count.

Defense & Hitting

Benson is a surehanded defender with quick reflexes and good athleticism on the mound. His pickoff move is decent, and he does an average job of holding runners with a quick delivery to the plate. At the same time, he can become easily distracted by baserunners, which can cause him to fall behind in the count. Offensively, Benson overcame an 0-for-30 showing at the plate in 2003 to post eight hits last year. He is a good bunter.

2005 Outlook

Benson re-signed with the Mets and received a healthy raise, inking a three-year deal worth $22.5 million with a club option for a fourth campaign at $7.5 million. For the deal to work for the Mets, Benson must continue to make refinements in his game while staying healthy enough to take the mound every fifth day. If he can do those two things while maintaining his solid repertoire and his overall stuff, Benson could be a solid middle-of-the-rotation pitcher for the length of the contract.

Position: SP
Bats: R **Throws:** R
Ht: 6' 4" **Wt:** 195

Opening Day Age: 30
Born: 11/7/74 in Superior, WI
ML Seasons: 5

Overall Statistics

	W	L	Pct.	ERA	G	GS	Sv	IP	H	BB	SO	HR	Avg
'04	12	12	.500	4.31	31	31	0	200.1	202	61	134	15	.263
Car.	47	53	.470	4.28	137	137	0	850.0	871	316	604	87	.266

2004 Pitching Profile

	Kris Benson	NL Average
Overall Strike %	63.6	62.5
1st Pitch Strike %	61.2	58.5
Ratio	1.31	1.39
Strikeouts per 9 IP	6.02	6.74
Walks per 9 IP	2.74	3.38
Home Runs per 9 IP	0.67	1.11
Strikeout/Walk Ratio	2.20	1.99
Groundball/Flyball Ratio	1.14	1.25

2004 Situational Stats

	W	L	ERA	Sv	IP		AB	H	HR	RBI	Avg
Home	5	5	4.18	0	97.0	LHB	362	100	8	46	.276
Road	7	7	4.44	0	103.1	RHB	407	102	7	44	.251
First Half	6	7	4.42	0	110.0	Sc Pos	193	55	5	69	.285
Scnd Half	6	5	4.18	0	90.1	Clutch	53	21	1	7	.396

2004 Rankings (National League)

- 3rd in sacrifice bunts (15)
- 8th in fewest home runs allowed per nine innings (.67)

Mike Cameron

2004 Season

After spending four seasons with Seattle, Mike Cameron signed a three-year deal with the Mets in December 2003 and provided his new employer with an uneven showing. Cameron set a New York franchise record for a center fielder by hitting a career best 30 home runs. He also added speed with 22 stolen bases, yet batted just .231, 17 points below his career norm and his lowest average since 1998.

Hitting

Cameron has been known as an all-or-nothing hitter for several years, and the trend does not appear to be on the brink of changing. He does not make consistent contact, resulting in high strikeout totals and low batting averages. Contrary to what his numbers might indicate, he is not a free swinger, however. He does a good job of working counts and is capable of drawing a decent number of walks, even though his 57 base on balls last year was his fewest since 1998. Cameron possesses above-average power, especially to left-center and center field. Lefthanded pitchers, particularly those adept at throwing sliders down and in to righthanded hitters, continue to frustrate him.

Baserunning & Defense

A two-time Gold Glove winner, Cameron was awful with the leather at times, with a sprained left wrist, a groin injury and a late-season viral infection contributing to his woes. Nevertheless, his overall glovework appeared to slip. On the basepaths, Cameron is capable of stealing 30 bases. He gets good jumps against righties but has trouble reading the moves of lefties. At full speed, he is one of the faster players in the game.

2005 Outlook

If the Mets have any hope of competing this year, Cameron needs to be a solid 30-30 candidate while rediscovering the nuances that made him a premier defensive center fielder in the American League. At age 32, he should be in the second half of his prime. With another year of experience in the NL under his belt (he played for the Reds in 1999), Cameron could improve upon all of his numbers if he remains healthy.

Position: CF
Bats: R **Throws:** R
Ht: 6' 2" **Wt:** 200

Opening Day Age: 32
Born: 1/8/73 in LaGrange, GA
ML Seasons: 10

Overall Statistics

G	AB	R	H	D	T	HR	RBI	SB	BB	SO	Avg	OBP	Slg
140	493	76	114	30	1	30	76	22	57	143	.231	.319	.479
1192	4021	643	996	215	37	161	586	216	529	1113	.248	.340	.440

Where He Hits the Ball

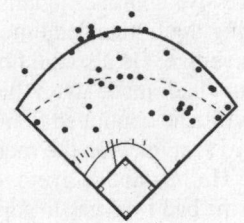
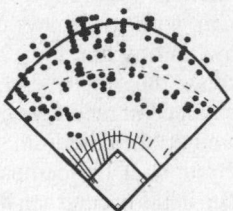

Vs. LHP   **Vs. RHP**

2004 Situational Stats

	AB	H	HR	RBI	Avg		AB	H	HR	RBI	Avg
Home	241	55	11	36	.228	LHP	102	22	5	12	.216
Road	252	59	19	40	.234	RHP	391	92	25	64	.235
First Half	275	63	14	34	.229	Sc Pos	127	29	5	43	.228
Scnd Half	218	51	16	42	.234	Clutch	90	15	2	7	.167

2004 Rankings (National League)

- 1st in errors in center field (8), lowest batting average, lowest groundball-flyball ratio (0.6) and lowest fielding percentage in center field (.978)
- 3rd in lowest batting average vs. righthanded pitchers
- 4th in lowest batting average at home
- 6th in lowest batting average in the clutch
- 7th in lowest batting average on the road
- 9th in steals of third (4)
- Led the Mets in home runs, at-bats, runs scored, total bases (236), RBI, stolen bases, caught stealing (6), strikeouts, pitches seen (2,278), plate appearances (562) and games played

Cliff Floyd

2004 Season

Injuries led to inconsistency and a disappointing season for Cliff Floyd. Bothered most of the year by a lingering ailing right heel and a strained right quadriceps that sidelined him from mid-April to mid-May, Floyd nearly matched his 2003 totals in doubles, homers and RBI, yet posted his lowest batting average since 1997. The Mets nearly traded him to Detroit in August after he irked the New York front office on several occasions with his negative comments.

Hitting

Floyd took little advantage of hitting around Mike Piazza and Richard Hidalgo in the Mets' lineup. Pitchers used Floyd's aggressive approach against him, with southpaws owning the lefthanded hitter by limiting him to a .239 average. He also did not show the improvement he had made with his patience in recent years. While he continued to hit well at Shea Stadium, Floyd struggled on the road throughout the campaign. He has above-average pop in his bat and can drive the ball from gap to gap.

Baserunning & Defense

Despite his chronic heel problems, Floyd maintains decent speed both on the basepaths and in the field. He reads pitchers well when attempting to steal and does a good job of taking an extra base. Floyd gets good jumps on flyballs in left field and is adept at holding runners to singles on balls hit down the line. His arm strength is above average for left. With his injuries, Floyd might benefit from a move to first base. Many scouts believe he would be best served as a designated hitter in the American League.

2005 Outlook

The Mets have made it known that Floyd is available, but the team has had difficulty finding a taker since he is owed $6.5 million in both 2005 and 2006. Floyd, meanwhile, has suggested that he will retire once his four-year deal expires because of the physical toll his body has experienced in the game. If not New York, his most likely destination is the AL.

Position: LF
Bats: L **Throws:** R
Ht: 6' 4" **Wt:** 230

Opening Day Age: 32
Born: 12/5/72 in Chicago, IL
ML Seasons: 12

Overall Statistics

	G	AB	R	H	D	T	HR	RBI	SB	BB	SO	Avg	OBP	Slg
'04	113	396	55	103	26	0	18	63	11	47	103	.260	.352	.462
Car.	1176	3893	622	1100	276	19	168	639	129	445	796	.283	.362	.493

Where He Hits the Ball

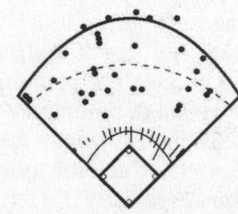 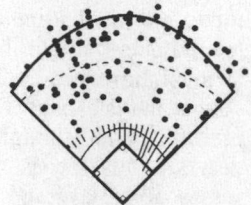

Vs. LHP   **Vs. RHP**

2004 Situational Stats

	AB	H	HR	RBI	Avg		AB	H	HR	RBI	Avg
Home	193	57	7	25	.295	LHP	113	27	1	14	.239
Road	203	46	11	38	.227	RHP	283	76	17	49	.269
First Half	213	60	13	42	.282	Sc Pos	92	25	7	49	.272
Scnd Half	183	43	5	21	.235	Clutch	63	9	0	2	.143

2004 Rankings (National League)

- 1st in lowest batting average in the clutch
- 4th in lowest percentage of swings put into play (33.8)
- 5th in lowest cleanup slugging percentage (.471)
- 9th in lowest percentage of pitches taken (48.2)
- 10th in lowest batting average vs. lefthanded pitchers
- Led the Mets in hit by pitch (11)

Tom Glavine

Position: SP
Bats: L **Throws:** L
Ht: 6' 0" **Wt:** 185

Opening Day Age: 39
Born: 3/25/66 in
Concord, MA
ML Seasons: 18
Pronunciation:
GLA-vin

2004 Season

The death of Tom Glavine as an elite pitcher was greatly exaggerated prior to the 2004 season. The lefthander proved that point with one of the better years of his storied career before injuries suffered in a car accident on August 10 sidelined him for 11 days. He accumulated 200 innings for the 12th time, and was selected to the NL All-Star team for the ninth time.

Pitching

Glavine remains one of the league's best pitchers because of his excellent control. Although he once hit 90 MPH on a regular basis with his fastball, his heater now resides in the 83-84 MPH range and tops out at 86. The lefthander subtracts from his two-seam fastball and throws primarily that pitch and his outstanding changeup, an offering with excellent depth and fade. He mixes in only a few breaking balls for show and to keep hitters guessing. He does not get the call on the outside part of the plate the way he did while with Atlanta. As a result, Glavine has become more adept at moving his pitches around the lower half of the strike zone.

Defense & Hitting

Glavine remains an excellent fielder with quick reflexes and soft hands. He has become craftier in holding runners on base in recent years. He will step off the back of the rubber with a quick throw and also employs a short slide step to home. Glavine also helps himself at the plate. He batted .204 last season and pinch-hit on two occasions. He leads all active players with 186 career sacrifice bunts.

2005 Outlook

While Glavine's style should enable him to pitch for a few more seasons, he will be 39 when the 2005 campaign begins, which should reduce the likelihood of his tossing 220 innings on an annual basis. His numbers in New York have been misleading due to the lack of offensive and defensive support he has received. A change in any of those scenarios this year would be a surprise.

Overall Statistics

W	L	Pct.	ERA	G	GS	Sv	IP	H	BB	SO	HR	Avg
11	14	.440	3.60	33	33	0	212.1	204	70	109	20	.252
262	171	.605	3.44	570	570	0	3740.1	3583	1276	2245	288	.254

2004 Pitching Profile

	Tom Glavine	NL Average
Overall Strike %	58.1	62.5
1st Pitch Strike %	50.4	58.5
Ratio	1.29	1.39
Strikeouts per 9 IP	4.62	6.74
Walks per 9 IP	2.97	3.38
Home Runs per 9 IP	0.85	1.11
Strikeout/Walk Ratio	1.56	1.99
Groundball/Flyball Ratio	1.67	1.25

2004 Situational Stats

	W	L	ERA	Sv	IP		AB	H	HR	RBI	Avg
Home	3	6	2.84	0	85.2	LHB	223	54	6	18	.242
Road	8	8	4.12	0	126.2	RHB	588	150	14	70	.255
First Half	7	7	2.66	0	128.2	Sc Pos	182	44	5	64	.242
Scnd Half	4	7	5.06	0	83.2	Clutch	44	12	0	2	.273

2004 Rankings (National League)

- 3rd in lowest stolen-base percentage allowed (46.7)
- 4th in losses
- 5th in fewest strikeouts per nine innings (4.6)
- 7th in pickoff throws (126) and runners caught stealing (8)
- 8th in highest groundball-flyball ratio allowed (1.7)
- 10th in innings pitched
- Led the Mets in losses, games started, innings pitched, hits allowed, batters faced (904), pitches thrown (3,395), runners caught stealing (8), highest strikeout-walk ratio (1.6), lowest on-base percentage allowed (.308), highest groundball-flyball ratio allowed (1.7), lowest stolen-base percentage allowed (46.7) and fewest walks per nine innings (3.0)

Richard Hidalgo

2004 Season

Richard Hidalgo began last year by earning National League Player of the Week honors for April 5-11 and hitting at a .341 clip during the season's first month. He then fell into an extended slump that led to a trade from Houston to the Mets on June 17 in exchange for pitchers David Weathers and Jeremy Griffiths. While his batting average failed to improve, Hidalgo tied the club record for reaching 10 home runs in the fewest amount of games (29) as a Met.

Hitting

Consistency has never been a major part of Hidalgo's game. After hitting the ball to the opposite field in 2003, he became pull-happy and intoxicated with trying to hit home runs over the short left-field porch at Houston's Minute Maid Park. He started rolling over his right wrist during his swing, resulting in a slew of weak groundball outs. The Mets tried to add more consistency and power to Hidalgo's swing by moving him closer to the plate. The initial results were impressive, but he fanned a career-high 129 times last year and showed little patience at the plate.

Baserunning & Defense

Few outfielders in either league have as strong an arm as Hidalgo. His reputation precedes him, and few teams are willing to run on the right fielder's cannon. He still managed to record a team-best 10 assists last summer and did an overall solid job of manning the right-field corner. Hidalgo's speed is a hair above average. While his legs enable him to make the occasional spectacular sliding catch, he rarely makes a positive impact on the basepaths.

2005 Outlook

The Mets said they wanted Hidalgo to return, but not for the $15 million option on his contract. They hoped to work out a new deal, but Hidalgo opted to sign a one-year, $5 million pact with Texas. He can be a prominent part in the middle of the Rangers' lineup when his entire game is in sync. Yet, his inconsistencies from year-to-year make his potential contributions hard to project.

Position: RF
Bats: R **Throws:** R
Ht: 6' 3" **Wt:** 220

Opening Day Age: 29
Born: 6/28/75 in Caracas, VZ
ML Seasons: 8
Pronunciation: huh-DAHL-go

Overall Statistics

	G	AB	R	H	D	T	HR	RBI	SB	BB	SO	Avg	OBP	Slg
'04	144	523	67	125	26	3	25	82	4	44	129	.239	.301	.444
Car.	899	3151	488	861	202	19	155	517	47	332	663	.273	.350	.497

Where He Hits the Ball

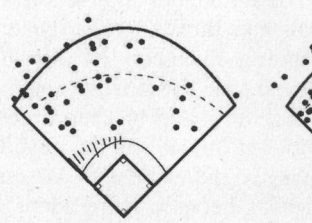 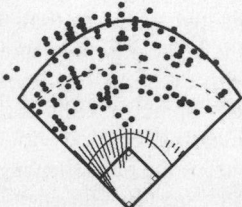

Vs. LHP **Vs. RHP**

2004 Situational Stats

	AB	H	HR	RBI	Avg		AB	H	HR	RBI	Avg
Home	253	61	13	43	.241	LHP	102	27	7	17	.265
Road	270	64	12	39	.237	RHP	421	98	18	65	.233
First Half	285	78	12	46	.274	Sc Pos	142	35	6	60	.246
Scnd Half	238	47	13	36	.197	Clutch	82	18	2	12	.220

2004 Rankings (National League)

- 2nd in lowest batting average vs. righthanded pitchers (.233) and lowest fielding percentage in right field (.978)
- 3rd in errors in right field (6)
- 4th in lowest batting average (.239) and lowest on-base percentage (.301)
- Led the Mets in HR frequency (15.4 ABs per HR)

Al Leiter

2004 Season

Last year was a tale of two seasons for Al Leiter. He pitched with a sore left shoulder during the first two months and owned a 1-2 record after losing to Arizona on May 11. The lefthander returned to action on June 1 after a stint on the disabled list and immediately tossed 15 consecutive scoreless innings. Leiter reached double digits in triumphs by allowing one earned run or less in 15 of his 30 starts.

Pitching

Leiter succeeds despite being one of the slowest-working and most deliberate pitchers in the majors. He had the highest pitches-per-batter average in the big leagues, and games he started had an average time of just under three hours. Even though he is not economical with his offerings, Leiter is an intelligent hurler who throws a hard, cut fastball that sits in the low 90s. He also throws a good changeup down in the strike zone that results in numerous groundball outs. Leiter attacks lefthanded hitters with fastballs and a sharp slider that can result in a half-dozen or so strikeouts per game.

Defense & Hitting

Not only does Leiter throw a lot of pitches, but he also throws over to first base more than just about any hurler in the game. Even so, he is not effective at holding runners on and surrenders as many stolen bases as any lefthander in recent memory due to his slow delivery. Leiter has good hands and defends his position well. He also is not adept with the lumber, but could be losing his reputation as the league's worst-hitting pitcher after recording five hits in 2004.

2005 Outlook

Even though he will celebrate his 40th birthday in October, Leiter remains one of the most reliable mid-level lefthanded starters in the game. He loves pitching in New York and anticipated returning to the Mets, but negotiations stalled and he wound up signing a one-year, $7 million deal with the Marlins, the team for which he pitched for two seasons before joining the Mets. Leiter was on the 1997 World Series team.

Position: SP
Bats: L **Throws:** L
Ht: 6' 3"   **Wt:** 220

Opening Day Age: 39
Born: 10/23/65 in Toms River, NJ
ML Seasons: 18
Pronunciation: LIGH-ter

Overall Statistics

W	L	Pct.	ERA	G	GS	Sv	IP	H	BB	SO	HR	Avg
10	8	.556	3.21	30	30	0	173.2	138	97	117	16	.218
155	120	.564	3.65	386	356	2	2248.2	1998	1065	1877	185	.240

2004 Pitching Profile

	Al Leiter	NL Average
Overall Strike %	56.2	62.5
1st Pitch Strike %	44.7	58.5
Ratio	1.35	1.39
Strikeouts per 9 IP	6.06	6.74
Walks per 9 IP	5.03	3.38
Home Runs per 9 IP	0.83	1.11
Strikeout/Walk Ratio	1.21	1.99
Groundball/Flyball Ratio	1.00	1.25

2004 Situational Stats

	W	L	ERA	Sv	IP		AB	H	HR	RBI	Avg
Home	5	2	2.61	0	86.1	LHB	137	28	2	10	.204
Road	5	6	3.81	0	87.1	RHB	495	110	14	52	.222
First Half	5	3	2.40	0	86.1	Sc Pos	162	28	5	44	.173
Scnd Half	5	5	4.02	0	87.1	Clutch	19	7	1	2	.368

2004 Rankings (National League)

- 1st in fielding percentage at pitcher (1.000), lowest batting average allowed with runners in scoring position and most pitches thrown per batter (4.33)
- 2nd in pickoff throws (189)
- 3rd in highest walks per nine innings (5.0)
- 4th in lowest strikeout-walk ratio (1.2) and least run support per nine innings (4.0)
- 5th in lowest batting average allowed (.218)
- 6th in walks allowed, hit batsmen (11) and lowest slugging percentage allowed (.354)
- Led the Mets in ERA, walks allowed, hit batsmen (11), strikeouts, winning percentage, lowest batting average allowed (.218), lowest slugging percentage allowed (.354), lowest ERA at home, lowest ERA on the road, lowest batting average allowed with runners in scoring position, fewest home runs allowed per nine innings (.83) and most strikeouts per nine innings (6.1)

New York (NL)

Kazuo Matsui

2004 Season

After arriving in the Big Apple amid worlds of hoopla, Kaz Matsui was nothing less than a flop for the Mets in his first major league season. Unproductive as a leadoff hitter and error-prone at shortstop, Matsui added injury to insult when he was sidelined for most of August and September with a lower back strain. He did manage to set a Mets club record and tie a National League rookie mark by hitting five leadoff home runs.

Hitting

It is hard to determine if Matsui was a worse leadoff hitter or shortstop. Opposing pitchers toyed with him with their two-seam fastballs, a pitch rarely seen in Japan. He also swung for the fences while leading off instead of focusing on reaching base. To his credit, Matsui shortened his swing after being a 30-30 performer in Japan. The shorter stroke allowed him to make more consistent contact. He still showed little patience, however, as evidenced by his 40 walks and 97 strikeouts.

Baserunning & Defense

Matsui tied Rafael Furcal for the most errors among NL shortstops with 24. Ironically, Matsui was compared with Furcal prior to last season for his fluidness afield. After playing all but nine games on artificial turf in Japan, Matsui had trouble making the adjustment to natural grass. He also made numerous miscues while trying to make throws on the run. A good baserunner with above-average speed, he stole just one base in his first 34 games before manager Art Howe pressured him into a more aggressive approach. Matsui appeared tentative on the basepaths, but should provide good speed near the top of the order if he settles into the second slot.

2005 Outlook

Unlike many of the Japanese players who preceded him to the United States, Matsui borders on being a marginal player in the major leagues. The Mets are hopeful the game will slow down for him when he moves to second base. With the spotlight considerably dimmer compared to his rookie campaign, Matsui could emerge as a steady contributor this year.

Position: SS
Bats: B **Throws:** R
Ht: 5'10" **Wt:** 185

Opening Day Age: 29
Born: 10/23/75 in Osaka, Japan
ML Seasons: 1
Pronunciation: mat-soo-ee

Overall Statistics

	G	AB	R	H	D	T	HR	RBI	SB	BB	SO	Avg	OBP	Slg
'04	114	460	65	125	32	2	7	44	14	40	97	.272	.331	.396
Car.	114	460	65	125	32	2	7	44	14	40	97	.272	.331	.396

Where He Hits the Ball

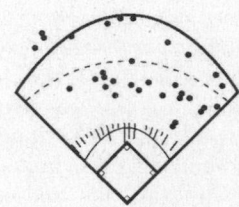 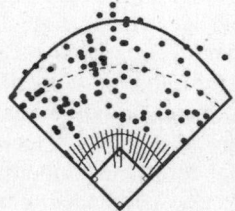

Vs. LHP   **Vs. RHP**

2004 Situational Stats

	AB	H	HR	RBI	Avg		AB	H	HR	RBI	Avg
Home	215	59	4	26	.274	LHP	98	30	3	11	.306
Road	245	66	3	18	.269	RHP	362	95	4	33	.262
First Half	350	94	7	32	.269	Sc Pos	108	32	1	35	.296
Scnd Half	110	31	0	12	.282	Clutch	82	22	0	4	.268

2004 Rankings (National League)

- 1st in lowest fielding percentage at shortstop (.956)
- 2nd in errors at shortstop (23)
- 7th in lowest on-base percentage for a leadoff hitter (.311)
- Led the Mets in hits, singles, doubles, triples, highest groundball-flyball ratio (1.5), bunts in play (13), batting average with runners in scoring position, batting average with the bases loaded (.286), batting average vs. left handed pitchers, and on-base percentage for a leadoff hitter (.311)

Mike Piazza

2004 Season

A left knee injury that cost him more than three weeks in August and an unsuccessful stint at first base led to another disappointing season for Mike Piazza. He batted a career-low .266, nearly 50 points lower than his career average, to mark the third straight year he has batted below .300. With a roundtripper on May 5, he became the all-time home-run leader among catchers.

Hitting

Piazza festered in an offensive funk early in the season when teams pitched around the Mets' cleanup hitter. He fell into the trap of taking huge swings, resulting in a 1-for-28 slump and a stretch of 74 at-bats without a home run at midseason. The situation failed to improve following his return from a knee injury in late August, with Piazza making poor pitch selections. He still has above-average power and is capable of driving the ball to all fields, yet there is no question that his bat is slowing with every passing season.

Baserunning & Defense

Piazza's calling-card never has been his defense nor his speed. His years behind the plate have robbed him of his once-average foot speed, although his intelligence when running the bases keeps him from being a clogger. Piazza looked like a Gold Glove catcher compared to his show-ing at first base, and the Mets have said that he will stay behind the dish as long as he is with the club. His arm strength and the accuracy of his throws are below average, and his footwork is poor.

2005 Outlook

Assuming he remains with the Mets, in part because of his $15 million salary, Piazza should catch in the neighborhood of 110 games this year if healthy. The wear and tear of catching means Piazza is not a young 36, and his decline is remi-niscent of what Johnny Bench endured at a rela-tively early age. But with Piazza apparently unable to make a change in position, his days as an offensive standout appear to be numbered.

Position: 1B/C
Bats: R **Throws:** R
Ht: 6' 3" **Wt:** 215

Opening Day Age: 36
Born: 9/4/68 in Norristown, PA
ML Seasons: 13
Pronunciation: pee-AH-zuh

Overall Statistics

G	AB	R	H	D	T	HR	RBI	SB	BB	SO	Avg	OBP	Slg
129	455	47	121	21	0	20	54	0	68	78	.266	.362	.444
1590	5805	935	1829	285	6	378	1161	17	666	919	.315	.385	.562

Where He Hits the Ball

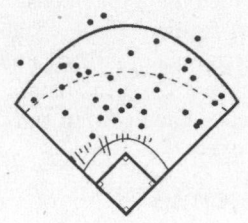
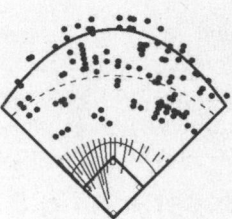

Vs. LHP   **Vs. RHP**

2004 Situational Stats

	AB	H	HR	RBI	Avg		AB	H	HR	RBI	Avg
Home	213	68	12	29	.319	LHP	89	27	4	15	.303
Road	242	53	8	25	.219	RHP	366	94	16	39	.257
First Half	310	92	16	40	.297	Sc Pos	102	24	2	33	.235
Scnd Half	145	29	4	14	.200	Clutch	76	17	3	11	.224

2004 Rankings (National League)

- 3rd in lowest batting average on the road
- 4th in intentional walks (14)
- 6th in errors at first base (8)
- 8th in errors at catcher (5)
- 9th in cleanup slugging percentage (.534)
- Led the Mets in walks, intentional walks (14), times on base (191), GDPs (14), on-base percentage, cleanup slugging percentage (.534) and batting average at home

Jose Reyes

2004 Season

Jose Reyes missed more than 100 games due to injury, including the first 66 contests because of a strained right hamstring and a sore back. He capped the campaign by spending half of August and most of September on the disabled list with a stress fracture of the left fibula. When on the field, Reyes hit safely in 25 of his last 32 games.

Hitting

The silver lining in Reyes' otherwise-disappointing season was his gradual improvements. He displayed more aggressiveness by trying to bunt for base hits and employed his outstanding speed by stealing bases. His at-bats also improved when he showed the ability to drive the ball to the opposite field. With the assistance of former hitting coach Don Baylor, Reyes went to the plate with a game plan instead of relying exclusively on his natural abilities. He still lacks patience and needs to work the count in his favor, however.

Baserunning & Defense

Reyes played well upon moving to second base, but he is headed back to shortstop in order to take full advantage of his great range and powerful arm. He has the natural athleticism to be one of the premier shortstops in the game, needing only to make the adjustments while completing the routine plays as well as the spectacular ones. Reyes is a good runner but tends to plod around the bases after sprinting to first. The Mets hired a chiropractor to alter his running style and take the pressure off his chronic hamstring problems, but the practice proved to be a failure. If he can stay healthy, Reyes should develop into a plus baserunner.

2005 Outlook

The Mets believe Reyes will be a different player this year while moving back to his natural position at short. The concern centers on his brittleness and being a notoriously slow healer. If he can remain on the field, Reyes will be a major improvement at the top of the New York lineup and should significantly upgrade one of the major leagues' most porous defenses.

Position: 2B/SS
Bats: B **Throws:** R
Ht: 6' 0" **Wt:** 160

Opening Day Age: 21
Born: 6/11/83 in Villa Gonzalez, DR
ML Seasons: 2
Pronunciation: RAY-ess

Overall Statistics

	G	AB	R	H	D	T	HR	RBI	SB	BB	SO	Avg	OBP	Slg
'04	53	220	33	56	16	2	2	14	19	5	31	.255	.271	.373
Car.	122	494	80	140	28	6	7	46	32	18	67	.283	.307	.407

Where He Hits the Ball

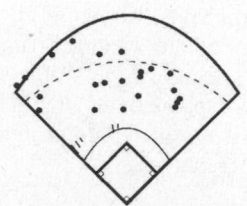 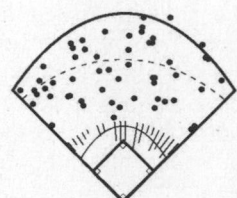

Vs. LHP   **Vs. RHP**

2004 Situational Stats

	AB	H	HR	RBI	Avg		AB	H	HR	RBI	Avg
Home	104	29	1	8	.279	LHP	43	14	1	3	.326
Road	116	27	1	6	.233	RHP	177	42	1	11	.237
First Half	88	19	2	7	.216	Sc Pos	40	12	1	13	.300
Scnd Half	132	37	0	7	.280	Clutch	38	8	0	3	.211

2004 Rankings (National League)

- 2nd in lowest on-base percentage for a lead-off hitter (.279)
- 3rd in stolen-base percentage (90.5)
- 4th in steals of third (6)
- Led the Mets in triples, stolen-base percentage (90.5), bunts in play (13) and steals of third (6)

Steve Trachsel

2004 Season

Steve Trachsel threw better than at any time in his career during the first half of the 2004 season. The righthander posted a 1.78 ERA from April 12-May 25 and put together a scoreless streak of 15 innings from May 14-30. He faltered after the All-Star break, but still managed to reach double digits in victories for the fourth consecutive season. Trachsel also allowed three earned runs or fewer in 24 of his 33 starts.

Pitching

Trachsel can make teammate Al Leiter look like a fast worker. The deliberate righthander visualizes every pitch before making it. Nevertheless, Trachsel is an innings-eater who went at least six frames in 25 of 33 starts last year. He focuses on throwing first-pitch strikes and is confident enough with his placement to try to coax hitters into putting the ball in play. He keeps his offerings down, and he moves his two-seam fastball that resides in the upper 80s, curveball and changeup throughout the strike zone. Unlike Leiter, Trachsel does not waste pitches, and prior to last season he kept runners off base by issuing few walks with his plus command.

Defense & Hitting

Stolen-base totals versus Trachsel can be misleading. He does a good job of holding runners for a righthander by employing a quick, spinning pickoff move. His tendency to hold the ball for long periods also is effective in upsetting a would-be basestealer's timing. Trachsel is one of the league's better fielders among pitchers, possessing good footwork and soft hands. He also is one of the top hitters among hurlers in the NL. Over the past two seasons, he has posted 22 hits and 22 sacrifices.

2005 Outlook

If Trachsel pitches 150 innings in 2005, his option for 2006 kicks in. He turned 34 in October, and he is at the point in his career where he is best suited as a fourth starter. The Mets envision him filling that role this year while making another 30-plus starts.

Position: SP
Bats: R **Throws:** R
Ht: 6' 4" **Wt:** 205

Opening Day Age: 34
Born: 10/31/70 in Oxnard, CA
ML Seasons: 12
Pronunciation: track-s'l

Overall Statistics

W	L	Pct.	ERA	G	GS	Sv	IP	H	BB	SO	HR	Avg
12	13	.480	4.00	33	33	0	202.2	203	83	117	25	.262
118	131	.474	4.23	345	344	0	2101.2	2136	750	1416	290	.265

2004 Pitching Profile

	Steve Trachsel	NL Average
Overall Strike %	60.8	62.5
1st Pitch Strike %	60.8	58.5
Ratio	1.41	1.39
Strikeouts per 9 IP	5.20	6.74
Walks per 9 IP	3.69	3.38
Home Runs per 9 IP	1.11	1.11
Strikeout/Walk Ratio	1.41	1.99
Groundball/Flyball Ratio	1.09	1.25

2004 Situational Stats

	W	L	ERA	Sv	IP		AB	H	HR	RBI	Avg
Home	9	6	3.06	0	129.1	LHB	380	93	8	34	.245
Road	3	7	5.65	0	73.1	RHB	394	110	17	56	.279
First Half	9	6	3.36	0	112.2	Sc Pos	205	42	4	60	.205
Scnd Half	3	7	4.80	0	90.0	Clutch	26	9	2	3	.346

2004 Rankings (National League)

- 1st in pickoff throws (194) and fielding percentage at pitcher (1.000)
- 2nd in balks (2)
- 6th in stolen bases allowed (19)
- 7th in walks allowed
- 9th in losses
- 10th in lowest groundball-flyball ratio allowed (1.1), fewest strikeouts per nine innings (5.2) and highest walks per nine innings (3.7)
- Led the Mets in sacrifice bunts (11), wins, games started, home runs allowed, strikeouts, wild pitches (4), balks (2), pickoff throws (194), stolen bases allowed (19) and most run support per nine innings (5.4)

2004 Season

David Wright gave Mets fans reason to care during the last two months of the season. After ranking ninth in the minors with a .341 batting average, Wright joined the Mets on July 21. He went on to hit 14 home runs, and in only 69 games, he tied for eighth among National League rookies in doubles, ranked ninth in extra-base hits, and ranked fourth in homers.

Hitting

Wright has a fluid, textbook swing that has produced base hits by the bunches since he was drafted in the first round out of a Virginia high school in 2001. He hits the ball to all fields, does equally well against righthanders and lefties, and hits for both power and average. He shows rare patience at the plate for a 22 year old. Big league pitchers do not intimidate Wright, and he does an excellent job of working deep into counts. He has a knack for getting big hits, and his power should increase as his body matures.

Baserunning & Defense

As good as Wright is at the plate, he is just as solid in the field. He has great hands for third base and an above-average arm. He can field bunts cleanly, and he moves well to his right and left with his outstanding range. Though not blessed with blazing speed, Wright is a heady baserunner who takes the extra base when available. In sum, he is a complete player and a student of the game who gets the most out of his abilities.

2005 Outlook

If last year proves to be a harbinger, Wright could be one of the best hitters in the NL for years to come. He was the Mets' best player down the stretch, and he finally could be the one to bring the revolving door that is third base at Shea Stadium to a permanent halt. Although he will have to make adjustments in his second season, Wright shows every indication that he is up to the task.

Position: 3B
Bats: R **Throws:** R
Ht: 6' 0" **Wt:** 200

Opening Day Age: 22
Born: 12/20/82 in Norfolk, VA
ML Seasons: 1

Overall Statistics

	G	AB	R	H	D	T	HR	RBI	SB	BB	SO	Avg	OBP	Slg
'04	69	263	41	77	17	1	14	40	6	14	40	.293	.332	.525
Car.	69	263	41	77	17	1	14	40	6	14	40	.293	.332	.525

Where He Hits the Ball

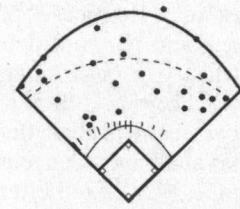 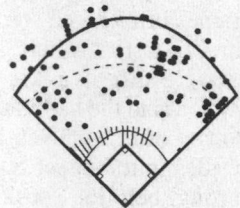

Vs. LHP **Vs. RHP**

2004 Situational Stats

	AB	H	HR	RBI	Avg		AB	H	HR	RBI	Avg
Home	134	40	8	23	.299	LHP	55	17	1	5	.309
Road	129	37	6	17	.287	RHP	208	60	13	35	.288
First Half	0	0	0	0	–	Sc Pos	64	18	4	28	.281
Scnd Half	263	77	14	40	.293	Clutch	44	15	2	4	.341

2004 Rankings (National League)

- 4th in home runs among rookies
- Led the Mets in slugging percentage, lowest percentage of swings that missed (14.9), batting average in the clutch and batting average with two strikes (.264)

Victor Zambrano

2004 Season

The catcalls were constant in New York after the Mets acquired Victor Zambrano in a deal that sent top pitching prospect Scott Kazmir to the Devil Rays on July 30. The volume increased when the hard-throwing righthander suffered a small tear in his flexor muscle during his third start with the Mets, causing him to miss the rest of the season. At the time of the trade, Zambrano was third in the American League with an opponent batting average of .230 and seventh with 109 strikeouts. He continues to reside atop the Tampa Bay all-time wins list with 35.

Pitching

The Mets saw untapped potential in Zambrano. He has a filthy repertoire, featuring a 92-94 MPH sinking fastball, an excellent changeup and an effective slider. He has trouble with his command and tends to finesse hitters by working the corners instead of challenging them with his nasty arsenal. His pitch counts can be outrageous because he falls behind in the count, which leads to an excessive number of walks. If he would trust his stuff and go after hitters on a consistent basis, Zambrano could be dominant.

Defense & Hitting

A former infielder, Zambrano is a good defender with above-average athleticism on the mound. His problem comes from allowing his emotions to carry over and affect his concentration. Runners can take advantage of that trait, although Zambrano does have an average pickoff move and is capable of holding runners on base. He is a good bunter and a better-than-average hitter for a pitcher because of his days as an everyday player.

2005 Outlook

Surgery was not required on Zambrano's injured flexor muscle, which doctors said was related to his bouts with tendinitis while toiling for Tampa. Provided that problem does not become chronic, Zambrano has the makings of a middle-of-the-rotation starter. Pitching in New York could be a difficult proposition for him, but his unbridled potential could lead to impressive returns. . . or a colossal failure that haunts the organization for years.

Position: SP
Bats: B **Throws:** R
Ht: 6' 0" **Wt:** 203

Opening Day Age: 29
Born: 8/6/75 in Los Teques, VZ
ML Seasons: 4

Overall Statistics

	W	L	Pct.	ERA	G	GS	Sv	IP	H	BB	SO	HR	Avg
'04	11	7	.611	4.37	26	25	0	142.0	119	102	123	13	.229
Car.	37	27	.578	4.45	138	64	3	495.2	442	294	386	55	.240

2004 Pitching Profile

	Victor Zambrano (NL)	NL Average
Overall Strike %	58.9	62.5
1st Pitch Strike %	57.1	58.5
Ratio	1.29	1.39
Strikeouts per 9 IP	9.00	6.74
Walks per 9 IP	3.86	3.38
Home Runs per 9 IP	0.00	1.11
Strikeout/Walk Ratio	2.33	1.99
Groundball/Flyball Ratio	2.88	1.25

2004 Situational Stats

	W	L	ERA	Sv	IP		AB	H	HR	RBI	Avg
Home	8	2	2.88	0	72.0	LHB	257	62	7	31	.241
Road	3	5	5.91	0	70.0	RHB	263	57	6	32	.217
First Half	9	5	4.46	0	113.0	Sc Pos	147	25	3	48	.170
Scnd Half	2	2	4.03	0	29.0	Clutch	25	4	0	0	.160

2004 Rankings (National League)

- Did not rank near the top or bottom in any category

Ricky Bottalico

Position: RP
Bats: L **Throws:** R
Ht: 6' 0" **Wt:** 215

Opening Day Age: 35
Born: 8/26/69 in New Britain, CT
ML Seasons: 11
Pronunciation: bo-TAL-e-koh

Overall Statistics

	W	L	Pct.	ERA	G	GS	Sv	IP	H	BB	SO	HR	Avg
'04	3	2	.600	3.38	60	0	0	69.1	54	34	61	3	.215
Car.	31	40	.437	3.96	522	0	114	587.0	518	297	546	64	.238

2004 Situational Stats

	W	L	ERA	Sv	IP		AB	H	HR	RBI	Avg
Home	2	1	4.11	0	35.0	LHB	78	16	0	7	.205
Road	1	1	2.62	0	34.1	RHB	173	38	3	18	.220
First Half	3	1	3.09	0	32.0	Sc Pos	68	13	1	18	.191
Scnd Half	0	1	3.62	0	37.1	Clutch	104	28	1	12	.269

2004 Season

The Mets purchased Ricky Bottalico's contract from Triple-A Norfolk on May 4 last season and watched him become the team's most dependable righthanded reliever. He did not surrender a run during a nine-game stretch from June 13-29, and gave up only one earned run over 9.2 frames from July 26 through August 8.

Pitching, Defense & Hitting

A sound arm enabled Bottalico to return to his aggressive ways by attacking hitters with his low-90s fastball, a sharp slider and a decent changeup. Once weak against lefthanded hitters, he limited lefties last year by moving the ball around in the strike zone. He is still a flyball pitcher, yet surrendered only three home runs in 69.1 innings. A converted catcher, Bottalico has quick defensive reflexes that allow him to man his position and hold runners on base. He is also a capable hitter.

2005 Outlook

Deemed a journeyman and fringe major league pitcher prior to the 2004 season, Bottalico was one of the more effective righthanded setup men in the league last year. His improved health, combined with a better idea of what it takes to retire major league hitters, have given this veteran an extended future in the bullpen.

Mike DeJean

Position: RP
Bats: R **Throws:** R
Ht: 6' 2" **Wt:** 219

Opening Day Age: 34
Born: 9/28/70 in Baton Rouge, LA
ML Seasons: 8
Pronunciation: DAY-zhan

Overall Statistics

	W	L	Pct.	ERA	G	GS	Sv	IP	H	BB	SO	HR	Avg
'04	0	5	.000	4.57	54	0	0	61.0	70	33	60	2	.290
Car.	24	29	.453	4.30	497	1	52	559.1	586	260	394	56	.273

2004 Situational Stats

	W	L	ERA	Sv	IP		AB	H	HR	RBI	Avg
Home	0	3	6.32	0	31.1	LHB	94	30	1	19	.319
Road	0	2	2.73	0	29.2	RHB	147	40	1	23	.272
First Half	0	5	6.57	0	37.0	Sc Pos	82	25	1	38	.305
Scnd Half	0	0	1.50	0	24.0	Clutch	82	31	0	14	.378

2004 Season

The Mets acquired Mike DeJean from Baltimore in exchange for outfielder Karim Garcia on July 19. He struggled with his control during the slate's first three-plus months with the Orioles, but he discovered the strike zone in New York. DeJean's season ended on August 30 when was placed on the DL with a fractured right tibia.

Pitching, Defense & Hitting

DeJean was at his best with the Mets because he was getting groundball outs with his low-90s sinker and strikeouts with his hard splitter. He had trouble throwing the splitter for strikes while in Baltimore. DeJean likes to challenge hitters and is not afraid to have the ball put into play. A steady fielder, he does not hold runners well, making second base an easy destination for any runner with average speed. DeJean rarely swings the bat.

2005 Outlook

DeJean has pitched for four teams in the past two seasons. He was not successful as Milwaukee's closer in 2003 after saving 27 games in 2002, and he appears better suited as a situational reliever between the sixth and eighth frames. If he can maintain the results he attained with the Mets in July and August, he will be a solid performer for them in 2005.

Aaron Heilman

Position: SP
Bats: R **Throws:** R
Ht: 6' 5" **Wt:** 220

Opening Day Age: 26
Born: 11/12/78 in Logansport, IN
ML Seasons: 2

Overall Statistics

	W	L	Pct.	ERA	G	GS	Sv	IP	H	BB	SO	HR	Avg
'04	1	3	.250	5.46	5	5	0	28.0	27	13	22	4	.257
Car.	3	10	.231	6.36	19	18	0	93.1	106	54	73	17	.288

2004 Situational Stats

	W	L	ERA	Sv	IP		AB	H	HR	RBI	Avg
Home	1	1	6.14	0	14.2	LHB	56	13	2	7	.232
Road	0	2	4.73	0	13.1	RHB	49	14	2	8	.286
First Half	0	0	—	0	0.0	Sc Pos	26	12	1	10	.462
Scnd Half	1	3	5.46	0	28.0	Clutch	6	3	0	2	.500

2004 Season

Aaron Heilman spent most of the year as a starter at Triple-A Norfolk before joining the Mets' rotation for five starts during the season's final six weeks. He tied for third in the IL in strikeouts and won seven of his last 10 decisions.

Pitching & Defense

Heilman tried to be too fine with his pitches, particularly early in the count, when he returned to the big leagues. Despite walking only one batter in his final start, he issued an average of 4.17 walks per nine. The key for Heilman is to keep his pitches down in the strike zone since he cannot overpower hitters, especially above the belt. His fastball sits in the low 90s, and his slider and changeup are above-average offerings, though inconsistent. Heilman is no better than an average fielder but holds runners well, allowing only one stolen base last year in the majors. He appears destined to replace Al Leiter as the game's worst hitter among pitchers.

2005 Outlook

Heilman needs more consistency with his pitches and a more aggressive approach in order to live up to his potential as a starter. He probably battles for a long-relief job in spring training with the Mets' stable of veteran starters.

Braden Looper (Rubber Arm)

Position: RP
Bats: R **Throws:** R
Ht: 6' 3" **Wt:** 220

Opening Day Age: 30
Born: 10/28/74 in Weatherford, OK
ML Seasons: 7

Overall Statistics

	W	L	Pct.	ERA	G	GS	Sv	IP	H	BB	SO	HR	Avg
'04	2	5	.286	2.70	71	0	29	83.1	86	16	60	5	.266
Car.	21	22	.488	3.53	443	0	75	474.2	476	171	306	36	.262

2004 Situational Stats

	W	L	ERA	Sv	IP		AB	H	HR	RBI	Avg
Home	2	4	3.86	12	44.1	LHB	151	47	3	20	.311
Road	0	1	1.38	17	39.0	RHB	172	39	2	12	.227
First Half	2	1	1.88	18	48.0	Sc Pos	89	24	1	26	.270
Scnd Half	0	4	3.82	11	35.1	Clutch	216	59	5	27	.273

2004 Season

Signed as a free agent from the Marlins prior to the season, Braden Looper was one of the NL's premier closers last year, his success limited only by the lack of save opportunities in New York. He established a career-high by recording 29 saves, with seven of the last eight preserving one-run victories.

Pitching, Defense & Hitting

Looper is a groundball pitcher who took another step last year in his development as a top-flight closer. After tiring toward the end of the 2003 slate with Florida, Looper maintained his strength as well as the velocity of his 93-96 MPH fastball. He showed more command of his cutter and split-finger fastball last year, which kept his walks to 1.73 per nine innings. Lefties continue to hit him well, but he limited righthanded hitters to a .227 norm. Looper is an average fielder with an above-average pickoff move for a righty. His hitting prowess, or lack thereof, is almost never a factor.

2005 Outlook

The Mets were pleased with the closing efforts Looper provided last year, with the reliever blowing just five saves in 34 opportunities. His services were acquired for little more than a song, and he remains a relative bargain for a solid closer.

Joe McEwing

Position: 2B/SS/1B
Bats: R **Throws:** R
Ht: 5'11" **Wt:** 210

Opening Day Age: 32
Born: 10/19/72 in Bristol, PA
ML Seasons: 7
Nickname: Super Joe

Overall Statistics

	G	AB	R	H	D	T	HR	RBI	SB	BB	SO	Avg	OBP	Slg
'04	75	138	17	35	3	1	1	16	4	9	32	.254	.297	.312
Car.	664	1581	201	400	82	10	24	152	29	107	315	.253	.307	.363

2004 Situational Stats

	AB	H	HR	RBI	Avg		AB	H	HR	RBI	Avg
Home	69	15	1	7	.217	LHP	44	11	0	2	.250
Road	69	20	0	9	.290	RHP	94	24	1	14	.255
First Half	83	19	1	10	.229	Sc Pos	31	11	1	16	.355
Scnd Half	55	16	0	6	.291	Clutch	25	6	0	3	.240

2004 Season

Joe McEwing finally got a chance to see some extended activity when both Jose Reyes and Kaz Matsui succumbed to injury in late July, and McEwing provided his typical yeoman's effort while giving the lineup a spark. His season ended on August 19 when he suffered a fractured left fibula during a slide by Colorado's J.D. Closser.

Hitting, Baserunning & Defense

McEwing played at least one game at every position last year except pitcher and catcher. His soft hands and decent range make him a solid fill-in at first, second and shortstop. His batting average has not been noteworthy since hitting .283 in 2001, but he remains a good fastball hitter who struggles against breaking balls after long stretches of inactivity. Though not blessed with great speed, McEwing is a good baserunner due to his instincts and ability to read balls off the bat.

2005 Outlook

The Mets considered trading McEwing to San Diego at midseason before they decided to keep him due to all of the team's injuries. A good guy in the clubhouse who knows and accepts his role, McEwing should keep his utility job with New York this spring provided he recovers as expected from his fractured fibula.

Jason Phillips

Position: C/1B
Bats: R **Throws:** R
Ht: 6' 1" **Wt:** 177

Opening Day Age: 28
Born: 9/27/76 in La Mesa, CA
ML Seasons: 4

Overall Statistics

	G	AB	R	H	D	T	HR	RBI	SB	BB	SO	Avg	OBP	Slg
'04	128	362	34	79	18	0	7	34	0	35	42	.218	.298	.326
Car.	264	791	85	207	44	0	19	95	0	75	94	.262	.337	.389

2004 Situational Stats

	AB	H	HR	RBI	Avg		AB	H	HR	RBI	Avg
Home	184	44	2	14	.239	LHP	85	19	2	12	.224
Road	178	35	5	20	.197	RHP	277	60	5	22	.217
First Half	229	49	5	25	.214	Sc Pos	78	16	0	25	.205
Scnd Half	133	30	2	9	.226	Clutch	67	12	2	5	.179

2004 Season

The fiasco that saw Mike Piazza move from catcher to first and back again affected Jason Phillips more than anyone. After putting together a solid season in '03, Phillips endured a difficult campaign as New York's primary receiver before showing signs of offensive production late in the slate.

Hitting, Baserunning & Defense

Phillips' aggressive approach at the plate cost him last season, especially when he tried to do too much to get out of his extended slump. When comfortable, Phillips has good power and is capable of hitting righthanders and lefties equally well. He also makes consistent contact and walks nearly as much as he strikes out. His speed was never a factor before, and if anything, Phillips appeared to lose a half-step while catching last year. Defensively, Phillips is a good catch-and-throw receiver who works well with pitchers. He also does a decent job controlling the running game.

2005 Outlook

Phillips' situation could be determined by what the Mets do with Piazza. If Piazza stays and a healthy Vance Wilson returns, Phillips could be relegated to first base, possibly in a platoon with rookie Craig Brazell. Otherwise, Phillips might be dangled as trade bait.

Jae Weong Seo

Position: SP
Bats: R **Throws:** R
Ht: 6' 1" **Wt:** 215

Opening Day Age: 27
Born: 5/24/77 in
Kwanju, South Korea
ML Seasons: 3
Pronunciation:
jay wong sew

Overall Statistics

	W	L	Pct.	ERA	G	GS	Sv	IP	H	BB	SO	HR	Avg
'04	5	10	.333	4.90	24	21	0	117.2	133	50	54	17	.299
Car.	14	22	.389	4.22	57	52	0	307.0	326	96	165	35	.274

2004 Situational Stats

	W	L	ERA	Sv	IP		AB	H	HR	RBI	Avg
Home	2	5	4.75	0	66.1	LHB	209	57	7	24	.273
Road	3	5	5.08	0	51.1	RHB	236	76	10	29	.322
First Half	4	5	4.76	0	79.1	Sc Pos	99	21	4	33	.212
Scnd Half	1	5	5.17	0	38.1	Clutch	15	6	0	1	.400

2004 Season

Jae Weong Seo spent the first four months of the 2004 season as the Mets' fifth starter before toiling at Triple-A Norfolk for most of August. He started only four games after New York acquired Victor Zambrano near the trading deadline, and did not start after a September 13 loss to Atlanta. Seo allowed three earned runs or fewer in 13 of his last 20 starts.

Pitching, Defense & Hitting

The Mets have become concerned that Seo does not trust his pitches, particularly when his low-90s fastball starts to get hit. His slider serves as his best and most consistent offering, and he throws an above-average changeup that he sits on when times get tough. He has good command of all his pitches, but tends to give hitters too much credit. Seo is a marginal fielder, but does a good job of holding runners with a quick pickoff move. He is a decent hitter but is not a good bunter.

2005 Outlook

Seo lost favor with former manager Art Howe, and he no longer seems to be in the Mets' plans. He wants to start but that isn't going to happen in New York. Over the winter, the Mets were exploring a deal to send Seo to a team in his native South Korea.

Mike Stanton

Traded To
YANKEES

Position: RP
Bats: L **Throws:** L
Ht: 6' 1" **Wt:** 215

Opening Day Age: 37
Born: 6/2/67 in
Houston, TX
ML Seasons: 16

Overall Statistics

	W	L	Pct.	ERA	G	GS	Sv	IP	H	BB	SO	HR	Avg
'04	2	6	.250	3.16	83	0	0	77.0	70	33	58	6	.237
Car.	57	50	.533	3.76	968	1	76	946.0	892	360	780	82	.250

2004 Situational Stats

	W	L	ERA	Sv	IP		AB	H	HR	RBI	Avg
Home	0	3	3.16	0	37.0	LHB	108	29	4	18	.269
Road	2	3	3.15	0	40.0	RHB	187	41	2	22	.219
First Half	0	3	3.59	0	47.2	Sc Pos	79	22	4	37	.278
Scnd Half	2	3	2.45	0	29.1	Clutch	133	32	3	18	.241

2004 Season

Mike Stanton was one of the league's most durable setup men. The lefthander was unscored upon in 19 of his last 21 games, and posted an 0.95 ERA during that span. He established a career-high and franchise record by pitching in 83 games, which tied for sixth in the National League.

Pitching, Defense & Hitting

Stanton's fastball has good movement while residing in the low 90s, and he does an excellent job of mixing his hard splitter and above-average slider. He is among the best in the game at retiring righthanded hitters, though he did not do as well as usual against them last year. His primary downfall can be an occasional lack of control. Stanton is good at freezing baserunners with a pickoff move that borders on a balk. He also employs a quick delivery. He fields his position well and is a good hitter.

2005 Outlook

Stanton, who has pitched for either the Yankees or Mets since 1997, returned to the Bronx in a November trade for Felix Heredia. He is better in the seventh and eighth innings than the ninth, with the lefthander failing in all six of his save opportunities last year. When placed in the right role, he is as dependable a lefty reliever as there is in the game.

New York (NL)

Eric Valent

Position: LF/1B/RF
Bats: L **Throws:** L
Ht: 5'11" **Wt:** 195

Opening Day Age: 27
Born: 4/4/77 in La Mirada, CA
ML Seasons: 4
Pronunciation: va-LENT

Overall Statistics

	G	AB	R	H	D	T	HR	RBI	SB	BB	SO	Avg	OBP	Slg
'04	130	270	39	72	15	2	13	34	0	28	61	.267	.337	.481
Car.	177	363	46	87	17	2	13	36	0	34	84	.240	.308	.405

2004 Situational Stats

	AB	H	HR	RBI	Avg		AB	H	HR	RBI	Avg
Home	129	30	5	16	.233	LHP	10	1	0	0	.100
Road	141	42	8	18	.298	RHP	260	71	13	34	.273
First Half	136	38	5	20	.279	Sc Pos	66	16	4	24	.242
Scnd Half	134	34	8	14	.254	Clutch	58	15	2	7	.259

2004 Season

The Mets' top reserve in 2004, Eric Valent posted three pinch-hit home runs, including two during a nine-day span in late August. He also became the eighth Met to hit for the cycle, accomplishing the feat on July 29 at Montreal when he posted a career-best four hits and equaled his career-high with three RBIs.

Hitting, Baserunning & Defense

Valent stands out as a solid pinch-hitter and valuable utilityman. He is a capable defender at both outfield corner positions and has good hands at first base, leading to only one error last year. His arm strength is slightly above average with good accuracy on his throws, and he has solid range at every position he plays. Valent provides good power from the left side of the plate. While he makes good contact against righthanded pitchers, lefties own him.

2005 Outlook

Valent bounced between the majors and minors with the Phillies and Reds in 2002 and 2003 before receiving his first extended taste of the big leagues with the Mets. He may have found a home in New York as a lefthanded bat off the bench. A repeat of last year's efforts would do nothing but solidify his hold on the job.

Vance Wilson

Position: C
Bats: R **Throws:** R
Ht: 5'11" **Wt:** 190

Opening Day Age: 32
Born: 3/17/73 in Mesa, AZ
ML Seasons: 6

Overall Statistics

	G	AB	R	H	D	T	HR	RBI	SB	BB	SO	Avg	OBP	Slg
'04	79	157	18	43	10	1	4	21	1	11	24	.274	.335	.427
Car.	286	649	68	165	29	2	17	92	2	33	130	.254	.308	.384

2004 Situational Stats

	AB	H	HR	RBI	Avg		AB	H	HR	RBI	Avg
Home	70	20	1	6	.286	LHP	40	8	0	3	.200
Road	87	23	3	15	.264	RHP	117	35	4	18	.299
First Half	76	18	2	11	.237	Sc Pos	39	12	1	15	.308
Scnd Half	81	25	2	10	.309	Clutch	37	9	1	3	.243

2004 Season

Vance Wilson battled injuries for much of last season. He missed three weeks at midseason with a strained right hamstring and underwent season-ending surgery to repair a torn tendon in his left hand in mid-September. His highlights included the second four-hit game of his career on July 26, and his first pinch-hit homer on June 1.

Hitting, Baserunning & Defense

The tendon problem in his hand made hitting difficult for Wilson. Nevertheless, he played through the pain and wound up hitting for a decent average and provided above-average punch in the lower half of the batting order. His speed is no better than average for a catcher, but his intelligence keeps him from hurting the team on the basepaths. Wilson's strengths center on his defensive efforts and his ability to call a game. He moves well behind the plate and has a strong arm.

2005 Outlook

With the Mets willing to bring Mike Piazza back and keep him behind the plate, Wilson's immediate future appears to be as a 50-game receiver on an annual basis with an occasional appearance at first base and as a pinch-hitter. He's capable of contributing more, but the opportunity does not appear to be there in New York.

James Baldwin (Pos: RHP, Age: 33)

	W	L	Pct.	ERA	G	GS	Sv	IP	H	BB	SO	HR	Avg
'04	0	2	.000	15.00	2	2	0	6.0	13	5	1	3	.448
Car.	79	72	.523	5.07	238	202	1	1266.0	1389	470	815	195	.279

The merry-go-round that has been Baldwin's career since 2000 shoulder surgery landed him in the Mets' organization to begin 2004. His audition for the fifth-starter role was disastrous, and he opted out of his contract instead of being sent down again. Detroit signed him in June. 2005 Outlook: C

Brian Buchanan (Pos: LF, Age: 31, Bats: R)

	G	AB	R	H	D	T	HR	RBI	SB	BB	SO	Avg	OBP	Slg
'04	40	63	7	12	2	0	2	6	0	7	20	.190	.278	.317
Car.	346	767	105	198	37	3	32	103	9	73	210	.258	.328	.439

Like James Baldwin, Buchanan was declared a free agent when he refused an August minor league assignment by the Padres. Buchanan, who owns an .845 career OPS versus lefthanders, was signed days later by the Mets only to appear in two games. 2005 Outlook: C

Vic Darensbourg (Pos: LHP, Age: 34)

	W	L	Pct.	ERA	G	GS	Sv	IP	H	BB	SO	HR	Avg
'04	0	1	.000	6.43	7	0	0	7.0	11	3	1	4	.423
Car.	7	16	.304	5.13	287	0	2	280.2	304	119	220	32	.279

Lefthanded specialists who can't get lefthanded hitters out usually don't last long. Darensbourg has fallen into this category, as lefties have hit .308/.355/.535 off him since the 2000 season. Compare this to a .202/.296/.306 line over his first three years in the big leagues. 2005 Outlook: C

Wilson Delgado (Pos: SS, Age: 32, Bats: B)

	G	AB	R	H	D	T	HR	RBI	SB	BB	SO	Avg	OBP	Slg
'04	42	130	11	38	4	1	2	13	1	15	29	.292	.366	.362
Car.	253	542	59	136	15	2	5	43	5	47	108	.251	.314	.314

Delgado provided the Mets with a lift at shortstop when Kaz Matsui and Jose Reyes went down with injuries in August. Playing for his fifth team in five years, he posted a respectable .366 OBP. The Mets' middle-infield log jam will force him to look for work elsewhere this year. 2005 Outlook: C

Jeff Duncan (Pos: LF, Age: 26, Bats: L)

	G	AB	R	H	D	T	HR	RBI	SB	BB	SO	Avg	OBP	Slg
'04	13	15	2	1	0	0	0	1	3	1	5	.067	.125	.067
Car.	69	154	15	28	0	2	1	11	7	18	46	.182	.276	.227

Duncan, a former Arizona State standout, burst onto the scene in 2003, making nice plays in the outfield while starting 14-for-35. Things have trended downward since then, however, as he was sent back to Double-A Binghamton to rediscover his stroke this past season. 2005 Outlook: C

Pedro Feliciano (Pos: LHP, Age: 28)

	W	L	Pct.	ERA	G	GS	Sv	IP	H	BB	SO	HR	Avg
'04	1	1	.500	5.40	22	0	0	18.1	14	12	14	2	.209
Car.	1	1	.500	4.21	51	0	0	72.2	75	34	61	7	.283

The door will be open for Feliciano to claim a bullpen spot with the departure of John Franco. The repertoire is not a concern for Feliciano, who possesses a curveball, changeup and low-90s fastball. The main issue always has been how it's used, and can he consistently throw strikes. 2005 Outlook: B

Bartolome Fortunato (Pos: RHP, Age: 30)

	W	L	Pct.	ERA	G	GS	Sv	IP	H	BB	SO	HR	Avg
'04	1	0	1.000	3.81	18	0	1	26.0	24	15	25	3	.247
Car.	1	0	1.000	3.81	18	0	1	26.0	24	15	25	3	.247

It was fortunate for the Mets that Fortunato was included in the July deal that sent Scott Kazmir and Jose Diaz to Tampa Bay for Victor Zambrano. Fortunato can still bring mid-90s heat, and his 10.4 SO/9 rate as a professional is outstanding. 2005 Outlook: C

John Franco (Pos: LHP, Age: 44)

	W	L	Pct.	ERA	G	GS	Sv	IP	H	BB	SO	HR	Avg
	2	7	.222	5.28	52	0	0	46.0	46	24	36	6	.258
	90	86	.511	2.84	1088	0	424	1230.2	1143	486	959	81	.248

Franco, who ranks second only to Jesse Orosco in pitching appearances, has thrown his final pitch for the Mets. The only question left to be answered is whether any other club will give the 44-year-old an opportunity to continue his craft. 2005 Outlook: C

Matt Ginter (Pos: RHP, Age: 27)

	W	L	Pct.	ERA	G	GS	Sv	IP	H	BB	SO	HR	Avg
'04	1	3	.250	4.54	15	14	0	69.1	82	20	38	8	.289
Car.	4	3	.571	5.32	78	14	1	176.0	195	63	105	22	.281

The Chicago White Sox did not know what to do with Ginter, shuffling him from starter to reliever during his five years with the organization. The Mets made it clear that Ginter would be a starter in 2004, as his 25 starts between Triple-A Norfolk and New York indicate. 2005 Outlook: C

Joe Hietpas (Pos: C, Age: 25, Bats: R)

	G	AB	R	H	D	T	HR	RBI	SB	BB	SO	Avg	OBP	Slg
'04	1	0	0	0	0	0	0	0	0	0	0	—	—	—
Car.	1	0	0	0	0	0	0	0	0	0	0	—	—	—

Hietpas is your typical defensive-minded catcher with little offensive punch. He should begin 2005 at Triple-A Norfolk, but it is imperative that he start producing with the bat. A strong showing in the Arizona Fall League would be a big boost to his career. 2005 Outlook: C

New York (NL)

Orber Moreno (Pos: RHP, Age: 27)

	W	L	Pct.	ERA	G	GS	Sv	IP	H	BB	SO	HR	Avg
'04	3	1	.750	3.38	33	0	1	34.2	29	11	29	0	.221
Car.	3	1	.750	4.44	47	0	1	50.2	43	20	41	2	.225

For the first time in 10 professional seasons, Moreno made the major league roster out of spring training. He got off to a shaky start, posting a 5.25 ERA through 12 games, but settled down nicely before recurring arm problems ended his season. Offseason shoulder surgery was needed. 2005 Outlook: C

Jose Parra (Pos: RHP, Age: 32)

	W	L	Pct.	ERA	G	GS	Sv	IP	H	BB	SO	HR	Avg
'04	1	0	1.000	3.21	13	0	0	14.0	14	6	14	2	.255
Car.	7	12	.368	6.09	82	19	0	181.2	225	79	117	33	.302

At one time Parra was a prized prospect in the Dodgers' system, but those days have long since passed. He never has been able to find a permanent home and was declared a free agent by the Mets after he cleared waivers in November. 2005 Outlook: C

Grant Roberts (Pos: RHP, Age: 27)

	W	L	Pct.	ERA	G	GS	Sv	IP	H	BB	SO	HR	Avg
'04	0	0	—	17.36	4	0	0	4.2	9	6	1	2	.429
Car.	4	4	.500	4.25	76	1	1	101.2	106	37	77	7	.267

It's been a rough couple of years for Roberts. First there was the much publicized marijuana photo in *Newsday*, followed by shoulder tendinitis that limited him in 2003. It got even worse this past season, when an MRI exam uncovered a torn labrum. He had surgery in May. 2005 Outlook: C

Esix Snead (Pos: LF, Age: 28, Bats: B)

	G	AB	R	H	D	T	HR	RBI	SB	BB	SO	Avg	OBP	Slg
'04	1	0	1	0	0	0	0	0	0	0	0	—	—	—
Car.	18	13	4	4	0	0	1	3	4	1	4	.308	.357	.538

What if Snead could hit? Many a coach and general manager likely has wondered this same question through the years. Snead can flat out run, and his 109 stolen bases for Class-A Potomac in 2000 still are a Carolina League record. Hitting .230/.321/.297 in the minors has hurt him. 2005 Outlook: C

Shane Spencer (Pos: LF/RF, Age: 33, Bats: R)

	G	AB	R	H	D	T	HR	RBI	SB	BB	SO	Avg	OBP	Slg
'04	74	185	21	52	10	1	4	26	6	13	37	.281	.332	.411
Car.	538	1671	208	438	84	8	59	242	13	152	357	.262	.326	.428

A tumultuous year for Spencer culminated in August, when he was released by the Mets. The parting of ways was sparked by several off-field incidents and a conspicuous loss of power from the corner outfielder. 2005 Outlook: C

Gerald Williams (Pos: LF/CF, Age: 38, Bats: R)

	G	AB	R	H	D	T	HR	RBI	SB	BB	SO	Avg	OBP	Slg
'04	57	129	17	30	8	2	4	11	2	8	26	.233	.277	.419
Car.	1129	3029	465	773	181	18	84	362	104	179	523	.255	.301	.410

The fact that the Mets even brought in an aging Williams in 2004 speaks volumes about the depleted state of the organization's outfield in the high minors. Williams spent half the year between Triple-A Norfolk and New York, but was credited with facilitating the emergence of Victor Diaz. 2005 Outlook: C

Tyler Yates (Pos: RHP, Age: 27)

	W	L	Pct.	ERA	G	GS	Sv	IP	H	BB	SO	HR	Avg
'04	2	4	.333	6.36	21	7	0	46.2	61	25	35	6	.311
Car.	2	4	.333	6.36	21	7	0	46.2	61	25	35	6	.311

It appears Yates may have found his niche as a setup man over the last month of the season. Past experiments as both a starter and closer have played to mixed results, but the setup role seems like a better fit. A 0.90 ERA in his final 10 games was a positive end to his year. 2005 Outlook: B

Todd Zeile (Pos: 1B/3B, Age: 39, Bats: R)

	G	AB	R	H	D	T	HR	RBI	SB	BB	SO	Avg	OBP	Slg
	137	348	30	81	16	0	9	35	0	44	83	.233	.319	.356
	2158	7573	986	2004	397	23	253	1110	53	945	1279	.265	.346	.423

Zeile capped off a fine career by hitting a three-run home run in his final major league at-bat. The 15-year veteran, who plans to retire, finishes his playing days with 2,004 hits and 253 home runs. Don't be surprised if you see him in a broadcast booth in the near future. 2005 Outlook : D

New York Mets Minor League Prospects

Organization Overview:

After making steady progress in rebuilding the farm system over the past few years, the Mets took a step back in 2004. While third baseman David Wright arrived in New York and looked to be every bit a long-term fixture, the acquisition of Victor Zambrano from Tampa Bay cost the Mets pitcher Scott Kazmir, one of the top lefthanded prospects in the minors. Also dealt away were catcher Justin Huber and righthander Matt Peterson in midseason trades that depleted much of the organization's core of top-tier prospects. At press time, the Mets were still trying to come to an agreement with pitcher Phillip Humber, the team's first-round pick last June. Overall, the 2004 draft added much-needed pitching depth, including early-rounders Matt Durkin and Gaby Hernandez.

Heath Bell

Position: P   **Opening Day Age:** 27
Bats: R **Throws:** R   **Born:** 9/29/77 in
Ht: 6' 2" **Wt:** 244   Oceanside, CA

Recent Statistics

	W	L	ERA	G	GS	Sv	IP	H	R	BB	SO	HR
2004 AA Binghamton	0	0	0.00	1	0	0	2.0	2	0	0	0	0
2004 AAA Norfolk	3	1	3.23	45	0	16	55.2	42	21	24	68	4
2004 NL New York	0	2	3.33	17	0	0	24.1	22	9	6	27	5

A former undrafted free agent, Bell received his first promotion to the major leagues last August and showed signs of becoming the Mets' most overpowering reliever since Armando Benitez. Bell displayed good command and the ability to punch out batters, resulting in 27 strikeouts in 24.1 innings, including six during a three-inning stint versus Philadelphia on September 3. He has a live fastball that resides in the low 90s, along with a consistent slider. His best pitch is a changeup that possesses both fade and depth and keeps hitters off balance. In addition to owning a deep repertoire for a reliever, Bell does a good job of keeping his pitches down in the zone while working both sides of the plate.

Craig Brazell

Position: 1B   **Opening Day Age:** 24
Bats: L **Throws:** R   **Born:** 5/10/80 in
Ht: 6' 3" **Wt:** 211   Montgomery, AL

Recent Statistics

	G	AB	R	H	D	T	HR	RBI	SB	BB	SO	Avg
2004 AAA Norfolk	121	475	66	126	22	2	23	67	1	21	99	.265
2004 NL New York	24	34	3	9	2	0	1	3	0	1	7	.265

Brazell made his major league debut last August before spending all of September with the team. The first baseman put a dagger in the hearts of Cubs fans with an 11th-inning, game-winning home run, his first in the big leagues, during a 4-3 victory on September 25.

Power serves as Brazell's calling card. He possesses a smooth swing from the left side that should allow him to become a solid run producer in the middle of the lineup. In seven minor league seasons, Brazell owns a career batting average of .285, and he should hit for average as well as power. Initially a catcher in the pro ranks, he has become a steady defensive player at first base with soft hands, good range and ever-improving footwork.

Victor Diaz

Position: 2B   **Opening Day Age:** 23
Bats: R **Throws:** R   **Born:** 12/10/81 in Santo
Ht: 6' 0" **Wt:** 200   Domingo, DR

Recent Statistics

	G	AB	R	H	D	T	HR	RBI	SB	BB	SO	Avg
2004 AAA Norfolk	141	528	81	154	31	1	24	94	6	31	133	.292
2004 NL New York	15	51	8	15	3	0	3	8	0	1	15	.294

A former third baseman in the Dodgers' organization prior to being acquired by the Mets in a deal for Jeromy Burnitz, Diaz received a look at second base before moving to the outfield last season. After failing to impress with the leather in previous defensive stints, he looked capable of handling himself sufficiently in the garden. Diaz' stocky body and his ability to put the bat on the ball attracted comparisons to Carlos Baerga or a miniature Manny Ramirez, only not with as much power. He won batting titles in his first two minor league seasons and is consistent enough to hit .300 in the majors. Diaz made his major league debut in September and hit safely in 12 of 15 games.

Danny Garcia

Position: 2B   **Opening Day Age:** 24
Bats: R **Throws:** R   **Born:** 4/12/80 in
Ht: 6' 1" **Wt:** 175   Riverside, CA

Recent Statistics

	G	AB	R	H	D	T	HR	RBI	SB	BB	SO	Avg
2004 AAA Norfolk	63	242	28	63	14	1	2	19	9	15	35	.260
2004 NL New York	58	138	23	32	7	1	3	17	3	22	34	.232

Garcia's all-out aggressiveness and combative attitude not only irritate other clubs, it also gives him the necessary edge his game requires to have success on the diamond. He spent 58 games with the Mets last year by filling in for the injured Jose Reyes at second base and did a laudable job of handling the chores at the keystone, displaying good range, a decent arm and the ability to turn the double play. Garcia possesses solid pop in his bat and puts the ball in play, even if he does not project to be a high-average hitter. Words being exchanged at second due to a takeout slide or low throw are not uncommon with Garcia, whose gritty approach is something the Mets have lacked of late.

Jeff Keppinger

Position: 2B   **Opening Day Age:** 24
Bats: R **Throws:** R   **Born:** 4/21/80 in Miami,
Ht: 6' 0" **Wt:** 180   FL

Recent Statistics

	G	AB	R	H	D	T	HR	RBI	SB	BB	SO	Avg
2004 AA Altoona	82	323	45	108	17	2	1	33	10	27	17	.334
2004 AA Binghamton	14	47	14	17	3	1	0	5	2	6	2	.362
2004 AAA Norfolk	6	19	1	6	1	0	0	2	0	4	2	.316
2004 NL New York	33	116	9	33	2	0	3	9	2	6	7	.284

The Mets acquired Keppinger along with Kris Benson from the Pirates in the deal that sent Ty Wigginton to Pittsburgh last July. What Keppinger may lack in tools he makes up with his approach. He is a gritty player who is fundamentally sound on defense with good range at second base. The Mets liked his footwork and arm at second so much that the team is considering giving him a look on the left side of the infield. At the plate, Keppinger makes consistent contact, which enabled him to win the Double-A Eastern League batting title last year. He also drives the ball to all fields and is a heady baserunner.

Wayne Lydon

Position: OF   **Opening Day Age:** 23
Bats: B **Throws:** R   **Born:** 4/17/81 in Fairfax,
Ht: 6' 2" **Wt:** 190   VA

Recent Statistics

	G	AB	R	H	D	T	HR	RBI	SB	BB	SO	Avg
2003 A St. Lucie	133	488	83	129	14	7	4	44	75	52	96	.264
2004 AA Binghamton	123	506	78	137	18	6	5	43	65	49	119	.271

Mookie Wilson is considered to be the last speed-oriented player developed in the Mets' organization who went on to become an everyday player in the major leagues. Lydon has the potential to fill that gap after ranking second in the minors last year with 65 stolen bases. He has made significant strides in his development over the past two seasons while discovering the nuances of switch-hitting. He does a good job of bunting for base hits, and his maturing body continues to add strength, allowing him to drive the ball into the gaps. Despite his spectacular speed, Lydon is limited to left field because of his modest throwing arm, although he does have a quick release and good accuracy.

Lastings Milledge

Position: OF   **Opening Day Age:** 19
Bats: R **Throws:** R   **Born:** 4/5/85 in
Ht: 6' 1" **Wt:** 180   Bradenton, FL

Recent Statistics

	G	AB	R	H	D	T	HR	RBI	SB	BB	SO	Avg
2003 R Kingsport	7	26	4	6	2	0	0	2	5	3	4	.231
2004 A St. Lucie	22	81	6	19	6	2	2	8	3	9	21	.235
2004 A Capital City	65	261	66	88	22	1	13	58	23	17	53	.337

The Mets' first-round draft pick in 2003, Milledge showed last season that his package of five-tool skills could enable him to move rapidly through the organization. He opened 2004 on the disabled list with a broken finger, yet earned a promotion to high Class-A St. Lucie. Milledge has outstanding bat speed and hits the ball with authority to all fields. He has leadoff capabilities with exceptional speed on the bases. While he tends to be overaggressive at the plate and in the field, he showed better patience with the bat by drawing more walks. Milledge also improved his routes on flyballs and displayed a strong arm.

Yusmeiro Petit

Position: P   **Opening Day Age:** 20
Bats: R **Throws:** R   **Born:** 11/22/84 in
Ht: 6' 0" **Wt:** 180   Maracaibo, VZ

Recent Statistics

	W	L	ERA	G	GS	Sv	IP	H	R	BB	SO	HR
2003 A Brooklyn	1	0	2.19	2	2	0	12.1	5	3	2	20	0
2003 R Kingsport	3	3	2.32	12	12	0	62.0	47	19	8	65	2
2004 A Capital City	9	2	2.39	15	15	0	83.0	47	29	22	122	1
2004 A St. Lucie	2	3	1.22	9	9	0	44.1	27	9	14	62	0
2004 AA Binghamton	1	1	4.50	2	2	0	12.0	10	6	5	16	0

New York officials justified the trade of Scott Kazmir and Matt Peterson by pointing to the rapid progress made by Petit last season as a 19-year-old. The Venezuelan ranked fifth in the minors with a 2.20 ERA while topping all starters with 12.92 strikeouts per nine innings and placing second with 200 whiffs. Petit limited Class-A South Atlantic League hitters to a .162 batting average, by displaying impeccable command of his 89-92 MPH fastball, solid slider and excellent changeup. He uses the entire plate with outstanding location, and employs deception with his low three-quarters delivery. The Mets became convinced that Petit could rise quickly after he struck out 10 batters and walked none in his Double-A debut on August 28.

Others to Watch

Aarom Baldiris (21) tied for the high Class-A Florida State League batting title and was named to the loop's year-end All-Star team. A career .308 hitter, Baldiris sprays line drives to all fields but has yet to demonstrate the power teams like to see from third basemen. Defensively, Baldiris has great range and good hands, and could make the move to second should his bat dictate a shift. . . **Jamar Hill** (22) had been deemed a two o'clock hitter after putting on power displays during batting practice. He took those performances to game situations last year in Class-A, where he hit at a .310 clip with 13 home runs in his last 57 games. The big outfielder is a raw talent, yet has outstanding bat speed and an improving idea of what he hopes to accomplish at the plate. . . The Mets signed Cuban defector **Alay Soler** (25) to a three-year, $2.8 million major league contract in July. Soler throws a fastball that touches the mid-90s as well as a solid split-finger pitch. He has had a history of shoulder problems, but the Mets feel confident those ailments are in the past.

Citizens Bank Park

Offense

When the Phillies were recruiting free-agent left-hander Tom Glavine, they tried to sell him on the fact that their new ballpark would favor pitching. They were spectacularly wrong. There were 228 home runs hit at Citizens Bank Park in its inaugural season, the second-highest total in the National League. The ball carries particularly well to left, although club officials say they won't draw any conclusions until they determine whether the wind patterns were a one-year aberration. It turned out, however, that the distances to left-center were shorter than marked on the fences.

Pitching & Defense

Phillies pitchers were openly unhappy with the cozy dimensions of their new home, where routine flyballs often end up as home runs. Interestingly, however, while the staff gave up more home runs at CBP (115) than on the road (99), the home ERA (4.31) was significantly lower than it was for road games (4.61). Head groundskeeper Mike Boekholder got high marks for the condition of the field. The small outfield made it more difficult for runners to take an extra base on balls hit to left.

Who It Helps the Most

Any pitcher who can keep the ball down will be at an advantage. The park's dimensions should help righthanded power hitters like Pat Burrell, but only if they don't alter their swings by trying to pull and uppercut everything.

Who It Hurts the Most

Lefthander Eric Milton, a flyball pitcher, gave up 43 homers. That was a career high and easily led the league. The conventional wisdom is that the Phillies will have difficulty signing free-agent pitchers, which also puts an added burden on the front office and farm system.

Rookies & Newcomers

Now that they know that Citizens Bank Park plays as small as any park in baseball, a premium will be placed on rebuilding the staff with more groundball pitchers. Rookie to watch: righthander Gavin Floyd.

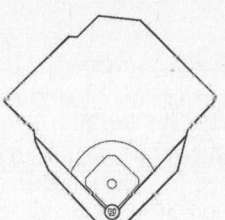

Dimensions: LF-329, LCF-369, CF-401, RCF-369, RF-330

Capacity: 43,500

Elevation: 20 feet

Surface: Grass

Foul Territory: Small

Park Factors

2004 Season

	Home Games			Away Games			
	Phillies	Opp	Total	Phillies	Opp	Total	Index
G	72	72	144	72	72	144	
Avg	.269	.259	.264	.264	.259	.261	101
AB	2438	2540	4978	2561	2413	4974	100
R	377	350	727	357	313	670	109
H	656	658	1314	675	625	1300	101
2B	129	128	257	142	143	285	90
3B	13	15	28	10	14	24	117
HR	100	102	202	85	79	164	123
BB	275	216	491	287	226	513	96
SO	462	495	957	524	448	972	98
E	35	40	75	38	46	84	89
E-Infield	29	34	63	30	42	72	88
LHB-Avg	.273	.283	.278	.273	.268	.270	103
LHB-HR	46	37	83	46	22	68	127
RHB-Avg	.267	.245	.255	.257	.254	.255	100
RHB-HR	54	65	119	39	57	96	121

2002-2003 (Veterans Stadium)

	Home Games			Away Games			
	Phillies	Opp	Total	Phillies	Opp	Total	Index
G	143	143	286	147	147	294	
Avg	.258	.234	.246	.265	.274	.269	91
AB	4717	4848	9565	5196	4934	10130	97
R	644	553	1197	720	734	1454	85
H	1216	1136	2352	1376	1351	2727	89
2B	282	245	527	305	304	609	92
3B	35	24	59	28	34	62	101
HR	141	121	262	153	149	302	92
BB	576	475	1051	573	511	1084	103
SO	983	1079	2062	1027	828	1855	118
E	71	73	144	99	94	193	77
E-Infield	61	60	121	81	73	154	81
LHB-Avg	.255	.234	.245	.273	.285	.278	88
LHB-HR	72	38	110	71	58	129	89
RHB-Avg	.260	.234	.246	.258	.267	.263	94
RHB-HR	69	83	152	82	91	173	94

2004 Rankings (National League)

- Third-highest run factor
- Third-highest home run factor
- Third-highest LHB home-run factor
- Third-highest RHB home-run factor
- Third-lowest double factor
- Third-lowest infield-error factor

Charlie Manuel

2004 Season

Charlie Manuel has spent the last two seasons as a special assistant to Phillies general manager Ed Wade, concentrating mostly on being a free-lance hitting instructor at every level of the organization. When Wade hired Manuel to succeed Larry Bowa as the Phillies' manager, he mentioned that a key factor that sold him on Manuel over the other seven candidates who interviewed was Manuel's inside knowledge of the team.

Offense

Manuel's previous experience in the majors was a two-and-a-half year stint with the Cleveland Indians from 2000-2002. In those days, the Tribe was a classic sit back and wait for the three-run homer American League team. Obviously, Manuel will have to learn to operate without the designated hitter. But with 41 years in baseball, including nine years as a minor league skipper, he shouldn't have a problem making the adjustment.

Pitching & Defense

Look for Manuel to rely heavily on his pitching coach, especially early in the season, since almost all of his experience has been on the offensive side of the game. As the year goes on, Manuel's handling of pitchers should be easier to assess. He also will have to pay more attention to defense than he was accustomed to with Cleveland teams that went to the playoffs six times in seven years from 1995-2001, largely on the basis of outslugging their opponents.

2005 Outlook

Manuel's primary responsibility will be to create a more productive atmosphere than existed during four years with the hard-driving Bowa. Last season, several players were quoted as saying they felt as though they had to walk on pins and needles. Manuel, who has a relentlessly upbeat and positive personality, should be the perfect antidote. But don't let his folksy manner and Southern drawl fool you. Manuel has demonstrated that he will draw a line if he believes players aren't applying themselves between the lines. His style, however, is to discipline players behind closed doors so that few know about it.

Born: 1/04/44 in Northfork, WV

Playing Experience: 1969-1975, Min, LA

Managerial Experience: 3 seasons

Manager Statistics

Year	Team, Lg	W	L	Pct	GB	Finish
2002	Cleveland, AL	39	47	.453	–	–
3 Seasons		220	190	.537	–	–

2004 Starting Pitchers by Days Rest

	<=3	4	5	6+
Phillies Starts	2	83	48	18
Phillies ERA	1.54	5.21	4.29	5.64
NL Avg Starts	2	82	46	23
NL ERA	4.58	4.35	4.28	4.73

2004 Situational Stats

	Larry Bowa	NL Average
Hit & Run Success %	40.0	38.0
Stolen Base Success %	78.7	71.7
Platoon Pct.	53.8	55.2
Defensive Subs	14	18
High-Pitch Outings	2	6
Quick/Slow Hooks	23/7	21/12
Sacrifice Attempts	78	99

2004 Rankings — Larry Bowa (National League)

- 1st in fewest caught stealings of third base (2)
- 2nd in stolen-base percentage
- 3rd in hit-and-run success percentage

Bobby Abreu

Position: RF
Bats: L **Throws:** R
Ht: 6' 0" **Wt:** 211

Opening Day Age: 31
Born: 3/11/74 in Aragua, VZ
ML Seasons: 9
Pronunciation: ah-BRAY-you

2004 Season

Bobby Abreu has begun to receive the national recognition that has eluded him for so much of his career. He made his first All Star team and became the first Phillies player in more than a decade to win a Silver Slugger Award. He had the second 30-30 season of his career and batted over .300 for the sixth time in his last seven seasons. And yet there are still those who believe he has batting champion or Most Valuable Player-type potential that he still hasn't begun to tap.

Hitting

Part of the puzzle of Bobby Abreu is that he is such a talented hitter that he's hard to categorize. He can hit for power and probably could hit 40 homers if he was willing to sacrifice his batting average. He has said repeatedly, though, that his goal is to win a batting title. He's patient, walking 127 times in 2004 and boasting a .412 lifetime on-base percentage. He has a good knowledge of the strike zone with no obvious weaknesses. He hits fastballs and breaking balls equally well and doesn't give in against lefthanders.

Baserunning & Defense

Abreu made his greatest strides in the field in 2004. He'd always had a rap as a player who was an indifferent fielder at best, especially going toward the wall. But he worked on that aspect of his game and made several catches on the warning track. His 13 outfield assists attest to his strong throwing arm. His above-average speed helps him both in the field and on the basepaths. He employs a quick popup slide that sometimes fools umpires into calling him out when he's actually beaten the throw.

2005 Outlook

Abreu is entering the third season of a five-year, $64 million extension and has firmly established himself as one of the league's best all-around hitters. What's interesting is that some club officials, primarily general manager Ed Wade, still believe he can be even better.

Overall Statistics

	G	AB	R	H	D	T	HR	RBI	SB	BB	SO	Avg	OBP	Slg
'04	159	574	118	173	47	1	30	105	40	127	116	.301	.428	.544
Car.	1167	4140	749	1264	297	41	166	674	210	762	909	.305	.412	.517

Where He Hits the Ball

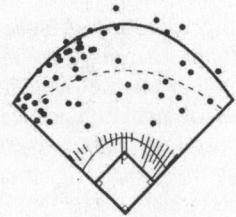
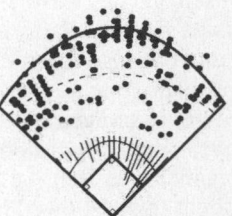

Vs. LHP **Vs. RHP**

2004 Situational Stats

	AB	H	HR	RBI	Avg		AB	H	HR	RBI	Avg
Home	277	87	13	48	.314	LHP	187	50	7	26	.267
Road	297	86	17	57	.290	RHP	387	123	23	79	.318
First Half	304	93	18	60	.306	Sc Pos	149	48	9	77	.322
Scnd Half	270	80	12	45	.296	Clutch	102	26	3	11	.255

2004 Rankings (National League)

- 1st in pitches seen (3,077) and most pitches seen per plate appearance (4.32)
- 2nd in walks
- 3rd in stolen bases and errors in right field (6)
- 4th in runs scored, doubles, times on base (305), plate appearances (713), stolen-base percentage (88.9), highest percentage of pitches taken (64.8) and lowest fielding percentage in right field (.982)
- Led the Phillies in batting average, doubles, total bases (312), RBI, sacrifice flies (7), games played, on-base percentage, stolen-base percentage (88.9), batting average with runners in scoring position, and lowest percentage of swings on the first pitch (14.7)
- Led NL right fielders in RBI

David Bell

2004 Season

In his second year with the Phillies, fans finally got to see the David Bell that the front office was so excited about signing as a free agent. Recovered from the back and hip problems that limited him to 85 games and a .195 average in 2003, Bell batted a career-high .291. Not only that, being healthy and productive allowed him to resume the kind of behind-the-scenes leadership role that made him such an integral part of the success of the Mariners and Giants.

Hitting

Unlike 2003, when back problems limited his follow-through, Bell was able to extend his arms and reach pitches on the outer half of the plate. He stays back well on breaking balls and offspeed stuff but also is quick enough to turn on inside fastballs, pitches that accounted for the majority of his 18 home runs. The son of former major leaguer Buddy Bell and grandson of former major leaguer Gus Bell, he knows the game. His situational savvy showed in the fact that he excelled in hitters' counts: .350 on 2-0, .529 on 3-1. He was also one of the team's best clutch hitters, batting .297 with runners in scoring position.

Baserunning & Defense

Known as a solid defensive player, Bell had a sub-par year in the field. He made 24 errors, second-highest among all National League third basemen. On the plus side, he was fourth in total chances, and that was on a team with several flyball pitchers. He has only an average arm but makes up for it with a quick release and accurate throws. He compensates for so-so speed with good instincts and awareness of his surroundings.

2005 Outlook

Bell has two years remaining on his contract, and the Phillies are counting on him to stabilize his position for at least that long. As long as he stays healthy, he'll be an important part of the team's plans.

Position: 3B
Bats: R **Throws:** R
Ht: 5'10" **Wt:** 181

Opening Day Age: 32
Born: 9/14/72 in Cincinnati, OH
ML Seasons: 10

Overall Statistics

	G	AB	R	H	D	T	HR	RBI	SB	BB	SO	Avg	OBP	Slg
'04	143	533	67	155	33	1	18	77	1	57	75	.291	.363	.458
Car.	1108	3765	474	965	209	13	103	465	16	331	550	.256	.319	.401

Where He Hits the Ball

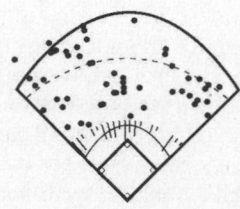
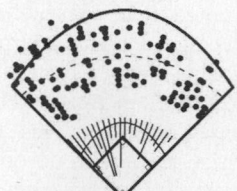

Vs. LHP   **Vs. RHP**

2004 Situational Stats

	AB	H	HR	RBI	Avg		AB	H	HR	RBI	Avg
Home	254	64	10	48	.252	LHP	125	37	2	16	.296
Road	279	91	8	29	.326	RHP	408	118	16	61	.289
First Half	292	80	12	45	.274	Sc Pos	138	41	4	57	.297
Scnd Half	241	75	6	32	.311	Clutch	89	33	4	16	.371

2004 Rankings (National League)

- 2nd in errors at third base (24)
- 3rd in lowest fielding percentage at third base (.943)
- 6th in batting average in the clutch
- 7th in batting average on the road
- Led the Phillies in batting average in the clutch and batting average on the road

Pat Burrell

Philadelphia

Position: LF
Bats: R **Throws:** R
Ht: 6' 4" **Wt:** 223

Opening Day Age: 28
Born: 10/10/76 in Eureka Springs, AR
ML Seasons: 5
Pronunciation: BURL

2004 Season

Pat Burrell is quietly becoming one of the Phillies' more pressing concerns. It's not just that he hasn't come close to matching his .282-37-116 breakout season of 2002. It's that he's still guaranteed $43.75 million over the next four years. If Burrell doesn't begin producing, the Phillies could be stuck, because the contract will be almost impossible to move. Last year he had an encouraging start, batting .276 in the first half, but slumped to .222 after the All-Star break.

Hitting

Power hitters are expected to strike out a lot, but Burrell whiffs too much for a guy who hasn't hit more than 24 homers in the past two years. In the second half of the season he reverted to bad habits—trying to pull everything for a home run and collapsing his back side in order to lift everything. That leaves him especially vulnerable to low, outside breaking balls. When Burrell first came up, he had a level swing and power to the opposite field. He also seems to have lost his sense of the strike zone, often taking fastballs down the middle and then swinging at pitches out of the zone.

Baserunning & Defense

Burrell has a strong arm, and opposing teams have learned to run on him at their own risk. While he doesn't have great speed, he generally makes the play on flyballs he gets to. The relatively small left field at Citizens Bank Park works to his advantage. On the bases, he runs hard and always is looking to take the extra base, but he is hardly a threat to steal.

2005 Outlook

Burrell is facing a pivotal season. Adding to the uncertainty is the fact that he decided against having offseason surgery on the sprained left wrist that landed him on the disabled list in August. For the Phillies' offense to click, it's vital that Burrell presents a legitimate threat as the cleanup hitter, breaking up lefthanded sluggers Bobby Abreu and Jim Thome.

Overall Statistics

	G	AB	R	H	D	T	HR	RBI	SB	BB	SO	Avg	OBP	Slg
'04	127	448	66	115	17	0	24	84	2	78	130	.257	.365	.455
Car.	696	2503	346	634	143	9	127	432	5	372	726	.253	.351	.470

Where He Hits the Ball

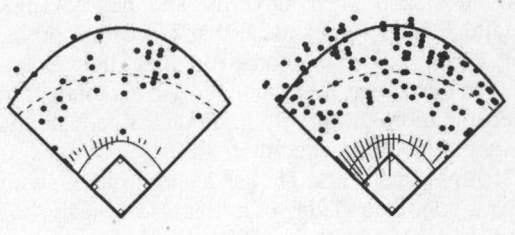

Vs. LHP   **Vs. RHP**

2004 Situational Stats

	AB	H	HR	RBI	Avg		AB	H	HR	RBI	Avg
Home	210	60	14	45	.286	LHP	96	26	3	17	.271
Road	238	55	10	39	.231	RHP	352	89	21	67	.253
First Half	286	79	15	62	.276	Sc Pos	133	35	2	53	.263
Scnd Half	162	36	9	22	.222	Clutch	72	16	2	15	.222

2004 Rankings (National League)

- 3rd in fielding percentage in left field (.983)

Mike Lieberthal

2004 Season

Mike Lieberthal didn't have a bad season, although you never would have known it from listening to the complaints from the fans. Lieberthal tied for the lead among National League catchers in homers and once again remained healthy. However, he was widely fingered as the primary cause for an offense that didn't produce as expected. That's because many focused on a single stat: Lieberthal batted just .142 with runners in scoring position. That was a surprise because, in the past, he's usually been one of the team's best clutch hitters.

Hitting

A half-dozen knee surgeries and nearly 1,000 major league games mean that Lieberthal probably never will be the home-run threat he was earlier in his career. He could increase his totals if he became more aware of turning on inside fastballs, especially with the short left-field fence at Citizens Bank Park. He has a short, quick swing and a good knowledge of hitting. He believes he's still capable of batting .300 and, if he does that, should also be good for 80 RBI.

Baserunning & Defense

Lieberthal, who won a Gold Glove in 1999, still possesses a strong, accurate arm. That hasn't been reflected in his success rate throwing out runners the past two seasons, in part a result of ex-pitching coach Joe Kerrigan's philosophy of focusing more on the hitter than the runners. They also weren't always on the same page in terms of pitch selection. Fortunately for Lieberthal, the Phillies will have a new pitching coach this season. No threat to steal, Lieberthal may be the slowest runner on the team.

2005 Outlook

Lieberthal remains an important cog for the Phillies, partly because his contract status almost guarantees that he'll be the primary receiver for at least the next two years. He's also important to the organization because, since the trade of Johnny Estrada, Philadelphia has no heir apparent in the farm system. Lieberthal's .290 batting average in the second half raises hope that he'll bounce back.

Position: C
Bats: R **Throws:** R
Ht: 6' 0" **Wt:** 190

Opening Day Age: 33
Born: 1/18/72 in Glendale, CA
ML Seasons: 11
Pronunciation: LEE-ber-thal

Overall Statistics

	G	AB	R	H	D	T	HR	RBI	SB	BB	SO	Avg	OBP	Slg
'04	131	476	58	129	31	1	17	61	1	37	69	.271	.335	.447
Car.	989	3540	458	977	216	10	129	526	8	288	506	.276	.340	.452

Where He Hits the Ball

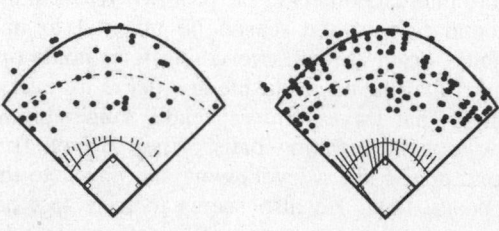

Vs. LHP   **Vs. RHP**

2004 Situational Stats

	AB	H	HR	RBI	Avg		AB	H	HR	RBI	Avg
Home	236	57	8	36	.242	LHP	102	29	4	13	.284
Road	240	72	9	25	.300	RHP	374	100	13	48	.267
First Half	262	67	11	36	.256	Sc Pos	134	19	3	35	.142
Scnd Half	214	62	6	25	.290	Clutch	78	18	3	12	.231

2004 Rankings (National League)

- 1st in lowest batting average with runners in scoring position
- 4th in lowest percentage of runners caught stealing as a catcher (20.4)
- 5th in errors at catcher (6)
- Led the Phillies in GDPs (19)
- Led NL catchers in home runs

Kevin Millwood

2004 Season

Kevin Millwood pitched his way out of the Phillies' plans in 2004. That was a crushing disappointment both for the team, which had made him the No. 1 starter for the second straight season, and for Millwood himself, who filed for free agency on the first allowable day after the World Series. He made only 25 starts, mostly due to elbow tendinitis that landed him on the disabled list. Conditioning became an issue—he never went deeper into a game than seven innings and only managed to pitch that long six times.

Pitching

Millwood has delicate mechanics and it doesn't take much to get him out of rhythm. When he was in Atlanta, pitching coach Leo Mazzone was able to keep him in synch, but he never developed the same kind of relationship with Joe Kerrigan in Philadelphia. While his fastball still hits 92 MPH consistently and his backdoor slider and sinker remain effective weapons, command has been a concern. In the last year and a half, he too often fell behind, raising his pitch count in the process. He's also been prone to leaving too many hittable pitches up in the strike zone.

Defense & Hitting

Millwood fields his position well, but is slow to the plate and vulnerable to the stolen base. He has just an average move to first and, when he tries to compensate by using a slide step, he loses something off his pitches. He isn't an automatic out at the plate, but doesn't often put the ball in play if he doesn't get a hit or sacrifice bunt.

2005 Outlook

When healthy, Millwood has shown the ability to pitch 200 innings. That alone should give him some value on the free-agent market after the Phillies declined to offer arbitration. There will be teams willing to take a chance that they can get him back on track, although it remains to be seen if he still can command the kind of four-year deal that he turned down from the Phillies in 2003.

Position: SP
Bats: R **Throws:** R
Ht: 6' 4" **Wt:** 235

Opening Day Age: 30
Born: 12/24/74 in Gastonia, NC
ML Seasons: 8

Overall Statistics

	W	L	Pct.	ERA	G	GS	Sv	IP	H	BB	SO	HR	Avg
'04	9	6	.600	4.85	25	25	0	141.0	155	51	125	14	.278
Car.	98	64	.605	3.89	228	220	0	1367.1	1283	422	1134	138	.247

2004 Pitching Profile

	Kevin Millwood	NL Average
Overall Strike %	62.1	62.5
1st Pitch Strike %	57.3	58.5
Ratio	1.46	1.39
Strikeouts per 9 IP	7.98	6.74
Walks per 9 IP	3.26	3.38
Home Runs per 9 IP	0.89	1.11
Strikeout/Walk Ratio	2.45	1.99
Groundball/Flyball Ratio	1.10	1.25

2004 Situational Stats

	W	L	ERA	Sv	IP		AB	H	HR	RBI	Avg
Home	4	1	4.95	0	63.2	LHB	269	83	6	38	.309
Road	5	5	4.77	0	77.1	RHB	288	72	8	35	.250
First Half	6	5	5.15	0	108.1	Sc Pos	149	43	4	55	.289
Scnd Half	3	1	3.86	0	32.2	Clutch	27	7	0	1	.259

2004 Rankings (National League)

- 7th in highest batting average allowed with runners in scoring position
- Led the Phillies in lowest slugging percentage allowed (.434), fewest home runs allowed per nine innings (.89) and most strikeouts per nine innings (8.0)

Eric Milton

2004 Season

Eric Milton was the Phillies' most dependable starter, the staff leader with 14 wins and the only member of the rotation to pitch at least 200 innings. Milton was on his way to a terrific season with 11 wins at the All-Star break. He held opposing hitters to a .227 batting average in the second half, but poor run support resulted in only three more victories. Milton always has been a flyball pitcher, and pitching in cozy Citizens Bank Park resulted in a league-leading 43 home runs allowed.

Pitching

While Milton's talent suggests a No. 2 or 3 starter, he has guts and competes well. With a full year of pitching behind him after missing most of the 2003 season following serious knee surgery, he could be expected to continue to improve. Milton throws a curve, a changeup and a 92-94 MPH fastball that he'll cut inside to a righthanded hitter. He is an aggressive pitcher who goes after the hitters. Even though he was a flyball pitcher in a park conducive to home runs, he never gave in and never made excuses. In doing so, he earned the respect of his teammates. One scout noted that he has a lot of "quality intangibles."

Defense & Hitting

Milton is above average in all aspects of his defensive game. He fields his position well and has a good move to first. At the plate, he batted .154 with five runs batted in and five sacrifice bunts.

2005 Outlook

Milton filed for free agency at the end of the season. The Phillies made an early offer, but Milton said he wanted to see who the next manager and pitching coach were going to be and also made it clear he wanted to test the market. The Phillies decided to not offer Milton arbitration, as they were unwilling to get into a bidding war when they would prefer to restock their staff with groundball pitchers.

Position: SP
Bats: L **Throws:** L
Ht: 6' 3" **Wt:** 208

Opening Day Age: 29
Born: 8/4/75 in State College, PA
ML Seasons: 7

Overall Statistics

	W	L	Pct.	ERA	G	GS	Sv	IP	H	BB	SO	HR	Avg
'04	14	6	.700	4.75	34	34	0	201.0	196	75	161	43	.255
Car.	71	57	.555	4.76	200	199	0	1188.1	1196	344	876	192	.258

2004 Pitching Profile

	Eric Milton	NL Average
Overall Strike %	64.3	62.5
1st Pitch Strike %	60.5	58.5
Ratio	1.35	1.39
Strikeouts per 9 IP	7.21	6.74
Walks per 9 IP	3.36	3.38
Home Runs per 9 IP	1.93	1.11
Strikeout/Walk Ratio	2.15	1.99
Groundball/Flyball Ratio	0.58	1.25

2004 Situational Stats

	W	L	ERA	Sv	IP		AB	H	HR	RBI	Avg
Home	6	3	4.40	0	104.1	LHB	119	30	6	16	.252
Road	8	3	5.12	0	96.2	RHB	649	166	37	84	.256
First Half	11	2	4.72	0	103.0	Sc Pos	157	42	10	56	.268
Scnd Half	3	4	4.78	0	98.0	Clutch	31	9	3	5	.290

2004 Rankings (National League)

- 1st in home runs allowed, fielding percentage at pitcher (1.000), lowest groundball-flyball ratio allowed (0.6) and most home runs allowed per nine innings (1.93)
- 2nd in highest slugging percentage allowed (.493) and most pitches thrown per batter (3.99)
- 3rd in most run support per nine innings (6.5)
- 5th in games started
- 6th in winning percentage, highest ERA, highest stolen-base percentage allowed (85.7) and highest ERA on the road
- Led the Phillies in wins, games started, innings pitched, hits allowed, batters faced (862), home runs allowed, walks allowed, strikeouts, pitches thrown (3,439), lowest batting average allowed (.255), lowest on-base percentage allowed (.320), lowest ERA at home and most run support per nine innings (6.5)

Brett Myers

Philadelphia

2004 Season

Though he's still only 24 with just two full big league seasons behind him, Brett Myers seems to be getting less, not more, consistent. Myers' 5.52 earned run average last year was the third highest among National League starters with at least 150 innings pitched, and he allowed 13.5 baserunners per nine innings. Late in the season, some questioned his conditioning. It was considered a positive sign when he asked for the ball on three days rest at the end of the season to even his record at .500.

Pitching

Everybody agrees that Myers has great stuff, and one scout compares his potential to Josh Beckett of the Marlins. Myers' fastball is above average, and he has a swing-and-miss curve that ranks among the best in baseball. He also has a splitter and a slider, and once he begins to throw his changeup effectively and with confidence, he could be a top-of-the-rotation starter. Even without the changeup, Myers can be dominant when he has command of his fastball and curve. He still has a tendency to simply try to throw harder with runners on base.

Defense & Hitting

Myers is an extremely athletic pitcher who is quick off the mound to field bunts or cover first. For a righthander, he has an excellent move to first. He has improved as a hitter, batting .196 last year while tying for the team lead with eight sacrifice bunts.

2005 Outlook

Myers is reaching a crossroad. At the end of this season, he'll be arbitration eligible for the first time. His salary figures to jump significantly, which means the organization can't afford to be as patient as it has been to this point. It's no secret that Myers clashed with former pitching coach Joe Kerrigan. That can no longer be offered as an excuse, and trying to get the former No. 1 draft pick straightened out will be a top priority for the club's new pitching coach.

Position: SP
Bats: R **Throws:** R
Ht: 6' 4" **Wt:** 223

Opening Day Age: 24
Born: 8/17/80 in Jacksonville, FL
ML Seasons: 3

Overall Statistics

	W	L	Pct.	ERA	G	GS	Sv	IP	H	BB	SO	HR	Avg
'04	11	11	.500	5.52	32	31	0	176.0	196	62	116	31	.281
Car.	29	25	.537	4.84	76	75	0	441.0	474	167	293	62	.276

2004 Pitching Profile

	Brett Myers	NL Average
Overall Strike %	64.3	62.5
1st Pitch Strike %	63.5	58.5
Ratio	1.47	1.39
Strikeouts per 9 IP	5.93	6.74
Walks per 9 IP	3.17	3.38
Home Runs per 9 IP	1.59	1.11
Strikeout/Walk Ratio	1.87	1.99
Groundball/Flyball Ratio	1.41	1.25

2004 Situational Stats

	W	L	ERA	Sv	IP		AB	H	HR	RBI	Avg
Home	5	7	5.77	0	73.1	LHB	338	94	12	42	.278
Road	6	4	5.35	0	102.2	RHB	360	102	19	63	.283
First Half	5	6	5.68	0	90.1	Sc Pos	177	51	3	68	.288
Scnd Half	6	5	5.36	0	85.2	Clutch	26	7	2	5	.269

2004 Rankings (National League)

- 1st in fielding percentage at pitcher (1.000)
- 2nd in highest ERA
- 3rd in highest slugging percentage allowed (.490)
- 4th in highest ERA on the road and most home runs allowed per nine innings (1.59)
- 5th in most run support per nine innings (6.2)
- 6th in home runs allowed and highest stolen-base percentage allowed (85.7)
- 7th in stolen bases allowed (18)
- 8th in highest batting average allowed (.281) and highest batting average allowed with runners in scoring position
- 9th in highest on-base percentage allowed (.343)
- Led the Phillies in sacrifice bunts (8), losses, hits allowed, pickoff throws (88), stolen bases allowed (18), GDPs induced (13) and highest groundball-flyball ratio allowed (1.4)

Vicente Padilla

2004 Season

Vicente Padilla was bothered by elbow tendinitis in 2004, but that still doesn't completely explain his puzzling lack of consistency. When healthy, he has one of the best arms in baseball. But that hasn't translated into wins. Over the last three years, Padilla is just five games over .500. Last year was more of the same, as he went 7-7 in 20 starts. His ERA also increased for the second straight year, from 3.28 in 2002 to 3.62 in 2003 to 4.53 last year.

Pitching

Sometimes Padilla looks like the All-Star he was in 2002. Sometimes he looks ordinary at best. At the top of his game he throws a heavy, boring fastball that sits comfortably at 96 MPH, a breaking ball that hits 94 MPH, a biting slider and an effective changeup. There are games, however, when he throws in the 87-88 MPH range for the first couple of innings for no apparent reason. There are other times when he stubbornly insists on throwing almost all fastballs, and games when his concentration seems to wander. He's not the kind of pitcher hitters feel comfortable facing— even though, as often as not, they can beat him in the end.

Defense & Hitting

Padilla is a switch-hitter who has little success from either side of the plate, normally operating on the theory that he should swing as hard as possible in case he connects. He is an average bunter at best and is only fair at holding runners and fielding his position.

2005 Outlook

Padilla remains stuck between potential and production. And that becomes an increasingly difficult position as he acquires the big league service time that drives his salary upward. At the end of this season, he'll be just a year away from free agency. While it's easy to be dazzled by his ability, he's at the point of his career where he has to start showing results.

Position: SP
Bats: R **Throws:** R
Ht: 6' 2" **Wt:** 219

Opening Day Age: 27
Born: 9/27/77 in Chinandega, Nicaragua
ML Seasons: 6
Pronunciation: pa-DEE-ya

Overall Statistics

	W	L	Pct.	ERA	G	GS	Sv	IP	H	BB	SO	HR	Avg
'04	7	7	.500	4.53	20	20	0	115.1	119	36	82	16	.267
Car.	42	39	.519	3.77	167	84	2	632.0	628	194	423	59	.261

2004 Pitching Profile

	Vicente Padilla	NL Average
Overall Strike %	65.2	62.5
1st Pitch Strike %	62.5	58.5
Ratio	1.34	1.39
Strikeouts per 9 IP	6.40	6.74
Walks per 9 IP	2.81	3.38
Home Runs per 9 IP	1.25	1.11
Strikeout/Walk Ratio	2.28	1.99
Groundball/Flyball Ratio	1.25	1.25

2004 Situational Stats

	W	L	ERA	Sv	IP		AB	H	HR	RBI	Avg
Home	4	5	4.96	0	69.0	LHB	242	70	10	34	.289
Road	3	2	3.88	0	46.1	RHB	203	49	6	27	.241
First Half	4	5	4.07	0	59.2	Sc Pos	95	28	5	47	.295
Scnd Half	3	2	5.01	0	55.2	Clutch	12	5	0	2	.417

2004 Rankings (National League)

- Led the Phillies in hit batsmen (10), lowest stolen-base percentage allowed (71.4) and fewest pitches thrown per batter (3.54)

Jimmy Rollins

2004 Season

Jimmy Rollins easily had the best season of his career, which is saying something for a fourth-year player who made the All-Star team his first two years in the league. He reached double figures in doubles, triples, homers and stolen bases for the third time in four years. He also set a record for runs by a Phillies shortstop (119) that had been held by Dick Bartell since 1932. He had more RBI (73) than any Phillies shortstop since Granny Hamner in 1952.

Hitting

A switch-hitter, Rollins is equally effective from both sides of the plate. He has improved dramatically in his approach. He no longer is prone to the uppercut swing that produced too many popups, concentrating instead on hitting on top of the ball and utilizing his speed. He can hit an outside pitch to the opposite field and also has begun bunting more often. Rollins has the discipline to look for a certain pitch—generally an inside fastball—and drive it. He drastically cut down on his strikeouts to 73 from triple-digits his first three seasons and had a .366 on-base percentage after the All-Star break. That allowed the Phillies to move him back to his preferred spot at the top of the order.

Baserunning & Defense

Rollins should be a Gold Glove candidate for years. He has great range, especially into the hole, and a strong enough arm to throw runners out from shallow left field. He has quick hands and turns the double play well. Recovered from nagging leg injuries that slowed him in 2003 and back in the leadoff spot, he again became a legitimate basestealing threat.

2005 Outlook

Rollins appears to have finally developed into the leadoff hitter the Phillies have been searching for since Lenny Dykstra retired. In doing so, he solidified himself as an up-the-middle asset that, as recently as a year earlier, some in the organization had begun to doubt he could be.

Position: SS
Bats: B **Throws:** R
Ht: 5' 8" **Wt:** 167

Opening Day Age: 26
Born: 11/27/78 in Oakland, CA
ML Seasons: 5

Overall Statistics

	G	AB	R	H	D	T	HR	RBI	SB	BB	SO	Avg	OBP	Slg
'04	154	657	119	190	43	12	14	73	30	57	73	.289	.348	.455
Car.	636	2631	388	708	148	41	47	254	130	215	404	.269	.325	.410

Where He Hits the Ball

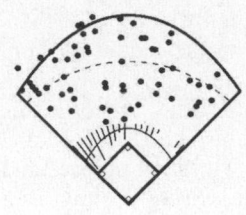
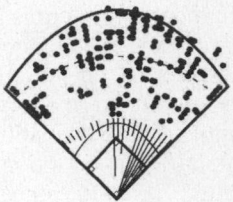

Vs. LHP   **Vs. RHP**

2004 Situational Stats

	AB	H	HR	RBI	Avg		AB	H	HR	RBI	Avg
Home	318	98	8	43	.308	LHP	165	50	5	26	.303
Road	339	92	6	30	.271	RHP	492	140	9	47	.285
First Half	344	93	3	30	.270	Sc Pos	134	42	4	58	.313
Scnd Half	313	97	11	43	.310	Clutch	105	31	2	12	.295

2004 Rankings (National League)

- 1st in triples
- 2nd in fielding percentage at shortstop (.986)
- 3rd in at-bats, runs scored and plate appearances (725)
- 6th in caught stealing (9) and fewest GDPs per GDP situation (4.4%)
- 7th in hits and on-base percentage for a lead off hitter (.360)
- 8th in stolen bases
- 9th in doubles and lowest stolen-base percentage (76.9)
- Led the Phillies in at-bats, runs scored, hits, singles, triples, caught stealing (9), plate appearances (725), bunts in play (24), steals of third (3) and on-base percentage for a leadoff hitter (.360)

Jim Thome

2004 Season

Jim Thome is coming off a disappointing season—at least, as disappointing as a 42-homer, 105-RBI season can be. The problems started in spring training when a bad-hop grounder during infield practice fractured the tip of his right middle finger. It ended with a bruised chest in September. Partly as a result, Thome hit only 14 homers in the second half. Despite that, he recorded the 400th home run of his career and had his sixth straight season with 100 walks and 100 RBI.

Hitting

Thome remains a pure power hitter who swings hard, even with two strikes. That results in a lot of home runs and a lot of strikeouts. He can carry a team but is also prone to lengthy slumps. Pitchers have some success going up the ladder on him. Last season, he showed more of a willingness to try to hit to the opposite field when teams employed an overshift against him. But Thome often tried to do too much with men on base and batted .203 with runners in scoring position as a result.

Baserunning & Defense

Thome never will win a Gold Glove, but he has turned himself into a more than adequate defensive player. He has the size to snag high throws and has worked hard to become dependable at digging the ball out of the dirt and handling short hops. He has a strong, accurate arm, which isn't surprising considering that he began his career as a third baseman. He has below-average speed, but always runs hard.

2005 Outlook

There's no doubt that Thome remains the key hitter in the Phillies' lineup, and the one player his teammates most look up to. He has the never-too-high, never-too-low approach to every game that's considered ideal for the daily grind of baseball. The Phillies believe that if Thome stays healthy and gets some protection around him, there's no reason he can't bounce back and have a terrific season.

Position: 1B
Bats: L **Throws:** R
Ht: 6' 4" **Wt:** 244

Opening Day Age: 34
Born: 8/27/70 in Peoria, IL
ML Seasons: 14
Pronunciation: TOE-mee

Overall Statistics

G	AB	R	H	D	T	HR	RBI	SB	BB	SO	Avg	OBP	Slg
143	508	97	139	28	1	42	105	0	104	144	.274	.396	.581
1679	5726	1125	1625	317	24	423	1163	18	1212	1703	.284	.410	.569

Where He Hits the Ball

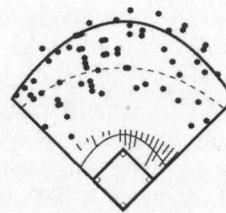 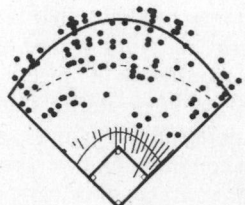

Vs. LHP　　　　**Vs. RHP**

2004 Situational Stats

	AB	H	HR	RBI	Avg		AB	H	HR	RBI	Avg
Home	235	57	19	39	.243	LHP	188	45	12	34	.239
Road	273	82	23	66	.300	RHP	320	94	30	71	.294
First Half	291	84	28	61	.289	Sc Pos	153	31	12	63	.203
Scnd Half	217	55	14	44	.253	Clutch	97	28	7	26	.289

2004 Rankings (National League)

- 2nd in intentional walks (26)
- 3rd in HR frequency (12.1 ABs per HR)
- 5th in home runs, cleanup slugging percentage (.577), fielding percentage at first base (.994), lowest percentage of swings put into play (33.8) and lowest batting average with runners in scoring position
- 7th in slugging percentage
- Led the Phillies in home runs, RBI, intentional walks (26), strikeouts, slugging percentage, HR frequency (12.1 ABs per HR) and cleanup slugging percentage (.577)

Billy Wagner

2004 Season

When healthy, Billy Wagner remains one of baseball's most automatic closers. The problem is that he wasn't healthy for almost half of last season, for reasons ranging from a strained groin to back spasms to shoulder tendinitis. That limited him to 45 games and 21 saves. Wagner still averaged 11 strikeouts per nine innings.

Pitching

Wagner's signature pitch is a 100-MPH fastball. That's what the crowds look for when the radar readings are posted on the scoreboard, cheering wildly when he reaches triple digits even if the pitch isn't a strike. And while his fastball can be almost unhittable when it's riding up in the strike zone, Wagner is more than just a thrower. He's developed a better sense of pitching in and out and also keeps hitters off balance with a slider that he usually throws between 86-90 MPH. More than just a change of pace, it can bite in or down and away, and makes him one of the best closers in baseball.

Defense & Hitting

Since Wagner's job description requires that he often protect one-run leads in the ninth, his primary defensive responsibility is to field bunts and cover first on balls hit to the right side of the infield. He executes both tasks well. Like most lefthanders, he has a good, quick move to first base. In a 10-year big league career, he's had only 17 at-bats and just one hit.

2005 Outlook

Wagner could have exercised his right to demand a trade after the Phillies exercised their $9 million option for 2005. But he made a commitment to return, partly because he might not have been able to command that kind of salary coming off a down season and partly, as he put it, because he thought the Phillies have "unfinished business." Wagner also said he would rededicate himself to conditioning to help prevent injuries in the future.

Position: RP
Bats: L **Throws:** L
Ht: 5'11" **Wt:** 195

Opening Day Age: 33
Born: 7/25/71 in Tannersville, VA
ML Seasons: 10

Overall Statistics

	W	L	Pct.	ERA	G	GS	Sv	IP	H	BB	SO	HR	Avg
'04	4	0	1.000	2.42	45	0	21	48.1	31	6	59	5	.181
Car.	30	29	.508	2.52	509	0	246	552.2	364	197	753	53	.186

2004 Pitching Profile

	Billy Wagner	NL Average
Overall Strike %	67.3	62.5
1st Pitch Strike %	63.4	58.5
Ratio	0.77	1.39
Strikeouts per 9 IP	10.99	6.74
Walks per 9 IP	1.12	3.38
Home Runs per 9 IP	0.93	1.11
Strikeout/Walk Ratio	9.83	1.99
Groundball/Flyball Ratio	1.17	1.25

2004 Situational Stats

	W	L	ERA	Sv	IP		AB	H	HR	RBI	Avg
Home	3	0	1.00	9	27.0	LHB	29	3	0	0	.103
Road	1	0	4.22	12	21.1	RHB	142	28	5	15	.197
First Half	3	0	3.52	13	30.2	Sc Pos	24	5	1	9	.208
Scnd Half	1	0	0.51	8	17.2	Clutch	94	16	3	7	.170

2004 Rankings (National League)

- 6th in lowest save percentage (84.0)
- 10th in first batter efficiency (.163)
- Led the Phillies in saves, games finished (38), lowest batting average allowed vs. righthanded batters and save percentage (84.0)

Randy Wolf

2004 Season

In 2003, Randy Wolf led all National League left-handers in wins, strikeouts, opponent batting average and innings pitched while making his first All-Star team. In 2004, Wolf had his worst season since making it to the big leagues for good in 2000. He was sidelined by elbow tendinitis, including two stints on the disabled list, helping end a streak of four straight years of reaching double-digit wins.

Pitching

One scout calls Wolf a poor man's Tom Glavine. Wolf has an extensive repertoire, throwing a fastball, curve, changeup, slider and cutter. He sets up his fastball with a big, looping curveball that is sometimes thrown in the mid-70s. He also features an above-average changeup. That makes his 90-MPH fastball appear to get on hitters more quickly than it actually does. Wolf has a deceptive motion and knows how to work hitters: up and down, in and out, soft and hard. Command is his key, as he walked just 2.4 batters per nine innings last year. Wolf almost always remains poised while on the mound, but he is a fierce competitor.

Defense & Hitting

Wolf is a good hitter who can not only help himself at the plate but also is occasionally used as a pinch-hitter in extra innings when all the available position players have been used. Last year, he batted .267 with three homers and eight RBI while tying for the team lead with eight sacrifice bunts. He's an excellent all-around athlete who fields his position well and pays attention to holding runners on with an above-average pickoff move and slide step.

2005 Outlook

As last season ended, the Phillies were braced for the departure of Kevin Millwood and Eric Milton as free agents. That would make Wolf the logical No. 1 starter. He has the ability, seniority and composure to handle the role as long as he's healthy. However, his elbow remains a concern.

Position: SP
Bats: L **Throws:** L
Ht: 6' 0" **Wt:** 200

Opening Day Age: 28
Born: 8/22/76 in Canoga Park, CA
ML Seasons: 6

Overall Statistics

	W	L	Pct.	ERA	G	GS	Sv	IP	H	BB	SO	HR	Avg
'04	5	8	.385	4.28	23	23	0	136.2	145	36	89	20	.271
Car.	59	56	.513	4.13	169	165	0	1038.1	979	378	866	130	.250

2004 Pitching Profile

	Randy Wolf	NL Average
Overall Strike %	65.1	62.5
1st Pitch Strike %	60.2	58.5
Ratio	1.32	1.39
Strikeouts per 9 IP	5.86	6.74
Walks per 9 IP	2.37	3.38
Home Runs per 9 IP	1.32	1.11
Strikeout/Walk Ratio	2.47	1.99
Groundball/Flyball Ratio	0.84	1.25

2004 Situational Stats

	W	L	ERA	Sv	IP		AB	H	HR	RBI	Avg
Home	3	6	4.95	0	76.1	LHB	122	31	5	8	.254
Road	2	2	3.43	0	60.1	RHB	413	114	15	51	.276
First Half	3	5	3.56	0	86.0	Sc Pos	117	31	4	40	.265
Scnd Half	2	3	5.51	0	50.2	Clutch	8	5	0	1	.625

2004 Rankings (National League)

- Led the Phillies in ERA, sacrifice bunts (8), GDPs induced (13), highest strikeout-walk ratio (2.5), lowest ERA on the road and fewest walks per nine innings (2.4)

Marlon Byrd

Position: CF
Bats: R **Throws:** R
Ht: 6' 0" **Wt:** 229

Opening Day Age: 27
Born: 8/30/77 in
Boynton Beach, FL
ML Seasons: 3

Overall Statistics

	G	AB	R	H	D	T	HR	RBI	SB	BB	SO	Avg	OBP	Slg
'04	106	346	48	79	13	2	5	33	2	22	68	.228	.287	.321
Car.	251	876	136	237	43	6	13	79	13	67	170	.271	.331	.378

2004 Situational Stats

	AB	H	HR	RBI	Avg		AB	H	HR	RBI	Avg
Home	167	36	3	13	.216	LHP	75	16	1	8	.213
Road	179	43	2	20	.240	RHP	271	63	4	25	.232
First Half	214	48	2	18	.224	Sc Pos	68	21	1	28	.309
Scnd Half	132	31	3	15	.235	Clutch	60	9	0	3	.150

2004 Season

No Phillies player has experienced a quicker, steeper fall than Marlon Byrd. He opened last season as the Phillies' regular center fielder and lead-off hitter. By June he was batting .224 and was sent to Triple-A to work on his swing. After being recalled, he batted only .235 and by the end of the season was rarely playing.

Hitting, Baserunning & Defense

Although the Phillies projected Byrd as a potential power hitter, his bat seems to have slowed since his breakthrough season at Double-A in 2001. While fast enough to beat out slow rollers and strong enough to muscle the ball over the infield when jammed, he doesn't work pitchers well and doesn't make the kind of consistent, solid contact that is needed to play regularly. Byrd can track down flyballs over his head or into the gaps. But he has lost his aggressiveness on the bases, attempting only four steals last season despite good speed. He has an average arm.

2005 Outlook

Byrd played his way out of the Phillies' plans, a fact that was underlined by the acquisitions of Kenny Lofton from the Yankees and Shane Victorino in the Rule 5 draft. It didn't help that Byrd ignored the suggestion to play winter ball.

Rheal Cormier

Position: RP
Bats: L **Throws:** L
Ht: 5'10" **Wt:** 195

Opening Day Age: 37
Born: 4/23/67 in
Moncton, NB, Canada
ML Seasons: 13
Pronunciation:
ree-AL cor-MEE-ay

Overall Statistics

	W	L	Pct.	ERA	G	GS	Sv	IP	H	BB	SO	HR	Avg
'04	4	5	.444	3.56	84	0	0	81.0	70	26	46	7	.237
Car.	65	59	.524	4.01	556	108	2	1123.1	1140	283	706	106	.264

2004 Situational Stats

	W	L	ERA	Sv	IP		AB	H	HR	RBI	Avg
Home	2	0	2.40	0	45.0	LHB	108	27	1	13	.250
Road	2	5	5.00	0	36.0	RHB	187	43	6	24	.230
First Half	4	3	4.36	0	43.1	Sc Pos	77	20	1	28	.260
Scnd Half	0	2	2.63	0	37.2	Clutch	152	34	4	19	.224

2004 Season

At age 37, Rheal Cormier set a franchise record for appearances by a lefthander by pitching in 84 games. And he got better as the year went on, posting a 2.28 earned run average after July 31 as the preferred lefthanded setup reliever in the bullpen. While he couldn't repeat his career best numbers (8-0, 1.70) from 2003, he remained an important member of the staff.

Pitching, Defense & Hitting

Cormier's stuff may not be as good as it once was. However, he has enough veteran's savvy to use his fastball (which routinely sits at around 88 MPH), slider and changeup to set hitters up for his out pitch, the splitter. He's equally effective against both righthanded and lefthanded hitters. He fields his position well and has a good pickoff move. Because of his role, he rarely is called on to bat.

2005 Outlook

Cormier had talked about retiring after the 2004 season, but his strong finish changed his mind and he signed a two-year, $5.25 million extension. While he's reaching the point of his career that may require him to be used more as a middle reliever than a setup man, he still projects as a valuable member of the bullpen.

Todd Jones

Position: RP
Bats: L **Throws:** R
Ht: 6' 3" **Wt:** 230

Opening Day Age: 36
Born: 4/24/68 in Marietta, GA
ML Seasons: 12

Overall Statistics

	W	L	Pct.	ERA	G	GS	Sv	IP	H	BB	SO	HR	Avg
'04	11	5	.688	4.15	78	0	2	82.1	84	33	59	7	.273
Car.	50	47	.515	4.07	744	1	186	832.0	827	377	731	79	.262

2004 Situational Stats

	W	L	ERA	Sv	IP		AB	H	HR	RBI	Avg
Home	7	3	4.76	1	39.2	LHB	132	33	3	13	.250
Road	4	2	3.59	1	42.2	RHB	176	51	4	27	.290
First Half	7	2	3.33	1	51.1	Sc Pos	88	27	3	36	.307
Scnd Half	4	3	5.52	1	31.0	Clutch	217	57	6	28	.263

2004 Season

Todd Jones was acquired from the Cincinnati Reds July 30 and was immediately put to work, pitching effectively in the first five games he wore a Phillies uniform. After that, he struggled. He ended up making 27 appearances for the Phillies and allowing 48 baserunners (35 hits, eight walks, five hit batters) in 25.1 innings.

Pitching, Defense & Hitting

Jones is a veteran durable reliever who throws a variety of pitches: fastball, curve, cutter and a fourth pitch that is somewhere between a change-up and a splitter. He's a good teammate who has been popular in the clubhouse wherever he's gone. When he's on, he can be very effective. When he's not, he walks too many batters and falls behind in the count. He's about average at fielding and holding runners.

2005 Outlook

Jones became a free agent at the end of the season and wasn't offered arbitration by the Phillies. He's far removed from his career-best 42 saves with the Tigers in 2000 and has been with four different organizations in the last two years. His leadership skills and intangibles, however, helped secure a one-year deal with Florida.

Cory Lidle

Position: SP
Bats: R **Throws:** R
Ht: 5'11" **Wt:** 192

Opening Day Age: 33
Born: 3/22/72 in Hollywood, CA
ML Seasons: 7
Pronunciation: LIE-dell

Overall Statistics

	W	L	Pct.	ERA	G	GS	Sv	IP	H	BB	SO	HR	Avg
'04	12	12	.500	4.90	34	34	0	211.1	224	61	126	27	.273
Car.	57	51	.528	4.52	215	138	2	967.1	1009	258	587	111	.269

2004 Situational Stats

	W	L	ERA	Sv	IP		AB	H	HR	RBI	Avg
Home	7	5	4.03	0	89.1	LHB	345	96	15	53	.278
Road	5	7	5.53	0	122.0	RHB	475	128	12	62	.269
First Half	6	7	4.82	0	121.1	Sc Pos	191	55	8	88	.288
Scnd Half	6	5	5.00	0	90.0	Clutch	42	10	1	7	.238

2004 Season

After Cory Lidle was acquired from the Reds in August, he didn't make a good first impression. In his first three starts, he went 0-2 with an 8.16 earned run average. After that, however, Lidle pitched back-to-back shutouts which turned out to be a springboard to a strong finish. In his last seven starts as a Phillie, he went 5-0, 2.63.

Pitching, Defense & Hitting

Lidle's stuff is only marginal, but he has decent control and a feel for pitching. He changes speeds well. His fastball usually sits in the 86-87 MPH range, but it sinks and his splitter has good downward movement as well. His curve does not break sharply. He also throws a cut fastball and change-up. Lidle has to keep the ball down and hit the corners to be effective, and he gets in trouble when he tries to be too fine. He does not hold runners well, but is an excellent fielder.

2005 Outlook

Lidle became a free agent at the end of the season and the Phillies, who are looking to rebuild their staff with groundball pitchers in cozy Citizens Bank Park, kept him with a two-year, $6.3 million contract. After being with six different organizations in parts of seven big league seasons, he projects as a No. 5 starter.

Ryan Madson

Position: RP
Bats: L **Throws:** R
Ht: 6' 6" **Wt:** 190

Opening Day Age: 24
Born: 8/28/80 in Long Beach, CA
ML Seasons: 2

Overall Statistics

	W	L	Pct.	ERA	G	GS	Sv	IP	H	BB	SO	HR	Avg
'04	9	3	.750	2.34	52	1	1	77.0	68	19	55	6	.238
Car.	9	3	.750	2.28	53	1	1	79.0	68	19	55	6	.233

2004 Situational Stats

	W	L	ERA	Sv	IP		AB	H	HR	RBI	Avg
Home	5	2	2.20	0	41.0	LHB	123	31	1	8	.252
Road	4	1	2.50	1	36.0	RHB	163	37	5	15	.227
First Half	6	2	2.03	1	53.1	Sc Pos	70	12	2	18	.171
Scnd Half	3	1	3.04	0	23.2	Clutch	108	22	2	10	.204

2004 Season

The Phillies debated long and hard at the end of spring training over whether to keep Ryan Madson as a reliever in the big leagues or have him return to Triple-A, where he had been the Red Barons' most effective starter in 2003. They kept him, and Madson almost immediately blossomed into one of the best middle relievers in baseball. He even worked himself into some late-inning situations as the year progressed.

Pitching, Defense & Hitting

Madson pitched much better in the big leagues than in the minors, mainly because his curveball, with a sharp 12-to-6 break, developed into his best pitch. Madson also has a swing-and-miss change-up that is reminiscent of Trevor Hoffman or Doug Jones, along with a decent fastball. His delivery is slightly unorthodox, but unlike many pitchers with long arms, he has no trouble getting his hands out and throwing downhill. Madson played well defensively but was just fair holding runners.

2005 Outlook

Madson appears to have a bright future. The next decision the Phillies must make is whether he can best help the team as a setup reliever or a starter. Scouts say he even has the trappings of a future closer.

Jason Michaels

Position: CF/LF/RF
Bats: R **Throws:** R
Ht: 6' 0" **Wt:** 204

Opening Day Age: 28
Born: 5/4/76 in Tampa, FL
ML Seasons: 4

Overall Statistics

	G	AB	R	H	D	T	HR	RBI	SB	BB	SO	Avg	OBP	Slg
'04	115	299	44	82	12	0	10	40	2	42	80	.274	.364	.415
Car.	278	519	80	147	33	3	17	69	3	70	137	.283	.370	.457

2004 Situational Stats

	AB	H	HR	RBI	Avg		AB	H	HR	RBI	Avg
Home	165	49	5	20	.297	LHP	84	24	5	14	.286
Road	134	33	5	20	.246	RHP	215	58	5	26	.270
First Half	95	26	3	10	.274	Sc Pos	81	23	1	27	.284
Scnd Half	204	56	7	30	.275	Clutch	70	19	2	8	.271

2004 Season

Jason Michaels got a chance to play center field regularly late in the season and hit well. Michaels batted .298 over the last two months of the season and also was one of the team's better situational hitters. He showed his versatility by batting at least once in every spot of the order and playing all three outfield positions.

Hitting, Baserunning & Defense

Michaels is a fastball hitter who likes to look for a pitch up in the strike zone. He handles righthanders almost as well as lefties. He's a free swinger who strikes out too much (80 times in 299 at-bats last season), but some of that could be due to lack of regular playing time. Michaels has decent range in the outfield but doesn't always make the play once he gets to the ball. He's an aggressive baserunner with slightly above-average speed.

2005 Outlook

Michaels probably could start as a corner outfielder for some teams, but he will end up sharing center field with new arrival Kenny Lofton. While Michaels didn't help himself when he declined the team's suggestion that he play winter ball after the 2004 season, he remains an asset off the bench.

Placido Polanco

Position: 2B/3B
Bats: R **Throws:** R
Ht: 5'10" **Wt:** 190

Opening Day Age: 29
Born: 10/10/75 in Santo Domingo, DR
ML Seasons: 7
Pronunciation: PLAH-si-doh poh-LAHN-co

Overall Statistics

	G	AB	R	H	D	T	HR	RBI	SB	BB	SO	Avg	OBP	Slg
'04	126	503	74	150	21	0	17	55	7	27	39	.298	.345	.441
Car.	790	2764	407	815	133	17	50	274	45	156	220	.295	.339	.410

2004 Situational Stats

	AB	H	HR	RBI	Avg		AB	H	HR	RBI	Avg
Home	265	84	10	35	.317	LHP	147	48	7	18	.327
Road	238	66	7	20	.277	RHP	356	102	10	37	.287
First Half	230	61	5	16	.265	Sc Pos	111	30	4	39	.270
Scnd Half	273	89	12	39	.326	Clutch	94	30	2	6	.319

2004 Season

Placido Polanco was considered one of the most important players in the Phillies' lineup at the beginning of the season, one of the club's few good situational hitters. Then he played his way into former manager Larry Bowa's doghouse by hitting .223 with just one RBI in his first 27 games, before going on to the disabled list with a strained left quadriceps. However, Polanco came back to hit .326 in 70 games after the break.

Hitting, Baserunning & Defense

Polanco is a professional hitter who maintains an excellent strikeout-to-at-bat ratio. While not a power hitter, he has the ability to look for a certain pitch in a zone and hit it out of the park. While best suited to batting second, he's a team player who will bat—or play in the field—wherever it helps the team most. He has an average arm but positions himself well and usually makes the play. He also is a heady baserunner.

2005 Outlook

The Phillies project Chase Utley as their everyday second baseman, and Polanco filed for free agency at season's end. However, there was some talk about him returning as a utility player, reprising the role he had with the Cardinals before being traded to Philadelphia.

Felix Rodriguez

Traded To YANKEES

Position: RP
Bats: R **Throws:** R
Ht: 6' 1" **Wt:** 198

Opening Day Age: 32
Born: 12/5/72 in Montecristi, DR
ML Seasons: 9

Overall Statistics

	W	L	Pct.	ERA	G	GS	Sv	IP	H	BB	SO	HR	Avg
'04	5	8	.385	3.29	76	0	1	65.2	61	29	59	8	.244
Car.	37	25	.597	3.41	498	1	11	524.2	461	247	479	43	.237

2004 Situational Stats

	W	L	ERA	Sv	IP		AB	H	HR	RBI	Avg
Home	1	3	3.49	0	28.1	LHB	99	19	1	6	.192
Road	4	5	3.13	1	37.1	RHB	151	42	7	22	.278
First Half	2	4	3.20	0	39.1	Sc Pos	74	15	1	19	.203
Scnd Half	3	4	3.42	1	26.1	Clutch	162	40	3	18	.247

2004 Season

The Giants traded Felix Rodriguez to the Phillies at a point in the season (July 30) when they desperately needed relief help. That wouldn't seem like a good omen, but Rodriguez pitched well enough in a setup role after the trade.

Pitching, Defense & Hitting

Rodriguez was somewhat of an enigma for the Giants, who traded him to the Phillies even though his four-seam fastball routinely hits 96 MPH. When he commands his pitches, he can be lights out, but he loses something when runners reach base. The Giants tried to convince him to throw a changeup, and he occasionally uses a slider while warming up. Once he gets into the game, though, he relies almost entirely on his fastball. On the rare occasions that he gets to bat he handles himself well. He is aware of runners and does a good job of holding them close. He also fields his position competently.

2005 Outlook

Rodriguez has the stuff to be a closer, but has never taken to that role. His future, then, is as an eighth-inning setup reliever. He'll do that for the Yankees after being traded by the Phillies for Kenny Lofton, after exercising his player option for $3.15 million in 2005.

Chase Utley

Position: 2B/1B
Bats: L **Throws:** R
Ht: 6' 1" **Wt:** 183

Opening Day Age: 26
Born: 12/17/78 in
Pasadena, CA
ML Seasons: 2

Overall Statistics

	G	AB	R	H	D	T	HR	RBI	SB	BB	SO	Avg	OBP	Slg
'04	94	267	36	71	11	2	13	57	4	15	40	.266	.308	.468
Car.	137	401	49	103	21	3	15	78	6	26	62	.257	.313	.436

2004 Situational Stats

	AB	H	HR	RBI	Avg		AB	H	HR	RBI	Avg
Home	128	33	8	32	.258	LHP	45	9	1	3	.200
Road	139	38	5	25	.273	RHP	222	62	12	54	.279
First Half	132	35	7	30	.265	Sc Pos	91	25	4	45	.275
Scnd Half	135	36	6	27	.267	Clutch	61	18	2	15	.295

2004 Season

Chase Utley demonstrated once and for all that he's ready to hit in the big leagues. The Phillies' No. 1 draft choice in 2000 made an immediate impact in May when he was put into the lineup after Placido Polanco was shelved with a strained quadriceps. While Utley suffered through some slumps, he demonstrated his potential by hitting 13 homers with 57 RBI in just 267 at-bats.

Hitting, Baserunning & Defense

Like many lefthanded hitters, Utley attacks low fastballs. He's a line-drive gap hitter with enough strength to hit the ball over the fence. Utley can be fooled by veteran pitchers who change speeds and move the ball around in the strike zone, but he's a smart hitter who should only get better as he gains experience. Utley's biggest improvement last season was in the field, where he went from being below average to adequate. He has above-average speed and is aggressive on the bases.

2005 Outlook

After breaking into the big leagues in 2003 and increasing his playing time in 2004, Utley is penciled in to play regularly this season. When he was drafted, he was advertised as having Jeff Kent-like tools, and to this point, he's living up to those comparisons.

Tim Worrell

Position: RP
Bats: R **Throws:** R
Ht: 6' 4" **Wt:** 230

Opening Day Age: 37
Born: 7/5/67 in
Pasadena, CA
ML Seasons: 12
Pronunciation:
wor-RELL

Overall Statistics

	W	L	Pct.	ERA	G	GS	Sv	IP	H	BB	SO	HR	Avg
'04	5	6	.455	3.68	77	0	19	78.1	75	21	64	10	.254
Car.	44	55	.444	3.88	604	49	64	904.2	876	347	707	90	.253

2004 Situational Stats

	W	L	ERA	Sv	IP		AB	H	HR	RBI	Avg
Home	2	4	4.23	7	38.1	LHB	129	40	1	16	.310
Road	3	2	3.15	12	40.0	RHB	166	35	9	26	.211
First Half	2	3	3.57	9	45.1	Sc Pos	80	18	2	31	.225
Scnd Half	3	3	3.82	10	33.0	Clutch	224	59	9	36	.263

2004 Season

Tim Worrell was signed to be Billy Wagner's primary setup reliever, and also to be available as insurance in case Wagner was injured. Unfortunately for the Phillies, Wagner missed two and a half months with a variety of injuries. Worrell filled in admirably and posted 19 saves.

Pitching, Defense & Hitting

At this point of his career, Worrell's stuff isn't as sharp as it once was. His fastball hit 90 MPH early in the season, but was more consistently in the 88-MPH range toward the end of the year. He also throws an average curveball and a splitter. Worrell's location has to be excellent for him to be effective. What makes him valuable, though, is that he's a tough veteran who is durable and takes the ball. He's a good influence on younger pitchers in the bullpen. Worrell is a good fielder but only so-so at holding runners.

2005 Outlook

Worrell is in the second year of a two-year deal and has talked about retiring at the end of the season. In the meantime, it's possible that he could be edged toward middle relief, especially if Ryan Madson remains a reliever instead of being moved into the rotation.

Other Philadelphia Phillies

Paul Abbott (Pos: RHP, Age: 37)

	W	L	Pct.	ERA	G	GS	Sv	IP	H	BB	SO	HR	Avg
'04	3	11	.214	6.47	20	19	0	96.0	106	58	46	22	.274
Car.	43	37	.538	4.92	162	112	0	720.2	682	393	496	101	.250

Abbott was equally as bad as he split time between the Devil Rays and Phillies last year. His 2.06 HR/9, 5.44 BB/9, and .79 K/BB ratio make it hard to believe he even won three games. His 2002 shoulder surgery seriously derailed his career. He was released in September. 2005 Outlook: D

Lou Collier (Pos: LF, Age: 31, Bats: R)

	G	AB	R	H	D	T	HR	RBI	SB	BB	SO	Avg	OBP	Slg
'04	32	36	7	10	1	0	1	4	1	5	10	.278	.381	.389
Car.	315	713	89	172	33	7	8	78	12	75	160	.241	.317	.341

If anyone is the Rodney Dangerfield of minor leaguers, it is Lou Collier. A Triple-A All-Star the past two seasons in the International League, Collier's success has only translated into a total of 37 major league at-bats. His .326/.383/.517 line in Scranton/Wilkes-Barre says it all. 2005 Outlook: C

Jim Crowell (Pos: LHP, Age: 30)

	W	L	Pct.	ERA	G	GS	Sv	IP	H	BB	SO	HR	Avg
'04	0	0	-	3.00	4	0	0	3.0	6	0	1	0	.333
Car.	0	1	.000	7.71	6	1	0	9.1	18	5	4	2	.383

It might have taken him nearly seven years, but Crowell finally made it back to the big leagues in 2004. In the process, he put together a solid Triple-A season, winning seven and saving 16, with a 2.40 ERA. Florida rewarded Crowell for his perseverance with an offseason contract. 2005 Outlook: C

Geoff Geary (Pos: RHP, Age: 28)

	W	L	Pct.	ERA	G	GS	Sv	IP	H	BB	SO	HR	Avg
'04	1	0	1.000	5.44	33	0	0	44.2	52	16	30	8	.292
Car.	1	0	1.000	5.33	38	0	0	50.2	60	19	33	8	.297

Geary struggled mightily at newly-opened Citizens Bank Park in his first extended stay in Philadelphia. His 6.66 home ERA paled in comparison to the staunch 3.79 mark he set on the road. He picked up his lone victory in August, against the Brewers. 2005 Outlook: B

Doug Glanville (Pos: CF/LF, Age: 34, Bats: R)

	G	AB	R	H	D	T	HR	RBI	SB	BB	SO	Avg	OBP	Slg
'04	87	162	21	34	1	1	2	14	8	8	21	.210	.244	.265
Car.	1115	3964	553	1100	166	32	59	333	168	208	502	.277	.315	.380

Glanville's return to Philadelphia did not go as planned, hitting a sparse .191/.217/.261 versus righthanders in 87 games as a fourth outfielder. It was the worst season in Glanville's nine-year career, as he posted numbers far below his .280/.318/.385 career level. 2005 Outlook: C

Roberto Hernandez (Pos: RHP, Age: 40)

	W	L	Pct.	ERA	G	GS	Sv	IP	H	BB	SO	HR	Avg
'04	3	5	.375	4.76	63	0	0	56.2	66	29	44	9	.297
Car.	56	59	.487	3.39	825	3	320	891.2	825	377	805	81	.245

The 40-year-old Hernandez has made a nice career for himself since his callup at age 26. The two seven-year spans, however, have been quite different. From 1991-97, he dominated with 9.18 K/9 and a 2.84 ERA. This has been replaced by 7.12 K/9 and a 3.92 ERA from 1998-04. 2005 Outlook: C

A.J. Hinch (Pos: C, Age: 30, Bats: R)

	G	AB	R	H	D	T	HR	RBI	SB	BB	SO	Avg	OBP	Slg
'04	4	11	1	2	1	0	0	0	0	0	4	.182	.182	.273
Car.	350	953	104	209	28	3	32	112	13	71	214	.219	.280	.356

Hinch spent most of 2004 at Triple-A Scranton/Wilkes-Barre after spending 2003 in the Detroit organization. He was declared a free agent in October, but re-signed with the Phillies a month later. If Todd Pratt does not return, Hinch could compete for the backup catching job. 2005 Outlook: C

Tomas Perez (Pos: 3B/2B, Age: 31, Bats: B)

	G	AB	R	H	D	T	HR	RBI	SB	BB	SO	Avg	OBP	Slg
'04	86	176	22	38	13	2	6	21	0	9	44	.216	.257	.415
Car.	588	1486	157	365	77	13	22	142	4	115	268	.246	.301	.359

Perez will be in Philadelphia through at least 2006 after agreeing on a two-year extension during the offseason. The switch-hitter is a good guy to have around over the course of a long season because of his versatility. He made starts at every infield position last season. 2005 Outlook: B

Brian Powell (Pos: RHP, Age: 31)

	W	L	Pct.	ERA	G	GS	Sv	IP	H	BB	SO	HR	Avg
'04	1	2	.333	5.03	17	2	0	39.1	39	16	24	5	.275
Car.	7	18	.280	5.94	59	34	0	219.2	251	90	120	45	.288

Lefthanded hitters pounded Powell all over the park in 2004. The .323/.410/.548 they hit off him was a byproduct of his inability to routinely locate his pitches, especially the changeup. Powell needs to refine his command if he hopes to find any lasting success. 2005 Outlook: C

Todd Pratt (Pos: C, Age: 38, Bats: R)

	G	AB	R	H	D	T	HR	RBI	SB	BB	SO	Avg	OBP	Slg
'04	45	128	16	33	5	0	3	16	0	18	38	.258	.351	.367
Car.	540	1302	163	332	74	3	38	182	5	177	361	.255	.352	.404

The day/night platoon arrangement between Pratt and starting catcher Mike Lieberthal worked once again this past season. Pratt hit .283/.363/.394 in day games while batting just .172/.314/.276 in 29 night at-bats. Pratt re-signed with the Phillies in early December. 2005 Outlook: B

Amaury Telemaco (Pos: RHP, Age: 31)

	W	L	Pct.	ERA	G	GS	Sv	IP	H	BB	SO	HR	Avg
'04	0	2	.000	4.31	42	0	0	54.1	51	19	32	12	.249
Car.	23	34	.404	4.96	212	64	0	550.1	567	190	356	90	.267

Telemaco overcame pre All-Star break right rotator cuff tendinitis to have a respectable second half. One must question, however, the quality of his stuff in a season which saw him give up home runs at a higher rate than Eric Milton. 2005 Outlook: B

Shawn Wooten (Pos: 1B, Age: 32, Bats: R)

	G	AB	R	H	D	T	HR	RBI	SB	BB	SO	Avg	OBP	Slg
'04	33	53	2	9	3	0	0	2	0	2	9	.170	.228	.226
Car.	266	668	66	182	28	1	18	86	4	37	120	.272	.314	.398

Wooten dropped some weight before the 2004 season at the urging of coaches, but he still played sparingly for the big club. A notoriously good pinch hitter, he hit only .118 in that capacity. This was a significant decline from the .359 mark he had compiled going into the year. 2005 Outlook: C

Philadelphia Phillies Minor League Prospects

Organization Overview:

The Phillies have sacrificed high draft picks as compensation for marquee free agents in recent years, most notably in 2003 when they gave up both their first- and second-round picks for signing Jim Thome and David Bell. And a steady stream of prospects just below the untouchable level (Johnny Estrada, Taylor Buchholz, Ezequiel Astacio, Anderson Machado, Alredo Simon, Elizardo Ramirez and Javon Moran to name just a few) have left in the last two years as Philadelphia pursued short-term moves in a futile attempt to win now. As a result, the farm system is thin at both the Double-A and Triple-A levels, especially in the areas of catching and middle infield. The strength of the Philadelphia system is now concentrated from high Class-A Clearwater down.

Michael Bourn

Position: OF **Opening Day Age:** 22
Bats: L **Throws:** R **Born:** 12/27/82 in
Ht: 5' 11" **Wt:** 180 Houston, TX

Recent Statistics

	G	AB	R	H	D	T	HR	RBI	SB	BB	SO	Avg
2003 A Batavia	35	125	12	35	0	1	0	4	23	23	28	.280
2004 A Lakewood	109	413	92	131	20	14	5	53	57	85	88	.317

The Phillies' fourth-round pick out of the University of Houston in 2003, Bourn projects as a Juan Pierre-type leadoff hitter. For a young player, Bourn shows exceptional plate discipline and is willing to take a walk. He not only has the instinct to run, but also the desire to steal bases. He's a good contact hitter who can hit an occasional home run, but he should be more of a doubles and triples guy. Defensively, he could play in the big leagues right now. While he has an average arm, he possesses above-average range. He probably will start the season at high Class-A Clearwater, but it wouldn't be a surprise to see him at Double-A Reading by the end of the summer.

Carlos Carrasco

Position: P **Opening Day Age:** 18
Bats: R **Throws:** R **Born:** 3/21/87 in
Ht: 6' 3" **Wt:** 180 Barquismento, VZ

Recent Statistics

	W	L	ERA	G	GS	Sv	IP	H	R	BB	SO	HR
2004 R GC Phillies	5	4	3.56	11	8	0	48.0	53	23	15	34	2

The first time Sal Artiaga, who directs the Phillies' Latin American scouting, saw Carrasco throw in Venezuela, he was impressed enough to want his bosses to take a look. At the second tryout, assistant GM Mike Arbuckle authorized an offer on the spot reported to be at least $300,000. For that, the Phillies got a high-ceiling pitcher whose fastball touched 93 MPH. Even though he was just 17 years old, Carrasco showed superior mound presence. He has solid mechanics and a good feel for pitching, and also demonstrates an aptitude for a power curve and a changeup. While his age and inexperience dictate that he won't start the season any higher than Class-A Lakewood, Carrasco has the physical tools to rise quickly through the system.

Gavin Floyd

Position: P **Opening Day Age:** 22
Bats: R **Throws:** R **Born:** 1/27/83 in
Ht: 6' 4" **Wt:** 212 Annapolis, MD

Recent Statistics

	W	L	ERA	G	GS	Sv	IP	H	R	BB	SO	HR
2004 AA Reading	6	6	2.57	20	20	0	119.0	93	39	46	94	5
2004 AAA Scran-WB	1	3	4.99	5	5	0	30.2	39	20	9	18	4
2004 NL Philadelphia	2	0	3.49	6	4	0	28.1	25	11	16	24	1

By the time Floyd got to the big leagues last September, his velocity was down after a long season that began at Double-A Reading. At that point, he was living with his curve. The breaking ball opened eyes but, at his best, he also throws a four-seam fastball that rests comfortably at 92 MPH and occasionally hits 95 MPH. By the end of the season, Floyd was throwing 88-89 MPH and using a lot of two-seamers to get extra movement. He also throws a solid changeup. The Phillies would like to see him develop a little better command of his fastball within the strike zone. Since injuries forced a premature big league debut last season, he could open 2005 at Triple-A to get more seasoning.

Greg Golson

Position: OF **Opening Day Age:** 19
Bats: R **Throws:** R **Born:** 9/17/85 in Austin,
Ht: 6' 0" **Wt:** 190 TX

Recent Statistics

	G	AB	R	H	D	T	HR	RBI	SB	BB	SO	Avg
2004 R GC Phillies	47	183	34	54	8	5	1	22	12	10	54	.295

Golson's favorite player is Torii Hunter, and the Phillies don't see any reason he can't become the same sort of player as the Twins' All-Star center fielder. Touted as a five-tool player, Golson was named to the *USA Today* All-USA team after batting .519 as a senior at Connally High School in Austin, Texas. The Phillies made him their No. 1 draft choice in 2004. His speed—he ran a 6.3 60—currently is his most notable skill, but he could grow into the kind of hitter who can bat at the top of the order or in the middle, as a run-producer. Golson also concentrates on his defense. He has great range, gets a good jump on the ball and loves throwing runners out.

Cole Hamels

Position: P
Opening Day Age: 21
Bats: L **Throws:** L
Born: 12/27/83 in San
Ht: 6' 3" **Wt:** 175
Diego, CA

Recent Statistics

	W	L	ERA	G	GS	Sv	IP	H	R	BB	SO	HR
2003 A Lakewood	6	1	0.84	13	13	0	74.2	32	8	25	115	0
2000 A Clearwater	0	2	2.70	5	5	0	20.1	23	9	14	32	0
2004 A Clearwater	1	0	1.13	4	4	0	16.0	10	2	4	24	0

Hamels, the Phillies' No. 1 draft choice in 2002, remains an untouchable prospect despite being slowed last season by elbow problems. He pulled a triceps muscle in spring training and then aggravated the injury rushing to get back. Despite rumors, there was no structural damage, and he's expected to be fully recovered. When healthy, Hamels has plus command of his 92-MPH fastball and curve, and also shows a quality changeup despite the fact that he was pitching in high school just three years ago. He could make up for lost time by starting the 2005 season at Double-A Reading, and has a chance to rise quickly after that.

Ryan Howard

Position: 1B
Opening Day Age: 25
Bats: L **Throws:** L
Born: 11/19/79 in
Ht: 6' 4" **Wt:** 230
St. Louis, MO

Recent Statistics

	G	AB	R	H	D	T	HR	RBI	SB	BB	SO	Avg
2004 AA Reading	102	374	73	111	18	1	37	102	1	46	129	.297
2004 AAA Scran-WB	29	111	21	30	10	0	9	29	0	14	37	.270
2004 NL Philadelphia	19	39	5	11	5	0	2	5	0	2	13	.282

Howard led all hitters in organized baseball in 2004 with 48 home runs between Double-A, Triple-A and a late-season cameo appearance in the big leagues. In so doing, he won the Paul Owens Award as the top position player in the system for the second straight year. Howard showed the ability to make adjustments at every level, a trend that projects him as a middle-of-the-order big league hitter once he learns to handle off-speed pitches a little better. He also is a solid defensive player. Because Howard's path to the parent club is blocked by Jim Thome, the Phillies have experimented with him in the outfield, but it remains likely that his future could be with another organization.

Scott Mathieson

Position: P
Opening Day Age: 21
Bats: R **Throws:** R
Born: 2/27/84 in
Ht: 6' 3" **Wt:** 190
Vancouver, British Columbia

Recent Statistics

	W	L	ERA	G	GS	Sv	IP	H	R	BB	SO	HR
2003 A Batavia	0	0	0.00	2	0	1	6.0	0	0	0	7	0
2003 R GC Phillies	2	7	5.52	11	11	0	58.2	59	42	13	51	5
2004 A Lakewood	8	9	4.32	25	25	0	131.1	130	73	50	112	7

If one diagramed the prototypical physique for a pitch-er, it would look a lot like Mathieson's lean build and long arms. His fastball occasionally hits 95-96 MPH, though it more typically settles in the 92-93 MPH range. He also has developed a pretty good changeup. He needs to work on his breaking ball, but the biggest thing holding him back at this point of his career is consistency. His command has a tendency to come and go from night to night, or even from inning to inning. His future role is yet to be determined. While Mathieson could end up as a power pitcher in the middle of the rotation, the Phillies haven't ruled out the possibility of trying to convert him into a closer someday.

Scott Mitchinson

Position: P
Opening Day Age: 20
Bats: R **Throws:** R
Born: 12/28/84 in Perth,
Ht: 6' 3" **Wt:** 185
Australia

Recent Statistics

	W	L	ERA	G	GS	Sv	IP	H	R	BB	SO	HR
2004 R GC Phillies	7	0	1.75	10	10	0	61.2	40	12	1	60	2

When Mitchinson was signed as an amateur free agent out of Australia in March 2003, his fastball was clocked at only 85 MPH. After one year in the Australian Summer League, he showed up at Rookie ball last season hitting 90 MPH consistently and tipping 92 MPH. The fastball is his strength, but he's also developed a good curve and has a feel for the changeup. His stuff is average, but his exceptional command projects him as a middle-of-the-rotation starter in the big leagues. His challenge now is to develop greater consistency with his secondary pitches. The Phillies expect him to get stronger as he matures, which could add even a few more ticks to his fastball.

Others to Watch

Righthander **Maximino Delacruz** (19) has a loose, spidery body that reminds scouts of Pascual Perez. His fastball hits 93 MPH, he spins his curve well and is developing a changeup. He's expected to improve as he matures physically; the basics are already there. . . Lefthander **J.A. Happ** (22) was the third-round draft pick last June out of Northwestern. Like Randy Wolf, his stuff doesn't grade out particularly well. All he does is get hitters out. His fastball sits at 88-90 MPH, but with his funky delivery, hitters tend to swing like it's 94. He also has a decent slider and changeup. . . Catcher **Jason Jaramillo** (22) is the most advanced of the Phillies' catching prospects after being selected out of Oklahoma State in the second round of the 2004 draft. He's a pretty good contact hitter with occasional power He throws well and has a good feel for calling a game. . . Catcher **Louis Marson** (18) isn't as far along as Jaramillo after being drafted out of Coronada High School in Scottsdale, Ariz. in the fourth round last year. However, Marson has plus power and a plus arm. He has a quick release and is considered to have a great makeup.

PNC Park

Offense

PNC Park has proven to be a fairly neutral park where runs are scored at a pace slightly above the league average but where home runs are harder to come by. Lefthanded batters fare better with the short 320-foot porch in right field and reachable gap in right-center. Righthanded batters, conversely, see many flyballs die in the spacious left-center gap that juts out to 410. Dead righthanded pull hitters, though, can take aim at the 325-mark down the left-field line. Because of wind patterns, the ball often seems to oddly carry better in cold weather than when it is warm.

Defense

Unlike most ballparks, it is advantageous to play a good defensive outfielder with a strong arm in left field than right at PNC Park. The alley is deep in left-center and the caroms are trickier in left with various angles along the fence. The infield surface has improved greatly since the park opened in 2001 but will still yield the occasional bad hop.

Who It Helps the Most

Lefthanded pitchers enjoy PNC Park. The three lefties who started games for the Pirates last season all had considerably better ERAs at home: Sean Burnett (3.79-6.61), Oliver Perez (2.21-3.98) and Dave Williams (3.08-7.30). Though a righthanded hitter, rookie Jason Bay took advantage of the spacious left-center gap to hit .303 at home.

Who It Hurts the Most

Free-agent bust Chris Stynes had a particularly tough time at home last season before being released, hitting .197. Ryan Vogelsong, trying to establish himself in the starting rotation, also pressed in front of the home crowd and posted a 7.77 ERA.

Rookies & Newcomers

Lefty Mark Redman may like PNC Park, while the two young pitchers on the verge of reaching the majors are righthanders, Bobby Bradley and Ian Snell. The Pirates' upper-level hitting prospects—Jose Bautista, J.R. House and Freddy Sanchez—won't gain a home-field advantage when they arrive because they bat righthanded.

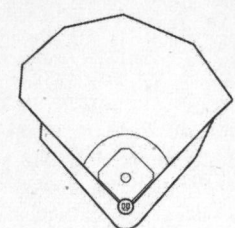

Dimensions: LF-325, LCF-389, CF-399, RCF-375, RF-320

Capacity: 38,496

Elevation: 730 feet

Surface: Grass

Foul Territory: Small

Park Factors

2004 Season

	Home Games Pirates	Opp	Total	Away Games Pirates	Opp	Total	Index
G	74	74	148	71	71	142	
Avg	.265	.263	.264	.261	.267	.264	100
AB	2474	2551	5025	2476	2348	4824	100
R	309	323	632	306	333	639	95
H	655	670	1325	646	627	1273	100
2B	125	148	273	125	118	243	108
3B	20	12	32	17	20	37	83
HR	67	56	123	56	79	135	87
BB	185	258	443	199	264	463	92
SO	459	489	948	509	480	989	92
E	41	46	87	51	39	90	93
E-Infield	31	36	67	42	31	73	88
LHB-Avg	.254	.291	.273	.249	.270	.259	105
LHB-HR	21	23	44	20	22	42	102
RHB-Avg	.271	.246	.258	.268	.265	.267	97
RHB-HR	46	33	79	36	57	93	81

2002-2004

	Home Games Pirates	Opp	Total	Away Games Pirates	Opp	Total	Index
G	223	223	446	221	221	442	
Avg	.265	.268	.266	.251	.266	.258	103
AB	7373	7782	15155	7614	7260	14874	101
R	968	1042	2010	935	1010	1945	102
H	1952	2085	4037	1912	1929	3841	104
2B	382	432	814	357	382	739	108
3B	43	38	81	54	44	98	81
HR	198	210	408	210	236	446	90
BB	685	736	1421	690	776	1466	95
SO	1352	1370	2722	1636	1329	2965	90
E	166	139	305	149	131	280	108
E-Infield	141	117	258	126	113	239	107
LHB-Avg	.273	.288	.281	.259	.272	.266	106
LHB-HR	80	78	158	80	88	168	93
RHB-Avg	.260	.255	.258	.247	.262	.254	102
RHB-HR	118	132	250	130	148	278	88

2004 Rankings (National League)

- Second-highest LHB batting-average factor
- Third-lowest walk factor
- Third-lowest strikeout factor

Lloyd McClendon

2004 Season

After many years of talking about it, the Pirates finally went to a youth movement as they opened the season with seven rookies on the roster and finished with 13. The Pirates' win total dropped from 75 to 72, but that was to be expected with such a young club. Knowing they were giving him a young roster, the Pirates exercised McClendon's option for 2005 on Opening Day and added a club option for 2006. McClendon's teams consistently play hard and take on his intense personality.

Offense

McClendon's teams have usually lacked power, so he tries to push things with steals, bunts and hit-and-run plays. He uses plenty of pinch-hitters and usually plays the platoon percentages. The Pirates have never stressed on-base percentage, but one of McClendon's best moves last season was to drop leadoff hitter Tike Redman, who rarely walks, to sixth in the batting order and move Jason Kendall, who always has high OBPs, to the No. 1 spot.

Pitching & Defense

McClendon has given his starting pitchers a little more leeway as they have gotten older but, for the most part, is cautious with pitch counts and cognizant of protecting young arms. He prefers a bullpen with set roles. That was the case last season and relief pitching was one of the Pirates' strengths as closer Jose Mesa had a big comeback year. McClendon tries to exploit platoon matchups and won't hesitate to make multiple pitching changes in an inning. He is a big proponent of pitching out to slow down the running game and intentional walks to set up the double play.

2005 Outlook

The Pirates have finally found the players they want to build around, but they're still not close to contending. Management understands what McClendon is up against as the skipper of a small-market team. His contract expires at the end of this season, but the Pirates hold an option for 2006 and will likely exercise it.

Born: 1/11/59 in Gary, IN

Playing Experience: 1987 1994, Cin, ChC, Pit

Managerial Experience: 4 seasons

Manager Statistics

Year	Team, Lg	W	L	Pct	GB	Finish
2004	Pittsburgh, NL	72	89	.447	32.5	5th Central
4 Seasons		281	365	.435	–	–

2004 Starting Pitchers by Days Rest

	<=3	4	5	6+
Pirates Starts	1	66	54	29
Pirates ERA	3.60	4.08	5.39	4.42
NL Avg Starts	2	82	46	23
NL ERA	4.58	4.35	4.28	4.73

2004 Situational Stats

	Lloyd McClendon	NL Average
Hit & Run Success %	32.7	38.0
Stolen Base Success %	61.2	71.7
Platoon Pct.	49.0	55.2
Defensive Subs	27	18
High-Pitch Outings	4	6
Quick/Slow Hooks	20/15	21/12
Sacrifice Attempts	102	99

2004 Rankings (National League)

- 2nd in hit-and-run attempts (98), pitchouts (64) and defensive substitutions
- 3rd in 2+ pitching changes in low-scoring games (38)

Jason Bay

2004 Season

Acquired from San Diego in the Brian Giles deal in August of 2003, Jason Bay did not make his 2004 major league debut until May 7. Bay, who had undergone arthroscopic surgery to repair torn cartilage in his right shoulder the previous November, quickly settled in as the starting left fielder. He set a club rookie record with 26 home runs and led all big league rookies in home runs, RBI (82) and slugging percentage (.550). In November, Bay was selected as the National League Rookie of the Year, becoming the first Pirate ever to win that honor.

Hitting

Bay showed somewhat surprising power in his rookie season, pulling balls to left field with good loft in his swing. He also used the gaps well, especially the spacious left-center one at PNC Park. Bay can handle the best fastballs and sliders, though he can be made to chase slow stuff out of the strike zone. He showed good plate discipline in the minor leagues but has not displayed that skill so far in the majors.

Baserunning & Defense

Bay has above-average speed, though he was often tentative in his rookie season. He struggled reading major league pitchers' pickoff moves after being a basestealing threat in the minor leagues, and also often hesitated in taking an extra base. Bay covers the big left-center gap with ease at PNC Park and has enough range to play center field, which some scouts feel is his best position. He was still regaining arm strength last season while recovering from surgery, but his throwing improved to average as the season went on.

2005 Outlook

Bay has established himself as a key building block for the Pirates and will again patrol left field and bat in the middle of the batting order. Bay proved to be an even better player than expected when the Pirates acquired him from San Diego.

Position: LF
Bats: R **Throws:** R
Ht: 6' 2" **Wt:** 200

Opening Day Age: 26
Born: 9/20/78 in Trail, BC, Canada
ML Seasons: 2

Overall Statistics

	G	AB	R	H	D	T	HR	RBI	SB	BB	SO	Avg	OBP	Slg
'04	120	411	61	116	24	4	26	82	4	41	129	.282	.358	.550
Car.	150	498	76	141	31	5	30	96	7	60	158	.283	.369	.546

Where He Hits the Ball

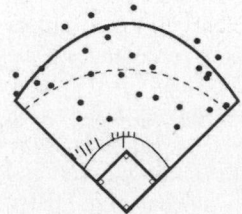
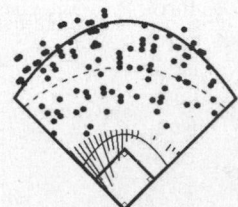

Vs. LHP   **Vs. RHP**

2004 Situational Stats

	AB	H	HR	RBI	Avg		AB	H	HR	RBI	Avg
Home	231	70	15	46	.303	LHP	83	22	7	17	.265
Road	180	46	11	36	.256	RHP	328	94	19	65	.287
First Half	148	45	12	39	.304	Sc Pos	111	36	9	61	.324
Scnd Half	263	71	14	43	.270	Clutch	58	14	4	7	.241

2004 Rankings (National League)

- 1st in home runs among rookies and RBI among rookies
- 2nd in fielding percentage in left field (.991)
- 3rd in highest percentage of swings that missed (31.7)
- 5th in batting average among rookies
- Led the Pirates in RBI, slugging percentage and HR frequency (15.8 ABs per HR)

Josh Fogg

2004 Season

In 2004, Josh Fogg became the first Pirates pitcher to win at least 10 games in three consecutive seasons since Jason Schmidt from 1997-99, despite having the 10th-highest ERA in the National League. Fogg salvaged his season with a good second half, going 5-3 with a 3.32 ERA in 15 starts after the All-Star break and winning four of his last five decisions.

Pitching

Fogg's stuff is nondescript, and he needs to have pinpoint control to be successful. His fastball rarely tops 90 MPH and sits in the 86-88 MPH range. Fogg's curveball is his best pitch, but he goes through spells where he has problems throwing it for strikes. He uses his slider primarily against lefthanded hitters, and his changeup is inconsistent. Fogg doesn't last deep into games and usually begins to lose his effectiveness in the fifth or sixth inning, leading some scouts to feel his best long-range role would be in middle relief. Fogg is an outstanding competitor, though, and will battle hitters despite his subpar arsenal. He also did a better job of keeping the ball in the park last season, giving up 17 homers after allowing 22 in 2003 and 28 in 2002.

Defense & Hitting

Fogg does a decent job of holding runners and will throw often to first base to keep them close. He is good defensively, particularly adept at stabbing balls up the middle and charging bunts. Fogg isn't very dangerous with the bat but is a good bunter.

2005 Outlook

This is a pivotal season for Fogg, as he will be in his second year of arbitration eligibility, which will make him an expensive player for a small-market club like the Pirates to retain. He gets his fair share of wins as a starter, primarily because he receives good run support. Yet, Fogg will need to step up his game to stay with the Pirates beyond 2005 and remain a long-term fixture in the rotation.

Position: SP
Bats: R **Throws:** R
Ht: 6' 0" **Wt:** 203

Opening Day Age: 28
Born: 12/13/76 in Lynn, MA
ML Seasons: 4

Overall Statistics

	W	L	Pct.	ERA	G	GS	Sv	IP	H	BB	SO	HR	Avg
'04	11	10	.524	4.64	32	32	0	178.1	193	66	82	17	.283
Car.	33	31	.516	4.64	102	91	0	528.0	568	178	283	67	.278

2004 Pitching Profile

	Josh Fogg	NL Average
Overall Strike %	61.3	62.5
1st Pitch Strike %	58.3	58.5
Ratio	1.45	1.39
Strikeouts per 9 IP	4.14	6.74
Walks per 9 IP	3.33	3.38
Home Runs per 9 IP	0.86	1.11
Strikeout/Walk Ratio	1.24	1.99
Groundball/Flyball Ratio	1.35	1.25

2004 Situational Stats

	W	L	ERA	Sv	IP		AB	H	HR	RBI	Avg
Home	7	2	4.48	0	86.1	LHB	326	92	8	34	.282
Road	4	8	4.79	0	92.0	RHB	355	101	9	51	.285
First Half	6	7	5.97	0	89.0	Sc Pos	178	47	3	63	.264
Scnd Half	5	3	3.32	0	89.1	Clutch	24	8	1	2	.333

2004 Rankings (National League)

- 2nd in GDPs induced (27)
- 3rd in fewest strikeouts per nine innings (4.1)
- 5th in lowest strikeout-walk ratio (1.2)
- 7th in highest batting average allowed (.283), highest on-base percentage allowed (.351) and highest ERA at home
- 9th in least run support per nine innings (4.3)
- 10th in highest ERA
- Led the Pirates in sacrifice bunts (11), games started, hits allowed, pickoff throws (94), stolen bases allowed (12), GDPs induced (27) and fewest pitches thrown per batter (3.63)

Jason Kendall

2004 Season

Jason Kendall again was one of the better catchers in the game as he hit .300 for the sixth time in his nine major league seasons. He led all big league catchers with 147 games, 86 runs scored and 183 hits. He was second with a .399 on-base percentage behind the Yankees' Jorge Posada. Kendall also moved up to 16th on the Pirates' career hit list with 1,409.

Hitting

Kendall hits from an open stance and sprays line drives and hard grounders from foul line to foul line. He used to have decent power, but lost some of it after undergoing reconstructive left thumb surgery following the 2001 season. Kendall won't hit many balls out of the park, but he can find the gaps for doubles. The Pirates used to think he would develop into an RBI guy but that hasn't happened. However, Kendall is a fine leadoff hitter because he will work the count, take a walk and make consistent contact. He can handle all types of pitching, but is particularly strong against offspeed pitches and in clutch situations.

Baserunning & Defense

Kendall once had excellent speed, but a dislocated right ankle suffered in 1999 has slowed him down. He still moves well for a catcher and looks to take the extra base whenever he can. Kendall will also steal an occasional base, though he has become more susceptible to being thrown out as he's gotten older. He had the best defensive season of his career in 2004 after extensive work with Pirates coach John Russell. Kendall threw better than at any point in his career and also improved his pitch blocking and calling.

2005 Outlook

Kendall has three years and $34 million left on his six-year, $60 million contract, and the cost-conscious Pirates found a way to shed his salary. In late November, Kendall was dealt to Oakland for lefthanders Mark Redman and Arthur Rhodes. With his impressive OBP, Kendall will bat near the top of the Oakland order and will continue to be one of the top hitting catchers in the major leagues. His improved defense is a bonus.

Position: C
Bats: R **Throws:** R
Ht: 6' 0" **Wt:** 195

Opening Day Age: 30
Born: 6/26/74 in San Diego, CA
ML Seasons: 9

Overall Statistics

	G	AB	R	H	D	T	HR	RBI	SB	BB	SO	Avg	OBP	Slg
'04	147	574	86	183	32	0	3	51	11	60	41	.319	.399	.390
Car.	1252	4606	706	1409	256	29	67	471	140	454	403	.306	.387	.418

Where He Hits the Ball

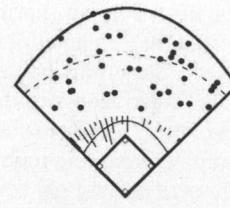
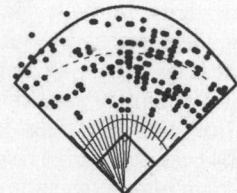

Vs. LHP   **Vs. RHP**

2004 Situational Stats

	AB	H	HR	RBI	Avg		AB	H	HR	RBI	Avg
Home	277	89	2	21	.321	LHP	103	30	0	5	.291
Road	297	94	1	30	.316	RHP	471	153	3	46	.325
First Half	313	95	2	31	.304	Sc Pos	107	37	1	47	.346
Scnd Half	261	88	1	20	.337	Clutch	94	24	2	14	.255

2004 Rankings (National League)

- 1st in on-base percentage for a leadoff hitter (.404), lowest percentage of swings on the first pitch (2.7), errors at catcher (10) and highest percentage of runners caught stealing as a catcher (32.3)
- 2nd in singles
- 3rd in hit by pitch (19) and lowest percentage of swings that missed (8.1)
- Led the Pirates in batting average, caught stealing (8), walks, times on base (262), pitches seen (2,773), most pitches seen per plate appearance (4.21), highest percentage of pitches taken (64.7), batting average with runners in scoring position, and batting average with two strikes (.266)
- Led NL catchers in batting average

Rob Mackowiak

2004 Season

Rob Mackowiak saw the most action of his four-year career and set career highs with 155 games, 17 home runs and 75 RBI. He also proved versatile by making 51 starts at third base, 40 in right field, 16 in left field and 15 in center field. Mackowiak saw most of his action at third base early in the season when veteran Chris Stynes struggled, then played primarily in the outfield after the Pirates acquired third baseman Ty Wigginton from the New York Mets in a July 30 trade.

Hitting

Mackowiak produces good power with a compact swing and is particularly adept at pulling pitches. He crushes low fastballs, especially from righthanders. Mackowiak is overly aggressive and often gets himself out on breaking balls and heaters out of the strike zone when he falls behind in the count. He likes to hit in big situations and has a tendency to show more patience and put the ball in play when the game is on the line.

Baserunning & Defense

Mackowiak has very good speed and uses it wisely. He is a high-percentage basestealer and adept at going from first to third and second to home on base hits. Mackowiak is an adequate third baseman with good reflexes and a very strong arm but only ordinary range. He is a better defender in the outfield with the speed to play center, though he is smoother playing on one of the corners.

2005 Outlook

Mackowiak, a former 53rd-round draft pick, got a chance to play regularly for the first time last season and was exposed as the season wore on. He hit just .165 in his last 48 games and only .164 against lefthanded pitchers. He is better suited to a super-utility role with his ability to play every position on the field but pitcher and shortstop. That will be his role this season, playing almost exclusively against righthanders.

Position: RF/3B/LF/CF
Bats: L **Throws:** R
Ht: 5'10" **Wt:** 195

Opening Day Age: 28
Born: 6/20/76 in Oak Lawn, IL
ML Seasons: 4
Pronunciation: mah-KOH-vee-ak

Pittsburgh

Overall Statistics

	G	AB	R	H	D	T	HR	RBI	SB	BB	SO	Avg	OBP	Slg
'04	155	491	65	121	22	6	17	75	13	50	114	.246	.319	.420
Car.	451	1264	172	319	63	12	43	163	32	122	339	.252	.325	.423

Where He Hits the Ball

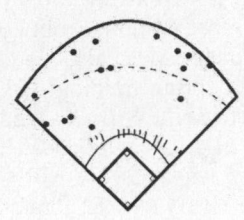
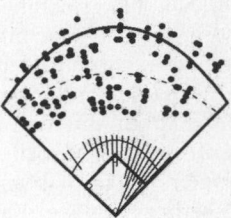

Vs. LHP   **Vs. RHP**

2004 Situational Stats

	AB	H	HR	RBI	Avg		AB	H	HR	RBI	Avg
Home	234	60	11	41	.256	LHP	61	10	0	5	.164
Road	257	61	6	34	.237	RHP	430	111	17	70	.258
First Half	277	73	12	43	.264	Sc Pos	122	34	6	57	.279
Scnd Half	214	48	5	32	.224	Clutch	82	23	3	18	.280

2004 Rankings (National League)

- 2nd in fewest GDPs per GDP situation (2.9%)
- 8th in lowest batting average and lowest batting average with two strikes (.142)
- 10th in lowest batting average on the road
- Led the Pirates in sacrifice flies (7), stolen-base percentage (76.5) and fewest GDPs per GDP situation (2.9%)

Jose Mesa

2004 Season

Jose Mesa proved to be one of the best free-agent bargains of the 2004 season. Signed by the Pirates to a minor league contract, he earned just $1.265 million, including performance bonuses, while finishing fifth in the National League with 43 saves. Mesa converted his first 18 save opportunities, setting a club record for one season, and became the sixth major leaguer with at least four 40-save seasons.

Pitching

Mesa began using all of his pitches again last season after relying almost entirely on his fastball during his dreadful 2003 season with Philadelphia. He relied on his split-finger pitch more and also gave hitters more to think about by mixing in curveballs and sliders. Mesa also made a mechanical adjustment in spring training with the help of pitching coach Spin Williams and improved his velocity to as high as 97 MPH, though his fastball usually sat at 93-94 MPH. Mesa has a tendency to tire easily and the Pirates were careful with him, allowing him to pitch more than one inning just twice in 2004.

Defense & Hitting

Mesa used to be easy to run on as he rarely paid attention to runners as a closer and was slow to the plate. However, he quickened his delivery last season and basestealers had a much more difficult time with him. Mesa stays in outstanding shape and still moves well in the field, committing just one error over the past five seasons. He has batted just once in his long career and, for what it's worth, walked and scored.

2005 Outlook

Mesa converted his final 10 save opportunities last season but started showing signs of his age late in the year. However, the Pirates very much wanted to bring him back, and they signed him to a one-year, $2.5 million contract in November. Mesa wants to continue closing, and the Pirates are one of the few teams willing to entrust that role to him at an advanced age.

Position: RP
Bats: R **Throws:** R
Ht: 6' 3" **Wt:** 232

Opening Day Age: 38
Born: 5/22/66 in Azua, DR
ML Seasons: 16
Pronunciation: MAY-sa
Nickname: Joe Table

Overall Statistics

	W	L	Pct.	ERA	G	GS	Sv	IP	H	BB	SO	HR	Avg
'04	5	2	.714	3.25	70	0	43	69.1	78	20	37	6	.291
Car.	75	93	.446	4.27	832	95	292	1369.0	1442	564	933	126	.272

2004 Pitching Profile

	Jose Mesa	NL Average
Overall Strike %	63.8	62.5
1st Pitch Strike %	57.1	58.5
Ratio	1.41	1.39
Strikeouts per 9 IP	4.80	6.74
Walks per 9 IP	2.60	3.38
Home Runs per 9 IP	0.78	1.11
Strikeout/Walk Ratio	1.85	1.99
Groundball/Flyball Ratio	1.22	1.25

2004 Situational Stats

	W	L	ERA	Sv	IP			AB	H	HR	RBI	Avg
Home	3	2	2.20	24	41.0	LHB		127	42	4	11	.331
Road	2	0	4.76	19	28.1	RHB		141	36	2	15	.255
First Half	2	0	2.45	22	36.2	Sc Pos		77	16	1	19	.208
Scnd Half	3	2	4.13	21	32.2	Clutch		196	56	5	22	.286

2004 Rankings (National League)

- 2nd in games finished (65)
- 4th in fewest strikeouts per nine innings in relief (4.8)
- 5th in saves and save percentage (89.6)
- 6th in highest batting average allowed in relief (.291)
- Led the Pirates in saves, games finished (65) and save percentage (89.6)

Oliver Perez

Position: SP
Bats: L **Throws:** L
Ht: 6' 0" **Wt:** 190

Opening Day Age: 23
Born: 8/15/81 in
Culiacan, Mexico
ML Seasons: 3

2004 Season

In his first full season with the Pirates, Oliver Perez had one of the finest seasons of any pitcher in club history, though his win total was depressed because Pittsburgh was shut out in four of his 30 starts and held to three runs or less 14 times. His 239 strikeouts were the third-highest total ever by a Pirate, trailing Bob Veale's 276 in 1965 and 250 in 1964. Perez led all major league starting pitchers with 11.0 strikeouts per nine innings.

Pitching

Perez can often be dominating with his power arsenal. He can throw his fastball as high as 97 MPH, though it is usually sits in the 90-94 MPH range. Perez has two kinds of sliders, one with a sharp late break against righthanded hitters and another that sweeps and eats up lefties. His changeup is developing, but he is erratic with the pitch at this stage of his career. Perez is still prone to walking people, but his command improved dramatically last season after pitching coach Spin Williams completely overhauled his mechanics in spring training. Perez is fragile looking with thin legs but has good stamina and keeps his stuff deep into games.

Defense & Hitting

Perez has the natural advantage of slowing down the running game as a lefthander, and he has continually improved his ability to hold runners. He also has good reflexes in the field and is a sure-handed fielder. At bat Perez is not an automatic out and usually comes through with a bunt in sacrifice situations.

2005 Outlook

Perez showed flashes of brilliance last season, and the best is yet to come. He will go into this season as the ace of the Pirates' rotation, and it is only a matter of time and gaining more experience before he becomes one of the best pitchers in the major leagues. That time could come as early as this year.

Overall Statistics

	W	L	Pct.	ERA	G	GS	Sv	IP	H	BB	SO	HR	Avg
'04	12	10	.545	2.98	30	30	0	196.0	145	81	239	22	.207
Car.	20	25	.444	3.86	70	69	0	412.2	345	206	474	57	.227

2004 Pitching Profile

	Oliver Perez	NL Average
Overall Strike %	64.4	62.5
1st Pitch Strike %	58.4	58.5
Ratio	1.15	1.39
Strikeouts per 9 IP	10.97	6.74
Walks per 9 IP	3.72	3.38
Home Runs per 9 IP	1.01	1.11
Strikeout/Walk Ratio	2.95	1.99
Groundball/Flyball Ratio	0.74	1.25

2004 Situational Stats

	W	L	ERA	Sv	IP		AB	H	HR	RBI	Avg
Home	6	7	2.21	0	110.0	LHB	132	29	3	10	.220
Road	6	3	3.98	0	86.0	RHB	569	116	19	56	.204
First Half	5	4	3.24	0	97.1	Sc Pos	128	23	5	41	.180
Scnd Half	7	6	2.74	0	98.2	Clutch	40	3	0	0	.075

2004 Rankings (National League)

- 1st in lowest ERA at home, most strikeouts per nine innings (11.0) and fielding percentage at pitcher (1.000)
- 3rd in lowest batting average allowed (.207), lowest batting average allowed vs. righthanded batters, lowest batting average allowed with runners in scoring position and lowest groundball-flyball ratio allowed (0.7)
- 4th in strikeouts and lowest stolen-base percentage allowed (50.0)
- 6th in ERA
- Led the Pirates in ERA, wins, complete games (2), innings pitched, batters faced (805), home runs allowed, walks allowed, pitches thrown (3,135), winning percentage, highest strikeout-walk ratio (3.0), lowest slugging percentage allowed (.359), lowest on-base percentage allowed (.295), lowest ERA on the road, and most strikeouts per nine innings (11.0)

Tike Redman

2004 Season

In his first full season in the major leagues, Tike Redman spent the year as the Pirates' starting center fielder. However, he was dropped from the leadoff spot in mid-May and hit No. 6 in the batting order for most the remainder of the season. Redman relaxed after being moved down, hitting .312 in his last 99 games after batting .223 in his first 56.

Hitting

Redman's game is to primarily hit the ball on the ground and take advantage of his speed. However, he has started to develop power and will occasionally turn on a mistake pitch and hit it into the gap or over the fence. Redman is going to have to greatly improve his plate discipline to ever be a plus offensive player. He tends to hit better the deeper he works the count but too often his at-bats are over after one or two pitches. Redman could also help his cause by bunting on a more consistent basis. Pitchers with good breaking balls give him trouble.

Baserunning & Defense

Redman has outstanding speed and is a stolen base threat, though he doesn't run as much, especially when hitting lower in the batting order. However, he sometimes gets bad jumps and doesn't always show the best instincts on the bases. Redman is improving defensively and his speed tends to cover up his mistakes. A strengthening program helped his throwing last season, though his arm is still below average. Redman also doesn't consistently take good routes to flyballs and can be fooled by balls hit over his head.

2005 Outlook

Redman will begin the season as the starter in center field, and he could assume leadoff duties with Jason Kendall traded to Oakland. However, he needs to show improvement this year if he wants to stay in the lineup on a long-term basis. Redman's weaknesses are likely to prevent him from being a career regular, but his speed and ability to play center field would make him an ideal fourth outfielder.

Position: CF
Bats: L **Throws:** L
Ht: 5'11" **Wt:** 172

Opening Day Age: 28
Born: 3/10/77 in Tuscaloosa, AL
ML Seasons: 4

Overall Statistics

	G	AB	R	H	D	T	HR	RBI	SB	BB	SO	Avg	OBP	Slg
'04	155	546	65	153	19	4	8	51	18	23	52	.280	.310	.374
Car.	257	919	111	263	40	10	13	75	29	42	102	.286	.319	.394

Where He Hits the Ball

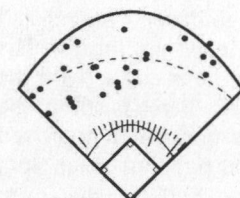 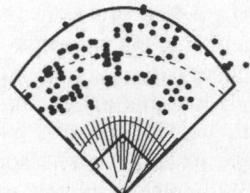

Vs. LHP   **Vs. RHP**

2004 Situational Stats

	AB	H	HR	RBI	Avg		AB	H	HR	RBI	Avg
Home	262	74	5	30	.282	LHP	109	29	1	13	.266
Road	284	79	3	21	.278	RHP	437	124	7	38	.284
First Half	287	72	4	32	.251	Sc Pos	136	36	1	42	.265
Scnd Half	259	81	4	19	.313	Clutch	85	21	4	12	.247

2004 Rankings (National League)

- 1st in lowest on-base percentage for a leadoff hitter (.250)
- 3rd in lowest fielding percentage in center field (.986)
- 4th in highest percentage of swings put into play (55.5) and errors in center field (5)
- 5th in highest groundball-flyball ratio (2.0) and fewest pitches seen per plate appearance (3.35)
- 7th in lowest on-base percentage
- 8th in lowest stolen-base percentage (75.0)
- Led the Pirates in stolen bases, bunts in play (19), highest percentage of swings put into play (55.5) and steals of third (2)

Daryle Ward

2004 Season

After struggling with the Dodgers in 2003, Daryle Ward started the season with the Pirates' Triple-A Nashville farm team. He was called up May 11 after Raul Mondesi jumped the club, and Ward hit .387 with seven homers in his first 19 games. He hit for the cycle on May 26 against the Cardinals, joining his father, Gary, as the first father and son combination to hit for the cycle in the big leagues. However, Ward was on the disabled list from June 26 to August 15 with a sprained right thumb, and batted just .202 in his last 60 games, with one homer in his final 25 contests.

Hitting

Ward's power potential has always been intriguing—he is the only player to hit a ball on the fly into the Allegheny River beyond the right-field stands at PNC Park—but has been short-circuited by his inability to lay off high fastballs and breaking balls outside the strike zone. He regained his stroke early last year, powering pitches low in the strike and always looking to pull the ball. He has had trouble with lefthanded pitchers but hung in better against them last season.

Baserunning & Defense

Ward has struggled to keep his weight down throughout his career, though he did lose 15 pounds at Nashville last season. The excess weight makes him a plodder on the basepaths. Ward's lack of agility also hurts him in the field. He has little range at first base and his footwork is subpar, though he shows decent hands. Ward is strictly a corner man in the outfield, where he gets to few balls and has a below-average arm.

2005 Outlook

Ward also battled a wrist injury late in the season, though he avoided surgery and rehabbed the ailment over the winter. Despite the thumb and wrist problems, he resurrected his career last year. His slow finish raises concerns that he may be best suited to be a platoon player, as he was overexposed when he saw regular duty. He will be a part-time player and pinch-hitter this season, a role for which Ward has value because of his power.

Position: 1B/RF
Bats: L **Throws:** L
Ht: 6' 2" **Wt:** 230

Opening Day Age: 29
Born: 6/27/75 in Lynwood, CA
ML Seasons: 7

Overall Statistics

	G	AB	R	H	D	T	HR	RBI	SB	BB	SO	Avg	OBP	Slg
'04	79	293	39	73	17	2	15	57	0	22	45	.249	.305	.474
Car.	549	1485	155	384	80	4	64	254	1	102	288	.259	.306	.447

Where He Hits the Ball

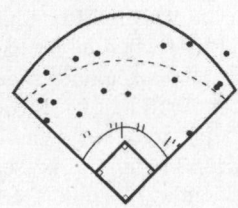 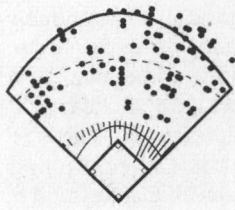

Vs. LHP   **Vs. RHP**

2004 Situational Stats

	AB	H	HR	RBI	Avg		AB	H	HR	RBI	Avg
Home	129	34	8	21	.264	LHP	54	16	1	7	.296
Road	164	39	7	36	.238	RHP	239	57	14	50	.238
First Half	163	45	10	33	.276	Sc Pos	77	21	6	44	.273
Scnd Half	130	28	5	24	.215	Clutch	45	10	3	6	.222

2004 Rankings (National League)

- Did not rank near the top or bottom in any category

Kip Wells

2004 Season

Kip Wells made his first career Opening Day start and beat Philadelphia. However, it went downhill from there as he won only four more games in 23 starts. Wells made just one start after August 14, one that lasted only 13 pitches, because of inflammation in his pitching elbow. He was bothered by the elbow and a blister on the middle finger of his pitching hand for much of the season, which partially accounted for him going 2-3 with 2.97 ERA in his first five starts but 3-4 with a 5.00 ERA thereafter.

Pitching

Wells has the arsenal to be a very successful starting pitcher in the major leagues. He has a lively fastball that routinely is in the 91-93 MPH range and can be dialed up to 96 MPH when he needs a little something extra. Wells also has a hard slider with good late bite and a curveball that he throws at varying speeds, though he sometimes has a problem controlling it. His changeup is serviceable and would be even better if he didn't tend to overthrow it in tight situations. Wells is not the innings-eater type you look for in a potential No. 1 starter, as he tends to lose his effectiveness around the 100-pitch mark.

Defense & Hitting

Wells has a slow delivery to the plate, which hampers his ability to hold runners. He is not a particularly good fielder and tends to rush his throws on bunts and toppers in front of the plate. Wells can't be taken lightly as a hitter because he has the ability to hit the ball out of the park. He is an adequate bunter.

2005 Outlook

Wells also experienced numbness in the middle finger of his pitching hand from time to time in 2004. His injury-riddled season ended with October surgery to alleviate the numbness problem. If he is healthy, Wells has the making of a front-line starter. It is time for him to fulfill that potential. The Pirates will give him another chance, but Wells is becoming expensive and this could be the end of the line in Pittsburgh if he doesn't rebound in 2005.

Position: SP
Bats: R **Throws:** R
Ht: 6' 3" **Wt:** 200

Opening Day Age: 27
Born: 4/21/77 in Houston, TX
ML Seasons: 6

Overall Statistics

	W	L	Pct.	ERA	G	GS	Sv	IP	H	BB	SO	HR	Avg
'04	5	7	.417	4.55	24	24	0	138.1	145	66	116	14	.270
Car.	47	51	.480	4.20	155	135	0	801.2	817	347	596	90	.265

2004 Pitching Profile

	Kip Wells	NL Average
Overall Strike %	61.3	62.5
1st Pitch Strike %	56.6	58.5
Ratio	1.53	1.39
Strikeouts per 9 IP	7.55	6.74
Walks per 9 IP	4.29	3.38
Home Runs per 9 IP	0.91	1.11
Strikeout/Walk Ratio	1.76	1.99
Groundball/Flyball Ratio	1.38	1.25

2004 Situational Stats

	W	L	ERA	Sv	IP		AB	H	HR	RBI	Avg
Home	1	3	4.47	0	58.1	LHB	247	74	6	31	.300
Road	4	4	4.61	0	80.0	RHB	291	71	8	31	.244
First Half	4	6	4.71	0	99.1	Sc Pos	144	31	5	50	.215
Scnd Half	1	1	4.15	0	39.0	Clutch	30	11	0	4	.367

2004 Rankings (National League)

- 3rd in errors at pitcher (3)
- Led the Pirates in runners caught stealing (6) and highest groundball-flyball ratio allowed (1.4)

Ty Wigginton

2004 Season

The Pirates acquired Ty Wiggington from the Mets on July 30 in a four-player trade that sent Kris Benson to New York. Wigginton was installed as the starting third baseman, but hit just .220 with five homers and 24 RBI in 58 games with the Pirates. However, after admittedly putting pressure on himself to justify the trade, he settled down and batted .283 with four homers and 17 RBI in his last 30 games.

Hitting

Wigginton is an extremely aggressive player, and that carries over into the batter's box. He can get himself out by being too overeager and swinging at pitches out of the strike zone, particularly with two outs or after falling behind in the count. Wigginton handles fastballs fairly well but can be made to chase low breaking pitches. He has decent pop but is a gap hitter who figures to hit more for average than power.

Baserunning & Defense

Wigginton is thick-legged and has only average speed. However, he always looks to take the extra base and is not afraid of contact as he flattened two rookie catchers, Arizona's Koyie Hill and St. Louis' Yadier Molina, in home-plate collisions last season. Wigginton isn't the smoothest third baseman around, but he fields the balls he gets to, though he'll occasionally airmail a throw to first base. He also played first base and second base for the Mets last season. He is adequate at first but his lack of range hurts him at second.

2005 Outlook

Wigginton will be the Pirates' starting third baseman this season, and they are curious to see if he can be a long-term piece to their puzzle as they try to build a winner after 12 straight losing seasons. It is doubtful Wigginton will ever become a superstar, but he has enough talent to be a solid major league regular. His hard-nosed approach figures to make him a crowd favorite in a blue-collar city like Pittsburgh.

Position: 3B/2B
Bats: R **Throws:** R
Ht: 6' 0" **Wt:** 200

Opening Day Age: 27
Born: 10/11/77 in San Diego, CA
ML Seasons: 3

Overall Statistics

	G	AB	R	H	D	T	HR	RBI	SB	BB	SO	Avg	OBP	Slg
'04	144	494	63	129	30	2	17	66	7	45	82	.261	.324	.433
Car.	346	1183	154	310	74	8	34	155	21	99	225	.262	.324	.424

Where He Hits the Ball

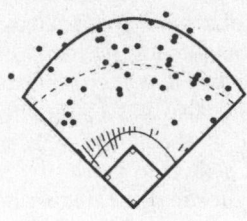

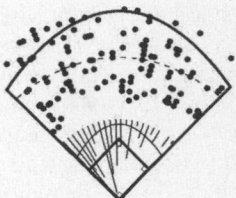

Vs. LHP   **Vs. RHP**

2004 Situational Stats

	AB	H	HR	RBI	Avg		AB	H	HR	RBI	Avg
Home	230	58	6	32	.252	LHP	108	24	4	11	.222
Road	264	71	11	34	.269	RHP	386	105	13	55	.272
First Half	262	72	12	39	.275	Sc Pos	125	27	2	38	.216
Scnd Half	232	57	5	27	.246	Clutch	85	20	2	16	.235

2004 Rankings (National League)

- 2nd in highest percentage of swings on the first pitch (42.7) and lowest fielding percentage at third base (.938)
- 4th in errors at third base (18) and fewest pitches seen per plate appearance (3.34)
- 9th in lowest batting average with runners in scoring position (.216)
- 10th in lowest percentage of pitches taken (48.4)
- Led the Pirates in batting average with the bases loaded (.500)

Craig Wilson

2004 Season

Craig Wilson got his first chance at regular playing time after three seasons as a productive role player and pinch-hitter. He made 78 starts in right field, 52 at first base, 17 in left field and one at catcher. Wilson was one of the hottest hitters in the National League for the first two months of the season, as his batting average stood at .360 on June 4. However, he hit just .213 in his last 105 games.

Hitting

Wilson has major power and can hit the ball out to all fields, though the majority of his home runs go to left. His swing tends to get long, causing him to strike out frequently. Though Wilson had more consistent at-bats with regular plate appearances, he can still be made to chase pitches, particularly breaking balls down and away. He will crush fastballs left over the plate and also has learned to stay back on changeups and hit them hard. Wilson crowds the plate and isn't scared to get hit by a pitch. He led the major leagues in that category in 2004 with 30 last year.

Baserunning & Defense

Wilson has below-average speed and rarely tries to steal a base. However, he is an alert and aggressive baserunner who will take an extra base if the defense naps. Wilson has split time between first base and the corner outfield positions. His best spot is first, where he makes up for a lack of range with surehandedness and improving footwork. He is adequate in right, particularly in cozy PNC Park, and catches the balls he reaches. His arm is a tick below average.

2005 Outlook

Wilson will get another opportunity to be an everyday player, but the only position that is open at the start of the 2005 season is first base. That's because the Pirates acquired potential leadoff man Matt Lawton to play right field. Wilson's second-half fade last year was disappointing, but his power still makes him an intriguing candidate to be a regular at first over Daryle Ward. He also could catch a few more games in 2005 with Jason Kendall traded to Oakland.

Position: RF/1B/LF
Bats: R **Throws:** R
Ht: 6' 2" **Wt:** 220

Opening Day Age: 28
Born: 11/30/76 in Fountain Valley, CA
ML Seasons: 4

Overall Statistics

	G	AB	R	H	D	T	HR	RBI	SB	BB	SO	Avg	OBP	Slg
'04	155	561	97	148	35	5	29	82	2	50	169	.264	.354	.499
Car.	490	1396	221	375	69	11	76	219	10	132	427	.269	.360	.497

Where He Hits the Ball

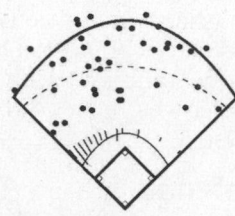
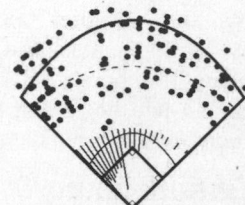

Vs. LHP   **Vs. RHP**

2004 Situational Stats

	AB	H	HR	RBI	Avg		AB	H	HR	RBI	Avg
Home	275	75	16	39	.273	LHP	108	28	6	14	.259
Road	286	73	13	43	.255	RHP	453	120	23	68	.265
First Half	318	91	17	48	.286	Sc Pos	143	36	4	54	.252
Scnd Half	243	57	12	34	.235	Clutch	88	24	7	16	.273

2004 Rankings (National League)

- 1st in hit by pitch (30) and highest percentage of swings that missed (32.4)
- 2nd in strikeouts and lowest cleanup slugging percentage (.437)
- 5th in highest percentage of swings on the first pitch (41.2)
- 6th in lowest percentage of swings put into play (33.8)
- Led the Pirates in home runs, runs scored, RBI, hit by pitch (30), strikeouts and cleanup slugging percentage (.437)

Jack Wilson

2004 Season

Jack Wilson easily had the finest season of his four-year career as he set career highs in almost every category. He also had the first 200-hit season by a Pirate since Dave Parker in 1977. Wilson became only the 14th shortstop (17 times) in National League history and just the second Pirates shortstop (Hall of Famer Honus Wagner was the other in 1908) to reach 200 hits. Wilson was also selected to his first All-Star Game.

Hitting

Wilson is a line-drive hitter who is starting to develop gap power as he gains experience and confidence at the major league level. He once was content to slap singles to all fields. However, Wilson has altered his approach and will now look to drive pitches he can handle. He will never be a big home-run hitter but looks capable of hitting 15 a year. Wilson got his long-awaited wish and batted No. 2 in order last year. Though his on-base percentage is low for that spot, he handles the bat well on hit-and-run plays and is a very good bunter.

Baserunning & Defense

Wilson is an average runner who is aggressive on the basepaths and will look to force the issue when possible. He does not attempt many steals from the No. 2 hole but has gotten better at reading pitchers' moves and will take off if the situation calls for it. Wilson has quietly become one of the better defensive shortstops in the game. He has outstanding range, particularly in the hole, and is an above-average thrower despite a short-arm motion. His hands are above average and he has excellent instincts.

2005 Outlook

Wilson had a breakthrough season in 2004 and will look to build on it this year. There is no reason he cannot continue at last year's pace or possibly even improve on it somewhat. Wilson, motivated to land a lucrative contract, is poised to take his place among the top NL shortstops.

Position: SS
Bats: R **Throws:** R
Ht: 6' 0"   **Wt:** 192

Opening Day Age: 27
Born: 12/29/77 in Westlake Village, CA
ML Seasons: 4

Overall Statistics

	G	AB	R	H	D	T	HR	RBI	SB	BB	SO	Avg	OBP	Slg
'04	157	652	82	201	41	12	11	59	8	26	71	.308	.335	.459
Car.	562	2127	261	564	101	20	27	193	19	115	289	.265	.305	.370

Where He Hits the Ball

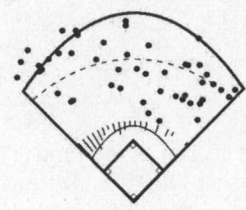

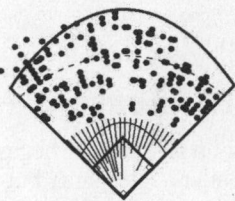

Vs. LHP   **Vs. RHP**

2004 Situational Stats

	AB	H	HR	RBI	Avg		AB	H	HR	RBI	Avg
Home	326	100	7	26	.307	LHP	115	30	5	12	.261
Road	326	101	4	33	.310	RHP	537	171	6	47	.318
First Half	355	118	8	35	.332	Sc Pos	141	38	0	43	.270
Scnd Half	297	83	3	24	.279	Clutch	103	39	2	15	.379

2004 Rankings (National League)

- 1st in triples
- 3rd in hits
- 4th in at-bats, batting average in the clutch and errors at shortstop (17)
- 6th in fielding percentage at shortstop (.977)
- Led the Pirates in at-bats, hits, doubles, triples, total bases (299), GDPs (15), plate appearances (693), games played and batting average in the clutch
- Led NL shortstops in batting average

Brian Boehringer

Position: RP
Bats: B **Throws:** R
Ht: 6' 2" **Wt:** 196

Opening Day Age: 35
Born: 1/8/70 in St. Louis, MO
ML Seasons: 10
Pronunciation: BOH-ring-uhr

Overall Statistics

	W	L	Pct.	ERA	G	GS	Sv	IP	H	BB	SO	HR	Avg
'04	1	1	.500	4.62	21	0	0	25.1	27	17	20	2	.293
Car.	26	32	.448	4.36	356	21	3	534.2	522	274	432	64	.257

2004 Situational Stats

	W	L	ERA	Sv	IP		AB	H	HR	RBI	Avg
Home	0	1	8.74	0	11.1	LHB	23	7	0	2	.304
Road	1	0	1.29	0	14.0	RHB	69	20	2	12	.290
First Half	1	1	4.62	0	25.1	Sc Pos	31	6	0	11	.194
Scnd Half	0	0	–	.0	0.0	Clutch	13	8	0	4	.615

2004 Season

Brian Boehringer began the season as the Pirates' primary setup man but lost that job after blowing a save in his first appearance. He did not pitch after June 1 because of a sore shoulder and eventually had surgery on August 12 to repair torn cartilage.

Pitching, Defense & Hitting

Boehringer challenges hitters with a fastball that is usually in the 90-91 MPH range and can top out at 94 MPH. He also has a slider and changeup but almost always goes with the fastball when he needs an out. Boehringer tends to sling the ball across his body, which makes him tough on righthanders. He is a good fielder who has made only one error in 356 career games and also does a decent job of holding runners. Boehringer isn't much of a hitter and has struck out in almost half his plate appearance.

2005 Outlook

Boehringer became a free agent when the Pirates failed to pick up his 2005 option. He will need to re-establish himself after two bad seasons during the life of a two-year, $3.8 million contract. He almost certainly will sign a minor league contract and try to make someone's bullpen as a non-roster player, if healthy.

Sean Burnett

Position: SP
Bats: L **Throws:** L
Ht: 5'11" **Wt:** 190

Opening Day Age: 22
Born: 9/17/82 in Dunedin, FL
ML Seasons: 1

Overall Statistics

	W	L	Pct.	ERA	G	GS	Sv	IP	H	BB	SO	HR	Avg
'04	5	5	.500	5.02	13	13	0	71.2	86	28	30	9	.301
Car.	5	5	.500	5.02	13	13	0	71.2	86	28	30	9	.301

2004 Situational Stats

	W	L	ERA	Sv	IP		AB	H	HR	RBI	Avg
Home	4	1	3.79	0	40.1	LHB	71	23	1	8	.324
Road	1	4	6.61	0	31.1	RHB	215	63	8	29	.293
First Half	3	2	2.35	0	38.1	Sc Pos	68	21	2	28	.309
Scnd Half	2	3	8.10	0	33.1	Clutch	8	3	0	1	.375

2004 Season

Highly-regarded prospect Sean Burnett made his major league debut May 30. Burnett, the Pirates' first-round draft pick in 2000, allowed one run in five innings to the Chicago Cubs, but wound up on an operating table less than four months later. Noted orthopedist James Andrews performed Tommy John reconstructive elbow surgery on Burnett on September 22. Burnett went 5-2 with a 2.84 ERA in his first eight starts but 0-3 with a 10.29 ERA in his last five.

Pitching, Defense & Hitting

Burnett proves that a young pitcher can be successful without great velocity. His fastball is usually in the 86-89 MPH range, though it will occasional touch 90 and even reach 93 MPH. He gets hitters out with a big-breaking curveball and a tantalizing changeup that drops off the table at the last second. Burnett has also added a slider but he is still gaining command of that pitch. He holds runners fairly well and is quick off the mound but was 0-for-23 in his first try as a major league hitter.

2005 Outlook

Burnett isn't likely to pitch before August after having his elbow rebuilt. The Pirates feel he is still a big part of their future, however, and will be cautious with his rehabilitation.

Jose Castillo

Position: 2B
Bats: R **Throws:** R
Ht: 6' 1" **Wt:** 200

Opening Day Age: 24
Born: 3/19/81 in Las Mercedes, VZ
ML Seasons: 1

Overall Statistics

	G	AB	R	H	D	T	HR	RBI	SB	BB	SO	Avg	OBP	Slg
'04	129	383	44	98	15	2	8	39	3	23	92	.256	.298	.368
Car.	129	383	44	98	15	2	8	39	3	23	92	.256	.298	.368

2004 Situational Stats

	AB	H	HR	RBI	Avg		AB	H	HR	RBI	Avg
Home	178	43	3	16	.242	LHP	90	24	1	8	.267
Road	205	55	5	23	.268	RHP	293	74	7	31	.253
First Half	185	46	3	15	.249	Sc Pos	88	25	3	33	.284
Scnd Half	198	52	5	24	.263	Clutch	68	13	1	6	.191

2004 Season

Rookie infielder Jose Castillo was the surprise of the Pirates' spring training camp and wound up making the jump from Double-A to the major leagues. Castillo began the season splitting time with Bobby Hill at second base but had claimed the starting job outright by June. Castillo hit .347 in August but batted just .221 in his last 25 games.

Hitting, Baserunning & Defense

Castillo concentrated mainly on making contact as a rookie, but he showed good power potential in the minor leagues and should add pop with experience. He added a leg kick last season that helped him stay back on breaking balls and changeups, but he can still be made to swing at bad pitches, particularly with two strikes. Castillo has good speed but did not run much as a rookie hitting out of the No. 8 spot of the batting order. He moved from shortstop to second base in 2003 and has made a smooth transition. Castillo is very adept at turning the double play and has above-average range and arm strength.

2005 Outlook

Castillo could start at second base this year, trying to build upon a decent rookie season. Prospect Freddy Sanchez could unseat him, but Castillo has the ability to forge a solid career.

Mike Gonzalez

Position: RP
Bats: R **Throws:** L
Ht: 6' 2" **Wt:** 205

Opening Day Age: 26
Born: 5/23/78 in Corpus Christi, TX
ML Seasons: 2

Overall Statistics

	W	L	Pct.	ERA	G	GS	Sv	IP	H	BB	SO	HR	Avg
'04	3	1	.750	1.25	47	0	1	43.1	32	6	55	2	.201
Car.	3	2	.600	2.26	63	0	1	51.2	39	12	61	6	.206

2004 Situational Stats

	W	L	ERA	Sv	IP		AB	H	HR	RBI	Avg
Home	3	0	1.17	0	23.0	LHB	61	13	0	3	.213
Road	0	1	1.33	1	20.1	RHB	98	19	2	10	.194
First Half	2	0	0.57	0	15.2	Sc Pos	36	6	1	11	.167
Scnd Half	1	1	1.63	1	27.2	Clutch	78	19	2	11	.244

2004 Season

Lefthander Mike Gonzalez began the season at Triple-A Nashville and was recalled twice before finally sticking with the Pirates for good on June 2. He proceeded to have one of the best seasons of any rookie relief pitcher in the major leagues. Gonzalez was scored on in just six of 47 relief appearances while striking out 11.42 batters per nine innings.

Pitching, Defense & Hitting

Gonzalez is often overpowering with his fastball-slider combination. He runs his fastball up to 98 MPH and regularly throws it at 93-95 MPH. Gonzalez' slider has a late break and is particularly tough on righthanded hitters. He struggles throwing his changeup for strikes at times, but it hardly matters working short stints in relief. Gonzalez began his professional career as a starting pitcher and has the ability to work multiple innings if needed. He often forgets about baserunners, making him easy to steal on, and is a subpar fielder. Gonzalez batted only once last season but belted a two-run double for his first hit since high school.

2005 Outlook

Gonzalez will be the primary lefthanded setup reliever in 2005. He has the ability to eventually close and will be eased into that role in the next few years.

John Grabow

Position: RP
Bats: L **Throws:** L
Ht: 6' 2" **Wt:** 210

Opening Day Age: 26
Born: 11/4/78 in Arcadia, CA
ML Seasons: 2
Pronunciation: GRAY-bo

Overall Statistics

	W	L	Pct.	ERA	G	GS	Sv	IP	H	BB	SO	HR	Avg
'04	2	5	.286	5.11	68	0	1	61.2	81	28	64	8	.323
Car.	2	5	.286	5.00	73	0	1	66.2	87	28	73	8	.319

2004 Situational Stats

	W	L	ERA	Sv	IP		AB	H	HR	RBI	Avg
Home	2	4	4.68	0	32.2	LHB	113	37	4	15	.327
Road	0	1	5.59	1	29.0	RHB	138	44	4	21	.319
First Half	0	3	4.17	0	36.2	Sc Pos	90	23	1	26	.256
Scnd Half	2	2	6.48	1	25.0	Clutch	82	31	4	22	.378

2004 Season

Lefthander John Grabow proved to be a workhorse in his first full major league season, setting a Pirates rookie record for a lefthanded reliever with 68 games pitched. He started off well, posting a 2.92 ERA in his first 28 games but then had a 6.57 mark in his last 40 appearances. Opponents batted .375 off Grabow after the All-Star break.

Pitching, Defense & Hitting

Grabow has the makings of a good array of pitches, topped by a fastball that routinely reaches 91-92 MPH. He also has a good curveball, and his changeup can be a plus pitch. However, Grabow needs better command of his pitches. He often struggles with his mechanics and leaves too many pitches up in the strike zone, where they get whacked. Grabow holds runners well and has a good pickoff move. He also fields his position soundly and is quick off the mound. He almost never bats in his relief role.

2005 Outlook

Grabow will be used as a middle reliever until he shows he is ready to handle a more expanded role, after blowing six of seven save opportunities last season. He has the chance to be an above-average reliever, but must become more consistent.

Bobby Hill

Position: 2B/3B
Bats: B **Throws:** R
Ht: 5' 9" **Wt:** 180

Opening Day Age: 26
Born: 4/3/78 in San Jose, CA
ML Seasons: 3

Overall Statistics

	G	AB	R	H	D	T	HR	RBI	SB	BB	SO	Avg	OBP	Slg
'04	126	233	28	62	7	2	2	27	0	20	39	.266	.353	.339
Car.	191	430	55	112	14	4	6	47	6	39	83	.260	.344	.353

2004 Situational Stats

	AB	H	HR	RBI	Avg		AB	H	HR	RBI	Avg
Home	119	35	1	12	.294	LHP	18	4	0	1	.222
Road	114	27	1	15	.237	RHP	215	58	2	26	.270
First Half	150	42	1	18	.280	Sc Pos	66	17	0	24	.258
Scnd Half	83	20	1	9	.241	Clutch	52	18	2	9	.346

2004 Season

Bobby Hill was the Pirates' Opening Day second baseman after a big spring training, but had lost the job to rookie Jose Castillo by the end of May. Hill wound up making only 31 starts at second and 19 at third base, and was in the lineup just twice after August 27.

Hitting, Baserunning & Defense

The switch-hitting Hill, who bucked a career trend by having better numbers from the left side last season, concentrates mainly on making contact, though he has the ability to hit for some power. Hill shows decent patience at the plate when he is playing regularly, but tends to become anxious when he gets infrequent starts. He was a big-time basestealer as an All-America at the University of Miami but rarely runs anymore, partially because he usually hits in the lower third of the batting order. Hill is surehanded at second base and third with a good arm but has a glaring lack of range.

2005 Outlook

Hill will be tried at the corner outfield spots this spring, a sure sign the Pirates feel his future is as a bench player. He could surprise if given the chance to play every day, but whether he will receive that opportunity is uncertain.

Brian Meadows

Position: RP
Bats: R **Throws:** R
Ht: 6' 4" **Wt:** 230

Opening Day Age: 29
Born: 11/21/75 in Montgomery, AL
ML Seasons: 7

Overall Statistics

	W	L	Pct.	ERA	G	GS	Sv	IP	H	BB	SO	HR	Avg
'04	2	4	.333	3.58	68	0	1	78.0	76	19	46	7	.259
Car.	41	55	.427	5.08	218	122	2	816.1	972	223	375	117	.299

2004 Situational Stats

	W	L	ERA	Sv	IP		AB	H	HR	RBI	Avg
Home	0	1	2.53	0	42.2	LHB	93	21	3	16	.226
Road	2	3	4.84	1	35.1	RHB	200	55	4	25	.275
First Half	2	2	3.14	1	43.0	Sc Pos	74	23	1	32	.311
Scnd Half	0	2	4.11	0	35.0	Clutch	94	34	2	13	.362

2004 Season

Brian Meadows made a career-high 68 appearances in middle relief in his first season working exclusively out of the bullpen. He had a fine 2.68 ERA at the end of July but then had a 5.20 mark in his last 25 games.

Pitching, Defense & Hitting

Meadows' stuff is average but he has a good idea of how to pitch and consistently keeps his pitches low in the strike zone. His fastball usually tops out at 90 MPH and sits in the high 80s as he works both sides of the plate with it. Meadows will also cut his fastball, giving it slider-like action as it bores in on lefthanded hitters. His curveball is solid, though he goes through spells where he uses it too often and hitters know it is coming. Meadows' changeup is serviceable. He is an adequate fielder but does not hold runners well. Meadows isn't much of a threat with the bat.

2005 Outlook

Meadows has found a home in the bullpen after struggling as a starter through much of his career. He is ideal to pitch the sixth or seventh inning and serve as a bridge between the starters and the setup men and closer.

Salomon Torres

Position: RP
Bats: R **Throws:** R
Ht: 5'11" **Wt:** 210

Opening Day Age: 33
Born: 3/11/72 in San Pedro de Macoris, DR
ML Seasons: 8

Overall Statistics

	W	L	Pct.	ERA	G	GS	Sv	IP	H	BB	SO	HR	Avg
'04	7	7	.500	2.64	84	0	0	92.0	87	22	62	6	.256
Car.	27	38	.415	4.78	198	64	2	526.2	551	225	317	65	.273

2004 Situational Stats

	W	L	ERA	Sv	IP		AB	H	HR	RBI	Avg
Home	4	4	2.22	0	52.2	LHB	126	32	2	17	.254
Road	3	3	3.20	0	39.1	RHB	214	55	4	21	.257
First Half	4	3	3.00	0	48.0	Sc Pos	97	23	3	33	.237
Scnd Half	3	4	2.25	0	44.0	Clutch	218	60	4	27	.275

2004 Season

Pitching out of the bullpen exclusively for the first time in his career, Salomon Torres had his finest season. His 84 relief appearances were the most by a Pirates pitcher since Kent Tekulve appeared in 85 games in 1982. Torres got stronger as the year went on, posting a 2.25 ERA in his final 37 games. He allowed runs in just 14 of his 57 games after June 1.

Pitching, Defense & Hitting

Torres has always had a great arm, but he finally figured out what to do with it after coming out of a four-season retirement in 2002. He has two types of fastballs, a four-seamer that reaches 94 MPH and a two-seamer that hits 91 and has great sinking action. Torres also throws a slider and curveball to keep hitters honest. Torres shows outstanding athleticism in the field and has made only one error in 198 major league games. He holds runners well and handles the bat decently.

2005 Outlook

Re-signed to a two-year contract in November, Torres will be the Pirates' primary setup reliever, a role he seems tailor-made for. He has pitched well enough in the eighth inning that it has led many to believe he could handle ninth-inning duties.

Ryan Vogelsong

Position: SP
Bats: R **Throws:** R
Ht: 6' 3" **Wt:** 213

Opening Day Age: 27
Born: 7/22/77 in
Charlotte, NC
ML Seasons: 4

Overall Statistics

	W	L	Pct.	ERA	G	GS	Sv	IP	H	BB	SO	HR	Avg
'04	6	13	.316	6.50	31	26	0	133.0	148	67	92	22	.285
Car.	8	20	.286	6.35	56	33	0	195.2	221	98	137	29	.285

2004 Situational Stats

	W	L	ERA	Sv	IP		AB	H	HR	RBI	Avg
Home	3	8	7.77	0	63.2	LHB	239	66	10	41	.276
Road	3	5	5.32	0	69.1	RHB	280	82	12	46	.293
First Half	2	7	6.93	0	74.0	Sc Pos	148	40	6	65	.270
Scnd Half	4	6	5.95	0	59.0	Clutch	12	3	1	1	.250

2004 Season

Ryan Vogelsong was dominant in spring training as he won an open spot in the starting rotation. However, he didn't carry that over into the regular season, as he became the first Pirates pitcher since 1900 to post an ERA over 6.00 while making 20 starts in a season. Vogelsong was demoted to the bullpen for a month at midseason but finished the year by winning three of his last four decisions.

Pitching, Defense & Hitting

Vogelsong has the makings of four above-average pitches. His fastball routinely exceeds 90 MPH, tops out at 95, and has good movement. When he keeps from bouncing it in the dirt, his curveball is a plus pitch and causes some funky swings. He also had a hard slider and a changeup with fading action. His problems are his inability to consistently command his pitches, and a quick loss of confidence when things go wrong. Vogelsong is a good athlete who fields his position and swings the bat well but struggles to hold runners.

2005 Outlook

Vogelsong is out of minor league options but will get one more chance to prove he is a major league starter. If it doesn't work out, he has enough ability to forge a career in relief.

Dave Williams

Position: SP
Bats: L **Throws:** L
Ht: 6' 2" **Wt:** 219

Opening Day Age: 26
Born: 3/12/79 in
Anchorage, AK
ML Seasons: 3

Overall Statistics

	W	L	Pct.	ERA	G	GS	Sv	IP	H	BB	SO	HR	Avg
'04	2	3	.400	4.42	10	6	0	38.2	31	13	33	4	.217
Car.	7	15	.318	4.13	41	33	0	196.0	169	82	123	28	.236

2004 Situational Stats

	W	L	ERA	Sv	IP		AB	H	HR	RBI	Avg
Home	2	1	3.08	0	26.1	LHB	39	11	1	6	.282
Road	0	2	7.30	0	12.1	RHB	104	20	3	17	.192
First Half	0	0	—	0	0.0	Sc Pos	33	11	1	20	.333
Scnd Half	2	3	4.42	0	38.2	Clutch	5	3	0	2	.600

2004 Season

More than two years after undergoing shoulder surgery, Dave Williams finally returned to the major leagues at the beginning of August when he was recalled from Triple-A Nashville. Williams first worked out of the bullpen, then shifted back to his normal starting role and went 2-3 with a 3.94 ERA in six starts to end the year.

Pitching, Defense & Hitting

Williams will never overpower anyone, but he has an advanced feel for pitching, something he honed while recovering from surgery. His fastball ranges from 84-92 MPH and he does a nice job of changing speeds and moving around the strike zone with it. Williams also has a knack for getting hitters to chase the heater up and out of the strike zone. He has an effective changeup that breaks away from righthanded hitters like a screwball and he also throws a curveball and slider. Williams needs to improve his pickoff move, fielding and bunting. However, he can drive the ball if the opposing pitcher doesn't take him seriously.

2005 Outlook

Williams will compete for a spot in the rotation in spring training. He showed promise as a rookie in 2001, and finally is regaining that form now that his shoulder woes are behind him.

Tony Alvarez (Pos: RF, Age: 25, Bats: R)

	G	AB	R	H	D	T	HR	RBI	SB	BB	SO	Avg	OBP	Slg
'04	24	38	5	8	2	0	1	8	0	4	7	.211	.289	.342
Car.	38	64	11	16	4	0	2	10	1	7	12	.250	.324	.406

The 25-year-old Alvarez spent his second consecutive season at Triple-A Nashville, waiting to fill any outfield vacancies in Pittsburgh. The Pirates' depth at those positions meant that few opportunities arose, which is a shame because Alvarez has proven he's ready to be a regular. 2005 Outlook: C

Jose Bautista (Pos: RF/3B, Age: 24, Bats: R)

	G	AB	R	H	D	T	HR	RBI	SB	BB	SO	Avg	OBP	Slg
'04	64	88	6	18	3	0	0	2	0	7	40	.205	.263	.239
Car.	64	88	6	18	3	0	0	2	0	7	40	.205	.263	.239

Pittsburgh GM Dave Littlefield took heat for losing Bautista to the Orioles in the 2003 Rule 5 draft. To Littlefield's credit, he never lost track of Bautista, as he journeyed through Baltimore, Tampa Bay and Kansas City in '04. A July trade eventually brought him back to Pittsburgh. 2005 Outlook: C

Jason Boyd (Pos: RHP, Age: 32)

	W	L	Pct.	ERA	G	GS	Sv	IP	H	BB	SO	HR	Avg
'04	1	0	1.000	5.54	12	0	0	13.0	13	8	12	4	.260
Car.	5	2	.714	5.74	113	0	0	133.1	128	75	97	16	.254

In February 2004, Boyd was ordered by an Illinois court to participate in an anger management course after two separate offseason fighting incidents. It appears the deep-breathing techniques didn't work for Boyd, who broke his pitching hand while punching the rubber in May. 2005 Outlook: D

Mark Corey (Pos: RHP, Age: 30)

	W	L	Pct.	ERA	G	GS	Sv	IP	H	BB	SO	HR	Avg
'04	1	2	.333	4.54	31	0	0	35.2	39	19	28	3	.275
Car.	2	7	.222	6.02	81	0	0	89.2	105	49	79	14	.290

Corey has experienced much minor league success since his complete bullpen conversion in 2001. His strikeout rate of 11.46 K/9, 2.79 ERA and 80 saves, are all outstanding numbers for this once shaky starter. He re-signed a minor league deal with the Pirates in December. 2005 Outlook: C

Humberto Cota (Pos: C, Age: 26, Bats: R)

	G	AB	R	H	D	T	HR	RBI	SB	BB	SO	Avg	OBP	Slg
'04	36	66	10	15	1	1	5	8	0	3	20	.227	.271	.500
Car.	60	108	13	26	3	1	5	10	0	5	34	.241	.281	.426

The injury sagas keep mounting for Cota. In 2003, he was suspended without pay for refusing to play, claiming his hand was sore. Two hand specialists were called in, with both independently confirming there was nothing wrong. A strained left oblique shelved him last year. 2005 Outlook: C

Nelson Figueroa (Pos: RHP, Age: 30)

	W	L	Pct.	ERA	G	GS	Sv	IP	H	BB	SO	HR	Avg
'04	0	3	.000	5.72	10	3	0	28.1	32	11	10	4	.302
Car.	7	17	.292	4.65	74	33	0	261.1	268	103	152	42	.270

The knock on Figueroa is that he lacks fastball velocity. Deception and command are the tools he has used to amass a 97-55 minor league record, but the large increase in home-run rates at the big league level give the critics some credence. 2005 Outlook: C

Mike Johnston (Pos: LHP, Age: 26)

	W	L	Pct.	ERA	G	GS	Sv	IP	H	BB	SO	HR	Avg
'04	0	3	.000	4.37	24	0	0	22.2	29	15	18	2	.315
Car.	0	3	.000	4.37	24	0	0	22.2	29	15	18	2	.315

Johnston made the leap to Pittsburgh last year, just two years removed from Class-A ball. His sudden rise is even more extraordinary when you factor in all the other capable lefties in the Pittsburgh organization. 2005 Outlook: C

Abraham O. Nunez (Pos: 2B/SS, Age: 29, Bats: B)

	G	AB	R	H	D	T	HR	RBI	SB	BB	SO	Avg	OBP	Slg
'04	112	182	17	43	9	0	2	13	1	10	36	.236	.275	.319
Car.	630	1489	156	354	55	14	11	117	35	142	278	.238	.306	.316

Nunez has established himself as a utility infielder. For a replacement infielder, his production from the left side is acceptable, but from the right side he has hit just a scant .212/.300/.253 over his career. 2005 Outlook: B

Carlos Rivera (Pos: 1B, Age: 26, Bats: L)

	G	AB	R	H	D	T	HR	RBI	SB	BB	SO	Avg	OBP	Slg
'04	7	15	1	3	0	0	0	1	0	1	3	.200	.250	.200
Car.	85	110	13	24	5	0	3	11	0	9	31	.218	.279	.345

Rivera is noted for his soft hands and excellent glovework at first base, but his 2004 Nashville offensive performance was what really intrigued Pirates brass. His .516 slugging percentage made the Pirates look smart for keeping Rivera on the 40-man roster. 2005: C

Willis Roberts (Pos: RHP, Age: 29)

	W	L	Pct.	ERA	G	GS	Sv	IP	H	BB	SO	HR	Avg
'04	0	0	–	5.25	9	0	0	12.0	12	9	7	0	.279
Car.	17	15	.531	4.64	148	18	7	259.2	277	112	179	27	.274

Manager Lloyd McClendon commented on Roberts' "heavy sinker" after seeing him perform in the spring of 2004. The "sinker" part may have been wanting, but the "heavy" part was accurate. It took Roberts until June to shed upwards of an excess 20 pounds and regain lost velocity. 2005 Outlook: C

Chris Stynes (Pos: 3B, Age: 32, Bats: R)

	G	AB	R	H	D	T	HR	RBI	SB	BB	SO	Avg	OBP	Slg
'04	74	162	16	35	10	0	1	16	0	9	23	.216	.266	.296
Car.	828	2326	351	640	118	9	51	265	49	191	308	.275	.335	.399

Stynes seriously underperformed as the starting third baseman. The acquisition of former Met Ty Wigginton signaled the end for Stynes in Pittsburgh. He was let go by the club in July. 2005 Outlook: C

Pittsburgh Pirates Minor League Prospects

Organization Overview:

The Pirates couldn't match their incredible 2003 season in which they sent all six farm clubs to the playoffs. However, they still had a solid year down on the farm in 2004 and, most importantly, sent a numbers of players to the major leagues. Pittsburgh's six farm clubs went a combined 354-339 in '04 for a solid .511 winning percentage, and Class-A Hickory won the South Atlantic League championship. The Pirates also had seven rookies on the Opening Day roster, and 13 by the time the season ended. They also began developing more hitting prospects after being top heavy with pitching for so long.

Frank Brooks

Position: P

Bats: L **Throws:** L

Ht: 6' 1" **Wt:** 200

Opening Day Age: 26

Born: 9/6/78 in Brooklyn, NY

Recent Statistics

	W	L	ERA	G	GS	Sv	IP	H	R	BB	SO	HR
2004 AAA Nashville	6	3	4.10	42	8	2	83.1	81	42	22	55	13
2004 NL Pittsburgh	0	1	4.67	11	1	0	17.1	13	10	9	18	5

Frank Brooks made his major league debut with the Pirates last August, but it took a long journey to get there. The Pirates acquired Brooks from Philadelphia in a July 2003 trade, then lost him to the Mets in the Rule 5 Draft. New York dealt him to Oakland, and he wound up in Boston's camp in spring training after failing to stick with the Athletics. The Red Sox then offered Brooks back to the Pirates. He has an average fastball and a decent curveball, but a tricky delivery makes his pitches tough for lefthanded hitters to pick up. Despite having trouble with walks at the major league level, command was one of his strengths in the minors. He was a swingman in the minors, but his future is likely to be out of the bullpen. Brooks was claimed off waivers by Los Angeles in mid-December.

J.J. Davis

Position: OF

Bats: R **Throws:** R

Ht: 6' 5" **Wt:** 250

Opening Day Age: 26

Born: 10/25/78 in Glendora, CA

Recent Statistics

	G	AB	R	H	D	T	HR	RBI	SB	BB	SO	Avg
2004 AAA Nashville	27	84	11	21	6	1	8	17	3	3	28	.250
2004 NL Pittsburgh	25	35	4	5	1	0	0	3	2	4	10	.143

Davis had a lost season in 2004. He was out of minor league options and the Pirates kept him in the major leagues all season despite feeling he needed more time at Triple-A. He was on the DL twice, and ended up with more at-bats for Nashville than the parent club. Davis has shown outstanding power potential in the upper levels of the minors, but he has been overmatched in his brief exposure to big league pitching. He has good speed and an above-average arm, but has yet to figure how to put all his tools to use. He has the potential to hit in the middle of the order, but his maturity has come into question throughout his career. Davis was dealt to Washington in late November.

Zach Duke

Position: P

Bats: L **Throws:** L

Ht: 6' 2" **Wt:** 212

Opening Day Age: 21

Born: 4/19/83 in Clifton, TX

Recent Statistics

	W	L	ERA	G	GS	Sv	IP	H	R	BB	SO	HR
2003 A Hickory	8	7	3.11	26	26	0	141.2	124	66	46	113	7
2004 A Lynchburg	10	5	1.39	17	17	0	97.0	73	24	20	106	3
2004 AA Altoona	5	1	1.58	9	9	0	51.1	41	11	10	36	2

Duke emerged as one of the game's top pitching prospects in 2004, his third professional season. He split the year between high Class-A Lynchburg and Double-A Altoona, and led the entire minor leagues with a 1.46 ERA in 148.1 innings while going 15-6. His best pitch is a curveball that sweeps through the strike zone and reminds some scouts of Barry Zito's bender. Duke's fastball has gained velocity as he's matured and is now in the 90-93 MPH range. His changeup is a work in progress but is getting better. Duke gets high marks for his poise and mound presence. He likely will start the 2005 season with Triple-A Indianapolis with an eye on making his major league debut later in the season.

Brad Eldred

Position: 1B

Bats: R **Throws:** R

Ht: 6' 5" **Wt:** 245

Opening Day Age: 24

Born: 7/12/80 in Fort Lauderdale, FL

Recent Statistics

	G	AB	R	H	D	T	HR	RBI	SB	BB	SO	Avg
2003 A Hickory	115	420	62	105	22	0	28	80	7	38	142	.250
2004 A Lynchburg	91	335	54	104	22	1	21	77	5	35	97	.310
2004 AA Altoona	39	147	24	41	9	0	17	60	0	6	51	.279

Eldred had a monstrous season split between high Class-A Lynchburg and Double-A Altoona, leading the minor leagues with 137 RBI—including a mind-boggling 50 in August in his first full month at Double-A. He has big-time power from the right side and is capable of hitting tape-measure homers. Eldred is a dead-fastball hitter, but is getting better at recognizing pitches and handling breaking balls. Despite his large frame, he shows decent athletic ability and is average in the field and on the bases. Eldred took a big step forward last year but must show he can handle pitching at higher levels. He certainly is an intriguing prospect in an organization that lacks power hitters.

J.R. House

Position: C
Bats: R **Throws:** R
Ht: 6' 0" **Wt:** 215

Opening Day Age: 25
Born: 11/11/79 in
Charleston, WV

Recent Statistics

	G	AB	R	H	D	T	HR	RBI	SB	BB	SO	Avg
2004 AAA Nashville	92	309	38	89	21	1	15	49	1	23	72	.288
2004 NL Pittsburgh	5	9	1	1	1	0	0	0	0	0	2	.111

House played a full season for the first time since 2001 after undergoing reconstructive elbow surgery and two hernia operations during the previous two years. He once was considered the organization's top prospect, and started flashing his old form last season at Triple-A Nashville. Hitting is House's best tool, as he is average at best defensively and a slow runner. Catcher remains his primary position, and he drew praise last season for his improved pitch-calling ability and work with pitchers. House also played some first base and left field, and his future could be as a multi-position player.

Freddy Sanchez

Position: SS-2B
Bats: R **Throws:** R
Ht: 5' 10" **Wt:** 192

Opening Day Age: 27
Born: 12/21/77 in
Hollywood, CA

Recent Statistics

	G	AB	R	H	D	T	HR	RBI	SB	BB	SO	Avg
2004 AAA Nashville	44	125	10	33	7	1	1	11	4	11	17	.264
2004 NL Pittsburgh	9	19	2	3	0	0	0	2	0	0	3	.158

Sanchez' tenure with the Pirates has been frustrating since he was acquired from Boston in a July 2003 trade. He missed the final two months of the 2003 season with a large bone chip in his right ankle, an injury that required surgery and kept him sidelined until June last year. Sanchez was rusty once he returned and did not show the hitting ability that made him a top prospect with the Red Sox—until late in the season. He has little power but makes consistent enough contact to be a .300 hitter. Sanchez runs fairly well and is adequate defensively at both middle-infield positions. He figures to make the Pirates this season as a utility infielder since he is out of minor league options.

Ian Snell

Position: P
Bats: R **Throws:** R
Ht: 5' 11" **Wt:** 170

Opening Day Age: 23
Born: 10/30/81 in Dover,
DE

Recent Statistics

	W	L	ERA	G	GS	Sv	IP	H	R	BB	SO	HR
2004 AA Altoona	11	7	3.16	26	26	0	151.0	147	54	40	142	16
2004 NL Pittsburgh	0	1	7.50	3	1	0	12.0	14	10	9	9	2

Snell draws comparisons to veteran reliever Tom "Flash" Gordon as a smallish righthander who has electric stuff. Snell has a live fastball that routinely sits at 93 MPH and tops out at 96 MPH. He also has an outstanding curveball that has such a sharp and late break that some scouts and opposing hitters swear it is a slider. Snell began throwing a slider last season with mixed results and must gain better command of his changeup. He has been a starting pitcher throughout his career and has posted an impressive 47-16 record in five minor league seasons. However, some scouts believe the lithe Snell's future would be better in relief because of the possibility he would wear down as a major league starter.

John Van Benschoten

Position: P
Bats: R **Throws:** R
Ht: 6' 4" **Wt:** 217

Opening Day Age: 24
Born: 4/14/80 in San
Diego, CA

Recent Statistics

	W	L	ERA	G	GS	Sv	IP	H	R	BB	SO	HR
2004 AAA Nashville	4	11	4.72	23	23	0	131.2	135	75	49	101	16
2004 NL Pittsburgh	1	3	6.91	6	5	0	28.2	33	27	19	18	3

Van Benschoten had a rough 2004. He struggled early at Triple-A Nashville, then had some tough outings late in the season with the Pirates as he was nursing a sore shoulder. He does not have a dominant pitch, but rather four offerings that have the chance to be above average. Van Benschoten's fastball comes in at 90-92 MPH but lacks consistent good movement. His curveball eventually could turn into a very good pitch if he sharpens up the break. He also throws a slider and change. Despite his age, he still needs pitching experience, as he served as a part-time closer in college at Kent State, where he hit 31 homers in 2001 as a first baseman/outfielder.

Others to Watch

Righthander **Bobby Bradley** (24) has had two elbow surgeries, including Tommy John, and one shoulder operation since 2001. However, he consistently gets people out when healthy with a big-breaking curveball and a 90-MPH fastball with good sink. . . Center fielder **Rajai Davis** (24) was extremely raw when he was drafted in the 38th round in 2001, but he has gotten better every year. He won the Carolina League batting title with a .314 average for high Class-A Lynchburg last season while leading the league with 57 stolen bases. He has a good eye at the plate and is willing to take a walk, which makes him an ideal leadoff hitter. . . Lefthander **Tom Gorzelanny** (22) might have the best stuff of anybody in the Pirates' farm system, with a fastball that routinely sits in the 91-93 MPH range and a sharp slider. He needs to improve his command and mound presence. . . Lefthander **Cory Stewart** (25) was the third player acquired from San Diego in 2003, along with Oliver Perez and Jason Bay, in the trade that sent Brian Giles to the Padres. Stewart struggled last season while pitching with a strained side muscle. However, he possesses a 92-MPH fastball with movement and a plus curveball. . . Catcher **Neil Walker** (19) was the Pirates' first-round draft pick last year. He is a switch-hitting catcher with power from both sides of the plate, along with the ability to hit for average. Walker has the potential to hit 40 homers a year.

Busch Stadium

Offense

Only one season remains for Busch Stadium, with construction of a new ballpark expected to be finished for the 2006 season. Formerly a spacious, artificial turf cookie-cutter, Busch remains a tough home-run park but fairly neutral in terms of batting average. The ball moves quickly through the infield, but weather or wind is rarely a factor. Over the long haul, few ballparks play more consistently.

Defense

Bad hops are a rarity at Busch, reducing the number of errors, and the quickness of the infield dirt makes it ideal for the outstanding Cardinals infielders to show their stuff. The outfield has deep alleys and requires above-average speed and range. The low fences also allow the athletic St. Louis outfielders to occasionally make home-run saving leaping grabs—especially center fielder Jim Edmonds.

Who It Helps the Most

Tony Womack was especially aided by the hard infield dirt, which he often employed to chop infield hits. And Jim Edmonds used the reachable left-center power alley to his advantage, hitting six more home runs at home than away. Cards pitchers had nearly a half run better ERA at home, with Steve Kline going the entire season without allowing an earned run at Busch Stadium.

Who It Hurts the Most

The Cardinals power was more prodigious on the road than at home, with Scott Rolen having significantly better all-around hitting numbers on the road. Jeff Suppan and Cal Eldred were two pitchers who also found their performance better away from Busch, where the fans can be tough on struggling St. Louis pitchers.

Rookies & Newcomers

Womack thrived playing at Busch Stadium. And after coming to St. Louis in an August trade, even a seasoned superstar like Larry Walker found out how appreciative the great Cards fans can be of talented players who give the maximum effort. That shouldn't change when the new ballpark opens next year.

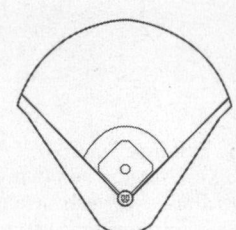

Dimensions: LF-330, LCF-372, CF-402, RCF-372, RF-330

Capacity: 50,345

Elevation: 535 feet

Surface: Grass

Foul Territory: Large

Park Factors

2004 Season

	Home Games			Away Games			
	Cardinals	Opp	Total	Cardinals	Opp	Total	Index
G	75	75	150	75	75	150	
Avg	.281	.252	.266	.270	.255	.263	101
AB	2501	2583	5084	2629	2487	5116	99
R	374	304	678	396	319	715	95
H	704	650	1354	709	634	1343	101
2B	150	137	287	144	136	280	103
3B	14	10	24	9	8	17	142
HR	87	71	158	113	86	199	80
BB	255	218	473	244	205	449	106
SO	481	515	996	523	447	970	103
E	39	46	85	49	61	110	77
E-Infield	31	39	70	39	55	94	74
LHB-Avg	.296	.236	.264	.273	.247	.260	102
LHB-HR	40	30	70	41	46	87	80
RHB-Avg	.272	.264	.268	.268	.261	.265	101
RHB-HR	47	41	88	72	40	112	79

2002-2004

	Home Games			Away Games			
	Cardinals	Opp	Total	Cardinals	Opp	Total	Index
G	222	222	444	222	222	444	
Avg	.276	.248	.262	.269	.267	.268	98
AB	7429	7676	15105	7816	7426	15242	99
R	1104	891	1995	1148	1008	2156	93
H	2053	1906	3959	2099	1986	4085	97
2B	437	404	841	418	401	819	104
3B	27	24	51	47	30	77	67
HR	244	213	457	288	256	544	85
BB	784	696	1480	745	694	1439	104
SO	1293	1464	2757	1425	1319	2744	101
E	115	148	263	132	162	294	89
E-Infield	93	126	219	104	139	243	90
LHB-Avg	.276	.245	.260	.268	.265	.267	98
LHB-HR	107	82	189	104	105	209	92
RHB-Avg	.276	.250	.263	.269	.269	.269	98
RHB-HR	137	131	268	184	151	335	80

2004 Rankings (National League)

- Second-lowest error factor
- Second-lowest infield-error factor
- Third-lowest home-run factor
- Third-lowest LHB home-run factor
- Third-lowest RHB home-run factor

Tony La Russa

Born: 10/04/44 in Tampa, FL

Playing Experience: 1963-1973, Oak, Atl, ChC

Managerial Experience: 26 seasons

2004 Season

A segment of the Cardinals' fan base has never seemed to accept Tony La Russa, but the number of critics was greatly reduced in 2004. With a team widely picked to finish no better than third in the strong National League Central, La Russa got the Cardinals rolling out of the gate, and the club went on to one of the most overpowering seasons in the proud history of St. Louis baseball. La Russa cleared one large hurdle by finally taking the Cards to the World Series. Unfortunately, the year ended with a four-game sweep at the hand of Boston.

Offense

The big bats in the middle of the Cardinals' order allow La Russa to often play for the big inning. However, he remains a hands-on skipper who loves to push the action with steals, hit-and-run plays and the occasional squeeze. La Russa is one of the best ever at extracting the maximum amount of production from his part-time players, displaying a great knack for placing them in situations that are the most advantageous to their abilities.

Pitching & Defense

No one in baseball wheels and deals his relievers more than La Russa. In 2004, he also was able to nurse a consistent and stable season from his deep five-man starting rotation. No team in baseball is better prepared than La Russa's Cardinals, who have hitters' and pitchers' meetings before every series. St. Louis' defensive placement is as skilled as any in baseball in terms of positioning and being on top of trends.

2005 Outlook

La Russa allowed the season to run its course without signing a contract extension, but it seems certain that the team of La Russa and general manager Walt Jocketty will remain intact for the next few years. La Russa has become very much imbued in the great Cardinals tradition, and would like nothing better than to lead the team to its first World Series title since 1982.

Manager Statistics

Year	Team, Lg	W	L	Pct	GB	Finish
2004	St. Louis, NL	105	57	.648	–	1st Central
26 Seasons		2114	1846	.534	–	–

2004 Starting Pitchers by Days Rest

	<=3	4	5	6+
Cardinals Starts	0	72	58	24
Cardinals ERA	-	3.91	3.85	3.98
NL Avg Starts	2	82	46	23
NL ERA	4.58	4.35	4.28	4.73

2004 Situational Stats

	Tony La Russa	NL Average
Hit & Run Success %	37.9	38.0
Stolen Base Success %	70.3	71.7
Platoon Pct.	50.5	55.2
Defensive Subs	23	18
High-Pitch Outings	6	6
Quick/Slow Hooks	19/16	21/12
Sacrifice Attempts	92	99

2004 Rankings (National League)

- 1st in double steals (3), squeeze plays (10), hit-and-run attempts (116) and saves with over 1 inning pitched (16)
- 2nd in stolen base attempts (158), steals of second base (96), steals of third base (15), mid-inning pitching changes (186), first-batter platoon percentage and one-batter pitcher appearances (54)
- 3rd in sacrifice-bunt percentage (85.9%) and slow hooks

St. Louis

Chris Carpenter

2004 Season

Though the end of his season was marred by nerve irritation in his right biceps muscle that sidelined him for the last two weeks of September and the entire postseason, Chris Carpenter made an impressive comeback from two years of arm trouble. Emerging as the Cardinals' No. 1 starter, Carpenter opened the year 7-1 and got more effective as the season went on. St. Louis was 20-8 in Carpenter's starts, despite providing him the lowest run support of any Cardinals starter.

Pitching

After a tentative beginning, Carpenter's stuff came all the way back as the season progressed. The velocity of both his two- and four-seam fastballs was consistently in the 93-95 MPH range, and he regained the sharpness on what has always been one of the better curveballs in baseball. Carpenter also developed excellent feel and command on his offspeed pitches. His control was outstanding, and his staying power increased with each passing week. Until his arm problem developed, Carpenter pitched into the seventh inning in all but four of his starts from May 28 on, one of those being a rain-delay situation.

Defense & Hitting

Carpenter pays close attention to runners and did not allow a stolen base all season (three runners were caught stealing). He is a good athlete who is an asset defensively. In his first major league season as a hitter, Carpenter was usually an automatic out, though he did manage five hits and four sacrifices.

2005 Outlook

Knowing Carpenter would likely miss an entire season after shoulder surgery, St. Louis gambled on signing him following the 2002 season, and the move paid off big time. Carpenter became the pitcher he has flirted with becoming since being drafted in the first round by Toronto in 1993. His physical troubles late last season were not serious, and the Cardinals feel they have a top-of-the-rotation pitcher who is entering his prime and capable of approaching 20 wins.

Position: SP
Bats: R **Throws:** R
Ht: 6' 6" **Wt:** 230

Opening Day Age: 29
Born: 4/27/75 in Exeter, NH
ML Seasons: 7

Overall Statistics

	W	L	Pct.	ERA	G	GS	Sv	IP	H	BB	SO	HR	Avg
'04	15	5	.750	3.46	28	28	0	182.0	169	38	152	24	.245
Car.	64	55	.538	4.59	180	163	0	1052.2	1153	369	764	135	.280

2004 Pitching Profile

	Chris Carpenter	NL Average
Overall Strike %	63.8	62.5
1st Pitch Strike %	61.0	58.5
Ratio	1.14	1.39
Strikeouts per 9 IP	7.52	6.74
Walks per 9 IP	1.88	3.38
Home Runs per 9 IP	1.19	1.11
Strikeout/Walk Ratio	4.00	1.99
Groundball/Flyball Ratio	1.93	1.25

2004 Situational Stats

	W	L	ERA	Sv	IP		AB	H	HR	RBI	Avg
Home	6	2	2.62	0	79.0	LHB	310	83	16	49	.268
Road	9	3	4.11	0	103.0	RHB	381	86	8	23	.226
First Half	9	4	3.87	0	111.2	Sc Pos	129	38	5	48	.295
Scnd Half	6	1	2.82	0	70.1	Clutch	74	17	2	6	.230

2004 Rankings (National League)

- 1st in lowest stolen-base percentage allowed (0.0)
- 2nd in winning percentage
- 4th in highest groundball-flyball ratio allowed (1.9)
- 5th in highest strikeout-walk ratio (4.0) and lowest on-base percentage allowed (.291)
- 6th in fewest walks per nine innings (1.9)
- 9th in wins
- Led the Cardinals in ERA, strikeouts, winning percentage, highest strikeout-walk ratio (4.0), lowest batting average allowed (.245), lowest slugging percentage allowed (.392), lowest on-base percentage allowed (.291), lowest stolen-base percentage allowed (0.0), fewest pitches thrown per batter (3.62), lowest ERA at home, most strikeouts per nine innings (7.5) and fewest walks per nine innings (1.9)

Jim Edmonds

2004 Season

With a strong second half, Jim Edmonds had another big season in St. Louis. Edmonds tied his career high in home runs and had a career-high RBI total while also hitting over .300 and placing among league leaders in walks. However, Edmonds finished his big year in a slump that included an 0-for-21 stretch and no homers over the last two weeks. Edmonds' late struggles at the plate carried over into the postseason when his only highlight was his walkoff home run to end the sixth game of the National League Championship Series.

Hitting

Edmonds is a complete hitter, equally dangerous against hard stuff and breaking balls. He has a good eye at the plate, and his exceptional oppo-site-field power makes him difficult to defense in the outfield. He loves to jump on first-pitch fast-balls and hit 12 first-pitch home runs last year. However, Boston's pitching in the World Series was able to underscore Edmonds' perennial flaw, a difficulty in laying off high fastballs and an at times haphazard approach. Boston also exposed Edmonds' career habit of giving away at bats by flailing on two-strike pitches out of the strike zone.

Baserunning & Defense

Last year, Edmonds had one of his better bases-stealing seasons, even though his baserunning habits are often sloppy. On a club that is noted for going hard on the bases, Edmonds at times can be an exception. He has meanwhile lost nothing in center field where he is one of the game's premier players, possessing remarkable range and flair to go with a strong and usually accurate throwing arm.

2005 Outlook

Edmonds' cocky, gliding style can sometimes grate on teammates and manager Tony La Russa. However, the Cardinals have little trouble looking the other way because the big picture with Edmonds is that he remains one of the game's elite players who should continue to contribute to one of baseball's best lineups.

Position: CF
Bats: L **Throws:** L
Ht: 6' 1" **Wt:** 212

Opening Day Age: 34
Born: 6/27/70 in Fullerton, CA
ML Seasons: 12
Pronunciation: ED-muns

St. Louis

Overall Statistics

G	AB	R	H	D	T	HR	RBI	SB	BB	SO	Avg	OBP	Slg
153	498	102	150	38	3	42	111	8	101	150	.301	.418	.643
1445	5090	975	1496	325	20	302	909	54	734	1272	.294	.384	.544

Where He Hits the Ball

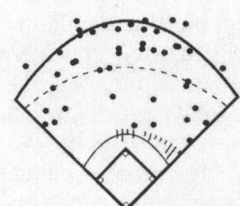

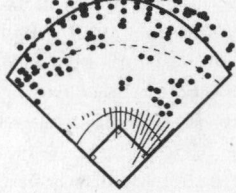

Vs. LHP   **Vs. RHP**

2004 Situational Stats

	AB	H	HR	RBI	Avg		AB	H	HR	RBI	Avg
Home	252	80	24	55	.317	LHP	106	35	5	23	.330
Road	246	70	18	56	.285	RHP	392	115	37	88	.293
First Half	278	79	21	56	.284	Sc Pos	144	36	9	66	.250
Scnd Half	220	71	21	55	.323	Clutch	77	18	4	10	.234

2004 Rankings (National League)

- 1st in lowest percentage of swings put into play (31.9)
- 2nd in HR frequency (11.9 ABs per HR)
- 3rd in slugging percentage
- 4th in most pitches seen per plate appearance (4.23), fewest GDPs per GDP situation (3.3%) and lowest fielding percentage in center field (.988)
- 5th in home runs
- Led the Cardinals in walks, intentional walks (12), strikeouts, pitches seen (2,587), on-base percentage, HR frequency (11.9 ABs per HR), most pitches seen per plate appearance (4.23) and fewest GDPs per GDP situation (3.3%)
- Led NL center fielders in home runs and RBI

Jason Isringhausen

2004 Season

A return to health by closer Jason Isringhausen was as important a factor as any in St. Louis' successful 2004 season. Isringhausen set career highs in saves, opportunities and games pitched on the way to tying for the NL saves lead. He also tied the Cardinals' club saves record set by Lee Smith in 1991. Isringhausen allowed an earned run in only 17 of his 74 appearances and only three of his seven blown saves came in the second half of the season. He was shaky earlier in the postseason, but came up big several times during the NLCS against Houston.

Pitching

Isringhausen sent a message to the Cardinals last spring by arriving in excellent physical condition. Though at times plagued by a tired shoulder, Isringhausen's best stuff largely held up over the balance of the season. His fastball, with excellent late movement, routinely was clocked in the 94-96 MPH range, offsetting his low-90s cutter. Isringhausen has also developed confidence in his command of a power curve that he now throws in any count. At times he has also shown an offspeed pitch, though it remains a third option. Isringhausen remains vulnerable when he does not get ahead of hitters and his command of the strike zone can occasionally become erratic.

Defense & Hitting

Like many closers, Isringhausen is easy to run on. However, it is rarely a factor in his success or failure. He is only a mediocre fielder. He has trouble coming off the mound and often is erratic when fielding bunts or trying to throw to second to begin double plays. Isringhausen rarely bats but is not an automatic out when he gets the chance.

2005 Outlook

Isringhausen underwent surgery to repair a torn labrum in his left hip in mid-November, but he was expected to be fully healthy by mid-January and ready for spring training. There may be more overpowering closers, but the Cardinals are more than satisfied with Isringhausen. He has become much better prepared and conditioned as he has reached his pitching prime, and the Cardinals can expect him to remain a consistent 40-plus saves closer.

Position: RP
Bats: R **Throws:** R
Ht: 6' 3" **Wt:** 230

Opening Day Age: 32
Born: 9/7/72 in Brighton, IL
ML Seasons: 9
Pronunciation: IS-ring-how-zin
Nickname: Izzy

Overall Statistics

	W	L	Pct.	ERA	G	GS	Sv	IP	H	BB	SO	HR	Avg
'04	4	2	.667	2.87	74	0	47	75.1	55	23	71	5	.199
Car.	35	34	.507	3.72	385	52	177	682.0	635	274	556	49	.247

2004 Pitching Profile

	Jason Isringhausen	NL Average
Overall Strike %	62.4	62.5
1st Pitch Strike %	55.8	58.5
Ratio	1.04	1.39
Strikeouts per 9 IP	8.48	6.74
Walks per 9 IP	2.75	3.38
Home Runs per 9 IP	0.60	1.11
Strikeout/Walk Ratio	3.09	1.99
Groundball/Flyball Ratio	1.36	1.25

2004 Situational Stats

	W	L	ERA	Sv	IP		AB	H	HR	RBI	Avg
Home	2	1	4.63	19	35.0	LHB	122	25	2	14	.205
Road	2	1	1.34	28	40.1	RHB	154	30	3	17	.195
First Half	3	2	2.83	21	41.1	Sc Pos	86	17	1	22	.198
Scnd Half	1	0	2.91	26	34.0	Clutch	179	29	2	18	.162

2004 Rankings (National League)

- 1st in saves and games finished (66)
- 3rd in fewest GDPs induced per GDP situation (2.6%)
- 4th in first batter efficiency (.116)
- 6th in blown saves (7) and fewest baserunners allowed per nine innings in relief (9.6)
- 7th in lowest batting average allowed in relief (.199)
- 8th in save percentage (87.0)
- Led the Cardinals in saves, games finished (66), lowest batting average allowed vs. righthanded batters, save percentage (87.0), lowest batting average allowed with runners in scoring position, blown saves (7), relief innings (75.1), most strikeouts per nine innings in relief (8.5) and fewest baserunners allowed per nine innings in relief (9.6)

Jason Marquis

2004 Season

A disappointing tease for several years with Atlanta, Jason Marquis turned around his career after being traded to St. Louis. In a breakthrough season, Marquis set a career high with 15 victories while going over 200 innings for the first time. He was a major factor when the Cardinals blew away the rest of the National League Central, putting together a 11-game winning streak stretching from Memorial Day to Labor Day. Marquis ended the year in disappointing fashion, struggling in most of his postseason appearances.

Pitching

Marquis has always had the equipment to be a successful major-league starter. However, until he took the advice of Cards pitching coach Dave Duncan and started using a two-seam, sinking fastball, he had always been inconsistent. Marquis throws the sinker in the low to mid-90s, along with a four-seam fastball and a cutter. He mixes in a decent curve and change. Marquis has always been stubborn about taking advice, and that remained the case late in the season when he ignored suggestions that he might have been tipping his pitches.

Defense & Hitting

Like most pitchers schooled in the Atlanta system, Marquis is a complete player who holds runners, fields his position well and makes all the fundamental plays. Marquis is also one of the best-hitting pitchers in baseball. He led all NL pitchers with 21 hits, along with six doubles and nine runs batted in. Marquis is also a good enough athlete to be used as a pinch-runner.

2005 Outlook

His strong 2004 season underscored how Marquis' ability makes him a legitimate candidate to be a consistent 15-17 game winner. The challenge always has been for him to accept instructions instead of insisting he had all the answers. Marquis made progress in that area last year, and at just 26 years old, there's no reason he should not be a major part of the Cardinals' rotation for years to come.

Position: SP
Bats: L **Throws:** R
Ht: 6' 1" **Wt:** 210

Opening Day Age: 26
Born: 8/21/78 in Manhasset, NY
ML Seasons: 5
Pronunciation: mar-KEE

Overall Statistics

	W	L	Pct.	ERA	G	GS	Sv	IP	H	BB	SO	HR	Avg
'04	15	7	.682	3.71	32	32	0	201.1	215	70	138	26	.275
Car.	29	22	.569	4.16	128	72	1	509.0	521	208	356	66	.266

2004 Pitching Profile

	Jason Marquis	NL Average
Overall Strike %	61.8	62.5
1st Pitch Strike %	58.4	58.5
Ratio	1.42	1.39
Strikeouts per 9 IP	6.17	6.74
Walks per 9 IP	3.13	3.38
Home Runs per 9 IP	1.16	1.11
Strikeout/Walk Ratio	1.97	1.99
Groundball/Flyball Ratio	2.17	1.25

2004 Situational Stats

	W	L	ERA	Sv	IP		AB	H	HR	RBI	Avg
Home	9	5	3.76	0	115.0	LHB	363	101	14	44	.278
Road	6	2	3.65	0	86.1	RHB	420	114	12	38	.271
First Half	9	4	3.88	0	106.2	Sc Pos	197	39	2	47	.198
Scnd Half	6	3	3.52	0	94.2	Clutch	34	8	1	3	.235

2004 Rankings (National League)

- 2nd in highest groundball-flyball ratio allowed (2.2)
- 3rd in errors at pitcher (3)
- 7th in lowest fielding percentage at pitcher (.945)
- 9th in wins, winning percentage and most run support per nine innings (5.9)
- 10th in hits allowed, GDPs induced (21), lowest batting average allowed with runners in scoring position and highest batting average allowed (.275)
- Led the Cardinals in games started, hits allowed, batters faced (874), walks allowed, hit batsmen (10), pitches thrown (3,328), highest groundball-flyball ratio allowed (2.2) and most run support per nine innings (5.9)

Matt Morris

2004 Season

Inconsistent stuff amid suspicions of arm trouble produced an inconsistent season for Matt Morris. Though he won 15 games, Morris' ERA was the highest of his career and nearly a full run higher than in 2003. Only one National League pitcher allowed more home runs. At the same time, Morris worked over 200 innings while leading his club in starts and winning 11 of his final 16 decisions. He was winless in four postseason starts.

Pitching

Whether it was due to shoulder weakness or mechanical troubles, Morris was no longer the power pitcher who could blow away opponents with his hard stuff. A tell-tale sign that he often could not get his shoulder loose was that three times in the second half, he was knocked out within the first two innings. Except on rare occasions, his fastball rarely topped the 90-92 MPH level. As a result, Morris had to rely more on his breaking stuff and sinker, which last year helped him induce 26 double plays, the third most among National League pitchers. Morris has developed an outstanding changeup over the last three years, and he is usually around the plate—sometimes too much, as evidenced by his high home-run total.

Defense & Hitting

Morris has worked to develop a better pickoff move, but he remains slow delivering to the plate and last year 11 of 14 basestealers were successful against him. Morris handles the other defensive chores very well, and swings the bat with above-average ability.

2005 Outlook

Morris entered the offseason as a free agent, but the Cardinals wanted him back and signed him to a one-year incentive-laden deal prior to the December deadline for offering players arbitration. Morris underwent shoulder surgery in November to clean up a frayed labrum, but the Cards expect him to be 100-percent healthy by early this season.

Position: SP
Bats: R **Throws:** R
Ht: 6' 5" **Wt:** 220

Opening Day Age: 30
Born: 8/9/74 in Middletown, NY
ML Seasons: 7

Overall Statistics

	W	L	Pct.	ERA	G	GS	Sv	IP	H	BB	SO	HR	Avg
'04	15	10	.600	4.72	32	32	0	202.0	205	56	131	35	.266
Car.	87	52	.626	3.53	206	175	4	1184.2	1159	341	869	107	.259

2004 Pitching Profile

	Matt Morris	NL Average
Overall Strike %	64.0	62.5
1st Pitch Strike %	62.7	58.5
Ratio	1.29	1.39
Strikeouts per 9 IP	5.84	6.74
Walks per 9 IP	2.50	3.38
Home Runs per 9 IP	1.56	1.11
Strikeout/Walk Ratio	2.34	1.99
Groundball/Flyball Ratio	1.59	1.25

2004 Situational Stats

	W	L	ERA	Sv	IP		AB	H	HR	RBI	Avg
Home	9	4	3.69	0	112.1	LHB	347	90	18	60	.259
Road	6	6	6.02	0	89.2	RHB	423	115	17	52	.272
First Half	9	6	4.33	0	124.2	Sc Pos	164	46	11	72	.280
Scnd Half	6	4	5.35	0	77.1	Clutch	55	10	0	2	.182

2004 Rankings (National League)

- 1st in highest ERA on the road
- 2nd in home runs allowed
- 3rd in shutouts (2) and GDPs induced (26)
- 5th in most home runs allowed per nine innings (1.56)
- 6th in complete games (3)
- 8th in highest ERA
- 9th in wins, highest slugging percentage allowed (.457) and highest stolen-base percentage allowed (78.6)
- Led the Cardinals in losses, games started, complete games (3), shutouts (2), innings pitched, home runs allowed, stolen bases allowed (11) and GDPs induced (26)

Albert Pujols

2004 Season

Maybe nothing sums up Albert Pujols better than the company he keeps. Another monster season left him with 504 career runs batted in over his first four seasons. The only other players with over 500 RBI in their first four seasons were Ted Williams and Joe DiMaggio. Pujols also became the only player ever with 30 or more homers in each of his first four years, and was third in the National League MVP voting. He finished the year with a strong postseason, though he failed to drive in a run in the World Series.

Hitting

National League pitchers find few ways to consistently retire Pujols. He can occasionally appear anxious on offspeed pitches away, a strategy Boston used with some success in the World Series. And it is sometimes possible to jam Pujols with high, hard stuff. However, he turns on the best hard stuff with amazing regularity, and pitching him away runs the risk of him using his remarkable power to the opposite field. Pujols has always been an outstanding breaking-ball hitter, and his mastery of the strike zone improves each year.

Baserunning & Defense

Pujols' below-average speed has been further impaired by planter fasciitis in his left foot, which he had surgically corrected over the winter. He is an aggressive baserunner who makes good decisions. After three years of moving between third base, first base and left field, the Cardinals made Pujols their everyday first baseman last year. Despite limited range, he grew into a solid defensive asset with an accurate arm and improving ability to pick low throws from the dirt.

2005 Outlook

It seems that the only person not impressed with Pujols' amazing production is Pujols himself. He constantly works on both his swing and his defense, and it is that attitude that firmly places him among the game's greatest players. The Cardinals were quick to recognize that fact last winter, signing Pujols to a contract that will keep him in St. Louis through the decade.

Position: 1B
Bats: R **Throws:** R
Ht: 6' 3" **Wt:** 225

Opening Day Age: 25
Born: 1/16/80 in Santo Domingo, DR
ML Seasons: 4
Pronunciation: POOH-holz

Overall Statistics

	G	AB	R	H	D	T	HR	RBI	SB	BB	SO	Avg	OBP	Slg
'04	154	592	133	196	51	2	46	123	5	84	52	.331	.415	.657
Car.	629	2363	500	787	189	9	160	504	13	304	279	.333	.413	.624

Where He Hits the Ball

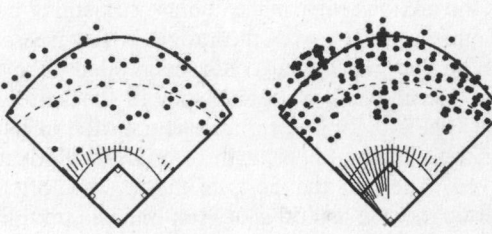

Vs. LHP   **Vs. RHP**

2004 Situational Stats

	AB	H	HR	RBI	Avg		AB	H	HR	RBI	Avg
Home	295	98	18	60	.332	LHP	116	44	9	34	.379
Road	297	98	28	63	.330	RHP	476	152	37	89	.319
First Half	312	95	22	60	.304	Sc Pos	143	49	10	71	.343
Scnd Half	280	101	24	63	.361	Clutch	79	26	8	18	.329

2004 Rankings (National League)

- 1st in runs scored, total bases (389) and batting average vs. lefthanded pitchers
- 2nd in home runs, doubles and slugging percentage
- 3rd in RBI
- 4th in errors at first base (10)
- 5th in batting average, hits, sacrifice flies (9), times on base (287), batting average with two strikes (.279) and lowest fielding percentage at first base (.994)
- Led the Cardinals in at-bats, intentional walks (12), times on base (287), GDPs (21), plate appearances (692), games played, highest percentage of swings put into play (51.1)
- Led NL first basemen in home runs and RBI

Edgar Renteria

2004 Season

A sluggish start, several shifts in the batting order, and some apparent discomfort about his contract status combined to produce some disappointing numbers for Edgar Renteria. The Cardinal shortstop hit under .300 with fewer than 80 RBI for the first time in three years. Even so, Renteria was among the top shortstops offensively in the National League and was the starting NL shortstop in the All-Star game.

Hitting

Renteria has good bat speed with his short stroke and the ability to spray balls with power to all fields. However, for much of last year, Renteria was too anxious early in the count—something he had grown out of over the previous few years. Part of the impatience could be related to his never settling into a regular spot in the batting order. The No. 2 hitter for an early portion of the year, he batted fifth or sixth after Larry Walker arrived. Then in the postseason, he was often inserted into the leadoff spot. Renteria had trouble making the adjustments in terms of pitch selection and working counts.

Baserunning & Defense

Always a good baserunner, Renteria had a poor basestealing season, getting caught 11 times in only 28 attempts. The Dodgers' Cesar Izturis supplanted him as the NL Gold Glove shortstop, but that was no indictment of Renteria, who is one of the game's most fluid and complete shortstops with excellent range, very soft hands and a strong arm.

2005 Outlook

St. Louis tried unsuccessfully to sign Renteria during spring training and then suspended talks during the season. As a result, he was a free agent this offseason, and few players were more coveted. St. Louis intended to do its best to keep one of the best in the business at his position. Whoever ends up with Renteria will get an outstanding performer who won't turn 30 until this summer, and who is a very positive personality in the clubhouse.

Position: SS
Bats: R **Throws:** R
Ht: 6' 1" **Wt:** 200

Opening Day Age: 29
Born: 8/7/75 in Barranquilla, Colombia
ML Seasons: 9
Pronunciation: ren-ter-EE-ah

Overall Statistics

	G	AB	R	H	D	T	HR	RBI	SB	BB	SO	Avg	OBP	Slg
'04	149	586	84	168	37	0	10	72	17	39	78	.287	.327	.401
Car.	1296	4922	734	1423	264	17	83	565	237	434	675	.289	.346	.400

Where He Hits the Ball

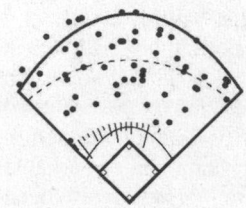
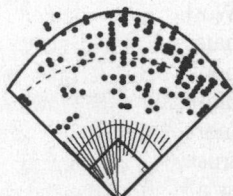

Vs. LHP   **Vs. RHP**

2004 Situational Stats

	AB	H	HR	RBI	Avg		AB	H	HR	RBI	Avg
Home	286	83	7	40	.290	LHP	131	48	4	20	.366
Road	300	85	3	32	.283	RHP	455	120	6	52	.264
First Half	315	89	6	40	.283	Sc Pos	140	40	3	58	.286
Scnd Half	271	79	4	32	.292	Clutch	85	14	1	5	.165

2004 Rankings (National League)

- 2nd in batting average vs. lefthanded pitchers and lowest stolen-base percentage (60.7)
- 3rd in sacrifice flies (10) and caught stealing (11)
- 4th in fielding percentage at shortstop (.983)
- 5th in lowest batting average in the clutch
- 7th in errors at shortstop (11)
- Led the Cardinals in sacrifice flies (10) and caught stealing (11)

Scott Rolen

2004 Season

Until leg problems sidelined him for much of September, Scott Rolen was a serious challenger for the National League Most Valuable Player award. Despite the discouraging finish which included a poor postseason (aside from his game-winning homer in the seventh game of the NLCS), Rolen batted better than .300 for the first time in his career and reached career highs in numerous other categories. Along the way, he reaffirmed his position as the game's premier defensive third baseman with his sixth Gold Glove Award.

Hitting

The Rolen who was shut down by Boston in the World Series was not the same hitter who dominated the NL for most of the regular season. The book on Rolen has always been to crowd him with high, hard stuff. He laid off those pitches much more effectively last season, until showing his frustration during the postseason. Rolen's growth as a hitter included working the strike zone to his benefit more consistently along with adding strength to increase his power. He ranked third in the NL in batting with runners in scoring position last year.

Baserunning & Defense

On a team loaded with excellent baserunners, manager Tony La Russa frequently singled out Rolen as being "one of the best baserunners I've ever seen." Rolen lacks basestealing speed, especially with his recently frequent leg troubles. However, no one is better at breaking up double plays or taking the extra base. As for his defense, suffice to say that his package of great range, soft hands, lightening-quick reactions and strong arm have baseball veterans seriously mentioning him in the same class as legendary third baseman such as Brooks Robinson and Mike Schmidt.

2005 Outlook

Rolen will be only 30 this spring, and his best years still could be ahead of him. He is already an All-Star fixture at his position and signed through the decade as an irreplaceable part of the Cardinals' organization.

Position: 3B
Bats: R **Throws:** R
Ht: 6' 4" **Wt:** 240

Opening Day Age: 29
Born: 4/4/75 in Jasper, IN
ML Seasons: 9
Pronunciation: ROH-len

St. Louis

Overall Statistics

	G	AB	R	H	D	T	HR	RBI	SB	BB	SO	Avg	OBP	Slg
'04	142	500	109	157	32	4	34	124	4	72	92	.314	.409	.598
Car.	1195	4389	777	1254	296	28	226	831	91	600	944	.286	.378	.520

Where He Hits the Ball

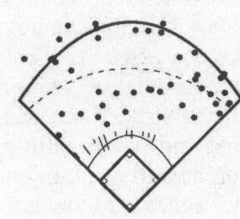

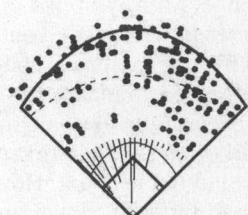

Vs. LHP   **Vs. RHP**

2004 Situational Stats

	AB	H	HR	RBI	Avg		AB	H	HR	RBI	Avg
Home	257	73	10	51	.284	LHP	89	33	6	27	.371
Road	243	84	24	73	.346	RHP	411	124	28	97	.302
First Half	304	103	18	80	.339	Sc Pos	151	54	14	95	.358
Scnd Half	196	54	16	44	.276	Clutch	69	15	4	12	.217

2004 Rankings (National League)

- 1st in batting average with the bases loaded (.583)
- 2nd in RBI
- 3rd in batting average with runners in scoring position
- 4th in cleanup slugging percentage (.604), batting average on the road and fielding percentage at third base (.977)
- 5th in lowest groundball-flyball ratio (0.7)
- 6th in slugging percentage
- Led the Cardinals in triples, RBI, hit by pitch (13), batting average with runners in scoring position, batting average with the bases loaded (.583), cleanup slugging percentage (.604) and batting average on the road

Reggie Sanders

2004 Season

Playing for his seventh different team in as many years, Reggie Sanders had an inconsistent, but overall solid season in St. Louis. Sanders got off to a blistering start with eight home runs in April, but struggled for the remainder of the first half of the season. His playing time during the second half was often limited, especially after the Cardinals acquired right fielder Larry Walker. However, Sanders still ended up with the fourth 20-20 season of his well-traveled career. He also reached the 20-homer mark for his sixth different team, an all-time record.

Hitting

Sanders always piles up the strikeouts, and has never failed to strike out at least 100 times in any of his full seasons. Though he possesses excellent bat speed, Sanders has big holes in his swing, especially on fastballs up in the strike zone. He will often swing at first pitches and end up falling behind in the count. However, he still can turn on most fastballs down in the zone, and he has always been a good mistake hitter as well as someone who bears down and produces in clutch situations. He also can do extra-base damage to the opposite field.

Baserunning & Defense

There are few 37 year olds in better physical condition than Sanders, who remains a high-percentage stolen-base threat and a solid all-around baserunner with smart aggressiveness on the bases. Sanders can play either corner outfield position with above-average range, though he will occasionally misjudge a ball. He has an above-average arm and will produce his share of assists because of the quickness with which he releases throws.

2005 Outlook

For the first time in a long while, Sanders entered the offseason not having to worry where he would play the next year. St. Louis already has him signed for 2005, and he should remain both a valuable part of the lineup and positive force in the clubhouse.

Position: RF/LF
Bats: R **Throws:** R
Ht: 6' 1" **Wt:** 205

Opening Day Age: 37
Born: 12/1/67 in Florence, SC
ML Seasons: 14

Overall Statistics

G	AB	R	H	D	T	HR	RBI	SB	BB	SO	Avg	OBP	Slg
135	446	64	116	27	3	22	67	21	33	118	.260	.315	.482
1572	5548	931	1483	297	57	271	869	283	607	1438	.267	.344	.488

Where He Hits the Ball

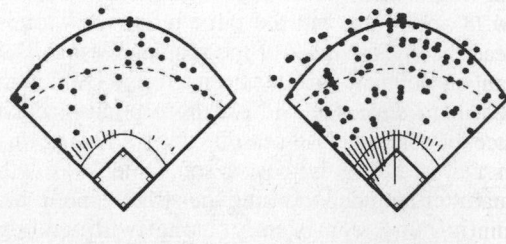

Vs. LHP   **Vs. RHP**

2004 Situational Stats

	AB	H	HR	RBI	Avg		AB	H	HR	RBI	Avg
Home	218	63	8	36	.289	LHP	113	26	3	14	.230
Road	228	53	14	31	.232	RHP	333	90	19	53	.270
First Half	265	68	14	43	.257	Sc Pos	125	35	4	44	.280
Scnd Half	181	48	8	24	.265	Clutch	83	21	3	16	.253

2004 Rankings (National League)

- 4th in steals of third (6)
- 5th in lowest batting average vs. lefthanded pitchers
- 8th in lowest percentage of swings put into play (34.5)
- 9th in highest percentage of swings that missed (29.7)
- 10th in fewest GDPs per GDP situation (4.7%)
- Led the Cardinals in steals of third (6)

Jeff Suppan

2004 Season

Jeff Suppan proved to be yet another shrewd acquisition by the Cardinals' canny general manager Walt Jocketty. Signed to a two-year contract plus a club option in December 2003, Suppan won a career-high 16 games, including 10 on the road—the second most in the National League. He finished strongly by winning 13 of his final 18 decisions, then becoming the Cardinals' best starter in an otherwise disappointing postseason rotation.

Pitching

Lacking one overpowering pitch, Suppan is successful by mixing speeds and locations. He will sink his fastball, which usually does not top the low 90s. He also shows a cutter, can often get ahead with his good curveball, and will also throw changeups in any count. Suppan has above-average control, though he can tend to nibble too much with runners on base. He rarely makes hitters miss the ball, and that hurts when he is in a situation that requires a strikeout. Suppan can eat innings, though he was under 200 innings last year for the first time in six years. At times he had trouble holding his best stuff much the past 100-pitch mark.

Defense & Hitting

Suppan fields his position well, but he lacks a decent pickoff move and is slow coming home. That makes him vulnerable to stolen bases, and basestealers were successful last year in 11 of 14 tries. He is not much of a threat batting, but he does handle the bat well enough to be serviceable in sacrifice bunt situations.

2005 Outlook

The Cardinals could not have expected more out of Suppan than they received. Signed for another season with an option in 2006, he would appear to be set in the St. Louis rotation unless the club elects to shop him to save money for use somewhere else. With a good all-around club like the Cardinals, Suppan should be able to win 13-15 games and be a durable asset to the rotation.

Position: SP
Bats: R **Throws:** R
Ht: 6' 2" **Wt:** 220

Opening Day Age: 30
Born: 1/2/75 in Oklahoma City, OK
ML Seasons: 10
Pronunciation: SOO-pahn

Overall Statistics

	W	L	Pct.	ERA	G	GS	Sv	IP	H	BB	SO	HR	Avg
'04	16	9	.640	4.16	31	31	0	188.0	192	65	110	25	.265
Car.	78	84	.481	4.80	253	237	0	1480.1	1616	480	830	202	.278

2004 Pitching Profile

	Jeff Suppan	NL Average
Overall Strike %	61.0	62.5
1st Pitch Strike %	59.3	58.5
Ratio	1.37	1.39
Strikeouts per 9 IP	5.27	6.74
Walks per 9 IP	3.11	3.38
Home Runs per 9 IP	1.20	1.11
Strikeout/Walk Ratio	1.69	1.99
Groundball/Flyball Ratio	1.59	1.25

2004 Situational Stats

	W	L	ERA	Sv	IP		AB	H	HR	RBI	Avg
Home	6	8	4.75	0	96.2	LHB	309	84	13	40	.272
Road	10	1	3.55	0	91.1	RHB	416	108	12	45	.260
First Half	8	5	3.33	0	105.1	Sc Pos	174	38	4	57	.218
Scnd Half	8	4	5.23	0	82.2	Clutch	30	6	0	4	.200

2004 Rankings (National League)
- 5th in wins and highest ERA at home
- 9th in highest stolen-base percentage allowed (78.6)
- Led the Cardinals in wins, stolen bases allowed (11) and lowest ERA on the road

Larry Walker

2004 Season

A once-great career seemingly cast adrift received new life when the Rockies traded Larry Walker to St. Louis last August. Inspired by his exuberant acceptance from the great Cardinals fans, Walker displayed regular flashes of the ability that had made him one of the game's best players. Walker had missed most of the first half of the season in Colorado with a strained left groin but stayed healthy in his two months with St. Louis. He finished with a strong postseason.

Hitting

Like anyone who has played in Colorado, Walker's offensive numbers have been inflated over the years. However, in his prime he had Triple Crown tools. Walker still has good bat speed, though he can be overpowered when crowded by hard stuff. He also has the ability to work counts into his favor. In recent years, Walker has been more prone to chasing breaking balls out of the strike zone, but he remains a dangerous mistake hitter with good power to all fields and the ability to hit both left- and righthanded pitching.

Baserunning & Defense

Though possessing only average speed at this stage of his career, Walker can steal bases in pressure situations, and he is aggressive as anybody in taking the extra base. Though he has lost a step or two of range in the field, Walker always seems to get a quick jump on the ball. He has strong and accurate arm, combined with a quick release that prevents most runners from taking extra bases against him.

2005 Outlook

Nagged by injuries and a seemingly declining desire for excellence, Walker's reputation has been in serious decline. However, the winning atmosphere in St. Louis could be the tonic he needs at his advanced baseball age. He vowed at the end of the season to work hard on offseason conditioning, and hitting amid the Cardinals' Murderer's Row could result in Walker putting up some major numbers for St. Louis this season.

Position: RF
Bats: L **Throws:** R
Ht: 6' 3" **Wt:** 235

Opening Day Age: 38
Born: 12/1/66 in Maple Ridge, BC, Canada
ML Seasons: 16

Overall Statistics

G	AB	R	H	D	T	HR	RBI	SB	BB	SO	Avg	OBP	Slg
82	258	51	77	16	4	17	47	6	49	57	.298	.424	.589
1888	6592	1289	2069	451	61	368	1259	228	872	1167	.314	.401	.568

Where He Hits the Ball

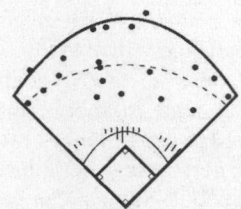 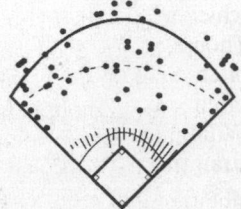

Vs. LHP   **Vs. RHP**

2004 Situational Stats

	AB	H	HR	RBI	Avg		AB	H	HR	RBI	Avg
Home	135	42	7	21	.311	LHP	76	24	1	12	.316
Road	123	35	10	26	.285	RHP	182	53	16	35	.291
First Half	45	14	3	10	.311	Sc Pos	59	10	3	24	.169
Scnd Half	213	63	14	37	.296	Clutch	48	13	2	9	.271

2004 Rankings (National League)

- Did not rank near the top or bottom in any category

Position: SP
Bats: R **Throws:** R
Ht: 6' 0" **Wt:** 200

Opening Day Age: 38
Born: 8/19/66 in
Houston, TX
ML Seasons: 12

2004 Season

After offseason shoulder surgery, Woody Williams pitched only sparingly in spring training and did not reach full strength until over a month into the season. After a 1-5 start, Williams went 10-3 the rest of the way, with opponents batting below .239 against him over his final 19 starts. With Chris Carpenter sidelined, Williams became the Cardinals' No. 1 starter in the postseason and pitched well until struggling in his one World Series start.

Pitching

Williams has an assortment of ways to get batters out. He relies heavily on a good cut fastball, which he can throw in the 89-92 MPH range. Though the cutter is often his bread and butter pitch, Williams also has an effective curve that he often employs as a strikeout pitch. In addition, Williams has outstanding command of a good straight change. He loses velocity and effectiveness in a hurry, so pitch counts are an issue with him. He pitched past the seventh inning only twice last year. Williams is a team leader who will battle in every start, even without his best stuff.

Defense & Hitting

Lacking a good pickoff move, Williams tries to vary his delivery in order to freeze runners. However, he was still nicked for 10 stolen bases last year. Williams is a poised, heady defensive player, but he did make three errors last year. He is also a good hitting pitcher, so confident with the bat that he tried to argue Tony La Russa out of using a designated hitter in Game 1 of the World Series in Boston.

2005 Outlook

The Cardinals declined their 2005 option on Williams, making him a free agent, and San Diego signed him to a one-year, $3.5 million contract that includes incentives and a 2006 option. San Diego GM Kevin Towers, who had Williams on the Padres' staff from 1999-2001, called trading Williams to the Cardinals "the worst deal I ever made."

Overall Statistics

	W	L	Pct.	ERA	G	GS	Sv	IP	H	BB	SO	HR	Avg
'04	11	8	.579	4.18	31	31	0	189.2	193	58	131	20	.262
Car.	103	84	.551	4.05	338	247	0	1723.1	1675	572	1201	229	.254

2004 Pitching Profile

	Woody Williams	NL Average
Overall Strike %	62.1	62.5
1st Pitch Strike %	58.9	58.5
Ratio	1.32	1.39
Strikeouts per 9 IP	6.22	6.74
Walks per 9 IP	2.75	3.38
Home Runs per 9 IP	0.95	1.11
Strikeout/Walk Ratio	2.26	1.99
Groundball/Flyball Ratio	0.93	1.25

2004 Situational Stats

	W	L	ERA	Sv	IP		AB	H	HR	RBI	Avg
Home	5	3	3.36	0	96.1	LHB	337	75	9	35	.223
Road	6	5	5.01	0	93.1	RHB	399	118	11	55	.296
First Half	6	6	4.09	0	103.1	Sc Pos	182	47	4	68	.258
Scnd Half	5	2	4.27	0	86.1	Clutch	33	8	0	1	.242

2004 Rankings (National League)

- 3rd in wild pitches (12) and errors at pitcher (3)
- 6th in lowest groundball-flyball ratio allowed (0.9) and lowest fielding percentage at pitcher (.944)
- 8th in highest ERA on the road and highest batting average allowed vs. righthanded batters
- Led the Cardinals in wild pitches (12), pick off throws (61), runners caught stealing (6) and fewest home runs allowed per nine innings (.95)

St. Louis

Marlon Anderson

Position: 2B/LF/RF
Bats: L **Throws:** R
Ht: 5'11" **Wt:** 200

Opening Day Age: 31
Born: 1/6/74 in Montgomery, AL
ML Seasons: 7

Overall Statistics

	G	AB	R	H	D	T	HR	RBI	SB	BB	SO	Avg	OBP	Slg
'04	113	253	31	60	12	0	8	28	6	12	38	.237	.269	.379
Car.	737	2453	285	647	136	16	40	277	55	167	332	.264	.311	.381

2004 Situational Stats

	AB	H	HR	RBI	Avg		AB	H	HR	RBI	Avg
Home	106	29	2	14	.274	LHP	25	4	0	1	.160
Road	147	31	6	14	.211	RHP	228	56	8	27	.246
First Half	150	39	5	17	.260	Sc Pos	50	11	1	20	.220
Scnd Half	103	21	3	11	.204	Clutch	58	16	2	11	.276

2004 Season

After failing to win the starting second base job in spring training, Marlon Anderson became a solid role player in his first year with St. Louis. Along with filling in effectively at second and occasionally in the outfield, Anderson became one of the National League's best pinch-hitters. He tied for the league lead in pinch-hits with 17.

Hitting, Baserunning & Defense

A free swinger, Anderson can hit the fastball. He tries to lift too many balls to stay consistent. He does not work counts effectively, and he is vulnerable to breaking balls. Anderson has above-average speed and can be a high-percentage basestealer. He remains a crude defensive player at second. His range is more than adequate, but he often throws without setting himself and is inconsistent in turning the double play. As an occasional outfielder, Anderson is adequate at best in left.

2005 Outlook

Anderson brings some offensive skills to his utility role, and manager Tony La Russa has a well-known fondness for players who can play both the infield and outfield. However, Anderson's lack of consistency both in the field and at bat could make him expendable if the Cardinals can find a better all-around alternative.

Kiko Calero

Position: RP
Bats: R **Throws:** R
Ht: 6' 1" **Wt:** 180

Opening Day Age: 30
Born: 1/9/75 in Santurce, PR
ML Seasons: 2

Overall Statistics

	W	L	Pct.	ERA	G	GS	Sv	IP	H	BB	SO	HR	Avg
'04	3	1	.750	2.78	41	0	2	45.1	27	10	47	5	.176
Car.	4	2	.667	2.80	67	1	3	83.2	56	30	98	10	.193

2004 Situational Stats

	W	L	ERA	Sv	IP		AB	H	HR	RBI	Avg
Home	2	0	4.18	1	23.2	LHB	57	10	3	8	.175
Road	1	1	1.25	1	21.2	RHB	96	17	2	6	.177
First Half	0	0	3.28	1	24.2	Sc Pos	35	8	2	10	.229
Scnd Half	3	1	2.18	1	20.2	Clutch	48	5	1	3	.104

2004 Season

Called up from the minors in early May, Kiko Calero gradually was given increasing responsibility in the busy and deep St. Louis bullpen. He produced an outstanding strikeout to walk ratio and earned either a win, save or hold in 16 of his final 35 appearances. After being sidelined for most of August with rotator cuff tendinitis, Calero played an important role in the first two rounds of the postseason, though he did not pitch well in the World Series.

Pitching, Defense & Hitting

Calero is tough to hit because of the sharp movement of his 90-plus cutter and his ability to mix in a hard curve and a change. He is usually around the plate and can be prone to the longball when he hangs his breaking pitches. He is a good athlete who handles himself well defensively and has shown signs in limited chances of being able to handle the bat.

2005 Outlook

One of the unrecognized factors in the Cardinals' disappointing 2003 collapse was the loss of Calero to a ruptured right patella tendon. He returned last year to become a very useful reliever for the Cardinals and should be a key part of the club's setup group this season.

Cal Eldred

Position: RP
Bats: R **Throws:** R
Ht: 6' 4" **Wt:** 240

Opening Day Age: 37
Born: 11/24/67 in
Cedar Rapids, IA
ML Seasons: 13
Pronunciation:
EL-dred

Overall Statistics

	W	L	Pct.	ERA	G	GS	Sv	IP	H	BB	SO	HR	Avg
'04	4	2	.667	3.76	52	0	1	67.0	71	17	54	11	.276
Car.	85	74	.535	4.48	310	191	9	1331.0	1305	558	910	170	.257

2004 Situational Stats

	W	L	ERA	Sv	IP		AB	H	HR	RBI	Avg
Home	1	0	4.15	0	30.1	LHB	96	26	5	15	.271
Road	3	2	3.44	1	36.2	RHB	161	45	6	20	.280
First Half	1	0	5.28	0	30.2	Sc Pos	52	16	1	21	.308
Scnd Half	3	2	2.48	1	36.1	Clutch	65	17	1	9	.262

2004 Season

In the wake of a brutal first half, the Cardinals were on the verge of releasing veteran righthander Cal Eldred. However, Eldred turned around his season with a second-half earned run average that was nearly three runs lower than his first-half showing. He permitted runs in only 13 of his final 41 appearances.

Pitching, Defense & Hitting

Eldred mostly lives and dies at this stage of his career with a cut fastball that he throws in the 87-91 MPH range. He will also mix in an occasional change. Eldred must be fine with his location or he becomes vulnerable to the long ball. Despite a somewhat slow delivery he has improved at holding runners, permitting only one stolen base last year, with four caught stealing. A competent fielder, Eldred has not committed an error since 1998. He is not a factor as a hitter.

2005 Outlook

With marginal stuff, Eldred is at the stage of his career when he needs to win his job back each season. The Cardinals like his competitiveness and veteran presence, and they re-signed him for 2005, but he probably can be counted on to be a middle reliever or long man at best.

Ray King

Position: RP
Bats: L **Throws:** L
Ht: 6' 1" **Wt:** 242

Opening Day Age: 31
Born: 1/15/74 in
Chicago, IL
ML Seasons: 6

Overall Statistics

	W	L	Pct.	ERA	G	GS	Sv	IP	H	BB	SO	HR	Avg
'04	5	2	.714	2.61	86	0	0	62.0	43	24	40	1	.197
Car.	14	14	.500	3.08	370	0	1	280.1	228	120	206	17	.225

2004 Situational Stats

	W	L	ERA	Sv	IP		AB	H	HR	RBI	Avg
Home	3	1	2.94	0	33.2	LHB	113	17	0	4	.150
Road	2	1	2.22	0	28.1	RHB	105	26	1	11	.248
First Half	2	0	1.41	0	32.0	Sc Pos	52	11	0	12	.212
Scnd Half	3	2	3.90	0	30.0	Clutch	100	20	1	11	.200

2004 Season

No reliever was more important for the Cardinals during their National League championship run than Ray King. The lefthander's 86 appearances were a career high and second-most in the league, as were his 31 holds. Along the way, King stranded 34 of his 44 inherited runners. He had a 21-inning scoreless stretch covering 30 games that stretched from early May into early July.

Pitching, Defense & Hitting

In this age of DLs and MRIs, King is a throwback who is willing to take the ball every day. He has averaged 81 appearances a year over his last four seasons. He throws a late-moving fastball in the low 90s and a big-breaking slider, making him very tough on lefthanded hitters. He is almost always down in the strike zone which is why he rarely is touched for a long ball. King holds runners well and is surprisingly agile coming off the mound. He rarely bats.

2005 Outlook

King was everything St. Louis could have expected after he was acquired from Atlanta, both on the mound and as an upbeat personality in the clubhouse. The Cardinals should get more of the same this year from King, who will remain a vital part of the Cards' bullpen mix.

St. Louis

Steve Kline

Position: RP
Bats: B **Throws:** L
Ht: 6' 1" **Wt:** 215

Opening Day Age: 32
Born: 8/22/72 in Sunbury, PA
ML Seasons: 8

Overall Statistics

	W	L	Pct.	ERA	G	GS	Sv	IP	H	BB	SO	HR	Avg
'04	2	2	.500	1.79	67	0	3	50.1	37	17	35	3	.209
Car.	27	30	.474	3.30	589	1	36	523.2	479	221	407	44	.246

2004 Situational Stats

	W	L	ERA	Sv	IP		AB	H	HR	RBI	Avg
Home	2	1	0.00	2	25.2	LHB	84	12	1	8	.143
Road	0	1	3.65	1	24.2	RHB	93	25	2	9	.269
First Half	2	1	1.97	2	32.0	Sc Pos	48	10	2	16	.208
Scnd Half	0	1	1.47	1	18.1	Clutch	74	14	1	10	.189

2004 Season

One of the best seasons of Steve Kline's career was spoiled at the end by injuries. Kline was sidelined for virtually all of September and most of the Cardinals' postseason run, first with a groin injury and then a torn tendon in his finger. Before the injuries, Kline was a key reliever for the National League champions, allowing runs in only eight of his 67 outings and going the entire season without allowing an earned run at home.

Pitching, Defense & Hitting

One of baseball's most effective lefthanded relievers, Kline mixes a hard slider and a sinking fastball. He is not afraid to run deep counts rather than throwing something over the heart of the plate, and he can also get key double plays with his sinker. Kline does a good job of holding runners and fielding his position. In his rare chances, Kline has shown he can handle the bat.

2005 Outlook

The Cardinals had a tough decision to make with Kline, a free agent after last season. They had several other contract priorities, so it was uncertain if Kline could be fitted into the budget and wasn't offered arbitration. Wherever he pitches in 2005, Kline will bring a tireless left arm and a great competitive spirit.

John Mabry

Position: LF/RF/3B/1B
Bats: L **Throws:** R
Ht: 6' 4" **Wt:** 210

Opening Day Age: 34
Born: 10/17/70 in Wilmington, DE
ML Seasons: 11
Pronunciation: MAY-bree

Overall Statistics

	G	AB	R	H	D	T	HR	RBI	SB	BB	SO	Avg	OBP	Slg
'04	87	240	32	71	11	0	13	40	0	26	63	.296	.363	.504
Car.	1075	2919	336	792	159	4	82	384	7	236	587	.271	.328	.413

2004 Situational Stats

	AB	H	HR	RBI	Avg		AB	H	HR	RBI	Avg
Home	98	32	7	19	.327	LHP	54	18	3	15	.333
Road	142	39	6	21	.275	RHP	186	53	10	25	.285
First Half	100	28	5	20	.280	Sc Pos	74	16	4	26	.216
Scnd Half	140	43	8	20	.307	Clutch	30	8	0	2	.267

2004 Season

John Mabry did not stick with the Cardinals out of spring training, but after coming from the minors at the end of May, he became one of the most valuable members of Tony La Russa's bench. Mabry started games in left, right, first and third, while matching his career high in home runs and finishing with his best batting average in eight years.

Hitting, Baserunning & Defense

Mabry is one lefthanded hitter who hangs in well against lefty pitchers. He is a good fastball hitter who is aggressive early in the count and thus can be prone to strikeouts. When he can get his arms extended, Mabry has very good power, including surprising pop to the opposite field. He is a solid defensive outfielder, a first baseman with good hands and a surprisingly adequate third baseman. Mabry is a below-average runner and no threat to steal.

2005 Outlook

Injuries and missed opportunities have robbed Mabry of a chance to be an everday player. But he is a very valuable bench player, and a manager like La Russa is a master at extracting the maximum from a versatile player like Mabry. The Cardinals re-signed him to a one-year, $725,000 deal, and he should be a valuable part-timer this year.

Mike Matheny

Position: C
Bats: R **Throws:** R
Ht: 6' 3" **Wt:** 220

Opening Day Age: 34
Born: 9/22/70 in
Reynoldsburg, OH
ML Seasons: 11
Pronunciation:
ma-THEE-nee

Overall Statistics

	G	AB	R	H	D	T	HR	RBI	SB	BB	SO	Avg	OBP	Slg
'04	122	385	28	95	22	1	5	50	0	23	83	.247	.292	.348
Car.	1124	3274	301	781	148	9	51	366	8	228	674	.239	.293	.336

2004 Situational Stats

	AB	H	HR	RBI	Avg		AB	H	HR	RBI	Avg
Home	187	49	4	25	.262	LHP	93	23	2	17	.247
Road	198	46	1	25	.232	RHP	292	72	3	33	.247
First Half	196	49	2	24	.250	Sc Pos	115	26	1	43	.226
Scnd Half	189	46	3	26	.243	Clutch	62	22	0	7	.355

2004 Season

It was another valuable all-around season for Mike Matheny, one of the game's most under-appreciated catchers. Matheny batted eight points above his career average and reached a career high with 50 RBI. In the field Matheny made only one error, that miscue snapping a catchers' all-time best 252 consecutive error-free streak.

Hitting, Baserunning & Defense

A shorter stroke has allowed Matheny to hang in better against good pitching, though he can still be blown away by quality hard stuff. Matheny is solid in the clutch, and he was one of the only Cardinals to meet expectations in the 2004 World Series. There are no better receivers in the game. Matheny handles pitchers well, blocks balls in the dirt and has a quick and accurate throwing arm. As a runner, he remains a catcher.

2005 Outlook

Matheny figured to be one of the Cardinals' toughest offseason decisions. He is like another coach on the field with his superb work behind the plate. Because the Cards love the potential of young catcher Yadier Molina and faced other signing priorities, Matheny slipped through their grasp and signed a three-year deal to join San Francisco. He's one of baseball's most solid catchers.

So Taguchi

Position: LF/CF/RF
Bats: R **Throws:** R
Ht: 5'10" **Wt:** 163

Opening Day Age: 35
Born: 7/2/69 in Hyogo
Prefecture, Japan
ML Seasons: 3
Pronunciation:
tah-gu-chee

Overall Statistics

	G	AB	R	H	D	T	HR	RBI	SB	BB	SO	Avg	OBP	Slg
'04	109	179	26	52	10	2	3	25	6	12	23	.291	.337	.419
Car.	171	248	39	72	13	3	6	40	7	18	35	.290	.339	.440

2004 Situational Stats

	AB	H	HR	RBI	Avg		AB	H	HR	RBI	Avg
Home	83	25	1	11	.301	LHP	94	25	2	10	.266
Road	96	27	2	14	.281	RHP	85	27	1	15	.318
First Half	92	24	1	11	.261	Sc Pos	41	14	0	21	.341
Scnd Half	87	28	2	14	.322	Clutch	26	7	1	4	.269

2004 Season

Invoking the immortal Sam and Dave hit, Tony La Russa often said last year that he was a "So Man." In his first full major league season after spending most of 2002-03 with Triple-A Memphis, So Taguchi developed into a very valuable bench player. The former Japanese League veteran batted nearly .300 while playing strong defense in a part-time role.

Hitting, Baserunning & Defense

When he first arrived from Japan in 2002, it looked like Taguchi could get the bat knocked out his hand by a hard-throwing Little Leaguer. However, he has added strength and shortened his swing, and he can now do damage with mistake pitches especially hanging breaking balls. Taguchi has excellent quickness on the bases and is not afraid to take the extra base. He gets good breaks on balls in the outfield while possessing an average but accurate arm.

2005 Outlook

An All-Star in Japan, Taguchi will never become an everyday outfielder with St. Louis. However, he has won the trust of his teammates and coaches with a great work ethic and has improved to the point where he figures to be the Cardinals' fourth outfielder this season.

St. Louis

Julian Tavarez

Position: RP
Bats: L **Throws:** R
Ht: 6' 2" **Wt:** 195

Opening Day Age: 31
Born: 5/22/73 in Santiago, DR
ML Seasons: 12
Pronunciation: JOOL-ee-en tah-VAR-rez

Overall Statistics

	W	L	Pct.	ERA	G	GS	Sv	IP	H	BB	SO	HR	Avg
'04	7	4	.636	2.38	77	0	4	64.1	57	19	48	1	.238
Car.	70	52	.574	4.39	568	79	17	1015.2	1104	394	579	77	.281

2004 Situational Stats

	W	L	ERA	Sv	IP			AB	H	HR	RBI	Avg
Home	3	0	1.69	2	32.0	LHB		83	21	1	8	.253
Road	4	4	3.06	2	32.1	RHB		156	36	0	14	.231
First Half	2	2	3.06	2	35.1	Sc Pos		64	14	0	21	.219
Scnd Half	5	2	1.55	2	29.0	Clutch		116	25	0	11	.216

2004 Season

When he wasn't punching dugout walls or getting suspended for having an oil well on the bill of his cap, Julian Tavarez was a big-time setup reliever for the Cardinals in 2004. He appeared in his most games since 1997, and over the season's last three months he allowed only five runs in 38 appearances.

Pitching, Defense & Hitting

Tavarez pounds the bottom of the strike zone with heavy mid-90s sinkers and a hard slider, a combination that is the reason why he has given up only two home runs in 141 regular-season appearances in 2003-04 (he did yield three home runs in the 2004 postseason). Tavarez also throws an occasional changeup, though it's a below-average pitch for him. He is an agile athlete who can help himself defensively while also holding runners well. He rarely is required to bat.

2005 Outlook

As long he avoids emotional outbursts and the occasional meltdowns on the mound, Tavarez can be as good a setup man as there is in any bullpen. The Cardinals for the most part kept a lid on his temper, and he will remain a key member of the pitching staff.

Tony Womack

Position: 2B
Bats: L **Throws:** R
Ht: 5' 9" **Wt:** 170

Opening Day Age: 35
Born: 9/25/69 in Danville, VA
ML Seasons: 11
Pronunciation: WO-mack

Overall Statistics

	G	AB	R	H	D	T	HR	RBI	SB	BB	SO	Avg	OBP	Slg
'04	145	553	91	170	22	3	5	38	26	36	60	.307	.349	.385
Car.	1167	4566	686	1253	179	58	35	348	335	288	593	.274	.319	.362

2004 Situational Stats

	AB	H	HR	RBI	Avg			AB	H	HR	RBI	Avg
Home	289	93	3	21	.322	LHP		123	35	0	8	.285
Road	264	77	2	17	.292	RHP		430	135	5	30	.314
First Half	288	92	4	25	.319	Sc Pos		116	32	1	34	.276
Scnd Half	265	78	1	13	.294	Clutch		80	25	0	10	.313

2004 Season

One of the biggest surprises for the Cardinals in 2004 was the emergence of Tony Womack as their everyday second baseman. Signed as a no-risk spring training gamble, Womack batted leadoff for the Cards while achieving career highs in both batting average and on-base percentage.

Hitting, Baserunning & Defense

Womack returned to the chop-and-run style that made him so valuable with the 2001 World Series champion Arizona club. He had 38 infield hits last year, but Womack can also pull inside fastballs for extra bases. Though he does not walk much, he can fashion long at bats with his ability to foul off pitches. Womack is a quick-starting baserunner who regained his high-percentage basestealing ability last year. Womack has good range at second base and is fearless, though at times erratic, in turning double plays.

2005 Outlook

St. Louis plucked Womack off the waiver wire from Boston last spring, and he filled a huge hole in the Cardinals' infield. His solid season produced a two-year, $2 million deal with the Yankees, the team he helped defeat in the 2001 World Series while with Arizona.

Other St. Louis Cardinals

Roger Cedeno (Pos: RF/LF, Age: 30, Bats: B)

	G	AB	R	H	D	T	HR	RBI	SB	BB	SO	Avg	OBP	Slg
'04	95	200	22	53	9	2	3	23	5	19	41	.265	.327	.375
Car.	1063	3117	474	856	126	32	40	266	213	317	607	.275	.342	.374

Traded to the Cardinals the day before the season began, Cedeno served the dual roles of reserve outfielder and lefthanded pinch-hitter. He hit .322 in his first four months with his new team, before slumping in the dog days of August. 2005 Outlook: B

Randy Flores (Pos: LHP, Age: 29)

	W	L	Pct.	ERA	G	GS	Sv	IP	H	BB	SO	HR	Avg
'04	1	0	1.000	1.93	9	1	0	14.0	13	3	7	0	.265
Car.	1	2	.333	5.65	37	3	1	43.0	53	19	21	7	.319

Flores has an unpleasant track record of rude introductions. Throughout his minor league career, his ERA initially skyrocketed, then stabilized, at every higher level. True to form, Flores' rookie ERA of 7.45 was lowered to 1.93 in his second big league audition. 2005 Outlook: C

Bo Hart (Pos: 2B, Age: 28, Bats: R)

	G	AB	R	H	D	T	HR	RBI	SB	BB	SO	Avg	OBP	Slg
'04	11	13	0	2	0	0	0	2	0	1	3	.154	.214	.154
Car.	88	309	46	84	13	5	4	30	3	13	67	.272	.313	.385

Hart exploded onto the scene in 2003 with 18 hits in his first seven games. The newfound fame was not enough to keep the newfound second-base job, though, and he spent 2004 back in Triple-A. 2005 Outlook: C

Ray Lankford (Pos: LF, Age: 37, Bats: L)

	G	AB	R	H	D	T	HR	RBI	SB	BB	SO	Avg	OBP	Slg
	92	200	36	51	14	1	6	22	2	29	55	.255	.349	.425
	1701	5747	968	1561	356	54	238	874	258	828	1550	.272	.364	.477

Lankford, who had played in just 212 games since 2000, returned to the Cardinals in 2004. He got 43 left-field starts before hamstring and wrist problems forced him to the disabled list. He had only 22 at-bats after the All-Star break. 2005 Outlook: D

Mike Lincoln (Pos: RHP, Age: 29)

	W	L	Pct.	ERA	G	GS	Sv	IP	H	BB	SO	HR	Avg
'04	3	2	.600	5.19	13	0	0	17.1	10	6	14	1	.164
Car.	13	24	.351	5.16	161	19	5	263.1	300	96	158	37	.289

You can add Lincoln to the growing ranks of Tommy John surgery recipients. Early season elbow discomfort was diagnosed as a torn ulnar collateral ligament that would need replacing. If everything goes right, he could be back by Opening Day 2005. 2005 Outlook: C

Hector Luna (Pos: SS/2B/3B, Age: 25, Bats: R)

	G	AB	R	H	D	T	HR	RBI	SB	BB	SO	Avg	OBP	Slg
'04	83	173	25	43	7	2	3	22	6	13	37	.249	.304	.364
Car.	83	173	25	43	7	2	3	22	6	13	37	.249	.304	.364

Rarely does a Rule 5 selection last the entire season in the big leagues, but that is exactly what Luna did in 2004. St. Louis had the luxury of keeping him around, using a variety of methods to make him useful, including playing him at five positions. 2005 Outlook: C

Cody McKay (Pos: C, Age: 31, Bats: L)

	G	AB	R	H	D	T	HR	RBI	SB	BB	SO	Avg	OBP	Slg
'04	35	74	7	17	2	0	0	6	0	2	14	.230	.269	.257
Car.	37	77	7	19	2	0	0	8	0	2	15	.247	.280	.273

McKay had many pondering the Old World notions of nepotism during some of his at-bats this past season. On the positive side, McKay was the personal catcher for Cardinals' starter Jeff Suppan, who had the best season of his career. 2005 Outlook: C

Josh Pearce (Pos: RHP, Age: 27)

	W	L	Pct.	ERA	G	GS	Sv	IP	H	BB	SO	HR	Avg
'04	0	0	—	3.86	3	0	0	2.1	3	0	0	0	.375
Car.	0	0	—	5.55	13	0	0	24.1	34	10	5	1	.351

Pearce has seen his career stall at Triple-A since 2001. He has been the victim of several shoulder-related injuries and a stacked bullpen in St. Louis. He must find a way to stay healthy if he has any designs on a big league job. 2005 Outlook: C

Colin Porter (Pos: RF, Age: 29, Bats: L)

	G	AB	R	H	D	T	HR	RBI	SB	BB	SO	Avg	OBP	Slg
'04	23	35	3	11	1	0	1	2	0	0	13	.314	.314	.429
Car.	47	67	8	17	1	0	1	2	1	1	30	.254	.265	.313

The crowded St. Louis outfield limited Porter to just one month of sporadic action at the major league level. Porter always has had a tendency to strike out, and this, coupled with his inability to hit home runs, made him expendable with St. Louis. But the Yankees signed him to a minor league contract in December. 2005 Outlook: D

Al Reyes (Pos: RHP, Age: 34)

	W	L	Pct.	ERA	G	GS	Sv	IP	H	BB	SO	HR	Avg
'04	0	0	—	0.75	12	2	0	12.0	3	2	11	0	.081
Car.	15	8	.652	3.92	232	2	3	282.2	232	144	266	33	.224

Reyes performed brilliantly after an August callup. He was so impressive, he earned a spot on the Cardinals' World Series roster. His 23 saves also led the Triple-A Memphis club. 2005 Outlook: B

Jason Simontacchi (Pos: RHP, Age: 31)

	W	L	Pct.	ERA	G	GS	Sv	IP	H	BB	SO	HR	Avg
'04	0	0	—	5.28	13	0	0	15.1	17	7	3	5	.304
Car.	20	10	.667	4.77	83	40	1	285.0	304	102	149	44	.277

Simontacchi was the 12th and final pitcher carried on the major league roster when the season began. Giving up four home runs in his first three appearances put him in the doghouse, and paved the way for Kiko Calero to eventually fill his spot in the bullpen. He was released in November. 2005 Outlook: C

St. Louis

St. Louis Cardinals Minor League Prospects

Organization Overview:

It's hard to quibble with the Cardinals' performance on the major league level in recent seasons. But much of that success has been paid for in the form of minor league prospects, leaving many observers to rank the system among the most barren in baseball. If the critics are right, the Cardinals soon could be placed in a precarious position, since many of their key performers were well into their 30s last season. Right now, most of the system's best upper-level prospects are pitchers. The front office appears to be taking a more analytical approach toward evaluating prospects, though that doesn't mean it's considering numbers only. Instead, the player's character, work ethic, makeup, and yes, tools, go into the process of assessing ability.

Rick Ankiel

Position: P	**Opening Day Age:** 25
Bats: L **Throws:** L	**Born:** 7/19/79 in Fort
Ht: 6' 1" **Wt:** 215	Pierce, FL

Recent Statistics

	W	L	ERA	G	GS	Sv	IP	H	R	BB	SO	HR
2004 A Palm Beach	0	1	2.08	3	3	0	8.2	5	4	0	11	0
2004 AA Tennessee	1	0	0.00	2	2	0	9.0	3	1	2	7	0
2004 AAA Memphis	1	0	0.00	1	1	0	6.0	1	1	0	5	0
2004 NL St. Louis	1	0	5.40	5	0	0	10.0	10	6	1	9	2

Ankiel's saga has been years in the making, yet he's still only 25 years old. Now, after living in baseball purgatory for the past four years, he's on the verge of making another splash on the Cardinals' staff. Ankiel still possesses very good stuff, with a 93-94 MPH fastball and big-breaking curveball that can buckle knees when he can control it. He didn't pitch a lot of innings last year after coming back from Tommy John surgery, so it's best not to get too excited. But he was impressive in his limited exposure. His role won't be determined until the spring, but he has chance to be a major weapon either in the rotation or out of the bullpen.

Daric Barton

Position: C	**Opening Day Age:** 19
Bats: L **Throws:** R	**Born:** 8/16/85 in
Ht: 5' 11" **Wt:** 195	Springfield, VT

Recent Statistics

	G	AB	R	H	D	T	HR	RBI	SB	BB	SO	Avg
2003 R Johnson City	54	170	29	50	10	0	4	29	0	37	48	.294
2004 A Peoria	90	313	63	98	23	0	13	77	4	69	44	.313

Barton was the Cardinals' first-round pick in the 2003 draft. There's little doubt that he has a chance to be a productive hitter, as he's shown the ability to hit for both average and power. In addition, his biggest offensive asset may be his plate discipline, as he's produced on-base percentages well above .400 in each of his first two pro seasons. However, his defense may be a question mark. He had elbow surgery after the 2003 campaign, which affected his throwing early last year. His blocking and receiving skills seemed to improve as the season wore on. For now, there's no thought of shifting Barton to another position, but his big bat makes such a move a possibility.

Danny Haren

Position: P	**Opening Day Age:** 24
Bats: R **Throws:** R	**Born:** 9/17/80 in
Ht: 6' 5" **Wt:** 220	Monterey Park, CA

Recent Statistics

	W	L	ERA	G	GS	Sv	IP	H	R	BB	SO	HR
2004 AAA Memphis	11	4	4.15	21	21	0	128.0	136	60	33	150	19
2004 NL St. Louis	3	3	4.50	14	5	0	46.0	45	23	17	32	4

Like Rick Ankiel, Haren no longer qualifies as a rookie. But he hasn't yet established himself on the Cardinals' staff, even after leading the Triple-A Pacific Coast League in strikeouts last season. Haren initially reached the majors in 2003, just a couple years after getting picked in the second round of the 2001 draft out of Pepperdine, so he had moved rather quickly through the system. His fastball touches the mid-90s, and he also throws a slider and a split that induces many of his strikeouts. He needs to work on repeating his delivery and remaining consistent. With the Cardinals' rotation a bit unsettled entering 2005, this could be the year the big righthander firmly secures his spot in it.

Blake Hawksworth

Position: P	**Opening Day Age:** 22
Bats: R **Throws:** R	**Born:** 3/1/83 in North
Ht: 6' 3" **Wt:** 195	Vancouver, BC

Recent Statistics

	W	L	ERA	G	GS	Sv	IP	H	R	BB	SO	HR
2003 A Peoria	5	1	2.30	10	10	0	54.2	37	16	12	57	0
2003 A Palm Beach	1	3	3.94	6	6	0	32.0	28	14	11	32	2
2004 A Palm Beach	1	0	5.91	2	2	0	10.2	10	7	3	11	2

Hawksworth possesses one of the most exciting arms in the Cardinals' system, even though he hasn't yet pitched as many as 90 innings in any season since signing as a draft-and-follow in 2002. An ankle spur ended his year early in 2003, while shoulder problems limited him to only two starts in 2004. He had the shoulder scoped and should be ready to go this spring. The Cardinals will be looking for the return of Hawksworth's mid-90s fastball and impressive change-up. His curveball has needed work in the past, and an injury-free season would provide an opportunity to improve the breaking ball. It also would give him a chance to show why he boasts one of the highest ceilings of any St. Louis pitching prospect.

Yadier Molina

Position: C
Bats: R **Throws:** R
Ht: 5' 11" **Wt:** 225

Opening Day Age: 22
Born: 7/13/82 in
Bayamon, PR

Recent Statistics

	G	AB	R	H	D	T	HR	RBI	SB	BB	SO	Avg
2004 AAA Memphis	37	129	19	39	6	0	1	14	0	17	14	.302
2004 NL St. Louis	51	135	12	36	6	0	2	15	0	13	20	.267

Molina hasn't hit for as high an average or as much power as Daric Barton, and Molina doesn't draw nearly as many walks. But Yadier clearly is a far superior defensive catcher at this point in his career. He works well with pitchers, is very intelligent, takes pride in his defense and is as tough as nails behind the plate. Those traits seem to come naturally, as two brothers are big league catchers. While Molina doesn't run well and needs to work for everything he gets at the plate, he is not an automatic out. He has improved offensively and does a nice job of hitting behind runners and going the other way. With Mike Matheny's departure as a free agent, Molina should get first crack at replacing him.

Anthony Reyes

Position: P
Bats: R **Throws:** R
Ht: 6' 2" **Wt:** 215

Opening Day Age: 23
Born: 10/16/81 in
Downey, CA

Recent Statistics

	W	L	ERA	G	GS	Sv	IP	H	R	BB	SO	HR
2004 A Palm Beach	3	0	4.66	7	7	0	36.2	41	21	7	38	5
2004 AA Tennessee	6	2	2.91	12	12	0	74.1	62	27	13	102	3

Elbow problems curtailed Reyes in college, where he pitched through his senior year for USC. But based upon his performance in his first professional season last year, he's stacking up as a steal. The elbow hasn't been an issue as a pro, and he's flashed the power arm that enticed scouts in the past. His fastball reaches 94-96 MPH, and he complements the heater with a slurvy type of breaking pitch that can be a decent offering when he stays on top of it. He's projected to begin 2005 at Triple-A Memphis, but it's quite likely he'll make an appearance in St. Louis at some point this season.

Brad Thompson

Position: P
Bats: R **Throws:** R
Ht: 6' 1" **Wt:** 190

Opening Day Age: 23
Born: 1/31/82 in Las
Vegas, NV

Recent Statistics

	W	L	ERA	G	GS	Sv	IP	H	R	BB	SO	HR
2003 A Peoria	5	3	2.91	30	4	0	65.0	70	23	10	43	2
2003 A Palm Beach	1	0	0.00	2	1	0	6.0	3	0	0	4	0
2004 AAA Memphis	1	0	5.52	3	3	0	14.2	20	10	3	10	3
2004 AA Tennessee	8	2	2.36	13	12	0	72.1	56	19	11	57	6

Thompson burst into prospect status early last season when he set the Double-A Southern League record for consecutive scoreless innings. It was quite a breakthrough for Thompson, considering he had been a 16th-round draft pick who began his pro career working out of the bullpen. Despite the less than sparkling resume, he rocketed to Triple-A by the end of his second pro season. Though not a soft tosser, Thompson is a groundball pitcher who succeeds with a 90-91 MPH fastball, slider and excellent sinker that serves as his out pitch. The scoreless-innings streak appeared to take a toll, as he missed a good chunk of last season due to a tired shoulder. But he should be good to go this spring.

Adam Wainwright

Position: P
Bats: R **Throws:** R
Ht: 6' 7" **Wt:** 205

Opening Day Age: 23
Born: 8/30/81 in
Brunswick, GA

Recent Statistics

	W	L	ERA	G	GS	Sv	IP	H	R	BB	SO	HR
2003 AA Greenville	10	8	3.37	27	27	0	149.2	133	59	37	128	9
2004 AAA Memphis	4	4	5.37	12	12	0	63.2	68	47	28	64	12

Wainwright arguably was the most important part of the J.D. Drew trade with the Braves that also landed Jason Marquis and Ray King. It isn't hard to understand why, considering Wainwright throws four serviceable pitches, including a 94-95 MPH fastball with good movement. But his 2004 campaign proved a bit disappointing, due in large measure to a very slight strain in his elbow. He struggled when the injury flared, and his ERA and home-run rates grew substantially compared to previous seasons. The elbow didn't require surgery and he's expected to be 100 percent in 2005. If so, he still has a chance to make the Drew trade look even better from the Cardinals' perspective.

Others to Watch

Carmen Cali (26) could be a quality lefthander in the Cardinals' bullpen, depending on what happens to last year's southpaws. He throws hard, features a good slider and has proven durable. He took a step forward in 2004 and reached the majors. . . **John Gall** (26) has hit at every level while displaying good but not great power. He's worked hard to improve as a left fielder and his ability to play first base adds some versatility. But his bat will dictate how much he plays. . . **Reid Gorecki** (24) is an outstanding defensive center fielder. His speed helps him track balls in the outfield, steal bases and accumulate extra-base hits. He'll hit some home runs but needs to use the entire field. . . Righthander **Rhett Parrott** (25) has stalled a bit at Triple-A, and shoulder surgery last year didn't help. His velocity still hits the low 90s, but it varied in 2004 and he had trouble with location. . . Righthander **Stuart Pomeranz** (20) is a 6-foot-7 high school product who was taken in the second round of the 2003 draft. His fastball features exploding action and good life. He pitches below the knees and induces lots of groundballs. . . Shortstop **Brendan Ryan** (23), a seventh-round pick in 2003, has good range, a strong arm and swings the bat well. He's fun to watch and figures to improve.

Petco Park

Offense

With a center-field fence less than 400 feet away, there was some concern before the season began that Petco Park would favor the hitters too much. It was the hitters who ended up crying "uncle," as Petco arguably was the park that most favored pitchers in 2004. No park did more to prevent home runs than Petco, and triples were the only offensive event on which it had a significantly positive effect.

Defense

Playing right field is a harrowing experience. Not only is it a huge area to cover, but the outfield wall is irregular, with a section of seats jutting out from the corner. One of the warmup mounds is only a couple of feet outside the foul line, and the wall along the line is only thigh high, which led to several nasty spills.

Who It Helps the Most

To quote legendary Dodgers broadcaster Vin Scully, "outfield defense was the missing front tooth in the Padres portrait." As long as the team has outfielders who can cover a lot of ground, fly-ball pitchers gain the most benefit from Petco's spacious outfield dimensions. Unfortunately, the Padres only had part of that equation in 2004. Adam Eaton stands to benefit the most from any upgrades.

Who It Hurts the Most

The Padres were second to the Royals with the fewest home runs hit at home. The team hit nearly 50 percent more longballs on the road. Power hitters, regardless of their ilk or style, suffer at Petco.

Rookies & Newcomers

Speedy Freddie Guzman may get another chance to showcase his talents in center field after a brief but poor showing in 2004. The Padres could use his speed to cover the expanse of the home park's outfield. Power off the bench could come from Xavier Nady, Jon Knott or Tagg Bozied, but Petco Park won't help them. Woody Williams, who has been more of a flyball pitcher in recent years, should enjoy pitching at home in his second go-round with the Padres.

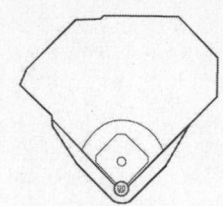

Dimensions: LF-334, LCF-367, CF-396, RCF-387, RF-322

Capacity: 42,445

Elevation: 20 feet

Surface: Grass

Foul Territory: Small

Park Factors

2004 Season

	Home Games Padres	Opp	Total	Away Games Padres	Opp	Total	Index
G	72	72	144	72	72	144	
Avg	.254	.263	.258	.293	.269	.281	92
AB	2353	2499	4852	2598	2438	5036	96
R	296	306	602	400	331	731	82
H	598	656	1254	760	655	1415	89
2B	117	142	259	154	141	295	91
3B	19	15	34	11	15	26	136
HR	48	65	113	77	100	177	66
BB	279	185	464	234	197	431	112
SO	392	492	884	409	472	881	104
E	36	44	80	59	54	113	71
E-Infield	30	33	63	48	45	93	68
LHB-Avg	.275	.262	.268	.287	.272	.279	96
LHB-HR	13	31	44	23	45	68	68
RHB-Avg	.241	.263	.252	.296	.266	.282	89
RHB-HR	35	34	69	54	55	109	65

2002-2003 (Qualcomm Stadium)

	Home Games Padres	Opp	Total	Away Games Padres	Opp	Total	Index
G	144	144	288	144	144	288	
Avg	.263	.259	.261	.251	.284	.267	98
AB	4844	5058	9902	4987	4806	9793	101
R	577	654	1231	608	834	1442	85
H	1273	1308	2581	1253	1363	2616	99
2B	198	235	433	239	284	523	82
3B	34	34	68	22	39	61	110
HR	105	160	265	127	192	319	82
BB	514	499	1013	465	564	1029	97
SO	911	1037	1948	1008	939	1947	99
E	99	99	198	100	87	187	106
E-Infield	84	76	160	85	70	155	103
LHB-Avg	.270	.270	.270	.257	.302	.277	97
LHB-HR	48	61	109	61	85	146	73
RHB-Avg	.256	.251	.253	.246	.271	.259	98
RHB-HR	57	99	156	66	107	173	90

2004 Rankings (National League)

- Highest walk factor
- Lowest run factor
- Lowest hit factor
- Lowest home-run factor
- Lowest error factor
- Lowest infield-error factor
- Lowest RHB batting-average factor
- Lowest RHB home-run factor

Bruce Bochy

2004 Season

The Padres had high hopes of competing for the division title after a last-place showing in 2003. They were moving into a new ballpark and had upgraded the rotation, the bullpen and several positions on the infield. However, they fell short of their goal and there weren't many obvious answers as to why. Whatever the reason, the fans didn't seem to mind too much, as attendance topped three million for the first time in team history.

Offense

Bruce Bochy is fairly laid back and lets his players play. Most of his lineup moves are made before the game begins. The players respond by playing hard almost to the point of being too aggressive at times. He doesn't employ many strategies, which is great when things are going well. But that may not be the best policy if the team is struggling, as it was in August when the Padres lost 14 of 27 games while in the thick of the division race.

Pitching & Defense

Bochy spends the first quarter of the season finding out which roles each pitcher is capable of handling and where they are most comfortable. Once he is comfortable with his conclusions, the pitchers remain in those roles until the end of the season. He generally doesn't let his starters throw more than 120 pitches, and he's become much more careful with young hurlers. He's not big on defensive substitutions with the exception of left fielder Ryan Klesko, whom he frequently takes out of games late.

2005 Outlook

For the most part, the Padres will remain intact this winter, giving Bochy and Co. another crack at the division title in 2005. The increased revenue stream of the new ballpark will help acquire more talent. However, the clock is ticking for Bochy, who no longer has the safety net of "small market" or "young team" to fall back on. This year will define his measure as a manager.

Born: 4/16/55 in Landes de Boussac, France

Playing Experience: 1978-1987, Hou, NYM, SD

Managerial Experience: 10 seasons

Manager Statistics

Year	Team, Lg	W	L	Pct	GB	Finish
2004	San Diego, NL	87	75	.537	6.0	3rd West
10 Seasons		781	821	.488	–	–

2004 Starting Pitchers by Days Rest

	<=3	4	5	6+
Padres Starts	6	93	39	15
Padres ERA	4.91	4.16	4.06	5.47
NL Avg Starts	2	82	46	23
NL ERA	4.58	4.35	4.28	4.73

2004 Situational Stats

	Bruce Bochy	NL Average
Hit & Run Success %	44.6	38.0
Stolen Base Success %	67.5	71.7
Platoon Pct.	53.1	55.2
Defensive Subs	26	18
High-Pitch Outings	2	6
Quick/Slow Hooks	24/9	21/12
Sacrifice Attempts	75	99

2004 Rankings (National League)

- 1st in starts on three days rest
- 2nd in hit-and-run success percentage
- 3rd in fewest caught stealings of second base (21), defensive substitutions and quick hooks

Sean Burroughs

2004 Season

Sean Burroughs got off to a strong start, hitting well above .300 in April and May, but he slumped in June as rumors swirled that he would be traded to Kansas City in exchange for Carlos Beltran. Once Padres GM Kevin Towers dispelled the notion, Burroughs hit well, but still didn't display the power that has been projected of him from his minor league success. His season ended prematurely in September when he tore the lateral meniscus in his right knee while sliding into second base. The highlight of his season, unfortunately, came in the first ever game at Petco Park, in which he drove in the first run as well as the winning run in extra innings.

Hitting

Burroughs' knee had been bothering him well before he injured it badly enough to require surgery, which could offer some explanation into his lack of power. Unable to plant comfortably, his weight wasn't shifting in his swing as it normally would. Another contributing factor was his position in the lineup. As a leadoff hitter, Burroughs made a conscious effort to see more pitches at the expense of trying to drive the ball. Despite the injury, he still showed tremendous ability to make contact and an improving eye at the plate.

Baserunning & Defense

Although he's one of the fastest guys on the team, Burroughs is not a basestealing threat. He's still learning pitchers and concentrating on staying healthy. The predictions of Gold Glove-caliber defense turned out to be premature in 2004, as he can be a bit tentative, but he has that kind of potential with his range and arm.

2005 Outlook

With Burroughs sometimes hailed as the next George Brett, Padres fans have been wondering if they don't instead have the next Joe Randa. In Burroughs' defense, he has been beset the last two years by the kind of injuries that tend to adversely affect power numbers, so a healthy season in 2005 just may be the tonic everyone is looking for.

Position: 3B
Bats: L **Throws:** R
Ht: 6' 2" **Wt:** 200

Opening Day Age: 24
Born: 9/12/80 in Atlanta, GA
ML Seasons: 3

Overall Statistics

	G	AB	R	H	D	T	HR	RBI	SB	BB	SO	Avg	OBP	Slg
'04	130	523	76	156	23	3	2	47	5	31	52	.298	.348	.365
Car.	339	1232	156	356	55	10	10	116	14	87	157	.289	.345	.374

Where He Hits the Ball

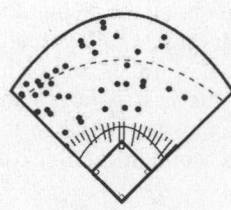
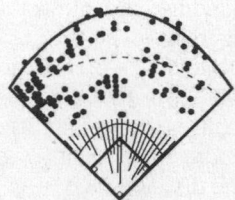

Vs. LHP　　　　**Vs. RHP**

2004 Situational Stats

	AB	H	HR	RBI	Avg		AB	H	HR	RBI	Avg
Home	253	71	0	20	.281	LHP	130	35	0	16	.269
Road	270	85	2	27	.315	RHP	393	121	2	31	.308
First Half	330	95	1	25	.288	Sc Pos	119	37	1	45	.311
Scnd Half	193	61	1	22	.316	Clutch	77	29	1	11	.377

2004 Rankings (National League)

- 2nd in lowest HR frequency (261.5 ABs per HR)
- 4th in highest groundball-flyball ratio (2.2)
- 5th in batting average in the clutch and lowest slugging percentage
- 6th in errors at third base (14) and lowest fielding percentage at third base (.957)
- Led the Padres in caught stealing (4), hit by pitch (9), highest groundball-flyball ratio (2.2), batting average in the clutch, on-base percentage for a leadoff hitter (.343) and lowest percentage of swings on the first pitch (15.4)

Adam Eaton

2004 Season

Both Adam Eaton and Jake Peavy were expected to have breakout seasons in 2004, but Eaton struggled with his mechanics for much of the year. It didn't help matters that no Padres starter was more dependent on his outfield defense—which turned out to be subpar—than Eaton. On the plus side, he fared very well against the Dodgers, against whom he was 4-1 with a 2.87 ERA in six starts.

Pitching

For all the tinkering that he and his coaches did with his mechanics—from lowering his arm angle to dropping a pitch altogether—what "fixed" Eaton was simply making smarter pitches. With a moving fastball ranging from 92-97 MPH, a very big-breaking slow curve, a good change and slider, it didn't make sense that he was getting hit as hard as he was. Making mistakes with his fastball, especially when ahead in the count, turned out to be his undoing. Most of the time it appeared that Eaton was thinking too much about the sequence rather than concentrating on making the next quality pitch.

Defense & Hitting

One of the things that Eaton will have to work on is not becoming too distracted by baserunners. There were occasions when he was more worried about a man on third with two outs than he was about the hitter. At the plate and in the field, he's "old school"—a good enough hitter to be used as a pinch-hitter and someone who runs the bases like an everyday player. He actually stole two bases last year.

2005 Outlook

Although Eaton struggled in his first full year after Tommy John surgery, there were plenty of positive signs to take into 2005: his strikeout-walk ratio was the best of his career, he was more efficient with his pitches and he pitched to the ballpark, even though his outfield defense wasn't tailored to it. With defensive upgrades likely in the offing, Eaton could be a big winner this year.

Position: SP
Bats: R **Throws:** R
Ht: 6' 2" **Wt:** 196

Opening Day Age: 27
Born: 11/23/77 in Seattle, WA
ML Seasons: 5

Overall Statistics

	W	L	Pct.	ERA	G	GS	Sv	IP	H	BB	SO	HR	Avg
'04	11	14	.440	4.61	33	33	0	199.1	204	52	153	28	.266
Car.	36	36	.500	4.36	109	109	0	667.1	647	238	523	87	.253

2004 Pitching Profile

	Adam Eaton	NL Average
Overall Strike %	67.1	62.5
1st Pitch Strike %	59.8	58.5
Ratio	1.28	1.39
Strikeouts per 9 IP	6.91	6.74
Walks per 9 IP	2.35	3.38
Home Runs per 9 IP	1.26	1.11
Strikeout/Walk Ratio	2.94	1.99
Groundball/Flyball Ratio	0.89	1.25

2004 Situational Stats

	W	L	ERA	Sv	IP		AB	H	HR	RBI	Avg
Home	3	8	4.99	0	101.0	LHB	384	100	11	40	.260
Road	8	6	4.21	0	98.1	RHB	383	104	17	66	.272
First Half	4	8	4.54	0	111.0	Sc Pos	187	55	9	79	.294
Scnd Half	7	6	4.69	0	88.1	Clutch	32	8	1	5	.250

2004 Rankings (National League)

- 4th in losses, lowest groundball-flyball ratio allowed (0.9) and highest ERA at home
- 5th in highest batting average allowed with runners in scoring position
- 6th in lowest stolen-base percentage allowed (54.5)
- 8th in lowest fielding percentage at pitcher (.946)
- 9th in fewest walks per nine innings (2.3) and most home runs allowed per nine innings (1.26)
- 10th in home runs allowed and highest strikeout-walk ratio (2.9)
- Led the Padres in losses, home runs allowed, wild pitches (5), pitches thrown (3,259), pickoff throws (60), runners caught stealing (5) and lowest stolen-base percentage allowed (54.5)

San Diego

2004 Season

When the Padres traded Oliver Perez and Jason Bay for Brian Giles in August 2003, they were hoping to get the player who was seventh in the majors in OPS (on-base plus slugging) from 1999-2002. Instead, they got more of a complementary player than a star who could carry the team for stretches. Giles' production was reasonably consistent, and he was one of the few hitters who's numbers were better at Petco, but his season has to be viewed as somewhat of a disappointment.

Hitting

High expectations may have played a role in Giles' struggles. Normally a very patient hitter with a discerning eye at the plate, his strikeout and walk numbers both trended in the wrong direction last year, and his groundball rate increased as well. From his open stance, he'll stride toward the pitch and try to pull anything on the inner half, or go to the opposite field with anything outside. In previous years, his homers went to all fields, but this year they went almost exclusively to right. Perhaps he was pressing, trying to justify the Padres trading two emerging stars for him.

Baserunning & Defense

While he isn't a speedy runner, Giles will steal a base if the pitcher isn't vigilant. He'll break up a double play or run over a catcher blocking the plate like a fullback taking out a safety. He positions himself well in the outfield and reads the ball off the bat better than most, but his average foot speed was exposed on grounders and liners that found Petco's deep alleys. Giles' arm is above average and quite accurate.

2005 Outlook

Giles undoubtedly will be focused on atoning for his 2004 showing, and a move to left field may help if the Padres can re-tool their outfield. They love his effort and quiet leadership, so regardless of whether Giles returns to his pre-2002 levels, they will feel bringing him home was a good deal.

Position: RF
Bats: L **Throws:** L
Ht: 5'10" **Wt:** 205

Opening Day Age: 34
Born: 1/20/71 in El Cajon, CA
ML Seasons: 10
Pronunciation: JYLES

Overall Statistics

	G	AB	R	H	D	T	HR	RBI	SB	BB	SO	Avg	OBP	Slg
'04	159	609	97	173	33	7	23	94	10	89	80	.284	.374	.475
Car.	1202	4111	771	1229	259	39	231	775	80	783	567	.299	.411	.550

Where He Hits the Ball

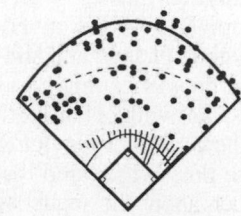
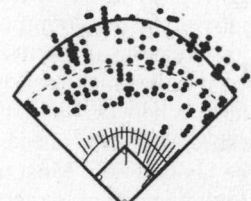

Vs. LHP   **Vs. RHP**

2004 Situational Stats

	AB	H	HR	RBI	Avg		AB	H	HR	RBI	Avg
Home	293	84	10	41	.287	LHP	211	50	5	25	.237
Road	316	89	13	53	.282	RHP	398	123	18	69	.309
First Half	328	96	14	55	.293	Sc Pos	165	44	7	71	.267
Scnd Half	281	77	9	39	.274	Clutch	82	29	1	9	.354

2004 Rankings (National League)

- 1st in errors in right field (7)
- 3rd in lowest fielding percentage in right field (.979)
- 5th in sacrifice flies (9)
- 6th in plate appearances (711)
- Led the Padres in triples, walks, pitches seen (2,625), plate appearances (711), games played, stolen-base percentage (76.9), highest percentage of pitches taken (61.2) and highest percentage of swings put into play (52.8)

Khalil Greene

Position: SS
Bats: R **Throws:** R
Ht: 5'11" **Wt:** 210

Opening Day Age: 25
Born: 10/21/79 in Butler, PA
ML Seasons: 2

2004 Season

The Padres drafted Khalil Greene in 2002 because of his offensive talent and makeup, but the team had some questions about his ability to handle shortstop. Those questions proved to be moot, as Greene might already be the best all-around shortstop the Padres have ever had. He made highlight reels with his glove almost weekly, and matched Rookie of the Year favorite Jason Bay stat for stat over the second half of the season. *Baseball America* did award Greene its rookie honor. His season had numerous standout moments, including two games in which he hit two homers, and culminated with a second-place finish in the National League Rookie of the Year vote.

Hitting

Greene faces pitchers with an open stance, stepping into the pitches to get good plate coverage on the outside. He stepped in too far once in September, resulting in a broken right index finger that ended his season two weeks prematurely. His approach is professional and fundamentally sound, going where the pitch is thrown and spraying line drives to all fields. All of his homers were down the line to left field.

Baserunning & Defense

Despite the highlights, Greene's range is only average, but he positions himself well, has a quick first step, never lacks for effort and has a decent enough arm to make plays in the hole. In college, he was a basestealing threat, but he really doesn't have the foot speed for that to translate to the majors. He is, however, a very intelligent baserunner.

2005 Outlook

Greene will be the Padres' shortstop at least until he's eligible for free agency. Padres fans and brass alike are excited by how quickly he has developed as a complete player, and are hoping they have an emerging star in the fold. He hit .293 with a near .900 OPS (on-base plus slugging) while cutting his strikeout rate in half after the break, so there's good reason for optimism.

Overall Statistics

	G	AB	R	H	D	T	HR	RBI	SB	BB	SO	Avg	OBP	Slg
'04	139	484	67	132	31	4	15	65	4	53	94	.273	.349	.446
Car.	159	549	75	146	35	5	17	71	4	57	113	.266	.340	.441

Where He Hits the Ball

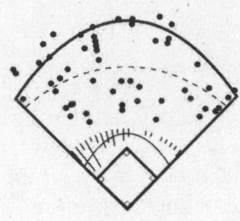
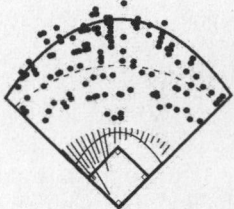

Vs. LHP **Vs. RHP**

2004 Situational Stats

	AB	H	HR	RBI	Avg		AB	H	HR	RBI	Avg
Home	228	55	3	29	.241	LHP	127	37	7	21	.291
Road	256	77	12	36	.301	RHP	357	95	8	44	.266
First Half	286	74	4	30	.259	Sc Pos	114	30	3	45	.263
Scnd Half	198	58	11	35	.293	Clutch	72	21	3	13	.292

2004 Rankings (National League)

- 2nd in home runs among rookies and RBI among rookies
- 3rd in errors at shortstop (20) and lowest fielding percentage at shortstop (.965)
- 7th in sacrifice flies (8)
- 8th in lowest batting average at home
- Led the Padres in intentional walks (10)

San Diego

Ramon Hernandez

2004 Season

The Padres have to be pleased with the November 2003 trade that brought them Ramon Hernandez and Terrence Long from the A's. In return for Mark Kotsay, they received their best all-around catcher since Terry Kennedy. Hernandez followed up his breakthrough 2003 season with another strong performance in '04, showing the previous year's power outburst was no fluke. An especially sweet bonus was that he was an RBI machine against the rival Dodgers, driving in 15 runs in 16 games. He missed a month of the season with a sprained left knee suffered in a collision at the plate, but showed no ill effects after his return. This was the first year since he became a starter in 2000 that Hernandez did not play at least 135 games.

Hitting

Hernandez has a good eye for balls and strikes and swings at the first pitch he can drive. He hits the ball from the right-field power alley to the left-field line, with all of his homers traveling to center or left. A good contact hitter capable of hitting behind the runner, he's also an excellent bunter. This year, he showed marked improvement in his walk and strikeout rates, so there's still some potential for an additional increase in his power numbers.

Baserunning & Defense

Easy going but in control behind the plate, his pitchers trust Hernandez' judgment and almost never shake him off. His glovework is excellent, buying extra strikes with his framing, and only a very small percentage of the balls in the dirt get by him. He has a strong arm with a quick release and is stalwart when blocking the plate.

2005 Outlook

The Padres have several young catchers on the way, but for the immediate future, Hernandez is their full-time starter. Catchers with his offensive and defensive skills are rare, so San Diego may opt to keep him beyond his current contract, which expires at the end of this season.

Position: C
Bats: R **Throws:** R
Ht: 6' 0" **Wt:** 210

Opening Day Age: 28
Born: 5/20/76 in Caracas, VZ
ML Seasons: 6
Pronunciation: ruh-MOWN

Overall Statistics

	G	AB	R	H	D	T	HR	RBI	SB	BB	SO	Avg	OBP	Slg
'04	111	384	45	106	23	0	18	63	1	35	45	.276	.341	.477
Car.	706	2278	286	586	118	1	78	326	4	204	331	.257	.325	.413

Where He Hits the Ball

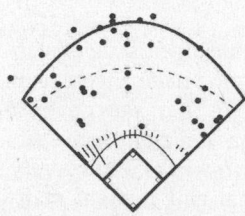 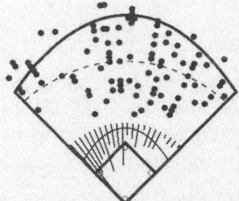

Vs. LHP   **Vs. RHP**

2004 Situational Stats

	AB	H	HR	RBI	Avg		AB	H	HR	RBI	Avg
Home	195	48	10	33	.246	LHP	100	31	7	19	.310
Road	189	58	8	30	.307	RHP	284	75	11	44	.264
First Half	184	49	7	25	.266	Sc Pos	114	26	5	43	.228
Scnd Half	200	57	11	38	.285	Clutch	68	15	0	3	.221

2004 Rankings (National League)

- 2nd in highest percentage of runners caught stealing as a catcher (25.4)
- 5th in errors at catcher (6)
- Led the Padres in GDPs (16)
- Led NL catchers in home runs

Trevor Hoffman

2004 Season

After missing almost all of 2003 recovering from shoulder surgery, Trevor Hoffman returned as the Padres' closer last season, racking up the sixth-most saves in the league. His 41 saves also marked the sixth time in his career that he's reached the 40 mark, and they moved him past Dennis Eckersley for third all-time at 393. One interesting note on Hoffman's year: all four of his blown saves came in David Wells' starts, and in all of them Wells was in line for the win when Hoffman entered the game.

Pitching

The rehab from his first shoulder surgery in 2002 did not go well, so a second visit to the operating table was necessary. The second time turned out to be the charm, as Hoffman came back and actually showed better velocity this year than he had since the late 1990s. Hoffman's fastball topped out around 90 MPH, which combined with his devastating changeup made him one of the most effective closers in the game—only Eric Gagne and Joe Nathan recorded more saves but fewer blown saves. He also showed a curve and a slider on occasion just to keep hitters from sitting on one of his two best pitches.

Defense & Hitting

A former shortstop in the minors, Hoffman is an excellent fielder, but there was a reason he was converted from infield to the bullpen—he is not a good hitter. Fortunately, as the closer he is rarely called upon to hit. His high leg kick can give basestealers the advantage, though he is rarely tested.

2005 Outlook

Hoffman will pass John Franco for second all-time with just 32 more saves. Only 37 years old, Hoffman also has a realistic chance of passing Lee Smith (478) within the next two or three years for the most ever. Pitching half his games in spacious Petco Park can only help extend his career, giving him an outside chance to surpass the 500 mark by the time his career is over.

Position: RP
Bats: R **Throws:** R
Ht: 6' 0" **Wt:** 215

Opening Day Age: 37
Born: 10/13/67 in Bellflower, CA
ML Seasons: 12

Overall Statistics

	W	L	Pct.	ERA	G	GS	Sv	IP	H	BB	SO	HR	Avg
'04	3	3	.500	2.30	55	0	41	54.2	42	8	53	5	.211
Car.	48	47	.505	2.74	696	0	393	764.2	575	225	861	71	.206

2004 Pitching Profile

	Trevor Hoffman	NL Average
Overall Strike %	67.9	62.5
1st Pitch Strike %	61.7	58.5
Ratio	0.91	1.39
Strikeouts per 9 IP	8.73	6.74
Walks per 9 IP	1.32	3.38
Home Runs per 9 IP	0.82	1.11
Strikeout/Walk Ratio	6.63	1.99
Groundball/Flyball Ratio	0.64	1.25

2004 Situational Stats

	W	L	ERA	Sv	IP		AB	H	HR	RBI	Avg
Home	3	3	2.61	20	31.0	LHB	106	27	3	7	.255
Road	0	0	1.90	21	23.2	RHB	93	15	2	7	.161
First Half	2	1	2.48	23	32.2	Sc Pos	46	4	0	5	.087
Scnd Half	1	2	2.05	18	22.0	Clutch	157	31	4	12	.197

2004 Rankings (National League)

- 2nd in fewest baserunners allowed per nine innings in relief (8.2)
- 3rd in save percentage (91.1)
- 6th in saves
- 9th in games finished (51)
- 10th in relief ERA (2.30)
- Led the Padres in saves, games finished (51), most GDPs induced per GDP situation (17.4%), save percentage (91.1), relief losses (3) and fewest baserunners allowed per nine innings in relief (8.2)

San Diego

Ryan Klesko

2004 Season

In September 2003, Ryan Klesko had surgery to repair damage in his right shoulder. Due to the restrictions of his rehab, he couldn't engage in his normal offseason weight-lifting regimen and as a result, his power stroke was missing in 2004. However, by the time the '04 campaign ended, Klesko had resumed training regularly, and the results were beginning to show—he hit .380 in September, with a slugging percentage of .582.

Hitting

In a game against the Giants in the opening series at Petco Park, Klesko crushed three pitches that in other years would have cleared the fences. But this year and in this park, all three fell short of the warning track. Klesko's big swing did not generate the home-run totals everyone had been expecting, and part of that was due to the deep power alleys. His road home-run total was double that of his Petco output, and it became an issue that festered for a good portion of the season. Thankfully, his approach did not change. He remains a patient hitter, but he will jump all over a first-pitch fastball inside.

Baserunning & Defense

Klesko has surprisingly good speed for a man his size, but he has not been given the green light the past couple of years in part because he can be too aggressive on the bases. However, it's hard to argue with the 81-percent success rate in 2000-2001, when he swiped 46 bases. He's a good athlete and has a strong enough arm to play right field, but he takes awkward routes, gets late reads and is a bit of a high-wire act on line drives. He frequently was replaced for defensive purposes in the later innings.

2005 Outlook

With the Padres looking to upgrade their outfield defense, it seems likely that they will move Klesko, either to first base if they can find a taker for Phil Nevin, or to another team. If Klesko is traded, some team could have a nice bargain on its hands if he is completely healthy.

Position: LF/1B
Bats: L **Throws:** L
Ht: 6' 3"   **Wt:** 220

Opening Day Age: 33
Born: 6/12/71 in Westminster, CA
ML Seasons: 13

Overall Statistics

	G	AB	R	H	D	T	HR	RBI	SB	BB	SO	Avg	OBP	Slg
'04	127	402	58	117	32	2	9	66	3	73	67	.291	.399	.448
Car.	1477	4802	762	1357	296	29	254	883	83	694	929	.283	.373	.515

Where He Hits the Ball

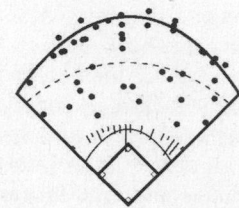 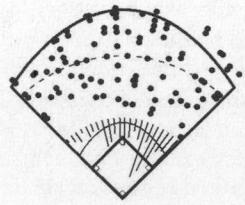

Vs. LHP   **Vs. RHP**

2004 Situational Stats

	AB	H	HR	RBI	Avg		AB	H	HR	RBI	Avg
Home	212	62	3	31	.292	LHP	114	37	1	18	.325
Road	190	55	6	35	.289	RHP	288	80	8	48	.278
First Half	192	52	2	30	.271	Sc Pos	120	36	2	52	.300
Scnd Half	210	65	7	36	.310	Clutch	53	19	1	20	.358

2004 Rankings (National League)

- 4th in batting average with the bases loaded (.500)
- 7th in batting average vs. lefthanded pitchers
- 9th in batting average in the clutch
- Led the Padres in on-base percentage

Brian Lawrence

2004 Season

Although Brian Lawrence won 15 games in 2004, his season was not dramatically different from his 2003 campaign that saw him drop 15 decisions. His home-run rate, walk rate and pitches per inning were all the same. Even the amount of run support he received was similar—4.88 versus 4.61. Given the ballpark he played in, it could be argued that he actually pitched worse in '04, but was simply the beneficiary of good luck. The year did have some bright moments: he threw a shutout versus the Mets in August and struck out 10 Brewers in a start in May, tying a career high.

Pitching

The velocity on Lawrence's fastball is slightly below average, but he can throw it with sink or as a cutter. He also throws a good slider and change-up, working down in the zone and inducing batters to put the ball on the ground. He still hasn't found a solution for lefties, who continue to rake him for a .300-plus batting average and an OPS (on-base plus slugging) far in excess of .800.

Defense & Hitting

Looks can be deceiving, as Lawrence is quick off the mound and has good range fielding his position. Basestealers were increasingly stymied by his pinpoint throws to first and quick delivery home. After his breakout season with the bat in 2003 in which he hit .224, he regressed badly in '04, looking much more like a pitcher at the plate. However, his bunting skills improved significantly, so he does have some value as a hitter.

2005 Outlook

There were some very minor encouraging signs of improvement for Lawrence in 2004, like slight upticks in groundball, strikeout and strikeout-walk rates. But at this point in his career, there's not much upside that can be expected. The Padres are hoping to get another year of 200 serviceable innings out of him before some of their young starters are ready to step up in 2006.

Position: SP
Bats: R **Throws:** R
Ht: 6' 0" **Wt:** 197

Opening Day Age: 28
Born: 5/14/76 in Fort Collins, CO
ML Seasons: 4

Overall Statistics

	W	L	Pct.	ERA	G	GS	Sv	IP	H	BB	SO	HR	Avg
'04	15	14	.517	4.12	34	34	0	203.0	226	55	121	26	.287
Car.	42	46	.477	3.91	129	113	0	738.1	769	198	470	79	.270

2004 Pitching Profile

	Brian Lawrence	NL Average
Overall Strike %	64.6	62.5
1st Pitch Strike %	62.4	58.5
Ratio	1.38	1.39
Strikeouts per 9 IP	5.36	6.74
Walks per 9 IP	2.44	3.38
Home Runs per 9 IP	1.15	1.11
Strikeout/Walk Ratio	2.20	1.99
Groundball/Flyball Ratio	1.81	1.25

2004 Situational Stats

	W	L	ERA	Sv	IP		AB	H	HR	RBI	Avg
Home	5	9	4.42	0	95.2	LHB	405	122	17	58	.301
Road	10	5	3.86	0	107.1	RHB	382	104	9	38	.272
First Half	10	6	3.89	0	111.0	Sc Pos	169	44	6	63	.260
Scnd Half	5	8	4.40	0	92.0	Clutch	32	13	2	6	.406

2004 Rankings (National League)

- 1st in fielding percentage at pitcher (1.000)
- 4th in losses and hits allowed
- 5th in games started, highest groundball-fly ball ratio allowed (1.8) and fewest pitches thrown per batter (3.47)
- 6th in highest batting average allowed (.287)
- 7th in complete games (2)
- 8th in GDPs induced (22) and highest slugging percentage allowed (.460)
- 9th in wins, lowest stolen-base percentage allowed (57.1) and highest ERA at home
- Led the Padres in sacrifice bunts (8), wins, losses, games started, complete games (2), innings pitched, hits allowed, batters faced (870), walks allowed, GDPs induced (22), highest groundball-flyball ratio allowed (1.8), fewest pitches thrown per batter (3.47) and bunts in play (11)

San Diego

Mark Loretta

2004 Season

Padres GM Kevin Towers was so impressed with Mark Loretta after 2003 that he inked him to a two-year deal through 2005. That may end up as one of Towers' best signings, as Loretta led all second basemen in batting average, on-base percentage, OPS, total bases and runs created, all while playing Gold Glove-caliber defense. He also earned his first All-Star appearance, while setting personal highs in hits, home runs, doubles, runs and RBI. Loretta became the first Padre not named Tony Gwynn to have 200 hits in a season.

Hitting

Loretta is a patient contact hitter with an excellent eye for balls and strikes. His smooth, level swing generates line drives to all fields with occasional home-run pop on pitches inside. Getting behind in the count isn't a problem for him, as he is one of the better two-strike hitters around. Loretta can hit-and-run, lay down a bunt, and this year he led the majors in sacrifice flies. Between he and Sean Burroughs fouling off pitches in the top two spots in the order, it was not uncommon for an opposing starter to throw more than 20 pitches before the first inning was over last season.

Baserunning & Defense

Although he doesn't have the range that many of the flashier glove men have, Loretta is fundamentally sound, positions himself well and turns the pivot as well as anyone. He was involved in 101 double plays in 2004, the high mark among all National League second basemen. Loretta has average speed, but is a smart enough runner to take as many bases as the defense will allow.

2005 Outlook

The Padres are looking forward to another year of the infield tandem of shortstop Khalil Greene and Loretta. They are so enamored of Loretta that they may seek to extend him beyond this year and move second-base prospect Josh Barfield to another position when he's ready. Regardless, the franchise will be extremely reluctant to let a good thing go when Loretta's contract expires after this season.

Position: 2B
Bats: R **Throws:** R
Ht: 6' 0" **Wt:** 186

Opening Day Age: 33
Born: 8/14/71 in Santa Monica, CA
ML Seasons: 10

Overall Statistics

	G	AB	R	H	D	T	HR	RBI	SB	BB	SO	Avg	OBP	Slg
'04	154	620	108	208	47	2	16	76	5	58	45	.335	.391	.495
Car.	1125	3871	541	1172	214	19	60	428	33	368	416	.303	.366	.414

Where He Hits the Ball

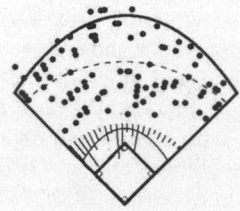
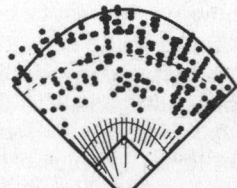

Vs. LHP **Vs. RHP**

2004 Situational Stats

	AB	H	HR	RBI	Avg		AB	H	HR	RBI	Avg
Home	278	82	11	36	.295	LHP	182	64	5	25	.352
Road	342	126	5	40	.368	RHP	438	144	11	51	.329
First Half	347	112	8	36	.323	Sc Pos	125	36	2	57	.288
Scnd Half	273	96	8	40	.352	Clutch	79	22	0	8	.278

2004 Rankings (National League)

- 1st in sacrifice flies (16) and batting average on the road
- 2nd in hits
- 3rd in batting average and batting average vs. lefthanded pitchers
- 4th in singles, doubles and lowest percentage of swings that missed (8.1)
- 5th in lowest fielding percentage at second base (.987)
- Led the Padres in at-bats, runs scored, total bases (307), hit by pitch (9), times on base (275), slugging percentage, batting average vs. righthanded pitchers, batting average at home, batting average on the road and batting average with two strikes (.271)
- Led NL second basemen in batting average

Phil Nevin

2004 Season

Despite missing just over two weeks due to surgery to repair torn cartilage in his right knee, Phil Nevin finished the 2004 season with more than 100 RBI for the third time in his career. His 26 home runs put him third all-time among Padres hitters and just 16 away from tying Nate Colbert for the franchise record. Not bad for a guy the Padres got six years ago for Andy Sheets.

Hitting

Like teammate Ryan Klesko, Nevin also had issues with Petco Park. But after clearing the air with GM Kevin Towers, Nevin refocused and hit .315 in June, .413 in July and .318 in August. His first choice is to pull the ball early in the count, but if he gets behind he'll try to go up the middle or away. Pitcher's usually try to get him to chase down and away out of the zone with breaking stuff. If they miss up and in trying to set up that pitch, they probably won't get a second chance because that is his favorite location.

Baserunning & Defense

A converted third baseman, Nevin has a strong, accurate arm, quick reactions and good range around the first-base bag. He occasionally does get lazy with his footwork and fails to position his body in front of a groundball. With his first full season at first behind him, Nevin still is learning the subtleties of digging throws out of the dirt. He doesn't have much speed, but no one breaks up a double play with more enthusiasm.

2005 Outlook

With the Padres looking to re-tool their outfield, Nevin may be on the block this winter. His no-trade clause makes him tricky to deal, but there are teams that would be interested in his services. Whether he's in San Diego in 2005 or elsewhere likely will be up to him. Whether a player who has been injured for more than a season's worth of games over the last three years can stay healthy probably is the biggest question.

Position: 1B
Bats: R **Throws:** R
Ht: 6' 2" **Wt:** 231

Opening Day Age: 34
Born: 1/19/71 in Fullerton, CA
ML Seasons: 10

Overall Statistics

	G	AB	R	H	D	T	HR	RBI	SB	BB	SO	Avg	OBP	Slg
'04	147	547	78	158	31	1	26	105	0	66	121	.289	.368	.492
Car.	986	3411	484	946	180	5	174	620	15	374	816	.277	.351	.486

Where He Hits the Ball

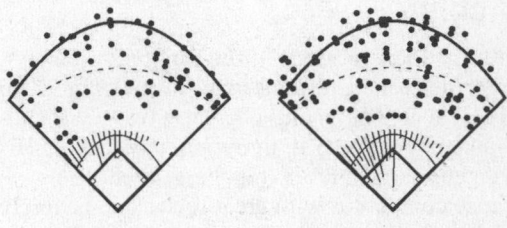

Vs. LHP   **Vs. RHP**

2004 Situational Stats

	AB	H	HR	RBI	Avg		AB	H	HR	RBI	Avg
Home	260	69	12	40	.265	LHP	170	55	10	28	.324
Road	287	89	14	65	.310	RHP	377	103	16	77	.273
First Half	296	87	14	53	.294	Sc Pos	177	56	8	80	.316
Scnd Half	251	71	12	52	.283	Clutch	75	22	2	12	.293

2004 Rankings (National League)

- 1st in errors at first base (13)
- 2nd in lowest fielding percentage at first base (.989)
- 3rd in batting average with the bases loaded (.556)
- 8th in batting average vs. lefthanded pitchers
- Led the Padres in home runs, RBI, strikeouts, GDPs (16), HR frequency (21.0 ABs per HR), most pitches seen per plate appearance (4.03), batting average with runners in scoring position, batting average with the bases loaded (.556), and cleanup slugging percentage (.493)

San Diego

Jake Peavy

2004 Season

Comparison's to Mark Prior or a young Greg Maddux seemed far-fetched after his 2003 showing, but Jake Peavy proved they were valid last year when he led the majors in ERA and was among the top 10 in strikeout rate. Peavy lost a month's worth of starts due to ligament inflammation in his right forearm in June, but he still managed to win 15 games and walk away with National League Pitcher of the Month honors in August. He also was the pitcher who ended Barry Bonds' consecutive games with a homer streak at seven. Twice Peavy struck out 11 batters in a game, and six times he struck out at least nine opponents.

Pitching

With a loose-armed, three-quarters delivery, Peavy delivers a fastball that ranges from 92-96 MPH. He also has a plus change, a two-plane slider and a curve he'll throw in any count. His changeup arguably is his best pitch. He's an intense competitor with great focus, and he rarely lets hitters escape with a mistake once he gets ahead.

Defense & Hitting

If Peavy has any flaw, it's that he sometimes focuses too much on the hitters and completely ignores the men on base. Big league basestealers are 26-for-28 when he is on the mound. He'll never win a Gold Glove, but he does an adequate job of fielding his position. When Peavy is at the plate, he takes good-looking swings although it's rare anything comes of it. He's an adequate bunter.

2005 Outlook

Padres GM Kevin Towers has been insisting for years that Peavy was the next Maddux. With his 2004 season as evidence, Peavy should get perennial consideration when it comes to the NL Cy Young discussion. His inflamed ligament gave the team a scare, especially with him being so young. But his pitch efficiency continues to improve every year, so concerns about serious injury are gradually fading, while the expectations of greatness grow.

Position: SP
Bats: R **Throws:** R
Ht: 6' 1" **Wt:** 180

Opening Day Age: 23
Born: 5/31/81 in Mobile, AL
ML Seasons: 3
Pronunciation: PEE-vee

Overall Statistics

	W	L	Pct.	ERA	G	GS	Sv	IP	H	BB	SO	HR	Avg
'04	15	6	.714	2.27	27	27	0	166.1	146	53	173	13	.236
Car.	33	24	.579	3.53	76	76	0	458.2	425	168	419	57	.245

2004 Pitching Profile

	Jake Peavy	NL Average
Overall Strike %	65.4	62.5
1st Pitch Strike %	60.6	58.5
Ratio	1.20	1.39
Strikeouts per 9 IP	9.36	6.74
Walks per 9 IP	2.87	3.38
Home Runs per 9 IP	0.70	1.11
Strikeout/Walk Ratio	3.26	1.99
Groundball/Flyball Ratio	1.18	1.25

2004 Situational Stats

	W	L	ERA	Sv	IP		AB	H	HR	RBI	Avg
Home	7	3	2.21	0	85.1	LHB	311	73	7	25	.235
Road	8	3	2.33	0	81.0	RHB	308	73	6	23	.237
First Half	5	3	2.43	0	63.0	Sc Pos	130	24	1	31	.185
Scnd Half	10	3	2.18	0	103.1	Clutch	20	3	0	0	.150

2004 Rankings (National League)

- 1st in ERA and lowest ERA on the road
- 2nd in lowest ERA at home and highest stolen-base percentage allowed (94.1)
- 4th in most run support per nine innings (6.4)
- 5th in winning percentage and lowest batting average allowed with runners in scoring position
- 6th in hit batsmen (11) and most strikeouts per nine innings (9.4)
- 7th in highest strikeout-walk ratio (3.3) and lowest slugging percentage allowed (.359)
- Led the Padres in ERA, wins, hit batsmen (11), strikeouts, stolen bases allowed (16), lowest batting average allowed (.236), lowest slugging percentage allowed (.359), lowest ERA at home, lowest ERA on the road, most run support per nine innings (6.4), fewest home runs allowed per nine innings (.70) and most strikeouts per nine innings (9.4)

David Wells

2004 Season

After building a distinguished record as a big-game pitcher, David Wells decided to return to his hometown San Diego at a substantial discount for one final year before possibly retiring. He dispelled any concerns about his back or his mobility by coming to camp in the best shape of his career. He missed four starts due to an accident at home in which he cut his hand, but that was about the only disappointing aspect of his season. His best start of the campaign came against the Mets on August 24, when he came within one out of a four-hitter, but he also tossed seven innings of shutout ball against the Yankees, Braves and Giants.

Pitching

Wells has excellent command of a 90-MPH fastball, a big-breaking slow curve and a plus change. He's fourth among active pitchers with the fewest walks per game, so when he misses, it's usually over the plate. He has very good instincts on the mound, usually working the outside of the plate. But he is unafraid to come inside with anything. One unexpected development last year was a change in pitching style, from a flyball pitcher to a borderline groundball pitcher despite the flyball-friendly dimensions of Petco Park.

Defense & Hitting

Despite his size, Wells proved to be a fairly decent fielder. He's not a good bunter but generally puts the ball in play. In previous years, he had been quite vulnerable to the running game, but National League thieves weren't quite as quick to figure him out, getting caught on three of eight attempts.

2005 Outlook

Wells' 2004 season was so encouraging that he filed for free agency instead of opting for retirement. The lefthander still had an eye open to the highest bidder, and he agreed to a two-year, $8 million deal, with tantalizing incentives, to join the Boston rotation. He re-enters the Red Sox-Yankees rivalry on the other side of the fence, but that works for a guy with a fondness for former Red Sox lefthander Babe Ruth.

Position: SP
Bats: L **Throws:** L
Ht: 6' 4" **Wt:** 248

Opening Day Age: 41
Born: 5/20/63 in Torrance, CA
ML Seasons: 18
Nickname: Boomer

Overall Statistics

W	L	Pct.	ERA	G	GS	Sv	IP	H	BB	SO	HR	Avg
12	8	.600	3.73	31	31	0	195.2	203	20	101	23	.266
212	136	.609	4.03	588	417	13	3022.1	3117	644	1974	353	.266

2004 Pitching Profile

	David Wells	NL Average
Overall Strike %	68.7	62.5
1st Pitch Strike %	62.3	58.5
Ratio	1.14	1.39
Strikeouts per 9 IP	4.65	6.74
Walks per 9 IP	0.92	3.38
Home Runs per 9 IP	1.06	1.11
Strikeout/Walk Ratio	5.05	1.99
Groundball/Flyball Ratio	1.52	1.25

2004 Situational Stats

	W	L	ERA	Sv	IP		AB	H	HR	RBI	Avg
Home	3	6	4.06	0	108.2	LHB	149	41	10	21	.275
Road	9	2	3.31	0	87.0	RHB	615	162	13	54	.263
First Half	4	5	3.09	0	96.0	Sc Pos	138	33	5	47	.239
Scnd Half	8	3	4.33	0	99.2	Clutch	40	9	0	1	.225

2004 Rankings (National League)

- 1st in fewest walks per nine innings (0.9)
- 3rd in highest strikeout-walk ratio (5.1)
- 4th in lowest on-base percentage allowed (.285)
- 6th in fewest pitches thrown per batter (3.49) and fewest strikeouts per nine innings (4.6)
- 9th in lowest ERA on the road
- Led the Padres in sacrifice bunts (8), highest strikeout-walk ratio (5.1), lowest on-base percentage allowed (.285), bunts in play (11) and fewest walks per nine innings (0.9)

San Diego

Rich Aurilia

Position: SS/3B
Bats: R **Throws:** R
Ht: 6' 1" **Wt:** 189

Opening Day Age: 33
Born: 9/2/71 in
Brooklyn, NY
ML Seasons: 10
Pronunciation:
uh-REEL-yuh

Overall Statistics

	G	AB	R	H	D	T	HR	RBI	SB	BB	SO	Avg	OBP	Slg
'04	124	399	49	98	21	2	6	44	1	37	71	.246	.314	.353
Car.	1117	3997	540	1100	211	16	132	517	17	319	618	.275	.329	.435

2004 Situational Stats

	AB	H	HR	RBI	Avg		AB	H	HR	RBI	Avg
Home	204	47	3	25	.230	LHP	136	35	3	19	.257
Road	195	51	3	19	.262	RHP	263	63	3	25	.240
First Half	261	63	4	28	.241	Sc Pos	102	24	0	31	.235
Scnd Half	138	35	2	16	.254	Clutch	73	14	0	4	.192

2004 Season

The Mariners thought they had their shortstop when they signed Rich Aurilia, but they soon discovered that he was not close to the same hitter who had averaged 21 homers per season the previous five years. The Padres traded for him to add veteran depth to their infield, and he proved to be a capable backup until third baseman Sean Burrough's knee injury forced Aurilia into full-time service during the final weeks of the season.

Hitting, Baserunning & Defense

Aurilia played mostly third base in San Diego and showed enough arm and range to have value as a utility player at any infield position. However, his bat speed had slowed, which may have been due to a sore groin and side that bothered him for much of the season. He had trouble handling pitches on the outside of the plate, and couldn't turn on hard stuff inside. He's no threat on the bases.

2005 Outlook

Aurilia will be looking for a starting job at shortstop, but that may be hard to come by with the number of high-profile free agents at that position. Concerns about his bat, which was his most notable asset during his peak years, will have to be answered. Aurilia may have to settle for a smaller role on his new team.

Scott Linebrink

Position: RP
Bats: R **Throws:** R
Ht: 6' 3" **Wt:** 208

Opening Day Age: 28
Born: 8/4/76 in Austin,
TX
ML Seasons: 5

Overall Statistics

	W	L	Pct.	ERA	G	GS	Sv	IP	H	BB	SO	HR	Avg
'04	7	3	.700	2.14	73	0	0	84.0	61	26	83	8	.209
Car.	10	5	.667	3.39	167	6	0	223.0	209	89	190	23	.253

2004 Situational Stats

	W	L	ERA	Sv	IP		AB	H	HR	RBI	Avg
Home	6	1	1.93	0	42.0	LHB	135	24	3	15	.178
Road	1	2	2.36	0	42.0	RHB	157	37	5	17	.236
First Half	4	1	2.22	0	48.2	Sc Pos	91	15	1	22	.165
Scnd Half	3	2	2.04	0	35.1	Clutch	147	39	6	18	.265

2004 Season

Petco turned out to be the perfect park for Scott Linebrink. He was dominating all season, posting ERAs under 2.00 in April, May, July and August. In July, batters hit just .088 off him, and he finished the month with an ERA of 0.82. He concluded the season with 28 holds, good for sixth best in the National League. He also set career highs in wins (seven) and strikeouts (83).

Pitching, Defense & Hitting

Linebrink likes to work up in the zone, with a fastball that runs 94-97 MPH. He'll sink it occasionally, and work in a decent change and splitter to keep hitters from getting on top of it. The result usually is a popup or a lazy flyball. When he needs a strikeout, he'll pitch to the bottom of the zone as well, using his splitter to entice batters to chase. At the plate, he swings hard in case he makes contact. His style of pitching generally takes him out of the play, but he is surehanded when the ball does find him.

2005 Outlook

Pitching in a park tailored to his skills, Linebrink should be optimistic about a repeat performance in 2005 as one of Trevor Hoffman's primary setup men.

Terrence Long

Traded To ROYALS

Position: LF/CF
Bats: L **Throws:** L
Ht: 6' 1" **Wt:** 200

Opening Day Age: 29
Born: 2/29/76 in
Montgomery, AL
ML Seasons: 6

Overall Statistics

	G	AB	R	H	D	T	HR	RBI	SB	BB	SO	Avg	OBP	Slg
'04	136	288	31	85	19	4	3	28	3	19	51	.295	.335	.420
Car.	741	2577	360	691	144	18	63	321	24	193	396	.268	.319	.411

2004 Situational Stats

	AB	H	HR	RBI	Avg		AB	H	HR	RBI	Avg
Home	118	35	1	10	.297	LHP	39	9	0	1	.231
Road	170	50	2	18	.294	RHP	249	76	3	27	.305
First Half	170	44	1	10	.259	Sc Pos	82	18	0	20	.220
Scnd Half	118	41	2	18	.347	Clutch	65	15	2	6	.231

2004 Season

Taking Terrence Long's contract was the cost of acquiring Ramon Hernandez, and it was an expense the Padres are glad they paid. Although his home-run power was absent the way it was for many Padres hitters, Long had a particularly good year, achieving a career high in batting average and hitting better than .300 in every month but May and June. He also supplied quality defense in the outfield.

Hitting, Baserunning & Defense

Although he has a big swing, Long is not really a home-run hitter. He spreads the ball around the field with line drives and increasingly hard grounders. Pitchers like to work him up with hard stuff and down and away with breaking pitches. He has good speed, although he rarely uses it to steal bases and when he has attempted, his success rate has not been good. His range in the outfield is rather average, considering his foot speed, and his arm is suited only to playing left or center.

2005 Outlook

The Padres were able to move Long to the Royals in exchange for Darrell May and Ryan Bukvich in early November. Long will provide insurance for the outfield youth movement in KC and be a solid veteran bat off the bench.

Xavier Nady

Position: LF
Bats: R **Throws:** R
Ht: 6' 2" **Wt:** 205

Opening Day Age: 26
Born: 11/14/78 in
Carmel, CA
ML Seasons: 3
Pronunciation:
ZAV-yer NAY-dee

Overall Statistics

	G	AB	R	H	D	T	HR	RBI	SB	BB	SO	Avg	OBP	Slg
'04	34	77	7	19	4	0	3	9	0	5	13	.247	.301	.416
Car.	145	449	58	119	21	1	12	48	6	29	87	.265	.319	.396

2004 Situational Stats

	AB	H	HR	RBI	Avg		AB	H	HR	RBI	Avg
Home	35	8	1	3	.229	LHP	32	11	2	4	.344
Road	42	11	2	6	.262	RHP	45	8	1	5	.178
First Half	26	6	1	4	.231	Sc Pos	21	5	1	7	.238
Scnd Half	51	13	2	5	.255	Clutch	12	2	1	1	.167

2004 Season

After playing a good portion of his season in the majors in 2003, Xavier Nady was back in Triple-A to further refine his skills in 2004. The Padres have to be pleased with the results: he hit .330 with 22 homers at Portland while showing a significantly improved eye at the plate.

Hitting, Baserunning & Defense

Even though his swing can get a little long and he still has to learn to lay off the breaking stuff outside, there were noticeable improvements in Nady's approach last year. He didn't give away as many at-bats and didn't try to yank everything. He came to the plate with a plan, and when the pitcher made a mistake, he hit it a mile. There still are questions about what position Nady will end up playing, but given the dimensions of Petco Park, he's probably best suited to first base. He's a smart baserunner, but with only station-to-station speed.

2005 Outlook

Nady has nothing left to prove in the minors, but the situation at his positions in San Diego is pretty crowded, so 2005 may not be the year he gets another chance to play every day. Until he does, he'll provide a quality power bat off the bench.

San Diego

Blaine Neal

Position: RP
Bats: L **Throws:** R
Ht: 6' 5" **Wt:** 248

Opening Day Age: 26
Born: 4/6/78 in Marlton, NJ
ML Seasons: 4

Overall Statistics

	W	L	Pct.	ERA	G	GS	Sv	IP	H	BB	SO	HR	Avg
'04	1	1	.500	4.07	40	0	0	42.0	49	11	36	6	.295
Car.	4	1	.800	4.62	94	0	0	101.1	126	39	82	9	.307

2004 Situational Stats

	W	L	ERA	Sv	IP		AB	H	HR	RBI	Avg
Home	1	0	3.20	0	25.1	LHB	68	17	2	11	.250
Road	0	1	5.40	0	16.2	RHB	98	32	4	15	.327
First Half	0	1	3.00	0	12.0	Sc Pos	47	16	2	21	.340
Scnd Half	1	0	4.50	0	30.0	Clutch	21	8	0	5	.381

2004 Season

The Padres sent hard-throwing righthander Ben Howard to the Marlins in exchange for Blaine Neal near the end of spring training in an effort to bolster their bullpen. Neal spent the first two months at Triple-A, then struggled when he was called up to the parent club in June. His season turned for the better in July, and for the next two months he pitched extremely well. He faded badly starting September, but rebounded with four scoreless innings in his final three outings.

Pitching, Defense & Hitting

Neal's fastball was good enough that he was considered a possible future closer when he was with the Marlins. The heater runs 94-95 MPH, and he also has a good slider. He needs to expand the zone up and down more to be consistently effective—most of his pitches were from the middle thigh to the belt. He's a power pitcher, so fielding his position is not a strong suit. He has never had a major league at-bat, and basestealers were 5-for-7 on his watch last year.

2005 Outlook

Fitting in behind Scott Linebrink and Akinori Otsuka will buy Neal time to grow into a setup role, and perhaps one day a shot at closing. For now, he will work in the middle innings.

Miguel Ojeda

Position: C
Bats: R **Throws:** R
Ht: 6' 2" **Wt:** 190

Opening Day Age: 30
Born: 1/29/75 in Sonora, Mexico
ML Seasons: 2

Overall Statistics

	G	AB	R	H	D	T	HR	RBI	SB	BB	SO	Avg	OBP	Slg
'04	62	156	23	40	3	0	8	26	0	15	34	.256	.322	.429
Car.	123	297	36	73	9	0	12	48	1	33	60	.246	.326	.397

2004 Situational Stats

	AB	H	HR	RBI	Avg		AB	H	HR	RBI	Avg
Home	73	19	1	7	.260	LHP	37	13	5	12	.351
Road	83	21	7	19	.253	RHP	119	27	3	14	.227
First Half	96	21	3	17	.219	Sc Pos	47	15	0	15	.319
Scnd Half	60	19	5	9	.317	Clutch	31	7	2	5	.226

2004 Season

One of the better hitting backup catchers in baseball, Miguel Ojeda batted .317 with a near .400 on-base and .600 slugging percentage after the All-Star break. He also filled in nicely when Ramon Hernandez was on the shelf with a knee injury. While Ismael Valdes was with the team, Ojeda was his personal catcher. A bruised left wrist from an errant pitch limited Ojeda's availability in August and September.

Hitting, Baserunning & Defense

Ojeda's bat is what originally caught the Padres' eye, and it is his all-around offensive game that will keep him in the majors for a few more years. He is an average contact hitter who also can yank the ball out of the park, with one homer every 25 at-bats for his career. It's not a problem for Ojeda to hit-and-run or lay down a bunt, either. Behind the plate he does an adequate job, but he needs a lot of help from his pitchers to control the running game.

2005 Outlook

Ojeda is better suited to a backup role, where his incomplete defensive game does not come into play too often while still allowing the team to take advantage of his obvious offensive skills. He again will be Hernandez' backup.

Akinori Otsuka

Position: RP
Bats: R **Throws:** R
Ht: 6' 0" **Wt:** 200

Opening Day Age: 33
Born: 1/13/72 in Chiba, Japan
ML Seasons: 1
Pronunciation: oats-kah

Overall Statistics

	W	L	Pct.	ERA	G	GS	Sv	IP	H	BB	SO	HR	Avg
'04	7	2	.778	1.75	73	0	2	77.1	56	26	87	6	.199
Car.	7	2	.778	1.75	73	0	2	77.1	56	26	87	6	.199

2004 Situational Stats

	W	L	ERA	Sv	IP			AB	H	HR	RBI	Avg
Home	4	0	2.15	1	37.2	LHB		140	30	1	9	.214
Road	3	2	1.36	1	39.2	RHB		142	26	5	12	.183
First Half	5	2	2.34	2	42.1	Sc Pos		68	13	1	15	.191
Scnd Half	2	0	1.03	0	35.0	Clutch		210	43	4	19	.205

2004 Season

Akinori Otsuka was one of the best relievers in Japanese League history when he signed with the Padres in December 2003. He welcomed what he called the ultimate challenge, to match skills against the best players in the world. He certainly can't be disappointed with his effort. Although Otsuka's role was not as high profile as other rookies, he placed third in the vote for NL Rookie of the Year.

Pitching, Defense & Hitting

Otsuka's unorthodox delivery caused some controversy early in the season. The claim was that the little tap in his glove with the ball he makes as he drives toward the plate was deceiving to the runners and therefore he was guilty of a balk. The league found no such problem. Otsuka throws a straight low-90s fastball, a change and a devastating slider with a sharp, late break. He spots the fastball in all quadrants, but uses his other pitches in the lower half of the zone. He's an average defender, but doesn't hold runners on very well.

2005 Outlook

Otsuka led the NL in holds, and figures to be among the leaders again next year. If something were to befall Trevor Hoffman, he would step in as the closer.

Jay Payton

Position: CF
Bats: R **Throws:** R
Ht: 5'10" **Wt:** 185

Opening Day Age: 32
Born: 11/22/72 in Zanesville, OH
ML Seasons: 7

Overall Statistics

	G	AB	R	H	D	T	HR	RBI	SB	BB	SO	Avg	OBP	Slg
'04	143	458	57	119	17	4	8	55	2	43	56	.260	.326	.367
Car.	715	2382	329	678	110	18	77	300	25	164	305	.285	.335	.443

2004 Situational Stats

	AB	H	HR	RBI	Avg		AB	H	HR	RBI	Avg
Home	227	55	0	20	.242	LHP	152	43	3	23	.283
Road	231	64	8	35	.277	RHP	306	76	5	32	.248
First Half	284	73	3	31	.257	Sc Pos	115	34	3	48	.296
Scnd Half	174	46	5	24	.264	Clutch	72	19	2	10	.264

2004 Season

The Padres signed Jay Payton for two years thinking they had a center fielder who could cover lots of ground and hit 20 homers a season. Payton was unable to do either. He strained his right hamstring in spring training and never showed the range the Padres had hoped for. As for his hitting, from June through August he batted .186. He did manage to hit .354 with power in September, but that was not enough to salvage the season.

Hitting, Baserunning & Defense

While Payton did show increased patience last year, it came at the expense of what he does well, which is make contact. For much of the season, he took pitches for the sake of taking them, rather than swinging at ones he would normally try to drive. His good speed serves him well in the outfield, but inefficient routes made a number of flyballs unnecessarily exciting. His arm is both strong and accurate, but mental lapses often gave the opposition additional opportunities.

2005 Outlook

Payton showed the kind of player he can be in September, and the Padres are hoping for a similar but more lengthy performance in 2005. He's only 32, so he still could have a couple of prime seasons left in the tank.

San Diego

Dennis Tankersley

Traded To ROYALS

Position: SP
Bats: R **Throws:** R
Ht: 6' 2" **Wt:** 185

Opening Day Age: 26
Born: 2/24/79 in Troy, MO
ML Seasons: 3
Pronunciation: TANK-ers-lee

Overall Statistics

	W	L	Pct.	ERA	G	GS	Sv	IP	H	BB	SO	HR	Avg
'04	0	5	.000	5.14	9	6	0	35.0	35	17	29	3	.254
Car.	1	10	.091	7.61	27	16	0	86.1	97	61	68	13	.290

2004 Situational Stats

	W	L	ERA	Sv	IP		AB	H	HR	RBI	Avg
Home	0	2	5.74	0	15.2	LHB	74	17	2	7	.230
Road	0	3	4.66	0	19.1	RHB	64	18	1	10	.281
First Half	0	3	3.20	0	25.1	Sc Pos	33	7	0	10	.212
Scnd Half	0	2	10.24	0	9.2	Clutch	2	2	0	2	1.000

2004 Season

Dennis Tankersley proved he could handle major league hitters when he was asked to fill in the rotation for Jake Peavy when the latter went on the DL in late May. Tankersley went 0-3 in those four starts, but posted an ERA of 2.82 and struck out 18 in 22.1 innings despite getting no run support. After a solid year in Triple-A (7-4, 3.15 ERA), he was called up for a couple of spot starts late, but he looked tired and wasn't as effective.

Pitching, Defense & Hitting

A hard-breaking slider is Tankersley's best pitch, but his fastball rates above average and he's working on his changeup. He still makes mistakes with the location of his fastball and sometimes will fall in love with his slider, overusing it and/or over-throwing it. He is a decent fielder and is better than most pitchers with a bat.

2005 Outlook

Tankersley's brief audition as a starter was enough to intrigue Kansas City, who traded lefty Darrell May and hard-throwing Ryan Bukvich for him and Terrence Long in early November. The Royals are in full rebuilding mode and desperate for young starting pitching, so Tankersley should have more freedom to learn on the job without fear of being sent down.

Jay Witasick

Position: RP
Bats: R **Throws:** R
Ht: 6' 4" **Wt:** 235

Opening Day Age: 32
Born: 8/28/72 in Baltimore, MD
ML Seasons: 9
Pronunciation: wi-TASS-ik

Overall Statistics

	W	L	Pct.	ERA	G	GS	Sv	IP	H	BB	SO	HR	Avg
'04	0	1	.000	3.21	44	0	1	61.2	57	26	57	8	.244
Car.	29	36	.446	4.72	289	56	4	614.0	666	287	531	88	.277

2004 Situational Stats

	W	L	ERA	Sv	IP		AB	H	HR	RBI	Avg
Home	0	1	3.24	0	33.1	LHB	100	33	5	16	.330
Road	0	0	3.18	1	28.1	RHB	134	24	3	12	.179
First Half	0	1	2.70	0	43.1	Sc Pos	66	13	2	21	.197
Scnd Half	0	0	4.42	1	18.1	Clutch	12	5	0	5	.417

2004 Season

Jay Witasick was one of the Padres' more effective relievers until a strained left oblique forced him to the trainer's table. From April until the All-Star break, his ERA was 2.70 with 41 strikeouts in 43.1 innings. After the break, he struggled until the Padres placed him on the DL in mid-August for all but the final week of the season.

Pitching, Defense & Hitting

Using a 94-MPH fastball that he can tail into righthanders or sink, Witasick sets up a nasty curve that breaks hard and late into lefties. Umpires are reluctant to call all the pitches he throws over the plate "strikes" because their movement is so violent. His fielding and batting skills are marginal, but he has improved considerably in keeping runners at bay if they reach.

2005 Outlook

The Padres released Witasick after the season in large part because they have a preponderance of quality righthanded short relievers. Witasick's 6.94 ERA versus the Giants and Dodgers made the decision easier. He is well suited to short relief and shouldn't have too much trouble finding takers. His best work has come in the NL, so it's likely that is where he will remain.

Other San Diego Padres

Andy Ashby (**Pos**: RHP, **Age**: 37)

	W	L	Pct.	ERA	G	GS	Sv	IP	H	BB	SO	HR	Avg
'04	0	0	–	0.00	2	0	0	2.0	1	0	2	0	.143
Car.	98	110	.471	4.12	309	285	1	1810.2	1857	540	1173	205	.268

Ashby fought all the way back from Tommy John surgery to make two relief appearances in September. He will have to prove that he is fully healthy to make a major league rotation this season. He needs two more wins to reach 100 for his career. 2005 Outlook: C

Rod Beck (**Pos**: RHP, **Age**: 36)

	W	L	Pct.	ERA	G	GS	Sv	IP	H	BB	SO	HR	Avg
'04	0	2	.000	6.38	26	0	0	24.0	27	9	15	8	.278
Car.	38	45	.458	3.30	704	0	286	768.0	703	191	644	97	.243

Beck began last season on the restricted list as he dealt with a mysterious family problem. When he finally made it back to the mound, "Shooter" was unable to repeat his amazing 2003 success, and the Padres released the 36-year-old in August. 2005 Outlook: D

Jeff Cirillo (**Pos**: 3B, **Age**: 35, **Bats**: R)

	G	AB	R	H	D	T	HR	RBI	SB	BB	SO	Avg	OBP	Slg
'04	33	75	12	16	3	0	1	7	0	5	14	.213	.259	.293
Car.	1350	4755	714	1414	299	19	103	654	56	500	620	.297	.368	.433

Cirillo spent the first month of the season on the DL with a broken right index finger, then rotted on the Padre bench until they released him in August. He hit .311 over his first eight seasons; in his last three, he has hit .232. 2005 Outlook: C

Robert Fick (**Pos**: DH/1B/LF, **Age**: 31, **Bats**: L)

	G	AB	R	H	D	T	HR	RBI	SB	BB	SO	Avg	OBP	Slg
'04	89	226	14	45	5	2	6	26	0	22	36	.199	.277	.319
Car.	575	1818	224	472	96	9	62	269	5	180	287	.260	.329	.425

Fick began the year with Tampa Bay, but was released in August after hitting just .201. After signing with the Padres, he hit .380 in 50 at-bats for Triple-A Portland and spent the last month on the big league bench. 2005 Outlook: C

Dave Hansen (**Pos**: 1B, **Age**: 36, **Bats**: L)

	G	AB	R	H	D	T	HR	RBI	SB	BB	SO	Avg	OBP	Slg
'04	86	106	15	26	5	0	2	12	0	21	21	.245	.367	.349
Car.	1170	1718	182	453	79	6	33	211	4	274	313	.264	.365	.374

After sending Hansen north in the previous offseason, the Padres re-acquired him for their bench down the stretch. Though he averaged just .157 as a pinch-hitter last season, he is a quality hitter and will find a job somewhere. 2005 Outlook: C

Sterling Hitchcock (**Pos**: LHP, **Age**: 33)

	W	L	Pct.	ERA	G	GS	Sv	IP	H	BB	SO	HR	Avg
'04	0	3	.000	6.33	4	4	0	21.1	22	8	14	5	.265
Car.	74	76	.493	4.80	281	200	3	1285.2	1374	471	997	181	.273

A stress fracture in his ribcage sidelined Hitchcock for most of last season. Then, after making just four August starts, his elbow finally gave out for good and he called it quits. He finished his career with exactly 200 starts. 2005 Outlook: D

Jon Knott (**Pos**: LF, **Age**: 26, **Bats**: R)

	G	AB	R	H	D	T	HR	RBI	SB	BB	SO	Avg	OBP	Slg
'04	9	14	1	3	2	0	0	1	0	1	5	.214	.267	.357
Car.	9	14	1	3	2	0	0	1	0	1	5	.214	.267	.357

Knott came up for a three-week cup of major league coffee in late May. Down in Triple-A Portland, he hit .290 with 26 homers and 85 RBI. With a good spring, the 26-year-old could find himself in the mix for at least a bench job. 2005 Outlook: C

Marty McLeary (**Pos**: RHP, **Age**: 30)

	W	L	Pct.	ERA	G	GS	Sv	IP	H	BB	SO	HR	Avg
'04	0	0	–	14.73	3	0	0	3.2	7	2	4	2	.438
Car.	0	0	–	14.73	3	0	0	3.2	7	2	4	2	.438

McLeary came over from the Marlins in a minor league deal in April. Pitching mostly out of the bullpen for Triple-A Portland, he posted a 2.99 ERA with 81 strikeouts in 84.1 IP, but allowed runs in each of his three big league appearances. 2005 Outlook: D

Eddie Oropesa (**Pos**: LHP, **Age**: 33)

	W	L	Pct.	ERA	G	GS	Sv	IP	H	BB	SO	HR	Avg
'04	2	1	.667	11.00	16	0	0	9.0	6	13	6	1	.188
Car.	8	4	.667	7.34	125	0	0	92.0	99	72	78	11	.274

Oropesa spent the first six weeks of last season with the Padres before they sent him down to Triple-A Portland, where he posted a 2.31 ERA and 54/19 K/W ratio. Released in mid-September, he has held lefties to a lifetime average of .242. 2005 Outlook: C

Antonio Osuna (**Pos**: RHP, **Age**: 31)

	W	L	Pct.	ERA	G	GS	Sv	IP	H	BB	SO	HR	Avg
'04	2	1	.667	2.45	31	0	0	36.2	32	11	36	3	.232
Car.	36	29	.554	3.50	407	0	21	486.1	423	202	501	42	.235

Osuna went on the DL twice last year, once with a strained right groin and the second with a bum elbow. When he was sound, the burly righthander was quite good, and he finished the season with 11 scoreless appearances. He will help someone's bullpen this season. 2005 Outlook: B

Brandon Puffer (Pos: RHP, Age: 29)

	W	L	Pct.	ERA	G	GS	Sv	IP	H	BB	SO	HR	Avg
'04	0	1	.000	5.50	14	0	0	18.0	24	11	12	0	.020
Car.	3	4	.429	4.75	82	0	0	108.0	115	65	70	8	.277

Puffer has been pitching professionally since 1994 and has a lifetime minor league ERA of 3.23. After shuttling back and forth between San Diego and Triple-A Portland, he was traded to the Red Sox. He ended the year as the closer at Triple-A Pawtucket. 2005 Outlook: C

Kerry Robinson (Pos: LF, Age: 31, Bats: L)

	G	AB	R	H	D	T	HR	RBI	SB	BB	SO	Avg	OBP	Slg
'04	80	92	20	27	4	0	0	5	11	5	8	.293	.330	.337
Car.	445	671	104	179	23	8	3	51	35	36	86	.267	.305	.338

Acquired from the Cardinals right before Opening Day, Robinson filled out the Padre bench in the first half of the season. The speedster has a .314 average and 265 stolen bases in 750 games in the minors, but has never gotten much of a shot in the bigs. 2005 Outlook: C

Ricky Stone (Pos: RHP, Age: 30)

	W	L	Pct.	ERA	G	GS	Sv	IP	H	BB	SO	HR	Avg
'04	2	2	.500	6.45	43	0	0	51.2	66	16	38	11	.307
Car.	11	9	.550	4.26	192	0	2	219.2	228	83	152	32	.269

After two fine years in Houston's bullpen, Stone struggled last year and was turned loose. The Padres gave him a shot, but he could not keep the ball in the yard. After the season, the Reds signed him and he will get a shot to turn it back around. 2005 Outlook: C

Brian Sweeney (Pos: RHP, Age: 30)

	W	L	Pct.	ERA	G	GS	Sv	IP	H	BB	SO	HR	Avg
'04	1	0	1.000	5.65	7	2	0	14.1	20	2	10	1	.328
Car.	1	0	1.000	4.18	12	2	0	23.2	27	3	17	1	.287

Sweeney came over from Seattle in the Jeff Cirillo deal and went 11-4 with a 3.83 ERA at Triple-A Portland. Now 30 years old, he has a 58-38 record in eight minor league seasons and will get a shot at making the Padre staff this year. 2005 Outlook: C

Jason Szuminski (Pos: RHP, Age: 26)

	W	L	Pct.	ERA	G	GS	Sv	IP	H	BB	SO	HR	Avg
'04	0	0		7.00	7	0	0	10.0	12	11	5	3	.286
Car.	0	0	—	7.20	7	0	0	10.0	12	11	5	3	.286

Szuminski was taken from the Cubs by the Royals in the Rule 5 draft, then traded to the Padres, who returned him to Chicago in early May. He walked more guys than he struck out in 51 innings for Triple-A Iowa and will have to prove himself there before getting another shot. 2005 Outlook: C

Ramon Vazquez (Pos: SS, Age: 28, Bats: L)

	G	AB	R	H	D	T	HR	RBI	SB	BB	SO	Avg	OBP	Slg
'04	52	115	12	27	3	2	1	13	1	11	24	.235	.297	.322
Car.	313	995	123	261	41	11	6	79	18	108	194	.262	.334	.344

The emergence of Khalil Greene sent Vazquez to the bench and ultimately the minors. He also spent a month on the DL last year with a strained right oblique. He can play anywhere in the infield and can hit a little, though his time may be short in San Diego. 2005 Outlook: C

Steve Watkins (Pos: RHP, Age: 26)

	W	L	Pct.	ERA	G	GS	Sv	IP	H	BB	SO	HR	Avg
'04	0	0	—	6.28	11	0	0	14.1	17	4	7	3	.293
Car.	0	0	—	6.28	11	0	0	14.1	17	4	7	3	.293

Splitting his time between two levels, Watkins went 9-6 with a 3.37 ERA and 115 strikeouts in the same number of innings last year. While he was unable to duplicate that success in the majors, he should get another shot at it in the spring with the Indians, who signed him to a minor league deal in early November. 2005 Outlook: C

Organization Overview:

With the No. 1 overall pick in the 2004 draft, the Padres passed on more heralded—but more expensive—college picks Jared Weaver and Stephen Drew, both the younger brothers of established major leaguers. Instead, they opted for local high-school product Matt Bush, who brought to the table excellent defense, projectable offense and one of the strongest arms in the draft, in addition to his outspoken passion to play for the Padres. Unfortunately, much of the goodwill was lost when the 18-year-old was busted in a bar scuffle that resulted in a month-long suspension. Despite the awkward start, the Padres still are optimistic they made the right pick after Bush's honest display of contrition and strong work ethic.

Brad Baker

Position: P **Opening Day Age:** 24
Bats: R **Throws:** R **Born:** 11/6/80 in
Ht: 6' 2" **Wt:** 180 Brattleboro, VT

Recent Statistics

	W	L	ERA	G	GS	Sv	IP	H	R	BB	SO	HR
2003 AA Mobile	1	6	5.68	17	9	0	50.2	50	34	36	53	3
2003 A Lk Elsinore	3	0	2.01	27	4	12	44.2	31	13	14	69	2
2004 AA Mobile	2	1	1.57	55	0	30	57.1	37	11	24	68	2
2004 AAA Portland	1	0	0.93	8	0	4	9.2	5	2	4	17	0

Frustrated by Baker's mixed success as a starter, the Padres moved him to the bullpen late in 2003, a move that has since restored the brilliant shine to his once-fading star. With a fastball that runs from 90-94 MPH, a two-plane curve and a superb changeup, Baker dominated Double-A Southern and Triple-A Pacific Coast League hitters in his first full season as a closer. He set the Mobile single-season record for saves with 30 and was named the Southern League's Most Outstanding Pitcher. Batters hit a collective .174 off him, and he continued his dominance in the Arizona Fall League. The Padres should give him a chance to make the team out of spring training, where he could become Trevor Hoffman's heir apparent.

Josh Barfield

Position: 2B **Opening Day Age:** 22
Bats: R **Throws:** R **Born:** 12/17/82 in
Ht: 6' 0" **Wt:** 185 Barquisimento, VZ

Recent Statistics

	G	AB	R	H	D	T	HR	RBI	SB	BB	SO	Avg
2003 A Lk Elsinore	135	549	99	185	46	6	16	128	16	50	122	.337
2004 AA Mobile	138	521	79	129	28	3	18	90	4	48	119	.248

Despite suffering a hamstring injury that cost him all of spring training, Barfield still was one of the Double-A Southern League's most productive players, leading the league with 90 RBI and placing among the leaders in homers and doubles. He has power to all fields, and opposing managers described him as the league's best situational hitter. His arm and range are only average, but they should be good enough to keep him at second. The hamstring injury kept his running in check last year, but when healthy, he has better than average speed and good basestealing instincts. The part of his game that needs the most attention is pitch recognition, as his walk and strikeout rates aren't particularly good.

Tagg Bozied

Position: 1B **Opening Day Age:** 25
Bats: R **Throws:** R **Born:** 7/24/79 in Sioux
Ht: 6' 3" **Wt:** 210 Falls, SD

Recent Statistics

	G	AB	R	H	D	T	HR	RBI	SB	BB	SO	Avg
2003 AAA Portland	119	450	59	123	25	2	14	59	1	38	80	.273
2004 AAA Portland	57	213	41	67	17	1	16	58	0	18	29	.315

Bozied was off to the best start of his career and on an emotional high when disaster struck on July 19. He ruptured the patella tendon in his left knee jumping toward home plate while celebrating his game-winning grand slam against Tacoma. Red hot at the time of the injury, he should be back to full strength by spring training. Not especially mobile or graceful, Bozied's only option defensively in the National League is at first base. For someone with his power, he makes contact more than might be expected, and his eye continues to improve. But there will be an adjustment period once he reaches the majors, as his swing can get a little long.

Justin Germano

Position: P **Opening Day Age:** 22
Bats: R **Throws:** R **Born:** 8/6/82 in
Ht: 6' 1" **Wt:** 190 Pasadena, CA

Recent Statistics

	W	L	ERA	G	GS	Sv	IP	H	R	BB	SO	HR
2004 AA Mobile	2	1	2.51	5	5	0	32.1	31	11	7	20	3
2004 AAA Portland	9	5	3.38	20	20	0	122.2	113	48	25	98	12
2004 NL San Diego	1	2	8.86	7	5	0	21.1	31	24	14	16	2

The Padres have been challenging Justin Germano from the day they drafted him, and last year was no different. After beginning the season in Double-A Mobile, Germano was called up to make his first major league start in Philadelphia, home to some of the most hostile fans in sports. He made his next start at Coors Field, and he held the Rockies without an earned run for six innings. The 13th-round pick in the 2000 draft spent most of the rest of the season at Triple-A Portland before being recalled in September. His fastball is consistently around 90 MPH, which he commands along with a curve, change and plus slider. If Germano has a weakness, it is that he throws *too* many strikes.

San Diego

Freddy Guzman

Position: OF
Bats. B Throws. R
Ht: 5' 10" **Wt:** 165

Opening Day Age: 24
Born: 1/20/81 in Santo Domingo, DR

Recent Statistics

	G	AB	R	H	D	T	HR	RBI	SB	BB	SO	Avg
2004 AA Mobile	35	138	21	39	5	2	1	7	17	16	28	.283
2004 AAA Portland	66	264	48	77	12	4	1	19	48	30	46	.292
2004 NL San Diego	20	76	8	16	3	0	0	5	5	3	13	.211

The word on Guzman was that he had tremendous speed, good on-base skills, excellent defensive range and a strong, accurate arm. But that wasn't the player the Padres saw when they called him up in mid-August. Despite excellent numbers at both Double-A and Triple-A, including a .363 on-base mark and 65 stolen bases at an 87-percent success rate, he looked overmatched at the plate and tentative in the outfield at Petco Park. Perhaps his struggles simply were a case of rookie jitters, and the Padres will give him another look in the spring. For Guzman to succeed, he'll need to do a much better job of laying off the pitches he can't handle. The rest should take care of itself.

Jon Knott

Position: OF
Bats: R **Throws:** R
Ht: 6' 3" **Wt:** 220

Opening Day Age: 26
Born: 8/4/78 in Manassas, VA

Recent Statistics

	G	AB	R	H	D	T	HR	RBI	SB	BB	SO	Avg
2003 AA Mobile	127	432	83	109	32	0	27	82	5	82	117	.252
2003 AAA Portland	7	26	5	9	1	0	1	5	0	4	3	.346
2004 AAA Portland	113	435	79	126	22	3	26	85	5	58	110	.290

There are plenty of 26-year-old hitters with sweet swings and tape-measure power floating around the minors. A few of them have solid on-base skills despite high strikeout totals. But none of them are MBAs who went undrafted out of college as Knott did. He also has another unique distinction: he has logged every professional at-bat he's ever had—the pitch type, the location, the name and arm angle of the pitcher and the result—in a written ledger. In addition to his intelligence, attention to detail and obvious hitting skills, he also is a pretty good athlete with a strong enough arm to play right field. His .407 average last spring caught Bruce Bochy's eye.

Humberto Quintero

Position: C
Bats: R **Throws:** R
Ht: 6' 1" **Wt:** 190

Opening Day Age: 25
Born: 8/8/79 in Maracaibo, VZ

Recent Statistics

	G	AB	R	H	D	T	HR	RBI	SB	BB	SO	Avg
2004 AAA Portland	68	259	36	82	25	0	5	30	0	8	18	.317
2004 NL San Diego	23	72	7	18	3	0	2	10	0	5	16	.250

Quintero got the callup when Ramon Hernandez went down with his knee injury and quickly became a fan favorite for his "defense first" style of play. It didn't hurt that he also got off to a hot start with the bat, hitting .400 with a .657 slugging percentage in his first 10 games. Quintero covers the plate well, has decent doubles power that could develop into home-run pop, but he's very hard to walk. He could develop into a Bengie Molina-type starter, but more likely will end up as a Jose Molina-type backup with exceptional defensive and handling skills, but only marginal offensive value.

Tim Stauffer

Position: P
Bats: R **Throws:** R
Ht: 6' 2" **Wt:** 205

Opening Day Age: 22
Born: 6/2/82 in Portland, ME

Recent Statistics

	W	L	ERA	G	GS	Sv	IP	H	R	BB	SO	HR
2004 A Lk Elsinore	2	0	1.78	6	6	0	35.1	28	10	9	30	0
2004 AA Mobile	3	2	2.63	8	8	0	51.1	56	17	13	33	3
2004 AAA Portland	6	3	3.54	14	14	0	81.1	83	46	26	50	15

The Padres' top pick in the 2003 draft and fourth player taken overall eased last year's concerns about his sore shoulder by tossing nearly 170 quality innings over three levels. Finishing the year in Triple-A Portland, Stauffer's strikeout rate was a little lower than anticipated, but his control and poise were as advertised. The two-time All-American, who currently is more famous for his honesty off the field than his prowess on it, has excellent command of a low-90s moving fastball, a hard curve and an above-average changeup. The Padres don't have an opening in their rotation, but Stauffer should get an opportunity to pitch in San Diego at some point this year.

Others to Watch

Mike Bynum (27) seems to have found his niche as a lefty specialist. The first-round pick in 1999 came into 62 games at Triple-A Portland: he saved six, won six and posted a 3.19 ERA with 75 strikeouts in 79 innings. . . Shortstop **J.J. Furmaniak** (25) enjoyed his best season at the plate after switching to a heavier bat, popping 17 homers and driving in 73 runs at Triple-A Portland. The 22nd-round pick in the 2000 draft is currently blocked at short, but he has experience playing third base and second, which opens the possibility of becoming a valuable utilityman. . . **Ben Johnson** (23) finally appears to be putting his considerable tools to good use after spending his third season in Double-A. The outfielder hit 23 homers and 28 doubles, but still needs to improve his walk and strikeout rates to take the next step. . . Aussie righthander **Chris Oxspring** (27) had a solid season at Triple-A Portland and continued his good work in the AFL. He has a good feel for pitching and his two best pitches—a 92-94 MPH fastball and a wicked breaking pitch that breaks more than a slider but harder than a curve—are good enough that he could contribute in a major league bullpen even if he never masters his changeup.

SBC Park

Offense

SBC Park can be a tough park for hitters, though most complaints come from lefthanded batters other than Barry Bonds. Although the 309-foot dimension down the right-field line is inviting, players find it difficult to hit homers because of a constant cross wind and high wall. Players have been more successful trying to hit balls into the big gaps, and it's easy for even slow runners to whack triples to right-center field.

Defense

Not many players have issues with the conditions of the SBC Park infield and outfield. Each year, the entire field is resodded after several non-baseball events have been staged at the park. However, the park can be a nightmare for a left fielder during day games due to the glare of the sun. Right field also can be a difficult position to play because of the nooks and crannies and the caroms balls take off various parts of the wall.

Who It Helps the Most

Bonds, obviously, flourishes at home. Second baseman Ray Durham had a lot of success at home in 2004, with a .323 batting average. J.T. Snow has complained about the park in the past, but he hit .355 at SBC last season. Reliever Jim Brower had the most success at home of any Giants pitcher last season based on ERA.

Who It Hurts the Most

Giants lefthanded hitters usually are at a disadvantage at their home park. Brett Tomko also had difficult times in his first season at home, with a 5.31 ERA, and was booed several times after being knocked out early.

Rookies & Newcomers

Rookie Noah Lowry flourished in his first season at SBC, with a 5-0 record and a 3.10 ERA in eight games. Shortstop Omar Vizquel, who was signed by the Giants in November, should not be impacted by the park. He's not a home-run hitter, and if he hits line drives into the gaps, he should have no problems adjusting to SBC.

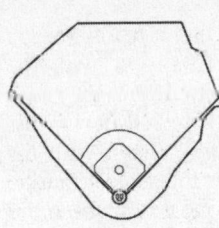

Dimensions: LF-339, LCF-382, CF-399, RCF-421, RF-309

Capacity: 41,584

Elevation: 0 feet

Surface: Grass

Foul Territory: Average

Park Factors

2004 Season

| | Home Games | | | Away Games | | | |
	Giants	Opp	Total	Giants	Opp	Total	Index
G	73	73	146	69	69	138	
Avg	.286	.273	.279	.259	.255	.257	109
AB	2441	2556	4997	2408	2321	4729	100
R	383	362	745	348	315	663	106
H	699	697	1396	624	592	1216	109
2B	152	148	300	130	126	256	111
3B	23	18	41	4	21	25	155
HR	76	69	145	82	74	156	88
BB	314	234	548	293	241	534	97
SO	367	466	833	402	407	809	97
E	47	49	96	41	35	76	119
E-Infield	37	38	75	38	30	68	104
LHB-Avg	.290	.279	.285	.279	.269	.274	104
LHB-HR	39	31	70	44	32	76	89
RHB-Avg	.283	.268	.276	.244	.245	.244	113
RHB-HR	37	38	75	38	42	80	87

2002-2003

| | Home Games | | | Away Games | | | |
	Giants	Opp	Total	Giants	Opp	Total	Index
G	144	144	288	143	143	286	
Avg	.267	.244	.255	.262	.254	.258	99
AB	4720	4930	9650	4979	4650	9629	100
R	673	508	1181	697	596	1293	91
H	1259	1204	2463	1305	1179	2484	98
2B	239	221	460	277	219	496	93
3B	39	30	69	20	21	41	168
HR	132	89	221	202	130	332	66
BB	555	449	1004	543	497	1040	96
SO	811	921	1732	934	827	1761	98
E	86	110	196	70	82	152	128
E-Infield	67	88	155	56	72	128	120
LHB-Avg	.262	.240	.249	.275	.264	.269	93
LHB-HR	50	27	77	73	47	120	64
RHB-Avg	.269	.248	.259	.256	.246	.252	103
RHB-HR	82	62	144	129	83	212	68

2004 Rankings (National League)

- Second-highest batting-average factor
- Second-highest hit factor
- Second-highest triple factor
- Second-highest RHB batting-average factor

San Francisco

Felipe Alou

2004 Season

In some regards, Felipe Alou had a better season in 2004 than he did in his first year with the Giants, when he guided them to 100 wins and a postseason berth. Alou was criticized during his first year for not communicating much with his players. Although he said after the season that he wasn't going to change, he appeared to be more communicative, meeting with players behind closed doors and spending more time in the clubhouse.

Offense

Alou once again squeezed the most out of a lineup built almost exclusively around Barry Bonds. The Giants were second in the league with 850 runs scored, five less than the mighty St. Louis lineup. Alou was handcuffed by a veteran team with little team speed, and opposing managers walking Bonds a record 232 times. Alou constantly tinkered with his lineup, which kept some players guessing as to where they would hit each day.

Pitching & Defense

The Giants won 91 games with a pitching staff and defense that was in the middle of the pack in the NL. Outside of Jason Schmidt, San Francisco did not have a dependable starter until the second half. One drawback was Alou's propensity to yank starters too early. He went to the bullpen 521 times, by far the most in baseball. The defense was, at times, sloppy. Only first baseman J.T. Snow had what could be considered a standout year in the field, though right fielders Michael Tucker and Dustan Mohr played solidly.

2005 Outlook

While the Giants have added a new shortstop, catcher and closer, Alou will have pretty much the same cast of characters that he did in 2004, so most players are familiar with his sometimes unique managing style. He has rubbed some the wrong way with his failure to communicate, but he improved in that area last year. Alou will turn 70 in May, and the rigors of managing seemed to take a toll on him last summer. His contract expires after the season, and managing general partner Peter Magowan has said this might be Alou's last season.

Born: 5/12/35 in Haina, Dominican Republic

Playing Experience: 1958-1974, SF, Atl, Oak, NYY, Mon, Mil

Managerial Experience: 11 seasons

Manager Statistics

Year	Team, Lg	W	L	Pct	GB	Finish
2004	San Fran, NL	91	71	.562	2.0	2nd West
11 Seasons		882	849	.510	–	–

2004 Starting Pitchers by Days Rest

	<=3	4	5	6+
Giants Starts	0	88	36	28
Giants ERA	–	4.35	3.55	4.22
NL Avg Starts	2	82	46	23
NL ERA	4.58	4.35	4.28	4.73

2004 Situational Stats

	Felipe Alou	NL Average
Hit & Run Success %	50.7	38.0
Stolen Base Success %	65.2	71.7
Platoon Pct.	63.9	55.2
Defensive Subs	29	18
High-Pitch Outings	13	6
Quick/Slow Hooks	19/7	21/12
Sacrifice Attempts	107	99

2004 Rankings (National League)

- 1st in fewest caught stealings of third base (2), hit-and-run success percentage, defensive substitutions, starting lineups used (138), starts with over 120 pitches (13), relief appearances (521), mid-inning pitching changes (247), first-batter platoon percentage and one-batter pitcher appearances (95)
- 2nd in fewest caught stealings of second base (20), sacrifice-bunt percentage (88.8%) and starts with over 140 pitches (1)

Edgardo Alfonzo

2004 Season

Once again, Edgardo Alfonzo started miserably, hitting .219 in April. But his slow start was not as pronounced as it was the year before, when he was hitting .216 as of June 28. Last season, Alfonzo rebounded by hitting .315 in May and .305 in June. However, he dipped to .217 in July, with just two home runs.

Hitting

For a player with a .288 lifetime batting average, Alfonzo goes into long slumps, particularly at the start of the season. He'll have confidence issues during those times, having no idea why he starts so slowly. There's a theory that Alfonzo, a native Venezuelan, is a warm-weather player who heats up in June. But it is rarely hot at his home stadium, SBC Park, which is not suited to Alfonzo's style of hitting. He'll never hit a lot of home runs at home, and once again his power numbers dropped.

Baserunning & Defense

Alfonzo did not have as good a season defensively as he did in 2003. He made 14 errors, his highest total in the majors and three more than last season. His range has steadily declined, possibly the result of a chronic bad back. Alfonzo, however, did what he was told, including moving to second base when Ray Durham was injured for a handful of games. He is one of the team's slowest runners and no threat on the bases, but he is considered an intelligent baserunner.

2005 Outlook

Although Alfonzo has been steady for two seasons, the Giants know he has not been worth the four-year, $26 million contract he was given. The front office privately would like to trade him and make room for Pedro Feliz at third base, but Alfonzo's contract has been hard to unload. There were reports as early as last season that the Giants were shopping him, but with no likely suitor, the club will have to keep Alfonzo for at least one more season, after which time he should be easier to deal.

Position: 3B
Bats: R **Throws:** R
Ht: 5'11" **Wt:** 226

Opening Day Age: 31
Born: 11/8/73 in Soapire, VZ
ML Seasons: 10

Overall Statistics

	G	AB	R	H	D	T	HR	RBI	SB	BB	SO	Avg	OBP	Slg
'04	139	519	66	150	26	1	11	77	1	46	40	.289	.350	.407
Car.	1367	4930	736	1419	263	17	144	696	51	562	579	.288	.362	.436

Where He Hits the Ball

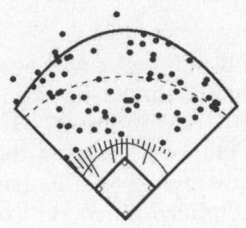
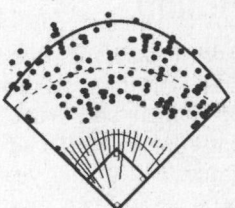

Vs. LHP   **Vs. RHP**

2004 Situational Stats

	AB	H	HR	RBI	Avg		AB	H	HR	RBI	Avg
Home	245	78	8	42	.318	LHP	154	49	5	27	.318
Road	274	72	3	35	.263	RHP	365	101	6	50	.277
First Half	305	86	6	49	.282	Sc Pos	150	44	2	59	.293
Scnd Half	214	64	5	28	.299	Clutch	83	23	3	18	.277

2004 Rankings (National League)

- 6th in fielding percentage at third base (.965)
- Led the Giants in singles and batting average with the bases loaded (.438)

San Francisco

2004 Season

Barry Bonds won his second batting title in three years, broke his own record with a .609 on-base percentage and walked a major league record 232 times, including 120 intentional walks. Managers went to greater lengths to avoid pitching to Bonds, yet he still won an unprecedented fourth straight MVP and his seventh overall. He accomplished all of this despite the swirl of his involvement in the Bay Area Laboratory Co-Operative (BALCO) scandal. Bonds constantly was reminded and questioned throughout the season about his rumored steroid use, but he has consistently denied any knowledge of using performance enhancing drugs.

Hitting

Like a fine wine, Bonds only gets better with age. Last season, a year in which he turned 40, he hit 45 homers and drove in 101 runs in just 373 at-bats. Bonds still had the quickest stroke in the game, and as the years have progressed, he has become an even more disciplined hitter. He has drawn an incredible 755 walks the past four seasons, an unparalleled achievement in baseball.

Baserunning & Defense

Bonds no longer plays the Gold Glove left field that made him a five-tool player. He has bulked up over the years, losing his agility. He rarely dives for balls, not wanting to risk injury. However, he positions himself well and keeps runners from taking the extra base with a quick release. Bonds was once a 40-steal man, but he hasn't reached double figures since 2001. When he does run, however, he's usually successful.

2005 Outlook

Many wait for Bonds to show signs of aging, but there seems no reason to think Bonds will be slowed by Father Time in 2005. He continues his high-energy training program during the offseason and is in better shape then most players in the game. With 703 home runs, Bonds will make a run at Babe Ruth's mark of 714, which he could top in May. After that, Hank Aaron's record 755 homers could be toppled in the early stages of the 2006 season.

Position: LF
Bats: L **Throws:** L
Ht: 6' 2" **Wt:** 228

Opening Day Age: 40
Born: 7/24/64 in Riverside, CA
ML Seasons: 19
Nickname: BB

Overall Statistics

G	AB	R	H	D	T	HR	RBI	SB	BB	SO	Avg	OBP	Slg
147	373	129	135	27	3	45	101	6	232	41	.362	.609	.812
2716	9098	2070	2730	563	77	703	1843	506	2302	1428	.300	.443	.611

Where He Hits the Ball

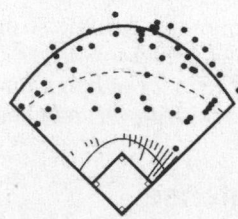 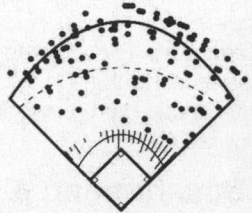

Vs. LHP **Vs. RHP**

2004 Situational Stats

	AB	H	HR	RBI	Avg		AB	H	HR	RBI	Avg
Home	182	75	26	51	.412	LHP	140	43	8	23	.307
Road	191	60	19	50	.314	RHP	233	92	37	78	.395
First Half	189	69	23	48	.365	Sc Pos	71	28	11	55	.394
Scnd Half	184	66	22	53	.359	Clutch	52	18	7	13	.346

2004 Rankings (National League)

- 1st in batting average, walks, intentional walks (120), times on base (376), slugging percentage, on-base percentage, HR frequency (8.3 ABs per HR), batting average with runners in scoring position, batting average vs. righthanded pitchers, cleanup slugging percentage (.817), batting average at home and highest percentage of pitches taken (71.9)
- 2nd in runs scored
- 3rd in batting average with two strikes (.286)
- 4th in home runs and fielding percentage in left field (.983)
- Led the Giants in runs scored, total bases (303), RBI, walks, pitches seen (2,425), plate appearances (617), games played, and batting average with runners in scoring position,

Ray Durham

Position: 2B
Bats: B **Throws:** R
Ht: 5' 8" **Wt:** 196

Opening Day Age: 33
Born: 11/30/71 in Charlotte, NC
ML Seasons: 10

2004 Season

Ray Durham once again endured an injury-plagued season, landing on the disabled list twice for the second straight year with an assortment of leg injuries. When he was in the lineup, Durham showed some of the skills the Giants believed he possessed when they signed him. He had to dig himself out of hole created when he was hurt most of May. He had only two home runs and eight RBI entering June, but he collected 31 RBI the next two months.

Hitting

There's no question about Durham's hitting when he's in the lineup. He hit the most homers since swatting 20 for the White Sox in 2001. Last year, he had a higher batting average from the right side, but more power from the left side. For a leadoff hitter, Durham strikes out too much. He struck out 60 times last year, three more than his walk total.

Baserunning & Defense

Once a threat to run, Durham's injuries have cut down his stolen-base totals. He is blessed with athletic genes, however, and the Giants once considered moving him to the outfield. That likely won't happen after Durham struggled so much to catch popups at his position last season. He had a horrible season in the field, with 16 errors. Furthermore, he was slow to turn what should have been easy double plays.

2005 Outlook

The Giants were candid about Durham's offseason regimen. They would like him to follow their training program to keep his tender legs in shape. Privately, they are not happy with his work ethic. The training staff was critical of him last season, as he spent most of May on the DL. Perhaps that motivated Durham, who was healthier in the second half. If Durham can't stay healthy, the Giants might try to trade him, though he still has two years and $13.5 million remaining on his contract.

Overall Statistics

	G	AB	R	H	D	T	HR	RBI	SB	BB	SO	Avg	OBP	Slg
'04	120	471	95	133	28	8	17	65	10	57	60	.282	.364	.484
Car.	1430	5579	983	1556	321	70	137	604	242	615	934	.279	.354	.435

Where He Hits the Ball

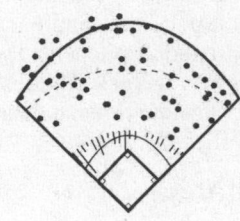
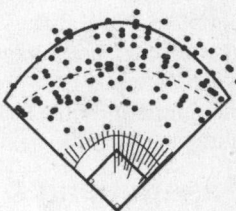

Vs. LHP   **Vs. RHP**

2004 Situational Stats

	AB	H	HR	RBI	Avg		AB	H	HR	RBI	Avg
Home	235	76	8	39	.323	LHP	132	44	4	23	.333
Road	236	57	9	26	.242	RHP	339	89	13	42	.263
First Half	195	56	7	27	.287	Sc Pos	92	28	1	43	.304
Scnd Half	276	77	10	38	.279	Clutch	58	14	2	9	.241

2004 Rankings (National League)

- 1st in errors at second base (16) and lowest fielding percentage at second base (.972)
- 5th in triples and batting average vs. lefthanded pitchers
- 6th in on-base percentage for a leadoff hitter (.365)
- 8th in batting average at home
- 10th in most pitches seen per plate appearance (4.07)
- Led the Giants in triples, stolen bases, caught stealing (4), stolen-base percentage (71.4), most pitches seen per plate appearance (4.07), steals of third (3) and batting average vs. left handed pitchers

San Francisco

Marquis Grissom

2004 Season

Marquis Grissom had a fast start and a fast finish, helping to conceal his subpar June and July numbers. But just when it appeared age might be catching up to him—he'll turn 38 in April—Grissom hit .287 in September with 12 RBI. While the Giants may have had doubts about picking up his option, his good finish provided enough evidence that he's still a capable center fielder.

Hitting

Grissom does not hide the fact that he's a free swinger, proving that by striking out 83 times and drawing just 37 walks. He will chase fastballs out of the strike zone and swing at breaking pitches off the plate. He's always been a pull hitter and once again flourished against lefthanded pitchers. He wasn't nearly as productive against righties, though he did hit 11 homers against righthanders, matching his total against lefties.

Baserunning & Defense

Grissom may have lost a step in the outfield, but he's still among the most skilled center fielders in the National League. He doesn't have the raw speed he had in his earlier days with Montreal, but he makes up for that deficiency with experience and positioning. He gets superior jumps on balls and his arm is adequate. However, for a second straight season, he dropped a couple of routine balls. Grissom's stolen-base totals have steadily declined. Nonetheless, he is smart and skilled while running the bases.

2005 Outlook

The Giants have gotten much more than they expected from Grissom after signing him to a two-year, $4.5 million contract. However, Father Time is catching up to a body that had been ravaged by injuries even before he joined the Giants. Manager Felipe Alou said he believed Grissom was tired at midseason, something Grissom did not agree with. He has played nearly 150 games in each of the last two seasons after platooning in Los Angeles the previous year. Alou will have to give Grissom more days off this season to avoid the slump that plagued him last year.

Position: CF
Bats: R **Throws:** R
Ht: 5'11" **Wt:** 208

Opening Day Age: 37
Born: 4/17/67 in Atlanta, GA
ML Seasons: 16
Pronunciation: mar-KEESE
Nickname: Grip

Overall Statistics

	G	AB	R	H	D	T	HR	RBI	SB	BB	SO	Avg	OBP	Slg
	145	562	78	157	26	2	22	90	3	37	83	.279	.323	.450
	2121	8138	1179	2222	382	56	225	952	428	546	1222	.273	.319	.417

Where He Hits the Ball

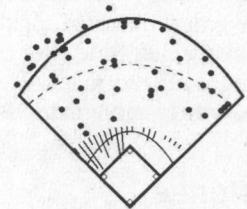
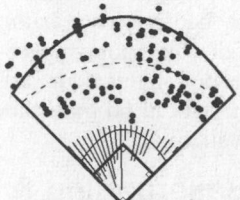

Vs. LHP   **Vs. RHP**

2004 Situational Stats

	AB	H	HR	RBI	Avg		AB	H	HR	RBI	Avg
Home	288	82	11	46	.285	LHP	149	47	11	34	.315
Road	274	75	11	44	.274	RHP	413	110	11	56	.266
First Half	326	93	14	51	.285	Sc Pos	157	43	7	69	.274
Scnd Half	236	64	8	39	.271	Clutch	92	19	2	10	.207

2004 Rankings (National League)

- 3rd in fielding percentage in center field (.994)
- 5th in GDPs (22)
- Led the Giants in at-bats and hits

Dustin Hermanson

Signed By
WHITE SOX

2004 Season

No one could have imagined the Giants' closer at the end of the season would have been Dustin Hermanson. He had not performed those duties since 2000, when he replaced Ugueth Urbina temporarily in Montreal. Hermanson was 4-4 with a 4.59 ERA in 18 starts before the team approached him in early August and asked if he'd to switch to closer. Hermanson, taking over for an ineffective Matt Herges, saved 17 of 20 games.

Pitching

Hermanson was drafted by San Diego as a closer who could throw in the high 90-MPH range. However, the Padres already had a closer, Trevor Hoffman, and Hermanson was dealt to the Expos via the Marlins. He was quickly converted to a starter by then-Expos manager Felipe Alou. Hermanson doesn't have the velocity he once had, but he can still throw in the mid-90s. With no need to pace himself after moving from the rotation, Hermanson was able to throw as hard as he could. He also used an effective slider while closing. Hermanson might not have the repertoire of other pitchers, but he's a competitor who isn't afraid to throw any pitch at any time.

Defense & Hitting

Hermanson did not make an error last season and doesn't hinder the team's defense when he's on the mound. He is paid to pitch, not hit. Although he's a good athlete, he had just three hits in 30 at-bats last season, and is an .093 career batter. Two of his 30 career hits are home runs, however.

2005 Outlook

Hermanson can be a competent closer, but will assume another role after signing a two-year, $5.5 million deal with the Chicago White Sox in December. He may work in a setup role for Sox closer Shingo Takatsu, or it's still possible that he could claim the last rotation spot if his new club doesn't sign another established starter during the offseason. Hermanson became a mentor to young Giants Jerome Williams and Jesse Foppert the past two seasons. He could assume a similar role with the Sox' young arms.

Position: RP/SP
Bats: R **Throws:** R
Ht: 6' 2" **Wt:** 200

Opening Day Age: 32
Born: 12/21/72 in Springfield, OH
ML Seasons: 10

Overall Statistics

	W	L	Pct.	ERA	G	GS	Sv	IP	H	BB	SO	HR	Avg
'04	6	9	.400	4.53	47	18	17	131.0	132	46	102	15	.262
Car.	71	74	.490	4.31	294	180	22	1219.0	1233	442	836	154	.265

2004 Pitching Profile

	Dustin Hermanson	NL Average
Overall Strike %	61.7	62.5
1st Pitch Strike %	62.4	58.5
Ratio	1.36	1.39
Strikeouts per 9 IP	7.01	6.74
Walks per 9 IP	3.16	3.38
Home Runs per 9 IP	1.03	1.11
Strikeout/Walk Ratio	2.22	1.99
Groundball/Flyball Ratio	1.06	1.25

2004 Situational Stats

	W	L	ERA	Sv	IP		AB	H	HR	RBI	Avg
Home	3	3	4.50	7	60.0	LHB	239	65	10	33	.285
Road	3	6	4.56	10	71.0	RHB	265	64	5	29	.242
First Half	3	3	4.34	0	87.0	Sc Pos	106	29	4	47	.274
Scnd Half	3	6	4.91	17	44.0	Clutch	84	23	3	15	.274

2004 Rankings (National League)
- 7th in lowest save percentage (85.0)
- 9th in lowest winning percentage
- Led the Giants in save percentage (85.0)

San Francisco

A.J. Pierzynski

2004 Season

A.J. Pierzynski had some memorable moments in his first season with the Giants, but the campaign will be remembered primarily for an unidentified teammate calling him a "cancer," home fans booing him in April and a propensity to ground into double plays. With his so-so year, and the fact that he will not be back in 2005, the trade that sent Joe Nathan to Minnesota for Pierzynski has to be considered a Twins victory.

Hitting

Pierzynski began and ended the season poorly. When he was struggling, he had trouble getting the ball in the air and was an easy out because of his lack of speed. He admitted that he was pressing, and the boos only made it worse. Pierzynski grounded into 27 double plays, a major league high and a new franchise record. He began to show the style that made him a career .300 hitter with the Twins when he hit .368 in June, the only month he batted over .300. The highlight of his season probably was the grand slam he hit in Puerto Rico that helped beat the Expos.

Baserunning & Defense

Pierzynski is one of the slowest runners on the Giants, and he doesn't get many infield hits. Although he was said to have improved defensively, Pierzynski didn't show those skills last season. He was charged with nine passed balls and an error, and threw out only 11 of 62 runners trying to steal. Pitchers privately grumbled about his defense, and his issues with pitcher Brett Tomko went public when another teammate called Pierzynski a "cancer."

2005 Outlook

Pierzynski's career with San Francisco got off to a rocky start when he and the Giants could not reach a deal and he took them to arbitration. He won his case and was awarded $3.5 million. Pierzynski is arbitration eligible again, but the Giants signed catcher Mike Matheny to a three-year deal in December. Pierzynski's days in San Francisco are over.

Position: C
Bats: L **Throws:** R
Ht: 6' 3" **Wt:** 245

Opening Day Age: 28
Born: 12/30/76 in Bridgehampton, NY
ML Seasons: 7
Pronunciation: PEER-zin-skee

Overall Statistics

	G	AB	R	H	D	T	HR	RBI	SB	BB	SO	Avg	OBP	Slg
'04	131	471	45	128	28	2	11	77	0	19	27	.272	.319	.410
Car.	561	1899	229	558	134	14	37	270	6	79	220	.294	.336	.438

Where He Hits the Ball

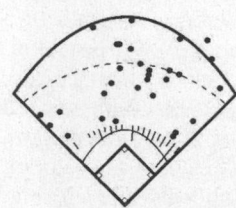 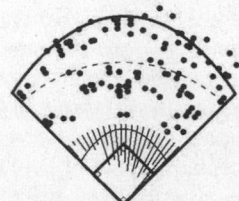

Vs. LHP **Vs. RHP**

2004 Situational Stats

	AB	H	HR	RBI	Avg		AB	H	HR	RBI	Avg
Home	233	66	3	31	.283	LHP	97	22	2	14	.227
Road	238	62	8	46	.261	RHP	374	106	9	63	.283
First Half	260	79	7	45	.304	Sc Pos	153	47	5	68	.307
Scnd Half	211	49	4	32	.232	Clutch	76	25	4	15	.329

2004 Rankings (National League)

- 1st in GDPs (27), fewest pitches seen per plate appearance (3.07), lowest percentage of pitches taken (41.6) and most GDPs per GDP situation (23.3%)
- 3rd in fielding percentage at catcher (.999)
- 4th in highest percentage of swings on the first pitch (41.7)
- 5th in hit by pitch (15)
- 10th in lowest on-base percentage
- Led the Giants in hit by pitch (15) and GDPs (27)

Kirk Rueter

2004 Season

Kirk Rueter had his second straight subpar season, and fans were wondering if it was time to take him out of the rotation. It wasn't learned until late in the year that he had been pitching most of the campaign with a sports hernia, a common injury to hockey players. Rueter insists that the injury did not contribute to his poor pitching, but it certainly could have been a factor, according to the team's training staff.

Pitching

The National League finally has caught on to Rueter's strategy. He lived on the outer half of the plate for most of his career. When umpires began following the rulebook strike zone at the behest of baseball officials several years ago, Rueter wasn't always getting the outside pitches. With a fastball that barely travels more than 86 MPH, Rueter can't afford to have location problems, and if he isn't getting the outside calls, he's very hittable. He began pitching more inside in the second half, when his numbers improved.

Defense & Hitting

With his boyish looks and country-boy vernacular, Rueter gives the impression that he's laid back. Actually, he's one of the toughest competitors on the team. He's one of the top fielding pitchers in baseball. He fields comebackers with grace and covers first base with ease. Although he has only a .152 lifetime batting average, Rueter takes hitting seriously. He always is among the team leaders in sacrifice bunts.

2005 Outlook

Rueter is signed through this season, but his days as a starter could end before then. The Giants have a deep rotation, with young pitchers such as Noah Lowry, Jerome Williams, Brad Hennessey and Matt Cain either on the starting staff or on the brink of joining it. Rueter is the senior member of the pitching staff. The front office adores him because of his success in big games and unselfish demeanor. He'll have to break out of his two-year funk or he might be pitching elsewhere, or in the bullpen, next season.

Position: SP
Bats: L **Throws:** L
Ht: 6' 2" **Wt:** 212

Opening Day Age: 34
Born: 12/1/70 in Centralia, IL
ML Seasons: 12
Pronunciation: REE-ter
Nickname: Woody

Overall Statistics

	W	L	Pct.	ERA	G	GS	Sv	IP	H	BB	SO	HR	Avg
'04	9	12	.429	4.73	33	33	0	190.1	225	66	56	21	.296
Car.	128	85	.601	4.18	320	318	0	1810.2	1961	535	793	208	.279

2004 Pitching Profile

	Kirk Rueter	NL Average
Overall Strike %	58.1	62.5
1st Pitch Strike %	52.5	58.5
Ratio	1.53	1.39
Strikeouts per 9 IP	2.65	6.74
Walks per 9 IP	3.12	3.38
Home Runs per 9 IP	0.99	1.11
Strikeout/Walk Ratio	0.85	1.99
Groundball/Flyball Ratio	1.60	1.25

2004 Situational Stats

	W	L	ERA	Sv	IP		AB	H	HR	RBI	Avg
Home	5	8	4.43	0	103.2	LHB	188	52	4	22	.277
Road	4	4	5.09	0	86.2	RHB	572	173	17	77	.302
First Half	5	6	4.85	0	104.0	Sc Pos	168	58	7	72	.345
Scnd Half	4	6	4.59	0	86.1	Clutch	26	9	1	3	.346

2004 Rankings (National League)

- 1st in lowest strikeout-walk ratio (0.8), highest batting average allowed with runners in scoring position and fewest strikeouts per nine innings (2.6)
- 2nd in lowest stolen-base percentage allowed (25.0) and highest batting average allowed (.296)
- 4th in GDPs induced (25) and most pitches thrown per batter (3.91)
- 5th in hits allowed, highest on-base percentage allowed (.351) and highest batting average allowed vs. righthanded batters
- 7th in highest ERA, highest slugging percentage allowed (.463) and highest ERA on the road
- Led the Giants in losses, games started, hits allowed, home runs allowed, runners caught stealing (3), GDPs induced (25), highest groundball-flyball ratio allowed (1.6) and lowest stolen-base percentage allowed (25.0)

San Francisco

Jason Schmidt

2004 Season

Jason Schmidt had two seasons. The first was a Cy Young Award campaign over the first four-plus months. The second was a disappointing, injury-plagued August and September. Schmidt was 15-4 with a 2.52 ERA on August 17, a heavy favorite to win his first Cy Young, when he hurt his right groin in a start against Montreal. Though not at full strength, he returned after an 11-day layoff, later admitting he wasn't ready to come back. Houston's Roger Clemens won the Cy Young, with Schmidt finishing a disappointing fourth. Clemens admitted when he won the award that Schmidt "was the Cy Young race" before he was injured.

Pitching

Many players call Schmidt the most feared starter in the National League. He not only throws hard and has a nasty slider, but he has developed a changeup that is among the best in the game. Rather than nibbling at the corners as he did earlier in his career in Pittsburgh, Schmidt comes at hitters with a fastball clocked as high as 98 MPH. Schmidt had a 12-game winning streak from April 26 to July 17 in which he established himself as the top starter in baseball. He threw two one-hitters during the streak, each against high-powered offenses (Cubs, Red Sox).

Defense & Hitting

If there is a drawback in Schmidt's game, it's his fielding. His 6-foot-5 frame and high-energy delivery put him at a disadvantage with the glove. He committed three errors last season. An elbow injury in 2003 hindered Schmidt at the plate. He has four homers in his career, however, with 17 RBI. Although at times he can look awkward at the plate, he has sneaky power.

2005 Outlook

Schmidt hasn't been healthy in two of the last three spring trainings. He underwent right elbow surgery before last year, then developed a sore shoulder in spring training and started the season on the disabled list. If he stays healthy, there's no doubt Schmidt can win 20 games and his elusive first Cy Young Award.

Position: SP
Bats: R **Throws:** R
Ht: 6' 5" **Wt:** 205

Opening Day Age: 32
Born: 1/29/73 in Lewiston, ID
ML Seasons: 10

Overall Statistics

	W	L	Pct.	ERA	G	GS	Sv	IP	H	BB	SO	HR	Avg
'04	18	7	.720	3.20	32	32	0	225.0	165	77	251	18	.202
Car.	104	74	.584	3.90	252	243	0	1567.2	1449	601	1383	142	.244

2004 Pitching Profile

	Jason Schmidt	NL Average
Overall Strike %	64.3	62.5
1st Pitch Strike %	61.6	58.5
Ratio	1.08	1.39
Strikeouts per 9 IP	10.04	6.74
Walks per 9 IP	3.08	3.38
Home Runs per 9 IP	0.72	1.11
Strikeout/Walk Ratio	3.26	1.99
Groundball/Flyball Ratio	1.15	1.25

2004 Situational Stats

	W	L	ERA	Sv	IP		AB	H	HR	RBI	Avg
Home	9	6	3.47	0	124.2	LHB	398	76	6	35	.191
Road	9	1	2.87	0	100.1	RHB	419	89	12	43	.212
First Half	11	2	2.51	0	122.0	Sc Pos	172	31	5	54	.180
Scnd Half	7	5	4.02	0	103.0	Clutch	72	15	5	12	.208

2004 Rankings (National League)

- 1st in shutouts (3) and lowest fielding percentage at pitcher (.900)
- 2nd in wins, stolen bases allowed (28), lowest batting average allowed (.202) and lowest slugging percentage allowed (.323)
- 3rd in strikeouts, pitches thrown (3,607), lowest on-base percentage allowed (.272), most strikeouts per nine innings (10.0), errors at pitcher (3), highest stolen-base percentage allowed (93.3) and most pitches thrown per batter (3.98)
- 4th in complete games (4), winning percentage and lowest batting average allowed with runners in scoring position
- Led the Giants in ERA, sacrifice bunts (13), complete games (4), innings pitched, batters faced (907), walks allowed, winning percentage, highest strikeout-walk ratio (3.3), fewest home runs allowed per nine innings (.72) and most strikeouts per nine innings (10.0)

J.T. Snow

2004 Season

The 2003 season was expected to be J.T. Snow's last with the Giants. They declined to exercise his $6.5 million contract after the season was over, making him a free agent. A few weeks later, with a chance to sign with either Baltimore, Pittsburgh or the New York Mets, Snow opted to return to San Francisco, agreeing to a $1.5 million contract with an option for 2005. He split time with Pedro Feliz at first base and had his best season since 2000. His batting average was a career-best .327.

Hitting

After injury-plagued seasons from 2001-03 and a drastic drop in production, he began hitting like the old Snow. He was spraying balls to all fields and regained his power. Although his homer total was just 12, it nearly equaled his output in the previous two seasons combined. He had a breakout game on August 13 in Philadelphia, hitting three home runs for the first time in his career. Snow hit nine of his homers in the second half, when he batted .387. Only Seattle's Ichiro Suzuki (.429) had a higher batting average after the All-Star break.

Baserunning & Defense

Snow hasn't won a Gold Glove since 2000, but that's not to say his defense has eroded. He continues to make spectacular plays seem routine. He hurt his knee at Wrigley Field making a diving catch just short of the bullpen mound, one of the best plays of the season. But as good as Snow is on defense, his lack of speed can sometimes be a drawback. This is not to insinuate that Snow is a bad baserunner. He doesn't make bonehead moves. He's just slow.

2005 Outlook

The Giants want Snow around for his defense, which saves untold runs every year. When he hits as he did last season, that's a bonus. Snow has been a fixture during the Giants' rise as a National League West power, and it appears he could be around for a few more years.

Position: 1B
Bats: L **Throws:** L
Ht: 6' 2" **Wt:** 209

Opening Day Age: 37
Born: 2/26/68 in Long Beach, CA
ML Seasons: 13
Nickname: Snowball

Overall Statistics

G	AB	R	H	D	T	HR	RBI	SB	BB	SO	Avg	OBP	Slg
107	346	62	113	32	1	12	60	4	58	61	.327	.429	.529
1560	5230	753	1399	276	17	185	833	19	720	1073	.267	.358	.433

Where He Hits the Ball

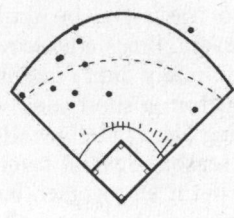 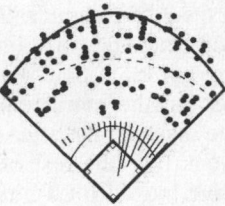

Vs. LHP   **Vs. RHP**

2004 Situational Stats

	AB	H	HR	RBI	Avg		AB	H	HR	RBI	Avg
Home	169	60	5	34	.355	LHP	47	12	1	9	.255
Road	177	53	7	26	.299	RHP	299	101	11	51	.338
First Half	165	43	3	16	.261	Sc Pos	83	30	2	43	.361
Scnd Half	181	70	9	44	.387	Clutch	51	18	1	12	.353

2004 Rankings (National League)

- 2nd in batting average with runners in scoring position
- Led the Giants in batting average in the clutch

Brett Tomko

2004 Season

Brett Tomko's start paralleled that of another San Francisco newcomer, catcher A.J. Pierzynski. Both began poorly and were booed by their home fans. But unlike Pierzynski, Tomko went on to have a very fine season. He was only 4-5 with a 4.98 ERA before the All-Star break, but was 7-2 with a 3.15 ERA in the second half. When Jason Schmidt hurt his right groin and was ineffective in mid-August and September, it coincided with Tomko's resurgence.

Pitching

With an explosive fastball, slider, changeup and curveball, Tomko was the team's best pitcher the final two months of the season, with all due respect to Schmidt. Tomko was awful in April, however, and was booed several times after leaving games at SBC Park. He really didn't get his act together until returning from a short stint on the disabled list after injuring his right elbow. He went 10-3 the rest of the season. Several teams have longed for Tomko to put it all together, but he bounced from team to team each season, with the Giants being his fourth stop in four years.

Defense & Hitting

Tomko isn't considered a good fielder or hitter. He has cut down on giving up homers and induces more groundballs, allowing him to make more plays in the field, but he committed a pair of errors last season. He can be run on, though he has worked on a slide step. Last season he hit .113 with no RBI. He did have 13 sacrifice bunts, tying Jason Schmidt for the team lead among pitchers.

2005 Outlook

With Tomko's poor start in 2004 and several young pitchers ready to break into the San Francisco rotation, it was assumed his $2.5 million option would not be picked up after the season. However, the way Tomko finished, the Giants didn't hesitate to bring him back. With a healthy Schmidt and Tomko, the Giants could have one of the best 1-2 tandems in the National League.

Position: SP
Bats: R **Throws:** R
Ht: 6' 4" **Wt:** 215

Opening Day Age: 31
Born: 4/7/73 in Euclid, OH
ML Seasons: 8
Pronunciation: TOM-koh

Overall Statistics

	W	L	Pct.	ERA	G	GS	Sv	IP	H	BB	SO	HR	Avg
'04	11	7	.611	4.04	32	31	0	194.0	196	64	108	19	.260
Car.	73	58	.557	4.53	229	186	1	1236.2	1273	407	818	173	.266

2004 Pitching Profile

	Brett Tomko	NL Average
Overall Strike %	62.9	62.5
1st Pitch Strike %	59.4	58.5
Ratio	1.34	1.39
Strikeouts per 9 IP	5.01	6.74
Walks per 9 IP	2.97	3.38
Home Runs per 9 IP	0.88	1.11
Strikeout/Walk Ratio	1.69	1.99
Groundball/Flyball Ratio	1.08	1.25

2004 Situational Stats

	W	L	ERA	Sv	IP		AB	H	HR	RBI	Avg
Home	6	4	5.31	0	79.2	LHB	333	98	9	39	.294
Road	5	3	3.15	0	114.1	RHB	420	98	10	49	.233
First Half	4	5	4.98	0	94.0	Sc Pos	171	51	4	66	.298
Scnd Half	7	2	3.15	0	100.0	Clutch	21	3	0	1	.143

2004 Rankings (National League)

- 4th in wild pitches (10) and highest batting average allowed with runners in scoring position
- 6th in sacrifice bunts (13)
- 7th in complete games (2) and lowest ERA on the road
- 8th in most run support per nine innings (6.0) and fewest strikeouts per nine innings (5.0)
- 9th in lowest stolen-base percentage allowed (57.1) and lowest groundball-flyball ratio allowed (1.1)
- 10th in lowest fielding percentage at pitcher (.950)
- Led the Giants in sacrifice bunts (13), wild pitches (10), pickoff throws (100), runners caught stealing (3), most run support per nine innings (6.0) and fewest walks per nine innings (3.0)

Michael Tucker

2004 Season

The Giants were criticized for not signing a free agent such as Vladimir Guerrero to fill their right-field hole. Instead, the cost-conscious team signed Michael Tucker, who platooned with Dustan Mohr. San Francisco got more than it could have expected from Tucker at the plate, and his defense also improved after a shaky start.

Hitting

Tucker is a prototypical hacker. He can be streaky, and his home runs come during those stretches. When he is hot, he can be a dangerous hitter. The Giants are aware of what he can do, since he had so much success against them during his many stops in the National League. Tucker hit .360 with eight homers against the Giants in 114 at-bats, prompting them to give him a budget-friendly, two-year contract before 2004.

Baserunning & Defense

Tucker runs the bases extremely well and has speed to take the extra base. He seemed lost in the difficult right field at SBC Park at the start of the season, running wrong routes to the ball and getting fooled with the quirky bounces off the wall. However, he quickly adjusted and played very well, following in the footsteps of predecessors Reggie Sanders and Jose Cruz Jr., who won a Gold Glove in 2003. Tucker made just six errors and got to many balls with his feet-first slides. His arm isn't strong, but it wasn't a major concern last season.

2005 Outlook

Tucker will be back for another season, but his role will be determined during the offseason. The Giants were looking at a few outfield options that could put Tucker on the bench, but their early activity focused on signing a catcher, shortstop and closer. With a .231 lifetime average as a pinch-hitter, Tucker may not be suited to pinch-hitting and spot starts, since he needs to play often to stay sharp.

Position: RF/CF
Bats: L **Throws:** R
Ht: 6' 2" **Wt:** 195

Opening Day Age: 33
Born: 6/25/71 in South Boston, VA
ML Seasons: 10

Overall Statistics

	G	AB	R	H	D	T	HR	RBI	SB	BB	SO	Avg	OBP	Slg
'04	140	464	77	119	21	6	13	62	5	70	106	.256	.353	.412
Car.	1256	3759	587	972	188	48	119	486	108	443	894	.259	.340	.429

Where He Hits the Ball

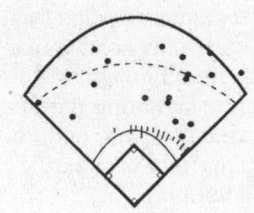 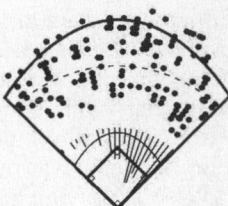

Vs. LHP   **Vs. RHP**

2004 Situational Stats

	AB	H	HR	RBI	Avg		AB	H	HR	RBI	Avg
Home	213	47	4	26	.221	LHP	64	15	1	8	.234
Road	251	72	9	36	.287	RHP	400	104	12	54	.260
First Half	258	71	7	35	.275	Sc Pos	109	28	1	46	.257
Scnd Half	206	48	6	27	.233	Clutch	65	19	2	9	.292

2004 Rankings (National League)

- 2nd in lowest batting average at home
- 6th in errors in right field (4)
- 8th in fewest GDPs per GDP situation (4.6%)
- Led the Giants in strikeouts and on-base percentage for a leadoff hitter (.413)

Jerome Williams

2004 Season

Jerome Williams came to camp overweight and out of shape and suffered through a miserable spring training. He started well, though, going 3-1 with a 3.93 ERA the first month of the season. That was his best month, and he was lost for all but one start the final two months of the season when he suffered a right elbow injury while pitching against St. Louis on July 30.

Pitching

Williams throws a low-90s fastball and a decent slider. He had a 5.10 ERA in June, but was settling down in July before he was sidelined. It's hard to fully evaluate his season after he missed most of the second half with his elbow injury. Williams returned in late September for his final start and beat San Diego. After his solid rookie season in 2003, the team's training staff wasn't happy that Williams took it easy during the off-season, and put him on a strenuous workout program. While he was rehabbing from his injury, he was also improving his conditioning.

Defense & Hitting

Williams is a gifted athlete who had been compared to a young Dwight Gooden when Williams was in the minor leagues. Williams is quick to field his position. The only problem is a nonchalant, sidearm pickoff throw to first base, which caused strain on his elbow and forced him to leave a game. His hitting isn't much to speak of. He batted just .139 last season and is a .123 lifetime hitter.

2005 Outlook

Williams had surgery in early August to remove bone chips and a bone spur from his right elbow. If the righthander shows up to camp in shape and stays healthy, the Giants expect him to win 15 or so games. However, he has to prove to the team he can get through a season without an injury. He is not considered a workhorse and must improve his conditioning if he wants to remain a legitimate major leaguer.

Position: SP
Bats: R **Throws:** R
Ht: 6' 3" **Wt:** 246

Opening Day Age: 23
Born: 12/4/81 in Honolulu, HI
ML Seasons: 2

Overall Statistics

	W	L	Pct.	ERA	G	GS	Sv	IP	H	BB	SO	HR	Avg
'04	10	7	.588	4.24	22	22	0	129.1	123	44	80	14	.254
Car.	17	12	.586	3.77	43	43	0	260.1	239	93	168	24	.248

2004 Pitching Profile

	Jerome Williams	NL Average
Overall Strike %	62.1	62.5
1st Pitch Strike %	55.9	58.5
Ratio	1.29	1.39
Strikeouts per 9 IP	5.57	6.74
Walks per 9 IP	3.06	3.38
Home Runs per 9 IP	0.97	1.11
Strikeout/Walk Ratio	1.82	1.99
Groundball/Flyball Ratio	1.59	1.25

2004 Situational Stats

	W	L	ERA	Sv	IP		AB	H	HR	RBI	Avg
Home	5	4	4.85	0	59.1	LHB	234	64	6	34	.274
Road	5	3	3.73	0	70.0	RHB	251	59	8	26	.235
First Half	8	6	4.66	0	102.1	Sc Pos	120	31	3	43	.258
Scnd Half	2	1	2.67	0	27.0	Clutch	16	2	1	1	.125

2004 Rankings (National League)

- 2nd in hit batsmen (17)
- Led the Giants in hit batsmen (17), pickoff throws (100) and fewest pitches thrown per batter (3.60)

Jim Brower

Position: RP
Bats: R **Throws:** R
Ht: 6' 3" **Wt:** 215

Opening Day Age: 32
Born: 12/29/72 in Edina, MN
ML Seasons: 6
Pronunciation: BROW-er

Overall Statistics

	W	L	Pct.	ERA	G	GS	Sv	IP	H	BB	SO	HR	Avg
'04	7	7	.500	3.29	89	0	1	93.0	90	36	63	6	.259
Car.	30	28	.517	4.22	264	28	4	490.1	483	208	329	57	.260

2004 Situational Stats

	W	L	ERA	Sv	IP		AB	H	HR	RBI	Avg
Home	3	1	2.96	1	48.2	LHB	133	45	2	22	.338
Road	4	6	3.65	0	44.1	RHB	215	45	4	20	.209
First Half	5	5	3.72	1	55.2	Sc Pos	112	27	2	36	.241
Scnd Half	2	2	2.65	0	37.1	Clutch	162	41	3	11	.253

2004 Season

Jim Brower arguably was the Giants' most valuable pitcher. He was transformed from a long reliever/spot starter to the club's primary setup man. He tied the franchise record with 89 appearances, and became manager Felipe Alou's most dependable reliever, often being used more than an inning per appearance.

Pitching, Defense & Hitting

Although he finished with a 3.29 ERA, Brower had a quick start, with a 2.93 ERA in April and a 2.45 mark in May over 30 games. The overuse took a toll in the middle of the season, but he had a 1.17 ERA in August and a 1.26 mark in the final month of the season. Brower earns his money pitching and is not a standout in the field or at the plate. He made two errors last season, and had just two at-bats.

2005 Outlook

Brower has proven his value to the team and received a two-year contract before last season. He has the body to pitch so many innings, but Alou cannot turn to him as much as he did last season. Brower was bothered by right elbow tightness late in the season, and was unavailable the next-to-last game of the season. Still, he never complains about overuse.

Dave Burba

Position: RP
Bats: R **Throws:** R
Ht: 6' 4" **Wt:** 255

Opening Day Age: 38
Born: 7/7/66 in Dayton, OH
ML Seasons: 15
Pronunciation: BUR-ba

Overall Statistics

	W	L	Pct.	ERA	G	GS	Sv	IP	H	BB	SO	HR	Avg
'04	4	1	.800	4.21	51	0	2	77.0	70	26	50	7	.241
Car.	115	87	.569	4.49	511	234	3	1777.2	1777	762	1398	201	.260

2004 Situational Stats

	W	L	ERA	Sv	IP		AB	H	HR	RBI	Avg
Home	3	0	3.11	0	37.2	LHB	121	32	5	15	.264
Road	1	1	5.26	2	39.1	RHB	170	38	2	20	.224
First Half	3	1	3.61	2	42.1	Sc Pos	82	20	1	28	.244
Scnd Half	1	0	4.93	0	34.2	Clutch	63	16	2	7	.254

2004 Season

Dave Burba spent most of the season with the Brewers, where he posted a 4.08 ERA in 45 games. The Giants acquired him on September 2 for minor league pitcher Josh Habel, making Burba ineligible for the postseason roster. Even if he had been eligible, he would have been unable to pitch after sustaining a separated left shoulder while covering first base in late September.

Pitching, Defense & Hitting

Burba proved his value quickly, pitching two scoreless innings of relief in his first game with the Giants a day after he was acquired. He was dependable in his short stay. His injury, however, put pressure on the team's bullpen. Burba did not distinguish himself hitting, going 0-for-4 last season. With his 6-foot-4 frame, Burba can be a little awkward fielding, as evidenced by his tumble while covering first when he sustained his injury.

2005 Outlook

The Giants did not tender Burba a contract before December 7, making him a free agent. He's always been considered a durable workhorse during his career, but the team's signing of closer Armando Benitez made him expendable. It was his second, and quite possibly his last, tour of duty with the Giants.

San Francisco

Deivi Cruz

Position: SS
Bats: R **Throws:** R
Ht: 6' 0" **Wt:** 207

Opening Day Age: 32
Born: 11/6/72 in Nizao de Bani, DR
ML Seasons: 8
Pronunciation: DAY-vee

Overall Statistics

	G	AB	R	H	D	T	HR	RBI	SB	BB	SO	Avg	OBP	Slg
'04	127	397	46	116	30	2	7	55	1	17	32	.292	.322	.431
Car.	1133	3864	414	1040	239	15	65	444	16	121	395	.269	.293	.389

2004 Situational Stats

	AB	H	HR	RBI	Avg		AB	H	HR	RBI	Avg
Home	192	59	2	24	.307	LHP	108	28	2	14	.259
Road	205	57	5	31	.278	RHP	289	88	5	41	.304
First Half	151	46	1	19	.305	Sc Pos	105	35	2	46	.333
Scnd Half	246	70	6	36	.285	Clutch	69	23	1	15	.333

2004 Season

Deivi Cruz was signed to a minor league deal on March 29 and wasn't called up to the big leagues until April 26, when regular shortstop Neifi Perez started poorly offensively. The move proved shrewd, as Cruz eventually became the everyday player and Perez was released.

Hitting, Baserunning & Defense

Cruz had his second highest batting average during a full season in the majors. He showed some power, but he couldn't match the 14 homers he hit the year before in Baltimore. His on-base percentage takes a hit because he walks so infrequently. Cruz isn't built in the classic mold of a shortstop and appears bulky and lacks range. However, he improved his defense late in the season.

2005 Outlook

The Giants re-signed Cruz, giving him an $800,000 contract in November, but he was quickly relegated to backup status with the signing of long-time Cleveland shortstop Omar Vizquel a couple of weeks later. Vizquel is an everyday player and a defensive gem, and the Giants could trade Cruz before the season, or he could ask for his release. If he sticks around, he could be a valuable player coming off the bench or starting when Vizquel needs a day off.

Scott Eyre

Position: RP
Bats: L **Throws:** L
Ht: 6' 1" **Wt:** 210

Opening Day Age: 32
Born: 5/30/72 in Inglewood, CA
ML Seasons: 8
Pronunciation: AIR

Overall Statistics

	W	L	Pct.	ERA	G	GS	Sv	IP	H	BB	SO	HR	Avg
'04	2	2	.500	4.10	83	0	1	52.2	43	27	49	8	.219
Car.	16	23	.410	4.83	322	32	4	411.2	441	218	300	61	.274

2004 Situational Stats

	W	L	ERA	Sv	IP		AB	H	HR	RBI	Avg
Home	2	1	4.63	0	23.1	LHB	100	20	4	11	.200
Road	0	1	3.68	1	29.1	RHB	96	23	4	12	.240
First Half	0	1	2.92	0	24.2	Sc Pos	51	10	0	13	.196
Scnd Half	2	1	5.14	1	28.0	Clutch	91	22	4	15	.242

2004 Season

Scott Eyre began the season on the DL with a lower back strain, but he returned April 21. He once again was a valuable member of the bullpen, appearing in a career-high 83 games. Eyre had a horrible August, but he arguably was the team's most valuable reliever the final month. He did not allow an earned run in his final 16 appearances.

Pitching, Defense & Hitting

With a devastating slider and a sneaky-fast fastball, Eyre can be tough to face when he's on. While he was once only a lefthanded specialist, manager Felipe Alou trusts him to face all hitters, sometimes using him more than an inning per appearance. Eyre is neither a standout nor a liability on defense, and he's no factor at the plate. He hasn't driven in a run in nine career at-bats.

2005 Outlook

Since he was claimed off waivers from Toronto on August 8, 2002, Eyre has resurrected his career. That turnaround can be traced to his focus after he was diagnosed with Attention Deficit Disorder. Eyre is less hyper on the mound and able to concentrate much better. With fellow lefthander Jason Christiansen a question mark to return in 2005, Eyre's role could be even more important.

Pedro Feliz

Position: 1B/3B/SS
Bats: R **Throws:** R
Ht: 6' 1" **Wt:** 205

Opening Day Age: 29
Born: 4/27/75 in Azua, DR
ML Seasons: 5

Overall Statistics

	G	AB	R	H	D	T	HR	RBI	SB	BB	SO	Avg	OBP	Slg
'04	144	503	72	139	33	3	22	84	5	23	85	.276	.305	.485
Car.	408	1111	141	286	55	8	47	167	9	49	216	.257	.288	.448

2004 Situational Stats

	AB	H	HR	RBI	Avg		AB	H	HR	RBI	Avg
Home	260	77	11	52	.296	LHP	172	50	7	31	.291
Road	243	62	11	32	.255	RHP	331	89	15	53	.269
First Half	297	76	13	51	.256	Sc Pos	167	41	2	58	.246
Scnd Half	206	63	9	33	.306	Clutch	95	27	7	23	.284

2004 Season

The Giants waited and waited for the talent to materialize at the big league level, and Pedro Feliz finally had his breakout year. He is still the player without a position, however, sharing time at first and third base, while making a few appearances at shortstop.

Hitting, Baserunning & Defense

Feliz once was an easy out, susceptible to off-speed pitches while trying to pull everything over the left-field fence. He still is a free swinger, but he now tries to go the opposite way and is better at recognizing offspeed pitches. He also has become a bit more patient, though he still strikes out too often. Defensively, he's become a solid first sacker. Third base is his natural position, and he could take over there full time when Edgardo Alfonzo moves on. The Giants started Feliz at shortstop for 14 games last season, but he's not a natural shortstop.

2005 Outlook

Feliz is on the verge of becoming a star. Look for him to receive more than 500 at-bats this season, mostly at first base in a platoon with J.T. Snow. Playing time and a little patience at the plate appear to be the only things keeping Feliz from realizing his immense potential.

Matt Herges

Position: RP
Bats: L **Throws:** R
Ht: 6' 0" **Wt:** 200

Opening Day Age: 35
Born: 4/1/70 in Champaign, IL
ML Seasons: 6
Pronunciation: hur-JISS

Overall Statistics

	W	L	Pct.	ERA	G	GS	Sv	IP	H	BB	SO	HR	Avg
'04	4	5	.444	5.23	70	0	23	65.1	90	21	39	8	.338
Car.	29	25	.537	3.61	350	4	34	443.1	459	170	326	41	.272

2004 Situational Stats

	W	L	ERA	Sv	IP		AB	H	HR	RBI	Avg
Home	2	1	4.35	14	39.1	LHB	112	41	3	23	.366
Road	2	4	6.58	9	26.0	RHB	154	49	5	27	.318
First Half	4	3	4.89	22	42.1	Sc Pos	77	28	1	35	.364
Scnd Half	0	2	5.87	1	23.0	Clutch	166	57	5	31	.343

2004 Season

Matt Herges was thrust into the closer's role when Robb Nen couldn't pitch for a second straight season with an injured right shoulder. It didn't take long to find out that Herges was miscast in his job. He blew eight saves and eventually lost his job to Dustin Hermanson, who was moved from the rotation to the bullpen.

Pitching, Defense & Hitting

Herges seemed psyched out in the closer role and never really recovered last season. His slider can be nasty, but he never seemed to control it and was forced to use only one pitch in most of his appearances. He was hit hard and often. Herges does not hurt the team in the field, and he's hard to run on because of his quick move to first base. He's a .222 lifetime hitter in the major leagues, though he did not bat last year.

2005 Outlook

The Giants signed Herges to a two-year contract before last season, a logical move based on his fine 2003 campaign. His days as a closer almost certainly are over, but he can be valuable in a less stressful role, as he proved the year before. He was always a dependable reliever—until last season.

Noah Lowry

Position: SP
Bats: R **Throws:** L
Ht: 6' 2" **Wt:** 210

Opening Day Age: 24
Born: 10/10/80 in Ventura, CA
ML Seasons: 2

Overall Statistics

	W	L	Pct.	ERA	G	GS	Sv	IP	H	BB	SO	HR	Avg
'04	6	0	1.000	3.82	16	14	0	92.0	91	28	72	10	.259
Car.	6	0	1.000	3.57	20	14	0	98.1	92	30	77	10	.247

2004 Situational Stats

	W	L	ERA	Sv	IP		AB	H	HR	RBI	Avg
Home	5	0	3.10	0	52.1	LHB	71	24	3	14	.338
Road	1	0	4.76	0	39.2	RHB	281	67	7	25	.238
First Half	0	0	3.48	0	20.2	Sc Pos	65	20	3	27	.308
Scnd Half	6	0	3.91	0	71.1	Clutch	9	1	0	0	.111

2004 Season

Noah Lowry, who rose from the Double-A ranks before a September callup the year before, moved into the rotation in 2004 because of injuries to Brett Tomko and Jerome Williams. Only 23, Lowry showed the poise of a veteran. In just his second start in the majors, he matched up against Pedro Martinez, outpitching the Boston ace in a 6-4 Giants win.

Pitching, Defense & Hitting

Lowry relies on a wicked changeup that quickly became one of the best in the National League. He kept hitters off balance in four June appearances, but had four no-decisions. Lowry fields his position well and keeps runners close with his above-average pickoff move. He did not distinguish himself at the plate, hitting only .182.

2005 Outlook

Lowry should earn a spot in the rotation and could be a fixture with the team for years. Manager Felipe Alou likes Lowry's easy-going, mature style, saying often, "This kid doesn't get rattled." The Giants pitched him in big games down the stretch last season, including a September 29 start against David Wells in San Diego. In his previous start, he faced Houston's Roy Oswalt, who finished third in the Cy Young Award voting.

Dustan Mohr

Position: RF/LF
Bats: R **Throws:** R
Ht: 6' 1" **Wt:** 214

Opening Day Age: 28
Born: 6/19/76 in Hattiesburg, MS
ML Seasons: 4

Overall Statistics

	G	AB	R	H	D	T	HR	RBI	SB	BB	SO	Avg	OBP	Slg
'04	117	263	52	72	20	1	7	28	0	46	64	.274	.394	.437
Car.	378	1045	163	274	67	3	29	113	12	115	273	.262	.339	.415

2004 Situational Stats

	AB	H	HR	RBI	Avg		AB	H	HR	RBI	Avg
Home	127	40	3	20	.315	LHP	115	28	2	10	.243
Road	136	32	4	8	.235	RHP	148	44	5	18	.297
First Half	136	33	3	12	.243	Sc Pos	53	12	2	21	.226
Scnd Half	127	39	4	16	.307	Clutch	52	13	0	3	.250

2004 Season

Dustan Mohr's hustle and blue-collar style of play made him a memorable part of the Giants. He made a game-saving catch in Arizona in early September by crashing into the fence, then getting up and throwing out a runner at second base. He also returned quickly from two injuries that were supposed to have sidelined him much longer.

Hitting, Baserunning & Defense

Mohr hit just .042 in April, but steadily improved. One of his homers was 425-foot blast that reached the second balcony of the Western Metal Supply Co. at San Diego's new Petco Park. Only Sammy Sosa and Ramon Hernandez hit homers into the second tier of the building. Although he's not the fastest outfielder, Mohr made several sensational plays last season. He never stops hustling on the field, sometimes to his detriment. He sometimes hurts himself with his reckless abandon.

2005 Outlook

Mohr should be the team's top backup outfielder, platooning with Michael Tucker in right field and replacing Barry Bonds on his days off. Although Mohr is arbitration eligible, the Giants want him back. He's become a good clubhouse presence and a good friend of Bonds, after bonding quickly with the slugger in spring training.

Cody Ransom

Position: SS/2B
Bats: R **Throws:** R
Ht: 6' 2" **Wt:** 211

Opening Day Age: 29
Born: 2/17/76 in Mesa, AZ
ML Seasons: 4

Overall Statistics

	G	AB	R	H	D	T	HR	RBI	SB	BB	SO	Avg	OBP	Slg
'04	78	68	13	17	6	0	1	11	2	6	20	.250	.320	.382
Car.	114	105	23	25	7	0	2	13	2	8	37	.238	.298	.362

2004 Situational Stats

	AB	H	HR	RBI	Avg		AB	H	HR	RBI	Avg
Home	30	7	0	5	.233	LHP	16	8	1	4	.500
Road	38	10	1	6	.263	RHP	52	9	0	7	.173
First Half	31	6	0	5	.194	Sc Pos	17	6	0	9	.353
Scnd Half	37	11	1	6	.297	Clutch	8	2	0	2	.250

2004 Season

Whatever good Cody Ransom did during the season evaporated with a costly error in the next-to-last game in Los Angeles. With one out, Ransom booted Cesar Izturis' bases-loaded grounder, cutting the Giants' lead to 3-2 in the ninth. The Dodgers won the game on Steve Finley's grand slam, clinching the NL West title. The Giants were eliminated from the wild-card race the next day.

Hitting, Baserunning & Defense

Ransom spent most of the second half with the Giants, hitting .250 with a home run. The club had kept him in the organization for his defense, hoping his offense would catch up. It never did. Baserunning wasn't a problem. Defense, which was supposed to be his strong suit, certainly was. His errors cost the team at least a pair of wins last season.

2005 Outlook

Ransom does not figure in the team's plans this season. Even if the Giants had not signed Omar Vizquel, it was doubtful Ransom would be retained. The Giants kept Ransom when he was out of options in August, but now that he is questionable on defense in the late innings, there seems to be no reason for the club to retain him.

Yorvit Torrealba

Position: C
Bats: R **Throws:** R
Ht: 5'11" **Wt:** 190

Opening Day Age: 26
Born: 7/19/78 in Caracas, VZ
ML Seasons: 4
Pronunciation:
yor-VEET tor-EE-all-buh

Overall Statistics

	G	AB	R	H	D	T	HR	RBI	SB	BB	SO	Avg	OBP	Slg
'04	64	172	19	39	7	3	6	23	2	17	31	.227	.302	.407
Car.	186	512	58	131	27	6	12	68	3	45	90	.256	.322	.402

2004 Situational Stats

	AB	H	HR	RBI	Avg		AB	H	HR	RBI	Avg
Home	87	20	3	13	.230	LHP	84	24	5	17	.286
Road	85	19	3	10	.224	RHP	88	15	1	6	.170
First Half	90	18	3	16	.200	Sc Pos	50	10	3	19	.200
Scnd Half	82	21	3	7	.256	Clutch	29	5	1	3	.172

2004 Season

Instead of making Yorvit Torrealba the successor to Benito Santiago, the Giants acquired catcher A.J. Pierzynski from Minnesota. Torrealba was relegated to backup duty for a third straight season. He performed commendably in his occasional starts as Santiago's backup, but he seemed to regress behind Pierzynski.

Hitting, Baserunning & Defense

Torrealba never got into much of a grove after going only 3-for-18 in April. He seemed to want to pull everything rather than taking controlled swings, a philosophy that helped him the previous two seasons. His defense also declined a bit. He threw out only 22.2 percent of baserunners (6 of 27), but his ability to block balls in the dirt was superior to Pierzynski's.

2005 Outlook

For a second straight year, the Giants brought in a catcher over the winter, rather than give Torrealba the starting job. It was Pierzynski a year ago and Mike Matheny in December. Matheny has signed a three-year deal and will start. The club believes Torrealba can handle a pitching staff, as he was the personal catcher for Jason Schmidt and Brett Tomko in stretches of 2004. The only question is whether Torrealba can provide enough offense to start.

San Francisco

663

Jason Christiansen (Pos: LHP, Age: 35)

	W	L	Pct.	ERA	G	GS	Sv	IP	H	BB	SO	HR	Avg
'04	4	3	.571	4.50	60	0	3	36.0	34	26	22	3	.250
Car.	21	25	.457	4.20	460	0	16	388.0	354	200	363	33	.243

Christiansen had a 3.07 ERA at the end of May before developing some tendinitis in his shoulder. Upon returning from a short DL stint, he was effective until running out of steam down the stretch. He has held lefties to a .230 average over his career. 2005 Outlook: C

Brian Cooper (Pos: RHP, Age: 30)

	W	L	Pct.	ERA	G	GS	Sv	IP	H	BB	SO	HR	Avg
'04	0	2	.000	8.78	5	2	0	13.1	15	5	7	4	.288
Car.	5	13	.278	6.12	34	25	0	150.0	167	66	68	32	.284

After starting the year with the big club, Cooper was outrighted to Triple-A Fresno at the end of April. In parts of 10 minor league seasons, he has a 76-63 record, but he has not been able to repeat that success at the major league level. 2005 Outlook: C

Brian Dallimore (Pos: 2B, Age: 31, Bats: R)

	G	AB	R	H	D	T	HR	RBI	SB	BB	SO	Avg	OBP	Slg
'04	20	43	8	12	2	0	1	7	0	4	7	.279	.347	.395
Car.	20	43	8	12	2	0	1	7	0	4	7	.279	.347	.395

Dallimore has been playing professionally since 1996, but got his first sip of major league coffee in three separate stints with the Giants. He has hit .336 over the last two years at Triple-A Fresno and can play a couple of infield spots. 2005 Outlook: C

Jason Ellison (Pos: CF, Age: 26, Bats: R)

	G	AB	R	H	D	T	HR	RBI	SB	BB	SO	Avg	OBP	Slg
'04	13	4	4	2	0	0	1	3	2	0	1	.500	.500	1.250
Car.	20	14	5	3	0	0	1	3	2	0	2	.214	.214	.429

Ellison has hit .295 and .315 in his last two seasons at Triple-A Fresno with 48 stolen bases in the two years combined. He showed in a September callup that he can handle himself in the outfield and could earn a bench role with a strong showing in the spring. 2005 Outlook: C

Leo Estrella (Pos: RHP, Age: 30)

	W	L	Pct.	ERA	G	GS	Sv	IP	H	BB	SO	HR	Avg
'04	0	0	—	27.00	2	0	0	1.1	8	1	0	0	.727
Car.	7	3	.700	4.88	62	0	3	72.0	92	22	28	11	.317

Estrella was acquired from the Brewers right before Opening Day and proceeded to post nearly identical lines (0.2 IP, 4 H, 2 ER) in two relief appearances before they sent him packing. The 30-year-old may have a hard time finding a job this spring. 2005 Outlook: D

Wayne Franklin (Pos: LHP, Age: 31)

	W	L	Pct.	ERA	G	GS	Sv	IP	H	BB	SO	HR	Avg
'04	2	1	.667	6.39	43	2	0	50.2	55	22	40	11	.281
Car.	14	15	.483	5.47	119	40	0	302.2	313	154	203	54	.268

After making 34 starts for Milwaukee in 2003, Franklin was acquired by the Giants in a late-spring deal. Pitching almost exclusively out of the bullpen, he held lefties to a .250 average and posted a fine 2.25 ERA in September. 2005 Outlook: C

Jeffrey Hammonds (Pos: RF, Age: 34, Bats: R)

	G	AB	R	H	D	T	HR	RBI	SB	BB	SO	Avg	OBP	Slg
'04	40	95	14	20	5	0	3	6	1	15	22	.211	.336	.358
Car.	944	3000	472	817	171	17	110	422	67	290	592	.272	.339	.451

After starting the season on the disabled list with a broken bone in his right thumb, Hammonds just never got untracked and was released in early June. He has accumulated just 227 at-bats over the last two seasons and will have to prove to the Nationals, who signed him to a minor league deal in December, that he has anything left. 2005 Outlook: D

Brad Hennessey (Pos: RHP, Age: 25)

	W	L	Pct.	ERA	G	GS	Sv	IP	H	BB	SO	HR	Avg
'04	2	2	.500	4.98	7	7	0	34.1	42	15	25	2	.294
Car.	2	2	.500	4.98	7	7	0	34.1	42	15	25	2	.294

For a guy who had never pitched above Class-A before last season began, Hennessey acquitted himself nicely in his seven big league outings. He posted a record of 9-6 with a 3.16 ERA in 23 starts between Double- and Triple-A, and could use a bit more seasoning. 2005 Outlook: C

Ricky Ledee (Pos: CF/RF, Age: 31, Bats: L)

	G	AB	R	H	D	T	HR	RBI	SB	BB	SO	Avg	OBP	Slg
'04	104	176	25	41	9	0	7	30	3	27	47	.233	.337	.403
Car.	666	1672	245	404	95	16	53	264	27	213	414	.242	.328	.413

Despite missing a couple of weeks due to hemorrhoidal surgery, Ledee was having a solid season as a bench player for the Phillies when he was traded to the Giants. He was a complete washout on the Left Coast, but will get another chance with the Dodgers, who signed him in December. 2005 Outlook: C

Damon Minor (Pos: 1B, Age: 31, Bats: L)

	G	AB	R	H	D	T	HR	RBI	SB	BB	SO	Avg	OBP	Slg
'04	24	58	8	14	2	0	0	6	0	12	18	.241	.405	.276
Car.	136	285	35	66	9	0	13	39	0	41	61	.232	.338	.400

After trading Minor to the Phillies in 2003, the Giants signed him again last season. In 338 AB for Triple-A Fresno, he hit .302 with 17 homers and 56 RBI. He has hit 179 longballs in parts of nine minor league seasons and should add to that total this year. The Pirates signed him to a minor league deal in December. 2005 Outlook: C

Tony Torcato (Pos: LF, **Age**: 25, **Bats**: L)

	G	AB	R	H	D	T	HR	RBI	SB	BB	SO	Avg	OBP	Slg
'04	13	9	1	5	0	0	0	2	0	1	0	.556	.583	.556
Car.	32	36	1	11	2	0	0	3	0	1	6	.306	.350	.361

Formerly a rising star in the Giants' organization, Torcato's career has stalled. He has played the last three seasons for Triple-A Fresno, hitting between .289 and .296 in each campaign. He may need a change of scenery. 2005 Outlook: C

Kevin Walker (Pos: LHP, **Age**: 28)

	W	L	Pct.	ERA	G	GS	Sv	IP	H	BB	SO	HR	Avg
'04	0	0	—	16.20	5	0	0	1.2	3	2	1	1	.429
Car.	7	2	.778	4.45	113	0	0	95.0	74	58	90	9	.213

Since undergoing elbow surgery in 2001, Walker has pitched just 16.1 major league innings. Last year, he posted a 4.26 ERA in 48 games at Triple-A, but the Giants let him go at the end of the campaign and the 28-year-old signed with the White Sox. 2005 Outlook: C

Tyler Walker (Pos: RHP, **Age**: 28)

	W	L	Pct.	ERA	G	GS	Sv	IP	H	BB	SO	HR	Avg
'04	5	1	.833	4.24	52	0	1	63.2	69	24	48	8	.288
Car.	6	1	.857	4.48	57	1	1	74.1	80	29	55	11	.282

Born in San Francisco and a star at Cal-Berkeley, Walker was a fan favorite from the moment he was called up in late April. Pitching exclusively out of the bullpen, he found his stride late in the campaign, posting a 3.09 ERA from August 1 on. 2005 Outlook: C

San Francisco Giants Minor League Prospects

Organization Overview:

When the Giants take the field on Opening Day, Edgardo Alfonzo, at age 31, likely will be the youngest player in San Francisco's starting lineup. And yet the Giants continue to gamble with golden oldies, such as shortstop Omar Vizquel. Such a strategy wouldn't be necessary if the system was cranking out position prospects. Instead, the organization continues to produce pitching prospects, many of which have been utilized as currency in past trades. Merkin Valdez and Matt Cain lead the next wave of Giants pitching talent, while others like Jesse Foppert, Kevin Correia and David Aardsma try to rebound from injuries or disappointing performances. There are a few position prospects bubbling up through the system, including outfielder Todd Linden.

David Aardsma

Position: P | **Opening Day Age:** 23
Bats: R **Throws:** R | **Born:** 12/27/81 in
Ht: 6' 5" **Wt:** 200 | Denver, CO

Recent Statistics

	W	L	ERA	G	GS	Sv	IP	H	R	BB	SO	HR
2004 AAA Fresno	6	4	3.09	44	0	11	55.1	46	21	29	53	2
2004 NL San Fran	1	0	6.75	11	0	0	10.2	20	8	10	5	1

Aardsma needed just 18.1 innings of minor league experience before opening last season in the Giants' bullpen. He had been San Francisco's first pick the previous June, and managed to earn the win in his major league debut last April. Unfortunately, he wound up riding a shuttle between Frisco and Fresno on five separate occasions. Perhaps the most discouraging aspect of his season was the lack of command he exhibited with the Giants. Aardsma has good stuff, with a hard breaking ball and a fastball that reaches 96-97 MPH. He has the talent to succeed as a major league closer, though San Francisco just signed Armando Benitez to a three-year deal. Aardsma's best chance for immediate success will be in a less demanding role.

Matt Cain

Position: P | **Opening Day Age:** 20
Bats: R **Throws:** R | **Born:** 10/1/84 in Dothan,
Ht: 6' 3" **Wt:** 185 | AL

Recent Statistics

	W	L	ERA	G	GS	Sv	IP	H	R	BB	SO	HR
2003 A Hagerstown	4	4	2.55	14	14	0	74.0	57	24	24	90	5
2004 A San Jose	7	1	1.86	13	13	0	72.2	58	25	17	89	5
2004 AA Norwich	6	4	3.35	15	15	0	86.0	73	44	40	72	7

Any time a pitcher like Cain reaches Double-A while still just a teenager, you know he possesses great promise. Similarly, you wonder about his long-term health, and Cain did miss a good part of 2003 due to a stress fracture in his elbow. But he showed few ill effects last season as he rose through the system. His mid-90s fastball, hard breaking ball and excellent changeup simply proved too challenging for most opposing hitters. A first-round selection in 2002 out of a Tennessee high school, Cain shows the aptitude to make adjustments. As long as he remains healthy, he looks like a future No. 1 starter. It isn't out of the question that he'll surface in San Francisco in 2005.

Kevin Correia

Position: P | **Opening Day Age:** 24
Bats: R **Throws:** R | **Born:** 8/24/80 in San
Ht: 6' 3" **Wt:** 200 | Diego, CA

Recent Statistics

	W	L	ERA	G	GS	Sv	IP	H	R	BB	SO	HR
2004 AAA Fresno	3	7	4.53	29	16	0	105.1	118	61	35	70	12
2004 NL San Fran	0	1	8.05	12	1	0	19.0	25	20	10	14	3

Correia was a fast riser who made his major league debut almost one year to the day after signing. But he just hasn't been able to solidify a spot on the Giants' staff and has been up and down between San Francisco and the minors like a yo-yo. He didn't enjoy the greatest of success at Triple-A Fresno last season, and clearly was lit up in 12 big league appearances. A starter in college and early in his professional career, he pitched primarily in relief in 2004. With a few other hurlers in the system appearing to have higher ceilings, Correia's best chance of sticking may be in the bullpen, and he'll compete for a spot somewhere this spring.

Jesse Foppert

Position: P | **Opening Day Age:** 24
Bats: R **Throws:** R | **Born:** 7/10/80 in
Ht: 6' 6" **Wt:** 210 | Reading, PA

Recent Statistics

	W	L	ERA	G	GS	Sv	IP	H	R	BB	SO	HR
2004 R Az Giants	0	0	9.00	1	1	0	1.0	3	1	0	2	0
2004 A San Jose	0	0	1.93	4	4	0	9.1	4	2	4	11	1
2004 AAA Fresno	0	2	5.52	4	4	0	14.2	14	11	9	13	2
2004 NL San Fran	0	0	0.00	1	0	0	1.0	1	0	0	2	0

Foppert looked like a future star when he conquered Double-A and Triple-A in 2002, averaging nearly 12 strikeouts per nine innings. He then held his own in the Giants' rotation in 2003, before elbow problems halted his rise and resulted in Tommy John surgery. Before the injury, Foppert featured a mid-90s fastball, hard slider and split-finger offering that was a strikeout pitch. At this point it looks like the surgery and rehab were successful, as Foppert was able to return in the second half of last season. He also worked in winter ball, and should be back to nearly full strength in spring training. If so, he'll battle for a starting spot and could provide a boost for San Francisco's rotation.

Fred Lewis

Position: OF
Bats: L **Throws:** R
Ht: 6' 2" **Wt:** 190

Opening Day Age: 24
Born: 12/9/80 in Hattiesburg, MS

Recent Statistics

	G	AB	R	H	D	T	HR	RBI	SB	BB	SO	Avg
2003 A Hagerstown	114	420	61	105	17	8	1	27	30	68	112	.250
2004 A San Jose	115	439	88	132	20	11	8	57	33	84	109	.301
2004 AAA Fresno	6	20	3	7	1	0	1	2	1	5	5	.304

Lewis took a nice step forward in 2004, when his batting average returned to the .300 level as he moved up in classification to the high Class-A California League. In the process, he not only continued to draw tons of walks and steal lots of bases, but also delivered much more power. Add it all up, and Lewis presents an exciting offensive package at the top of a lineup. He was the Giants' second-round pick in the 2002 draft out of Southern University, and clearly is turning his impressive tools into skills. After finishing last year in Triple-A, Lewis likely will return there in 2005, and soon could be knocking on the door for a major league job.

Todd Linden

Position: OF
Bats: B **Throws:** R
Ht: 6' 3" **Wt:** 210

Opening Day Age: 24
Born: 6/30/80 in Edmonds, WA

Recent Statistics

	G	AB	R	H	D	T	HR	RBI	SB	BB	SO	Avg
2004 AAA Fresno	130	489	93	127	28	2	23	75	8	63	149	.260
2004 NL San Fran	16	32	6	5	1	0	0	1	0	5	7	.156

Linden is an impressive physical specimen with enticing power. The Giants clearly have recognized his potential, as they haven't hesitated to challenge him. A supplemental first-round pick in 2001, he debuted in Double-A the following year and reached the majors by the end of 2003. He possesses power from both sides of the plate and surprising speed. Last year at Triple-A, he exhibited the home-run ability that draws notice, but too often failed to make contact. While he does draw his share of walks, he may need to sharpen his approach at the plate. A return to Triple-A may be his likely destination when 2005 begins, but he may surface in San Francisco's outfield at some point this season.

Daniel Ortmeier

Position: OF
Bats: B **Throws:** L
Ht: 6' 4" **Wt:** 220

Opening Day Age: 23
Born: 5/11/81 in Chattanooga, TN

Recent Statistics

	G	AB	R	H	D	T	HR	RBI	SB	BB	SO	Avg
2003 A San Jose	115	408	62	124	32	6	8	56	13	39	89	.304
2004 AA Norwich	106	377	55	95	23	6	10	48	18	47	110	.252

Like Linden, Ortmeier is a switch-hitting outfielder with impressive size. He also was thought to have nice power potential, which is one reason the Giants selected Ortmeier in the third round of the 2002 draft. That power may yet come, but he still hasn't hit more than 10 homers in any of three professional seasons. Part of the problem may be injuries that repeatedly have hampered him. While they likely contributed to a large batting average decline last summer, he also struck out at an alarming rate. The Giants will be looking for his average to rebound. If he's healthy and his swing is consistent, he again could become a .300 hitter.

Merkin Valdez

Position: P
Bats: R **Throws:** R
Ht: 6' 5" **Wt:** 208

Opening Day Age: 23
Born: 11/10/81 in San Cristobal, DR

Recent Statistics

	W	L	ERA	G	GS	Sv	IP	H	R	BB	SO	HR
2004 AAA Fresno	0	0	7.20	1	1	0	5.0	6	4	4	5	0
2004 A San Jose	3	1	2.52	7	7	0	35.2	30	12	5	44	4
2004 AA Norwich	1	4	4.32	10	7	1	41.2	35	21	15	31	3
2004 NL San Fran	0	0	27.00	2	0	0	1.2	4	5	2	1	1

Valdez was part of the package the Giants received when they traded Russ Ortiz to Atlanta following the 2002 season. At the time, Valdez had yet to pitch above Rookie-level, but since then he's shown enough ability to more than justify the deal. After dominating the Class-A South Atlantic League in 2003, leading it in strikeouts, he zoomed through four levels last season. His delivery, arm strength and poise have drawn heaps of praise in the past. His fastball can reach 97 MPH and he boasts a good slider. It's a package that might be unstoppable in a relief role. But there's also no reason to think he can't emerge as a top-of-the-rotation starter.

Others to Watch

The Giants had to pay nearly $1 million to sign first baseman **Travis Ishikawa** (21) in 2002. A highly touted football prospect, he has improved defensively and supposedly has just scratched the surface of his power potential. . . **Justin Knoedler** (24) began his pro career by fashioning a 1.26 ERA over 13 relief appearances in 2001. But he was moved behind the plate the following year and has made nice progress. As you might suspect, his arm may be his best defensive asset. . . Lefthander **Pat Misch** (23) was taken in the seventh round of the 2003 draft. He's crafted an ERA under three over his two minor league seasons while posting a nice strikeout-walk ratio. . . **Lance Niekro** (26) just hasn't fulfilled the promise predicted by his talent and pedigree, although he did hit for more power last year than he had previously. He can play either corner-infield position and has a nice swing. . . Third baseman **Nate Schierholtz** (21) was picked in the second round of the 2003 draft. His lefthanded stroke delivered a .295 batting average and lots of extra-base hits in at two levels of Class-A ball last year. . . Righthander **Craig Whitaker** (20) was a supplemental first-round pick in 2003. He was a bit crude entering the pro ranks, but possessed an excellent fastball, curveball and an outstanding arm.

Offense

It's been 33 years since a regular-season game was played at RFK Stadium, but only five years since the Expos played spring exhibition games there. It remains to be seen exactly which configuration will be used, but in either case the park will have some pitcher-friendly dimensions. The left-field dimensions could be the same as in right, unless the configuration from the exhibitions are used, which featured a 24-foot high "mini-Green Monster" at 260 feet down the left-field line.

Defense

The infield probably will be the worst in the majors because there simply isn't time to rebuild it using all the latest technologies. However, the grass will be slow so bad hops shouldn't occur too frequently.

Who It Helps the Most

Righthanded pull hitters could have a field day with a short porch in left. Otherwise, flyball pitchers should reap the most benefits. RFK played as a pitchers' park, and with the infield a question mark, a pitcher's best friend might be a trio of speedy outfielders. Also working in the pitcher's favor is the likelihood that the lighting for night games won't be up to the latest standard.

Who It Hurts the Most

The dimensions and climate will be similar to that of Busch Stadium, which has played slightly biased against hitters, especially so against home runs. A lefty power hitter like Brad Wilkerson might see a minor drop in his longball totals.

Rookies & Newcomers

New third baseman Vinny Castilla won't confuse RFK with Coors Field, unless that mini-Green Monster is erected as part of the park's renovation. Both Castilla and shortstop Cristian Guzman will have to deal with the potentially rugged infield terrain. Ryan Church will try to force his way into the outfield picture after being named the Expos' Minor League Player of the Year in 2004. Righthander Jon Rauch may benefit from the park's spacious dimensions.

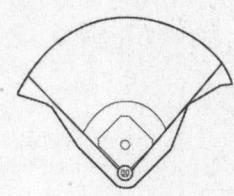

Dimensions: LF-335, LCF-385, CF-410, RCF-385, RF-335

Capacity: 56,000

Elevation: 20 feet

Surface: Grass

Foul Territory: Small

Park Factors

2004 Season (Olympic Stadium)

	Home Games			Away Games			
	Expos	Opp	Total	Expos	Opp	Total	Index
G	53	53	106	73	73	146	
Avg	.248	.260	.254	.252	.273	.262	97
AB	1733	1837	3570	2556	2485	5041	98
R	211	227	438	312	368	680	89
H	430	477	907	643	679	1322	94
2B	108	98	206	119	124	243	120
3B	10	8	18	12	14	26	98
HR	56	56	112	75	99	174	91
BB	176	196	372	225	265	490	107
SO	266	347	613	450	461	911	95
E	28	32	60	52	48	100	83
E-Infield	25	29	54	44	41	85	88
LHB-Avg	.259	.264	.261	.261	.280	.269	97
LHB-HR	34	20	54	43	42	85	93
RHB-Avg	.236	.256	.248	.241	.268	.256	97
RHB-HR	22	36	58	32	57	89	89

2002-2004 (Olympic Stadium)

	Home Games			Away Games			
	Expos	Opp	Total	Expos	Opp	Total	Index
G	181	181	362	217	217	434	
Avg	.267	.260	.264	.247	.271	.259	102
AB	5985	6320	12305	7489	7292	14781	100
R	859	787	1646	864	996	1860	106
H	1599	1644	3243	1853	1973	3826	102
2B	388	369	757	346	374	720	126
3B	39	29	68	36	42	78	105
HR	182	189	371	201	232	433	103
BB	621	546	1167	701	735	1436	98
SO	1030	1205	2235	1472	1367	2839	95
E	123	125	248	155	148	303	98
E-Infield	99	110	209	132	120	252	99
LHB-Avg	.271	.262	.267	.247	.281	.262	102
LHB-HR	85	71	156	89	97	186	104
RHB-Avg	.264	.259	.261	.248	.263	.256	102
RHB-HR	97	118	215	112	135	247	102

2004 Rankings (National League)
- Second-highest double factor
- Third-lowest error factor

Frank Robinson

2004 Season

After consecutive winning seasons in 2002-03, the talent exodus finally caught up to Frank Robinson and the Expos. Inundated by injuries and inexperienced players, it was clear very early that last season was going to be about teaching, not winning. To his credit, the team played hard until the final day, winning two of three in the final series in New York. They were also just three games under .500 at Stade Olympique.

Offense

Despite all the injuries, Robinson actually used fewer lineups than he did in 2003. The main reason was that he decided to give his young players a chance to show what they could do on a regular basis. He was rewarded for his patience with solid years from Juan Rivera and Termel Sledge. What didn't change was his affinity for the hit-and-run and advancing runners via the sacrifice, two strategies that he historically has been among the most prolific users.

Pitching & Defense

Robinson is not one to suffer walks or lack of focus on the mound, so there were occasions when he showed his displeasure with a starter by yanking him before he was eligible for the win. Ironically, he was second in the majors in issuing intentional walks. Combined with concerns about young starters' pitch counts, Robinson used his bullpen as much as any manager in the game. The one pitcher whom he didn't concern himself with pitch counts was Livan Hernandez, who once again racked up nearly 4,000 pitches in a season.

2005 Outlook

Interim GM Jim Bowden has said he won't change managers, so the job is Robinson's, at least until an ownership group is announced and a new front office appointed. Robinson has done a remarkable job given the circumstances, so he'll get serious consideration once the team is fully settled. Unless the new owner has someone specific in mind, it's hard to imagine him finding a candidate who could do a better job than Robby, especially now that the team will have more financial wherewithal.

Born: 8/31/35 in Beaumont, TX

Playing Experience: 1956-1976, Cin, Bal, LA, Ana, Cle

Managerial Experience: 14 seasons

Manager Statistics

Year	Team, Lg	W	L	Pct	GB	Finish
2004	Montreal, NL	67	95	.414	29.0	5th East
14 Seasons		913	1004	.476	–	–

2004 Starting Pitchers by Days Rest

	<=3	4	5	6+
Expos Starts	0	79	43	29
Expos ERA	–	4.32	4.59	5.00
NL Avg Starts	2	82	46	23
NL ERA	4.58	4.35	4.28	4.73

2004 Situational Stats

	Frank Robinson	NL Average
Hit & Run Success %	38.6	38.0
Stolen Base Success %	74.1	71.7
Platoon Pct.	63.5	55.2
Defensive Subs	16	18
High-Pitch Outings	13	6
Quick/Slow Hooks	30/14	21/12
Sacrifice Attempts	124	99

2004 Rankings (National League)

- 1st in steals of third base (21), double steals (3), sacrifice-bunt percentage (89.5%), quick hooks, starts with over 120 pitches (13) and starts with over 140 pitches (2)
- 2nd in sacrifice bunt attempts and intentional walks (57)
- 3rd in stolen base attempts (147) and hit-and-run attempts (83)

Tony Armas

2004 Season

Due to his sore shoulder, Tony Armas never did get going in 2004. Sidelined for the first two months following May 2003 surgery, even when he returned to action he wasn't more than a five-inning starter. In addition to his shoulder problems, Armas was hit on his plant leg by a liner which affected his ability to go deep into games. He had several outstanding outings, the best of which was no-hitting the Astros for five innings before being pulled for precautionary reasons. He was shut down for good in the middle of September.

Pitching

Armas throws a heavy sinking fastball around 90 MPH, mixing in a good slider, curve and change. He has very good pitching instincts, so even when he doesn't have his best command, he keeps his team in games. With a slider that tails away from righthanders but a fastball that tails in to them, opposing teams go through plenty of bats when he's on the mound. He has no fear of pitching inside to either batter's box.

Defense & Hitting

Although he's a decent bunter, it's clear that Armas didn't inherit any of his father's hitting prowess. Injuries have affected his tendency to induce groundballs, so his athletic ability off the mound did not have as much impact as it has in previous years. While his move to first isn't exceptional, he's very good at keeping runners honest by getting to the plate quickly and varying his timing. He has allowed just six stolen bases in 103 innings during the past two seasons.

2005 Outlook

The team hopes that Armas finally will be completely healthy going into the 2005 campaign. He showed tremendous potential at the start of the 2003 season before the shoulder injury, when he was among the league leaders in ERA and strikeouts. With the team bolstering its offense over the winter, he could be one of the bigger surprises of 2005.

Position: SP
Bats: R **Throws:** R
Ht: 6' 3" **Wt:** 225

Opening Day Age: 26
Born: 4/29/78 in Puerto Piritu, VZ
ML Seasons: 6
Pronunciation: ar-MUS

Overall Statistics

	W	L	Pct.	ERA	G	GS	Sv	IP	H	BB	SO	HR	Avg
'04	2	4	.333	4.88	16	16	0	72.0	66	45	54	13	.247
Car.	32	41	.438	4.21	102	102	0	565.0	502	274	445	67	.241

2004 Pitching Profile

	Tony Armas	NL Average
Overall Strike %	58.5	62.5
1st Pitch Strike %	54.2	58.5
Ratio	1.54	1.39
Strikeouts per 9 IP	6.75	6.74
Walks per 9 IP	5.63	3.38
Home Runs per 9 IP	1.63	1.11
Strikeout/Walk Ratio	1.20	1.99
Groundball/Flyball Ratio	0.73	1.25

2004 Situational Stats

	W	L	ERA	Sv	IP		AB	H	HR	RBI	Avg
Home	2	1	3.05	0	44.1	LHB	108	25	5	12	.231
Road	0	3	7.81	0	27.2	RHB	159	41	8	22	.258
First Half	1	3	4.46	0	34.1	Sc Pos	62	13	2	19	.210
Scnd Half	1	1	5.26	0	37.2	Clutch	6	2	0	0	.333

2004 Rankings (National League)

- Did not rank near the top or bottom in any category

Tony Batista

Position: 3B
Bats: R **Throws:** R
Ht: 6' 0" **Wt:** 208

Opening Day Age: 31
Born: 12/9/73 in Puerto Plata, DR
ML Seasons: 9
Pronunciation: bah-TEESE-tah

2004 Season

The Expos got a late gift when they signed Tony Batista for $1.5 million the day after Christmas in 2003. He not only drove in more than 100 runs for a team with one of the worst on-base percentages in the league, but he also solidified the infield and gave a young team some much-needed leadership. Batista saved his best for division rivals, smacking 19 of his 32 homers and driving in 57 of his 110 RBI against National League East foes.

Hitting

Batista often is noted for his exaggerated open stance that allows him to see the ball better. He's an extreme pull hitter who will lunge at outside pitches in an effort to get around them. This leaves him susceptible to pitches low and away, down and in, as well as up and in on his hands. Batista also has a long swing, so he can be overpowered by good fastballs. Working in his favor is that he crushes mistakes over the heart of the plate, and he's a smart hitter who anticipates what pitchers are trying to do with him.

Baserunning & Defense

Batista was surprisingly effective stealing bases last year largely because he was ignored by opposing pitchers. It wasn't so long ago that the third baseman came to the majors as a shortstop, and he's only 31 years old, but his range has deteriorated to below average. If he gets to the ball, however, the batter will be out as he has one of the most accurate arms at the hot corner and an extremely quick release.

2005 Outlook

While his feast-or-famine style of hitting and decreasing lack of range in the field are not overly appealing, Batista should be able to find a regular job in the majors. Since 1999, he has averaged 31 homers a season, and he has some value as a defensive player. The Nationals opted to make a splash before their inaugural season in Washington, and they signed Vinny Castilla to play third base for the next two seasons. Batista will be looking for a new team over the winter.

Overall Statistics

	G	AB	R	H	D	T	HR	RBI	SB	BB	SO	Avg	OBP	Slg
'04	157	606	76	146	30	2	32	110	14	26	78	.241	.272	.455
Car.	1179	4289	591	1078	211	17	214	681	47	260	749	.251	.298	.458

Where He Hits the Ball

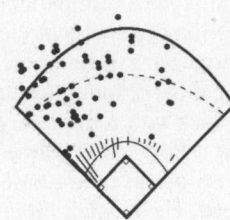
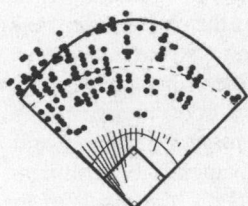

Vs. LHP   **Vs. RHP**

2004 Situational Stats

	AB	H	HR	RBI	Avg		AB	H	HR	RBI	Avg
Home	284	68	13	48	.239	LHP	165	38	13	25	.230
Road	322	78	19	62	.242	RHP	441	108	19	85	.245
First Half	302	70	11	42	.232	Sc Pos	166	41	8	76	.247
Scnd Half	304	76	21	68	.250	Clutch	96	23	7	25	.240

2004 Rankings (National League)

- 2nd in lowest on-base percentage
- 3rd in sacrifice flies (10) and errors at third base (19)
- 4th in batting average with the bases loaded (.500) and lowest cleanup slugging percentage (.463)
- 5th in lowest batting average and lowest fielding percentage at third base (.954)
- 6th in lowest percentage of swings on the first pitch (12.3), lowest stolen-base percentage (70.0), lowest batting average vs. lefthanded pitchers, lowest batting average vs. righthanded pitchers and lowest batting average at home
- Led the Expos in home runs, at-bats, hits, RBI, GDPs (14) and lowest percentage of swings on the first pitch (12.3)

Endy Chavez

2004 Season

Endy Chavez began his season as the Expos' lead-off man, but he slumped badly in his first month with the parent club because his skills were not suited to the role. When he was moved one spot down in the order to No. 2, Chavez found his game, hitting .296 with a .400 slugging percentage there. He slumped late in the season, possibly due to some shoulder soreness. The Expos began and ended their run as a major league club at Shea Stadium, and it was Chavez who made their final out.

Hitting

While many might look at his speed and think of Chavez as a leadoff hitter, he is far too impatient for the role. Quite frankly, he likes to swing at the first "strike" he sees. If he was a little more patient, he might be the perfect No. 2 hitter, as he is a good bunter, makes contact with a high percentage of pitches and does a very good job of advancing baserunners. Most of his extra-base hits are the result of his speed. He's a slap hitter who hasn't yet learned to drive the ball.

Baserunning & Defense

Speed is Chavez' primary tool. In addition to being an excellent basestealer, he puts pressure on opposing defenses the moment he makes contact, taking an extra base when any opportunity presents itself. He covers a lot of ground in center and usually can outrun his mistakes. His strong, accurate arm helped him rank seventh in the majors in 2004 in assists for a center fielder.

2005 Outlook

With Terrmel Sledge and Jose Guillen already in the outfield and Brad Wilkerson expected to return there, Chavez' playing time likely will be cut back. While his speed and defense certainly are appealing, his other skills indicate that he probably is better suited to coming off the bench.

Position: CF
Bats: L **Throws:** L
Ht: 5'10" **Wt:** 189

Opening Day Age: 27
Born: 2/7/78 in Valencia, VZ
ML Seasons: 4
Pronunciation: shah-VEZ

Overall Statistics

	G	AB	R	H	D	T	HR	RBI	SB	BB	SO	Avg	OBP	Slg
'04	132	502	65	139	20	6	5	34	32	30	40	.277	.318	.371
Car.	338	1187	155	313	55	16	11	95	53	69	123	.264	.303	.365

Where He Hits the Ball

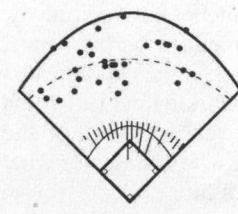 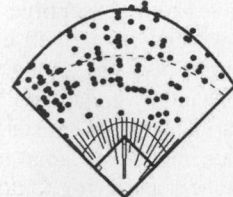

Vs. LHP   **Vs. RHP**

2004 Situational Stats

	AB	H	HR	RBI	Avg		AB	H	HR	RBI	Avg
Home	241	65	4	17	.270	LHP	137	33	2	12	.241
Road	261	74	1	17	.284	RHP	365	106	3	22	.290
First Half	251	70	4	12	.279	Sc Pos	98	23	2	28	.235
Scnd Half	251	69	1	22	.275	Clutch	77	23	2	10	.299

2004 Rankings (National League)

- 2nd in highest percentage of swings put into play (57.1) and lowest fielding percentage in center field (.984)
- 4th in bunts in play (36), errors in center field (5) and lowest on-base percentage for a lead off hitter (.291)
- 6th in stolen bases, highest groundball-flyball ratio (2.0) and steals of third (5)
- 9th in sacrifice bunts (12), stolen-base percentage (82.1), lowest slugging percentage and lowest on-base percentage
- Led the Expos in singles, triples, stolen bases, caught stealing (7), highest groundball-flyball ratio (2.0), stolen-base percentage (82.1), bunts in play (36), and steals of third (5)

Chad Cordero

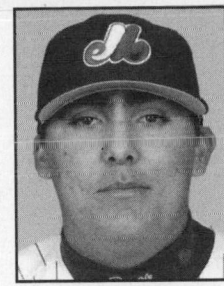

Position: RP
Bats: R **Throws:** R
Ht: 6' 0" **Wt:** 198

Opening Day Age: 23
Born: 3/18/82 in
Upland, CA
ML Seasons: 2

2004 Season

When the Expos drafted and signed Chad Cordero last year, it was with an eye toward making him the closer eventually. What they probably didn't anticipate was that "eventually" would come in June of last year. Even more surprising was that he was more dominating as a closer than he was as a setup man, improving both his strikeout and walk rates. Not surprisingly, Cordero was the last Expos pitcher on the mound in their final game in Montreal, and the result of the final opposition at-bat was a strikeout.

Pitching

Although Cordero has a good fastball, it's his excellent slider that makes him so effective. He'll spot the fastball in all quadrants, but he likes to use the upper part of the zone to set up the slider for strikes. The drawback is that pitching up in the zone leaves him susceptible to the longball. Hitters tend to look for the slider and try to foul off the fastball, which tails very slightly into righthanders at around 92 MPH. Even after Cordero was named closer, Robinson was unafraid of using him for more than one inning or in non-save situations.

Defense & Hitting

Cordero has a decent move to first, but he isn't a real threat to pick off anyone who's paying attention. Like many closers, he doesn't have much range off the mound, but he is surehanded when he can make a play. He very rarely gets to wield a bat, but he did lay down a sacrifice bunt the one time he was asked.

2005 Outlook

Washington has found its closer, at least until Cordero becomes arbitration eligible. Whether he will be used exclusively in save situations or for just one inning at a time will depend upon the team's manager. Regardless, he has proven he can handle the extra work, and because of that will be one of the more valuable closers in the league.

Overall Statistics

	W	L	Pct.	ERA	G	GS	Sv	IP	H	BB	SO	HR	Avg
'04	7	3	.700	2.94	69	0	14	82.2	68	43	83	8	.221
Car.	8	3	.727	2.79	81	0	15	93.2	72	46	95	9	.210

2004 Pitching Profile

	Chad Cordero	NL Average
Overall Strike %	61.2	62.5
1st Pitch Strike %	60.5	58.5
Ratio	1.34	1.39
Strikeouts per 9 IP	9.04	6.74
Walks per 9 IP	4.68	3.38
Home Runs per 9 IP	0.87	1.11
Strikeout/Walk Ratio	1.93	1.99
Groundball/Flyball Ratio	0.60	1.25

2004 Situational Stats

	W	L	ERA	Sv	IP		AB	H	HR	RBI	Avg
Home	2	0	2.81	9	41.2	LHB	136	33	4	13	.243
Road	5	3	3.07	5	41.0	RHB	171	35	4	12	.205
First Half	2	1	2.87	7	47.0	Sc Pos	66	11	2	18	.167
Scnd Half	5	2	3.03	7	35.2	Clutch	207	43	7	19	.208

2004 Rankings (National League)

- 2nd in wins among rookies
- 4th in relief wins (7)
- 9th in relief innings (82.2) and most strikeouts per nine innings in relief (9.0)
- Led the Expos in saves, games finished (40), winning percentage, lowest batting average allowed vs. righthanded batters, save percentage (77.8), relief wins (7), lowest batting average allowed in relief (.221), and most strikeouts per nine innings in relief (9.0)

Zach Day

2004 Season

Much like 2003, Zach Day's season was abbreviated by injury after a very strong start. Through the first three months his ERA was 3.40, but shoulder tendinitis followed by a broken finger suffered in a bunt attempt ended his season before August. Before the final injury, Day had been the victim of the worst run support in the majors (2.47 per game). It was the primary reason his won-lost record was as unimpressive as it was.

Pitching

Day uses his excellent sinking fastball to great effect, inducing groundballs at better than twice the rate he gives up flies. He works quickly, mixing in a curve, change and slider to keep hitters off-balance and his infielders on their toes. His command and strikeout rate improved over 2003, both good signs for continued development. One alarming trend is an increased home-run rate, which was in part due to a big drop in his groundball rate. While in '03 most of his mistakes were with his fastball low, last year they were in the zone with his secondary pitches.

Defense & Hitting

Like most sinkerballers, Day fields his position well. Even though he is capable of making big plays with his glove, he usually defers to the excellent glove men he's had behind him. His below-average bunting skills cost him a trip to the DL when bad technique put his right hand between the bat and the ball. Basrunners don't take too many liberties with him because he doesn't have much of a leg kick and is reasonably quick to the plate.

2005 Outlook

Barring any spring surprises, Day is a lock for the rotation and the favorite to win the No. 3 starter spot. It remains to be seen how RFK Stadium will play, but the grass infield almost assuredly will work in his favor. However, Day will need to reverse the decrease in his groundball rate in 2004 to reap the benefits of playing in a park that just may be tailor-made for his skills.

Position: SP
Bats: R **Throws:** R
Ht: 6' 4" **Wt:** 216

Opening Day Age: 26
Born: 6/15/78 in Cincinnati, OH
ML Seasons: 3

Overall Statistics

	W	L	Pct.	ERA	G	GS	Sv	IP	H	BB	SO	HR	Avg
'04	5	10	.333	3.93	19	19	0	116.2	117	45	61	13	.265
Car.	18	19	.486	4.01	61	44	1	285.1	277	119	147	24	.256

2004 Pitching Profile

	Zach Day	NL Average
Overall Strike %	61.1	62.5
1st Pitch Strike %	58.1	58.5
Ratio	1.39	1.39
Strikeouts per 9 IP	4.71	6.74
Walks per 9 IP	3.47	3.38
Home Runs per 9 IP	1.00	1.11
Strikeout/Walk Ratio	1.36	1.99
Groundball/Flyball Ratio	2.09	1.25

2004 Situational Stats

	W	L	ERA	Sv	IP		AB	H	HR	RBI	Avg
Home	2	7	4.52	0	63.2	LHB	190	53	8	26	.279
Road	3	3	3.23	0	53.0	RHB	252	64	5	20	.254
First Half	5	9	4.04	0	104.2	Sc Pos	98	24	4	34	.245
Scnd Half	0	1	3.00	0	12.0	Clutch	27	9	2	4	.333

2004 Rankings (National League)

- 6th in lowest winning percentage
- Led the Expos in highest groundball-flyball ratio allowed (2.1) and lowest ERA on the road

Alex Gonzalez

2004 Season

When the season began, Alex Gonzalez was hoping to return Chicago to the NLCS. But his .217 batting average at the trading deadline marked him as one of the scapegoats for the Cubs' struggles last year, so he was dealt to the Expos in the four-team trade that brought Nomar Garicaparra to the Cubs and sent Orlando Cabrera to the Red Sox. Little more than a month later, Gonzalez was shipped off to the Padres to replace the injured Khalil Greene for the final stretch run.

Hitting

Gonzalez is a first-ball fastball hitter and if he doesn't get it, he hopes to somehow get ahead in the count so he can look for the fastball again. He's a pull conscious hitter with some power, so pitching him on the inside is a dangerous proposition. Most pitchers work him away with breaking balls. About the best he can do with those is foul off the ones that are left up. As someone who swings and misses as much as he does, Gonzalez simply cannot be trusted near the top of the batting order.

Baserunning & Defense

A smooth fielder with soft hands and good range, Gonzalez is one of the better fielding shortstops in the majors. He doesn't have any problems charging balls or going back on pops, and his strong, accurate arm allows him to make plays in the hole that few shortstops can. It's been four years since he was asked to steal regularly, but he has enough speed to swipe 15-20 bases a season. What holds him back is his inability to consistently read pitchers.

2005 Outlook

Good glove men who can hit the longball always are in demand, so some team may give Gonzalez a starting job. Very likely it will be a team that has a good young shortstop prospect that's not quite ready, like Cleveland or Seattle.

Position: SS
Bats: R **Throws:** R
Ht: 6' 0" **Wt:** 200

Opening Day Age: 31
Born: 4/8/73 in Miami, FL
ML Seasons: 11

Overall Statistics

	G	AB	R	H	D	T	HR	RBI	SB	BB	SO	Avg	OBP	Slg
'04	83	285	36	64	18	1	7	27	2	14	64	.225	.263	.368
Car.	1267	4592	572	1111	254	26	128	497	95	364	1081	.242	.302	.392

Where He Hits the Ball

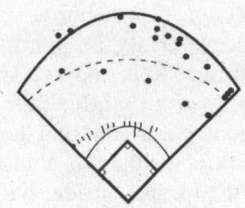

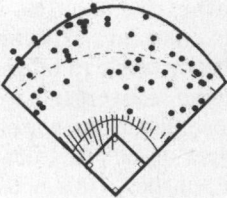

Vs. LHP   **Vs. RHP**

2004 Situational Stats

	AB	H	HR	RBI	Avg		AB	H	HR	RBI	Avg
Home	118	26	2	8	.220	LHP	61	11	2	11	.180
Road	167	38	5	19	.228	RHP	224	53	5	16	.237
First Half	90	22	3	7	.244	Sc Pos	75	17	2	20	.227
Scnd Half	195	42	4	20	.215	Clutch	52	11	2	4	.212

2004 Rankings (National League)

- 1st in lowest batting average with the bases loaded (.000)
- 7th in errors at shortstop (11)

Livan Hernandez

2004 Season

Livan Hernandez continues to baffle pitch-count mavens who swear his arm eventually will fall off. Yet he keeps plugging away. He threw 229 more pitches than anyone in the majors last year and nearly doubled the complete-game totals of his next closest competitors. Had he been afforded better than the sixth-worst run support in baseball, he might have won 15 games. As it is, he will have to content himself with being the major league leader in innings pitched.

Pitching

With the same easy motion, Hernandez delivers a fastball in the upper 80s, a slow curve, slider and plus changeup. He'll alter the speeds on any of his pitches and has great instincts for throwing what the hitter isn't expecting. Occasionally, he'll drop his arm angle to offer a different look and to add lateral movement to his fastball and slider. Generally, Hernandez has good control around the edges of the plate, but when it's off the hits come in bunches. He's not afraid to come inside, but anything he doesn't bury tends to get crushed.

Defense & Hitting

For someone of his weight and body build, Hernandez is a surprisingly agile fielder. In fact, he's one of the best fielding pitchers in baseball. He has a good move to first and is reasonably quick getting the ball to the plate. Hernandez can do much more with a bat in his hands than simply lay down a good bunt. He's hit as high as .296 in a season, and last year set career highs with seven doubles and 10 RBI.

2005 Outlook

Hernandez is one of those rare starters who takes the mound with the intent of completing the game, regardless of his pitch count. Every year he is among the league leaders in complete games and pitches thrown. The Expos were not phased by his high pitch totals, signing him to a three-year, $23 million extension in April 2004. He'll be the Nationals' Opening Day starter in 2005.

Position: SP
Bats: R **Throws:** R
Ht: 6' 2" **Wt:** 245

Opening Day Age: 30
Born: 2/20/75 in Villa Clara, Cuba
ML Seasons: 9
Pronunciation: lee-VAHN her-NAN-dezz

Overall Statistics

	W	L	Pct.	ERA	G	GS	Sv	IP	H	BB	SO	HR	Avg
'04	11	15	.423	3.60	35	35	0	255.0	234	83	186	26	.248
Car.	95	94	.503	4.13	249	248	0	1704.1	1788	589	1181	183	.272

2004 Pitching Profile

	Livan Hernandez	NL Average
Overall Strike %	62.0	62.5
1st Pitch Strike %	58.1	58.5
Ratio	1.24	1.39
Strikeouts per 9 IP	6.56	6.74
Walks per 9 IP	2.93	3.38
Home Runs per 9 IP	0.92	1.11
Strikeout/Walk Ratio	2.24	1.99
Groundball/Flyball Ratio	1.29	1.25

2004 Situational Stats

	W	L	ERA	Sv	IP		AB	H	HR	RBI	Avg
Home	7	7	3.32	0	116.2	LHB	450	116	16	49	.258
Road	4	8	3.84	0	138.1	RHB	495	118	10	38	.238
First Half	6	8	3.58	0	135.2	Sc Pos	194	48	5	59	.247
Scnd Half	5	7	3.62	0	119.1	Clutch	122	39	3	11	.320

2004 Rankings (National League)

- 1st in games started, complete games (9), innings pitched, batters faced (1,053) and pitches thrown (3,926)
- 2nd in losses and hits allowed
- 3rd in sacrifice bunts (15), shutouts (2) and least run support per nine innings (4.0)
- 5th in runners caught stealing (9)
- Led the Expos in ERA, sacrifice bunts (15), wins, losses, games started, shutouts (2), innings pitched, batters faced (1,053), home runs allowed, walks allowed, strikeouts, pick off throws (89), stolen bases allowed (16), runners caught stealing (9), GDPs induced (22), highest strikeout-walk ratio (2.2), lowest batting average allowed (.248), lowest slugging percentage allowed (.387), lowest on-base percentage allowed (.314), fewest home runs allowed per nine innings (.92) and fewest walks per nine innings (2.9)

Nick Johnson

2004 Season

It's unclear whether Nick Johnson had a tougher time adjusting to a new league or trying to stay healthy for more than a month at a time in 2004. Whatever it was, it's probably a year he'd like to forget. His season began on the disabled list with a sore back and it ended on the DL in August when his cheekbone was broken by a bad-hop grounder in Colorado. In between, Johnson had a couple of good months where he showed his typical ability to get on base, but also a couple stretches where he was alarmingly ineffective at the plate.

Hitting

Johnson's calling card is his understanding of the strike zone, but he does have decent home-run power. His problem has been staying healthy long enough for his power to fully develop. He's been in the majors now for four years, and he finally topped 1,000 career at-bats just last year before his season ended. When healthy, he forces pitchers to throw strikes, smoking line drives to all fields when they do. He's been used primarily as a No. 2 hitter because of his on-base skills and ability to make contact, but he should move down in the order as his power develops.

Baserunning & Defense

Although he's not particularly graceful around the first-base bag, Johnson has quick feet and better-than-average range. In fact, his zone rating was among the top five in the majors in 2004. He's not a threat to steal, but he will take a base if left unattended.

2005 Outlook

Moving from the hard turfs in Montreal and Puerto Rico to a grass field in D.C. should help Johnson's back stay healthier, but it remains to be seen if he can kick the injury bug completely. If he can stay on the field for 140 or more games, he finally should justify the high praise he received in 2000-01 as one of the top prospects in baseball.

Position: 1B
Bats: L **Throws:** L
Ht: 6' 3" **Wt:** 224

Opening Day Age: 26
Born: 9/19/78 in Sacramento, CA
ML Seasons: 4

Overall Statistics

	G	AB	R	H	D	T	HR	RBI	SB	BB	SO	Avg	OBP	Slg
'04	73	251	35	63	16	0	7	33	6	40	58	.251	.359	.398
Car.	321	1020	157	260	52	0	38	146	12	165	228	.255	.372	.418

Where He Hits the Ball

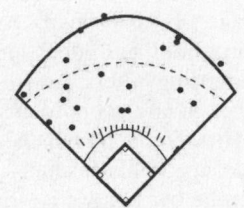 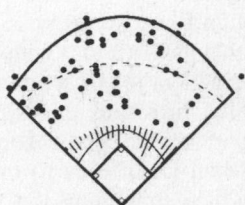

Vs. LHP   **Vs. RHP**

2004 Situational Stats

	AB	H	HR	RBI	Avg		AB	H	HR	RBI	Avg
Home	115	28	4	19	.243	LHP	62	20	1	9	.323
Road	136	35	3	14	.257	RHP	189	43	6	24	.228
First Half	143	36	4	16	.252	Sc Pos	63	16	4	27	.254
Scnd Half	108	27	3	17	.250	Clutch	38	12	1	3	.316

2004 Rankings (National League)

- Led the Expos in highest percentage of pitches taken (62.5), batting average in the clutch, batting average with the bases loaded (.750) and batting average vs. lefthanded pitchers

Tomo Ohka

2004 Season

After a rough April, Tomo Ohka looked like a world beater through May and June, posting ERAs of 1.51 and 2.79, respectively. His best start of the season came on May 8, when he held the Cardinals scoreless on three hits for eight innings. But on June 10, his renaissance came to an abrupt end when a liner off the bat of Carlos Beltran broke his right forearm, sending Ohka to the disabled list for most of the rest of the season. Although he was able to return during the final weeks of September, he was not effective.

Pitching

Ohka throws a fastball, curve, slider and change, though none of these offerings can be described as significantly above average. In his favor, he changes speeds with everything and does an excellent job of scouting opposing hitters. He will also throw any of his pitches in any count to any part of the strike zone. Hits come in bunches when Ohka tries to muscle up on his fastball—which straightens out when he overthrows it—or when he tries to be too fine around the edges of the plate.

Defense & Hitting

Ohka is quick off the mound and makes the plays on balls he reaches. His move to first is average, so he must keep runners in check by varying his timing to home. At the plate, he moves his feet in the box almost as much as Ichiro, but with nowhere near the same results. Still, Ohka puts the ball in play and usually helps himself when he needs to lay down a bunt.

2005 Outlook

Ohka will be in the mix for the rotation in 2005. His dominance in May and June opened some eyes that he could become more than an innings-eating fourth starter, but his margin for error is so small that there's probably not much upside beyond that. Assuming he's fully recovered, he should repeat the 190-plus innings he gave the Expos in each of the two years previous to 2004.

Position: SP
Bats: R **Throws:** R
Ht: 6' 1" **Wt:** 200

Opening Day Age: 29
Born: 3/18/76 in Kyoto, Japan
ML Seasons: 6
Pronunciation: toe-mo oh-kah

Overall Statistics

	W	L	Pct.	ERA	G	GS	Sv	IP	H	BB	SO	HR	Avg
'04	3	7	.300	3.40	15	15	0	84.2	98	20	38	11	.288
Car.	33	44	.429	3.92	124	115	0	665.2	750	171	390	78	.285

2004 Pitching Profile

	Tomo Ohka	NL Average
Overall Strike %	66.1	62.5
1st Pitch Strike %	64.1	58.5
Ratio	1.39	1.39
Strikeouts per 9 IP	4.04	6.74
Walks per 9 IP	2.13	3.38
Home Runs per 9 IP	1.17	1.11
Strikeout/Walk Ratio	1.90	1.99
Groundball/Flyball Ratio	1.13	1.25

2004 Situational Stats

	W	L	ERA	Sv	IP		AB	H	HR	RBI	Avg
Home	3	4	3.14	0	48.2	LHB	162	45	5	11	.278
Road	0	3	3.75	0	36.0	RHB	178	53	6	26	.298
First Half	3	5	3.01	0	71.2	Sc Pos	88	20	1	25	.227
Scnd Half	0	2	5.54	0	13.0	Clutch	21	4	0	1	.190

2004 Rankings (National League)

- Led the Expos in lowest ERA at home

Brian Schneider

2004 Season

The Expos weren't disappointed when they handed Brian Schneider the full-time job behind the plate last year. He posted career highs in nearly all his counting categories while improving his strikeout rate and walk total. Defensively, he fostered a young pitching staff beset by injuries, yet he was able to post the fifth-best catcher's ERA (3.86) in baseball. He also led the majors in throwing out would-be basestealers, with a nearly 50-percent success rate.

Hitting

Schneider is a good contact hitter, spraying line-drives to all fields. He's a versatile batter capable of executing hit-and-run plays and going the other way when he's worked to the outside. Like most lefties, he'll turn on a pitch low and inside. He covers the plate well, but as last season wore on he showed an increased tendency to get himself out on pitches that were off the plate outside.

Baserunning & Defense

Schneider's greatest gains this season were at the plate, but his calling card is his work behind it. Rarely do his pitchers shake him off, and he'll usually get them an extra strike or two over the course of the game with his framing. No one picks errant pitches out of the dirt better and his technique for blocking the plate is textbook. It's amazing that as many teams try to run on him as they do because he has such a strong, accurate arm. Over the last three years, he's thrown out 45.9 percent of runners trying to steal.

2005 Outlook

Schneider is young for a catcher, so it's likely he still hasn't peaked offensively. He's already one of the best backstops in baseball, but because he hasn't put up gaudy home-run numbers and he's been playing many of his games outside the U.S., he hasn't been recognized as such. This year, with the team moving to a more media-intense market, that will change.

Position: C
Bats: L **Throws:** R
Ht: 6' 1" **Wt:** 196

Opening Day Age: 28
Born: 11/26/76 in Jacksonville, FL
ML Seasons: 5

Overall Statistics

	G	AB	R	H	D	T	HR	RBI	SB	BB	SO	Avg	OBP	Slg
'04	135	436	40	112	20	3	12	49	0	42	63	.257	.325	.399
Car.	388	1134	105	286	74	6	27	141	1	113	206	.252	.321	.399

Where He Hits the Ball

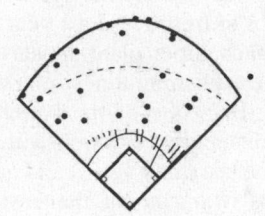 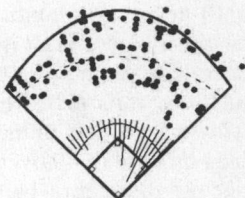

Vs. LHP   **Vs. RHP**

2004 Situational Stats

	AB	H	HR	RBI	Avg		AB	H	HR	RBI	Avg
Home	205	55	5	21	.268	LHP	86	21	2	8	.244
Road	231	57	7	28	.247	RHP	350	91	10	41	.260
First Half	232	59	9	23	.254	Sc Pos	106	25	6	40	.236
Scnd Half	204	53	3	26	.260	Clutch	90	23	3	10	.256

2004 Rankings (National League)

- 5th in fielding percentage at catcher (.998)
- Led the Expos in intentional walks (10)

Jose Vidro

2004 Season

For the second consecutive season, a knee injury took its toll on Jose Vidro's production. Last year, it ended his campaign a month early and required surgery. Also ending was his streak of five consecutive seasons of hitting at least .300. Despite a slow start and a premature finish, he nearly matched his home-run and RBI totals from 2003 in 34 fewer games. From the beginning of June until the end of August when he opted for surgery, Vidro hit .342 with 10 homers and 45 RBI.

Hitting

Vidro makes contact with a level, easy swing from both sides of the plate, hitting line drives to all fields. He covers the plate well and his eye for balls and strikes continues to improve. Last year, he set a career high in pitches per plate appearance, and came close to establishing a new mark in home runs per at-bat. He's one of the better two-strike hitters in the game, hits very well with men on base (.349 over the last three years) and is one of those rare batters who can hit the best pitchers' best pitches. He's not asked to do it much, but Vidro is an accomplished bunter.

Baserunning & Defense

Vidro's slow foot speed prevents him from being a stolen-base threat, but he's a smart runner who takes advantage of defensive miscues and lazy play. He doesn't have the same raw quickness to move laterally that most middle infielders have, but his strong arm allows him to play deeper to make up for a lack of side-to-side range. His arm also makes him one of the better pivot men on the double play.

2005 Outlook

The September surgery on his knee went well and all indications are that Vidro will be ready to play by the start of spring training. Moving to a grass field should help him stay healthier, and with a number of his trends on the rise, a big season could be in store in 2005.

Position: 2B
Bats: B **Throws:** R
Ht: 5'11" **Wt:** 193

Opening Day Age: 30
Born: 8/27/74 in Mayaguez, PR
ML Seasons: 8
Pronunciation: VEE-droe

Overall Statistics

	G	AB	R	H	D	T	HR	RBI	SB	BB	SO	Avg	OBP	Slg
'04	110	412	51	121	24	0	14	60	3	49	43	.294	.367	.454
Car.	973	3485	524	1061	257	9	101	471	20	325	385	.304	.367	.470

Where He Hits the Ball

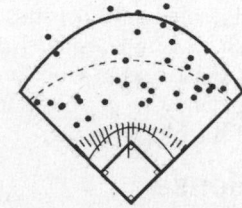 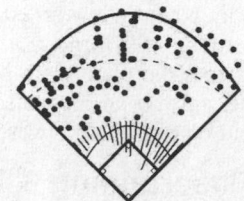

Vs. LHP   **Vs. RHP**

2004 Situational Stats

	AB	H	HR	RBI	Avg		AB	H	HR	RBI	Avg
Home	175	51	6	29	.291	LHP	131	35	2	13	.267
Road	237	70	8	31	.295	RHP	281	86	12	47	.306
First Half	299	87	10	39	.291	Sc Pos	105	31	2	42	.295
Scnd Half	113	34	4	21	.301	Clutch	70	22	2	9	.314

2004 Rankings (National League)

• Led the Expos in GDPs (14)

Brad Wilkerson

2004 Season

After Endy Chavez failed to get on base consistently, manager Frank Robinson once again turned to Brad Wilkerson to be his team's leadoff man. Wilkerson responded by leading the National League in leadoff homers and ranking second in pitches per plate appearance. He and Tony Batista became the first tandem of Expos hitters to top 30 home runs in a season. On two different occasions, Wilkerson hit two home runs in a game, and 2004 also marked the third consecutive year that both his strikeout and walk rates improved.

Hitting

Wilkerson generally is very patient, but he will swing at a first-ball fastball if it's left over the inner half. He has as many personality ticks as Nomar Garciaparra when he approaches the plate, but is quiet once he's set in the batter's box. Wilkerson is somewhat susceptible to pitches on the outer half, usually down and away, but he will make contact if it's in the strike zone. This year, he concentrated on pulling the ball more, hammering pitches down and in especially. His power comes from his strong, quick wrists, so even on bad swings Wilkerson can hit the ball for extra bases. His contact rate went down some, but he can get a bunt down when needed.

Baserunning & Defense

Although not a particularly fast runner, Wilkerson is very good at taking as many bases as the defense will allow and is very aggressive in breaking up double plays. He's a versatile outfielder who gets good jumps, takes smart routes and possesses a strong, accurate arm. At first base, his range is above average, and he shows surprisingly soft hands.

2005 Outlook

The Expos should try to find a suitable leadoff hitter, allowing Wilkerson to be more productive in the third spot. If they don't, he's probably their best option to handle the duties at the top of the order. Either way, his star should remain on the rise.

Position: 1B/LF/CF/RF
Bats: L **Throws:** L
Ht: 6' 0" **Wt:** 206

Opening Day Age: 27
Born: 6/1/77 in Daviess, KY
ML Seasons: 4

Overall Statistics

	G	AB	R	H	D	T	HR	RBI	SB	BB	SO	Avg	OBP	Slg
'04	160	572	112	146	39	2	32	67	13	106	152	.255	.374	.498
Car.	506	1700	293	440	107	16	72	208	35	293	509	.259	.370	.468

Where He Hits the Ball

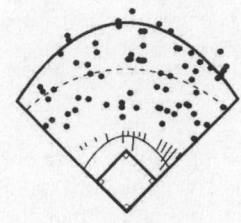
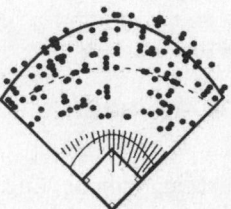

Vs. LHP   **Vs. RHP**

2004 Situational Stats

	AB	H	HR	RBI	Avg		AB	H	HR	RBI	Avg
Home	271	71	15	28	.262	LHP	176	49	9	21	.278
Road	301	75	17	39	.249	RHP	396	97	23	46	.245
First Half	293	68	16	34	.232	Sc Pos	112	26	4	35	.232
Scnd Half	279	78	16	33	.280	Clutch	88	22	3	8	.250

2004 Rankings (National League)

- 2nd in pitches seen (2,954) and most pitches seen per plate appearance (4.29)
- 3rd in lowest groundball-flyball ratio (0.6)
- 4th in strikeouts and on-base percentage for a leadoff hitter (.382)
- 5th in games played
- Led the Expos in home runs, runs scored, hits, doubles, total bases (285), walks, times on base (256), strikeouts, pitches seen (2,954), plate appearances (688), games played, slugging percentage, on-base percentage, HR frequency (17.9 ABs per HR), most pitches seen per plate appearance (4.29) and on-base percentage for a leadoff hitter (.382)

Washington

Luis Ayala

Position: RP
Bats: R **Throws:** R
Ht: 6' 2" **Wt:** 186

Opening Day Age: 27
Born: 1/12/78 in Los Mochis, Mexico
ML Seasons: 2
Pronunciation: eye-YA-lah

Overall Statistics

	W	L	Pct.	ERA	G	GS	Sv	IP	H	BB	SO	HR	Avg
'04	6	12	.333	2.69	81	0	2	90.1	92	15	63	6	.268
Car.	16	15	.516	2.79	146	0	7	161.1	157	28	109	14	.258

2004 Situational Stats

	W	L	ERA	Sv	IP		AB	H	HR	RBI	Avg
Home	3	4	2.60	2	45.0	LHB	134	33	3	14	.246
Road	3	8	2.78	0	45.1	RHB	209	59	3	36	.282
First Half	1	6	2.89	0	46.2	Sc Pos	95	27	0	40	.284
Scnd Half	5	6	2.47	2	43.2	Clutch	177	55	1	34	.311

2004 Season

Even though he was only a long shot to close out of spring training, Luis Ayala's woeful April (5.25 ERA) assured he would be no more than the team's primary setup man. After the rough start, however, he pitched brilliantly the rest of the way, showing excellent control and posting an ERA of 2.30. His biggest improvement this year was against lefthanders, who hit him hard in 2003 but were held in check in '04.

Pitching, Defense & Hitting

Ayala is not overpowering, but he has superb command, works quickly and will drop down sidearm to give hitters a couple of different looks with his low-90s fastball and slider. The fastball has natural movement toward righthanders, and he aggressively pitches inside to both sides of the plate. He has a decent move to first and his delivery is quick and compact, so baserunners generally have a tough time getting good jumps. He's an average fielder who rarely gets to bat.

2005 Outlook

The back-end of the Washington bullpen is set, with Chad Cordero closing and Ayala setting him up. Both pitchers are young and improving, so it should get even tougher to beat Washington late in games.

Rocky Biddle

Position: RP
Bats: R **Throws:** R
Ht: 6' 3" **Wt:** 221

Opening Day Age: 28
Born: 5/21/76 in Las Vegas, NV
ML Seasons: 5

Overall Statistics

	W	L	Pct.	ERA	G	GS	Sv	IP	H	BB	SO	HR	Avg
'04	4	8	.333	6.92	47	9	11	78.0	98	31	51	15	.307
Car.	20	30	.400	5.47	198	41	46	378.2	409	170	261	59	.274

2004 Situational Stats

	W	L	ERA	Sv	IP		AB	H	HR	RBI	Avg
Home	2	4	6.07	6	46.0	LHB	137	42	6	28	.307
Road	2	4	8.16	5	32.0	RHB	182	56	9	36	.308
First Half	1	4	7.09	11	39.1	Sc Pos	80	31	5	48	.388
Scnd Half	3	4	6.75	0	38.2	Clutch	63	19	5	13	.302

2004 Season

Entering last season, Rocky Biddle's hold on the closer's job was precarious, as his second-half performance in 2003 (5.81 ERA) did not inspire much confidence. Unfortunately, that turned into a trend—7.09 in the first half last year—and he was out of the closer's spot by June. He did not find much success as a starter, either, and his worst major league season mercifully came to an end for all intents and purposes in August when he was hit on the ankle by a Lance Berkman line drive.

Pitching, Defense & Hitting

Biddle spots a straight fastball in the low 90s to set up a big-breaking curve. He works quickly and gets hitters to put the ball on the ground, where he can help himself with his glove. He is literally an automatic out when he's at the plate, having appeared 13 times in his career with no hits and nine strikeouts. Opposing basestealers have been nabbed eight times in 12 attempts on his watch during the past two seasons.

2005 Outlook

Biddle made nearly $2 million in a dreadful 2004, and he was released in early November. He most likely will be relegated to middle relief and mopup work wherever he ends up in 2005.

Jamey Carroll

Position: 2B/3B/SS
Bats: R **Throws:** R
Ht: 5' 9" **Wt:** 170

Opening Day Age: 31
Born: 2/18/74 in Evansville, IN
ML Seasons: 3

Overall Statistics

	G	AB	R	H	D	T	HR	RBI	SB	BB	SO	Avg	OBP	Slg
'04	102	218	36	63	14	2	0	16	5	32	21	.289	.378	.372
Car.	223	516	83	144	29	6	2	32	11	55	72	.279	.350	.370

2004 Situational Stats

	AB	H	HR	RBI	Avg		AB	H	HR	RBI	Avg
Home	113	29	0	8	.257	LHP	76	19	0	5	.250
Road	105	34	0	8	.324	RHP	142	44	0	11	.310
First Half	96	25	0	9	.260	Sc Pos	44	8	0	14	.182
Scnd Half	122	38	0	7	.311	Clutch	30	8	0	3	.267

2004 Season

Probably no current Washington player is more popular than Jamey Carroll. Fans love his do-anything-for-the-team attitude and his 110-percent effort despite the fact that he's not that athletically gifted. He rewarded them for their affection by playing very good ball in the second half, hitting .311 with a .408 on-base percentage in limited duty.

Hitting, Baserunning & Defense

Carroll has no power to speak of, so he chokes up on the bat and slashes at pitches, hoping they'll find a crease in the infield defense. He's a prototypical small-ball player: excellent bunter, can hit-and-run, makes contact, fouls balls off by the boxful and generally finds a way to get on base. Once on base, he's aggressive but smart and will steal a sack when given the chance. His best defensive position is second, but he has quick enough reactions to play third and enough range to occasionally sub at shortstop, although his arm isn't quite strong enough to play there regularly.

2005 Outlook

The fact that the team is moving to a new city simply means that there will be a new audience for Carroll's infectious style of play. He'll be Washington's infield utility player, designated bunter and primary late-inning pinch-hitter.

Joey Eischen

Position: RP
Bats: L **Throws:** L
Ht: 6' 0" **Wt:** 214

Opening Day Age: 34
Born: 5/25/70 in West Covina, CA
ML Seasons: 8
Pronunciation: EYE-shen

Overall Statistics

	W	L	Pct.	ERA	G	GS	Sv	IP	H	BB	SO	HR	Avg
'04	0	1	.000	3.93	21	0	0	18.1	16	8	17	2	.232
Car.	9	7	.563	3.45	245	0	3	245.1	245	101	196	22	.262

2004 Situational Stats

	W	L	ERA	Sv	IP		AB	H	HR	RBI	Avg
Home	0	1	5.91	0	10.2	LHB	24	4	1	5	.167
Road	0	0	1.17	0	7.2	RHB	45	12	1	5	.267
First Half	0	0	—	0	0.0	Sc Pos	21	2	0	7	.095
Scnd Half	0	1	3.93	0	18.1	Clutch	17	3	1	3	.176

2004 Season

Surgery at the beginning of spring training to remove bone chips in his left elbow delayed Joey Eischen's start to 2004. In total, he missed 104 games while rehabbing and returned to the majors noticeably lighter than he was the previous year. Despite the setback, he pitched reasonably well as the Expos finished their final season in Montreal.

Pitching, Defense & Hitting

Although Eischen was declared fully recovered when he returned, his fastball had lost some life and about 3-4 MPH of velocity. Likewise, his two-plane slider didn't have as much velocity or break. Despite the decreases, he was able to disguise his release point enough with his delivery—an exaggerated crouch swooping upward to holding the ball in the glove high over his head—to keep batters guessing. Eischen occasionally showed the changeup and curve leftover from his days as a starter in the minors. He's not particularly adept as a fielder, nor as a hitter. Basestealers are just 2-for-8 against him the past two years.

2005 Outlook

From 2002-03, Eischen was one of the better lefty relievers in the league. Over the final two months of the 2004 season, he demonstrated that he is well on his way back to that level.

Sun-Woo Kim

Position: RP/SP
Bats: R **Throws:** R
Ht: 6' 1" **Wt:** 185

Opening Day Age: 27
Born: 9/4/77 in Inchon, South Korea
ML Seasons: 4

Overall Statistics

	W	L	Pct.	ERA	G	GS	Sv	IP	H	BB	SO	HR	Avg
'04	4	6	.400	4.58	43	17	0	135.2	145	55	87	17	.275
Car.	7	9	.438	5.05	86	27	0	240.2	275	98	148	29	.290

2004 Situational Stats

	W	L	ERA	Sv	IP		AB	H	HR	RBI	Avg
Home	2	4	4.87	0	68.1	LHB	229	69	6	35	.301
Road	2	2	4.28	0	67.1	RHB	298	76	11	39	.255
First Half	3	4	4.92	0	71.1	Sc Pos	133	38	1	52	.286
Scnd Half	1	2	4.20	0	64.1	Clutch	8	1	0	0	.125

2004 Season

After a terrible 2003 campaign in which manager Frank Robinson questioned whether he would ever become a major league pitcher, Sun-Woo Kim rebounded with a decent season capped by a surprisingly strong September. It might have been even better had nervousness not gotten to him in his final start—the final game played in Montreal.

Pitching, Defense & Hitting

Kim is a versatile pitcher, capable of starting or relieving. His numbers indicate he's probably better suited to the bullpen because his rate of surrendering longballs is much better there. The velocity on his fastball drops a little after the first inning of work, from 92 MPH to consistently around 88. None of his pitches—fastball, curve, slider and change—are significantly above average, so he must mix his selection and locate around the edges. When situations get sticky he has a tendency to overthrow. He takes good hacks at the plate and fields his position reasonably well.

2005 Outlook

The Nationals hope that Kim will build on his strong finish and contend for a spot in their rotation in 2005, if for no other reason than to provide incentive for the team's more talented starting prospects.

John Patterson

Position: SP
Bats: R **Throws:** R
Ht: 6' 5" **Wt:** 208

Opening Day Age: 27
Born: 1/30/78 in Orange, TX
ML Seasons: 3

Overall Statistics

	W	L	Pct.	ERA	G	GS	Sv	IP	H	BB	SO	HR	Avg
'04	4	7	.364	5.03	19	19	0	98.1	100	46	99	18	.260
Car.	7	11	.389	5.04	42	32	1	184.0	188	83	173	32	.262

2004 Situational Stats

	W	L	ERA	Sv	IP		AB	H	HR	RBI	Avg
Home	2	3	5.75	0	36.0	LHB	162	37	2	13	.228
Road	2	4	4.62	0	62.1	RHB	223	63	16	38	.283
First Half	1	2	3.57	0	22.2	Sc Pos	84	17	5	31	.202
Scnd Half	3	5	5.47	0	75.2	Clutch	7	0	0	0	.000

2004 Season

John Patterson began the season like a house afire, even though his won-lost record didn't reflect it. A groin strain at the end of April sent him to the sidelines for two months, and he was not nearly as effective when he returned. However, he will be the answer to a trivia question: Who was the last pitcher to start a game in a Montreal Expos uniform?

Pitching, Defense & Hitting

As he showed in April, Patterson can be dominating with his four-pitch repertoire—a 90-MPH fastball complemented by a slider, slow curve and a developing changeup. With his height, he's most effective when he pitches on a downward plane to the bottom of the strike zone. He has confidence throwing any of his pitches to the outside part of the plate on any count. Problems occur with men on base, when he tends to rush his delivery and elevate his offerings. He has a decent swing for a pitcher but isn't a good bunter. Nor does he stand out with his glove.

2005 Outlook

Patterson will fall into the fourth spot in the rotation. If he can learn to relax more on the mound, he should develop into a solid 200-inning starter with excellent strikeout totals.

Juan Rivera

Traded To ANGELS

Position: RF/CF/LF
Bats: R **Throws:** R
Ht: 6' 2" **Wt:** 205

Opening Day Age: 26
Born: 7/3/78 in
Guarenas, VZ
ML Seasons: 4

Overall Statistics

	G	AB	R	H	D	T	HR	RBI	SB	BB	SO	Avg	OBP	Slg
'04	134	391	48	120	24	1	12	49	6	34	45	.307	.364	.465
Car.	222	651	79	188	43	1	20	81	7	50	82	.289	.339	.450

2004 Situational Stats

	AB	H	HR	RBI	Avg		AB	H	HR	RBI	Avg
Home	192	58	6	26	.302	LHP	156	43	6	21	.276
Road	199	62	6	23	.312	RHP	235	77	6	28	.328
First Half	176	43	5	23	.244	Sc Pos	90	28	1	31	.311
Scnd Half	215	77	7	26	.358	Clutch	56	17	1	7	.304

2004 Season

Juan Rivera came to the Expos as part of the trade that sent Javier Vazquez to the Yankees in December 2003. Rivera finally got a chance to play every day after Carl Everett was traded, and he proved that he deserved a regular job in the majors. After the All-Star break, he hit .358 with seven homers and more walks than strikeouts.

Hitting, Baserunning & Defense

Rivera always has been a pretty good contact hitter, but he is learning to be a little more selective. Breaking stuff away gave him trouble, but he is showing signs of laying off pitches he can't handle. He still has a strong affinity for first-pitch fastballs. Once on the bases, he has good speed but tends to be overly aggressive, leading to some unnecessary outs. He has good enough range to play center and a strong enough arm to play right. He tied for the major league lead in outfield assists despite not playing regularly until the second half of the season.

2005 Outlook

The Angels were impressed enough with Rivera's second-half performance that they traded Jose Guillen for him in November. Rivera will compete with Jeff DaVanon for the fourth outfielder spot with the Angels.

Terrmel Sledge

Position: LF/RF/1B
Bats: L **Throws:** L
Ht: 6' 0" **Wt:** 185

Opening Day Age: 28
Born: 3/18/77 in
Fayetteville, NC
ML Seasons: 1

Overall Statistics

	G	AB	R	H	D	T	HR	RBI	SB	BB	SO	Avg	OBP	Slg
'04	133	398	45	107	20	6	15	62	3	40	66	.269	.336	.462
Car.	133	398	45	107	20	6	15	62	3	40	66	.269	.336	.462

2004 Situational Stats

	AB	H	HR	RBI	Avg		AB	H	HR	RBI	Avg
Home	192	48	6	25	.250	LHP	87	21	2	16	.241
Road	206	59	9	37	.286	RHP	311	86	13	46	.277
First Half	180	47	8	24	.261	Sc Pos	95	32	4	44	.337
Scnd Half	218	60	7	38	.275	Clutch	71	18	2	16	.254

2004 Season

After being named the Expos' Minor League Player of the Year in 2003, there were plenty of expectations for Terrmel Sledge in 2004. Starting the season 1-for-34 wasn't exactly what the Expos or Sledge had in mind. Nor was an episode where he threw his bat near an umpire. But he recovered from both to hit .286 from May on. Montreal fans will remember him as the final out at Stade Olympique.

Hitting, Baserunning & Defense

It appeared that Sledge began the season trying to live up to the minor league hype and got himself into some bad habits. Pitchers worked him on the outer half with breaking stuff and changeups because he was trying to pull everything. As the season wore on, he learned to be more patient and drive the ball alley-to-alley. He has decent speed, but isn't much of a threat to steal. The two strikes against his defense are an average arm and a tendency to glide to the ball rather than get to it and position himself to make plays. The latter resulted in a few balls dropping in for hits that might otherwise have been caught had he been hustling.

2005 Outlook

Sledge will open 2005 as the starting left fielder and will hit in the bottom half of the Washington lineup.

Washington

T.J. Tucker

Position: RP
Bats: R **Throws:** R
Ht: 6' 3" **Wt:** 266

Opening Day Age: 26
Born: 8/20/78 in
Clearwater, FL
ML Seasons: 4

Overall Statistics

	W	L	Pct.	ERA	G	GS	Sv	IP	H	BB	SO	HR	Avg
'04	4	2	.667	3.72	54	1	0	67.2	73	17	44	5	.275
Car.	12	9	.571	4.46	158	10	4	216.0	243	71	135	23	.283

2004 Situational Stats

	W	L	ERA	Sv	IP		AB	H	HR	RBI	Avg
Home	3	0	2.65	0	34.0	LHB	103	29	1	11	.282
Road	1	2	4.81	0	33.2	RHB	162	44	4	20	.272
First Half	0	1	3.99	0	29.1	Sc Pos	73	22	3	28	.301
Scnd Half	4	1	3.52	0	38.1	Clutch	33	11	2	5	.333

2004 Season

T.J. Tucker experienced somewhat of a breakthrough year in 2004, posting his best ERA yet, although most of his other numbers weren't significantly better than previous years. The biggest changes came in an improved strikeout-walk rate and using fewer pitches per batter. He was particularly effective in July, posting an ERA of 0.63.

Pitching, Defense & Hitting

Tucker uses an 89-MPH fastball and a changeup to set up a sharp breaking slider. His fastball doesn't have much movement, so if he doesn't have command, it gets hit pretty hard. He'll pitch up in the zone on both sides of the plate to set up the slider for strikes, and work down to get hitters to swing at it out of the zone. He has a tendency to nibble, especially with runners on base, which commonly gets him into more trouble. As one might expect of a pitcher who weighs 260-plus pounds, Tucker is not agile and isn't much help in the field or at the plate. He does a good job of limiting stolen bases.

2005 Outlook

While he'll never be an impact pitcher, Tucker appears to have found his niche as a solid middle reliever, capable of giving one, two or even three innings of dependable work when called upon.

Claudio Vargas

Position: RP/SP
Bats: R **Throws:** R
Ht: 6' 3" **Wt:** 228

Opening Day Age: 26
Born: 6/19/78 in
Valverde Mao, DR
ML Seasons: 2

Overall Statistics

	W	L	Pct.	ERA	G	GS	Sv	IP	H	BB	SO	HR	Avg
'04	5	5	.500	5.25	45	14	0	118.1	120	64	89	26	.266
Car.	11	13	.458	4.80	68	34	0	232.1	231	105	151	42	.260

2004 Situational Stats

	W	L	ERA	Sv	IP		AB	H	HR	RBI	Avg
Home	2	4	5.72	0	61.1	LHB	196	59	11	38	.301
Road	3	1	4.74	0	57.0	RHB	255	61	15	38	.239
First Half	4	4	5.87	0	79.2	Sc Pos	95	28	6	50	.295
Scnd Half	1	1	3.96	0	38.2	Clutch	20	8	1	3	.400

2004 Season

Claudio Vargas began the season with a spot in the rotation but inconsistency drove manager Frank Robinson to move him to the bullpen. With Rocky Biddle's early struggles, Vargas was considered an option at closer, but his control issues and the emergence of the reliable Chad Cordero put that idea on the shelf.

Pitching, Defense & Hitting

When he comes out of the pen, Vargas can let loose with a fastball that occasionally touches 97 MPH. As a starter, it's consistently around 91-92 MPH, and he complements it with a tight breaking pitch and a change. He was far more hittable than someone with his stuff should be due to his inability to maintain a consistent release point. His fastball straightens out when he overthrows, and he'll try to aim the ball when he gets behind. He's average in the field and with the bat.

2005 Outlook

Vargas showed considerable promise in the high minors, so there's still hope that he could emerge as a decent starter. The upside is there, as he showed when he shut out the Diamondbacks for seven innings in May, then four-hit the Giants for seven in his next start. In the meantime, he will work on his consistency out of the bullpen.

Other Washington Nationals

Rigo Beltran (**Pos**: LHP, **Age**: 35)

	W	L	Pct.	ERA	G	GS	Sv	IP	H	BB	SO	HR	Avg
'04	0	0	−	13.50	2	0	0	0.2	1	0	0	0	.333
Car.	2	3	.400	4.40	78	5	1	106.1	110	43	106	13	.268

Beltran is the soft lefty type who drives hitters crazy. He nibbles the corners with offspeed stuff and sneaks the fastball by you when least expected. He probably is best known as the winning pitcher for Mexico in their 2004 Olympic qualifying upset over the United States. He signed a minor league deal with the Brewers over the winter. 2005 Outlook: C

Chad Bentz (**Pos**: LHP, **Age**: 24)

	W	L	Pct.	ERA	G	GS	Sv	IP	H	BB	SO	HR	Avg
'04	0	3	.000	5.86	36	0	0	27.2	23	23	18	5	.228
Car.	0	3	.000	5.86	36	0	0	27.2	23	23	18	5	.228

Born without a right hand, Bentz followed in the footsteps of Jim Abbott by making it to the major leagues last year. It was not a fairy tale beginning, however, as Bentz had difficulty finding the plate. His 7.61 BB/9 led to a Double-A demotion to work on control issues. 2005 Outlook: C

Peter Bergeron (**Pos**: CF, **Age**: 27, **Bats**: L)

	G	AB	R	H	D	T	HR	RBI	SB	BB	SO	Avg	OBP	Slg
'04	11	42	2	9	0	0	0	1	0	2	16	.214	.250	.214
Car.	308	1103	171	249	41	13	8	56	31	119	252	.226	.303	.308

It was Bergeron's fourth and final chance to earn an everyday outfield job with the Expos in 2004. After opening the season as Montreal's starting center-fielder, he futilely battled to keep his strikeouts down. He was traded to Milwaukee in June. 2005 Outlook: C

Ron Calloway (**Pos**: RF, **Age**: 28, **Bats**: L)

	G	AB	R	H	D	T	HR	RBI	SB	BB	SO	Avg	OBP	Slg
'04	46	84	4	14	2	0	1	10	2	5	22	.167	.211	.226
Car.	172	424	40	95	19	1	10	62	11	25	102	.224	.268	.344

Calloway hit himself right off the team with his 3-for-43 showing to begin the year. He was sent to Triple-A Edmonton, where he responded by hitting .290/.390/.452 in 186 at-bats, before being recalled to Montreal. He will compete for a reserve outfield spot this year. 2005 Outlook: C

Matt Cepicky (**Pos**: LF, **Age**: 27, **Bats**: L)

	G	AB	R	H	D	T	HR	RBI	SB	BB	SO	Avg	OBP	Slg
'04	32	60	4	13	4	0	1	3	1	1	18	.217	.230	.333
Car.	69	142	11	31	8	0	4	18	1	5	41	.218	.245	.359

In 2003, Cepicky did what management had asked of him and cut back on his strikeouts. But his power production plummeted. The power returned in 2004, as Cepicky consciously tried to lift more pitches. But the strikeouts also returned. 2005 Outlook: C

Roy Corcoran (**Pos**: RHP, **Age**: 24)

	W	L	Pct.	ERA	G	GS	Sv	IP	H	BB	SO	HR	Avg
'04	0	0	−	6.75	5	0	0	5.1	7	5	4	0	.304
Car.	0	0	−	3.55	10	0	0	12.2	14	8	6	0	.275

Corcoran, signed as an undrafted free agent, was remarkable in 2003. His 1.23 cumulative ERA through all three minor league levels, perfectly matched his major league earned run average. Walks were the problem last season, as he spent most of his time in Edmonton. 2005 Outlook: C

Einar Diaz (**Pos**: C, **Age**: 32, **Bats**: R)

	G	AB	R	H	D	T	HR	RBI	SB	BB	SO	Avg	OBP	Slg
'04	55	139	9	31	6	1	1	11	2	11	10	.223	.293	.302
Car.	612	1928	208	494	110	6	20	185	21	91	187	.256	.305	.351

The Nationals declined to pick up the 2005 option on Diaz after a dismal 2004 season. Serving as Brian Schneider's backup, Diaz did not hit his first home run until nearly September and managed to throw out less than 19 percent of basestealers. 2005 Outlook: C

Scott Downs (**Pos**: LHP, **Age**: 29)

	W	L	Pct.	ERA	G	GS	Sv	IP	H	BB	SO	HR	Avg
'04	3	6	.333	5.14	12	12	0	63.0	79	23	38	9	.310
Car.	7	10	.412	5.41	32	32	0	163.0	206	66	105	24	.312

Downs missed almost all of 2001-02 after undergoing Tommy John surgery. His return to prolonged major league action last year did not go off without a hitch. He posted a 8.38 road ERA in seven games, averaging just over four innings per start. 2005 Outlook: C

Jeremy Fikac (**Pos**: RHP, **Age**: 29)

	W	L	Pct.	ERA	G	GS	Sv	IP	H	BB	SO	HR	Avg
'04	1	2	.333	5.40	19	0	0	25.0	26	13	22	5	.274
Car.	7	10	.412	4.56	121	0	0	136.1	129	63	116	24	.248

A bullpen usually has at least one plus-minus guy who comes in to finish games out. Fikac was that guy for Montreal in 2004, except his appearances commonly occurred in minus games. The Expos lost 18 of 19 games in which Fikac pitched, and he was sent down the day after his only win. The Giants signed him to a minor league deal in December. 2005 Outlook: C

Shawn Hill (**Pos**: RHP, **Age**: 23)

	W	L	Pct.	ERA	G	GS	Sv	IP	H	BB	SO	HR	Avg
'04	1	2	.333	16.00	3	3	0	9.0	17	7	10	1	.415
Car.	1	2	.333	16.00	3	3	0	9.0	17	7	10	1	.415

Hill was destroyed in two of his three 2004 major league starts, lasting a total of four innings in the two appearances. It got worse when he learned he would need Tommy John surgery. The lone bright spot for the Canadian was his July victory over the Blue Jays. 2005 Outlook: D

Joe Horgan (Pos: LHP, Age: 27)

	W	L	Pct.	ERA	G	GS	Sv	IP	H	BB	SO	HR	Avg
'04	4	1	.800	3.15	47	0	2	40.0	35	22	30	5	.230
Car.	4	1	.800	3.15	47	0	2	40.0	35	22	30	5	.230

Horgan might have been the most pleasant surprise for the Expos. Traded from the Cardinals in May, he posted an ERA over a run and a half lower than his 4.77 minor league career mark. His hard slider frustrated left- and righthanded hitters alike. They hit only .230. 2005 Outlook: B

Josh Labandeira (Pos: SS, Age: 26, Bats: R)

	G	AB	R	H	D	T	HR	RBI	SB	BB	SO	Avg	OBP	Slg
'04	7	14	0	0	0	0	0	0	0	0	4	.000	.000	.000
Car.	7	14	0	0	0	0	0	0	0	0	4	.000	.000	.000

The Nationals solidified the shortstop position with the signing of Cristian Guzman. Labandeira had a two-week mini audition last September, but failed to get a hit or draw a walk in limited duty. He was not protected and was eligible for the Rule 5 draft. 2005 Outlook: C

Luis Lopez (Pos: 1B, Age: 31, Bats: R)

	G	AB	R	H	D	T	HR	RBI	SB	BB	SO	Avg	OBP	Slg
'04	11	26	0	4	0	0	0	0	0	0	9	.154	.185	.154
Car.	52	145	10	33	4	0	3	10	0	0	23	.228	.270	.317

A team leading 14 RBI during spring training earned Lopez a reserve spot on the Opening Day roster. A quick 4-for-26 to begin the season was enough to warrant a move the other way. He was sent packing for Edmonton and ended up in the Braves' organization by June. 2005 Outlook: C

Henry Mateo (Pos: 2B, Age: 28, Bats: B)

	G	AB	R	H	D	T	HR	RBI	SB	BB	SO	Avg	OBP	Slg
'04	40	44	3	12	2	0	0	0	2	1	9	.273	.289	.318
Car.	167	230	34	56	6	2	0	7	15	14	54	.243	.296	.287

Mateo suffered all season through chronic shoulder pain and the lingering effects of a broken hand in April. His second-half callup was unremarkable, with most of his at-bats coming as a pinch-hitter. Dr. James Andrews repaired the torn shoulder cartilage in September, and Mateo will play in South Korea in 2005. 2005 Outlook: D

Washington Nationals Minor League Prospects

Organization Overview:

The Nationals have done a pretty remarkable job with their system, considering their shoestring budget and the exodus of talent they've had to accommodate over the last decade. With the smallest scouting staff of any big league team, their amateur drafts have focused on players who can help them quickly, like 2003 draftee and current closer Chad Cordero. Southpaw Bill Bray topped their draft list this year and figures to ascend quickly. The team bolstered its system with several trades, and a number of these youngsters will compete for starting jobs. It hasn't been all good news, however, as top pitching prospect Clint Everts underwent Tommy John surgery in September and will miss all of 2005.

Francis Beltran

Position: P
Bats: R **Throws:** R
Ht: 6' 6" **Wt:** 230

Opening Day Age: 25
Born: 11/29/79 in Santo Domingo, DR

Recent Statistics

	W	L	ERA	G	GS	Sv	IP	H	R	BB	SO	HR
2004 AAA Iowa	0	0	2.84	6	0	4	6.1	5	2	1	6	1
2004 AAA Edmonton	0	0	1.80	5	0	3	5.0	4	1	2	6	0
2004 NL Chicago	2	2	4.63	34	0	0	35.0	27	19	22	40	8
2004 NL Montreal	0	0	7.53	11	0	1	14.1	20	12	5	8	3

Beltran spent most of the season in the Cubs' bullpen, but finished it in Montreal as a result of the four-team deal that sent Nomar Garciaparra to the Cubs and Orlando Cabrera to the Red Sox. Shoulder tendinitis reduced Beltran's effectiveness after the deal and ultimately sent him to the DL. He returned in September and was the last pitcher to throw a pitch in an Expos uniform. He has two fastballs—a four-seamer that can touch 95 MPH and a sinker around 89—as well as a curve, slider and change. He's worked out of the pen since 2001 and is viewed as a potential closer. The buzz surrounding his excellent strikeout rate is tempered by his struggles with the longball.

Larry Broadway

Position: 1B
Bats: L **Throws:** L
Ht: 6' 4" **Wt:** 225

Opening Day Age: 24
Born: 12/17/80 in Miami, FL

Recent Statistics

	G	AB	R	H	D	T	HR	RBI	SB	BB	SO	Avg
2003 A Savannah	83	290	56	89	25	4	14	51	3	44	70	.307
2003 A Brevard Cty	25	76	8	17	7	1	1	7	0	18	20	.224
2003 AA Harrisburg	21	78	13	25	3	0	5	18	0	7	15	.321
2004 AA Harrisburg	131	477	70	129	20	0	22	72	2	68	103	.270

Broadway regressed slightly at the plate after climbing three levels in 2003, but his tape-measure power has continued to develop. Although he's a decent fielder with a strong arm, he probably doesn't have enough speed to make the move to the outfield. With as many young players as the Nationals have at the corners, there's certainly no urgency to rush the 2002 third-round pick out of Duke University. Nick Johnson's frequent trips to the disabled list could provide Broadway an opportunity to enter the first-base picture this year, although it probably will be 2006 before he makes the majors for good.

Ryan Church

Position: OF
Bats: L **Throws:** L
Ht: 6' 1" **Wt:** 190

Opening Day Age: 26
Born: 10/14/78 in Santa Barbara, CA

Recent Statistics

	G	AB	R	H	D	T	HR	RBI	SB	BB	SO	Avg
2004 AAA Edmonton	98	347	74	119	29	8	17	78	0	51	62	.343
2004 NL Montreal	30	63	6	11	1	0	1	6	0	7	16	.175

Cleveland traded both Church and Maicer Izturis to the Expos for lefthander Scott Stewart in January 2004. After a disappointing '03, the 14th-round pick from 2000 finished third in the batting race in the Triple-A Pacific Coast League, good enough to be named the Expos' top minor leaguer. Shortly after his callup in late August, he was sidelined with a severe case of the flu. Sapped of his strength, he never got back on track. He's a good contact hitter with excellent bat speed and a good eye, but was overprotective of the outer edge of the plate, often getting himself out when pitchers went outside. He is fundamentally sound in the outfield, with average range but a very strong and accurate arm.

Brendan Harris

Position: 3B
Bats: R **Throws:** R
Ht: 6' 1" **Wt:** 200

Opening Day Age: 24
Born: 8/26/80 in Albany, NY

Recent Statistics

	G	AB	R	H	D	T	HR	RBI	SB	BB	SO	Avg
2004 AAA Iowa	69	254	48	79	21	1	11	35	0	16	40	.311
2004 AAA Edmonton	33	123	20	35	6	0	6	24	0	10	21	.285
2004 NL Chicago	3	9	0	2	1	0	0	1	0	1	1	.222
2004 NL Montreal	20	50	4	8	2	0	1	2	0	2	11	.160

Like Francis Beltran, Harris also came to the Expos in the Nomar Garciaparra deadline deal. Initially it was a great trade for Harris, but Washington more recently has signed Vinny Castilla to play third base. Harris is a patient hitter who looked very comfortable at the plate for a rookie. Pitchers were successful working him away with breaking pitches, but he's a discerning hitter who will learn when to lay off. The Expos tried him both at second and third, but he didn't look especially comfortable at either spot, especially on the pivot at second. He has the arm and range to become a good third baseman but needs to play more aggressively.

Mike Hinckley

Position: P **Opening Day Age:** 22
Bats: R **Throws:** L **Born:** 10/5/82 in
Ht: 6' 3" **Wt:** 170 Oklahoma City, OK

Recent Statistics

	W	L	ERA	G	GS	Sv	IP	H	R	BB	SO	HR
2003 A Savannah	9	5	3.64	23	23	0	121.0	124	54	41	111	4
2003 A Brevard Cty	4	0	0.72	4	4	0	25.0	14	2	1	23	1
2004 A Brevard Cty	6	2	2.61	10	10	0	62.0	47	23	18	51	6
2004 AA Harrisburg	5	2	2.87	16	16	0	94.0	83	34	23	80	5

With Clint Everts going down for the 2005 season, Hinckley will be the focus of attention as the Nationals' top pitching prospect. The third-round pick in 2001 went 11-4 with an ERA of 2.77, spending the year at high Class-A and Double-A. Known for his near-obsessive preparation that includes visualizing every pitch from the first batter to the postgame handshake, Hinckley has good command of a low-90s fastball, a two-plane curve and a change. As good as Hinckley's command and stuff are, scouts are even more impressed by his confidence pitching to the inside corner. Barring any setbacks, the lefty should figure in the Nationals' starting picture by the end of 2005.

Gary Majewski

Position: P **Opening Day Age:** 25
Bats: R **Throws:** R **Born:** 2/26/80 in
Ht: 6' 1" **Wt:** 215 Houston, TX

Recent Statistics

	W	L	ERA	G	GS	Sv	IP	H	R	BB	SO	HR
2004 AAA Charlotte	3	3	3.19	35	0	14	42.1	30	16	16	41	2
2004 AAA Edmonton	1	2	4.11	14	0	1	15.1	18	8	8	17	0
2004 NL Montreal	0	1	3.86	16	0	1	21.0	28	15	5	12	2

Majewski was another of the many young players the Expos acquired last year, as he and Jon Rauch came to Montreal in exchange for Carl Everett. With a compact three-quarters delivery, he throws a fastball in the mid-90s, a hard slider and an occasional changeup. He likes to pitch inside and work his fastball up and down to set up the slider. While he's been used primarily as a reliever, he might be able to make the transition to starter—he pitched most effectively with at least two days' rest, and he has a decent move to first base. He also can close, having saved 15 games in Triple-A last year as well as the Expos' final win of the season.

Val Pascucci

Position: OF **Opening Day Age:** 26
Bats: R **Throws:** R **Born:** 11/17/78 in
Ht: 6' 6" **Wt:** 235 Bellflower, CA

Recent Statistics

	G	AB	R	H	D	T	HR	RBI	SB	BB	SO	Avg
2004 AAA Edmonton	109	392	83	117	32	1	25	92	9	78	95	.298
2004 NL Montreal	32	62	6	11	1	0	2	6	1	10	22	.177

The 15th-round pick from the 1999 draft got a month-long callup at the end of April before returning to Triple-A Edmonton for his second tour there. In September, he was again recalled, but was largely relegated to a part-time/pinch-hitting role as the season concluded. Pascucci is a tremendously patient hitter with power. However, he offers pitchers a tall strike zone and doesn't have a strong command of the outer half of the plate. In addition, his swing can get a little long. He doesn't have good range in the outfield, but he does have a gun for an arm. In December, Pascucci was released and signed to play in Japan.

Jon Rauch

Position: P **Opening Day Age:** 26
Bats: R **Throws:** R **Born:** 9/27/78 in
Ht: 6' 11" **Wt:** 260 Louisville, KY

Recent Statistics

	W	L	ERA	G	GS	Sv	IP	H	R	BB	SO	HR
2004 AAA Charlotte	6	3	3.11	14	13	0	72.1	57	27	25	61	9
2004 AAA Edmonton	1	1	4.50	3	3	0	18.0	17	9	2	13	3
2004 AL Chicago	1	1	6.23	2	2	0	8.2	16	6	4	4	0
2004 NL Montreal	3	0	1.54	9	2	0	23.1	14	4	7	18	1

Rauch is the tallest player to ever put on a major league uniform. His release point is almost over the infield grass, making his low-90s fastball seem 1-2 MPH faster than it actually is. He also delivers a curve, slider and change over the top on a downward plane, giving current batters a taste of what hitting was like in 1968, before the mounds were lowered. His biggest issue is maintaining consistent mechanics. He tends to leave the ball up when he doesn't follow through. As one might expect, he has a huge wingspan when it comes to fielding, but he also moves surprisingly well. He takes good-looking hacks at the plate, and his first career homer came off Roger Clemens last year.

Others to Watch

Lefthander **Bill Bray** (21) signed too late to do much in any of the regular-season leagues, but he pitched reasonably well in the Arizona Fall League. With good command of a fastball that reaches 95 MPH, he has struck out a batter per inning against tough competition. . . 2002 top draft pick **Clint Everts** (20) figured to make his major league debut no later than 2006 after dominating Class-A and high Class-A hitters last year. But the righthander will miss all of 2005 recovering from surgery to repair a damaged ligament in his elbow. . . RHP **Josh Karp's** (25) season was a mixed bag. The Expos' top pick in 2001 showed significant improvement in his strikeout rate while advancing to Triple-A, but he was hit quite hard and finished with an ERA of 5.95. His combination of a mid-90s fastball, biting curve and plus change should yield better results. . . Outfielder **Jerry Owens** (24) doesn't have much power, but he does have a good eye at the plate, makes contact and gets on base enough to take advantage of very good speed. He posted a .365 on-base percentage and stole 30 bases last season in the Class-A Sally League, then continued the good work in the Arizona Fall League.

2004 American League Leaders

Batters

Batting Average
minimum 502 PA

Ichiro Suzuki	.372
Melvin Mora	.340
Vladimir Guerrero	.337

Home Runs

Manny Ramirez	43
Paul Konerko	41
David Ortiz	41

Runs Batted In

Miguel Tejada	150
David Ortiz	139
Manny Ramirez	130

Games Played

Hideki Matsui	162
Miguel Tejada	162
Ichiro Suzuki	161

At-Bats

Ichiro Suzuki	704
Michael Young	690
Miguel Tejada	653

Runs Scored

Vladimir Guerrero	124
Johnny Damon	123
Gary Sheffield	117

Hits

Ichiro Suzuki	262
Michael Young	216
Vladimir Guerrero	206

Singles

Ichiro Suzuki	225
Michael Young	152
Mark Kotsay	135

Doubles

Brian Roberts	50
Ronnie Belliard	48
David Ortiz	47

Triples

Carl Crawford	19
Chone Figgins	17
Carlos Guillen	10

Stolen Bases

Carl Crawford	59
Ichiro Suzuki	36
Chone Figgins	34

Caught Stealing

Carl Crawford	15
3 players tied with	13

Walks

Eric Chavez	95
Gary Sheffield	92
3 players tied with	88

Intentional Walks

Ichiro Suzuki	19
Rafael Palmeiro	15
Manny Ramirez	15

Hit by Pitch

Travis Hafner	17
Kevin Millar	17
Jose Guillen	15

Strikeouts

Mark Bellhorn	177
Hank Blalock	149
Carlos Pena	146

GDP

Jorge Posada	24
Miguel Tejada	24
2 players tied with	23

Sacrifice Hits

Omar Vizquel	20
Derek Jeter	16
Brian Roberts	15

Sacrifice Flies

Miguel Tejada	14
Carlos Delgado	11
Rafael Palmeiro	9

Plate Appearances

Ichiro Suzuki	762
Michael Young	739
Brian Roberts	736

Times on Base

Ichiro Suzuki	315
Gary Sheffield	269
Johnny Damon	267

Total Bases

Vladimir Guerrero	366
David Ortiz	351
Miguel Tejada	349

Slugging Percentage
minimum 502 PA

Manny Ramirez	.613
David Ortiz	.603
Vladimir Guerrero	.598

Slugging vs. LHP
minimum 125 PA

Vladimir Guerrero	.723
Alex Rodriguez	.659
Kevin Mench	.646

Slugging vs. RHP
minimum 377 PA

Travis Hafner	.690
David Ortiz	.671
Manny Ramirez	.605

Cleanup Slugging
minimum 150 PA

Manny Ramirez	.621
Miguel Tejada	.591
David Ortiz	.570

On-Base Percentage
minimum 502 PA

Melvin Mora	.419
Ichiro Suzuki	.414
Travis Hafner	.410

OBP vs. LHP
minimum 125 PA

Manny Ramirez	.446
Ichiro Suzuki	.444
Vladimir Guerrero	.434

OBP vs. RHP
minimum 377 PA

Travis Hafner	.433
Melvin Mora	.419
Erubiel Durazo	.419

Leadoff Hitters OBP
minimum 150 PA

Ichiro Suzuki	.418
Johnny Damon	.385
Ronnie Belliard	.384

AB per HR
minimum 502 PA

Manny Ramirez	13.2
Paul Konerko	13.7
David Ortiz	14.2

Ground/Fly Ratio
minimum 502 PA

Ichiro Suzuki	3.31
Reed Johnson	2.12
Larry Bigbie	2.08

% Extra Bases Taken
minimum 40 Opp to Advance

Laynce Nix	67.5
Carlos Guillen	66.7
Vladimir Guerrero	65.4

% Runs/Time on Base
minimum 502 PA

Jose Valentin	51.0
Aaron Rowand	49.2
Carlos Pena	47.1

SB Success %
minimum 20 SB Attempts

Lew Ford	90.9
Alex Rodriguez	87.5
Jeff DaVanon	85.7

Steals of Third

Derek Jeter	12
Chone Figgins	10
Carl Crawford	9

AVG Scoring Position
minimum 100 PA

Ichiro Suzuki	.372
Ivan Rodriguez	.361
Shannon Stewart	.359

AVG Late & Close
minimum 50 PA

Ichiro Suzuki	.393
Hideki Matsui	.378
Chris Gomez	.370

AVG Bases Loaded
minimum 10 PA

Carlos Guillen	.667
Ben Broussard	.636
2 players tied with	.615

GDP/GDP Opp
minimum 50 PA

Eric Munson	0.02
Gary Matthews Jr.	0.02
Dee Brown	0.02

AVG vs. LHP
minimum 125 PA

Ichiro Suzuki	.404
Jason Varitek	.350
Alex Sanchez	.348

AVG vs. RHP
minimum 377 PA

Ichiro Suzuki	.359
Melvin Mora	.352
Travis Hafner	.344

AVG at Home
minimum 251 PA

Melvin Mora	.356
Ivan Rodriguez	.354
Kevin Millar	.350

AVG on the Road
minimum 251 PA

Ichiro Suzuki	.405
Vladimir Guerrero	.335
Hideki Matsui	.327

AVG on 3-1 Count
minimum 10 PA

Jorge Cantu	.833
Ross Gload	.833
Eric Munson	.750

AVG with Two Strikes
minimum 150 PA

Melvin Mora	.293
Ichiro Suzuki	.284
Jerry Hairston Jr.	.280

AVG on 0-2 Count
minimum 20 PA

Ken Harvey	.354
Jerry Hairston Jr.	.343
Chone Figgins	.333

AVG on Full Count
minimum 40 PA

Angel Berroa	.500
Hideki Matsui	.375
Omar Vizquel	.368

Pitches Seen

Brian Roberts	2908
Johnny Damon	2893
Casey Blake	2844

Pitches per PA
minimum 502 PA

Casey Blake	4.26
Jermaine Dye	4.25
Bobby Crosby	4.17

% Pitches Taken
minimum 1500 Pitches Seen

John Olerud	64.7
Scott Hatteberg	63.9
Bobby Higginson	62.5

% Swings that Missed
minimum 1500 Pitches Seen

David Eckstein	7.6
Scott Hatteberg	7.9
David DeJesus	8.5

% Swings Put in Play
minimum 1500 Pitches Seen

Scott Hatteberg	55.6
Eric Young	55.3
Cristian Guzman	54.7

Bunts in Play

Alex Sanchez	72
Chone Figgins	31
2 players tied with	29

Pitchers

Earned Run Average
minimum 162 IP

Johan Santana	2.61
Curt Schilling	3.26
Jake Westbrook	3.38

Wins

Curt Schilling	21
Johan Santana	20
2 players tied with	18

Losses

Darrell May	19
Ryan Franklin	16
3 players tied with	15

Won-Lost Percentage
minimum 15 decisions

Curt Schilling	.778
Johan Santana	.769
Mark Mulder	.680

Games

Paul Quantrill	86
Tom Gordon	80
Juan Rincon	77

Games Started

Mark Buehrle	35
Kenny Rogers	35
5 players tied with	34

Complete Games

Mark Mulder	5
Sidney Ponson	5
Jake Westbrook	5

Shutouts

Jeremy Bonderman	2
Tim Hudson	2
Sidney Ponson	2

Games Finished

Mariano Rivera	69
Francisco Cordero	63
Joe Nathan	63

Innings Pitched

Mark Buehrle	245.1
Johan Santana	228.0
Curt Schilling	226.2

Hits Allowed

Sidney Ponson	265
Mark Buehrle	257
Carlos Silva	255

Batters Faced

Mark Buehrle	1016
Sidney Ponson	954
Mark Mulder	952

Runs Allowed

Derek Lowe	138
Sidney Ponson	136
Darrell May	130

Earned Runs Allowed

Sidney Ponson	127
Jon Garland	118
Jamie Moyer	117

Home Runs Allowed

Jamie Moyer	44
Bartolo Colon	38
Darrell May	38

Walks Allowed

Miguel Batista	96
Victor Zambrano	96
2 players tied with	89

Hit Batsmen

Bronson Arroyo	20
3 players tied with	16

Strikeouts

Johan Santana	265
Pedro Martinez	227
Curt Schilling	203

Wild Pitches

Jose Contreras	17
Kevin Gregg	13
3 players tied with	12

Balks

Ted Lilly	4
3 players tied with	3

Run Support per 9 IP
minimum 162 IP

Curt Schilling	7.54
Derek Lowe	7.29
Bartolo Colon	7.00

Baserunners per 9 IP
minimum 162 IP

Johan Santana	8.6
Curt Schilling	9.8
Brad Radke	10.7

Opposition AVG
minimum 162 IP

Johan Santana	.192
Ted Lilly	.230
Pedro Martinez	.238

Opposition SLG
minimum 162 IP

Johan Santana	.315
Rich Harden	.366
Tim Hudson	.366

Opposition OBP
minimum 162 IP

Johan Santana	.249
Curt Schilling	.271
Brad Radke	.291

Home Runs per 9 IP
minimum 162 IP

Tim Hudson	0.38
Ryan Drese	0.69
Derek Lowe	0.74

Strikeouts per 9 IP
minimum 162 IP

Johan Santana	10.46
Pedro Martinez	9.41
Kelvim Escobar	8.25

Walks per 9 IP
minimum 162 IP

Jon Lieber	0.9
Brad Radke	1.1
Curt Schilling	1.4

K/BB Ratio
minimum 162 IP

Curt Schilling	5.80
Jon Lieber	5.67
Brad Radke	5.50

Steals Allowed

Derek Lowe	34
Tim Wakefield	33
Jose Contreras	29

Caught Stealing Off

Mark Mulder	13
4 players tied with	11

SB % Allowed
minimum 162 IP

Brian Anderson	20.0
Kenny Rogers	28.6
Javier Vazquez	28.6

GDPs Induced

Mark Mulder	37
Sidney Ponson	36
Mark Buehrle	33

GDPs per 9 IP
minimum 162 IP

Sidney Ponson	1.50
Mark Mulder	1.48
Derek Lowe	1.38

GDP/GDP Opp
minimum 30 BFP

Todd Williams	21.9
Matt Miller	21.2
Mark Mulder	20.0

Ground/Fly Ratio Off
minimum 162 IP

Derek Lowe	2.9
Jake Westbrook	2.7
Tim Hudson	2.5

AVG Allowed Sc Pos
minimum 125 BFP

Victor Zambrano	.157
Johan Santana	.165
Pedro Martinez	.197

Pitches Thrown

Mark Buehrle	3697
Barry Zito	3688
Kenny Rogers	3506

Pitches per Batter
minimum 162 IP

Carlos Silva	3.33
Jon Lieber	3.40
Ryan Drese	3.46

Pickoff Throws

Ryan Franklin	219
Barry Zito	151
Kelvim Escobar	150

ERA at Home
minimum 81 IP

Jake Westbrook	2.36
Johan Santana	2.62
Dewon Brazelton	2.90

ERA on the Road
minimum 81 IP

Johan Santana	2.58
Mark Buehrle	2.63
Mark Redman	2.90

AVG vs. LHB
minimum 125 BFP

Juan Rincon	.148
Keith Foulke	.185
Tom Gordon	.185

AVG vs. RHB
minimum 225 BFP

Johan Santana	.191
Victor Zambrano	.219
Jeremy Bonderman	.223

Relief ERA
minimum 50 relief IP

Joe Nathan	1.62
Francisco Rodriguez	1.82
Mariano Rivera	1.94

Relief Wins

Juan Rincon	11
Tom Gordon	9
Scot Shields	8

Relief Losses

Justin Speier	8
3 players tied with	7

Saves

Mariano Rivera	53
Francisco Cordero	49
Joe Nathan	44

Blown Saves

Esteban Yan	10
Jason Grimsley	9
6 players tied with	7

Save Opportunities

Mariano Rivera	57
Francisco Cordero	54
Joe Nathan	47

Save Percentage
minimum 20 SvOp

Shingo Takatsu	95.0
Joe Nathan	93.6
Mariano Rivera	93.0

Holds

Tom Gordon	36
Francisco Rodriguez	27
Paul Quantrill	22

Relief Innings

Scot Shields	105.1
Justin Duchscherer	96.1
Paul Quantrill	95.1

Relief AVG Allowed
minimum 50 relief IP

F. Rodriguez	.172
Tom Gordon	.180
Juan Rincon	.181

Relief Runners/9 IP
minimum 50 relief IP

Tom Gordon	8.0
Joe Nathan	9.1
Shingo Takatsu	9.1

Relief Strikeouts/9 IP
minimum 50 relief IP

F. Rodriguez	13.2
Octavio Dotel	12.8
B.J. Ryan	12.6

% Inh Runners Scored
minimum 30 inh runners

Nate Field	14.3
Doug Brocail	15.2
Tom Gordon	16.2

1st Batter AVG
minimum 40 relief first BFP

Ron Villone	.093
Shingo Takatsu	.143
Chad Bradford	.145

Fielding

Errors by Pitcher

John Parrish	6
3 players tied with	5

Errors by Catcher

Ivan Rodriguez	11
Jorge Posada	9
Gregg Zaun	8

Errors by First Base

Scott Hatteberg	10
Mark Teixeira	10
Rafael Palmeiro	8

Errors by Second Base

Alfonso Soriano	23
Ronnie Belliard	14
Bret Boone	14

Errors by Third Base

Casey Blake	26
Melvin Mora	21
Hank Blalock	17

Errors by Shortstop

Angel Berroa	28
Julio Lugo	25
Miguel Tejada	24

Errors by Left Field

Craig Monroe	8
Hideki Matsui	7
Manny Ramirez	7

Errors by Center Field

Alex Sanchez	9
Rocco Baldelli	8
2 players tied with	6

Errors by Right Field

Jose Cruz Jr.	10
Vladimir Guerrero	9
Bobby Higginson	6

% CS by Catchers
minimum 70 SB Attempts

Gregg Zaun	25.9
Jorge Posada	25.6
Javy Lopez	22.7

2004 National League Leaders

Batters

Batting Average
minimum 502 PA

Barry Bonds	.362
Todd Helton	.347
Mark Loretta	.335

Home Runs

Adrian Beltre	48
Adam Dunn	46
Albert Pujols	46

Runs Batted In

Vinny Castilla	131
Scott Rolen	124
Albert Pujols	123

Games Played

Steve Finley	162
Juan Pierre	162
2 players tied with	161

At-Bats

Juan Pierre	678
Cesar Izturis	670
Jimmy Rollins	657

Runs Scored

Albert Pujols	133
Barry Bonds	129
Jimmy Rollins	119

Hits

Juan Pierre	221
Mark Loretta	208
Jack Wilson	201

Singles

Juan Pierre	184
Cesar Izturis	148
Jason Kendall	148

Doubles

Lyle Overbay	53
Albert Pujols	51
Todd Helton	49

Triples

Juan Pierre	12
Jimmy Rollins	12
Jack Wilson	12

Stolen Bases

Scott Podsednik	70
Juan Pierre	45
Bobby Abreu	40

Caught Stealing

Juan Pierre	24
Scott Podsednik	13
2 players tied with	11

Walks

Barry Bonds	232
3 players tied with	127

Intentional Walks

Barry Bonds	120
Jim Thome	26
Todd Helton	19

Hit by Pitch

Craig Wilson	30
Jason LaRue	24
Jason Kendall	19

Strikeouts

Adam Dunn	195
Craig Wilson	169
Corey Patterson	168

GDP

A.J. Pierzynski	27
Aramis Ramirez	25
Andruw Jones	24

Sacrifice Hits

Royce Clayton	24
Adam Everett	22
3 players tied with	15

Sacrifice Flies

Mark Loretta	16
Jeff Kent	11
2 players tied with	10

Plate Appearances

Juan Pierre	748
Cesar Izturis	728
Jimmy Rollins	725

Times on Base

Barry Bonds	376
Todd Helton	320
Lance Berkman	309

Total Bases

Albert Pujols	389
Adrian Beltre	376
Todd Helton	339

Slugging Percentage
minimum 502 PA

Barry Bonds	.812
Albert Pujols	.657
Jim Edmonds	.643

Slugging vs. LHP
minimum 125 PA

Albert Pujols	.741
Mike Lowell	.672
Jose Hernandez	.627

Slugging vs. RHP
minimum 377 PA

Barry Bonds	.957
Adrian Beltre	.672
Todd Helton	.669

Cleanup Slugging
minimum 150 PA

Barry Bonds	.817
Adrian Beltre	.657
Moises Alou	.612

On-Base Percentage
minimum 502 PA

Barry Bonds	.609
Todd Helton	.469
Lance Berkman	.450

OBP vs. LHP
minimum 125 PA

Barry Bonds	.524
Albert Pujols	.465
Phil Nevin	.431

OBP vs. RHP
minimum 377 PA

Barry Bonds	.652
Todd Helton	.492
Lance Berkman	.463

Leadoff Hitters OBP
minimum 150 PA

Jason Kendall	.404
Ryan Freel	.389
Juan Pierre	.382

AB per HR
minimum 502 PA

Barry Bonds	8.3
Jim Edmonds	11.9
Jim Thome	12.1

Ground/Fly Ratio
minimum 502 PA

Luis Castillo	3.63
Juan Pierre	2.36
Royce Clayton	2.34

% Extra Bases Taken
minimum 40 Opp to Advance

Rafael Furcal	73.2
Aaron Miles	71.4
Matt Holliday	70.7

% Runs/Time on Base
minimum 502 PA

Ray Durham	48.5
Rafael Furcal	47.7
Jimmy Rollins	47.6

SB Success %
minimum 20 SB Attempts

Carlos Beltran	100.0
Dave Roberts	97.1
Jose Reyes	90.5

Steals of Third

Carlos Beltran	11
Scott Podsednik	10
Juan Pierre	8

AVG Scoring Position
minimum 100 PA

Barry Bonds	.394
J.T. Snow	.361
Scott Rolen	.358

AVG Late & Close
minimum 50 PA

M. Grudzielanek	.457
Danny Bautista	.386
Morgan Ensberg	.383

AVG Bases Loaded
minimum 10 PA

Scott Rolen	.583
Paul Lo Duca	.563
Phil Nevin	.556

GDP/GDP Opp
minimum 50 PA

Jayson Werth	0.01
Rob Mackowiak	0.03
Terrmel Sledge	0.03

AVG vs. LHP
minimum 125 PA

Albert Pujols	**.379**
Edgar Renteria	.366
Mark Loretta	.352

AVG vs. RHP
minimum 377 PA

Barry Bonds	**.395**
Todd Helton	.360
Adrian Beltre	.347

AVG at Home
minimum 251 PA

Barry Bonds	**.412**
Todd Helton	.368
Shea Hillenbrand	.347

AVG on the Road
minimum 251 PA

Mark Loretta	**.368**
Sean Casey	.361
Johnny Estrada	.351

AVG on 3-1 Count
minimum 10 PA

Robin Ventura	**1.000**
Johnny Estrada	**1.000**
2 players tied with	.800

AVG with Two Strikes
minimum 150 PA

Shea Hillenbrand	**.302**
Tony Womack	.294
Barry Bonds	.286

AVG on 0-2 Count
minimum 20 PA

Jesse Garcia	**.364**
Jason Kendall	.341
Mark Loretta	.311

AVG on Full Count
minimum 40 PA

Shea Hillenbrand	**.444**
Sean Burroughs	.388
Juan Pierre	.381

Pitches Seen

Bobby Abreu	**3077**
Brad Wilkerson	2954
Adam Dunn	2888

Pitches per PA
minimum 502 PA

Bobby Abreu	**4.32**
Brad Wilkerson	4.29
Adam Dunn	4.24

% Pitches Taken
minimum 1500 Pitches Seen

Barry Bonds	**71.9**
Todd Zeile	66.4
D'Angelo Jimenez	65.1

% Swings that Missed
minimum 1500 Pitches Seen

Juan Pierre	**5.6**
Placido Polanco	7.2
Jason Kendall	8.1

% Swings Put in Play
minimum 1500 Pitches Seen

Juan Pierre	**59.1**
Endy Chavez	57.1
Placido Polanco	57.1

Bunts in Play

Juan Pierre	**66**
Royce Clayton	52
Adam Everett	43

Pitchers

Earned Run Average
minimum 162 IP

Jake Peavy	**2.27**
Randy Johnson	2.60
Ben Sheets	2.70

Wins

Roy Oswalt	**20**
3 players tied with	18

Losses

Brandon Webb	**16**
Casey Fossum	15
Livan Hernandez	15

Won-Lost Percentage
minimum 15 decisions

Roger Clemens	**.818**
Chris Carpenter	.750
Jose Lima	.722

Games

Jim Brower	**89**
Ray King	86
3 players tied with	84

Games Started

4 players tied with	**35**

Complete Games

Livan Hernandez	**9**
Cory Lidle	5
Ben Sheets	5

Shutouts

Cory Lidle	**3**
Jason Schmidt	**3**
6 players tied with	2

Games Finished

Jason Isringhausen	**66**
Jose Mesa	65
John Smoltz	61

Innings Pitched

Livan Hernandez	**255.0**
Randy Johnson	245.2
2 players tied with	237.0

Hits Allowed

Jason Jennings	**241**
Livan Hernandez	234
Roy Oswalt	233

Batters Faced

Livan Hernandez	**1053**
Roy Oswalt	983
Randy Johnson	964

Runs Allowed

Shawn Estes	**133**
Jason Jennings	125
Cory Lidle	123

Earned Runs Allowed

Shawn Estes	**131**
Jason Jennings	123
Cory Lidle	115

Home Runs Allowed

Eric Milton	**43**
Greg Maddux	35
Matt Morris	35

Walks Allowed

Brandon Webb	**119**
Russ Ortiz	112
Shawn Estes	105

Hit Batsmen

Carlos Zambrano	**20**
Jerome Williams	17
Jeff Weaver	14

Strikeouts

Randy Johnson	**290**
Ben Sheets	264
Jason Schmidt	251

Wild Pitches

Brandon Webb	**17**
Matt Clement	14
Woody Williams	12

Balks

Carl Pavano	**3**
7 players tied with	2

Run Support per 9 IP
minimum 162 IP

Kazuhisa Ishii	**6.70**
Shawn Estes	6.55
Eric Milton	6.54

Baserunners per 9 IP
minimum 162 IP

Randy Johnson	**8.5**
Ben Sheets	9.0
Jason Schmidt	9.8

Opposition AVG
minimum 162 IP

Randy Johnson	**.197**
Jason Schmidt	.202
Oliver Perez	.207

Opposition SLG
minimum 162 IP

Randy Johnson	**.315**
Jason Schmidt	.323
Roger Clemens	.329

Opposition OBP
minimum 162 IP

Randy Johnson	**.241**
Ben Sheets	.255
Jason Schmidt	.272

Home Runs per 9 IP
minimum 162 IP

Jaret Wright	**0.53**
Carlos Zambrano	0.60
Doug Davis	0.61

Strikeouts per 9 IP
minimum 162 IP

Oliver Perez	**10.97**
Randy Johnson	10.62
Jason Schmidt	10.04

Walks per 9 IP
minimum 162 IP

David Wells	**0.9**
Ben Sheets	1.2
Greg Maddux	1.4

K/BB Ratio
minimum 162 IP

Ben Sheets	**8.25**
Randy Johnson	6.59
David Wells	5.05

Steals Allowed

Brandon Webb	**31**
Jason Schmidt	28
Greg Maddux	26

Caught Stealing Off

Greg Maddux	**12**
3 players tied with	10

SB % Allowed
minimum 162 IP

Chris Carpenter	**0.0**
Kirk Rueter	25.0
Tom Glavine	46.7

GDPs Induced

Shawn Estes	**34**
Josh Fogg	27
Matt Morris	26

GDPs per 9 IP
minimum 162 IP

Shawn Estes	**1.5**
Josh Fogg	1.4
Kirk Rueter	1.2

GDP/GDP Opp
minimum 30 BFP

Amaury Telemaco	**22.6**
Matt Wise	21.9
Chad Harville	20.9

Ground/Fly Ratio Off
minimum 162 IP

Brandon Webb	**3.6**
Jason Marquis	2.2
Mike Hampton	2.0

AVG Allowed Sc Pos
minimum 125 BFP

Al Leiter	**.173**
Carlos Zambrano	.179
Oliver Perez	.180

Pitches Thrown

Livan Hernandez	**3926**
Randy Johnson	3633
Jason Schmidt	3606

Pitches per Batter
minimum 162 IP

Greg Maddux	**3.35**
Jose Lima	3.44
Cory Lidle	3.44

Pickoff Throws

Steve Trachsel	**194**
Al Leiter	189
Russ Ortiz	161

ERA at Home
minimum 81 IP

Oliver Perez	**2.21**
Jake Peavy	2.21
Carlos Zambrano	2.38

ERA on the Road
minimum 81 IP

Jake Peavy	**2.33**
Randy Johnson	2.77
Ben Sheets	2.81

AVG vs. LHB
minimum 125 BFP

Ray King	**.150**
Luis Vizcaino	.163
Randy Johnson	.163

AVG vs. RHB
minimum 225 BFP

Josh Beckett	**.192**
Randy Johnson	.204
Oliver Perez	.204

Relief ERA
minimum 50 relief IP

Armando Benitez	**1.29**
Ryan Madson	1.65
Akinori Otsuka	1.75

Relief Wins

Todd Jones	**11**
Ryan Madson	9
Guillermo Mota	9

Relief Losses

Luis Ayala	**12**
Shawn Chacon	9
3 players tied with	8

Saves

Armando Benitez	**47**
Jason Isringhausen	**47**
Eric Gagne	45

Blown Saves

Shawn Chacon	**9**
Danny Graves	**9**
LaTroy Hawkins	**9**

Save Opportunities

Jason Isringhausen	**54**
Armando Benitez	51
Danny Graves	50

Save Percentage
minimum 20 SvOp

Eric Gagne	**95.7**
Armando Benitez	92.2
Trevor Hoffman	91.1

Holds

Akinori Otsuka	**34**
Ray King	31
Chris Reitsma	31

Relief Innings

Guillermo Mota	**96.2**
Brad Lidge	94.2
Jim Brower	93.0

Relief AVG Allowed
minimum 50 relief IP

Armando Benitez	**.152**
Brad Lidge	.174
Eric Gagne	.181

Relief Runners/9 IP
minimum 50 relief IP

Armando Benitez	**7.4**
Trevor Hoffman	8.2
Eric Gagne	8.7

Relief Strikeouts/9 IP
minimum 50 relief IP

Brad Lidge	**14.9**
Eric Gagne	12.5
Darren Dreifort	11.2

% Inh Runners Scored
minimum 30 inh runners

Brad Lidge	**6.7**
Javier Lopez	13.0
Scott Eyre	15.6

1st Batter AVG
minimum 40 relief first BFP

Joe Horgan	**.100**
Kiko Calero	.108
Brad Lidge	.113

Fielding

Errors by Pitcher

Brandon Webb	**5**
Joe Kennedy	4
10 players tied with	3

Errors by Catcher

Jason Kendall	**10**
Johnny Estrada	9
Jason LaRue	8

Errors by First Base

Shea Hillenbrand	**13**
Phil Nevin	**13**
Lyle Overbay	11

Errors by Second Base

Ray Durham	**16**
Tony Womack	15
Marcus Giles	12

Errors by Third Base

Chad Tracy	**25**
David Bell	24
Tony Batista	19

Errors by Shortstop

Rafael Furcal	**24**
Kazuo Matsui	23
Khalil Greene	20

Errors by Left Field

Craig Biggio	**9**
Moises Alou	8
Adam Dunn	8

Errors by Center Field

Mike Cameron	**8**
Luis Terrero	6
Preston Wilson	6

Errors by Right Field

Miguel Cabrera	**7**
Brian Giles	**7**
3 players tied with	6

% CS by Catchers
minimum 70 SB Attempts

Jason Kendall	**32.3**
Ramon Hernandez	25.4
Paul Lo Duca	23.8

Projections for 2005 Batters

Batter projections based on transactions through December 19, 2004. Age as of June 30, 2005.

Batter	Age	Avg	G	AB	R	H	2B	3B	HR	RBI	BB	SO	SB	CS	OBP	SLG
Abreu,Bobby, Phi	31	.307	156	566	109	174	41	4	25	101	114	119	28	11	.424	.527
Alfonzo,Edgardo, SF	31	.293	142	516	70	151	28	1	14	72	57	47	3	1	.363	.432
Alomar,Roberto, CWS	37	.278	102	363	50	101	20	2	6	40	37	57	8	3	.345	.394
Alomar Jr.,Sandy, Tex	39	.264	48	110	10	29	7	0	2	13	4	11	0	0	.289	.382
Alou,Moises, ChC	38	.288	137	511	73	147	28	2	25	85	55	67	3	1	.357	.497
Anderson,Garret, Ana	33	.297	142	566	71	168	35	2	22	100	30	81	5	3	.332	.482
Anderson,Marlon, StL	31	.267	109	318	40	85	17	3	6	37	24	43	6	2	.319	.396
Aurilia,Rich, SD	33	.264	112	349	45	92	18	1	9	39	27	61	1	1	.316	.398
Ausmus,Brad, Hou	36	.251	124	395	42	99	17	2	4	38	35	61	3	2	.312	.334
Bagwell,Jeff, Hou	37	.275	146	538	93	148	32	1	29	92	87	122	6	3	.376	.500
Baldelli,Rocco, TB	23	.297	87	333	49	99	17	2	8	44	15	64	11	6	.328	.432
Barajas,Rod, Tex	29	.243	119	383	40	93	25	0	12	52	18	66	2	1	.277	.402
Barrett,Michael, ChC	28	.263	126	437	53	115	29	2	15	55	40	69	3	2	.325	.442
Batista,Tony, Was	31	.252	155	600	80	151	29	2	30	100	34	94	6	4	.292	.457
Bautista,Danny, Ari	33	.277	103	357	39	99	13	2	7	41	24	52	4	3	.323	.384
Bay,Jason, Pit	26	.280	138	457	79	128	21	3	25	81	62	125	18	9	.366	.503
Bell,David, Phi	32	.254	140	500	66	127	28	1	15	67	56	72	1	1	.329	.404
Bellhorn,Mark, Bos	30	.245	134	425	67	104	20	3	15	59	76	135	5	3	.359	.412
Belliard,Ronnie, Cle	30	.266	146	518	74	138	34	3	9	56	49	82	4	3	.330	.396
Beltran,Carlos, Hou	28	.286	155	587	116	168	32	8	32	103	82	106	35	5	.374	.532
Beltre,Adrian, Sea	26	.282	158	582	83	164	31	3	34	98	45	93	7	4	.333	.521
Bennett,Gary, Was	33	.251	71	199	18	50	11	0	2	24	15	31	1	1	.304	.337
Berg,Dave, Tor	34	.263	42	99	12	26	6	0	2	10	6	17	0	0	.305	.384
Berkman,Lance, Hou	29	.304	114	395	77	120	29	2	23	79	85	78	5	4	.427	.562
Berroa,Angel, KC	27	.247	147	546	80	135	28	6	12	61	26	118	14	7	.281	.386
Bigbie,Larry, Bal	27	.280	131	454	72	127	26	2	13	61	47	107	6	2	.347	.432
Biggio,Craig, Hou	39	.269	138	558	90	150	31	2	16	55	44	101	6	3	.322	.418
Blake,Casey, Cle	31	.261	133	476	71	124	27	2	19	64	45	104	5	6	.324	.445
Blalock,Hank, Tex	24	.292	156	613	107	179	43	3	32	118	65	122	3	3	.360	.529
Blanco,Henry, ChC	33	.217	88	226	22	49	14	1	6	25	17	43	1	1	.272	.367
Bloomquist,Willie, Sea	27	.216	99	204	27	44	13	1	1	18	16	45	6	2	.273	.304
Blum,Geoff, SD	32	.253	101	300	36	76	17	1	7	37	25	48	2	1	.311	.387
Bonds,Barry, SF	40	.305	129	354	94	108	25	2	36	81	174	46	5	2	.534	.692
Boone,Bret, Sea	36	.261	145	570	82	149	29	1	24	94	55	118	8	4	.326	.442
Borchard,Joe, CWS	26	.267	85	266	41	71	14	0	12	38	19	67	2	2	.316	.455
Bradley,Milton, LA	27	.274	136	485	72	133	29	2	15	62	67	98	20	8	.362	.435
Branyan,Russell, Mil	29	.244	117	393	56	96	17	1	24	63	57	151	2	2	.340	.476
Brito,Juan, Ari	27	.235	63	187	19	44	6	0	3	19	8	33	1	1	.267	.316
Broussard,Ben, Cle	28	.262	139	450	62	118	25	1	17	70	45	99	5	2	.329	.436
Brown,Dee, KC	27	.261	73	238	29	62	12	1	7	35	15	53	2	2	.304	.408
Buck,John, KC	24	.250	113	400	44	100	23	1	11	60	22	89	1	1	.289	.395
Burke,Jamie, CWS	33	.254	74	201	21	51	7	0	2	22	10	26	0	1	.289	.318
Burnitz,Jeromy, Col	36	.244	138	472	70	115	24	2	27	78	47	124	4	4	.312	.475
Burrell,Pat, Phi	28	.263	141	506	74	133	33	2	29	91	82	138	1	0	.366	.508
Burroughs,Sean, SD	24	.289	142	533	73	154	32	3	4	56	45	61	4	2	.344	.383
Byrd,Marlon, Phi	27	.283	100	322	49	91	17	3	5	34	24	58	4	2	.332	.401
Byrnes,Eric, Oak	29	.255	143	538	80	137	35	2	16	64	42	93	12	3	.309	.416
Cabrera,Jolbert, Sea	32	.262	105	309	43	81	16	1	4	31	21	54	6	5	.309	.359
Cabrera,Miguel, Fla	22	.306	148	555	88	170	41	3	26	109	56	130	7	5	.370	.532
Cabrera,Orlando, Bos	30	.268	162	613	73	164	39	3	12	73	48	59	18	6	.321	.400
Cairo,Miguel, NYY	31	.261	119	291	40	76	16	2	5	32	16	43	4	3	.300	.381
Cameron,Mike, NYM	32	.237	147	518	80	123	27	3	24	82	69	153	21	7	.327	.440
Cantu,Jorge, TB	23	.263	104	358	44	94	26	1	8	43	14	60	2	2	.290	.408
Carroll,Jamey, Was	31	.250	94	188	23	47	14	1	0	12	22	26	3	2	.329	.335
Casey,Sean, Cin	30	.309	150	569	84	176	37	1	17	90	51	51	2	1	.366	.467
Cash,Kevin, TB	27	.235	84	243	25	57	18	0	5	26	18	64	0	0	.287	.370
Castilla,Vinny, Was	37	.264	138	522	67	138	25	1	23	84	31	87	1	1	.306	.448
Castillo,Jose, Pit	24	.266	105	350	43	93	16	2	5	40	22	70	7	4	.309	.366
Castillo,Luis, Fla	29	.303	154	604	94	183	18	5	3	48	69	70	30	14	.374	.364
Castro,Juan, Min	33	.228	103	303	28	69	14	1	5	27	15	54	1	1	.264	.330
Catalanotto,Frank, Tor	31	.294	107	360	54	106	22	3	6	39	28	46	6	3	.345	.422
Cedeno,Roger, StL	30	.275	103	258	36	71	10	2	4	23	22	48	13	5	.332	.376
Chavez,Endy, Was	27	.287	142	512	75	147	29	4	4	43	34	51	21	10	.332	.383
Chavez,Eric, Oak	27	.279	142	537	92	150	33	2	32	100	75	98	7	3	.368	.527
Choi,Hee Seop, LA	26	.238	119	349	54	83	18	1	17	54	61	104	3	2	.351	.441

698

Batter	Age	Avg	G	AB	R	H	2B	3B	HR	RBI	BB	SO	SB	CS	OBP	SLG
Cintron,Alex, Ari	26	.289	109	349	44	101	20	3	5	38	21	28	2	1	.330	.407
Clark,Brady, Mil	32	.270	120	367	45	99	23	1	5	47	30	46	8	4	.325	.379
Clark,Tony, NYY	33	.240	98	225	29	54	16	1	11	40	21	66	0	0	.305	.467
Clayton,Royce, Ari	35	.243	133	456	59	111	22	2	8	44	38	97	6	3	.302	.353
Closser,J.D., Col	25	.309	59	191	25	59	15	1	7	29	20	33	1	1	.374	.508
Conine,Jeff, Fla	39	.284	121	422	50	120	22	1	12	66	33	61	4	2	.336	.427
Cora,Alex, LA	29	.258	147	415	45	107	19	4	7	41	34	50	3	2	.314	.373
Counsell,Craig, Ari	34	.260	119	415	58	108	18	2	2	32	49	61	8	5	.338	.328
Crawford,Carl, TB	23	.292	154	638	97	186	28	9	9	61	33	89	59	14	.326	.406
Crede,Joe, CWS	27	.280	150	521	78	146	34	0	25	85	35	78	1	1	.326	.489
Crisp,Coco, Cle	25	.302	158	557	89	168	31	4	9	61	45	68	27	14	.354	.420
Crosby,Bobby, Oak	25	.254	151	551	74	140	33	2	21	74	52	131	14	6	.318	.436
Cruz,Deivi, SF	32	.267	86	240	25	64	14	1	4	29	9	23	1	1	.293	.383
Cruz Jr.,Jose, TB	31	.249	146	519	78	129	28	3	21	72	78	116	12	6	.347	.435
Cuddyer,Michael, Min	26	.269	122	401	54	108	26	4	11	57	47	96	7	6	.346	.436
Damon,Johnny, Bos	31	.286	150	616	116	176	32	6	15	70	71	72	23	9	.360	.430
DaVanon,Jeff, Ana	31	.282	100	280	41	79	19	3	8	39	37	57	9	5	.366	.457
Davis,Ben, Chi	28	.236	105	331	36	78	19	0	9	46	26	81	1	1	.291	.375
DeJesus,David, KC	25	.287	139	508	86	146	29	5	10	58	54	70	11	10	.356	.423
Delgado,Carlos, Tor	33	.278	143	504	92	140	34	1	34	109	93	127	1	0	.390	.552
Delgado,Wilson, Fla	32	.233	49	116	10	27	6	1	1	11	10	24	1	1	.294	.328
Dellucci,David, Tex	31	.232	112	340	49	79	16	4	12	51	43	89	7	3	.319	.409
DeRosa,Mark, Atl	30	.261	103	280	37	73	18	1	4	27	19	39	3	2	.308	.375
DeVore,Doug, Ari	27	.244	44	127	13	31	7	2	4	15	8	31	1	1	.289	.425
Diaz,Einar, StL	32	.253	57	150	16	38	10	0	1	15	7	13	1	0	.287	.340
Drew,J.D., Atl	29	.286	150	548	109	157	24	4	31	88	99	120	11	4	.396	.515
Dunn,Adam, Cin	25	.262	156	557	109	146	31	1	44	98	122	177	12	5	.395	.558
Durazo,Erubiel, Oak	30	.303	150	502	90	152	31	1	23	89	79	103	1	1	.398	.506
Durham,Ray, SF	33	.277	130	487	87	135	29	5	14	54	62	82	13	7	.359	.444
Dye,Jermaine, CWS	31	.255	121	443	67	113	25	1	18	71	47	99	3	1	.327	.438
Easley,Damion, Fla	35	.245	90	245	31	60	15	1	7	31	22	35	3	2	.307	.400
Eckstein,David, Ana	30	.273	142	553	83	151	25	2	4	44	43	47	17	7	.326	.347
Edmonds,Jim, StL	35	.270	140	456	83	123	30	1	31	86	84	138	3	3	.383	.544
Encarnacion,Juan, Fla	29	.268	135	507	69	136	27	4	19	75	39	85	12	6	.321	.450
Ensberg,Morgan, Hou	29	.287	138	422	67	121	26	1	17	64	58	73	7	4	.373	.474
Erstad,Darin, Ana	31	.292	122	480	73	140	26	2	7	57	29	62	14	4	.332	.398
Escobar,Alex, CWS	26	.249	65	213	29	53	11	1	9	32	14	65	4	2	.295	.437
Estrada,Johnny, Atl	29	.282	140	497	51	140	33	0	10	71	41	54	0	0	.336	.408
Everett,Adam, Hou	28	.256	125	422	68	108	20	3	7	45	26	67	9	3	.299	.367
Everett,Carl, CWS	34	.280	110	361	53	101	20	1	15	58	32	65	4	2	.338	.465
Feliz,Pedro, SF	30	.256	136	391	49	100	25	2	17	60	18	74	2	2	.289	.460
Fick,Robert, SD	31	.261	80	245	29	64	15	1	7	35	22	37	0	0	.322	.416
Figgins,Chone, Ana	27	.273	153	594	84	162	27	11	5	57	50	88	27	13	.329	.380
Finley,Steve, Ana	40	.264	138	493	71	130	23	4	22	72	54	77	9	5	.336	.460
Flaherty,John, NYY	37	.236	48	123	12	29	7	0	3	14	6	23	0	0	.271	.366
Floyd,Cliff, NYM	32	.276	128	442	74	122	29	2	21	71	61	97	10	4	.364	.493
Ford,Lew, Min	28	.281	150	558	81	157	36	3	12	69	50	75	13	8	.340	.421
Fordyce,Brook, TB	35	.244	41	90	8	22	6	0	1	7	5	15	0	0	.284	.344
Franco,Julio, Atl	46	.259	107	247	28	64	15	1	4	30	29	56	1	1	.337	.377
Freel,Ryan, Cin	29	.254	123	437	67	111	24	3	4	34	48	69	26	10	.328	.350
Fullmer,Brad, Tex	30	.280	77	246	40	69	19	1	11	38	24	29	3	2	.344	.500
Furcal,Rafael, Atl	26	.287	151	620	112	178	31	6	14	61	56	84	29	9	.346	.424
Garcia,Danny, NYM	25	.242	67	194	25	47	13	1	2	20	19	36	4	3	.310	.351
Garcia,Karim, Bal	29	.257	76	237	27	61	11	1	9	33	12	52	2	1	.293	.426
Garciaparra,Nomar, ChC	31	.318	136	553	94	176	41	5	21	93	36	54	7	3	.360	.524
Gerut,Jody, Cle	27	.276	110	355	55	98	25	2	14	55	37	48	7	4	.344	.476
Giambi,Jason, NYY	34	.269	100	334	60	90	21	0	23	67	71	80	1	1	.398	.539
Gibbons,Jay, Bal	28	.272	113	412	54	112	28	0	18	64	36	61	1	1	.330	.471
Giles,Brian, SD	34	.291	144	515	91	150	30	3	25	84	108	71	9	4	.414	.507
Giles,Marcus, Atl	27	.297	138	499	88	148	32	1	14	69	54	78	13	6	.365	.449
Ginter,Keith, Oak	29	.281	129	395	57	111	28	2	19	63	41	100	4	2	.349	.506
Glanville,Doug, Phi	34	.259	51	116	13	30	7	1	2	10	5	16	3	1	.289	.388
Glaus,Troy, Ari	28	.259	136	491	90	127	29	1	33	95	78	119	7	3	.360	.523
Gload,Ross, CWS	29	.293	107	341	49	100	22	3	11	46	21	45	2	2	.334	.472
Gomez,Chris, Phi	34	.262	55	164	18	43	7	0	2	18	10	20	1	1	.305	.341
Gonzalez,Alex, Fla	28	.243	158	556	64	135	33	5	20	74	34	117	3	2	.286	.428
Gonzalez,Alex S., SD	32	.235	111	353	44	83	20	2	11	39	29	88	4	3	.293	.397
Gonzalez,Juan, KC	35	.281	102	349	50	98	20	1	18	67	19	74	1	1	.318	.499
Gonzalez,Luis, Ari	37	.276	131	471	75	130	29	2	23	79	81	66	3	2	.382	.493
Gonzalez,Luis A., Col	26	.283	92	304	47	86	15	2	8	35	18	45	2	2	.323	.424

Batter	Age	Avg	G	AB	R	H	2B	3B	HR	RBI	BB	SO	SB	CS	OBP	SLG
Grabowski,Jason, LA	29	.258	80	194	27	50	17	1	6	29	21	45	2	2	.330	.448
Graffanino,Tony, KC	33	.267	103	311	51	83	19	3	7	37	31	51	7	2	.????	.401
Green,Andy, Ari	27	.258	64	209	25	54	15	1	2	20	13	28	4	3	.302	.368
Green,Nick, Atl	26	.256	88	246	27	63	15	1	5	30	15	50	3	3	.299	.386
Green,Shawn, LA	32	.278	154	579	93	161	36	2	29	96	77	112	8	4	.363	.497
Greene,Khalil, SD	25	.272	147	526	75	143	33	2	17	72	60	100	4	3	.346	.439
Greene,Todd, Col	34	.253	81	217	26	55	14	0	10	35	8	44	1	0	.280	.456
Grieve,Ben, ChC	29	.262	93	248	34	65	15	0	8	34	41	64	2	1	.367	.419
Griffey Jr.,Ken, Cin	35	.266	110	349	54	93	18	1	22	60	52	83	1	1	.362	.513
Grissom,Marquis, SF	38	.262	129	470	61	123	22	2	17	65	25	76	5	2	.299	.426
Gross,Gabe, Tor	25	.261	123	414	57	108	26	2	9	57	53	87	4	3	.345	.399
Grudzielanek,Mark, ChC	35	.277	121	430	53	119	25	2	6	38	22	65	3	2	.312	.386
Guerrero,Vladimir, Ana	29	.330	149	561	106	185	35	4	36	110	72	68	23	11	.406	.599
Guillen,Carlos, Det	29	.281	137	505	86	142	26	4	14	72	56	87	6	4	.353	.432
Guillen,Jose, Was	29	.290	153	558	80	162	31	2	27	101	30	98	4	4	.327	.498
Guzman,Cristian, Was	27	.275	151	601	86	165	28	9	8	58	28	75	16	9	.307	.391
Hafner,Travis, Cle	28	.289	146	501	84	145	34	1	26	97	72	126	3	2	.379	.517
Hairston,Scott, Ari	25	.253	91	316	41	80	17	5	10	35	19	77	3	3	.296	.434
Hairston Jr.,Jerry, Bal	29	.271	98	332	44	90	18	2	3	30	31	40	16	7	.333	.364
Hall,Bill, Mil	25	.240	130	441	53	106	22	1	8	43	27	108	10	9	.284	.349
Hall,Toby, TB	29	.285	133	481	54	137	30	0	11	72	24	45	1	1	.319	.416
Hammock,Robby, Ari	28	.251	88	267	30	67	15	1	5	30	18	49	3	3	.298	.371
Harris,Willie, CWS	27	.265	125	344	57	91	19	2	5	30	44	68	17	7	.348	.375
Harvey,Ken, KC	27	.280	134	492	63	138	30	1	14	74	31	94	2	1	.323	.431
Hatteberg,Scott, Oak	35	.268	140	508	65	136	26	1	12	62	65	53	0	0	.351	.394
Hawpe,Brad, Col	26	.302	94	311	46	94	20	1	22	60	26	78	2	2	.356	.585
Helms,Wes, Mil	29	.253	88	249	26	63	12	1	8	32	21	64	1	1	.311	.406
Helton,Todd, Col	31	.338	155	554	116	187	46	2	32	111	113	78	3	2	.450	.601
Hernandez,Jose, Cle	35	.235	102	319	37	75	13	2	11	38	31	114	2	2	.303	.392
Hernandez,Ramon, SD	29	.256	131	425	55	109	21	1	16	61	39	63	0	0	.319	.424
Hidalgo,Richard, Tex	30	.266	145	516	76	137	34	2	25	81	54	116	5	4	.335	.484
Higginson,Bobby, Det	34	.264	123	435	58	115	24	2	12	59	55	67	8	6	.347	.411
Hill,Bobby, Pit	27	.255	104	239	27	61	11	1	2	22	21	43	7	5	.315	.335
Hillenbrand,Shea, Ari	29	.284	149	578	72	164	36	2	17	81	26	72	2	2	.315	.441
Hinske,Eric, Tor	27	.263	147	540	84	142	29	3	18	75	67	116	12	5	.344	.428
Hollandsworth,Todd, ChC	32	.272	102	276	38	75	17	2	9	35	28	62	4	3	.339	.446
Holliday,Matt, Col	25	.292	133	469	73	137	29	3	16	67	43	84	8	5	.352	.469
Hudson,Orlando, Tor	27	.268	144	497	67	133	34	6	12	64	49	94	5	3	.333	.433
Huff,Aubrey, TB	28	.306	160	618	94	189	45	2	29	100	55	74	3	2	.363	.526
Hummel,Tim, Bos	26	.261	64	157	16	41	13	1	1	18	12	27	1	0	.314	.376
Hunter,Torii, Min	29	.275	148	557	86	153	34	3	27	94	44	109	14	7	.328	.492
Ibanez,Raul, Sea	33	.279	139	546	71	147	24	2	18	80	42	79	3	3	.333	.435
Infante,Omar, Det	23	.250	152	519	70	130	21	5	10	49	45	92	25	11	.310	.368
Inge,Brandon, Det	28	.236	132	424	43	100	25	3	11	51	36	95	4	5	.296	.387
Izturis,Cesar, LA	25	.252	160	588	63	148	26	4	2	48	30	61	14	8	.288	.320
Izturis,Maicer, Ana	24	.262	57	191	24	50	9	2	1	17	16	20	6	4	.319	.346
Jacobsen,Bucky, Sea	29	.270	104	348	54	94	20	0	21	67	38	91	1	1	.342	.509
Jenkins,Geoff, Mil	30	.274	158	576	89	158	36	3	28	94	53	145	2	2	.335	.493
Jeter,Derek, NYY	31	.314	145	592	108	186	31	3	18	73	56	100	20	5	.373	.468
Jimenez,D'Angelo, Cin	27	.269	153	576	83	155	30	3	14	62	79	85	10	8	.357	.405
Johnson,Charles, Col	33	.238	111	324	39	77	19	0	14	52	47	87	1	1	.334	.426
Johnson,Nick, Was	26	.278	99	309	51	86	18	1	12	47	53	67	4	2	.384	.460
Johnson,Reed, Tor	28	.278	102	309	48	86	16	1	6	36	16	50	3	3	.314	.395
Jones,Andruw, Atl	28	.263	157	581	96	153	32	3	33	102	73	136	7	4	.346	.499
Jones,Chipper, Atl	33	.292	146	513	87	150	31	2	29	96	95	90	4	3	.403	.530
Jones,Jacque, Min	30	.283	145	547	76	155	32	2	22	76	33	117	9	6	.324	.470
Jordan,Brian, Tex	38	.268	55	168	21	45	9	1	5	24	13	29	1	1	.320	.423
Kata,Matt, Ari	27	.257	81	303	38	78	18	5	5	31	19	49	3	3	.301	.399
Kearns,Austin, Cin	25	.278	114	389	66	108	21	2	17	69	59	91	7	5	.373	.473
Kendall,Jason, Oak	31	.313	148	569	79	178	31	3	5	54	54	37	11	9	.372	.404
Kennedy,Adam, Ana	29	.276	130	417	57	115	23	3	9	44	33	73	13	5	.329	.410
Kent,Jeff, LA	37	.286	135	524	76	150	32	2	24	89	43	92	5	3	.340	.492
Kielty,Bobby, Oak	28	.259	102	286	45	74	22	1	10	42	49	61	3	1	.367	.448
Klesko,Ryan, SD	34	.279	132	444	67	124	26	2	18	76	72	81	6	3	.380	.468
Konerko,Paul, CWS	29	.279	152	552	81	154	29	1	33	103	57	80	0	0	.346	.514
Koskie,Corey, Tor	32	.268	134	470	76	126	29	2	20	75	69	119	12	6	.362	.466
Kotsay,Mark, Oak	29	.284	148	573	78	163	30	4	13	61	61	83	9	6	.353	.419
Laird,Gerald, Tex	25	.261	77	245	37	64	12	2	5	32	23	50	4	3	.325	.388
Lamb,Mike, Hou	29	.279	104	301	44	84	24	2	10	48	35	53	1	0	.354	.472
Lane,Jason, Hou	28	.299	99	231	34	69	24	1	8	39	25	31	1	1	.367	.515

Batter	Age	Avg	G	AB	R	H	2B	3B	HR	RBI	BB	SO	SB	CS	OBP	SLG
Larkin,Barry, Cin	41	.269	107	349	50	94	20	2	5	35	32	42	4	2	.331	.381
LaRoche,Adam, Atl	25	.282	128	433	61	122	31	0	17	62	43	101	1	1	.347	.471
Larson,Brandon, TB	29	.279	36	111	14	31	6	0	7	21	9	30	0	0	.333	.523
LaRue,Jason, Cin	31	.229	124	397	46	91	27	1	14	53	31	120	2	2	.285	.408
Lawton,Matt, Pit	33	.257	126	471	77	121	25	1	16	60	62	60	13	6	.343	.416
LeCroy,Matthew, Min	29	.283	103	315	39	89	17	0	14	57	23	71	1	1	.331	.470
Ledee,Ricky, LA	31	.249	97	177	29	44	15	1	7	31	27	44	1	1	.348	.463
Lee,Carlos, Mil	29	.289	157	591	97	171	35	1	31	101	60	87	11	5	.355	.509
Lee,Derrek, ChC	29	.269	160	576	94	155	32	2	30	88	89	141	12	6	.367	.488
Leone,Justin, Sea	27	.247	56	174	34	43	11	1	9	30	22	50	4	2	.332	.477
Lieberthal,Mike, Phi	33	.277	133	491	58	136	29	1	15	63	39	64	0	0	.330	.432
Lo Duca,Paul, Fla	33	.279	144	551	66	154	32	1	12	70	38	45	2	2	.326	.407
Lofton,Kenny, Phi	38	.289	116	426	77	123	21	3	8	41	46	50	15	7	.358	.408
Logan,Nook, Det	25	.249	55	189	24	47	6	3	1	14	13	40	11	5	.297	.328
Long,Terrence, KC	29	.268	144	444	58	119	28	3	10	57	34	70	4	2	.320	.412
Lopez,Felipe, Cin	25	.257	95	334	52	86	17	3	7	37	37	88	8	4	.332	.389
Lopez,Javy, Bal	34	.283	131	460	60	130	22	1	23	77	36	87	0	0	.335	.485
Lopez,Jose, Sea	21	.241	125	432	58	104	27	0	12	51	18	52	7	5	.271	.387
Loretta,Mark, SD	33	.302	156	559	76	169	30	2	11	59	55	56	3	2	.365	.422
Lowell,Mike, Fla	31	.282	149	561	81	158	37	0	27	97	63	83	3	2	.354	.492
Lugo,Julio, TB	29	.275	154	560	85	154	28	3	12	62	53	112	14	7	.338	.400
Luna,Hector, StL	25	.280	82	161	27	45	10	1	1	16	13	25	4	2	.333	.373
Mabry,John, StL	34	.259	100	220	27	57	14	0	11	38	23	51	0	0	.329	.473
Macias,Jose, ChC	33	.233	108	249	27	58	14	3	4	25	12	45	5	3	.268	.361
Mackowiak,Rob, Pit	29	.244	123	389	48	95	22	2	11	47	38	103	7	3	.311	.396
Marrero,Eli, KC	31	.249	110	329	45	82	16	1	11	46	29	61	6	3	.310	.404
Martinez,Ramon, ChC	32	.264	108	269	30	71	16	1	3	31	24	43	1	1	.324	.364
Martinez,Tino, TB	37	.262	135	455	60	119	25	1	19	72	55	70	2	1	.341	.446
Martinez,Victor, Cle	26	.311	143	524	76	163	42	0	18	95	52	65	3	4	.373	.494
Mateo,Ruben, KC	27	.266	85	256	35	68	18	1	9	35	18	53	2	1	.314	.449
Matheny,Mike, SF	34	.236	123	368	34	87	16	1	5	42	33	71	1	1	.299	.326
Matos,Luis, Bal	26	.251	95	358	48	90	17	2	8	43	29	73	12	5	.307	.377
Matsui,Hideki, NYY	31	.295	162	601	96	177	39	1	25	110	77	92	2	1	.375	.488
Matsui,Kazuo, NYM	29	.274	126	504	72	138	36	2	8	54	46	104	12	5	.335	.401
Matthews Jr.,Gary, Tex	30	.252	102	301	44	76	15	1	8	34	34	63	7	4	.328	.389
Mauer,Joe, Min	22	.318	118	387	60	123	25	1	8	53	28	41	0	0	.364	.450
Mayne,Brent, LA	37	.244	98	271	25	66	12	0	3	27	28	49	1	1	.314	.321
McCracken,Quinton, Ari	34	.274	85	186	25	51	15	2	1	18	16	33	3	2	.332	.392
McEwing,Joe, NYM	32	.240	71	129	15	31	11	1	1	14	9	29	2	1	.290	.364
McLemore,Mark, Oak	40	.244	90	271	36	66	11	1	3	29	42	52	9	4	.345	.325
Melhuse,Adam, Oak	33	.266	82	214	26	57	15	0	8	29	23	49	1	1	.338	.449
Mench,Kevin, Tex	27	.253	133	455	67	115	33	1	21	70	50	91	1	1	.327	.468
Menechino,Frank, Tor	34	.244	78	197	30	48	10	1	5	23	30	37	1	1	.344	.381
Merloni,Lou, Cle	34	.255	88	200	27	51	15	0	3	20	19	41	1	1	.320	.375
Michaels,Jason, Phi	29	.268	117	231	33	62	21	2	7	34	33	57	2	2	.360	.468
Mientkiewicz,Doug, Bos	31	.284	109	345	46	98	25	1	7	45	51	47	2	2	.376	.423
Miles,Aaron, Col	28	.290	134	518	74	150	29	2	7	59	28	50	7	7	.326	.394
Millar,Kevin, Bos	33	.278	141	492	65	137	31	2	18	75	52	96	1	1	.347	.459
Miller,Damian, Mil	35	.249	118	393	40	98	24	0	10	48	42	104	0	0	.322	.387
Mirabelli,Doug, Bos	34	.243	73	173	21	42	12	0	8	27	17	44	0	0	.311	.451
Moeller,Chad, Mil	30	.248	96	290	33	72	16	1	7	35	28	68	1	1	.314	.383
Mohr,Dustan, SF	29	.278	112	281	46	78	20	1	9	34	33	72	3	2	.354	.452
Molina,Bengie, Ana	30	.268	119	407	38	109	19	0	10	59	16	35	0	0	.296	.388
Molina,Jose, Ana	30	.248	90	218	19	54	11	0	2	22	7	50	1	1	.271	.326
Molina,Yadier, StL	22	.271	122	395	38	107	15	0	2	46	33	51	1	1	.327	.324
Mondesi,Raul, Ana	34	.266	52	169	25	45	10	1	7	26	18	33	5	3	.337	.462
Monroe,Craig, Det	28	.279	137	462	67	129	33	3	21	77	31	90	3	2	.325	.500
Mora,Melvin, Bal	33	.279	131	488	81	136	24	1	19	68	62	95	9	6	.360	.449
Morneau,Justin, Min	24	.273	141	502	71	137	28	1	27	82	41	100	2	1	.328	.494
Mueller,Bill, Bos	34	.287	126	428	65	123	26	1	12	56	55	59	1	2	.369	.437
Munson,Eric, Det	27	.242	120	360	40	87	23	2	24	65	38	84	2	1	.314	.517
Nevin,Phil, SD	34	.275	133	488	65	134	25	0	23	88	51	106	2	1	.343	.467
Newhan,David, Bal	31	.294	86	303	47	89	13	2	5	31	21	54	5	3	.340	.399
Nix,Laynce, Tex	24	.249	120	404	62	108	25	1	18	66	29	101	5	2	.316	.468
Nixon,Trot, Bos	31	.280	140	453	75	127	28	4	22	79	59	93	3	2	.363	.506
Nunez,Abraham, KC	28	.242	120	376	48	91	17	4	10	48	45	104	7	5	.323	.388
Nunez,Abraham O., Pit	29	.234	110	239	25	56	10	1	2	19	21	46	5	3	.296	.310
Ojeda,Miguel, SD	30	.245	87	204	26	50	6	0	9	30	23	40	1	1	.322	.407
Olerud,John, NYY	36	.287	118	404	53	116	26	0	11	64	64	54	0	0	.385	.433
Olivo,Miguel, Sea	26	.248	119	391	52	97	25	4	15	58	26	101	6	4	.295	.448

Batter	Age	Avg	G	AB	R	H	2B	3B	HR	RBI	BB	SO	SB	CS	OBP	SLG
Ordonez,Magglio, CWS	31	.307	129	489	80	150	32	2	25	92	45	61	8	5	.365	.534
Ortiz,David, Bos	29	.301	159	570	99	180	41	1	47	116	73	130	1	1	.365	.554
Overbay,Lyle, Mil	28	.295	149	567	77	167	43	1	14	76	87	123	1	1	.388	.448
Palmeiro,Orlando, Hou	36	.272	58	92	12	25	5	0	1	10	10	10	1	1	.343	.359
Palmeiro,Rafael, Bal	40	.252	138	492	74	124	27	1	22	92	81	72	1	1	.358	.445
Patterson,Corey, ChC	25	.256	151	594	82	152	30	4	21	70	32	142	23	7	.294	.426
Payton,Jay, SD	32	.285	145	498	71	142	24	3	16	64	39	63	4	3	.337	.442
Pena,Carlos, Det	27	.254	144	493	73	125	35	2	25	79	59	139	4	2	.333	.485
Pena,Wily Mo, Cin	23	.265	139	378	62	100	22	1	26	72	28	113	4	3	.315	.534
Perez,Eddie, Atl	37	.245	61	151	12	37	8	0	4	13	8	25	0	0	.283	.377
Perez,Neifi, ChC	32	.261	116	337	39	88	15	4	3	31	15	32	3	3	.293	.356
Perez,Timo, CWS	30	.296	96	280	37	83	16	2	5	32	15	24	7	4	.332	.421
Perez,Tomas, Phi	31	.242	75	153	17	37	11	1	3	17	12	31	0	0	.297	.386
Phelps,Josh, Cle	27	.278	80	252	38	70	17	0	14	46	21	67	0	0	.333	.512
Phillips,Jason, NYM	28	.262	131	408	42	107	23	0	12	63	35	44	0	0	.321	.407
Piazza,Mike, NYM	36	.297	125	462	63	137	22	0	25	77	61	83	1	1	.379	.506
Pickering,Calvin, KC	28	.257	58	175	26	45	8	0	11	35	33	58	0	0	.375	.491
Pierre,Juan, Fla	27	.315	162	660	105	208	25	7	2	50	47	41	50	19	.361	.383
Pierzynski,A.J., SF	28	.290	140	490	59	142	33	2	10	69	21	50	2	2	.319	.427
Podsednik,Scott, CWS	29	.259	156	606	96	157	26	4	10	54	61	99	41	12	.327	.365
Polanco,Placido, Phi	29	.291	134	519	83	151	23	2	13	53	33	40	8	3	.333	.418
Posada,Jorge, NYY	33	.269	140	476	73	128	29	1	23	93	88	117	2	2	.383	.479
Pratt,Todd, Phi	38	.245	43	94	11	23	5	0	2	10	17	28	0	0	.360	.362
Pujols,Albert, StL	25	.341	157	593	136	202	49	2	45	136	83	60	3	3	.422	.658
Quinlan,Robb, Ana	28	.284	78	236	30	67	15	2	5	33	14	41	2	2	.324	.428
Ramirez,Aramis, ChC	27	.284	153	573	81	163	35	1	32	104	43	86	2	2	.334	.517
Ramirez,Manny, Bos	33	.313	141	508	93	159	34	1	36	111	85	104	1	1	.411	.596
Randa,Joe, KC	35	.279	114	390	48	109	22	2	8	53	32	55	1	1	.334	.408
Redman,Tike, Pit	28	.267	126	408	51	109	16	5	4	31	26	35	19	8	.311	.360
Redmond,Mike, Min	34	.269	91	234	19	63	12	0	2	23	16	30	0	0	.316	.346
Reese,Pokey, Bos	32	.234	95	316	35	74	14	1	4	34	28	72	11	3	.297	.323
Relaford,Desi, KC	31	.250	101	320	43	80	16	2	5	35	29	47	8	4	.312	.359
Renteria,Edgar, Bos	29	.302	154	577	82	174	33	2	12	81	54	64	22	8	.361	.428
Reyes,Jose, NYM	22	.262	79	301	46	79	15	5	2	26	15	47	24	8	.297	.365
Rios,Alexis, Tor	24	.304	117	431	56	131	26	6	5	49	27	78	9	3	.345	.427
Rivas,Luis, Min	25	.257	129	428	60	110	29	5	9	45	24	62	15	6	.296	.411
Rivera,Juan, Ana	26	.303	122	350	47	106	28	1	10	50	23	47	2	1	.346	.474
Roberts,Brian, Bal	27	.269	151	606	91	163	27	3	4	49	72	73	39	14	.347	.343
Roberts,Dave, Bos	33	.272	122	389	62	106	16	4	3	30	45	49	28	10	.348	.357
Rodriguez,Alex, NYY	29	.300	158	606	122	182	35	2	47	125	88	125	15	4	.389	.597
Rodriguez,Ivan, Det	33	.292	132	487	70	142	31	2	17	70	42	88	7	4	.348	.468
Rolen,Scott, StL	30	.294	154	544	100	160	39	3	31	113	76	100	9	4	.381	.548
Rollins,Jimmy, Phi	26	.261	157	648	98	169	34	9	12	63	58	94	32	11	.322	.397
Rolls,Damian, TB	27	.244	61	193	27	47	8	1	3	21	12	39	6	2	.288	.342
Ross,David, LA	28	.222	67	180	20	40	7	0	7	26	16	61	0	1	.286	.378
Rowand,Aaron, CWS	27	.276	139	464	75	128	29	2	18	61	28	73	6	3	.317	.463
Sanchez,Alex, Det	28	.282	116	440	50	124	15	3	1	32	22	65	33	16	.316	.336
Sanchez,Rey, TB	37	.260	86	265	27	69	10	1	1	21	12	28	2	1	.292	.317
Sanders,Reggie, StL	37	.257	130	447	66	115	23	3	24	75	37	116	13	6	.314	.483
Santiago,Benito, Pit	40	.259	114	402	41	104	17	1	10	48	24	69	2	2	.300	.381
Schneider,Brian, Was	28	.246	135	415	40	102	31	1	11	53	45	75	1	1	.320	.405
Scutaro,Marco, Oak	29	.278	121	367	48	102	22	2	8	40	32	53	6	4	.336	.414
Sexson,Richie, Sea	30	.275	149	552	91	152	29	2	39	113	81	136	1	2	.368	.547
Sheffield,Gary, NYY	36	.293	149	549	99	161	28	1	32	105	83	66	9	4	.386	.523
Sierra,Ruben, NYY	39	.258	94	275	34	71	17	1	11	45	22	47	1	0	.313	.447
Simon,Randall, TB	30	.278	66	209	20	58	10	0	6	29	9	17	0	1	.307	.411
Sizemore,Grady, Cle	22	.277	124	430	69	119	22	6	9	57	36	76	9	8	.333	.419
Sledge,Terrmel, Was	28	.268	107	314	44	84	17	4	8	37	31	61	7	4	.333	.424
Smith,Jason, Det	27	.250	71	228	29	57	10	3	4	23	10	53	4	2	.282	.373
Snow,J.T., SF	37	.261	118	360	48	94	19	1	8	48	56	70	1	1	.361	.386
Soriano,Alfonso, Tex	29	.279	152	659	102	184	38	3	33	93	33	135	31	10	.314	.496
Sosa,Sammy, ChC	36	.264	134	497	88	131	20	2	38	95	70	140	0	0	.354	.541
Spencer,Shane, NYY	33	.245	98	282	29	69	16	1	6	33	30	65	2	1	.317	.372
Spiezio,Scott, Sea	32	.259	101	317	43	82	18	2	9	44	35	42	3	2	.332	.413
Spivey,Junior, Mil	30	.262	97	343	51	90	19	3	10	45	37	73	7	5	.334	.423
Stairs,Matt, KC	37	.255	119	330	43	84	19	1	16	52	44	69	1	1	.342	.464
Stewart,Shannon, Min	31	.305	130	531	85	162	34	3	12	55	54	60	11	5	.369	.448
Stynes,Chris, Pit	32	.256	55	117	17	30	7	0	2	15	12	19	1	1	.326	.368
Surhoff,B.J., Bal	40	.272	85	268	32	73	15	1	5	33	25	30	2	2	.334	.392
Suzuki,Ichiro, Sea	31	.336	157	687	114	231	30	6	9	61	53	66	35	13	.384	.437

Batter	Age	Avg	G	AB	R	H	2B	3B	HR	RBI	BB	SO	SB	CS	OBP	SLG
Sweeney,Mark, Col	35	.252	88	155	17	39	13	0	4	27	23	39	1	1	.348	.413
Sweeney,Mike, KC	31	.302	123	453	72	137	28	0	22	86	55	53	5	3	.378	.510
Taguchi,So, StL	35	.241	72	112	12	27	9	0	1	13	8	18	3	1	.292	.348
Teixeira,Mark, Tex	25	.287	148	543	94	156	33	5	36	101	62	117	4	3	.360	.565
Tejada,Miguel, Bal	29	.291	162	650	106	189	36	2	32	126	49	74	7	2	.340	.500
Terrero,Luis, Ari	25	.265	101	347	44	92	17	6	5	31	18	85	13	10	.301	.392
Thames,Marcus, Det	28	.242	79	248	36	60	17	1	9	37	25	57	2	2	.311	.427
Thomas,Charles, Oak	26	.290	82	255	40	74	14	3	4	32	22	46	4	4	.347	.416
Thomas,Frank, CWS	37	.274	124	424	70	116	27	0	29	82	81	97	1	1	.390	.542
Thome,Jim, Phi	34	.272	145	504	94	137	27	1	43	112	111	156	1	1	.403	.585
Torrealba,Yorvit, SF	26	.248	89	238	28	59	14	1	7	31	22	41	1	0	.312	.403
Tracy,Chad, Ari	25	.302	134	461	57	139	30	3	7	55	30	49	1	2	.344	.425
Tucker,Michael, SF	34	.253	121	387	58	98	19	3	11	50	49	91	10	6	.337	.403
Upton,B.J., TB	20	.287	95	328	59	94	20	1	9	41	40	92	10	5	.364	.436
Uribe,Juan, CWS	25	.275	129	473	75	130	35	8	17	65	29	89	7	5	.317	.490
Utley,Chase, Phi	26	.271	136	458	68	124	31	1	18	73	39	86	6	3	.328	.461
Valent,Eric, NYM	28	.225	110	222	28	50	21	1	7	27	25	53	0	0	.304	.423
Valentin,Javier, Cin	29	.266	94	233	24	62	21	1	7	31	16	46	0	0	.313	.455
Valentin,Jose, CWS	35	.230	98	317	47	73	17	1	18	47	30	84	4	3	.297	.461
Varitek,Jason, Bos	33	.261	138	459	58	120	30	1	17	69	52	112	4	2	.337	.442
Vazquez,Ramon, SD	28	.259	77	220	29	57	12	1	2	20	27	42	3	1	.340	.350
Vidro,Jose, Was	30	.305	139	515	81	157	39	1	16	73	61	56	2	1	.378	.478
Vina,Fernando, Det	36	.271	34	107	14	29	5	1	1	9	7	8	2	1	.316	.364
Vizcaino,Jose, Hou	37	.274	122	369	40	101	14	2	4	31	20	40	2	2	.311	.355
Vizquel,Omar, SF	38	.265	135	514	73	136	22	2	6	48	52	56	12	6	.332	.350
Walker,Larry, StL	38	.299	129	428	79	128	28	2	22	81	75	81	6	3	.404	.528
Walker,Todd, ChC	32	.289	143	523	80	151	32	2	14	68	48	63	3	3	.349	.438
Ward,Daryle, Pit	30	.270	93	296	30	80	16	0	11	48	18	53	0	0	.312	.436
Wells,Vernon, Tor	26	.283	148	591	95	167	38	4	27	94	41	78	6	3	.329	.497
Werth,Jayson, LA	26	.238	111	366	61	87	21	1	16	55	29	108	8	3	.294	.432
White,Rondell, Det	33	.277	131	470	64	130	26	2	20	76	33	84	1	1	.324	.468
Wigginton,Ty, Pit	27	.260	152	538	68	140	30	2	15	63	48	102	7	4	.321	.407
Wilkerson,Brad, Was	28	.251	157	561	94	141	36	2	25	80	103	164	13	8	.367	.456
Williams,Bernie, NYY	36	.290	136	514	89	149	29	3	18	79	75	83	5	3	.380	.463
Wilson,Craig, Pit	28	.265	150	550	85	146	25	2	29	81	55	164	4	2	.332	.476
Wilson,Dan, Sea	36	.249	92	281	25	70	13	1	3	31	16	57	1	1	.290	.335
Wilson,Enrique, NYY	31	.237	72	139	16	33	10	0	3	19	9	16	1	1	.284	.374
Wilson,Jack, Pit	27	.276	157	598	80	165	30	6	9	56	36	74	5	4	.317	.391
Wilson,Preston, Col	30	.272	108	393	60	107	23	1	20	67	40	99	11	6	.339	.489
Wilson,Vance, NYM	32	.232	86	185	18	43	12	0	4	25	10	36	0	1	.272	.362
Winn,Randy, Sea	31	.295	154	604	89	178	37	6	13	77	50	105	19	8	.349	.440
Wise,Dewayne, Det	27	.226	79	234	31	53	13	3	8	29	13	53	6	2	.267	.410
Womack,Tony, NYY	35	.268	132	488	68	131	19	4	4	36	29	64	19	8	.309	.348
Woodward,Chris, Tor	29	.261	85	268	34	70	17	2	7	34	22	58	1	1	.317	.418
Youkilis,Kevin, Bos	26	.285	77	249	46	71	16	0	5	33	45	39	3	2	.395	.410
Young,Dmitri, Det	31	.284	133	489	70	139	33	3	22	71	44	102	3	2	.343	.499
Young,Eric, SD	38	.270	110	371	56	100	20	2	5	25	39	32	16	8	.339	.375
Young,Michael, Tex	28	.294	161	650	97	191	36	6	17	85	43	101	8	5	.338	.446
Zaun,Gregg, Tor	34	.236	100	254	27	60	14	1	4	29	29	46	1	1	.314	.346

Projections for 2005 Pitchers

Projections based on transactions through Dec. 19, 2004; pitchers with 150 games or 500 IP in the majors. Age as of June 30, 2005.

Pitcher	Age	ERA	W	L	Sv	G	GS	IP	H	HR	BB	SO	BR/9
Abbott,Paul, Phi	37	6.19	4	7	0	17	15	80	85	17	48	43	15.0
Adams,Terry, Bos	32	3.91	5	3	0	63	0	69	72	5	28	51	13.0
Alfonseca,Antonio, Fla	33	4.06	4	4	0	73	0	71	74	5	30	55	13.2
Almanzar,Carlos, Tex	31	3.33	6	3	0	67	0	73	66	8	21	44	10.7
Alvarez,Wilson, LA	35	3.46	5	4	0	34	14	112	104	12	35	93	11.2
Anderson,Brian, KC	33	5.29	8	12	0	34	28	177	205	29	56	76	13.3
Appier,Kevin, KC	37	6.61	3	8	0	18	18	83	91	15	62	41	16.6
Armas,Tony, Was	27	4.84	5	7	0	18	18	93	84	11	58	70	13.7
Baez,Danys, TB	27	3.55	2	4	31	66	0	71	63	7	31	57	11.9
Batista,Miguel, Tor	34	4.27	12	10	2	37	32	200	195	16	93	120	13.0
Bell,Rob, TB	28	5.04	6	8	0	22	19	116	127	20	39	52	12.9
Benitez,Armando, SF	32	2.79	3	3	39	66	0	71	51	7	29	69	10.1
Benson,Kris, NYM	30	4.50	10	12	0	29	29	182	201	20	55	120	12.7
Biddle,Rocky, Was	29	4.97	3	5	0	56	6	76	81	12	37	56	14.0
Boehringer,Brian, Pit	35	4.03	2	2	0	35	0	38	35	4	18	30	12.6
Borowski,Joe, ChC	34	3.41	3	2	0	37	0	37	34	4	13	36	11.4
Bottalico,Ricky, NYM	35	3.64	3	2	0	41	0	47	43	3	23	41	12.6
Bradford,Chad, Oak	30	3.32	5	3	0	69	0	65	61	5	21	47	11.4
Brocail,Doug, Tex	38	3.63	4	2	0	43	0	52	54	2	20	43	12.8
Brower,Jim, SF	32	3.69	6	5	0	76	2	95	89	9	37	65	11.9
Brown,Kevin, NYY	40	3.19	13	6	0	25	25	158	146	12	42	124	10.7
Buehrle,Mark, CWS	26	3.68	17	11	0	35	35	240	239	27	50	143	10.8
Burba,Dave, SF	38	3.68	4	3	0	40	1	66	61	7	25	46	11.7
Burnett,A.J., Fla	28	2.89	13	7	0	27	27	168	135	14	53	157	10.1
Byrd,Paul, Ana	34	4.22	9	8	0	24	24	143	156	21	23	99	11.3
Carpenter,Chris, StL	30	4.05	13	9	0	28	28	182	188	25	38	152	11.2
Carrara,Giovanni, LA	37	4.20	2	3	0	36	0	45	47	4	19	34	13.2
Chen,Bruce, Bal	28	4.95	2	2	0	11	5	40	40	8	13	29	11.9
Choate,Randy, Ari	29	3.34	3	2	0	51	0	35	31	1	20	30	13.1
Christiansen,Jason, SF	35	4.36	3	3	0	53	0	33	32	3	19	22	13.9
Clemens,Roger, Hou	42	3.46	15	9	0	33	33	213	184	20	79	204	11.1
Clement,Matt, Bos	30	3.97	13	9	0	31	31	188	176	18	79	171	12.2
Colon,Bartolo, Ana	32	4.13	14	12	0	34	34	220	213	28	75	161	11.8
Cordero,Francisco, Tex	30	2.76	3	2	47	69	0	75	62	3	31	79	11.2
Cormier,Rheal, Phi	38	2.41	8	2	0	78	0	82	62	5	25	56	9.5
D'Amico,Jeff, Cle	29	4.67	5	5	0	14	14	79	91	12	15	44	12.1
Davis,Doug, Mil	29	4.47	10	11	0	30	29	175	187	16	67	126	13.1
DeJean,Mike, NYM	34	4.10	4	4	0	61	0	68	67	6	35	61	13.5
Dempster,Ryan, ChC	28	4.85	2	2	11	23	7	52	56	6	27	39	14.4
Dessens,Elmer, LA	34	4.53	4	6	0	45	17	129	141	18	38	78	12.5
Dotel,Octavio, Oak	31	2.41	4	2	38	77	0	86	59	8	29	107	9.2
Dreifort,Darren, LA	33	4.17	3	3	0	43	3	54	50	6	30	63	13.3
Eaton,Adam, SD	27	3.90	12	10	0	32	32	194	187	27	51	152	11.0
Eischen,Joey, Was	35	3.30	2	2	0	37	0	30	28	2	9	26	11.1
Elarton,Scott, Cle	29	5.85	6	9	0	23	23	123	137	29	48	72	13.5
Eldred,Cal, StL	37	4.30	4	3	3	55	0	67	66	10	24	60	12.1
Embree,Alan, Bos	35	3.06	5	2	0	69	0	53	46	6	15	51	10.4
Escobar,Kelvim, Ana	29	3.75	13	10	0	36	31	199	184	18	73	179	11.6
Estes,Shawn, Col	32	5.16	11	12	0	32	32	185	200	20	96	115	14.4
Eyre,Scott, SF	33	4.17	4	4	0	80	0	54	54	5	26	42	13.3
Farnsworth,Kyle, ChC	29	3.86	5	4	0	74	0	70	61	8	34	80	12.2
Fassero,Jeff, SF	42	5.08	4	5	0	48	10	101	120	11	41	61	14.3
Fogg,Josh, Pit	28	4.77	8	13	0	30	30	166	179	21	62	79	13.1
Foulke,Keith, Bos	32	2.14	4	2	36	72	0	84	62	7	16	76	8.4
Franco,John, NYM	44	4.50	2	2	0	37	0	32	32	4	15	21	13.2
Franklin,Ryan, Sea	32	4.46	12	12	0	32	32	204	206	32	62	101	11.8
Fuentes,Brian, Col	29	3.76	4	3	0	56	0	55	49	6	25	63	12.1
Fultz,Aaron, Phi	31	4.34	4	3	0	58	0	56	56	7	25	43	13.0
Gagne,Eric, LA	29	2.30	3	3	48	72	0	82	60	8	19	122	8.7
Garcia,Freddy, CWS	30	3.74	14	10	0	32	32	207	193	23	63	165	11.1
Garland,Jon, CWS	25	4.48	13	12	0	33	33	209	210	29	73	113	12.2
Glavine,Tom, NYM	39	4.21	11	13	0	33	33	203	209	21	67	98	12.2
Gordon,Tom, NYY	37	2.14	8	2	3	75	0	84	58	5	28	96	9.2
Graves,Danny, Cin	31	4.43	2	4	40	65	0	69	77	9	16	32	12.1
Grimsley,Jason, Bal	37	4.57	4	4	0	74	0	67	72	5	34	47	14.2

Pitcher	Age	ERA	W	L	Sv	G	GS	IP	H	HR	BB	SO	BR/9
Groom,Buddy, Bal	39	5.22	3	4	0	60	0	50	64	7	15	34	14.2
Gryboski,Kevin, Atl	31	4.41	4	3	2	67	0	49	49	4	28	30	14.1
Guardado,Eddie, Sea	34	2.61	3	2	33	64	0	62	46	7	16	61	9.0
Halama,John, Bos	33	4.93	4	4	0	34	14	115	136	17	34	61	13.3
Halladay,Roy, Tor	28	3.46	16	9	0	32	32	213	204	15	62	160	11.2
Hammond,Chris, Oak	39	3.47	4	2	0	48	0	57	59	4	12	38	11.2
Hampton,Mike, Atl	32	4.96	10	12	0	30	30	178	203	20	67	97	13.7
Harper,Travis, TB	29	4.23	4	4	0	55	0	83	86	11	26	59	12.1
Hasegawa,Chigetoshi, Sea	00	0.21	5	0	0	00	0	70	02	5	20	09	11.3
Hawkins,LaTroy, ChC	32	2.81	7	3	9	76	0	80	72	6	15	69	9.8
Haynes,Jimmy, TB	32	5.27	2	3	0	9	9	41	46	5	19	22	14.3
Hentgen,Pat, Tor	36	5.47	5	7	0	21	18	107	110	19	56	59	14.0
Heredia,Felix, NYM	30	4.09	3	4	0	54	0	55	54	6	25	30	12.9
Herges,Matt, SF	35	4.63	4	5	0	69	0	70	80	7	25	53	13.5
Hermanson,Dustin, CWS	32	5.09	4	4	0	56	0	69	74	14	24	48	12.8
Hernandez,Livan, Was	30	4.17	14	14	0	34	34	248	255	26	81	185	12.2
Hernandez,Orlando, NYY	35	3.92	6	4	0	15	15	85	75	10	36	84	11.8
Hernandez,Roberto, Phi	40	5.59	3	4	0	64	0	58	63	9	36	44	15.4
Hitchcock,Sterling, SD	34	5.23	2	3	0	14	5	43	51	6	16	33	14.0
Hoffman,Trevor, SD	37	2.31	2	1	43	40	0	39	30	4	7	40	8.5
Howry,Bob, Cle	31	4.20	2	2	0	26	0	30	31	4	9	23	12.0
Hudson,Tim, Atl	29	3.01	17	8	0	31	31	221	201	14	52	135	10.3
Isringhausen,Jason, StL	32	2.25	3	1	45	63	0	64	47	3	21	63	9.6
Jackson,Mike, CWS	40	4.98	3	3	0	45	0	47	55	7	15	26	13.4
Jarvis,Kevin, Pit	35	5.71	1	2	0	12	5	41	50	7	15	23	14.3
Jennings,Jason, Col	26	5.52	10	13	0	33	33	194	223	24	98	128	14.9
Jimenez,Jose, Cle	31	4.50	3	3	0	42	2	58	69	6	16	31	13.2
Johnson,Jason, Det	31	4.55	11	12	0	33	33	194	210	25	59	122	12.5
Johnson,Randy, Ari	41	2.67	15	8	0	29	29	202	169	19	36	233	9.1
Jones,Todd, Fla	37	4.96	4	5	3	72	0	78	93	8	33	61	14.5
Julio,Jorge, Bal	26	4.16	4	4	6	65	0	67	61	9	34	60	12.8
Kennedy,Joe, Col	26	4.88	9	9	0	29	25	153	164	19	63	100	13.4
Kim,Byung-Hyun, Bos	26	2.60	3	1	0	23	6	52	40	5	15	47	9.5
King,Ray, StL	31	2.95	6	2	0	84	0	61	50	4	25	44	11.1
Kline,Steve, Bal	32	3.11	5	3	0	71	0	55	46	4	21	33	11.0
Koch,Billy, Fla	30	4.32	3	3	0	50	0	50	47	6	28	48	13.5
Kolb,Dan, Atl	30	3.12	2	2	42	55	0	52	45	3	22	31	11.6
Koplove,Mike, Ari	28	3.21	5	3	0	61	0	70	62	5	26	48	11.3
Lackey,John, Ana	26	4.50	12	12	0	33	32	200	216	25	61	147	12.5
Lawrence,Brian, SD	29	4.06	12	12	0	34	34	206	214	22	56	118	11.8
Leiter,Al, Fla	39	4.19	11	11	0	30	30	176	155	15	98	133	12.9
Leskanic,Curtis, Bos	37	4.11	3	3	0	52	0	46	41	5	28	42	13.5
Levine,Al, Det	37	4.56	4	4	0	61	0	71	75	9	26	31	12.8
Lidge,Brad, Hou	28	2.47	4	3	40	79	0	91	63	7	39	129	10.1
Lidle,Cory, Phi	33	4.13	13	11	0	33	33	205	210	24	59	121	11.8
Lieber,Jon, Phi	35	3.80	13	10	0	31	31	199	221	21	21	118	10.9
Ligtenberg,Kerry, Tor	34	4.02	4	3	0	61	0	56	55	6	22	46	12.4
Lilly,Ted, Tor	29	4.48	12	11	0	32	32	191	178	27	86	160	12.4
Lima,Jose, LA	32	4.89	6	9	0	29	21	138	156	25	28	71	12.0
Linebrink,Scott, SD	28	3.52	5	4	0	66	2	87	79	8	32	76	11.5
Loaiza,Esteban, NYY	33	5.03	12	11	0	32	29	197	222	25	77	156	13.7
Lohse,Kyle, Min	26	5.10	11	13	0	34	34	196	216	29	77	120	13.5
Looper,Braden, NYM	30	3.29	3	4	34	72	0	82	78	6	24	56	11.2
Lopez,Rodrigo, Bal	29	4.31	9	9	0	33	24	163	166	22	52	115	12.0
Lowe,Derek, Bos	32	4.12	13	10	0	33	33	190	193	14	74	106	12.6
Maddux,Greg, ChC	39	3.85	14	11	0	34	34	215	221	29	33	137	10.6
Mahay,Ron, Tex	34	3.45	4	3	0	52	0	60	49	7	27	50	11.4
Maroth,Mike, Det	27	4.65	11	13	0	33	33	209	237	26	57	99	12.7
Marquis,Jason, StL	26	4.45	12	10	0	30	30	188	193	24	65	122	12.4
Marte,Damaso, CWS	30	2.84	7	3	2	73	0	76	56	7	31	81	10.3
Martin,Tom, Atl	35	4.02	4	3	0	77	0	47	43	6	21	40	12.3
Martinez,Pedro, NYM	33	2.35	17	7	0	32	32	207	152	14	59	226	9.2
Matthews,Mike, Cin	31	4.29	3	3	0	49	0	42	39	5	22	28	13.1
May,Darrell, SD	33	4.41	11	12	0	32	31	194	195	30	58	124	11.7
Meadows,Brian, Pit	29	4.32	4	5	0	57	2	77	87	10	16	41	12.0
Mecir,Jim, Oak	35	4.09	4	3	0	57	0	44	44	4	19	37	12.9
Mendoza,Ramiro, Bos	33	3.98	3	2	0	30	2	43	46	4	10	25	11.7
Mercker,Kent, Cin	37	3.33	5	3	0	70	0	54	42	5	29	48	11.8
Mesa,Jose, Pit	39	4.91	2	5	42	67	0	66	77	7	26	43	14.0
Miceli,Dan, Hou	34	4.14	5	4	0	68	0	74	71	11	26	69	11.8

Pitcher	Age	ERA	W	L	Sv	G	GS	IP	H	HR	BB	SO	BR/9
Miller,Trever, TB	32	3.78	4	3	2	66	0	50	46	5	21	43	12.1
Miller,Wade, Hou	28	4.20	8	7	0	21	21	122	108	14	60	103	12.4
Millwood,Kevin, Phi	30	3.91	11	9	0	28	28	168	161	17	61	136	11.9
Milton,Eric, Phi	29	4.74	11	12	0	32	32	188	187	32	70	145	12.3
Morris,Matt, StL	30	3.84	14	9	0	30	30	192	191	20	53	129	11.4
Mota,Guillermo, Fla	31	2.93	3	3	44	77	0	80	64	7	27	71	10.2
Moyer,Jamie, Sea	42	4.37	13	12	0	34	33	206	206	31	64	126	11.8
Mulder,Mark, StL	27	3.59	15	9	0	31	31	213	194	17	79	138	11.5
Mulholland,Terry, Min	42	5.40	4	5	0	41	11	115	145	18	36	53	14.2
Mussina,Mike, NYY	36	3.73	14	8	0	28	28	181	176	21	44	156	10.9
Myers,Mike, Bos	36	4.61	4	3	0	71	0	41	43	4	21	29	14.0
Nathan,Joe, Min	30	2.04	4	2	46	75	0	75	48	5	27	84	9.0
Nelson,Jeff, Tex	38	3.71	3	2	0	43	0	34	29	3	19	39	12.7
Nomo,Hideo, LA	36	4.40	7	9	0	23	23	129	116	17	64	98	12.6
Ohka,Tomo, Was	29	4.48	10	12	0	31	31	183	207	22	43	101	12.3
Oliver,Darren, Hou	34	5.04	6	7	0	29	17	109	128	15	38	58	13.7
Ortiz,Ramon, Cin	32	4.25	10	10	0	31	28	163	159	26	53	105	11.7
Ortiz,Russ, Ari	31	4.26	11	14	0	34	34	207	190	17	113	144	13.2
Osuna,Antonio, SD	32	3.73	3	2	0	37	0	41	42	3	16	40	12.7
Oswalt,Roy, Hou	27	3.33	15	9	0	31	30	200	187	17	52	173	10.8
Padilla,Vicente, Phi	27	3.81	12	9	0	29	29	175	170	17	55	116	11.6
Park,Chan Ho, Tex	32	4.11	8	6	0	20	20	114	107	16	39	72	11.5
Patterson,Danny, StL	34	3.97	2	2	0	31	0	34	34	3	12	24	12.2
Pavano,Carl, NYY	29	4.31	14	10	0	32	31	215	240	25	47	135	12.0
Penny,Brad, LA	27	3.86	10	9	0	27	27	161	157	16	51	118	11.6
Percival,Troy, Det	35	3.06	2	2	34	52	0	50	36	6	22	47	10.4
Perez,Odalis, LA	28	3.54	12	10	0	31	31	193	182	23	43	136	10.5
Perisho,Matt, Fla	30	5.55	3	4	0	66	0	47	56	6	26	37	15.7
Pettitte,Andy, Hou	33	4.30	10	9	0	26	26	155	165	12	58	138	12.9
Pineiro,Joel, Sea	26	3.64	13	9	0	28	28	183	169	19	56	136	11.1
Politte,Cliff, CWS	31	3.88	4	3	0	54	0	51	47	6	19	47	11.6
Ponson,Sidney, Bal	28	4.50	12	13	0	32	32	216	234	25	69	124	12.6
Powell,Jay, Tex	33	5.00	2	2	0	32	0	36	38	4	19	25	14.3
Quantrill,Paul, NYY	36	3.34	7	3	0	87	0	89	95	3	21	48	11.7
Radke,Brad, Min	32	3.73	15	11	0	34	34	217	232	25	26	132	10.7
Redman,Mark, Pit	31	4.24	10	13	0	31	31	191	198	18	69	120	12.6
Reed,Steve, Col	40	4.15	5	3	0	66	0	65	66	8	22	39	12.2
Reitsma,Chris, Atl	27	4.44	5	5	0	75	0	81	89	11	23	53	12.4
Remlinger,Mike, ChC	39	3.83	4	3	5	56	0	47	39	6	25	53	12.3
Reyes,Dennys, SD	28	4.38	3	3	0	32	8	76	76	7	40	67	13.7
Reynolds,Shane, Ari	37	7.26	2	5	0	11	10	57	66	7	57	32	19.4
Rhodes,Arthur, Cle	35	3.35	4	2	2	55	0	51	45	5	16	53	10.8
Riedling,John, Cin	29	4.13	5	4	0	65	3	85	85	7	43	53	13.6
Rincon,Ricardo, Oak	35	3.38	5	2	0	66	0	48	42	3	20	40	11.6
Riske,David, Cle	28	3.79	5	4	2	71	0	76	63	10	36	84	11.7
Rivera,Mariano, NYY	35	2.25	4	2	47	71	0	76	63	4	16	66	9.4
Rodriguez,Felix, NYY	32	3.46	6	3	0	73	0	65	56	6	29	53	11.8
Rogers,Kenny, Tex	40	4.85	12	12	0	34	34	206	241	23	64	123	13.3
Romero,J.C., Min	29	3.93	5	4	0	74	0	71	65	6	37	63	12.9
Rueter,Kirk, SF	34	4.65	10	12	0	31	31	176	194	20	61	51	13.0
Rusch,Glendon, ChC	30	4.68	8	9	0	33	22	154	178	18	51	107	13.4
Ryan,B.J., Bal	29	3.24	6	3	24	76	0	75	62	5	37	93	11.9
Sabathia,C.C., Cle	24	3.82	13	9	0	30	30	191	176	18	73	139	11.7
Santana,Johan, Min	26	2.64	18	7	0	33	33	218	169	22	52	245	9.1
Schilling,Curt, Bos	38	2.87	17	7	0	29	29	207	184	21	32	208	9.4
Schmidt,Jason, SF	32	2.88	17	8	0	31	31	219	172	17	75	233	10.2
Schoeneweis,Scott, CWS	31	4.92	5	6	0	33	13	97	104	11	42	68	13.5
Seanez,Rudy, SD	36	3.97	2	2	0	29	0	34	30	4	19	35	13.0
Sele,Aaron, Ana	35	5.30	7	9	0	27	24	129	152	17	50	53	14.1
Sheets,Ben, Mil	26	3.53	15	11	0	34	34	232	234	27	31	213	10.3
Shouse,Brian, Tex	36	3.24	4	2	0	56	0	50	47	3	17	35	11.5
Silva,Carlos, Min	26	4.15	13	11	0	32	32	195	227	18	34	83	12.0
Smoltz,John, Atl	38	2.36	15	5	0	28	28	160	135	11	23	173	8.9
Sparks,Steve, Ari	39	5.04	4	7	0	36	12	116	129	16	43	57	13.3
Speier,Justin, Tor	31	3.86	5	3	9	65	0	70	64	10	23	56	11.2
Stanton,Mike, NYY	38	3.68	5	3	0	72	0	66	60	7	28	51	12.0
Stewart,Scott, LA	29	4.22	2	2	0	40	0	32	33	3	11	29	12.4
Stone,Ricky, Cin	30	4.79	3	4	0	50	0	62	64	11	24	43	12.8
Sturtze,Tanyon, NYY	34	4.89	4	3	0	32	5	81	90	11	34	51	13.8
Sullivan,Scott, KC	34	4.35	4	4	0	54	0	62	62	8	26	54	12.8

Pitcher	Age	ERA	W	L	Sv	G	GS	IP	H	HR	BB	SO	BR/9
Suppan,Jeff, StL	30	4.62	12	11	0	31	31	193	204	25	67	109	12.6
Tavarez,Julian, StL	32	3.93	5	4	0	73	0	71	75	4	28	36	13.1
Telemaco,Amaury, Phi	31	4.24	3	2	0	31	3	51	50	9	15	31	11.5
Thomson,John, Atl	31	4.30	13	34	0	34	34	205	216	27	54	132	11.9
Timlin,Mike, Bos	39	3.30	6	3	0	75	0	79	75	9	14	60	10.1
Tomko,Brett, SF	32	4.93	10	13	0	32	31	197	217	29	65	110	12.9
Torres,Salomon, Pit	33	3.88	5	5	0	70	5	102	102	11	32	66	11.8
Trachsel,Steve, NYM	34	4.48	11	13	0	33	33	203	201	26	83	114	12.6
Tucker,T. J., Was	26	4.25	4	4	0	51	2	72	80	6	22	46	12.9
Urbina,Ugueth, Det	31	3.19	5	3	10	60	0	62	47	8	27	67	10.7
Valdez,Ismael, Fla	31	4.91	8	11	0	30	28	152	170	24	44	61	12.7
Van Poppel,Todd, Cin	33	4.65	4	4	0	37	9	93	99	16	30	75	12.5
Vazquez,Javier, NYY	28	3.88	15	9	0	33	33	209	197	27	63	191	11.2
Villone,Ron, Sea	35	3.95	5	4	0	44	13	114	103	13	52	83	12.2
Vizcaino,Luis, CWS	30	4.30	5	4	0	74	0	69	63	13	25	64	11.5
Wagner,Billy, Phi	33	2.03	3	2	40	66	0	71	46	7	17	85	8.0
Wakefield,Tim, Bos	38	4.29	13	10	0	33	31	193	193	26	65	141	12.0
Walker,Jamie, Det	33	3.60	5	4	0	73	0	65	61	10	14	52	10.4
Wasdin,John, Tex	32	6.40	2	3	0	11	7	45	58	10	16	26	14.8
Washburn,Jarrod, Ana	30	3.99	11	9	0	27	27	169	166	22	45	96	11.2
Weathers,David, Cin	35	4.07	5	4	0	70	1	84	81	9	38	64	12.8
Weaver,Jeff, LA	28	4.14	11	12	0	33	31	200	212	17	61	130	12.3
Weber,Ben, Cin	35	3.86	3	2	0	33	0	42	42	4	14	23	12.0
Wells,David, Bos	42	4.30	13	10	0	31	31	201	238	26	20	98	11.6
Wells,Kip, Pit	28	4.56	8	11	0	26	26	158	156	17	75	124	13.2
Wendell,Turk, Col	38	4.22	2	2	0	27	0	32	30	4	16	15	12.9
White,Gabe, Cin	33	4.25	4	3	2	58	0	55	57	10	10	38	11.0
White,Rick, Cle	36	4.68	4	4	0	56	0	75	80	11	25	50	12.6
Wickman,Bob, Cle	36	4.80	1	2	28	30	0	30	35	3	9	29	13.2
Williams,Woody, SD	38	3.87	13	11	0	32	32	200	199	19	61	138	11.7
Williamson,Scott, Bos	29	2.70	4	1	0	41	0	40	27	3	21	45	10.8
Wilson,Paul, Cin	32	4.90	10	12	0	29	29	178	196	26	61	107	13.0
Witasick,Jay, SD	32	3.70	3	3	0	45	0	56	52	6	23	49	12.1
Wolf,Randy, Phi	28	3.51	13	8	0	29	29	177	160	21	47	140	10.5
Wood,Kerry, ChC	28	3.15	15	8	0	30	30	197	153	21	72	230	10.3
Worrell,Tim, Phi	37	3.58	6	4	4	77	0	78	74	7	24	64	11.3
Wright,Jamey, Col	30	5.13	9	10	0	27	27	149	152	18	85	86	14.3
Wright,Jaret, NYY	29	4.72	9	8	0	38	21	143	162	13	53	126	13.5
Yan,Esteban, Ana	30	4.72	4	5	2	64	0	80	88	11	30	64	13.3
Zambrano,Carlos, ChC	24	3.28	15	9	0	31	31	211	183	13	82	177	11.3
Zito,Barry, Oak	27	3.58	16	10	0	34	34	219	190	22	83	152	11.2